REGULATIONS

IRS Centr

Ogden, UT 84201

Title 44
Emergency Management and
Assistance

Revised as of October 1, 2011

Containing a codification of documents
of general applicability and future effect

As of October 1, 2011

Published by the Office of the Federal Register
National Archives and Records Administration
as a Special Edition of the Federal Register

U.S. GOVERNMENT PRINTING OFFICE

U.S. Superintendent of Documents • Washington, DC 20402–0001

http://bookstore.gpo.gov

Phone: toll-free (866) 512-1800; DC area (202) 512-1800

Table of Contents

Cite this Code: CFR

To cite the regulations in this volume use title, part and section number. Thus, 44 CFR 1.1 refers to title 44, part 1, section 1.

Explanation

The Code of Federal Regulations is a codification of the general and permanent rules published in the Federal Register by the Executive departments and agencies of the Federal Government. The Code is divided into 50 titles which represent broad areas subject to Federal regulation. Each title is divided into chapters which usually bear the name of the issuing agency. Each chapter is further subdivided into parts covering specific regulatory areas.

Each volume of the Code is revised at least once each calendar year and issued on a quarterly basis approximately as follows:

The appropriate revision date is printed on the cover of each volume.

LEGAL STATUS

The contents of the Federal Register are required to be judicially noticed (44 U.S.C. 1507). The Code of Federal Regulations is prima facie evidence of the text of the original documents (44 U.S.C. 1510).

HOW TO USE THE CODE OF FEDERAL REGULATIONS

The Code of Federal Regulations is kept up to date by the individual issues of the Federal Register. These two publications must be used together to determine the latest version of any given rule.

To determine whether a Code volume has been amended since its revision date (in this case, October 1, 2011), consult the "List of CFR Sections Affected (LSA)," which is issued monthly, and the "Cumulative List of Parts Affected," which appears in the Reader Aids section of the daily Federal Register. These two lists will identify the Federal Register page number of the latest amendment of any given rule.

EFFECTIVE AND EXPIRATION DATES

Each volume of the Code contains amendments published in the Federal Register since the last revision of that volume of the Code. Source citations for the regulations are referred to by volume number and page number of the Federal Register and date of publication. Publication dates and effective dates are usually not the same and care must be exercised by the user in determining the actual effective date. In instances where the effective date is beyond the cut-off date for the Code a note has been inserted to reflect the future effective date. In those instances where a regulation published in the Federal Register states a date certain for expiration, an appropriate note will be inserted following the text.

OMB CONTROL NUMBERS

The Paperwork Reduction Act of 1980 (Pub. L. 96–511) requires Federal agencies to display an OMB control number with their information collection request.

Many agencies have begun publishing numerous OMB control numbers as amendments to existing regulations in the CFR. These OMB numbers are placed as close as possible to the applicable recordkeeping or reporting requirements.

OBSOLETE PROVISIONS

Provisions that become obsolete before the revision date stated on the cover of each volume are not carried. Code users may find the text of provisions in effect on a given date in the past by using the appropriate numerical list of sections affected. For the period before April 1, 2001, consult either the List of CFR Sections Affected, 1949–1963, 1964–1972, 1973–1985, or 1986–2000, published in eleven separate volumes. For the period beginning April 1, 2001, a "List of CFR Sections Affected" is published at the end of each CFR volume.

"[RESERVED]" TERMINOLOGY

The term "[Reserved]" is used as a place holder within the Code of Federal Regulations. An agency may add regulatory information at a "[Reserved]" location at any time. Occasionally "[Reserved]" is used editorially to indicate that a portion of the CFR was left vacant and not accidentally dropped due to a printing or computer error.

INCORPORATION BY REFERENCE

What is incorporation by reference? Incorporation by reference was established by statute and allows Federal agencies to meet the requirement to publish regulations in the Federal Register by referring to materials already published elsewhere. For an incorporation to be valid, the Director of the Federal Register must approve it. The legal effect of incorporation by reference is that the material is treated as if it were published in full in the Federal Register (5 U.S.C. 552(a)). This material, like any other properly issued regulation, has the force of law.

What is a proper incorporation by reference? The Director of the Federal Register will approve an incorporation by reference only when the requirements of 1 CFR part 51 are met. Some of the elements on which approval is based are:

(a) The incorporation will substantially reduce the volume of material published in the Federal Register.

(b) The matter incorporated is in fact available to the extent necessary to afford fairness and uniformity in the administrative process.

(c) The incorporating document is drafted and submitted for publication in accordance with 1 CFR part 51.

What if the material incorporated by reference cannot be found? If you have any problem locating or obtaining a copy of material listed as an approved incorporation by reference, please contact the agency that issued the regulation containing that incorporation. If, after contacting the agency, you find the material is not available, please notify the Director of the Federal Register, National Archives and Records Administration, 8601 Adelphi Road, College Park, MD 20740-6001, or call 202-741-6010.

CFR INDEXES AND TABULAR GUIDES

A subject index to the Code of Federal Regulations is contained in a separate volume, revised annually as of January 1, entitled CFR INDEX AND FINDING AIDS. This volume contains the Parallel Table of Authorities and Rules. A list of CFR titles, chapters, subchapters, and parts and an alphabetical list of agencies publishing in the CFR are also included in this volume.

An index to the text of "Title 3—The President" is carried within that volume.

vi

The Federal Register Index is issued monthly in cumulative form. This index is based on a consolidation of the "Contents" entries in the daily Federal Register.

A List of CFR Sections Affected (LSA) is published monthly, keyed to the revision dates of the 50 CFR titles.

REPUBLICATION OF MATERIAL

There are no restrictions on the republication of material appearing in the Code of Federal Regulations.

INQUIRIES

For a legal interpretation or explanation of any regulation in this volume, contact the issuing agency. The issuing agency's name appears at the top of odd-numbered pages.

For inquiries concerning CFR reference assistance, call 202–741–6000 or write to the Director, Office of the Federal Register, National Archives and Records Administration, 8601 Adelphi Road, College Park, MD 20740-6001 or e-mail fedreg.info@nara.gov.

SALES

The Government Printing Office (GPO) processes all sales and distribution of the CFR. For payment by credit card, call toll-free, 866-512-1800, or DC area, 202-512-1800, M-F 8 a.m. to 4 p.m. e.s.t. or fax your order to 202-512-2104, 24 hours a day. For payment by check, write to: US Government Printing Office – New Orders, P.O. Box 979050, St. Louis, MO 63197-9000.

ELECTRONIC SERVICES

The full text of the Code of Federal Regulations, the LSA (List of CFR Sections Affected), The United States Government Manual, the Federal Register, Public Laws, Public Papers of the Presidents of the United States, Compilation of Presidential Documents and the Privacy Act Compilation are available in electronic format via www.ofr.gov. For more information, contact the GPO Customer Contact Center, U.S. Government Printing Office. Phone 202-512-1800, or 866-512-1800 (toll-free). E-mail, gpo@custhelp.com.

The Office of the Federal Register also offers a free service on the National Archives and Records Administration's (NARA) World Wide Web site for public law numbers, Federal Register finding aids, and related information. Connect to NARA's web site at www.archives.gov/federal-register.

RAYMOND A. MOSLEY,
Director,
Office of the Federal Register.
October 1, 2011.

THIS TITLE

Title 44—EMERGENCY MANAGEMENT AND ASSISTANCE is composed of one volume. The contents of this volume represent all current regulations codified under this title of the CFR as of October 1, 2011.

For this volume, Bonnie Fritts was Chief Editor. The Code of Federal Regulations publication program is under the direction of Michael L. White, assisted by Ann Worley.

Title 44—Emergency Management and Assistance

1

CHAPTER I—FEDERAL EMERGENCY MANAGEMENT AGENCY, DEPARTMENT OF HOMELAND SECURITY

EDITORIAL NOTE: Nomenclature changes to chapter I appear at 74 FR 15331, Apr. 3, 2009.

SUBCHAPTER A—GENERAL

4

SUBCHAPTER A—GENERAL

PART 0—GENERAL STATEMENTS OF POLICY [RESERVED]

PART 1—RULEMAKING; POLICY AND PROCEDURES

Subpart A—General

Sec.
1.1 Purpose.
1.2 Definitions.
1.3 Scope.
1.4 Policy and procedures.
1.5 Rules docket.
1.6 Ex parte communications.
1.7 Regulations agendas.
1.8 Regulations review.
1.9 Regulatory impact analyses.

Subpart B—Procedures for Rulemaking

1.10 Initiation of rulemaking.
1.11 Advance notice of proposed rulemaking.
1.12 Notice of proposed rulemaking.
1.13 Participation by interested persons.
1.14 Additional rulemaking proceedings.
1.15 Hearings.
1.16 Adoption of a final rule.
1.17 Petitions for reconsideration.
1.18 Petition for rulemaking.

AUTHORITY: 5 U.S.C. 551, 552, 553; 5 U.S.C. 601, *et seq.*; E.O. 12291. Reorganization Plan No. 3 of 1978; E.O. 12127; E.O. 12148.

SOURCE: 46 FR 32584, June 24, 1981, unless otherwise noted.

Subpart A—General

§ 1.1 Purpose.

(a) This part contains the basic policies and procedures of the Federal Emergency Management Agency (FEMA) for adoption of rules. These policies and procedures incorporate those provisions of section 4 of the Administrative Procedure Act (APA) (5 U.S.C. 553) which FEMA will follow. This part and internal FEMA Manuals implement Executive Order 12291.

(b) Rules which must be published are described in section 3(a) of the APA, 5 U.S.C. 552(a). FEMA implementation of paragraph (a) is contained in 44 CFR part 5, subpart B.

(c) This part contains policies and procedures for implementation of the Regulatory Flexibility Act which took effect January 1, 1981.

(d) A FEMA Manual No. 1140.1, "The Formulation, Drafting, Clearance, and Publication of FEDERAL REGISTER Documents" has been issued describing the internal procedures including policy level oversight of FEMA for:

(1) Publishing the semiannual agenda of significant regulations under development and review;

(2) Making initial determinations with respect to significance of proposed rulemaking;

(3) Determining the need for regulatory analyses; and

(4) Reviewing existing regulations, including the reviews required by the Regulatory Flexibility Act.

(e) As the FEMA Manual deals with internal management it is not subject to the requirements either of 5 U.S.C. 552 or 553. Its provisions are not part of this rule and reference to it is informative only.

[46 FR 32584, June 24, 1981, as amended at 49 FR 33878, Aug. 27, 1984]

§ 1.2 Definitions.

(a) *Rule* or *regulation* means the whole or a part of any agency statement of general applicability and future effect designed to (1) implement, interpret, or prescribe law or policy, or (2) describe procedures or practice requirements. It includes any rule of general applicability governing Federal grants to State and local governments for which the agency provides an opportunity for notice and public comment, except that the term *rule* does not include a rule of particular applicability relating to rates, wages, prices, facilities, appliances, services, or allowances therefor or to valuations, costs or accounting, or practices relating to such rates, wages, structures, prices, appliances, services, or allowances. For purposes of this part the term *rule* does not include regulations issued with respect to a military or foreign affairs function of the United States.

(b) *Rulemaking* means the FEMA process for considering and formulating the issuance, amendment or repeal of a rule.

(c) *Administrator* means the Administrator, FEMA, or an official to whom the Administrator has expressly delegated authority to issue rules.

(d) *FEMA* means Federal Emergency Management Agency.

(e) *Major rule* means any regulation that is likely to result in:

(1) An annual effect on the economy of $100 million or more;

(2) A major increase in costs or prices for consumers, individual industries, Federal, State, or local government agencies, or geographic regions; or

(3) Significant adverse effects on competition, employment, investment, productivity, innovation, or on the ability of United States-based enterprises to compete with foreign-based enterprises in domestic or export markets.

[46 FR 32584, June 24, 1981, as amended at 49 FR 38118, Sept. 27, 1984]

§ 1.3 Scope.

(a) This part prescribes general rulemaking procedures for the issuance, amendment, or repeal of rules in which participation by interested persons is required by 5 U.S.C. 553 or other statutes, by Executive Order 12291, by FEMA policy, or by § 1.4 of this part.

(b) Any delegation by the Administrator of authority to issue rules may not be further redelegated, unless expressly provided for in the delegation.

(c) This part does not apply to rules issued in accordance with the formal rulemaking provisions of the Administrative Procedure Act (5 U.S.C. 556, 557).

§ 1.4 Policy and procedures.

(a) In promulgating new regulations, reviewing existing regulations, and developing legislative proposals concerning regulation, FEMA, to the extent permitted by law, shall adhere to the following requirements:

(1) Administrative decisions shall be based on adequate information concerning the need for and consequences of proposed government action;

(2) Regulatory action shall not be undertaken unless the potential benefits to society for the regulation outweigh the potential costs to society;

(3) Regulatory objectives shall be chosen to maximize the net benefits to society;

(4) Among alternative approaches to any given regulatory objective, the alternative involving the least net cost to society shall be chosen; and

(5) FEMA shall set regulatory priorities with the aim of maximizing the aggregate net benefits to society, taking into account the condition of the particular entities affected by regulations, the condition of the national economy, and other regulatory actions contemplated for the future.

(b) It is the policy of FEMA to provide for public participation in rulemaking regarding its programs and functions, including matters that relate to public property, loans, grants, or benefits, or contracts, even though these matters are not subject to a requirement for notice and public comment rulemaking by law.

(c) FEMA will publish notices of proposed rulemaking in the FEDERAL REGISTER and will give interested persons an opportunity to participate in the rulemaking through submission of written data, views, and arguments with or without opportunity for oral presentation.

(d) In order to give the public, including small entities and consumer groups, an early and meaningful opportunity to participate in the development of rules, for a number of regulations the Administrator will employ additional methods of inviting public participation. These methods include, but are not limited to, publishing advance Notices of Proposed Rulemaking (ANPR), which can include a statement with respect to the impact of the proposed rule on small entities; holding open conferences; convening public forums or panels, sending notices of proposed regulations to publications likely to be read by those affected and soliciting comment from interested parties by such means as direct mail. An ANPR should be used to solicit public comment early in the rulemaking process for significant rules.

(e) It is the policy of FEMA that its notices of proposed rulemaking are to afford the public at least sixty days for submission of comments unless the Administrator makes an exception and sets forth the reasons for the exception in the preamble to the notice of proposed rulemaking. This period shall also include any period of review required by the Office of Management and Budget in accordance with the Paperwork Reduction Act of 1980.

(f) Unless required by statute or Executive Order, notice and public procedure may be omitted if the Administrator, for good cause, determines in a particular case or class of cases that notice and public procedure is impractical, unnecessary or contrary to the public interest and sets forth the reason for the determination in the rulemaking document or, for a class of cases, in a published rule or statement of policy. In a particular case, the reasons for the determination will be stated in the rulemaking document. Notice and public procedure may also be omitted with respect to statements of policy, interpretative rules, rules governing FEMA's organization or its own internal practices or procedures, or if a statute expressly authorizes omission.

(g) A final substantive rule will be published not less than 30 days before its effective date unless it grants or recognizes an exemption or relieves a restriction or unless the rulemaking document states good cause for its taking effect less than 30 days after publication. Statements of policy and interpretative rules will usually be made effective on the date of publication.

(h) This part shall not apply to any regulation that responds to an emergency situation, provided that, any such regulation shall be reported to the Director, Office of Management and Budget, as soon as is practicable. FEMA shall publish in the FEDERAL REGISTER a statement of the reasons why it is impracticable for the agency to follow the procedures of Executive Order 12866 with respect to such a rule, and the agency shall prepare and transmit, if needed, as soon as is practicable a Regulatory Impact Analysis of any such major rule.

[46 FR 32584, June 24, 1981, as amended at 49 FR 38119, Sept. 27, 1984; 50 FR 40004, Oct. 1, 1985]

§ 1.5 Rules docket.

(a) Documents which are public records and which are a part of a specific rulemaking procedure, including but not limited to, advance notices of proposed rulemaking, notices of proposed rulemaking, written comments addressed to the merits of a proposed rule, and comments received in response to notices, or withdrawals or terminations of proposed rulemaking, petitions for rulemaking, requests for oral argument in public participation cases, requests for extension of time, grants or denials of petitions or requests, transcripts or minutes of informal hearings, final rules and general notices shall be maintained in the Office of Chief Counsel. All public rulemaking comments should refer to the docket number which appears in the heading of the rule and should be addressed to the Rule Docket Clerk, Federal Emergency Management Agency, Office of Chief Counsel.

(b) Documents which are a part of a specific rulemaking proceeding are public records. After a docket is established, any person may examine docketed material at any time during established hours of business and may obtain a copy of any docketed material upon payment of the prescribed fee. (See part 5 of this chapter.)

[46 FR 32584, June 24, 1981, as amended at 48 FR 44542, Sept. 29, 1983]

§ 1.6 Ex parte communications.

In rulemaking proceedings subject only to the procedural requirements of 5 U.S.C. 553:

(a) All oral communications from outside FEMA of significant information and argument respecting the merits of a proposed rule, received after notice of proposed informal rulemaking and in its course by FEMA or its offices and divisions or their personnel participating in the decision, should be summarized in writing and placed promptly in the Rules Docket File available for public inspection.

(b) FEMA may conclude that restrictions on ex parte communications in particular rulemaking proceedings are necessitated by consideration of fairness or for other reasons.

§ 1.7 Regulations agendas.

(a) The FEMA semi-annual agenda called for by Executive Order 12291 will be part of the Unified Agenda of Federal Regulations published in April and October of each year.

(b) In accordance with 5 U.S.C. 605, the regulatory flexibility agenda required by 5 U.S.C. 602 and the list of rules, if any, to be reviewed pursuant to 5 U.S.C. 610 shall be included in the FEMA semiannual agenda described in paragraph (a) of this section.

(c) The semiannual agenda shall, among other items, include:

(1) A summary of the nature of each major rule being considered, the objectives and legal basis for the issuance of the rule, and an approximate schedule for completing action on any major rule for which the agency has issued a notice of proposed rulemaking.

(2) The name and telephone number of a knowledgeable agency official for each item on the agenda; and

(3) A list of existing regulations to be reviewed under the terms of the Order and a brief discussion of each such regulation.

[46 FR 32584, June 24, 1981, as amended at 49 FR 33878, Aug. 27, 1984]

§ 1.8 Regulations review.

(a) As part of the semiannual agenda described in § 1.7 of this part, FEMA will publish in the FEDERAL REGISTER and keep updated a plan for periodic review of existing rules at least within 10 years from date of publication of a rule as final. This includes those that have significant impact on a substantial number of small entities.

(b) The purpose of the review shall be to determine whether such rules should be continued without change, or should be amended or rescinded, consistent with the stated objectives of applicable statutes, including minimizing any significant economic impact of the rules upon a substantial number of small entities.

(c) In reviewing rules FEMA shall consider the following factors:

(1) The continued need for the rule;

(2) The nature, type and number of complaints or comments received concerning the rule from the public;

(3) The complexity of the rule, including need for review of language for clarity;

(4) The extent to which the rule overlaps, duplicates or conflicts with other Federal rules, and, to the extent feasible, with State and local governmental rules; and

(5) The length of time since the rule has been evaluated or the degree to which technology, economic conditions, or other factors have changed in the area affected by the rule.

§ 1.9 Regulatory impact analyses.

(a) FEMA shall, in connection with any major rule, prepare and consider a Regulatory Impact Analysis. Such analysis may be combined with the Regulatory Flexibility Analysis described in §§ 1.12(f) and 1.16(c) of this part.

(b) FEMA shall initially determine whether a rule it intends to propose or to issue is a major rule and, if a major rule, shall prepare Regulatory Impact Analyses and transmit them, along with all notices of proposed rulemaking and all final rules, to the Director, Office of Management and Budget, as follows:

(1) If no notice of proposed rulemaking is to be published for a proposed major rule that is not an emergency rule, the agency shall prepare only a final Regulatory Impact Analysis, which shall be transmitted, along with the proposed rule, to the Director, Office of Management and Budget, at least 60 days prior to the publication of the major rule as a final rule;

(2) With respect to all other major rules, FEMA shall prepare a preliminary Regulatory Impact Analysis, which shall be transmitted, along with a notice of proposed rulemaking, to the Director, Office of Management and Budget, at least 60 days prior to the publication of a notice of proposed rulemaking, and a final Regulatory Impact Analysis, which shall be transmitted along with the final rule at least 30 days prior to the publication of the major rule as a final rule;

(3) For all rules other than major rules, FEMA shall, unless an exemption has been granted, submit to the Director, Office of Management and

Budget, at least 10 days prior to publication, every notice of proposed rulemaking and final rule.

(c) To permit each major rule to be analyzed in light of the requirements stated in section 2 of Executive Order 12291, each preliminary and final Regulatory Impact Analysis shall contain the following information:

(1) A description of the potential benefits of the rule, including any beneficial effects that cannot be quantified in monetary terms, and the identification of those likely to receive the benefits;

(2) A description of the potential costs of the rule, including any adverse effects that cannot be quantified in monetary terms, and the identification of those likely to bear the costs;

(3) A determination of the potential net benefits of the rule, including an evaluation of effects that cannot be quantified in monetary terms;

(4) A description of alternative approaches that could substantially achieve the same regulatory goal at lower cost, together with an analysis of this potential benefit and costs and a brief explanation of the legal reasons why such alternatives, if proposed, could not be adopted; and

(5) Unless covered by the description required under paragraph (c)(4) of this section, an explanation of any legal reasons why the rule cannot be based on the requirements set forth in section 2 of Executive Order 12291.

Subpart B—Procedures for Rulemaking

§1.10 Initiation of rulemaking.

Rulemaking may be initiated on the Administrator's motion or upon motion of an official to whom rulemaking authority has been delegated. Rulemaking may also be initiated on the petition of any interested person in accordance with the provisions of §1.18. Interested person includes a Federal, State, or local government or government agency.

§1.11 Advance notice of proposed rulemaking.

An Advance Notice of Proposed Rulemaking will be published in the FEDERAL REGISTER and contains:

(a) A description of the proposed new program or program changes, and why they are needed;

(b) A presentation of the major policy issues involved;

(c) A request for comments, both specific and general, on the need for the proposed rule and the provisions that the rule might include;

(d) If appropriate, a list of questions about the proposal which seeks to bring out detailed comments;

(e) If known, an estimate of the reporting or recordkeeping requirements, if any, that the rule would impose; and

(f) The time within which comments may be submitted to the Rules Docket Clerk, Federal Emergency Management Agency, Washington, DC 20472.

[46 FR 32584, June 24, 1981, as amended at 48 FR 44542, Sept. 29, 1983; 49 FR 33879, Aug. 27, 1984]

§1.12 Notice of proposed rulemaking.

Each notice of proposed rulemaking required by statute, executive order, or by §1.4 will be published in the FEDERAL REGISTER and will include:

(a) The substance or terms of the proposed rule or a description of the subject matter and issues involved.

(b) A statement of how and to what extent interested persons may participate in the proceeding.

(c) Where participation is limited to written comments, a statement of the time within which such comments must be submitted.

(d) A reference to the legal authority under which the proposal is issued.

(e) In a proceeding which has provided Advance Notice of Proposed Rulemaking, an analysis of the principal issues and recommendations raised by the comments, and the manner in which they have been addressed in the proposed rulemaking.

(f)(1) A brief statement setting forth the agency's initial determination whether the proposed rule is a major rule, together with the reasons underlying that determination;

(2) For each proposed major rule, a brief summary of the agency's preliminary Regulatory Impact Analysis; and

(3) The initial regulatory flexibility analysis or a summary thereof as required by the Regulatory Flexibility

Act (5 U.S.C. 601, *et seq.*), or a certification that the rule, if promulgated, will not have a significant economic impact on a significant number of small entities pursuant to 5 U.S.C. 605. Such certification may be made by any FEMA official with rulemaking authority.

(g) It is desirable, but not required, that the notices contain a target deadline for issuance of the regulation, and that to the extent feasible, this deadline be met.

(h) If the rule is one which contains a requirement for collection of information, a copy of the rule will be furnished OMB in accordance with 44 U.S.C. 3504(h).

[46 FR 32584, June 24, 1981, as amended at 49 FR 38119, Sept. 27, 1984]

§ 1.13　Participation by interested persons.

(a) Unless the notice otherwise provides, any interested person may participate in rulemaking proceedings by submitting written data, views or arguments within the comment time stated in the notice. In addition, the Administrator may permit the filing of comments in response to original comments.

(b) In appropriate cases, the Administrator may provide for oral presentation of views in additional proceedings described in § 1.14.

(c) Copies of regulatory flexibility analyses shall be furnished the Chief Counsel for Advocacy of the Small Business Administration.

§ 1.14　Additional rulemaking proceedings.

The Administrator may invite interested persons to present oral arguments, appear at informal hearings, or participate in any other procedure affording opportunity for oral presentation of views. The transcript or minutes of such meetings, as appropriate, will be kept and filed in the Rules Docket.

§ 1.15　Hearings.

(a) The provisions of 5 U.S.C. 556 and 557, which govern formal hearings in adjudicatory proceedings, do not apply to informal rulemaking proceedings described in this part. When opportunity is afforded for oral presentation, the informal "hearing" is a nonadversary, fact-finding proceeding. Any rule issued in a proceeding under this part in which a hearing is held need not be based exclusively on the record of such hearing.

(b) When a hearing is provided, the Administrator will designate a representative to conduct the hearing.

§ 1.16　Adoption of a final rule.

(a) All timely comments will be considered in taking final action on a proposed rule. Each preamble to a final rule will contain a short analysis and evaluation of the relevant significant issues set forth in the comments submitted, and a clear concise statement of the basis and purpose of the rule.

(b) When determined necessary by the Administrator in accordance with the provisions of 1 CFR 18.12, the preamble shall contain the following information:

(1) A discussion of the background and major issues involved;

(2) In the case of a final rule, any significant differences between it and the proposed rule;

(3) A response to substantive public comments received; and

(4) Any other information the Administrator considers appropriate.

(c) At the time of publication of the final rule, a statement shall be published describing how the public may obtain copies of the final regulatory flexibility analysis which must be prepared in accordance with 5 U.S.C. 604 unless the procedure for waiver or delay of completion under 5 U.S.C. 608 is followed.

(d) Before approving any final major rule FEMA will:

(1) Make a determination that the regulation is clearly within the authority delegated by law and consistent with congressional intent and include in the FEDERAL REGISTER at the time of promulgation a memorandum of law supporting that determination; and

(2) Make a determination that the factual conclusions upon which the rule is based have substantial support in the agency record, viewed as a whole, with full attention to public

comments in general and the comments of persons directly affected by the rule in particular.

§ 1.17 Petitions for reconsideration.

Petitions for reconsideration of a final rule will not be considered. Such petitions, if filed, will be treated as petitions for rulemaking in accordance with § 1.18.

§ 1.18 Petition for rulemaking.

(a) Any interested person may petition the Administrator for the issuance, amendment, or repeal of a rule. For purposes of this section the term *person* includes a Federal, State or local government or government agency. Each petition shall:

(1) Be submitted to the Rules Docket Clerk;

(2) Set forth the substance of the rule or amendment proposed or specify the rule sought to be repealed or amended;

(3) Explain the interest of the petitioner in support of the action sought; and

(4) Set forth all data and arguments available to the petitioner in support of the action sought.

(b) No public procedures will be held directly on the petition before its disposition. If the Administrator finds that the petition contains adequate justification, a rulemaking proceeding will be initiated or a final rule will be issued as appropriate. If the Administrator finds that the petition does not

contain adequate justification, the petition will be denied by letter or other notice, with a brief statement of the ground for denial. The Administrator may consider new evidence at any time; however, repetitious petitions for rulemaking will not be considered.

PART 2—OMB CONTROL NUMBERS

Sec.
2.1 Purpose.
2.2 OMB control numbers assigned to information collections.

AUTHORITY: 5 U.S.C. 552; 42 U.S.C. 3507; Reorganization Plan No. 3 of 1978, 5 U.S.C. App. 1; E.O. 12127, 3 CFR, 1979 Comp., p. 376; E.O. 12148, as amended, 3 CFR, 1979 Comp., p. 412.

SOURCE: 74 FR 15332, Apr. 3, 2009, unless otherwise noted.

§ 2.1 Purpose.

This part collects and displays the control numbers assigned to information collection requirements of FEMA by the Office of Management and Budget (OMB) pursuant to the Paperwork Reduction Act of 1980 (44 U.S.C. 3501 *et seq.*). FEMA intends that this part comply with the requirements of section 3507(f) of the Paperwork Reduction Act, which requires that agencies display a current control number assigned by the Director of OMB for each agency information collection requirement.

§ 2.2 OMB control numbers assigned to information collections.

44 CFR part or section where identified or described	Current OMB Control No.
59	1660–0023
59.22	1660–0003, 1660–0004
59 subpart C	1660–0045
60.6, 60.3	1660–0033
61.13	1660–0006
62 subpart B	1660–0005,1660–0095
62.23(l)	1660–0086
62.24	1660–0020, 1660–0038
65, 70 generally	1660–0037
71.4	1660–0010
72	1660–0015, 1660–0016
75.11	1660–0013
78	1660–0062, 1660–0072,1660–0075
79.7(d)	1660–0104
80	1660–0103
151.11	1660–0014
152.4, 152.7	1660–0069
201	1660–0062, 1660–0072, 1660–0103
204	1660–0058
206 subpart B: 206.34, 206.35, 206.36, 206.46, 206.47	1660–0009
206 subpart D: 206.101(e), 202.110, 206.117, 206.119	1660–0002
206.112, 206.114, 206.115	1660–0061
206.171	1660–0085
206.202(f)(2), 206.203(c), 206.203(d)(i), 206.204(f)	1660–0017

44 CFR part or section where identified or described	Current OMB Control No.
206 subpart K	1660–0082, 1660–0083
206 subpart N	1660–0076
206.437	1660–0026
206.440	1660–0076
208	1660–0073
352	1660–0024

PART 3 [RESERVED]

PART 4—INTERGOVERNMENTAL REVIEW OF FEDERAL EMERGENCY MANAGEMENT AGENCY (FEMA) PROGRAMS AND ACTIVITIES

Sec.
4.1 What is the purpose of these regulations?
4.2 What definitions apply to these regulations?
4.3 What programs and activities of FEMA are subject to these regulations?
4.4 [Reserved]
4.5 What is the Administrator's obligation with respect to Federal interagency coordination?
4.6 What procedures apply to the selection of programs and activities under these regulations?
4.7 How does the Administrator communicate with State and local officials concerning FEMA's programs and activities?
4.8 How does the Administrator provide an opportunity to comment on proposed Federal financial assistance and direct Federal development?
4.9 How does the Administrator receive and respond to comments?
4.10 How does the Administrator make efforts to accommodate intergovernmental concerns?
4.11 What are the Administrator's obligations in interstate situations?
4.12 How may a State simplify, consolidate, or substitute federally required State plans?
4.13 May the Administrator waive any provision of these regulations?

AUTHORITY: E.O. 12372, July 14, 1982 (47 FR 30959), as amended April 8, 1983 (48 FR 15887); sec. 401, Intergovernmental Cooperation Act of 1968, as amended (31 U.S.C. 6506); sec. 204, Demonstration Cities and Metropolitan Development Act of 1966, as amended (42 U.S.C. 3334).

SOURCE: 48 FR 29316, June 24, 1983, unless otherwise noted.

EDITORIAL NOTE: For additional information, see related documents published at 47 FR 57369, Dec. 23, 1982; 48 FR 17101, Apr. 21, 1983; and 48 FR 29096, June 24, 1983.

§ 4.1 What is the purpose of these regulations?

(a) The regulations in this part implement Executive Order 12372, "Intergovernmental Review of Federal Programs," issued July 14, 1982 and amended on April 8, 1983. These regulations also implement applicable provisions of section 401 of the Intergovernmental Cooperation Act of 1968 and section 204 of the Demonstration Cities and Metropolitan Development Act of 1966.

(b) These regulations are intended to foster an intergovernmental partnership and a strengthened Federalism by relying on state processes and on State, areawide, regional and local coordination for review of proposed Federal financial assistance and direct Federal development.

(c) These regulations are intended to aid the internal management of FEMA, and are not intended to create any right or benefit enforceable at law by a party against FEMA or its officers.

§ 4.2 What definitions apply to these regulations?

Administrator means the Administrator of FEMA or an official or employee of FEMA acting for the Administrator of FEMA under a delegation of authority.

FEMA means the Federal Emergency Management Agency.

Order means Executive Order 12372, issued July 14, 1982, and amended April 8, 1983 and titled "Intergovernmental Review of Federal Programs."

State means any of the 50 states, the District of Columbia, the Commonwealth of Puerto Rico, the Commonwealth of Northern Mariana Islands, Guam, American Samoa, the U.S. Virgin Islands, or the Trust Territory of the Pacific Islands.

[48 FR 29316, June 24, 1983, as amended at 74 FR 15332, Apr. 3, 2009]

§4.3 What programs and activities of FEMA are subject to these regulations?

The Administrator publishes in the FEDERAL REGISTER a list of FEMA's programs and activities that are subject to these regulations and identifies which of these are subject to the requirements of section 204 of the Demonstration Cities and Metropolitan Development Act.

§4.4 [Reserved]

§4.5 What is the Administrator's obligation with respect to Federal interagency coordination?

The Administrator, to the extent practicable, consults with and seeks advice from all other substantially affected Federal departments and agencies in an effort to assure full coordination between such agencies and FEMA regarding programs and activities covered under these regulations.

§4.6 What procedures apply to the selection of programs and activities under these regulations?

(a) A State may select any program or activity published in the FEDERAL REGISTER in accordance with §4.3 of this part for intergovernmental review under these regulations. Each State, before selecting programs and activities, shall consult with local elected officials.

(b) Each State that adopts a process shall notify the Administrator of FEMA's programs and activities selected for that process.

(c) A State may notify the Administrator of changes in its selections at any time. For each change, the State shall submit to the Administrator an assurance that the State has consulted with local elected officials regarding the change. FEMA may establish deadlines by which States are required to inform the Administrator of changes in their program selections.

(d) The Administrator uses a State's process as soon as feasible, depending on individual programs and activities, after the Administrator is notified of its selections.

§4.7 How does the Administrator communicate with State and local officials concerning FEMA's programs and activities?

(a) For those programs and activities covered by a state process under §4.6, the Administrator, to the extent permitted by law:

(1) Uses the state process to determine views of State and local elected officials; and,

(2) Communicates with State and local elected officials, through the state process, as early in a program planning cycle as is reasonably feasible to explain specific plans and actions.

(b) The Administrator provides notice to directly affected State, areawide, regional, and local entities in a State of proposed Federal financial assistance or direct Federal development if:

(1) The State has not adopted a process under the Order; or

(2) The assistance or development involves a program or activity not selected for the State process.

This notice may be made by publication in the FEDERAL REGISTER or other appropriate means, which FEMA in its discretion deems appropriate.

§4.8 How does the Administrator provide an opportunity to comment on proposed Federal financial assistance and direct Federal development?

(a) Except in unusual circumstances, the Administrator gives state processes or directly affected State, areawide, regional and local officials and entities at least 60 days from the date established by the Administrator to comment on proposed direct Federal development or Federal financial assistance.

(b) This section also applies to comments in cases in which the review, coordination, and communication with FEMA have been delegated.

(c) Applicants for programs and activities subject to section 204 of the Demonstration Cities and Metropolitan Act shall allow areawide agencies a 60-day opportunity for review and comment.

§4.9 How does the Administrator receive and respond to comments?

(a) The Administrator follows the procedures in §4.10 if:

(1) A State office or official is designated to act as a single point of contact between a state process and all Federal agencies, and

(2) That office or official transmits a state process recommendation for a program selected under §4.6.

(b)(1) The single point of contact is not obligated to transmit comments from State, areawide, regional or local officials and entities where there is no state process recommendation.

(2) If a state process recommendation is transmitted by a single point of contact, all comments from state, areawide, regional, and local officials and entities that differ from it must also be transmitted.

(c) If a State has not established a process, or is unable to submit a state process recommendation, State, areawide, regional and local officials and entities may submit comments to FEMA.

(d) If a program or activity is not selected for a state process, State, areawide, regional and local officials and entities may submit comments to FEMA. In addition, if a state process recommendation for a nonselected program or activity is transmitted to FEMA by the single point of contact, the Administrator follows the procedures of §4.10 of this part.

(e) The Administrator considers comments which do not constitute a state process recommendation submitted under these regulations and for which the Administrator is not required to apply the procedures of §4.10 of this part, when such comments are provided by a single point of contact, by the applicant or directly to FEMA by a commenting party.

§4.10 How does the Administrator make efforts to accommodate intergovernmental concerns?

(a) If a state process provides a state process recommendation to FEMA through its single point of contact, the Administrator either:

(1) Accepts the recommendation;

(2) Reaches a mutually agreeable solution with the state process; or

(3) Provides the single point of contact with such written explanation of the decision, as the Administrator in his or her discretion deems appropriate. The Administrator may also supplement the written explanation by providing the explanation to the single point of contact by telephone, other telecommunication, or other means.

(b) In any explanation under paragraph (a)(3) of this section, the Administrator informs the single point of contact that:

(1) FEMA will not implement its decision for at least ten days after the single point of contact receives the explanation; or

(2) The Administrator has reviewed the decision and determined that, because of unusual circumstances, the waiting period of at least ten days is not feasible.

(c) For purposes of computing the waiting period under paragraph (b)(1) of this section, a single point of contact is presumed to have received written notification 5 days after the date of mailing of such notification.

§4.11 What are the Administrator's obligations in interstate situations?

(a) The Administrator is responsible for:

(1) Identifying proposed Federal financial assistance and direct Federal development that have an impact on interstate areas;

(2) Notifying appropriate officials and entities in states which have adopted a process and which select FEMA's program or activity;

(3) Making efforts to identify and notify the affected State, areawide, regional, and local officials and entities in those States that have not adopted a process under the Order or do not select FEMA's program or activity;

(4) Responding pursuant to §4.10 of this part if the Administrator receives a recommendation from a designated areawide agency transmitted by a single point of contact, in cases in which the review, coordination, and communication with FEMA have been delegated.

(b) The Administrator uses the procedures in §4.10 if a state process provides a state process recommendation to FEMA through a single point of contact.

§ 4.12 How may a State simplify, consolidate, or substitute federally required State plans?

(a) As used in this section:

(1) *Simplify* means that a State may develop its own format, choose its own submission date, and select the planning period for a State plan.

(2) *Consolidate* means that a State may meet statutory and regulatory requirements by combining two or more plans into one document and that the State can select the format, submission date, and planning period for the consolidated plan.

(3) *Substitute* means that a State may use a plan or other document that it has developed for its own purposes to meet Federal requirements.

(b) If not inconsistent with law, a State may decide to try to simplify, consolidate, or substitute federally required state plans without prior approval by the Administrator.

(c) The Administrator reviews each state plan that a State has simplified, consolidated, or substituted and accepts the plan only if its contents meet Federal requirements.

§ 4.13 May the Administrator waive any provision of these regulations?

In an emergency, the Administrator may waive any provision of these regulations.

PART 5—PRODUCTION OR DISCLOSURE OF INFORMATION

Subpart A—General Provisions

Subpart B—Publication of or Availability of General Agency Information, Rules, Orders, Policies, and Similar Material

Subpart C—Fees

Subpart D—Described Records

Subpart E—Exemptions

Subpart F—Subpoenas or Other Legal Demands for Testimony or the Production or Disclosure of Records or Other Information

AUTHORITY: 5 U.S.C. 552; 5 U.S.C. 301; 6 U.S.C. 101 *et seq*; Reorganization Plan No. 3 of 1978; E.O. 12127; and E.O. 12148.

SOURCE: 44 FR 50287, Aug. 27, 1979, unless otherwise noted.

Subpart A—General Provisions

§ 5.1 Scope and purposes of part.

This part sets forth policies and procedures concerning the availability of and disclosure of records and information held by the Federal Emergency Management Agency (FEMA) in accordance with 5 U.S.C. 552, popularly known as the "Freedom of Information Act," (FOIA).

§ 5.2 Application.

This part applies to all records and information materials generated, developed, or held by FEMA at Headquarters, in Regions, or in the field, or any component thereof.

§ 5.3 Definitions.

For purposes of this part, the following terms have the meanings ascribed to them in this section:

(a) *Records. Records* means all books, papers, maps, photographs, or other documentary materials, regardless of physical form or characteristics made or received by FEMA in pursuance of Federal Law or in connection with the transaction of public business and preserved, or appropriate for preservation, as evidence of the organization, functions, policies, decisions, procedures, operations, or other activities of FEMA or because of the information value of data contained therein. The term does not include:

(1) Material made or acquired and preserved solely for reference or exhibition purposes, extra copies of documents preserved only for convenience of reference, and stocks of publications and of processed documents; or

(2) Objects or articles, such as structures, furniture, paintings, sculpture, models, vehicles or equipment; or

(3) Formulae, designs, drawings, research data, computer programs, technical data packages, and the like, which are not considered *records* within the Congressional intent of reference because of development costs, utilization, or value. These items are considered exploitable resources to be utilized in the best interest of *all* the public and are not preserved for informational value nor as evidence of agency functions. Requests for copies of such material shall be evaluated in accordance with policies expressly directed to the appropriate dissemination or use of these resources. Requests to inspect this material to determine its content for informational purposes shall normally be granted, unless inspection is inconsistent with the obligation to protect the property value of the material, as, for example, may be true for patent information and certain formulae, or is inconsistent with another significant and legitimate governmental purpose.

(b) *Reasonably Described. Reasonably described*, when applied to a request record, means identifying it to the extent that it will permit the location of the particular document with a reasonable effort.

(c) *Agency. Agency*, as defined in section 552(e) of title 5 U.S.C., includes any executive department, military department, government corporation, or other establishment in the executive branch of the Government (including the Executive Office of the President), or any independent regulatory agency.

(d) *Headquarters FOIA Officer.* The FOIA/Privacy Act Specialist or his/her designee.

(e) *Regional FOIA Officer.* The Regional Administrator, or his/her designee.

[44 FR 50287, Aug. 27, 1979, as amended at 45 FR 1421, Jan. 7, 1980; 51 FR 34604, Sept. 30, 1986]

§5.4 Availability of records.

(a) FEMA records are available to the greatest extent possible in keeping with the spirit and intent of FOIA and will be furnished promptly to any member of the public upon request addressed to the office designated in §5.26. The person making the request need not have a particular interest in the subject matter, nor must he provide justification for the request.

(b) The requirement of 5 U.S.C. 552 that records be available to the public refers only to records in being at the time the request for them is made. FOIA imposes no obligation to compile a record in response to a request.

§5.5 Exemptions.

Requests for FEMA records may be denied if disclosure is exempted under the provisions of 5 U.S.C. 552, as outlined in subpart E. Usually, except when a record is classified, or when disclosure would violate any other Federal statute, the authority to withhold a record from disclosure is permissive rather than mandatory. The authority for nondisclosure will not be invoked unless there is compelling reason to do so.

§5.6 Congressional information.

Nothing in this part authorizes withholding information from the Congress except when executive privilege is invoked by the President.

§5.7 Records of other agencies.

If a request is submitted to FEMA to make available current records which are the primary responsibility of another agency, FEMA will refer the request to the agency concerned for appropriate action. FEMA will advise the requester that the request has been forwarded to the responsible agency.

§5.8 Records involved in litigation or other judicial process.

Where there is reason to believe that any records requested may be involved in litigation or other judicial process in which the United States is a party, including discovery procedures pursuant to the Federal Rules of Civil Procedure or Federal Rules of Criminal Procedure, the request shall be referred to the Chief Counsel.

§5.9 Inconsistent issuances of FEMA and its predecessor agencies superseded.

Policies and procedures of any of FEMA's predecessor agencies inconsistent with this regulation are superseded to the extent of that inconsistency.

Subpart B—Publication of or Availability of General Agency Information, Rules, Orders, Policies, and Similar Material

§5.20 Publication of rules and general policies.

In accordance with 5 U.S.C. 552(a)(1), there are separately stated and currently published, or from time to time there will be published, in the FEDERAL REGISTER for the guidance of the public, the following general information concerning FEMA:

(a) Description of the organization of the Headquarters Office and regional and other offices and the established places at which, the employees from whom, and the methods whereby the public may obtain information, make submittals or requests, or obtain decisions.

(b) Statement of the general course and method by which FEMA functions are channeled and determined, including the nature and requirements of all formal and informal procedures available.

(c) Rules of procedure, descriptions of forms available or the places at which forms may be obtained, and instructions as to the scope and contents of all papers, reports, or examinations.

(d) Substantive rules of general applicability adopted as authorized by law, and statements of general policy or interpretations of general applicability formulated and adopted by FEMA.

(e) Each amendment, revision, or repeal of the materials described in this section. Much of this information will also be codified in this subchapter A.

§ 5.21 Effect of failure to publish.

5 U.S.C. 552(a)(1) provides that, except to the extent that a person has actual and timely notice of the terms thereof, a person may not in any manner be required to resort to, or to be adversely affected by, a matter required to be published in the FEDERAL REGISTER and not so published.

§ 5.22 Coordination of publication.

The Chief Counsel, FEMA, is responsible for coordination of FEMA materials required to be published in the FEDERAL REGISTER.

§ 5.23 Incorporation by reference.

When deemed appropriate, matter covered by this subpart, which is reasonably available to the class of persons affected thereby may be incorporated by reference in the FEDERAL REGISTER in accordance with standards prescribed from time to time by the Director of the Federal Register (see 1 CFR part 51).

§ 5.24 Availability of opinions, orders, policies, interpretations, manuals, and instructions.

FEMA will make available for public inspection and copying the material described in 5 U.S.C. 552(a)(2) as enumerated in § 5.25 and an index of those materials as described in § 5.28, at convenient places and times.

§ 5.25 Available materials.

FEMA materials which are available under this subpart are as follows:

(a) Final opinions and orders made in the adjudication of cases.

(b) Those statements of policy and interpretations which have been adopted by FEMA and are not published in the FEDERAL REGISTER.

(c) Administrative staff manuals and instructions to staff that affect a member of the public, unless such materials are promptly published and copies offered for sale.

§ 5.26 Rules for public inspection and copying.

(a) *Location.* Materials are available for public inspection and copying at the following locations:

(1) Headquarters:

Federal Center Plaza, 500 C Street, SW, Washington, DC 20472

(2) *Regional Offices*

Region I: 99 High Street, 6th Floor, Boston, Massachusetts 02110.

Region II: 26 Federal Plaza, Suite 1337, New York, New York 10278.

Region III: 615 Chestnut Street, One Independence Mall, 6th Floor, Philadelphia, Pennsylvania 19106.

Region IV: 3003 Chamblee Tucker Road, Atlanta, Georgia 30341.

Region V: 536 South Clark Street, 6th Floor, Chicago, Illinois 60605.

Region VI: Federal Regional Center, 800 North Loop 288, Denton, Texas 76209.

Region VII: 9221 Ward Parkway, Suite 300, Kansas City, Missouri 64114.

Region VIII: Denver Federal Center, Building 710, Box 25267, Denver, Colorado 80255.

Region IX: 1111 Broadway, Suite 1200, Oakland, California 94607.

Region X: Federal Regional Center, 130 228th Street SW, Bothell, Washington 98021.

(b) *Time.* Materials will be made available for public inspection and copying during the normal hours of business.

(c) FEMA will furnish reasonable copying services at fees specified in subpart C. Such reproduction services as are required will be arranged by the Office of Administrative Support in the headquarters or by regional offices as appropriate.

(d) *Handling of materials.* The unlawful removal or mutilation of materials is forbidden by law and is punishable by fine or imprisonment or both. FEMA personnel making materials available will ensure that all materials provided for inspection and copying are returned in the same condition as provided.

[44 FR 50287, Aug. 27, 1979, as amended at 47 FR 13149, Mar. 29, 1982; 48 FR 44542, Sept. 29, 1983; 50 FR 40006, Oct. 1, 1985; 74 FR 15333, Apr. 3, 2009]

§ 5.27 Deletion of identifying details.

To the extent required to prevent a clearly unwarranted invasion of personal privacy, FEMA may delete identifying details when making available or publishing an opinion, statement of policy, interpretation, or staff manual or instruction. However, the justification for each deletion will be explained fully in writing, and will require the concurrence of the Chief Counsel. A copy of the justification will be attached to the material containing the deletion and a copy will also be furnished to the Headquarters FOIA Officer or appropriate Regional Administrator.

§ 5.28 Indexes.

FEMA will maintain and make available for public inspection and copying current indexes arranged by subject matter providing identifying information for the public regarding any matter issued, adopted, or promulgated after July 4, 1967, and described in § 5.25. FEMA will publish quarterly and make available copies of each index or supplements thereto. The indexes will be maintained for public inspection at the location described in § 5.26.

§ 5.29 Effect of failure to make information materials available.

Materials requested to be made available pursuant to § 5.24 that affect a member of the public may be relied upon, used, or cited as precedent by FEMA against any private party only if (a) they have been indexed and either made available or published as required by 5 U.S.C. 552(a)(2), or (b) the private party has actual and timely notice of their terms.

Subpart C—Fees

§ 5.40 Copies of FEMA records available at a fee.

One copy of FEMA records not available free of charge will be provided at a fee as provided in § 5.46. A reasonable number of additional copies will be provided for the applicable fee where reproduction services are not readily obtainable from private commercial sources.

§ 5.41 FEMA publications.

Anyone may obtain FEMA publications without charge from the FEMA Headquarters, Regional Offices, the FEMA Library at www. FEMA.gov, or from the FEMA Distribution Center at P.O. Box 2012, 8231 Stayton Drive, Jessup, Maryland 20794 in accordance with standard operating procedures, including limitation on numbers of specific individual publications. FEMA Films may be obtained on loan or certain of these films may be purchased, in which case fees will be charged as set out in a FEMA catalogue. Non-exempt FEMA research reports are available from the National Technical Information Service, United States Department of Commerce, which establishes its own fee schedule. Charges, if any, for these items and similar user charges are established in accordance with other provisions of law as, for example, 31 U.S.C. 9701 and are not deemed search and duplication charges hereunder.

[44 FR 50287, Aug. 27, 1979, as amended at 48 FR 44542, Sept. 29, 1983; 50 FR 40006, Oct. 1, 1985]

§ 5.42 Fees to be charged—categories of requesters.

(a) There are four categories of FOIA requesters: Commercial use requesters; representatives of news media; educational and noncommercial scientific institutions; and all other requesters. The time limits for processing requests shall only begin upon receipt of a proper request which reasonably identifies records being sought. The Freedom of Information Reform Act of 1986 prescribes specific levels of fees for each of these categories:

(1) When records are being requested for commercial use, the fee policy of FEMA is to levy full allowable direct cost of searching for, reviewing for release, and duplicating the records sought. Commercial users are not entitled to two hours of free search time nor 100 free pages of reproduction of documents. The full allowable direct cost of searching for and reviewing records will be charged even if there is ultimately no disclosure of records. Commercial use is defined as a use that furthers the commercial, trade or profit interests of the requester or person on whose behalf the request is made. In determining whether a requester falls within the commercial use category, FEMA will look to the use to which a requester will put the documents requested. Where a requester does not explain his/her use, or where his/her explanation is insufficient to permit a determination of the nature of the use, FEMA shall require the requester to provide information regarding the use to be made of the information and if

the request does not include an agreement to pay all appropriate fees, FEMA will process such request only up to the $30.00 threshold which is the estimated cost to FEMA to collect fees which we are prohibited from charging by law. Requesters must reasonably describe the records sought.

(2) When records are being requested by representatives of the news media, the fee policy of FEMA is to levy reproduction charges only, excluding charges for the first 100 pages. Representatives of the news media refers to any person actively gathering news for an entity that is organized and operated to publish or broadcast news to the public. The term *news* means information that is about current events or that would be of current interest to the public. Examples of news media entities include television or radio stations broadcasting to the public at large, and publishers of periodicals (but only in those instances where they can qualify as disseminators of "news") who make their products available for purchase or subscription by the general public. These examples are not intended to be all-inclusive. As traditional methods of news delivery evolve (i.e., electronic dissemination of newspapers through telecommunications services), such alternative media would be included in this category. In the case of "freelance" journalists, they may be regarded as working for a news organization if they can demonstrate a solid basis for expecting publication through that organization, even though not actually employed by it. For example, a publication contract would be the clearest proof, but FEMA may also look to the past publication record, press accreditation, guild membership, business registration, Federal Communications Commission licensing, or similar credentials of a requester in making this determination. To be eligible for inclusion in this category, requesters must meet the criteria specified in this section and his or her request must not be made for a commercial use basis as that term is defined under paragraph (a)(1) of this section. A request for records supporting the news dissemination function of the requester shall not be considered to be a request that is for a commercial use.

Requesters must reasonably describe the records sought.

(3) When records are being requested by an educational or noncommercial scientific institution whose purpose is scholarly or scientific research, the fee policy of FEMA is to levy reproduction charges only, excluding charges for the first 100 pages. Educational institution refers to a preschool, a public or private elementary or secondary school, an institution of graduate higher education, an institution of undergraduate higher education, an institution of professional education and an institution of vocational education, which operates a program or programs of scholarly research. Noncommercial scientific institution refers to an institution that is not operated on a commercial basis as that term is defined under paragraph (a)(1) of this section and which is operated solely for the purpose of conducting scientific research, the results of which are not intended to promote any particular product or industry. To be eligible for inclusion in this category, requesters must show that the request is being made under the auspices of a qualifying institution and that the records are not sought for a commercial use, but are sought in furtherance of scholarly (if the request is from an educational institution) or scientific (if the request is from a noncommercial scientific institution) research. Requesters must reasonably describe the records sought.

(4) For any other request which does not meet the criteria contained in paragraphs (a)(1) through (3) of this section, the fee policy of FEMA is to levy full reasonable direct cost of searching for and duplicating the records sought, except that the first 100 pages of reproduction and the first two hours of search time shall be furnished without charge. The first two hours of computer search time is based on the hourly cost of operating the central processing unit and the operator's hourly salary plus 16 percent. When the cost of the computer search, including the operator time and the cost of operating the computer to process the request, equals the equivalent dollar amount of two hours of the salary of the person performing the search, i.e.,

the operator, FEMA shall begin assessing charges for computer search. Requests from individuals requesting records about themselves filed in FEMA's systems of records shall continue to be treated under the fee provisions of the Privacy Act of 1974 which permit fees only for reproduction. Requesters must reasonably describe the records sought.

(b) Except for requests that are for a commercial use, FEMA may not charge for the first two hours of search time or for the first 100 pages of reproduction. However, a requester may not file multiple requests at the same time, each seeking portions of a document or documents, solely in order to avoid payment of fees. When FEMA believes that a requester or, on rare occasions, a group of requesters acting in concert, is attempting to break a request down into a series of requests for the purpose of evading the assessment of fees, FEMA may aggregate any such requests and charge accordingly. For example, it would be reasonable to presume that multiple requests of this type made within a 30-day period had been made to avoid fees. For requests made over a longer period, however, FEMA must have a solid basis for determining that aggregation is warranted in such cases. Before aggregating requests from more than one requester, FEMA must have a concrete basis on which to conclude that the requesters are acting in concert and are acting specifically to avoid payment of fees. In no case may FEMA aggregate multiple requests on unrelated subjects from one requester.

(c) In accordance with the prohibition of section (4)(A)(iv) of the Freedom of Information Act, as amended, FEMA shall not charge fees to any requester, including commercial use requesters, if the cost of collecting a fee would be equal to or greater than the fee itself.

(1) For commercial use requesters, if the direct cost of searching for, reviewing for release, and duplicating the records sought would not exceed $30.00, FEMA shall not charge the requester any costs.

(2) For requests from representatives of news media or educational and noncommercial scientific institutions, ex-cluding the first 100 pages which are provided at no charge, if the duplication cost would not exceed $30.00, FEMA shall not charge the requester any costs.

(3) For all other requests not falling within the category of commercial use requests, representatives of news media, or educational and noncommercial scientific institutions, if the direct cost of searching for and duplicating the records sought, excluding the first two hours of search time and first 100 pages which are free of charge, would not exceed $30.00, FEMA shall not charge the requester any costs.

[52 FR 13677, Apr. 24, 1987]

§5.43 **Waiver or reduction of fees.**

(a) FEMA may waive all fees or levy a reduced fee when disclosure of the information requested is deemed to be in the public interest because it is likely to contribute significantly to public understanding of the operations or activities of the Federal Government and is not primarily in the commercial interest of the requester.

(b) A fee waiver request shall indicate how the information will be used, to whom it will be provided, whether the requester intends to use the information for resale at a fee above actual cost, any personal or commercial benefits that the requester reasonably expects to receive by the disclosure, provide justification to support how release would benefit the general public, the requester's and/or intended user's identity and qualifications, expertise in the subject area and ability and intention to disseminate the information to the public.

[52 FR 13678, Apr. 24, 1987]

§5.44 **Prepayment of fees.**

(a) When FEMA estimates or determines that allowable charges that a requester may be required to pay are likely to exceed $250.00, FEMA may require a requester to make an advance payment of the entire fee before continuing to process the request.

(b) When a requester has previously failed to pay a fee charged in a timely fashion (i.e., within 30 days of the date of the billing), FEMA may require the requester to pay the full amount owed plus any applicable interest as provided in § 5.46(d), and to make an advance payment of the full amount of the estimated fee before the agency begins to process a new request or a pending request from that requester.

(c) When FEMA acts under paragraphs (a) or (b) of this section, the administrative time limits prescribed in subsection (a)(6) of the FOIA (i.e., 10 working days from the receipt of initial requests and 20 working days from receipt of appeals from initial denial, plus permissible extensions of these time limits) will begin only after FEMA has received fee payments described under paragraphs (a) or (b) of this section.

[52 FR 13678, Apr. 24, 1987]

§ 5.45   Form of payment.

Payment shall be by check or money order payable to the Federal Emergency Management Agency and shall be addressed to the official designated by FEMA in correspondence with the requestor or to the Headquarters FOIA Officer or Regional FOIA Officer, as appropriate.

[44 FR 50287, Aug. 27, 1979, as amended at 48 FR 44542, Sept. 29, 1983]

§ 5.46   Fee schedule.

(a) *Manual searches for records.* FEMA will charge at the salary rate(s), (i.e., basic hourly pay rate plus 16 percent) of the employee(s) conducting the search. FEMA may assess charges for time spent searching, even if the agency fails to locate the records or if records located are determined to be exempt from disclosure. FEMA may assess charges for time spent searching, even if FEMA fails to locate the records or if records located are determined to be exempt from disclosure.

(b) *Computer searches for records.* FEMA will charge the actual direct cost of providing the service. This will include the cost of operating the central processing unit (CPU) for that portion of operating time that is directly attributable to searching for records responsive to a FOIA request and operator/programmer salary apportionable to the search. FEMA may assess charges for time spent searching, even if FEMA fails to locate the records or

if records located are determined to be exempt from disclosure.

(c) *Duplication costs.* (1) For copies of documents reproduced on a standard office copying machine in sizes up to 8½ x 14 inches, the charge will be $.15 per page.

(2) The fee for reproducing copies of records over 8½ x 14 inches or whose physical characteristics do not permit reproduction by routine electrostatic copying shall be the direct cost of reproducing the records through government or commercial sources. If FEMA estimates that the allowable duplication charges are likely to exceed $25, it shall notify the requester of the estimated amount of fees, unless the requester has indicated in advance his/her willingness to pay fees as high as those anticipated. Such a notice shall offer a requester the opportunity to confer with agency personnel with the objective of reformulating the request to meet his/her needs at a lower cost.

(3) For copies prepared by computer, such as tapes or printouts, FEMA shall charge the actual cost, including operator time, of production of the tape or printout. If FEMA estimates that the allowable duplication charges are likely to exceed $25, it shall notify the requester of the estimated amount of fees, unless the requester has indicated in advance his/her willingness to pay fees as high as those anticipated. Such a notice shall offer a requester the opportunity to confer with agency personnel with the objective of reformulating the request to meet his/her needs at a lower cost.

(4) For other methods of reproduction or duplication, FEMA shall charge the actual direct costs of producing the document(s). If FEMA estimates that the allowable duplication charges are likely to exceed $25, it shall notify the requester of the estimated amount of fees, unless the requester has indicated in advance his/her willingness to pay fees as high as those anticipated. Such a notice shall offer a requester the opportunity to confer with agency personnel with the objective of reformulating the request to meet his/her needs at a lower cost.

(d) Interest may be charged to those requesters who fail to pay fees charged. FEMA may begin assessing interest charges on the amount billed starting on the 31st day following the day on which the billing was sent. Interest will be at the rate prescribed in section 3717 of Title 31 U.S.C. and will accrue from the date of the billing.

(e) FEMA shall use the most efficient and least costly methods to comply with requests for documents made under the FOIA. FEMA may choose to contract with private sector services to locate, reproduce and disseminate records in response to FOIA requests when that is the most efficient and least costly method. When documents responsive to a request are maintained for distribution by agencies operating statutory-based fee schedule programs, such as but not limited to the Government Printing Office or the National Technical Information Service, FEMA will inform requesters of the steps necessary to obtain records from those sources.

[52 FR 13678, Apr.24, 1987, as amended at 52 FR 33410, Sept. 3, 1987]

§5.47   Appeals regarding fees.

A requestor whose application for a fee waiver or a fee reduction is denied may appeal that decision to the Deputy Administrator in the manner prescribed in subpart D.

Subpart D—Described Records

§5.50   General.

(a) Except for records made available pursuant to subpart B, FEMA shall promptly make records available to a requestor pursuant to a request which reasonably described such records unless FEMA invokes an exemption pursuant to subpart E. Although the burden of reasonable description of the records rests with the requestor, FEMA will assist in identification to the extent practicable. Where requested records may be involved in litigation or other judicial proceedings in which the United States is a party, the procedures set forth under §5.8 shall be followed.

(b) Upon receipt of a request which does not reasonably describe the records requested, FEMA may contact the requestor to seek a more specific description. The 10-day time limit set

forth in §5.52 will not start until a request reasonably describing the records is received in the office of the appropriate official identified in §5.51.

§5.51   Submission of requests for described records.

(a) For records located in the FEMA Headquarters, requests shall be submitted in writing, to the Headquarters FOIA Officer, Federal Emergency Management Agency, Washington, DC 20472. For records located in the FEMA Regional Offices, requests shall be submitted to the appropriate Regional FOIA Officer, at the address listed in §5.26. Requests should bear the legend "Freedom of Information Request" prominently marked on both the face of the request letter and the envelope. The 10-day time limit for agency determinations set forth in §5.52 shall not start until a request is received in the office of the appropriate official identified in this paragraph.

(b) The Headquarters FOIA Officer shall respond to questions concerning the proper office to which Freedom of Information requests should be addressed.

§5.52   Review of requests.

(a) Upon receipt of a request for information, the Headquarters FOIA Officer, or the Regional FOIA Officer for a regional office, will forward the request to the FEMA office which has custody of the record.

(b) Upon any request for records made pursuant to §5.20, §5.24, or §5.51, the office having custody of the records shall determine within 10 workdays, after receipt of any such request in the office of the appropriate official identified in §5.51 whether to comply with the request. If the request is approved, the office having custody of the record shall notify the requestor and the Headquarters FOIA Officer whether request originated in Headquarters, Region or field.

[44 FR 50287, Aug. 27, 1979, as amended at 50 FR 40006, Oct. 1, 1985; 53 FR 2740, Feb. 1, 1988]

§5.53   Approval of request.

When a request is approved, records will be made available promptly in accordance with the terms of the regulation. Copies may be furnished or the records may be inspected and copied as provided in § 5.26.

§ 5.54 Denial of request of records.

(a) Each of the following officials within FEMA, any official designated to act for the official, or any official redelegated authority by such officials shall have the authority to make initial denials of requests for disclosure of records in his or her custody, and shall, in accordance with 5 U.S.C. 552(a)(6)(C) be the responsible official for denial of records under this part.

(1) Deputy Administrator(s).

(2) [Reserved]

(3) Federal Insurance Administrator.

(4) Assistant Administrators.

(5) United States Fire Administrator.

(6) Chief of Staff.

(7) Office Directors.

(8) Chief Counsel.

(9) [Reserved]

(10) Chief Financial Officer.

(11) Regional Administrators.

(b) If a request is denied, the appropriate official listed in paragraph (a) of this section shall except as provided in § 5.56 advise the requestor within 10 workdays of receipt of the request by the official specified in § 5.51 and furnish written reasons for the denial. The denial will (1) describe the record or records requested, (2) state the reasons for nondisclosure pursuant to subpart E, (3) state the name and title or position of the official responsible for the denial of such request, and (4) state the requestor's appeal rights.

(c) In the event FEMA cannot locate requested records the appropriate official specified in paragraph (a) of this section will inform the requestor (1) that the agency has determined at the present time to deny the request because the records have not yet been found or examined, but (2) that the agency will review the request within a specified number of days, when the search or examination is expected to be complete. The denial letter will state the name and title or position of the official responsible for the denial of such request. In such event, the re-

questor may file an agency appeal immediately, pursuant to § 5.55.

[44 FR 50287, Aug. 27, 1979, as amended at 48 FR 44542, Sept. 29, 1983; 50 FR 40006, Oct. 1, 1985; 51 FR 34604, Sept. 30, 1986; 74 FR 15333, Apr. 3, 2009]

§ 5.55 Appeal within FEMA of denial of request.

(a) A requestor denied access, in whole or in part, to FEMA records may appeal that decision within FEMA. All appeals should be addressed to the Headquarters FOIA Officer, Federal Emergency Management Agency, Washington, DC, 20472 regardless of whether the denial being appealed was made at Headquarters, in a field office, or by a Regional Administrator.

(b) An appeal must be received in the Headquarters FOIA Office no later than thirty calendar days after receipt by the requestor of the initial denial.

(c) An appeal must be in writing and should contain a brief statement of the reasons why the records should be released and enclose copies of the initial request and denial. The appeal letter should bear the legend, "FREEDOM OF INFORMATION APPEAL," conspicuously marked on both the face of the appeal letter and on the envelope. FEMA has twenty workdays after the receipt of an appeal to make a determination with respect to such appeal. The twenty day time limit shall not begin to run until the appeal is received by the Headquarters FOIA Officer. Misdirected appeals should be promptly forwarded to that office.

(d) The Headquarters FOIA Officer will submit the appeal to the Deputy Administrator for final administrative determination.

(e) The Deputy Administrator shall be the deciding official on all appeals except in those cases in which the initial denial was made by him/her. If the Deputy Administrator made the initial denial, the Administrator will be the deciding official on any appeal from that denial. In the absence of the Deputy Administrator, or in case of a vacancy in that office, the Administrator may designate another FEMA official to perform the Deputy Administrator's functions.

(f) If an appeal is filed in response to a tentative denial pending locating and/or examination of records, as described in §5.53(c), FEMA will continue to search for and/or examine the requested records and will issue a response immediately upon completion of the search and/or examination. Such action in no way suspends the time for FEMA's response to the requestor's appeal which FEMA will continue to process regardless of the response under this paragraph.

(g) If a requestor files suit pending an agency appeal, FEMA nonetheless will continue to process the appeal, and will furnish a response within the twenty day time limit set out in paragraph (c) of this section.

(h) If, on appeal, the denial of the request for records is in whole or in part upheld, the Deputy Administrator will promptly furnish the requestor a copy of the ruling in writing within the twenty day time limit set out in paragraph (c) of this section except as provided in §5.55. The notification letter shall contain:

(1) A brief description of the record or records requested;

(2) A statement of the legal basis for nondisclosure;

(3) A statement of the name and title or position of the official or officials responsible for the denial of the initial request as described in §5.54 and the denial of the appeal as described in paragraph (f) of this section, and

(4) A statement of the requestor's rights of judicial review.

[44 FR 50287, Aug. 27, 1979, as amended at 45 FR 1422, Jan. 7, 1980; 50 FR 40006, Oct. 1, 1985]

§5.56 Extension of time limits.

In unusual circumstances as specified in this section, the time limits prescribed in §§5.52 and 5.55 may be extended by an official named in §5.54(a) who will provide written notice to the requestor setting forth the reasons for such extension and the date on which a determination is expected. Such notice will specify no date that would result in an extension of more than ten work days. In unusual circumstances, the Headquarters FOIA Officer may authorize more than one extension, divided between the initial request stage and the appeals stage, but in no event will the combined periods of extension exceed ten work days. As used in this section, "unusual circumstances" include only those circumstances where extension of time is reasonably necessary to the proper processing of the particular request. Examples include:

(a) The need to search for and collect the requested records from field facilities or other establishments that are separate from the office processing the request; or

(b) The need to search for, collect, and appropriately examine a voluminous amount of separate and distinct records which are demanded in a single request; or

(c) The need for consultation, which shall be conducted with all practicable speed, with another agency or with a non-Federal source having a substantial interest in the determination of the request or among two or more components of FEMA having substantial subject matter interest therein.

§5.57 Predisclosure notification procedures for confidential commercial information.

(a) *In general.* Business information provided to FEMA by a business submitter shall not be disclosed pursuant to a Freedom of Information Act (FOIA) request except in accordance with this section. For purposes of this section, the following definitions apply:

(1) *Confidential commercial information* means records provided to the government by a submitter that arguably contain material exempt from release under Exemption 4 of the Freedom of Information Act, 5 U.S.C 552(b)(4), because disclosure could reasonably be expected to cause substantial competitive harm.

(2) *Submitter* means any person or entity who provides confidential commercial information to the government. The term *submitter* includes, but is not limited to, corporations, State governments, and foreign governments.

(b) *Notice to business submitters.* FEMA shall provide a submitter with prompt notice of receipt of a Freedom of Information Act request encompassing its business information whenever required in accordance with paragraph (c) of this section, and except as provided in paragraph (g) of this section. The written notice shall either describe

27

the exact nature of the business information requested or provide copies of the records or portions of records containing the business information.

(c) *When notice is required.* (1) For confidential commercial information submitted prior to January 1, 1988, FEMA shall provide a submitter with notice of receipt of a FOIA request whenever:

(i) The records are less than 10 years old and the information has been designated by the submitter as confidential commercial information;

(ii) FEMA has reason to believe that disclosure of the information could reasonably result in commercial or financial injury to the submitter; or

(iii) The information is subject to prior express commitment of confidentiality given by FEMA to the submitter.

(2) For confidential commercial information submitted to FEMA on or after January 1, 1988, FEMA shall provide a submitter with notice of receipt of a FOIA request whenever:

(i) The submitter has in good faith designated the information as commercially or financially sensitive information; or

(ii) FEMA has reason to believe that disclosure of the information could reasonably result in commercial or financial injury to the submitter.

(3) Notice of a request for confidential commercial information falling within paragraph (c)(2)(i) of this section shall be required for a period of not more than 10 years after the date of submission unless the submitter requests, and provides acceptable justification for, a specific notice period of greater duration.

(4) Whenever possible, the submitter's claim of confidentiality shall be supported by a statement or certification by an officer or authorized representative of the company that the information in question is in fact confidential commercial or financial information and has not been disclosed to the public.

(d) *Opportunity to object to disclosure.* (1) Through the notice described in paragraph (b) of this section, FEMA shall afford a submitter 7 working days within which to provide FEMA with a detailed statement of any objection to disclosure. Such statement shall specify all grounds for withholding any of the information under any exemptions of the Freedom of Information Act and, in the case of Exemption 4, shall demonstrate why the information is contended to be a trade secret or commercial or financial information which is considered privileged or confidential. Information provided by a submitter pursuant to this paragraph may itself be subject to disclosure under the FOIA.

(2) When notice is given to a submitter under this section, FEMA shall notify the requester that such notice has been given to the submitter. The requester will be further advised that a delay in responding to the request, i.e., 10 working days after receipt of the request by FEMA or 20 working days after receipt of the request by FEMA if the time limits are extended under unusual circumstances permitted by the FOIA, may be considered a denial of access to records and the requester may proceed with an administrative appeal or seek judicial review, if appropriate.

(e) *Notice of intent to disclose.* FEMA shall consider carefully a submitter's objections and specific grounds for nondisclosure prior to determining whether to disclose business information. Whenever FEMA decides to disclose business information over the objection of a submitter, FEMA shall forward to the submitter a written notice which shall include:

(1) A statement of the reasons for which the submitter's disclosure objections were not sustained;

(2) A description of the business information to be disclosed; and

(3) A specified disclosure date, which is 7 working days after the notice of the final decision to release the requested information has been mailed to the submitter. FEMA shall inform the submitter that disclosure will be made by the specified disclosure date, unless the submitter seeks a court injunction to prevent its release by the date. When notice is given to a submitter under this section, FEMA shall notify the requester that such notice has been given to the submitter and the proposed date for disclosure.

(f) *Notice of lawsuit.* (1) Whenever a requester brings legal action seeking to compel disclosure of business information covered by paragraph (c) of this section, FEMA shall promptly notify the submitter.

(2) Whenever a submitter brings legal action seeking to prevent disclosure of business information covered by paragraph (c) of this section, FEMA shall promptly notify the requester.

(g) *Exception to notice requirement.* The notice requirements of this section shall not apply if:

(1) FEMA determines that the information shall not be disclosed;

(2) The information has been published or otherwise officially made available to the public;

(3) Disclosure of the information is required by law (other than 5 U.S.C. 552); or

(4) The information was required in the course of a lawful investigation of a possible violation of criminal law.

[53 FR 2740, Feb. 1, 1988]

§5.58 Exhaustion of administrative remedies.

Any person making a request to FEMA for records under this part shall be deemed to have exhausted his administrative remedies with respect to the request if the agency fails to comply with the applicable time limit provisions set forth in §§5.52 and 5.55.

[44 FR 50287, Aug. 27, 1979. Redesignated at 53 FR 2740, Feb. 1, 1988]

§5.59 Judicial relief available to the public.

Upon denial of a requestor's appeal by the Deputy Administrator the requester may file a complaint in a district court of the United States in the district in which the complainant resides, or has his principal place of business, or in which the agency records are situated, or in the District of Columbia, pursuant to 5 U.S.C. 552(a)(4)(B).

[44 FR 50287, Aug. 27, 1979. Redesignated at 53 FR 2740, Feb. 1, 1988]

§5.60 Disciplinary action against employees for "arbitrary or capricious" denial.

Pursuant to 5 U.S.C. 552(a)(4)(F), whenever the district court, described in §5.59 orders the production of any FEMA records improperly withheld from the complainant and assesses against the United States reasonable attorney fees and other litigation costs, and the court additionally issues a written finding that the circumstances surrounding the withholding raise questions whether FEMA personnel acted arbitrarily or capriciously with respect to the withholding, the Special Counsel in the Merit Systems Protection Board is required to initiate a proceeding to determine whether disciplinary action is warranted against the officer or employee who primarily was responsible for the withholding. The Special Counsel after investigation and consideration of the evidence submitted, submits findings and recommendations to the Administrator of FEMA and sends copies of the findings and recommendations to the officer or employee or his or her representative. The law requires the Administrator to take any corrective action which the Special Counsel recommends.

[44 FR 50287, Aug. 27, 1979, as amended at 45 FR 1422, Jan. 7, 1980. Redesignated and amended at 53 FR 2740, Feb. 1, 1988]

§5.61 Contempt for noncompliance.

In the event of noncompliance by FEMA with an order of a district court pursuant to §5.60, the district court may punish for contempt the FEMA employee responsible for the noncompliance, pursuant to 5 U.S.C. 552(a)(4)(G).

[44 FR 50287, Aug. 27, 1979, as amended at 45 FR 1422, Jan. 7, 1980; 50 FR 40006, Oct. 1, 1985. Redesignated and amended at 53 FR 2740, Feb. 1, 1988]

Subpart E—Exemptions

§5.70 General.

The exemptions enumerated in 5 U.S.C. 552(b), under which the provisions for availability of records and informational materials will not apply, are general in nature. FEMA will decide each case on its merits in accordance with the FEMA policy expressed in subpart A.

§ 5.71 Categories of records exempt from disclosure under 5 U.S.C. 552.

5 U.S.C. 552(b) provides that the requirements of the statute do not apply to matters that are:

(a) Specifically authorized under criteria established by an Executive Order to be kept secret in the interest of national defense or foreign policy and are, in fact, properly classified pursuant to such Executive Order.

(b) Related solely to the internal personnel rules and practices of an agency.

(c) Specifically exempted from disclosure by statute other than section 552(b) of title 5, provided that such statute (1) requires that the matters be withheld from the public in such a manner as to leave no discretion on the issue or (2) establishes particular criteria for withholding or refers to particular types of matter to be withheld.

(d) Trade secrets and commercial or financial information obtained from a person and privileged or confidential.

(e) Inter-agency or intra-agency memoranda or letters which would not be available by law to a party other than an agency in litigation with the agency.

(f) Personnel and medical files and similar files the disclosure of which would constitute a clearly unwarranted invasion of personal privacy.

(g) Records or information compiled for law enforcement purposes, but only to the extent that the production of such law enforcement records or information:

(1) Could reasonably be expected to interfere with enforcement proceedings;

(2) Would deprive a person of a right to a fair trial or an impartial adjudication;

(3) Could reasonably be expected to constitute an unwarranted invasion of personal privacy;

(4) Could reasonably be expected to disclose the identity of a confidential source, including a State, local, or foreign agency or authority or any private institution which furnished information on a confidential basis, and, in the case of a record or information compiled by a criminal law enforcement authority in the course of a criminal investigation, or by an agency conducting a lawful national security intelligence investigation, information furnished by a confidential source;

(5) Would disclose techniques and procedures for law enforcement investigations or prosecutions, or would disclose guidelines for law enforcement investigations or prosecutions if such disclosure could reasonably be expected to risk circumvention of the law; or

(6) Could reasonably be expected to endanger the life or physical safety of any individual.

(h) Contained in or related to examination, operating, or condition reports prepared by, on behalf of, or for the use of any agency responsible for the regulation or supervision of financial institutions.

(i) Geological and geophysical information and data, including maps, concerning wells. Any reasonably segregable portion of a record shall be provided to any person requesting the record after deletion of the portions which are exempt under this section.

(j) Whenever a request is made which involves access to records described in paragraph (g)(1) of this section and the investigation or proceeding involves a possible violation of criminal law; and there is reason to believe that the subject of the investigation or proceeding is not aware of its pendency, and disclosure of the existence of the records could reasonably be expected to interfere with enforcement proceedings, FEMA may, during only such time as that circumstance continues, treat the records as not subject to the requirements of 5 U.S.C. 552 and this subpart.

[44 FR 50287, Aug. 27, 1979, as amended at 52 FR 13679, Apr. 24, 1987]

§ 5.72 Executive privilege exemption.

Where application of the executive privilege exemption is desired, the matter shall be forwarded to the Administrator for consideration. If the request for information is Congressional, only the President may invoke the exemption. Presidential approval is not necessarily required if the request for information is in connection with judicial or adjudicatory proceedings or otherwise. In connection with judicial proceedings, the response shall be coordinated with the Department of Justice.

Subpart F—Subpoenas or Other Legal Demands for Testimony or the Production or Disclosure of Records or Other Information

Source: 54 FR 11715, Mar. 22, 1989, unless otherwise noted.

§5.80 Scope and applicability.

(a) This subpart sets forth policies and procedures with respect to the disclosure or production by FEMA employees, in response to a subpoena, order or other demand of a court or other authority, of any material contained in the files of the Agency or any information relating to material contained in the files of the Agency or any information acquired by an employee as part of the performance of that person's official duties or because of that person's official status.

(b) This subpart applies to State and local judicial, administrative and legislative proceedings, and Federal judicial and administrative proceedings.

(c) This subpart does not apply to Congressional requests or subpoenas for testimony or documents, or to an employee making an appearance solely in his or her private capacity in judicial or administrative proceedings that do not relate to the Agency (such as cases arising out of traffic accidents, domestic relations, etc.).

(d) The Department of Homeland Security's regulations, 6 CFR 5.41 through 5.49, apply to any subject matter not already covered by this subpart, including but not limited to demands or requests directed to current or former FEMA contractors.

[54 FR 11715, Mar. 22, 1989, as amended at 72 FR 43546, Aug. 6, 2007]

§5.81 Statement of policy.

(a) It is the policy of FEMA to make its records available to private litigants to the same extent and in the same manner as such records are made available to members of the general public, except where protected from disclosure by litigation procedural authority (e.g., Federal Rules of Civil Procedure) or other applicable law.

(b) It is FEMA's policy and responsibility to preserve its human resources for performance of the official functions of the Agency and to maintain strict impartiality with respect to private litigants. Participation by FEMA employees in private litigation in their official capacities is generally contrary to this policy.

§5.82 Definitions.

For purposes of this subpart, the following terms have the meanings ascribed to them in this section:

(a) *Demand* refers to a subpoena, order, or other demand of a court of competent jurisdiction, or other specific authority (e.g., an administrative or State legislative body), signed by the presiding officer, for the production, disclosure, or release of FEMA records or information or for the appearance and testimony of FEMA personnel as witnesses in their official capacities.

(b) *Employee of the Agency* includes all officers and employees of the United States appointed by or subject to the supervision, jurisdiction or control of the Administrator of FEMA.

(c) *Private litigation* refers to any legal proceeding which does not involve as a named party the United States Government, or the Federal Emergency Management Agency, or any official thereof in his or her official capacity.

§5.83 Authority to accept service of subpoenas.

In all legal proceedings between private litigants, a subpoena duces tecum or subpoena ad testificandum or other demand by a court or other authority for the production of records held by FEMA Regional offices or for the oral or written testimony of FEMA Regional employees should be addressed to the appropriate Regional Administrator listed in §5.26. For all other records or testimony, the subpoena should be addressed to the Chief Counsel, FEMA, 500 C Street SW., Washington, DC 20472 Washington, DC 20472. No other official or employee of FEMA is authorized to accept service of subpoenas on behalf of the Agency.

§ 5.84 Production of documents in private litigation.

(a) The production of records held by FEMA in response to a subpoena duces tecum or other demand issued pursuant to private litigation, whether or not served in accordance with the provisions of § 5.83 of this subpart, is prohibited absent authorization by the Chief Counsel.

(b) Whenever an official or employee of FEMA, including any Regional Administrator, receives a subpoena or other demand for the production of Agency documents or material, he or she shall immediately notify and provide a copy of the demand to the Chief Counsel.

(c) The Chief Counsel, after consultation with other appropriate officials as deemed necessary, shall promptly determine whether to disclose the material or documents identified in the subpoena or other demand. Generally, authorization to furnish the requested material or documents shall not be withheld unless their disclosure is prohibited by relevant law or for other compelling reasons.

(d) Whenever a subpoena or demand commanding the production of any record is served upon any Agency employee other than as provided in § 5.83 of this subpart, or the response to a demand is required before the receipt of instructions from the Chief Counsel, such employee shall appear in response thereto, respectfully decline to produce the record(s) on the ground that it is prohibited by this section and state that the demand has been referred for the prompt consideration of the Chief Counsel.

(e) Where the release of documents in response to a subpoena duces tecum is authorized by the Chief Counsel, the official having custody of the requested records will furnish, upon the request of the party seeking disclosure, authenticated copies of the documents. No official or employee of FEMA shall respond in strict compliance with the terms of a subpoena duces tecum unless specifically authorized by the Chief Counsel.

§ 5.85 Authentication and attestation of copies.

The Administrator, Deputy Administrators, Regional Administrators, Assistant Administrators, United States Fire Administrator, Federal Insurance Administrator, Chief Counsel, and their designees, and other heads of offices having possession of records are authorized in the name of the Administrator to authenticate and attest for copies or reproductions of records. Appropriate fees will be charged for such copies or reproductions based on the fee schedule set forth in section 5.46 of this part.

[74 FR 15334, Apr. 3, 2009]

§ 5.86 Production of documents in litigation or other adjudicatory proceeding in which the United States is a party.

Subpoenas duces tecum issued pursuant to litigation or any other adjudicatory proceeding in which the United States is a party shall be handled as provided at § 5.8.

§ 5.87 Testimony of FEMA employees in private litigation.

(a) No FEMA employee shall testify in response to a subpoena or other demand in private litigation as to any information relating to material contained in the files of the Agency, or any information acquired as part of the performance of that person's official duties or because of that person's official status, including the meaning of Agency documents.

(b) Whenever a demand is made upon a FEMA employee, for the disclosure of information described in paragraph (a) of this section, that employee shall immediately notify the Office of Chief Counsel. The Chief Counsel, upon receipt of such notice and absent waiver of the general prohibition against employee testimony at his or her discretion, shall arrange with the appropriate United States Attorney the taking of such steps as are necessary to quash the subpoena or seek a protective order.

(c) In the event that an immediate demand for testimony or disclosure is made in circumstances which would preclude prior notice to and consultation with the Chief Counsel, the employee shall respectfully request from the demanding authority a stay in the proceedings to allow sufficient time to obtain advice of counsel.

(d) If the court or other authority declines to stay the effect of the demand in response to a request made in accordance with paragraph (c) of this section pending consultation with counsel, or if the court or other authority rules that the demand must be complied with irrespective of instructions not to testify or disclose the information sought, the employee upon whom the demand has been made shall respectfully decline to comply with the demand, citing these regulations and *United States ex rel. Touhy* v. *Ragen*, 340 U.S. 462 (1951).

§ 5.88 Testimony in litigation in which the United States is a party.

(a) Whenever, in any legal proceeding in which the United States is a party, the attorney in charge of presenting the case for the United States requests it, the Chief Counsel shall arrange for an employee of the Agency to testify as a witness for the United States.

(b) The attendance and testimony of named employees of the Agency may not be required in any legal proceeding by the judge or other presiding officer, by subpoena or otherwise. However, the judge or other presiding officer may, upon a showing of exceptional circumstances (such as a case in which a particular named FEMA employee has direct personal knowledge of a material fact not known to the witness made available by the Agency) require the attendance and testimony of named FEMA personnel.

§ 5.89 Waiver.

The Chief Counsel may grant, in writing, a waiver of any policy or procedure prescribed by this subpart, where waiver is considered necessary to promote a significant interest of the Agency or for other good cause. In granting such waiver, the Chief Counsel shall attach to the waiver such reasonable conditions and limitations as are deemed appropriate in order that a response in strict compliance with the terms of a subpoena duces tecum or the

providing of testimony will not interfere with the duties of the employee and will otherwise conform to the policies of this part. The Administrator may, in his or her discretion, review any decision to authorize a waiver of any policy or procedure prescribed by this subpart.

PART 6—IMPLEMENTATION OF THE PRIVACY ACT OF 1974

Subpart A—General

6.72 Effective date of new system of records or alteration of an existing system of records.

Subpart F—Fees

6.80 Records available at fee.
6.81 Additional copies.
6.82 Waiver of fee.
6.83 Prepayment of fees.
6.84 Form of payment.
6.85 Reproduction fees.

Subpart G—Exempt Systems of Records

6.86 General exemptions.
6.87 Specific exemptions.

AUTHORITY: 5 U.S.C. 552a; Reorganization Plan No. 3 of 1978; and E.O. 12127.

SOURCE: 44 FR 50293, Aug. 27, 1979, unless otherwise noted.

Subpart A—General

§6.1 Purpose and scope of part.

This part sets forth policies and procedures concerning the collection, use and dissemination of records maintained by the Federal Emergency Management Agency (FEMA) which are subject to the provision of 5 U.S.C. 552a, popularly known as the "Privacy Act of 1974" (hereinafter referred to as the Act). These policies and procedures govern only those records as defined in §6.2. Policies and procedures governing the disclosure and availability of records in general are in part 5 of this chapter. This part also covers: (a) Procedures for notification to individuals of a FEMA system of records pertaining to them; (b) guidance to individuals in obtaining information, including inspections of, and disagreement with, the content of records; (c) accounting of disclosure; (d) special requirements for medical records; and (e) fees.

§6.2 Definitions.

For the purpose of this part:

(a) *Agency* includes any executive department, military department, Government corporation, Government controlled corporation, or other establishment in the executive branch of the Government (including the Executive Office of the President), or any independent regulatory agency (see 5 U.S.C. 552(e)).

(b) *Individual* means a citizen of the United States or an alien lawfully admitted for permanent residence.

(c) *Maintain* includes maintain, collect, use, and disseminate.

(d) *Record* means any item, collection, or grouping of information about an individual that is maintained by an agency, including, but not limited to those concerning education, financial transactions, medical history, and criminal or employment history, and that contains the name or other identifying particular assigned to the individual, such as a fingerprint, voiceprint, or photograph.

(e) *System of records* means a group of any records under the control of an agency from which information is retrieved by the name of the individual or by some identifying number, symbol, or other identification assigned to that individual.

(f) *Statistical record* means a record in a system of records maintained for statistical research or reporting purposes only and not used in whole or in part in making any determination about an identifiable individual, except as provided by 13 U.S.C. 8.

(g) *Routine use* means, with respect to the disclosure of a record, the use of that record for a purpose which is compatible with the purpose for which it was collected.

(h) *System manager* means the employee of FEMA who is responsible for the maintenance of a system of records and for the collection, use, and dissemination of information therein.

(i) *Subject individual* means the individual named or discussed in a record of the individual to whom a record otherwise pertains.

(j) *Disclosure* means a transfer of a record, a copy of a record, or any or all of the information contained in a record to a recipient other than the subject individual, or the review of a record by someone other than the subject individual.

(k) *Access* means a transfer of a record, a copy of a record, or the information in a record to the subject individual, or the review of a record by the subject individual.

(l) *Solicitation* means a request by an officer or employee of FEMA that an individual provide information about himself or herself.

(m) *Administrator* means the Administrator, FEMA.

(n) *Deputy Administrator* means the Deputy Administrator, FEMA, or, in the case of the absence of the Deputy Administrator, or a vacancy in that office, a person designated by the Administrator to perform the functions under this regulation of the Deputy Administrator.

(o) *Privacy Appeals Officer* means the FOIA/Privacy Act Specialist or his/her designee.

[44 FR 50293, Aug. 27, 1979, as amended at 45 FR 17152, Mar. 18, 1980; 51 FR 34604, Sept. 30, 1986]

§6.3 Collection and use of information (Privacy Act statements).

(a) *General.* Any information used in whole or in part in making a determination about an individual's rights, benefits, or privileges under FEMA programs will be collected directly from the subject individual to the extent practicable. The system manager also shall ensure that information collected is used only in conformance with the provisions of the Act and these regulations.

(b) *Solicitation of information.* System managers shall ensure that at the time information is solicited the solicited individual is informed of the authority for collecting that information, whether providing the information is mandatory or voluntary, the purpose for which the information will be used, the routine uses to be made of the information, and the effects on the individual, if any, of not providing the information. The Director, Records Management Division, Office of Management and Regional Administrators shall ensure that forms used to solicit information are in compliance with the Act and these regulations.

(c) *Solicitation of Social Security numbers.* Before an employee of FEMA can deny to any individual a right, benefit, or privilege provided by law because such individual refuses to disclose his/her social security account number, the employee of FEMA shall ensure that either:

(1) The disclosure is required by Federal statute; or

(2) The disclosure of a social security number was required under a statute or regulation adopted before January 1, 1975, to verify the identity of an individual, and the social security number will become a part of a system of records in existence and operating before January 1, 1975.

If solicitation of the social security number is authorized under paragraph (c) (1) or (2) of this section, the FEMA employee who requests an individual to disclose the social security account number shall first inform that individual whether that disclosure is mandatory or voluntary, by what statutory or other authority the number is solicited, and the use that will be made of it.

(d) *Soliciting information from third parties.* An employee of FEMA shall inform third parties who are requested to provide information about another individual of the purposes for which the information will be used.

[44 FR 50293, Aug. 27, 1979, as amended at 47 FR 13149, Mar. 29, 1982; 48 FR 12091, Mar. 23, 1983; 50 FR 40006, Oct. 1, 1985]

§6.4 Standards of accuracy.

The system manager shall ensure that all records which are used by FEMA to make determinations about any individual are maintained with such accuracy, relevance, timeliness, and completeness as is reasonably necessary to ensure fairness to the individual.

§6.5 Rules of conduct.

Employees of FEMA involved in the design, development, operation, or maintenance of any system of records or in maintaining any record, shall conduct themselves in accordance with the rules of conduct concerning the protection of personal information in §3.25 of this chapter.

§6.6 Safeguarding systems of records.

(a) Systems managers shall ensure that appropriate administrative, technical, and physical safeguards are established to ensure the security and confidentiality of records and to protect against any anticipated threats or hazards to their security or integrity which could result in substantial harm, embarrassment, inconvenience, or unfairness to any individual on whom information is maintained.

(b) Personnel information contained in both manual and automated systems of records shall be protected by implementing the following safeguards:

(1) Official personnel folders, authorized personnel operating or work folders and other records of personnel actions effected during an employee's Federal service or affecting the employee's status and service, including information on experience, education, training, special qualification, and skills, performance appraisals, and conduct, shall be stored in a lockable metal filing cabinet when not in use by an authorized person. A system manager may employ an alternative storage system providing that it furnished an equivalent degree of physical security as storage in a lockable metal filing cabinet.

(2) System managers, at their discretion, may designate additional records of unusual sensitivity which require safeguards similar to those described in paragraph (a) of this section.

(3) A system manager shall permit access to and use of automated or manual personnel records only to persons whose official duties require such access, or to a subject individual or his or her representative as provided by this part.

§ 6.7 Records of other agencies.

If FEMA receives a request for access to records which are the primary responsibility of another agency, but which are maintained by or in the temporary possession of FEMA on behalf of that agency, FEMA will advise the requestor that the request has been forwarded to the responsible agency. Records in the custody of FEMA which are the primary responsibility of the Office of Personnel Management are governed by the rules promulgated by it pursuant to the Privacy Act.

§ 6.8 Subpoena and other legal demands.

Access to records in systems of records by subpoena or other legal process shall be in accordance with the provisions of part 5 of this chapter.

§ 6.9 Inconsistent issuances of FEMA and/or its predecessor agencies superseded.

Any policies and procedures in any issuances of FEMA or any of its predecessor agencies which are inconsistent with the policies and procedures in this part are superseded to the extent of that inconsistency.

§ 6.10 Assistance and referrals.

Requests for assistance and referral to the responsible system manager or other FEMA employee charged with implementing these regulations should be made to the Privacy Appeals Officer, Federal Emergency Management Agency, Washington, DC 20472.

[45 FR 17152, Mar. 18, 1980]

Subpart B—Disclosure of Records

§ 6.20 Conditions of disclosure.

No employee of FEMA shall disclose any record to any person or to another agency without the express written consent of the subject individual unless the disclosure is:

(a) To officers or employees of FEMA who have a need for the information in the official performance of their duties;

(b) Required by the provisions of the Freedom of Information Act, 5 U.S.C. 552.

(c) For a routine use as published in the notices in the FEDERAL REGISTER;

(d) To the Bureau of the Census for use pursuant to title 13, United States Code;

(e) To a recipient who has provided FEMA with advance adequate written assurance that the record will be used solely as a statistical research or reporting record subject to the following: The record shall be transferred in a form that is not individually identifiable. The written statement should include as a minimum (1) a statement of the purpose for requesting the records; and (2) certification that the records will be used only for statistical purposes. These written statements should be maintained as accounting records. In addition to deleting personal identifying information from records released for statistical purposes, the system manager shall ensure that the identity of the individual cannot reasonably be deduced by combining various statistical records;

(f) To the National Archives of the United States as a record which has sufficient historical or other value to warrant its continued preservation by the United States Government, or for evaluation by the Administrator of The National Archives and Records Administration or his designee to determine whether the record has such value;

(g) To another agency or instrumentality of any governmental jurisdiction within or under the control of the United States for civil or criminal law enforcement activity, if the activity is authorized by law, and if the head of the agency or instrumentality or his designated representative has made a written request to the Administrator specifying the particular portion desired and the law enforcement activity for which the record is sought;

(h) To a person showing compelling circumstances affecting the health and safety of an individual to whom the record pertains. (Upon such disclosure, a notification must be sent to the last known address of the subject individual.)

(i) To either House of Congress or to a subcommittee or committee (joint or of either House, to the extent that the subject matter falls within their jurisdiction;

(j) To the Comptroller General or any duly authorized representatives of the Comptroller General in the course of the performance of the duties of the Government Accountability Office; or

(k) Pursuant to the order of a court of competent jurisdiction.

(l) To consumer reporting agencies as defined in the Fair Credit Reporting Act (35 U.S.C. 1681a(f) or the Debt Collection Act of 1982 (31 U.S.C. 3711(d)(4)).

[44 FR 50293, Aug. 27, 1979, as amended at 48 FR 44543, Sept. 29, 1983; 50 FR 40006, Oct. 1, 1985]

§6.21 Procedures for disclosure.

(a) Upon receipt of a request for disclosure, the system manager shall verify the right of the requestor to obtain disclosure pursuant to §6.20. Upon that verification and subject to other requirements of this part, the system manager shall make the requested records available.

(b) If the system manager determines that the disclosure is not permitted under the provisions of §6.20 or other provisions of this part, the system manager shall deny the request in writing and shall inform the requestor of the right to submit a request for review and final determination to the Administrator or designee.

§6.22 Accounting of disclosures.

(a) Except for disclosures made pursuant to §6.20 (a) and (b), an accurate accounting of each disclosure shall be made and retained for 5 years after the disclosure or for the life of the record, whichever is longer. The accounting shall include the date, nature, and purpose of each disclosure, and the name and address of the person or agency to whom the disclosure is made;

(b) The system manager also shall maintain in conjunction with the accounting of disclosures;

(1) A full statement of the justification for the disclosure.

(2) All documentation surrounding disclosure of a record for statistical or law enforcement purposes; and

(3) Evidence of written consent to a disclosure given by the subject individual.

(c) Except for the accounting of disclosures made to agencies or instrumentalities in law enforcement activities in accordance with §6.20 (g) or of disclosures made from exempt systems the accounting of disclosures shall be made available to the individual upon request. Procedures for requesting access to the accounting are in subpart C of this part.

Subpart C—Individual Access to Records

§6.30 Form of requests.

(a) An individual who seeks access to his or her record or to any information pertaining to the individual which is contained in a system of records should notify the system manager at the address indicated in the FEDERAL REGISTER notice describing the pertinent system. The notice should bear the legend "Privacy Act Request" both on the request letter and on the envelope. It will help in the processing of a request if the request letter contains the complete name and identifying number of the system as published in the FEDERAL REGISTER; the full name and address of the subject individual; a brief description of the nature, time, place, and circumstances of the individual's association with FEMA; and any other information which the individual believes would help the system manager to determine whether the information about the individual is included in the system of records. The system manager shall answer or acknowledge the request within 10 workdays of its receipt by FEMA.

(b) The system manager, at his discretion, may accept oral requests for access subject to verification of identity.

§6.31 Special requirements for medical records.

(a) A system manager who receives a request from an individual for access to those official medical records which belong to the U.S. Office of Personnel Management and are described in Chapter 339, Federal Personnel Manual (medical records about entrance qualifications or fitness for duty, or medical records which are otherwise filed in the Official Personnel Folder), shall refer the pertinent system of records to a Federal Medical Officer for review and determination in accordance with this section. If no Federal Medical Officer is available to make the determination required by this section, the system manager shall refer the request and the medical reports concerned to the Office of Personnel Management for determination.

(b) If, in the opinion of a Federal Medical Officer, medical records requested by the subject individual indicate a condition about which a prudent physician would hesitate to inform a person suffering from such a condition of its exact nature and probable outcome, the system manager shall not release the medical information to the subject individual nor to any person other than a physician designated in writing by the subject individual, or the guardian or conservator of the individual.

(c) If, in the opinion of a Federal Medical Officer, the medical information does not indicate the presence of any condition which would cause a prudent physician to hesitate to inform a person suffering from such a condition of its exact nature and probable outcome, the system manager shall release it to the subject individual or to any person, firm, or organization which the individual authorizes in writing to receive it.

§6.32 Granting access.

(a) Upon receipt of a request for access to non-exempt records, the system manager shall make these records available to the subject individual or shall acknowledge the request within 10 workdays of its receipt by FEMA. The acknowledgment shall indicate when the system manager will make the records available.

(b) If the system manager anticipates more than a 10 day delay in making a record available, he or she also shall include in the acknowledgment specific reasons for the delay.

(c) If a subject individual's request for access does not contain sufficient information to permit the system manager to locate the records, the system manager shall request additional information from the individual and shall have 10 workdays following receipt of the additional information in which to make the records available or to acknowledge receipt of the request and indicate when the records will be available.

(d) Records will be available for authorized access during normal business hours at the offices where the records are located. A requestor should be prepared to identify himself or herself by signature; i.e., to note by signature the date of access and/or produce other identification verifying the signature.

(e) Upon request, a system manager shall permit an individual to examine the original of a non-exempt record, shall provide the individual with a copy of the record, or both. Fees shall be charged in accordance with subpart F.

(f) An individual may request to pick up a record in person or to receive it by mail, directed to the name and address provided by the individual in the request. A system manager shall not make a record available to a third party for delivery to the subject individual except for medical records as outlined in § 6.31.

(g) An individual who selects another person to review, or to accompany the individual in reviewing or obtaining a copy of the record must, prior to the disclosure, sign a statement authorizing the disclosure of the record. The system manager shall maintain this statement with the record.

(h) The procedure for access to an accounting of disclosure is identical to the procedure for access to a record as set forth in this section.

§ 6.33 Denials of access.

(a) A system manager may deny an individual access to that individual's record only upon the grounds that FEMA has published the rules in the FEDERAL REGISTER exempting the pertinent system of records from the access requirement. These exempt systems of records are described in subpart G of this part.

(b) Upon receipt of a request for access to a record which the system manager believes is contained within an exempt system of records he or she shall forward the request to the appropriate official listed below or to his or her delegate through normal supervisory channels.

(1) Deputy Administrators.
(2) [Reserved]
(3) Federal Insurance Administrator.
(4) Assistant Administrators.
(5) United States Fire Administrator.
(6) Chief of Staff.
(7) Office Directors.
(8) Chief Counsel.
(9) [Reserved]
(10) Chief Financial Officer.
(11) Regional Administrators.

(c) In the event that the system manager serves in one of the positions listed in paragraph (b) of this section, he or she shall retain the responsibility for denying or granting the request.

(d) The appropriate official listed in paragraph (b) of this section shall, in consultation with the Office of Chief Counsel and such other officials as deemed appropriate, determine if the request record is contained within an exempt system of records and:

(1) If the record is not contained within an exempt system of records, the above official shall notify the system manager to grant the request in accordance with § 6.32, or

(2) If the record is contained within an exempt system said official shall:

(i) Notify the requestor that the request is denied, including a statement justifying the denial and advising the requestor of a right to judicial review of that decision as provided in § 6.57, or

(ii) Notify the system manager to make record available to the requestor in accordance with § 6.31, notwithstanding the record's inclusion within an exempt system.

(e) The appropriate official listed in paragraph (b) of this section shall provide the Privacy Appeals Office with a copy of any denial of a requested access.

[44 FR 50293, Aug. 27, 1979, as amended at 48 FR 44543, Sept. 29, 1983; 50 FR 40006, Oct. 1, 1985; 51 FR 34604, Sept. 30, 1986; 74 FR 15334, Apr. 3, 2009]

§ 6.34 Appeal of denial of access within FEMA.

A requestor denied access in whole or in part, to records pertaining to that individual, exclusive of those records for which the system manager is the Administrator, may file an administrative appeal of that denial. Appeals of denied access will be processed in the same manner as processing for appeals from a denial of a request to amend a record set out in § 6.55, regardless whether the denial being appealed is made at headquarters or by a regional official.

Subpart D—Requests To Amend Records

§ 6.50 Submission of requests to amend records.

An individual who desires to amend any record containing personal information about the individual should direct a written request to the system manager specified in the pertinent FEDERAL REGISTER notice concerning FEMA's systems of records. A current FEMA employee who desires to amend personnel records should submit a written request to the Director, Human Capital Division, Washington, DC 20472. Each request should include evidence of and justification for the need to amend the pertinent record. Each request should bear the legend "Privacy Act—Request to Amend Record" prominently marked on both the face of the request letter and the envelope.

§ 6.51 Review of requests to amend records.

(a) The system manager shall acknowledge the receipt of a request to amend a record within 10 workdays. If possible, the acknowledgment shall include the system manager's determination either to amend the record or to deny the request to amend as provided in § 6.53.

(b) When reviewing a record in response to a request to amend, the system manager shall assess the accuracy, relevance, timeliness, and completeness of the existing record in light of the proposed amendment and shall determine whether the request for the amendment is justified. With respect to a request to delete information, the system manager also shall review the request and the existing record to determine whether the information is relevant and necessary to accomplish an agency purpose required to be accomplished by statute or Executive Order.

§ 6.52 Approval of requests to amend records.

If the system manager determines that amendment of a record is proper in accordance with the request to amend, he or she promptly shall make the necessary corrections to the record and shall send a copy of the corrected record to the individual. Where an accounting of disclosure has been maintained, the system manager shall advise all previous recipients of the record of the fact that a correction has been made and the substance of the correction. Where practicable, the system manager shall advise the Privacy Appeals Officer that a request to amend has been approved.

§ 6.53 Denial of requests to amend records.

(a) If the system manager determines that an amendment of a record is improper or that the record should be amended in a manner other than that requested by an individual, he shall refer the request to amend and his determinations and recommendations to the appropriate official listed in § 6.33(b) through normal supervisory channels.

(b) If the official listed in § 6.33, after reviewing the request to amend a record, determines to amend the record in accordance with the request, said official promptly shall return the request to the system manager with instructions to make the requested amendments in accordance with § 6.52.

(c) If the appropriate official listed in § 6.33, after reviewing the request to amend a record, determines not to amend the record in accordance with the request, the requestor shall be promptly advised in writing of the determination. The refusal letter (1) shall state the reasons for the denial of the request to amend; (2) shall include proposed alternative amendments, if appropriate; (3) shall state the requestor's right to appeal the denial of the request to amend; and (4) shall state the procedures for appealing and the name and title of the official to whom the appeal is to be addressed.

(d) The appropriate official listed in § 6.33 shall furnish the Privacy Appeals Officer a copy of each initial denial of a request to amend a record.

[44 FR 50293, Aug. 27, 1979, as amended at 45 FR 17152, Mar. 18, 1980]

§ 6.54 Agreement to alternative amendments.

If the denial of a request to amend a record includes proposed alternative amendments, and if the requestor agrees to accept them, he or she must notify the official who signed the denial. That official immediately shall instruct the system manager to make the necessary amendments in accordance with § 6.52.

§ 6.55 Appeal of denial of request to amend a record.

(a) A requestor who disagrees with a denial of a request to amend a record may file an administrative appeal of that denial. The requestor should address the appeal to the FEMA Privacy Appeals Officer, Washington, DC 20472. If the requestor is an employee of FEMA and the denial to amend involves a record maintained in the employee's Official Personnel Folder covered by an Office of Personnel Management Government-wide system notice, the appeal should be addressed to the Assistant Director, Information Systems, Agency Compliance and Evaluation Group, Office of Personnel Management, Washington, DC 20415.

(b) Each appeal to the Privacy Act Appeals Officer shall be in writing and must be received by FEMA no later than 30 calendar days from the requestor's receipt of a denial of a request to amend a record. The appeal should bear the legend "Privacy Act—Appeal," both on the face of the letter and the envelope.

(c) Upon receipt of an appeal, the Privacy Act Appeals Officer shall consult with the system manager, the official who made the denial, the Chief Counsel or a member of that office, and such other officials as may be appropriate. If the Privacy Act Appeals Officer in consultation with these officials, determines that the record should be amended, as requested, the system manager shall be instructed immediately to amend the record in accordance with §6.52 and shall notify the requestor of that action.

(d) If the Privacy Act Appeals Officer, in consultation with the officials specified in paragraph (c) of this section, determines that the appeal should be rejected, the Privacy Act Appeals Officer shall submit the file on the request and appeal, including findings and recommendations, to the Deputy Administrator for a final administrative determination.

(e) If the Deputy Administrator determines that the record should be amended as requested, he or she immediately shall instruct the system manager in writing to amend the record in accordance with §6.52. The Deputy Administrator shall send a copy of those instructions to the Privacy Act Appeals Officer, who shall notify the requester of that action.

(f) If the Deputy Administrator determines to reject the appeal, the requestor shall immediately be notified in writing of that determination. This action shall constitute the final administrative determination on the request to amend the record and shall include:

(1) The reasons for the rejection of the appeal.

(2) Proposed alternative amendments, if appropriate, which the requestor subsequently may accept in accordance with §6.54.

(3) Notice of the requestor's right to file a Statement of Disagreement for distribution in accordance with §6.56.

(4) Notice of the requestor's right to seek judicial review of the final administrative determination, as provided in §6.57.

(g) The final agency determination must be made no later than 30 workdays from the date on which the appeal is received by the Privacy Act Appeals Officer.

(h) In extraordinary circumstances, the Administrator may extend this time limit by notifying the requestor in writing before the expiration of the 30 workdays. The Administrator's notification will include a justification for the extension.

[44 FR 50293, Aug. 27, 1979, as amended at 45 FR 17152, Mar. 18, 1980]

§6.56 Statement of disagreement.

Upon receipt of a final administrative determination denying a request to amend a record, the requestor may file a Statement of Disagreement with the appropriate system manager. The Statement of Disagreement should include an explanation of why the requestor believes the record to be inaccurate, irrelevant, untimely, or incomplete. The system manager shall maintain the Statement of Disagreement in conjunction with the pertinent record, and shall include a copy of the Statement of Disagreement in any disclosure of the pertinent record. The system manager shall provide a copy of the Statement of Disagreement to any person or agency to whom the record has been disclosed only if the disclosure was subject to the accounting requirements of §6.22.

§ 6.57 Judicial review.

Within 2 years of receipt of a final administrative determination as provided in § 6.34 or § 6.55, a requestor may seek judicial review of that determination. A civil action must be filed in the Federal District Court in which the requestor resides or has his or her principal place of business or in which the agency records are situated, or in the District of Columbia.

Subpart E—Report on New Systems and Alterations of Existing Systems

§ 6.70 Reporting requirement.

(a) No later than 90 calendar days prior to the establishment of a new system of records, the prospective system manager shall notify the Privacy Appeals Officer of the proposed new system. The prospective system manager shall include with the notification a completed FEMA Form 11-2, System of Records Covered by the Privacy Act of 1974, and a justification for each system of records proposed to be established. If the Privacy Appeals Officer determines that the establishment of the proposed system is in the best interest of the Government, then no later than 60 calendar days prior to the establishment of that system of records, a report of the proposal shall be submitted by the Administrator or a designee thereof, to the President of the Senate, the Speaker of the House of Representatives, and the Administrator, Office of Information and Regulatory Affairs, Office of Management and Budget for their evaluation of the probable or potential effect of that proposal on the privacy and other personal or property rights of individuals.

(b) No later than 90 calendar days prior to the alteration of a system of records, the system manager responsible for the maintenance of that system of records shall notify the Privacy Appeals Officer of the proposed alteration. The system manager shall include with the notification a completed FEMA Form 11-2. System of Records. Covered by the Privacy Act of 1974, and a justification for each system of records he proposes to alter. If it is determined that the proposed alteration

is in the best interest of the Government, then, the Administrator, or a designee thereof, shall submit, no later than 60 calendar days prior to the establishment of that alteration, a report of the proposal to the President of the Senate, the Speaker of the House of Representatives, and the Administrator, Office of Information and Regulatory Affairs, Office of Management and Budget for their evaluation of the probable or potential effect of that proposal on the privacy and other personal or property rights of individuals.

(c) The reports required by this regulation are exempt from reports control.

(d) The Administrator, Office of Information and Regulatory Affairs, Office of Management and Budget may waive the time requirements set out in this section upon a finding that a delay in the establishing or amending the system would not be in the public interest and showing how the public interest would be adversely affected if the waiver were not granted and otherwise complying with OMB Circular A-130.

[44 FR 50293, Aug. 27, 1979, as amended at 45 FR 17152, Mar. 18, 1980; 51 FR 34604, Sept. 30, 1986]

§ 6.71 Federal Register notice of establishment of new system or alteration of existing system.

Notice of the proposed establishment or alteration of a system of records shall be published in the FEDERAL REGISTER, in accordance with FEMA procedures when:

(a) Notice is received that the Senate, the House of Representatives, and the Office of Management and Budget do not object to the establishment of a new system or records or to the alteration of an existing system of records, or

(b) No fewer than 30 calendar days elapse from the date of submission of the proposal to the Senate, the House of Representatives, and the Office of Management and Budget without receipt of an objection to the proposal. The notice shall include all of the information required to be provided in FEMA Form 11-2, System of Records Covered by the Privacy Act of 1974, and such other information as the Administrator deems necessary.

§ 6.72 Effective date of new system of records or alteration of an existing system of records.

Systems of records proposed to be established or altered in accordance with the provisions of this subpart shall be effective no sooner than 30 calendar days from the publication of the notice required by § 6.71.

Subpart F—Fees

§ 6.80 Records available at fee.

The system manager shall provide a copy of a record to a requestor at a fee prescribed in § 6.85 unless the fee is waived under § 6.82.

[44 FR 50293, Aug. 27, 1979, as amended at 45 FR 17152, Mar. 18, 1980]

§ 6.81 Additional copies.

A reasonable number of additional copies shall be provided for the applicable fee to a requestor who indicates that he has no access to commercial reproduction services.

§ 6.82 Waiver of fee.

The system manager shall make one copy of a record, up to 300 pages, available without charge to a requestor who is an employee of FEMA. The system manager may waive the fee requirement for any other requestor if the cost of collecting the fee is an unduly large part of, or greater than, the fee, or when furnishing the record without charge conforms to generally established business custom or is in the public interest.

[44 FR 50287, Aug. 27, 1979, as amended at 52 FR 13679, Apr. 24, 1987]

§ 6.83 Prepayment of fees.

(a) When FEMA estimates or determines that allowable charges that a requester may be required to pay are likely to exceed $250.00, FEMA may require a requester to make an advance payment of the entire fee before continuing to process the request.

(b) When a requester has previously failed to pay a fee charged in a timely fashion (i.e., within 30 days of the date of the billing), FEMA may require the requester to pay the full amount owed plus any applicable interest as provided in § 6.85(d), and to make an advance

payment of the full amount of the estimated fee before the agency begins to process a new request or a pending request from that requester.

(c) When FEMA acts under § 5.44 (a) or (b), the administrative time limits prescribed in subsection (a)(6) of the FOIA (i.e., 10 working days from the receipt of initial requests and 20 working days from receipt of appeals from initial denial, plus permissible extensions of these time limits) will begin only after FEMA has received fee payments described under § 5.44 (a) or (b).

[52 FR 13679, Apr. 24, 1987]

§ 6.84 Form of payment.

Payment shall be by check or money order payable to The Federal Emergency Management Agency and shall be addressed to the system manager.

§ 6.85 Reproduction fees.

(a) *Duplication costs.* (1) For copies of documents reproduced on a standard office copying machine in sizes up to 8½ x 14 inches, the charge will be $.15 per page.

(2) The fee for reproducing copies of records over 8½ x 14 inches or whose physical characteristics do not permit reproduction by routine electrostatic copying shall be the direct cost of reproducing the records through Government or commercial sources. If FEMA estimates that the allowable duplication charges are likely to exceed $25, it shall notify the requester of the estimated amount of fees, unless the requester has indicated in advance his/her willingness to pay fees as high as those anticipated. Such a notice shall offer a requester the opportunity to confer with agency personnel with the objective of reformulating the request to meet his/her needs at a lower cost.

(3) For other methods of reproduction or duplication, FEMA shall charge the actual direct costs of producing the document(s). If FEMA estimates that the allowable duplication charges are likely to exceed $25, it shall notify the requester of the estimated amount of fees, unless the requester has indicated in advance his/her willingness to pay fees as high as those anticipated. Such

a notice shall offer a requester the opportunity to confer with agency personnel with the objective of reformulating the request to meet his/her needs at a lower cost.

(b) Interest may be charge to those requesters who fail to pay fees charged. FEMA may begin assessing interest charges on the amount billed starting on the 31st day following the day on which the billing was sent. Interest will be at the rate prescribed in section 3717 of title 31 U.S.C.

[52 FR 13679, Apr. 24, 1987]

Subpart G—Exempt Systems of Records

§ 6.86 General exemptions.

(a) Whenever the Administrator, Federal Emergency Management Agency, determines it to be necessary and proper, with respect to any system of records maintained by the Federal Emergency Management Agency, to exercise the right to promulgate rules to exempt such systems in accordance with the provisions of 5 U.S.C. 552a (j) and (k), each specific exemption, including the parts of each system to be exempted, the provisions of the Act from which they are exempted, and the justification for each exemption shall be published in the FEDERAL REGISTER as part of FEMA's Notice of Systems of Records.

(b) Exempt under 5 U.S.C. 552a(j)(2) from the requirements of 5 U.S.C. 552a(c) (3) and (4), (d), (e) (1), (2), (3), (e)(4) (G), (H), and (I), (e) (5) and (8) (f) and (g) of the Privacy Act.

(1) *Exempt systems.* The following systems of records, which contain information of the type described in 5 U.S.C. 552(j)(2), shall be exempt from the provisions of 5 U.S.C. 552a listed in paragraph (b) of this section.

General Investigative Files (FEMA/IG-2)— Limited Access

(2) *Reasons for exemptions.* (i) 5 U.S.C. 552a (e)(4)(G) and (f)(1) enable individuals to be notified whether a system of records contains records pertaining to them. The Federal Emergency Management Agency believes that application of these provisions to the above-listed system of records would give individuals an opportunity to learn whether

they are of record either as suspects or as subjects of a criminal investigation; this would compromise the ability of the Federal Emergency Management Agency to complete investigations and identify or detect violators of laws administered by the Federal Emergency Management Agency or other Federal agencies. Individuals would be able (A) to take steps to avoid detection, (B) to inform co-conspirators of the fact that an investigation is being conducted, (C) to learn the nature of the investigation to which they are being subjected, (D) to learn the type of surveillance being utilized, (E) to learn whether they are only suspects or identified law violators, (F) to continue to resume their illegal conduct without fear of detection upon learning that they are not in a particular system of records, and (G) to destroy evidence needed to prove the violation.

(ii) 5 U.S.C. 552a (d)(1), (e)(4)(H) and (f)(2), (3) and (5) enable individuals to gain access to records pertaining to them. The Federal Emergency Management Agency believes that application of these provisions to the above-listed system of records would compromise its ability to complete or continue criminal investigations and to detect or identify violators of laws administered by the Federal Emergency Management Agency or other Federal agencies. Permitting access to records contained in the above-listed system of records would provide individuals with significant information concerning the nature of the investigation, and this could enable them to avoid detection or apprehension in the following ways:

(A) By discovering the collection of facts which would form the basis for their arrest, (B) by enabling them to destroy evidence of criminal conduct which would form the basis for their arrest, and (C) by learning that the criminal investigators had reason to believe that a crime was about to be committed, they could delay the commission of the crime or change the scene of the crime to a location which might not be under surveillance. Granting access to ongoing or closed investigative files would also reveal investigative techniques and procedures, the knowledge of which could enable individuals planning criminal activity to structure their future operations in such a way as to avoid detection or apprehension, thereby neutralizing law enforcement officers' established investigative tools and procedures. Further, granting access to investigative files and records could disclose the identity of confidential sources and other informers and the nature of the information which they supplied, thereby endangering the life or physical safety of those sources of information by exposing them to possible reprisals for having provided information relating to the criminal activities of those individuals who are the subjects of the investigative files and records; confidential sources and other informers might refuse to provide criminal investigators with valuable information if they could not be secure in the knowledge that their identities would not be revealed through disclosure of either their names or the nature of the information they supplied, and this would seriously impair the ability of the Federal Emergency Management Agency to carry out its mandate to enforce criminal and related laws. Additionally, providing access to records contained in the above-listed system of records could reveal the identities of undercover law enforcement personnel who compiled information regarding individual's criminal activities, thereby endangering the life or physical safety of those undercover personnel or their families by exposing them to possible reprisals.

(iii) 5 U.S.C. 552a(d) (2), (3) and (4), (e)(4)(H) and (f)(4), which are dependent upon access having been granted to records pursuant to the provisions cited in paragraph (b)(2)(ii) of this section, enable individuals to contest (seek amendment to) the content of records contained in a system of records and require an agency to note an amended record and to provide a copy of an individual's statement (of disagreement with the agency's refusal to amend a record) to persons or other agencies to whom the record has been disclosed. The Federal Emergency Management Agency believes that the reasons set forth in paragraph (b)(2)(ii) of this section are equally applicable to this paragraph and, accordingly, those reasons are hereby incorporated herein by reference.

(iv) 5 U.S.C. 552a(c)(3) requires that an agency make accountings of disclosures of records available to individuals named in the records at their request; such accountings must state the date, nature and purpose of each disclosure of a record and the name and address of the recipient. The Federal Emergency Management Agency believes that application of this provision to the above-listed system of records would impair the ability of other law enforcement agencies to make effective use of information provided by the Federal Emergency Management Agency in connection with the investigation, detection and apprehension of violators of the criminal laws enforced by those other law enforcement agencies. Making accountings of disclosure available to violators or possible violators would alert those individuals to the fact that another agency is conducting an investigation into their criminal activities, and this could reveal the geographic location of the other agency's investigation, the nature and purpose of that investigation, and the dates on which that investigation was active. Violators possessing such knowledge would thereby be able to take appropriate measures to avoid detection or apprehension by altering their operations, by transferring their criminal activities to other geographic areas or by destroying or concealing evidence which would form the basis for their arrest. In addition, providing violators with accountings of disclosure would alert those individuals to the fact that the Federal Emergency Management Agency has information regarding their criminal activities and could inform those individuals of the general nature of that information; this, in turn, would afford those individuals a better opportunity to take appropriate steps to avoid detection or apprehension for violations of criminal and related laws.

(v) 5 U.S.C. 552a(c)(4) requires that an agency inform any person or other agency about any correction or notation of dispute made by the agency in accordance with 5 U.S.C. 552a(d) of any record that has been disclosed to the person or agency if an accounting of the disclosure was made. Since this provision is dependent on an individual's having been provided an opportunity to contest (seek amendment to) records pertaining to him/her, and since the above-listed system of records is proposed to be exempt from those provisions of 5 U.S.C. 552a relating to amendments of records as indicated in paragraph (b)(2)(iii) of this section, the Federal Emergency Management Agency believes that this provision should not be applicable to the above system of records.

(vi) 5 U.S.C. 552a(e)(4)(I) requires that an agency publish a public notice listing the categories of sources for information contained in a system of records. The categories of sources of this system of records have been published in the FEDERAL REGISTER in broad generic terms in the belief that this is all that subsection (e)(4)(I) of the Act requires. In the event, however, that this subsection should be interpreted to require more detail as to the identity of sources of the records in this system, exemption from this provision is necessary in order to protect the confidentiality of the sources of criminal and other law enforcement information. Such exemption is further necessary to protect the privacy and physical safety of witnesses and informants.

(vii) 5 U.S.C. 552a(e)(1) requires that an agency maintain in its records only such information about an individual as is relevant and necessary to accomplish a purpose of the agency required to be accomplished by statute or executive order. The term *maintain* as defined in 5 U.S.C. 552a(a)(3) includes "collect" and "disseminate." At the time that information is collected by the Federal Emergency Management Agency, there is often insufficient time to determine whether the information is relevant and necessary to accomplish a purpose of the Federal Emergency Management Agency; in many cases information collected may not be immediately susceptible to a determination of whether the information is relevant and necessary, particularly in the early stages of an investigation, and in many cases, information which initially appears to be irrelevant or unnecessary may, upon further evaluation or upon continuation of the inves-

tigation, prove to have particular relevance to an enforcement program of the Federal Emergency Management Agency. Further, not all violations of law discovered during a criminal investigation fall within the investigative jurisdiction of the Federal Emergency Management Agency; in order to promote effective law enforcement, it often becomes necessary and desirable to disseminate information pertaining to such violations to other law enforcement agencies which have jurisdiction over the offense to which the information relates. The Federal Emergency Management Agency should not be placed in a position of having to ignore information relating to violations of law not within its jurisdiction when that information comes to the attention of the Federal Emergency Management Agency through the conduct of a lawful FEMA investigation. The Federal Emergency Management Agency, therefore, believes that it is appropriate to exempt the above-listed system of records from the provisions of 5 U.S.C. 552a(e)(1).

(viii) 5 U.S.C. 552a(e)(2) requires that an agency collect information to the greatest extent practicable directly from the subject individual when the information may result in adverse determinations about an individual's rights, benefits, and privileges under Federal programs. The Federal Emergency Management Agency believes that application of this provision to the above-listed system of records would impair the ability of the Federal Emergency Management Agency to conduct investigations and to identify or detect violators of criminal or related laws for the following reasons:

(A) Most information collected about an individual under criminal investigations is obtained from third parties such as witnesses and informers, and it is usually not feasible to rely upon the subject of the investigation as a source for information regarding his/her criminal activities, (B) an attempt to obtain information from the subject of a criminal investigation will often alert that individual to the existence of an investigation, thereby affording the individual an opportunity to attempt to conceal his/her criminal activities so as to avoid apprehension, (C) in certain instances, the subject of a criminal investigation is not required to supply information to criminal investigators as a matter of legal duty, and (D) during criminal investigations it is often a matter of sound investigative procedures to obtain information from a variety of sources in order to verify information already obtained.

(ix) 5 U.S.C. 552a(e)(3) requires that an agency inform each individual whom it asks to supply information, either on the form which the agency uses to collect the information or on a separate form which can be retained by the individual, with the following information: The authority which authorizes the solicitation of the information and whether disclosure of such information is mandatory or voluntary; the principal purposes for which the information is intended to be used; the routine uses which may be made of the information; and the effects on the individual of not providing all or part of the requested information. The Federal Emergency Management Agency believes that the above-listed system of records should be exempted from this provision in order to avoid adverse effects on its ability to identify or detect violators of criminal or related laws. In many cases, information is obtained by confidential sources, other informers or undercover law enforcement officers under circumstances where it is necessary that the true purpose of their actions be kept secret so as to avoid alerting the subject of the investigation or his/her associates that a criminal investigation is in process. Further, if it became known that the undercover officer was assisting in a criminal investigation, that officer's life or physical safety could be endangered through reprisal, and, under such circumstances it may not be possible to continue to utilize that officer in the investigation. In many cases, individuals, for personal reasons, would feel inhibited in talking to a person representing a criminal law enforcement agency but would be willing to talk to a confidential source or undercover officer who they believe is not involved in law enforcement activities. In addition, providing a source of information with written evidence that he

was a source, as required by this provision, could increase the likelihood that the source of information would be the subject of retaliatory action by the subject of the investigation. Further, application of this provision could result in an unwarranted invasion of the personal privacy of the subject of the criminal investigation, particularly where further investigation would result in a finding that the subject was not involved in any criminal activity.

(x) 5 U.S.C. 552a(e)(5) requires that an agency maintain all records used by the agency in making any determination about any individual with such accuracy, relevance, timeliness and completeness as is reasonably necessary to assure fairness to the individual in the determination. Since 5 U.S.C. 552a(a)(3) defines "maintain" to include "collect" and "disseminate," application of this provision to the above-listed system of records would hinder the initial collection of any information which could not, at the moment of collection, be determined to be accurate, relevant, timely and complete. Similarly, application of this provision would seriously restrict the necessary flow of information from the Federal Emergency Management Agency to other law enforcement agencies when a FEMA investigation revealed information pertaining to a violation of law which was under investigative jurisdiction of another agency. In collecting information during the course of a criminal investigation, it is not possible or feasible to determine accuracy, relevance, timeliness or completeness prior to collection of the information; in disseminating information to other law enforcement agencies it is often not possible to determine accuracy, relevance, timeliness or completeness prior to dissemination because the disseminating agency may not have the expertise with which to make such determinations. Further, information which may initially appear to be inaccurate, irrelevant, untimely or incomplete may, when gathered, grouped, and evaluated with other available information, become more pertinent as an investigation progresses. In addition, application of this provision could seriously impede criminal investigators and intelligence analysts in the exercise of their judgment in reporting on results obtained during criminal investigations. The Federal Emergency Management Agency believes that it is appropriate to exempt the above-listed system of records from the provisions of 5 U.S.C. 552a(e)(5).

(xi) 5 U.S.C. 552a(e)(8) requires that an agency make reasonable effort to serve notice on an individual when any record on the individual is made available to any person under compulsory legal process when such process becomes a matter of public record. The Federal Emergency Management Agency believes that the above-listed system of records should be exempt from this provision in order to avoid revealing investigative techniques and procedures outlined in those records and in order to prevent revelation of the existence on an on-going investigation where there is a need to keep the existence of the investigation secret.

(xii) 5 U.S.C. 552a(g) provides civil remedies to an individual for an agency's refusal to amend a record or to make a review of a request for amendment; for an agency's refusal to grant access to a record; for an agency's failure to maintain accurate, relevant, timely and complete records which are used to make a determination which is adverse to the individual; and for an agency's failure to comply with any other provision of 5 U.S.C. 552a in such a way as to have an adverse effect on an individual. The Federal Emergency Management Agency believes that the above-listed system of records should be exempted from this provision to the extent that the civil remedies provided therein may relate to provisions of 5 U.S.C. 552a from which the above-listed system of records is proposed to be exempt. Since the provisions of 5 U.S.C. 552a enumerated in paragraphs (b)(2)(i) through (xi) of this section are proposed to be inapplicable to the above-listed systems of records for the reasons stated therein, there should be no corresponding civil remedies for failure to comply with the requirements of those provisions to which the exemption is proposed to apply. Further, the Federal Emergency Management Agency believes that application of this provision to the above-listed system of records would adversely affect its abil-

ity to conduct criminal investigations by exposing to civil court action every stage of the criminal investigative process in which information is compiled or used in order to identify, detect, or otherwise investigate persons suspected or known to be engaged in criminal conduct.

(xiii) Individuals may not have access to another agency's records, which are contained in files maintained by the Federal Emergency Management Agency, when that other agency's regulations provide that such records are subject to general exemption under 5 U.S.C. 552a(j). If such exempt records are within a request for access, FEMA will advise the individual of their existence and of the name and address of the source agency. For any further information concerning the record and the exemption, the individual must contact that source agency.

[45 FR 64580, Sept. 30, 1980]

§ 6.87   Specific exemptions.

(a) *Exempt under 5 U.S.C. 552a(k)(1).* The Administrator, Federal Emergency Management Agency has determined that certain systems of records may be exempt from the requirements of (c)(3) and (d) pursuant to 5 U.S.C. 552a(k)(1) to the extent that the system contains any information properly classified under Executive Order 12356 or any subsequent Executive order and which are required to be kept secret in the interest of national defense or foreign policy. To the extent that this occurs, such records in the following systems would be exempt:

Claims (litigation) (FEMA/GC–1)—Limited Access
FEMA Enforcement (Compliance) (FEMA/GC–2)—Limited Access
General Investigative Files (FEMA/IG–1)—Limited Access
Security Management Information System (FEMA/SEC–1)—Limited Access

(b) *Exempt under 5 U.S.C. 552a(k)(2) from the requirements of 5 U.S.C. 552a (c)(3), (d), (e)(1), (e)(4) (G), (H), and (I), and (f).* The Federal Emergency Management Agency will not deny individuals access to information which has been used to deny them a right, privilege, or benefit to which they would otherwise be entitled.

(1) *Exempt systems.* The following systems of records, which contain information of the type described in 5 U.S.C. 552a(k)(2), shall be exempt from the provisions of 5 U.S.C. 552a(k)(2) listed in paragraph (b) of this section.

Claims (litigation) (FEMA/GC–1)—Limited Access

FEMA Enforcement (Compliance) (FEMA/ GC–2)—Limited Access

General Investigative Files (FEMA/IG–1)— Limited Access

Equal Employment Opportunity Complaints of Discrimination Files (FEMA/PER–2)— Limited Access

(2) *Reasons for exemptions.* (i) 5 U.S.C. 552a (e)(4)(G) and (f)(1) enable individuals to be notified whether a system of records contains records pertaining to them. The Federal Emergency Management Agency believes that application of these provisions to the above-listed systems of records would impair the ability of FEMA to successfully complete investigations and inquiries of suspected violators of civil and criminal laws and regulations under its jurisdiction. In many cases investigations and inquiries into violations of civil and criminal laws and regulations involve complex and continuing patterns of behavior. Individuals, if informed, that they have been identified as suspected violators of civil or criminal laws and regulations, would have an opportunity to take measures to prevent detection of illegal action so as to avoid prosecution or the imposition of civil sanctions. They would also be able to learn the nature and location of the investigation or inquiry, the type of surveillance being utilized, and they would be able to transmit this knowledge to co-conspirators. Finally, violators might be given the opportunity to destroy evidence needed to prove the violation under investigation or inquiry.

(ii) 5 U.S.C. 552a (d)(1), (e)(4)(H) and (f)(2), (3) and (5) enable individuals to gain access to records pertaining to them. The Federal Emergency Management Agency believes that application of these provisions to the above-listed systems of records would impair its ability to complete or continue civil or criminal investigations and inquiries and to detect violators of civil or criminal laws. Permitting access to

records contained in the above-listed systems of records would provide violators with significant information concerning the nature of the civil or criminal investigation or inquiry. Knowledge of the facts developed during an investigation or inquiry would enable violators of criminal and civil laws and regulations to learn the extent to which the investigation or inquiry has progressed, and this could provide them with an opportunity to destroy evidence that would form the basis for prosecution or the imposition of civil sanctions. In addition, knowledge gained through access to investigatory material could alert a violator to the need to temporarily postpone commission of the violation or to change the intended point where the violation is to be committed so as to avoid detection or apprehension. Further, access to investigatory material would disclose investigative techniques and procedures which, if known, could enable violators to structure their future operations in such a way as to avoid detection or apprehension, thereby neutralizing investigators' established and effective investigative tools and procedures. In addition, investigatory material may contain the identity of a confidential source of information or other informer who would not want his/her identity to be disclosed for reasons of personal privacy or for fear of reprisal at the hands of the individual about whom he/she supplied information. In some cases mere disclosure of the information provided by an informer would reveal the identity of the informer either through the process of elimination or by virtue of the nature of the information supplied. If informers cannot be assured that their identities (as sources for information) will remain confidential, they would be very reluctant in the future to provide information pertaining to violations of criminal and civil laws and regulations, and this would seriously compromise the ability of the Federal Emergency Management Agency to carry out its mission. Further, application of 5 U.S.C. 552a (d)(1), (e)(4)(H) and (f)(2), (3) and (5) to the above-listed systems of records would make available attorney's work product and other documents which contain evaluations, recommendations, and discussions of ongoing civil and criminal legal proceedings; the availability of such documents could have a chilling effect on the free flow of information and ideas within the Federal Emergency Management Agency which is vital to the agency's predecisional deliberative process, could seriously prejudice the agency's or the Government's position in a civil or criminal litigation, and could result in the disclosure of investigatory material which should not be disclosed for the reasons stated above. It is the belief of the Federal Emergency Management Agency that, in both civil actions and criminal prosecutions, due process will assure that individuals have a reasonable opportunity to learn of the existence of, and to challenge, investigatory records and related materials which are to be used in legal proceedings.

(iii) 5 U.S.C. 552a (d)(2), (3) and (4), (e)(4)(H) and (f)(4) which are dependent upon access having been granted to records pursuant to the provisions cited in paragraph (b)(2)(ii) of this section, enable individuals to contest (seek amendment to) the content of records contained in a system of records and require an agency to note an amended record and to provide a copy of an individual's statement (of disagreement with the agency's refusal to amend a record) to persons or other agencies to whom the record has been disclosed. The Federal Emergency Management Agency believes that the reasons set forth in paragraphs (b)(2)(i) of this section are equally applicable to this paragraph, and, accordingly, those reasons are hereby incorporated herein by reference.

(iv) 5 U.S.C. 552a(c)(3) requires that an agency make accountings of disclosures of records available to individuals named in the records at their request; such accountings must state the date, nature, and purpose of each disclosure of a record and the name and address of the recipient. The Federal Emergency Management Agency believes that application of this provision to the above-listed systems of records would impair the ability of the Federal Emergency Management Agency and other law enforcement agencies to conduct investigations and inquiries into civil and criminal violations under their respective jurisdictions. Making accountings available to violators would alert those individuals to the fact that the Federal Emergency Management Agency or another law enforcement authority is conducting an investigation or inquiry into their activities, and such accountings could reveal the geographic location of the investigation or inquiry, the nature and purpose of the investigation or inquiry and the nature of the information disclosed, and the date on which that investigation or inquiry was active. Violators possessing such knowledge would thereby be able to take appropriate measures to avoid detection or apprehension by altering their operations, transferring their activities to other locations or destroying or concealing evidence which would form the basis for prosecution or the imposition of civil sanctions.

(v) 5 U.S.C. 552a(e)(1) requires that an agency maintain in its records only such information about an individual as is relevant and necessary to accomplish a purpose of the agency required to be accomplished by statute or executive order. The term *maintain* as defined in 5 U.S.C. 552a(a)(3) includes "collect" and "disseminate." At the time that information is collected by the Federal Emergency Management Agency there is often insufficient time to determine whether the information is relevant and necessary to accomplish a purpose of the Federal Emergency Management Agency; in many cases information collected may not be immediately susceptible to a determination of whether the information is relevant and necessary, particularly in the early stages of investigation or inquiry, and in many cases information which initially appears to be irrelevant or unnecessary may, upon further evaluation or upon continuation of the investigation or inquiry, prove to have particular relevance to an enforcement program of the Federal Emergency Management Agency. Further, not all violations of law uncovered during a Federal Emergency Management Agency inquiry fall within the civil or criminal jurisdiction of the Federal

Emergency Management Agency; in order to promote effective law enforcement, it often becomes necessary and desirable to disseminate information pertaining to such violations to other law enforcement agencies which have jurisdiction over the offense to which the information relates. The Federal Emergency Management Agency should not be placed in a position of having to ignore information relating to violations of law not within its jurisdiction when that information comes to the attention of the Federal Emergency Management Agency through the conduct of a lawful FEMAs civil or criminal investigation or inquiry. The Federal Emergency Management Agency therefore believes that it is appropriate to exempt the above-listed systems of records from the provisions of 5 U.S.C. 552a(e)(1).

(c) *Exempt under 5 U.S.C. 552a(k)(5)*. The Administrator, Federal Emergency Management Agency has determined that certain systems of records are exempt from the requirements of (c)(3) and (d) of 5 U.S.C. 552a.

(1) *Exempt systems*. The following systems of records, which contain information of the type described in 5 U.S.C. 552a(k)(5), shall be exempted from the provisions of 5 U.S.C. 552a listed in paragraph (c) of this section.

Claims (litigation) (FEMA/GC–1)—Limited Access
FEMA Enforcement (Compliance) (FEMA/GC–2)—Limited Access
General Investigative Files (FEMA/IG–2)—Limited Access
Security Management Information Systems (FEMA/SEC–1)—Limited Access

(2) *Reasons for exemptions*. All information about individuals in these records that meet the criteria stated in 5 U.S.C. 552a(k)(5) is exempt from the requirements of 5 U.S.C. 552a (c)(3) and (d). These provisions of the Privacy Act relate to making accountings of disclosure available to the subject and access to and amendment of records. These exemptions are claimed because the system of records entitled, FEMA/SEC–1, Security Management Information System, contains investigatory material compiled solely for the purpose of determining suitability, ·eligibility, or qualifications for access to classified information or classified Federal con-

tracts, but only to the extent that the disclosure would reveal the identity of a source who furnished information to the Government under an express promise or, prior to September 27, 1975, under an implied promise that the identity of the source would be held in confidence. During the litigation process and investigations, it is possible that certain records from the system of records entitled, FEMA/SEC–1, Security Management System may be necessary and relevant to the litigation or investigation and included in these systems of records. To the extent that this occurs, the Administrator, FEMA, has determined that the records would also be exempted from subsections (c)(3) and (d) pursuant to 5 U.S.C. 552a(k)(5) to protect such records. A determination will be made at the time of the request for a record concerning whether specific information would reveal the identity of a source. This exemption is required in order to protect the confidentiality of the sources of information compiled for the purpose of determining access to classified information. This confidentiality helps maintain the Government's continued access to information from persons who would otherwise refuse to give it.

[45 FR 64580, Sept. 30, 1980, as amended at 47 FR 54816, Dec. 6, 1982; 52 FR 5114, Feb. 19, 1987]

PART 7—NONDISCRIMINATION IN FEDERALLY-ASSISTED PROGRAMS (FEMA REG. 5)

Subpart A—Nondiscrimination in FEMA-Assisted Programs—General

7.16 Effect on other regulations; forms and instructions.

Subparts B–D [Reserved]

Subpart E—Nondiscrimination on the Basis of Age in Programs or Activities Receiving Federal Financial Assistance From FEMA

SOURCE: 30 FR 321, Jan. 9, 1965, unless otherwise noted. Redesignated at 45 FR 44575, July 1, 1980.

Subpart A—Nondiscrimination in FEMA-Assisted Programs—General

AUTHORITY: FEMA Reg. 5 issued under sec. 602, 78 Stat. 252; 42 U.S.C. 2000 d–1; 42 U.S.C. 1855–1885g; 50 U.S.C. 404.

SOURCE: 30 FR 321, Jan. 9, 1965, unless otherwise noted. Redesignated at 45 FR 44575, July 1, 1980, and further redesignated at 55 FR 23078, June 6, 1990.

§ 7.1 Purpose.

The purpose of this regulation is to effectuate the provisions of title VI of the Civil Rights Act of 1964 (hereafter referred to as the "Act") to the end that no person in the United States shall, on the ground of race, color, or national origin, be excluded from participation in, be denied the benefits of, or be otherwise subjected to discrimination under any program or activity receiving Federal financial assistance from the Federal Emergency Management Agency.

§ 7.2 Definitions.

As used in this regulation:

(a) The term *responsible agency official* with respect to any program receiving Federal financial assistance means the Administrator of the Federal Emergency Management Agency or other official of the agency who by law or by delegation has the principal responsibility within the agency for the administration of the law extending such assistance.

(b) The term *United States* means the States of the United States, the District of Columbia, Puerto Rico, the Virgin Islands, American Samoa, Guam, Wake Island, the Canal Zone, and the territories and possessions of the United States, and the term *State* means any one of the foregoing.

(c) The term *Federal financial assistance* includes (1) grants and loans of Federal funds, (2) the grant or donation of Federal property and interests in property, (3) the detail of Federal personnel, (4) the sale and lease of, and the permission to use (on other than a casual or transient basis), Federal property or any interest in such property without consideration or at a nominal consideration, or at a consideration which is reduced for the purpose of assisting the recipient, or in recognition of the public interest to be served by such sale or lease to the recipient, and (5) any Federal agreement, arrangement, or other contract which has as one of its purposes the provision of assistance.

(d) The terms *program or activity* and *program* mean all of the operations of any entity described in paragraphs (d)(1) through (4) of this section, any part of which is extended Federal financial assistance:

(1)(i) A department, agency, special purpose district, or other instrumentality of a State or of a local government; or

(ii) The entity of such State or local government that distributes such assistance and each such department or agency (and each other State or local government entity) to which the assistance is extended, in the case of assistance to a State or local government;

(2)(i) A college, university, or other postsecondary institution, or a public system of higher education; or

(ii) A local educational agency (as defined in 20 U.S.C. 7801), system of vocational education, or other school system;

(3)(i) An entire corporation, partnership, or other private organization, or an entire sole proprietorship—

(A) If assistance is extended to such corporation, partnership, private organization, or sole proprietorship as a whole; or

(B) Which is principally engaged in the business of providing education, health care, housing, social services, or parks and recreation; or

(ii) The entire plant or other comparable, geographically separate facility to which Federal financial assistance is extended, in the case of any other corporation, partnership, private organization, or sole proprietorship; or

(4) Any other entity which is established by two or more of the entities described in paragraph (d)(1), (2), or (3) of this section.

(e) The term *facility* includes all or any portion of structure, equipment, or other real or personal property or interests therein, and the provision of facilities includes the construction, expansion, renovation, remodeling, alteration or acquisition of facilities.

(f) The term *recipient* means any State, political subdivision of any State, or instrumentality of any State or political subdivision, any public or private agency, institution, or organization, or other entity, or any individual, in any State, to whom Federal financial assistance is extended, directly or through another recipient, including any successor, assign, or transferee thereof, but such term does not include any ultimate beneficiary.

(g) The term *primary recipient* means any recipient which is authorized or required to extend Federal financial assistance to another recipient.

(h) The term *applicant* means one who submits an application, request, or plan required to be approved by a responsible agency official, or by a primary recipient, as a condition to eligibility for Federal financial assistance, and the term *application* means such an application, request, or plan.

[30 FR 321, Jan. 9, 1965. Redesignated at 45 FR 44575, July 1, 1980, and further redesignated at 55 FR 23078, June 6, 1990. 68 FR 51379, Aug. 26, 2003]

§7.3 Application of this regulation.

No person in the United States shall, on the ground of race, color, or national origin, be excluded from participation in, be denied the benefits of, or be otherwise subjected to discrimination under any program to which this regulation applies.

[68 FR 51379, Aug. 26, 2003]

§7.4 Further application of this regulation.

This regulation applies to any program for which Federal financial assistance is authorized under a law administered by the Federal Emergency Management Agency. It applies to money paid, property transferred, or other Federal financial assistance extended after the effective date of the regulation pursuant to an application approved prior to such effective date. This regulation does not apply to (a) any Federal financial assistance by way of insurance or guaranty contracts, (b) money paid, property transferred, or other assistance extended before the effective date of this regulation, (c) any assistance to any individual who is the ultimate beneficiary, or (d) any employment practice, under such program, of any employer, employment agency, or labor organization.

(Reorganization Plan No. 3 of 1978, E.O. 12127 and E.O. 12148)

[30 FR 321, Jan. 9, 1965. Redesignated at 45 FR 44575, July 1, 1980, as amended at 48 FR 44543, Sept. 29, 1983; 68 FR 51379, Aug. 26, 2003]

§ 7.5 Specific discriminatory actions prohibited.

(a) A recipient to which this regulation applies may not, directly or through contractual or other arrangements, on ground of race, color, or national origin:

(1) Deny any individual any service, financial aid, or other benefit provided under the program;

(2) Provide any service, financial aid, or other benefit to an individual which is different, or is provided in a different manner, from that provided to others under the program;

(3) Subject an individual to segregation or separate treatment in any matter related to his receipt of any service, financial aid, or other benefit under the program;

(4) Restrict an individual in any way in the enjoyment of any advantage or privilege enjoyed by others receiving any service, financial aid, or other benefit under the program;

(5) Treat an individual differently from others in determining whether he satisfies any admission, enrollment, quota, eligibility, membership or other requirement or condition which individuals must meet in order to be provided any service, financial aid, or other benefit provided under the program;

(6) Deny an individual an opportunity to participate in the program through the provision of services or otherwise or afford him an opportunity to do so which is different from that afforded others under the program.

(b) A recipient, in determining the types of services, financial aid, or other benefits, or facilities which will be provided under any such program, or the class of individuals to whom, or the situations in which, such services, financial aid, other benefits, or facilities will be provided under any such program, or the class of individuals to be afforded an opportunity to participate in any such program, may not, directly or through contractual or other arrangements, utilize criteria or methods of administration which have the effect of subjecting individuals to discrimination because of their race, color, or national origin, or have the effect of defeating or substantially impairing accomplishment of the objectives of the program as respect individuals of a particular race, color, or national origin.

(c) As used in this section the services, financial aid, or other benefits provided under a program receiving Federal financial assistance shall be deemed to include any service, financial aid, or other benefit provided in or through a facility provided with the aid of Federal financial assistance.

(d) The enumeration of specific forms of prohibited discrimination in this section does not limit the generality of the prohibition in section 4.

[30 FR 321, Jan. 9, 1965. Redesignated at 45 FR 44575, July 1, 1980, and further redesignated at 55 FR 23078, June 6, 1990. 68 FR 51379, Aug. 26, 2003]

§ 7.6 Life, health, and safety.

Notwithstanding the provisions of section 5, a recipient of Federal financial assistance shall not be deemed to have failed to comply with section 3, if immediate provision of a service or other benefit to an individual is necessary to prevent his death or serious impairment of his health or safety.

§ 7.7 Assurances required.

Every application for Federal financial assistance to which this regulation applies, and every application for Federal financial assistance to provide a facility shall, as a condition to its approval and the extension of any Federal financial assistance pursuant to the application, contain or be accompanied by an assurance that the program will be conducted or the facility operated in compliance with all requirements imposed by or pursuant to this regulation. In the case of an application for Federal financial assistance to provide real property or structures thereon, the assurance shall obligate the recipient, or, in the case of a subsequent transfer, the transferee, for the period during which the real property or structures are used for a purpose for which the Federal financial assistance is extended or for another purpose involving the provision of similar services or benefits. In the case of personal property the assurance shall obligate the recipient for the period during which he retains ownership or possession of the property. In all other cases the assurance shall obligate the recipient for the period during which Federal financial assistance is extended pursuant to the application. The responsible agency official shall specify the form of the foregoing assurances and the extent to which like assurances will be required of subgrantee, contractors and subcontractors, transferees, successors in interest, and other participants. Any such assurance shall include provisions which give the United States a right to seek its judicial enforcement.

[30 FR 321, Jan. 9, 1965. Redesignated at 45 FR 44575, July 1, 1980, and further redesignated at 55 FR 23078, June 6, 1990. 68 FR 51379, Aug. 26, 2003]

§7.8 Elementary and secondary schools.

The requirements of section 7 with respect to any elementary or secondary school or school system shall be deemed to be satisfied if such school or school system (a) is subject to a final order of a court of the United States for the desegregation of such school or school system, and provides an assurance that it will comply with such order, including any future modification of such order, or (b) submits a plan for the desegregation of such school or school system which the United States Commissioner of Education determines is adequate to accomplish the purpose of the Act and this regulation, and provides reasonable assurance that it will carry out such plans; in any case of continuing Federal financial assistance the responsible agency official may reserve the right to redetermine, after such period as may be specified by him, the adequacy of the plan to accomplish the purposes of the Act and this regulation. In any case to which a final order of a court of the United States for the desegregation of such school or school system is entered after submission of such a plan, such plan shall be revised to conform to such final order, includ-

ing any future modification of such order.

§7.9 Assurances from institutions.

(a) In the case of any application for Federal financial assistance to an institution of higher education, the assurance required by section 7 shall extend to admission practices and to all other practices relating to the treatment of students.

(b) The assurances required with respect to an institution of higher education, hospital, or any other institution, insofar as the assurance relates to the institution's practices with respect to admission or other treatment of individuals as students, patients, or clients of the institutions or to the opportunity to participate in the provision of services or other benefits to such individuals, shall be applicable to the entire institution.

[30 FR 321, Jan. 9, 1965. Redesignated at 45 FR 44575, July 1, 1980, and further redesignated at 55 FR 23078, June 6, 1990. 68 FR 51379, Aug. 26, 2003]

§7.10 Compliance information.

(a) *Cooperation and assistance.* The responsible official in the Federal Emergency Management Agency shall to the fullest extent practicable seek the cooperation of recipients in obtaining compliance with this regulation and shall provide assistance and guidance to recipients to help them comply voluntarily with this regulation.

(b) *Compliance reports.* Each recipient shall keep such records and submit to the responsible agency official or his designee timely, complete, and accurate compliance reports at such times, and in such form and containing such information, as the responsible agency official or his designee may determine to be necessary to enable him to ascertain whether the recipient has complied or is complying with this regulation. In the case in which a primary recipient extends Federal financial assistance to any other recipient, such other recipient shall also submit such compliance reports to the primary recipient as may be necessary to enable the primary recipient to carry out its obligations under this regulation.

(c) *Access to sources of information.* Each recipient shall permit access by the responsible agency official or his designee during normal business hours to such of its books, records, accounts, and other sources of information, and its facilities as may be pertinent to ascertain compliance with this regulation. Where any information required of a recipient is in the exclusive possession of any other agency, institution or person and this agency, institution or person shall fail or refuse to furnish this information, the recipient shall so certify in its report and shall set forth what efforts it has made to obtain the information.

(d) *Information to beneficiaries and participants.* Each recipient shall make available to participants, beneficiaries, and other interested persons such information regarding the provisions of this regulation and its applicability to the program for which the recipient receives Federal financial assistance, and make such information available to them in such manner, as the responsible agency official finds necessary to apprise such persons of the protection against discrimination assured them by the Act and this regulation.

[30 FR 321, Jan. 9, 1965. Redesignated at 45 FR 44575, July 1, 1980, and further redesignated at 55 FR 23078, June 6, 1990. 68 FR 51379, Aug. 26, 2003]

§7.11 Conduct of investigations.

(a) *Periodic compliance reviews.* The responsible agency official or his designee shall from time to time review the practices of recipients to determine whether they are complying with this regulation.

(b) *Complaints.* Any person who believes himself or any specific class of individuals to be subjected to discrimination prohibited by this regulation may by himself or by a representative file a written complaint with the National Headquarters or any Regional Office of the Federal Emergency Management Agency. A complaint must be filed not later than 180 days from the date of the alleged discrimination, unless the time for filing is extended by the responsible agency official or his designee.

(c) *Investigations.* The responsible agency official or his designee will make a prompt investigation whenever a compliance review, report, complaint, or any other information indicates a possible failure to comply with this regulation. The investigation should include, where appropriate, a review of the pertinent practices and policies of the recipient, the circumstances under which the possible noncompliance with this regulation occurred, and other factors relevant to a determination as to whether the recipient has failed to comply with this regulation.

(d) *Resolution of matters.* (1) If an investigation pursuant to paragraph (c) of this section indicates a failure to comply with this regulation, the responsible agency official or his designee will so inform the recipient and the matter will be resolved by informal means whenever possible. If it has been determined that the matter cannot be resolved by informal means, action will be taken as provided for in section 12.

(2) If an investigation does not warrant action pursuant to paragraph (d)(1) of this section the responsible agency official or his designee will so inform the recipient and the complainant, if any, in writing.

(e) *Intimidatory or retaliatory acts prohibited.* No recipient or other person shall intimidate, threaten, coerce, or discriminate against any individual for the purpose of interfering with any right or privilege secured by section 601 of the Act or this regulation, or because he has made a complaint, testified, assisted, or participated in any manner in an investigation, proceeding, or hearing under this regulation. The identity of complainants shall be kept confidential except to the extent necessary to carry out the purposes of this regulation, including the conduct of any investigation, hearing, or judicial proceeding arising thereunder.

[30 FR 321, Jan. 9, 1965. Redesignated at 45 FR 44575, July 1, 1980, and further redesignated at 55 FR 23078, June 6, 1990, as amended at 64 FR 38309, July 16, 1999]

§7.12 Procedure for effecting compliance.

(a) *General.* If there appears to be a failure or threatened failure to comply with this regulation, and if the noncompliance or threatened noncompliance cannot be corrected by informal means, compliance with this regulation may be effected by the suspension or termination of or refusal to grant or to continue Federal financial assistance or by any other means authorized by law. Such other means may include, but are not limited to, (1) a reference to the Department of Justice with a recommendation that appropriate proceedings be brought to enforce any rights of the United States under any law of the United States (including other titles of the Act), or any assurance or other contractual undertaking, and (2) any applicable proceeding under state or local law.

(b) *Noncompliance with section 7.* If an applicant fails or refuses to furnish an assurance required under section 7 or otherwise fails or refuses to comply with a requirement imposed by or pursuant to that section Federal financial assistance may be refused in accordance with the procedures of paragraph (c) of this section. The agency shall not be required to provide assistance in such a case during the pendency of the administrative proceedings under such paragraph except that the agency shall continue assistance during the pendency of such proceedings where such assistance is due and payable pursuant to an application thereof approved prior to the effective date of this regulation.

(c) *Termination of or refusal to grant or to continue Federal financial assistance.* No order suspending, terminating or refusing to grant or continue Federal financial assistance shall become effective until (1) the responsible agency official has advised the applicant or recipient of his failure to comply and has determined that compliance cannot be secured by voluntary means, (2) there has been an express finding on the record, after opportunity for hearing, of a failure by the applicant or recipient to comply with a requirement imposed by or pursuant to this regulation, (3) the action has been approved by the Administrator of the Federal Emergency Management Agency pursuant to section 14, and (4) the expiration of 30 days after the Administrator has filed with the committee of the House and the committee of the Senate having legislative jurisdiction over the program involved, a full written report

of the circumstances and the grounds for such action. Any action to suspend or terminate or to refuse to grant or to continue Federal financial assistance shall be limited to the particular political entity, or part thereof, or other applicant or recipient as to whom such a finding has been made and shall be limited in its effect to the particular program, or part thereof, in which such noncompliance has been so found.

(d) *Other means authorized by law.* No action to effect compliance by any other means authorized by law shall be taken until (1) the responsible agency official has determined that compliance cannot be secured by voluntary means, (2) the action has been approved by the Administrator of the Federal Emergency Management Agency, (3) the recipient or other person has been notified of its failure to comply and of the action to be taken to effect compliance, and (4) the expiration of at least 10 days from the mailing of such notice to the recipient or other person. During this period of at least 10 days additional efforts shall be made to persuade the recipient or other person to comply with the regulation and to take such corrective action as may be appropriate.

§7.13 **Hearings.**

(a) *Opportunity for hearing.* Whenever an opportunity for a hearing is required by section 12(c), reasonable notice shall be given by registered or certified mail, return receipt requested, to the affected applicant or recipient. This notice shall advise the applicant or recipient of the action proposed to be taken, the specific provision under which the proposed action against it is to be taken, and the matters of fact or law asserted as the basis for this action, and either (1) fix a date not less than 20 days after the date of such notice within which the applicant or recipient may request of the responsible agency official that the matter be scheduled for hearing or (2) advise the applicant or recipient that the matter in question has been set down for hearing at a stated place and time. The time and place so fixed shall be reasonable and shall be subject to change for cause. The complainant, if any, shall be advised of the time and place of the

57

hearing. An applicant or recipient may waive a hearing and submit written information and argument for the record. The failure of an applicant or recipient to request a hearing under this subsection or to appear at a hearing for which a date has been set shall be deemed to be a waiver of the right to a hearing under section 602 of the Act and section 12(c) of this regulation and consent to the making of a decision on the basis of such information as is available.

(b) *Time and place of hearing.* Hearings shall be held at the National Headquarters of the Federal Emergency Management Agency in Washington, DC, at a time fixed by the responsible agency official unless he determines that the convenience of the applicant or recipient or of the agency requires that another place be selected. Hearings shall be held before the responsible agency official or, at his discretion, before a hearing examiner designated in accordance with section 11 of the Administrative Procedure Act.

(c) *Right to counsel.* In all proceedings under this section, the applicant or recipient and the agency shall have the right to be represented by counsel.

(d) *Procedures, evidence, and record.* (1) The hearing, decision, and any administrative review thereof shall be conducted in conformity with sections 5–8 of the Administrative Procedure Act, and in accordance with such rules of procedure as are proper (and not inconsistent with this section) relating to the conduct of the hearing, giving of notices subsequent to those provided for in paragraph (a) of this section, taking of testimony, exhibits, arguments and briefs, requests for findings, and other related matters. Both the agency and the applicant or recipient shall be entitled to introduce all relevant evidence on the issues as stated in the notice for hearing or as determined by the officer conducting the hearing at the outset of or during the hearing.

(2) Technical rules of evidence shall not apply to hearings conducted pursuant to this regulation, but rules or principles designed to assure production of the most credible evidence available and to subject testimony to test by cross-examination shall be ap-plied where reasonably necessary by the officer conducting the hearing. The hearing officer may exclude irrelevant, immaterial, or unduly repetitious evidence. All documents and other evidence offered or taken for the record shall be open to examination by the parties and opportunity shall be given to refute facts and arguments advanced on either side of the issues. A transcript shall be made of the oral evidence except to the extent the substance thereof is stipulated for the record. All decisions shall be based upon the hearing record and written findings shall be made.

(e) *Consolidated or joint hearings.* In cases in which the same or related facts are asserted to constitute noncompliance with this regulation with respect to two or more Federal statutes, authorities, or other means by which Federal financial assistance is extended and to which this regulation applies, or noncompliance with this regulation and the regulations of one or more other Federal departments or agencies issued under title VI of the Act, the Administrator of the Federal Emergency Management Agency may, by agreement with such other departments or agencies where applicable, provide for the conduct of consolidated or joint hearings, and for the application to such hearings of rules of procedures not inconsistent with this regulation. Final decisions in such cases, insofar as this regulation is concerned, shall be made in accordance with section 14.

[30 FR 321, Jan. 9, 1965. Redesignated at 45 FR 44575, July 1, 1980, and further redesignated at 55 FR 23078, June 6, 1990. 68 FR 51379, Aug. 26, 2003]

§ 7.14   Decisions and notices.

(a) *Decision by person other than the responsible agency official.* If the hearing is held by a hearing examiner such hearing examiner shall either make an initial decision, if so authorized, or certify the entire record including his recommended findings and proposed decision to the responsible agency official for a final decision, and a copy of such initial decision or certification shall be mailed to the applicant or recipient. Where the initial decision is made by the hearing examiner the applicant or recipient may within 30 days of the mailing of such notice of initial decision file with the responsible agency official his exceptions to the initial decision, with his reasons therefor. In the absence of exceptions, the responsible agency official may on his own motion within 45 days after the initial decision serve on the applicant or recipient a notice that he will review the decision. Upon the filing of such exceptions or of such notice of review the responsible agency official shall review the initial decision and issue his own decision thereon including the reasons therefor. In the absence of either exceptions or a notice of review the initial decision shall constitute the final decision of the responsible agency official.

(b) *Decisions on record or review by the responsible agency official.* Whenever a record is certified to the responsible agency official for decision or he reviews the decision of a hearing examiner pursuant to paragraph (a) of this section, or whenever he conducts the hearing, the applicant or recipient shall be given reasonable opportunity to file with him briefs or other written statements of its contentions, and a copy of his final decision shall be given in writing to the applicant or recipient and to the complainant, if any.

(c) *Decisions on record where a hearing is waived.* Whenever a hearing is waived pursuant to section 13(a) a decision shall be made by the responsible agency official on the record and a copy of such decision shall be given in writing to the applicant or recipient, and to the complainant, if any.

(d) *Rulings required.* Each decision of a hearing officer or responsible agency official shall set forth his ruling on each finding, conclusion, or exception presented, and shall identify the requirement or requirements imposed by or pursuant to this regulation with which it is found that the applicant or recipient has failed to comply.

(e) *Approval by Administrator.* Any final decision of a responsible agency official (other than the Director of the agency) which provides for the suspension or termination of, or the refusal to grant or continue Federal financial assistance, or the imposition of any other

sanction available under this regulation or the Act, shall promptly be transmitted to the Administrator of the Federal Emergency Management Agency who may approve such decision, may vacate it, or remit or mitigate any sanction imposed.

(f) *Content of orders.* The final decision may provide for suspension or termination of, or refusal to grant or continue Federal financial assistance, in whole or in part, to which this regulation applies, and may contain such terms, conditions, and other provisions as are consistent with and will effectuate the purposes of the Act and this regulation, including provisions designed to assure that no Federal financial assistance to which this regulation applies will thereafter be extended to the applicant or recipient determined by such decision to be in default in its performance of an assurance given by it pursuant to this regulation, or to have otherwise failed to comply with this regulation, unless and until it corrects its noncompliance and satisfies the Administrator of the Federal Emergency Management Agency that it will fully comply with this regulation.

[30 FR 321, Jan. 9, 1965. Redesignated at 45 FR 44575, July 1, 1980, and further redesignated at 55 FR 23078, June 6, 1990. 68 FR 51379, Aug. 26, 2003]

§7.15 Judicial review.

Action taken pursuant to section 602 of the Act is subject to judicial review as provided in section 603 of the Act.

§7.16 Effect on other regulations; forms and instructions.

(a) *Effect on other regulations.* All regulations, orders, or like directions heretofore issued by any officer of the Federal Emergency Management Agency which impose requirements designed to prohibit any discrimination against individuals on the ground of race, color, or national origin under any program to which this regulation applies, and which authorize the suspension or termination of or refusal to grant or to continue Federal financial assistance to any applicant for or recipient of such assistance for failure to comply with such requirements, are hereby superseded to the extent that such discrimination is prohibited by this regulation, except that nothing in this regulation shall be deemed to relieve any person of any obligation assumed or imposed under any such superseded regulation, order, instruction, or like direction prior to the effective date of this regulation. Nothing in this regulation, however, shall be deemed to supersede Executive Orders 10925 and 11114 (including future amendments thereof) and regulations issued thereunder, or any other regulations or instructions, insofar as such regulations or instructions prohibit discrimination on the ground of race, color, or national origin in any program or situation to which this regulation is inapplicable, or prohibit discrimination on any other ground.

(b) *Forms and instructions.* Each responsible agency official shall issue and promptly make available to interested persons forms and detailed instructions and procedures for effectuating this regulation as applied to programs to which this regulation applies and for which he is responsible.

(c) *Supervision and coordination.* The Administrator of the Federal Emergency Management Agency may from time to time assign to officials of other departments or agencies of the Government with the consent of such departments or agencies, responsibilities in connection with the effectuation of the purposes of title VI of the Act and this regulation (other than responsibility for final decision as provided in section 14), including the achievement of effective coordination and maximum uniformity within the agency and within the Executive Branch of the Government in the application of title VI and this regulation to similar programs and in similar situations.

[30 FR 321, Jan. 9, 1965. Redesignated at 45 FR 44575, July 1, 1980, and further redesignated at 55 FR 23078, June 6, 1990. 68 FR 51379, Aug. 26, 2003]

Subparts B–D [Reserved]

Subpart E—Nondiscrimination on the Basis of Age in Programs or Activities Receiving Federal Financial Assistance From FEMA

AUTHORITY: Age Discrimination Act of 1975, as amended (42 U.S.C. 6101 *et seq.*); 45 CFR part 90.

SOURCE: 55 FR 23078, June 6, 1990, unless otherwise noted.

GENERAL

§ 7.910 What is the purpose of the Age Discrimination Act of 1975?

The Age Discrimination Act of 1975 (the "Act"), as amended, is designed to prohibit discrimination on the basis of age in programs or activities receiving Federal financial assistance. The Act also permits federally-assisted programs or activities, and recipients of Federal funds, to continue to use certain age distinctions and factors other than age which meet the requirements of the Act and this regulation.

[55 FR 23078, June 6, 1990, as amended at 68 FR 51380, Aug. 26, 2003]

§ 7.911 What is the purpose of FEMA's age discrimination regulation?

The purpose of this regulation is to set out FEMA's policies and procedures under the Age Discrimination Act of 1975 and the general governmentwide regulations, 45 CFR part 90. The Act and the general regulations prohibit discrimination on the basis of age in programs or activities receiving Federal financial assistance. The Act and the general regulations permit federally-assisted programs or activities, and recipients of Federal funds, to continue to use age distinctions and factors other than age which meet the requirements of the Act and its implementing regulations.

[55 FR 23078, June 6, 1990, as amended at 68 FR 51380, Aug. 26, 2003]

§ 7.912 To what programs or activities does this regulation apply?

(a) The Act and this regulation apply to each FEMA recipient and to each program or activity operated by the recipient which receives Federal financial assistance provided by FEMA.

(b) The Act and this regulation do not apply to:

(1) An age distinction contained in that part of a Federal, State or local statute or ordinance adopted by an elected, general purpose legislative body which:

(i) Provides any benefits or assistance to persons based on age; or

(ii) Establishes criteria for participation in age-related terms; or

(iii) Describes intended beneficiaries or target groups in age-related terms.

(2) Any employment practice of any employer, employment agency, labor organization, or any labor-management joint apprenticeship training program, except for any program or activity receiving Federal financial assistance for public service employment under the Job Training Partnership Act (29 U.S.C. 150, *et seq.*)

[55 FR 23078, June 6, 1990, as amended at 68 FR 51380, Aug. 26, 2003]

§ 7.913 Definition of terms used in this regulation.

As used in this regulation, the term *Act* means the Age Discrimination Act of 1975 as amended (title III of Pub. L. 94–135).

Action means any act, activity, policy, rule, standard, or method of administration; or the use of any policy, rule, standard or method of administration.

Administrator means the Administrator of the Federal Emergency Management Agency.

Age means how old a person is, or the number of years from the date of a person's birth.

Age distinction means any action using age or an age-related term.

Age-related term means a word or words which necessarily imply a particular age or range of ages (for example, *children, older persons,* but not *student*).

Agency means the Federal Emergency Management Agency.

Federal financial assistance means any grant, entitlement, loan, cooperative agreement, contract (other than a procurement contract or a contract of insurance or guaranty), or any other arrangement by which the agency provides or otherwise makes available assistance in the form of:

(a) Funds; or

(b) Services or Federal personnel; or

(c) Real and personal property or any interest in or use of property, including:

(1) Transfers or leases of property for less than fair market value or for reduced consideration; and

(2) Proceeds from a subsequent transfer or lease of property if the Federal share of its fair market value is not returned to the Federal Government.

Normal operation means the operation of a program or activity without significant changes that would impair its ability to meet its objective.

Program or activity means all of the operations of any entity described in paragraphs (1) through (4) of this definition, any part of which is extended Federal financial assistance:

(1)(i) A department, agency, special purpose district, or other instrumentality of a State or of a local government; or

(ii) The entity of such State or local government that distributes such assistance and each such department or agency (and each other State or local government entity) to which the assistance is extended, in the case of assistance to a State or local government;

(2)(i) A college, university, or other postsecondary institution, or a public system of higher education; or

(ii) A local educational agency (as defined in 20 U.S.C. 7801), system of vocational education, or other school system;

(3)(i) An entire corporation, partnership, or other private organization, or an entire sole proprietorship—

(A) If assistance is extended to such corporation, partnership, private organization, or sole proprietorship as a whole; or

(B) Which is principally engaged in the business of providing education, health care, housing, social services, or parks and recreation; or

(ii) The entire plant or other comparable, geographically separate facility to which Federal financial assistance is extended, in the case of any other corporation, partnership, private organization, or sole proprietorship; or

(4) Any other entity which is established by two or more of the entities

described in paragraph (1), (2), or (3) of this definition.

Recipient means any State or its political subdivision, any instrumentality of a State or its political subdivision, institution, organization, or other entity, or any person to which Federal financial assistance is extended, directly or through another recipient. Recipient includes any successor, assignee, or transferee, but excludes the ultimate beneficiary of the assistance.

Statutory objective means any purpose of a program or activity expressly stated in any Federal statute, State statute or local statute or ordinance adopted by an elected, general purpose legislative body.

Subrecipient means any of the entities in the definition of "recipient" to which a recipient extends or passes on Federal financial assistance. A subrecipient is generally regarded as a recipient of Federal financial assistance and has all the duties of a recipient in these regulations.

United States includes the States of the United States, the District of Columbia, the Commonwealth of Puerto Rico, the Virgin Islands, American Samoa, Guam, the Commonwealth of the Northern Mariana Islands, Wake Island, the Canal Zone, the Trust Territory of the Pacific Islands and all other territories and possessions of the United States. The term "State" also includes any one of the foregoing.

[55 FR 23078, June 6, 1990, as amended at 68 FR 51380, Aug. 26, 2003; 74 FR 15335, Apr. 3, 2009]

STANDARDS FOR DETERMINING AGE DISCRIMINATION

§ 7.920 Rules against discrimination.

The rules stated in this section are limited by the exceptions contained in §§ 7.921 and 7.922 of these regulations.

(a) *General rule:* No person in the United States shall, on the basis of age, be excluded from participation in, be denied the benefits of, or be subjected to discrimination under, any program or activity receiving Federal financial assistance.

(b) *Specific rules:* A recipient may not, in any program or activity receiving Federal financial assistance, directly

or through contractual licensing, or other arrangements, use age distinctions or take any other actions which have the effect, on the basis of age, of:

(1) Excluding individuals from, denying them the benefits of, subjecting them to discrimination under, a program or activity receiving Federal financial assistance; or

(2) Denying or limiting individuals in their opportunity to participate in any program or activity receiving Federal financial assistance. The specific forms of age discrimination listed in paragraph (b) of this section do not necessarily constitute a complete list.

§ 7.921 Exceptions to the rules against age discrimination: Normal operation or statutory objective of any program or activity.

A recipient is permitted to take an action, otherwise prohibited by § 7.920, if the action reasonably takes into account age as a factor necessary to the normal operation of the achievement of any statutory objective of a program or activity. An action reasonably takes into account age as a factor necessary to the normal operation or the achievement of any statutory objective of a program or activity, if:

(a) Age is used as a measure or approximation of one or more other characteristics; and

(b) The other characteristic(s) must be measured or approximated in order for the normal operation of the program or activity to continue, or to achieve any statutory objective of the program or activity; and

(c) The other characteristic(s) can be reasonably measured or approximated by the use of age; and

(d) The other characteristic(s) are impractical to measure directly on an individual basis.

§ 7.922 Exceptions to the rules against age discrimination: Reasonable factors other than age.

A recipient is permitted to take an action otherwise prohibited by § 7.920 which is based on a factor other than age, even though that action may have a disproportionate effect on persons of different ages only if the factor bears a direct and substantial relationship to the normal operation of the program or activity or to the achievement of a statutory objective.

§7.923 Burden of proof for exceptions.

The burden of proving that an age distinction or other action falls within the exceptions outlined in §§7.921 and 7.922 is on the recipient of Federal financial assistance.

§7.924 Affirmative action by recipient.

Even in the absence of a finding of discrimination, a recipient may take affirmative action to overcome the effects of conditions that resulted in the limited participation in the recipient's program or activity on the basis of age.

§7.925 Special benefits for children and the elderly.

If a recipient operating a program or activity provides special benefits to the elderly or to children, such use of age distinctions shall be presumed to be necessary to the normal operation of the program or activity, notwithstanding the provisions of §7.921.

[55 FR 23078, June 6, 1990, as amended at 68 FR 51380, Aug. 26, 2003]

§7.926 Age distinctions contained in FEMA regulations.

Any age distinctions contained in a rule or regulation issued by FEMA shall be presumed to be necessary to the achievement of a statutory objective of the program or activity to which the rule or regulation applies, notwithstanding the provisions of §7.921.

[55 FR 23078, June 6, 1990, as amended at 68 FR 51380, Aug. 26, 2003]

Duties of FEMA Recipients

§7.930 General responsibilities.

Each FEMA recipient has primary responsibility to ensure that its programs or activities are in compliance with the Act and this regulation, and shall take steps to eliminate violations of the Act. A recipient also has responsibility to maintain records, provide information, and to afford FEMA access to its records to the extent FEMA finds necessary to determine whether the recipient is in compliance with the Act and this regulation.

[55 FR 23078, June 6, 1990, as amended at 68 FR 51380, Aug. 26, 2003]

§7.931 Notice to subrecipients and beneficiaries.

(a) Where a recipient passes on Federal financial assistance from FEMA to subrecipients, the recipient shall provide the subrecipients written notice of their obligations under the Act and this regulation.

(b) Each recipient shall make necessary information about the Act and this regulation available to its beneficiaries in order to inform them about the protection against discrimination provided by the Act and this regulation.

[55 FR 23078, June 6, 1990, as amended at 68 FR 51380, Aug. 26, 2003]

§7.932 Assurance of compliance and recipient assessment of age distinctions.

(a) Each recipient of Federal financial assistance from FEMA shall sign a written assurance as specified by FEMA that it will comply with Act and this regulation.

(b) Recipient assessment of age distinctions. (1) As part of the compliance review under §7.940 or complaint investigation under §7.943, FEMA may require a recipient employing the equivalent of fifteen or more employees to complete written evaluation, in a manner specified by the responsible Agency official, of any age distinction imposed in its program or activity receiving Federal financial assistance from FEMA to assess the recipient's compliance with the Act.

(2) Whenever an assessment indicates a violation of the Act and the FEMA regulations, the recipient shall take corrective action.

§7.933 Information requirement.

Each recipient shall:

(a) Keep records in a form acceptable to FEMA and containing information which FEMA determines are necessary to ascertain whether the recipient is complying with the Act and this regulation.

(b) Provide to FEMA, upon request, information and reports which FEMA determines are necessary to ascertain whether the recipient is complying with the Act and this regulation.

(c) Permit FEMA reasonable access to the books, records, accounts, and other recipient facilities and sources of information to the extent FEMA determines is necessary to ascertain whether the recipient is complying with the Act and this regulation.

INVESTIGATION, CONCILIATION, AND ENFORCEMENT PROCEDURES

§ 7.940 Compliance reviews.

(a) FEMA may conduct compliance reviews and preaward reviews or use other similar procedures that will permit it to investigate and correct violations of the Act and this regulation. FEMA may conduct these reviews even in the absence of a complaint against a recipient. The reviews may be as comprehensive as necessary to determine whether a violation of the Act and this regulation has occurred.

(b) If a compliance review or preaward review indicates a violation of the Act or this regulation, FEMA will attempt to achieve voluntary compliance with the Act. If voluntary compliance cannot be achieved, FEMA will arrange for enforcement as described in § 7.945.

§ 7.941 Complaints.

(a) Any person, individually or as a member of a class or on behalf of others, may file a complaint with FEMA, alleging discrimination prohibited by the Act or these regulations occurring after the date of final adoption of this rule. A complaint shall file a complaint within 180 days from the date the complainant first had knowledge of the alleged act of discrimination. However, for good cause showing, FEMA may extend this time limit.

(b) FEMA will consider the date a complaint is filed to be the date upon which the complaint is sufficient to be processed. A complaint is deemed "sufficient" when it contains particulars (e.g., names, addresses, and telephone numbers of parties involved; date(s) of alleged discrimination; kind(s) of alleged discrimination) upon which to begin an investigation.

(c) FEMA will attempt to facilitate the filing of complaints wherever possible, including taking the following measures:

(1) Accepting as a sufficient complaint any written statement which identifies the parties involved and the date the complainant first had knowledge of the alleged violation, describes generally the action or practice complained of, and is signed by the complainant.

(2) Freely permitting a complainant to add information to the complaint to meet the requirements of a sufficient complaint.

(3) Notifying the complainant and the recipient of their rights and obligations under the complaint procedure, including the right to have a representative at all stages of the complaint procedure.

(4) Notifying the complainant and the recipient (or their representatives) of their right to contact FEMA for information and assistance regarding the complaint resolution process.

(d) FEMA will return to the complainant any complaint outside the jurisdiction of this regulation, and will state the reason(s) why it is outside the jurisdiction of this regulation.

§ 7.942 Mediation.

(a) FEMA will promptly refer to a mediation agency designated by the Administrator all sufficient complaints that:

(1) Fall within the jurisdiction of the Act and this regulation, unless the age distinction complained of is clearly within an exception; and,

(2) Contain all information necessary for further processing.

(b) Both the complainant and the recipient shall participate in the mediation process to the extent necessary to reach an agreement or for the mediator to make an informed judgment that an agreement is not possible.

(c) If the complainant and the recipient reach an agreement, the mediator shall prepare a written statement of the agreement and have the complainant and the recipient sign it. The mediator shall send a copy of the agreement to FEMA. FEMA will take no further action on the complaint unless the complainant or the recipient fails to comply with the agreement.

(d) The mediator shall protect the confidentiality of all information obtained in the course of the mediation process. No mediator shall testify in any adjudicative proceeding, produce any document, or otherwise disclose any information obtained in the course of the mediation process without prior approval of the head of the mediation agency.

(e) The mediation will proceed for a maximum of 60 days after a complaint is filed with FEMA. Mediation ends if:

(1) Sixty days elapse from the time the complaint is filed; or

(2) Prior to the end of that 60 day period, an agreement is reached; or

(3) Prior to the end of that 60 day period, the mediator determines that an agreement cannot be reached. This 60 day period may be extended by the mediator, with the concurrence of FEMA, for not more than 30 days if the mediator determines agreement will likely be reached during such extended period.

(f) The mediator shall return unresolved complaints to FEMA.

§7.943 Investigation.

(a) *Informal investigation.* (1) FEMA will investigate complaints that are unresolved after mediation or are reopened because of a violation of a mediation agreement.

(2) As part of the initial investigation, FEMA will use informal fact finding methods, including joint or separate discussion with the complainant and recipient, to establish the facts and, if possible, settle the complaint on terms that are mutually agreeable to the parties. FEMA may seek the assistance of any involved state agency.

(3) FEMA will put any agreement in writing and have it signed by the parties and an authorized official at FEMA.

(4) The settlement shall not affect the operation of any other enforcement effort of FEMA, including compliance reviews and investigation of other complaints which may involve the recipient.

(5) The settlement is not a finding of discrimination against a recipient.

(b) *Formal investigation.* If FEMA cannot resolve the complaint through informal investigation, it will begin to develop formal findings through further investigation of the complaint. If the investigation indicates a violation of this regulation, FEMA will attempt to obtain voluntary compliance, it will begin enforcement as described in §7.945.

[55 FR 23078, June 6, 1990, as amended at 68 FR 51380, Aug. 26, 2003]

§7.944 Prohibition against intimidation or retaliation.

A recipient may not engage in acts of intimidation or retaliation against any person who:

(a) Attempts to assert a right protected by the Act or this regulation; or

(b) Cooperates in any mediation, investigation, hearing, or other part of FEMA's investigation, conciliation and enforcement process.

§7.945 Compliance procedure.

(a) FEMA may enforce the Act and this regulation through:

(1) Termination of a recipient's Federal financial assistance from FEMA under the program or activity involved where the recipient has violated the Act or this regulation. The determination of the recipient's violation may be made only after a recipient has had an opportunity for a hearing on the record before an administrative law judge.

(2) Any other means authorized by law including but not limited to:

(i) Referral to the Department of Justice for proceedings to enforce any rights of the United States or obligations of the recipient created by the Act or this regulation.

(ii) Use of any requirement of or referral to any Federal, State or local government agency that will have the effect of correcting a violation of the Act or this regulation.

(b) FEMA will limit any termination under §7.945(a)(1) to the particular recipient and particular program or activity or part of such program or activity FEMA finds in violation of this regulation. FEMA will not base any part of a termination on a finding with respect to any program or activity of the recipient which does not receive Federal financial assistance from FEMA.

(c) FEMA will take no action under paragraph (a) until:

(1) The Administrator has advised the recipient of its failure to comply with the Act and this regulation and has determined that voluntary compliance cannot be obtained.

(2) Thirty days have elapsed after the Administrator has sent a written report of the circumstances and grounds of the action to the committees of the Congress having legislative jurisdiction over the program or activity involved. The Administrator will file a report whenever any action is taken under paragraph (a).

(d) FEMA also may defer granting new Federal financial assistance from FEMA to a recipient when a hearing under §7.945(a)(1) is initiated.

(1) New Federal financial assistance from FEMA includes all assistance for which FEMA requires an application or approval, including renewal or continuation of existing activities, or authorization of new activities, during the deferral period. New Federal financial assistance from FEMA does not include increases in funding as a result of changed computation of formula awards or assistance approved prior to the beginning of a hearing under §7.945(a)(1).

(2) FEMA will not begin a deferral until the recipient has received a notice of an opportunity for a hearing under §7.945(a)(1). FEMA will not continue a deferral for more than 60 days unless a hearing has begun within that time or the time for beginning the hearing has been extended by mutual consent of the recipient for more than 30 days after the close of the hearing, unless the hearing results in a finding against the recipient.

(3) FEMA will limit any deferral to the particular recipient and particular program or activity or part of such program or activity FEMA finds in violation of this regulation. FEMA will not base any part of a deferral on a finding with respect to any program or activity of the recipient which does not and would not, in connection with new funds, receive Federal financial assistance from FEMA.

[55 FR 23078, June 6, 1990, as amended at 68 FR 51380, Aug. 26, 2003]

§ 7.946 Hearings, decisions, post-termination proceedings.

Certain FEMA procedural provisions applicable to title VI of the Civil Rights Act of 1964 apply to FEMA enforcement of this regulation. They are found at 44 CFR 7.10 through 7.16.

§ 7.947 Remedial action by recipient.

Where FEMA finds a recipient has discriminated on the basis of age, the recipient shall take any remedial action that FEMA may require to overcome the effects of the discrimination. If another recipient exercises control over the recipient that had discriminated, FEMA may require both recipients to take remedial action.

§ 7.948 Alternate funds disbursal procedure.

(a) When FEMA withholds funds from recipient under this regulation, the Administrator may, if allowable under the statute governing the assistance, disburse the withheld funds directly to an alternate recipient: Any public or nonprofit private organization or agency, or State or political subdivision of the State.

(b) The Administrator will require any alternate recipient to demonstrate:

(1) The ability to comply with this regulation; and

(2) The ability to achieve the goals of the Federal statute authorizing the Federal financial assistance.

[55 FR 23078, June 6, 1990, as amended at 68 FR 51380, Aug. 26, 2003]

§ 7.949 Exhaustion of administrative remedies.

(a) A complainant may file a civil action following the exhaustion of administrative remedies under the Act. Administrative remedies are exhausted if:

(1) 180 days have elapsed since the complainant filed the complaint and FEMA had made no finding with regard to the complaint; or

(2) FEMA issues any finding in favor of the recipient.

(b) If FEMA fails to make a finding within 180 days or issues a finding in favor of the recipient, FEMA shall:

(1) Promptly advise the complainant in writing of this fact; and

(2) Advise the complainant of his or her right to bring a civil action for injunctive relief; and

(3) Inform the complainant:

(i) That the complainant may bring a civil action only in a United States District Court for the district in which the recipient is located or transacts business;

(ii) That a complainant prevailing in a civil action has the right to be awarded the costs of the action, including reasonable attorney's fees, but that the complainant must demand these costs in the complaint at the time it is filed.

(iii) That before commencing the action, the complainant shall give 30 days notice by registered mail to the Administrator, the Attorney General of the United States, and the recipient;

(iv) That the notice must state: The alleged violation of the Act; the relief requested; the court in which the complainant is bringing the action; and whether or not attorney's fees are demanded in the event the complainant prevails; and

(v) That the complainant may not bring an action if the same alleged violation of the Act by the same recipient is the subject of a pending action in any court (Federal or State) of the United States.

PART 8—NATIONAL SECURITY INFORMATION

Sec.
8.1 Purpose.
8.2 Original classification authority.
8.3 Senior FEMA official responsible for the information security program.
8.4 Mandatory declassification review procedures.

AUTHORITY: Reorganization Plan No. 3 of 1978, E.O. 12148 and E.O. 12356.

§8.1 Purpose.

(a) Section 5.3(b) of Executive Order (EO) 12356, "National Security Information" requires agencies to promulgate implementing policies and regulations. To the extent that these regulations affect members of the public, these policies are to be published in the FEDERAL REGISTER.

(b) This regulation provides public notification of the FEMA procedures for processing requests for the mandatory review of classified information pursuant to section 3.4(d) of E.O. 12356.

[49 FR 24518, June 14, 1984, as amended at 49 FR 38119, Sept. 27, 1984; 50 FR 40006, Oct. 1, 1985]

§8.2 Original classification authority.

(a) The Administrator, Federal Emergency Management Agency (FEMA), has the authority to classify information originally as TOP SECRET, as designated by the President in the FEDERAL REGISTER, Vol 47, No. 91, May 11, 1982, in accordance with section 1.2(a)(2), E.O. 12356.

(b) In accordance with section 1.2(d)(2), E.O. 12356, the following positions have been delegated ORIGINAL TOP SECRET CLASSIFICATION AUTHORITY by the Administrator, FEMA:

(1) Deputy Administrator, FEMA

(2) Deputy Administrator, National Preparedness Directorate

(3) Director, Office of Security

(c) The positions delegated original Top Secret Classification Authority in paragraph (b) of this section, are also delegated Original Secret and Confidential Classification Authority by virtue of this delegation. The following positions have been delegated Original Secret and Original Confidential Classification Authority:

(1) Associate Director, State and Local Programs and Support.

(2) Regional Administrators.

(d) Any further delegation of original classification authority, for any classification level, will be accomplished only by the Director of the Federal Emergency Management Agency.

(e) The positions delegated ORIGINAL TOP SECRET CLASSIFICATION AUTHORITY in paragraph (b) of this section, are also delegated ORIGINAL SECRET and CONFIDENTIAL CLASSIFICATION AUTHORITY by virtue of this delegation. The positions delegated ORIGINAL SECRET CLASSIFICATION AUTHORITY in paragraph (c) of this section, are also delegated ORIGINAL CONFIDENTIAL CLASSIFICATION AUTHORITY by virtue of this delegation. Any further delegation of original classification authority, for any classification level, will be accomplished only by the Administrator of FEMA.

[49 FR 24518, June 14, 1984 as amended at 51 FR 34605, Sept. 30, 1986; 53 FR 47210, Nov. 22, 1989; 56 FR 32328, July 16, 1991; 74 FR 15335, Apr. 3, 2009]

§ 8.3 Senior FEMA official responsible for the information security program.

The Director of the Security Division, has been designated as the senior official to direct and administer the FEMA information security program, in accordance with section 5.3(a), E.O. 12356.

[49 FR 24518, June 14, 1984]

§ 8.4 Mandatory declassification review procedures.

(a) All information classified by FEMA under E.O. 12356 or predecessor orders shall be subject to a review for declassification if such a review is requested by a United States citizen or permanent resident alien, a Federal agency or a State or local government.

(b) Requests for declassification review shall be submitted to the Security Division, Federal Emergency Management Agency, Washington, DC 20472. All requests shall be in writing and reasonably describe the information sought with sufficient clarity to enable the appropriate FEMA component to identify the information sought. Any requests that do not sufficiently identify the information sought shall be returned to the requestor and he or she shall be asked to clarify the request and/or provide additional information.

(c) If within 30 days the requestor does not respond to the agency's request for clarification or additional information, the FEMA Security Division shall notify the requestor that no further action can be taken on the request. If the requestor's response to the agency's request for clarification and/or additional information is inadequate, the Office of Security shall notify him or her that no further action will be taken until such time as the agency is provided with adequate information concerning the request. In addition, the agency's response will set forth the agency's explanation of the deficiencies of the request.

(d) Once a request meets the foregoing requirements for processing, it will be acted upon as follows:

(1) Receipt of all requests shall be acknowledged within ten (10) working days.

(2) FEMA action upon a request shall be completed within sixty (60) calendar days.

(e) The Director of the Security Division shall designate a FEMA component to conduct the declassification review. This will normally be the originating component. The designated program or staff office shall conduct the review and forward its recommendation(s) to the Security Division. Information no longer requiring protection under E.O. 12356 shall be declassified and released unless withholding is otherwise authorized under applicable law. When information cannot be declassified in its entirety, FEMA will make a reasonable effort to release those declassified portions of the requested information that constitute a coherent segment. If the information may not be released in whole or part, the requestor shall be given a brief statement as to the reason for the denial, a notice of the right to appeal the determination to the Administrator of FEMA and a notice that such an appeal must be filed within sixty (60) calendar days to be considered.

(f) If the request requires the rendering of services for which fees may be charged under 31 U.S.C. 9701, such fees may be imposed in accordance with the provisions of 44 CFR part 5, subpart C.

(g) The following procedures shall be followed when denials of requests for declassification are appealed:

(1) The Administrator shall, within fifteen (15) working days of receipt of the appeal, convene a meeting of the FEMA Information Security Oversight Committee (ISOC). Representation on the FEMA ISOC shall include the Director of the Security Division or his/her representative, a representative of the component that denied the original request, a representative from the Office of Chief Counsel, a representative from the Office of External Affairs and the Chief of Staff or his/her representative.

(2) If the ISOC upholds the appeal in its entirety, the information will be released in accordance with the provisions of paragraph (e) of this section.

(3) If the ISOC denies the appeal, in part or in its entirety, then it will forward the appeal with its recommendation(s) to the Administrator of FEMA, for a final determination. A reply will be forwarded to the requestor enclosing the declassified releasable information if any, and an explanation for denying the request in whole or in part.

(4) Final action on appeals shall be completed within thirty (30) working days of receipt of appeal.

[49 FR 24518, June 14, 1984, as amended at 49 FR 38119, Sept. 27, 1984; 50 FR 40006, Oct. 1, 1985; 51 FR 34605, Sept. 30, 1986]

PART 9—FLOODPLAIN MANAGEMENT AND PROTECTION OF WETLANDS

AUTHORITY: E.O. 11988 of May 24, 1977. 3 CFR, 1977 Comp., p. 117; E.O. 11990 of May 24 1977, 3 CFR, 1977 Comp. p. 121; Reorganization Plan No. 3 of 1978, 43 FR 41943, 3 CFR, 1978 Comp., p. 329; E.O. 12127 of March 31, 1979, 44 FR 19367, 3 CFR, 1979 Comp., p. 376; E.O. 12148 of July 20, 1979, 44 FR 43239, 3 CFR, 1979 Comp., p. 412, as amended.; E.O. 12127; E.O. 12148; 42 U.S.C. 5201.

SOURCE: 45 FR 59526, Sept. 9, 1980, unless otherwise noted.

§9.1 Purpose of part.

This regulation sets forth the policy, procedure and responsibilities to implement and enforce Executive Order 11988, Floodplain Management, and Executive Order 11990, Protection of Wetlands.

§9.2 Policy.

(a) FEMA shall take no action unless and until the requirements of this regulation are complied with.

(b) It is the policy of the Agency to provide leadership in floodplain management and the protection of wetlands. Further, the Agency shall integrate the goals of the Orders to the greatest possible degree into its procedures for implementing NEPA. The Agency shall take action to:

(1) Avoid long- and short-term adverse impacts associated with the occupancy and modification of floodplains and the destruction and modification of wetlands;

(2) Avoid direct and indirect support of floodplain development and new construction in wetlands wherever there is a practicable alternative;

(3) Reduce the risk of flood loss;

(4) Promote the use of nonstructural flood protection methods to reduce the risk of flood loss;

(5) Minimize the impact of floods on human health, safety and welfare;

(6) Minimize the destruction, loss or degradation of wetlands;

(7) Restore and preserve the natural and beneficial values served by floodplains;

(8) Preserve and enhance the natural values of wetlands;

(9) Involve the public throughout the floodplain management and wetlands protection decision-making process;

(10) Adhere to the objectives of the Unified National Program for Floodplain Management; and

(11) Improve and coordinate the Agency's plans, programs, functions and resources so that the Nation may attain the widest range of beneficial uses of the environment without degradation or risk to health and safety.

§9.3 Authority.

The authority for these regulations is (a) Executive Order 11988, May 24, 1977, which replaced Executive Order

11296, August 10, 1966, (b) Executive Order 11990, May 24, 1977, (c) Reorganization Plan No. 3 of 1978 (43 FR 41943); and (d) Executive Order 12127, April 1, 1979 (44 FR 1936). E.O. 11988 was issued in furtherance of the National Flood Insurance Act of 1968, as amended (Pub. L. 90–488); the Flood Disaster Protection Act of 1973, as amended (Pub. L. 93–234); and the National Environmental Policy Act of 1969 (NEPA) (Pub. L. 91–190). Section 2(d) of Executive Order 11988 requires issuance of new or amended regulations and procedures to satisfy its substantive and procedural provisions. E.O. 11990 was issued in furtherance of NEPA, and at section 6 required issuance of new or amended regulations and procedures to satisfy its substantive and procedural provisions.

[45 FR 59526, Sept. 9, 1980, as amended at 48 FR 44543, Sept. 29, 1983]

§ 9.4 Definitions.

The following definitions shall apply throughout this regulation.

Action means any action or activity including: (a) Acquiring, managing and disposing of Federal lands and facilities; (b) providing federally undertaken, financed or assisted construction and improvements; and (c) conducting Federal activities and programs affecting land use, including, but not limited to, water and related land resources, planning, regulating and licensing activities.

Actions Affecting or Affected by Floodplains or Wetlands means actions which have the potential to result in the long- or short-term impacts associated with (a) the occupancy or modification of floodplains, and the direct or indirect support of floodplain development, or (b) the destruction and modification of wetlands and the direct or indirect support of new construction in wetlands.

Administrator means the Administrator of the Federal Emergency Management Agency.

Agency means the Federal Emergency Management Agency (FEMA).

Agency Assistance means grants for projects or planning activities, loans, and all other forms of financial or technical assistance provided by the Agency.

Base Flood means the flood which has a one percent chance of being equalled or exceeded in any given year (also known as a 100-year flood). This term is used in the National Flood Insurance Program (NFIP) to indicate the minimum level of flooding to be used by a community in its floodplain management regulations.

Base Floodplain means the 100-year floodplain (one percent chance floodplain).

Coastal High Hazard Area means the areas subject to high velocity waters including but not limited to hurricane wave wash or tsunamis. On a Flood Insurance Rate Map (FIRM), this appears as zone V1–30, VE or V.

Critical Action means an action for which even a slight chance of flooding is too great. The minimum floodplain of concern for critical actions is the 500-year floodplain, i.e., critical action floodplain. Critical actions include, but are not limited to, those which create or extend the useful life of structures or facilities:

(a) Such as those which produce, use or store highly volatile, flammable, explosive, toxic or water-reactive materials;

(b) Such as hospitals and nursing homes, and housing for the elderly, which are likely to contain occupants who may not be sufficiently mobile to avoid the loss of life or injury during flood and storm events;

(c) Such as emergency operation centers, or data storage centers which contain records or services that may become lost or inoperative during flood and storm events; and

(d) Such as generating plants, and other principal points of utility lines.

Direct Impacts means changes in floodplain or wetland values and functions and changes in the risk to lives and property caused or induced by an action or related activity. Impacts are caused whenever these natural values and functions are affected as a direct result of an action. An action which would result in the discharge of polluted storm waters into a floodplain or wetland, for example, would directly affect their natural values and functions. Construction-related activities, such as dredging and filling operations within the floodplain or a wetland would be another example of impacts caused by an action.

Emergency Actions means emergency work essential to save lives and protect property and public health and safety performed under sections 305 and 306 of the Disaster Relief Act of 1974 (42 U.S.C. 5145 and 5146). See 44 CFR part 205, subpart E.

Enhance means to increase, heighten, or improve the natural and beneficial values associated with wetlands.

Facility means any man-made or man-placed item other than a structure.

FEMA means the Federal Emergency Management Agency.

FIA means the Federal Insurance Administration.

Five Hundred Year Floodplain (the 500-year floodplain or 0.2 percent change floodplain) means that area, including the base floodplain, which is subject to inundation from a flood having a 0.2 percent chance of being equalled or exceeded in any given year.

Flood or *flooding* means a general and temporary condition of partial or complete inundation of normally dry land areas from the overflow of inland and/or tidal waters, and/or the unusual and rapid accumulation or runoff of surface waters from any source.

Flood Fringe means that portion of the floodplain outside of the floodway (often referred to as "floodway fringe").

Flood Hazard Boundary Map (FHBM) means an official map of a community, issued by the Administrator, where the boundaries of the flood, mudslide (i.e., mudflow) and related erosion areas having special hazards have been designated as Zone A, M, or E.

Flood Insurance Rate Map (FIRM) means an official map of a community on which the Administrator has delineated both the special hazard areas and the risk premium zones applicable to the community. FIRMs are also available digitally, and are called Digital Flood Insurance Rate Maps (DFIRM).

Flood Insurance Study (FIS) means an examination, evaluation and determination of flood hazards and, if appropriate, corresponding water surface elevations or an examination, evaluation and determination of mudslide (i.e.,

mudflow) and/or flood-related erosion hazards.

Floodplain means the lowland and relatively flat areas adjoining inland and coastal waters including, at a minimum, that area subject to a one percent or greater chance of flooding in any given year. Wherever in this regulation the term "floodplain" is used, if a critical action is involved, "floodplain" shall mean the area subject to inundation from a flood having a 0.2 percent chance of occurring in any given year (500-year floodplain). "Floodplain" does not include areas subject only to mudflow until FIA adopts maps identifying "M" Zones.

Floodproofing means the modification of individual structures and facilities, their sites, and their contents to protect against structural failure, to keep water out, or to reduce effects of water entry.

Floodway means that portion of the floodplain which is effective in carrying flow, within which this carrying capacity must be preserved and where the flood hazard is generally highest, i.e., where water depths and velocities are the greatest. It is that area which provides for the discharge of the base flood so the cumulative increase in water surface elevation is no more than one foot.

Functionally Dependent Use means a use which cannot perform its intended purpose unless it is located or carried out in close proximity to water, (e.g., bridges, and piers).

Indirect Impacts means an indirect result of an action whenever the action induces or makes possible related activities which effect the natural values and functions of floodplains or wetlands or the risk to lives and property. Such impacts occur whenever these values and functions are potentially affected, either in the short- or long-term, as a result of undertaking an action.

Minimize means to reduce to the smallest amount or degree possible.

Mitigation means all steps necessary to minimize the potentially adverse effects of the proposed action, and to restore and preserve the natural and beneficial floodplain values and to preserve and enhance natural values of wetlands.

Mitigation Directorate means the Mitigation Directorate of the Federal Emergency Management Agency.

Natural Values of Floodplains and Wetlands means the qualities of or functions served by floodplains and wetlands which include but are not limited to: (a) Water resource values (natural moderation of floods, water quality maintenance, groundwater recharge); (b) living resource values (fish, wildlife, plant resources and habitats); (c) cultural resource values (open space, natural beauty, scientific study, outdoor education, archeological and historic sites, recreation); and (d) cultivated resource values (agriculture, aquaculture, forestry).

New Construction means the construction of a new structure (including the placement of a mobile home) or facility or the replacement of a structure or facility which has been totally destroyed.

New Construction in Wetlands includes draining, dredging, channelizing, filling, diking, impounding, and related activities and any structures or facilities begun or authorized after the effective dates of the Orders, May 24, 1977.

Orders means Executive Orders 11988, Floodplain Management, and 11990, Protection of Wetlands.

Practicable means capable of being done within existing constraints. The test of what is practicable depends upon the situation and includes consideration of all pertinent factors, such as environment, cost and technology.

Preserve means to prevent alterations to natural conditions and to maintain the values and functions which operate the floodplains or wetlands in their natural states.

Regional Administrator means the Regional Administrator of the Federal Emergency Management Agency for the Region in which FEMA is acting, or the Disaster Recovery Manager when one is designated.

Regulatory Floodway means the area regulated by federal, State or local requirements to provide for the discharge of the base flood so the cumulative increase in water surface elevation is no more than a designated amount (not to exceed one foot as set by the National Flood Insurance Program).

Restore means to reestablish a setting or environment in which the natural functions of the floodplain can again operate.

Structures means walled or roofed buildings, including mobile homes and gas or liquid storage tanks.

Substantial Improvement means any repair, reconstruction or other improvement of a structure or facility, which has been damaged in excess of, or the cost of which equals or exceeds, 50% of the market value of the structure or replacement cost of the facility (including all "public facilities" as defined in the Disaster Relief Act of 1974) (a) before the repair or improvement is started, or (b) if the structure or facility has been damaged and is proposed to be restored, before the damage occurred. If a facility is an essential link in a larger system, the percentage of damage will be based on the relative cost of repairing the damaged facility to the replacement cost of the portion of the system which is operationally dependent on the facility. The term "substantial improvement" does not include any alteration of a structure or facility listed on the National Register of Historic Places or a State Inventory of Historic Places.

Support means to encourage, allow, serve or otherwise facilitate floodplain or wetland development. Direct support results from actions within a floodplain or wetland, and indirect support results from actions outside of floodplains or wetlands.

Wetlands means those areas which are inundated or saturated by surface or ground water with a frequency sufficient to support, or that under normal hydrologic conditions does or would support, a prevalence of vegetation or aquatic life typically adapted for life in saturated or seasonally saturated soil conditions. Examples of wetlands include, but are not limited to, swamps, fresh and salt water marshes, estuaries, bogs, beaches, wet meadows, sloughs, potholes, mud flats, river overflows and other similar areas. This definition includes those wetlands areas separated from their natural supply of water as a result of activities such as the construction of structural flood protection methods or solid-fill road beds and activities such as mineral extraction and navigation improvements. This definition is intended to be consistent with the definition utilized by the U.S. Fish and Wildlife Service in the publication entitled *Classification of Wetlands and Deep Water Habitats of the United States* (Cowardin, et al., 1977).

[45 FR 59526, Sept. 9, 1980, as amended at 47 FR 13149, Mar. 29, 1982; 50 FR 40006, Oct. 1, 1985; 74 FR 15335, Apr. 3, 2009]

§9.5 Scope.

(a) *Applicability.* (1) These regulations apply to all Agency actions which have the potential to affect floodplains or wetlands or their occupants, or which are subject to potential harm by location in floodplains or wetlands.

(2) The basic test of the potential of an action to affect floodplains or wetlands is the action's potential (both by itself and when viewed cumulatively with other proposed actions) to result in the long- or short-term adverse impacts associated with:

(i) The occupancy or modification of floodplains, and the direct and indirect support of floodplain development; or

(ii) The destruction or modification of wetlands and the direct or indirect support of new construction in wetlands.

(3) This regulation applies to actions that were, on the effective date of the Orders (May 24, 1977), ongoing, in the planning and/or development stages, or undergoing implementation, and are incomplete as of the effective date of these regulations. The regulation also applies to proposed (new) actions. The Agency shall:

(i) Determine the applicable provisions of the Orders by analyzing whether the action in question has progressed beyond critical stages in the floodplain management and wetlands protection decision-making process, as set out below in §9.6. This determination need only be made at the time that followup actions are being taken to complete or implement the action in question; and

(ii) Apply the provisions of the Orders and of this regulation to all such actions to the fullest extent practicable.

(b) *Limited exemption of ongoing actions involving wetlands located outside the floodplains.* (1) Executive Order 11990, Protection of Wetlands, contains a limited exemption not found in Executive Order 11988, Floodplain Management. Therefore, this exemption applies only to actions affecting wetlands which are located outside the floodplains, and which have no potential to result in harm to or within floodplains or to support floodplain development.

(2) The following proposed actions that impact wetlands located outside of floodplains are exempt from this regulation:

(i) Agency-assisted or permitted projects which were under construction before May 24, 1977; and

(ii) Projects for which the Agency has proposed a draft of a final environmental impact statement (EIS) which adequately analyzes the action and which was filed before October 1, 1977. Proposed actions that impact wetlands outside of floodplains are not exempt if the EIS:

(A) Only generally covers the proposed action;

(B) Is devoted largely to related activities; or

(C) Treats the project area or program without an adequate and specific analysis of the floodplain and wetland implications of the proposed action.

(c) *Decision-making involving certain categories of actions.* The provisions set forth in this regulation are *not applicable* to the actions enumerated below except that the Regional Administrators shall comply with the spirit of the Order to the extent practicable. For any action which is excluded from the actions enumerated below, the full 8-step process applies (see §9.6) (except as indicated at paragraphs (d), (f) and (g) of this section regarding other categories of partial or total exclusions). The provisions of these regulations do not apply to the following (all references are to the Disaster Relief Act of 1974, Pub. L. 93–288, as amended, except as noted):

(1) Assistance provided for emergency work essential to save lives and protect property and public health and safety performed pursuant to sections 305 and 306;

(2) Emergency Support Teams (section 304);

(3) Unemployment Assistance (section 407);

(4) Emergency Communications (section 415);

(5) Emergency Public Transportation (section 416);

(6) Fire Management Assistance (Section 420);

(7) Community Disaster Loans (section 414), except to the extent that the proceeds of the loan will be used for repair of facilities or structures or for construction of additional facilities or structures;

(8) The following Individual and Family Grant Program (section 408) actions:

(i) Housing needs or expenses, except for restoring, repairing or building private bridges, purchase of mobile homes and provision of structures as minimum protective measures;

(ii) Personal property needs or expenses;

(iii) Transportation expenses;

(iv) Medical/dental expenses;

(v) Funeral expenses;

(vi) Limited home repairs;

(vii) Flood insurance premium;

(viii) Cost estimates;

(ix) Food expenses; and

(x) Temporary rental accommodations.

(9) Mortgage and rental assistance under section 404(b);

(10) Use of existing resources in the temporary housing assistance program [section 404(a)], except that Step 1 (§ 9.7) shall be carried out;

(11) Minimal home repairs [section 404(c)];

(12) Debris removal (section 403), except those grants involving non-emergency disposal of debris within a floodplain or wetland;

(13) Repairs or replacements under section 402, of less than $5,000 to damaged structures or facilities.

(14) Placement of families in existing resources and Temporary Relocation Assistance provided to those families so placed under the Comprehensive Environmental Response, Compensation, and Liability Act of 1980, Public Law 96–510.

(d) For each action enumerated below, the Regional Administrator *shall apply steps 1, 2, 4, 5 and 8* of the decision-making process (§§ 9.7, 9.8, 9.10 and 9.11, see § 9.6). Steps 3 and 6 (§ 9.9) shall be carried out except that alternative sites outside the floodplain or wetland need not be considered. After assessing impacts of the proposed action on the floodplain or wetlands and of the site on the proposed action, alternative actions to the proposed action, if any, and the "no action" alternative shall be considered. The Regional Administrator may also require certain other portions of the decision-making process to be carried out for individual actions as is deemed necessary. For any action which is excluded from the actions listed below. (except as indicated in paragraphs (c), (f) and (g) of this section regarding other categories of partial or total exclusion), the full 8-step process applies (see § 9.6). The references are to the Disaster Relief Act of 1974, Public Law 93–288, as amended.

(1) Actions performed under the Individual and Family Grant Program (section 408) for restoring or repairing a private bridge, except where two or more individuals or families are authorized to pool their grants for this purpose.

(2) Small project grants (section 419), except to the extent that Federal funding involved is used for construction of new facilities or structures.

(3) Replacement of building contents, materials and equipment. (sections 402 and 419).

(4) Repairs under section 402 to damaged facilities or structures, except any such action for which one or more of the following is applicable:

(i) FEMA estimated cost of repairs is more than 50% of the estimated reconstruction cost of the entire facility or structure, or is more than $100,000, or

(ii) The action is located in a floodway or coastal high hazard area, or

(iii) The facility or structure is one which has previously sustained structural damage from flooding due to a major disaster or emergency or on which a flood insurance claim has been paid, or

(iv) The action is a critical action.

(e) *Other categories of actions.* Based upon the completion of the 8-step decision-making process (§9.6), the Director may find that a specific category of actions either offers no potential for carrying out the purposes of the Orders and shall be treated as those actions listed in §9.5(c), or has no practicable alternative sites and shall be treated as those actions listed in §9.5(d), or has no practicable alternative actions or sites and shall be treated as those actions listed in §9.5(g). This finding will be made in consultation with the Federal Insurance Administration and the Council on Environmental Quality as provided in section 2(d) of E.O. 11988. Public notice of each of these determinations shall include publication in the FEDERAL REGISTER and a 30-day comment period.

(f) *The National Flood Insurance Program (NFIP).* (1) Most of what is done by FIA or the Mitigation Directorate, in administering the National Flood Insurance Program is performed on a program-wide basis. For all regulations, procedures or other issuances making or amending program policy, FIA or the Mitigation Directorate, shall apply the 8-step decision-making process to that program-wide action. The action to which the 8-step process must be applied is the establishment of programmatic standards or criteria, not the application of programmatic standards or criteria to specific situations. Thus, for example, FIA or the Mitigation Directorate, would apply the 8-step process to a programmatic determination of categories of structures to be insured, but not to whether to insure each individual structure. The two prime examples of where FIA or the Mitigation Directorate, does take site specific actions which would require individual application of the 8-step process are property acquisition under section 1362 of the National Flood Insurance Act of 1968, as amended, and the issuance of an exception to a community under 44 CFR 60.6(b). (See also §9.9(e)(6) and §9.11(e).)

(2) The provisions set forth in this regulation are not applicable to the actions enumerated below except that the Federal Insurance Administrator or the Assistant Administrator for Mitigation, as appropriate shall comply with the spirit of the Orders to the extent practicable:

(i) The issuance of individual flood insurance policies and policy interpretations;

(ii) The adjustment of claims made under the Standard Flood Insurance Policy;

(iii) The hiring of independent contractors to assist in the implementation of the National Flood Insurance Program;

(iv) The issuance of individual flood insurance maps, Map Information Facility map determinations, and map amendments; and

(v) The conferring of eligibility for emergency or regular program (NFIP) benefits upon communities.

(g) For the action listed below, the Regional Administrator *shall apply steps 1, 4, 5 and 8* of the decision-making process (§§9.7, 9.10 and 9.11). For any action which is excluded from the actions listed below, (except as indicated in paragraphs (c), (d) and (f) of this section regarding other categories of partial or total exclusion), the full 8-step process applies (See §9.6). The Regional Administrator may also require certain other portions of the decision-making process to be carried out for individual actions as is deemed necessary. The references are to the Disaster Relief Act of 1974, Public Law 93–288. The above requirements apply to repairs, under section 402, between $5,000 and $25,000 to damaged structures of facilities except for:

(1) Actions in a floodway or coastal high hazard area; or

(2) New or substantially improved structures or facilities; or

(3) Facilities or structures which have previously sustained structural damage from flooding due to a major disaster or emergency.

[45 FR 59526, Sept. 9, 1980, as amended at 47 FR 13149, Mar. 29, 1982; 49 FR 35583, Sept. 10, 1984; 50 FR 40006, Oct. 1, 1985; 51 FR 39531, Oct. 29, 1986; 66 FR 57347, Nov. 14, 2001]

§9.6 Decision-making process.

(a) *Purpose.* The purpose of this section is to set out the floodplain management and wetlands protection decision-making process to be followed by the Agency in applying the Orders to its actions. While the decision-making process was initially designed to address the floodplain Order's requirements, the process will also satisfy the wetlands Order's provisions due to the close similarity of the two directives. The numbering of Steps 1 through 8 does not firmly require that the steps be followed sequentially. As information is gathered throughout the decision-making process and as additional information is needed, reevaluation of lower numbered steps may be necessary.

(b) Except as otherwise provided in §9.5 (c), (d), (f), and (g) regarding categories of partial or total exclusion when proposing an action, the Agency shall apply the 8-step decision-making process. FEMA shall:

Step 1. Determine whether the proposed action is located in a wetland and/or the 100-year floodplain (500-year floodplain for critical actions); and whether it has the potential to affect or be affected by a floodplain or wetland (see §9.7);

Step 2. Notify the public at the earliest possible time of the intent to carry out an action in a floodplain or wetland, and involve the affected and interested public in the decision-making process (see §9.8);

Step 3. Identify and evaluate practicable alternatives to locating the proposed action in a floodplain or wetland (including alternative sites, actions and the "no action" option) (see §9.9). If a practicable alternative exists outside the floodplain or wetland FEMA must locate the action at the alternative site.

Step 4. Identify the potential direct and indirect impacts associated with the occupancy or modification of floodplains and wetlands and the potential direct and indirect support of floodplain and wetland development that could result from the proposed action (see §9.10);

Step 5. Minimize the potential adverse impacts and support to or within floodplains and wetlands to be identified under Step 4, restore and preserve the natural and beneficial values served by floodplains, and preserve and enhance the natural and beneficial values served by wetlands (see §9.11);

Step 6. Reevaluate the proposed action to determine first, if it is still

practicable in light of its exposure to flood hazards, the extent to which it will aggravate the hazards to others, and its potential to disrupt floodplain and wetland values and second, if alternatives preliminarily rejected at Step 3 are practicable in light of the information gained in Steps 4 and 5. FEMA shall not act in a floodplain or wetland unless it is the only practicable location (see §9.9);

Step 7. Prepare and provide the public with a finding and public explanation of any final decision that the floodplain or wetland is the only practicable alternative (see §9.12); and

Step 8. Review the implementation and post-implementation phases of the proposed action to ensure that the requirements stated in §9.11 are fully implemented. Oversight responsibility shall be integrated into existing processes.

[45 FR 59526, Sept. 9, 1980, as amended at 49 FR 35583, Sept. 10, 1984; 50 FR 40006, Oct. 1, 1985]

§ 9.7 Determination of proposed action's location.

(a) The purpose of this section is to establish Agency procedures for determining whether any action as proposed is located in or affects (1) the base floodplain (the Agency shall substitute the 500-year floodplain for the base floodplain where the action being proposed involves a critical action), or (2) a wetland.

(b) *Information needed.* The Agency shall obtain enough information so that it can fulfill the requirements of the Orders to (1) avoid floodplain and wetland locations unless they are the only practicable alternatives; and (2) minimize harm to and within floodplains and wetlands. In all cases, FEMA shall determine whether the proposed action is located in a floodplain or wetland. In the absence of a finding to the contrary, FEMA may assume that a proposed action involving a facility or structure that has been flooded is in the floodplain. Information about the 100-year and 500-year floods and location of floodways and coastal high hazard areas may also be needed to comply with these regulations, especially §9.11. The following additional flooding characteristics shall be identified by the Regional Administrator as appropriate:

(i) Velocity of floodwater;

(ii) Rate of rise of floodwater;

(iii) Duration of flooding;

(iv) Available warning and evacuation time and routes;

(v) Special problems:

(A) Levees;

(B) Erosion;

(C) Subsidence;

(D) Sink holes;

(E) Ice jams;

(F) Debris load;

(G) Pollutants;

(H) Wave heights;

(I) Groundwater flooding;

(J) Mudflow.

(c) *Floodplain determination.* (1) In the search for flood hazard information, FEMA shall follow the sequence below:

(i) The Regional Administrator shall consult the FEMA Flood Insurance Rate Map (FIRM) the Flood Boundary Floodway Map (FBFM) and the Flood Insurance Study (FIS).

(ii) If a detailed map (FIRM or FBFM) is not available, the Regional Administrator shall consult an FEMA Flood Hazard Boundary Map (FHBM) . If data on flood elevations, floodways, or coastal high hazard areas are needed, or if the map does not delineate the flood hazard boundaries in the vicinity of the proposed site, the Regional Administrator shall seek the necessary detailed information and assistance from the sources listed below.

SOURCES OF MAPS AND TECHNICAL
INFORMATION

Department of Agriculture: Soil Conservation Service

Department of the Army: Corps of Engineers

Department of Commerce: National Oceanic and Atmospheric Administration

Federal Insurance Administration

FEMA Regional Offices/Natural and Technological Hazards Division

Department of the Interior:

Geological Survey

Bureau of Land Management

Bureau of Reclamation

Tennessee Valley Authority

Delaware River Basin Commission

Susquehanna River Basin Commission

States

(iii) If the sources listed do not have. or know of the information necessary to comply with the Orders' requirements, the Regional Administrator shall seek the services of a Federal or other engineer experienced in this type of work.

(2) If a decision involves an area or location within extensive Federal or state holdings or a headwater area, and an FIS, FIRM, FBFM, or FHBM is not available, the Regional Administrator shall seek information from the land administering agency before information and/or assistance is sought from the sources listed in this section. If none of these sources has information or can provide assistance, the services of an experienced Federal or other engineer shall be sought as described above.

(d) *Wetland determination.* The following sequence shall be followed by the Agency in making the wetland determination.

(1) The Agency shall consult with the U.S. Fish and Wildlife Service (FWS) for information concerning the location, scale and type of wetlands within the area which could be affected by the proposed action.

(2) If the FWS does not have adequate information upon which to base the determination, the Agency shall consult wetland inventories maintained by the Army Corps of Engineers, the Environmental Protection Agency, various states, communities and others.

(3) If state or other sources do not have adequate information upon which to base the determination, the Agency shall carry out an on-site analysis performed by a representative of the FWS or other qualified individual for wetlands characteristics based on the performance definition of what constitutes a wetland.

(4) If an action is in a wetland but not in a floodplain, and the action is new construction, the provisions of this regulation shall apply. Even if the action is not in a wetland, the Regional Administrator shall determine if the action has the potential to result in indirect impacts on wetlands. If so, all adverse impacts shall be minimized. For actions which are in a wetland and the floodplain, completion of the decision-making process is required. (See §9.6.) In such a case the wetland will be

considered as one of the natural and beneficial values of floodplain.

[45 FR 59526, Sept. 9, 1980, as amended at 47 FR 13149, Mar. 29, 1982; 49 FR 33879, Aug. 27, 1984; 50 FR 40006, Oct. 1, 1985; 51 FR 34605, Sept. 30, 1986]

§ 9.8 Public notice requirements.

(a) *Purpose.* The purpose of this section is to establish the initial notice procedures to be followed when proposing any action in or affecting floodplains or wetlands.

(b) *General.* The Agency shall provide adequate information to enable the public to have impact on the decision outcome for all actions having potential to affect, adversely, or be affected by floodplains or wetlands that it proposes. To achieve this objective, the Agency shall:

(1) Provide the public with adequate information and opportunity for review and comment at the earliest possible time and throughout the decision-making process; and upon completion of this process, provide the public with an accounting of its final decisions (see § 9.12); and

(2) Rely on its environmental assessment processes, to the extent possible, as vehicles for public notice, involvement and explanation.

(c) *Early public notice.* The Agency shall provide opportunity for public involvement in the decision-making process through the provision of public notice upon determining that the proposed action can be expected to affect or be affected by floodplains or wetlands. Whenever possible, notice shall precede major project site identification and analysis in order to preclude the foreclosure of options consistent with the Orders.

(1) For an action for which an environmental impact statement is being prepared, the Notice of Intent to File an EIS is adequate to constitute the early public notice, if it includes the information required under paragraph (c)(5) of this section.

(2) For each action having national significance for which notice is being provided, the Agency shall use the FEDERAL REGISTER as the minimum means for notice, and shall provide notice by mail to national organizations reasonably expected to be interested in the

action. The additional notices listed in paragraph (c)(4) of this section shall be used in accordance with the determination made under paragraph (c)(3) of this section.

(3) The Agency shall base its determination of appropriate notices, adequate comment periods, and whether to issue cumulative notices (paragraphs (c)(4), (6) and (7) of this section) on factors which include, but are not limited to:

(i) Scale of the action;

(ii) Potential for controversy;

(iii) Degree of public need;

(iv) Number of affected agencies and individuals; and

(v) Its anticipated potential impact.

(4) For each action having primarily local importance for which notice is being provided, notice shall be made in accordance with the criteria under paragraph (c)(3) of this section, and shall entail as appropriate:

(i) [Reserved]

(ii) Notice to Indian tribes when effects may occur on reservations.

(iii) Information required in the affected State's public notice procedures for comparable actions.

(iv) Publication in local newspapers (in papers of general circulation rather than legal papers).

(v) Notice through other local media.

(vi) Notice to potentially interested community organizations.

(vii) Publication in newsletters that may be expected to reach potentially interested persons.

(viii) Direct mailing to owners and occupants of nearby or affected property.

(ix) Posting of notice on and off site in the area where the action is to be located.

(x) Holding a public hearing.

(5) The notice shall include:

(i) A description of the action, its purpose and a statement of the intent to carry out an action affecting or affected by a floodplain or wetland;

(ii) Based on the factors in paragraph (c)(3) of this section, a map of the area or other indentification of the floodplain and/or wetland areas which is of adequate scale and detail so that the location is discernible; instead of publication of such map, FEMA may state that such map is available for public inspection, including the location at which such map may be inspected and a telephone number to call for information;

(iii) Based on the factors in paragraph (c)(3) of this section, a description of the type, extent and degree of hazard involved and the floodplain or wetland values present; and

(iv) Identification of the responsible official or organization for implementing the proposed action, and from whom further information can be obtained.

(6) The Agency shall provide for an adequate comment period.

(7) In a post-disaster situation in particular, the requirement for early public notice may be met in a cumulative manner based on the factors set out in paragraph (c)(3) of this section. Several actions may be addressed in one notice or series of notices. For some actions involving limited public interest a single notice in a local newspaper or letter to interested parties may suffice.

(d) *Continuing public notice.* The Agency shall keep the public informed of the progress of the decision-making process through additional public notices at key points in the process. The preliminary information provided under paragraph (c)(5) of this section shall be augmented by the findings of the adverse effects of the proposed actions and steps necessary to mitigate them. This responsibility shall be performed for actions requiring the preparation of an EIS, and all other actions having the potential for major adverse impacts, or the potential for harm to the health and safety of the general public.

[45 FR 59526, Sept. 9, 1980, as amended at 48 FR 29318, June 24, 1983]

§ 9.9 Analysis and reevaluation of practicable alternatives.

(a) *Purpose.* (1) The purpose of this section is to expand upon the directives set out in §9.6, of this part, in order to clarify and emphasize the Orders' key requirements to avoid floodplains and wetlands unless there is no practicable alternative.

(2) Step 3 is a preliminary determination as to whether the floodplain is the only practicable location for the action. It is a preliminary determination

because it comes early in the decision-making process when the Agency has a limited amount of information. If it is clear that there is a practicable alternative, or the floodplain or wetland is itself not a practicable location, FEMA shall then act on that basis. Provided that the location outside the floodplain or wetland does not indirectly impact floodplains or wetlands or support development therein (see §9.10), the remaining analysis set out by this regulation is not required. If such location does indirectly impact floodplains or wetlands or support development therein, the remaining analysis set out by this regulation is required. If the preliminary determination is to act in the floodplain, FEMA shall gather the additional information required under Steps 4 and 5 and then reevaluate all the data to determine if the floodplain or wetland is the only practicable alternative.

(b) *Analysis of practicable alternatives.* The Agency shall identify and evaluate practicable alternatives to carrying out a proposed action in floodplains or wetlands, including:

(1) Alternative sites outside the floodplain or wetland;

(2) Alternative actions which serve essentially the same purpose as the proposed action, but which have less potential to affect or be affected by the floodplain or wetlands; and

(3) *No action.* The floodplain and wetland site itself must be a practicable location in light of the factors set out in this section.

(c) The Agency shall analyze the following factors in determining the practicability of the alternatives set out in paragraph (b) of this section:

(1) Natural environment (topography, habitat, hazards, etc.);

(2) Social concerns (aesthetics, historical and cultural values, land patterns, etc.);

(3) Economic aspects (costs of space, construction, services, and relocation); and

(4) Legal constraints (deeds, leases, etc.).

(d) *Action following the analysis of practicable alternatives.* (1) The Agency shall not locate the proposed action in the floodplain or in a wetland if a practicable alternative exists outside the floodplain or wetland.

(2) For critical actions, the Agency shall not locate the proposed action in the 500-year floodplain if a practicable alternative exists outside the 500-year floodplain.

(3) Even if no practicable alternative exists outside the floodplain or wetland, in order to carry out the action the floodplain or wetland must itself be a practicable location in light of the review required in this section.

(e) *Reevaluation of alternatives.* Upon determination of the impact of the proposed action to or within the floodplain or wetland and of what measures are necessary to comply with the requirement to minimize harm to and within floodplains and wetlands (§ 9.11), FEMA shall:

(1) Determine whether:

(i) The action is still practicable at a floodplain or wetland site in light of the exposure to flood risk and the ensuing disruption of natural values;

(ii) The floodplain or wetland site is the only practicable alternative;

(iii) There is a potential for limiting the action to increase the practicability of previously rejected non-floodplain or wetland sites and alternative actions; and

(iv) Minimization of harm to or within the floodplain can be achieved using all practicable means.

(2) Take no action in a floodplain unless the importance of the floodplain site clearly outweighs the requirement of E.O. 11988 to:

(i) Avoid direct or indirect support of floodplain development;

(ii) Reduce the risk of flood loss;

(iii) Minimize the impact of floods on human safety, health and welfare; and

(iv) Restore and preserve floodplain values.

(3) Take no action in a wetland unless the importance of the wetland site clearly outweighs the requirements of E.O. 11990 to:

(i) Avoid the destruction or modification of the wetlands;

(ii) Avoid direct or indirect support of new construction in wetlands;

(iii) Minimize the destruction, loss or degradation of wetlands; and

(iv) Preserve and enhance the natural and beneficial values of wetlands.

(4) In carrying out this balancing process, give the factors in paragraphs (e)(2) and (3) of this section, the great weight intended by the Orders.

(5) Choose the "no action" alternative where there are no practicable alternative actions or sites and where the floodplain or wetland is not itself a practicable alternative. In making the assessment of whether a floodplain or wetland location is itself a practicable alternative, the practicability of the floodplain or wetland location shall be balanced against the practicability of not carrying out the action at all. That is, even if there is no practicable alternative outside of the floodplain or wetland, the floodplain or wetland itself must be a practicable location in order for the action to be carried out there. To be a practicable location, the importance of carrying out the action must clearly outweigh the requirements of the Orders listed in paragraphs (e)(2) and (e)(3) of this section. Unless the importance of carrying out the action clearly outweighs those requirements, the "no action" alternative shall be selected.

(6) In any case in which the Regional Director has selected the "no action" option, FIA may not provide a new or renewed contract of flood insurance for that structure.

EFFECTIVE DATE NOTE: At 45 FR 79070, Nov. 28, 1980, § 9.9(e)(6) was temporarily suspended until further notice.

§ 9.10   Identify impacts of proposed actions.

(a) *Purpose.* The purpose of this section is to ensure that the effects of proposed Agency actions are identified.

(b) The Agency shall identify the potential direct and indirect adverse impacts associated with the occupancy and modification of floodplains and wetlands and the potential direct and indirect support of floodplain and wetland development that could result from the proposed action. Such identification of impacts shall be to the extent necessary to comply with the requirements of the Orders to avoid floodplain and wetland locations unless they are the only practicable alternatives and to minimize harm to and within floodplains and wetlands.

(c) This identification shall consider whether the proposed action will result in an increase in the useful life of any structure or facility in question, maintain the investment at risk and exposure of lives to the flood hazard or forego an opportunity to restore the natural and beneficial values served by floodplains or wetlands. Regional Offices of the U.S. Fish and Wildlife Service may be contacted to aid in the identification and evaluation of potential impacts of the proposed action on natural and beneficial floodplain and wetland values.

(d) In the review of a proposed or alternative action, the Regional Administrator shall specifically consider and evaluate: impacts associated with modification of wetlands and floodplains regardless of its location; additional impacts which may occur when certain types of actions may support subsequent action which have additional impacts of their own; adverse impacts of the proposed actions on lives and property and on natural and beneficial floodplain and wetland values; and the three categories of factors listed below:

(1) *Flood hazard-related factors.* These include for example, the factors listed in §9.7(b)(2);

(2) *Natural values-related factors.* These include, for example, the following: Water resource values (natural moderation of floods, water quality maintenance, and ground water recharge); living resource values (fish and wildlife and biological productivity); cultural resource values (archeological and historic sites, and open space recreation and green belts); and agricultural, aquacultural and forestry resource values.

(3) *Factors relevant to a proposed action's effects on the survival and quality of wetlands.* These include, for example, the following: Public health, safety, and welfare, including water supply, quality, recharge and discharge; pollution; flood and storm hazards; and sediment and erosion; maintenance of natural systems, including conservation and long term productivity of existing flora and fauna, species and habitat diversity and stability, hydrologic utility, fish, wildlife, timber, and food and fiber resources; and other uses of wetlands in the public interest, including recreational, scientific, and cultural uses.

§9.11 Mitigation.

(a) *Purpose.* The purpose of this section is to expand upon the directives set out in §9.6 of this part, and to set out the mitigative actions required if the preliminary determination is made to carry out an action that affects or is in a floodplain or wetland.

(b) *General provisions.* (1) The Agency shall design or modify its actions so as to minimize harm to or within the floodplain;

(2) The Agency shall minimize the destruction, loss or degradation of wetlands;

(3) The Agency shall restore and preserve natural and beneficial floodplain values; and

(4) The Agency shall preserve and enhance natural and beneficial wetland values.

(c) *Minimization provisions.* The Agency shall minimize:

(1) Potential harm to lives and the investment at risk from the base flood, or, in the case of critical actions, from the 500-year flood;

(2) Potential adverse impacts the action may have on others; and

(3) Potential adverse impact the action may have on floodplain and wetland values.

(d) *Minimization Standards.* In its implementation of the Disaster Relief Act of 1974, the Agency shall apply at a minimum, the following standards to its actions to comply with the requirements of paragraphs (b) and (c), of this section, (except as provided in §9.5 (c), (d), and (g) regarding categories of partial or total exclusion). Any Agency action to which the following specific requirements do not apply, shall nevertheless be subject to the full 8-step process (§9.6) including the general requirement to minimize harm to and within floodplains:

(1) There shall be no new construction or substantial improvement in a floodway, and no new construction in a coastal high hazard area, except for:

(i) A functionally dependent use; or

(ii) A structure or facility which facilitates an open space use.

(2) For a structure which is a functionally dependent use, or which facilitates an open space use, the following applies. There shall be no construction of a new or substantially improved structure in a coastal high hazard area unless it is elevated on adequately anchored pilings or columns, and securely anchored to such piles or columns so that the lowest portion of the structural members of the lowest floor (excluding the pilings or columns) is elevated to or above the base flood level (the 500-year flood level for critical actions) (including wave height). The structure shall be anchored so as to withstand velocity waters and hurricane wave wash. The Regional Administrator shall be responsible for determining the base flood level, including the wave height, in all cases. Where there is a FIRM in effect, it shall be the basis of the Regional Administrator's determination. If the FIRM does not reflect wave heights, or if there is no FIRM in effect, the Regional Administrator is responsible for delineating the base flood level, including wave heights.

(3) *Elevation of structures.* (i) There shall be no new construction or substantial improvement of structures unless the lowest floor of the structures (including basement) is at or above the level of the base flood.

(ii) There shall be no new construction or substantial improvement of structures involving a critical action unless the lowest floor of the structure (including the basement) is at or above the level of the 500-year flood.

(iii) If the subject structure is non-residential, FEMA may, instead of elevating the structure to the 100-year or 500-year level, as appropriate, approve the design of the structure and its attendant utility and sanitary facilities so that below the flood level the structure is water tight with walls substantially impermeable to the passage of water and with structural components having the capability of resisting hydrostatic and hydrodynamic loads and effects of buoyancy.

(iv) The provisions of paragraphs (d)(3)(i), (ii), and (iii) of this section do not apply to the extent that the Fed-

eral Insurance Administration has granted an exception under 44 CFR § 60.6(b) (formerly 24 CFR 1910.6(b)), or the community has granted a variance which the Regional Administrator determines is consistent with 44 CFR 60.6(a) (formerly 24 CFR 1910.6(a)). In a community which does not have a FIRM in effect, FEMA may approve a variance from the standards of paragraphs (d)(3)(i), (ii), and (iii) of this section, after compliance with the standards of 44 CFR 60.6(a).

(4) There shall be no encroachments, including fill, new construction, substantial improvements of structures or facilities, or other development within a designated regulatory floodway that would result in any increase in flood levels within the community during the occurrence of the base flood discharge. Until a regulatory floodway is designated, no new construction, substantial improvements, or other development (including fill) shall be permitted within the base floodplain unless it is demonstrated that the cumulative effect of the proposed development, when combined with all other existing and anticipated development, will not increase the water surface elevation of the base flood more than one foot at any point within the community.

(5) Even if an action is a functionally dependent use or facilitates open space uses (under paragraph (d) (1) or (2) of this section) and does not increase flood heights (under paragraph (d)(4) of this section), such action may only be taken in a floodway or coastal high hazard area if:

(i) Such site is the only practicable alternative; and

(ii) Harm to and within the floodplain is minimized.

(6) In addition to standards (d)(1) through (d)(5) of this section, no action may be taken if it is inconsistent with the criteria of the National Flood Insurance Program (44 CFR part 59 *et seq.*) or any more restrictive Federal, State or local floodplain management standards.

(7) New construction and substantial improvement of structures shall be elevated on open works (walls, columns, piers, piles, etc.) rather than on fill, in

all cases in coastal high hazard areas and elsewhere, where practicable.

(8) To minimize the effect of floods on human health, safety and welfare, the Agency shall:

(i) Where appropriate, integrate all of its proposed actions in floodplains into existing flood warning and preparedness plans and ensure that available flood warning time is reflected;

(ii) Facilitate adequate access and egress to and from the site of the proposed action; and

(iii) Give special consideration to the unique hazard potential in flash flood, rapid-rise or tsunami areas.

(9) In the replacement of building contents, materials and equipment, the Regional Administrator shall require as appropriate, disaster proofing of the building and/or elimination of such future losses by relocation of those building contents, materials and equipment outside or above the base floodplain or the 500-year floodplain for critical actions.

(e) *In the implementation of the National Flood Insurance Program.* (1) The Federal Insurance Administration shall make identification of all coastal high hazard areas a priority;

(2) Beginning October 1, 1981, the Federal Insurance Administration of FEMA may only provide flood insurance for new construction or substantial improvements in a coastal high hazard area if:

(i) Wave heights have been designated for the site of the structure either by the Administrator of FEMA based upon data generated by FEMA or by another source, satisfactory to the Administrator; and

(ii) The structure is rated by FEMA-FIA based on a system which reflects the capacity to withstand the effects of the 100-year frequency flood including, but not limited to, the following factors:

(A) Wave heights;

(B) The ability of the structure to withstand the force of waves.

(3)(i) FEMA shall accept and take fully into account information submitted by a property owner indicating that the rate for a particular structure is too high based on the ability of the structure to withstand the force of waves. In order to obtain a rate adjust-

ment, a property owner must submit to FEMA specific information regarding the structure and its immediate environment. Such information must be certified by a registered professional architect or engineer who has demonstrable experience and competence in the fields of foundation, soils, and structural engineering. Such information should include:

(A) Elevation of the structure (bottom of lowest floor beam) in relation to the Base Flood Elevation including wave height;

(B) Distance of the structure from the shoreline;

(C) Dune protection and other environmental factors;

(D) Description of the building support system; and

(E) Other relevant building details.

Adequate completion of the "V-Zone Risk Factor Rating Form" is sufficient for FEMA to determine whether a rate adjustment is appropriate. The form is available from and applications for rate adjustments should be submitted to:

National Flood Insurance Program
Attention: V-Zone Underwriting Specialist
9901–A George Palmer Highway
Lanham, MD 20706

Pending a determination on a rate adjustment, insurance will be issued at the class rate. If the rate adjustment is granted, a refund of the appropriate portion of the premium will be made. *Unless a property owner is seeking an adjustment of the rate prescribed by FEMA-FIA, this information need not be submitted.*

(ii) FIA shall notify communities with coastal high hazard areas and federally related lenders in such communities, of the provisions of this paragraph. Notice to the lenders may be accomplished by the Federal instrumentalities to which the lenders are related.

(4) In any case in which the Regional Director has been, pursuant to §9.11(d)(1), precluded from providing assistance for a new or substantially improved structure in a floodway, FIA may not provide a new or renewed policy of flood insurance for that structure.

(f) *Restore and preserve.* (1) For any action taken by the Agency which affects the floodplain or wetland and which has resulted in, or will result in, harm to the floodplain or wetland, the Agency shall act to restore and preserve the natural and beneficial values served by floodplains and wetlands.

(2) Where floodplain or wetland values have been degraded by the proposed action, the Agency shall identify, evaluate and implement measures to restore the values.

(3) If an action will result in harm to or within the floodplain or wetland, the Agency shall design or modify the action to preserve as much of the natural and beneficial floodplain and wetland values as is possible.

[45 FR 59526, Sept. 9, 1980, as amended at 46 FR 51752, Oct. 22, 1981; 48 FR 44543, Sept. 29, 1983; 49 FR 33879, Aug. 27, 1984; 49 FR 35584, Sept. 10, 1984; 50 FR 40006, Oct. 1, 1985]

EFFECTIVE DATE NOTE: At 45 FR 79070, Nov. 28, 1980, § 9.11(e)(4) was temporarily suspended until further notice.

§ 9.12 Final public notice.

If the Agency decides to take an action in or affecting a floodplain or wetland, it shall provide the public with a statement of its final decision and shall explain the relevant factors considered by the Agency in making this determination.

(a) In addition, those sent notices under § 9.8 shall also be provided the final notice.

(b) For actions for which an environmental impact statement is being prepared, the FEIS is adequate to constitute final notice in all cases except where:

(1) Significant modifications are made in the FEIS after its initial publication;

(2) Significant modifications are made in the development plan for the proposed action; or

(3) Significant new information becomes available in the interim between issuance of the FEIS and implementation of the proposed action.

If any of these situations develop, the Agency shall prepare a separate final notice that contains the contents of paragraph (e) of this section and shall make it available to those who received the FEIS. A minimum of 15 days shall, without good cause shown, be allowed for comment on the final notice.

(c) For actions for which an environmental assessment was prepared, the Notice of No Significant Impact is adequate to constitute final public notice, if it includes the information required under paragraph (e) of this section.

(d) For all other actions, the finding shall be made in a document separate from those described in paragraphs (a), (b), and (c) of this section. Based on an assessment of the following factors, the requirement for final notice may be met in a cumulative manner:

(1) Scale of the action;

(2) Potential for controversy;

(3) Degree of public need;

(4) Number of affected agencies and individuals;

(5) Its anticipated potential impact; and

(6) Similarity of the actions, i.e., to the extent that they are susceptible of common descriptions and assessments.

When a damaged structure or facility is already being repaired by the State or local government at the time of the Damage Survey Report, the requirements of Steps 2 and 7 (§§ 9.8 and 9.12) may be met by a single notice. Such notice shall contain all the information required by both sections.

(e) The final notice shall include the following:

(1) A statement of why the proposed action must be located in an area affecting or affected by a floodplain or a wetland;

(2) A description of all significant facts considered in making this determination;

(3) A list of the alternatives considered;

(4) A statement indicating whether the action conforms to applicable state and local floodplain protection standards;

(5) A statement indicating how the action affects or is affected by the floodplain and/or wetland, and how mitigation is to be achieved;

(6) Identification of the responsible official or organization for implementation and monitoring of the proposed action, and from whom further information can be obtained; and

(7) A map of the area or a statement that such map is available for public

inspection, including the location at which such map may be inspected and a telephone number to call for information.

(f) After providing the final notice, the Agency shall, without good cause shown, wait at least 15 days before carrying out the action.

[45 FR 59526, Sept. 9, 1980, as amended at 48 FR 29318, June 24, 1983]

§9.13 Particular types of temporary housing.

(a) The purpose of this section is to set forth the procedures whereby the Agency will provide certain specified types of temporary housing.

(b) Prior to providing the types of temporary housing enumerated in paragraph (c) of this section, the Agency shall comply with the provisions of this section. For all temporary housing not enumerated below, the full 8-step process (see §9.6) applies.

(c) The following temporary housing actions are subject to the provisions of this section and not the full 8-step process:

(1) [Reserved]

(2) Placing a mobile home or readily fabricated dwelling on a private or commercial site, but not a group site.

(d) The actions set out in paragraph (c) of this section are subject to the following decision-making process:

(1) The temporary housing action shall be evaluated in accordance with the provisions of §9.7 to determine if it is in or affects a floodplain or wetland.

(2) No mobile home or readily fabricated dwelling may be placed on a private or commercial site in a floodway or coastal high hazard area.

(3) An individual or family shall not be housed in a floodplain or wetland unless the Regional Administrator has complied with the provisions of §9.9 to determine that such site is the only practicable alternative. The following factors shall be substituted for the factors in §9.9 (c) and (e) (2) through (4):

(i) Speedy provision of temporary housing;

(ii) Potential flood risk to the temporary housing occupant;

(iii) Cost effectiveness;

(iv) Social and neighborhood patterns;

(v) Timely availability of other housing resources; and

(vi) Potential harm to the floodplain or wetland.

(4) An individual or family shall not be housed in a floodplain or wetland (except in existing resources) unless the Regional Administrator has complied with the provisions of §9.11 to minimize harm to and within floodplains and wetlands. The following provisions shall be substituted for the provisions of §9.11(d) for mobile homes:

(i) No mobile home or readily fabricated dwelling may be placed on a private or commercial site unless it is elevated to the fullest extent practicable up to the base flood level and adequately anchored.

(ii) No mobile home or readily fabricated dwelling may be placed if such placement is inconsistent with the criteria of the National Flood Insurance Program (44 CFR part 59 *et seq.*) or any more restrictive Federal, State or local floodplain management standard. Such standards may require elevation to the base flood level in the absence of a variance.

(iii) Mobile homes shall be elevated on open works (walls, columns, piers, piles, etc.) rather than on fill where practicable.

(iv) To minimize the effect of floods on human health, safety and welfare, the Agency shall:

(A) Where appropriate, integrate all of its proposed actions in placing mobile homes for temporary housing in floodplains into existing flood warning and preparedness plans and ensure that available flood warning time is reflected;

(B) Provide adequate access and egress to and from the proposed site of the mobile home; and

(C) Give special consideration to the unique hazard potential in flash flood and rapid-rise areas.

(5) FEMA shall comply with Step 2 Early Public Notice (§9.8(c)) and Step 7 Final Public Notice (§9.12). In providing these notices, the emergency nature of temporary housing shall be taken into account.

(e) FEMA shall not sell or otherwise dispose of mobile homes or other readily fabricated dwellings which would be located in floodways or coastal high hazard areas. FEMA shall not sell or otherwise dispose of mobile homes or other readily fabricated dwellings which would be located in floodplains or wetlands unless there is full compliance with the 8-step process. Given the vulnerability of mobile homes to flooding, a rejection of a non-floodplain location alternative and of the no-action alternative shall be based on (1) a compelling need of the family or individual to buy a mobile home for permanent housing, and (2) a compelling requirement to locate the unit in a floodplain. Further, FEMA shall not sell or otherwise dispose of mobile homes or other readily fabricated dwellings in a floodplain unless they are elevated at least to the level of the 100-year flood. The Regional Administrator shall notify the Assistant Administrator for Mitigation of each instance where a floodplain location has been found to be the only practicable alternative for a mobile home sale.

[45 FR 59526, Sept. 9, 1980, as amended at 47 FR 13149, Mar. 29, 1982; 49 FR 35584, Sept. 10, 1984; 50 FR 40006, Oct. 1, 1985]

§ 9.14 Disposal of Agency property.

(a) The purpose of this section is to set forth the procedures whereby the Agency shall dispose of property.

(b) Prior to its disposal by sale, lease or other means of disposal, property proposed to be disposed of by the Agency shall be reviewed according to the decision-making process set out in § 9.6 of this part, as follows:

(1) The property shall be evaluated in accordance with the provisions of § 9.7 to determine if it affects or is affected by a floodplain or wetland;

(2) The public shall be notified of the proposal and involved in the decision-making process in accordance with the provisions of § 9.8;

(3) Practicable alternatives to disposal shall be evaluated in accordance with the provisions of § 9.9. For disposals, this evaluation shall focus on alternative actions (conveyance for an alternative use that is more consistent with the floodplain management and wetland protection policies set out in § 9.2 than the one proposed, e.g., open space use for park or recreational purposes rather than high intensity uses),

and on the "no action" option (retain the property);

(4) Identify the potential impacts and support associated with the disposal of the property in accordance with § 9.10;

(5) Identify the steps necessary to minimize, restore, preserve and enhance in accordance with § 9.11. For disposals, this analysis shall address all four of these components of mitigation where unimproved property is involved, but shall focus on minimization through floodproofing and restoration of natural values where improved property is involved;

(6) Reevaluate the proposal to dispose of the property in light of its exposure to the flood hazard and its natural values-related impacts, in accordance with § 9.9. This analysis shall focus on whether it is practicable in light of the findings from §§ 9.10 and 9.11 to dispose of the property, or whether it must be retained. If it is determined that it is practicable to dispose of the property, this analysis shall identify the practicable alternative that best achieves all of the components of the Orders' mitigation responsibility;

(7) To the extent that it would decrease the flood hazard to lives and property, the Agency shall, wherever practicable, dispose of the properties according to the following priorities:

(i) Properties located outside the floodplain;

(ii) Properties located in the flood fringe; and

(iii) Properties located in a floodway, regulatory floodway or coastal high hazard area.

(8) The Agency shall prepare and provide the public with a finding and public explanation in accordance with § 9.12.

(9) The Agency shall ensure that the applicable mitigation requirements are fully implemented in accordance with § 9.11.

(c) At the time of disposal, for all disposed property, the Agency shall reference in the conveyance uses that are restricted under existing Federal, State and local floodplain management and wetland protection standards relating to flood hazards and floodplain and wetland values.

§ 9.15 Planning programs affecting land use.

The Agency shall take floodplain management into account when formulating or evaluating any water and land use plans. No plan may be approved unless it:

(a) Reflects consideration of flood hazards and floodplain management and wetlands protection; and

(b) Prescribes planning procedures to implement the policies and requirements of the Orders and this regulation.

§ 9.16 Guidance for applicants.

(a) The Agency shall encourage and provide adequate guidance to applicants for agency assistance to evaluate the effects of their plans and proposals in or affecting floodplains and wetlands.

(b) This shall be accomplished primarily through amendment of all Agency instructions to applicants, e.g., program handbooks, contracts, application and agreement forms, etc., and also through contact made by agency staff during the normal course of their activities, to fully inform prospective applicants of:

(1) The Agency's policy on floodplain management and wetlands protection as set out in § 9.2;

(2) The decision-making process to be used by the Agency in making the determination of whether to provide the required assistance as set out in § 9.6;

(3) The nature of the Orders' practicability analysis as set out in § 9.9;

(4) The nature of the Orders' mitigation responsibilities as set out in § 9.11;

(5) The nature of the Orders' public notice and involvement process as set out in §§ 9.8 and 9.12; and

(6) The supplemental requirements applicable to applications for the lease or other disposal of Agency owned properties set out in § 9.14.

(c) Guidance to applicants shall be provided where possible, prior to the time of application in order to minimize potential delays in process application due to failure of applicants to recognize and reflect the provisions of the Orders and this regulation.

§ 9.17 Instructions to applicants.

(a) *Purpose.* In accordance with Executive Orders 11988 and 11990, the Federal executive agencies must respond to a number of floodplain management and wetland protection responsibilities before carrying out any of their activities, including the provision of Federal financial and technical assistance. The purpose of this section is to put applicants for Agency assistance on notice concerning both the criteria that it is required to follow under the Orders, and applicants' responsibilities under this regulation.

(b) *Responsibilities of Applicants.* Based upon the guidance provided by the Agency under § 9.16, that guidance included in the U.S. Water Resources Council's *Guidance for Implementing E.O. 11988,* and based upon the provisions of the Orders and this regulation, applicants for Agency assistance shall recognize and reflect in their application:

(1) The Agency's policy on floodplain management and wetlands protection as set out in § 9.2;

(2) The decision-making process to be used by the Agency in making the determination of whether to provide the requested assistance as set out in § 9.6;

(3) The nature of the Orders' practicability analysis as set out in § 9.9;

(4) The nature of the Orders' mitigation responsibilities as set out in § 9.11;

(5) The nature of the Orders' public and involvement process as set out in §§ 9.8 and 9.12; and

(6) The supplemental requirements for application for the lease or other disposal of Agency-owned properties, as set out in § 9.13.

(c) *Provision of supporting information.* Applicants for Agency assistance may be called upon to provide supporting information relative to the various responsibilities set out in paragraph (b) of this section as a prerequisite to the approval of their applications.

(d) *Approval of applications.* Applications for Agency assistance shall be reviewed for the recognition and reflection of the provisions of this regulation in addition to the Agency's existing approval criteria.

§9.18 Responsibilities.

(a) *Regional Administrators' responsibilities.* Regional Administrators shall, for all actions falling within their respective jurisdictions:

(1) Implement the requirements of the Orders and this regulation. Anywhere in §§9.2, 9.6 through 9.13, and 9.15 where a direction is given to the Agency, it is the responsibility of the Regional Administrator.

(2) Consult with the Chief Counsel regarding any question of interpretation concerning this regulation or the Orders.

(b) The Heads of the Offices, Directorates and Administrations of FEMA shall:

(1) Implement the requirements of the Orders and this regulation. When a decision of a Regional Administrator relating to disaster assistance is appealed, the Assistant Administrator for Mitigation may make determinations under these regulations on behalf of the Agency.

(2) Prepare and submit to the Office of Chief Counsel reports to the Office of Management and Budget in accordance with section 2(b) of E.O. 11988 and section 3 of E.O. 11990. If a proposed action is to be located in a floodplain or wetland, any requests to the Office of Management and Budget for new authorizations or appropriations shall be accompanied by a report indicating whether the proposed action is in accord with the Orders and these regulations.

[45 FR 59526, Sept. 9, 1980, as amended at 49 FR 33879, Aug. 27, 1984; 74 FR 15336, Apr. 3, 2009]

APPENDIX A TO PART 9—DECISION-MAKING PROCESS FOR E.O. 11988

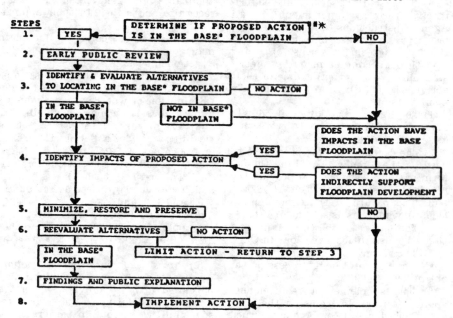

* FOR CRITICAL ACTIONS SUBSTITUTE "500 YEAR" FOR "BASE" AND
 FOR WETLANDS DELETE "BASE FLOODPLAIN" AND
 SUBSTITUTE " WETLANDS".

** FOR WETLANDS "ACTION" INCLUDES "NEW CONSTRUCTION" ONLY.

PART 10—ENVIRONMENTAL CONSIDERATIONS

Subpart A—General

AUTHORITY: 42 U.S.C. 4321 *et seq.*; E.O. 11514 of March 7, 1970, 35 FR 4247, as amended by E. O. 11991 of March 24, 1977, 3 CFR, 1977 Comp., p. 123; Reorganization Plan No. 3 of 1978, 43 FR 41943, 3 CFR, 1978 Comp., p. 329; E.O. 12127 of March 31, 1979, 44 FR 19367, 3 CFR, 1979 Comp., p. 376; E.O. 12148 of July 20, 1979, 44 FR 43239, 3 CFR, 1979 Comp., p. 412, as amended.

SOURCE: 45 FR 41142, June 18, 1980, unless otherwise noted.

Subpart A—General

§ 10.1 Background and purpose.

(a) This part implements the Council on Environmental Quality (CEQ) regulations (National Environmental Policy Act Regulations, 43 FR 55978 (1978)) and provides policy and procedures to enable Federal Emergency Management Agency (FEMA) officials to be informed of and take into account environmental considerations when authorizing or approving major FEMA actions that significantly affect the environment in the United States. The Council on Environmental Quality Regulations implement the procedural provisions, section 102(2), of the National Environmental Policy Act of 1969, as amended (hereinafter NEPA) (Pub. L. 91–190, 42 U.S.C. 4321 *et seq.*), and Executive Order 11991, 42 FR 26967 (1977).

(b) Section 1507.3, Council on Environmental Quality Regulations (National Environmental Policy Act Regulations, 43 FR 55978 (1978)) directs that Federal agencies shall adopt procedures to supplement the CEQ regulations. This regulation provides detailed FEMA implementing procedures to supplement the CEQ regulations.

(c) The provisions of this part must be read together with those of the CEQ regulations and NEPA as a whole when applying the NEPA process.

§ 10.2 Applicability and scope.

The provisions of this part apply to the Federal Emergency Management Agency, (hereinafter referred to as FEMA) including any office or administration of FEMA, and the FEMA regional offices.

§ 10.3 Definitions.

(a) Regional Administrator means the Regional Administrator of the Federal Emergency Management Agency for the region in which FEMA is acting.

(b) The other terms used in this part are defined in the CEQ regulations (40 CFR part 1508).

(c) Environmental Officer means the Director, Office of Environmental Planning and Historic Preservation, Mitigation Directorate, or his or her designee.

[45 FR 41142, June 18, 1980, as amended at 47 FR 13149, Mar. 29, 1982; 50 FR 40006, Oct. 1, 1985; 74 FR 15336, Apr. 3, 2009]

§ 10.4 Policy.

(a) FEMA shall act with care to assure that, in carrying out its responsibilities, including disaster planning, response and recovery and hazard mitigation and flood insurance, it does so in a manner consistent with national environmental policies. Care shall be taken to assure, consistent with other considerations of national policy, that all practical means and measures are used to protect, restore, and enhance the quality of the environment, to avoid or minimize adverse environmental consequences, and to attain the objectives of:

(1) Achieving use of the environment without degradation, or undesirable and unintended consequences;

(2) Preserving historic, cultural and natural aspects of national heritage and maintaining, wherever possible, an environment that supports diversity and variety of individual choice;

(3) Achieving a balance between resource use and development within the sustained carrying capacity of the ecosystem involved; and

(4) Enhancing the quality of renewable resources and working toward the maximum attainable recycling of depletable resources.

(b) *FEMA shall:*

(1) Assess environmental consequences of FEMA actions in accordance with §§ 10.9 and 10.10 of this part and parts 1500 through 1508 of the CEQ regulations;

(2) Use a systematic, interdisciplinary approach that will ensure the integrated use of the natural and social sciences, and environmental considerations, in planning and decisionmaking where there is a potential for significant environmental impact;

(3) Ensure that presently unmeasured environmental amenities are considered in the decisionmaking process;

(4) Consider reasonable alternatives to recommended courses of action in any proposal that involves conflicts concerning alternative uses of resources; and

(5) Make available to States, counties, municipalities, institutions and individuals advice and information useful in restoring, maintaining, and enhancing the quality of the environment.

Subpart B—Agency Implementing Procedures

§ 10.5 Responsibilities.

(a) *The Regional Administrators shall,* for each action not categorically excluded from this regulation and falling within their respective jurisdictions:

(1) Prepare an environmental assessment and submit such assessment to the Environmental Officer and the Office of Chief Counsel (OCC);

(2) Prepare a finding of no significant impact, or prepare an environmental impact statement;

(3) Coordinate and provide information regarding environmental review with applicants for FEMA assistance;

(4) Prepare and maintain an administrative record for each proposal that is determined to be categorically excluded from this regulation;

(5) Involve environmental agencies, applicants, and the public to the extent practicable in preparing environmental assessments;

(6) Prepare, as required, a supplement to either the draft or final environmental impact statement;

(7) Circulate draft and final environmental impact statements;

(8) Ensure that decisions are made in accordance with the policies and procedures of NEPA and this part, and prepare a concise public record of such decisions;

(9) Consider mitigating measures to avoid or minimize environmental harm, and, in particular, harm to and within floodplains and wetlands; and

(10) Review and comment upon, as appropriate, environmental assessments and impact statements of other Federal agencies and of State and local entities within their respective regions.

(b) *The Environmental Officer shall:*

(1) Determine, on the basis of the environmental assessment whether an environmental impact statement is required, or whether a finding of no significant impact shall be prepared;

(2) Review all proposed changes or additions to the list of categorical exclusions;

(3) Review all findings of no significant impact;

(4) Review all proposed draft and final environmental statements;

(5) Publish the required notices in the FEDERAL REGISTER;

(6) Provide assistance in the preparation of environmental assessments and impact statements and assign lead agency responsibility when more than one FEMA office or administration is involved;

(7) Direct the preparation of environmental documents for specific actions when required;

(8) Comply with the requirements of this part when the Administrator of FEMA promulgates regulations, procedures or other issuances making or amending Agency policy;

(9) Provide, when appropriate, consolidated FEMA comments on draft

and final impact statements prepared for the issuance of regulations and procedures of other agencies;

(10) Review FEMA issuances that have environmental implications;

(11) Maintain liaison with the Council on Environmental Quality, the Environmental Protection Agency, the Office of Management and Budget, other Federal agencies, and State and local groups, with respect to environmental analysis for FEMA actions affecting the environment.

(c) *The Heads of the Offices, Directorates, and Administrations of FEMA shall:*

(1) Assess environmental consequences of proposed and on-going programs within their respective organizational units;

(2) Prepare and process environmental assessments and environmental impact statements for all regulations, procedures and other issuances making or amending program policy related to actions which do not qualify for categorical exclusions;

(3) Integrate environmental considerations into their decisionmaking processes;

(4) Ensure that regulations, procedures and other issuances making or amending program policy are reviewed for consistency with the requirements of this part;

(5) Designate a single point of contact for matters pertaining to this part;

(6) Provide applicants for FEMA assistance with technical assistance regarding FEMA's environmental review process.

(d) *The Office of Chief Counsel of FEMA shall:*

(1) Provide advice and assistance concerning the requirements of this part;

(2) Review all proposed changes or additions to the list of categorical exclusions;

(3) Review all findings of no significant impact; and

(4) Review all proposed draft and final environmental impact statements.

[45 FR 41142, June 18, 1980, as amended at 47 FR 13149, Mar. 29, 1982]

§10.6 Making or amending policy.

For all regulations, procedures, or other issuances making or amending policy, the head of the FEMA office or administration establishing such policy shall be responsible for application of this part to that action. This does not apply to actions categorically excluded. For all policy-making actions not categorically excluded, the head of the office or administration shall comply with the requirements of this part. Thus, for such actions, the office or administration head shall assume the responsibilities that a Regional Administrator assumes for a FEMA action in his/her respective region. For such policy-making actions taken by the Administrator of FEMA, the Environmental Officer shall assume the responsibilities that a Regional Administrator assumes for a FEMA action in his/her respective region.

[45 FR 41142, June 18, 1980, as amended at 47 FR 13149, Mar. 29, 1982]

§10.7 Planning.

(a) *Early planning.* The Regional Administrator shall integrate the NEPA process with other planning at the earliest possible time to ensure that planning decisions reflect environmental values, to avoid delays later in the process, and to head off potential conflicts.

(b) *Lead agency.* To determine the lead agency for policy-making in which more than one FEMA office or administration is involved or any action in which another Federal agency is involved, FEMA offices and administrations shall apply criteria defined in §1501.5 of the CEQ regulation. If there is disagreement, the FEMA offices and/or administrations shall forward a request for lead agency determination to the Environmental Officer;

(1) The Environmental Officer will determine lead agency responsibility among FEMA offices and administration.

(2) In those cases involving a FEMA office or administration and another Federal agency, the Environmental Officer will attempt to resolve the differences. If unsuccessful, the Environmental Officer will file the request

with the Council on Environmental Quality for determination.

(c) *Technical assistance to applicants.* (1) Section 1501.2(d) of the CEQ regulations requires agencies to provide for early involvement in actions which, while planned by private applicants or other non-Federal entities, require some form of Federal approval. To implement the requirements of § 1501.2(d),

(i) The heads of the FEMA offices and administration shall prepare where practicable, generic guidelines describing the scope and level of environmental information required from applicants as a basis for evaluating their proposed actions, and make these guidelines available upon request.

(ii) The Regional Administrator shall provide such guidance on a project-by-project basis to applicants seeking assistance from FEMA.

(iii) Upon receipt of an application for agency approval, or notification that an application will be filed, the Regional Administrator shall consult as required with other appropriate parties to initiate and coordinate the necessary environmental analyses.

(2) To facilitate compliance with the requirements of paragraph (a) of this section, applicants and other non-Federal entities are expected to:

(i) Contact the Regional Administrator as early as possible in the planning process for guidance on the scope and level of environmental information required to be submitted in support of their application;

(ii) Conduct any studies which are deemed necessary and appropriate by FEMA to determine the impact of the proposed action on the human environment;

(iii) Consult with appropriate Federal, regional, State, and local agencies and other potentially interested parties during preliminary planning stages to ensure that all environmental factors are identified;

(iv) Submit applications for all Federal, regional, State, and local approvals as early as possible in the planning process;

(v) Notify the Regional Administrator as early as possible of all other Federal, regional, State, local, and Indian tribe actions required for project completion so that FEMA may coordinate all Federal environmental reviews; and

(vi) Notify the Regional Administrator of all known parties potentially affected by or interested in the proposed action.

[45 FR 41142, June 18, 1980, as amended at 47 FR 13149, Mar. 29, 1982]

§ 10.8   Determination of requirement for environmental review.

The first step in applying the NEPA process is to determine whether to prepare an environmental assessment or an environmental impact statement. Early determination will help ensure that necessary environmental documentation is prepared and integrated into the decision-making process. Environmental impact statements will be prepared for all major Agency actions (see 40 CFR 1508.18) significantly (see 40 CFR 1508.27) affecting the quality of the human environment.

(a) In determining whether to prepare an environmental impact statement (EIS) the Regional Administrator will first determine whether the proposal is one which:

(1) Normally requires an environmental impact statement; or

(2) Normally does not require either an environmental impact statement or an environmental assessment (categorical exclusion).

(b) *Actions that normally require an EIS.* (1) In some cases, it will be readily apparent that a proposed action will have significant impact on the environment. In that event, the Regional Administrator will, pursuant to § 10.9(g) of this part, submit the notice of preparation of an environmental impact statement to the Environmental Officer.

(2) To assist in determining those actions that normally do require an environmental impact statement, the following criteria apply:

(i) If an action will result in an extensive change in land use or the commitment of a large amount of land;

(ii) If an action will result in a land use change which is incompatible with the existing or planned surrounding area;

(iii) If many people will be affected;

(iv) If the environmental impact of the project is likely to be controversial;

(v) If an action will affect, in large measure, wildlife populations and their habitats, important natural resources, floodplains, wetlands, estuaries, beaches, dunes, unstable soils, steep slopes, aquifer recharge areas, or delicate or rare ecosystems, including endangered species;

(vi) If an action will result in a major adverse impact upon air or water quality;

(vii) If an action will adversely affect a property listed on the National Register of Historic Places or eligible for listing on the Register if, after consultation with the Advisory Council on Historic Preservation an environmental assessment is not deemed sufficient;

(viii) If an action is one of several actions underway or planned for an area and the cumulative impact of these projects is considered significant in terms of the above criteria;

(ix) If an action holds potential for threat or hazard to the public; or

(x) If an action is similar to previous actions determined to require an environmental impact statement.

(3) In any case involving an action that normally does require an environmental impact statement, the Regional Administrator may prepare an environmental assessment to determine if an environmental impact statement is required.

(c) *Statutory exclusions.* The following actions are statutorily excluded from NEPA and the preparation of environmental impact statements and environmental assessments by section 316 of the Robert T. Stafford Disaster Relief and Emergency Assistance Act (Stafford Act), as amended, 42 U.S.C. 5159;

(1) Action taken or assistance provided under sections 402, 403, 407, or 502 of the Stafford Act; and

(2) Action taken or assistance provided under section 406 of the Stafford Act that has the effect of restoring facilities substantially as they existed before a major disaster or emergency.

(d) *Categorical Exclusions (CATEXs).* CEQ regulations at 40 CFR 1508.4 provide for the categorical exclusion of actions that do not individually or cumulatively have a significant impact on the human environment and for which, therefore, neither an environmental as-

sessment nor an environmental impact statement is required. Full implementation of this concept will help FEMA avoid unnecessary or duplicate effort and concentrate resources on significant environmental issues.

(1) *Criteria.* The criteria used for determination of those categories of actions that normally do not require either an environmental impact statement or an environmental assessment include:

(i) Minimal or no effect on environmental quality;

(ii) No significant change to existing environmental conditions; and

(iii) No significant cumulative environmental impact.

(2) *List of exclusion categories.* FEMA has determined that the following categories of actions have no significant effect on the human environment and are, therefore, categorically excluded from the preparation of environmental impact statements and environmental assessments except where extraordinary circumstances as defined in paragraph (d)(5) of this section exist. If the action is of an emergency nature as described in §316 of the Stafford Act (42 U.S.C. 5159), it is statutorily excluded and is noted with [SE].

(i) Administrative actions such as personnel actions, travel, procurement of supplies, etc., in support of normal day-to-day activities and disaster related activities;

(ii) Preparation, revision, and adoption of regulations, directives, manuals, and other guidance documents related to actions that qualify for categorical exclusions;

(iii) Studies that involve no commitment of resources other than manpower and associated funding;

(iv) Inspection and monitoring activities, granting of variances, and actions to enforce Federal, state, or local codes, standards or regulations;

(v) Training activities and both training and operational exercises utilizing existing facilities in accordance with established procedures and land use designations;

(vi) Procurement of goods and services for support of day-to-day and emergency operational activities, and the temporary storage of goods other than hazardous materials, so long as storage occurs on previously disturbed land or in existing facilities;

(vii) The acquisition of properties and the associated demolition/removal [see paragraph (d)(2)(xii) of this section] or relocation of structures [see paragraph (d)(2)(xiii) of this section] under any applicable authority when the acquisition is from a willing seller, the buyer coordinated acquisition planning with affected authorities, and the acquired property will be dedicated in perpetuity to uses that are compatible with open space, recreational, or wetland practices.

(viii) Acquisition or lease of existing facilities where planned uses conform to past use or local land use requirements;

(ix) Acquisition, installation, or operation of utility and communication systems that use existing distribution systems or facilities, or currently used infrastructure rights-of-way;

(x) Routine maintenance, repair, and grounds-keeping activities at FEMA facilities;

(xi) Planting of indigenous vegetation;

(xii) Demolition of structures and other improvements or disposal of uncontaminated structures and other improvements to permitted off-site locations, or both;

(xiii) Physical relocation of individual structures where FEMA has no involvement in the relocation site selection or development;

(xiv) Granting of community-wide exceptions for floodproofed residential basements meeting the requirements of 44 CFR 60.6(c) under the National Flood Insurance Program;

(xv) Repair, reconstruction, restoration, elevation, retrofitting, upgrading to current codes and standards, or replacement of any facility in a manner that substantially conforms to the pre-existing design, function, and location; [SE, in part]

(xvi) Improvements to existing facilities and the construction of small scale hazard mitigation measures in existing developed areas with substantially completed infrastructure, when the immediate project area has already been disturbed, and when those actions do not alter basic functions, do not exceed capacity of other system components,

or modify intended land use; provided the operation of the completed project will not, of itself, have an adverse effect on the quality of the human environment;

(xvii) Actions conducted within enclosed facilities where all airborne emissions, waterborne effluent, external radiation levels, outdoor noise, and solid and bulk waste disposal practices comply with existing Federal, state, and local laws and regulations;

(xviii) The following planning and administrative activities in support of emergency and disaster response and recovery:

(A) Activation of the Emergency Support Team and convening of the Catastrophic Disaster Response Group at FEMA headquarters;

(B) Activation of the Regional Operations Center and deployment of the Emergency Response Team, in whole or in part;

(C) Deployment of Urban Search and Rescue teams;

(D) Situation Assessment including ground and aerial reconnaissance;

(E) Information and data gathering and reporting efforts in support of emergency and disaster response and recovery and hazard mitigation; and

(xix) The following emergency and disaster response, recovery and hazard mitigation activities under the Stafford Act:

(A) General Federal Assistance (§ 402); [SE]

(B) Essential Assistance (§ 403); [SE]

(C) Debris Removal (§ 407) [SE]

(D) Temporary Housing (§ 408), except locating multiple mobile homes or other readily fabricated dwellings on sites, other than private residences, not previously used for such purposes;

(E) Unemployment Assistance (§ 410);

(F) Individual and Family Grant Programs (§ 411), except for grants that will be used for restoring, repairing or building private bridges, or purchasing mobile homes or other readily fabricated dwellings;

(G) Food Coupons and Distribution (§ 412);

(H) Food Commodities (§ 413);

(I) Legal Services (§ 415);

(J) Crisis Counseling Assistance and Training (§ 416);

(K) Community Disaster Loans (§417);

(L) Emergency Communications (§418);

(M) Emergency Public Transportation (§419);

(N) Fire Management Assistance Grants; and

(O) Federal Emergency Assistance (§502) [SE].

(3) *Extraordinary circumstances.* If extraordinary circumstances exist within an area affected by an action, such that an action that is categorically excluded from NEPA compliance may have a significant adverse environmental impact, an environmental assessment shall be prepared. Extraordinary circumstances that may have a significant environmental impact include:

(i) Greater scope or size than normally experienced for a particular category of action;

(ii) Actions with a high level of public controversy;

(iii) Potential for degradation, even though slight, of already existing poor environmental conditions;

(iv) Employment of unproven technology with potential adverse effects or actions involving unique or unknown environmental risks;

(v) Presence of endangered or threatened species or their critical habitat, or archaeological, cultural, historical or other protected resources;

(vi) Presence of hazardous or toxic substances at levels which exceed Federal, state or local regulations or standards requiring action or attention;

(vii) Actions with the potential to affect special status areas adversely or other critical resources such as wetlands, coastal zones, wildlife refuge and wilderness areas, wild and scenic rivers, sole or principal drinking water aquifers;

(viii) Potential for adverse effects on health or safety; and

(ix) Potential to violate a Federal, State, local or tribal law or requirement imposed for the protection of the environment.

(x) Potential for significant cumulative impact when the proposed action is combined with other past, present and reasonably foreseeable future actions, even though the impacts of the proposed action may not be significant by themselves.

(4) *Documentation.* The Regional Administrator will prepare and maintain an administrative record of each proposal that is determined to be categorically excluded from the preparation of an environmental impact statement or an environmental assessment.

(5) *Revocation.* The Regional Administrator shall revoke a determination of categorical exclusion and shall require a full environmental review if, subsequent to the granting an exclusion, the Regional Administrator determines that due to changes in the proposed action or in light of new findings, the action no longer meets the requirements for a categorical exclusion.

(6) *Changes to the list of exclusion categories.* (i) The FEMA list of exclusion categories will be continually reviewed and refined as additional categories are identified and experience is gained in the categorical exclusion process. An office, directorate, or administration of FEMA may, at any time, recommend additions or changes to the FEMA list of exclusion categories.

(ii) Offices, directorates, and administrations of FEMA are encouraged to develop additional categories of exclusions necessary to meet their unique operational and mission requirements.

(iii) If an office, directorate, or administration of FEMA proposes to change or add to the list of exclusion categories, it shall first:

(A) Obtain the approval of the Environmental Officer and the Office of the Chief Counsel; and

(B) Publish notice of such proposed change or addition in the FEDERAL REGISTER at least 60 days before the effective date of such change or addition.

(e) *Actions that normally require an environmental assessment.* When a proposal is not one that normally requires an environmental impact statement and does not qualify as a categorical exclusion, the Regional Administrator shall prepare an environmental assessment.

(f) *Documentation.* The Regional Administrator will prepare and maintain an administrative record of each proposal that is determined to be categorically excluded from the preparation of an environmental impact statement or an environmental assessment.

(g) *Actions that normally require an environmental assessment.* When a proposal is not one that normally requires an environmental impact statement and does not qualify as a categorical exclusion, the Regional Administrator shall prepare an environmental assessment.

[45 FR 41142, June 18, 1980, as amended at 46 FR 2049, Jan. 8, 1981; 46 FR 54346, Nov. 3, 1981; 47 FR 13149, Mar. 29, 1982; 52 FR 5285, Feb. 20, 1987; 59 FR 954, Jan. 7, 1994; 61 FR 4230, Feb. 5, 1996; 61 FR 10688, Mar. 15, 1996; 66 FR 57347, Nov. 14, 2001]

§ 10.9 Preparation of environmental assessments.

(a) *When to prepare.* The Regional Administrator shall begin preparation of an environmental assessment as early as possible after the determination that an assessment is required. The Regional Administrator may prepare an environmental assessment at any time to assist planning and decision-making.

(b) *Content and format.* The environmental assessment is a concise public document to determine whether to prepare an environmental impact statement, aiding in compliance with NEPA when no EIS is necessary, and facilitating preparation of a statement when one is necessary. Preparation of an environmental assessment generally will not require extensive research or lengthy documentation. The environmental assessment shall contain brief discussion of the following:

(1) Purpose and need for the proposed action.

(2) Description of the proposed action.

(3) Alternatives considered.

(4) Environmental impact of the proposed action and alternatives.

(5) Listing of agencies and persons consulted.

(6) Conclusion of whether to prepare an environmental impact statement.

(c) *Public participation.* The Regional Administrator shall involve environmental agencies, applicants, and the public, to the extent practicable, in preparing environmental assessments. In determining "to the extent practicable," the Regional Administrator shall consider:

(1) Magnitude of the proposal;

(2) Likelihood of public interest;

(3) Need to act quickly;

(4) Likelihood of meaningful public comment;

(5) National security classification issues;

(6) Need for permits; and

(7) Statutory authority of environmental agency regarding the proposal.

(d) *When to prepare an EIS.* The Regional Administrator shall prepare an environmental impact statement for all major Agency actions significantly affecting the quality of the human environment. The test of what is a "significant" enough impact to require an EIS is found in the CEQ regulations at 40 CFR 1508.27.

(e) *Finding of No Significant Impact.* If the Regional Administrator determines on the basis of the environmental assessment not to prepare an environmental impact statement, the Regional Administrator shall prepare a finding of no significant impact in accordance with 40 CFR 1501.4(e) of the CEQ regulations. The assessment and the finding shall be submitted to the Environmental Officer and the Office of Chief Counsel (OCC) for approval. If Environmental Officer and OGC approval is obtained, the Regional Administrator shall then make the finding of no significant impact available to the public as specified in § 1506.6 of the CEQ regulations. A finding of no significant impact is not required when the decision not to prepare an environmental impact statement is based on a categorical exclusion.

(f) *Environmental Officer or OCC Disallowance.* If the Environmental Officer or OCC disagrees with the finding of no significant impact, the Regional Administrator shall prepare an environmental impact statement. Prior to preparation of an EIS, the Regional Administrator shall forward a notice of intent to prepare the EIS to the Environmental Officer who shall publish such notice in the FEDERAL REGISTER.

(g) *EIS determination of Regional Administrator.* The Regional Director may decide on his/her own to prepare an environmental impact statement. In such case, the Regional Administrator shall forward a notice of intent to prepare the EIS to the Environmental Officer who shall publish such notice in the FEDERAL REGISTER. The notice of intent shall be published before initiation of the scoping process.

[45 FR 41142, June 18, 1980, as amended at 47 FR 13149, Mar. 29, 1982]

§ 10.10 Preparation of environmental impact statements.

(a) *Scoping.* After determination that an environmental impact statement will be prepared and publication of the notice of intent, the Regional Administrator will initiate the scoping process in accordance with § 1501.7 of the CEQ regulations.

(b) *Preparation.* Based on the scoping process, the Regional Administrator will begin preparation of the environmental impact statement. Detailed procedures for preparation of the environmental impact statement are provided in part 1502 of the CEQ regulations.

(c) *Supplemental Environmental Impact Statements.* The Regional Administrator may at any time supplement a draft or final environmental impact statement. The Regional Administrator shall prepare a supplement to either the draft or final environmental impact statement when required under the criteria set forth in § 1502.9(2). The Regional Administrator will prepare, circulate, and file a supplement to a statement in the same fashion (exclusive of scoping) as a draft or final statement and will introduce the supplement into their formal administrative record.

(d) *Circulation of Environmental Impact Statements.* The Regional Administrator shall circulate draft and final environmental impact statements as prescribed in § 1502.19 of CEQ regulations. Prior to signing off on a draft or final impact statement, the Regional Administrator shall obtain the approval of the Environmental Officer and OCC.

[45 FR 41142, June 18, 1980, as amended at 47 FR 13149, Mar. 29, 1982]

§ 10.11 Environmental information.

Interested persons may contact the Environmental Officer or the Regional Administrator for information regarding FEMA's compliance with NEPA.

[45 FR 41142, June 18, 1980, as amended at 47 FR 13149, Mar. 29, 1982]

§ 10.12 Pre-implementation actions.

(a) *Decision-making.* The Regional Administrator shall ensure that decisions are made in accordance with the policies and procedures of the Act and that the NEPA process is integrated into the decision-making process. Because of the diversity of FEMA, it is not feasible to describe in this part the decision-making process for each of the various FEMA programs. Proposals and actions may be initiated at any level. Similarly, review and approval authority may be exercised at various levels depending on the nature of the action, available funding, and statutory authority. FEMA offices and administrations shall provide further guidance, commensurate with their programs and organization, for integration of environmental considerations into the decision-making process. The Regional Administrator shall:

(1) Consider all relevant environmental documents in evaluating proposals for Agency action;

(2) Make all relevant environmental documents, comments, and responses part of the record in formal rulemaking or adjudicatory proceedings;

(3) Ensure that all relevant environmental documents, comments and responses accompany the proposal through existing Agency review processes;

(4) Consider only those alternatives encompassed by the range of alternatives discussed in the relevant environmental documents when evaluating proposals for Agency action;

(5) Where an EIS has been prepared, consider the specific alternatives analyzed in the EIS when evaluating the proposal which is the subject of the EIS.

(b) *Record of decision.* In those cases requiring environmental impact statements, the Regional Administrator at the time of his/her decision, or if appropriate, his/her recommendation to Congress, shall prepare a concise public record of that decision. The record of decision is not intended to be an extensive, detailed document for the purpose of justifying the decision. Rather it is a concise document that sets forth the decision and describes the alternatives and relevant factors considered as specified in 40 CFR 1505.2. The record of decision will normally be less than three pages in length.

(c) *Mitigation.* Throughout the NEPA process, the Regional Administrator shall consider mitigating measures to avoid or minimize environmental harm and, in particular, harm to or within flood plains and wetlands. Mitigation measures or programs will be identified in the environmental impact statement and made available to decision-makers. Mitigation and other conditions established in the environmental impact statement or during its review and committed as part of the decision shall be implemented by the Regional Administrator.

(d) *Monitoring.* If a Regional Administrator determines that monitoring is applicable for established mitigation, a monitoring program will be adopted to assure the mitigation measures are accomplished. The Regional Administrator shall provide monitoring information, upon request, as specified in 40 CFR 1505.3. This does not, however, include standing or blanket requests for periodic reporting.

§ 10.13   Emergencies.

In the event of an emergency, the Regional Administrator may be required to take immediate action with significant environmental impact. The Regional Administrator shall notify the Environmental Officer of the emergency action at the earliest possible time so that the Environmental Officer may consult with the Council on Environmental Quality. In no event shall any Regional Administrator delay an emergency action necessary to the preservation of human life for the purpose of complying with the provision of this directive or the CEQ regulations.

[45 FR 41142, June 18, 1980, as amended at 47 FR 13149, Mar. 29, 1982]

§ 10.14   Flood plains and wetlands.

For any action taken by FEMA in a flood plain or wetland, the provisions of this part are supplemental to, and not instead of, the provisions of the FEMA regulation implementing Executive Order 11988, Flood Plain Management, and Executive Order 11990, Protection of Wetlands (44 CFR part 9).

PART 11—CLAIMS

Subpart A—General

AUTHORITY: 31 U.S.C. 3701 *et seq.*

SOURCE: 45 FR 15930, Mar. 12, 1980, unless otherwise noted.

Subpart A—General

§ 11.1   General collection standards.

The general standards and procedures governing the collection, compromise, termination and referral to the Department of Justice of claims for money and property that are prescribed in the regulations issued jointly by the Government Accountability Office and the Department of Justice pursuant to the Federal Claims Collection Act of 1966 (4 CFR part 101 *et seq.*), apply to the administrative claim collection activities of the Federal Emergency Management Agency (FEMA).

§11.2 Delegations of authority.

Any and all claims that arise under subchapter III of chapter 83, chapter 87 and chapter 88 of title 5, the United States Code, the Retired Federal Employees Health Benefits Act (74 Stat. 849), the Panama Canal Construction Annuity Act (58 Stat. 257), and the Lighthouse Service Widow's Annuity Act (64 Stat. 465) shall be referred to the Director of the Bureau of Retirement and Insurance, Office of Personnel Management, for handling. The Chief Counsel, FEMA shall act on all other claims against FEMA for money and property.

Subpart B—Administrative Claims Under Federal Tort Claims Act

§11.10 Scope of regulation.

This regulation applies to claims asserted under the Federal Tort Claims Act against the Federal Emergency Management Agency (FEMA). It does not include any contractor with FEMA.

§11.11 Administrative claim; when presented; appropriate FEMA office.

(a) For the purpose of this part, and the provisions of the Federal Tort Claims Act a claim is deemed to have been presented when FEMA receives, at a place designated in paragraph (b) or (c) of this section, an executed "Claim for Damage or Injury," Standard Form 95, or other written notification of an incident, accompanied by a claim for money damages in a sum certain for injury to or loss of property, for personal injury, or for death alleged to have occurred by reason of the incident. A claim which should have been presented to FEMA, but which was mistakenly addressed to or filed with another Federal agency, is deemed to be presented to FEMA as of the date that the claim is received by FEMA. If a claim is mistakenly addressed to or filed with FEMA, the claim shall forthwith be transferred to the appropriate Federal Agency, if ascertainable, or returned to the claimant.

(b) Except as provided in paragraph (c) of this section, a claimant shall mail or deliver his or her claim to the Office of Chief Counsel, Federal Emergency Management Agency, Washington, DC, 20472.

(c) When a claim is for $200 or less, does not involve a personal injury, and involves a FEMA regional employee, the claimant shall mail or deliver the claim to the Administrator of the FEMA Regional Office in which is employed the FEMA employee whose negligence or wrongful act or omission is alleged to have caused the loss or injury complained of. The addresses of the Regional Offices of FEMA are set out in part 2 of this chapter.

(d) A claim presented in compliance with paragraph (a) of this section may be amended by the claimant at any time prior to final FEMA action or prior to the exercise of the claimant's option under 28 U.S.C. 2675(a). Amendments shall be submitted in writing and signed by the claimant or his or her duly authorized agent or legal representative. Upon the timely filing of an amendment to a pending claim, FEMA shall have six months in which to make a final disposition of the claim as amended and the claimant's option under 28 U.S.C. 2675(a) shall not accrue until six months after the filing of an amendment.

[45 FR 15930, Mar. 12, 1980, as amended at 48 FR 6711, Feb. 15, 1983; 49 FR 33879, Aug. 27, 1984]

§11.12 Administrative claim; who may file.

(a) A claim for injury to or loss of property may be presented by the owner of the property interest which is the subject of the claim, his or her authorized agent, or legal representative.

(b) A claim for personal injury may be presented by the injured person or, his or her authorized agent or legal representative.

(c) A claim based on death may be presented by the executor or administrator of the decedent's estate or by any other person legally entitled to assert such a claim under applicable State law.

(d) A claim for loss wholly compensated by an insurer with the rights of a subrogee may be presented by the insurer or the insured individually, as their respective interests appear, or jointly. When an insurer presents a claim asserting the rights of a subrogee, he or she shall present with the claim appropriate evidence that he or she has the rights of a subrogee.

(e) A claim presented by an agent or legal representative shall be presented in the name of the claimant, be signed by the agent or legal representative, show the title of legal capacity of the person signing, and be accompanied by evidence of his or her authority to present a claim on behalf of the claimant as agent, executor, administrator, parent, guardian, or other representative.

§ 11.13 Investigations.

FEMA may investigate, or may request any other Federal agency to investigate, a claim filed under this part.

§ 11.14 Administrative claim; evidence and information to be submitted.

(a) *Death.* In support of a claim based on death the claimant may be required to submit the following evidence or information:

(1) An authenticated death certificate or other competent evidence showing cause of death, date of death, and age of the decedent.

(2) Decedent's employment or occupation at time of death, including his or her monthly or yearly salary or earnings (if any), and the duration of his or her last employment or occupation.

(3) Full names, addresses, birth dates, kinship, and marital status of the decedent's survivors, including identification of those survivors who were dependent for support on the decedent at the time of his or her death.

(4) Degree of support afforded by the decedent to each survivor dependent on him or her for support at the time of death.

(5) Decedent's general physical and mental condition before death.

(6) Itemized bills or medical and burial expenses incurred by reason of the incident causing death, or itemized receipts of payment for such expenses.

(7) If damages for pain and suffering before death are claimed, a physician's detailed statement specifying the injuries suffered, duration of pain and suffering, any drugs administered for pain, and the decedent's physical condition in the interval between injury and death.

(8) Any other evidence or information which may have a bearing on either the responsibility of the United States for the death or the amount of damages claimed.

(b) *Personal injury.* In support of a claim for personal injury, including pain and suffering, the claimant may be required to submit the following evidence or information:

(1) A written report by his or her attending physician or dentist setting forth the nature and extent of the injury, nature and extent of treatment, any degree of temporary or permanent disability, the prognosis, period of hospitalization, and any diminished earning capacity. In addition, the claimant may be required to submit to a physical or mental examination by a physician employed by FEMA or another Federal agency. FEMA shall make available to the claimant a copy of the report of the examining physician on written request by the claimant, if he or she has, on request, furnished the report referred to in the first sentence of this subparagraph and has made or agrees to make available to FEMA any other physician's reports previously or thereafter made of the physical or mental condition which is the subject matter of the claim.

(2) Itemized bills for medical, dental, and hospital expenses incurred, or itemized receipts of payment of such expenses.

(3) If the prognosis reveals the necessity for future treatment, a statement of expected expenses for such treatment.

(4) If a claim is made for loss of time from employment, a written statement from the employer showing actual time lost from employment, whether he or she is a full- or part-time employee, and wages or salary actually lost.

(5) If a claim is made for loss of income and the claimant is self-employed, documentary evidence showing the amount of earnings actually lost.

(6) Any other evidence or information which may have a bearing on either the responsibility of the United States for the personal injury or the damages claimed.

(c) *Property damage.* In support of a claim for injury to or loss of property, real or personal, the claimant may be required to submit the following evidence or information:

(1) Proof of ownership of the property interest which is the subject of the claim.

(2) A detailed statement of the amount claimed with respect to each item of property.

(3) An itemized receipt of payment for necessary repairs or itemized written estimates of the cost of such repairs.

(4) A statement listing date of purchase, purchase price, and salvage value, where repair is not economical.

(5) Any other evidence or information which may have a bearing on either the responsibility of the United States for the injury to or loss of property or the damages claimed.

§11.15 Authority to adjust, determine, compromise and settle.

(a) The Chief Counsel of FEMA, or a designee of the Chief Counsel, is delegated authority to consider, ascertain, adjust, determine, compromise, and settle claims under the provisions of section 2672 of title 28, United States Code, and this part.

(b) Notwithstanding the delegation of authority in paragraph (a) of this section, a Regional Administrator is delegated authority to be exercised in his or her discretion, to consider, ascertain, adjust, determine, compromise, and settle under the provisions of section 2672 of title 28, United States Code, and this part, any claim for $200 or less which is based on alleged negligence or wrongful act or omission of an employee of the appropriate Region, except when:

(1) There are personal injuries to either Government personnel or individuals not employed by the Government; or

(2) All damage to Government property or to property being used by FEMA, or both, is more than $200, or all damage to non-Government property being used by individuals not employed by the Government is more than $200.

[45 FR 15930, Mar. 12, 1980, as amended at 48 FR 6711, Feb. 15, 1983]

§11.16 Limitations on authority.

(a) An award, compromise, or settlement of a claim under this part in excess of $25,000 may be effected only with the advance written approval of the Attorney General or his or her designee. For the purpose of this paragraph, a principal claim and any derivative or subrogated claim shall be treated as a single claim.

(b) An administrative claim may be adjusted, determined, compromised, or settled under this part only after consultation with the Department of Justice, when, in the opinion of the Chief Counsel of FEMA or his or her designee:

(1) A new precedent or a new point of law is involved; or

(2) A question of policy is or may be involved; or

(3) The United States is or may be entitled to indemnity or contribution from a third party and FEMA is unable to adjust the third party claim; or

(4) The compromise of a particular claim, as a practical matter, will or may control the disposition of a related claim in which the amount to be paid may exceed $25,000.

(c) An administrative claim may be adjusted, determined, compromised or settled under this part only after consultation with the Department of Justice when FEMA is informed or is otherwise aware that the United States or an employee, agent or cost-type contractor of the United States is involved in litigation based on a claim arising out of the same incident or transaction.

§11.17 Referral to Department of Justice.

When Department of Justice approval or consultation is required under §11.16, the referral or request shall be transmitted to the Department of Justice by the Chief Counsel or his or her designee.

§11.18 Final denial of claim.

(a) Final denial of an administrative claim under this part shall be in writing and sent to the claimant, his or her attorney, or legal representative by certified or registered mail. The notification of final denial may include a statement of the reasons for the denial and shall include a statement that, if the claimant is dissatisfied with the FEMA action, he or she may file suit in an appropriate U.S. District Court not later than 6 months after the date of mailing of the notification.

(b) Prior to the commencement of suit and prior to the expiration of the 6-month period provided in 28 U.S.C. 2401(b), a claimant, his or her duly authorized agent, or legal representative, may file a written request with FEMA for reconsideration of a final denial of a claim under paragraph (a) of this section. Upon the timely filing of a request for reconsideration the FEMA shall have 6 months from the date of filing in which to make a final FEMA disposition of the claim and the claimant's option under 28 U.S.C. 2675(a) shall not accrue until 6 months after the filing of a request for reconsideration. Final FEMA action on a request for reconsideration shall be effected in accordance with the provisions of paragraph (a) of this section.

§ 11.19 Action on approved claim.

(a) Payment of a claim approved under this part is contingent on claimant's execution of (1) a "Claim for Damage or Injury," Standard Form 95, or a claims settlement agreement, and (2) a "Voucher for Payment," Standard Form 1145, as appropriate. When a claimant is represented by an attorney, the voucher for payment shall designate both the claimant and his or her attorney as payees, and the check shall be delivered to the attorney, whose address shall appear on the voucher.

(b) Acceptance by the claimant, his or her agent, or legal representative, of an award, compromise, or settlement made under section 2672 or 2677 of title 28, United States Code, is final and conclusive on the claimant, his or her agent or legal representative, and any other person on whose behalf or for whose benefit the claim has been presented, and constitutes a complete release of any claim against the United States and against any employee of the Government whose act or omission gave rise to the claim, by reason of the same subject matter.

Subpart C [Reserved]

Subpart D—Personnel Claims Regulations

AUTHORITY: 31 U.S.C. 3721.

SOURCE: 50 FR 8112, Feb. 28, 1985, unless otherwise noted.

§ 11.70 Scope and purpose.

(a) The Administrator, Federal Emergency Management Agency (FEMA), is authorized by 31 U.S.C. 3721 to settle and pay (including replacement in kind) claims of officers and employees of FEMA, amounting to not more than $25,000 for damage to or loss of personal property incident to their service. Property may be replaced in-kind at the option of the Government. Claims are payable only for such types, quantities, or amounts of tangible personal property (including money) as the approving authority shall determine to be reasonable, useful, or proper under the circumstances existing at the time and place of the loss. In determining what is reasonable, useful, or proper, the approving authority will consider the type and quantity of property involved, circumstances attending acquisition and use of the property, and whether possession or use by the claimant at the time of damage or loss was incident to service.

(b) The Government does not underwrite all personal property losses that a claimant may sustain and it does not underwrite individual tastes. While the Government does not attempt to limit possession of property by an individual, payment for damage or loss is made only to the extent that the possession of the property is determined to be reasonable, useful, or proper. If individuals possess excessive quantities of items, or expensive items, they should have such property privately insured. Failure of the claimant to comply with these procedures may reduce or preclude payment of the claim under this subpart.

§ 11.71 Claimants.

(a) A claim pursuant to this subpart may only be made by: (1) An employee of FEMA; (2) a former employee of

FEMA whose claim arises out of an incident occurring before his/her separation from FEMA; (3) survivors of a person named in paragraph (a) (1) or (2) of this section, in the following order of precedence: (i) Spouse; (ii) children; (iii) father or mother, or both or (iv) brothers or sisters, or both; (4) the authorized agent or legal representative of a person named in paragraphs (a) (1), (2), and (3) of this section.

(b) A claim may not be presented by or for the benefit of a subrogee, assignee, conditional vendor, or other third party.

§ 11.72 Time limitations.

(a) A claim under this part may be allowed only if it is in writing, specifies a sum certain and is received in the Office of Chief Counsel, Federal Emergency Management Agency, Washington, DC 20472: (1) Within 2 years after it accrues; (2) or if it cannot be filed within the time limits of paragraph (a)(1) of this section because it accrues in time of war or in time of armed conflict in which any armed force of the United States is engaged or if such a war or armed conflict intervenes within 2 years after the claim accrues, when the claimant shows good cause, the claim may be filed within 2 years after the cause ceases to exist but not more than 2 years after termination of the war or armed conflict.

(b) For purposes of this subpart, a claim accrues at the time of the accident or incident causing the loss or damage, or at such time as the loss or damage should have been discovered by the claimant by the exercise of due diligence.

§ 11.73 Allowable claims.

(a) A claim may be allowed only if: (1) The damage or loss was not caused wholly or partly by the negligent or wrongful act of the claimant, his/her agent, the members of his/her family, or his/her private employee (the standard to be applied is that of reasonable care under the circumstances); and (2) the possession of the property lost or damaged and the quantity possessed is determined to have been reasonable, useful, or proper under the circumstances; and (3) the claim is substantiated by proper and convincing evidence.

(b) Claims which are otherwise allowable under this subpart shall not be disallowed solely because the property was not in the possession of the claimant at the time of the damage or loss, or solely because the claimant was not the legal owner of the property for which the claim is made. For example, borrowed property may be the subject of a claim.

(c) Subject to the conditions in paragraph (a) of this section, and the other provisions of this subpart, any claim for damage to, or loss of, personal property incident to service with FEMA may be considered and allowed. The following are examples of the principal types of claims which may be allowed, unless excluded by § 11.74.

(1) *Property loss or damage in quarters or other authorized places.* Claims may be allowed for damage to, or loss of, property arising from fire, flood, hurricane, other natural disaster, theft, or other unusual occurrence, while such property is located at:

(i) Quarters within the 50 states or the District of Columbia that were assigned to the claimant or otherwise provided in-kind by the United States; or

(ii) Any warehouse, office, working area, or other place (except quarters) authorized for the reception or storage of property.

(2) *Transportation or travel losses.* Claims may be allowed for damage to, or loss of, property incident to transportation or storage pursuant to orders, or in connection with travel under orders, including property in the custody of a carrier, an agent or agency of the Government, or the claimant.

(3) *Motor vehicles.* Claims may be allowed for automobiles and other motor vehicles damaged or lost by overseas shipments provided by the Government. "Shipments provided by the Government" means via Government vessels, charter of commercial vessels, or by Government bills of lading on commercial vessels, and includes storage, unloading, and offloading incident thereto. Other claims for damage to or loss of automobiles and other major vehicles may be allowed when use of the vehicles on a nonreimbursable basis

was required by the claimant's supervisor, but these claims shall be limited to a maximum of $1,000.00.

(4) *Mobile homes.* Claims may be allowed for damage to or loss of mobile homes and their content under the provisions of paragraph (c)(2) of this section. Claims for structural damage to mobile homes resulting from such structural damage must contain conclusive evidence that the damage was not caused by structural deficiency of the mobile home and that it was not overloaded. Claims for damage to or loss of tires mounted on mobile homes may be allowed only in cases of collision, theft, or vandalism.

(5) *Money.* Claims for money in an amount that is determined to be reasonable for the claimant to possess at the time of the loss are payable:

(i) Where personal funds were accepted by responsible Government personnel with apparent authority to receive them for safekeeping, deposit, transmittal, or other authorized disposition, but were neither applied as directed by the owner nor returned;

(ii) When lost incident to a marine or aircraft disaster;

(iii) When lost by fire, flood, hurricane, or other natural disaster;

(iv) When stolen from the quarters of the claimant where it is conclusively shown that the money was in a locked container and that the quarters themselves were locked. Exceptions to the foregoing "double lock" rule are permitted when the adjudicating authority determines that the theft loss was not caused wholly or partly by the negligent or wrongful act of the claimant, their agent, or their employee. The adjudicating authority should use the test of whether the claimant did their best under the circumstances to protect the property; or

(v) When taken by force from the claimant's person.

(6) *Clothing.* Claims may be allowed for clothing and accessories customarily worn on the person which are damaged or lost:

(i) During the performance of official duties in an unusual or extraordinary-risk situation;

(ii) In cases involving emergency action required by natural disaster such as fire, flood, hurricane, or by enemy or other belligerent action;

(iii) In cases involving faulty equipment or defective furniture maintained by the Government and used by the claimant required by the job situation; or

(iv) When using a motor vehicle.

(7) *Property used for benefit of the Government.* Claims may be allowed for damage to or loss of property (except motor vehicles, see §§ 11.73(c)(3) and 11.74(b)(13)) used for the benefit of the Government at the request of, or with the knowledge and consent of, superior authority or by reason of necessity.

(8) *Enemy action or public service.* Claims may be allowed for damage to or loss of property as a direct consequence of:

(i) Enemy action or threat thereof, or combat, guerrilla, brigandage, or other belligerent activity, or unjust confiscation by a foreign power or its nation;

(ii) Action by the claimant to quiet a civil disturbance or to alleviate a public disaster; or

(iii) Efforts by the claimant to save human life or Government property.

(9) *Marine or aircraft disaster.* Claims may be allowed for personal property damaged or lost as a result of marine or aircraft disaster or accident.

(10) *Government property.* Claims may be allowed for property owned by the United States only when the claimant is financially responsible to an agency of the Government other than FEMA.

(11) *Borrowed property.* Claims may be allowed for borrowed property that has been damaged or lost.

(12)(i) A claim against the Government may be made for not more than $40,000 by an officer or employee of the agency for damage to, or loss of, personal property in a foreign country that was incurred incident to service, and—

(A) The officer, or employee was evacuated from the country on a recommendation or order of the Secretary of State or other competent authority that was made in responding to an incident of political unrest or hostile act by people in that country; and the damage or loss resulted from the evacuation, incident, or hostile act; or

(B) The damage or loss resulted from a hostile act directed against the Government or its officers, or employees.

(ii) On paying the claim under this section, the Government is subrogated for the amount of the payment to a right or claim that the claimant may have against the foreign country for the damage or loss for which the Government made the payment.

(iii) Amounts may be obligated or expended for claims under this section only to the extent provided in advance in appropriation laws.

§11.74 Claims not allowed.

(a) A claim is not allowable if:

(1) The damage or loss was caused wholly or partly by the negligent or wrongful act of the claimant, claimant's agent, claimant's employee, or a member of claimant's family;

(2) The damage or loss occurred in quarters occupied by the claimant within the 50 states and the District of Columbia that were not assigned to the claimant or otherwise provided in-kind by the United States;

(3) Possession of the property lost or damaged was not incident to service or not reasonable or proper under the circumstances.

(b) In addition to claims falling within the categories of paragraph (a) of this section, the following are examples of claims which are not payable:

(1) *Claims not incident to service.* Claims which arose during the conduct of personal business are not payable.

(2) *Subrogation claims.* Claims based upon payment or other consideration to a proper claimant are not payable.

(3) *Assigned claims.* Claims based upon assignment of a claim by a proper claimant are not payable.

(4) *Conditional vendor claims.* Claims asserted by or on behalf of a conditional vendor are not payable.

(5) *Claims by improper claimants.* Claims by persons not designated in §11.71 are not payable.

(6) *Articles of extraordinary value.* Claims are not payable for valuable or expensive articles, such as cameras, watches, jewelry, furs, or other articles of extraordinary value, when shipped with household goods or as unaccompanied baggage (shipment includes storage). This prohibition does not apply to articles in the personal custody of the claimant or articles properly checked, provided that reasonable protection or security measures have been taken, by the claimant.

(7) *Articles acquired for other persons.* Claims are not payable for articles intended directly or indirectly for persons other than the claimant or members of the claimants' immediate household. This prohibition includes articles acquired at the request of others and articles for sale.

(8) *Property used for business.* Claims are not payable for property normally used for business or profit.

(9) *Unserviceable property.* Claims are not payable for wornout or unserviceable property.

(10) *Violation of law or directive.* Claims are not payable for property acquired, possessed, or transported in violation of law, regulation, or other directive. This does not apply to limitation imposed on the weight of shipments of household goods.

(11) *Intangible property.* Claims are not payable for intangible property such as bank books, checks, promissory notes, stock certificates, bonds, bills of lading, warehouse receipts, baggage checks, insurance policies, money orders, and traveler's checks.

(12) *Government property.* Claims are not payable for property owned by the United States unless the claimant is financially responsible for the property to an agency of the Government other than FEMA.

(13) *Motor vehicles.* Claims for motor vehicles, except as provided for by §11.73(c)(3), will ordinarily not be paid. However, in exceptional cases, meritorious claims for damage to or loss of motor vehicles, limited to a maximum of $1,000.00, may be recommended to the Office of Chief Counsel for consideration and approval for payment.

(14) *Enemy property.* Claims are not payable for enemy property, including war trophies.

(15) *Losses recoverable from carrier, insurer or contractor.* Claims are not payable for losses, or any portion thereof, which have been recovered or are recoverable from a carrier, insurer or under contract except as permitted under §11.75.

(16) *Fees for estimates.* Claims are not normally payable for fees paid to obtain estimates of repair in conjunction with submitting a claim under this subpart. However, where, in the opinion of the adjudicating authority, the claimant could not obtain an estimate without paying a fee, such a claim may be considered in an amount reasonable in relation to the value for the cost of repairs of the articles involved, provided that the evidence furnished clearly indicates that the amount of the fee paid will not be deducted from the cost of repairs if the work is accomplished by the estimator.

(17) *Items fraudulently claimed.* Claims are not payable for items fraudulently claimed. When investigation discloses that a claimant, claimant's agent, claimant's employee, or member of claimant's family has intentionally misrepresented an item claimed as to cost, condition, costs to repair, etc., the item will be disallowed in its entirety even though some actual damage has been sustained. However, if the remainder of the claim is proper, it may be paid. This does not preclude appropriate disciplinary action if warranted.

(18) *Minimum amount.* Loss or damage amounting to less than $10.

§ 11.75 Claims involving carriers and insurers.

In the event the property which is the subject of a claim was lost or damaged while in the possession of a carrier or was insured, the following procedures will apply:

(a) Whenever property is damaged, lost, or destroyed while being shipped pursuant to authorized travel orders, the owner must file a written claim for reimbursement with the last commercial carrier known or believed to have handled the goods, or the carrier known to be in possession of the property when the damage or loss occurred, according to the terms of its bill of lading or contract, before submitting a claim against the Government under this subpart.

(1) If more than one bill of lading or contract was issued, a separate demand should be made against the last carrier on each such document.

(2) The demand should be made within the time limit provided in the policy and prior to the filing of a claim against the Government.

(3) If it is apparent that the damage or loss is attributable to packing, storage, or unpacking while in the custody of the Government, no demand need be made against the carrier.

(b) Whenever property which is damaged, lost, or destroyed incident to the claimant's service is insured in whole or in part, the claimant must make demand in writing against the insurer for reimbursement under terms and conditions of the insurance coverage, prior to the filing of the concurrent claim against the Government.

(c) Failure to make a demand on a carrier or insurer or to make all reasonable efforts to protect and prosecute rights available against a carrier or insurer and to collect the amount recoverable from the carrier or insurer may result in reducing the amount recoverable from the Government by the maximum amount which would have been recoverable from the carrier or insurer, had the claim been timely or diligently prosecuted. However, no deduction will be made where the circumstances of the claimant's service preclude reasonable filing of such a claim or diligent prosecution, or the evidence indicates a demand was impracticable or would have been unavailing.

(d) Following the submission of the claim against the carrier or insurer, the claimant may immediately submit a claim against the Government in accordance with the provisions of this subpart, without waiting until either final approval or denial of the claim is made by the carrier or insurer.

(1) Upon submission of a claim to the Government, the claimant must certify in the claim that no recovery (or the amount of recovery) has been gained from a carrier or insurer, and enclose all correspondence pertinent thereto.

(2) If the carrier or insurer has not taken final action on the claim against them, by the time the claimant submits a claim to the Government, the claimant will immediately notify them to address all correspondence in regard to the claim to him/her, in care of the Chief Counsel of FEMA.

(3) The claimant shall timely advise the Chief Counsel in writing, of any action which is taken by the carrier or insurer on the claim. On request, the claimant also will furnish such evidence as may be required to enable the United States to enforce the claim.

(e) When a claim is paid by FEMA, the claimant will assign to the United States, to the extent of any payment on the claim accepted by claimant, all rights, title, and interest in any claim against the carrier, insurer, or other party arising out of the incident on which the claim against the Government is based. After payment of the claim by the Government, the claimant will, upon receipt of any payment from a carrier or insurer, pay the proceeds to the United States to the extent of the payment received by the claimant from the United States.

(f) When a claimant recovers for the loss from the carrier or insurer before the claim against the Government under this subpart is settled, the amount or recovery shall be applied to the claim as follows:

(1) When the amount recovered from a carrier, insurer, or other third party is greater than or equal to the claimant's total loss as determined under this subpart, no compensation is allowable under this subpart.

(2) When the amount recovered is less than such total loss, the allowable amount is determined by deducting the recovery from the amount of such total loss;

(3) For the purpose of this paragraph (f) the claimant's total loss is to be determined without regard to the $25,000 maximum set forth above. However, if the resulting amount, after making this deduction, exceeds $25,000, the claimant will be allowed only $25,000.

§ 11.76 Claims procedures.

(a) *Filing a claim.* Applicants shall file claims in writing with the Chief Counsel, Federal Emergency Management Agency, Washington, DC 20472. Each written claim shall contain, as a minimum:

(1) Name, address, and place of employment of the claimant;

(2) Place and date of the damage or loss;

(3) A brief statement of the facts and circumstances surrounding the damage or loss;

(4) Cost, date, and place of acquisition of each price of property damaged or lost;

(5) Two itemized repair estimates, or value estimates, whichever is applicable;

(6) Copies of police reports, if applicable;

(7) A statement from the claimant's supervisor that the loss was incident to service;

(8) A statement that the property was or was not insured;

(9) With respect to claims involving thefts or losses in quarters or other places where the property was reasonably kept, a statement as to what security precautions were taken to protect the property involved;

(10) With respect to claims involving property being used for the benefit of the Government, a statement by the claimant's supervisor that the claimant was required to provide such property or that the claimant's providing it was in the interest of the Government; and

(11) Other evidence as may be required.

(b) *Single claim.* A single claim shall be presented for all lost or damaged property resulting from the same incident. If this procedure causes a hardship, the claimant may present an initial claim with notice that it is a partial claim, an explanation of the circumstances causing the hardship, and an estimate of the balance of the claim and the date it will be submitted. Payment may be made on a partial claim if the adjudicating authority determines that a genuine hardship exists.

(c) *Loss in quarters.* Claims for property loss in quarters or other authorized places should be accompanied by a statement indicating:

(1) Geographical location;

(2) Whether the quarters were assigned or provided in-kind by the Government;

(3) Whether the quarters are regularly occupied by the claimant;

(4) Names of the authority, if any, who designated the place of storage of the property if other than quarters;

(5) Measures taken to protect the property; and

(6) Whether the claimant is a local inhabitant.

(d) *Loss by theft or robbery.* Claims for property loss by theft or robbery should be accompanied by a statement indicating:

(1) Geographical location;

(2) Facts and circumstances surrounding the loss, including evidence of the crime such as breaking and entering, capture of the thief or robber, or recovery of part of the stolen goods; and

(3) Evidence that the claimant exercised due care in protecting the property prior to the loss, including information as to the degree of care normally exercised in the locale of the loss due to any unusual risks involved.

(e) *Transportation losses.* Claims for transportation losses should be accompanied by the following:

(1) Copies of orders authorizing the travel, transportation, or shipment or a certificate explaining the absence of orders and stating their substance;

(2) Statement in cases where property was turned over to a shipping officer, supply officer, or contract packer indicating:

(i) Name (or designation) and address of the shipping officer, supply officer, or contract packer indicating;

(ii) Date the property was turned over;

(iii) Inventoried condition when the property was turned over;

(iv) When and where the property was packed and by whom;

(v) Date of shipment;

(vi) Copies of all bills of lading, inventories, and other applicable shipping documents;

(vii) Date and place of delivery to the claimant;

(viii) Date the property was unpacked by the carrier, claimant, or Government;

(ix) Statement of disinterested witnesses as to the condition of the property when received and delivered, or as to handling or storage;

(x) Whether the negligence of any Government employee acting within the scope of his/her employment caused the damage or loss;

(xi) Whether the last common carrier or local carrier was given a clear receipt, except for concealed damages;

(xii) Total gross, tare, and new weight of shipment;

(xiii) Insurance certificate or policy if losses are privately insured;

(xiv) Copy of the demand on carrier or insured, or both, when required, and the reply, if any;

(xv) Action taken by the claimant to locate missing baggage or household effects, including related correspondence.

(f) *Marine or aircraft disaster.* Claims for property losses due to marine or aircraft disaster should be accompanied by a copy of orders or other evidence to establish the claimant's right to be, or to have property on board.

(g) *Enemy action, public disaster, or public service.* Claims for property losses due to enemy action, public disaster, or public service should be accompanied by:

(1) Copies of orders or other evidence establishing the claimant's required presence in the area involved; and

(2) A detailed statement of facts and circumstances showing an applicable case enumerated in § 11.73(c)(8).

(h) *Money.* Claims for loss of money deposited for safekeeping, transmittal, or other authorized disposition should be accompanied by:

(1) Name, grade, and address of the person or persons who received money and any others involved;

(2) Name and designation of the authority who authorized such person or persons to accept personal funds and the disposition required; and

(3) Receipts and written sworn statements explaining the failure to account for funds or return them to the claimant.

(i) *Motor vehicles or mobile homes in transit.* Claims for damage to motor vehicles or mobile homes in transit should be accompanied by a copy of orders or other available evidence to establish the claimant's lawful right to have the property shipped and evidence to establish damage in transit.

§ 11.77 Settlement of claims.

(a) The Chief Counsel, FEMA, is authorized to settle (consider, ascertain, adjust, determine, and dispose of, whether by full or partial allowance or disallowance) any claim under this subpart.

(b) The Chief Counsel may formulate such procedures and make such redelegations as may be required to fulfill the objectives of this subpart.

(c) The Chief Counsel shall conduct or request the Office of Inspector General to conduct such investigation as may be appropriate in order to determine the validity of a claim.

(d) The Chief Counsel shall notify a claimant in writing of action taken on their claim, and if partial or full disallowance is made, the reasons therefor.

(e) In the event a claim submitted against a carrier under § 11.75 has not been settled, before settlement of the claim against the Government pursuant to this subpart, the Chief Counsel shall notify such carrier or insurer to pay the proceeds of the claim to FEMA to the extent FEMA has paid such to claimant in settlement.

(f) The settlement of a claim under this subpart, whether by full or partial allowance or disallowance, is final and conclusive.

§ 11.78 Computation of amount of award.

(a) The amount allowed for damage to or loss of any items of property may not exceed the cost of the item (either the price paid in cash or property, or the value at the time of acquisition if not acquired by purchase or exchange), and there will be no allowance for replacement cost or for appreciation in the value of the property. Subject to these limitations, the amount allowable is either:

(1) The depreciated value, immediately prior to the loss or damage, of property lost or damaged beyond economical repair, less any salvage value; or

(2) The reasonable cost or repairs, when property is economically repairable, provided that the cost of repairs does not exceed the amount allowable under paragraph (a)(1) of this section.

(b) Depreciation in value is determined by considering the type of article involved, its costs, its conditions when damaged or lost, and the time elapsed between the date of acquisition and the date of damage or loss.

(c) Replacement of lost or damaged property may be made in-kind whenever appropriate.

§ 11.79 Attorney's fees.

No more than 10 per centum of the amount paid in settlement of each individual claim submitted and settled under this subpart shall be paid or delivered to or received by any agent or attorney on account of services rendered in connection with that claim. A person violating this section shall be fined not more than $1,000.

[45 FR 15930, Mar. 12, 1980, as amended at 74 FR 15337, Apr. 3, 2009]

PART 12—ADVISORY COMMITTEES

AUTHORITY: Federal Advisory Committee Act, 5 U.S.C. app. 1; Reorganization Plan No. 3 of 1978; E.O. 12127; E.O. 12148; E.O. 12024.

SOURCE: 45 FR 64180, Sept. 29, 1980, unless otherwise noted.

§ 12.1 Purpose and applicability.

(a) The regulations in this part implement the Federal Advisory Committee Act, Executive Order 12024 and General Services Administration Regulation 41 CFR part 101–6. The provisions of the Federal Advisory Committee Act in this part shall apply to all advisory committees established by the Federal Emergency Management Agency (FEMA), including advisory committees created pursuant to any act of Congress relating to the United States Fire Administration, Federal Insurance Administration, or any other component of the Federal Emergency Management Agency, except to the extent that any act of Congress establishing an advisory committee reporting to the agencies specifically provides otherwise.

(b) This part does not apply to interagency advisory committees or advisory committees established by the President unless specifically made applicable by the establishing authority.

(c) This part does not apply to any local group, contractor, grantee, or other organization whose primary function is to render public service with respect to a Federal program, or any state or local committee, counsel, board, commission, or similar group established to advise or make recommendations to State or local officials or agencies.

[45 FR 64180, Sept. 29, 1980, as amended at 48 FR 44543, Sept. 29, 1983; 50 FR 40007, Oct. 1, 1985]

§ 12.2 Definitions.

As used in this part—

Act means the Federal Advisory Committee Act (86 Stat. 770).

Administrator means the Administrator of the Federal Emergency Management Agency.

Advisory Committee is used as per the meaning set forth in section 3(2) of the Act.

Agency means the Federal Emergency Management Agency, established by Presidential Reorganization Plan No. 3 of 1978, or any component thereof.

Administrator, GSA means the Administrator of General Services.

FEMA means the Federal Emergency Management Agency.

GSA means the General Services Administration.

Presidential Advisory Committee means an advisory committee which advises the President of the United States.

Secretariat means the Committee Management Secretariat of the General Services Administration.

Any officer of the Federal Government means any agency official or employee of the Federal government designated to perform duties with respect to an advisory committee established under this part.

Nonstatutory advisory committee means an advisory committee not established by statute or reorganization plan.

[45 FR 64180, Sept. 29, 1980, as amended at 74 FR 15337, Apr. 3, 2009]

§ 12.3 Policy.

In determining whether an advisory committee should be created, and in reviewing the functions of operating advisory committees, the Agency will:

(a) Establish new advisory committees only when they are determined to be essential, keeping their number to the minimum necessary to accomplish the assigned mission of the agency or its components;

(b) Provide standards and uniform procedures to govern the establishment, operation, administration, and duration of the advisory committees;

(c) Terminate the advisory committees when they are no longer necessary to carry out the purposes for which they were established; and

(d) Keep the Congress and the public informed with respect to the number, purpose, membership, activity, and cost of the advisory committees.

§ 12.4 Interpretations.

Except as specifically authorized in writing by the Administrator, including internal instructions, no interpretation of the meaning of the regulations in this part by any employee or officer of the Agency, other than a written interpretation by the Chief Counsel, will be recognized to be binding upon the Agency.

§ 12.5 Advisory committee management officer.

(a) The Director, Records Management Division, Office of Management serves as FEMA's advisory committee management officer and shall:

(1) Exercise control and supervision over the establishment, procedures, and accomplishments of the advisory committees established by the Director; and

(2) Assemble and maintain the reports, records, and other papers of any advisory committee during its existence.

(b) The name of the Advisory Committee Management Officer designated in accordance with this part shall be provided to the Secretariat.

[45 FR 64180, Sept. 29, 1980, as amended at 47 FR 13149, Mar. 29, 1982; 48 FR 44543, Sept. 29, 1983; 49 FR 33879, Aug. 27, 1984; 74 FR 15338, Apr. 3, 2009]

§12.6 Establishment of advisory committees.

(a) No advisory committee shall be established under this part unless such establishment is:

(1) Specifically authorized by statute or the President of the United States; or

(2) Determined as a matter of formal record by the Administrator after consultation with the Secretariat, with timely notice published in the FEDERAL REGISTER as a matter of the public interest, in connection with the performance of duties imposed on the agency by law.

(b) The determination required by paragraph (a)(2) of this section shall:

(1) Contain a clearly defined purpose for the advisory committee;

(2) Require the membership of the advisory committee to be fairly balanced in terms of the points of view represented in the functions performed by the advisory committee;

(3) Contain appropriate provisions to assure that the advice and recommendations of the advisory committee will not be inappropriately influenced by the appointing authority or by any special interest, but will instead be the result of the advisory committee's independent judgment;

(4) Contain provisions dealing with the date for submission of reports (if any), the duration of the advisory committee, and the publication of reports and other materials, to the extent that the agency determines the provisions of §12.16 of this part to be inadequate; and

(5) Contain provisions which will assure that the advisory committee will have adequate staff (either supplied by the Agency or employed by it), will be provided adequate quarters, and will have funds available to meet its other necessary expenses.

(c) Consultation with the Secretariat may be in the form of a letter from the Agency describing the nature and purpose of the proposed advisory committee, including an explanation of why the functions of the proposed committee could not be performed by FEMA or by an existing committee. The letter should describe the Agency's plan to attain balanced membership on the proposed committee, as prescribed in paragraph (b)(2) of this section. If the Secretariat is satisfied that the establishment of the advisory committee will be in accord with the Act, the Agency shall certify in writing that creation of the advisory committee is in the public interest.

(d) Unless otherwise specifically provided by statute or Presidential directive, advisory committees shall be utilized solely for advisory functions.

§12.7 Charter.

(a) No advisory committee established under this part shall meet or take any action until an advisory committee charter has been filed with the Agency and the standing Committee or Committees of the Senate and House of Representatives having legislative jurisdiction over the FEMA component to which the advisory committee renders its advice.

(b) The charter required by paragraph (a) of this section shall contain at least the following information:

(1) The committee's official designations;

(2) The committee's objectives and the scope of its activities;

(3) The period of time necessary for the committee to carry out its purposes;

(4) The FEMA component and official to whom the committee reports;

(5) The FEMA component responsible for providing the necessary support for the committee;

(6) A description of the duties for which the committee is responsible, and, if such duties are not solely advisory, specification of the authority for such functions;

(7) The estimated annual operating cost in dollars and man years for the committee;

(8) The estimated number in frequency of committee meetings;

(9) The committee's termination date, if less than 2 years from the date of committee's establishment; and

(10) The date the charter is filed.

(c) A copy of the charter required by paragraph (a) of this section shall also be furnished at the time of filing to the Library of Congress, Exchange and Gift Division, Federal Advisory Committee, Washington, DC 20540.

(d) An amendment to the charter may be filed whenever there is a substantial change regarding matters stated in the original charter.

(e) The requirements of this section shall also apply to committees utilized as advisory committees, even though not expressly established for that purpose.

§ 12.8 Meetings.

(a) Advisory committees established under this part shall not hold any meetings, nor shall they render any advice, except at the call of, or with the advice and approval of, the Federal Officer or employee designated in accordance with § 12.10 of this part, who shall also approve the agenda of such meetings. Timely notice of each meeting shall be provided in accordance with § 12.11 of this part.

(b) The agenda required by paragraph (a) of this section shall list the matters to be considered at the meeting. It shall also indicate when any part of the meeting will concern matters within the exceptions of the (Government) Sunshine Act, 5 U.S.C. 552b, and § 12.9 of this part.

(c) Subject to the provisions of § 12.9 of this part, each advisory committee meeting shall be open to the public. Meetings which are completely or partly open to the public shall be held at reasonable times and at such a place that is reasonably accessible to the public. The size of the meeting room should be determined by such factors as the size of the committee, the number of members of the public who could reasonably be expected to attend, the number of persons who attended similar meetings in the past, and the resource facilities available.

(d) Any member of the public shall be permitted to file a written statement with the committee related to any meeting that is completely or partly open to the public. Interested persons may also be permitted by the committee chairman to speak at such meetings in accordance with the procedures established by the committee.

§ 12.9 Closed meetings.

(a) The requirements of § 12.8 (c) and (d) of this part that meetings shall be open to the public and that the public shall be afforded an opportunity to participate in such meetings shall not apply to any advisory committee meeting which the President or the Administrator determines is concerned with matters listed in 5 U.S.C. 552b(c).

(b) An advisory committee which seeks to have all or part of its meetings closed shall notify the Administrator before the scheduled date of the meeting. The notification shall be in writing and shall specify the reasons why any part of the meeting should be closed.

(c) A request that the meeting be closed will be granted upon determination by the Administrator that the request is in accordance with the policies of this part. The Administrator's determination will be in writing and will state the specific reasons for closing all or part of the meeting. The determination will be made available to the public upon request.

(d) The Administrator may delegate responsibility for making the determination required by paragraph (c) of this section. In any case where the determination to close the meeting is made by the Administrator's delegate, the determination will be reviewed by the Chief Counsel.

(e) When a meeting is closed to the public, the advisory committee shall issue a report, at least annually, setting forth a summary of its activities in such meetings, addressing those related matters as would be informative to the public and consistent with the policy of 5 U.S.C. 552b(c) and of this part. Notice of the availability of such annual reports shall be published in accordance with § 12.11 of this part.

§12.10 Designated Federal officer or employee.

(a) The Agency will designate an officer or employee of the Federal Government to chair or attend each meeting of each advisory committee established under this part.

(b) No advisory committee shall conduct any meeting in the absence of the Federal employee or officer designated in accordance with paragraph (a) of this section.

(c) The Federal officer or employee designated in accordance with paragraph (a) of this section is authorized, whenever he/she determines it to be in the public interest, to adjourn any committee meeting he/she is designated to chair or attend.

§12.11 Public notice.

(a) The Agency's determination procedure described by §12.6 of this part for the creation of the advisory committee, and a description of the nature and purpose of the committee, should be published in the FEDERAL REGISTER at least 15 days prior to the filing of the committee's charter, unless the Secretariat, for good cause, authorizes a shorter period of time between publication of the notice and the filing of the charter.

(b) Except when the Administrator GSA determines contrarily for reasons of national security, timely notice of each advisory committee meeting, whether open or closed to the public, shall be published in the FEDERAL REGISTER at least 15 days before the meeting date. Such notice should state the name of the advisory committee, the time, place and purpose of the meeting, and should include, where appropriate, a summary of the meeting agenda. Notice ordinarily should state that the meeting is open to the public or explain why the meeting or any portion of the meeting is to be closed. Notices shorter than the time prescribed by this paragraph may be provided in emergency situations, and the reasons for such emergency exceptions should be made part of the meeting notice. *Due to the emergency nature of FEMA's many programs, it is contemplated that advisory committees may have to be established or meetings called on fairly short notice; however, every effort should be*
made to comply with the notice requirement, except in cases where delay may result in harm to individuals or damage to property. A request for a determination that notice of a meeting should not be published for reasons of national security shall be submitted to the Administrator GSA with a statement of reasons supporting such request at least 30 days before the meeting is scheduled. Where, however, there is a significant likelihood of severe damage to property or injury to individuals, the notice period may be reduced as necessary to minimize such damage or injury.

(c) In addition to the notice required by paragraph (b) of this section, other forms of notice such as public releases and notices by mail should be used to inform the public of advisory committee meetings.

(d) The Committee Management Officer, in coordination with the Office of External Affairs, should, where practical, maintain lists of people and organizations interested in advisory committees and notify them of meetings by mail.

(e) Notice of the availability of the annual reports required by §12.9(e) of this part will be published in the FEDERAL REGISTER no later than 60 days after their completion. Notice will include instructions which will allow the public access to the reports.

§12.12 Minutes.

(a) Detailed minutes of each advisory committee meeting shall be kept and shall contain a record of the persons present, a complete summary of matters discussed and conclusions reached, and copies of all reports received, issued, or approved by the advisory committee. The record of persons present shall include the time and place of the meeting, a list of advisory committee members and staff and agency employees present at the meeting, a list of members of the public who presented oral or written statements, and an estimated number of members of the public who attended the meeting. The minutes shall describe the extent to which the meeting was open to the public and the extent of public participation. If it is impracticable to attach to the minutes of the meeting any report received, issued, or approved by the advisory committee, then the minutes will describe the report in sufficient detail to enable any person requesting the report to readily identify it.

(b) The accuracy of all minutes shall be certified by the chairperson of the advisory committee concerned, except in the case of a subcommittee or subgroup of the advisory committee, in which case the accuracy of the minutes shall be certified by the chairperson of the subcommittee or subgroup concerned *and co-signed by the chairperson of the advisory committee.*

§ 12.13 Transcripts of the advisory committee meetings and agency proceedings.

Copies of transcripts of advisory committee meetings which have been prepared will be made available to any person at the actual cost of duplication, as prescribed in § 12.17 of this part.

§ 12.14 Annual comprehensive review.

(a) The Agency will conduct an annual comprehensive review of the activities and responsibilities of each advisory committee to determine:

(1) Whether such committee is carrying out its purpose;

(2) Whether, consistent with the provisions of applicable statutes, the responsibilities assigned to it should be revised;

(3) Whether it should be merged with any other advisory committee or committees; or

(4) Whether it should be abolished.

(b) Pertinent factors to be considered in the comprehensive review required by paragraph (a) of this section includes the following:

(1) The number of times the committee has met in the past year;

(2) The number of reports or recommendations submitted by the committee;

(3) An evaluation of the substance of the reports or recommendations submitted by the committee, regarding the Agency's programs or operations;

(4) An evaluation of the utilization by the Agency of the committee's policy formation recommendations in: program planning, decision making, more effective achievement of program objectives, and more economical accomplishment of programs in general, with emphasis in such evaluation on the preceding 12 month period of the committee's work;

(5) Whether information or recommendations could be obtained from sources within the Agency or from other advisory committees already in existence;

(6) The degree of duplication of effort by the committee as compared with that of other parts of the Agency or other advisory committees; and

(7) The estimated annual cost of the committee.

(c) The annual review required by this section shall be conducted on a calendar year basis, and results of the review shall be included in the annual report to the Secretariat required by § 12.16(b) of this part. The report shall contain a justification of each advisory committee which the Agency determines should be continued, making reference, as appropriate, to the factors specified in paragraph (b) of this section.

(d) The review will examine all advisory committees, and committees found to be no longer needed shall be terminated. Advisory committees established by act of Congress or the President of the United States will be reviewed, and if appropriate, their termination will be recommended.

§ 12.15 Termination and renewal of advisory committees.

(a) Each advisory committee shall terminate not later than the expiration of the 2 year period beginning on the date of its establishment, unless:

(1) In the case of an advisory committee established by the President or an officer of the Federal Government, such advisory committee is renewed by the President or such officer by appropriate action prior to the end of such period; or

(2) In the case of an advisory committee established by an Act of Congress, its duration is otherwise provided by law.

(b) Any advisory committee which is renewed by the President or any officer of the Federal Government may be continued only for successive 2-year periods by appropriate action taken by the

President or such officer prior to the date on which the advisory committee would otherwise terminate.

(c) Before it renews a non-statutory advisory committee in accordance with paragraph (a) or (b) of this section, the Agency will inform the Secretariat by letter, not more than 60 days nor less than 30 days before the committee expires, of the following:

(1) Its determination that a renewal is necessary and is in the public interest;

(2) The reasons for its determination;

(3) The Agency's plan to attain balanced membership on the committee;

(4) An explanation of why the committee's functions cannot be performed by the Agency or by an existing advisory committee.

(d) After concurrence by the Secretariat, the Agency will certify in writing that the renewal of the advisory committee is in the public interest, and will publish a notice of the renewal in the FEDERAL REGISTER, and will file a new charter in accordance with §12.7 of this part.

(e) Any advisory committee established by an Act of Congress shall file a charter in accordance with §12.7 of this part upon the expiration of each successive 2-year period following the date of enactment of the Act establishing such advisory committee.

(f) No advisory committee required under this section to file a charter shall take any action, other than preparation and filing of such charter, between the date the new charter is required and the date on which such charter is actually filed.

§12.16 Reports about the advisory committees.

(a) The Agency will furnish a report of the activities of the FEMA advisory committees annually to the Administrator, General Services Administration, in accordance with the Federal Property Management Regulations.

(b) The Agency will furnish a report of the activities of FEMA advisory committees annually to the Secretariat.

(c) The Agency will inform the Secretariat, by letter, of the termination of, or other significant changes with respect to, its advisory committees no later than 10 working days following the end of the month in which the committee is changed. If no changes are made during any given month the report of the Secretariat is not required.

[45 FR 64180, Sept. 29, 1980, as amended at 48 FR 44543, Sept. 29, 1983]

§12.17 Availability of documents and information on advisory committees.

(a) Subject to the provisions of §§12.12 and 12.13 of this part, the records, reports, transcripts, minutes, appendices, working papers, drafts, studies, agenda, or other documents which were made available to or prepared for by each advisory committee shall be available for public inspection and copying at a single location in the FEMA Headquarters, Washington, DC, in accordance with the regulations in part 5 of this chapter.

(b) The Agency will maintain systematic information on the nature, functions, and operations of each of its advisory committees. A complete set of the charters of the Agency's advisory committees and copies of the annual reports required by §12.16 will be maintained for public inspection in the FEMA Headquarters.

[45 FR 64180, Sept. 29, 1980, as amended at 47 FR 13150, Mar. 29, 1982]

§12.18 Uniform pay guidelines.

(a) *Members.* Subject to the provisions of this section, the pay of any member of an advisory committee shall be fixed at the daily equivalent rate of the FEMA general salary schedule unless the member is appointed as a consultant, to be compensated as provided in paragraph (c) of this section. In determining an appropriate rate of pay for the members of an advisory committee, consideration shall be given to the significance, scope and technical complexity of the matters with which the advisory committee is concerned, and the qualifications required of the members of the advisory committee. The pay of the members of an advisory committee shall not be fixed at a rate higher than the daily equivalent of the maximum rate for GS–15 unless the Director has determined that, under the factors set forth in this paragraph, a higher rate of pay is justified and necessary. Such a determination will be reviewed annually by the Administrator.

(b) *Advisory committee staff.* The pay of each member of the staff of an advisory committee shall be fixed at a rate of the general salary schedule in which the staff member's position would be appropriately compensated for in the FEMA evaluation system applicable to the position. Pay of the member of the staff of an advisory committee shall not be fixed at a rate higher than the daily equivalent of the maximum rate for a GS–15 unless the Director or his designee has determined that, under its evaluation system, the staff member's position would appropriately be placed in the General Salary Schedule at a grade higher than GS–15. Such a determination will be reviewed by the Administrator annually.

(c) *Consultants.* The rate of pay of a consultant to an advisory committee shall not exceed the maximum rate of pay which FEMA may pay experts and consultants under 5 U.S.C. 3109. Consideration shall be given to the qualifications required of the consultant and the significance, scope, and technical complexity of the work in fixing the rate of pay for the consultants.

(d) *Voluntary services.* The provisions of this section shall not prevent FEMA from accepting the voluntary services of a member of an advisory committee, or a member of the staff of an advisory committee, provided that FEMA has the authority to accept such services without compensation.

(e) *Reimbursable travel expenses.* The members of an advisory committee and the staff thereof, while engaged in the performance of their duties away from their home or regular places of business, may be allowed travel expenses, including per diem and in lieu of subsistences, as authorized by 5 U.S.C. 5703 for persons employed intermittently in the government service.

§ 12.19 **Fiscal and administrative responsibilities.**

(a) The Chief Financial Officer, shall keep such records as will fully disclose the disposition of any funds which may be at the disposal of any FEMA advisory committee.

(b) The FEMA Advisory Committee management officer or designee shall keep such records as are necessary to fully disclose the nature and extent of the activities of the FEMA advisory committees.

(c) Support services shall be provided by FEMA for each advisory committee established by or reporting to it, unless the establishing authority provides otherwise. Where such advisory committee reports to more than one agency, only one agency or component thereof shall be responsible for support services at any one time, and the establishing authority shall designate the agency responsible for providing such services.

[45 FR 64180, Sept. 29, 1980, as amended at 48 FR 44543, Sept. 29, 1983]

PART 13—UNIFORM ADMINISTRATIVE REQUIREMENTS FOR GRANTS AND COOPERATIVE AGREEMENTS TO STATE AND LOCAL GOVERNMENTS

Subpart A—General

13.35 Subawards to debarred and suspended parties.
13.36 Procurement.
13.37 Subgrants.

REPORTS, RECORDS RETENTION, AND ENFORCEMENT

13.40 Monitoring and reporting program performance.
13.41 Financial reporting.
13.42 Retention and access requirements for records.
13.43 Enforcement.
13.44 Termination for convenience.

Subpart D—After-the-Grant Requirements

13.50 Closeout.
13.51 Later disallowances and adjustments.
13.52 Collection of amounts due.

Subpart E—Entitlement [Reserved]

AUTHORITY: Reorganization Plan No. 3 of 1978; 43 FR 41943, 3 CFR, 1978 Comp., p. 329; E.O. 12148, 44 FR 43239, 3 CFR, 1979 Comp., p. 412.

SOURCE: 53 FR 8078, 8087, Mar. 11, 1988, unless otherwise noted.

EDITORIAL NOTE: For additional information, see related documents published at 49 FR 24958, June 18, 1984; 52 FR 20178, May 29, 1987; and 53 FR 8028, Mar. 11, 1988.

Subpart A—General

§13.1 Purpose and scope of this part.

This part establishes uniform administrative rules for Federal grants and cooperative agreements and subawards to State, local and Indian tribal governments.

§13.2 Scope of subpart.

This subpart contains general rules pertaining to this part and procedures for control of exceptions from this part.

§13.3 Definitions.

As used in this part:

Accrued expenditures mean the charges incurred by the grantee during a given period requiring the provision of funds for:

(1) Goods and other tangible property received;

(2) Services performed by employees, contractors, subgrantees, subcontractors, and other payees; and

(3) Other amounts becoming owed under programs for which no current services or performance is required, such as annuities, insurance claims, and other benefit payments.

Accrued income means the sum of: (1) Earnings during a given period from services performed by the grantee and goods and other tangible property delivered to purchasers, and (2) amounts becoming owed to the grantee for which no current services or performance is required by the grantee.

Acquisition cost of an item of purchased equipment means the net invoice unit price of the property including the cost of modifications, attachments, accessories, or auxiliary apparatus necessary to make the property usable for the purpose for which it was acquired. Other charges such as the cost of installation, transportation, taxes, duty or protective in-transit insurance, shall be included or excluded from the unit acquisition cost in accordance with the grantee's regular accounting practices.

Administrative requirements mean those matters common to grants in general, such as financial management, kinds and frequency of reports, and retention of records. These are distinguished from "programmatic" requirements, which concern matters that can be treated only on a program-by-program or grant-by-grant basis, such as kinds of activities that can be supported by grants under a particular program.

Awarding agency means (1) with respect to a grant, the Federal agency, and (2) with respect to a subgrant, the party that awarded the subgrant.

Cash contributions means the grantee's cash outlay, including the outlay of money contributed to the grantee or subgrantee by other public agencies and institutions, and private organizations and individuals. When authorized by Federal legislation, Federal funds received from other assistance agreements may be considered as grantee or subgrantee cash contributions.

Contract means (except as used in the definitions for *grant* and *subgrant* in this section and except where qualified by *Federal*) a procurement contract under a grant or subgrant, and means a procurement subcontract under a contract.

Cost sharing or matching means the value of the third party in-kind contributions and the portion of the costs of a federally assisted project or program not borne by the Federal Government.

Cost-type contract means a contract or subcontract under a grant in which the contractor or subcontractor is paid on the basis of the costs it incurs, with or without a fee.

Equipment means tangible, non-expendable, personal property having a useful life of more than one year and an acquisition cost of $5,000 or more per unit. A grantee may use its own definition of equipment provided that such definition would at least include all equipment defined above.

Expenditure report means: (1) For non-construction grants, the SF–269 "Financial Status Report" (or other equivalent report); (2) for construction grants, the SF–271 "Outlay Report and Request for Reimbursement" (or other equivalent report).

Federally recognized Indian tribal government means the governing body or a governmental agency of any Indian tribe, band, nation, or other organized group or community (including any Native village as defined in section 3 of the Alaska Native Claims Settlement Act, 85 Stat 688) certified by the Secretary of the Interior as eligible for the special programs and services provided by him through the Bureau of Indian Affairs.

Government means a State or local government or a federally recognized Indian tribal government.

Grant means an award of financial assistance, including cooperative agreements, in the form of money, or property in lieu of money, by the Federal Government to an eligible grantee. The term does not include technical assistance which provides services instead of money, or other assistance in the form of revenue sharing, loans, loan guarantees, interest subsidies, insurance, or direct appropriations. Also, the term does not include assistance, such as a fellowship or other lump sum award, which the grantee is not required to account for.

Grantee means the government to which a grant is awarded and which is accountable for the use of the funds provided. The grantee is the entire legal entity even if only a particular component of the entity is designated in the grant award document.

Local government means a county, municipality, city, town, township, local public authority (including any public and Indian housing agency under the United States Housing Act of 1937) school district, special district, intrastate district, council of governments (whether or not incorporated as a nonprofit corporation under state law), any other regional or interstate government entity, or any agency or instrumentality of a local government.

Obligations means the amounts of orders placed, contracts and subgrants awarded, goods and services received, and similar transactions during a given period that will require payment by the grantee during the same or a future period.

OMB means the United States Office of Management and Budget.

Outlays (expenditures) mean charges made to the project or program. They may be reported on a cash or accrual basis. For reports prepared on a cash basis, outlays are the sum of actual cash disbursement for direct charges for goods and services, the amount of indirect expense incurred, the value of in-kind contributions applied, and the amount of cash advances and payments made to contractors and subgrantees. For reports prepared on an accrued expenditure basis, outlays are the sum of actual cash disbursements, the amount of indirect expense incurred, the value of inkind contributions applied, and the new increase (or decrease) in the amounts owed by the grantee for goods and other property received, for services performed by employees, contractors, subgrantees, subcontractors, and other payees, and other amounts becoming owed under programs for which no current services or performance are required, such as annuities, insurance claims, and other benefit payments.

Percentage of completion method refers to a system under which payments are made for construction work according to the percentage of completion of the work, rather than to the grantee's cost incurred.

Prior approval means documentation evidencing consent prior to incurring specific cost.

Real property means land, including land improvements, structures and appurtenances thereto, excluding movable machinery and equipment.

Share, when referring to the awarding agency's portion of real property, equipment or supplies, means the same percentage as the awarding agency's portion of the acquiring party's total costs under the grant to which the acquisition costs under the grant to which the acquisition cost of the property was charged. Only costs are to be counted—not the value of third-party in-kind contributions.

State means any of the several States of the United States, the District of Columbia, the Commonwealth of Puerto Rico, any territory or possession of the United States, or any agency or instrumentality of a State exclusive of local governments. The term does not include any public and Indian housing agency under United States Housing Act of 1937.

Subgrant means an award of financial assistance in the form of money, or property in lieu of money, made under a grant by a grantee to an eligible subgrantee. The term includes financial assistance when provided by contractual legal agreement, but does not include procurement purchases, nor does it include any form of assistance which is excluded from the definition of *grant* in this part.

Subgrantee means the government or other legal entity to which a subgrant is awarded and which is accountable to the grantee for the use of the funds provided.

Supplies means all tangible personal property other than *equipment* as defined in this part.

Suspension means depending on the context, either (1) temporary withdrawal of the authority to obligate grant funds pending corrective action by the grantee or subgrantee or a decision to terminate the grant, or (2) an action taken by a suspending official in accordance with agency regulations implementing E.O. 12549 to immediately exclude a person from participating in grant transactions for a period, pending completion of an investigation and such legal or debarment proceedings as may ensue.

Termination means permanent withdrawal of the authority to obligate previously-awarded grant funds before that authority would otherwise expire. It also means the voluntary relinquishment of that authority by the grantee or subgrantee. "Termination" does not include: (1) Withdrawal of funds awarded on the basis of the grantee's underestimate of the unobligated balance in a prior period; (2) Withdrawal of the unobligated balance as of the expiration of a grant; (3) Refusal to extend a grant or award additional funds, to make a competing or noncompeting continuation, renewal, extension, or supplemental award; or (4) voiding of a grant upon determination that the award was obtained fraudulently, or was otherwise illegal or invalid from inception.

Terms of a grant or subgrant mean all requirements of the grant or subgrant, whether in statute, regulations, or the award document.

Third party in-kind contributions mean property or services which benefit a federally assisted project or program and which are contributed by non-Federal third parties without charge to the grantee, or a cost-type contractor under the grant agreement.

Unliquidated obligations for reports prepared on a cash basis mean the amount of obligations incurred by the grantee that has not been paid. For reports prepared on an accrued expenditure basis, they represent the amount of obligations incurred by the grantee for which an outlay has not been recorded.

Unobligated balance means the portion of the funds authorized by the Federal agency that has not been obligated by the grantee and is determined by deducting the cumulative obligations from the cumulative funds authorized.

§ 13.4 Applicability.

(a) *General.* Subparts A through D of this part apply to all grants and subgrants to governments, except where inconsistent with Federal statutes or with regulations authorized in accordance with the exception provision of section 13.6, or:

(1) Grants and subgrants to State and local institutions of higher education or State and local hospitals.

(2) The block grants authorized by the Omnibus Budget Reconciliation Act of 1981 (Community Services; Preventive Health and Health Services; Alcohol, Drug Abuse, and Mental Health Services; Maternal and Child Health Services; Social Services; Low-Income Home Energy Assistance; States' Program of Community Development Block Grants for Small Cities; and Elementary and Secondary Education other than programs administered by the Secretary of Education under title V, subtitle D, Chapter 2, Section 583—the Secretary's discretionary grant program) and titles I–III of the Job Training Partnership Act of 1982 and under the Public Health Services Act (section 1921), Alcohol and Drug Abuse Treatment and Rehabilitation Block Grant and Part C of title V, Mental Health Service for the Homeless Block Grant).

(3) Entitlement grants to carry out the following programs of the Social Security Act:

(i) Aid to Needy Families with Dependent Children (Title IV-A of the Act, not including the Work Incentive Program (WIN) authorized by section 402(a)19(G); HHS grants for WIN are subject to this part);

(ii) Child Support Enforcement and Establishment of Paternity (Title IV-D of the Act);

(iii) Foster Care and Adoption Assistance (Title IV-E of the Act);

(iv) Aid to the Aged, Blind, and Disabled (Titles I, X, XIV, and XVI-AABD of the Act); and

(v) Medical Assistance (Medicaid) (Title XIX of the Act) not including the State Medicaid Fraud Control program authorized by section 1903(a)(6)(B).

(4) Entitlement grants under the following programs of The National School Lunch Act:

(i) School Lunch (section 4 of the Act),

(ii) Commodity Assistance (section 6 of the Act),

(iii) Special Meal Assistance (section 11 of the Act),

(iv) Summer Food Service for Children (section 13 of the Act), and

(v) Child Care Food Program (section 17 of the Act).

(5) Entitlement grants under the following programs of The Child Nutrition Act of 1966:

(i) Special Milk (section 3 of the Act), and

(ii) School Breakfast (section 4 of the Act).

(6) Entitlement grants for State Administrative expenses under The Food Stamp Act of 1977 (section 16 of the Act).

(7) A grant for an experimental, pilot, or demonstration project that is also supported by a grant listed in paragraph (a)(3) of this section;

(8) Grant funds awarded under subsection 412(e) of the Immigration and Nationality Act (8 U.S.C. 1522(e)) and subsection 501(a) of the Refugee Education Assistance Act of 1980 (Pub. L. 96–422, 94 Stat. 1809), for cash assistance, medical assistance, and supplemental security income benefits to refugees and entrants and the administrative costs of providing the assistance and benefits;

(9) Grants to local education agencies under 20 U.S.C. 236 through 241–1(a), and 242 through 244 (portions of the Impact Aid program), except for 20 U.S.C. 238(d)(2)(c) and 240(f) (Entitlement Increase for Handicapped Children); and

(10) Payments under the Veterans Administration's State Home Per Diem Program (38 U.S.C. 641(a)).

(b) *Entitlement programs.* Entitlement programs enumerated above in § 13.4(a) (3) through (8) are subject to subpart E.

§ 13.5 Effect on other issuances.

All other grants administration provisions of codified program regulations, program manuals, handbooks and other nonregulatory materials which are inconsistent with this part are superseded, except to the extent they are required by statute, or authorized in accordance with the exception provision in § 13.6.

§ 13.6 Additions and exceptions.

(a) For classes of grants and grantees subject to this part, Federal agencies may not impose additional administrative requirements except in codified regulations published in the FEDERAL REGISTER.

(b) Exceptions for classes of grants or grantees may be authorized only by OMB.

(c) Exceptions on a case-by-case basis and for subgrantees may be authorized by the affected Federal agencies.

Subpart B—Pre-Award Requirements

§13.10 Forms for applying for grants.

(a) *Scope.* (1) This section prescribes forms and instructions to be used by governmental organizations (except hospitals and institutions of higher education operated by a government) in applying for grants. This section is not applicable, however, to formula grant programs which do not require applicants to apply for funds on a project basis.

(2) This section applies only to applications to Federal agencies for grants, and is not required to be applied by grantees in dealing with applicants for subgrants. However, grantees are encouraged to avoid more detailed or burdensome application requirements for subgrants.

(b) *Authorized forms and instructions for governmental organizations.* (1) In applying for grants, applicants shall only use standard application forms or those prescribed by the granting agency with the approval of OMB under the Paperwork Reduction Act of 1980.

(2) Applicants are not required to submit more than the original and two copies of preapplications or applications.

(3) Applicants must follow all applicable instructions that bear OMB clearance numbers. Federal agencies may specify and describe the programs, functions, or activities that will be used to plan, budget, and evaluate the work under a grant. Other supplementary instructions may be issued only with the approval of OMB to the extent required under the Paperwork Reduction Act of 1980. For any standard form, except the SF–424 facesheet, Federal agencies may shade out or instruct the applicant to disregard any line item that is not needed.

(4) When a grantee applies for additional funding (such as a continuation or supplemental award) or amends a previously submitted application, only the affected pages need be submitted. Previously submitted pages with information that is still current need not be resubmitted.

§13.11 State plans.

(a) *Scope.* The statutes for some programs require States to submit plans before receiving grants. Under regulations implementing Executive Order 12372, "Intergovernmental Review of Federal Programs," States are allowed to simplify, consolidate and substitute plans. This section contains additional provisions for plans that are subject to regulations implementing the Executive Order.

(b) *Requirements.* A State need meet only Federal administrative or programmatic requirements for a plan that are in statutes or codified regulations.

(c) *Assurances:* In each plan the State will include an assurance that the State shall comply with all applicable Federal statutes and regulations in effect with respect to the periods for which it receives grant funding. For this assurance and other assurances required in the plan, the State may:

(1) Cite by number the statutory or regulatory provisions requiring the assurances and affirm that it gives the assurances required by those provisions,

(2) Repeat the assurance language in the statutes or regulations, or

(3) Develop its own language to the extent permitted by law.

(d) *Amendments.* A State will amend a plan whenever necessary to reflect: (1) New or revised Federal statutes or regulations or (2) a material change in any State law, organization, policy, or State agency operation. The State will obtain approval for the amendment and its effective date but need submit for approval only the amended portions of the plan.

§13.12 Special grant or subgrant conditions for "high-risk" grantees.

(a) A grantee or subgrantee may be considered "high risk" if an awarding agency determines that a grantee or subgrantee:

(1) Has a history of unsatisfactory performance, or

(2) Is not financially stable, or

(3) Has a management system which does not meet the management standards set forth in this part, or

(4) Has not conformed to terms and conditions of previous awards, or

(5) Is otherwise not responsible; and if the awarding agency determines that an award will be made, special conditions and/or restrictions shall correspond to the high risk condition and shall be included in the award.

(b) Special conditions or restrictions may include:

(1) Payment on a reimbursement basis;

(2) Withholding authority to proceed to the next phase until receipt of evidence of acceptable performance within a given funding period;

(3) Requiring additional, more detailed financial reports;

(4) Additional project monitoring;

(5) Requiring the grante or subgrantee to obtain technical or management assistance; or

(6) Establishing additional prior approvals.

(c) If an awarding agency decides to impose such conditions, the awarding official will notify the grantee or subgrantee as early as possible, in writing, of:

(1) The nature of the special conditions/restrictions;

(2) The reason(s) for imposing them;

(3) The corrective actions which must be taken before they will be removed and the time allowed for completing the corrective actions and

(4) The method of requesting reconsideration of the conditions/restrictions imposed.

Subpart C—Post-Award Requirements

FINANCIAL ADMINISTRATION

§ 13.20 Standards for financial management systems.

(a) A State must expand and account for grant funds in accordance with State laws and procedures for expending and accounting for its own funds. Fiscal control and accounting procedures of the State, as well as its sub-

grantees and cost-type contractors, must be sufficient to—

(1) Permit preparation of reports required by this part and the statutes authorizing the grant, and

(2) Permit the tracing of funds to a level of expenditures adequate to establish that such funds have not been used in violation of the restrictions and prohibitions of applicable statutes.

(b) The financial management systems of other grantees and subgrantees must meet the following standards:

(1) *Financial reporting.* Accurate, current, and complete disclosure of the financial results of financially assisted activities must be made in accordance with the financial reporting requirements of the grant or subgrant.

(2) *Accounting records.* Grantees and subgrantees must maintain records which adequately identify the source and application of funds provided for financially-assisted activities. These records must contain information pertaining to grant or subgrant awards and authorizations, obligations, unobligated balances, assets, liabilities, outlays or expenditures, and income.

(3) *Internal control.* Effective control and accountability must be maintained for all grant and subgrant cash, real and personal property, and other assets. Grantees and subgrantees must adequately safeguard all such property and must assure that it is used solely for authorized purposes.

(4) *Budget control.* Actual expenditures or outlays must be compared with budgeted amounts for each grant or subgrant. Financial information must be related to performance or productivity data, including the development of unit cost information whenever appropriate or specifically required in the grant or subgrant agreement. If unit cost data are required, estimates based on available documentation will be accepted whenever possible.

(5) *Allowable cost.* Applicable OMB cost principles, agency program regulations, and the terms of grant and subgrant agreements will be followed in determining the reasonableness, allowability, and allocability of costs.

(6) *Source documentation.* Accounting records must be supported by such source documentation as cancelled

checks, paid bills, payrolls, time and attendance records, contract and subgrant award documents, etc.

(7) *Cash management.* Procedures for minimizing the time elapsing between the transfer of funds from the U.S. Treasury and disbursement by grantees and subgrantees must be followed whenever advance payment procedures are used. Grantees must establish reasonable procedures to ensure the receipt of reports on subgrantees' cash balances and cash disbursements in sufficient time to enable them to prepare complete and accurate cash transactions reports to the awarding agency. When advances are made by letter-of-credit or electronic transfer of funds methods, the grantee must make drawdowns as close as possible to the time of making disbursements. Grantees must monitor cash drawdowns by their subgrantees to assure that they conform substantially to the same standards of timing and amount as apply to advances to the grantees.

(c) An awarding agency may review the adequacy of the financial management system of any applicant for financial assistance as part of a preaward review or at any time subsequent to award.

§ 13.21 **Payment.**

(a) *Scope.* This section prescribes the basic standard and the methods under which a Federal agency will make payments to grantees, and grantees will make payments to subgrantees and contractors.

(b) *Basic standard.* Methods and procedures for payment shall minimize the time elapsing between the transfer of funds and disbursement by the grantee or subgrantee, in accordance with Treasury regulations at 31 CFR part 205.

(c) *Advances.* Grantees and subgrantees shall be paid in advance, provided they maintain or demonstrate the willingness and ability to maintain procedures to minimize the time elapsing between the transfer of the funds and their disbursement by the grantee or subgrantee.

(d) *Reimbursement.* Reimbursement shall be the preferred method when the requirements in paragraph (c) of this section are not met. Grantees and sub-

grantees may also be paid by reimbursement for any construction grant. Except as otherwise specified in regulation, Federal agencies shall not use the percentage of completion method to pay construction grants. The grantee or subgrantee may use that method to pay its construction contractor, and if it does, the awarding agency's payments to the grantee or subgrantee will be based on the grantee's or subgrantee's actual rate of disbursement.

(e) *Working capital advances.* If a grantee cannot meet the criteria for advance payments described in paragraph (c) of this section, and the Federal agency has determined that reimbursement is not feasible because the grantee lacks sufficient working capital, the awarding agency may provide cash or a working capital advance basis. Under this procedure the awarding agency shall advance cash to the grantee to cover its estimated disbursement needs for an initial period generally geared to the grantee's disbursing cycle. Thereafter, the awarding agency shall reimburse the grantee for its actual cash disbursements. The working capital advance method of payment shall not be used by grantees or subgrantees if the reason for using such method is the unwillingness or inability of the grantee to provide timely advances to the subgrantee to meet the subgrantee's actual cash disbursements.

(f) *Effect of program income, refunds, and audit recoveries on payment.* (1) Grantees and subgrantees shall disburse repayments to and interest earned on a revolving fund before requesting additional cash payments for the same activity.

(2) Except as provided in paragraph (f)(1) of this section, grantees and subgrantees shall disburse program income, rebates, refunds, contract settlements, audit recoveries and interest earned on such funds before requesting additional cash payments.

(g) *Withholding payments.* (1) Unless otherwise required by Federal statute, awarding agencies shall not withhold payments for proper charges incurred by grantees or subgrantees unless—

(i) The grantee or subgrantee has failed to comply with grant award conditions or

123

(ii) The grantee or subgrantee is indebted to the United States.

(2) Cash withheld for failure to comply with grant award condition, but without suspension of the grant, shall be released to the grantee upon subsequent compliance. When a grant is suspended, payment adjustments will be made in accordance with § 13.43(c).

(3) A Federal agency shall not make payment to grantees for amounts that are withheld by grantees or subgrantees from payment to contractors to assure satisfactory completion of work. Payments shall be made by the Federal agency when the grantees or subgrantees actually disburse the withheld funds to the contractors or to escrow accounts established to assure satisfactory completion of work.

(h) *Cash depositories.* (1) Consistent with the national goal of expanding the opportunities for minority business enterprises, grantees and subgrantees are encouraged to use minority banks (a bank which is owned at least 50 percent by minority group members). A list of minority owned banks can be obtained from the Minority Business Development Agency, Department of Commerce, Washington, DC 20230.

(2) A grantee or subgrantee shall maintain a separate bank account only when required by Federal-State agreement.

(i) *Interest earned on advances.* Except for interest earned on advances of funds exempt under the Intergovernmental Cooperation Act (31 U.S.C. 6501 *et seq.)* and the Indian Self-Determination Act (23 U.S.C. 450), grantees and subgrantees shall promptly, but at least quarterly, remit interest earned on advances to the Federal agency. The grantee or subgrantee may keep interest amounts up to $100 per year for administrative expenses.

§ 13.22 Allowable costs.

(a) *Limitation on use of funds.* Grant funds may be used only for:

(1) The allowable costs of the grantees, subgrantees and cost-type contractors, including allowable costs in the form of payments to fixed-price contractors; and

(2) Reasonable fees or profit to cost-type contractors but not any fee or profit (or other increment above allowable costs) to the grantee or subgrantee.

(b) *Applicable cost principles.* For each kind of organization, there is a set of Federal principles for determining allowable costs. Allowable costs will be determined in accordance with the cost principles applicable to the organization incurring the costs. The following chart lists the kinds of organizations and the applicable cost principles.

For the costs of a—	Use the principles in—
State, local or Indian tribal government.	OMB Circular A–87.
Private nonprofit organization other than an (1) institution of higher education, (2) hospital, or (3) organization named in OMB Circular A–122 as not subject to that circular.	OBM Circular A–122.
Educational institutions.	OMB Circular A–21.
For-profit organization other than a hospital and an organization named in OBM Circular A–122 as not subject to that circular.	48 CFR part 31. Contract Cost Principles and Procedures, or uniform cost accounting standards that comply with cost principles acceptable to the Federal agency.

§ 13.23 Period of availability of funds.

(a) *General.* Where a funding period is specified, a grantee may charge to the award only costs resulting from obligations of the funding period unless carryover of unobligated balances is permitted, in which case the carryover balances may be charged for costs resulting from obligations of the subsequent funding period.

(b) *Liquidation of obligations.* A grantee must liquidate all obligations incurred under the award not later than 90 days after the end of the funding period (or as specified in a program regulation) to coincide with the submission of the annual Financial Status Report (SF–269). The Federal agency may extend this deadline at the request of the grantee.

§ 13.24 Matching or cost sharing.

(a) *Basic rule: Costs and contributions acceptable.* With the qualifications and exceptions listed in paragraph (b) of this section, a matching or cost sharing requirement may be satisfied by either or both of the following:

(1) Allowable costs incurred by the grantee, subgrantee or a cost-type contractor under the assistance agreement. This includes allowable costs borne by non-Federal grants or by others cash donations from non-Federal third parties.

(2) The value of third party in-kind contributions applicable to the period to which the cost sharing or matching requirements applies.

(b) *Qualifications and exceptions*—(1) *Costs borne by other Federal grant agreements.* Except as provided by Federal statute, a cost sharing or matching requirement may not be met by costs borne by another Federal grant. This prohibition does not apply to income earned by a grantee or subgrantee from a contract awarded under another Federal grant.

(2) *General revenue sharing.* For the purpose of this section, general revenue sharing funds distributed under 31 U.S.C. 6702 are not considered Federal grant funds.

(3) *Cost or contributions counted towards other Federal costs-sharing requirements.* Neither costs nor the values of third party in-kind contributions may count towards satisfying a cost sharing or matching requirement of a grant agreement if they have been or will be counted towards satisfying a cost sharing or matching requirement of another Federal grant agreement, a Federal procurement contract, or any other award of Federal funds.

(4) *Costs financed by program income.* Costs financed by program income, as defined in §13.25, shall not count towards satisfying a cost sharing or matching requirement unless they are expressly permitted in the terms of the assistance agreement. (This use of general program income is described in §13.25(g).)

(5) *Services or property financed by income earned by contractors.* Contractors under a grant may earn income from the activities carried out under the contract in addition to the amounts earned from the party awarding the contract. No costs of services or property supported by this income may count toward satisfying a cost sharing or matching requirement unless other provisions of the grant agreement expressly permit this kind of income to be used to meet the requirement.

(6) *Records.* Costs and third party in-kind contributions counting towards satisfying a cost sharing or matching requirement must be verifiable from the records of grantees and subgrantee or cost-type contractors. These records must show how the value placed on third party in-kind contributions was derived. To the extent feasible, volunteer services will be supported by the same methods that the organization uses to support the allocability of regular personnel costs.

(7) *Special standards for third party in-kind contributions.* (i) Third party in-kind contributions count towards satisfying a cost sharing or matching requirement only where, if the party receiving the contributions were to pay for them, the payments would be allowable costs.

(ii) Some third party in-kind contributions are goods and services that, if the grantee, subgrantee, or contractor receiving the contribution had to pay for them, the payments would have been an indirect costs. Costs sharing or matching credit for such contributions shall be given only if the grantee, subgrantee, or contractor has established, along with its regular indirect cost rate, a special rate for allocating to individual projects or programs the value of the contributions.

(iii) A third party in-kind contribution to a fixed-price contract may count towards satisfying a cost sharing or matching requirement only if it results in:

(A) An increase in the services or property provided under the contract (without additional cost to the grantee or subgrantee) or

(B) A cost savings to the grantee or subgrantee.

(iv) The values placed on third party in-kind contributions for cost sharing or matching purposes will conform to the rules in the succeeding sections of this part. If a third party in-kind contribution is a type not treated in those sections, the value placed upon it shall be fair and reasonable.

(c) *Valuation of donated services*—(1) *Volunteer services.* Unpaid services provided to a grantee or subgrantee by individuals will be valued at rates consistent with those ordinarily paid for similar work in the grantee's or subgrantee's organization. If the grantee or subgrantee does not have employees performing similar work, the rates will be consistent with those ordinarily paid by other employers for similar work in the same labor market. In either case, a reasonable amount for fringe benefits may be included in the valuation.

(2) *Employees of other organizations.* When an employer other than a grantee, subgrantee, or cost-type contractor furnishes free of charge the services of an employee in the employee's normal line of work, the services will be valued at the employee's regular rate of pay exclusive of the employee's fringe benefits and overhead costs. If the services are in a different line of work, paragraph (c)(1) of this section applies.

(d) *Valuation of third party donated supplies and loaned equipment or space.* (1) If a third party donates supplies, the contribution will be valued at the market value of the supplies at the time of donation.

(2) If a third party donates the use of equipment or space in a building but retains title, the contribution will be valued at the fair rental rate of the equipment or space.

(e) *Valuation of third party donated equipment, buildings, and land.* If a third party donates equipment, buildings, or land, and title passes to a grantee or subgrantee, the treatment of the donated property will depend upon the purpose of the grant or subgrant, as follows:

(1) *Awards for capital expenditures.* If the purpose of the grant or subgrant is to assist the grantee or subgrantee in the acquisition of property, the market value of that property at the time of donation may be counted as cost sharing or matching,

(2) *Other awards.* If assisting in the acquisition of property is not the purpose of the grant or subgrant, paragraphs (e)(2) (i) and (ii) of this section apply:

(i) If approval is obtained from the awarding agency, the market value at the time of donation of the donated equipment or buildings and the fair rental rate of the donated land may be counted as cost sharing or matching. In the case of a subgrant, the terms of the grant agreement may require that the approval be obtained from the Federal agency as well as the grantee. In all cases, the approval may be given only if a purchase of the equipment or rental of the land would be approved as an allowable direct cost. If any part of the donated property was acquired with Federal funds, only the non-Federal share of the property may be counted as cost-sharing or matching.

(ii) If approval is not obtained under paragraph (e)(2)(i) of this section, no amount may be counted for donated land, and only depreciation or use allowances may be counted for donated equipment and buildings. The depreciation or use allowances for this property are not treated as third party in-kind contributions. Instead, they are treated as costs incurred by the grantee or subgrantee. They are computed and allocated (usually as indirect costs) in accordance with the cost principles specified in § 13.22, in the same way as depreciation or use allowances for purchased equipment and buildings. The amount of depreciation or use allowances for donated equipment and buildings is based on the property's market value at the time it was donated.

(f) *Valuation of grantee or subgrantee donated real property for construction/acquisition.* If a grantee or subgrantee donates real property for a construction or facilities acquisition project, the current market value of that property may be counted as cost sharing or matching. If any part of the donated property was acquired with Federal funds, only the non-Federal share of the property may be counted as cost sharing or matching.

(g) *Appraisal of real property.* In some cases under paragraphs (d), (e) and (f) of this section, it will be necessary to establish the market value of land or a building or the fair rental rate of land or of space in a building. In these cases, the Federal agency may require the market value or fair rental value be set by an independent appraiser, and that the value or rate be certified by the

126

grantee. This requirement will also be imposed by the grantee on subgrantees.

§13.25 Program income.

(a) *General.* Grantees are encouraged to earn income to defray program costs. Program income includes income from fees for services performed, from the use or rental of real or personal property acquired with grant funds, from the sale of commodities or items fabricated under a grant agreement, and from payments of principal and interest on loans made with grant funds. Except as otherwise provided in regulations of the Federal agency, program income does not include interest on grant funds, rebates, credits, discounts, refunds, etc. and interest earned on any of them.

(b) *Definition of program income.* Program income means gross income received by the grantee or subgrantee directly generated by a grant supported activity, or earned only as a result of the grant agreement during the grant period. *During the grant period* is the time between the effective date of the award and the ending date of the award reflected in the final financial report.

(c) *Cost of generating program income.* If authorized by Federal regulations or the grant agreement, costs incident to the generation of program income may be deducted from gross income to determine program income.

(d) *Governmental revenues.* Taxes, special assessments, levies, fines, and other such revenues raised by a grantee or subgrantee are not program income unless the revenues are specifically identified in the grant agreement or Federal agency regulations as program income.

(e) *Royalties.* Income from royalties and license fees for copyrighted material, patents, and inventions developed by a grantee or subgrantee is program income only if the revenues are specifically identified in the grant agreement or Federal agency regulations as program income. (See §13.34.)

(f) *Property.* Proceeds from the sale of real property or equipment will be handled in accordance with the requirements of §§13.31 and 13.32.

(g) *Use of program income.* Program income shall be deducted from outlays which may be both Federal and non-Federal as described below, unless the Federal agency regulations or the grant agreement specify another alternative (or a combination of the alternatives). In specifying alternatives, the Federal agency may distinguish between income earned by the grantee and income earned by subgrantees and between the sources, kinds, or amounts of income. When Federal agencies authorize the alternatives in paragraphs (g) (2) and (3) of this section, program income in excess of any limits stipulated shall also be deducted from outlays.

(1) *Deduction.* Ordinarily program income shall be deducted from total allowable costs to determine the net allowable costs. Program income shall be used for current costs unless the Federal agency authorizes otherwise. Program income which the grantee did not anticipate at the time of the award shall be used to reduce the Federal agency and grantee contributions rather than to increase the funds committed to the project.

(2) *Addition.* When authorized, program income may be added to the funds committed to the grant agreement by the Federal agency and the grantee. The program income shall be used for the purposes and under the conditions of the grant agreement.

(3) *Cost sharing or matching.* When authorized, program income may be used to meet the cost sharing or matching requirement of the grant agreement. The amount of the Federal grant award remains the same.

(h) *Income after the award period.* There are no Federal requirements governing the disposition of program income earned after the end of the award period (i.e., until the ending date of the final financial report, see paragraph (a) of this section), unless the terms of the agreement or the Federal agency regulations provide otherwise.

§13.26 Non-Federal audit.

(a) *Basic rule.* Grantees and subgrantees are responsible for obtaining audits in accordance with the Single Audit Act Amendments of 1996 (31 U.S.C. 7501–7507); 31 U.S.C. 503, 1111; Executive Order 8248; Executive Order 11541; and revised OMB Circular A–133, "Audits of States, Local Governments, and Non-Profit Organizations." The audits shall be made by an independent auditor in accordance with generally accepted government auditing standards covering financial audits.

(b) *Subgrantees.* State or local governments, as those terms are defined for purposes of the Single Audit Act Amendments of 1996, that provide Federal awards to a subgrantee, which expends $500,000 or more (or other amount as specified by OMB) in Federal awards in a fiscal year, shall:

(1) Determine whether State or local subgrantees have met the audit requirements of the Act and whether subgrantees covered by OMB Circular A–110, "Uniform Administrative Requirements for Grants and Agreements with Institutions of Higher Education, Hospitals, and Other Non-Profit Organizations," have met the audit requirements of the Act. Commercial contractors (private for-profit and private and governmental organizations) providing goods and services to State and local governments are not required to have a single audit performed. State and local governments should use their own procedures to ensure that the contractor has complied with laws and regulations affecting the expenditure of Federal funds;

(2) Determine whether the subgrantee spent Federal assistance funds provided in accordance with applicable laws and regulations. This may be accomplished by reviewing an audit of the subgrantee made in accordance with the Act, Circular A–110, or through other means (e.g., program reviews) if the subgrantee has not had such an audit;

(3) Ensure that appropriate corrective action is taken within six months after receipt of the audit report in instance of noncompliance with Federal laws and regulations;

(4) Consider whether subgrantee audits necessitate adjustment of the grantee's own records; and

(5) Require each subgrantee to permit independent auditors to have access to the records and financial statements.

(c) *Auditor selection.* In arranging for audit services, § 13.36 shall be followed.

[53 FR 8079, 887, Mar. 11, 1988, as amended at 62 FR 45939, 45945, Aug. 29, 1997; 74 FR 15338, Apr. 3, 2009]

CHANGES, PROPERTY, AND SUBAWARDS

§ 13.30 Changes.

(a) *General.* Grantees and subgrantees are permitted to rebudget within the approved direct cost budget to meet unanticipated requirements and may make limited program changes to the approved project. However, unless waived by the awarding agency, certain types of post-award changes in budgets and projects shall require the prior written approval of the awarding agency.

(b) *Relation to cost principles.* The applicable cost principles (see § 13.22) contain requirements for prior approval of certain types of costs. Except where waived, those requirements apply to all grants and subgrants even if paragraphs (c) through (f) of this section do not.

(c) *Budget changes*—(1) *Nonconstruction projects.* Except as stated in other regulations or an award document, grantees or subgrantees shall obtain the prior approval of the awarding agency whenever any of the following changes is anticipated under a nonconstruction award:

(i) Any revision which would result in the need for additional funding.

(ii) Unless waived by the awarding agency, cumulative transfers among direct cost categories, or, if applicable, among separately budgeted programs, projects, functions, or activities which exceed or are expected to exceed ten percent of the current total approved budget, whenever the awarding agency's share exceeds $100,000.

(iii) Transfer of funds allotted for training allowances (i.e., from direct payments to trainees to other expense categories).

(2) *Construction projects.* Grantees and subgrantees shall obtain prior written approval for any budget revision which would result in the need for additional funds.

(3) *Combined construction and nonconstruction projects.* When a grant or subgrant provides funding for both construction and nonconstruction activities, the grantee or subgrantee must obtain prior written approval from the awarding agency before making any

fund or budget transfer from non-construction to construction or vice versa.

(d) *Programmatic changes.* Grantees or subgrantees must obtain the prior approval of the awarding agency whenever any of the following actions is anticipated:

(1) Any revision of the scope or objectives of the project (regardless of whether there is an associated budget revision requiring prior approval).

(2) Need to extend the period of availability of funds.

(3) Changes in key persons in cases where specified in an application or a grant award. In research projects, a change in the project director or principal investigator shall always require approval unless waived by the awarding agency.

(4) Under nonconstruction projects, contracting out, subgranting (if authorized by law) or otherwise obtaining the services of a third party to perform activities which are central to the purposes of the award. This approval requirement is in addition to the approval requirements of §13.36 but does not apply to the procurement of equipment, supplies, and general support services.

(e) *Additional prior approval requirements.* The awarding agency may not require prior approval for any budget revision which is not described in paragraph (c) of this section.

(f) *Requesting prior approval.* (1) A request for prior approval of any budget revision will be in the same budget formal the grantee used in its application and shall be accompanied by a narrative justification for the proposed revision.

(2) A request for a prior approval under the applicable Federal cost principles (see §13.22) may be made by letter.

(3) A request by a subgrantee for prior approval will be addressed in writing to the grantee. The grantee will promptly review such request and shall approve or disapprove the request in writing. A grantee will not approve any budget or project revision which is inconsistent with the purpose or terms and conditions of the Federal grant to the grantee. If the revision, requested by the subgrantee would result in a change to the grantee's approved project which requires Federal prior approval, the grantee will obtain the Federal agency's approval before approving the subgrantee's request.

§13.31 **Real property.**

(a) *Title.* Subject to the obligations and conditions set forth in this section, title to real property acquired under a grant or subgrant will vest upon acquisition in the grantee or subgrantee respectively.

(b) *Use.* Except as otherwise provided by Federal statutes, real property will be used for the originally authorized purposes as long as needed for that purposes, and the grantee or subgrantee shall not dispose of or encumber its title or other interests.

(c) *Disposition.* When real property is no longer needed for the originally authorized purpose, the grantee or subgrantee will request disposition instructions from the awarding agency. The instructions will provide for one of the following alternatives:

(1) *Retention of title.* Retain title after compensating the awarding agency. The amount paid to the awarding agency will be computed by applying the awarding agency's percentage of participation in the cost of the original purchase to the fair market value of the property. However, in those situations where a grantee or subgrantee is disposing of real property acquired with grant funds and acquiring replacement real property under the same program, the net proceeds from the disposition may be used as an offset to the cost of the replacement property.

(2) *Sale of property.* Sell the property and compensate the awarding agency. The amount due to the awarding agency will be calculated by applying the awarding agency's percentage of participation in the cost of the original purchase to the proceeds of the sale after deduction of any actual and reasonable selling and fixing-up expenses. If the grant is still active, the net proceeds from sale may be offset against the original cost of the property. When a grantee or subgrantee is directed to sell property, sales procedures shall be followed that provide for competition to the extent practicable and result in the highest possible return.

(3) *Transfer of title.* Transfer title to the awarding agency or to a third-party designated/approved by the awarding agency. The grantee or subgrantee shall be paid an amount calculated by applying the grantee or subgrantee's percentage of participation in the purchase of the real property to the current fair market value of the property.

§ 13.32 Equipment.

(a) *Title.* Subject to the obligations and conditions set forth in this section, title to equipment acquired under a grant or subgrant will vest upon acquisition in the grantee or subgrantee respectively.

(b) *States.* A State will use, manage, and dispose of equipment acquired under a grant by the State in accordance with State laws and procedures. Other grantees and subgrantees will follow paragraphs (c) through (e) of this section.

(c) *Use.* (1) Equipment shall be used by the grantee or subgrantee in the program or project for which it was acquired as long as needed, whether or not the project or program continues to be supported by Federal funds. When no longer needed for the original program or project, the equipment may be used in other activities currently or previously supported by a Federal agency.

(2) The grantee or subgrantee shall also make equipment available for use on other projects or programs currently or previously supported by the Federal Government, providing such use will not interfere with the work on the projects or program for which it was originally acquired. First preference for other use shall be given to other programs or projects supported by the awarding agency. User fees should be considered if appropriate.

(3) Notwithstanding the encouragement in § 13.25(a) to earn program income, the grantee or subgrantee must not use equipment acquired with grant funds to provide services for a fee to compete unfairly with private companies that provide equivalent services, unless specifically permitted or contemplated by Federal statute.

(4) When acquiring replacement equipment, the grantee or subgrantee may use the equipment to be replaced as a trade-in or sell the property and use the proceeds to offset the cost of the replacement property, subject to the approval of the awarding agency.

(d) *Management requirements.* Procedures for managing equipment (including replacement equipment), whether acquired in whole or in part with grant funds, until disposition takes place will, as a minimum, meet the following requirements:

(1) Property records must be maintained that include a description of the property, a serial number or other identification number, the source of property, who holds title, the acquisition date, and cost of the property, percentage of Federal participation in the cost of the property, the location, use and condition of the property, and any ultimate disposition data including the date of disposal and sale price of the property.

(2) A physical inventory of the property must be taken and the results reconciled with the property records at least once every two years.

(3) A control system must be developed to ensure adequate safeguards to prevent loss, damage, or theft of the property. Any loss, damage, or theft shall be investigated.

(4) Adequate maintenance procedures must be developed to keep the property in good condition.

(5) If the grantee or subgrantee is authorized or required to sell the property, proper sales procedures must be established to ensure the highest possible return.

(e) *Disposition.* When original or replacement equipment acquired under a grant or subgrant is no longer needed for the original project or program or for other activities currently or previously supported by a Federal agency, disposition of the equipment will be made as follows:

(1) Items of equipment with a current per-unit fair market value of less than $5,000 may be retained, sold or otherwise disposed of with no further obligation to the awarding agency.

(2) Items of equipment with a current per unit fair market value in excess of $5,000 may be retained or sold and the awarding agency shall have a right to an amount calculated by multiplying

the current market value or proceeds from sale by the awarding agency's share of the equipment.

(3) In cases where a grantee or subgrantee fails to take appropriate disposition actions, the awarding agency may direct the grantee or subgrantee to take excess and disposition actions.

(f) *Federal equipment.* In the event a grantee or subgrantee is provided federally-owned equipment:

(1) Title will remain vested in the Federal Government.

(2) Grantees or subgrantees will manage the equipment in accordance with Federal agency rules and procedures, and submit an annual inventory listing.

(3) When the equipment is no longer needed, the grantee or subgrantee will request disposition instructions from the Federal agency.

(g) *Right to transfer title.* The Federal awarding agency may reserve the right to transfer title to the Federal Government or a third part named by the awarding agency when such a third party is otherwise eligible under existing statutes. Such transfers shall be subject to the following standards:

(1) The property shall be identified in the grant or otherwise made known to the grantee in writing.

(2) The Federal awarding agency shall issue disposition instruction within 120 calendar days after the end of the Federal support of the project for which it was acquired. If the Federal awarding agency fails to issue disposition instructions within the 120 calendar-day period the grantee shall follow §13.32(e).

(3) When title to equipment is transferred, the grantee shall be paid an amount calculated by applying the percentage of participation in the purchase to the current fair market value of the property.

§13.33 **Supplies.**

(a) *Title.* Title to supplies acquired under a grant or subgrant will vest, upon acquisition, in the grantee or subgrantee respectively.

(b) *Disposition.* If there is a residual inventory of unused supplies exceeding $5,000 in total aggregate fair market value upon termination or completion of the award, and if the supplies are

not needed for any other federally sponsored programs or projects, the grantee or subgrantee shall compensate the awarding agency for its share.

§13.34 **Copyrights.**

The Federal awarding agency reserves a royalty-free, nonexclusive, and irrevocable license to reproduce, publish or otherwise use, and to authorize others to use, for Federal Government purposes:

(a) The copyright in any work developed under a grant, subgrant, or contract under a grant or subgrant; and

(b) Any rights of copyright to which a grantee, subgrantee or a contractor purchases ownership with grant support.

§13.35 **Subawards to debarred and suspended parties.**

Grantees and subgrantees must not make any award or permit any award (subgrant or contract) at any tier to any party which is debarred or suspended or is otherwise excluded from or ineligible for participation in Federal assistance programs under Executive Order 12549, "Debarment and Suspension."

§13.36 **Procurement.**

(a) *States.* When procuring property and services under a grant, a State will follow the same policies and procedures it uses for procurements from its non-Federal funds. The State will ensure that every purchase order or other contract includes any clauses required by Federal statutes and executive orders and their implementing regulations. Other grantees and subgrantees will follow paragraphs (b) through (i) in this section.

(b) *Procurement standards.* (1) Grantees and subgrantees will use their own procurement procedures which reflect applicable State and local laws and regulations, provided that the procurements conform to applicable Federal law and the standards identified in this section.

(2) Grantees and subgrantees will maintain a contract administration system which ensures that contractors perform in accordance with the terms,

131

conditions, and specifications of their contracts or purchase orders.

(3) Grantees and subgrantees will maintain a written code of standards of conduct governing the performance of their employees engaged in the award and administration of contracts. No employee, officer or agent of the grantee or subgrantee shall participate in selection, or in the award or administration of a contract supported by Federal funds if a conflict of interest, real or apparent, would be involved. Such a conflict would arise when:

(i) The employee, officer or agent,

(ii) Any member of his immediate family,

(iii) His or her partner, or

(iv) An organization which employs, or is about to employ, any of the above, has a financial or other interest in the firm selected for award. The grantee's or subgrantee's officers, employees or agents will neither solicit nor accept gratuities, favors or anything of monetary value from contractors, potential contractors, or parties to subagreements. Grantee and subgrantees may set minimum rules where the financial interest is not substantial or the gift is an unsolicited item of nominal intrinsic value. To the extent permitted by State or local law or regulations, such standards or conduct will provide for penalties, sanctions, or other disciplinary actions for violations of such standards by the grantee's and subgrantee's officers, employees, or agents, or by contractors or their agents. The awarding agency may in regulation provide additional prohibitions relative to real, apparent, or potential conflicts of interest.

(4) Grantee and subgrantee procedures will provide for a review of proposed procurements to avoid purchase of unnecessary or duplicative items. Consideration should be given to consolidating or breaking out procurements to obtain a more economical purchase. Where appropriate, an analysis will be made of lease versus purchase alternatives, and any other appropriate analysis to determine the most economical approach.

(5) To foster greater economy and efficiency, grantees and subgrantees are encouraged to enter into State and local intergovernmental agreements for procurement or use of common goods and services.

(6) Grantees and subgrantees are encouraged to use Federal excess and surplus property in lieu of purchasing new equipment and property whenever such use is feasible and reduces project costs.

(7) Grantees and subgrantees are encouraged to use value engineering clauses in contracts for construction projects of sufficient size to offer reasonable opportunities for cost reductions. Value engineering is a systematic and creative analysis of each contract item or task to ensure that its essential function is provided at the overall lower cost.

(8) Grantees and subgrantees will make awards only to responsible contractors possessing the ability to perform successfully under the terms and conditions of a proposed procurement. Consideration will be given to such matters as contractor integrity, compliance with public policy, record of past performance, and financial and technical resources.

(9) Grantees and subgrantees will maintain records sufficient to detail the significant history of a procurement. These records will include, but are not necessarily limited to the following: rationale for the method of procurement, selection of contract type, contractor selection or rejection, and the basis for the contract price.

(10) Grantees and subgrantees will use time and material type contracts only—

(i) After a determination that no other contract is suitable, and

(ii) If the contract includes a ceiling price that the contractor exceeds at its own risk.

(11) Grantees and subgrantees alone will be responsible, in accordance with good administrative practice and sound business judgment, for the settlement of all contractual and administrative issues arising out of procurements. These issues include, but are not limited to source evaluation, protests, disputes, and claims. These standards do not relieve the grantee or subgrantee of any contractual responsibilities under its contracts. Federal agencies will not substitute their judgment for

that of the grantee or subgrantee unless the matter is primarily a Federal concern. Violations of law will be referred to the local, State, or Federal authority having proper jurisdiction.

(12) Grantees and subgrantees will have protest procedures to handle and resolve disputes relating to their procurements and shall in all instances disclose information regarding the protest to the awarding agency. A protestor must exhaust all administrative remedies with the grantee and subgrantee before pursuing a protest with the Federal agency. Reviews of protests by the Federal agency will be limited to:

(i) Violations of Federal law or regulations and the standards of this section (violations of State or local law will be under the jurisdiction of State or local authorities) and

(ii) Violations of the grantee's or subgrantee's protest procedures for failure to review a complaint or protest. Protests received by the Federal agency other than those specified above will be referred to the grantee or subgrantee.

(c) *Competition.* (1) All procurement transactions will be conducted in a manner providing full and open competition consistent with the standards of section 13.36. Some of the situations considered to be restrictive of competition include but are not limited to:

(i) Placing unreasonable requirements on firms in order for them to qualify to do business,

(ii) Requiring unnecessary experience and excessive bonding,

(iii) Noncompetitive pricing practices between firms or between affiliated companies,

(iv) Noncompetitive awards to consultants that are on retainer contracts,

(v) Organizational conflicts of interest,

(vi) Specifying only a "brand name" product instead of allowing "an equal" product to be offered and describing the performance of other relevant requirements of the procurement, and

(vii) Any arbitrary action in the procurement process.

(2) Grantees and subgrantees will conduct procurements in a manner that prohibits the use of statutorily or administratively imposed in-State or local geographical preferences in the evaluation of bids or proposals, except in those cases where applicable Federal statutes expressly mandate or encourage geographic preference. Nothing in this section preempts State licensing laws. When contracting for architectural and engineering (A/E) services, geographic location may be a selection criteria provided its application leaves an appropriate number of qualified firms, given the nature and size of the project, to compete for the contract.

(3) Grantees will have written selection procedures for procurement transactions. These procedures will ensure that all solicitations:

(i) Incorporate a clear and accurate description of the technical requirements for the material, product, or service to be procured. Such description shall not, in competitive procurements, contain features which unduly restrict competition. The description may include a statement of the qualitative nature of the material, product or service to be procured, and when necessary, shall set forth those minimum essential characteristics and standards to which it must conform if it is to satisfy its intended use. Detailed product specifications should be avoided if at all possible. When it is impractical or uneconomical to make a clear and accurate description of the technical requirements, a "brand name or equal" description may be used as a means to define the performance or other salient requirements of a procurement. The specific features of the named brand which must be met by offerors shall be clearly stated; and

(ii) Identify all requirements which the offerors must fulfill and all other factors to be used in evaluating bids or proposals.

(4) Grantees and subgrantees will ensure that all prequalified lists of persons, firms, or products which are used in acquiring goods and services are current and include enough qualified sources to ensure maximum open and free competition. Also, grantees and subgrantees will not preclude potential bidders from qualifying during the solicitation period.

(d) *Methods of procurement to be followed*—(1) *Procurement by small purchase procedures.* Small purchase procedures are those relatively simple and informal procurement methods for securing services, supplies, or other property that do not cost more than the simplified acquisition threshold fixed at 41 U.S.C. 403(11) (currently set at $100,000). If small purchase procedures are used, price or rate quotations shall be obtained from an adequate number of qualified sources.

(2) Procurement by *sealed bids* (formal advertising). Bids are publicly solicited and a firm-fixed-price contract (lump sum or unit price) is awarded to the responsible bidder whose bid, conforming with all the material terms and conditions of the invitation for bids, is the lowest in price. The sealed bid method is the preferred method for procuring construction, if the conditions in § 13.36(d)(2)(i) apply.

(i) In order for sealed bidding to be feasible, the following conditions should be present:

(A) A complete, adequate, and realistic specification or purchase description is available;

(B) Two or more responsible bidders are willing and able to compete effectively and for the business; and

(C) The procurement lends itself to a firm fixed price contract and the selection of the successful bidder can be made principally on the basis of price.

(ii) If sealed bids are used, the following requirements apply:

(A) The invitation for bids will be publicly advertised and bids shall be solicited from an adequate number of known suppliers, providing them sufficient time prior to the date set for opening the bids;

(B) The invitation for bids, which will include any specifications and pertinent attachments, shall define the items or services in order for the bidder to properly respond;

(C) All bids will be publicly opened at the time and place prescribed in the invitation for bids;

(D) A firm fixed-price contract award will be made in writing to the lowest responsive and responsible bidder. Where specified in bidding documents, factors such as discounts, transportation cost, and life cycle costs shall be considered in determining which bid is lowest. Payment discounts will only be used to determine the low bid when

prior experience indicates that such discounts are usually taken advantage of; and

(E) Any or all bids may be rejected if there is a sound documented reason.

(3) Procurement by *competitive proposals.* The technique of competitive proposals is normally conducted with more than one source submitting an offer, and either a fixed-price or cost-reimbursement type contract is awarded. It is generally used when conditions are not appropriate for the use of sealed bids. If this method is used, the following requirements apply:

(i) Requests for proposals will be publicized and identify all evaluation factors and their relative importance. Any response to publicized requests for proposals shall be honored to the maximum extent practical;

(ii) Proposals will be solicited from an adequate number of qualified sources;

(iii) Grantees and subgrantees will have a method for conducting technical evaluations of the proposals received and for selecting awardees;

(iv) Awards will be made to the responsible firm whose proposal is most advantageous to the program, with price and other factors considered; and

(v) Grantees and subgrantees may use competitive proposal procedures for qualifications-based procurement of architectural/engineering (A/E) professional services whereby competitors' qualifications are evaluated and the most qualified competitor is selected, subject to negotiation of fair and reasonable compensation. The method, where price is not used as a selection factor, can only be used in procurement of A/E professional services. It cannot be used to purchase other types of services though A/E firms are a potential source to perform the proposed effort.

(4) Procurement by *noncompetitive proposals* is procurement through solicitation of a proposal from only one source, or after solicitation of a number of sources, competition is determined inadequate.

(i) Procurement by noncompetitive proposals may be used only when the award of a contract is infeasible under small purchase procedures, sealed bids or competitive proposals and one of the following circumstances applies:

(A) The item is available only from a single source;

(B) The public exigency or emergency for the requirement will not permit a delay resulting from competitive solicitation;

(C) The awarding agency authorizes noncompetitive proposals; or

(D) After solicitation of a number of sources, competition is determined inadequate.

(ii) Cost analysis, i.e., verifying the proposed cost data, the projections of the data, and the evaluation of the specific elements of costs and profits, is required.

(iii) Grantees and subgrantees may be required to submit the proposed procurement to the awarding agency for pre-award review in accordance with paragraph (g) of this section.

(e) *Contracting with small and minority firms, women's business enterprise and labor surplus area firms.* (1) The grantee and subgrantee will take all necessary affirmative steps to assure that minority firms, women's business enterprises, and labor surplus area firms are used when possible.

(2) Affirmative steps shall include:

(i) Placing qualified small and minority businesses and women's business enterprises on solicitation lists;

(ii) Assuring that small and minority businesses, and women's business enterprises are solicited whenever they are potential sources;

(iii) Dividing total requirements, when economically feasible, into smaller tasks or quantities to permit maximum participation by small and minority business, and women's business enterprises;

(iv) Establishing delivery schedules, where the requirement permits, which encourage participation by small and minority business, and women's business enterprises;

(v) Using the services and assistance of the Small Business Administration, and the Minority Business Development Agency of the Department of Commerce; and

(vi) Requiring the prime contractor, if subcontracts are to be let, to take the affirmative steps listed in paragraphs (e)(2) (i) through (v) of this section.

(f) *Contract cost and price.* (1) Grantees and subgrantees must perform a cost or price analysis in connection with every procurement action including contract modifications. The method and degree of analysis is dependent on the facts surrounding the particular procurement situation, but as a starting point, grantees must make independent estimates before receiving bids or proposals. A cost analysis must be performed when the offeror is required to submit the elements of his estimated cost, e.g., under professional, consulting, and architectural engineering services contracts. A cost analysis will be necessary when adequate price competition is lacking, and for sole source procurements, including contract modifications or change orders, unless price resonableness can be established on the basis of a catalog or market price of a commercial product sold in substantial quantities to the general public or based on prices set by law or regulation. A price analysis will be used in all other instances to determine the reasonableness of the proposed contract price.

(2) Grantees and subgrantees will negotiate profit as a separate element of the price for each contract in which there is no price competition and in all cases where cost analysis is performed. To establish a fair and reasonable profit, consideration will be given to the complexity of the work to be performed, the risk borne by the contractor, the contractor's investment, the amount of subcontracting, the quality of its record of past performance, and industry profit rates in the surrounding geographical area for similar work.

(3) Costs or prices based on estimated costs for contracts under grants will be allowable only to the extent that costs incurred or cost estimates included in negotiated prices are consistent with Federal cost principles (see §13.22). Grantees may reference their own cost principles that comply with the applicable Federal cost principles.

(4) The cost plus a percentage of cost and percentage of construction cost methods of contracting shall not be used.

§ 13.36

. (1) Grant-
, make avail-
the awarding
cifications on pro-
s where the award-
eves such review is
ure that the item and/or
ified is the one being pro-
p   purchase. This review gen-
era. will take place prior to the time
the specification is incorporated into a
solicitation document. However, if the
grantee or subgrantee desires to have
the review accomplished after a solicitation has been developed, the awarding agency may still review the specifications, with such review usually limited to the technical aspects of the proposed purchase.

(2) Grantees and subgrantees must on
request make available for awarding
agency pre-award review procurement
documents, such as requests for proposals or invitations for bids, independent cost estimates, etc. when:

(i) A grantee's or subgrantee's procurement procedures or operation fails
to comply with the procurement standards in this section; or

(ii) The procurement is expected to
exceed the simplified acquisition
threshold and is to be awarded without
competition or only one bid or offer is
received in response to a solicitation;
or

(iii) The procurement, which is expected to exceed the simplified acquisition threshold, specifies a "brand
name" product; or

(iv) The proposed award is more than
the simplified acquisition threshold
and is to be awarded to other than the
apparent low bidder under a sealed bid
procurement; or

(v) A proposed contract modification
changes the scope of a contract or increases the contract amount by more
than the simplified acquisition threshold.

(3) A grantee or subgrantee will be
exempt from the pre-award review in
paragraph (g)(2) of this section if the
awarding agency determines that its
procurement systems comply with the
standards of this section.

(i) A grantee or subgrantee may request that its procurement system be
reviewed by the awarding agency to determine whether its system meets

these standards in order for its system
to be certified. Generally, these reviews shall occur where there is a continuous high-dollar funding, and third-
party contracts are awarded on a regular basis.

(ii) A grantee or subgrantee may self-
certify its procurement system. Such
self-certification shall not limit the
awarding agency's right to survey the
system. Under a self-certification procedure, awarding agencies may wish to
rely on written assurances from the
grantee or subgrantee that it is complying with these standards. A grantee
or subgrantee will cite specific procedures, regulations, standards, etc., as
being in compliance with these requirements and have its system available
for review.

(h) *Bonding requirements.* For construction or facility improvement contracts or subcontracts exceeding the
simplified acquisition threshold, the
awarding agency may accept the bonding policy and requirements of the
grantee or subgrantee provided the
awarding agency has made a determination that the awarding agency's
interest is adequately protected. If
such a determination has not been
made, the minimum requirements shall
be as follows:

(1) *A bid guarantee from each bidder
equivalent to five percent of the bid price.*
The "bid guarantee" shall consist of a
firm commitment such as a bid bond,
certified check, or other negotiable instrument accompanying a bid as assurance that the bidder will, upon acceptance of his bid, execute such contractual documents as may be required
within the time specified.

(2) *A performance bond on the part of
the contractor for 100 percent of the contract price.* A "performance bond" is
one executed in connection with a contract to secure fulfillment of all the
contractor's obligations under such
contract.

(3) *A payment bond on the part of the
contractor for 100 percent of the contract
price.* A "payment bond" is one executed in connection with a contract to
assure payment as required by law of
all persons supplying labor and material in the execution of the work provided for in the contract.

(i) *Contract provisions.* A grantee's and subgrantee's contracts must contain provisions in paragraph (i) of this section. Federal agencies are permitted to require changes, remedies, changed conditions, access and records retention, suspension of work, and other clauses approved by the Office of Federal Procurement Policy.

(1) Administrative, contractual, or legal remedies in instances where contractors violate or breach contract terms, and provide for such sanctions and penalties as may be appropriate. (Contracts more than the simplified acquisition threshold)

(2) Termination for cause and for convenience by the grantee or subgrantee including the manner by which it will be effected and the basis for settlement. (All contracts in excess of $10,000)

(3) Compliance with Executive Order 11246 of September 24, 1965, entitled "Equal Employment Opportunity," as amended by Executive Order 11375 of October 13, 1967, and as supplemented in Department of Labor regulations (41 CFR chapter 60). (All construction contracts awarded in excess of $10,000 by grantees and their contractors or subgrantees)

(4) Compliance with the Copeland "Anti-Kickback" Act (18 U.S.C. 874) as supplemented in Department of Labor regulations (29 CFR Part 3). (All contracts and subgrants for construction or repair)

(5) Compliance with the Davis-Bacon Act (40 U.S.C. 276a to 276a–7) as supplemented by Department of Labor regulations (29 CFR part 5). (Construction contracts in excess of $2000 awarded by grantees and subgrantees when required by Federal grant program legislation)

(6) Compliance with Sections 103 and 107 of the Contract Work Hours and Safety Standards Act (40 U.S.C. 327–330) as supplemented by Department of Labor regulations (29 CFR Part 5). (Construction contracts awarded by grantees and subgrantees in excess of $2000, and in excess of $2500 for other contracts which involve the employment of mechanics or laborers)

(7) Notice of awarding agency requirements and regulations pertaining to reporting.

(8) Notice of awarding agency requirements and regulations pertaining to patent rights with respect to any discovery or invention which arises or is developed in the course of or under such contract.

(9) Awarding agency requirements and regulations pertaining to copyrights and rights in data.

(10) Access by the grantee, the subgrantee, the Federal grantor agency, the Comptroller General of the United States, or any of their duly authorized representatives to any books, documents, papers, and records of the contractor which are directly pertinent to that specific contract for the purpose of making audit, examination, excerpts, and transcriptions.

(11) Retention of all required records for three years after grantees or subgrantees make final payments and all other pending matters are closed.

(12) Compliance with all applicable standards, orders, or requirements issued under section 306 of the Clean Air Act (42 U.S.C. 1857(h)), section 508 of the Clean Water Act (33 U.S.C. 1368), Executive Order 11738, and Environmental Protection Agency regulations (40 CFR part 15). (Contracts, subcontracts, and subgrants of amounts in excess of $100,000)

(13) Mandatory standards and policies relating to energy efficiency which are contained in the state energy conservation plan issued in compliance with the Energy Policy and Conservation Act (Pub. L. 94–163, 89 Stat. 871).

[53 FR 8078, 8087, Mar. 11, 1988, as amended at 60 FR 19639, 19645, Apr. 19, 1995]

§13.37 Subgrants.

(a) *States.* States shall follow state law and procedures when awarding and administering subgrants (whether on a cost reimbursement or fixed amount basis) of financial assistance to local and Indian tribal governments. States shall:

(1) Ensure that every subgrant includes any clauses required by Federal statute and executive orders and their implementing regulations;

(2) Ensure that subgrantees are aware of requirements imposed upon them by Federal statute and regulation;

(3) Ensure that a provision for compliance with § 13.42 is placed in every cost reimbursement subgrant; and

(4) Conform any advances of grant funds to subgrantees substantially to the same standards of timing and amount that apply to cash advances by Federal agencies.

(b) *All other grantees.* All other grantees shall follow the provisions of this part which are applicable to awarding agencies when awarding and administering subgrants (whether on a cost reimbursement or fixed amount basis) of financial assistance to local and Indian tribal governments. Grantees shall:

(1) Ensure that every subgrant includes a provision for compliance with this part;

(2) Ensure that every subgrant includes any clauses required by Federal statute and executive orders and their implementing regulations; and

(3) Ensure that subgrantees are aware of requirements imposed upon them by Federal statutes and regulations.

(c) *Exceptions.* By their own terms, certain provisions of this part do not apply to the award and administration of subgrants:

(1) Section 13.10;

(2) Section 13.11;

(3) The letter-of-credit procedures specified in Treasury Regulations at 31 CFR part 205, cited in § 13.21; and

(4) Section 13.50.

REPORTS, RECORDS RETENTION, AND
ENFORCEMENT

§ 13.40 Monitoring and reporting program performance.

(a) *Monitoring by grantees.* Grantees are responsible for managing the day-to-day operations of grant and subgrant supported activities. Grantees must monitor grant and subgrant supported activities to assure compliance with applicable Federal requirements and that performance goals are being achieved. Grantee monitoring must cover each program, function or activity.

(b) *Nonconstruction performance reports.* The Federal agency may, if it decides that performance information available from subsequent applications contains sufficient information to meet its programmatic needs, require the grantee to submit a performance report only upon expiration or termination of grant support. Unless waived by the Federal agency this report will be due on the same date as the final Financial Status Report.

(1) Grantees shall submit annual performance reports unless the awarding agency requires quarterly or semi-annual reports. However, performance reports will not be required more frequently than quarterly. Annual reports shall be due 90 days after the grant year, quarterly or semi-annual reports shall be due 30 days after the reporting period. The final performance report will be due 90 days after the expiration or termination of grant support. If a justified request is submitted by a grantee, the Federal agency may extend the due date for any performance report. Additionally, requirements for unnecessary performance reports may be waived by the Federal agency.

(2) Performance reports will contain, for each grant, brief information on the following:

(i) A comparison of actual accomplishments to the objectives established for the period. Where the output of the project can be quantified, a computation of the cost per unit of output may be required if that information will be useful.

(ii) The reasons for slippage if established objectives were not met.

(iii) Additional pertinent information including, when appropriate, analysis and explanation of cost overruns or high unit costs.

(3) Grantees will not be required to submit more than the original and two copies of performance reports.

(4) Grantees will adhere to the standards in this section in prescribing performance reporting requirements for subgrantees.

(c) *Construction performance reports.* For the most part, on-site technical inspections and certified percentage-of-completion data are relied on heavily by Federal agencies to monitor progress under construction grants and subgrants. The Federal agency will require additional formal performance reports only when considered necessary, and never more frequently than quarterly.

(d) *Significant developments.* Events may occur between the scheduled performance reporting dates which have significant impact upon the grant or subgrant supported activity. In such cases, the grantee must inform the Federal agency as soon as the following types of conditions become known:

(1) Problems, delays, or adverse conditions which will materially impair the ability to meet the objective of the award. This disclosure must include a statement of the action taken, or contemplated, and any assistance needed to resolve the situation.

(2) Favorable developments which enable meeting time schedules and objectives sooner or at less cost than anticipated or producing more beneficial results than originally planned.

(e) Federal agencies may make site visits as warranted by program needs.

(f) *Waivers, extensions.* (1) Federal agencies may waive any performance report required by this part if not needed.

(2) The grantee may waive any performance report from a subgrantee when not needed. The grantee may extend the due date for any performance report from a subgrantee if the grantee will still be able to meet its performance reporting obligations to the Federal agency.

§13.41 **Financial reporting.**

(a) *General.* (1) Except as provided in paragraphs (a) (2) and (5) of this section, grantees will use only the forms specified in paragraphs (a) through (e) of this section, and such supplementary or other forms as may from time to time be authorized by OMB, for:

(i) Submitting financial reports to Federal agencies, or

(ii) Requesting advances or reimbursements when letters of credit are not used.

(2) Grantees need not apply the forms prescribed in this section in dealing with their subgrantees. However, grantees shall not impose more burdensome requirements on subgrantees.

(3) Grantees shall follow all applicable standard and supplemental Federal agency instructions approved by OMB to the extend required under the Paperwork Reduction Act of 1980 for use in connection with forms specified in paragraphs (b) through (e) of this section. Federal agencies may issue substantive supplementary instructions only with the approval of OMB. Federal agencies may shade out or instruct the grantee to disregard any line item that the Federal agency finds unnecessary for its decisionmaking purposes.

(4) Grantees will not be required to submit more than the original and two copies of forms required under this part.

(5) Federal agencies may provide computer outputs to grantees to expedite or contribute to the accuracy of reporting. Federal agencies may accept the required information from grantees in machine usable format or computer printouts instead of prescribed forms.

(6) Federal agencies may waive any report required by this section if not needed.

(7) Federal agencies may extend the due date of any financial report upon receiving a justified request from a grantee.

(b) *Financial Status Report*—(1) *Form.* Grantees will use Standard Form 269 or 269A, Financial Status Report, to report the status of funds for all nonconstruction grants and for construction grants when required in accordance with paragraph (e)(2)(iii) of this section.

(2) *Accounting basis.* Each grantee will report program outlays and program income on a cash or accrual basis as prescribed by the awarding agency. If the Federal agency requires accrual information and the grantee's accounting records are not normally kept on the accural basis, the grantee shall not be required to convert its accounting system but shall develop such accrual information through and analysis of the documentation on hand.

(3) *Frequency.* The Federal agency may prescribe the frequency of the report for each project or program. However, the report will not be required more frequently than quarterly. If the Federal agency does not specify the frequency of the report, it will be submitted annually. A final report will be required upon expiration or termination of grant support.

(4) *Due date.* When reports are required on a quarterly or semiannual

basis, they will be due 30 days after the reporting period. When required on an annual basis, they will be due 90 days after the grant year. Final reports will be due 90 days after the expiration or termination of grant support.

(c) *Federal Cash Transactions Report*— (1) *Form.* (i) For grants paid by letter or credit, Treasury check advances or electronic transfer of funds, the grantee will submit the Standard Form 272, Federal Cash Transactions Report, and when necessary, its continuation sheet, Standard Form 272a, unless the terms of the award exempt the grantee from this requirement.

(ii) These reports will be used by the Federal agency to monitor cash advanced to grantees and to obtain disbursement or outlay information for each grant from grantees. The format of the report may be adapted as appropriate when reporting is to be accomplished with the assistance of automatic data processing equipment provided that the information to be submitted is not changed in substance.

(2) *Forecasts of Federal cash requirements.* Forecasts of Federal cash requirements may be required in the "Remarks" section of the report.

(3) *Cash in hands of subgrantees.* When considered necessary and feasible by the Federal agency, grantees may be required to report the amount of cash advances in excess of three days' needs in the hands of their subgrantees or contractors and to provide short narrative explanations of actions taken by the grantee to reduce the excess balances.

(4) *Frequency and due date.* Grantees must submit the report no later than 15 working days following the end of each quarter. However, where an advance either by letter of credit or electronic transfer of funds is authorized at an annualized rate of one million dollars or more, the Federal agency may require the report to be submitted within 15 working days following the end of each month.

(d) *Request for advance or reimbursement*—(1) *Advance payments.* Requests for Treasury check advance payments will be submitted on Standard Form 270, Request for Advance or Reimbursement. (This form will not be used for drawdowns under a letter of credit,

electronic funds transfer or when Treasury check advance payments are made to the grantee automatically on a predetermined basis.)

(2) *Reimbursements.* Requests for reimbursement under nonconstruction grants will also be submitted on Standard Form 270. (For reimbursement requests under construction grants, see paragraph (e)(1) of this section.)

(3) The frequency for submitting payment requests is treated in paragraph (b)(3) of this section.

(e) *Outlay report and request for reimbursement for construction programs.* (1) Grants that support construction activities paid by reimbursement method.

(i) Requests for reimbursement under construction grants will be submitted on Standard Form 271, Outlay Report and Request for Reimbursement for Construction Programs. Federal agencies may, however, prescribe the Request for Advance or Reimbursement form, specified in paragraph (d) of this section, instead of this form.

(ii) The frequency for submitting reimbursement requests is treated in paragraph (b)(3) of this section.

(2) Grants that support construction activities paid by letter of credit, electronic funds transfer or Treasury check advance.

(i) When a construction grant is paid by letter of credit, electronic funds transfer or Treasury check advances, the grantee will report its outlays to the Federal agency using Standard Form 271, Outlay Report and Request for Reimbursement for Construction Programs. The Federal agency will provide any necessary special instruction. However, frequency and due date shall be governed by paragraphs (b) (3) and (4) of this section.

(ii) When a construction grant is paid by Treasury check advances based on periodic requests from the grantee, the advances will be requested on the form specified in paragraph (d) of this section.

(iii) The Federal agency may substitute the Financial Status Report specified in paragraph (b) of this section for the Outlay Report and Request for Reimbursement for Construction Programs.

(3) *Accounting basis.* The accounting basis for the Outlay Report and Request for Reimbursement for Construction Programs shall be governed by paragraph (b)(2) of this section.

§ 13.42 Retention and access requirements for records.

(a) *Applicability.* (1) This section applies to all financial and programmatic records, supporting documents, statistical records, and other records of grantees or subgrantees which are:

(i) Required to be maintained by the terms of this part, program regulations or the grant agreement, or

(ii) Otherwise reasonably considered as pertinent to program regulations or the grant agreement.

(2) This section does not apply to records maintained by contractors or subcontractors. For a requirement to place a provision concerning records in certain kinds of contracts, see § 13.36(i)(10).

(b) *Length of retention period.* (1) Except as otherwise provided, records must be retained for three years from the starting date specified in paragraph (c) of this section.

(2) If any litigation, claim, negotiation, audit or other action involving the records has been started before the expiration of the 3-year period, the records must be retained until completion of the action and resolution of all issues which arise from it, or until the end of the regular 3-year period, whichever is later.

(3) To avoid duplicate recordkeeping, awarding agencies may make special arrangements with grantees and subgrantees to retain any records which are continuously needed for joint use. The awarding agency will request transfer of records to its custody when it determines that the records possess long-term retention value. When the records are transferred to or maintained by the Federal agency, the 3-year retention requirement is not applicable to the grantee or subgrantee.

(c) *Starting date of retention period*—(1) *General.* When grant support is continued or renewed at annual or other intervals, the retention period for the records of each funding period starts on the day the grantee or subgrantee submits to the awarding agency its single or last expenditure report for that period. However, if grant support is continued or renewed quarterly, the retention period for each year's records starts on the day the grantee submits its expenditure report for the last quarter of the Federal fiscal year. In all other cases, the retention period starts on the day the grantee submits its final expenditure report. If an expenditure report has been waived, the retention period starts on the day the report would have been due.

(2) *Real property and equipment records.* The retention period for real property and equipment records starts from the date of the disposition or replacement or transfer at the direction of the awarding agency.

(3) *Records for income transactions after grant or subgrant support.* In some cases grantees must report income after the period of grant support. Where there is such a requirement, the retention period for the records pertaining to the earning of the income starts from the end of the grantee's fiscal year in which the income is earned.

(4) *Indirect cost rate proposals, cost allocations plans, etc.* This paragraph applies to the following types of documents, and their supporting records: indirect cost rate computations or proposals, cost allocation plans, and any similar accounting computations of the rate at which a particular group of costs is chargeable (such as computer usage chargeback rates or composite fringe benefit rates).

(i) *If submitted for negotiation.* If the proposal, plan, or other computation is required to be submitted to the Federal Government (or to the grantee) to form the basis for negotiation of the rate, then the 3-year retention period for its supporting records starts from the date of such submission.

(ii) *If not submitted for negotiation.* If the proposal, plan, or other computation is not required to be submitted to the Federal Government (or to the grantee) for negotiation purposes, then the 3-year retention period for the proposal plan, or computation and its supporting records starts from end of the fiscal year (or other accounting period) covered by the proposal, plan, or other computation.

(d) *Substitution of microfilm.* Copies made by microfilming, photocopying, or similar methods may be substituted for the original records.

(e) *Access to records*—(1) *Records of grantees and subgrantees.* The awarding agency and the Comptroller General of the United States, or any of their authorized representatives, shall have the right of access to any pertinent books, documents, papers, or other records of grantees and subgrantees which are pertinent to the grant, in order to make audits, examinations, excerpts, and transcripts.

(2) *Expiration of right of access.* The rights of access in this section must not be limited to the required retention period but shall last as long as the records are retained.

(f) *Restrictions on public access.* The Federal Freedom of Information Act (5 U.S.C. 552) does not apply to records Unless required by Federal, State, or local law, grantees and subgrantees are not required to permit public access to their records.

§ 13.43 Enforcement.

(a) *Remedies for noncompliance.* If a grantee or subgrantee materially fails to comply with any term of an award, whether stated in a Federal statute or regulation, an assurance, in a State plan or application, a notice of award, or elsewhere, the awarding agency may take one or more of the following actions, as appropriate in the circumstances:

(1) Temporarily withhold cash payments pending correction of the deficiency by the grantee or subgrantee or more severe enforcement action by the awarding agency,

(2) Disallow (that is, deny both use of funds and matching credit for) all or part of the cost of the activity or action not in compliance,

(3) Wholly or partly suspend or terminate the current award for the grantee's or subgrantee's program,

(4) Withhold further awards for the program, or

(5) Take other remedies that may be legally available.

(b) *Hearings, appeals.* In taking an enforcement action, the awarding agency will provide the grantee or subgrantee an opportunity for such hearing, appeal, or other administrative proceeding to which the grantee or subgrantee is entitled under any statute or regulation applicable to the action involved.

(c) *Effects of suspension and termination.* Costs of grantee or subgrantee resulting from obligations incurred by the grantee or subgrantee during a suspension or after termination of an award are not allowable unless the awarding agency expressly authorizes them in the notice of suspension or termination or subsequently. Other grantee or subgrantee costs during suspension or after termination which are necessary and not reasonably avoidable are allowable if:

(1) The costs result from obligations which were properly incurred by the grantee or subgrantee before the effective date of suspension or termination, are not in anticipation of it, and, in the case of a termination, are noncancellable, and,

(2) The costs would be allowable if the award were not suspended or expired normally at the end of the funding period in which the termination takes effect.

(d) *Relationship to Debarment and Suspension.* The enforcement remedies identified in this section, including suspension and termination, do not preclude grantee or subgrantee from being subject to "Debarment and Suspension" under E.O. 12549 (see § 13.35).

§ 13.44 Termination for convenience.

Except as provided in § 13.43 awards may be terminated in whole or in part only as follows:

(a) By the awarding agency with the consent of the grantee or subgrantee in which case the two parties shall agree upon the termination conditions, including the effective date and in the case of partial termination, the portion to be terminated, or

(b) By the grantee or subgrantee upon written notification to the awarding agency, setting forth the reasons for such termination, the effective date, and in the case of partial termination, the portion to be terminated. However, if, in the case of a partial termination, the awarding agency determines that the remaining portion of the award will not accomplish the purposes for which the award was made, the awarding agency may terminate the award in its entirety under either §13.43 or paragraph (a) of this section.

Subpart D—After-The-Grant Requirements

§13.50 Closeout.

(a) *General.* The Federal agency will close out the award when it determines that all applicable administrative actions and all required work of the grant has been completed.

(b) *Reports.* Within 90 days after the expiration or termination of the grant, the grantee must submit all financial, performance, and other reports required as a condition of the grant. Upon request by the grantee, Federal agencies may extend this timeframe. These may include but are not limited to:

(1) *Final performance or progress report.*

(2) *Financial Status Report (SF 269) or Outlay Report and Request for Reimbursement for Construction Programs (SF–271) (as applicable.)*

(3) *Final request for payment (SF–270) (if applicable).*

(4) *Invention disclosure (if applicable).*

(5) *Federally-owned property report:*

In accordance with §13.32(f), a grantee must submit an inventory of all federally owned property (as distinct from property acquired with grant funds) for which it is accountable and request disposition instructions from the Federal agency of property no longer needed.

(c) *Cost adjustment.* The Federal agency will, within 90 days after receipt of reports in paragraph (b) of this section, make upward or downward adjustments to the allowable costs.

(d) *Cash adjustments.* (1) The Federal agency will make prompt payment to the grantee for allowable reimbursable costs.

(2) The grantee must immediately refund to the Federal agency any balance of unobligated (unencumbered) cash advanced that is not authorized to be retained for use on other grants.

§13.51 Later disallowances and adjustments.

The closeout of a grant does not affect:

(a) The Federal agency's right to disallow costs and recover funds on the basis of a later audit or other review;

(b) The grantee's obligation to return any funds due as a result of later refunds, corrections, or other transactions;

(c) Records retention as required in §13.42;

(d) Property management requirements in §§13.31 and 13.32; and

(e) Audit requirements in §13.26.

§13.52 Collection of amounts due.

(a) Any funds paid to a grantee in excess of the amount to which the grantee is finally determined to be entitled under the terms of the award constitute a debt to the Federal Government. If not paid within a reasonable period after demand, the Federal agency may reduce the debt by:

(1) Making an administrative offset against other requests for reimbursements,

(2) Withholding advance payments otherwise due to the grantee, or

(3) Other action permitted by law.

(b) Except where otherwise provided by statutes or regulations, the Federal agency will charge interest on an overdue debt in accordance with the Federal Claims Collection Standards (4 CFR Chapter II). The date from which interest is computed is not extended by litigation or the filing of any form of appeal.

Subpart E—Entitlement [Reserved]

PART 14 [RESERVED]

PART 15—CONDUCT AT THE MT. WEATHER EMERGENCY ASSISTANCE CENTER AND AT THE NATIONAL EMERGENCY TRAINING CENTER

15.6   Compliance with signs and directions.
15.7   Disturbances.
15.8   Gambling.
15.9   Alcoholic beverages and narcotics.
15.10 Soliciting, vending, and debt collection.
15.11 Distribution of handbills.
15.12 Photographs and other depictions.
15.13 Dogs and other animals.
15.14 Vehicular and pedestrian traffic.
15.15 Weapons and explosives.
15.16 Penalties.
15.17 Other laws.

AUTHORITY: Reorganization Plan No. 3 of 1978, 43 FR 41943, 3 CFR, 1978 Comp., p. 329; E.O. 12127 of Mar. 31, 1979, 44 FR 19367, 3 CFR, 1979 Comp., p. 376; E.O. 12148, 44 FR 13239, 3 CFR, 1979 Comp., p. 412; Federal Fire Prevention and Control Act of 1974, 15 U.S.C. 2201 *et seq.*; delegation of authority from the Administrator of General Services, dated July 18, 1979; Pub. L. 80-566, approved June 1, 1948, 40 U.S.C. 318-318d; and the Federal Property and Administrative Services Act of 1949, 40 U.S.C. 271 *et seq.*

SOURCE: 64 FR 31137, June 10, 1999, unless otherwise noted.

§ 15.1 Applicability.

The rules and regulations in this part apply to all persons entering, while on, or leaving all the property known as the Mt. Weather Emergency Operations Center (Mt. Weather) located at 19844 Blue Ridge Mountain Road, Bluemont, Virginia 20135, and all the property known as the National Emergency Training Center (NETC), located on 16825 South Seton Avenue in Emmitsburg, Maryland, which the Federal Emergency Management Agency (FEMA) owns, operates and controls.

§ 15.2 Definitions.

Terms used in part 15 have these meanings:

Administrator means the Administrator of the Federal Emergency Management Agency.

Assistant Administrator means the Assistant Administrator, United States Fire Administration, FEMA.

FEMA means the Federal Emergency Management Agency.

Mt. Weather means the Mt. Weather Emergency Operations Center, Bluemont, Virginia.

Mt. Weather Executive Director means the Executive Director of the Mt. Weather Emergency Operations Center.

NETC means the National Emergency Training Center, Emmitsburg, MD.

We means the Federal Emergency Management Agency or FEMA.

[64 FR 31137, June 10, 1999, as amended at 74 FR 15338, April 3, 2009]

§ 15.3 Access to Mt. Weather.

Mt. Weather contains classified material and areas that we must protect in the interest of national security. The facility is a restricted area. We deny access to Mt. Weather to the general public and limit access to those persons having official business related to the missions and operations of Mt. Weather. The Administrator or the Mt. Weather Executive Director must approve all persons and vehicles entering Mt. Weather. All persons must register with the Mt. Weather Police/Security Force and must receive a Mt. Weather identification badge and vehicle parking decal or permit to enter or remain on the premises. No person will enter or remain on Mt. Weather premises unless he or she has received permission from the Administrator or the Mt. Weather Executive Director and has complied with these procedures.

§ 15.4 Inspection.

(a) *In general.* All vehicles, packages, handbags, briefcases, and other containers being brought into, while on or being removed from Mt. Weather or the NETC are subject to inspection by the Police/Security Force and other authorized officials. A full search of a vehicle or person may accompany an arrest.

(b) *Inspection at Mt. Weather.* We authorize inspection at Mt. Weather to prevent the possession and use of items prohibited by these rules and regulations or by other applicable laws, to prevent theft of property and to prevent the wrongful obtaining of defense information under 18 U.S.C. 793. If individuals object to such inspections they must tell the officer on duty at the entrance gate before entering Mt. Weather. The Police/Security Force and other authorized officials must not authorize or allow individuals who refuse to permit an inspection of their vehicle or possessions to enter the premises of Mt. Weather.

§15.5 Preservation of property.

At both Mt. Weather and NETC we prohibit:

(a) The improper disposal of rubbish;

(b) Willful destruction of or damage to property;

(c) Theft of property;

(d) Creation of any hazard on the property to persons or things;

(e) Throwing articles of any kind from or at a building;

(f) Climbing upon a fence; or

(g) Climbing upon the roof or any part of a building.

§15.6 Compliance with signs and directions.

Persons at Mt. Weather and the NETC must comply at all times with official signs that prohibit, regulate, or direct, and with the directions of the Police/Security Force and other authorized officials.

§15.7 Disturbances.

At both Mt. Weather and NETC we prohibit any unwarranted loitering, disorderly conduct, or other conduct at Mt. Weather and NETC that:

(a) Creates loud or unusual noise or a nuisance;

(b) Unreasonably obstructs the usual use of classrooms, dormitory rooms, entrances, foyers, lobbies, corridors, offices, elevators, stairways, roadways or parking lots;

(c) Otherwise impedes or disrupts the performance of official duties by government employees or government contractors;

(d) Interferes with the delivery of educational or other programs; or

(e) Prevents persons from obtaining in a timely manner the administrative services provided at both facilities.

§15.8 Gambling.

We prohibit participating in games for money or other personal property, including the operation of gambling devices, the conduct of a lottery or pool, or the sale or purchase of numbers tickets at both facilities.

§15.9 Alcoholic beverages and narcotics.

At both Mt. Weather and the NETC we prohibit:

(a) Operating a motor vehicle by any person under the influence of alcoholic beverages, narcotic drugs, hallucinogens, marijuana, barbiturates or amphetamines as defined in Title 21 of the Annotated Code of Maryland, Transportation, sec. 21–902 or in Title 18.2, ch. 7, Art. 2 of the Code of Virginia, secs. 18.2–266 and 18.2–266.1, as applicable;

(b) Entering upon or while on either property being under the influence of or using or possessing any narcotic drug, marijuana, hallucinogen, barbiturate or amphetamine. This prohibition does not apply in cases where a licensed physician has prescribed the drug for the person;

(c) Entering upon either property or being on either property under the influence of alcoholic beverages;

(d) Bringing alcoholic beverages, narcotic drugs, hallucinogens, marijuana, barbiturates or amphetamines onto the premises unless the Assistant Administrator, the Mt. Weather Executive Director, or the Administrator or designee for the NETC authorizes it in writing; and

(e) Use of alcoholic beverages on the property except:

(1) In the Balloon Shed Lounge at Mt. Weather and in other locations that the Administrator or the Mt. Weather Executive Director authorizes in writing; and

(2) In the NETC Recreation Association and other locations that the Assistant Administrator for the United States Fire Administration or the Administrator, or designee, authorizes in writing.

§15.10 Soliciting, vending, and debt collection.

(a) We prohibit soliciting alms and contributions, commercial or political soliciting and vending of all kinds, displaying or distributing commercial advertising, or collecting private debts unless the Assistant Administrator for the United States Fire Administration or the Mt. Weather Executive Director approve the activities in writing and in advance.

(b) The prohibitions of this section do not apply to:

(1) National or local drives for funds for welfare, health, or other purposes

as authorized by 5 CFR part 950, Solicitation of Federal Civilian and Uniformed Service Personnel for Contributions to Private Voluntary Organizations. The Administrator, or the Senior Resident Manager, or the Assistant Administrator for the United States Fire Administration or designee, must approve all such national or local drives before they are conducted on either premises;

(2) Authorized concessions;

(3) Personal notices posted by employees on authorized bulletin boards; and

(4) Solicitation of labor organization membership or dues authorized by occupant agencies under the Civil Service Reform Act of 1978, 5 U.S.C. 7101 *et seq.*

§ 15.11 Distribution of handbills.

We prohibit the distribution of materials such as pamphlets, handbills or flyers, and the displaying of placards or posting of materials on bulletin boards or elsewhere at Mt. Weather and the NETC unless the Administrator, the Mt. Weather Executive Director, or the Deputy Assistant Administrator for the United States Fire Administration or designee, approves such distribution or display, or when such distribution or display is conducted as part of authorized government activities.

§ 15.12 Photographs and other depictions.

(a) *Photographs and other depictions at Mt. Weather.* We prohibit taking photographs and making notes, sketches, or diagrams of buildings, grounds or other features of Mt. Weather, or the possession of a camera while at Mt. Weather except when the Administrator or Mt. Weather Executive Director approves in advance.

(b) *Photographs and other depictions at the NETC.* (1) Photographs may be taken inside classroom or office areas of the NETC only with the consent of the occupants. Except where security regulations apply or a Federal court order or rule prohibits it, photographs may be taken in entrances, lobbies, foyers, corridors, or auditoriums when used for public meetings.

(2) Subject to the foregoing prohibitions, photographs for advertising and commercial purposes may be taken

only with written permission of the Director of Management Operations and Systems Support, United States Fire Administration, Federal Emergency Management Agency, Emmitsburg, MD 21727, (telephone) (301) 447–1223, (facsimile) (301) 447–1052, or other authorized official where photographs are to be taken.

§ 15.13 Dogs and other animals.

Dogs and other animals, except seeing-eye dogs, must not be brought onto Mt. Weather grounds or into the buildings at NETC for other than official purposes.

§ 15.14 Vehicular and pedestrian traffic.

(a) Drivers of all vehicles entering or while at Mt. Weather or the NETC must drive carefully and safely at all times and must obey the signals and directions of the Police/Security Force or other authorized officials and all posted traffic signs;

(b) Drivers must comply with NETC parking requirements and vehicle registration requirements;

(c) At both Mt. Weather and the NETC we prohibit:

(1) Blocking entrances, driveways, walks, loading platforms, or fire hydrants on the property; and

(2) Parking without authority, parking in unauthorized locations or in locations reserved for other persons, or parking contrary to the direction of posted signs.

(3) Where warning signs are posted vehicles parked in violation may be removed at the owners' risk and expense.

(d) The Administrator, Mt. Weather Executive Director, or the Assistant Administrator for the United States Fire Administration or designee may issue and post specific supplemental traffic directives if needed. When issued and posted supplemental traffic directives will have the same force and effect as if they were in these rules. Proof that a parked motor vehicle violated these rules or directives may be taken as prima facie evidence that the registered owner was responsible for the violation.

§ 15.15 Weapons and explosives.

No person entering or while at Mt. Weather or the NETC will carry or possess firearms, other dangerous or deadly weapons, explosives or items intended to be used or that could reasonably be used to fabricate an explosive or incendiary device, either openly or concealed, except:

(a) For official purposes if the Administrator, Mt. Weather Executive Director, or the Assistant Administrator for the United States Fire Administration or designee approves; and

(b) In accordance with FEMA policy governing the possession of firearms.

§ 15.16 Penalties.

(a) *Misconduct.* (1) Whoever is found guilty of violating any of these rules and regulations is subject to a fine of not more than $50 or imprisonment for not more than 30 days, or both. (See 40 U.S.C. 318c.)

(2) We will process any misconduct at NETC according to FEMA/NETC policy or instructions.

(b) *Parking violations.* We may tow at the owner's expense any vehicles parked in violation of State law, FEMA, Mt. Weather, or NETC instructions.

§ 15.17 Other laws.

Nothing in the rules and regulations in this part will be construed to abolish any other Federal laws or any State and local laws and regulations applicable to Mt. Weather or NETC premises. The rules and regulations in this part supplement penal provisions of Title 18, United States Code, relating to Crimes and Criminal Procedure, which apply without regard to the place of the offense and to those penal provisions that apply in areas under the special maritime and territorial jurisdiction of the United States, as defined in 18 U.S.C. 7. They supersede provisions of State law, however, that Federal law makes criminal offenses under the Assimilated Crimes Act (18 U.S.C. 13) to the extent that State laws conflict with these regulations. State and local criminal laws apply as such only to the extent that the State reserved such authority to itself by the State consent or cession statute or that a Federal statute vests such authority in the State.

PART 16—ENFORCEMENT OF NON-DISCRIMINATION ON THE BASIS OF HANDICAP IN PROGRAMS OR ACTIVITIES CONDUCTED BY THE FEDERAL EMERGENCY MANAGEMENT AGENCY

AUTHORITY: 29 U.S.C. 794.

SOURCE: 53 FR 25885, July 8, 1988, unless otherwise noted.

§ 16.101 Purpose.

The purpose of this regulation is to effectuate section 119 of the Rehabilitation, Comprehensive Services, and Developmental Disabilities Amendments of 1978, which amended section 504 of the Rehabilitation Act of 1973 to prohibit discrimination on the basis of handicap in programs or activities conducted by Executive agencies or the United States Postal Service.

§ 16.102 Application.

This regulation (§§ 16.101 through 16.170) applies to all programs or activities conducted by the agency, except for programs or activities conducted outside the United States that do not involve individuals with handicaps in the United States.

§ 16.103 Definitions.

For purposes of this regulation, the term—

Assistant Attorney General means the Assistant Attorney General, Civil Rights Division, United States Department of Justice.

Auxiliary aids means services or devices that enable persons with impaired sensory, manual, or speaking skills to have an equal opportunity to participate in, and enjoy the benefits of, programs or activities conducted by the agency. For example, auxiliary aids useful for persons with impaired vision include readers, Brailled materials, audio recordings, and other similar services and devices. Auxiliary aids useful for persons with impaired hearing include telephone handset amplifiers, telephones compatible with hearing aids, telecommunication devices for deaf persons (TDD's), interpreters, notetakers, written materials, and other similar services and devices.

Complete complaint means a written statement that contains the complainant's name and address and describes the agency's alleged discriminatory action in sufficient detail to inform the agency of the nature and date of the alleged violation of section 504. It shall be signed by the complainant or by someone authorized to do so on his or her behalf. Complaints filed on behalf of classes or third parties shall describe or identify (by name, if possible) the alleged victims of discrimination.

Facility means all or any portion of buildings, structures, equipment, roads, walks, parking lots, rolling stock or other conveyances, or other real or personal property.

Historic preservation programs means programs conducted by the agency that have preservation of historic properties as a primary purpose.

Historic properties means those properties that are listed or eligible for listing in the National Register of Historic Places or properties designated as historic under a statute of the appropriate State or local government body.

Individual with handicaps means any person who has a physical or mental impairment that substantially limits one or more major life activities, has a record of such an impairment, or is regarded as having such an impairment.

As used in this definition, the phrase:

(1) *Physical or mental impairment* includes—

(i) Any physiological disorder or condition, cosmetic disfigurement, or anatomical loss affecting one or more of the following body systems: Neurological; musculoskeletal; special sense organs; respiratory, including speech organs; cardiovascular; reproductive; digestive; genitourinary; hemic and lymphatic; skin; and endocrine; or

(ii) Any mental or psychological disorder, such as mental retardation, organic brain syndrome, emotional or mental illness, and specific learning disabilities. The term *physical or mental impairment* includes, but is not limited to, such diseases and conditions as orthopedic, visual, speech, and hearing impairments, cerebral palsy, epilepsy, muscular dystrophy, multiple sclerosis, cancer, heart disease, diabetes, mental retardation, emotional illness, and drug addiction and alcoholism.

(2) *Major life activities* includes functions such as caring for one's self, performing manual tasks, walking, seeing, hearing, speaking, breathing, learning, and working.

(3) *Has a record of such an impairment* means has a history of, or has been misclassified as having, a mental or physical impairment that substantially limits one or more major life activities.

(4) *Is regarded as having an impairment* means—

(i) Has a physical or mental impairment that does not substantially limit major life activities but is treated by the agency as constituting such a limitation;

(ii) Has a physical or mental impairment that substantially limits major life activities only as a result of the attitudes of others toward such impairment; or

(iii) Has none of the impairments defined in paragraph (1) of this definition but is treated by the agency as having such an impairment.

Qualified individual with handicaps means—

(1) With respect to preschool, elementary, or secondary education services provided by the agency, an individual with handicaps who is a member of a class of persons otherwise entitled by

statute, regulation, or agency policy to receive education services from the agency;

(2) With respect to any other agency program or activity under which a person is required to perform services or to achieve a level of accomplishment, an individual with handicaps who meets the essential eligibility requirements and who can achieve the purpose of the program or activity without modifications in the program or activity that the agency can demonstrate would result in a fundamental alteration in its nature;

(3) With respect to any other program or activity, an individual with handicaps who meets the essential eligibility requirements for participation in, or receipt of benefits from, that program or activity; and

(4) *Qualified handicapped person* as that term is defined for purposes of employment in 29 CFR 1613.702(f), which is made applicable to this regulation by §16.140.

Section 504 means section 504 of the Rehabilitation Act of 1973 (Pub. L. 93–112, 87 Stat. 394 (29 U.S.C. 794)), as amended by the Rehabilitation Act Amendments of 1974 (Pub. L. 93–516, 88 Stat. 1617); the Rehabilitation, Comprehensive Services, and Developmental Disabilities Amendments of 1978 (Pub. L. 95–602, 92 Stat. 2955); and the Rehabilitation Act Amendments of 1986 (Pub. L. 99–506, 100 Stat. 1810). As used in this regulation, section 504 applies only to programs or activities conducted by Executive agencies and not to federally assisted programs.

Substantial impairment means a significant loss of the integrity of finished materials, design quality, or special character resulting from a permanent alteration.

§§16.104–16.109 [Reserved]

§16.110 Self-evaluation.

(a) The agency shall, by September 6, 1989, evaluate its current policies and practices, and the effects thereof, that do not or may not meet the requirements of this regulation and, to the extent modification of any such policies and practices is required, the agency shall proceed to make the necessary modifications.

(b) The agency shall provide an opportunity to interested persons, including individuals with handicaps or organizations representing individuals with handicaps, to participate in the self-evaluation process by submitting comments (both oral and written).

(c) The agency shall, for at least three years following completion of the self-evaluation, maintain on file and make available for public inspection:

(1) A description of areas examined and any problems identified; and

(2) A description of any modifications made.

§16.111 Notice.

The agency shall make available to employees, applicants, participants, beneficiaries, and other interested persons such information regarding the provisions of this regulation and its applicability to the programs or activities conducted by the agency, and make such information available to them in such manner as the head of the agency finds necessary to apprise such persons of the protections against discrimination assured them by section 504 and this regulation.

§§16.112–16.129 [Reserved]

§16.130 General prohibitions against discrimination.

(a) No qualified individual with handicaps shall, on the basis of handicap, be excluded from participation in, be denied the benefits of, or otherwise be subjected to discrimination under any program or activity conducted by the agency.

(b)(1) The agency, in providing any aid, benefit, or service, may not, directly or through contractual, licensing, or other arrangements, on the basis of handicap—

(i) Deny a qualified individual with handicaps the opportunity to participate in or benefit from the aid, benefit, or service;

(ii) Afford a qualified individual with handicaps an opportunity to participate in or benefit from the aid, benefit, or service that is not equal to that afforded others;

(iii) Provide a qualified individual with handicaps with an aid, benefit, or service that is not as effective in affording equal opportunity to obtain the same result, to gain the same benefit, or to reach the same level of achievement as that provided to others;

(iv) Provide different or separate aid, benefits, or services to individuals with handicaps or to any class of individuals with handicaps than is provided to others unless such action is necessary to provide qualified individuals with handicaps with aid, benefits, or services that are as effective as those provided to others;

(v) Deny a qualified individual with handicaps the opportunity to participate as a member of planning or advisory boards;

(vi) Otherwise limit a qualified individual with handicaps in the enjoyment of any right, privilege, advantage, or opportunity enjoyed by others receiving the aid, benefit, or service.

(2) The agency may not deny a qualified individual with handicaps the opportunity to participate in programs or activities that are not separate or different, despite the existence of permissibly separate or different programs or activities.

(3) The agency may not, directly or through contractual or other arrangements, utilize criteria or methods of administration the purpose or effect of which would—

(i) Subject qualified individuals with handicaps to discrimination on the basis of handicap; or

(ii) Defeat or substantially impair accomplishment of the objectives of a program or activity with respect to individuals with handicaps.

(4) The agency may not, in determining the site or location of a facility, make selections the purpose or effect of which would—

(i) Exclude individuals with handicaps from, deny them the benefits of, or otherwise subject them to discrimination under any program or activity conducted by the agency; or

(ii) Defeat or substantially impair the accomplishment of the objectives of a program or activity with respect to individuals with handicaps.

(5) The agency, in the selection of procurement contractors, may not use criteria that subject qualified individuals with handicaps to discrimination on the basis of handicap.

(6) The agency may not administer a licensing or certification program in a manner that subjects qualified individuals with handicaps to discrimination on the basis of handicap, nor may the agency establish requirements for the programs or activities of licensees or certified entities that subject qualified individuals with handicaps to discrimination on the basis of handicap. However, the programs or activities of entities that are licensed or certified by the agency are not, themselves, covered by this regulation.

(c) The exclusion of nonhandicapped persons from the benefits of a program limited by Federal statute or Executive order to individuals with handicaps or the exclusion of a specific class of individuals with handicaps from a program limited by Federal statute or Executive order to a different class of individuals with handicaps is not prohibited by this regulation.

(d) The agency shall administer programs and activities in the most integrated setting appropriate to the needs of qualified individuals with handicaps.

§§ 16.131–16.139　[Reserved]

§ 16.140　Employment.

No qualified individual with handicaps shall, on the basis of handicap, be subject to discrimination in employment under any program or activity conducted by the agency. The definitions, requirements, and procedures of section 501 of the Rehabilitation Act of 1973 (29 U.S.C. 791), as established by the Equal Employment Opportunity Commission in 29 CFR part 1613, shall apply to employment in federally conducted programs or activities.

§§ 16.141–16.148　[Reserved]

§ 16.149　Program accessibility: Discrimination prohibited.

Except as otherwise provided in § 16.150, no qualified individual with handicaps shall, because the agency's facilities are inaccessible to or unusable by individuals with handicaps, be denied the benefits of, be excluded from participation in, or otherwise be subjected to discrimination under any program or activity conducted by the agency.

§16.150 Program accessibility: Existing facilities.

(a) *General.* The agency shall operate each program or activity so that the program or activity, when viewed in its entirety, is readily accessible to and usable by individuals with handicaps. This paragraph does not—

(1) Necessarily require the agency to make each of its existing facilities accessible to and usable by individuals with handicaps;

(2) In the case of historic preservation programs, require the agency to take any action that would result in a substantial impairment of significant historic features of an historic property; or

(3) Require the agency to take any action that it can demonstrate would result in a fundamental alteration in the nature of a program or activity or in undue financial and administrative burdens. In those circumstances where agency personnel believe that the proposed action would fundamentally alter the program or activity or would result in undue financial and administrative burdens, the agency has the burden of proving that compliance with §16.150(a) would result in such alteration or burdens. The decision that compliance would result in such alteration or burdens must be made by the agency head or his or her designee after considering all agency resources available for use in the funding and operation of the conducted program or activity, and must be accompanied by a written statement of the reasons for reaching that conclusion. If an action would result in such an alteration or such burdens, the agency shall take any other action that would not result in such an alteration or such burdens but would nevertheless ensure that individuals with handicaps receive the benefits and services of the program or activity.

(b) *Methods*—(1) *General.* The agency may comply with the requirements of this section through such means as redesign of equipment, reassignment of services to accessible buildings, assignment of aides to beneficiaries, home visits, delivery of services at alternate accessible sites, alteration of existing facilities and construction of new facilities, use of accessible rolling stock, or any other methods that result in making its programs or activities readily accessible to and usable by individuals with handicaps. The agency is not required to make structural changes in existing facilities where other methods are effective in achieving compliance with this section. The agency, in making alterations to existing buildings, shall meet accessibility requirements to the extent compelled by the Architectural Barriers Act of 1968, as amended (42 U.S.C. 4151 through 4157), and any regulations implementing it. In choosing among available methods for meeting the requirements of this section, the agency shall give priority to those methods that offer programs and activities to qualified individuals with handicaps in the most integrated setting appropriate.

(2) *Historic preservation programs.* In meeting the requirements of §16.150(a) in historic preservation programs, the agency shall give priority to methods that provide physical access to individuals with handicaps. In cases where a physical alteration to an historic property is not required because of §16.150(a) (2) or (3), alternative methods of achieving program accessibility include—

(i) Using audio-visual materials and devices to depict those portions of an historic property that cannot otherwise be made accessible;

(ii) Assigning persons to guide individuals with handicaps into or through portions of historic properties that cannot otherwise be made accessible; or

(iii) Adopting other innovative methods.

(c) *Time period for compliance.* The agency shall comply with the obligations established under this section by November 7, 1988, except that where structural changes in facilities are undertaken, such changes shall be made by September 6, 1991, but in any event as expeditiously as possible.

(d) *Transition plan.* In the event that structural changes to facilities will be undertaken to achieve program accessibility, the agency shall develop, by March 6, 1989, a transition plan setting forth the steps necessary to complete such changes. The agency shall provide an opportunity to interested persons, including individuals with handicaps or organizations representing individuals with handicaps, to participate in the development of the transition plan by submitting comments (both oral and written). A copy of the transition plan shall be made available for public inspection. The plan shall, at a minimum—

(1) Identify physical obstacles in the agency's facilities that limit the accessibility of its programs or activities to individuals with handicaps;

(2) Describe in detail the methods that will be used to make the facilities accessible;

(3) Specify the schedule for taking the steps necessary to achieve compliance with this section and, if the time period of the transition plan is longer than one year, identify steps that will be taken during each year of the transition period; and

(4) Indicate the official responsible for implementation of the plan.

§ 16.151 Program accessibility: New construction and alterations.

Each building or part of a building that is constructed or altered by, on behalf of, or for the use of the agency shall be designed, constructed, or altered so as to be readily accessible to and usable by individuals with handicaps. The definitions, requirements, and standards of the Architectural Barriers Act (42 U.S.C. 4151–4157), as established in 41 CFR 101–19.600 to 101–19.607, apply to buildings covered by this section.

§§ 16.152–16.159 [Reserved]

§ 16.160 Communications.

(a) The agency shall take appropriate steps to ensure effective communication with applicants, participants, personnel of other Federal entities, and members of the public.

(1) The agency shall furnish appropriate auxiliary aids where necessary to afford an individual with handicaps an equal opportunity to participate in, and enjoy the benefits of, a program or activity conducted by the agency.

(i) In determining what type of auxiliary aid is necessary, the agency shall give primary consideration to the requests of the individual with handicaps.

(ii) The agency need not provide individually prescribed devices, readers for personal use or study, or other devices of a personal nature.

(2) Where the agency communicates with applicants and beneficiaries by telephone, telecommunication devices for deaf persons (TDD's) or equally effective telecommunication systems shall be used to communicate with persons with impaired hearing.

(b) The agency shall ensure that interested persons, including persons with impaired vision or hearing, can obtain information as to the existence and location of accessible services, activities, and facilities.

(c) The agency shall provide signage at a primary entrance to each of its inaccessible facilities, directing users to a location at which they can obtain information about accessible facilities. The international symbol for accessibility shall be used at each primary entrance of an accessible facility.

(d) This section does not require the agency to take any action that it can demonstrate would result in a fundamental alteration in the nature of a program or activity or in undue financial and administrative burdens. In those circumstances where agency personnel believe that the proposed action would fundamentally alter the program or activity or would result in undue financial and administrative burdens, the agency has the burden of proving that compliance with § 16.160 would result in such alteration or burdens. The decision that compliance would result in such alteration or burdens must be made by the agency head or his or her designee after considering all agency resources available for use in the funding and operation of the conducted program or activity and must be accompanied by a written statement of the reasons for reaching that conclusion. If an action required to comply with this section would result in such an alteration or such burdens, the agency shall take any other action that would not result in such an alteration or such burdens but would nevertheless ensure that, to the maximum extent possible, individuals with handicaps receive the benefits and services of the program or activity.

§§ 16.161–16.169 [Reserved]

§ 16.170 Compliance procedures.

(a) Except as provided in paragraph (b) of this section, this section applies to all allegations of discrimination on the basis of handicap in programs and activities conducted by the agency.

(b) The agency shall process complaints alleging violations of section 504 with respect to employment according to the procedures established by the Equal Employment Opportunity Commission in 29 CFR part 1613 pursuant to section 501 of the Rehabilitation Act of 1973 (29 U.S.C. 791).

(c) The Director of the Office of Equal Rights shall be responsible for coordinating implementation of this section. Complaints may be sent to Director of the Office of Equal Rights, Room 810, Federal Emergency Management Agency, 500 C Street, SW., Washington, DC 20472.

(d) The agency shall accept and investigate all complete complaints for which it has jurisdiction. All complete complaints must be filed within 180 days of the alleged act of discrimination. The agency may extend this time period for good cause.

(e) If the agency receives a complaint over which it does not have jurisdiction, it shall promptly notify the complainant and shall make reasonable efforts to refer the complaint to the appropriate Government entity.

(f) The agency shall notify the Architectural and Transportation Barriers Compliance Board upon receipt of any complaint alleging that a building or facility that is subject to the Architectural Barriers Act of 1968, as amended (42 U.S.C. 4151–4157), is not readily accessible to and usable by individuals with handicaps.

(g) Within 180 days of the receipt of a complete complaint for which it has jurisdiction, the agency shall notify the complainant of the results of the investigation in a letter containing—

(1) Findings of fact and conclusions of law;

(2) A description of a remedy for each violation found; and

(3) A notice of the right to appeal.

(h) Appeals of the findings of fact and conclusions of law or remedies must be filed by the complainant within 90 days of receipt from the agency of the letter required by paragraph (g) of this section. The agency may extend this time for good cause.

(i) Timely appeals shall be accepted and processed by the head of the agency.

(j) The head of the agency shall notify the complainant of the results of the appeal within 60 days of the receipt of the request. If the head of the agency determines that additional information is needed from the complainant, he or she shall have 60 days from the date of receipt of the additional information to make his or her determination on the appeal.

(k) The time limits cited in paragraphs (g) and (j) of this section may be extended with the permission of the Assistant Attorney General.

(l) The agency may delegate its authority for conducting complaint investigations to other Federal agencies, except that the authority for making the final determination may not be delegated to another agency.

§§ 16.171–16.999 [Reserved]

PART 17 [RESERVED]

PART 18—NEW RESTRICTIONS ON LOBBYING

Subpart A—General

Subpart D—Penalties and Enforcement

18.400 Penalties.
18.405 Penalty procedures.
18.410 Enforcement.

Subpart E—Exemptions

18.500 Secretary of Defense.

Subpart F—Agency Reports

18.600 Semi-annual compilation.
18.605 Inspector General report.
APPENDIX A TO PART 18—CERTIFICATION RE-
GARDING LOBBYING
APPENDIX B TO PART 18—DISCLOSURE FORM
TO REPORT LOBBYING

AUTHORITY: Section 319, Public Law 101–121
(31 U.S.C. 1352); 5 U.S.C. 551, 552, 553; 5 U.S.C.
601, *et seq.;* E.O. 12291. Reorganization Plan
No. 3 of 1978, E.O. 12127, E.O. 12148, E.O. 12657,
E.O. 12699.

SOURCE: 55 FR 6737, 6754, Feb. 26, 1990, unless otherwise noted.

CROSS REFERENCE: See also Office of Management and Budget notice published at 54
FR 52306, December 20, 1989.

Subpart A—General

§ 18.100 Conditions on use of funds.

(a) No appropriated funds may be expended by the recipient of a Federal
contract, grant, loan, or cooperative
agreement to pay any person for influencing or attempting to influence an
officer or employee of any agency, a
Member of Congress, an officer or employee of Congress, or an employee of a
Member of Congress in connection with
any of the following covered Federal
actions: the awarding of any Federal
contract, the making of any Federal
grant, the making of any Federal loan,
the entering into of any cooperative
agreement, and the extension, continuation, renewal, amendment, or modification of any Federal contract, grant,
loan, or cooperative agreement.

(b) Each person who requests or receives from an agency a Federal contract, grant, loan, or cooperative
agreement shall file with that agency a
certification, set forth in appendix A,
that the person has not made, and will
not make, any payment prohibited by
paragraph (a) of this section.

(c) Each person who requests or receives from an agency a Federal contract, grant, loan, or a cooperative
agreement shall file with that agency a
disclosure form, set forth in appendix
B, if such person has made or has
agreed to make any payment using
nonappropriated funds (to include profits from any covered Federal action),
which would be prohibited under paragraph (a) of this section if paid for with
appropriated funds.

(d) Each person who requests or receives from an agency a commitment
providing for the United States to insure or guarantee a loan shall file with
that agency a statement, set forth in
appendix A, whether that person has
made or has agreed to make any payment to influence or attempt to influence an officer or employee of any
agency, a Member of Congress, an officer or employee of Congress, or an employee of a Member of Congress in connection with that loan insurance or
guarantee.

(e) Each person who requests or receives from an agency a commitment
providing for the United States to insure or guarantee a loan shall file with
that agency a disclosure form, set forth
in appendix B, if that person has made
or has agreed to make any payment to
influence or attempt to influence an officer or employee of any agency, a
Member of Congress, an officer or employee of Congress, or an employee of a
Member of Congress in connection with
that loan insurance or guarantee.

§ 18.105 Definitions.

For purposes of this part:

(a) *Agency*, as defined in 5 U.S.C.
552(f), includes Federal executive departments and agencies as well as independent regulatory commissions and
Government corporations, as defined in
31 U.S.C. 9101(1).

(b) *Covered Federal action* means any
of the following Federal actions:

(1) The awarding of any Federal contract;

(2) The making of any Federal grant;

(3) The making of any Federal loan;

(4) The entering into of any cooperative agreement; and,

(5) The extension, continuation, renewal, amendment, or modification of
any Federal contract, grant, loan, or
cooperative agreement.

Covered Federal action does not include receiving from an agency a commitment providing for the United States to insure or guarantee a loan. Loan guarantees and loan insurance are addressed independently within this part.

(c) *Federal contract* means an acquisition contract awarded by an agency, including those subject to the Federal Acquisition Regulation (FAR), and any other acquisition contract for real or personal property or services not subject to the FAR.

(d) *Federal cooperative agreement* means a cooperative agreement entered into by an agency.

(e) *Federal grant* means an award of financial assistance in the form of money, or property in lieu of money, by the Federal Government or a direct appropriation made by law to any person. The term does not include technical assistance which provides services instead of money, or other assistance in the form of revenue sharing, loans, loan guarantees, loan insurance, interest subsidies, insurance, or direct United States cash assistance to an individual.

(f) *Federal loan* means a loan made by an agency. The term does not include loan guarantee or loan insurance.

(g) *Indian tribe* and *tribal organization* have the meaning provided in section 4 of the Indian Self-Determination and Education Assistance Act (25 U.S.C. 450B). Alaskan Natives are included under the definitions of Indian tribes in that Act.

(h) *Influencing or attempting to influence* means making, with the intent to influence, any communication to or appearance before an officer or employee or any agency, a Member of Congress, an officer or employee of Congress, or an employee of a Member of Congress in connection with any covered Federal action.

(i) *Loan guarantee* and *loan insurance* means an agency's guarantee or insurance of a loan made by a person.

(j) *Local government* means a unit of government in a State and, if chartered, established, or otherwise recognized by a State for the performance of a governmental duty, including a local public authority, a special district, an intrastate district, a council of govern-

ments, a sponsor group representative organization, and any other instrumentality of a local government.

(k) *Officer or employee of an agency* includes the following individuals who are employed by an agency:

(1) An individual who is appointed to a position in the Government under title 5, U.S. Code, including a position under a temporary appointment;

(2) A member of the uniformed services as defined in section 101(3), title 37, U.S. Code;

(3) A special Government employee as defined in section 202, title 18, U.S. Code; and,

(4) An individual who is a member of a Federal advisory committee, as defined by the Federal Advisory Committee Act, title 5, U.S. Code appendix 2.

(l) *Person* means an individual, corporation, company, association, authority, firm, partnership, society, State, and local government, regardless of whether such entity is operated for profit or not for profit. This term excludes an Indian tribe, tribal organization, or any other Indian organization with respect to expenditures specifically permitted by other Federal law.

(m) *Reasonable compensation* means, with respect to a regularly employed officer or employee of any person, compensation that is consistent with the normal compensation for such officer or employee for work that is not furnished to, not funded by, or not furnished in cooperation with the Federal Government.

(n) *Reasonable payment* means, with respect to professional and other technical services, a payment in an amount that is consistent with the amount normally paid for such services in the private sector.

(o) *Recipient* includes all contractors, subcontractors at any tier, and subgrantees at any tier of the recipient of funds received in connection with a Federal contract, grant, loan, or cooperative agreement. The term excludes an Indian tribe, tribal organization, or any other Indian organization with respect to expenditures specifically permitted by other Federal law.

(p) *Regularly employed* means, with respect to an officer or employee of a

155

person requesting or receiving a Federal contract, grant, loan, or cooperative agreement or a commitment providing for the United States to insure or guarantee a loan, an officer or employee who is employed by such person for at least 130 working days within one year immediately preceding the date of the submission that initiates agency consideration of such person for receipt of such contract, grant, loan, cooperative agreement, loan insurance commitment, or loan guarantee commitment. An officer or employee who is employed by such person for less than 130 working days within one year immediately preceding the date of the submission that initiates agency consideration of such person shall be considered to be regularly employed as soon as he or she is employed by such person for 130 working days.

(q) *State* means a State of the United States, the District of Columbia, the Commonwealth of Puerto Rico, a territory or possession of the United States, an agency or instrumentality of a State, and a multi-State, regional, or interstate entity having governmental duties and powers.

§ 18.110 Certification and disclosure.

(a) Each person shall file a certification, and a disclosure form, if required, with each submission that initiates agency consideration of such person for:

(1) Award of a Federal contract, grant, or cooperative agreement exceeding $100,000; or

(2) An award of a Federal loan or a commitment providing for the United States to insure or guarantee a loan exceeding $150,000.

(b) Each person shall file a certification, and a disclosure form, if required, upon receipt by such person of:

(1) A Federal contract, grant, or cooperative agreement exceeding $100,000; or

(2) A Federal loan or a commitment providing for the United States to insure or guarantee a loan exceeding $150,000, unless such person previously filed a certification, and a disclosure form, if required, under paragraph (a) of this section.

(c) Each person shall file a disclosure form at the end of each calendar quarter in which there occurs any event that requires disclosure or that materially affects the accuracy of the information contained in any disclosure form previously filed by such person under paragraphs (a) or (b) of this section. An event that materially affects the accuracy of the information reported includes:

(1) A cumulative increase of $25,000 or more in the amount paid or expected to be paid for influencing or attempting to influence a covered Federal action; or

(2) A change in the person(s) or individual(s) influencing or attempting to influence a covered Federal action; or,

(3) A change in the officer(s), employee(s), or Member(s) contacted to influence or attempt to influence a covered Federal action.

(d) Any person who requests or receives from a person referred to in paragraphs (a) or (b) of this section:

(1) A subcontract exceeding $100,000 at any tier under a Federal contract;

(2) A subgrant, contract, or subcontract exceeding $100,000 at any tier under a Federal grant;

(3) A contract or subcontract exceeding $100,000 at any tier under a Federal loan exceeding $150,000; or,

(4) A contract or subcontract exceeding $100,000 at any tier under a Federal cooperative agreement,

shall file a certification, and a disclosure form, if required, to the next tier above.

(e) All disclosure forms, but not certifications, shall be forwarded from tier to tier until received by the person referred to in paragraphs (a) or (b) of this section. That person shall forward all disclosure forms to the agency.

(f) Any certification or disclosure form filed under paragraph (e) of this section shall be treated as a material representation of fact upon which all receiving tiers shall rely. All liability arising from an erroneous representation shall be borne solely by the tier filing that representation and shall not be shared by any tier to which the erroneous representation is forwarded. Submitting an erroneous certification or disclosure constitutes a failure to file the required certification or disclosure, respectively. If a person fails to file a required certification or disclosure, the United States may pursue all available remedies, including those authorized by section 1352, title 31, U.S. Code.

(g) For awards and commitments in process prior to December 23, 1989, but not made before that date, certifications shall be required at award or commitment, covering activities occurring between December 23, 1989, and the date of award or commitment. However, for awards and commitments in process prior to the December 23, 1989 effective date of these provisions, but not made before December 23, 1989, disclosure forms shall not be required at time of award or commitment but shall be filed within 30 days.

(h) No reporting is required for an activity paid for with appropriated funds if that activity is allowable under either subpart B or C.

Subpart B—Activities by Own Employees

§ 18.200 Agency and legislative liaison.

(a) The prohibition on the use of appropriated funds, in § 18.100 (a), does not apply in the case of a payment of reasonable compensation made to an officer or employee of a person requesting or receiving a Federal contract, grant, loan, or cooperative agreement if the payment is for agency and legislative liaison activities not directly related to a covered Federal action.

(b) For purposes of paragraph (a) of this section, providing any information specifically requested by an agency or Congress is allowable at any time.

(c) For purposes of paragraph (a) of this section, the following agency and legislative liaison activities are allowable at any time only where they are not related to a specific solicitation for any covered Federal action:

(1) Discussing with an agency (including individual demonstrations) the qualities and characteristics of the person's products or services, conditions or terms of sale, and service capabilities; and,

(2) Technical discussions and other activities regarding the application or adaptation of the person's products or services for an agency's use.

(d) For purposes of paragraph (a) of this section, the following agencies and legislative liaison activities are allowable only where they are prior to formal solicitation of any covered Federal action:

(1) Providing any information not specifically requested but necessary for an agency to make an informed decision about initiation of a covered Federal action;

(2) Technical discussions regarding the preparation of an unsolicited proposal prior to its official submission; and,

(3) Capability presentations by persons seeking awards from an agency pursuant to the provisions of the Small Business Act, as amended by Public Law 95–507 and other subsequent amendments.

(e) Only those activities expressly authorized by this section are allowable under this section.

§ 18.205 Professional and technical services.

(a) The prohibition on the use of appropriated funds, in § 18.100 (a), does not apply in the case of a payment of reasonable compensation made to an officer or employee of a person requesting or receiving a Federal contract, grant, loan, or cooperative agreement or an extension, continuation, renewal, amendment, or modification of a Federal contract, grant, loan, or cooperative agreement if payment is for professional or technical services rendered directly in the preparation, submission, or negotiation of any bid, proposal, or application for that Federal contract, grant, loan, or cooperative agreement or for meeting requirements imposed by or pursuant to law as a condition for receiving that Federal contract, grant, loan, or cooperative agreement.

(b) For purposes of paragraph (a) of this section, "professional and technical services" shall be limited to advice and analysis directly applying any professional or technical discipline. For example, drafting of a legal document accompanying a bid or proposal by a lawyer is allowable. Similarly, technical advice provided by an engineer on the performance or operational

157

capability of a piece of equipment rendered directly in the negotiation of a contract is allowable. However, communications with the intent to influence made by a professional (such as a licensed lawyer) or a technical person (such as a licensed accountant) are not allowable under this section unless they provide advice and analysis directly applying their professional or technical expertise and unless the advice or analysis is rendered directly and solely in the preparation, submission or negotiation of a covered Federal action. Thus, for example, communications with the intent to influence made by a lawyer that do not provide legal advice or analysis directly and solely related to the legal aspects of his or her client's proposal, but generally advocate one proposal over another are not allowable under this section because the lawyer is not providing professional legal services. Similarly, communications with the intent to influence made by an engineer providing an engineering analysis prior to the preparation or submission of a bid or proposal are not allowable under this section since the engineer is providing technical services but not directly in the preparation, submission or negotiation of a covered Federal action.

(c) Requirements imposed by or pursuant to law as a condition for receiving a covered Federal award include those required by law or regulation, or reasonably expected to be required by law or regulation, and any other requirements in the actual award documents.

(d) Only those services expressly authorized by this section are allowable under this section.

§ 18.210   Reporting.

No reporting is required with respect to payments of reasonable compensation made to regularly employed officers or employees of a person.

Subpart C—Activities by Other Than Own Employees

§ 18.300   Professional and technical services.

(a) The prohibition on the use of appropriated funds, in § 18.100 (a), does not apply in the case of any reasonable payment to a person, other than an officer or employee of a person requesting or receiving a covered Federal action, if the payment is for professional or technical services rendered directly in the preparation, submission, or negotiation of any bid, proposal, or application for that Federal contract, grant, loan, or cooperative agreement or for meeting requirements imposed by or pursuant to law as a condition for receiving that Federal contract, grant, loan, or cooperative agreement.

(b) The reporting requirements in § 18.110 (a) and (b) regarding filing a disclosure form by each person, if required, shall not apply with respect to professional or technical services rendered directly in the preparation, submission, or negotiation of any commitment providing for the United States to insure or guarantee a loan.

(c) For purposes of paragraph (a) of this section, "professional and technical services" shall be limited to advice and analysis directly applying any professional or technical discipline. For example, drafting or a legal document accompanying a bid or proposal by a lawyer is allowable. Similarly, technical advice provided by an engineer on the performance or operational capability of a piece of equipment rendered directly in the negotiation of a contract is allowable. However, communications with the intent to influence made by a professional (such as a licensed lawyer) or a technical person (such as a licensed accountant) are not allowable under this section unless they provide advice and analysis directly applying their professional or technical expertise and unless the advice or analysis is rendered directly and solely in the preparation, submission or negotiation of a covered Federal action. Thus, for example, communications with the intent to influence made by a lawyer that do not provide legal advice or analysis directly and solely related to the legal aspects of his or her client's proposal, but generally advocate one proposal over another are not allowable under this section because the lawyer is not providing professional legal services. Similarly, communications with the intent to influence made by an engineer providing an engineering analysis prior to the preparation or submission of a bid or proposal are not allowable under this section since the engineer is providing technical services but not directly in the preparation, submission or negotiation of a covered Federal action.

(d) Requirements imposed by or pursuant to law as a condition for receiving a covered Federal award include those required by law or regulation, or reasonably expected to be required by law or regulation, and any other requirements in the actual award documents.

(e) Persons other than officers or employees of a person requesting or receiving a covered Federal action include consultants and trade associations.

(f) Only those services expressly authorized by this section are allowable under this section.

Subpart D—Penalties and Enforcement

§ 18.400 Penalties.

(a) Any person who makes an expenditure prohibited herein shall be subject to a civil penalty of not less than $10,000 and not more than $100,000 for each such expenditure.

(b) Any person who fails to file or amend the disclosure form (see appendix B) to be filed or amended if required herein, shall be subject to a civil penalty of not less than $10,000 and not more than $100,000 for each such failure.

(c) A filing or amended filing on or after the date on which an administrative action for the imposition of a civil penalty is commenced does not prevent the imposition of such civil penalty for a failure occurring before that date. An administrative action is commenced with respect to a failure when an investigating official determines in writing to commence an investigation of an allegation of such failure.

(d) In determining whether to impose a civil penalty, and the amount of any such penalty, by reason of a violation by any person, the agency shall consider the nature, circumstances, extent, and gravity of the violation, the

effect on the ability of such person to continue in business, any prior violations by such person, the degree of culpability of such person, the ability of the person to pay the penalty, and such other matters as may be appropriate.

(e) First offenders under paragraphs (a) or (b) of this section shall be subject to a civil penalty of $10,000, absent aggravating circumstances. Second and subsequent offenses by persons shall be subject to an appropriate civil penalty between $10,000 and $100,000, as determined by the agency head or his or her designee.

(f) An imposition of a civil penalty under this section does not prevent the United States from seeking any other remedy that may apply to the same conduct that is the basis for the imposition of such civil penalty.

§ 18.405 Penalty procedures.

Agencies shall impose and collect civil penalties pursuant to the provisions of the Program Fraud and Civil Remedies Act, 31 U.S.C. 3803 (except subsection (c)), 3804, 3805, 3806, 3807, 3808, and 3812, insofar as these provisions are not inconsistent with the requirements herein.

§ 18.410 Enforcement.

The head of each agency shall take such actions as are necessary to ensure that the provisions herein are vigorously implemented and enforced in that agency.

Subpart E—Exemptions

§ 18.500 Secretary of Defense.

(a) The Secretary of Defense may exempt, on a case-by-case basis, a covered Federal action from the prohibition whenever the Secretary determines, in writing, that such an exemption is in the national interest. The Secretary shall transmit a copy of each such written exemption to Congress immediately after making such a determination.

(b) The Department of Defense may issue supplemental regulations to implement paragraph (a) of this section.

Subpart F—Agency Reports

§ 18.600 Semi-annual compilation.

(a) The head of each agency shall collect and compile the disclosure reports (see appendix B) and, on May 31 and November 30 of each year, submit to the Secretary of the Senate and the Clerk of the House of Representatives a report containing a compilation of the information contained in the disclosure reports received during the six-month period ending on March 31 or September 30, respectively, of that year.

(b) The report, including the compilation, shall be available for public inspection 30 days after receipt of the report by the Secretary and the Clerk.

(c) Information that involves intelligence matters shall be reported only to the Select Committee on Intelligence of the Senate, the Permanent Select Committee on Intelligence of the House of Representatives, and the Committees on Appropriations of the Senate and the House of Representatives in accordance with procedures agreed to by such committees. Such information shall not be available for public inspection.

(d) Information that is classified under Executive Order 12356 or any successor order shall be reported only to the Committee on Foreign Relations of the Senate and the Committee on Foreign Affairs of the House of Representatives or the Committees on Armed Services of the Senate and the House of Representatives (whichever such committees have jurisdiction of matters involving such information) and to the Committees on Appropriations of the Senate and the House of Representatives in accordance with procedures agreed to by such committees. Such information shall not be available for public inspection.

(e) The first semi-annual compilation shall be submitted on May 31, 1990, and shall contain a compilation of the disclosure reports received from December 23, 1989 to March 31, 1990.

(f) Major agencies, designated by the Office of Management and Budget (OMB), are required to provide machine-readable compilations to the Secretary of the Senate and the Clerk of the House of Representatives no later than with the compilations due on May 31, 1991. OMB shall provide detailed specifications in a memorandum to these agencies.

(g) Non-major agencies are requested to provide machine-readable compilations to the Secretary of the Senate and the Clerk of the House of Representatives.

(h) Agencies shall keep the originals of all disclosure reports in the official files of the agency.

§ 18.605 Inspector General report.

(a) The Inspector General, or other official as specified in paragraph (b) of this section, of each agency shall prepare and submit to Congress each year, commencing with submission of the President's Budget in 1991, an evaluation of the compliance of that agency with, and the effectiveness of, the requirements herein. The evaluation may include any recommended changes that may be necessary to strengthen or improve the requirements.

(b) In the case of an agency that does not have an Inspector General, the agency official comparable to an Inspector General shall prepare and submit the annual report, or, if there is no such comparable official, the head of the agency shall prepare and submit the annual report.

(c) The annual report shall be submitted at the same time the agency submits its annual budget justifications to Congress.

(d) The annual report shall include the following: All alleged violations relating to the agency's covered Federal actions during the year covered by the report, the actions taken by the head of the agency in the year covered by the report with respect to those alleged violations and alleged violations in previous years, and the amounts of civil penalties imposed by the agency in the year covered by the report.

APPENDIX A TO PART 18—CERTIFICATION REGARDING LOBBYING

CERTIFICATION FOR CONTRACTS, GRANTS, LOANS, AND COOPERATIVE AGREEMENTS

The undersigned certifies, to the best of his or her knowledge and belief, that:

(1) No Federal appropriated funds have been paid or will be paid, by or on behalf of

the undersigned, to any person for influencing or attempting to influence an officer or employee of an agency, a Member of Congress, an officer or employee of Congress, or an employee of a Member of Congress in connection with the awarding of any Federal contract, the making of any Federal grant, the making of any Federal loan, the entering into of any cooperative agreement, and the extension, continuation, renewal, amendment, or modification of any Federal contract, grant, loan, or cooperative agreement.

(2) If any funds other than Federal appropriated funds have been paid or will be paid to any person for influencing or attempting to influence an officer or employee of any agency, a Member of Congress, an officer or employee of Congress, or an employee of a Member of Congress in connection with this Federal contract, grant, loan, or cooperative agreement, the undersigned shall complete and submit Standard Form-LLL, "Disclosure Form to Report Lobbying," in accordance with its instructions.

(3) The undersigned shall require that the language of this certification be included in the award documents for all subawards at all tiers (including subcontracts, subgrants, and contracts under grants, loans, and cooperative agreements) and that all subrecipients shall certify and disclose accordingly.

This certification is a material representation of fact upon which reliance was placed when this transaction was made or entered into. Submission of this certification is a prerequisite for making or entering into this transaction imposed by section 1352, title 31, U.S. Code. Any person who fails to file the required certification shall be subject to a civil penalty of not less than $10,000 and not more than $100,000 for each such failure.

STATEMENT FOR LOAN GUARANTEES AND LOAN INSURANCE

The undersigned states, to the best of his or her knowledge and belief, that:

If any funds have been paid or will be paid to any person for influencing or attempting to influence an officer or employee of any agency, a Member of Congress, an officer or employee of Congress, or an employee of a Member of Congress in connection with this commitment providing for the United States to insure or guarantee a loan, the undersigned shall complete and submit Standard Form-LLL, "Disclosure Form to Report Lobbying," in accordance with its instructions.

Submission of this statement is a prerequisite for making or entering into this transaction imposed by section 1352, title 31, U.S. Code. Any person who fails to file the required statement shall be subject to a civil penalty of not less than $10,000 and not more than $100,000 for each such failure.

APPENDIX B TO PART 18—DISCLOSURE FORM TO REPORT LOBBYING

DISCLOSURE OF LOBBYING ACTIVITIES

Approved by OMB
0348-0046

Complete this form to disclose lobbying activities pursuant to 31 U.S.C. 1352
(See reverse for public burden disclosure.)

1. Type of Federal Action:	2. Status of Federal Action:	3. Report Type:
☐ a. contract b. grant c. cooperative agreement d. loan e. loan guarantee f. loan insurance	☐ a. bid/offer/application b. initial award c. post-award	☐ a. initial filing b. material change **For Material Change Only:** year _____ quarter _____ date of last report _____

4. Name and Address of Reporting Entity: ☐ Prime ☐ Subawardee Tier _____ , if known: Congressional District, if known:	5. If Reporting Entity in No. 4 is Subawardee, Enter Name and Address of Prime: Congressional District, if known:
6. Federal Department/Agency:	7. Federal Program Name/Description: CFDA Number, if applicable: _____
8. Federal Action Number, if known:	9. Award Amount, if known: $
10. a. Name and Address of Lobbying Entity (if individual, last name, first name, MI):	b. Individuals Performing Services (including address if different from No. 10a) (last name, first name, MI):

(attach Continuation Sheet(s) SF-LLL-A, if necessary)

11. Amount of Payment (check all that apply): $ _____ ☐ actual ☐ planned 12. Form of Payment (check all that apply): ☐ a. cash ☐ b. in-kind; specify: nature _____ value _____	13. Type of Payment (check all that apply): ☐ a. retainer ☐ b. one-time fee ☐ c. commission ☐ d. contingent fee ☐ e. deferred ☐ f. other; specify: _____

14. Brief Description of Services Performed or to be Performed and Date(s) of Service, including officer(s), employee(s), or Member(s) contacted, for Payment Indicated in Item 11:

(attach Continuation Sheet(s) SF-LLL-A, if necessary)

15. Continuation Sheet(s) SF-LLL-A attached: ☐ Yes   ☐ No

16. Information requested through this form is authorized by title 31 U.S.C. section 1352. This disclosure of lobbying activities is a material representation of fact upon which reliance was placed by the tier above when this transaction was made or entered into. This disclosure is required pursuant to 31 U.S.C. 1352. This information will be reported to the Congress semi-annually and will be available for public inspection. Any person who fails to file the required disclosure shall be subject to a civil penalty of not less than $10,000 and not more than $100,000 for each such failure.	Signature: _____ Print Name: _____ Title: _____ Telephone No.: _____ Date: _____
Federal Use Only:	Authorized for Local Reproduction Standard Form - LLL

162

INSTRUCTIONS FOR COMPLETION OF SF-LLL, DISCLOSURE OF LOBBYING ACTIVITIES

This disclosure form shall be completed by the reporting entity, whether subawardee or prime Federal recipient, at the initiation or receipt of a covered Federal action, or a material change to a previous filing, pursuant to title 31 U.S.C. section 1352. The filing of a form is required for each payment or agreement to make payment to any lobbying entity for influencing or attempting to influence an officer or employee of any agency, a Member of Congress, an officer or employee of Congress, or an employee of a Member of Congress in connection with a covered Federal action. Use the SF-LLL-A Continuation Sheet for additional information if the space on the form is inadequate. Complete all items that apply for both the initial filing and material change report. Refer to the implementing guidance published by the Office of Management and Budget for additional information.

1. Identify the type of covered Federal action for which lobbying activity is and/or has been secured to influence the outcome of a covered Federal action.

2. Identify the status of the covered Federal action.

3. Identify the appropriate classification of this report. If this is a followup report caused by a material change to the information previously reported, enter the year and quarter in which the change occurred. Enter the date of the last previously submitted report by this reporting entity for this covered Federal action.

4. Enter the full name, address, city, state and zip code of the reporting entity. Include Congressional District, if known. Check the appropriate classification of the reporting entity that designates if it is, or expects to be, a prime or subaward recipient. Identify the tier of the subawardee, e.g., the first subawardee of the prime is the 1st tier. Subawards include but are not limited to subcontracts, subgrants and contract awards under grants.

5. If the organization filing the report in item 4 checks "Subawardee", then enter the full name, address, city, state and zip code of the prime Federal recipient. Include Congressional District, if known.

6. Enter the name of the Federal agency making the award or loan commitment. Include at least one organizational level below agency name, if known. For example, Department of Transportation, United States Coast Guard.

7. Enter the Federal program name or description for the covered Federal action (item 1). If known, enter the full Catalog of Federal Domestic Assistance (CFDA) number for grants, cooperative agreements, loans, and loan commitments.

8. Enter the most appropriate Federal identifying number available for the Federal action identified in item 1 (e.g., Request for Proposal (RFP) number; Invitation for Bid (IFB) number; grant announcement number; the contract, grant, or loan award number; the application/proposal control number assigned by the Federal agency). Include prefixes, e.g., "RFP-DE-90-001."

9. For a covered Federal action where there has been an award or loan commitment by the Federal agency, enter the Federal amount of the award/loan commitment for the prime entity identified in item 4 or 5.

10. (a) Enter the full name, address, city, state and zip code of the lobbying entity engaged by the reporting entity identified in item 4 to influence the covered Federal action.

    (b) Enter the full names of the individual(s) performing services, and include full address if different from 10 (a). Enter Last Name, First Name, and Middle Initial (MI).

11. Enter the amount of compensation paid or reasonably expected to be paid by the reporting entity (item 4) to the lobbying entity (item 10). Indicate whether the payment has been made (actual) or will be made (planned). Check all boxes that apply. If this is a material change report, enter the cumulative amount of payment made or planned to be made.

12. Check the appropriate box(es). Check all boxes that apply. If payment is made through an in-kind contribution, specify the nature and value of the in-kind payment.

13. Check the appropriate box(es). Check all boxes that apply. If other, specify nature.

14. Provide a specific and detailed description of the services that the lobbyist has performed, or will be expected to perform, and the date(s) of any services rendered. Include all preparatory and related activity, not just time spent in actual contact with Federal officials. Identify the Federal official(s) or employee(s) contacted or the officer(s), employee(s), or Member(s) of Congress that were contacted.

15. Check whether or not a SF-LLL-A Continuation Sheet(s) is attached.

16. The certifying official shall sign and date the form, print his/her name, title, and telephone number.

Public reporting burden for this collection of information is estimated to average 30 mintues per response, including time for reviewing instructions, searching existing data sources, gathering and maintaining the data needed, and completing and reviewing the collection of information. Send comments regarding the burden estimate or any other aspect of this collection of information, including suggestions for reducing this burden, to the Office of Management and Budget, Paperwork Reduction Project (0348-0046), Washington, D.C. 20503.

DISCLOSURE OF LOBBYING ACTIVITIES
CONTINUATION SHEET

Approved by OMB
0348-0046

Reporting Entity: _____ Page _____ of _____

Authorized for Local Reproduction
Standard Form - LLL-A

PART 19—NONDISCRIMINATION ON THE BASIS OF SEX IN EDUCATION PROGRAMS OR ACTIVITIES RECEIVING FEDERAL FINANCIAL ASSISTANCE

AUTHORITY: 20 U.S.C. 1681, 1682, 1683, 1685, 1686, 1687, 1688.

SOURCE: 65 FR 52865, 52892, Aug. 30, 2000, unless otherwise noted.

Subpart A—Introduction

§ 19.100 Purpose and effective date.

The purpose of these Title IX regulations is to effectuate Title IX of the Education Amendments of 1972, as amended (except sections 904 and 906 of those Amendments) (20 U.S.C. 1681, 1682, 1683, 1685, 1686, 1687, 1688), which is designed to eliminate (with certain exceptions) discrimination on the basis of sex in any education program or activity receiving Federal financial assistance, whether or not such program or activity is offered or sponsored by an educational institution as defined in these Title IX regulations. The effective date of these Title IX regulations shall be September 29, 2000.

§ 19.105 Definitions.

As used in these Title IX regulations, the term:

Administratively separate unit means a school, department, or college of an educational institution (other than a local educational agency) admission to which is independent of admission to any other component of such institution.

Admission means selection for part-time, full-time, special, associate, transfer, exchange, or any other enrollment, membership, or matriculation in or at an education program or activity operated by a recipient.

Applicant means one who submits an application, request, or plan required to be approved by an official of the Federal agency that awards Federal financial assistance, or by a recipient, as a condition to becoming a recipient.

Designated agency official means Director, Office of Equal Rights.

Educational institution means a local educational agency (LEA) as defined by 20 U.S.C. 8801(18), a preschool, a private elementary or secondary school, or an applicant or recipient that is an institution of graduate higher education, an institution of undergraduate higher education, an institution of professional education, or an institution of vocational education, as defined in this section.

Federal financial assistance means any of the following, when authorized or extended under a law administered by the Federal agency that awards such assistance:

(1) A grant or loan of Federal financial assistance, including funds made available for:

(i) The acquisition, construction, renovation, restoration, or repair of a building or facility or any portion thereof; and

(ii) Scholarships, loans, grants, wages, or other funds extended to any entity for payment to or on behalf of students admitted to that entity, or extended directly to such students for payment to that entity.

(2) A grant of Federal real or personal property or any interest therein, including surplus property, and the proceeds of the sale or transfer of such property, if the Federal share of the fair market value of the property is not, upon such sale or transfer, properly accounted for to the Federal Government.

(3) Provision of the services of Federal personnel.

(4) Sale or lease of Federal property or any interest therein at nominal consideration, or at consideration reduced for the purpose of assisting the recipient or in recognition of public interest to be served thereby, or permission to use Federal property or any interest therein without consideration.

(5) Any other contract, agreement, or arrangement that has as one of its purposes the provision of assistance to any education program or activity, except a contract of insurance or guaranty.

Institution of graduate higher education means an institution that:

(1) Offers academic study beyond the bachelor of arts or bachelor of science degree, whether or not leading to a certificate of any higher degree in the liberal arts and sciences;

(2) Awards any degree in a professional field beyond the first professional degree (regardless of whether the first professional degree in such field is awarded by an institution of undergraduate higher education or professional education); or

(3) Awards no degree and offers no further academic study, but operates ordinarily for the purpose of facilitating research by persons who have received the highest graduate degree in any field of study.

Institution of professional education means an institution (except any institution of undergraduate higher education) that offers a program of academic study that leads to a first professional degree in a field for which there is a national specialized accrediting agency recognized by the Secretary of Education.

Institution of undergraduate higher education means:

(1) An institution offering at least two but less than four years of college-level study beyond the high school level, leading to a diploma or an associate degree, or wholly or principally creditable toward a baccalaureate degree; or

(2) An institution offering academic study leading to a baccalaureate degree; or

(3) An agency or body that certifies credentials or offers degrees, but that may or may not offer academic study.

Institution of vocational education means a school or institution (except an institution of professional or graduate or undergraduate higher education) that has as its primary purpose preparation of students to pursue a technical, skilled, or semiskilled occupation or trade, or to pursue study in a technical field, whether or not the school or institution offers certificates, diplomas, or degrees and whether or not it offers full-time study.

Recipient means any State or political subdivision thereof, or any instrumentality of a State or political subdivision thereof, any public or private agency, institution, or organization, or other entity, or any person, to whom Federal financial assistance is extended directly or through another recipient and that operates an education program or activity that receives such assistance, including any subunit, successor, assignee, or transferee thereof.

Student means a person who has gained admission.

Title IX means Title IX of the Education Amendments of 1972, Public Law 92–318, 86 Stat. 235, 373 (codified as amended at 20 U.S.C. 1681–1688) (except sections 904 and 906 thereof), as amended by section 3 of Public Law 93–568, 88 Stat. 1855, by section 412 of the Education Amendments of 1976, Public Law 94–482, 90 Stat. 2234, and by Section 3 of Public Law 100–259, 102 Stat. 28, 28–29 (20 U.S.C. 1681, 1682, 1683, 1685, 1686, 1687, 1688).

Title IX regulations means the provisions set forth at §§ 19.100 through 19.605.

Transition plan means a plan subject to the approval of the Secretary of Education pursuant to section 901(a)(2) of the Education Amendments of 1972, 20 U.S.C. 1681(a)(2), under which an educational institution operates in making the transition from being an educational institution that admits only students of one sex to being one that admits students of both sexes without discrimination.

§ 19.110 Remedial and affirmative action and self-evaluation.

(a) *Remedial action.* If the designated agency official finds that a recipient has discriminated against persons on the basis of sex in an education program or activity, such recipient shall take such remedial action as the designated agency official deems necessary to overcome the effects of such discrimination.

(b) *Affirmative action.* In the absence of a finding of discrimination on the basis of sex in an education program or activity, a recipient may take affirmative action consistent with law to overcome the effects of conditions that resulted in limited participation therein by persons of a particular sex. Nothing in these Title IX regulations shall be interpreted to alter any affirmative action obligations that a recipient may have under Executive Order 11246, 3 CFR, 1964–1965 Comp., p. 339; as amended by Executive Order 11375, 3 CFR, 1966–1970 Comp., p. 684; as amended by Executive Order 11478, 3 CFR, 1966–1970 Comp., p. 803; as amended by Executive Order 12086, 3 CFR, 1978 Comp., p. 230; as amended by Executive Order 12107, 3 CFR, 1978 Comp., p. 264.

(c) *Self-evaluation.* Each recipient education institution shall, within one year of September 29, 2000:

(1) Evaluate, in terms of the requirements of these Title IX regulations, its current policies and practices and the effects thereof concerning admission of students, treatment of students, and employment of both academic and non-academic personnel working in connection with the recipient's education program or activity;

(2) Modify any of these policies and practices that do not or may not meet the requirements of these Title IX regulations; and

(3) Take appropriate remedial steps to eliminate the effects of any discrimination that resulted or may have resulted from adherence to these policies and practices.

(d) *Availability of self-evaluation and related materials.* Recipients shall maintain on file for at least three years following completion of the evaluation required under paragraph (c) of this section, and shall provide to the designated agency official upon request, a description of any modifications made pursuant to paragraph (c)(2) of this section and of any remedial steps taken pursuant to paragraph (c)(3) of this section.

§ 19.115 Assurance required.

(a) *General.* Either at the application stage or the award stage, Federal agencies must ensure that applications for Federal financial assistance or awards of Federal financial assistance contain, be accompanied by, or be covered by a specifically identified assurance from the applicant or recipient, satisfactory to the designated agency official, that each education program or activity operated by the applicant or recipient and to which these Title IX regulations apply will be operated in compliance with these Title IX regulations. An assurance of compliance with these Title IX regulations shall not be satisfactory to the designated agency official if the applicant or recipient to whom such assurance applies fails to commit itself to take whatever remedial action is necessary in accordance with § 19.110(a) to eliminate existing discrimination on the basis of sex or to eliminate the effects of past discrimination whether occurring prior to or subsequent to the submission to the designated agency official of such assurance.

(b) *Duration of obligation.* (1) In the case of Federal financial assistance extended to provide real property or structures thereon, such assurance shall obligate the recipient or, in the case of a subsequent transfer, the transferee, for the period during which the real property or structures are used to provide an education program or activity.

(2) In the case of Federal financial assistance extended to provide personal property, such assurance shall obligate the recipient for the period during which it retains ownership or possession of the property.

(3) In all other cases such assurance shall obligate the recipient for the period during which Federal financial assistance is extended.

(c) *Form.* (1) The assurances required by paragraph (a) of this section, which may be included as part of a document that addresses other assurances or obligations, shall include that the applicant or recipient will comply with all applicable Federal statutes relating to nondiscrimination. These include but are not limited to: Title IX of the Education Amendments of 1972, as amended (20 U.S.C. 1681–1683, 1685–1688).

(2) The designated agency official will specify the extent to which such assurances will be required of the applicant's or recipient's subgrantees, contractors, subcontractors, transferees, or successors in interest.

§ 19.120 Transfers of property.

If a recipient sells or otherwise transfers property financed in whole or in part with Federal financial assistance to a transferee that operates any education program or activity, and the Federal share of the fair market value of the property is not upon such sale or transfer properly accounted for to the Federal Government, both the transferor and the transferee shall be deemed to be recipients, subject to the provisions of §§ 19.205 through 19.235(a).

§ 19.125 Effect of other requirements.

(a) *Effect of other Federal provisions.* The obligations imposed by these Title IX regulations are independent of, and do not alter, obligations not to discriminate on the basis of sex imposed by Executive Order 11246, 3 CFR, 1964–1965 Comp., p. 339; as amended by Executive Order 11375, 3 CFR, 1966–1970 Comp., p. 684; as amended by Executive Order 11478, 3 CFR, 1966–1970 Comp., p. 803; as amended by Executive Order 12087, 3 CFR, 1978 Comp., p. 230; as amended by Executive Order 12107, 3 CFR, 1978 Comp., p. 264; sections 704 and 855 of the Public Health Service Act (42 U.S.C. 295m, 298b-2); Title VII of the Civil Rights Act of 1964 (42 U.S.C. 2000e *et seq.*); the Equal Pay Act of 1963 (29 U.S.C. 206); and any other Act of Congress or Federal regulation.

(b) *Effect of State or local law or other requirements.* The obligation to comply with these Title IX regulations is not obviated or alleviated by any State or local law or other requirement that would render any applicant or student ineligible, or limit the eligibility of any applicant or student, on the basis of sex, to practice any occupation or profession.

(c) *Effect of rules or regulations of private organizations.* The obligation to comply with these Title IX regulations is not obviated or alleviated by any rule or regulation of any organization, club, athletic or other league, or association that would render any applicant or student ineligible to participate or limit the eligibility or participation of any applicant or student, on the basis of sex, in any education program or activity operated by a recipient and that receives Federal financial assistance.

§19.130 Effect of employment opportunities.

The obligation to comply with these Title IX regulations is not obviated or alleviated because employment opportunities in any occupation or profession are or may be more limited for members of one sex than for members of the other sex.

§19.135 Designation of responsible employee and adoption of grievance procedures.

(a) *Designation of responsible employee.* Each recipient shall designate at least one employee to coordinate its efforts to comply with and carry out its responsibilities under these Title IX regulations, including any investigation of any complaint communicated to such recipient alleging its noncompliance with these Title IX regulations or alleging any actions that would be prohibited by these Title IX regulations. The recipient shall notify all its students and employees of the name, office address, and telephone number of the employee or employees appointed pursuant to this paragraph.

(b) *Complaint procedure of recipient.* A recipient shall adopt and publish grievance procedures providing for prompt and equitable resolution of student and employee complaints alleging any action that would be prohibited by these Title IX regulations.

§19.140 Dissemination of policy.

(a) *Notification of policy.* (1) Each recipient shall implement specific and continuing steps to notify applicants for admission and employment, students and parents of elementary and secondary school students, employees, sources of referral of applicants for admission and employment, and all unions or professional organizations holding collective bargaining or professional agreements with the recipient, that it does not discriminate on the basis of sex in the educational programs or activities that it operates, and that it is required by Title IX and these Title IX regulations not to discriminate in such a manner. Such notification shall contain such information, and be made in such manner, as the designated agency official finds necessary to apprise such persons of the protections against discrimination assured them by Title IX and these Title IX regulations, but shall state at least that the requirement not to discriminate in education programs or activities extends to employment therein, and to admission thereto unless §§19.300 through 19.310 do not apply to the recipient, and that inquiries concerning the application of Title IX and these Title IX regulations to such recipient may be referred to the employee designated pursuant to §19.135, or to the designated agency official.

(2) Each recipient shall make the initial notification required by paragraph (a)(1) of this section within 90 days of September 29, 2000 or of the date these Title IX regulations first apply to such recipient, whichever comes later, which notification shall include publication in:

(i) Newspapers and magazines operated by such recipient or by student, alumnae, or alumni groups for or in connection with such recipient; and

(ii) Memoranda or other written communications distributed to every student and employee of such recipient.

(b) *Publications.* (1) Each recipient shall prominently include a statement of the policy described in paragraph (a) of this section in each announcement, bulletin, catalog, or application form that it makes available to any person of a type, described in paragraph (a) of this section, or which is otherwise used in connection with the recruitment of students or employees.

(2) A recipient shall not use or distribute a publication of the type described in paragraph (b)(1) of this section that suggests, by text or illustration, that such recipient treats applicants, students, or employees differently on the basis of sex except as such treatment is permitted by these Title IX regulations.

(c) *Distribution.* Each recipient shall distribute without discrimination on the basis of sex each publication described in paragraph (b)(1) of this section, and shall apprise each of its admission and employment recruitment representatives of the policy of nondiscrimination described in paragraph (a) of this section, and shall require such representatives to adhere to such policy.

Subpart B—Coverage

§ 19.200 Application.

Except as provided in §§ 19.205 through 19.235(a), these Title IX regulations apply to every recipient and to each education program or activity operated by such recipient that receives Federal financial assistance.

§ 19.205 Educational institutions and other entities controlled by religious organizations.

(a) *Exemption.* These Title IX regulations do not apply to any operation of an educational institution or other entity that is controlled by a religious organization to the extent that application of these Title IX regulations would not be consistent with the religious tenets of such organization.

(b) *Exemption claims.* An educational institution or other entity that wishes to claim the exemption set forth in paragraph (a) of this section shall do so by submitting in writing to the designated agency official a statement by the highest-ranking official of the institution, identifying the provisions of these Title IX regulations that conflict with a specific tenet of the religious organization.

§ 19.210 Military and merchant marine educational institutions.

These Title IX regulations do not apply to an educational institution whose primary purpose is the training of individuals for a military service of the United States or for the merchant marine.

§ 19.215 Membership practices of certain organizations.

(a) *Social fraternities and sororities.* These Title IX regulations do not apply to the membership practices of social fraternities and sororities that are exempt from taxation under section 501(a) of the Internal Revenue Code of 1954, 26 U.S.C. 501(a), the active membership of which consists primarily of students in attendance at institutions of higher education.

(b) *YMCA, YWCA, Girl Scouts, Boy Scouts, and Camp Fire Girls.* These Title IX regulations do not apply to the membership practices of the Young Men's Christian Association (YMCA), the Young Women's Christian Association (YWCA), the Girl Scouts, the Boy Scouts, and Camp Fire Girls.

(c) *Voluntary youth service organizations.* These Title IX regulations do not apply to the membership practices of a voluntary youth service organization that is exempt from taxation under section 501(a) of the Internal Revenue Code of 1954, 26 U.S.C. 501(a), and the membership of which has been traditionally limited to members of one sex and principally to persons of less than nineteen years of age.

§ 19.220 Admissions.

(a) Admissions to educational institutions prior to June 24, 1973, are not covered by these Title IX regulations.

(b) *Administratively separate units.* For the purposes only of this section, §§ 19.225 and 19.230, and §§ 19.300 through 19.310, each administratively separate unit shall be deemed to be an educational institution.

(c) *Application of §§ 19.300 through .310.* Except as provided in paragraphs (d) and (e) of this section, §§ 19.300 through 19.310 apply to each recipient. A recipient to which §§ 19.300 through 19.310 apply shall not discriminate on the basis of sex in admission or recruitment in violation of §§ 19.300 through 19.310.

(d) *Educational institutions.* Except as provided in paragraph (e) of this section as to recipients that are educational institutions, §§ 19.300 through 19.310 apply only to institutions of vocational education, professional education, graduate higher education, and public institutions of undergraduate higher education.

(e) *Public institutions of undergraduate higher education.* §§ 19.300 through 19.310 do not apply to any public institution of undergraduate higher education that traditionally and continually from its establishment has had a policy of admitting students of only one sex.

§ 19.225 Educational institutions eligible to submit transition plans.

(a) *Application.* This section applies to each educational institution to which §§ 19.300 through 19.310 apply that:

(1) Admitted students of only one sex as regular students as of June 23, 1972; or

(2) Admitted students of only one sex as regular students as of June 23, 1965, but thereafter admitted, as regular students, students of the sex not admitted prior to June 23, 1965.

(b) *Provision for transition plans.* An educational institution to which this section applies shall not discriminate on the basis of sex in admission or recruitment in violation of §§ 19.300 through 19.310.

§ 19.230 Transition plans.

(a) *Submission of plans.* An institution to which § 19.225 applies and that is composed of more than one administratively separate unit may submit either a single transition plan applicable to all such units, or a separate transition plan applicable to each such unit.

(b) *Content of plans.* In order to be approved by the Secretary of Education, a transition plan shall:

(1) State the name, address, and Federal Interagency Committee on Education Code of the educational institution submitting such plan, the administratively separate units to which the plan is applicable, and the name, address, and telephone number of the person to whom questions concerning the plan may be addressed. The person who submits the plan shall be the chief administrator or president of the institution, or another individual legally authorized to bind the institution to all actions set forth in the plan.

(2) State whether the educational institution or administratively separate unit admits students of both sexes as regular students and, if so, when it began to do so.

(3) Identify and describe with respect to the educational institution or administratively separate unit any obstacles to admitting students without discrimination on the basis of sex.

(4) Describe in detail the steps necessary to eliminate as soon as practicable each obstacle so identified and indicate the schedule for taking these steps and the individual directly responsible for their implementation.

(5) Include estimates of the number of students, by sex, expected to apply for, be admitted to, and enter each class during the period covered by the plan.

(c) *Nondiscrimination.* No policy or practice of a recipient to which § 19.225 applies shall result in treatment of applicants to or students of such recipient in violation of §§ 19.300 through 19.310 unless such treatment is necessitated by an obstacle identified in paragraph (b)(3) of this section and a schedule for eliminating that obstacle has been provided as required by paragraph (b)(4) of this section.

(d) *Effects of past exclusion.* To overcome the effects of past exclusion of students on the basis of sex, each educational institution to which § 19.225 applies shall include in its transition plan, and shall implement, specific steps designed to encourage individuals of the previously excluded sex to apply for admission to such institution. Such steps shall include instituting recruitment programs that emphasize the institution's commitment to enrolling students of the sex previously excluded.

§ 19.235 Statutory amendments.

(a) This section, which applies to all provisions of these Title IX regulations, addresses statutory amendments to Title IX.

(b) These Title IX regulations shall not apply to or preclude:

(1) Any program or activity of the American Legion undertaken in connection with the organization or operation of any Boys State conference, Boys Nation conference, Girls State conference, or Girls Nation conference;

(2) Any program or activity of a secondary school or educational institution specifically for:

(i) The promotion of any Boys State conference, Boys Nation conference, Girls State conference, or Girls Nation conference; or

(ii) The selection of students to attend any such conference;

(3) Father-son or mother-daughter activities at an educational institution or in an education program or activity, but if such activities are provided for students of one sex, opportunities for reasonably comparable activities shall be provided to students of the other sex;

(4) Any scholarship or other financial assistance awarded by an institution of higher education to an individual because such individual has received such award in a single-sex pageant based upon a combination of factors related to the individual's personal appearance, poise, and talent. The pageant, however, must comply with other nondiscrimination provisions of Federal law.

(c) *Program or activity* or *program* means:

(1) All of the operations of any entity described in paragraphs (c)(1)(i) through (iv) of this section, any part of which is extended Federal financial assistance:

(i)(A) A department, agency, special purpose district, or other instrumentality of a State or of a local government; or

(B) The entity of such State or local government that distributes such assistance and each such department or agency (and each other State or local government entity) to which the assistance is extended, in the case of assistance to a State or local government;

(ii)(A) A college, university, or other postsecondary institution, or a public system of higher education; or

(B) A local educational agency (as defined in section 8801 of title 20), system of vocational education, or other school system;

(iii)(A) An entire corporation, partnership, or other private organization, or an entire sole proprietorship—

(*1*) If assistance is extended to such corporation, partnership, private organization, or sole proprietorship as a whole; or

(*2*) Which is principally engaged in the business of providing education, health care, housing, social services, or parks and recreation; or

(B) The entire plant or other comparable, geographically separate facility to which Federal financial assistance is extended, in the case of any other corporation, partnership, private organization, or sole proprietorship; or

(iv) Any other entity that is established by two or more of the entities described in paragraphs (c)(1)(i), (ii), or (iii) of this section.

(2)(i) *Program or activity* does not include any operation of an entity that is controlled by a religious organization if the application of 20 U.S.C. 1681 to such operation would not be consistent with the religious tenets of such organization.

(ii) For example, all of the operations of a college, university, or other postsecondary institution, including but not limited to traditional educational operations, faculty and student housing, campus shuttle bus service, campus restaurants, the bookstore, and other commercial activities are part of a "program or activity" subject to these Title IX regulations if the college, university, or other institution receives Federal financial assistance.

(d)(1) Nothing in these Title IX regulations shall be construed to require or prohibit any person, or public or private entity, to provide or pay for any benefit or service, including the use of facilities, related to an abortion. Medical procedures, benefits, services, and the use of facilities, necessary to save the life of a pregnant woman or to address complications related to an abortion are not subject to this section.

(2) Nothing in this section shall be construed to permit a penalty to be imposed on any person or individual because such person or individual is seeking or has received any benefit or service related to a legal abortion. Accordingly, subject to paragraph (d)(1) of this section, no person shall be excluded from participation in, be denied the benefits of, or be subjected to discrimination under any academic, extracurricular, research, occupational training, employment, or other educational program or activity operated by a recipient that receives Federal financial assistance because such individual has sought or received, or is seeking, a legal abortion, or any benefit or service related to a legal abortion.

Subpart C—Discrimination on the Basis of Sex in Admission and Recruitment Prohibited

§ 19.300 Admission.

(a) *General.* No person shall, on the basis of sex, be denied admission, or be subjected to discrimination in admission, by any recipient to which §§ 19.300 through §§ 19.310 apply, except as provided in §§ 19.225 and §§ 19.230.

(b) *Specific prohibitions.* (1) In determining whether a person satisfies any policy or criterion for admission, or in making any offer of admission, a recipient to which §§ 19.300 through 19.310 apply shall not:

(i) Give preference to one person over another on the basis of sex, by ranking applicants separately on such basis, or otherwise;

(ii) Apply numerical limitations upon the number or proportion of persons of either sex who may be admitted; or

(iii) Otherwise treat one individual differently from another on the basis of sex.

(2) A recipient shall not administer or operate any test or other criterion for admission that has a disproportionately adverse effect on persons on the basis of sex unless the use of such test or criterion is shown to predict validly success in the education program or activity in question and alternative tests or criteria that do not have such a disproportionately adverse effect are shown to be unavailable.

(c) *Prohibitions relating to marital or parental status.* In determining whether a person satisfies any policy or criterion for admission, or in making any offer of admission, a recipient to which §§ 19.300 through 19.310 apply:

(1) Shall not apply any rule concerning the actual or potential parental, family, or marital status of a student or applicant that treats persons differently on the basis of sex;

(2) Shall not discriminate against or exclude any person on the basis of pregnancy, childbirth, termination of pregnancy, or recovery therefrom, or establish or follow any rule or practice that so discriminates or excludes;

(3) Subject to § 19.235(d), shall treat disabilities related to pregnancy, childbirth, termination of pregnancy, or recovery therefrom in the same manner and under the same policies as any other temporary disability or physical condition; and

(4) Shall not make pre-admission inquiry as to the marital status of an applicant for admission, including whether such applicant is "Miss" or "Mrs."

A recipient may make pre-admission inquiry as to the sex of an applicant for admission, but only if such inquiry is made equally of such applicants of both sexes and if the results of such inquiry are not used in connection with discrimination prohibited by these Title IX regulations.

§ 19.305 **Preference in admission.**

A recipient to which §§ 19.300 through 19.310 apply shall not give preference to applicants for admission, on the basis of attendance at any educational institution or other school or entity that admits as students only or predominantly members of one sex, if the giving of such preference has the effect of discriminating on the basis of sex in violation of §§ 19.300 through 19.310.

§ 19.310 **Recruitment.**

(a) *Nondiscriminatory recruitment.* A recipient to which §§ 19.300 through 19.310 apply shall not discriminate on the basis of sex in the recruitment and admission of students. A recipient may be required to undertake additional recruitment efforts for one sex as remedial action pursuant to § 19.110(a), and may choose to undertake such efforts as affirmative action pursuant to § 19.110(b).

(b) *Recruitment at certain institutions.* A recipient to which §§ 19.300 through 19.310 apply shall not recruit primarily or exclusively at educational institutions, schools, or entities that admit as students only or predominantly members of one sex, if such actions have the effect of discriminating on the basis of sex in violation of §§ 19.300 through 19.310.

Subpart D—Discrimination on the Basis of Sex in Education Programs or Activities Prohibited

§ 19.400 **Education programs or activities.**

(a) *General.* Except as provided elsewhere in these Title IX regulations, no person shall, on the basis of sex, be excluded from participation in, be denied the benefits of, or be subjected to discrimination under any academic, extracurricular, research, occupational training, or other education program or activity operated by a recipient that receives Federal financial assistance. Sections 19.400 through 19.455 do not apply to actions of a recipient in connection with admission of its students to an education program or activity of a recipient to which §§ 19.300 through 19.310 do not apply, or an entity, not a recipient, to which §§ 19.300 through 19.310 would not apply if the entity were a recipient.

(b) *Specific prohibitions.* Except as provided in §§ 19.400 through 19.455, in providing any aid, benefit, or service to a student, a recipient shall not, on the basis of sex:

(1) Treat one person differently from another in determining whether such person satisfies any requirement or condition for the provision of such aid, benefit, or service;

(2) Provide different aid, benefits, or services or provide aid, benefits, or services in a different manner;

(3) Deny any person any such aid, benefit, or service;

(4) Subject any person to separate or different rules of behavior, sanctions, or other treatment;

(5) Apply any rule concerning the domicile or residence of a student or applicant, including eligibility for instate fees and tuition;

(6) Aid or perpetuate discrimination against any person by providing significant assistance to any agency, organization, or person that discriminates on the basis of sex in providing any aid, benefit, or service to students or employees;

(7) Otherwise limit any person in the enjoyment of any right, privilege, advantage, or opportunity.

(c) *Assistance administered by a recipient educational institution to study at a foreign institution.* A recipient educational institution may administer or assist in the administration of scholarships, fellowships, or other awards established by foreign or domestic wills, trusts, or similar legal instruments, or by acts of foreign governments and restricted to members of one sex, that are designed to provide opportunities to study abroad, and that are awarded to students who are already matriculating at or who are graduates of the recipient institution; *Provided,* that a recipient educational institution that administers or assists in the adminis-

tration of such scholarships, fellowships, or other awards that are restricted to members of one sex provides, or otherwise makes available, reasonable opportunities for similar studies for members of the other sex. Such opportunities may be derived from either domestic or foreign sources.

(d) *Aids, benefits or services not provided by recipient.* (1) This paragraph (d) applies to any recipient that requires participation by any applicant, student, or employee in any education program or activity not operated wholly by such recipient, or that facilitates, permits, or considers such participation as part of or equivalent to an education program or activity operated by such recipient, including participation in educational consortia and cooperative employment and student-teaching assignments.

(2) Such recipient:

(i) Shall develop and implement a procedure designed to assure itself that the operator or sponsor of such other education program or activity takes no action affecting any applicant, student, or employee of such recipient that these Title IX regulations would prohibit such recipient from taking; and

(ii) Shall not facilitate, require, permit, or consider such participation if such action occurs.

§ 19.405 Housing.

(a) *Generally.* A recipient shall not, on the basis of sex, apply different rules or regulations, impose different fees or requirements, or offer different services or benefits related to housing, except as provided in this section (including housing provided only to married students).

(b) *Housing provided by recipient.* (1) A recipient may provide separate housing on the basis of sex.

(2) Housing provided by a recipient to students of one sex, when compared to that provided to students of the other sex, shall be as a whole:

(i) Proportionate in quantity to the number of students of that sex applying for such housing; and

(ii) Comparable in quality and cost to the student.

(c) *Other housing.* (1) A recipient shall not, on the basis of sex, administer different policies or practices concerning occupancy by its students of housing other than that provided by such recipient.

(2)(i) A recipient which, through solicitation, listing, approval of housing, or otherwise, assists any agency, organization, or person in making housing available to any of its students, shall take such reasonable action as may be necessary to assure itself that such housing as is provided to students of one sex, when compared to that provided to students of the other sex, is as a whole:

(A) Proportionate in quantity; and

(B) Comparable in quality and cost to the student.

(ii) A recipient may render such assistance to any agency, organization, or person that provides all or part of such housing to students of only one sex.

§ 19.410   Comparable facilities.

A recipient may provide separate toilet, locker room, and shower facilities on the basis of sex, but such facilities provided for students of one sex shall be comparable to such facilities provided for students of the other sex.

§ 19.415   Access to course offerings.

(a) A recipient shall not provide any course or otherwise carry out any of its education program or activity separately on the basis of sex, or require or refuse participation therein by any of its students on such basis, including health, physical education, industrial, business, vocational, technical, home economics, music, and adult education courses.

(b)(1) With respect to classes and activities in physical education at the elementary school level, the recipient shall comply fully with this section as expeditiously as possible but in no event later than one year from September 29, 2000. With respect to physical education classes and activities at the secondary and post-secondary levels, the recipient shall comply fully with this section as expeditiously as possible but in no event later than three years from September 29, 2000.

(2) This section does not prohibit grouping of students in physical education classes and activities by ability as assessed by objective standards of individual performance developed and applied without regard to sex.

(3) This section does not prohibit separation of students by sex within physical education classes or activities during participation in wrestling, boxing, rugby, ice hockey, football, basketball, and other sports the purpose or major activity of which involves bodily contact.

(4) Where use of a single standard of measuring skill or progress in a physical education class has an adverse effect on members of one sex, the recipient shall use appropriate standards that do not have such effect.

(5) Portions of classes in elementary and secondary schools, or portions of education programs or activities, that deal exclusively with human sexuality may be conducted in separate sessions for boys and girls.

(6) Recipients may make requirements based on vocal range or quality that may result in a chorus or choruses of one or predominantly one sex.

§ 19.420   Access to schools operated by LEAs.

A recipient that is a local educational agency shall not, on the basis of sex, exclude any person from admission to:

(a) Any institution of vocational education operated by such recipient; or

(b) Any other school or educational unit operated by such recipient, unless such recipient otherwise makes available to such person, pursuant to the same policies and criteria of admission, courses, services, and facilities comparable to each course, service, and facility offered in or through such schools.

§ 19.425   Counseling and use of appraisal and counseling materials.

(a) *Counseling.* A recipient shall not discriminate against any person on the basis of sex in the counseling or guidance of students or applicants for admission.

(b) *Use of appraisal and counseling materials.* A recipient that uses testing or other materials for appraising or counseling students shall not use different materials for students on the basis of their sex or use materials that permit or require different treatment of students on such basis unless such different materials cover the same occupations and interest areas and the use of such different materials is shown to be essential to eliminate sex bias. Recipients shall develop and use internal procedures for ensuring that such materials do not discriminate on the basis of sex. Where the use of a counseling test or other instrument results in a substantially disproportionate number of members of one sex in any particular course of study or classification, the recipient shall take such action as is necessary to assure itself that such disproportion is not the result of discrimination in the instrument or its application.

(c) *Disproportion in classes.* Where a recipient finds that a particular class contains a substantially disproportionate number of individuals of one sex, the recipient shall take such action as is necessary to assure itself that such disproportion is not the result of discrimination on the basis of sex in counseling or appraisal materials or by counselors.

§ 19.430 Financial assistance.

(a) *General.* Except as provided in paragraphs (b) and (c) of this section, in providing financial assistance to any of its students, a recipient shall not:

(1) On the basis of sex, provide different amounts or types of such assistance, limit eligibility for such assistance that is of any particular type or source, apply different criteria, or otherwise discriminate;

(2) Through solicitation, listing, approval, provision of facilities, or other services, assist any foundation, trust, agency, organization, or person that provides assistance to any of such recipient's students in a manner that discriminates on the basis of sex; or

(3) Apply any rule or assist in application of any rule concerning eligibility for such assistance that treats persons of one sex differently from persons of the other sex with regard to marital or parental status.

(b) *Financial aid established by certain legal instruments.* (1) A recipient may administer or assist in the administration of scholarships, fellowships, or other forms of financial assistance established pursuant to domestic or foreign wills, trusts, bequests, or similar legal instruments or by acts of a foreign government that require that awards be made to members of a particular sex specified therein; *Provided,* that the overall effect of the award of such sex-restricted scholarships, fellowships, and other forms of financial assistance does not discriminate on the basis of sex.

(2) To ensure nondiscriminatory awards of assistance as required in paragraph (b)(1) of this section, recipients shall develop and use procedures under which:

(i) Students are selected for award of financial assistance on the basis of nondiscriminatory criteria and not on the basis of availability of funds restricted to members of a particular sex;

(ii) An appropriate sex-restricted scholarship, fellowship, or other form of financial assistance is allocated to each student selected under paragraph (b)(2)(i) of this section; and

(iii) No student is denied the award for which he or she was selected under paragraph (b)(2)(i) of this section because of the absence of a scholarship, fellowship, or other form of financial assistance designated for a member of that student's sex.

(c) *Athletic scholarships.* (1) To the extent that a recipient awards athletic scholarships or grants-in-aid, it must provide reasonable opportunities for such awards for members of each sex in proportion to the number of students of each sex participating in interscholastic or intercollegiate athletics.

(2) A recipient may provide separate athletic scholarships or grants-in-aid for members of each sex as part of separate athletic teams for members of each sex to the extent consistent with this paragraph (c) and § 19.450.

§ 19.435 Employment assistance to students.

(a) *Assistance by recipient in making available outside employment.* A recipient that assists any agency, organization, or person in making employment available to any of its students:

(1) Shall assure itself that such employment is made available without discrimination on the basis of sex; and

(2) Shall not render such services to any agency, organization, or person that discriminates on the basis of sex in its employment practices.

(b) *Employment of students by recipients.* A recipient that employs any of its students shall not do so in a manner that violates §§ 19.500 through 19.550.

§ 19.440 Health and insurance benefits and services.

Subject to § 19.235(d), in providing a medical, hospital, accident, or life insurance benefit, service, policy, or plan to any of its students, a recipient shall not discriminate on the basis of sex, or provide such benefit, service, policy, or plan in a manner that would violate §§ 19.500 through 19.550 if it were provided to employees of the recipient. This section shall not prohibit a recipient from providing any benefit or service that may be used by a different proportion of students of one sex than of the other, including family planning services. However, any recipient that provides full coverage health service shall provide gynecological care.

§ 19.445 Marital or parental status.

(a) *Status generally.* A recipient shall not apply any rule concerning a student's actual or potential parental, family, or marital status that treats students differently on the basis of sex.

(b) *Pregnancy and related conditions.* (1) A recipient shall not discriminate against any student, or exclude any student from its education program or activity, including any class or extracurricular activity, on the basis of such student's pregnancy, childbirth, false pregnancy, termination of pregnancy, or recovery therefrom, unless the student requests voluntarily to participate in a separate portion of the program or activity of the recipient.

(2) A recipient may require such a student to obtain the certification of a physician that the student is physically and emotionally able to continue participation as long as such a certification is required of all students for other physical or emotional conditions requiring the attention of a physician.

(3) A recipient that operates a portion of its education program or activity separately for pregnant students, admittance to which is completely voluntary on the part of the student as provided in paragraph (b)(1) of this section, shall ensure that the separate portion is comparable to that offered to non-pregnant students.

(4) Subject to § 19.235(d), a recipient shall treat pregnancy, childbirth, false pregnancy, termination of pregnancy and recovery therefrom in the same manner and under the same policies as any other temporary disability with respect to any medical or hospital benefit, service, plan, or policy that such recipient administers, operates, offers, or participates in with respect to students admitted to the recipient's educational program or activity.

(5) In the case of a recipient that does not maintain a leave policy for its students, or in the case of a student who does not otherwise qualify for leave under such a policy, a recipient shall treat pregnancy, childbirth, false pregnancy, termination of pregnancy, and recovery therefrom as a justification for a leave of absence for as long a period of time as is deemed medically necessary by the student's physician, at the conclusion of which the student shall be reinstated to the status that she held when the leave began.

§ 19.450 Athletics.

(a) *General.* No person shall, on the basis of sex, be excluded from participation in, be denied the benefits of, be treated differently from another person, or otherwise be discriminated against in any interscholastic, intercollegiate, club, or intramural athletics offered by a recipient, and no recipient shall provide any such athletics separately on such basis.

(b) *Separate teams.* Notwithstanding the requirements of paragraph (a) of this section, a recipient may operate or sponsor separate teams for members of each sex where selection for such teams is based upon competitive skill or the activity involved is a contact sport. However, where a recipient operates or sponsors a team in a particular sport for members of one sex but operates or sponsors no such team for members of the other sex, and athletic opportunities for members of that sex have previously been limited, members of the excluded sex must be allowed to try out for the team offered unless the sport involved is a contact sport. For the purposes of these Title IX regulations, contact sports include boxing, wrestling, rugby, ice hockey, football, basketball, and other sports the purpose or major activity of which involves bodily contact.

(c) *Equal opportunity.* (1) A recipient that operates or sponsors interscholastic, intercollegiate, club, or intramural athletics shall provide equal athletic opportunity for members of both sexes. In determining whether equal opportunities are available, the designated agency official will consider, among other factors:

(i) Whether the selection of sports and levels of competition effectively accommodate the interests and abilities of members of both sexes;

(ii) The provision of equipment and supplies;

(iii) Scheduling of games and practice time;

(iv) Travel and per diem allowance;

(v) Opportunity to receive coaching and academic tutoring;

(vi) Assignment and compensation of coaches and tutors;

(vii) Provision of locker rooms, practice, and competitive facilities;

(viii) Provision of medical and training facilities and services;

(ix) Provision of housing and dining facilities and services;

(x) Publicity.

(2) For purposes of paragraph (c)(1) of this section, unequal aggregate expenditures for members of each sex or unequal expenditures for male and female teams if a recipient operates or sponsors separate teams will not constitute noncompliance with this section, but the designated agency official may consider the failure to provide necessary funds for teams for one sex in assessing equality of opportunity for members of each sex.

(d) *Adjustment period.* A recipient that operates or sponsors interscholastic, intercollegiate, club, or intramural athletics at the elementary school level shall comply fully with this section as expeditiously as possible but in no event later than one year from September 29, 2000. A recipient that operates or sponsors interscholastic, intercollegiate, club, or intramural athletics at the secondary or postsecondary school level shall comply fully with this section as expeditiously as possible but in no event later than three years from September 29, 2000.

§ 19.455 **Textbooks and curricular material.**

Nothing in these Title IX regulations shall be interpreted as requiring or prohibiting or abridging in any way the use of particular textbooks or curricular materials.

Subpart E—Discrimination on the Basis of Sex in Employment in Education Programs or Activities Prohibited

§ 19.500 **Employment.**

(a) *General.* (1) No person shall, on the basis of sex, be excluded from participation in, be denied the benefits of, or be subjected to discrimination in employment, or recruitment, consideration, or selection therefor, whether full-time or part-time, under any education program or activity operated by a recipient that receives Federal financial assistance.

(2) A recipient shall make all employment decisions in any education program or activity operated by such recipient in a nondiscriminatory manner and shall not limit, segregate, or classify applicants or employees in any way that could adversely affect any applicant's or employee's employment opportunities or status because of sex.

(3) A recipient shall not enter into any contractual or other relationship which directly or indirectly has the effect of subjecting employees or students to discrimination prohibited by §§ 19.500 through 19.550, including relationships with employment and referral agencies, with labor unions, and

with organizations providing or administering fringe benefits to employees of the recipient.

(4) A recipient shall not grant preferences to applicants for employment on the basis of attendance at any educational institution or entity that admits as students only or predominantly members of one sex, if the giving of such preferences has the effect of discriminating on the basis of sex in violation of these Title IX regulations.

(b) *Application.* The provisions of §§ 19.500 through 19.550 apply to:

(1) Recruitment, advertising, and the process of application for employment;

(2) Hiring, upgrading, promotion, consideration for and award of tenure, demotion, transfer, layoff, termination, application of nepotism policies, right of return from layoff, and rehiring;

(3) Rates of pay or any other form of compensation, and changes in compensation;

(4) Job assignments, classifications, and structure, including position descriptions, lines of progression, and seniority lists;

(5) The terms of any collective bargaining agreement;

(6) Granting and return from leaves of absence, leave for pregnancy, childbirth, false pregnancy, termination of pregnancy, leave for persons of either sex to care for children or dependents, or any other leave;

(7) Fringe benefits available by virtue of employment, whether or not administered by the recipient;

(8) Selection and financial support for training, including apprenticeship, professional meetings, conferences, and other related activities, selection for tuition assistance, selection for sabbaticals and leaves of absence to pursue training;

(9) Employer-sponsored activities, including social or recreational programs; and

(10) Any other term, condition, or privilege of employment.

§ 19.505 **Employment criteria.**

A recipient shall not administer or operate any test or other criterion for any employment opportunity that has a disproportionately adverse effect on persons on the basis of sex unless:

(a) Use of such test or other criterion is shown to predict validly successful performance in the position in question; and

(b) Alternative tests or criteria for such purpose, which do not have such disproportionately adverse effect, are shown to be unavailable.

§ 19.510 **Recruitment.**

(a) *Nondiscriminatory recruitment and hiring.* A recipient shall not discriminate on the basis of sex in the recruitment and hiring of employees. Where a recipient has been found to be presently discriminating on the basis of sex in the recruitment or hiring of employees, or has been found to have so discriminated in the past, the recipient shall recruit members of the sex so discriminated against so as to overcome the effects of such past or present discrimination.

(b) *Recruitment patterns.* A recipient shall not recruit primarily or exclusively at entities that furnish as applicants only or predominantly members of one sex if such actions have the effect of discriminating on the basis of sex in violation of §§ 19.500 through 19.550.

§ 19.515 **Compensation.**

A recipient shall not make or enforce any policy or practice that, on the basis of sex:

(a) Makes distinctions in rates of pay or other compensation;

(b) Results in the payment of wages to employees of one sex at a rate less than that paid to employees of the opposite sex for equal work on jobs the performance of which requires equal skill, effort, and responsibility, and that are performed under similar working conditions.

§ 19.520 **Job classification and structure.**

A recipient shall not:

(a) Classify a job as being for males or for females;

(b) Maintain or establish separate lines of progression, seniority lists, career ladders, or tenure systems based on sex; or

(c) Maintain or establish separate lines of progression, seniority systems, career ladders, or tenure systems for similar jobs, position descriptions, or job requirements that classify persons on the basis of sex, unless sex is a bona fide occupational qualification for the positions in question as set forth in § 19.550.

§ 19.525 Fringe benefits.

(a) *"Fringe benefits" defined.* For purposes of these Title IX regulations, *fringe benefits* means: Any medical, hospital, accident, life insurance, or retirement benefit, service, policy or plan, any profit-sharing or bonus plan, leave, and any other benefit or service of employment not subject to the provision of § 19.515.

(b) *Prohibitions.* A recipient shall not:

(1) Discriminate on the basis of sex with regard to making fringe benefits available to employees or make fringe benefits available to spouses, families, or dependents of employees differently upon the basis of the employee's sex;

(2) Administer, operate, offer, or participate in a fringe benefit plan that does not provide for equal periodic benefits for members of each sex and for equal contributions to the plan by such recipient for members of each sex; or

(3) Administer, operate, offer, or participate in a pension or retirement plan that establishes different optional or compulsory retirement ages based on sex or that otherwise discriminates in benefits on the basis of sex.

§ 19.530 Marital or parental status.

(a) *General.* A recipient shall not apply any policy or take any employment action:

(1) Concerning the potential marital, parental, or family status of an employee or applicant for employment that treats persons differently on the basis of sex; or

(2) Which is based upon whether an employee or applicant for employment is the head of household or principal wage earner in such employee's or applicant's family unit.

(b) *Pregnancy.* A recipient shall not discriminate against or exclude from employment any employee or applicant for employment on the basis of pregnancy, childbirth, false pregnancy, termination of pregnancy, or recovery therefrom.

(c) *Pregnancy as a temporary disability.* Subject to § 19235(d), a recipient shall treat pregnancy, childbirth, false pregnancy, termination of pregnancy, recovery therefrom, and any temporary disability resulting therefrom as any other temporary disability for all job-related purposes, including commencement, duration, and extensions of leave, payment of disability income, accrual of seniority and any other benefit or service, and reinstatement, and under any fringe benefit offered to employees by virtue of employment.

(d) *Pregnancy leave.* In the case of a recipient that does not maintain a leave policy for its employees, or in the case of an employee with insufficient leave or accrued employment time to qualify for leave under such a policy, a recipient shall treat pregnancy, childbirth, false pregnancy, termination of pregnancy, and recovery therefrom as a justification for a leave of absence without pay for a reasonable period of time, at the conclusion of which the employee shall be reinstated to the status that she held when the leave began or to a comparable position, without decrease in rate of compensation or loss of promotional opportunities, or any other right or privilege of employment.

§ 19.535 Effect of state or local law or other requirements.

(a) *Prohibitory requirements.* The obligation to comply with §§ 19.500 through 19.550 is not obviated or alleviated by the existence of any State or local law or other requirement that imposes prohibitions or limits upon employment of members of one sex that are not imposed upon members of the other sex.

(b) *Benefits.* A recipient that provides any compensation, service, or benefit to members of one sex pursuant to a State or local law or other requirement shall provide the same compensation, service, or benefit to members of the other sex.

§ 19.540 Advertising.

A recipient shall not in any advertising related to employment indicate preference, limitation, specification, or discrimination based on sex unless sex is a bona fide occupational qualification for the particular job in question.

§ 19.545 **Pre-employment inquiries.**

(a) *Marital status.* A recipient shall not make pre-employment inquiry as to the marital status of an applicant for employment, including whether such applicant is "Miss" or "Mrs."

(b) *Sex.* A recipient may make pre-employment inquiry as to the sex of an applicant for employment, but only if such inquiry is made equally of such applicants of both sexes and if the results of such inquiry are not used in connection with discrimination prohibited by these Title IX regulations.

§ 19.550 **Sex as a bona fide occupational qualification.**

A recipient may take action otherwise prohibited by §§ 19.500 through 19.550 provided it is shown that sex is a bona fide occupational qualification for that action, such that consideration of sex with regard to such action is essential to successful operation of the employment function concerned. A recipient shall not take action pursuant to this section that is based upon alleged comparative employment characteristics or stereotyped characterizations of one or the other sex, or upon preference based on sex of the recipient, employees, students, or other persons, but nothing contained in this section shall prevent a recipient from considering an employee's sex in relation to employment in a locker room or toilet facility used only by members of one sex.

Subpart F—Procedures

§ 19.600 **Notice of covered programs.**

Within 60 days of September 29, 2000, each Federal agency that awards Federal financial assistance shall publish in the FEDERAL REGISTER a notice of the programs covered by these Title IX regulations. Each such Federal agency shall periodically republish the notice of covered programs to reflect changes in covered programs. Copies of this notice also shall be made available upon request to the Federal agency's office that enforces Title IX.

§ 19.605 **Enforcement procedures.**

The investigative, compliance, and enforcement procedural provisions of Title VI of the Civil Rights Act of 1964 (42 U.S.C. 2000d) ("Title VI") are hereby adopted and applied to these Title IX regulations. These procedures may be found at 32 CFR 195.7 through 195.12.

PARTS 20–24 [RESERVED]

PART 25—UNIFORM RELOCATION ASSISTANCE AND REAL PROPERTY ACQUISITION FOR FEDERAL AND FEDERALLY ASSISTED PROGRAMS

AUTHORITY: Sec. 213, Uniform Relocation Assistance and Real Property Acquisition Policies Act of 1970, Pub. L. 91–646, 84 Stat. 1894 (42 U.S.C. 4601) as amended by the Surface Transportation and Uniform Relocation Assistance Act of 1987, title IV of Pub. L. 100–17, 101 Stat. 246–256 (42 U.S.C. 4601 note).

§ 25.1 **Uniform relocation assistance and real property acquisition.**

Regulations and procedures for complying with the Uniform Relocation Assistance and Real Property Acquisition Policies Act of 1970 (Pub. L. 91–646, 84 Stat. 1894, 42 U.S.C. 4601), as amended by the Surface Transportation and Uniform Relocation Assistance Act of 1987 (title IV of Pub. L. 100–17, 101 Stat. 246–256, 42 U.S.C. 4601 note) are set forth in 49 CFR part 24.

[52 FR 48026, Dec. 17, 1987 and 54 FR 8912, Mar. 2, 1989]

PARTS 26–49 [RESERVED]

SUBCHAPTER B—INSURANCE AND HAZARD MITIGATION

PARTS 50-54 [RESERVED]

NATIONAL INSURANCE DEVELOPMENT PROGRAM

PARTS 55-58 [RESERVED]

NATIONAL FLOOD INSURANCE PROGRAM

PART 59—GENERAL PROVISIONS

Subpart A—General

AUTHORITY: 42 U.S.C. 4001 et seq.; Reorganization Plan No. 3 of 1978, 43 FR 41943, 3 CFR, 1978 Comp., p. 329; E.O. 12127 of Mar. 31, 1979, 44 FR 19367, 3 CFR, 1979 Comp., p. 376.

Subpart A—General

§ 59.1 Definitions.

As used in this subchapter—

Act means the statutes authorizing the National Flood Insurance Program that are incorporated in 42 U.S.C. 4001–4128.

Actuarial rates—see *risk premium rates.*

Administrator means the Administrator of the Federal Emergency Management Agency.

Agency means the Federal Emergency Management Agency, Washington DC.

Alluvial fan flooding means flooding occurring on the surface of an alluvial fan or similar landform which originates at the apex and is characterized by high-velocity flows; active processes of erosion, sediment transport, and deposition; and, unpredictable flow paths.

Apex means a point on an alluvial fan or similar landform below which the flow path of the major stream that formed the fan becomes unpredictable and alluvial fan flooding can occur.

Applicant means a community which indicates a desire to participate in the Program.

Appurtenant structure means a structure which is on the same parcel of property as the principal structure to be insured and the use of which is incidental to the use of the principal structure.

Area of future-conditions flood hazard means the land area that would be inundated by the 1-percent-annual-chance (100-year) flood based on future-conditions hydrology.

Area of shallow flooding means a designated AO, AH, AR/AO, AR/AH, or VO zone on a community's Flood Insurance Rate Map (FIRM) with a 1 percent or greater annual chance of flooding to an average depth of 1 to 3 feet where a clearly defined channel does not exist, where the path of flooding is unpredictable, and where velocity flow may be evident. Such flooding is characterized by ponding or sheet flow.

Area of special flood-related erosion hazard is the land within a community which is most likely to be subject to severe flood-related erosion losses. The area may be designated as Zone E on the Flood Hazard Boundary Map (FHBM). After the detailed evaluation of the special flood-related erosion hazard area in preparation for publication of the FIRM, Zone E may be further refined.

Area of special flood hazard is the land in the flood plain within a community subject to a 1 percent or greater chance of flooding in any given year. The area may be designated as Zone A on the FHBM. After detailed ratemaking has been completed in preparation for publication of the flood insurance rate map, Zone A usually is refined into Zones A, AO, AH, A1–30, AE, A99, AR, AR/A1–30, AR/AE, AR/AO, AR/AH, AR/A, VO, or V1–30, VE, or V. For purposes of these regulations, the term "special flood hazard area" is synonymous in

182

meaning with the phrase "area of special flood hazard".

Area of special mudslide (i.e., mudflow) hazard is the land within a community most likely to be subject to severe mudslides (i.e., mudflows). The area may be designated as Zone M on the FHBM. After the detailed evaluation of the special mudslide (i.e., mudflow) hazard area in preparation for publication of the FIRM, Zone M may be further refined.

Base flood means the flood having a one percent chance of being equalled or exceeded in any given year.

Basement" means any area of the building having its floor subgrade (below ground level) on all sides.

Breakaway wall means a wall that is not part of the structural support of the building and is intended through its design and construction to collapse under specific lateral loading forces, without causing damage to the elevated portion of the building or supporting foundation system.

Building—see *structure*.

Chargeable rates mean the rates established by the Federal Insurance Administrator pursuant to section 1308 of the Act for first layer limits of flood insurance on existing structures.

Chief Executive Officer of the community *(CEO)* means the official of the community who is charged with the authority to implement and administer laws, ordinances and regulations for that community.

Coastal high hazard area means an area of special flood hazard extending from offshore to the inland limit of a primary frontal dune along an open coast and any other area subject to high velocity wave action from storms or seismic sources.

Community means any State or area or political subdivision thereof, or any Indian tribe or authorized tribal organization, or Alaska Native village or authorized native organization, which has authority to adopt and enforce flood plain management regulations for the areas within its jurisdiction.

Contents coverage is the insurance on personal property within an enclosed structure, including the cost of debris removal, and the reasonable cost of removal of contents to minimize damage. Personal property may be household goods usual or incidental to residential occupancy, or merchandise, furniture, fixtures, machinery, equipment and supplies usual to other than residential occupancies.

Criteria means the comprehensive criteria for land management and use for flood-prone areas developed under 42 U.S.C. 4102 for the purposes set forth in part 60 of this subchapter.

Critical feature means an integral and readily identifiable part of a flood protection system, without which the flood protection provided by the entire system would be compromised.

Curvilinear Line means the border on either a FHBM or FIRM that delineates the special flood, mudslide (i.e., mudflow) and/or flood-related erosion hazard areas and consists of a curved or contour line that follows the topography.

Deductible means the fixed amount or percentage of any loss covered by insurance which is borne by the insured prior to the insurer's liability.

Developed area means an area of a community that is:

(a) A primarily urbanized, built-up area that is a minimum of 20 contiguous acres, has basic urban infrastructure, including roads, utilities, communications, and public facilities, to sustain industrial, residential, and commercial activities, and

(1) Within which 75 percent or more of the parcels, tracts, or lots contain commercial, industrial, or residential structures or uses; or

(2) Is a single parcel, tract, or lot in which 75 percent of the area contains existing commercial or industrial structures or uses; or

(3) Is a subdivision developed at a density of at least two residential structures per acre within which 75 percent or more of the lots contain existing residential structures at the time the designation is adopted.

(b) Undeveloped parcels, tracts, or lots, the combination of which is less than 20 acres and contiguous on at least 3 sides to areas meeting the criteria of paragraph (a) at the time the designation is adopted.

(c) A subdivision that is a minimum of 20 contiguous acres that has obtained all necessary government approvals, provided that the actual "start of construction" of structures has occurred on at least 10 percent of the lots or remaining lots of a subdivision or 10 percent of the maximum building coverage or remaining building coverage allowed for a single lot subdivision at the time the designation is adopted and construction of structures is underway. Residential subdivisions must meet the density criteria in paragraph (a)(3).

Development means any man-made change to improved or unimproved real estate, including but not limited to buildings or other structures, mining, dredging, filling, grading, paving, excavation or drilling operations or storage of equipment or materials.

Eligible community or *participating community* means a community for which the Federal Insurance Administrator has authorized the sale of flood insurance under the National Flood Insurance Program..

Elevated building means, for insurance purposes, a nonbasement building which has its lowest elevated floor raised above ground level by foundation walls, shear walls, posts, piers, pilings, or columns.

Emergency Flood Insurance Program or *emergency program* means the Program as implemented on an emergency basis in accordance with section 1336 of the Act. It is intended as a program to provide a first layer amount of insurance on all insurable structures before the effective date of the initial FIRM.

Erosion means the process of the gradual wearing away of land masses. This peril is not per se covered under the Program.

Exception means a waiver from the provisions of part 60 of this subchapter directed to a community which relieves it from the requirements of a rule, regulation, order or other determination made or issued pursuant to the Act.

Existing construction, means for the purposes of determining rates, structures for which the "start of construction" commenced before the effective date of the FIRM or before January 1, 1975, for FIRMs effective before that date. "Existing construction" may also be referred to as "existing structures."

Existing manufactured home park or subdivision means a manufactured home park or subdivision for which the construction of facilities for servicing the lots on which the manufactured homes are to be affixed (including, at a minimum, the installation of utilities, the construction of streets, and either final site grading or the pouring of concrete pads) is completed before the effective date of the floodplain management regulations adopted by a community.

Existing structures see *existing construction.*

Expansion to an existing manufactured home park or subdivision means the preparation of additional sites by the construction of facilities for servicing the lots on which the manufacturing homes are to be affixed (including the installation of utilities, the construction of streets, and either final site grading or the pouring of concrete pads).

Federal agency means any department, agency, corporation, or other entity or instrumentality of the executive branch of the Federal Government, and includes the Federal National Mortgage Association and the Federal Home Loan Mortgage Corporation.

Federal instrumentality responsible for the supervision, approval, regulation, or insuring of banks, savings and loan associations, or similar institutions means the Board of Governors of the Federal Reserve System, the Federal Deposit Insurance Corporation, the Comptroller of the Currency, the Federal Home Loan Bank Board, the Federal Savings and Loan Insurance Corporation, and the National Credit Union Administration.

Financial assistance means any form of loan, grant, guaranty, insurance, payment, rebate, subsidy, disaster assistance loan or grant, or any other form of direct or indirect Federal assistance, other than general or special revenue sharing or formula grants made to States.

Financial assistance for acquisition or construction purposes means any form of financial assistance which is intended in whole or in part for the acquisition, construction, reconstruction, repair, or improvement of any publicly or privately owned building or mobile home, and for any machinery, equipment, fixtures, and furnishings contained or to be contained therein, and shall include the purchase or subsidization of mortgages or mortgage loans but shall exclude assistance pursuant to the Disaster Relief Act of 1974 other than assistance under such Act in connection with a flood. It includes only financial assistance insurable under the Standard Flood Insurance Policy.

First-layer coverage is the maximum amount of structural and contents insurance coverage available under the Emergency Program.

Flood or *Flooding* means:

(a) A general and temporary condition of partial or complete inundation of normally dry land areas from:

(1) The overflow of inland or tidal waters.

(2) The unusual and rapid accumulation or runoff of surface waters from any source.

(3) Mudslides (i.e., mudflows) which are proximately caused by flooding as defined in paragraph (a)(2) of this definition and are akin to a river of liquid and flowing mud on the surfaces of normally dry land areas, as when earth is carried by a current of water and deposited along the path of the current.

(b) The collapse or subsidence of land along the shore of a lake or other body of water as a result of erosion or undermining caused by waves or currents of water exceeding anticipated cyclical levels or suddenly caused by an unusually high water level in a natural body of water, accompanied by a severe storm, or by an unanticipated force of nature, such as flash flood or an abnormal tidal surge, or by some similarly unusual and unforeseeable event which results in flooding as defined in paragraph (a)(1) of this definition.

Flood elevation determination means a determination by the Federal Insurance Administrator of the water surface elevations of the base flood, that is, the flood level that has a one percent or greater chance of occurrence in any given year.

Flood elevation study means an examination, evaluation and determination of flood hazards and, if appropriate, corresponding water surface elevations, or an examination, evaluation and determination of mudslide (i.e., mudflow) and/or flood-related erosion hazards.

Flood Hazard Boundary Map means an official map of a community, issued by the Federal Insurance Administrator, where the boundaries of the flood, mudslide (i.e., mudflow) related erosion areas having special hazards have been designated as Zones A, M, and/or E.

Flood insurance means the insurance coverage provided under the Program.

Flood Insurance Rate Map (FIRM) means an official map of a community, on which the Federal Insurance Administrator has delineated both the special hazard areas and the risk premium zones applicable to the community. A FIRM that has been made available digitally is called a Digital Flood Insurance Rate Map (DFIRM).

Flood Insurance Study see *flood elevation study*.

Flood plain or *flood-prone area* means any land area susceptible to being inundated by water from any source (see definition of "flooding").

Flood plain management means the operation of an overall program of corrective and preventive measures for reducing flood damage, including but not limited to emergency preparedness plans, flood control works and flood plain management regulations.

Flood plain management regulations means zoning ordinances, subdivision regulations, building codes, health regulations, special purpose ordinances (such as a flood plain ordinance, grading ordinance and erosion control ordinance) and other applications of police power. The term describes such state or local regulations, in any combination thereof, which provide standards for the purpose of flood damage prevention and reduction.

Flood protection system means those physical structural works for which funds have been authorized, appropriated, and expended and which have been constructed specifically to modify flooding in order to reduce the extent of the area within a community subject to a "special flood hazard" and the extent of the depths of associated flooding. Such a system typically includes hurricane tidal barriers, dams, reservoirs, levees or dikes. These specialized flood modifying works are those constructed in conformance with sound engineering standards.

Flood proofing means any combination of structural and non-structural additions, changes, or adjustments to structures which reduce or eliminate flood damage to real estate or improved real property, water and sanitary facilities, structures and their contents.

Flood-related erosion means the collapse or subsidence of land along the shore of a lake or other body of water as a result of undermining caused by waves or currents of water exceeding anticipated cyclical levels or suddenly caused by an unusually high water level in a natural body of water, accompanied by a severe storm, or by an unanticipated force of nature, such as a flash flood or an abnormal tidal surge, or by some similarly unusual and unforeseeable event which results in flooding.

Flood-related erosion area or *flood-related erosion prone area* means a land area adjoining the shore of a lake or other body of water, which due to the composition of the shoreline or bank and high water levels or wind-driven currents, is likely to suffer flood-related erosion damage.

Flood-related erosion area management means the operation of an overall program of corrective and preventive measures for reducing flood-related erosion damage, including but not limited to emergency preparedness plans, flood-related erosion control works, and flood plain management regulations.

Floodway—see *regulatory floodway.*

Floodway encroachment lines mean the lines marking the limits of floodways on Federal, State and local flood plain maps.

Freeboard means a factor of safety usually expressed in feet above a flood level for purposes of flood plain management. "Freeboard" tends to compensate for the many unknown factors that could contribute to flood heights greater than the height calculated for a selected size flood and floodway conditions, such as wave action, bridge openings, and the hydrological effect of urbanization of the watershed.

Functionally dependent use means a use which cannot perform its intended purpose unless it is located or carried out in close proximity to water. The term includes only docking facilities, port facilities that are necessary for the loading and unloading of cargo or passengers, and ship building and ship repair facilities, but does not include long-term storage or related manufacturing facilities.

Future-conditions flood hazard area, or *future-conditions floodplain*—see *Area of future-conditions flood hazard.*

Future-conditions hydrology means the flood discharges associated with projected land-use conditions based on a community's zoning maps and/or comprehensive land-use plans and without consideration of projected future construction of flood detention structures or projected future hydraulic modifications within a stream or other waterway, such as bridge and culvert construction, fill, and excavation.

Highest adjacent grade means the highest natural elevation of the ground surface prior to construction next to the proposed walls of a structure.

Historic Structure means any structure that is:

(a) Listed individually in the National Register of Historic Places (a listing maintained by the Department of Interior) or preliminarily determined by the Secretary of the Interior as meeting the requirements for individual listing on the National Register;

(b) Certified or preliminarily determined by the Secretary of the Interior as contributing to the historical significance of a registered historic district or a district preliminarily determined by the Secretary to qualify as a registered historic district;

(c) Individually listed on a state inventory of historic places in states with historic preservation programs which have been approved by the Secretary of the Interior; or

(d) Individually listed on a local inventory of historic places in communities with historic preservation programs that have been certified either:

(1) By an approved state program as determined by the Secretary of the Interior or

(2) Directly by the Secretary of the Interior in states without approved programs.

Independent scientific body means a non-Federal technical or scientific organization involved in the study of land use planning, flood plain management, hydrology, geology, geography, or any other related field of study concerned with flooding.

Insurance adjustment organization means any organization or person engaged in the business of adjusting loss claims arising under the Standard Flood Insurance Policy.

Insurance company or *insurer* means any person or organization authorized to engage in the insurance business under the laws of any State.

Levee means a man-made structure, usually an earthen embankment, designed and constructed in accordance with sound engineering practices to contain, control, or divert the flow of water so as to provide protection from temporary flooding.

Levee System means a flood protection system which consists of a levee, or levees, and associated structures, such as closure and drainage devices, which are constructed and operated in accordance with sound engineering practices.

Lowest Floor means the lowest floor of the lowest enclosed area (including basement). An unfinished or flood resistant enclosure, usable solely for parking of vehicles, building access or storage in an area other than a basement area is not considered a building's lowest floor; *Provided*, that such enclosure is not built so as to render the structure in violation of the applicable non-elevation design requirements of §60.3.

Mangrove stand means an assemblage of mangrove trees which are mostly low trees noted for a copious development of interlacing adventitious roots above the ground and which contain one or more of the following species: Black mangrove (Avicennia Nitida); red mangrove (Rhizophora Mangle); white mangrove (Languncularia Racemosa); and buttonwood (Conocarpus Erecta).

Manufactured home means a structure, transportable in one or more sections, which is built on a permanent chassis and is designed for use with or without a permanent foundation when attached to the required utilities. The term "manufactured home" does not include a "recreational vehicle".

Manufactured home park or subdivision" means a parcel (or contiguous parcels) of land divided into two or more manufactured home lots for rent or sale.

Map means the Flood Hazard Boundary Map (FHBM) or the Flood Insurance Rate Map (FIRM) for a community issued by the Agency.

Mean sea level means, for purposes of the National Flood Insurance Program, the National Geodetic Vertical Datum (NGVD) of 1929 or other datum, to which base flood elevations shown on a community's Flood Insurance Rate Map are referenced.

Mudslide (i.e., mudflow) describes a condition where there is a river, flow or inundation of liquid mud down a hillside usually as a result of a dual condition of loss of brush cover, and the subsequent accumulation of water on the ground preceded by a period of unusually heavy or sustained rain. A mudslide (i.e., mudflow) may occur as a distinct phenomenon while a landslide is in progress, and will be recognized as such by the Administrator only if the mudflow, and not the landslide, is the proximate cause of damage that occurs.

Mudslide (i.e., mudflow) area management means the operation of an overall program of corrective and preventive measures for reducing mudslide (i.e., mudflow) damage, including but not limited to emergency preparedness plans, mudslide control works, and flood plain management regulations.

Mudslide (i.e., mudflow) prone area means an area with land surfaces and slopes of unconsolidated material where the history, geology and climate indicate a potential for mudflow.

New construction means, for the purposes of determining insurance rates, structures for which the "start of construction" commenced on or after the effective date of an initial FIRM or after December 31, 1974, whichever is later, and includes any subsequent improvements to such structures. For floodplain management purposes, *new construction* means structures for which the *start of construction* commenced on or after the effective date of a floodplain management regulation adopted by a community and includes any subsequent improvements to such structures.

187

New manufactured home park or subdivision means a manufactured home park or subdivision for which the construction of facilities for servicing the lots on which the manufactured homes are to be affixed (including at a minimum, the installation of utilities, the construction of streets, and either final site grading or the pouring of concrete pads) is completed on or after the effective date of floodplain management regulations adopted by a community.

100-year flood see *base flood.*

Participating community, also known as an *eligible community*, means a community in which the Administrator has authorized the sale of flood insurance.

Person includes any individual or group of individuals, corporation, partnership, association, or any other entity, including State and local governments and agencies.

Policy means the Standard Flood Insurance Policy.

Premium means the total premium payable by the insured for the coverage or coverages provided under the policy. The calculation of the premium may be based upon either chargeable rates or risk premium rates, or a combination of both.

Primary frontal dune means a continuous or nearly continuous mound or ridge of sand with relatively steep seaward and landward slopes immediately landward and adjacent to the beach and subject to erosion and overtopping from high tides and waves during major coastal storms. The inland limit of the primary frontal dune occurs at the point where there is a distinct change from a relatively steep slope to a relatively mild slope.

Principally above ground means that at least 51 percent of the actual cash value of the structure, less land value, is above ground.

Program means the National Flood Insurance Program authorized by 42 U.S.C. 4001 through 4128.

Program deficiency means a defect in a community's flood plain management regulations or administrative procedures that impairs effective implementation of those flood plain management regulations or of the standards in §§ 60.3, 60.4, 60.5, or 60.6.

Project cost means the total financial cost of a flood protection system (including design, land acquisition, construction, fees, overhead, and profits), unless the Federal Insurance Administrator determines a given "cost" not to be a part of such project cost.

Recreational vehicle means a vehicle which is:

(a) Built on a single chassis;

(b) 400 square feet or less when measured at the largest horizontal projection;

(c) Designed to be self-propelled or permanently towable by a light duty truck; and

(d) Designed primarily not for use as a permanent dwelling but as temporary living quarters for recreational, camping, travel, or seasonal use.

Reference feature is the receding edge of a bluff or eroding frontal dune, or if such a feature is not present, the normal high-water line or the seaward line of permanent vegetation if a high-water line cannot be identified.

Regular Program means the Program authorized by the Act under which risk premium rates are required for the first half of available coverage (also known as "first layer" coverage) for all new construction and substantial improvements started on or after the effective date of the FIRM, or after December 31, 1974, for FIRM's effective on or before that date. All buildings, the construction of which started before the effective date of the FIRM, or before January 1, 1975, for FIRMs effective before that date, are eligible for first layer coverage at either subsidized rates or risk premium rates, whichever are lower. Regardless of date of construction, risk premium rates are always required for the second layer coverage and such coverage is offered only after the Administrator has completed a risk study for the community.

Regulatory floodway means the channel of a river or other watercourse and the adjacent land areas that must be reserved in order to discharge the base flood without cumulatively increasing the water surface elevation more than a designated height.

Remedy a violation means to bring the structure or other development into compliance with State or local flood plain management regulations, or, if this is not possible, to reduce the impacts of its noncompliance. Ways that impacts may be reduced include protecting the structure or other affected development from flood damages, implementing the enforcement provisions of the ordinance or otherwise deterring future similar violations, or reducing Federal financial exposure with regard to the structure or other development.

Risk premium rates means those rates established by the Federal Insurance Administrator pursuant to individual community studies and investigations which are undertaken to provide flood insurance in accordance with section 1307 of the Act and the accepted actuarial principles. "Risk premium rates" include provisions for operating costs and allowances.

Riverine means relating to, formed by, or resembling a river (including tributaries), stream, brook, etc.

Sand dunes mean naturally occurring accumulations of sand in ridges or mounds landward of the beach.

Scientifically incorrect. The methodology(ies) and/or assumptions which have been utilized are inappropriate for the physical processes being evaluated or are otherwise erroneous.

Second layer coverage means an additional limit of coverage equal to the amounts made available under the Emergency Program, and made available under the Regular Program.

Servicing company means a corporation, partnership, association, or any other organized entity which contracts with the Federal Insurance Administration to service insurance policies under the National Flood Insurance Program for a particular area.

Sheet flow area—see *area of shallow flooding.*

60-year setback means a distance equal to 60 times the average annual long term recession rate at a site, measured from the reference feature.

Special flood hazard area—see "area of special flood hazard".

Special hazard area means an area having special flood, mudslide (i.e., mudflow), or flood-related erosion hazards, and shown on an FHBM or FIRM as Zone A, AO, A1–30, AE, AR, AR/A1–30, AR/AE, AR/AO, AR/AH, AR/A, A99, AH, VO, V1–30, VE, V, M, or E.

Standard Flood Insurance Policy means the flood insurance policy issued by the Federal Insurance Adminis-

trator or an insurer pursuant to an arrangement with the Federal Insurance Administrator pursuant to Federal statutes and regulations.

Start of Construction (for other than new construction or substantial improvements under the Coastal Barrier Resources Act (Pub. L. 97–348)), includes substantial improvement, and means the date the building permit was issued, provided the actual start of construction, repair, reconstruction, rehabilitation, addition placement, or other improvement was within 180 days of the permit date. The actual start means either the first placement of permanent construction of a structure on a site, such as the pouring of slab or footings, the installation of piles, the construction of columns, or any work beyond the stage of excavation; or the placement of a manufactured home on a foundation. Permanent construction does not include land preparation, such as clearing, grading and filling; nor does it include the installation of streets and/or walkways; nor does it include excavation for a basement, footings, piers, or foundations or the erection of temporary forms; nor does it include the installation on the property of accessory buildings, such as garages or sheds not occupied as dwelling units or not part of the main structure. For a substantial improvement, the actual start of construction means the first alteration of any wall, ceiling, floor, or other structural part of a building, whether or not that alteration affects the external dimensions of the building.

State means any State of the United States, the District of Columbia, Puerto Rico, the Virgin Islands, Guam, American Samoa, and the Commonwealth of the Northern Mariana Islands.

State Coordinating Agency means the agency of the state government (or other office designated by the Governor of the state or by state statute) that, at the request of the Federal Insurance Administrator, assists in the implementation of the National Flood Insurance Program in that state.

Storm cellar means a space below grade used to accommodate occupants of the structure and emergency supplies as a means of temporary shelter against severe tornado or similar wind storm activity.

Structure means, for floodplain management purposes, a walled and roofed building, including a gas or liquid storage tank, that is principally above ground, as well as a manufactured home. *Structure*, for insurance purposes, means:

(1) A building with two or more outside rigid walls and a fully secured roof, that is affixed to a permanent site;

(2) A manufactured home ("a manufactured home," also known as a mobile home, is a structure: built on a permanent chassis, transported to its site in one or more sections, and affixed to a permanent foundation); or

(3) A travel trailer without wheels, built on a chassis and affixed to a permanent foundation, that is regulated under the community's floodplain management and building ordinances or laws.

For the latter purpose, "structure" does not mean a recreational vehicle or a park trailer or other similar vehicle, except as described in paragraph (3) of this definition, or a gas or liquid storage tank.

Subsidized rates mean the rates established by the Federal Insurance Administrator involving in the aggregate a subsidization by the Federal Government.

Substantial damage means damage of any origin sustained by a structure whereby the cost of restoring the structure to its before damaged condition would equal or exceed 50 percent of the market value of the structure before the damage occurred.

Substantial improvement means any reconstruction, rehabilitation, addition, or other improvement of a structure, the cost of which equals or exceeds 50 percent of the market value of the structure before the "start of construction" of the improvement. This term includes structures which have incurred "substantial damage", regardless of the actual repair work performed. The term does not, however, include either:

(1) Any project for improvement of a structure to correct existing violations of state or local health, sanitary, or safety code specifications which have

been identified by the local code enforcement official and which are the minimum necessary to assure safe living conditions or

(2) Any alteration of a "historic structure", provided that the alteration will not preclude the structure's continued designation as a "historic structure".

30-year setback means a distance equal to 30 times the average annual long term recession rate at a site, measured from the reference feature.

Technically incorrect. The methodology(ies) utilized has been erroneously applied due to mathematical or measurement error, changed physical conditions, or insufficient quantity or quality of input data.

V Zone—see "coastal high hazard area."

Variance means a grant of relief by a community from the terms of a flood plain management regulation.

Violation means the failure of a structure or other development to be fully compliant with the community's flood plain management regulations. A structure or other development without the elevation certificate, other certifications, or other evidence of compliance required in § 60.3(b)(5), (c)(4), (c)(10), (d)(3), (e)(2), (e)(4), or (e)(5) is presumed to be in violation until such time as that documentation is provided.

Water surface elevation means the height, in relation to the National Geodetic Vertical Datum (NGVD) of 1929, (or other datum, where specified) of floods of various magnitudes and frequencies in the flood plains of coastal or riverine areas.

Zone of imminent collapse means an area subject to erosion adjacent to the shoreline of an ocean, bay, or lake and within a distance equal to 10 feet plus 5 times the average annual long-term erosion rate for the site, measured from the reference feature.

[41 FR 46968, Oct. 26, 1976]

EDITORIAL NOTE: For FEDERAL REGISTER citations affecting § 59.1, see the List of CFR Sections Affected, which appears in the Finding Aids section of the printed volume and at *www.fdsys.gov.*

§59.2 Description of program.

(a) The National Flood Insurance Act of 1968 was enacted by title XIII of the Housing and Urban Development Act of 1968 (Pub. L. 90–448, August 1, 1968) to provide previously unavailable flood insurance protection to property owners in flood-prone areas. Mudslide (as defined in §59.1) protection was added to the Program by the Housing and Urban Development Act of 1969 (Pub. L. 91–152, December 24, 1969). Flood-related erosion (as defined in §59.1) protection was added to the Program by the Flood Disaster Protection Act of 1973 (Pub. L. 93–234, December 31, 1973). The Flood Disaster Protection Act of 1973 requires the purchase of flood insurance on and after March 2, 1974, as a condition of receiving any form of Federal or federally-related financial assistance for acquisition or construction purposes with respect to insurable buildings and mobile homes within an identified special flood, mudslide (i.e., mudflow), or flood-related erosion hazard area that is located within any community participating in the Program. The Act also requires that on and after July 1, 1975, or one year after a community has been formally notified by the Federal Insurance Administrator. of its identification as community containing one or more special flood, mudslide (i.e., mudflow), or flood-related erosion hazard areas, no such Federal financial assistance, shall be provided within such an area unless the community in which the area is located is then participating in the Program, subject to certain exceptions. See FIA published Guidelines at §59.4(c).

(b) To qualify for the sale of federally-subsidized flood insurance a community must adopt and submit to the Federal Insurance Administrator. as part of its application, flood plain management regulations, satisfying at a minimum the criteria set forth at part 60 of this subchapter, designed to reduce or avoid future flood, mudslide (i.e., mudflow) or flood-related erosion damages. These regulations must include effective enforcement provisions.

(c) Minimum requirements for adequate flood plain management regulations are set forth in §60.3 for flood-prone areas, in §60.4 for mudslide (i.e.,

mudflow) areas and in §60.5 for flood-related erosion areas. Those applicable requirements and standards are based on the amount of technical information available to the community.

[41 FR 46968, Oct. 26, 1976, as amended at 43 FR 7140, Feb. 17, 1978. Redesignated at 44 FR 31177, May 31, 1979, and amended at 48 FR 44552, Sept. 29, 1983; 49 FR 4751, Feb. 8, 1984]

§59.3 Emergency program.

The 1968 Act required a risk study to be undertaken for each community before it could become eligible for the sale of flood insurance. Since this requirement resulted in a delay in providing insurance, the Congress, in section 408 of the Housing and Urban Development Act of 1969 (Pub. L. 91–152, December 24, 1969), established an Emergency Flood Insurance Program as a new section 1336 of the National Flood Insurance Act (42 U.S.C. 4056) to permit the early sale of insurance in flood-prone communities. The emergency program does not affect the requirement that a community must adopt adequate flood plain management regulations pursuant to part 60 of this subchapter but permits insurance to be sold before a study is conducted to determine risk premium rates for the community. The program still requires upon the effective date of a FIRM the charging of risk premium rates for all new construction and substantial improvements and for higher limits of coverage for existing structures.

[43 FR 7140, Feb. 17, 1978. Redesignated at 44 FR 31177, May 31, 1979, and amended at 48 FR 44543, Sept. 29, 1983]

§59.4 References.

(a) The following are statutory references for the National Flood Insurance Program, under which these regulations are issued:

(1) National Flood Insurance Act of 1968 (title XIII of the Housing and Urban Development Act of 1968), Pub. L. 90–448, approved August 1, 1968, 42 U.S.C. 4001 et seq.

(2) Housing and Urban Development Act of 1969 (Pub. L. 91–152, approved December 24, 1969).

(3) Flood Disaster Protection Act of 1973 (87 Stat. 980), Public Law 93–234, approved December 31, 1973.

(4) Section 816 of the Housing and Community Development Act of 1974 (87 Stat. 975), Public Law 93–383, approved August 22, 1974.

(5) Public Law 5–128 (effective October 12, 1977).

(6) The above statutes are included in 42 U.S.C. 4001 et seq.

(b) The following are references relevant to the National Flood Insurance Program:

(1) Executive Order 11988 (Floodplain Management, dated May 24, 1977 (42 FR 26951, May 25, 1977)).

(2) The Flood Control Act of 1960 (Pub. L. 86–645).

(3) Title II, section 314 of title III and section 406 of title IV of the Disaster Relief Act of 1974 (Pub. L. 93–288).

(4) Coastal Zone Management Act (Pub. L. 92–583), as amended Public Law 94–370.

(5) Water Resources Planning Act (Pub. L. 89–90), as amended Public Law 94–112 (October 16, 1975).

(6) Title I, National Environmental Policy Act (Pub. L. 91–190).

(7) Land and Water Conservation Fund Act (Pub. L. 89–578), and subsequent amendments thereto.

(8) Water Resources Council, Principals and Standards for Planning, Water and Related Land Resources (38 FR 24778–24869, September 10, 1973).

(9) Executive Order 11593 (Protection and Enchancement of the Cultural Environment), dated May 13, 1971 (36 FR 8921, May 15, 1971).

(10) 89th Cong., 2nd Session, H.D. 465.

(11) Required land use element for comprehensive planning assistance under section 701 of the Housing Act of 1954, as amended by the Housing and Community Development Act of 1974 (24 CFR 600.72).

(12) Executive Order 11990 (Protection of Wetlands, dated May 24, 1977 (42 FR 26951, May 25, 1977)).

(13) Water Resources Council (Guidance for Floodplain Management) (42 FR 52590, September 30, 1977).

(14) Unified National Program for Floodplain Management of the United States Water Resources Council, July 1976.

(c) The following reference guidelines represent the views of the Federal Insurance Administration with respect to the mandatory purchase of flood insurance under section 102 of the Flood Disaster Protection Act of 1973: Mandatory Purchase of Flood Insurance Guidelines (54 FR 29666–29695, July 13, 1989).

[41 FR 46968, Oct. 26, 1976, as amended at 43 FR 7140, Feb. 17, 1978. Redesignated at 44 FR 31177, May 31, 1979, and amended at 57 FR 19540, May 7, 1992]

Subpart B—Eligibility Requirements

§ 59.21　Purpose of subpart.

This subpart lists actions that must be taken by a community to become eligible and to remain eligible for the Program.

[41 FR 46968, Oct. 26, 1976. Redesignated at 44 FR 31177, May 31, 1979]

§ 59.22　Prerequisites for the sale of flood insurance.

(a) To qualify for flood insurance availability a community shall apply for the entire area within its jurisdiction, and shall submit:

(1) Copies of legislative and executive actions indicating a local need for flood insurance and an explicit desire to participate in the National Flood Insurance Program;

(2) Citations to State and local statutes and ordinances authorizing actions regulating land use and copies of the local laws and regulations cited;

(3) A copy of the flood plain management regulations the community has adopted to meet the requirements of §§ 60.3, 60.4 and/or § 60.5 of this subchapter. This submission shall include copies of any zoning, building, and subdivision regulations, health codes, special purpose ordinances (such as a flood plain ordinance, grading ordinance, or flood-related erosion control ordinance), and any other corrective and preventive measures enacted to reduce or prevent flood, mudslide (i.e., mudflow) or flood-related erosion damage;

(4) A list of the incorporated communities within the applicant's boundaries;

(5) Estimates relating to the community as a whole and to the flood, mudslide (i.e., mudflow) and flood-related erosion prone areas concerning:

(i) Population;

(ii) Number of one to four family residences;

(iii) Number of small businesses; and

(iv) Number of all other structures.

(6) Address of a local repository, such as a municipal building, where the Flood Hazard Boundary Maps (FHBM's) and Flood Insurance Rate Maps (FIRM's) will be made available for public inspection;

(7) A summary of any State or Federal activities with respect to flood plain, mudslide (i.e., mudflow) or flood-related erosion area management within the community, such as federally-funded flood control projects and State-administered flood plain management regulations;

(8) A commitment to recognize and duly evaluate flood, mudslide (i.e., mudflow) and/or flood-related erosion hazards in all official actions in the areas having special flood, mudslide (i.e., mudflow) and/or flood-related erosion hazards and to take such other official action reasonably necessary to carry out the objectives of the program; and

(9) A commitment to:

(i) Assist the Federal Insurance Administrator at his/her request, in his/her delineation of the limits of the areas having special flood, mudslide (i.e., mudflow) or flood-related erosion hazards;

(ii) Provide such information concerning present uses and occupancy of the flood plain, mudslide (i.e., mudflow) or flood-related erosion areas as the Federal Insurance Administrator may request;

(iii) Maintain for public inspection and furnish upon request, for the determination of applicable flood insurance risk premium rates within all areas having special flood hazards identified on a FHBM or FIRM, any certificates of floodproofing, and information on the elevation (in relation to mean sea level) of the level of the lowest floor (including basement) of all new or substantially improved structures, and include whether or not such structures contain a basement, and if the structure has been floodproofed, the elevation (in relation to mean sea level) to which the structure was floodproofed;

(iv) Cooperate with Federal, State, and local agencies and private firms which undertake to study, survey, map, and identify flood plain, mudslide (i.e., mudflow) or flood-related erosion areas, and cooperate with neighboring communities with respect to the management of adjoining flood plain, mudslide (i.e., mudflow) and/or flood-related erosion areas in order to prevent aggravation of existing hazards;

(v) Upon occurrence, notify the Federal Insurance Administrator in writing whenever the boundaries of the community have been modified by annexation or the community has otherwise assumed or no longer has authority to adopt and enforce flood plain management regulations for a particular area. In order that all FHBM's and FIRM's accurately represent the community's boundaries, include within such notification a copy of a map of the community suitable for reproduction, clearly delineating the new corporate limits or new area for which the community has assumed or relinquished flood plain management regulatory authority.

(b) An applicant shall legislatively:

(1) Appoint or designate the agency or official with the responsibility, authority, and means to implement the commitments made in paragraph (a) of this section, and

(2) Designate the official responsible to submit a report to the Federal Insurance Administrator concerning the community participation in the Program, including, but not limited to the development and implementation of flood plain management regulations. This report shall be submitted annually or biennially as determined by the Federal Insurance Administrator.

(c) The documents required by paragraph (a) of this section and evidence of the actions required by paragraph (b) of this section shall be submitted to the Federal Emergency Management Agency, Washington DC 20472.

[41 FR 46968, Oct. 26, 1976. Redesignated at 44 FR 31177, May 31, 1979 and amended at 48 FR 29318, June 24, 1983; 48 FR 44543 and 44552, Sept. 29, 1983; 49 FR 4751, Feb. 8, 1984; 49 FR 33656, Aug. 24, 1984; 50 FR 36023, Sept. 4, 1985]

§ 59.23 Priorities for the sale of flood insurance under the regular program.

Flood-prone, mudslide (i.e., mudflow) and flood-related erosion prone communities are placed on a register of areas eligible for ratemaking studies and then selected from this register for ratemaking studies on the basis of the following considerations—

(a) Recommendations of State officials;

(b) Location of community and urgency of need for flood insurance;

(c) Population of community and intensity of existing or proposed development of the flood plain, the mudslide (i.e., mudflow) and the flood-related erosion area;

(d) Availability of information on the community with respect to its flood, mudslide (i.e., mudflow) and flood-related erosion characteristics and previous losses;

(e) Extent of State and local progress in flood plain, mudslide (i.e., mudflow) area and flood-related erosion area management, including adoption of flood plain management regulations consistent with related ongoing programs in the area.

[41 FR 46968, Oct. 26, 1976. Redesignated at 44 FR 31177, May 31, 1979]

§ 59.24 Suspension of community eligibility.

(a) A community eligible for the sale of flood insurance shall be subject to suspension from the Program for failing to submit copies of adequate flood plain management regulations meeting the minimum requirements of paragraphs (b), (c), (d), (e) or (f) of § 60.3 or paragraph (b) of §§ 60.4 or 60.5, within six months from the date the Federal Insurance Administrator provides the data upon which the flood plain regulations for the applicable paragraph shall be based. Where there has not been any submission by the community, the Federal Insurance Administrator shall notify the community that 90 days remain in the six month period in order to submit adequate flood plain management regulations. Where there has been an inadequate submission, the Federal Insurance Administrator shall notify the community of the specific deficiencies in its submitted flood plain management regulations and inform the community of the amount of time remaining within the six month period. If, subsequently, copies of adequate flood plain management regulations are not received by the Administrator, no later than 30 days before the expiration of the original six month period the Federal Insurance Administrator shall provide written notice to the community and to the state and assure publication in the FEDERAL REGISTER under part 64 of this subchapter of the community's loss of eligibility for the sale of flood insurance, such suspension to become effective upon the expiration of the six month period. Should the community remedy the defect and the Federal Insurance Administrator receive copies of adequate flood plain management regulations within the notice period, the suspension notice shall be rescinded by the Federal Insurance Administrator. If the Federal Insurance Administrator receives notice from the State that it has enacted adequate flood plain management regulations for the community within the notice period, the suspension notice shall be rescinded by the Federal Insurance Administrator. The community's eligibility shall remain terminated after suspension until copies of adequate flood plain management regulations have been received and approved by the Federal Insurance Administrator.

(b) A community eligible for the sale of flood insurance which fails to adequately enforce flood plain management regulations meeting the minimum requirements set forth in §§ 60.3, 60.4 and/or 60.5 shall be subject to probation. Probation shall represent formal notification to the community that the Federal Insurance Administrator regards the community's flood plain management program as not compliant with NFIP criteria. Prior to imposing probation, the Federal Insurance Administrator (1) shall inform the community upon 90 days prior written notice of the impending probation and of the specific program deficiencies and violations relative to the failure to enforce, (2) shall, at least 60 days before probation is to begin, issue a press release to local media explaining the reasons for and the effects of probation, and (3) shall, at least 90 days before probation is to begin, advise all policy-holders in the community of the impending probation and the additional premium that will be charged, as provided in this paragraph, on policies sold or renewed during the period of probation. During this 90-day period the community shall have the opportunity to avoid probation by demonstrating compliance with Program requirements, or by correcting Program deficiencies and remedying all violations to the maximum extent possible. If, at the end of the 90-day period, the Federal Insurance Administrator determines that the community has failed to do so, the probation shall go into effect. Probation may be continued for up to one year after the community corrects all Program deficiencies and remedies all violations to the maximum extent possible. Flood insurance may be sold or renewed in the community while it is on probation. Where a policy covers property located in a community placed on probation on or after October 1, 1986, but prior to October 1, 1992, an additional premium of $25.00 shall be charged on each such policy newly issued or renewed during the one-year period beginning on the date the community is placed on probation and during any successive one-year periods that begin prior to October 1, 1992. Where a community's probation begins on or after October 1, 1992, the additional premium described in the preceding sentence shall be $50.00, which shall also be charged during any successive one-year periods during which the community remains on probation for any part thereof. This $50.00 additional premium shall further be charged during any successive one-year periods that begin on or after October 1, 1992, where the preceding one-year probation period began prior to October 1, 1992.

(c) A community eligible for the sale of flood insurance which fails to adequately enforce its flood plain management regulations meeting the minimum requirements set forth in §§ 60.3, 60.4 and/or 60.5 and does not correct its Program deficiencies and remedy all violations to the maximum extent possible in accordance with compliance deadlines established during a period of probation shall be subject to suspension of its Program eligibility. Under such circumstances, the Federal Insurance Administrator shall grant the community 30 days in which to show cause why it should not be suspended. The Federal Insurance Administrator may conduct a hearing, written or oral, before commencing suspensive action. If a community is to be suspended, the Federal Insurance Administrator shall inform it upon 30 days prior written notice and upon publication in the FEDERAL REGISTER under part 64 of this subchapter of its loss of eligibility for the sale of flood insurance. In the event of impending suspension, the Federal Insurance Administrator shall issue a press release to the local media explaining the reasons and effects of the suspension. The community's eligibility shall only be reinstated by the Federal Insurance Administrator upon his receipt of a local legislative or executive measure reaffirming the community's formal intent to adequately enforce the flood plain management requirements of this subpart, together with evidence of action taken by the community to correct Program deficiencies and remedy to the maximum extent possible those violations which caused the suspension. In certain cases, the Federal Insurance Administrator, in order to evaluate the community's performance under the terms of its submission, may withhold reinstatement for a period not to exceed one year from the date of his receipt of the satisfactory submission or place the community on probation as provided for in paragraph (b) of this section.

(d) A community eligible for the sale of flood insurance which repeals its flood plain management regulations, allows its regulations to lapse, or amends its regulations so that they no longer meet the minimum requirements set forth in §§ 60.3, 60.4 and/or 60.5 shall be suspended from the Program. If a community is to be suspended, the Federal Insurance Administrator shall inform it upon 30 days prior written notice and upon publication in the FEDERAL REGISTER under part 64 of this subchapter of its loss of eligibility for the sale of flood insurance. The community eligibility shall remain terminated after suspension until copies of adequate flood plain management regulations have been received and approved by the Federal Insurance Administrator.

(e) A community eligible for the sale of flood insurance may withdraw from the Program by submitting to theFederal Insurance Administrator a copy of a legislative action that explicitly states its desire to withdraw from the National Flood Insurance Program. Upon receipt of a certified copy of a final legislative action, the Federal Insurance Administrator shall withdraw the community from the Program and publish in the FEDERAL REGISTER under part 64 of this subchapter its loss of eligibility for the sale of flood insurance. A community that has withdrawn from the Program may be reinstated if its submits the application materials specified in § 59.22(a).

(f) If during a period of ineligibility under paragraphs (a), (d), or (e) of this section, a community has permitted actions to take place that have aggravated existing flood plain, mudslide (i.e., mudflow) and/or flood related erosion hazards, the Federal Insurance Administrator may withhold reinstatement until the community submits evidence that it has taken action to remedy to the maximum extent possible the increased hazards. The Administrator may also place the reinstated community on probation as provided for in paragraph (b) of this section.

(g) The Federal Insurance Administrator shall promptly notify the servicing company and any insurers issuing flood insurance pursuant to an arrangement with the Federal Insurance Administrator of those communities whose eligibility has been suspended or which have withdrawn from the program. Flood insurance shall not be sold or renewed in those communities. Policies sold or renewed within a community during a period of ineligibility are deemed to be voidable by the Federal Insurance Administrator whether or not the parties to sale or renewal had actual notice of the ineligibility.

[41 FR 46968, Oct. 26, 1976. Redesignated at 44 FR 31177, May 31, 1979, and amended at 48 FR 44543 and 44552, Sept. 29, 1983; 49 FR 4751, Feb. 8, 1984; 50 FR 36023, Sept. 4, 1985; 57 FR 19540, May 7, 1992; 59 FR 53598, Oct. 25, 1994; 62 FR 55715, Oct. 27, 1997]

Subpart C—Pilot Inspection Program

§ 59.30 A pilot inspection procedure.

(a) *Purpose.* This section sets forth the criteria for implementing a pilot inspection procedure in Monroe County and the Village of Islamorada, Florida. Areas within Monroe County that become communities by incorporating on or after January 1, 1999, are required to implement the pilot inspection procedure as a condition of participating in the NIP. The criteria will also be used to implement the pilot inspection procedure in these communities. The purpose of this inspection procedure is to provide the communities participating in the pilot inspection procedure with an additional means to identify whether structures built in Special Flood Hazard Areas (SFHAs) after the effective date of the initial Flood Insurance Rate Map (FIRM) comply with the community's floodplain management regulations. The pilot inspection procedure will also assist FEMA in verifying that structures insured under the National Flood Insurance Program's Standard Flood Insurance Policy are properly rated. FEMA will publish notices in the FEDERAL REGISTER when communities in Monroe County incorporate, agree to implement the pilot inspection procedure, and become eligible for the sale of flood insurance.

(b) *Procedures and requirements for implementation.* Each community must establish procedures and requirements for implementing the pilot inspection procedure consistent with the criteria established in this section.

(c) *Inspection procedure—*(1) *Starting and termination dates.* The Federal Insurance Administrator will establish the starting date and the termination date for implementing the pilot inspection procedure upon the recommendation of the Regional Administrator. The Regional Director will consult with each community.

(2) *Extension.* TheFederal Insurance Administrator may extend the implementation of the inspection procedure with a new termination date upon the

recommendation of the Regional Administrator. The Regional Administrator will consult with the community. An extension will be granted based on good cause.

(3) *Notices.* Before the starting date of the inspection procedure, each community must publish a notice in a prominent local newspaper and publish other notices as appropriate. The Federal Insurance Administrator will publish a notice in the FEDERAL REGISTER that the community will undertake an inspection procedure. Published notices will include the purpose for implementing the inspection procedure and the effective period of time that the inspection procedure will cover.

(4) *Community reviews.* The communities participating in the pilot inspection procedure must review a list of all pre-FIRM and post-FIRM flood insurance policies in SFHAs to confirm that the start of construction or substantial improvement of insured pre-FIRM buildings occurred on or before December 31, 1974, and to identify possible violations of insured post-FIRM buildings. The community will provide to FEMA a list of insured buildings incorrectly rated as pre-FIRM and a list of insured post-FIRM buildings that the community identifies as possible violations.

(5) *SFIP endorsement.* In the communities that undertake the pilot inspection procedure, all new and renewed flood insurance policies that become effective on and after the date that we and the community establish for the start of the inspection procedure will contain an endorsement to the Standard Flood Insurance Policy that an inspection may be necessary before a subsequent policy renewal [see Part 61, Appendices A(4), (5), and (6)].

(6) *Notice from insurer.* For a building identified as a possible violation under paragraph (c)(4) of this section, the insurer will send a notice to the policyholder that an inspection is necessary in order to renew the policy and that the policyholder must submit a community inspection report as part of the policy renewal process, which includes the payment of the premium. The insurer will send this notice about 6 months before the Standard Flood Insurance Policy expires.

(7) *Conditions for renewal.* If a policyholder receives a notice under paragraph (c)(6) of this section that an inspection is necessary in order to renew the Standard Flood Insurance Policy the following conditions apply:

(i) If the policyholder obtains an inspection from the community and the policyholder sends the community inspection report to the insurer as part of the renewal process, which includes the payment of the premium, the insurer will renew the policy and will verify the flood insurance rate, or

(ii) If the policyholder does not obtain and submit a community inspection report the insurer will not renew the policy.

(8) *Community responsibilities.* For insured post-FIRM buildings that the community inspects and determines to violate the community's floodplain management regulations, the community must demonstrate to FEMA that the community is undertaking measures to remedy the violation to the maximum extent possible. Nothing in this section modifies the community's responsibility under the NFIP to enforce floodplain management regulations adequately that meet the minimum requirements in § 60.3 for all new construction and substantial improvements within the community's SFHAs. The community's responsibility also includes the insured buildings where the policyholder did not obtain an inspection report, and non-insured buildings that this procedure does not cover.

(d) *Restoration of flood insurance coverage.* Insurers will not provide new flood insurance on any building if a property owner does not obtain a community inspection report or if the property owner obtains a community inspection report but does not submit the report with the renewal premium payment. Flood insurance policies sold on a building ineligible in accordance with paragraph (c)(6)(ii) of this section are void under the Standard Flood Insurance Policy inspection endorsements [44 CFR part 61, Appendices (A)(4), (A)(5), and (A)(6)]. When the property owner applies for a flood insurance policy and submits a completed community inspection report by the community with an application and renewal premium payment, the insurer will issue a flood insurance policy.

[65 FR 39748, June 27, 2000, as amended at 67 FR 10633, Mar. 8, 2002; 74 FR 15339, Apr. 3, 2009]

PART 60—CRITERIA FOR LAND MANAGEMENT AND USE

Subpart A—Requirements for Flood Plain Management Regulations

Sec.
60.1 Purpose of subpart.
60.2 Minimum compliance with flood plain management criteria.
60.3 Flood plain management criteria for flood-prone areas.
60.4 Flood plain management criteria for mudslide (i.e., mudflow)-prone areas.
60.5 Flood plain management criteria for flood-related erosion-prone areas.
60.6 Variances and exceptions.
60.7 Revisions of criteria for flood plain management regulations.
60.8 Definitions.

Subpart B—Requirements for State Flood Plain Management Regulations

60.11 Purpose of this subpart.
60.12 Flood plain management criteria for State-owned properties in special hazard areas.
60.13 Noncompliance.

Subpart C—Additional Considerations in Managing Flood-Prone, Mudslide (i.e., Mudflow)-Prone, and Flood-Related Erosion-Prone Areas

60.21 Purpose of this subpart.
60.22 Planning considerations for flood-prone areas.
60.23 Planning considerations for mudslide (i.e., mudflow)-prone areas.
60.24 Planning considerations for flood-related erosion-prone areas.
60.25 Designation, duties, and responsibilities of State Coordinating Agencies.
60.26 Local coordination.

AUTHORITY: 42 U.S.C. 4001 et seq.; Reorganization Plan No. 3 of 1978, 43 FR 41943, 3 CFR, 1978 Comp., p. 329; E.O. 12127 of Mar. 31, 1979, 44 FR 19367, 3 CFR, 1979 Comp., p. 376.

SOURCE: 41 FR 46975, Oct. 26, 1976, unless otherwise noted. Redesignated at 44 FR 31177, May 31, 1979.

Subpart A—Requirements for Flood Plain Management Regulations

§ 60.1 Purpose of subpart.

(a) The Act provides that flood insurance shall not be sold or renewed under the program within a community, unless the community has adopted adequate flood plain management regulations consistent with Federal criteria. Responsibility for establishing such criteria is delegated to the Federal Insurance Administrator.

(b) This subpart sets forth the criteria developed in accordance with the Act by which the Federal Insurance Administrator will determine the adequacy of a community's flood plain management regulations. These regulations must be legally-enforceable, applied uniformly throughout the community to all privately and publicly owned land within flood-prone, mudslide (i.e., mudflow) or flood-related erosion areas, and the community must provide that the regulations take precedence over any less restrictive conflicting local laws, ordinances or codes. Except as otherwise provided in § 60.6, the adequacy of such regulations shall be determined on the basis of the standards set forth in § 60.3 for flood-prone areas, § 60.4 for mudslide areas and § 60.5 for flood-related erosion areas.

(c) Nothing in this subpart shall be construed as modifying or replacing the general requirement that all eligible communities must take into account flood, mudslide (i.e., mudflow) and flood-related erosion hazards, to the extent that they are known, in all official actions relating to land management and use.

(d) The criteria set forth in this subpart are minimum standards for the adoption of flood plain management regulations by flood-prone, mudslide (i.e., mudflow)-prone and flood-related erosion-prone communities. Any community may exceed the minimum criteria under this part by adopting more comprehensive flood plain management regulations utilizing the standards such as contained in subpart C of this part. In some instances, community officials may have access to information or knowledge of conditions that require, particularly for human safety, higher standards than the minimum criteria set forth in subpart A of this part. Therefore, any flood plain management regulations adopted by a State or a community which are more restrictive than the criteria set forth in this part are encouraged and shall take precedence.

[41 FR 46975, Oct. 26, 1976. Redesignated at 44 FR 31177, May 31, 1979, as amended at 48 FR 44552, Sept. 29, 1983; 49 FR 4751, Feb. 8, 1984]

§60.2 Minimum compliance with flood plain management criteria.

(a) A flood-prone community applying for flood insurance eligibility shall meet the standards of §60.3(a) in order to become eligible if a FHBM has not been issued for the community at the time of application. Thereafter, the community will be given a period of six months from the date the Federal Insurance Administrator provides the data set forth in §60.3 (b), (c), (d), (e) or (f), in which to meet the requirements of the applicable paragraph. If a community has received a FHBM, but has not yet applied for Program eligibility, the community shall apply for eligibility directly under the standards set forth in §60.3(b). Thereafter, the community will be given a period of six months from the date the Federal Insurance Administrator provides the data set forth in §60.3 (c), (d), (e) or (f) in which to meet the requirements of the applicable paragraph.

(b) A mudslide (i.e., mudflow)-prone community applying for flood insurance eligibility shall meet the standards of §60.4(a) to become eligible. Thereafter, the community will be given a period of six months from the date the mudslide (i.e., mudflow) areas having special mudslide hazards are delineated in which to meet the requirements of §60.4(b).

(c) A flood-related erosion-prone community applying for flood insurance eligibility shall meet the standards of §60.5(a) to become eligible. Thereafter, the community will be given a period of six months from the date the flood-related erosion areas having special erosion hazards are delineated in which to meet the requirements of §60.5(b).

(d) Communities identified in part 65 of this subchapter as containing more than one type of hazard (e.g., any combination of special flood, mudslide (i.e., mudflow), and flood-related erosion hazard areas) shall adopt flood plain management regulations for each type of hazard consistent with the requirements of §§60.3, 60.4 and 60.5.

(e) Local flood plain management regulations may be submitted to the State Coordinating Agency designated pursuant to §60.25 for its advice and concurrence. The submission to the State shall clearly describe proposed enforcement procedures.

(f) The community official responsible for submitting annual or biennial reports to the Federal Insurance Administrator pursuant to §59.22(b)(2) of this subchapter shall also submit copies of each annual or biennial report to any State Coordinating Agency.

(g) A community shall assure that its comprehensive plan is consistent with the flood plain management objectives of this part.

(h) The community shall adopt and enforce flood plain management regulations based on data provided by the Federal Insurance Administrator. Without prior approval of the Federal Insurance Administrator, the community shall not adopt and enforce flood plain management regulations based upon modified data reflecting natural or man-made physical changes.

[41 FR 46975, Oct. 26, 1976. Redesignated at 44 FR 31177, May 31, 1979, as amended at 48 FR 29318, June 24, 1983; 48 FR 44552, Sept. 29, 1983; 49 FR 4751, Feb. 8, 1984; 50 FR 36024, Sept. 4, 1985; 59 FR 53598, Oct. 25, 1994; 62 FR 55716, Oct. 27, 1997]

§60.3 Flood plain management criteria for flood-prone areas.

The Federal Insurance Administrator will provide the data upon which flood plain management regulations shall be based. If the Federal Insurance Administrator has not provided sufficient data to furnish a basis for these regulations in a particular community, the community shall obtain, review and reasonably utilize data available from other Federal, State or other sources pending receipt of data from the Federal Insurance Administrator. However, when special flood hazard area designations and water surface elevations have been furnished by the Federal Insurance Administrator, they shall apply. The symbols defining such special flood hazard designations are set forth in § 64.3 of this subchapter. In all cases the minimum requirements governing the adequacy of the flood plain management regulations for flood-prone areas adopted by a particular community depend on the amount of technical data formally provided to the community by the Federal Insurance Administrator. Minimum standards for communities are as follows:

(a) When the Federal Insurance Administrator has not defined the special flood hazard areas within a community, has not provided water surface elevation data, and has not provided sufficient data to identify the floodway or coastal high hazard area, but the community has indicated the presence of such hazards by submitting an application to participate in the Program, the community shall:

(1) Require permits for all proposed construction or other development in the community, including the placement of manufactured homes, so that it may determine whether such construction or other development is proposed within flood-prone areas;

(2) Review proposed development to assure that all necessary permits have been received from those governmental agencies from which approval is required by Federal or State law, including section 404 of the Federal Water Pollution Control Act Amendments of 1972, 33 U.S.C. 1334;

(3) Review all permit applications to determine whether proposed building sites will be reasonably safe from flooding. If a proposed building site is in a flood-prone area, all new construction and substantial improvements shall (i) be designed (or modified) and adequately anchored to prevent flotation, collapse, or lateral movement of the structure resulting from hydrodynamic and hydrostatic loads, including the effects of buoyancy, (ii) be constructed with materials resistant to flood damage, (iii) be constructed by methods and practices that minimize flood damages, and (iv) be constructed with electrical, heating, ventilation,

plumbing, and air conditioning equipment and other service facilities that are designed and/or located so as to prevent water from entering or accumulating within the components during conditions of flooding.

(4) Review subdivision proposals and other proposed new development, including manufactured home parks or subdivisions, to determine whether such proposals will be reasonably safe from flooding. If a subdivision proposal or other proposed new development is in a flood-prone area, any such proposals shall be reviewed to assure that (i) all such proposals are consistent with the need to minimize flood damage within the flood-prone area, (ii) all public utilities and facilities, such as sewer, gas, electrical, and water systems are located and constructed to minimize or eliminate flood damage, and (iii) adequate drainage is provided to reduce exposure to flood hazards;

(5) Require within flood-prone areas new and replacement water supply systems to be designed to minimize or eliminate infiltration of flood waters into the systems; and

(6) Require within flood-prone areas (i) new and replacement sanitary sewage systems to be designed to minimize or eliminate infiltration of flood waters into the systems and discharges from the systems into flood waters and (ii) onsite waste disposal systems to be located to avoid impairment to them or contamination from them during flooding.

(b) When the Federal Insurance Administrator has designated areas of special flood hazards (A zones) by the publication of a community's FHBM or FIRM, but has neither produced water surface elevation data nor identified a floodway or coastal high hazard area, the community shall:

(1) Require permits for all proposed construction and other developments including the placement of manufactured homes, within Zone A on the community's FHBM or FIRM;

(2) Require the application of the standards in paragraphs (a) (2), (3), (4), (5) and (6) of this section to development within Zone A on the community's FHBM or FIRM;

(3) Require that all new subdivision proposals and other proposed developments (including proposals for manufactured home parks and subdivisions) greater than 50 lots or 5 acres, whichever is the lesser, include within such proposals base flood elevation data;

(4) Obtain, review and reasonably utilize any base flood elevation and floodway data available from a Federal, State, or other source, including data developed pursuant to paragraph (b)(3) of this section, as criteria for requiring that new construction, substantial improvements, or other development in Zone A on the community's FHBM or FIRM meet the standards in paragraphs (c)(2), (c)(3), (c)(5), (c)(6), (c)(12), (c)(14), (d)(2) and (d)(3) of this section;

(5) Where base flood elevation data are utilized, within Zone A on the community's FHBM or FIRM:

(i) Obtain the elevation (in relation to mean sea level) of the lowest floor (including basement) of all new and substantially improved structures, and

(ii) Obtain, if the structure has been floodproofed in accordance with paragraph (c)(3)(ii) of this section, the elevation (in relation to mean sea level) to which the structure was floodproofed, and

(iii) Maintain a record of all such information with the official designated by the community under §59.22 (a)(9)(iii);

(6) Notify, in riverine situations, adjacent communities and the State Coordinating Office prior to any alteration or relocation of a watercourse, and submit copies of such notifications to the Federal Insurance Administrator;

(7) Assure that the flood carrying capacity within the altered or relocated portion of any watercourse is maintained;

(8) Require that all manufactured homes to be placed within Zone A on a community's FHBM or FIRM shall be installed using methods and practices which minimize flood damage. For the purposes of this requirement, manufactured homes must be elevated and anchored to resist flotation, collapse, or lateral movement. Methods of anchoring may include, but are not to be limited to, use of over-the-top or frame

ties to ground anchors. This requirement is in addition to applicable State and local anchoring requirements for resisting wind forces.

(c) When the Federal Insurance Administrator has provided a notice of final flood elevations for one or more special flood hazard areas on the community's FIRM and, if appropriate, has designated other special flood hazard areas without base flood elevations on the community's FIRM, but has not identified a regulatory floodway or coastal high hazard area, the community shall:

(1) Require the standards of paragraph (b) of this section within all A1–30 zones, AE zones, A zones, AH zones, and AO zones, on the community's FIRM;

(2) Require that all new construction and substantial improvements of residential structures within Zones A1–30, AE and AH zones on the community's FIRM have the lowest floor (including basement) elevated to or above the base flood level, unless the community is granted an exception by the Federal Insurance Administrator for the allowance of basements in accordance with §60.6 (b) or (c);

(3) Require that all new construction and substantial improvements of non-residential structures within Zones A1–30, AE and AH zones on the community's firm (i) have the lowest floor (including basement) elevated to or above the base flood level or, (ii) together with attendant utility and sanitary facilities, be designed so that below the base flood level the structure is watertight with walls substantially impermeable to the passage of water and with structural components having the capability of resisting hydrostatic and hydrodynamic loads and effects of buoyancy;

(4) Provide that where a non-residential structure is intended to be made watertight below the base flood level, (i) a registered professional engineer or architect shall develop and/or review structural design, specifications, and plans for the construction, and shall certify that the design and methods of

construction are in accordance with accepted standards of practice for meeting the applicable provisions of paragraph (c)(3)(ii) or (c)(8)(ii) of this section, and (ii) a record of such certificates which includes the specific elevation (in relation to mean sea level) to which such structures are floodproofed shall be maintained with the official designated by the community under § 59.22(a)(9)(iii);

(5) Require, for all new construction and substantial improvements, that fully enclosed areas below the lowest floor that are usable solely for parking of vehicles, building access or storage in an area other than a basement and which are subject to flooding shall be designed to automatically equalize hydrostatic flood forces on exterior walls by allowing for the entry and exit of floodwaters. Designs for meeting this requirement must either be certified by a registered professional engineer or architect or meet or exceed the following minimum criteria: A minimum of two openings having a total net area of not less than one square inch for every square foot of enclosed area subject to flooding shall be provided. The bottom of all openings shall be no higher than one foot above grade. Openings may be equipped with screens, louvers, valves, or other coverings or devices provided that they permit the automatic entry and exit of floodwaters.

(6) Require that manufactured homes that are placed or substantially improved within Zones A1–30, AH, and AE on the community's FIRM on sites

(i) Outside of a manufactured home park or subdivision,

(ii) In a new manufactured home park or subdivision,

(iii) In an expansion to an existing manufactured home park or subdivision, or

(iv) In an existing manufactured home park or subdivision on which a manufactured home has incurred "substantial damage" as the result of a flood, be elevated on a permanent foundation such that the lowest floor of the manufactured home is elevated to or above the base flood elevation and be securely anchored to an adequately anchored foundation system to resist floatation collapse and lateral movement.

(7) Require within any AO zone on the community's FIRM that all new construction and substantial improvements of residential structures have the lowest floor (including basement) elevated above the highest adjacent grade at least as high as the depth number specified in feet on the community's FIRM (at least two feet if no depth number is specified);

(8) Require within any AO zone on the community's FIRM that all new construction and substantial improvements of nonresidential structures (i) have the lowest floor (including basement) elevated above the highest adjacent grade at least as high as the depth number specified in feet on the community's FIRM (at least two feet if no depth number is specified), or (ii) together with attendant utility and sanitary facilities be completely floodproofed to that level to meet the floodproofing standard specified in § 60.3(c)(3)(ii);

(9) Require within any A99 zones on a community's FIRM the standards of paragraphs (a)(1) through (a)(4)(i) and (b)(5) through (b)(9) of this section;

(10) Require until a regulatory floodway is designated, that no new construction, substantial improvements, or other development (including fill) shall be permitted within Zones A1–30 and AE on the community's FIRM, unless it is demonstrated that the cumulative effect of the proposed development, when combined with all other existing and anticipated development, will not increase the water surface elevation of the base flood more than one foot at any point within the community.

(11) Require within Zones AH and AO, adequate drainage paths around structures on slopes, to guide floodwaters around and away from proposed structures.

(12) Require that manufactured homes to be placed or substantially improved on sites in an existing manufactured home park or subdivision within Zones A–1–30, AH, and AE on the community's FIRM that are not subject to the provisions of paragraph (c)(6) of this section be elevated so that either

(i) The lowest floor of the manufactured home is at or above the base flood elevation, or

(ii) The manufactured home chassis is supported by reinforced piers or other foundation elements of at least equivalent strength that are no less than 36 inches in height above grade and be securely anchored to an adequately anchored foundation system to resist floatation, collapse, and lateral movement.

(13) Notwithstanding any other provisions of §60.3, a community may approve certain development in Zones A1–30, AE, and AH, on the community's FIRM which increase the water surface elevation of the base flood by more than one foot, provided that the community first applies for a conditional FIRM revision, fulfills the requirements for such a revision as established under the provisions of §65.12, and receives the approval of the Federal Insurance Administrator.

(14) Require that recreational vehicles placed on sites within Zones A1–30, AH, and AE on the community's FIRM either

(i) Be on the site for fewer than 180 consecutive days,

(ii) Be fully licensed and ready for highway use, or

(iii) Meet the permit requirements of paragraph (b)(1) of this section and the elevation and anchoring requirements for "manufactured homes" in paragraph (c)(6) of this section.

A recreational vehicle is ready for highway use if it is on its wheels or jacking system, is attached to the site only by quick disconnect type utilities and security devices, and has no permanently attached additions.

(d) When the Federal Insurance Administrator has provided a notice of final base flood elevations within Zones A1–30 and/or AE on the community's FIRM and, if appropriate, has designated AO zones, AH zones, A99 zones, and A zones on the community's FIRM, and has provided data from which the community shall designate its regulatory floodway, the community shall:

(1) Meet the requirements of paragraphs (c) (1) through (14) of this section;

(2) Select and adopt a regulatory floodway based on the principle that the area chosen for the regulatory floodway must be designed to carry the waters of the base flood, without increasing the water surface elevation of that flood more than one foot at any point;

(3) Prohibit encroachments, including fill, new construction, substantial improvements, and other development within the adopted regulatory floodway unless it has been demonstrated through hydrologic and hydraulic analyses performed in accordance with standard engineering practice that the proposed encroachment would not result in any increase in flood levels within the community during the occurrence of the base flood discharge;

(4) Notwithstanding any other provisions of §60.3, a community may permit encroachments within the adopted regulatory floodway that would result in an increase in base flood elevations, provided that the community first applies for a conditional FIRM and floodway revision, fulfills the requirements for such revisions as established under the provisions of §65.12, and receives the approval of the Federal Insurance Administrator.

(e) When the Federal Insurance Administrator has provided a notice of final base flood elevations within Zones A1–30 and/or AE on the community's FIRM and, if appropriate, has designated AH zones, AO zones, A99 zones, and A zones on the community's FIRM, and has identified on the community's FIRM coastal high hazard areas by designating Zones V1–30, VE, and/or V, the community shall:

(1) Meet the requirements of paragraphs (c)(1) through (14) of this section;

(2) Within Zones V1–30, VE, and V on a community's FIRM, (i) obtain the elevation (in relation to mean sea level) of the bottom of the lowest structural member of the lowest floor (excluding pilings and columns) of all new and substantially improved structures, and whether or not such structures contain a basement, and (ii) maintain a record of all such information with the official designated by the community under §59.22(a)(9)(iii);

(3) Provide that all new construction within Zones V1–30, VE, and V on the community's FIRM is located landward of the reach of mean high tide;

(4) Provide that all new construction and substantial improvements in Zones V1–30 and VE, and also Zone V if base flood elevation data is available, on the community's FIRM, are elevated on pilings and columns so that (i) the bottom of the lowest horizontal structural member of the lowest floor (excluding the pilings or columns) is elevated to or above the base flood level; and (ii) the pile or column foundation and structure attached thereto is anchored to resist flotation, collapse and lateral movement due to the effects of wind and water loads acting simultaneously on all building components. Water loading values used shall be those associated with the base flood. Wind loading values used shall be those required by applicable State or local building standards. A registered professional engineer or architect shall develop or review the structural design, specifications and plans for the construction, and shall certify that the design and methods of construction to be used are in accordance with accepted standards of practice for meeting the provisions of paragraphs (e)(4) (i) and (ii) of this section.

(5) Provide that all new construction and substantial improvements within Zones V1–30, VE, and V on the community's FIRM have the space below the lowest floor either free of obstruction or constructed with non-supporting breakaway walls, open wood latticework, or insect screening intended to collapse under wind and water loads without causing collapse, displacement, or other structural damage to the elevated portion of the building or supporting foundation system. For the purposes of this section, a breakaway wall shall have a design safe loading resistance of not less than 10 and no more than 20 pounds per square foot. Use of breakaway walls which exceed a design safe loading resistance of 20 pounds per square foot (either by design or when so required by local or State codes) may be permitted only if a registered professional engineer or architect certifies that the designs proposed meet the following conditions:

(i) Breakaway wall collapse shall result from a water load less than that which would occur during the base flood; and,

(ii) The elevated portion of the building and supporting foundation system shall not be subject to collapse, displacement, or other structural damage due to the effects of wind and water loads acting simultaneously on all building components (structural and non-structural). Water loading values used shall be those associated with the base flood. Wind loading values used shall be those required by applicable State or local building standards.

Such enclosed space shall be useable solely for parking of vehicles, building access, or storage.

(6) Prohibit the use of fill for structural support of buildings within Zones V1–30, VE, and V on the community's FIRM;

(7) Prohibit man-made alteration of sand dunes and mangrove stands within Zones V1–30, VE, and V on the community's FIRM which would increase potential flood damage.

(8) Require that manufactured homes placed or substantially improved within Zones V1–30, V, and VE on the community's FIRM on sites

(i) Outside of a manufactured home park or subdivision,

(ii) In a new manufactured home park or subdivision,

(iii) In an expansion to an existing manufactured home park or subdivision, or

(iv) In an existing manufactured home park or subdivision on which a manufactured home has incurred "substantial damage" as the result of a flood, meet the standards of paragraphs (e)(2) through (7) of this section and that manufactured homes placed or substantially improved on other sites in an existing manufactured home park or subdivision within Zones VI–30, V, and VE on the community's FIRM meet the requirements of paragraph (c)(12) of this section.

(9) Require that recreational vehicles placed on sites within Zones V1–30, V, and VE on the community's FIRM either

(i) Be on the site for fewer than 180 consecutive days,

(ii) Be fully licensed and ready for highway use, or

(iii) Meet the requirements in paragraphs (b)(1) and (e) (2) through (7) of this section.

A recreational vehicle is ready for highway use if it is on its wheels or jacking system, is attached to the site only by quick disconnect type utilities and security devices, and has no permanently attached additions.

(f) When the Federal Insurance Administrator has provided a notice of final base flood elevations within Zones A1–30 or AE on the community's FIRM, and, if appropriate, has designated AH zones, AO zones, A99 zones, and A zones on the community's FIRM, and has identified flood protection restoration areas by designating Zones AR, AR/A1–30, AR/AE, AR/AH, AR/AO, or AR/A, the community shall:

(1) Meet the requirements of paragraphs (c)(1) through (14) and (d)(1) through (4) of this section.

(2) Adopt the official map or legal description of those areas within Zones AR, AR/A1–30, AR/AE, AR/AH, AR/A, or AR/AO that are designated developed areas as defined in § 59.1 in accordance with the eligibility procedures under § 65.14.

(3) For all new construction of structures in areas within Zone AR that are designated as developed areas and in other areas within Zone AR where the AR flood depth is 5 feet or less:

(i) Determine the lower of either the AR base flood elevation or the elevation that is 3 feet above highest adjacent grade; and

(ii) Using this elevation, require the standards of paragraphs (c)(1) through (14) of this section.

(4) For all new construction of structures in those areas within Zone AR that are not designated as developed areas where the AR flood depth is greater than 5 feet:

(i) Determine the AR base flood elevation; and

(ii) Using that elevation require the standards of paragraphs (c)(1) through (14) of this section.

(5) For all new construction of structures in areas within Zone AR/A1–30, AR/AE, AR/AH, AR/AO, and AR/A:

(i) Determine the applicable elevation for Zone AR from paragraphs (a)(3) and (4) of this section;

(ii) Determine the base flood elevation or flood depth for the underlying A1–30, AE, AH, AO and A Zone; and

(iii) Using the higher elevation from paragraphs (a)(5)(i) and (ii) of this section require the standards of paragraphs (c)(1) through (14) of this section.

(6) For all substantial improvements to existing construction within Zones AR/A1–30, AR/AE, AR/AH, AR/AO, and AR/A:

(i) Determine the A1–30 or AE, AH, AO, or A Zone base flood elevation; and

(ii) Using this elevation apply the requirements of paragraphs (c)(1) through (14) of this section.

(7) Notify the permit applicant that the area has been designated as an AR, AR/A1–30, AR/AE, AR/AH, AR/AO, or AR/A Zone and whether the structure will be elevated or protected to or above the AR base flood elevation.

[41 FR 46975, Oct. 26, 1976]

EDITORIAL NOTE: For FEDERAL REGISTER citations affecting § 60.3, see the List of CFR Sections Affected, which appears in the Finding Aids section of the printed volume and at *www.fdsys.gov*.

§ 60.4 Flood plain management criteria for mudslide (i.e., mudflow)-prone areas.

The Federal Insurance Administrator will provide the data upon which flood plain management regulations shall be based. If the Federal Insurance Administrator has not provided sufficient data to furnish a basis for these regulations in a particular community, the community shall obtain, review, and reasonably utilize data available from other Federal, State or other sources pending receipt of data from the Federal Insurance Administrator. However, when special mudslide (i.e., mudflow) hazard area designations have been furnished by the Federal Insurance Administrator, they shall apply. The symbols defining such special mudslide (i.e., mudflow) hazard designations are set forth in § 64.3 of this subchapter. In all cases, the minimum requirements for mudslide (i.e., mudflow)-prone areas adopted by a particular community depend on the amount of technical data provided to the community by the Federal Insurance Administrator. Minimum standards for communities are as follows:

(a) When the Federal Insurance Administrator has not yet identified any area within the community as an area having special mudslide (i.e., mudflow) hazards, but the community has indicated the presence of such hazards by submitting an application to participate in the Program, the community shall

(1) Require permits for all proposed construction or other development in the community so that it may determine whether development is proposed within mudslide (i.e., mudflow)-prone areas;

(2) Require review of each permit application to determine whether the proposed site and improvements will be reasonably safe from mudslides (i.e., mudflows). Factors to be considered in making such a determination should include but not be limited to (i) the type and quality of soils, (ii) any evidence of ground water or surface water problems, (iii) the depth and quality of any fill, (iv) the overall slope of the site, and (v) the weight that any proposed structure will impose on the slope;

(3) Require, if a proposed site and improvements are in a location that may have mudslide (i.e., mudflow) hazards, that (i) a site investigation and further review be made by persons qualified in geology and soils engineering, (ii) the proposed grading, excavations, new construction, and substantial improvements are adequately designed and protected against mudslide (i.e., mudflow) damages, (iii) the proposed grading, excavations, new construction and substantial improvements do not aggravate the existing hazard by creating either on-site or off-site disturbances, and (iv) drainage, planting, watering, and maintenance be such as not to endanger slope stability.

(b) When the Federal Insurance Administrator has delineated Zone M on the community's FIRM, the community shall:

(1) Meet the requirements of paragraph (a) of this section; and

(2) Adopt and enforce a grading ordinance or regulation in accordance with data supplied by the Federal Insurance Administrator which (i) regulates the location of foundation systems and utility systems of new construction and substantial improvements, (ii) regulates the location, drainage and main-

tenance of all excavations, cuts and fills and planted slopes, (iii) provides special requirements for protective measures including but not necessarily limited to retaining walls, buttress fills, sub-drains, diverter terraces, benchings, etc., and (iv) requires engineering drawings and specifications to be submitted for all corrective measures, accompanied by supporting soils engineering and geology reports. Guidance may be obtained from the provisions of the 1973 edition and any subsequent edition of the Uniform Building Code, sections 7001 through 7006, and 7008 through 7015. The Uniform Building Code is published by the International Conference of Building Officials, 50 South Los Robles, Pasadena, California 91101.

[41 FR 46975, Oct. 26, 1976. Redesignated at 44 FR 31177, May 31, 1979, as amended at 48 FR 44552, Sept. 29, 1983; 49 FR 4751, Feb. 8, 1984]

§ 60.5 **Flood plain management criteria for flood-related erosion-prone areas.**

The Federal Insurance Administrator will provide the data upon which flood plain management regulations for flood-related erosion-prone areas shall be based. If the Federal Insurance Administrator has not provided sufficient data to furnish a basis for these regulations in a particular community, the community shall obtain, review, and reasonably utilize data available from other Federal, State or other sources, pending receipt of data from the Federal Insurance Administrator. However, when special flood-related erosion hazard area designations have been furnished by the Federal Insurance Administrator they shall apply. The symbols defining such special flood-related erosion hazard designations are set forth in §64.3 of this subchapter. In all cases the minimum requirements governing the adequacy of the flood plain management regulations for flood-related erosion-prone areas adopted by a particular community depend on the amount of technical data provided to the community by the Federal Insurance Administrator. Minimum standards for communities are as follows:

(a) When the Federal Insurance Administrator has not yet identified any area within the community as having special flood-related erosion hazards, but the community has indicated the presence of such hazards by submitting an application to participate in the Program, the community shall

(1) Require the issuance of a permit for all proposed construction, or other development in the area of flood-related erosion hazard, as it is known to the community;

(2) Require review of each permit application to determine whether the proposed site alterations and improvements will be reasonably safe from flood-related erosion and will not cause flood-related erosion hazards or otherwise aggravate the existing flood-related erosion hazard; and

(3) If a proposed improvement is found to be in the path of flood-related erosion or to increase the erosion hazard, require the improvement to be relocated or adequate protective measures to be taken which will not aggravate the existing erosion hazard.

(b) When the Federal Insurance Administrator has delineated Zone E on the community's FIRM, the community shall

(1) Meet the requirements of paragraph (a) of this section; and

(2) Require a setback for all new development from the ocean, lake, bay, riverfront or other body of water, to create a safety buffer consisting of a natural vegetative or contour strip. This buffer will be designated by the Federal Insurance Administrator according to the flood-related erosion hazard and erosion rate, in conjunction with the anticipated "useful life" of structures, and depending upon the geologic, hydrologic, topographic and climatic characteristics of the community's land. The buffer may be used for suitable open space purposes, such as for agricultural, forestry, outdoor recreation and wildlife habitat areas, and for other activities using temporary and portable structures only.

[41 FR 46975, Oct. 26, 1976. Redesignated at 44 FR 31177, May 31, 1979, as amended at 48 FR 44552, Sept. 29, 1983; 49 FR 4751, Feb. 8, 1984]

§ 60.6 **Variances and exceptions.**

(a) The Federal Insurance Administrator does not set forth absolute criteria for granting variances from the criteria set forth in §§ 60.3, 60.4, and 60.5. The issuance of a variance is for flood plain management purposes only. Insurance premium rates are determined by statute according to actuarial risk and will not be modified by the granting of a variance. The community, after examining the applicant's hardships, shall approve or disapprove a request. While the granting of variances generally is limited to a lot size less than one-half acre (as set forth in paragraph (a)(2) of this section), deviations from that limitation may occur. However, as the lot size increases beyond one-half acre, the technical justification required for issuing a variance increases. The Federal Insurance Administrator may review a community's findings justifying the granting of variances, and if that review indicates a pattern inconsistent with the objectives of sound flood plain management, the Federal Insurance Administrator may take appropriate action under § 59.24(b) of this subchapter. Variances may be issued for the repair or rehabilitation of historic structures upon a determination that the proposed repair or rehabilitation will not preclude the structure's continued designation as a historic structure and the variance is the minimum necessary to preserve the historic character and design of the structure. Procedures for the granting of variances by a community are as follows:

(1) Variances shall not be issued by a community within any designated regulatory floodway if any increase in flood levels during the base flood discharge would result;

(2) Variances may be issued by a community for new construction and substantial improvements to be erected on a lot of one-half acre or less in size contiguous to and surrounded by lots with existing structures constructed below the base flood level, in conformance with the procedures of paragraphs (a) (3), (4), (5) and (6) of this section;

(3) Variances shall only be issued by a community upon (i) a showing of good and sufficient cause, (ii) a determination that failure to grant the variance would result in exceptional hardship to the applicant, and (iii) a determination that the granting of a variance will not result in increased flood heights, additional threats to public

safety, extraordinary public expense, create nuisances, cause fraud on or victimization of the public, or conflict with existing local laws or ordinances;

(4) Variances shall only be issued upon a determination that the variance is the minimum necessary, considering the flood hazard, to afford relief;

(5) A community shall notify the applicant in writing over the signature of a community official that (i) the issuance of a variance to construct a structure below the base flood level will result in increased premium rates for flood insurance up to amounts as high as $25 for $100 of insurance coverage and (ii) such construction below the base flood level increases risks to life and property. Such notification shall be maintained with a record of all variance actions as required in paragraph (a)(6) of this section; and

(6) A community shall (i) maintain a record of all variance actions, including justification for their issuance, and (ii) report such variances issued in its annual or biennial report submitted to the Federal Insurance Administrator.

(7) Variances may be issued by a community for new construction and substantial improvements and for other development necessary for the conduct of a functionally dependent use provided that (i) the criteria of paragraphs (a)(1) through (a)(4) of this section are met, and (ii) the structure or other development is protected by methods that minimize flood damages during the base flood and create no additional threats to public safety.

(b)(1) The requirement that each flood-prone, mudslide (i.e., mudflow)-prone, and flood-related erosion prone community must adopt and submit adequate flood plain management regulations as a condition of initial and continued flood insurance eligibility is statutory and cannot be waived, and such regulations shall be adopted by a community within the time periods specified in §§ 60.3, 60.4 or § 60.5. However, certain exceptions from the standards contained in this subpart may be permitted where the Federal Insurance Administrator recognizes that, because of extraordinary circumstances, local conditions may render the application of certain standards the cause for severe hardship and

gross inequity for a particular community. Consequently, a community proposing the adoption of flood plain management regulations which vary from the standards set forth in §§ 60.3, 60.4, or § 60.5, shall explain in writing to the Federal Insurance Administrator the nature and extent of and the reasons for the exception request and shall include sufficient supporting economic, environmental, topographic, hydrologic, and other scientific and technical data, and data with respect to the impact on public safety and the environment.

(2) The Federal Insurance Administrator shall prepare a Special Environmental Clearance to determine whether the proposal for an exception under paragraph (b)(1) of this section will have significant impact on the human environment. The decision whether an Environmental Impact Statement or other environmental document will be prepared, will be made in accordance with the procedures set out in 44 CFR part 10. Ninety or more days may be required for an environmental quality clearance if the proposed exception will have significant impact on the human environment thereby requiring an EIS.

(c) A community may propose flood plain management measures which adopt standards for floodproofed residential basements below the base flood level in zones A1–30, AH, AO, and AE which are not subject to tidal flooding. Notwithstanding the requirements of paragraph (b) of this section the Federal Insurance Administrator may approve the proposal provided that:

(1) The community has demonstrated that areas of special flood hazard in which basements will be permitted are subject to shallow and low velocity flooding and that there is adequate flood warning time to ensure that all residents are notified of impending floods. For the purposes of this paragraph flood characteristics must include:

(i) Flood depths that are five feet or less for developable lots that are contiguous to land above the base flood level and three feet or less for other lots;

(ii) Flood velocities that are five feet per second or less; and

(iii) Flood warning times that are 12 hours or greater. Flood warning times of two hours or greater may be approved if the community demonstrates that it has a flood warning system and emergency plan in operation that is adequate to ensure safe evacuation of flood plain residents.

(2) The community has adopted flood plain management measures that require that new construction and substantial improvements of residential structures with basements in zones A1–30, AH, AO, and AE shall:

(i) Be designed and built so that any basement area, together with attendant utilities and sanitary facilities below the floodproofed design level, is watertight with walls that are impermeable to the passage of water without human intervention. Basement walls shall be built with the capacity to resist hydrostatic and hydrodynamic loads and the effects of buoyancy resulting from flooding to the floodproofed design level, and shall be designed so that minimal damage will occur from floods that exceed that level. The floodproofed design level shall be an elevation one foot above the level of the base flood where the difference between the base flood and the 500-year flood is three feet or less and two feet above the level of the base flood where the difference is greater than three feet.

(ii) Have the top of the floor of any basement area no lower than five feet below the elevation of the base flood;

(iii) Have the area surrounding the structure on all sides filled to or above the elevation of the base flood. Fill must be compacted with slopes protected by vegetative cover;

(iv) Have a registered professional engineer or architect develop or review the building's structural design, specifications, and plans, including consideration of the depth, velocity, and duration of flooding and type and permeability of soils at the building site, and certify that the basement design and methods of construction proposed are in accordance with accepted standards of practice for meeting the provisions of this paragraph;

(v) Be inspected by the building inspector or other authorized representative of the community to verify that the structure is built according to its design and those provisions of this section which are verifiable.

[41 FR 46975, Oct. 26, 1976. Redesignated at 44 FR 31177, May 31, 1979, as amended at 48 FR 44543 and 44552, Sept. 29, 1983; 49 FR 4751, Feb. 8, 1984; 50 FR 36025, Sept. 4, 1985; 51 FR 30308, Aug. 25, 1986; 54 FR 33550, Aug. 15, 1989]

§ 60.7 Revisions of criteria for flood plain management regulations.

From time to time part 60 may be revised as experience is acquired under the Program and new information becomes available. Communities will be given six months from the effective date of any new regulation to revise their flood plain management regulations to comply with any such changes.

§ 60.8 Definitions.

The definitions set forth in part 59 of this subchapter are applicable to this part.

Subpart B—Requirements for State Flood Plain Management Regulations

§ 60.11 Purpose of this subpart.

(a) A State is considered a "community" pursuant to §59.1 of this subchapter; and, accordingly, the Act provides that flood insurance shall not be sold or renewed under the Program unless a community has adopted adequate flood plain management regulations consistent with criteria established by the Federal Insurance Administrator.

(b) This subpart sets forth the flood plain management criteria required for State-owned properties located within special hazard areas identified by the Federal Insurance Administrator. A State shall satisfy such criteria as a condition to the purchase of a Standard Flood Insurance Policy for a State-owned structure or its contents, or as a condition to the approval by the Federal Insurance Administrator, pursuant to part 75 of this subchapter, of its plan of self-insurance.

[41 FR 46975, Oct. 26, 1976. Redesignated at 44 FR 31177, May 31, 1979, as amended at 48 FR 44552, Sept. 29, 1983; 49 FR 4751, Feb. 8, 1984]

§ 60.12 Flood plain management criteria for State-owned properties in special hazard areas.

(a) The State shall comply with the minimum flood plain management criteria set forth in §§ 60.3, 60.4, and 60.5. A State either shall:

(1) Comply with the flood plain management requirements of all local communities participating in the program in which State-owned properties are located; or

(2) Establish and enforce flood plain management regulations which, at a minimum, satisfy the criteria set forth in §§ 60.3, 60.4, and 60.5.

(b) The procedures by which a state government adopts and administers flood plain management regulations satisfying the criteria set forth in §§ 60.3, 60.4 and 60.5 may vary from the procedures by which local governments satisfy the criteria.

(c) If any State-owned property is located in a non-participating local community, then the State shall comply with the requirements of paragraph (a)(2) of this section for the property.

§ 60.13 Noncompliance.

If a State fails to submit adequate flood plain management regulations applicable to State-owned properties pursuant to § 60.12 within six months of the effective date of this regulation, or fails to adequately enforce such regulations, the State shall be subject to suspensive action pursuant to § 59.24. Where the State fails to adequately enforce its flood plain management regulations, the Federal Insurance Administrator shall conduct a hearing before initiating such suspensive action.

[41 FR 46975, Oct. 26, 1976. Redesignated at 44 FR 31177, May 31, 1979, as amended at 48 FR 44552, Sept. 29, 1983; 49 FR 4751, Feb. 8, 1984]

Subpart C—Additional Considerations in Managing Flood-Prone, Mudslide (i.e., Mudflow)-Prone and Flood-Related Erosion-Prone Areas

§ 60.21 Purpose of this subpart.

The purpose of this subpart is to encourage the formation and adoption of overall comprehensive management plans for flood-prone, mudslide (i.e., mudflow)-prone and flood-related erosion-prone areas. While adoption by a community of the standards in this subpart is not mandatory, the community shall completely evaluate these standards.

§ 60.22 Planning considerations for flood-prone areas.

(a) The flood plain management regulations adopted by a community for flood-prone areas should:

(1) Permit only that development of flood-prone areas which (i) is appropriate in light of the probability of flood damage and the need to reduce flood losses, (ii) is an acceptable social and economic use of the land in relation to the hazards involved, and (iii) does not increase the danger to human life;

(2) Prohibit nonessential or improper installation of public utilities and public facilities in flood-prone areas.

(b) In formulating community development goals after the occurrence of a flood disaster, each community shall consider—

(1) Preservation of the flood-prone areas for open space purposes;

(2) Relocation of occupants away from flood-prone areas;

(3) Acquisition of land or land development rights for public purposes consistent with a policy of minimization of future property losses;

(4) Acquisition of frequently flood-damaged structures;

(c) In formulating community development goals and in adopting flood plain management regulations, each community shall consider at least the following factors—

(1) Human safety;

(2) Diversion of development to areas safe from flooding in light of the need to reduce flood damages and in light of the need to prevent environmentally incompatible flood plain use;

(3) Full disclosure to all prospective and interested parties (including but not limited to purchasers and renters) that (i) certain structures are located within flood-prone areas, (ii) variances have been granted for certain structures located within flood-prone areas, and (iii) premium rates applied to new structures built at elevations below the

base flood substantially increase as the elevation decreases;

(4) Adverse effects of flood plain development on existing development;

(5) Encouragement of floodproofing to reduce flood damage;

(6) Flood warning and emergency preparedness plans;

(7) Provision for alternative vehicular access and escape routes when normal routes are blocked or destroyed by flooding;

(8) Establishment of minimum floodproofing and access requirements for schools, hospitals, nursing homes, orphanages, penal institutions, fire stations, police stations, communications centers, water and sewage pumping stations, and other public or quasi-public facilities already located in the flood-prone area, to enable them to withstand flood damage, and to facilitate emergency operations;

(9) Improvement of local drainage to control increased runoff that might increase the danger of flooding to other properties;

(10) Coordination of plans with neighboring community's flood plain management programs;

(11) The requirement that all new construction and substantial improvements in areas subject to subsidence be elevated above the base flood level equal to expected subsidence for at least a ten year period;

(12) For riverine areas, requiring subdividers to furnish delineations for floodways before approving a subdivision;

(13) Prohibition of any alteration or relocation of a watercourse, except as part of an overall drainage basin plan. In the event of an overall drainage basin plan, provide that the flood carrying capacity within the altered or relocated portion of the watercourse is maintained;

(14) Requirement of setbacks for new construction within Zones V1–30, VE, and V on a community's FIRM;

(15) Requirement of additional elevation above the base flood level for all new construction and substantial improvements within Zones A1–30, AE, V1–30, and VE on the community's FIRM to protect against such occurrences as wave wash and floating debris, to provide an added margin of

safety against floods having a magnitude greater than the base flood, or to compensate for future urban development;

(16) Requirement of consistency between state, regional and local comprehensive plans and flood plain management programs;

(17) Requirement of pilings or columns rather than fill, for the elevation of structures within flood-prone areas, in order to maintain the storage capacity of the flood plain and to minimize the potential for negative impacts to sensitive ecological areas;

(18) Prohibition, within any floodway or coastal high hazard area, of plants or facilities in which hazardous substances are manufactured.

(19) Requirement that a plan for evacuating residents of all manufactured home parks or subdivisions located within flood prone areas be developed and filed with and approved by appropriate community emergency management authorities.

[41 FR 46975, Oct. 26, 1976. Redesignated at 44 FR 31177, May 31, 1979, as amended at 50 FR 36025, Sept. 4, 1985; 54 FR 40284, Sept. 29, 1989]

§ 60.23 Planning considerations for mudslide (i.e., mudflow)-prone areas.

The planning process for communities identified under part 65 of this subchapter as containing Zone M, or which indicate in their applications for flood insurance pursuant to §59.22 of this subchapter that they have mudslide (i.e., mudflow) areas, should include—

(a) The existence and extent of the hazard;

(b) The potential effects of inappropriate hillside development, including

(1) Loss of life and personal injuries, and

(2) Public and private property losses, costs, liabilities, and exposures resulting from potential mudslide (i.e., mudflow) hazards;

(c) The means of avoiding the hazard including the (1) availability of land which is not mudslide (i.e., mudflow)-prone and the feasibility of developing such land instead of further encroaching upon mudslide (i.e., mudflow) areas, (2) possibility of public acquisition of land, easements, and development rights to assure the proper development of hillsides, and (3) advisability of preserving mudslide (i.e., mudflow) areas as open space;

(d) The means of adjusting to the hazard, including the (1) establishment by ordinance of site exploration, investigation, design, grading, construction, filing, compacting, foundation, sewerage, drainage, subdrainage, planting, inspection and maintenance standards and requirements that promote proper land use, and (2) provision for proper drainage and subdrainage on public property and the location of public utilities and service facilities, such as sewer, water, gas and electrical systems and streets in a manner designed to minimize exposure to mudslide (i.e., mudflow) hazards and prevent their aggravation;

(e) Coordination of land use, sewer, and drainage regulations and ordinances with fire prevention, flood plain, mudslide (i.e., mudflow), soil, land, and water regulation in neighboring communities;

(f) Planning subdivisions and other developments in such a manner as to avoid exposure to mudslide (i.e., mudflow) hazards and the control of public facility and utility extension to discourage inappropriate development;

(g) Public facility location and design requirements with higher site stability and access standards for schools, hospitals, nursing homes, orphanages, correctional and other residential institutions, fire and police stations, communication centers, electric power transformers and substations, water and sewer pumping stations and any other public or quasi-public institutions located in the mudslide (i.e., mudflow) area to enable them to withstand mudslide (i.e., mudflow) damage and to facilitate emergency operations; and

(h) Provision for emergencies, including:

(1) Warning, evacuation, abatement, and access procedures in the event of mudslide (i.e., mudflow),

(2) Enactment of public measures and initiation of private procedures to limit danger and damage from continued or future mudslides (i.e., mudflow),

(3) Fire prevention procedures in the event of the rupture of gas or electrical distribution systems by mudslides,

(4) Provisions to avoid contamination of water conduits or deterioration of slope stability by the rupture of such systems,

(5) Similar provisions for sewers which in the event of rupture pose both health and site stability hazards and

(6) Provisions for alternative vehicular access and escape routes when normal routes are blocked or destroyed by mudslides (i.e., mudflow);

(i) The means for assuring consistency between state, areawide, and local comprehensive plans with the plans developed for mudslide (i.e., mudflow)-prone areas;

(j) Deterring the nonessential installation of public utilities and public facilities in mudslide (i.e., mudflow)-prone areas.

§ 60.24 Planning considerations for flood-related erosion-prone areas.

The planning process for communities identified under part 65 of this subchapter as containing Zone E or which indicate in their applications for flood insurance coverage pursuant to § 59.22 of this subchapter that they have flood-related erosion areas should include—

(a) The importance of directing future developments to areas not exposed to flood-related erosion;

(b) The possibility of reserving flood-related erosion-prone areas for open space purposes;

(c) The coordination of all planning for the flood-related erosion-prone areas with planning at the State and Regional levels, and with planning at the level of neighboring communities;

(d) Preventive action in E zones, including setbacks, shore protection works, relocating structures in the path of flood-related erosion, and community acquisition of flood-related erosion-prone properties for public purposes;

(e) Consistency of plans for flood-related erosion-prone areas with comprehensive plans at the state, regional and local levels.

§ 60.25 Designation, duties, and responsibilities of State Coordinating Agencies.

(a) States are encouraged to demonstrate a commitment to the minimum flood plain management criteria set forth in §§ 60.3, 60.4, and 60.5 as evidenced by the designation of an agency of State government to be responsible for coordinating the Program aspects of flood plain management in the State.

(b) State participation in furthering the objectives of this part shall include maintaining capability to perform the appropriate duties and responsibilities as follows:

(1) Enact, whenever necessary, legislation enabling counties and municipalities to regulate development within flood-prone areas;

(2) Encourage and assist communities in qualifying for participation in the Program;

(3) Guide and assist county and municipal public bodies and agencies in developing, implementing, and maintaining local flood plain management regulations;

(4) Provide local governments and the general public with Program information on the coordination of local activities with Federal and State requirements for managing flood-prone areas;

(5) Assist communities in disseminating information on minimum elevation requirements for development within flood-prone areas;

(6) Assist in the delineation of riverine and coastal flood-prone areas, whenever possible, and provide all relevant technical information to the Federal Insurance Administrator;

(7) Recommend priorities for Federal flood plain management activities in relation to the needs of county and municipal localities within the State;

(8) Provide notification to the Federal Insurance Administrator in the event of apparent irreconcilable differences between a community's local flood plain management program and the minimum requirements of the Program;

(9) Establish minimum State flood plain management regulatory standards consistent with those established in this part and in conformance with other Federal and State environmental and water pollution standards for the prevention of pollution during periods of flooding;

(10) Assure coordination and consistency of flood plain management activities with other State, areawide, and local planning and enforcement agencies;

(11) Assist in the identification and implementation of flood hazard mitigation recommendations which are consistent with the minimum flood plain management criteria for the Program;

(12) Participate in flood plain management training opportunities and other flood hazard preparedness programs whenever practicable.

(c) Other duties and responsibilities, which may be deemed appropriate by the State and which are to be officially designated as being conducted in the capacity of the State Coordinating Agency for the Program, may be carried out with prior notification of the Federal Insurance Administrator.

(d) For States which have demonstrated a commitment to and experience in application of the minimum flood plain management criteria set forth in §§ 60.3, 60.4, and 60.5 as evidenced by the establishment and implementation of programs which substantially encompass the activities described in paragraphs (a), (b), and (c) of this section, the Federal Insurance Administrator shall take the foregoing into account when:

(1) Considering State recommendations prior to implementing Program activities affecting State communities;

(2) Considering State approval or certifications of local flood plain management regulations as meeting the requirements of this part.

[51 FR 30309, Aug. 25, 1986]

§ 60.26 Local coordination.

(a) Local flood plain, mudslide (i.e., mudflow) and flood-related erosion area management, forecasting, emergency preparedness, and damage abatement programs should be coordinated with relevant Federal, State, and regional programs;

(b) A community adopting flood plain management regulations pursuant to these criteria should coordinate with the appropriate State agency to promote public acceptance and use of effective flood plain, mudslide, (i.e., mudflow) and flood-related erosion regulations;

(c) A community should notify adjacent communities prior to substantial commercial developments and large subdivisions to be undertaken in areas having special flood, mudslide (i.e., mudflow) and/or flood-related erosion hazards.

PART 61—INSURANCE COVERAGE AND RATES

Sec.

AUTHORITY: 42 U.S.C. 4001 et seq.; Reorganization Plan No. 3 of 1978, 43 FR 41943, 3 CFR, 1978 Comp., p. 329; E.O. 12127 of Mar. 31, 1979, 44 FR 19367, 3 CFR, 1979 Comp., p. 376.

SOURCE: 43 FR 2570, Jan. 17, 1978, unless otherwise noted. Redesignated at 44 FR 31177, May 31, 1979.

§ 61.1   Purpose of part.

This part describes the types of properties eligible for flood insurance coverage under the Program, the limits of such coverage, and the premium rates actually to be paid by insureds. The specific communities eligible for coverage are designated by the Federal Insurance Administrator from time to time as applications are approved under the emergency program and as ratemaking studies of communities are completed prior to the regular program. Lists of such communities are periodically published under part 64 of this subchapter.

[43 FR 2570, Jan. 17, 1978. Redesignated at 44 FR 31177, May 31, 1979, as amended at 48 FR 39068, Aug. 29, 1983; 49 FR 4751, Feb. 8, 1984; 49 FR 5621, Feb. 14, 1984]

§ 61.2   Definitions.

The definitions set forth in part 59 of this subchapter are applicable to this part.

§ 61.3   Types of coverage.

Insurance coverage under the Program is available for structures and their contents. Coverage for each may be purchased separately.

[43 FR 2570, Jan. 17, 1978. Redesignated at 44 FR 31177, May 31, 1979, as amended at 48 FR 39068, Aug. 29, 1983; 50 FR 36025, Sept. 4, 1985; 51 FR 30309, Aug. 25, 1986; 58 FR 62424, Nov. 26, 1993]

§ 61.4   Limitations on coverage.

All flood insurance made available under the Program is subject:

(a) To the Act, the Amendments thereto, and the Regulations issued under the Act;

(b) To the terms and conditions of the Standard Flood Insurance Policy, which shall be promulgated by the Federal Insurance Administrator for substance and form, and which is subject to interpretation by the Federal Insurance Administrator as to scope of coverage pursuant to the applicable statutes and regulations;

(c) To the specified limits of coverage set forth in the Application and Declarations page of the policy; and

(d) To the maximum limits of coverage set forth in §61.6.

[43 FR 2570, Jan. 17, 1978. Redesignated at 44 FR 31177, May 31, 1979, as amended at 48 FR 39068, Aug. 29, 1983; 50 FR 36025, Sept. 4, 1985; 53 FR 16277, May 6, 1988; 58 FR 62424, Nov. 26, 1993]

§61.5 Special terms and conditions.

(a) No new flood insurance or renewal of flood insurance policies shall be written for properties declared by a duly constituted State or local zoning or other authority to be in violation of any flood plain, mudslide (i.e., mudflow) or flood-related erosion area management or control law, regulation, or ordinance.

(b) In order to reduce the administrative costs of the Program, of which the Federal Government pays a major share, payment of the full policyholder premium must be made at the time of application.

(c) Because of the seasonal nature of flooding, refunds of premiums upon cancellation of coverage by the insured are permitted only if the insurer ceases to have an ownership interest in the covered property at the location described in the policy. Refunds of premiums for any other reason are subject to the conditions set forth in §62.5 of this subchapter.

(d) Optional Deductibles, All Zones, are available as follows:

CATEGORY ONE—1 TO 4 FAMILY BUILDING AND CONTENTS COVERAGE POLICIES

Options	Building/contents
	$500/$500
	1,000/1,000
	2,000/1,000
	3,000/1,000
	4,000/2,000
	5,000/2,000

CATEGORY TWO—1 TO 4 FAMILY BUILDING COVERAGE ONLY OR CONTENTS COVERAGE ONLY POLICIES

Options	Building	Contents[1]
	$500	$500
	1,000	1,000
	2,000	2,000
	3,000	3,000
	4,000	4,000

CATEGORY TWO—1 TO 4 FAMILY BUILDING COVERAGE ONLY OR CONTENTS COVERAGE ONLY POLICIES—Continued

Options	Building	Contents[1]
	5,000	5,000

[1] Also applies to residential unit contents in other residential building or in multi-unit condominium building.

CATEGORY THREE—OTHER RESIDENTIAL AND NONRESIDENTIAL POLICIES

Options	Policy combining building and contents	Single coverage only policy (either building or contents)
	$500/$500	$500
	1,000/1,000	1,000
	2,000/2,000	2,000
	3,000/3,000	3,000
	4,000/4,000	4,000
	5,000/5,000	5,000

CATEGORY FOUR—RESIDENTIAL CONDOMINIUM BUILDING POLICIES

Options	Policy combining building and contents	Single coverage only policy (either building or contents)
	$10,000/$10,000	$10,000
	25,000/10,000	25,000

NOTE: Any other combination may be submitted for rating to the NFIP.

(e) The standard flood insurance policy is authorized only under terms and conditions established by Federal statute, the program's regulations, the Administrator's interpretations and the express terms of the policy itself. Accordingly, representations regarding the extent and scope of coverage which are not consistent with the National Flood Insurance Act of 1968, as amended, or the Program's regulations, are void, and the duly licensed property or casualty agent acts for the insured and does not act as agent for the Federal Government, the Federal Emergency Management Agency, or the servicing agent.

[43 FR 2570, Jan. 17, 1978. Redesignated at 44 FR 31177, May 31, 1979, as amended at 47 FR 19140, May 4, 1982; 48 FR 39068, Aug. 29, 1983; 49 FR 33656, Aug. 23, 1984; 50 FR 36025, Sept. 4, 1985; 51 FR 30309, Aug. 25, 1986; 53 FR 16277, May 6, 1988; 53 FR 27991, July 26, 1988; 57 FR 19541, May 7, 1992; 58 FR 62424, Nov. 26, 1993]

§ 61.6 Maximum amounts of coverage available.

(a) Pursuant to section 1306 of the Act, the following are the limits of coverage available under the emergency program and under the regular program.

	Regular program		
	Emergency program [1] first layer	Second layer	Total amount available
Single Family Residential			
Except in Hawaii, Alaska, Guam, U.S. Virgin Islands	$35,000	$215,000	$250,000
In Hawaii, Alaska, Guam, U.S. Virgin Islands	50,000	200,000	250,000
Other Residential			
Except in Hawaii, Alaska, Guam, U.S. Virgin Islands	100,000	150,000	250,000
In Hawaii, Alaska, Guam, U.S. Virgin Islands	150,000	100,000	250,000
Nonresidential			
Small business	100,000	400,000	500,000
Churches and other properties	100,000	400,000	500,000
Contents [2]			
Residential	10,000	90,000	100,000
Small business	100,000	400,000	500,000
Churches, other properties	100,000	400,000	500,000

[1] Only first layer available under emergency program.
[2] Per unit.

(b) In the insuring of a residential condominium building in a regular program community, the maximum limit of building coverage is $250,000 times the number of units in the building (not to exceed the building's replacement cost).

[60 FR 5585, Jan. 30, 1995]

§ 61.7 Risk premium rate determinations.

(a) Pursuant to section 1307 of the Act, the Federal Insurance Administrator is authorized to undertake studies and investigations to enable him/her to estimate the risk premium rates necessary to provide flood insurance in accordance with accepted actuarial principles, including applicable operating costs and allowances. Such rates are also referred to in this subchapter as "actuarial rates."

(b) The Federal Insurance Administrator is also authorized to prescribe by regulation the rates which can reasonably be charged to insureds in order to encourage them to purchase the flood insurance made available under the Program. Such rates are referred to in this subchapter as "chargeable rates." For areas having special flood, mudslide (i.e., mudflow), and flood-related erosion hazards, chargeable rates are usually lower than actuarial rates.

§ 61.8 Applicability of risk premium rates.

Risk premium rates are applicable to all flood insurance made available for:

(a) Any structure, the construction or substantial improvement of which was started after December 31, 1974 or on or after the effective date of the initial FIRM, whichever is later.

(b) Coverage which exceeds the following limits:

(1) For dwelling properties in States other than Alaska, Hawaii, the Virgin Islands, and Guam (i) $35,000 aggregate liability for any property containing only one unit, (ii) $100,000 for any property containing more than one unit, and (iii) $10,000 liability per unit for any contents related to such unit.

(2) For dwelling properties in Alaska, Hawaii, the Virgin Islands, and Guam (i) $50,000 aggregate liability for any property containing only one unit, (ii) $150,000 for property containing more than one unit, and (iii) $10,000 aggregate liability per unit for any contents related to such unit.

(3) For churches and other properties (i) $100,000 for the structure and (ii) $100,000 for contents of any such unit.

(c) Any structure or the contents thereof for which the chargeable rates prescribed by this part would exceed the risk premium rates.

§61.9 Establishment of chargeable rates.

(a) Under section 1308 of the Act, we are establishing annual chargeable rates for each $100 of flood insurance coverage as follows for Pre-FIRM, A zone properties, Pre-FIRM, V-zone properties, and emergency program properties.

Type of structure	A zone[1] rates per year per $100 coverage on:				V zone[2] rates per year per $100 coverage on:			
	structure			Contents	Structure			Contents
	RCBAP[3]		All other		RCBAP[3]		All other	
	High rise	Low rise			High rise	Low rise		
1. Residential:								
No Basement or Enclosure	.85	.70	.76	.96	1.08	.93	.99	1.23
With Basement or Enclosure	.90	.75	.81	.96	1.15	1.00	1.06	1.23
2. All other including hotels and motels with normal occupancy of less than 6 months duration:								
No Basement or Enclosure	N/A	N/A	.83	1.62	N/A	N/A	1.10	2.14
With Basement or Enclosure	N/A	N/A	.88	1.62	N/A	N/A	1.16	2.14

[1] A zones are zones A1–A30, AE, AO, AH, and unnumbered A zones.
[2] V zones are zones V1–V30, VE, and unnumbered V zones.
[3] Residential Condominium Building Association Policies (RCBAP) are distinguished between High Rise (those structures that have 3 or more floors and 5 or more units) and Low Rise (those structures that have either less than 3 floors or less than 5 units).

(b) We will charge rates for contents in pre-FIRM buildings according to the use of the building.

(c) A-zone rates for buildings without basements or enclosures apply uniformly to all buildings throughout emergency program communities.

(d) Properties that meet the definition of Severe Repetitive Loss properties as defined in §79.2(g) of this subchapter, and who refuse an offer of mitigation pursuant to §79.7 of this subchapter are not eligible for the rates identified in paragraphs (a) through (c) of this section.

(e) Properties leased from the Federal Government and located either on the river-facing side of a dike, levee, or other riverine flood control structure, or seaward of any seawall or other coastal flood control structure are not eligible for the rates identified in paragraphs (a) through (c) of this section.

[64 FR 13116, Mar. 17, 1999, as amended at 67 FR 8905, Feb. 27, 2002; 68 FR 15668, Apr. 1, 2003; 72 FR 61737, Oct. 31, 2007]

§61.11 Effective date and time of coverage under the Standard Flood Insurance Policy—New Business Applications and Endorsements.

(a) During the 13-month period beginning on the effective date of a revised Flood Hazard Boundary Map or Flood Insurance Rate Map for a community, the effective date and time of any initial flood insurance coverage shall be 12:01 a.m. (local time) on the first calendar day after the application date and the presentment of payment of premium; for example, a flood insurance policy applied for with the payment of the premium on May 1 will become effective at 12:01 a.m. on May 2.

(b) Where the initial purchase of flood insurance is in connection with the making, increasing, extension, or renewal of a loan, the coverage with respect to the property which is the subject of the loan shall be effective as of the time of the loan closing, provided the written request for the coverage is received by the NFIP and the flood insurance policy is applied for and the presentment of payment of premium is made at or prior to the loan closing.

(c) Except as provided by paragraphs (a) and (b) of this section, the effective date and time of any new policy or added coverage or increase in the amount of coverage shall be 12:01 a.m. (local time) on the 30th calendar day after the application date and the presentment of payment of premium; for example, a flood insurance policy applied for with the payment of the premium on May 1 will become effective at 12:01 a.m. on May 31.

(d) Adding new coverage or increasing the amount of coverage in force is permitted during the term of any policy. The additional premium for any new coverage or increase in the amount of coverage shall be calculated pro rata in accordance with the rates currently in force.

(e) With respect to any submission of an application in connection with new business, the payment by an insured to an agent or the issuance of premium payment by the agent, does not constitute payment to the NFIP, except where a WYO Company receives an application and premium payment from one of its agents and elects to refer the business to the NFIP Servicing Agent because the WYO Company does not wish to write the business, in which case any applicable waiting period under this section shall be calculated in accordance with the first sentence of paragraph (f) of this section. Therefore, it is important that an application for Flood Insurance and its premium be mailed to the NFIP promptly in order to have the effective date of the coverage based on the application date plus the waiting period. If the application and the premium payment are received at the office of the NFIP within ten (10) days from the date of application, the waiting period will be calculated from the date of application. Also, as an alternative, in those cases where the application and premium payment are mailed by certified mail within four (4) days from the date of application, the waiting period will be calculated from the date of application even though the application and premium payment are received at the office of the NFIP after ten (10) days following the date of application. Thus, if the application and premium payment are received after ten (10) days from the date of the application or are not mailed by certified mail within four (4) days from the date of application, the waiting period will be calculated from the date of receipt at the office of the NFIP. To determine the effective date of any coverage added by endorsement to a flood insurance policy already in effect, substitute the term *endorsement* for the term *application* in this paragraph (e).

(f) With respect to the submission of an application in connection with new business, a renewal of a policy in effect and an endorsement to a policy in effect, the payment by an insured to an agent or the issuance of premium payment to a Write-Your-Own (WYO) Company by the agent, accompanied by a properly completed application, renewal or endorsement form, as appropriate, shall commence the calculation of any applicable waiting period under this section, provided that the agent is acting in the capacity of an agent of a Write-Your-Own (WYO) Company authorized by 44 CFR 62.23, is under written contract to or is an employee of such Company, and such WYO Company is, at the time of such submission of an application in connection with new business or a renewal of or endorsement to flood insurance coverage, engaged in WYO business under an arrangement entered into by the Federal Insurance Administrator and the WYO Company pursuant to § 62.23.

(g) Subject to the provisions of paragraph (f) of this section, the rules set forth in paragraphs (a), (b), (c), (d) and (e) of this section apply to WYO Companies, except that premium payments and accompanying applications and endorsements shall be mailed to and received by the WYO Company, rather than the NFIP.

[43 FR 50427, Oct. 30, 1978. Redesignated at 44 FR 31177, May 31, 1979, as amended at 46 FR 13514, Feb. 23, 1981; 48 FR 39069, Aug. 29, 1983; 48 FR 44544, Sept. 29, 1983; 49 FR 33656, Aug. 24, 1984; 50 FR 16242, Apr. 25, 1985; 50 FR 36026, Sept. 4, 1985; 51 FR 30309, Aug. 25, 1986; 53 FR 15211, Apr. 28, 1988; 60 FR 5585, 5586, Jan. 30, 1995]

§ 61.12 Rates based on a flood protection system involving Federal funds.

(a) Where the Federal Insurance Administrator determines that a community has made adequate progress on the construction of a flood protection system involving Federal funds which will significantly limit the area of special flood hazards, the applicable risk premium rates for any property, located within a special flood hazard area intended to be protected directly by such system will be those risk premium rates which would be applicable when the system is complete.

(b) Adequate progress in paragraph (a) of this section means that the community has provided information to the Federal Insurance Administrator sufficient to determine that substantial completion of the flood protection system has been effected because:

(1) 100 percent of the total financial project cost of the completed flood protection system has been authorized;

(2) At least 60 percent of the total financial project cost of the completed flood protection system has been appropriated;

(3) At least 50 percent of the total financial project cost of the completed flood protection system has been expended;

(4) All critical features of the flood protection system, as identified by the Federal Insurance Administrator, are under construction, and each critical feature is 50 percent completed as measured by the actual expenditure of the estimated construction budget funds; and

(5) The community has not been responsible for any delay in the completion of the system.

(c) Each request by a community for a determination must be submitted in writing to the Risk Analysis Division, Mitigation Directorate, Federal Emergency Management Agency, Washington DC, and contain a complete statement of all relevant facts relating to the flood protection system, including, but not limited to, supporting technical data (e.g., U.S. Army Corps of Engineers flood protection project data), cost schedules, budget appropriation data and the extent of Federal funding of the system's construction. Such facts shall include information sufficient to identify all persons affected by such flood protection system or by such request: A full and precise statement of intended purposes of the flood protection system; and a carefully detailed description of such project, including construction completion target dates. In addition, true copies of all contracts, agreements, leases, instruments, and other documents involved must be submitted with the request. Relevant facts reflected in documents, however, must be included in the statement and not merely incorporated by reference, and must be accompanied by an analysis of their bearing on the requirements of paragraph (b) of this section, specifying the perti-

nent provisions. The request must contain a statement whether, to the best of the knowledge of the person responsible for preparing the application for the community, the flood protection system is currently the subject matter of litigation before any Federal, State or local court or administrative agency, and the purpose of that litigation. The request must also contain a statement as to whether the community has previously requested a determination with respect to the same subject matter from the Federal Insurance Administrator, detailing the disposition of such previous request. As documents become part of the file and cannot be returned, the original documents should not be submitted.

(d) The effective date for any risk premium rates established under this section shall be the date of final determination by the Federal Insurance Administrator that adequate progress toward completion of a flood protection system has been made in a community.

(e) A responsible official of a community which received a determination that adequate progress has been made towards completion of a flood protection system shall certify to the Federal Insurance Administrator annually on the anniversary date of receipt of such determination that no present delay in completion of the system is attributable to local sponsors of the system, and that a good faith effort is being made to complete the project.

(f) A community for which risk premium rates have been made available under section 1307(e) of the National Flood Insurance Act of 1968, as amended, shall notify the Federal Insurance Administrator if, at any time, all progress on the completion of the flood protection system has been halted or if the project for the completion of the flood protection system has been canceled.

[43 FR 2570, Jan. 17, 1978, Redesignated at 44 FR 31177, May 31, 1979, as amended at 47 FR 43061 Sept. 30, 1982; 48 FR 39069, Aug. 29, 1983; 48 FR 44552, Sept. 29, 1983; 49 FR 4751, Feb. 8, 1984; 51 FR 30310, Aug. 25, 1986]

§ 61.13 Standard Flood Insurance Policy.

(a) *Incorporation of forms.* Each of the Standard Flood Insurance Policy forms included in appendix "A" hereto (General Property, Dwelling, and Residential Condominium Building Association) and by reference incorporated herein shall be incorporated into the Standard Flood Insurance Policy.

(b) *Endorsements.* All endorsements to the Standard Flood Insurance Policy shall be final upon publication in the FEDERAL REGISTER for inclusion in appendix A.

(c) *Applications.* The application and renewal application forms utilized by the National Flood Insurance Program shall be the only application forms used in connection with the Standard Flood Insurance Policy.

(d) *Waivers.* The Standard Flood Insurance Policy and required endorsements must be used in the Flood Insurance Program, and no provision of the said documents shall be altered, varied, or waived other than by the express written consent of the Federal Insurance Administrator through the issuance of an appropriate amendatory endorsement, approved by the Federal Insurance Administrator as to form and substance for uniform use.

(e) *Oral and written binders.* No oral binder or contract shall be effective. No written binder shall be effective unless issued with express authorization of the Federal Insurance Administrator.

(f) The Standard Flood Insurance Policy and endorsements may be issued by private sector "Write-Your-Own" (WYO) property insurance companies, based upon flood insurance applications and renewal forms, all of which instruments of flood insurance may bear the name, as Insurer, of the issuing WYO Company. In the case of any Standard Flood Insurance Policy, and its related forms, issued by a WYO Company, wherever the names "Federal Emergency Management Agency" and "Federal Insurance Administration" appear, the WYO Company is authorized to substitute its own name therefor. Standard Flood Insurance Policies issued by WYO Companies may be executed by the issuing WYO Company as Insurer, in the place and

stead of the Federal Insurance Federal Insurance Administrator.

[43 FR 2570, Jan. 17, 1978. Redesignated at 44 FR 31177, May 31, 1979, as amended at 44 FR 62517, Oct. 31, 1979; 48 FR 46791, Oct. 14, 1983; 58 FR 62424, Nov. 26, 1993]

§ 61.14   Standard Flood Insurance Policy Interpretations.

(a) *Definition.* A Standard Flood Insurance Policy Interpretation is a written determination by the Federal Insurance Administrator construing the scope of the flood insurance coverage that has been and is provided under the policy.

(b) *Publication and requests for interpretation.* The Federal Insurance Administrator shall, pursuant to these regulations from time to time, issue interpretative rulings regarding the provisions of the Standard Flood Insurance Policy. Such Interpretations shall be published in the FEDERAL REGISTER, made a part of appendix C to these regulations, and incorporated by reference as part of these regulations. Any policyholder or person in privity with a policyholder may file a request for an interpretation in writing with the Federal Insurance Administration, Federal Emergency Management Agency, Washington, DC 20472.

[43 FR 2570, Jan. 17, 1978. Redesignated at 44 FR 31177, May 31, 1979, as amended at 48 FR 39072, Aug. 29, 1983]

§ 61.16   Probation additional premium.

The additional premium charged pursuant to § 59.24(b) on each policy sold or renewed within a community placed on probation prior to October 1, 1992, is $25.00. Where the community was placed on probation on or after October 1, 1992, the additional premium charge is $50.00."

[50 FR 36026, Sept. 4, 1985, as amended at 57 FR 19541, May 7, 1992; 74 FR 15340, Apr. 3, 2009]

§ 61.17   Group Flood Insurance Policy.

(a) A Group Flood Insurance Policy (GFIP) is a policy covering all individuals named by a State as recipients under section 408 of the Stafford Act (42 U.S.C. 5174) of an Individuals and Households Program (IHP) award for flood damage as a result of major disaster declaration by the President.

(b) The premium for the GFIP is a flat fee of $600 per insured. We may adjust the premium to reflect NFIP loss experience and any adjustment of benefits under the IHP program.

(c) The amount of coverage is equivalent to the maximum grant amount established under section 408 of the Stafford Act (42 U.S.C. 5174).

(d) The term of the GFIP is for 36 months and begins 60 days after the date of the disaster declaration.

(e) Coverage for individual grantees begins on the thirtieth day after the NFIP receives the required data for individual grantees and their premium payments.

(f) We will send a Certificate of Flood Insurance to each individual insured under the GFIP.

(g) The GFIP is the Standard Flood Insurance Policy Dwelling Form (a copy of which is included in Appendix A(1) of this part), except that:

(1) VI. DEDUCTIBLES does not apply to the GFIP. A special deductible of $200 (applicable separately to any building loss and any contents loss) applies to insured flood-damage losses sustained by the insured property in the course of any subsequent flooding event during the term of the GFIP. The deductible does not apply to:

(i) III.C.2. Loss Avoidance Measures; or

(ii) III. C.3. Condominium Loss Assessments coverage.

(2) VII. GENERAL CONDITIONS, E. Cancellation of Policy by You, does not apply to the GFIP.

(3) VII. GENERAL CONDITIONS, H. Policy Renewal, does not apply to the GFIP.

(h) We will send a notice to the GFIP certificate holders approximately 60 days before the end of the thirty-six month term of the GFIP. The notice will encourage them to contact a local insurance agent or producer or a private insurance company selling NFIP policies under the Write Your Own program of the NFIP Standard Flood Insurance Policy, and advise them as to the amount of coverage they must maintain in order not to jeopardize their eligibility for future disaster assistance. The IHP program will provide the NFIP the amount of flood insurance coverage to be maintained by certificate holders.

[65 FR 60769, Oct. 12, 2000, as amended at 67 FR 61462, Sept. 30, 2002]

APPENDIX A(1) TO PART 61

FEDERAL EMERGENCY MANAGEMENT AGENCY, FEDERAL INSURANCE ADMINISTRATION

STANDARD FLOOD INSURANCE POLICY

DWELLING FORM

Please read the policy carefully. The flood insurance provided is subject to limitations, restrictions, and exclusions. This policy covers only:

1. A non-condominium residential building designed for principal use as a dwelling place of one to four families, or

2. A single family dwelling unit in a condominium building.

I. AGREEMENT

The Federal Emergency Management Agency (FEMA) provides flood insurance under the terms of the National Flood Insurance Act of 1968 and its Amendments, and Title 44 of the Code of Federal Regulations. We will pay you for direct physical loss by or from flood to your insured property if you:

1. Have paid the correct premium;

2. Comply with all terms and conditions of this policy; and

3. Have furnished accurate information and statements.

We have the right to review the information you give us at any time and to revise your policy based on our review.

II. DEFINITIONS

A. In this policy, "you" and "your" refer to the insured(s) shown on the Declarations Page of this policy and your spouse, if a resident of the same household. Insured(s) includes: Any mortgagee and loss payee named in the Application and Declarations Page, as well as any other mortgagee or loss payee determined to exist at the time of loss in the order of precedence. "We," "us," and "our" refer to the insurer.

Some definitions are complex because they are provided as they appear in the law or regulations, or result from court cases. The precise definitions are intended to protect you.

Flood, as used in this flood insurance policy, means:

1. A general and temporary condition of partial or complete inundation of two or more acres of normally dry land area or of two or more properties (one of which is your property) from:

a. Overflow of inland or tidal waters,

b. Unusual and rapid accumulation or run-off of surface waters from any source,

c. Mudflow.

2. Collapse or subsidence of land along the shore of a lake or similar body of water as a result of erosion or undermining caused by waves or currents of water exceeding anticipated cyclical levels that result in a flood as defined in A.1.a. above.

B. The following are the other key definitions we use in this policy:

1. *Act.* The National Flood Insurance Act of 1968 and any amendments to it.

2. *Actual Cash Value.* The cost to replace an insured item of property at the time of loss, less the value of its physical depreciation.

3. *Application.* The statement made and signed by you or your agent in applying for this policy. The application gives information we use to determine the eligibility of the risk, the kind of policy to be issued, and the correct premium payment. The application is part of this flood insurance policy. For us to issue you a policy, the correct premium payment must accompany the application.

4. *Base Flood.* A flood having a one percent chance of being equaled or exceeded in any given year.

5. *Basement.* Any area of the building, including any sunken room or sunken portion of a room, having its floor below ground level (subgrade) on all sides.

6. *Building.*

a. A structure with two or more outside rigid walls and a fully secured roof, that is affixed to a permanent site;

b. A manufactured home (a "manufactured home," also known as a mobile home, is a structure: built on a permanent chassis, transported to its site in one or more sections, and affixed to a permanent foundation); or

c. A travel trailer without wheels, built on a chassis and affixed to a permanent foundation, that is regulated under the community's floodplain management and building ordinances or laws.

Building does not mean a gas or liquid storage tank or a recreational vehicle, park trailer or other similar vehicle, except as described in B.6.c. above.

7. *Cancellation.* The ending of the insurance coverage provided by this policy before the expiration date.

8. *Condominium.* That form of ownership of real property in which each unit owner has an undivided interest in common elements.

9. *Condominium Association.* The entity made up of the unit owners responsible for the maintenance and operation of:

a. Common elements owned in undivided shares by unit owners; and

b. Other real property in which the unit owners have use rights; where membership in the entity is a required condition of unit ownership.

10. *Declarations Page.* A computer-generated summary of information you provided in the application for insurance. The Declarations Page also describes the term of the policy, limits of coverage, and displays the premium and our name. The Declarations Page is a part of this flood insurance policy.

11. *Described Location.* The location where the insured building(s) or personal property are found. The described location is shown on the Declarations Page.

12. *Direct Physical Loss By or From Flood.* Loss or damage to insured property, directly caused by a flood. There must be evidence of physical changes to the property.

13. *Dwelling.* A building designed for use as a residence for no more than four families or a single-family unit in a building under a condominium form of ownership.

14. *Elevated Building.* A building that has no basement and that has its lowest elevated floor raised above ground level by foundation walls, shear walls, posts, piers, pilings, or columns.

15. *Emergency Program.* The initial phase of a community's participation in the National Flood Insurance Program. During this phase, only limited amounts of insurance are available under the Act.

16. *Expense Constant.* A flat charge you must pay on each new or renewal policy to defray the expenses of the Federal Government related to flood insurance.

17. *Federal Policy Fee.* A flat charge you must pay on each new or renewal policy to defray certain administrative expenses incurred in carrying out the National Flood Insurance Program. This fee covers expenses not covered by the Expense Constant.

18. *Improvements.* Fixtures, alterations, installations, or additions comprising a part of the insured dwelling or the apartment in which you reside.

19. *Mudflow.* A river of liquid and flowing mud on the surface of normally dry land areas, as when earth is carried by a current of water. Other earth movements, such as landslide, slope failure, or a saturated soil mass moving by liquidity down a slope, are not mudflows.

20. *National Flood Insurance Program (NFIP).* The program of flood insurance coverage and floodplain management administered under the Act and applicable Federal regulations in Title 44 of the Code of Federal Regulations, Subchapter B.

21. *Policy.* The entire written contract between you and us. It includes:

a. This printed form;

b. The application and Declarations Page;

c. Any endorsement(s) that may be issued; and

d. Any renewal certificate indicating that coverage has been instituted for a new policy and new policy term.

Only one dwelling, which you specifically described in the application, may be insured under this policy.

22. *Pollutants.* Substances that include, but are not limited to, any solid, liquid, gaseous, or thermal irritant or contaminant, including smoke, vapor, soot, fumes, acids, alkalis, chemicals, and waste. "Waste" includes, but is not limited to, materials to be recycled, reconditioned, or reclaimed.

23. *Post-FIRM Building.* A building for which construction or substantial improvement occurred after December 31, 1974, or on or after the effective date of an initial Flood Insurance Rate Map (FIRM), whichever is later.

24. *Probation Premium.* A flat charge you must pay on each new or renewal policy issued covering property in a community the NFIP has placed on probation under the provisions of 44 CFR 59.24.

25. *Regular Program.* The final phase of a community's participation in the National Flood Insurance Program. In this phase, a Flood Insurance Rate Map is in effect and full limits of coverage are available under the Act.

26. *Special Flood Hazard Area.* An area having special flood or mudflow, and/or flood-related erosion hazards, and shown on a Flood Hazard Boundary Map or Flood Insurance Rate Map as Zone A, AO, A1–A30, AE, A99, AH, AR, AR/A, AR/AE, AR/AH, AR/AO, AR/A1–A30, V1–V30, VE, or V.

27. *Unit.* A single-family unit you own in a condominium building.

28. *Valued Policy.* A policy in which the insured and the insurer agree on the value of the property insured, that value being payable in the event of a total loss. The Standard Flood Insurance Policy is not a valued policy.

III. PROPERTY COVERED

A. Coverage A—Building Property

We insure against direct physical loss by or from flood to:

1. The dwelling at the described location, or for a period of 45 days at another location as set forth in III.C.2.b., Property Removed to Safety.

2. Additions and extensions attached to and in contact with the dwelling by means of a rigid exterior wall, a solid load-bearing interior wall, a stairway, an elevated walkway, or a roof. At your option, additions and extensions connected by any of these methods may be separately insured. Additions and extensions attached to and in contact with the building by means of a common interior wall that is not a solid load-bearing wall are always considered part of the dwelling and cannot be separately insured.

3. A detached garage at the described location. Coverage is limited to no more than 10% of the limit of liability on the dwelling.

Use of this insurance is at your option but reduces the building limit of liability. We do not cover any detached garage used or held for use for residential (i.e., dwelling), business, or farming purposes.

4. Materials and supplies to be used for construction, alteration, or repair of the dwelling or a detached garage while the materials and supplies are stored in a fully enclosed building at the described location or on an adjacent property.

5. A building under construction, alteration, or repair at the described location.

a. If the structure is not yet walled or roofed as described in the definition for building (see II.B.6.a.) then coverage applies:

(1) Only while such work is in progress; or

(2) If such work is halted, only for a period of up to 90 continuous days thereafter.

b. However, coverage does not apply until the building is walled and roofed if the lowest floor, including the basement floor, of a non-elevated building or the lowest elevated floor of an elevated building is:

(1) Below the base flood elevation in Zones AH, AE, A1–A30, AR, AR/AE, AR/AH, AR/A1–A30, AR/A, AR/AO; or

(2) Below the base flood elevation adjusted to include the effect of wave action in Zones VE or V1–V30.

The lowest floor levels are based on the bottom of the lowest horizontal structural member of the floor in Zones VE or V1–V30 and the top of the floor in Zones AH, AE, A1–A30, AR, AR/AE, AR/AH, AR/A1–A30, AR/A, AR/AO.

6. A manufactured home or a travel trailer as described in the Definitions section (see II.B.6.b. and II.B.6.c.).

If the manufactured home or travel trailer is in a special flood hazard area, it must be anchored in the following manner at the time of the loss:

a. By over-the-top or frame ties to ground anchors; or

b. In accordance with the manufacturer's specifications; or

c. In compliance with the community's floodplain management requirements unless it has been continuously insured by the NFIP at the same described location since September 30, 1982.

7. The following items of property which are covered under Coverage A only:

a. Awnings and canopies;

b. Blinds;

c. Built-in dishwashers;

d. Built-in microwave ovens;

e. Carpet permanently installed over unfinished flooring;

f. Central air conditioners;

g. Elevator equipment;

h. Fire sprinkler systems;

i. Walk-in freezers;

j. Furnaces and radiators;

k. Garbage disposal units;

l. Hot water heaters, including solar water heaters;

m. Light fixtures;

n. Outdoor antennas and aerials fastened to buildings;

o. Permanently installed cupboards, bookcases, cabinets, paneling, and wallpaper;

p. Plumbing fixtures;

q. Pumps and machinery for operating pumps;

r. Ranges, cooking stoves, and ovens;

s. Refrigerators; and

t. Wall mirrors, permanently installed.

8. Items of property in a building enclosure below the lowest elevated floor of an elevated post-FIRM building located in Zones A1–A30, AE, AH, AR, AR/A, AR/AE, AR/AH, AR/A1–A30, V1–V30, or VE, or in a basement, regardless of the zone. Coverage is limited to the following:

a. Any of the following items, if installed in their functioning locations and, if necessary for operation, connected to a power source:

(1) Central air conditioners;

(2) Cisterns and the water in them;

(3) Drywall for walls and ceilings in a basement and the cost of labor to nail it, unfinished and unfloated and not taped, to the framing;

(4) Electrical junction and circuit breaker boxes;

(5) Electrical outlets and switches;

(6) Elevators, dumbwaiters and related equipment, except for related equipment installed below the base flood elevation after September 30, 1987;

(7) Fuel tanks and the fuel in them;

(8) Furnaces and hot water heaters;

(9) Heat pumps;

(10) Nonflammable insulation in a basement;

(11) Pumps and tanks used in solar energy systems;

(12) Stairways and staircases attached to the building, not separated from it by elevated walkways;

(13) Sump pumps;

(14) Water softeners and the chemicals in them, water filters, and faucets installed as an integral part of the plumbing system;

(15) Well water tanks and pumps;

(16) Required utility connections for any item in this list; and

(17) Footings, foundations, posts, pilings, piers, or other foundation walls and anchorage systems required to support a building.

b. Clean-up.

B. Coverage B—Personal Property

1. If you have purchased personal property coverage, we insure against direct physical loss by or from flood to personal property inside a building at the described location, if:

a. The property is owned by you or your household family members; and

b. At your option, the property is owned by guests or servants.

Personal property is also covered for a period of 45 days at another location as set forth in III.C.2.b., Property Removed to Safety.

Personal property in a building that is not fully enclosed must be secured to prevent flotation out of the building. If the personal property does float out during a flood, it will be conclusively presumed that it was not reasonably secured. In that case there is no coverage for such property.

2. Coverage for personal property includes the following property, subject to B.1. above, which is covered under Coverage B only:

a. Air conditioning units, portable or window type;

b. Carpets, not permanently installed, over unfinished flooring;

c. Carpets over finished flooring;

d. Clothes washers and dryers;

e. "Cook-out" grills;

f. Food freezers, other than walk-in, and food in any freezer; and

g. Portable microwave ovens and portable dishwashers.

3. Coverage for items of property in a building enclosure below the lowest elevated floor of an elevated post-FIRM building located in Zones A1–A30, AE, AH, AR, AR/A, AR/AE, AR/AH, AR/A1–A30, V1–V30, or VE, or in a basement, regardless of the zone, is limited to the following items, if installed in their functioning locations and, if necessary for operation, connected to a power source:

a. Air conditioning units, portable or window type;

b. Clothes washers and dryers; and

c. Food freezers, other than walk-in, and food in any freezer.

4. If you are a tenant and have insured personal property under Coverage B in this policy, we will cover such property, including your cooking stove or range and refrigerator. The policy will also cover improvements made or acquired solely at your expense in the dwelling or apartment in which you reside, but for not more than 10% of the limit of liability shown for personal property on the Declarations Page. Use of this insurance is at your option but reduces the personal property limit of liability.

5. If you are the owner of a unit and have insured personal property under Coverage B in this policy, we will also cover your interior walls, floor, and ceiling (not otherwise covered under a flood insurance policy purchased by your condominium association) for not more than 10% of the limit of liability shown for personal property on the Declarations Page. Use of this insurance is at your option but reduces the personal property limit of liability.

6. Special Limits. We will pay no more than $2,500 for any one loss to one or more of the following kinds of personal property:

224

a. Artwork, photographs, collectibles, or memorabilia, including but not limited to, porcelain or other figures, and sports cards;

b. Rare books or autographed items;

c. Jewelry, watches, precious and semi-precious stones, or articles of gold, silver, or platinum;

d. Furs or any article containing fur which represents its principal value; or

e. Personal property used in any business.

7. We will pay only for the functional value of antiques.

C. Coverage C—Other Coverages

1. *Debris Removal.*

a. We will pay the expense to remove non-owned debris that is on or in insured property and debris of insured property anywhere.

b. If you or a member of your household perform the removal work, the value of your work will be based on the Federal minimum wage.

c. This coverage does not increase the Coverage A or Coverage B Limit of Liability.

2. *Loss Avoidance Measures*

a. Sandbags, Supplies, and Labor

(1) We will pay up to $1,000 for costs you incur to protect the insured building from a flood or imminent danger of flood, for the following:

(a) Your reasonable expenses to buy:

(i) Sandbags, including sand to fill them;

(ii) Fill for temporary levees;

(iii) Pumps; and

(iv) Plastic sheeting and lumber used in connection with these items.

(b) The value of work, at the Federal minimum wage, that you or a member of your household perform.

(2) This coverage for Sandbags, Supplies and Labor only applies if damage to insured property by or from flood is imminent and the threat of flood damage is apparent enough to lead a person of common prudence to anticipate flood damage. One of the following must also occur:

(a) A general and temporary condition of flooding in the area near the described location must occur, even if the flood does not reach the building; or

(b) A legally authorized official must issue an evacuation order or other civil order for the community in which the building is located calling for measures to preserve life and property from the peril of flood.

This coverage does not increase the Coverage A or Coverage B Limit of Liability.

b. Property Removed to Safety

(1) We will pay up to $1,000 for the reasonable expenses you incur to move insured property to a place other than the described location that contains the property in order to protect it from flood or the imminent danger of flood.

Reasonable expenses include the value of work, at the Federal minimum wage, you or a member of your household perform.

(2) If you move insured property to a location other than the described location that contains the property, in order to protect it from flood or the imminent danger of flood, we will cover such property while at that location for a period of 45 consecutive days from the date you begin to move it there. The personal property that is moved must be placed in a fully enclosed building or otherwise reasonably protected from the elements.

Any property removed, including a moveable home described in II.6.b.and c., must be placed above ground level or outside of the special flood hazard area.

This coverage does not increase the Coverage A or Coverage B Limit of Liability.

3. *Condominium Loss Assessments.*

a. If this policy insures a unit, we will pay, up to the Coverage A limit of liability, your share of loss assessments charged against you by the condominium association in accordance with the condominium association's articles of association, declarations and your deed.

The assessment must be made as a result of direct physical loss by or from flood during the policy term, to the building's common elements.

b. We will not pay any loss assessment charged against you:

(1) And the condominium association by any governmental body;

(2) That results from a deductible under the insurance purchased by the condominium association insuring common elements;

(3) That results from a loss to personal property, including contents of a condominium building;

(4) That results from a loss sustained by the condominium association that was not reimbursed under a flood insurance policy written in the name of the association under the Act because the building was not, at the time of loss, insured for an amount equal to the lesser of:

(a) 80% or more of its full replacement cost; or

(b) The maximum amount of insurance permitted under the Act;

(5) To the extent that payment under this policy for a condominium building loss, in combination with payments under any other NFIP policies for the same building loss, exceeds the maximum amount of insurance permitted under the Act for that kind of building; or

(6) To the extent that payment under this policy for a condominium building loss, in combination with any recovery available to you as a tenant in common under any NFIP condominium association policies for the

225

same building loss, exceeds the amount of insurance permitted under the Act for a single-family dwelling.

Loss assessment coverage does not increase the Coverage A Limit of Liability.

D. Coverage D—Increased Cost of Compliance

1. *General.*

This policy pays you to comply with a State or local floodplain management law or ordinance affecting repair or reconstruction of a structure suffering flood damage. Compliance activities eligible for payment are: elevation, floodproofing, relocation, or demolition (or any combination of these activities) of your structure. Eligible floodproofing activities are limited to:

a. Non-residential structures.

b. Residential structures with basements that satisfy FEMA's standards published in the Code of Federal Regulations [44 CFR 60.6 (b) or (c)].

2. *Limit of Liability.*

We will pay you up to $30,000 under this Coverage D—Increased Cost of Compliance, which only applies to policies with building coverage (Coverage A). Our payment of claims under Coverage D is in addition to the amount of coverage which you selected on the application and which appears on the Declarations Page. But the maximum you can collect under this policy for both Coverage A—Building Property and Coverage D—Increased Cost of Compliance cannot exceed the maximum permitted under the Act. We do not charge a separate deductible for a claim under Coverage D.

3. *Eligibility*

a. A structure covered under Coverage A—Building Property sustaining a loss caused by a flood as defined by this policy must:

(1) Be a "repetitive loss structure." A repetitive loss structure is one that meets the following conditions:

(a) The structure is covered by a contract of flood insurance issued under the NFIP.

(b) The structure has suffered flood damage on two occasions during a 10-year period which ends on the date of the second loss.

(c) The cost to repair the flood damage, on average, equaled or exceeded 25% of the market value of the structure at the time of each flood loss.

(d) In addition to the current claim, the NFIP must have paid the previous qualifying claim, and the State or community must have a cumulative, substantial damage provision or repetitive loss provision in its floodplain management law or ordinance being enforced against the structure; or

(2) Be a structure that has had flood damage in which the cost to repair equals or exceeds 50% of the market value of the structure at the time of the flood. The State or community must have a substantial damage provision in its floodplain management law

or ordinance being enforced against the structure.

b. This Coverage D pays you to comply with State or local floodplain management laws or ordinances that meet the minimum standards of the National Flood Insurance Program found in the Code of Federal Regulations at 44 CFR 60.3. We pay for compliance activities that exceed those standards under these conditions:

(1) 3.a.(1) above.

(2) Elevation or floodproofing in any risk zone to preliminary or advisory base flood elevations provided by FEMA which the State or local government has adopted and is enforcing for flood-damaged structures in such areas. (This includes compliance activities in B, C, X, or D zones which are being changed to zones with base flood elevations. This also includes compliance activities in zones where base flood elevations are being increased, and a flood-damaged structure must comply with the higher advisory base flood elevation.) Increased Cost of Compliance coverage does not apply to situations in B, C, X, or D zones where the community has derived its own elevations and is enforcing elevation or floodproofing requirements for flood-damaged structures to elevations derived solely by the community.

(3) Elevation or floodproofing above the base flood elevation to meet State or local "freeboard" requirements, *i.e.*, that a structure must be elevated above the base flood elevation.

c. Under the minimum NFIP criteria at 44 CFR 60.3(b)(4), States and communities must require the elevation or floodproofing of structures in unnumbered A zones to the base flood elevation where elevation data is obtained from a Federal, State, or other source. Such compliance activities are also eligible for Coverage D.

d. This coverage will also pay for the incremental cost, after demolition or relocation, of elevating or floodproofing a structure during its rebuilding at the same or another site to meet State or local floodplain management laws or ordinances, subject to Exclusion D.5.g. below.

e. This coverage will also pay to bring a flood-damaged structure into compliance with state or local floodplain management laws or ordinances even if the structure had received a variance before the present loss from the applicable floodplain management requirements.

4. *Conditions.*

a. When a structure covered under Coverage A—Building Property sustains a loss caused by a flood, our payment for the loss under this Coverage D will be for the increased cost to elevate, floodproof, relocate, or demolish (or any combination of these activities) caused by the enforcement of current State or local floodplain management ordinances or laws. Our payment for eligible demolition activities will be for the cost to demolish and clear the site of the building debris or a portion thereof caused by the enforcement of current State or local floodplain management ordinances or laws. Eligible activities for the cost of clearing the site will include those necessary to discontinue utility service to the site and ensure proper abandonment of on-site utilities.

b. When the building is repaired or rebuilt, it must be intended for the same occupancy as the present building unless otherwise required by current floodplain management ordinances or laws.

5. *Exclusions.*

Under this Coverage D (Increased Cost of Compliance) we will not pay for:

a. The cost to comply with any floodplain management law or ordinance in communities participating in the Emergency Program.

b. The cost associated with enforcement of any ordinance or law that requires any insured or others to test for, monitor, clean up, remove, contain, treat, detoxify or neutralize, or in any way respond to, or assess the effects of pollutants.

c. The loss in value to any insured building or other structure due to the requirements of any ordinance or law.

d. The loss in residual value of the undamaged portion of a building demolished as a consequence of enforcement of any State or local floodplain management law or ordinance.

e. Any Increased Cost of Compliance under this Coverage D:

(1) Until the building is elevated, floodproofed, demolished, or relocated on the same or to another premises; and

(2) Unless the building is elevated, floodproofed, demolished, or relocated as soon as reasonably possible after the loss, not to exceed two years.

f. Any code upgrade requirements, *e.g.*, plumbing or electrical wiring, not specifically related to the State or local floodplain management law or ordinance.

g. Any compliance activities needed to bring additions or improvements made after the loss occurred into compliance with State or local floodplain management laws or ordinances.

h. Loss due to any ordinance or law that you were required to comply with before the current loss.

i. Any rebuilding activity to standards that do not meet the NFIP's minimum requirements. This includes any situation where the insured has received from the State or community a variance in connection with the current flood loss to rebuild the property to an elevation below the base flood elevation.

j. Increased Cost of Compliance for a garage or carport.

k. Any structure insured under an NFIP Group Flood Insurance Policy.

l. Assessments made by a condominium association on individual condominium unit owners to pay increased costs of repairing commonly owned buildings after a flood in compliance with State or local floodplain management ordinances or laws.

6. *Other Provisions.*

a. Increased Cost of Compliance coverage will not be included in the calculation to determine whether coverage meets the 80% insurance-to-value requirement for replacement cost coverage as set forth in VII. General Conditions, V. Loss Settlement.

b. All other conditions and provisions of the policy apply.

IV. PROPERTY NOT COVERED

We do not cover any of the following:

1. Personal property not inside a building;

2. A building, and personal property in it, located entirely in, on, or over water or seaward of mean high tide if it was constructed or substantially improved after September 30, 1982;

3. Open structures, including a building used as a boathouse or any structure or building into which boats are floated, and personal property located in, on, or over water;

4. Recreational vehicles other than travel trailers described in the Definitions section (see II.B.6.c.) whether affixed to a permanent foundation or on wheels;

5. Self-propelled vehicles or machines, including their parts and equipment. However, we do cover self-propelled vehicles or machines not licensed for use on public roads that are:

a. Used mainly to service the described location or

b. Designed and used to assist handicapped persons, while the vehicles or machines are inside a building at the described location;

6. Land, land values, lawns, trees, shrubs, plants, growing crops, or animals;

7. Accounts, bills, coins, currency, deeds, evidences of debt, medals, money, scrip, stored value cards, postage stamps, securities, bullion, manuscripts, or other valuable papers;

8. Underground structures and equipment, including wells, septic tanks, and septic systems;

9. Those portions of walks, walkways, decks, driveways, patios and other surfaces, all whether protected by a roof or not, located outside the perimeter, exterior walls of the insured building or the building in which the insured unit is located;

10. Containers, including related equipment, such as, but not limited to, tanks containing gases or liquids;

11. Buildings or units and all their contents if more than 49% of the actual cash value of the building is below ground, unless

the lowest level is at or above the base flood elevation and is below ground by reason of earth having been used as insulation material in conjunction with energy efficient building techniques;

12. Fences, retaining walls, seawalls, bulkheads, wharves, piers, bridges, and docks;

13. Aircraft or watercraft, or their furnishings and equipment;

14. Hot tubs and spas that are not bathroom fixtures, and swimming pools, and their equipment, such as, but not limited to, heaters, filters, pumps, and pipes, wherever located;

15. Property not eligible for flood insurance pursuant to the provisions of the Coastal Barrier Resources Act and the Coastal Barrier Improvement Act and amendments to these Acts;

16. Personal property you own in common with other unit owners comprising the membership of a condominium association.

V. EXCLUSIONS

A. We only pay for direct physical loss by or from flood, which means that we do not pay you for:

1. Loss of revenue or profits;

2. Loss of access to the insured property or described location;

3. Loss of use of the insured property or described location;

4. Loss from interruption of business or production;

5. Any additional living expenses incurred while the insured building is being repaired or is unable to be occupied for any reason;

6. The cost of complying with any ordinance or law requiring or regulating the construction, demolition, remodeling, renovation, or repair of property, including removal of any resulting debris. This exclusion does not apply to any eligible activities we describe in Coverage D—Increased Cost of Compliance; or

7. Any other economic loss you suffer.

B. We do not insure a loss directly or indirectly caused by a flood that is already in progress at the time and date:

1. The policy term begins; or

2. Coverage is added at your request.

C. We do not insure for loss to property caused directly by earth movement even if the earth movement is caused by flood. Some examples of earth movement that we do not cover are:

1. Earthquake;

2. Landslide;

3. Land subsidence;

4. Sinkholes;

5. Destabilization or movement of land that results from accumulation of water in subsurface land area; or

6. Gradual erosion.

We do, however, pay for losses from mudflow and land subsidence as a result of erosion that are specifically covered under our definition of flood (see II.A.1.c. and II.A.2.).

D. We do not insure for direct physical loss caused directly or indirectly by any of the following:

1. The pressure or weight of ice;

2. Freezing or thawing;

3. Rain, snow, sleet, hail, or water spray;

4. Water, moisture, mildew, or mold damage that results primarily from any condition:

a. Substantially confined to the dwelling; or

b. That is within your control, including but not limited to:

(1) Design, structural, or mechanical defects;

(2) Failure, stoppage, or breakage of water or sewer lines, drains, pumps, fixtures, or equipment; or

(3) Failure to inspect and maintain the property after a flood recedes;

5. Water or water-borne material that:

a. Backs up through sewers or drains;

b. Discharges or overflows from a sump, sump pump or related equipment; or

c. Seeps or leaks on or through the covered property;

unless there is a flood in the area and the flood is the proximate cause of the sewer or drain backup, sump pump discharge or overflow, or the seepage of water;

6. The pressure or weight of water unless there is a flood in the area and the flood is the proximate cause of the damage from the pressure or weight of water;

7. Power, heating, or cooling failure unless the failure results from direct physical loss by or from flood to power, heating, or cooling equipment on the described location;

8. Theft, fire, explosion, wind, or windstorm;

9. Anything you or any member of your household do or conspires to do to deliberately cause loss by flood; or

10. Alteration of the insured property that significantly increases the risk of flooding.

E. We do not insure for loss to any building or personal property located on land leased from the Federal Government, arising from or incident to the flooding of the land by the Federal Government, where the lease expressly holds the Federal Government harmless under flood insurance issued under any Federal Government program.

F. We do not pay for the testing for or monitoring of pollutants unless required by law or ordinance.

VI. DEDUCTIBLES

A. When a loss is covered under this policy, we will pay only that part of the loss that exceeds your deductible amount, subject to the limit of liability that applies. The deductible amount is shown on the Declarations Page.

However, when a building under construction, alteration, or repair does not have at least two rigid exterior walls and a fully secured roof at the time of loss, your deductible amount will be two times the deductible that would otherwise apply to a completed building.

B. In each loss from flood, separate deductibles apply to the building and personal property insured by this policy.

C. The deductible does NOT apply to:

1. III.C.2. Loss Avoidance Measures;

2. III.C.3. Condominium Loss Assessments; or

3. III.D. Increased Cost of Compliance.

VII. GENERAL CONDITIONS

A. Pair and Set Clause

In case of loss to an article that is part of a pair or set, we will have the option of paying you:

1. An amount equal to the cost of replacing the lost, damaged, or destroyed article, minus its depreciation, or

2. The amount that represents the fair proportion of the total value of the pair or set that the lost, damaged, or destroyed article bears to the pair or set.

B. Concealment or Fraud and Policy Voidance

1. With respect to all insureds under this policy, this policy:

a. Is void;

b. Has no legal force or effect;

c. Cannot be renewed; and

d. Cannot be replaced by a new NFIP policy, if, before or after a loss, you or any other insured or your agent have at any time:

(1) Intentionally concealed or misrepresented any material fact or circumstance;

(2) Engaged in fraudulent conduct; or

(3) Made false statements; relating to this policy or any other NFIP insurance.

2. This policy will be void as of the date wrongful acts described in B.1.above were committed.

3. Fines, civil penalties, and imprisonment under applicable Federal laws may also apply to the acts of fraud or concealment described above.

4. This policy is also void for reasons other than fraud, misrepresentation, or wrongful act. This policy is void from its inception and has no legal force under the following conditions:

a. If the property is located in a community that was not participating in the NFIP on the policy's inception date and did not join or reenter the program during the policy term and before the loss occurred; or

b. If the property listed on the application is otherwise not eligible for coverage under the NFIP.

C. Other Insurance

1. If a loss covered by this policy is also covered by other insurance that includes flood coverage not issued under the Act, we will not pay more than the amount of insurance you are entitled to for lost, damaged, or destroyed property insured under this policy subject to the following:

a. We will pay only the proportion of the loss that the amount of insurance that applies under this policy bears to the total amount of insurance covering the loss, unless C.1.b. or c. immediately below applies.

b. If the other policy has a provision stating that it is excess insurance, this policy will be primary.

c. This policy will be primary (but subject to its own deductible) up to the deductible in the other flood policy (except another policy as described in C.1.b. above). When the other deductible amount is reached, this policy will participate in the same proportion that the amount of insurance under this policy bears to the total amount of both policies, for the remainder of the loss.

2. If there is other insurance in the name of your condominium association covering the same property covered by this policy, then this policy will be in excess over the other insurance.

D. Amendments, Waivers, Assignment

This policy cannot be changed nor can any of its provisions be waived without the express written consent of the Federal Insurance Administrator. No action we take under the terms of this policy constitutes a waiver of any of our rights. You may assign this policy in writing when you transfer title of your property to someone else except under these conditions:

1. When this policy covers only personal property; or

2. When this policy covers a structure during the course of construction.

E. Cancellation of the Policy by You

1. You may cancel this policy in accordance with the applicable rules and regulations of the NFIP.

2. If you cancel this policy, you may be entitled to a full or partial refund of premium also under the applicable rules and regulations of the NFIP.

F. Non-Renewal of the Policy by Us

Your policy will not be renewed:

1. If the community where your covered property is located stops participating in the NFIP, or

2. If your building has been declared ineligible under section 1316 of the Act.

G. Reduction and Reformation of Coverage

1. If the premium we received from you was not enough to buy the kind and amount of coverage you requested, we will provide only the amount of coverage that can be purchased for the premium payment we received.

2. The policy can be reformed to increase the amount of coverage resulting from the reduction described in G.1. above to the amount you requested as follows:

a. Discovery of Insufficient Premium or Incomplete Rating Information Before a Loss:

(1) If we discover before you have a flood loss that your premium payment was not enough to buy the requested amount of coverage, we will send you and any mortgagee or trustee known to us a bill for the required additional premium for the current policy term (or that portion of the current policy term following any endorsement changing the amount of coverage). If you or the mortgagee or trustee pay the additional premium within 30 days from the date of our bill, we will reform the policy to increase the amount of coverage to the originally requested amount effective to the beginning of the current policy term (or subsequent date of any endorsement changing the amount of coverage).

(2) If we determine before you have a flood loss that the rating information we have is incomplete and prevents us from calculating the additional premium, we will ask you to send the required information. You must submit the information within 60 days of our request. Once we determine the amount of additional premium for the current policy term, we will follow the procedure in G.2.a.(1) above.

(3) If we do not receive the additional premium (or additional information) by the date it is due, the amount of coverage can only be increased by endorsement subject to any appropriate waiting period.

b. Discovery of Insufficient Premium or Incomplete Rating Information After a Loss:

(1) If we discover after you have a flood loss that your premium payment was not enough to buy the requested amount of coverage, we will send you and any mortgagee or trustee known to us a bill for the required additional premium for the current and the prior policy terms. If you or the mortgagee or trustee pay the additional premium within 30 days of the date of our bill, we will reform the policy to increase the amount of coverage to the originally requested amount effective to the beginning of the prior policy term.

(2) If we discover after you have a flood loss that the rating information we have is incomplete and prevents us from calculating the additional premium, we will ask you to send the required information. You must submit the information before your claim

can be paid. Once we determine the amount of additional premium for the current and prior policy terms, we will follow the procedure in G.2.b.(1) above.

(3) If we do not receive the additional premium by the date it is due, your flood insurance claim will be settled based on the reduced amount of coverage. The amount of coverage can only be increased by endorsement subject to any appropriate waiting period.

3. However, if we find that you or your agent intentionally did not tell us, or falsified, any important fact or circumstance or did anything fraudulent relating to this insurance, the provisions of Condition B. Concealment or Fraud and Policy Voidance apply.

H. Policy Renewal

1. This policy will expire at 12:01 a.m. on the last day of the policy term.

2. We must receive the payment of the appropriate renewal premium within 30 days of the expiration date.

3. If we find, however, that we did not place your renewal notice into the U.S. Postal Service, or if we did mail it, we made a mistake, e.g., we used an incorrect, incomplete, or illegible address, which delayed its delivery to you before the due date for the renewal premium, then we will follow these procedures:

a. If you or your agent notified us, not later than one year after the date on which the payment of the renewal premium was due, of non-receipt of a renewal notice before the due date for the renewal premium, and we determine that the circumstances in the preceding paragraph apply, we will mail a second bill providing a revised due date, which will be 30 days after the date on which the bill is mailed.

b. If we do not receive the premium requested in the second bill by the revised due date, then we will not renew the policy. In that case, the policy will remain an expired policy as of the expiration date shown on the Declarations Page.

4. In connection with the renewal of this policy, we may ask you during the policy term to recertify, on a Recertification Questionnaire we will provide to you, the rating information used to rate your most recent application for or renewal of insurance.

I. Conditions Suspending or Restricting Insurance

We are not liable for loss that occurs while there is a hazard that is increased by any means within your control or knowledge.

J. Requirements in Case of Loss

In case of a flood loss to insured property, you must:

1. Give prompt written notice to us;

2. As soon as reasonably possible, separate the damaged and undamaged property, putting it in the best possible order so that we may examine it;

3. Prepare an inventory of damaged property showing the quantity, description, actual cash value, and amount of loss. Attach all bills, receipts, and related documents;

4. Within 60 days after the loss, send us a proof of loss, which is your statement of the amount you are claiming under the policy signed and sworn to by you, and which furnishes us with the following information:

a. The date and time of loss;

b. A brief explanation of how the loss happened;

c. Your interest (for example, "owner") and the interest, if any, of others in the damaged property;

d. Details of any other insurance that may cover the loss;

e. Changes in title or occupancy of the covered property during the term of the policy;

f. Specifications of damaged buildings and detailed repair estimates;

g. Names of mortgagees or anyone else having a lien, charge, or claim against the insured property;

h. Details about who occupied any insured building at the time of loss and for what purpose; and

i. The inventory of damaged personal property described in J.3. above.

5. In completing the proof of loss, you must use your own judgment concerning the amount of loss and justify that amount.

6. You must cooperate with the adjuster or representative in the investigation of the claim.

7. The insurance adjuster whom we hire to investigate your claim may furnish you with a proof of loss form, and she or he may help you complete it. However, this is a matter of courtesy only, and you must still send us a proof of loss within 60 days after the loss even if the adjuster does not furnish the form or help you complete it.

8. We have not authorized the adjuster to approve or disapprove claims or to tell you whether we will approve your claim.

9. At our option, we may accept the adjuster's report of the loss instead of your proof of loss. The adjuster's report will include information about your loss and the damages you sustained. You must sign the adjuster's report. At our option, we may require you to swear to the report.

K. Our Options After a Loss

Options we may, in our sole discretion, exercise after loss include the following:

1. At such reasonable times and places that we may designate, you must:

a. Show us or our representative the damaged property;

b. Submit to examination under oath, while not in the presence of another insured, and sign the same; and

c. Permit us to examine and make extracts and copies of:

(1) Any policies of property insurance insuring you against loss and the deed establishing your ownership of the insured real property;

(2) Condominium association documents including the Declarations of the condominium, its Articles of Association or Incorporation, Bylaws, rules and regulations, and other relevant documents if you are a unit owner in a condominium building; and

(3) All books of accounts, bills, invoices and other vouchers, or certified copies pertaining to the damaged property if the originals are lost.

2. We may request, in writing, that you furnish us with a complete inventory of the lost, damaged or destroyed property, including:

a. Quantities and costs;

b. Actual cash values or replacement cost (whichever is appropriate);

c. Amounts of loss claimed;

d. Any written plans and specifications for repair of the damaged property that you can reasonably make available to us; and

e. Evidence that prior flood damage has been repaired.

3. If we give you written notice within 30 days after we receive your signed, sworn proof of loss, we may:

a. Repair, rebuild, or replace any part of the lost, damaged, or destroyed property with material or property of like kind and quality or its functional equivalent; and

b. Take all or any part of the damaged property at the value that we agree upon or its appraised value.

L. No Benefit to Bailee

No person or organization, other than you, having custody of covered property will benefit from this insurance.

M. Loss Payment

1. We will adjust all losses with you. We will pay you unless some other person or entity is named in the policy or is legally entitled to receive payment. Loss will be payable 60 days after we receive your proof of loss (or within 90 days after the insurance adjuster files the adjuster's report signed and sworn to by you in lieu of a proof of loss) and:

a. We reach an agreement with you;

b. There is an entry of a final judgment; or

c. There is a filing of an appraisal award with us, as provided in VII. P.

2. If we reject your proof of loss in whole or in part you may:

a. Accept our denial of your claim;

b. Exercise your rights under this policy; or

c. File an amended proof of loss as long as it is filed within 60 days of the date of the loss.

N. Abandonment

You may not abandon to us damaged or undamaged property insured under this policy.

O. Salvage

We may permit you to keep damaged property insured under this policy after a loss, and we will reduce the amount of the loss proceeds payable to you under the policy by the value of the salvage.

P. Appraisal

If you and we fail to agree on the actual cash value or, if applicable, replacement cost of your damaged property to settle upon the amount of loss, then either may demand an appraisal of the loss. In this event, you and we will each choose a competent and impartial appraiser within 20 days after receiving a written request from the other. The two appraisers will choose an umpire. If they cannot agree upon an umpire within 15 days, you or we may request that the choice be made by a judge of a court of record in the state where the covered property is located. The appraisers will separately state the actual cash value, the replacement cost, and the amount of loss to each item. If the appraisers submit a written report of an agreement to us, the amount agreed upon will be the amount of loss. If they fail to agree, they will submit their differences to the umpire. A decision agreed to by any two will set the amount of actual cash value and loss, or if it applies, the replacement cost and loss.

Each party will:

1. Pay its own appraiser; and
2. Bear the other expenses of the appraisal and umpire equally.

Q. Mortgage Clause

The word "mortgagee" includes trustee.

Any loss payable under Coverage A—Building Property will be paid to any mortgagee of whom we have actual notice, as well as any other mortgagee or loss payee determined to exist at the time of loss, and you, as interests appear. If more than one mortgagee is named, the order of payment will be the same as the order of precedence of the mortgages.

If we deny your claim, that denial will not apply to a valid claim of the mortgagee, if the mortgagee:

1. Notifies us of any change in the ownership or occupancy, or substantial change in risk of which the mortgagee is aware;
2. Pays any premium due under this policy on demand if you have neglected to pay the premium; and

3. Submits a signed, sworn proof of loss within 60 days after receiving notice from us of your failure to do so.

All of the terms of this policy apply to the mortgagee.

The mortgagee has the right to receive loss payment even if the mortgagee has started foreclosure or similar action on the building.

If we decide to cancel or not renew this policy, it will continue in effect for the benefit of the mortgagee only for 30 days after we notify the mortgagee of the cancellation or non-renewal.

If we pay the mortgagee for any loss and deny payment to you, we are subrogated to all the rights of the mortgagee granted under the mortgage on the property. Subrogation will not impair the right of the mortgagee to recover the full amount of the mortgagee's claim.

R. Suit Against Us

You may not sue us to recover money under this policy unless you have complied with all the requirements of the policy. If you do sue, you must start the suit within one year after the date of the written denial of all or part of the claim, and you must file the suit in the United States District Court of the district in which the covered property was located at the time of loss. This requirement applies to any claim that you may have under this policy and to any dispute that you may have arising out of the handling of any claim under the policy.

S. Subrogation

Whenever we make a payment for a loss under this policy, we are subrogated to your right to recover for that loss from any other person. That means that your right to recover for a loss that was partly or totally caused by someone else is automatically transferred to us, to the extent that we have paid you for the loss. We may require you to acknowledge this transfer in writing. After the loss, you may not give up our right to recover this money or do anything that would prevent us from recovering it. If you make any claim against any person who caused your loss and recover any money, you must pay us back first before you may keep any of that money.

T. Continuous Lake Flooding

1. If an insured building has been flooded by rising lake waters continuously for 90 days or more and it appears reasonably certain that a continuation of this flooding will result in a covered loss to the insured building equal to or greater than the building policy limits plus the deductible or the maximum payable under the policy for any one building loss, we will pay you the lesser of these two amounts without waiting for the

further damage to occur if you sign a release agreeing:

a. To make no further claim under this policy;

b. Not to seek renewal of this policy;

c. Not to apply for any flood insurance under the Act for property at the described location; and

d. Not to seek a premium refund for current or prior terms.

If the policy term ends before the insured building has been flooded continuously for 90 days, the provisions of this paragraph T.1. will apply when the insured building suffers a covered loss before the policy term ends.

2. If your insured building is subject to continuous lake flooding from a closed basin lake, you may elect to file a claim under either paragraph T.1. above or T.2. (A "closed basin lake" is a natural lake from which water leaves primarily through evaporation and whose surface area now exceeds or has exceeded one square mile at any time in the recorded past. Most of the nation's closed basin lakes are in the western half of the United States where annual evaporation exceeds annual precipitation and where lake levels and surface areas are subject to considerable fluctuation due to wide variations in the climate. These lakes may overtop their basins on rare occasions.) Under this paragraph T.2., we will pay your claim as if the building is a total loss even though it has not been continuously inundated for 90 days, subject to the following conditions:

a. Lake flood waters must damage or imminently threaten to damage your building.

b. Before approval of your claim, you must:

(1) Agree to a claim payment that reflects your buying back the salvage on a negotiated basis; and

(2) Grant the conservation easement described in FEMA's "Policy Guidance for Closed Basin Lakes" to be recorded in the office of the local recorder of deeds. FEMA, in consultation with the community in which the property is located, will identify on a map an area or areas of special consideration (ASC) in which there is a potential for flood damage from continuous lake flooding. FEMA will give the community the agreed-upon map showing the ASC. This easement will only apply to that portion of the property in the ASC. It will allow certain agricultural and recreational uses of the land. The only structures it will allow on any portion of the property within the ASC are certain simple agricultural and recreational structures. If any of these allowable structures are insurable buildings under the NFIP and are insured under the NFIP, they will not be eligible for the benefits of this paragraph T.2. If a U.S. Army Corps of Engineers certified flood control project or otherwise certified flood control project later protects the property, FEMA will, upon request, amend the ASC to remove areas protected by

those projects. The restrictions of the easement will then no longer apply to any portion of the property removed from the ASC; and

(3) Comply with paragraphs T.1.a. through T.1.d. above.

c. Within 90 days of approval of your claim, you must move your building to a new location outside the ASC. FEMA will give you an additional 30 days to move if you show there is sufficient reason to extend the time.

d. Before the final payment of your claim, you must acquire an elevation certificate and a floodplain development permit from the local floodplain administrator for the new location of your building.

e. Before the approval of your claim, the community having jurisdiction over your building must:

(1) Adopt a permanent land use ordinance, or a temporary moratorium for a period not to exceed 6 months to be followed immediately by a permanent land use ordinance, that is consistent with the provisions specified in the easement required in paragraph T.2.b. above.

(2) Agree to declare and report any violations of this ordinance to FEMA so that under Section 1316 of the National Flood Insurance Act of 1968, as amended, flood insurance to the building can be denied; and

(3) Agree to maintain as deed-restricted, for purposes compatible with open space or agricultural or recreational use only, any affected property the community acquires an interest in. These deed restrictions must be consistent with the provisions of paragraph T.2.b. above, except that, even if a certified project protects the property, the land use restrictions continue to apply if the property was acquired under the Hazard Mitigation Grant Program or the Flood Mitigation Assistance Program. If a non-profit land trust organization receives the property as a donation, that organization must maintain the property as deed-restricted, consistent with the provisions of paragraph T.2.b. above.

f. Before the approval of your claim, the affected State must take all action set forth in FEMA's "Policy Guidance for Closed Basin Lakes."

g. You must have NFIP flood insurance coverage continuously in effect from a date established by FEMA until you file a claim under paragraph T.2. If a subsequent owner buys NFIP insurance that goes into effect within 60 days of the date of transfer of title, any gap in coverage during that 60-day period will not be a violation of this continuous coverage requirement. For the purpose of honoring a claim under this paragraph T.2, we will not consider to be in effect any increased coverage that became effective after the date established by FEMA. The exception to this is any increased coverage in the amount suggested by your insurer as an inflation adjustment.

h. This paragraph T.2. will be in effect for a community when the FEMA Regional Administrator for the affected region provides to the community, in writing, the following:

(1) Confirmation that the community and the State are in compliance with the conditions in paragraphs T.2.e. and T.2.f. above, and

(2) The date by which you must have flood insurance in effect.

U. Duplicate Policies Not Allowed

1. We will not insure your property under more than one NFIP policy.

If we find that the duplication was not knowingly created, we will give you written notice. The notice will advise you that you may choose one of several options under the following procedures:

a. If you choose to keep in effect the policy with the earlier effective date, you may also choose to add the coverage limits of the later policy to the limits of the earlier policy. The change will become effective as of the effective date of the later policy.

b. If you choose to keep in effect the policy with the later effective date, you may also choose to add the coverage limits of the earlier policy to the limits of the later policy. The change will be effective as of the effective date of the later policy.

In either case, you must pay the pro rata premium for the increased coverage limits within 30 days of the written notice. In no event will the resulting coverage limits exceed the permissible limits of coverage under the Act or your insurable interest, whichever is less. We will make a refund to you, according to applicable NFIP rules, of the premium for the policy not being kept in effect.

2. Your option under Condition U. Duplicate Policies Not Allowed to elect which NFIP policy to keep in effect does not apply when duplicates have been knowingly created. Losses occurring under such circumstances will be adjusted according to the terms and conditions of the earlier policy. The policy with the later effective date must be canceled.

V. Loss Settlement

1. Introduction

This policy provides three methods of settling losses: Replacement Cost, Special Loss Settlement, and Actual Cash Value. Each method is used for a different type of property, as explained in a-c. below.

a. Replacement Cost Loss Settlement, described in V.2. below, applies to a single-family dwelling provided:

(1) It is your principal residence, which means that, at the time of loss, you or your spouse lived there for 80% of:

(a) The 365 days immediately preceding the loss; or

(b) The period of your ownership, if you owned the dwelling for less than 365 days; and

(2) At the time of loss, the amount of insurance in this policy that applies to the dwelling is 80% or more of its full replacement cost immediately before the loss, or is the maximum amount of insurance available under the NFIP.

b. Special Loss Settlement, described in V.3. below, applies to a single-family dwelling that is a manufactured or mobile home or a travel trailer.

c. Actual Cash Value loss settlement applies to a single-family dwelling not subject to replacement cost or special loss settlement, and to the property listed in V.4. below.

2. Replacement Cost Loss Settlement

The following loss settlement conditions apply to a single-family dwelling described in V.1.a. above:

a. We will pay to repair or replace the damaged dwelling after application of the deductible and without deduction for depreciation, but not more than the least of the following amounts:

(1) The building limit of liability shown on your Declarations Page;

(2) The replacement cost of that part of the dwelling damaged, with materials of like kind and quality and for like use; or

(3) The necessary amount actually spent to repair or replace the damaged part of the dwelling for like use.

b. If the dwelling is rebuilt at a new location, the cost described above is limited to the cost that would have been incurred if the dwelling had been rebuilt at its former location.

c. When the full cost of repair or replacement is more than $1,000, or more than 5% of the whole amount of insurance that applies to the dwelling, we will not be liable for any loss under V.2.a. above or V.4.a.(2) below unless and until actual repair or replacement is completed.

d. You may disregard the replacement cost conditions above and make claim under this policy for loss to dwellings on an actual cash value basis. You may then make claim for any additional liability according to V.2.a., b., and c. above, provided you notify us of your intent to do so within 180 days after the date of loss.

e. If the community in which your dwelling is located has been converted from the Emergency Program to the Regular Program during the current policy term, then we will consider the maximum amount of available NFIP insurance to be the amount that was available at the beginning of the current policy term.

3. Special Loss Settlement

a. The following loss settlement conditions apply to a single-family dwelling that:

(1) is a manufactured or mobile home or a travel trailer, as defined in II.B.6.b. and c.,

(2) is at least 16 feet wide when fully assembled and has an area of at least 600 square feet within its perimeter walls when fully assembled, and

(3) is your principal residence as specified in V.1.a.(1) above.

b. If such a dwelling is totally destroyed or damaged to such an extent that, in our judgment, it is not economically feasible to repair, at least to its pre-damage condition, we will, at our discretion pay the least of the following amounts:

(1) The lesser of the replacement cost of the dwelling or 1.5 times the actual cash value, or

(2) The building limit of liability shown on your Declarations Page.

c. If such a dwelling is partially damaged and, in our judgment, it is economically feasible to repair it to its pre-damage condition, we will settle the loss according to the Replacement Cost conditions in V.2.above.

4. Actual Cash Value Loss Settlement

The types of property noted below are subject to actual cash value (or in the case of V.4.a.(2), below, proportional) loss settlement.

a. A dwelling, at the time of loss, when the amount of insurance on the dwelling is both less than 80% of its full replacement cost immediately before the loss and less than the maximum amount of insurance available under the NFIP. In that case, we will pay the greater of the following amounts, but not more than the amount of insurance that applies to that dwelling:

(1) The actual cash value, as defined in II.B.2., of the damaged part of the dwelling; or

(2) A proportion of the cost to repair or replace the damaged part of the dwelling, without deduction for physical depreciation and after application of the deductible.

This proportion is determined as follows: If 80% of the full replacement cost of the dwelling is less than the maximum amount of insurance available under the NFIP, then the proportion is determined by dividing the actual amount of insurance on the dwelling by the amount of insurance that represents 80% of its full replacement cost. But if 80% of the full replacement cost of the dwelling is greater than the maximum amount of insurance available under the NFIP, then the proportion is determined by dividing the actual amount of insurance on the dwelling by the maximum amount of insurance available under the NFIP.

b. A two-, three-, or four-family dwelling.

c. A unit that is not used exclusively for single-family dwelling purposes.

d. Detached garages.

e. Personal property.

f. Appliances, carpets, and carpet pads.

g. Outdoor awnings, outdoor antennas or aerials of any type, and other outdoor equipment.

h. Any property covered under this policy that is abandoned after a loss and remains as debris anywhere on the described location.

i. A dwelling that is not your principal residence.

5. Amount of Insurance Required

To determine the amount of insurance required for a dwelling immediately before the loss, we do not include the value of:

a. Footings, foundations, piers, or any other structures or devices that are below the undersurface of the lowest basement floor and support all or part of the dwelling;

b. Those supports listed in V.5.a. above, that are below the surface of the ground inside the foundation walls if there is no basement; and

c. Excavations and underground flues, pipes, wiring, and drains.

NOTE: The Coverage D—Increased Cost of Compliance limit of liability is not included in the determination of the amount of insurance required.

VIII. LIBERALIZATION CLAUSE

If we make a change that broadens your coverage under this edition of our policy, but does not require any additional premium, then that change will automatically apply to your insurance as of the date we implement the change, provided that this implementation date falls within 60 days before or during the policy term stated on the Declarations Page.

IX. WHAT LAW GOVERNS

This policy and all disputes arising from the handling of any claim under the policy are governed exclusively by the flood insurance regulations issued by FEMA, the National Flood Insurance Act of 1968, as amended (42 U.S.C. 4001, et seq.), and Federal common law.

In Witness Whereof, we have signed this policy below and hereby enter into this Insurance Agreement.

Administrator, Federal Insurance
Administration.

[65 FR 60769, Oct. 12, 2000, as amended at 68 FR 9897, Mar. 3, 2003]

APPENDIX A(2) TO PART 61

FEDERAL EMERGENCY MANAGEMENT AGENCY,
FEDERAL INSURANCE ADMINISTRATION

STANDARD FLOOD INSURANCE POLICY

GENERAL PROPERTY FORM

Please read the policy carefully. The flood insurance coverage provided is subject to limitations, restrictions, and exclusions.

This policy provides no coverage:

1. In a regular program community, for a residential condominium building, as defined in this policy; and

2. Except for personal property coverage, for a unit in a condominium building.

I. AGREEMENT

The Federal Emergency Management Agency (FEMA) provides flood insurance under the terms of the National Flood Insurance Act of 1968 and its Amendments, and Title 44 of the Code of Federal Regulations. We will pay you for direct physical loss by or from flood to your insured property if you:

1. Have paid the correct premium;

2. Comply with all terms and conditions of this policy; and

3. Have furnished accurate information and statements.

We have the right to review the information you give us at any time and to revise your policy based on our review.

II. DEFINITIONS

A. In this policy, "you" and "your" refer to the insured(s) shown on the Declarations Page of this policy. Insured(s) includes: Any mortgagee and loss payee named in the Application and Declarations page, as well as any other mortgagee or loss payee determined to exist at the time of loss in the order of precedence. "We," "us," and "our" refer to the insurer.

Some definitions are complex because they are provided as they appear in the law or regulations, or result from court cases. The precise definitions are intended to protect you.

Flood, as used in this flood insurance policy, means:

1. A general and temporary condition of partial or complete inundation of two or more acres of normally dry land area or of two or more properties (one of which is your property) from:

a. Overflow of inland or tidal waters;

b. Unusual and rapid accumulation or run-off of surface waters from any source;

c. Mudflow.

2. The collapse or subsidence of land along the shore of a lake or similar body of water as a result of erosion or undermining caused by waves or currents of water exceeding an-ticipated cyclical levels which result in a flood as defined in A.1.a. above.

B. The following are the other key definitions we use in this policy:

1. *Act.* The National Flood Insurance Act of 1968 and any amendments to it.

2. *Actual Cash Value.* The cost to replace an insured item of property at the time of loss, less the value of its physical depreciation.

3. *Application.* The statement made and signed by you or your agent in applying for this policy. The application gives information we use to determine the eligibility of the risk, the kind of policy to be issued, and the correct premium payment. The application is part of this flood insurance policy. For us to issue you a policy, the correct premium payment must accompany the application.

4. *Base Flood.* A flood having a one percent chance of being equaled or exceeded in any given year.

5. *Basement.* Any area of the building, including any sunken room or sunken portion of a room, having its floor below ground level (subgrade) on all sides.

6. *Building.*

a. A structure with two or more outside rigid walls and a fully secured roof, that is affixed to a permanent site;

b. A manufactured home ("a manufactured home," also known as a mobile home, is a structure: built on a permanent chassis, transported to its site in one or more sections, and affixed to a permanent foundation); or

c. A travel trailer without wheels, built on a chassis and affixed to a permanent foundation, that is regulated under the community's floodplain management and building ordinances or laws.

Building does not mean a gas or liquid storage tank or a recreational vehicle, park trailer, or other similar vehicle, except as described in B.6.c., above.

7. *Cancellation.* The ending of the insurance coverage provided by this policy before the expiration date.

8. *Condominium.* That form of ownership of real property in which each unit owner has an undivided interest in common elements.

9. *Condominium Association.* The entity, formed by the unit owners, responsible for the maintenance and operation of:

a. Common elements owned in undivided shares by unit owners; and

b. Other real property in which the unit owners have use rights where membership in the entity is a required condition of unit ownership.

10. *Declarations Page.* A computer-generated summary of information you provided in the application for insurance. The Declarations Page also describes the term of the policy, limits of coverage, and displays the premium and our name. The Declarations Page is a part of this flood insurance policy.

11. *Described Location.* The location where the insured building or personal property is found. The described location is shown on the Declarations Page.

12. *Direct Physical Loss By or From Flood.* Loss or damage to insured property, directly caused by a flood. There must be evidence of physical changes to the property.

13. *Elevated Building.* A building that has no basement and that has its lowest elevated floor raised above ground level by foundation walls, shear walls, posts, piers, pilings, or columns.

14. *Emergency Program.* The initial phase of a community's participation in the National Flood Insurance Program. During this phase, only limited amounts of insurance are available under the Act.

15. *Expense Constant.* A flat charge you must pay on each new or renewal policy to defray the expenses of the Federal Government related to flood insurance.

16. *Federal Policy Fee.* A flat charge you must pay on each new or renewal policy to defray certain administrative expenses incurred in carrying out the National Flood Insurance Program. This fee covers expenses not covered by the expense constant.

17. *Improvements.* Fixtures, alterations, installations, or additions comprising a part of the insured building.

18. *Mudflow.* A river of liquid and flowing mud on the surfaces of normally dry land areas, as when earth is carried by a current of water. Other earth movements, such as landslide, slope failure, or a saturated soil mass moving by liquidity down a slope, are not mudflows.

19. *National Flood Insurance Program (NFIP).* The program of flood insurance coverage and floodplain management administered under the Act and applicable Federal regulations in Title 44 of the Code of Federal Regulations, Subchapter B.

20. *Policy.* The entire written contract between you and us. It includes:

a. This printed form;

b. The application and Declarations Page;

c. Any endorsement(s) that may be issued; and,

d. Any renewal certificate indicating that coverage has been instituted for a new policy and new policy term.

Only one building, which you specifically described in the application, may be insured under this policy.

21. *Pollutants.* Substances that include, but that are not limited to, any solid, liquid, gaseous or thermal irritant or contaminant, including smoke, vapor, soot, fumes, acids, alkalis, chemicals, and waste. "Waste" includes, but is not limited to, materials to be recycled, reconditioned, or reclaimed.

22. *Post-FIRM Building.* A building for which construction or substantial improvement occurred after December 31, 1974, or on or after the effective date of an initial Flood Insurance Rate Map (FIRM), whichever is later.

23. *Probation Premium.* A flat charge you must pay on each new or renewal policy issued covering property in a community that has been placed on probation under the provisions of 44 CFR 59.24.

24. *Regular Program.* The final phase of a community's participation in the National Flood Insurance Program. In this phase, a Flood Insurance Rate Map is in effect and full limits of coverage are available under the Act.

25. *Residential Condominium Building.* A building, owned and administered as a condominium, containing one or more family units and in which at least 75% of the floor area is residential.

26. *Special Flood Hazard Area.* An area having special flood or mudflow, and/or flood-related erosion hazards, and shown on a Flood Hazard Boundary Map or Flood Insurance Rate Map as Zone A, AO, A1–A30, AE, A99, AH, AR, AR/A, AR/AE, AR/AH, AR/AO, AR/A1–A30, V1–V30, VE, V.

27. *Stock* means merchandise held in storage or for sale, raw materials, and in-process or finished goods, including supplies used in their packing or shipping.

Stock does not include any property not covered under Section IV. Property Not Covered, except the following:

a. Parts and equipment for self-propelled vehicles;

b. Furnishings and equipment for watercraft;

c. Spas and hot-tubs, including their equipment; and

d. Swimming pool equipment.

28. *Unit.* A unit in a condominium building.

29. *Valued Policy.* A policy in which the insured and the insurer agree on the value of the property insured, that value being payable in the event of a total loss. The Standard Flood Insurance Policy is not a valued policy.

III. PROPERTY COVERED

A. Coverage A—Building Property

We insure against direct physical loss by or from flood to:

1. The building described on the Declarations Page at the described location. If the building is a condominium building and the named insured is the condominium association, Coverage A includes all units within the building and the improvements within the units, provided the units are owned in common by all unit owners.

2. We also insure building property for a period of 45 days at another location, as set forth in III.C.2.b., Property Removed to Safety.

3. Additions and extensions attached to and in contact with the building by means of

237

a rigid exterior wall, a solid load-bearing interior wall, a stairway, an elevated walkway, or a roof. At your option, additions and extensions connected by any of these methods may be separately insured. Additions and extensions attached to and in contact with the building by means of a common interior wall that is not a solid load-bearing wall are always considered part of the building and cannot be separately insured.

4. The following fixtures, machinery, and equipment, which are covered under Coverage A only:

   a. Awnings and canopies;

   b. Blinds;

   c. Carpet permanently installed over unfinished flooring;

   d. Central air conditioners;

   e. Elevator equipment;

   f. Fire extinguishing apparatus;

   g. Fire sprinkler systems;

   h. Walk-in freezers;

   i. Furnaces;

   j. Light fixtures;

   k. Outdoor antennas and aerials attached to buildings;

   l. Permanently installed cupboards, bookcases, paneling, and wallpaper;

   m. Pumps and machinery for operating pumps;

   n. Ventilating equipment; and

   o. Wall mirrors, permanently installed;

   p. In the units within the building, installed:

     (1) Built-in dishwashers;

     (2) Built-in microwave ovens;

     (3) Garbage disposal units;

     (4) Hot water heaters, including solar water heaters;

     (5) Kitchen cabinets;

     (6) Plumbing fixtures;

     (7) Radiators;

     (8) Ranges;

     (9) Refrigerators; and

     (10) Stoves.

5. Materials and supplies to be used for construction, alteration, or repair of the insured building while the materials and supplies are stored in a fully enclosed building at the described location or on an adjacent property.

6. A building under construction, alteration, or repair at the described location.

   a. If the structure is not yet walled or roofed as described in the definition for building (see II. 6.a.), then coverage applies:

     (1) Only while such work is in progress; or

     (2) If such work is halted, only for a period of up to 90 continuous days thereafter.

   b. However, coverage does not apply until the building is walled and roofed if the lowest floor, including the basement floor, of a non-elevated building or the lowest elevated floor of an elevated building is:

     (1) Below the base flood elevation in Zones AH, AE, A1–A30, AR, AR/AE, AR/AH, AR/A1–A30, AR/A, AR/AO; or

(2) Below the base flood elevation adjusted to include the effect of wave action in Zones VE or V1–V30.

The lowest floor levels are based on the bottom of the lowest horizontal structural member of the floor in Zones VE or V1–V30 and the top of the floor in Zones AH, AE, A1–A30, AR, AR/AE, AR/AH, AR/A1–A30, AR/A, AR/AO.

7. A manufactured home or a travel trailer as described in the Definitions

Section (see II.B.6.b.and II.B.6.c.).

If the manufactured home or travel trailer is in a special flood hazard area, it must be anchored in the following manner at the time of the loss:

   a. By over-the-top or frame ties to ground anchors; or

   b. In accordance with the manufacturer's specifications; or

   c. In compliance with the community's floodplain management requirements unless it has been continuously insured by the NFIP at the same described location since September 30, 1982.

8. Items of property in a building enclosure below the lowest elevated floor of an elevated post-FIRM building located in zones A1–A30, AE, AH, AR, AR/A, AR/AE, AR/AH, AR/A1–A30, V1–V30, or VE, or in a basement, regardless of the zone. Coverage is limited to the following:

   a. Any of the following items, if installed in their functioning locations and, if necessary for operation, connected to a power source:

     (1) Central air conditioners;

     (2) Cisterns and the water in them;

     (3) Drywall for walls and ceilings in a basement and the cost of labor to nail it, unfinished and unfloated and not taped, to the framing;

     (4) Electrical junction and circuit breaker boxes;

     (5) Electrical outlets and switches;

     (6) Elevators, dumbwaiters, and related equipment, except for related equipment installed below the base flood elevation after September 30, 1987;

     (7) Fuel tanks and the fuel in them;

     (8) Furnaces and hot water heaters;

     (9) Heat pumps;

     (10) Nonflammable insulation in a basement;

     (11) Pumps and tanks used in solar energy systems;

     (12) Stairways and staircases attached to the building, not separated from it by elevated walkways;

     (13) Sump pumps;

     (14) Water softeners and the chemicals in them, water filters, and faucets installed as an integral part of the plumbing system;

     (15) Well water tanks and pumps;

     (16) Required utility connections for any item in this list; and

(17) Footings, foundations, posts, pilings, piers, or other foundation walls and anchorage systems required to support a building.

b. Clean-up.

B. Coverage B—Personal Property

1. If you have purchased personal property coverage, we insure, subject to B. 2., 3., and 4. below, against direct physical loss by or from flood to personal property inside the fully enclosed insured building:

a. Owned solely by you, or in the case of a condominium, owned solely by the condominium association and used exclusively in the conduct of the business affairs of the condominium association; or

b. Owned in common by the unit owners of the condominium association.

We also insure such personal property for 45 days while stored at a temporary location, as set forth in III.C.2.b., Property Removed to Safety.

2. When this policy covers personal property, coverage will be either for household personal property or other than household personal property, while within the insured building, but not both.

a. If this policy covers household personal property, it will insure household personal property usual to a living quarters, that:

(1) Belongs to you, or a member of your household, or at your option:

(a) Your domestic worker;

(b) Your guest; or

(2) You may be legally liable for.

b. If this policy covers other than household personal property, it will insure your:

(1) Furniture and fixtures;

(2) Machinery and equipment;

(3) Stock; and

(4) Other personal property owned by you and used in your business, subject to IV. Property Not Covered.

3. Coverage for personal property includes the following property, subject to B.1.a. and B.1.b. above, which is covered under Coverage B. only:

a. Air conditioning units installed in the building;

b. Carpet, not permanently installed, over unfinished flooring;

c. Carpets over finished flooring;

d. Clothes washers and dryers;

e. "Cook-out" grills;

f. Food freezers, other than walk-in, and the food in any freezer;

g. Outdoor equipment and furniture stored inside the insured building;

h. Ovens and the like; and

i. Portable microwave ovens and portable dishwashers.

4. Coverage for items of property in a building enclosure below the lowest elevated floor of an elevated post-FIRM building located in zones A1–A30, AE, AH, AR, AR/A, AR/AE, AR/AH, AR/A1–A30, V1–V30, or VE, or in a basement, regardless of the zone, is limited to the following items, if installed in their functioning locations and, if necessary for operation, connected to a power source:

a. Air conditioning units—portable or window type;

b. Clothes washers and dryers; and

c. Food freezers, other than walk-in, and food in any freezer.

5. Special Limits. We will pay no more than $2,500 for any loss to one or more of the following kinds of personal property:

a. Artwork, photographs, collectibles, or memorabilia, including but not limited to, porcelain or other figures, and sports cards;

b. Rare books or autographed items;

c. Jewelry, watches, precious and semi-precious stones, articles of gold, silver, or platinum;

d. Furs or any article containing fur which represents its principal value; or

6. We will pay only for the functional value of antiques.

7. If you are a tenant, you may apply up to 10% of the Coverage B limit to improvements:

a. Made a part of the building you occupy; and

b. You acquired, or made at your expense, even though you cannot legally remove.

This coverage does not increase the amount of insurance that applies to insured personal property.

8. If you are a condominium unit owner, you may apply up to 10% of the Coverage B limit to cover loss to interior:

a. walls,

b. floors, and

c. ceilings,

that are not covered under a policy issued to the condominium association insuring the condominium building.

This coverage does not increase the amount of insurance that applies to insured personal property.

9. If you are a tenant, personal property must be inside the fully enclosed building.

C. Coverage C—Other Coverages

1. *Debris Removal.*

a. We will pay the expense to remove non-owned debris that is on or in insured property and debris of insured property anywhere.

b. If you or a member of your household perform the removal work, the value of your work will be based on the Federal minimum wage.

c. This coverage does not increase the Coverage A or Coverage B limit of liability.

2. *Loss Avoidance Measures.*

a. Sandbags, Supplies, and Labor

(1) We will pay up to $1,000 for the costs you incur to protect the insured building from a flood or imminent danger of flood, for the following:

(a) Your reasonable expenses to buy:

(i) Sandbags, including sand to fill them;

(ii) Fill for temporary levees;

(iii) Pumps; and

(iv) Plastic sheeting and lumber used in connection with these items; and

(b) The value of work, at the Federal minimum wage, that you perform.

(2) This coverage for Sandbags, Supplies, and Labor only applies if damage to insured property by or from flood is imminent and the threat of flood damage is apparent enough to lead a person of common prudence to anticipate flood damage. One of the following must also occur:

(a) A general and temporary condition of flooding in the area near the described location must occur, even if the flood does not reach the insured building; or

(b) A legally authorized official must issue an evacuation order or other civil order for the community in which the insured building is located calling for measures to preserve life and property from the peril of flood.

This coverage does not increase the Coverage A or Coverage B limit of liability.

b. Property Removed to Safety

(1) We will pay up to $1,000 for the reasonable expenses you incur to move insured property to a place other than the described location that contains the property in order to protect it from flood or the imminent danger of flood.

Reasonable expenses include the value of work, at the Federal minimum wage, that you perform.

(2) If you move insured property to a place other than the described location that contains the property, in order to protect it from flood or the imminent danger of flood, we will cover such property while at that location for a period of 45 consecutive days from the date you begin to move it there. The personal property that is moved must be placed in a fully enclosed building, or otherwise reasonably protected from the elements.

Any property removed, including a moveable home described in II.6.b. and c., must be placed above ground level or outside of the special flood hazard area.

This coverage does not increase the Coverage A or Coverage B limit of liability.

3. *Pollution Damage.*

We will pay for damage caused by pollutants to covered property if the discharge, seepage, migration, release, or escape of the pollutants is caused by or results from flood. The most we will pay under this coverage is $10,000. This coverage does not increase the Coverage A or Coverage B limits of liability. Any payment under this provision when combined with all other payments for the same loss cannot exceed the replacement cost or actual cash value, as appropriate, of the covered property. This coverage does not include the testing for or monitoring of pollutants unless required by law or ordinance.

D. Coverage D—Increased Cost of Compliance

1. *General.*

This policy pays you to comply with a State or local floodplain management law or ordinance affecting repair or reconstruction of a structure suffering flood damage. Compliance activities eligible for payment are: elevation, floodproofing, relocation, or demolition (or any combination of these activities) of your structure. Eligible floodproofing activities are limited to:

a. Non-residential structures. b. Residential structures with basements that satisfy FEMA's standards published in the Code of Federal Regulations [44 CFR 60.6 (b) or (c)].

2. *Limit of Liability.*

We will pay you up to $30,000 under this Coverage D—Increased Cost of Compliance, which only applies to policies with building coverage (Coverage A). Our payment of claims under Coverage D is in addition to the amount of coverage which you selected on the application and which appears on the Declarations Page. But the maximum you can collect under this policy for both Coverage A (Building Property) and Coverage D (Increased Cost of Compliance) cannot exceed the maximum permitted under the Act. We do NOT charge a separate deductible for a claim under Coverage D.

3. *Eligibility.*

a. A structure covered under Coverage A— Building Property sustaining a loss caused by a flood as defined by this policy must:

(1) Be a "repetitive loss structure." A "repetitive loss structure" is one that meets the following conditions:

(a) The structure is covered by a contract of flood insurance issued under the NFIP.

(b) The structure has suffered flood damage on 2 occasions during a 10-year period which ends on the date of the second loss.

(c) The cost to repair the flood damage, on average, equaled or exceeded 25% of the market value of the structure at the time of each flood loss.

(d) In addition to the current claim, the NFIP must have paid the previous qualifying claim, and the State or community must have a cumulative, substantial damage provision or repetitive loss provision in its floodplain management law or ordinance being enforced against the structure; or

(2) Be a structure that has had flood damage in which the cost to repair equals or exceeds 50% of the market value of the structure at the time of the flood. The State or community must have a substantial damage provision in its floodplain management law or ordinance being enforced against the structure.

b. This Coverage D pays you to comply with State or local floodplain management laws or ordinances that meet the minimum standards of the National Flood Insurance

Program found in the Code of Federal Regulations at 44 CFR 60.3. We pay for compliance activities that exceed those standards under these conditions:

(1) 3.a.(1) above.

(2) Elevation or floodproofing in any risk zone to preliminary or advisory base flood elevations provided by FEMA which the State or local government has adopted and is enforcing for flood-damaged structures in such areas. (This includes compliance activities in B, C, X, or D zones which are being changed to zones with base flood elevations. This also includes compliance activities in zones where base flood elevations are being increased, and a flood-damaged structure must comply with the higher advisory base flood elevation.) Increased Cost of Compliance coverage does not apply to situations in B, C, X, or D zones where the community has derived its own elevations and is enforcing elevation or floodproofing requirements for flood-damaged structures to elevations derived solely by the community.

(3) Elevation or floodproofing above the base flood elevation to meet State or local "freeboard" requirements, i.e., that a structure must be elevated above the base flood elevation.

c. Under the minimum NFIP criteria at 44 CFR 60.3(b)(4), States and communities must require the elevation or floodproofing of structures in unnumbered A zones to the base flood elevation where elevation data is obtained from a Federal, State, or other source. Such compliance activities are also eligible for Coverage D.

d. This coverage will also pay for the incremental cost, after demolition or relocation, of elevating or floodproofing a structure during its rebuilding at the same or another site to meet State or local floodplain management laws or ordinances, subject to Exclusion D.5.g. below.

e. This coverage will also pay to bring a flood-damaged structure into compliance with State or local floodplain management laws or ordinances even if the structure had received a variance before the present loss from the applicable floodplain management requirements.

4. *Conditions.*

a. When a structure covered under Coverage A—Building Property sustains a loss caused by a flood, our payment for the loss under this Coverage D will be for the increased cost to elevate, floodproof, relocate, or demolish (or any combination of these activities) caused by the enforcement of current State or local floodplain management ordinances or laws. Our payment for eligible demolition activities will be for the cost to demolish and clear the site of the building debris or a portion thereof caused by the enforcement of current State or local floodplain management ordinances or laws. Eligible activities for the cost of clearing the site will include those necessary to discontinue utility service to the site and ensure proper abandonment of on-site utilities.

b. When the building is repaired or rebuilt, it must be intended for the same occupancy as the present building unless otherwise required by current floodplain management ordinances or laws.

5. *Exclusions.*

Under this Coverage D—Increased Cost of Compliance, we will not pay for:

a. The cost to comply with any floodplain management law or ordinance in communities participating in the Emergency Program.

b. The cost associated with enforcement of any ordinance or law that requires any insured or others to test for, monitor, clean up, remove, contain, treat, detoxify or neutralize, or in any way respond to, or assess the effects of pollutants.

c. The loss in value to any insured building or other structure due to the requirements of any ordinance or law.

d. The loss in residual value of the undamaged portion of a building demolished as a consequence of enforcement of any State or local floodplain management law or ordinance.

e. Any Increased Cost of Compliance under this Coverage D:

(1) Until the building is elevated, floodproofed, demolished, or relocated on the same or to another premises; and

(2) Unless the building is elevated, floodproofed, demolished, or relocated as soon as reasonably possible after the loss, not to exceed two years.

f. Any code upgrade requirements, e.g., plumbing or electrical wiring, not specifically related to the State or local floodplain management law or ordinance.

g. Any compliance activities needed to bring additions or improvements made after the loss occurred into compliance with State or local floodplain management laws or ordinances.

h. Loss due to any ordinance or law that you were required to comply with before the current loss.

i. Any rebuilding activity to standards that do not meet the NFIP's minimum requirements. This includes any situation where the insured has received from the State or community a variance in connection with the current flood loss to rebuild the property to an elevation below the base flood elevation.

j. Increased Cost of Compliance for a garage or carport.

k. Any structure insured under an NFIP Group Flood Insurance Policy.

l. Assessments made by a condominium association on individual condominium unit owners to pay increased costs of repairing commonly owned buildings after a flood in compliance with State or local floodplain management ordinances or laws.

6. *Other Provisions.*

All other conditions and provisions of the policy apply.

IV. PROPERTY NOT COVERED

A. We do not cover any of the following property:

1. Personal property not inside the fully enclosed building;

2. A building, and personal property in it, located entirely in, on, or over water or seaward of mean high tide, if it was constructed or substantially improved after September 30, 1982;

3. Open structures, including a building used as a boathouse or any structure or building into which boats are floated, and personal property located in, on, or over water;

4. Recreational vehicles other than travel trailers described in the II.B.6.c., whether affixed to a permanent foundation or on wheels;

5. Self-propelled vehicles or machines, including their parts and equipment. However, we do cover self-propelled vehicles or machines, provided they are not licensed for use on public roads and are:

a. Used mainly to service the described location; or

b. Designed and used to assist handicapped persons, while the vehicles or machines are inside a building at the described location;

6. Land, land values, lawns, trees, shrubs, plants, growing crops, or animals;

7. Accounts, bills, coins, currency, deeds, evidences of debt, medals, money, scrip, stored value cards, postage stamps, securities, bullion, manuscripts, or other valuable papers;

8. Underground structures and equipment, including wells, septic tanks, and septic systems;

9. Those portions of walks, walkways, decks, driveways, patios, and other surfaces, all whether protected by a roof or not, located outside the perimeter, exterior walls of the insured building;

10. Containers including related equipment, such as, but not limited to, tanks containing gases or liquids;

11. Buildings or units and all their contents if more than 49% of the actual cash value of the building or unit is below ground, unless the lowest level is at or above the base flood elevation and is below ground by reason of earth having been used as insulation material in conjunction with energy efficient building techniques;

12. Fences, retaining walls, seawalls, bulkheads, wharves, piers, bridges, and docks;

13. Aircraft or watercraft, or their furnishings and equipment;

14. Hot tubs and spas that are not bathroom fixtures, and swimming pools, and

their equipment such as, but not limited to, heaters, filters, pumps, and pipes, wherever located;

15. Property not eligible for flood insurance pursuant to the provisions of the Coastal Barrier Resources Act and the Coastal Barrier Improvement Act of 1990 and amendments to these Acts;

16. Personal property owned by or in the care, custody or control of a unit owner, except for property of the type and under the circumstances set forth under III. Coverage B—Personal Property of this policy;

17. A residential condominium building located in a Regular Program community.

V. EXCLUSIONS

A. We only provide coverage for direct physical loss by or from flood, which means that we do not pay you for:

1. Loss of revenue or profits;

2. Loss of access to the insured property or described location;

3. Loss of use of the insured property or described location;

4. Loss from interruption of business or production;

5. Any additional expenses incurred while the insured building is being repaired or is unable to be occupied for any reason;

6. The cost of complying with any ordinance or law requiring or regulating the construction, demolition, remodeling, renovation or repair of property, including removal of any resulting debris. This exclusion does not apply to any eligible activities that we describe in Coverage D—Increased Cost of Compliance; or

7. Any other economic loss you suffer.

B. We do not insure a loss directly or indirectly caused by a flood that is already in progress at the time and date:

1. The policy term begins; or

2. Coverage is added at your request.

C. We do not insure for loss to property caused directly by earth movement even if the earth movement is caused by flood. Some examples of earth movement that we do not cover are:

1. Earthquake;

2. Landslide;

3. Land subsidence;

4. Sinkholes;

5. Destabilization or movement of land that results from accumulation of water in subsurface land areas; or

6. Gradual erosion.

We do, however, pay for losses from mudflow and land subsidence as a result of erosion that are specifically covered under our definition of flood (see A.1.c. and II.A.2.).

D. We do not insure for direct physical loss caused directly or indirectly by:

1. The pressure or weight of ice;

2. Freezing or thawing;

3. Rain, snow, sleet, hail, or water spray;

4. Water, moisture, mildew, or mold damage that results primarily from any condition:

a. Substantially confined to the insured building; or

b. That is within your control including, but not limited to:

(1) Design, structural, or mechanical defects;

(2) Failures, stoppages, or breakage of water or sewer lines, drains, pumps, fixtures, or equipment; or

(3) Failure to inspect and maintain the property after a flood recedes;

5. Water or water-borne material that:

a. Backs up through sewers or drains;

b. Discharges or overflows from a sump, sump pump, or related equipment; or

c. Seeps or leaks on or through the covered property;

unless there is a flood in the area and the flood is the proximate cause of the sewer or drain backup, sump pump discharge or overflow, or the seepage of water;

6. The pressure or weight of water unless there is a flood in the area and the flood is the proximate cause of the damage from the pressure or weight of water;

7. Power, heating, or cooling failure unless the failure results from direct physical loss by or from flood to power, heating, or cooling equipment situated on the described location;

8. Theft, fire, explosion, wind, or windstorm;

9. Anything that you or your agents do or conspire to do to cause loss by flood deliberately; or

10. Alteration of the insured property that significantly increases the risk of flooding.

E. We do not insure for loss to any building or personal property located on land leased from the Federal Government, arising from or incident to the flooding of the land by the Federal Government, where the lease expressly holds the Federal Government harmless under flood insurance issued under any Federal Government program.

VI. DEDUCTIBLES

A. When a loss is covered under this policy, we will pay only that part of the loss that exceeds the applicable deductible amount, subject to the limit of liability that applies. The deductible amount is shown on the Declarations Page.

However, when a building under construction, alteration, or repair does not have at least two rigid exterior walls and a fully secured roof at the time of loss, your deductible amount will be two times the deductible that would otherwise apply to a completed building.

B. In each loss from flood, separate deductibles apply to the building and personal property insured by this policy.

C. No deductible applies to:

1. III.C.2. Loss Avoidance Measures; or
2. III.D. Increased Cost of Compliance.

VII. GENERAL CONDITIONS

A. Pair and Set Clause

In case of loss to an article that is part of a pair or set, we will have the option of paying you:

1. An amount equal to the cost of replacing the lost, damaged, or destroyed article, less depreciation, or

2. An amount which represents the fair proportion of the total value of the pair or set that the lost, damaged, or destroyed article bears to the pair or set.

B. Concealment or Fraud and Policy Voidance

1. With respect to all insureds under this policy, this policy:

a. Is void,

b. Has no legal force or effect,

c. Cannot be renewed, and

d. Cannot be replaced by a new NFIP policy, if, before or after a loss, you or any other insured or your agent have at any time:

(1) Intentionally concealed or misrepresented any material fact or circumstance,

(2) Engaged in fraudulent conduct, or

(3) Made false statements relating to this policy or any other NFIP insurance.

2. This policy will be void as of the date wrongful acts described in B.1. above were committed.

3. Fines, civil penalties, and imprisonment under applicable Federal laws may also apply to the acts of fraud or concealment described above.

4. This policy is also void for reasons other than fraud, misrepresentation, or wrongful act. This policy is void from its inception and has no legal force under the following conditions:

a. If the property is located in a community that was not participating in the NFIP on the policy's inception date and did not join or re-enter the program during the policy term and before the loss occurred; or

b. If the property listed on the application is otherwise not eligible for coverage under the NFIP.

C. Other Insurance

1. If a loss covered by this policy is also covered by other insurance that includes flood coverage not issued under the Act, we will not pay more than the amount of insurance that you are entitled to for lost, damaged, or destroyed property insured under this policy subject to the following:

a. We will pay only the proportion of the loss that the amount of insurance that applies under this policy bears to the total amount of insurance covering the loss, unless C.1.b. or c. below applies.

b. If the other policy has a provision stating that it is excess insurance, this policy will be primary.

c. This policy will be primary (but subject to its own deductible) up to the deductible in the other flood policy (except another policy as described in C.1.b. above). When the other deductible amount is reached, this policy will participate in the same proportion that the amount of insurance under this policy bears to the total amount of both policies, for the remainder of the loss.

2. Where this policy covers a condominium association and there is a flood insurance policy in the name of a unit owner that covers the same loss as this policy, then this policy will be primary.

D. Amendments, Waivers, Assignment

This policy cannot be changed nor can any of its provisions be waived without the express written consent of the Federal Insurance Administrator. No action that we take under the terms of this policy can constitute a waiver of any of our rights. You may assign this policy in writing when you transfer title of your property to someone else except under these conditions:

1. When this policy covers only personal property; or

2. When this policy covers a structure during the course of construction.

E. Cancellation of Policy by You

1. You may cancel this policy in accordance with the applicable rules and regulations of the NFIP.

2. If you cancel this policy, you may be entitled to a full or partial refund of premium also under the applicable rules and regulations of the NFIP.

F. Non-Renewal of the Policy by Us

Your policy will not be renewed:

1. If the community where your covered property is located stops participating in the NFIP; or

2. If your building has been declared ineligible under section 1316 of the Act.

G. Reduction and Reformation of Coverage

1. If the premium we received from you was not enough to buy the kind and amount of coverage that you requested, we will provide only the amount of coverage that can be purchased for the premium payment we received.

2. The policy can be reformed to increase the amount of coverage resulting from the reduction described in G.1. above to the amount you requested as follows:

a. Discovery of Insufficient Premium or Incomplete Rating Information Before a Loss.

(1) If we discover before you have a flood loss that your premium payment was not enough to buy the requested amount of coverage, we will send you and any mortgagee or trustee known to us a bill for the required additional premium for the current policy term (or that portion of the current policy term following any endorsement changing the amount of coverage). If you or the mortgagee or trustee pay the additional premium within 30 days from the date of our bill, we will reform the policy to increase the amount of coverage to the originally requested amount effective to the beginning of the current policy term (or subsequent date of any endorsement changing the amount of coverage).

(2) If we determine before you have a flood loss that the rating information we have is incomplete and prevents us from calculating the additional premium, we will ask you to send the required information. You must submit the information within 60 days of our request. Once we determine the amount of additional premium for the current policy term, we will follow the procedure in G.2.a.(1) above.

(3) If we do not receive the additional premium (or additional information) by the date it is due, the amount of coverage can only be increased by endorsement subject to any appropriate waiting period.

b. Discovery of Insufficient Premium or Incomplete Rating Information After a Loss.

(1) If we discover after you have a flood loss that your premium payment was not enough to buy the requested amount of coverage, we will send you and any mortgagee or trustee known to us a bill for the required additional premium for the current and the prior policy terms. If you or the mortgagee or trustee pay the additional premium within 30 days of the date of our bill, we will reform the policy to increase the amount of coverage to the originally requested amount effective to the beginning of the prior policy term.

(2) If we discover after you have a flood loss that the rating information we have is incomplete and prevents us from calculating the additional premium, we will ask you to send the required information. You must submit the information before your claim can be paid. Once we determine the amount of additional premium for the current and prior policy terms, we will follow the procedure in G.2.b.(1) above.

(3) If we do not receive the additional premium by the date it is due, your flood insurance claim will be settled based on the reduced amount of coverage. The amount of coverage can only be increased by endorsement subject to any appropriate waiting period.

3. However, if we find that you or your agent intentionally did not tell us, or falsified, any important fact or circumstance or did anything fraudulent relating to this insurance, the provisions of Condition B. above apply.

H. Policy Renewal

1. This policy will expire at 12:01 a.m. on the last day of the policy term.

2. We must receive the payment of the appropriate renewal premium within 30 days of the expiration date.

3. If we find, however, that we did not place your renewal notice into the U.S. Postal Service, or if we did mail it, we made a mistake, e.g., we used an incorrect, incomplete, or illegible address, which delayed its delivery to you before the due date for the renewal premium, then we will follow these procedures:

a. If you or your agent notified us, not later than one year after the date on which the payment of the renewal premium was due, of nonreceipt of a renewal notice before the due date for the renewal premium, and we determine that the circumstances in the preceding paragraph apply, we will mail a second bill providing a revised due date, which will be 30 days after the date on which the bill is mailed.

b. If we do not receive the premium requested in the second bill by the revised due date, then we will not renew the policy. In that case, the policy will remain as an expired policy as of the expiration date shown on the Declarations Page.

4. In connection with the renewal of this policy, we may ask you during the policy term to re-certify, on a Recertification Questionnaire that we will provide to you, the rating information used to rate your most recent application for or renewal of insurance.

I. Conditions Suspending or Restricting Insurance

We are not liable for loss that occurs while there is a hazard that is increased by any means within your control or knowledge.

J. Requirements in Case of Loss

In case of a flood loss to insured property, you must:

1. Give prompt written notice to us;

2. As soon as reasonably possible, separate the damaged and undamaged property, putting it in the best possible order so that we may examine it;

3. Prepare an inventory of damaged property showing the quantity, description, actual cash value, and amount of loss. Attach all bills, receipts, and related documents;

4. Within 60 days after the loss, send us a proof of loss, which is your statement of the amount you are claiming under the policy signed and sworn to by you, and which furnishes us with the following information:

a. The date and time of loss;

b. A brief explanation of how the loss happened;

c. Your interest (for example, "owner") and the interest, if any, of others in the damaged property;

d. Details of any other insurance that may cover the loss;

e. Changes in title or occupancy of the insured property during the term of the policy;

f. Specifications of damaged buildings and detailed repair estimates;

g. Names of mortgagees or anyone else having a lien, charge, or claim against the insured property;

h. Details about who occupied any insured building at the time of loss and for what purpose; and

i. The inventory of damaged property described in J.3. above.

5. In completing the proof of loss, you must use your own judgment concerning the amount of loss and justify that amount.

6. You must cooperate with the adjuster or representative in the investigation of the claim.

7. The insurance adjuster whom we hire to investigate your claim may furnish you with a proof of loss form, and she or he may help you complete it. However, this is a matter of courtesy only, and you must still send us a proof of loss within sixty days after the loss even if the adjuster does not furnish the form or help you complete it.

8. We have not authorized the adjuster to approve or disapprove claims or to tell you whether we will approve your claim.

9. At our option, we may accept the adjuster's report of the loss instead of your proof of loss. The adjuster's report will include information about your loss and the damages you sustained. You must sign the adjuster's report. At our option, we may require you to swear to the report.

K. Our Options After a Loss

Options we may, in our sole discretion, exercise after loss include the following:

1. At such reasonable times and places that we may designate, you must:

a. Show us or our representative the damaged property;

b. Submit to examination under oath, while not in the presence of another insured, and sign the same; and

c. Permit us to examine and make extracts and copies of:

(1) Any policies of property insurance insuring you against loss and the deed establishing your ownership of the insured real property;

(2) Condominium association documents including the Declarations of the condominium, its Articles of Association or Incorporation, Bylaws, and rules and regulations; and

(3) All books of accounts, bills, invoices, and other vouchers, or certified copies pertaining to the damaged property if the originals are lost.

2. We may request, in writing, that you furnish us with a complete inventory of the lost, damaged, or destroyed property, including:

   a. Quantities and costs;

   b. Actual cash values;

   c. Amounts of loss claimed;

   d. Any written plans and specifications for repair of the damaged property that you can reasonably make available to us; and

   e. Evidence that prior flood damage has been repaired.

3. If we give you written notice within 30 days after we receive your signed, sworn proof of loss, we may:

   a. Repair, rebuild, or replace any part of the lost, damaged, or destroyed property with material or property of like kind and quality or its functional equivalent; and

   b. Take all or any part of the damaged property at the value that we agree upon or its appraised value.

L. No Benefit to Bailee

No person or organization, other than you, having custody of covered property will benefit from this insurance.

M. Loss Payment

1. We will adjust all losses with you. We will pay you unless some other person or entity is named in the policy or is legally entitled to receive payment. Loss will be payable 60 days after we receive your proof of loss (or within 90 days after the insurance adjuster files an adjuster's report signed and sworn to by you in lieu of a proof of loss) and:

   a. We reach an agreement with you;

   b. There is an entry of a final judgment; or

   c. There is a filing of an appraisal award with us, as provided in VII. P.

2. If we reject your proof of loss in whole or in part you may:

   a. Accept such denial of your claim;

   b. Exercise your rights under this policy; or

   c. File an amended proof of loss as long as it is filed within 60 days of the date of the loss.

N. Abandonment

You may not abandon damaged or undamaged insured property to us.

O. Salvage

We may permit you to keep damaged insured property after a loss, and we will reduce the amount of the loss proceeds payable to you under the policy by the value of the salvage.

P. Appraisal

If you and we fail to agree on the actual cash value of the damaged property so as to determine the amount of loss, either may demand an appraisal of the loss. In this event,

you and we will each choose a competent and impartial appraiser within 20 days after receiving a written request from the other. The two appraisers will choose an umpire. If they cannot agree upon an umpire within 15 days, you or we may request that the choice be made by a judge of a court of record in the state where the insured property is located. The appraisers will separately state the actual cash value and the amount of loss to each item. If the appraisers submit a written report of an agreement to us, the amount agreed upon will be the amount of loss. If they fail to agree, they will submit their differences to the umpire. A decision agreed to by any two will set the amount of actual cash value and loss.

Each party will:

1. Pay its own appraiser; and

2. Bear the other expenses of the appraisal and umpire equally.

Q. Mortgage Clause

The word "mortgagee" includes trustee.

Any loss payable under Coverage A—Building Property will be paid to any mortgagee of whom we have actual notice, as well as any other mortgagee or loss payee determined to exist at the time of loss, and you, as interests appear. If more than one mortgagee is named, the order of payment will be the same as the order of precedence of the mortgages. If we deny your claim, that denial will not apply to a valid claim of the mortgagee, if the mortgagee:

1. Notifies us of any change in the ownership or occupancy, or substantial change in risk of which the mortgagee is aware;

2. Pays any premium due under this policy on demand if you have neglected to pay the premium; and

3. Submits a signed, sworn proof of loss within 60 days after receiving notice from us of your failure to do so.

All terms of this policy apply to the mortgagee.

The mortgagee has the right to receive loss payment even if the mortgagee has started foreclosure or similar action on the building.

If we decide to cancel or not renew this policy, it will continue in effect for the benefit of the mortgagee only for 30 days after we notify the mortgagee of the cancellation or non-renewal.

If we pay the mortgagee for any loss and deny payment to you, we are subrogated to all the rights of the mortgagee granted under the mortgage on the property. Subrogation will not impair the right of the mortgagee to recover the full amount of the mortgagee's claim.

R. Suit Against Us

You may not sue us to recover money under this policy unless you have complied with all the requirements of the policy. If you do sue, you must start the suit within one year of the date of the written denial of all or part of the claim, and you must file the suit in the United States District Court of the district in which the insured property was located at the time of loss. This requirement applies to any claim that you may have under this policy and to any dispute that you may have arising out of the handling of any claim under the policy.

S. Subrogation

Whenever we make a payment for a loss under this policy, we are subrogated to your right to recover for that loss from any other person. That means that your right to recover for a loss that was partly or totally caused by someone else is automatically transferred to us, to the extent that we have paid you for the loss. We may require you to acknowledge this transfer in writing. After the loss, you may not give up our right to recover this money or do anything that would prevent us from recovering it. If you make any claim against any person who caused your loss and recover any money, you must pay us back first before you may keep any of that money.

T. Continuous Lake Flooding

1. If an insured building has been flooded by rising lake waters continuously for 90 days or more and it appears reasonably certain that a continuation of this flooding will result in a covered loss to the insured building equal to or greater than the building policy limits plus the deductible or the maximum payable under the policy for any one building loss, we will pay you the lesser of these two amounts without waiting for the further damage to occur if you sign a release agreeing:

a. To make no further claim under this policy;

b. Not to seek renewal of this policy;

c. Not to apply for any flood insurance under the Act for property at the described location; and

d. Not to seek a premium refund for current or prior terms.

If the policy term ends before the insured building has been flooded continuously for 90 days, the provisions of this paragraph T.1. will apply when as the insured building suffers a covered loss before the policy term ends.

2. If your insured building is subject to continuous lake flooding from a closed basin lake, you may elect to file a claim under either paragraph T.1. above or this paragraph T.2. (A "closed basin lake" is a natural lake from which water leaves primarily through evaporation and whose surface area now exceeds or has exceeded one square mile at any time in the recorded past. Most of the nation's closed basin lakes are in the western

half of the United States, where annual evaporation exceeds annual precipitation and where lake levels and surface areas are subject to considerable fluctuation due to wide variations in the climate. These lakes may overtop their basins on rare occasions.) Under this paragraph T.2 we will pay your claim as if the building is a total loss even though it has not been continuously inundated for 90 days, subject to the following conditions:

a. Lake flood waters must damage or imminently threaten to damage your building.

b. Before approval of your claim, you must:

(1) Agree to a claim payment that reflects your buying back the salvage on a negotiated basis; and

(2) Grant the conservation easement described in FEMA's "Policy Guidance for Closed Basin Lakes," to be recorded in the office of the local recorder of deeds. FEMA, in consultation with the community in which the property is located, will identify on a map an area or areas of special consideration (ASC) in which there is a potential for flood damage from continuous lake flooding. FEMA will give the community the agreed-upon map showing the ASC. This easement will only apply to that portion of the property in the ASC. It will allow certain agricultural and recreational uses of the land. The only structures that it will allow on any portion of the property within the ASC are certain, simple agricultural and recreational structures. If any of these allowable structures are insurable buildings under the NFIP and are insured under the NFIP, they will not be eligible for the benefits of this paragraph T.2. If a U.S. Army Corps of Engineers certified flood control project or otherwise certified flood control project later protects the property, FEMA will, upon request, amend the ASC to remove areas protected by those projects. The restrictions of the easement will then no longer apply to any portion of the property removed from the ASC; and

(3) Comply with paragraphs T.1.a. through T.1.d. above.

c. Within 90 days of approval of your claim, you must move your building to a new location outside the ASC. FEMA will give you an additional 30 days to move if you show that there is sufficient reason to extend the time.

d. Before the final payment of your claim, you must acquire an elevation certificate and a floodplain development permit from the local floodplain administrator for the new location of your building.

e. Before the approval of your claim, the community having jurisdiction over your building must:

(1) Adopt a permanent land use ordinance, or a temporary moratorium for a period not to exceed 6 months to be followed immediately by a permanent land use ordinance,

that is consistent with the provisions specified in the easement required in paragraph T.2.b. above.

(2) Agree to declare and report any violations of this ordinance to FEMA so that under Sec. 1316 of the National Flood Insurance Act of 1968, as amended, flood insurance to the building can be denied; and

(3) Agree to maintain as deed-restricted, for purposes compatible with open space or agricultural or recreational use only, any affected property the community acquires an interest in. These deed restrictions must be consistent with the provisions of paragraph T.2.b. above except that even if a certified project protects the property, the land use restrictions continue to apply if the property was acquired under the Hazard Mitigation Grant Program or the Flood Mitigation Assistance Program. If a non-profit land trust organization receives the property as a donation, that organization must maintain the property as deed-restricted, consistent with the provisions of paragraph T.2.b. above.

f. Before the approval of your claim, the affected State must take all action set forth in FEMA's "Policy Guidance for Closed Basin Lakes."

g. You must have NFIP flood insurance coverage continuously in effect from a date established by FEMA until you file a claim under this paragraph T.2. If a subsequent owner buys NFIP insurance that goes into effect within 60 days of the date of transfer of title, any gap in coverage during that 60-day period will not be a violation of this continuous coverage requirement. For the purpose of honoring a claim under this paragraph T.2, we will not consider to be in effect any increased coverage that became effective after the date established by FEMA. The exception to this is any increased coverage in the amount suggested by your insurer as an inflation adjustment.

h. This paragraph T.2. will be in effect for a community when the FEMA Regional Administrator for the affected region provides to the community, in writing, the following:

(1) Confirmation that the community and the State are in compliance with the conditions in paragraphs T.2.e. and T.2.f. above, and

(2) The date by which you must have flood insurance in effect.

U. Duplicate Policies Not Allowed

1. Property may not be insured under more than one NFIP policy.

If we find that the duplication was not knowingly created, we will give you written notice. The notice will advise you that you may choose one of several options under the following procedures:

a. If you choose to keep in effect the policy with the earlier effective date, you may also choose to add the coverage limits of the later policy to the limits of the earlier policy. The change will become effective as of the effective date of the later policy.

b. If you choose to keep in effect the policy with the later effective date, you may also choose to add the coverage limits of the earlier policy to the limits of the later policy. The change will be effective as of the effective date of the later policy.

In either case, you must pay the pro rata premium for the increased coverage limits within 30 days of the written notice. In no event will the resulting coverage limits exceed the permissible limits of coverage under the Act or your insurable interest, whichever is less. We will make a refund to you, according to applicable NFIP rules, of the premium for the policy not being kept in effect.

2. Your option under this Condition U. Duplicate Policies Not Allowed to elect which NFIP policy to keep in effect does not apply when duplicates have been knowingly created. Losses occurring under such circumstances will be adjusted according to the terms and conditions of the earlier policy. The policy with the later effective date must be canceled.

V. Loss Settlement

We will pay the least of the following amounts after application of the deductible:

1. The applicable amount of insurance under this policy;

2. The actual cash value; or

3. The amount it would cost to repair or replace the property with material of like kind and quality within a reasonable time after the loss.

VIII. LIBERALIZATION CLAUSE

If we make a change that broadens your coverage under this edition of our policy, but does not require any additional premium, then that change will automatically apply to your insurance as of the date we implement the change, provided that this implementation date falls within 60 days before or during the policy term stated on the Declarations Page.

IX. WHAT LAW GOVERNS

This policy and all disputes arising from the handling of any claim under the policy are governed exclusively by the flood insurance regulations issued by FEMA, the National Flood Insurance Act of 1968, as amended (42 U.S.C. 4001, *et seq.*), and Federal common law.

In Witness Whereof, we have signed this policy below and hereby enter into this Insurance Agreement.

Administrator, Federal Insurance Administration.

[65 FR 60778, Oct. 12, 2000, as amended at 68 FR 9897, Mar. 3, 2003; 76 FR 7510, Feb. 10, 2011]

APPENDIX A(3) TO PART 61

FEDERAL EMERGENCY MANAGEMENT AGENCY
FEDERAL INSURANCE ADMINISTRATION

STANDARD FLOOD INSURANCE POLICY

RESIDENTIAL CONDOMINIUM BUILDING
ASSOCIATION POLICY

I. AGREEMENT

Please read the policy carefully. The flood insurance provided is subject to limitations, restrictions, and exclusions.

This policy covers only a residential condominium building in a regular program community. If the community reverts to emergency program status during the policy term and remains as an emergency program community at time of renewal, this policy cannot be renewed.

The Federal Emergency Management Agency (FEMA) provides flood insurance under the terms of the National Flood Insurance Act of 1968 and its Amendments, and Title 44 of the Code of Federal Regulations.

We will pay you for direct physical loss by or from flood to your insured property if you:

1. Have paid the correct premium;

2. Comply with all terms and conditions of this policy; and

3. Have furnished accurate information and statements.

We have the right to review the information you give us at any time and to revise your policy based on our review.

II. DEFINITIONS

A. In this policy, "you" and "your" refer to the insured(s) shown on the Declarations Page of this policy. Insured(s) includes: any mortgagee and loss payee named in the Application and Declarations Page, as well as any other mortgagee or loss payee determined to exist at the time of loss in the order of precedence. "We," "us," and "our" refer to the insurer.

Some definitions are complex because they are provided as they appear in the law or regulations, or result from court cases. The precise definitions are intended to protect you.

"Flood", as used in this flood insurance policy, means:

1. A general and temporary condition of partial or complete inundation of two or more acres of normally dry land area or of two or more properties (one of which is your property) from:

a. Overflow of inland or tidal waters;

b. Unusual and rapid accumulation or run-off of surface waters from any source;

c. Mudflow.

2. Collapse or subsidence of land along the shore of a lake or similar body of water as a result of erosion or undermining caused by waves or currents of water exceeding anticipated cyclical levels which result in a flood as defined in A.1.a above.

B. The following are the other key definitions we use in this policy:

1. *Act*. The National Flood Insurance Act of 1968 and any amendments to it.

2. *Actual Cash Value*. The cost to replace an insured item of property at the time of loss, less the value of its physical depreciation.

3. *Application*. The statement made and signed by you or your agent in applying for this policy. The application gives information we use to determine the eligibility of the risk, the kind of policy to be issued, and the correct premium payment. The application is part of this flood insurance policy. For us to issue you a policy, the correct premium payment must accompany the application.

4. *Base Flood*. A flood having a one percent chance of being equaled or exceeded in any given year.

5. *Basement*. Any area of the building, including any sunken room or sunken portion of a room, having its floor below ground level (subgrade) on all sides.

6. *Building*.

a. A structure with two or more outside rigid walls and a fully secured roof, that is affixed to a permanent site;

b. A manufactured home ("a manufactured home," also known as a mobile home, is a structure: built on a permanent chassis, transported to its site in one or more sections, and affixed to a permanent foundation); or

c. A travel trailer without wheels, built on a chassis and affixed to a permanent foundation, that is regulated under the community's floodplain management and building ordinances or laws.

Building does not mean a gas or liquid storage tank or a recreational vehicle, park trailer or other similar vehicle, except as described in B.6.c., above.

7. *Cancellation*. The ending of the insurance coverage provided by this policy before the expiration date.

8. *Condominium*. That form of ownership of real property in which each unit owner has an undivided interest in common elements.

9. *Condominium Association*. The entity, formed by the unit owners, responsible for the maintenance and operation of:

a. Common elements owned in undivided shares by unit owners; and

b. Other real property in which the unit owners have use rights; where membership in the entity is a required condition of unit ownership.

10. *Declarations Page*. A computer-generated summary of information you provided in the application for insurance. The Declarations Page also describes the term of the policy, limits of coverage, and displays the

premium and our name. The Declarations Page is a part of this flood insurance policy.

11. *Described Location.* The location where the insured building or personal property is found. The described location is shown on the Declarations Page.

12. *Direct Physical Loss By or From Flood.* Loss or damage to insured property, directly caused by a flood. There must be evidence of physical changes to the property.

13. *Elevated Building.* A building that has no basement and that has its lowest elevated floor raised above ground level by foundation walls, shear walls, posts, piers, pilings, or columns.

14. *Emergency Program.* The initial phase of a community's participation in the National Flood Insurance Program. During this phase, only limited amounts of insurance are available under the Act.

15. *Expense Constant.* A flat charge you must pay on each new or renewal policy to defray the expenses of the Federal Government related to flood insurance.

16. *Federal Policy Fee.* A flat charge you must pay on each new or renewal policy to defray certain administrative expenses incurred in carrying out the National Flood Insurance Program. This fee covers expenses not covered by the expense constant.

17. *Improvements.* Fixtures, alterations, installations, or additions comprising a part of the residential condominium building, including improvements in the units.

18. *Mudflow.* A river of liquid and flowing mud on the surfaces of normally dry land areas, as when earth is carried by a current of water. Other earth movements, such as landslide, slope failure, or a saturated soil mass moving by liquidity down a slope, are not mudflows.

19. *National Flood Insurance Program (NFIP).* The program of flood insurance coverage and floodplain management administered under the Act and applicable Federal regulations in Title 44 of the Code of Federal Regulations, Subchapter B.

20. *Policy.* The entire written contract between you and us. It includes:

a. This printed form;

b. The application and Declarations Page;

c. Any endorsement(s) that may be issued; and

d. Any renewal certificate indicating that coverage has been instituted for a new policy and new policy term.

Only one building, which you specifically described in the application, may be insured under this policy.

21. *Pollutants.* Substances that include, but are not limited to, any solid, liquid, gaseous, or thermal irritant or contaminant, including smoke, vapor, soot, fumes, acids, alkalis, chemicals, and waste. Waste includes, but is not limited to, materials to be recycled, reconditioned, or reclaimed.

22. *Post-FIRM Building.* A building for which construction or substantial improvement occurred after December 31, 1974, or on or after the effective date of an initial Flood Insurance Rate Map (FIRM), whichever is later.

23. *Probation Premium.* A flat charge you must pay on each new or renewal policy issued covering property in a community that the NFIP has placed on probation under the provisions of 44 CFR 59.24.

24. *Regular Program.* The final phase of a community's participation in the National Flood Insurance Program. In this phase, a Flood Insurance Rate Map is in effect and full limits of coverage are available under the Act.

25. *Residential Condominium Building.* A building, owned and administered as a condominium, containing one or more family units and in which at least 75% of the floor area is residential.

26. *Special Flood Hazard Area.* An area having special flood or mudflow, and/or flood-related erosion hazards, and shown on a Flood Hazard Boundary Map or Flood Insurance Rate Map as Zone A, AO, A1–A30, AE, A99, AH, AR, AR/A, AR/AE, AR/AH, AR/AO, AR/A1–A30, V1–V30, VE, or V.

27. *Unit.* A single-family unit in a residential condominium building.

28. *Valued Policy.* A policy in which the insured and the insurer agree on the value of the property insured, that value being payable in the event of a total loss. The Standard Flood Insurance Policy is not a valued policy.

III. PROPERTY COVERED

A. Coverage A—Building Property

We insure against direct physical loss by or from flood to:

1. The residential condominium building described on the Declarations Page at the described location, including all units within the building and the improvements within the units.

2. We also insure such building property for a period of 45 days at another location, as set forth in III.C.2.b., Property Removed to Safety.

3. Additions and extensions attached to and in contact with the building by means of a rigid exterior wall, a solid load-bearing interior wall, a stairway, an elevated walkway, or a roof. At your option, additions and extensions connected by any of these methods may be separately insured. Additions and extensions attached to and in contact with the building by means of a common interior wall that is not a solid load-bearing wall are always considered part of the building and cannot be separately insured.

4. The following fixtures, machinery and equipment, including its units, which are covered under Coverage A only:

a. Awnings and canopies;
b. Blinds;
c. Carpet permanently installed over unfinished flooring;
d. Central air conditioners;
e. Elevator equipment;
f. Fire extinguishing apparatus;
g. Fire sprinkler systems;
h. Walk-in freezers;
i. Furnaces;
j. Light fixtures;
k. Outdoor antennas and aerials fastened to buildings;
l. Permanently installed cupboards, bookcases, paneling, and wallpaper;
m. Pumps and machinery for operating pumps;
n. Ventilating equipment;
o. Wall mirrors, permanently installed; and
p. In the units within the building, installed:
(1) Built-in dishwashers;
(2) Built-in microwave ovens;
(3) Garbage disposal units;
(4) Hot water heaters, including solar water heaters;
(5) Kitchen cabinets;
(6) Plumbing fixtures;
(7) Radiators;
(8) Ranges;
(9) Refrigerators; and
(10) Stoves.
5. Materials and supplies to be used for construction, alteration or repair of the insured building while the materials and supplies are stored in a fully enclosed building at the described location or on an adjacent property.
6. A building under construction, alteration or repair at the described location.
a. If the structure is not yet walled or roofed as described in the definition for building (see II.B.6.a.), then coverage applies:
(1) Only while such work is in progress; or
(2) If such work is halted, only for a period of up to 90 continuous days thereafter.
b. However, coverage does not apply until the building is walled and roofed if the lowest floor, including the basement floor, of a non-elevated building or the lowest elevated floor of an elevated building is:
(1) Below the base flood elevation in Zones AH, AE, A1–30, AR, AR/AE, AR/AH, AR/A1–30, AR/A, AR/AO; or
(2) Below the base flood elevation adjusted to include the effect of wave action in Zones VE or V1–30.
The lowest floor levels are based on the bottom of the lowest horizontal structural member of the floor in Zones VE or V1–V30 and the top of the floor in Zones AH, AE, A1–A30, AR, AR/AE, AR/AH, AR/A1–A30, AR/A, AR/AO.
7. A manufactured home or a travel trailer as described in the Definitions Section (See II.B.b. and c.).

If the manufactured home is in a special flood hazard area, it must be anchored in the following manner at the time of the loss:
a. By over-the-top or frame ties to ground anchors; or
b. In accordance with the manufacturer's specifications; or
c. In compliance with the community's floodplain management requirements unless it has been continuously insured by the NFIP at the same described location since September 30, 1982.
8. Items of property in a building enclosure below the lowest elevated floor of an elevated post-FIRM building located in zones A1–A30, AE, AH, AR, AR/A, AR/AE, AR/AH, AR/A1–A30, V1–V30, or VE, or in a basement, regardless of the zone. Coverage is limited to the following:
a. Any of the following items, if installed in their functioning locations and, if necessary for operation, connected to a power source:
(1) Central air conditioners;
(2) Cisterns and the water in them;
(3) Drywall for walls and ceilings in a basement and the cost of labor to nail it, unfinished and unfloated and not taped, to the framing;
(4) Electrical junction and circuit breaker boxes;
(5) Electrical outlets and switches;
(6) Elevators, dumbwaiters, and related equipment, except for related equipment installed below the base flood elevation after September 30, 1987;
(7) Fuel tanks and the fuel in them;
(8) Furnaces and hot water heaters;
(9) Heat pumps;
(10) Nonflammable insulation in a basement;
(11) Pumps and tanks used in solar energy systems;
(12) Stairways and staircases attached to the building, not separated from it by elevated walkways;
(13) Sump pumps;
(14) Water softeners and the chemicals in them, water filters and faucets installed as an integral part of the plumbing system;
(15) Well water tanks and pumps;
(16) Required utility connections for any item in this list; and
(17) Footings, foundations, posts, pilings, piers, or other foundation walls and anchorage systems required to support a building.
b. Clean-up.

B. Coverage B—Personal Property

1. If you have purchased personal property coverage, we insure, subject to B.2. and B.3. below, against direct physical loss by or from flood to personal property that is inside the fully enclosed insured building and is:
a. Owned by the unit owners of the condominium association in common, meaning

251

property in which each unit owner has an un-divided ownership interest; or

b. Owned solely by the condominium asso-ciation and used exclusively in the conduct of the business affairs of the condominium association.

We also insure such personal property for 45 days while stored at a temporary location, as set forth in III.C.2.b., Property Removed to Safety.

2. Coverage for personal property includes the following property, subject to B.1. above, which is covered under Coverage B only:

a. Air conditioning units—portable or win-dow type;

b. Carpet, not permanently installed, over unfinished flooring;

c. Carpets over finished flooring;

d. Clothes washers and dryers;

e. "Cook-out" grills;

f. Food freezers, other than walk-in, and the food in any freezer;

g. Outdoor equipment and furniture stored inside the insured building;

h. Ovens and the like; and

i. Portable microwave ovens and portable dishwashers.

3. Coverage for items of property in a building enclosure below the lowest elevated floor of an elevated post-FIRM building lo-cated in zones A1-A30, AE, AH, AR, AR/A, AR/AE, AR/AH, AR/A1-A30, V1-V30, or VE, or in a basement, regardless of the zone, is lim-ited to the following items, if installed in their functioning locations and, if necessary for operation, connected to a power source:

a. Air conditioning units—portable or win-dow type;

b. Clothes washers and dryers; and

c. Food freezers, other than walk-in, and food in any freezer.

4. Special Limits. We will pay no more than $2,500 for any one loss to one or more of the following kinds of personal property:

a. Artwork, photographs, collectibles, or memorabilia, including but not limited to, porcelain or other figures, and sports cards;

b. Rare books or autographed items;

c. Jewelry, watches, precious and semi-pre-cious stones, or articles of gold, silver, or platinum;

d. Furs or any article containing fur which represents its principal value.

5. We will pay only for the functional value of antiques.

C. Coverage C—Other Coverages

1. *Debris Removal*

a. We will pay the expense to remove non-owned debris that is on or in insured prop-erty and debris of insured property any-where.

b. If you or a member of your household perform the removal work, the value of your work will be based on the Federal minimum wage.

c. This coverage does not increase the Cov-erage A or Coverage B limit of liability.

2. *Loss Avoidance Measures*

a. Sandbags, Supplies, and Labor

(1) We will pay up to $1,000 for the costs you incur to protect the insured building from a flood or imminent danger of flood, for the following:

(a) Your reasonable expenses to buy:

(i) Sandbags, including sand to fill them;

(ii) Fill for temporary levees;

(iii) Pumps; and

(iv) Plastic sheeting and lumber used in connection with these items; and

(b) The value of work, at the Federal min-imum wage, that you perform.

(2) This coverage for Sandbags, Supplies, and Labor applies only if damage to insured property by or from flood is imminent and the threat of flood damage is apparent enough to lead a person of common prudence to anticipate flood damage. One of the fol-lowing must also occur:

(a) A general and temporary condition of flooding in the area near the described loca-tion must occur, even if the flood does not reach the insured building; or

(b) A legally authorized official must issue an evacuation order or other civil order for the community in which the insured building is located calling for measures to preserve life and property from the peril of flood. This coverage does not increase the Coverage A or Coverage B limit of liability.

b. Property Removed to Safety

(1) We will pay up to $1,000 for the reason-able expenses you incur to move insured property to a place other than the described location that contains the property in order to protect it from flood or the imminent dan-ger of flood.

Reasonable expenses include the value of work, at the Federal minimum wage, that you perform.

(2) If you move insured property to a loca-tion other than the described location that contains the property, in order to protect it from flood or the imminent danger of flood, we will cover such property while at that lo-cation for a period of 45 consecutive days from the date you begin to move it there. The personal property that is moved must be placed in a fully enclosed building, or other-wise reasonably protected from the ele-ments.

Any property removed, including a move-able home described in II.6.b. and c., must be placed above ground level or outside of the special flood hazard area.

This coverage does not increase the Cov-erage A or Coverage B limit of liability.

D. Coverage D—Increased Cost of Compliance

1. *General.*

This policy pays you to comply with a State or local floodplain management law or ordinance affecting repair or reconstruction of a structure suffering flood damage. Compliance activities eligible for payment are: elevation, floodproofing, relocation, or demolition (or any combination of these activities) of your structure. Eligible floodproofing activities are limited to:

a. Non-residential structures.

b. Residential structures with basements that satisfy FEMA's standards published in the Code of Federal Regulations [44 CFR 60.6 (b) or (c)].

2. *Limit of Liability.*

We will pay you up to $30,000 under this Coverage D—Increased Cost of Compliance, which only applies to policies with building coverage (Coverage A). Our payment of claims under Coverage D is in addition to the amount of coverage which you selected on the application and which appears on the Declarations Page. But the maximum you can collect under this policy for both Coverage A—Building Property and Coverage D—Increased Cost of Compliance cannot exceed the maximum permitted under the Act. We do not charge a separate deductible for a claim under Coverage D.

3. *Eligibility.*

a. A structure covered under Coverage A—Building Property sustaining a loss caused by a flood as defined by this policy must:

(1) Be a "repetitive loss structure." A "repetitive loss structure" is one that meets the following conditions:

(a) The structure is covered by a contract of flood insurance issued under the NFIP.

(b) The structure has suffered flood damage on 2 occasions during a 10-year period which ends on the date of the second loss.

(c) The cost to repair the flood damage, on average, equaled or exceeded 25% of the market value of the structure at the time of each flood loss.

(d) In addition to the current claim, the NFIP must have paid the previous qualifying claim, and the State or community must have a cumulative, substantial damage provision or repetitive loss provision in its floodplain management law or ordinance being enforced against the structure; or

(2) Be a structure that has had flood damage in which the cost to repair equals or exceeds 50% of the market value of the structure at the time of the flood. The State or community must have a substantial damage provision in its floodplain management law or ordinance being enforced against the structure.

b. This Coverage D pays you to comply with State or local floodplain management laws or ordinances that meet the minimum standards of the National Flood Insurance Program found in the Code of Federal Regulations at 44 CFR 60.3. We pay for compliance activities that exceed those standards under these conditions:

(1) 3.a.(1) above.

(2) Elevation or floodproofing in any risk zone to preliminary or advisory base flood elevations provided by FEMA which the State or local government has adopted and is enforcing for flood-damaged structures in such areas. (This includes compliance activities in B, C, X, or D zones which are being changed to zones with base flood elevations. This also includes compliance activities in zones where base flood elevations are being increased, and a flood-damaged structure must comply with the higher advisory base flood elevation.) Increased Cost of Compliance coverage does not apply to situations in B, C, X, or D zones where the community has derived its own elevations and is enforcing elevation or floodproofing requirements for flood-damaged structures to elevations derived solely by the community.

(3) Elevation or floodproofing above the base flood elevation to meet State or local "freeboard" requirements, i.e., that a structure must be elevated above the base flood elevation.

c. Under the minimum NFIP criteria at 44 CFR 60.3(b)(4), States and communities must require the elevation or floodproofing of structures in unnumbered A zones to the base flood elevation where elevation data is obtained from a Federal, State, or other source. Such compliance activities are also eligible for Coverage D.

d. This coverage will also pay for the incremental cost, after demolition or relocation, of elevating or floodproofing a structure during its rebuilding at the same or another site to meet State or local floodplain management laws or ordinances, subject to Exclusion D.5.g. below relating to improvements.

e. This coverage will also pay to bring a flood-damaged structure into compliance with State or local floodplain management laws or ordinances even if the structure had received a variance before the present loss from the applicable floodplain management requirements.

4. *Conditions.*

a. When a structure covered under Coverage A—Building Property sustains a loss caused by a flood, our payment for the loss under this Coverage D will be for the increased cost to elevate, floodproof, relocate, or demolish (or any combination of these activities) caused by the enforcement of current State or local floodplain management ordinances or laws. Our payment for eligible demolition activities will be for the cost to demolish and clear the site of the building debris or a portion thereof caused by the enforcement of current State or local floodplain management ordinances or laws. Eligible activities for the cost of clearing the site will include those necessary to discontinue utility service to the site and ensure proper abandonment of on-site utilities.

b. When the building is repaired or rebuilt, it must be intended for the same occupancy as the present building unless otherwise required by current floodplain management ordinances or laws.

5. *Exclusions.*

Under this Coverage D—Increased Cost of Compliance, we will not pay for:

a. The cost to comply with any floodplain management law or ordinance in communities participating in the Emergency Program.

b. The cost associated with enforcement of any ordinance or law that requires any insured or others to test for, monitor, clean up, remove, contain, treat, detoxify or neutralize, or in any way respond to, or assess the effects of pollutants.

c. The loss in value to any insured building or other structure due to the requirements of any ordinance or law.

d. The loss in residual value of the undamaged portion of a building demolished as a consequence of enforcement of any State or local floodplain management law or ordinance.

e. Any Increased Cost of Compliance under this Coverage D:

(1) Until the building is elevated, floodproofed, demolished, or relocated on the same or to another premises; and

(2) Unless the building is elevated, floodproofed, demolished, or relocated as soon as reasonably possible after the loss, not to exceed two years.

f. Any code upgrade requirements, e.g., plumbing or electrical wiring, not specifically related to the State or local floodplain management law or ordinance.

g. Any compliance activities needed to bring additions or improvements made after the loss occurred into compliance with State or local floodplain management laws or ordinances.

h. Loss due to any ordinance or law that you were required to comply with before the current loss.

i. Any rebuilding activity to standards that do not meet the NFIP's minimum requirements. This includes any situation where the insured has received from the State or community a variance in connection with the current flood loss to rebuild the property to an elevation below the base flood elevation.

j. Increased Cost of Compliance for a garage or carport.

k. Any structure insured under an NFIP Group Flood Insurance Policy.

l. Assessments made by a condominium association on individual condominium unit owners to pay increased costs of repairing commonly owned buildings after a flood in compliance with State or local floodplain management ordinances or laws.

6. *Other Provisions.*

a. Increased Cost of Compliance coverage will not be included in the calculation to determine whether coverage meets the coinsurance requirement for replacement cost coverage under VIII. General Conditions, V. Loss Settlement.

b. All other conditions and provisions of this policy apply.

IV. PROPERTY NOT COVERED

We do not cover any of the following:

1. Personal property not inside the fully enclosed building;

2. A building, and personal property in it, located entirely in, on, or over water or seaward of mean high tide, if constructed or substantially improved after September 30, 1982;

3. Open structures, including a building used as a boathouse or any structure or building into which boats are floated, and personal property located in, on, or over water;

4. Recreational vehicles other than travel trailers described in the Definitions Section (see II.B.6.c.) whether affixed to a permanent foundation or on wheels;

5. Self-propelled vehicles or machines, including their parts and equipment.

However, we do cover self-propelled vehicles or machines, provided they are not licensed for use on public roads and are:

a. Used mainly to service the described location, or

b. Designed and used to assist handicapped persons, while the vehicles or machines are inside a building at the described location;

6. Land, land values, lawns, trees, shrubs, plants, growing crops, or animals;

7. Accounts, bills, coins, currency, deeds, evidences of debt, medals, money, scrip, stored value cards, postage stamps, securities, bullion, manuscripts, or other valuable papers;

8. Underground structures and equipment, including wells, septic tanks, and septic systems;

9. Those portions of walks, walkways, decks, driveways, patios, and other surfaces, all whether protected by a roof or not, located outside the perimeter, exterior walls of the insured building;

10. Containers, including related equipment, such as, but not limited to, tanks containing gases or liquids;

11. Buildings and all their contents if more than 49% of the actual cash value of the building is below ground, unless the lowest level is at or above the base flood elevation and is below ground by reason of earth having been used as insulation material in conjunction with energy efficient building techniques;

12. Fences, retaining walls, seawalls, bulkheads, wharves, piers, bridges, and docks;

13. Aircraft or watercraft, or their furnishings and equipment;

14. Hot tubs and spas that are not bathroom fixtures, and swimming pools, and their equipment such as, but not limited to,

heaters, filters, pumps, and pipes, wherever located;

15. Property not eligible for flood insurance pursuant to the provisions of the Coastal Barrier Resources Act and the Coastal Barrier Improvements Act of 1990 and amendments to these Acts;

16. Personal property used in connection with any incidental commercial occupancy or use of the building.

V. EXCLUSIONS

A. We only pay for direct physical loss by or from flood, which means that we do not pay you for:

1. Loss of revenue or profits;
2. Loss of access to the insured property or described location;
3. Loss of use of the insured property or described location;
4. Loss from interruption of business or production;
5. Any additional living expenses incurred while the insured building is being repaired or is unable to be occupied for any reason;
6. The cost of complying with any ordinance or law requiring or regulating the construction, demolition, remodeling, renovation, or repair of property, including removal of any resulting debris. This exclusion does not apply to any eligible activities that we describe in Coverage D—Increased Cost of Compliance; or
7. Any other economic loss.

B. We do not insure a loss directly or indirectly caused by a flood that is already in progress at the time and date:

1. The policy term begins; or
2. Coverage is added at your request.

C. We do not insure for loss to property caused directly by earth movement even if the earth movement is caused by flood. Some examples of earth movement that we do not cover are:

1. Earthquake;
2. Landslide;
3. Land subsidence;
4. Sinkholes;
5. Destabilization or movement of land that results from accumulation of water in subsurface land areas; or
6. Gradual erosion.

We do, however, pay for losses from mudflow and land subsidence as a result of erosion that are specifically covered under our definition of flood (see II.A.1.c. and II.A.2.).

D. We do not insure for direct physical loss caused directly or indirectly by:

1. The pressure or weight of ice;
2. Freezing or thawing;
3. Rain, snow, sleet, hail, or water spray;
4. Water, moisture, mildew, or mold damage that results primarily from any condition:

a. Substantially confined to the insured building; or

b. That is within your control including, but not limited to:

(1) Design, structural, or mechanical defects;

(2) Failures, stoppages, or breakage of water or sewer lines, drains, pumps, fixtures, or equipment; or

(3) Failure to inspect and maintain the property after a flood recedes;

5. Water or water-borne material that:

a. Backs up through sewers or drains;

b. Discharges or overflows from a sump, sump pump, or related equipment; or

c. Seeps or leaks on or through insured property;

unless there is a flood in the area and the flood is the proximate cause of the sewer, drain, or sump pump discharge or overflow, or the seepage of water;

6. The pressure or weight of water unless there is a flood in the area and the flood is the proximate cause of the damage from the pressure or weight of water.

7. Power, heating, or cooling failure unless the failure results from direct physical loss by or from flood to power, heating or cooling equipment situated on the described location;

8. Theft, fire, explosion, wind, or windstorm;

9. Anything you or your agents do to conspire to do to cause loss by flood deliberately; or

10. Alteration of the insured property that significantly increases the risk of flooding.

E. We do not insure for loss to any building or personal property located on land leased from the Federal Government, arising from or incident to the flooding of the land by the Federal Government, where the lease expressly holds the Federal Government harmless under flood insurance issued under any Federal Government program.

F. We do not pay for the testing for or monitoring of pollutants unless required by law or ordinance.

VI. DEDUCTIBLES

A. When a loss is covered under this policy, we will pay only that part of the loss that exceeds the applicable deductible amount, subject to the limit of insurance that applies. The deductible amount is shown on the Declarations Page.

However, when a building under construction, alteration, or repair does not have at least two rigid exterior walls and a fully secured roof at the time of loss, your deductible amount will be two times the deductible that would otherwise apply to a completed building.

B. In each loss from flood, separate deductibles apply to the building and personal property insured by this policy.

C. No deductible applies to:

1. III.C.2. Loss Avoidance Measures; or
2. III.D. Increased Cost of Compliance.

VII. COINSURANCE

A. This Coinsurance Section applies only to coverage on the building.

B. We will impose a penalty on loss payment unless the amount of insurance applicable to the damaged building is:

1. At least 80% of its replacement cost; or
2. The maximum amount of insurance available for that building under the NFIP, whichever is less.

C. If the actual amount of insurance on the building is less than the required amount in accordance with the terms of VII. B. above, then loss payment is determined as follows (subject to all other relevant conditions in this policy, including those pertaining to valuation, adjustment, settlement, and payment of loss):

1. Divide the actual amount of insurance carried on the building by the required amount of insurance.
2. Multiply the amount of loss, before application of the deductible, by the figure determined in C.1. above.
3. Subtract the deductible from the figure determined in C.2. above.

We will pay the amount determined in C.3. above, or the amount of insurance carried, whichever is less. The amount of insurance carried, if in excess of the applicable maximum amount of insurance available under the NFIP, is reduced accordingly.

Examples

Example #1 (Inadequate Insurance)

Replacement value of the building—$250,000
Required amount of insurance—$200,000
  (80% of replacement value of $250,000)
Actual amount of insurance carried—$180,000
Amount of the loss—$150,000
Deductible—$500
Step 1: $180,000 \div 200,000 = .90$
  (90% of what should be carried.)
Step 2: $150,000 \times .90 = 135,000$
Step 3: $135,000 - 500 = 134,500$

We will pay no more than $134,500. The remaining $15,500 is not covered due to the coinsurance penalty ($15,000) and application of the deductible ($500).

Example #2 (Adequate Insurance)

Replacement value of the building—$500,000
Required amount of insurance—$400,000
  (80% of replacement value of $500,000)
Actual amount of insurance carried—$400,000
Amount of the loss—$200,000
Deductible—$500

In this example there is no coinsurance penalty, because the actual amount of insurance carried meets the required amount. We will pay no more than $199,500 ($200,000 amount of loss minus the $500 deductible).

D. In calculating the full replacement cost of a building:

1. The replacement cost value of any covered building property will be included;
2. The replacement cost value of any building property not covered under this policy will not be included; and
3. Only the replacement cost value of improvements installed by the condominium association will be included.

VIII. GENERAL CONDITIONS

A. *Pair and Set Clause.*

In case of loss to an article that is part of a pair or set, we will have the option of paying you:

1. An amount equal to the cost of replacing the lost, damaged, or destroyed article, less depreciation; or
2. An amount which represents the fair proportion of the total value of the pair or set that the lost, damaged, or destroyed article bears to the pair or set.

B. *Concealment or Fraud and Policy Voidance.*

1. With respect to all insureds under this policy, this policy:
a. Is void,
b. Has no legal force or effect,
c. Cannot be renewed, and
d. Cannot be replaced by a new NFIP policy, if, before or after a loss, you or any other insured or your agent have at any time:
(1) Intentionally concealed or misrepresented any material fact or circumstance,
(2) Engaged in fraudulent conduct, or
(3) Made false statements,
relating to this policy or any other NFIP insurance.

2. This policy will be void as of the date the wrongful acts described in B.1. above were committed.

3. Fines, civil penalties, and imprisonment under applicable Federal laws may also apply to the acts of fraud or concealment described above.

4. This policy is also void for reasons other than fraud, misrepresentation, or wrongful act. This policy is void from its inception and has no legal force under the following conditions:

a. If the property is located in a community that was not participating in the NFIP on the policy's inception date and did not join or re-enter the program during the policy term and before the loss occurred; or

b. If the property listed on the application is not otherwise eligible for coverage under the NFIP.

C. *Other Insurance.*

1. If a loss covered by this policy is also covered by other insurance that includes flood coverage not issued under the Act, we will not pay more than the amount of insurance that you are entitled to for lost, damaged or destroyed property insured under this policy subject to the following:

a. We will pay only the proportion of the loss that the amount of insurance that applies under this policy bears to the total amount of insurance covering the loss, unless C.1.b. or c. immediately below applies.

b. If the other policy has a provision stating that it is excess insurance, this policy will be primary.

c. This policy will be primary (but subject to its own deductible) up to the deductible in the other flood insurance policy (except another policy as described in C.1.b. above). When the other deductible amount is reached, this policy will participate in the same proportion that the amount of insurance under this policy bears to the total amount of both policies, for the remainder of the loss.

2. If there is a flood insurance policy in the name of a unit owner that covers the same loss as this policy, then this policy will be primary.

D. *Amendments, Waivers, Assignment.*

This policy cannot be changed nor can any of its provisions be waived without the express written consent of the Federal Insurance Administrator. No action that we take under the terms of this policy constitutes a waiver of any of our rights. You may assign this policy in writing when you transfer title of your property to someone else except under these conditions:

1. When this policy covers only personal property; or

2. When this policy covers a structure during the course of construction.

E. *Cancellation of Policy by You.*

1. You may cancel this policy in accordance with the applicable rules and regulations of the NFIP.

2. If you cancel this policy, you may be entitled to a full or partial refund of premium also under the applicable rules and regulations of the NFIP.

F. *Non-Renewal of the Policy by Us.*

Your policy will not be renewed:

1. If the community where your covered property is located stops participating in the NFIP, or

2. Your building has been declared ineligible under section 1316 of the Act.

G. *Reduction and Reformation of Coverage.*

1. If the premium we received from you was not enough to buy the kind and amount of coverage you requested, we will provide only the amount of coverage that can be purchased for the premium payment we received.

2. The policy can be reformed to increase the amount of coverage resulting from the reduction described in G.1. above the amount that you requested as follows:

a. Discovery of Insufficient Premium or Incomplete Rating Information Before a Loss.

(1) If we discover before you have a flood loss that your premium payment was not enough to buy the requested amount of coverage, we will send you and any mortgagee or trustee known to us a bill for the required additional premium for the current policy term (or that portion of the current policy term following any endorsement changing the amount of coverage). If you or the mortgagee or trustee pay the additional premium within 30 days from the date of our bill, we will reform the policy to increase the amount of coverage to the originally requested amount effective to the beginning of the current policy term (or subsequent date of any endorsement changing the amount of coverage).

(2) If we determine before you have a flood loss that the rating information we have is incomplete and prevents us from calculating the additional premium, we will ask you to send the required information. You must submit the information within 60 days of our request. Once we determine the amount of additional premium for the current policy term, we will follow the procedure in G.2.a.(1) above.

(3) If we do not receive the additional premium (or additional information) by the date it is due, the amount of coverage can only be increased by endorsement subject to any appropriate waiting period.

b. Discovery of Insufficient Premium or Incomplete Rating Information After a Loss.

(1) If we discover after you have a flood loss that your premium payment was not enough to buy the requested amount of coverage, we will send you and any mortgagee or trustee known to us a bill for the required additional premium for the current and the prior policy terms. If you or the mortgagee or trustee pay the additional premium within 30 days of the date of our bill, we will reform the policy to increase the amount of coverage to the originally requested amount effective to the beginning of the prior policy term.

(2) If we discover after you have a flood loss that the rating information we have is incomplete and prevents us from calculating the additional premium, we will ask you to send the required information. You must submit the information before your claim can be paid. Once we determine the amount of additional premium for the current and prior policy terms, we will follow the procedure in G.2.b.(1) above.

(3) If we do not receive the additional premium by the date it is due, your flood insurance claim will be settled based on the reduced amount of coverage. The amount of coverage can only be increased by endorsement subject to any appropriate waiting period.

3. However, if we find that you or your agent intentionally did not tell us, or falsified, any important fact or circumstance or did anything fraudulent relating to this insurance, the provisions of Condition B. Concealment or Fraud and Policy Voidance above apply.

257

H. *Policy Renewal.*

1. This policy will expire at 12:01 a.m. on the last day of the policy term.

2. We must receive the payment of the appropriate renewal premium within 30 days of the expiration date.

3. If we find, however, that we did not place your renewal notice into the U.S. Postal Service, or if we did mail it, we made a mistake, *e.g.,* we used an incorrect, incomplete, or illegible address, which delayed its delivery to you before the due date for the renewal premium, then we will follow these procedures:

a. If you or your agent notified us, not later than one year after the date on which the payment of the renewal premium was due, of nonreceipt of a renewal notice before the due date for the renewal premium, and we determine that the circumstances in the preceding paragraph apply, we will mail a second bill providing a revised due date, which will be 30 days after the date on which the bill is mailed.

b. If we do not receive the premium requested in the second bill by the revised due date, then we will not renew the policy. In that case, the policy will remain as an expired policy as of the expiration date shown on the Declarations Page.

4. In connection with the renewal of this policy, we may ask you during the policy term to re-certify, on a Recertification Questionnaire that we will provide you, the rating information used to rate your most recent application for or renewal of insurance.

I. *Conditions Suspending or Restricting Insurance.*

We are not liable for loss that occurs while there is a hazard that is increased by any means within your control or knowledge.

J. *Requirements in Case of Loss.*

In case of a flood loss to insured property, you must:

1. Give prompt written notice to us;

2. As soon as reasonably possible, separate the damaged and undamaged property, putting it in the best possible order so that we may examine it;

3. Prepare an inventory of damaged personal property showing the quantity, description, actual cash value, and amount of loss. Attach all bills, receipts, and related documents;

4. Within 60 days after the loss, send us a proof of loss, which is your statement of the amount you are claiming under the policy signed and sworn to by you, and which furnishes us with the following information:

a. The date and time of loss;

b. A brief explanation of how the loss happened;

c. Your interest (for example, "owner") and the interest, if any, of others in the damaged property;

d. Details of any other insurance that may cover the loss;

e. Changes in title or occupancy of the insured property during the term of the policy;

f. Specifications of damaged insured buildings and detailed repair estimates;

g. Names of mortgagees or anyone else having a lien, charge, or claim against the insured property;

h. Details about who occupied any insured building at the time of loss and for what purpose; and

i. The inventory of damaged personal property described in J.3. above.

5. In completing the proof of loss, you must use your own judgment concerning the amount of loss and justify that amount.

6. You must cooperate with the adjuster or representative in the investigation of the claim.

7. The insurance adjuster whom we hire to investigate your claim may furnish you with a proof of loss form, and she or he may help you complete it. However, this is a matter of courtesy only, and you must still send us a proof of loss within sixty days after the loss even if the adjuster does not furnish the form or help you complete it.

8. We have not authorized the adjuster to approve or disapprove claims or to tell you whether we will approve your claim.

9. At our option, we may accept the adjuster's report of the loss instead of your proof of loss. The adjuster's report will include information about your loss and the damages you sustained. You must sign the adjuster's report. At our option, we may require you to swear to the report.

K. *Our Options After a Loss.*

Options that we may, in our sole discretion, exercise after loss include the following:

1. At such reasonable times and places that we may designate, you must:

a. Show us or our representative the damaged property;

b. Submit to examination under oath, while not in the presence of another insured, and sign the same; and

c. Permit us to examine and make extracts and copies of:

(1) Any policies of property insurance insuring you against loss and the deed establishing your ownership of the insured real property;

(2) Condominium association documents including the Declarations of the condominium, its Articles of Association or Incorporation, Bylaws, and rules and regulations; and

(3) All books of accounts, bills, invoices and other vouchers, or certified copies pertaining to the damaged property if the originals are lost.

2. We may request, in writing, that you furnish us with a complete inventory of the lost, damaged, or destroyed property, including:

a. Quantities and costs;

b. Actual cash values or replacement cost (whichever is appropriate);

c. Amounts of loss claimed;

d. Any written plans and specifications for repair of the damaged property that you can make reasonably available to us; and

e. Evidence that prior flood damage has been repaired.

3. If we give you written notice within 30 days after we receive your signed, sworn proof of loss, we may:

a. Repair, rebuild, or replace any part of the lost, damaged, or destroyed property with material or property of like kind and quality or its functional equivalent; and

b. Take all or any part of the damaged property at the value we agree upon or its appraised value.

L. *No Benefit to Bailee.*

No person or organization, other than you, having custody of covered property will benefit from this insurance.

M. *Loss Payment.*

1. We will adjust all losses with you. We will pay you unless some other person or entity is named in the policy or is legally entitled to receive payment. Loss will be payable 60 days after we receive your proof of loss (or within 90 days after the insurance adjuster files an adjuster's report signed and sworn to by you in lieu of a proof of loss) and:

a. We reach an agreement with you;

b. There is an entry of a final judgment; or

c. There is a filing of an appraisal award with us, as provided in VIII. P.

2. If we reject your proof of loss in whole or in part you may:

a. Accept such denial of your claim;

b. Exercise your rights under this policy; or

c. File an amended proof of loss as long as it is filed within 60 days of the date of the loss.

N. *Abandonment.*

You may not abandon damaged or undamaged insured property to us.

O. *Salvage.*

We may permit you to keep damaged insured property after a loss, and we will reduce the amount of the loss proceeds payable to you under the policy by the value of the salvage.

P. *Appraisal.*

If you and we fail to agree on the actual cash value or, if applicable, replacement cost of the damaged property so as to determine the amount of loss, then either may demand an appraisal of the loss. In this event, you and we will each choose a competent and impartial appraiser within 20 days after receiving a written request from the other. The two appraisers will choose an umpire. If they cannot agree upon an umpire within 15 days, you or we may request that the choice be made by a judge of a court of record in the state where the insured property is located. The appraisers will separately state the ac-

tual cash value, the replacement cost, and the amount of loss to each item. If the appraisers submit a written report of an agreement to us, the amount agreed upon will be the amount of loss. If they fail to agree, they will submit their differences to the umpire. A decision agreed to by any two will set the amount of actual cash value and loss, or if it applies, the replacement cost and loss.

Each party will:

1. Pay its own appraiser; and

2. Bear the other expenses of the appraisal and umpire equally.

Q. *Mortgage Clause.*

The word "mortgagee" includes trustee.

Any loss payable under Coverage A—Building will be paid to any mortgagee of whom we have actual notice, as well as any other mortgagee or loss payee determined to exist at the time of loss, and you, as interests appear. If more than one mortgagee is named, the order of payment will be the same as the order of precedence of the mortgages.

If we deny your claim, that denial will not apply to a valid claim of the mortgagee, if the mortgagee:

1. Notifies us of any change in the ownership or occupancy, or substantial change in risk, of which the mortgagee is aware;

2. Pays any premium due under this policy on demand if you have neglected to pay the premium; and

3. Submits a signed, sworn proof of loss within 60 days after receiving notice from us of your failure to do so.

All of the terms of this policy apply to the mortgagee.

The mortgagee has the right to receive loss payment even if the mortgagee has started foreclosure or similar action on the building.

If we decide to cancel or not renew this policy, it will continue in effect for the benefit of the mortgagee only for 30 days after we notify the mortgagee of the cancellation or non-renewal.

If we pay the mortgagee for any loss and deny payment to you, we are subrogated to all the rights of the mortgagee granted under the mortgage on the property. Subrogation will not impair the right of the mortgagee to recover the full amount of the mortgagee's claim.

R. *Suit Against Us.*

You may not sue us to recover money under this policy unless you have complied with all the requirements of the policy. If you do sue, you must start the suit within one year of the date of the written denial of all or part of the claim and you must file the suit in the United States District Court of the district in which the insured property was located at the time of loss. This requirement applies to any claim that you may have under this policy and to any dispute that you may have arising out of the handling of any claim under the policy.

S. *Subrogation.*

Whenever we make a payment for a loss under this policy, we are subrogated to your right to recover for that loss from any other person. That means that your right to recover for a loss that was partly or totally caused by someone else is automatically transferred to us, to the extent that we have paid you for the loss. We may require you to acknowledge this transfer in writing. After the loss, you may not give up our right to recover this money or do anything that would prevent us from recovering it. If you make any claim against any person who caused your loss and recover any money, you must pay us back first before you may keep any of that money.

T. *Continuous Lake Flooding.*

1. If an insured building has been flooded by rising lake waters continuously for 90 days or more and it appears reasonably certain that a continuation of this flooding will result in a covered loss to the insured building equal to or greater than the building policy limits plus the deductible or the maximum payable under the policy for any one building loss, we will pay you the lesser of these two amounts without waiting for the further damage to occur if you sign a release agreeing:

a. To make no further claim under this policy;

b. Not to seek renewal of this policy;

c. Not to apply for any flood insurance under the Act for property at the described location; and

d. Not to seek a premium refund for current or prior terms.

If the policy term ends before the insured building has been flooded continuously for 90 days, the provisions of this paragraph T.1. will apply as long as the insured building suffers a covered loss before the policy term ends.

2. If your insured building is subject to continuous lake flooding from a closed basin lake, you may elect to file a claim under either paragraph T.1. above or this paragraph T.2. (A "closed basin lake" is a natural lake from which water leaves primarily through evaporation and whose surface area now exceeds or has exceeded one square mile at any time in the recorded past. Most of the nation's closed basin lakes are in the western half of the United States where annual evaporation exceeds annual precipitation and where lake levels and surface areas are subject to considerable fluctuation due to wide variations in the climate. These lakes may overtop their basins on rare occasions.) Under this paragraph T.2, we will pay your claim as if the building is a total loss even though it has not been continuously inundated for 90 days, subject to the following conditions:

a. Lake flood waters must damage or imminently threaten to damage your building.

b. Before approval of your claim, you must:

(1) Agree to a claim payment that reflects your buying back the salvage on a negotiated basis; and

(2) Grant the conservation easement contained in FEMA's "Policy Guidance for Closed Basin Lakes," to be recorded in the office of the local recorder of deeds. FEMA, in consultation with the community in which the property is located, will identify on a map an area or areas of special consideration (ASC) in which there is a potential for flood damage from continuous lake flooding. FEMA will give the community the agreed-upon map showing the ASC. This easement will only apply to that portion of the property in the ASC. It will allow certain agricultural and recreational uses of the land. The only structures that it will allow on any portion of the property within the ASC are certain simple agricultural and recreational structures. If any of these allowable structures are insurable buildings under the NFIP and are insured under the NFIP, they will not be eligible for the benefits of this paragraph T.2. If a U.S. Army Corps of Engineers certified flood control project or otherwise certified flood control project later protects the property, FEMA will, upon request, amend the ASC to remove areas protected by those projects. The restrictions of the easement will then no longer apply to any portion of the property removed from the ASC; and

(3) Comply with paragraphs T.1.a. through T.1.d. above.

c. Within 90 days of approval of your claim, you must move your building to a new location outside the ASC. FEMA will give you an additional 30 days to move if you show there is sufficient reason to extend the time.

d. Before the final payment of your claim, you must acquire an elevation certificate and a floodplain development permit from the local floodplain administrator for the new location of your building.

e. Before the approval of your claim, the community having jurisdiction over your building must:

(1) Adopt a permanent land use ordinance, or a temporary moratorium for a period not to exceed 6 months to be followed immediately by a permanent land use ordinance, that is consistent with the provisions specified in the easement required in paragraph T.2.b. above;

(2) Agree to declare and report any violations of this ordinance to FEMA so that under Sec. 1316 of the National Flood Insurance Act of 1968, as amended, flood insurance to the building can be denied; and

(3) Agree to maintain as deed-restricted, for purposes compatible with open space or agricultural or recreational use only, any affected property the community acquires an interest in. These deed restrictions must be consistent with the provisions of paragraph T.2.b. above, except that even if a certified

project protects the property, the land use restrictions continue to apply if the property was acquired under the Hazard Mitigation Grant Program or the Flood Mitigation Assistance Program. If a non-profit land trust organization receives the property as a donation, that organization must maintain the property as deed-restricted, consistent with the provisions of paragraph T.2.b. above.

f. Before the approval of your claim, the affected State must take all action set forth in FEMA's "Policy Guidance for Closed Basin Lakes."

g. You must have NFIP flood insurance coverage continuously in effect from a date established by FEMA until you file a claim under this paragraph T.2. If a subsequent owner buys NFIP insurance that goes into effect within 60 days of the date of transfer of title, any gap in coverage during that 60-day period will not be a violation of this continuous coverage requirement. For the purpose of honoring a claim under this paragraph T.2., we will not consider to be in effect any increased coverage that became effective after the date established by FEMA. The exception to this is any increased coverage in the amount suggested by your insurer as an inflation adjustment.

h. This paragraph T.2. will be in effect for a community when the FEMA Regional Director for the affected region provides to the community, in writing, the following:

(1) Confirmation that the community and the State are in compliance with the conditions in paragraphs T.2.e. and T.2.f. above, and

(2) The date by which you must have flood insurance in effect.

U. *Duplicate Policies Not Allowed.*

1. We will not insure your property under more than one NFIP policy.

If we find that the duplication was not knowingly created, we will give you written notice. The notice will advise you that you may choose one of several options under the following procedures:

a. If you choose to keep in effect the policy with the earlier effective date, you may also choose to add the coverage limits of the later policy to the limits of the earlier policy. The change will become effective as of the effective date of the later policy.

b. If you choose to keep in effect the policy with the later effective date, you may also choose to add the coverage limits of the earlier policy to the limits of the later policy. The change will be effective as of the effective date of the later policy.

In either case, you must pay the pro rata premium for the increased coverage limits within 30 days of the written notice. In no event will the resulting coverage limits exceed the permissible limits of coverage under the Act or your insurable interest, whichever is less. We will make a refund to you, according to applicable NFIP rules, of the premium for the policy not being kept in effect.

2. The insured's option under this condition U. Duplicate Policies Not Allowed to elect which NFIP policy to keep in effect does not apply when duplicates have been knowingly created. Losses occurring under such circumstances will be adjusted according to the terms and conditions of the earlier policy. The policy with the later effective date must be canceled.

V. *Loss Settlement.*

1. Introduction

This policy provides three methods of settling losses: Replacement Cost, Special Loss Settlement, and Actual Cash Value. Each method is used for a different type of property, as explained in a.-c. below.

a. Replacement Cost Loss Settlement described in V.2. below applies to buildings other than manufactured homes or travel trailers.

b. Special Loss Settlement described in V.3. below applies to a residential condominium building that is a travel trailer or a manufactured home.

c. Actual Cash Value loss settlement applies to all other property covered under this policy, as outlined in V.4. below.

2. Replacement Cost Loss Settlement

a. We will pay to repair or replace a damaged or destroyed building, after application of the deductible and without deduction for depreciation, but not more than the least of the following amounts:

(1) The amount of insurance in this policy that applies to the building;

(2) The replacement cost of that part of the building damaged, with materials of like kind and quality, and for like occupancy and use; or

(3) The necessary amount actually spent to repair or replace the damaged part of the building for like occupancy and use.

b. We will not be liable for any loss on a Replacement Cost Coverage basis unless and until actual repair or replacement of the damaged building or parts thereof, is completed.

c. If a building is rebuilt at a location other than the described location, we will pay no more than it would have cost to repair or rebuild at the described location, subject to all other terms of Replacement Cost Loss Settlement.

3. Special Loss Settlement

a. The following loss settlement conditions apply to a residential condominium building that is: (1) a manufactured home or travel trailer, as defined in II.B.6.b. and c., and (2) at least 16 feet wide when fully assembled and has at least 600 square feet within its perimeter walls when fully assembled.

b. If such a building is totally destroyed or damaged to such an extent that, in our judgment, it is not economically feasible to repair, at least to its pre-damaged condition, we will, at our discretion, pay the least of the following amounts:

(1) The lesser of the replacement cost of the manufactured home or travel trailer or 1.5 times the actual cash value; or

(2) The Building Limit of liability shown on your Declarations Page.

c. If such a manufactured home or travel trailer is partially damaged and, in our judgment, it is economically feasible to repair it to its pre-damaged condition, we will settle the loss according to the Replacement Cost Loss Settlement conditions in V.2. above.

4. Actual Cash Value Loss Settlement

a. The types of property noted below are subject to actual cash value loss settlement:

(1) Personal property;

(2) Insured property abandoned after a loss and that remains as debris at the described location;

(3) Outside antennas and aerials, awning, and other outdoor equipment;

(4) Carpeting and pads;

(5) Appliances; and

(6) A manufactured home or mobile home or a travel trailer as defined in II.B.6.b. or c. that does not meet the conditions for special loss settlement in V.3. above.

b. We will pay the least of the following amounts:

(1) The applicable amount of insurance under this policy;

(2) The actual cash value (as defined in II.B.2.); or

(3) The amount it would cost to repair or replace the property with material of like kind and quality within a reasonable time after the loss.

IX. LIBERALIZATION CLAUSE

If we make a change that broadens your coverage under this edition of our policy, but does not require any additional premium, then that change will automatically apply to your insurance as of the date we implement the change, provided that this implementation date falls within 60 days before or during the policy term stated on the Declarations Page.

X. WHAT LAW GOVERNS

This policy and all disputes arising from the handling of any claim under the policy are governed exclusively by the flood insurance regulations issued by FEMA, the National Flood Insurance Act of 1968, as amended (42 U.S.C. 4001, *et seq.*), and Federal common law.

In Witness Whereof, we have signed this policy below and hereby enter into this Insurance Agreement.

Administrator, Federal Insurance Administration.

[65 FR 60785, Oct. 12, 2000, as amended at 68 FR 9897, Mar. 3, 2003]

APPENDIX A(4) TO PART 61

FEDERAL EMERGENCY MANAGEMENT AGENCY, FEDERAL INSURANCE ADMINISTRATION

Standard Flood Insurance Policy Endorsement to Dwelling Form

This endorsement replaces the provisions of VII.B.4 and VII.H.2, and also adds a new paragraph, VII.H.5. This endorsement applies in Monroe County and the Village of Islamorada, Florida, This endorsement also applies to communities within Monroe County, Florida that incorporate on or after January 1, 1999, agree to participate in the inspection procedure, and become eligible for the sale of flood insurance.

VII.B.4. This policy is also void for reasons other than fraud, misrepresentation, or wrongful act. This policy is void from its inception and has no legal force under the following conditions:

a. If the property is located in a community that was not participating in the NFIP on the policy's inception date and did not join or re-enter the program during the policy term and before the loss occurred.

b. If you have not submitted a community inspection report, referred to in "H. Policy Renewal" below, that was required in a notice sent to you in conjunction with the community inspection procedure established under 44 CFR 59.30.

c. If the property listed on the application is not otherwise eligible for coverage under the NFIP

VII.H.2. We must receive the payment of the appropriate renewal premium and when applicable, the community inspection report referred to in H.5 below within 30 days of the expiration date.

VII.H.5. Your community has been approved by the Federal Emergency Management Agency to participate in an inspection procedure set forth in National Flood Insurance Program Regulations (44 CFR 59.30). During the several years that this inspection procedure will be in place, you may be required to obtain and submit an inspection report from your community certifying whether or not your insured property is in compliance with the community's floodplain management ordinance before you can renew your policy. You will be notified in writing of this requirement approximately 6 months before a renewal date and again at the time your renewal bill is sent.

[65 FR 60793, Oct. 12, 2000, as amended at 67 FR 10634, Mar. 8, 2002]

APPENDIX A(5) TO PART 61

FEDERAL EMERGENCY MANAGEMENT AGENCY,
FEDERAL INSURANCE ADMINISTRATION

*Standard Flood Insurance Policy Endorsement
to General Property Form*

This endorsement replaces the provisions of VII.B.4 and VII.H.2, and also adds a new paragraph, VII.H.5. This endorsement applies in Monroe County and the Village of Islamorada, Florida. This endorsement also applies to communities within Monroe County, Florida that incorporate on or after January 1, 1999, agree to participate in the inspection procedure, and become eligible for the sale of flood insurance.

VII.B.4. This policy is also void for reasons other than fraud, misrepresentation, or wrongful act. This policy is void from its inception and has no legal force under the following conditions:

a. If the property is located in a community that was not participating in the NFIP on the policy's inception date and did not join or re-enter the program during the policy term and before the loss occurred.

b. If you have not submitted a community inspection report, referred to in "H. Policy Renewal" below, that was required in a notice sent to you in conjunction with the community inspection procedure established under 44 CFR 59.30.

c. If the property listed on the application is not otherwise eligible for coverage under the NFIP

VII.H.2. We must receive the payment of the appropriate renewal premium and when applicable, the community inspection report referred to in H.5 below within 30 days of the expiration date.

VII.H.5. Your community has been approved by the Federal Emergency Management Agency to participate in an inspection procedure set forth in National Flood Insurance Program Regulations (44 CFR 59.30). During the several years that this inspection procedure will be in place, you may be required to obtain and submit an inspection report from your community certifying whether or not your insured property is in compliance with the community's floodplain management ordinance before you can renew your policy. You will be notified in writing of this requirement approximately 6 months before a renewal date and again at the time your renewal bill is sent.

[65 FR 60793, Oct. 12, 2000, as amended at 67 FR 10634, Mar. 8, 2002]

APPENDIX A(6) TO PART 61

FEDERAL EMERGENCY MANAGEMENT AGENCY,
FEDERAL INSURANCE ADMINISTRATION

*Standard Flood Insurance Policy Endorsement
to Residential Condominium Building Association Policy*

This endorsement replaces the provisions of VIII.B.4 and VIII.H.2, and also adds a new paragraph, VIII.H.5. This endorsement applies in Monroe County and the Village of Islamorada, Florida. This endorsement also applies to communities within Monroe County, Florida and incorporate on or after January 1, 1999, agree to participate in the inspection procedure, and become eligible for the sale of flood insurance.

VIII.B.4. This policy is also void for reasons other than fraud, misrepresentation, or wrongful act. This policy is void from its inception and has no legal force under the following conditions:

a. If the property is located in a community that was not participating in the NFIP on the policy's inception date and did not join or re-enter the program during the policy term and before the loss occurred.

b. If you have not submitted a community inspection report, referred to in "H. Policy Renewal" below, that was required in a notice sent to you in conjunction with the community inspection procedure established under 44 CFR 59.30.

c. If the property listed on the application is not otherwise eligible for coverage under the NFIP

VIII.H.2. We must receive the payment of the appropriate renewal premium and when applicable, the community inspection report referred to in H.5 below within 30 days of the expiration date.

VIII.H.5. Your community has been approved by the Federal Emergency Management Agency to participate in an inspection procedure set forth in National Flood Insurance Program Regulations (44 CFR 59.30). During the several years that this inspection procedure will be in place, you may be required to obtain and submit an inspection report from your community certifying whether or not your insured property is in compliance with the community's floodplain management ordinance before you can renew your policy. You will be notified in writing of this requirement approximately 6 months before a renewal date and again at the time your renewal bill is sent.

[65 FR 60794, Oct. 12, 2000, as amended at 67 FR 10634, Mar. 8, 2002]

PART 62—SALE OF INSURANCE AND ADJUSTMENT OF CLAIMS

Subpart A—Issuance of Policies

Subpart B—Claims Adjustment, Claims Appeals, and Judicial Review

Subpart C—Write-Your-Own (WYO) Companies

AUTHORITY: 42 U.S.C. 4001 *et seq.*,; Reorganization Plan No. 3 of 1978, 43 FR 41943, 3 CFR, 1978 Comp., p. 329; E.O. 12127 of Mar. 31, 1979, 44 FR 19367, 3 CFR, 1979 Comp., p. 376.

SOURCE: 43 FR 2573, Jan. 17, 1978, unless otherwise noted. Redesignated at 44 FR 31177, May 31, 1979.

Subpart A—Issuance of Policies

§ 62.1   Purpose of part.

The purpose of this part is to set forth the manner in which flood insurance under the Program is made available to the general public in those communities designated as eligible for the sale of insurance under part 64 of this subchapter, and to prescribe the general method by which the Federal Insurance Administrator exercises his/her responsibility regarding the manner in which claims for losses are paid.

§ 62.2   Definitions.

The definitions set forth in part 59 of this subchapter are applicable to this part.

§ 62.3   Servicing agent.

(a) Pursuant to sections 1345 and 1346 of the Act, the Federal Insurance Ad-

ministrator has entered into the Agreement with a servicing agent to authorize it to assist in issuing flood insurance policies under the Program in communities designated by the Federal Insurance Administrator and to accept responsibility for delivery of policies and payment of claims for losses as prescribed by and at the discretion of the Federal Insurance Administrator.

(b) National Con-Serv, Inc., whose offices are located in Rockville, Maryland, is the servicing agent for the Federal Insurance Administration.

(c) The servicing agent will arrange for the issuance of flood insurance to any person qualifying for such coverage under parts 61 and 64 of this subchapter who submits an application to the servicing agent in accordance with the terms and conditions of the contract between the Agency and the servicing agent.

[43 FR 2573, Jan. 17, 1978. Redesignated at 44 FR 31177, May 31, 1979, as amended at 48 FR 44544, Sept. 29, 1983; 49 FR 4751, Feb. 8, 1984; 58 FR 62447, Nov. 26, 1993]

§ 62.4   Limitations on sale of policies.

(a) The servicing agent shall be deemed to have agreed, as a condition of its contract that it shall not offer flood insurance under any authority or auspices in any amount within the maximum limits of coverage specified in § 61.6 of this subchapter, in any area the Federal Insurance Administrator designates in part 64 of this subchapter as eligible for the sale of flood insurance under the Program, other than in accordance with this part, and the Standard Flood Insurance Policy.

(b) The agreement and all activities thereunder are subject to title VI of the Civil Rights Act of 1964, 42 U.S.C. 2000d, and to the applicable Federal regulations and requirements issued from time to time pursuant thereto. No person shall be excluded from participation in, denied the benefits of, or subjected to discrimination under the Program, on the ground of race, color, sex, creed or national origin. Any complaint or information concerning the existence of any such unlawful discrimination in any matter within the purview of this part should be referred to the Federal Insurance Administrator.

[43 FR 2573, Jan. 17, 1978. Redesignated at 44 FR 31177, May 31, 1979, as amended at 48 FR 44544, Sept. 29, 1983; 49 FR 4751, Feb. 8, 1984]

§ 62.5 Premium refund.

A Standard Flood Insurance Policyholder whose property has been determined not to be in a special hazard area after the map revision or a Letter of Map Amendment under part 70 of this subchapter may cancel the policy within the current policy year provided (a) he was required to purchase or to maintain flood insurance coverage, or both, as a condition for financial assistance, and (b) his property was located in an identified special hazard area as represented on an effective FHBM or FIRM when the financial assistance was provided. If no claim under the policy has been paid or is pending, the full premium shall be refunded for the current policy year, and for an additional policy year where the insured had been required to renew the policy during the period when a revised map was being reprinted. A Standard Flood Insurance Policyholder may cancel a policy having a term of three (3) years, on an anniversary date, where the reason for the cancellation is that a policy of flood insurance has been obtained or is being obtained in substitution for the NFIP policy and the NFIP obtains a written concurrence in the cancellation from any mortgage of which the NFIP has actual notice; or the policyholder has extinguishing the insured mortgage debt and is no longer required by the mortgagee to maintain the coverage. In such event, the premium refund shall be pro rata but with retention of the expense constant.

[43 FR 2573, Jan. 17, 1978. Redesignated at 44 FR 31177, May 31, 1979, as amended at 49 FR 33658, Aug. 24, 1984; 53 FR 16279, May 6, 1988]

§ 62.6 Minimum commissions.

(a) The earned commission which shall be paid to any property or casualty insurance agent or broker duly licensed by a state insurance regulatory authority, with respect to each policy or renewal the agent duly procures on behalf of the insured, in connection with policies of flood insurance placed with the NFIP at the offices of its servicing agent, but not with respect to policies of flood insurance issued pursuant to Subpart C of this part, shall not be less than $10 and is computed as follows:

(1) In the case of a new or renewal policy, the following commissions shall apply based on the total premiums paid for the policy term:

Premium amount	Commissions (percent)
First $2,000 of Premium	15
Excess of $2,000	5

(2) In the case of mid-term increases in amounts of insurance added by endorsements, the following commissions shall apply based on the total premiums paid for the increased amounts of insurance:

Premium amount	Commissions (percent)
First $2,000 of Premium	15
Excess of $2,000	5

(b) Any refunds of premiums authorized under this subchapter shall not affect a previously earned commission; and no agent shall be required to return that earned commission, unless the refund is made to establish a common policy term anniversary date with other insurance providing coverage against loss by other perils in which case a return of commission will be required by the agent on a pro rata basis. In such cases, the policy shall be immediately rewritten for a new term with the same amount(s) of coverage and with premium calculated at the then current rate and, as to return premium, returned, pro rata, to the insured based on the former policy's premium rate.

[46 FR 13515, Feb. 23, 1981, as amended at 53 FR 15221, Apr. 28, 1988; 57 FR 19541, May 7, 1992]

Subpart B—Claims Adjustment, Claims Appeals, and Judicial Review

§ 62.20 Claims appeals.

(a) *Definitions.*

Appeal decision means the disposition of the appeal by the Federal Insurance Administrator.

Decision means the insurer's final claim determination, which is the insurer's written denial, in whole or in part, of the insured's claim.

(b) *Appeal.* A National Flood Insurance Program (NFIP) policyholder, whether insured by a participating Write-Your-Own (WYO) Company or directly by the Federal Emergency Management Agency (FEMA), may appeal a *decision*, including a determination of any insurance agent, adjuster, insurance company, or any FEMA employee or contractor with respect to a claim, proof of loss, and loss estimate. In order to file an appeal, the insured must comply with all requirements set out in the Standard Flood Insurance Policy (SFIP). This appeals process is available after the issuance of the insurer's final claim determination, which is the insurer's written denial, in whole or in part, of the insured's claim. Once the final claim determination is issued, an insured may appeal any action taken by the insurer, FEMA employee, FEMA contractor, insurance adjuster, or insurance agent.

(c) *Limitations on Appeals.* The appeals process is intended to resolve claim issues and is not intended to grant coverage or limits that are not provided by the SFIP. Filing an appeal does not waive any of the requirements for perfecting a claim under the SFIP or extend any of the time limitations set forth in the SFIP.

(1) Disputes that are or have been subject to appraisal as provided for in the SFIP cannot be appealed under this section.

(2) When a policyholder files an appeal on any issue, that issue is no longer subject to resolution by appraisal or other pre-litigation remedies.

(d) *Litigation preclusion.* An insured who files suit against an insurer on the flood insurance claim issue is prohibited from filing an appeal under this section. All appeals submitted for decision but not yet resolved shall be terminated upon notice of the commencement of litigation regarding the claim.

(e) *Procedures.* To pursue an appeal under this section a policyholder must:

(1) Submit a written appeal to FEMA within 60 days from the date of the decision. The appeal should be sent to:

DHS/FEMA, Mitigation Directorate, Federal Insurance Administrator, 1800 South Bell Street, Arlington, VA 20598-MS3010;

(2) Provide a copy of the insurer's written denial, in whole or in part, of the claim;

(3) Identify relevant policy and claim information and state the basis for the appeal; and

(4) Submit relevant documentation to support the appeal. The policyholder should submit only the documentation that pertains to his or her claim. The following are examples of the kinds of documentation which FEMA will require to adjudicate the appeal: A copy of the proof of loss submitted to the insurer as required in the policy; room by room itemized estimates from the adjuster (includes contractors' estimates), detailing unit cost and quantities for the items needing repair or replacement; replacement cost proofs of loss; Preliminary Report; Final Report; detailed damaged personal property inventories that include the approximate age of the items; completed Mobile Home Worksheet; Mobile Home Title, including Salvage Titles; real estate appraisals that exclude land values; advance payment information; clear photographs (exterior and interior) confirming damage resulted from direct physical loss by or from flood; proof of prior repair; evidence of insurance and policy information , *i.e.* declarations page; Elevation Certificate, if the risk is an elevated building; the community's determination made concerning substantial damage; information regarding substantial improvement; zone determinations; pre-loss and post-loss inventories; financial statements; tax records, lease agreements, sales contracts, settlement papers, deed, *etc.*; emergency (911) address change information; salvage information (proceeds and sales); condominium association by-laws; proof of other insurance, including homeowners or wind policies and any claim information submitted to the other companies; Waiver, Letter of Map Revision (LOMR) or Letter of Map Amendment (LOMA) information; paid receipts and invoices including cancelled checks that support an insured's out-of-pocket

expenses pertaining to the claim; underwriting decisions; architectural plans and drawings; death certificates; a copy of the will; divorce decree, power of attorney; current lienholder information; current loss payee information; paid receipts and invoices documenting damaged stock; detailed engineering reports specifically addressing flood-related damage and pre-existing damage; engineering surveys; market values; documentation of Flood Insurance Rate Maps (FIRM) dates; documentation reflecting date(s) of construction and substantial improvement; loan documents including closings; evidence of insurability as a Residential Condominium Association; Franchise Agreements; letters of representation, *i.e.* attorneys and public adjusters; any assignment of interest in a claim; and, any other pertinent information which FEMA may request in processing a claim.

(f) *Appeal resolution.* (1) FEMA will acknowledge, in writing, receipt of a policyholder's appeal and include in the acknowledgement contact information for a FEMA point of contact who can advise the policyholder as to the status of his or her claim.

(2) The *Federal Insurance Administrator* will review the appeal documents and may notify the policyholder in writing of the need for additional information. A request for the additional information will include the date by which the information must be provided, and shall in no case be less than 14 calendar days. Failure to provide the requested information in full, or to request an extension by the due date, may result in a dismissal of the appeal. A re-inspection of the policyholder's property may be conducted at the discretion of the *Federal Insurance Administrator* to gather more information. The *Federal Insurance Administrator* will ensure that all information necessary to rule on the appeal has been provided prior to making an *appeal decision.*

(3) The *Federal Insurance Administrator* will review the appeal documents, including any reinspection report, if appropriate. The Federal Insurance Administrator will provide specific information on what grounds the claim was denied initially. The Federal Insurance Administrator will provide an *appeal decision* in writing to the policyholder and insurer within 90 days from the date that all information has been submitted by the policyholder and include specific information for the resolution of the appeal. No further administrative review will be provided to the insured.

(4) A policyholder who does not agree with FEMA's appeal decision should refer to the SFIP, for options for further action (*see* Part 61, App. A(1) VII.R., Part 61, App. A(2) VII.R., and Part 61, App. A(3) VIII.R.). The one-year period to file suit commences with the written denial from the insurer and is not extended by the appeals process.

[71 FR 30298, May 26, 2006, as amended at 71 FR 60438, Oct. 13, 2006; 74 FR 56123, Oct. 30, 2009]

§ 62.21 Claims adjustment.

(a) In accordance with the Agreement, the servicing agent shall arrange for the prompt adjustment and settlement and payment of all claims arising from policies of insurance issued under the program. Investigation of such claims may be made through the facilities of its subcontractors or insurance adjustment organizations, to the extent required and appropriate for the expeditious processing of such claims.

(b) All adjustment of losses and settlements of claims shall be made in accordance with the terms and conditions of the policy and parts 61 and 62 of this subchapter.

§ 62.22 Judicial review.

(a) Upon the disallowance by the Federal Insurance Administration, a participating Write-Your-Own Company, or the servicing agent of any claim on grounds other than failure to file a proof of loss, or upon the refusal of the claimant to accept the amount allowed upon any claim after appraisal pursuant to policy provisions, the claimant within one year after the date of mailing by the Federal Insurance Administration, the participating Write-Your-Own Company, or the servicing agent of the notice of disallowance or partial disallowance of the claim may, pursuant to 42 U.S.C. 4072, institute an action on such claim against the insurer only in the U.S. District Court for the district in which the insured property or the major portion thereof shall have been situated, without regard to the amount in controversy.

(b) Service of process for all judicial proceedings where a claimant is suing the Administrator of FEMA pursuant to 42 U.S.C. 4071 shall be made upon the appropriate United States Attorney, the Attorney General of the United States, and the Federal Insurance Administrator of the Federal Emergency Management Agency.

[43 FR 2573, Jan. 17, 1978. Redesignated at 44 FR 31177, May 31, 1979, as amended at 47 FR 43061 Sept. 30, 1982; 49 FR 33879, Aug. 27, 1984; 69 FR 45610, July 30, 2004]

Subpart C—Write-Your-Own (WYO) Companies

§ 62.23   WYO Companies authorized.

(a) Pursuant to section 1345 of the Act, the Federal Insurance Administrator may enter into arrangements with individual private sector property insurance companies or other insurers, such as public entity risk sharing organizations. Under these arrangements, such companies or other insurers may offer flood insurance coverage under the program to eligible applicants. Such WYO companies may offer flood coverage to policyholders insured by them under their own property business lines of insurance, pursuant to their customary business practices, including their usual arrangements with agents and producers. WYO companies may sell flood insurance coverage in any State in which the WYO company is authorized to engage in the business of property insurance. Other WYO insurers may offer flood insurance coverage to their pool members insured by them under their own property business lines of coverage, pursuant to their customary business practices. These other WYO insurers may provide flood coverage in any State that has authorized the other insurer to provide property coverage to its members. Arrangements entered into by WYO Companies or other insurers under this subpart must be in the form and substance of the standard arrangement, titled "Financial Assistance/Subsidy Arrangement," a copy of which is included in appendix A of this part and made a part of these regulations.

(b) Any duly authorized insurer so engaged in the Program shall be a WYO Company. (The term "WYO Company" shall include the following kinds of insurers: Public entity risk-sharing organizations, an association of local governments, a State association of political subdivisions, a State-sponsored municipal league, and other intergovernmental risk-sharing pool for covering public entity structures.)

(c) A WYO Company is authorized to arrange for the issuance of flood insurance in any amount within the maximum limits of coverage specified in § 61.6 of this subchapter, as Insurer, to any person qualifying for such coverage under parts 61 and 64 of this subchapter who submits an application to the WYO Company; coverage shall be issued under the Standard Flood Insurance Policy.

(d) A WYO Company issuing flood insurance coverage shall arrange for the adjustment, settlement, payment and defense of all claims arising from policies of flood insurance it issues under the Program, based upon the terms and conditions of the Standard Flood Insurance Policy.

(e) In carrying out its functions under this subpart, a WYO Company shall use its own customary standards, staff and independent contractor resources, as it would in the ordinary and necessary conduct of its own business affairs, subject to the Act and regulations prescribed by the Federal Insurance Administrator under the Act.

(f) To facilitate the marketing of flood insurance coverage under the Program to policyholders of WYO Companies, the Federal Insurance Administrator will enter into arrangements with such companies whereby the Federal Government will be a guarantor in which the primary relationship between the WYO Company and the Federal Government will be one of a fiduciary nature, i.e., to assure that any taxpayer funds are accounted for and appropriately expended. In furtherance of this end, the Federal Insurance Administrator has established "A Plan to Maintain Financial Control for Business Written Under the Write Your

Own Program", a copy of which is included in appendix B of this part and made a part of these regulations.

(g) A WYO Company shall act as a fiscal agent of the Federal Government, but not as its general agent. WYO Companies are solely responsible for their obligations to their insured under any flood insurance policies issued under agreements entered into with the Federal Insurance Administrator, such that the Federal Government is not a proper party defendant in any lawsuit arising out of such policies.

(h) To facilitate the underwriting of flood insurance coverage by WYO Companies, the following procedures will be used by WYO Companies:

(1) To expedite business growth, the WYO Company will encourage its present property insurance policyholders to purchase flood insurance through the NFIP WYO Program.

(2) To conform its underwriting practices to the underwriting rules and rates in effect as to the NFIP, the WYO Company will establish procedures to carry out the NFIP rating system and provide its policyholders with the same coverage as is afforded under the NFIP.

(3) The WYO Company may follow its customary billing practices to meet the Federal rules on the presentment of premium and net premium deposits to a Letter of Credit bank account authorized by the Federal Insurance Administrator and reduction of coverage when an underpayment is discovered.

(4) The WYO Company is expected to meet the recording and reporting requirements of the WYO Transaction Record Reporting and Processing Plan. Transactions reported by the WYO Company under the WYO Transaction Record Reporting and Processing Plan will be analyzed by the NFIP Bureau & Statistical Agent. A monthly report will be submitted to the WYO Company and the FIA. The analysis will cover the timeliness of WYO Company submissions, the disposition of transactions that have not passed systems edits and the reconciliation of the totals generated from transaction reports with those submitted on the WYO Company's reconciliation reports.

(5) If a WYO Company rejects an application from an agent or a producer, the agent or producer shall be notified so that the business can be placed through the NFIP Servicing Agent, or another WYO Company.

(6) Flood insurance coverage will be issued by the WYO Company on a separate policy form and will not be added, by endorsement, to the Company's other property insurance forms.

(7) Premium payment plans can be offered by the WYO Company so long as the net premium depository requirements specified under the NFIP/WYO Program accounting procedures are met. A cancellation by the WYO Company for non-payment of premium will not produce a pro rata return of the net premium deposit to the WYO Company.

(8) NFIP business will not be assumed by the WYO Companies at any time other than at renewal time, at which time the insurance producer may submit the business to the WYO Company as new business. However, it is permissible to cancel and rewrite flood policies to obtain concurrent expiration dates with other policies covering the property.

(i) To facilitate the adjustment of flood insurance claims by WYO Companies, the following procedures will be used by WYO Companies.

(1) Under the terms of the Arrangement set forth at appendix A of this part, WYO Companies will adjust claims in accordance with general Company standards, guided by NFIP Claims manuals. The Arrangement also provides that claim adjustments shall be binding upon the FIA. For example, the entire responsibility for providing a proper adjustment for both combined wind and water claims and flood-alone claims is the responsibility of the WYO Company. The responsibility for providing a proper adjustment for combined wind and water claims is to be conducted by listing in concert with the Single Adjuster provisions listed in appendix A.

(2) The WYO Company may use its staff adjusters, independent adjusters, or both. It is important that the Company's Claims Department verifies the correctness of the coverage interpretations and reasonableness of the payments recommended by the adjusters.

(3) An established loss adjustment Fee Schedule is part of the Arrangement and cannot be changed during an Arrangement year. This is the expense allowance to cover costs of independent or WYO Company adjusters.

(4) The normal catastrophe claims procedure currently operated by a WYO Company should be implemented in the event of a claim catastrophe situation. Flood claims will be handled along with other catastrophe claims.

(5) It will be the WYO Company's responsibility to try to detect fraud (as it does in the case of property insurance) and coordinate its findings with FIA.

(6) Pursuant to the Arrangement, the responsibility for defending claims will be upon the Write Your Own Company and defense costs will be part of the unallocated or allocated claim expense allowance, depending on whether a staff counsel or an outside attorney handles the defense of the matter. Claims in litigation will be reported by WYO Companies to FIA upon joinder of issue and FIA may inquire and be advised of the disposition of such litigation.

(7) The claim reserving procedures of the individual WYO Company can be used.

(8) Regarding the handling of subrogation, if a WYO Company prefers to forego pursuit of subrogation recovery, it may do so by referring the matter, with a complete copy of the claim file, to FIA. Subrogation initiatives may be truncated at any time before suit is commenced (after commencing an action, special arrangement must bemade). FIA, after consultation with FEMA's Office of the Chief Counsel (OCC), will forward the cause of action to OCC or to the NFIP Bureau and Statistical Agent for prosecution. Any funds received will be deposited, less expenses, in the National Flood Insurance Fund.

(9) Special allocated loss adjustment expenses will include such items as: nonstaff attorney fees, engineering fees and special investigation fees over and above normal adjustment practices.

(10) The customary content of claim files will include coverage verification, normal adjuster investigations, including statements where necessary, police reports, building reports and investiga-

tions, damage verification and other documentation relevant to the adjustment of claims under the NFIP's and the WYO Company's traditional claim adjustment practices and procedures. The WYO Company's claim examiners and managers will supervise the adjustment of flood insurance claims by staff and independent claims adjusters.

(11) The WYO Company will extend reasonable cooperation to FEMA's Office of the Chief Counsel on matters pertaining to litigation and subrogation, under paragraph (i)(8) of this section.

(j) To facilitate establishment of financial controls under the WYO Program, the WYO Company will:

(1) Have a biennial audit of the flood insurance financial statements conducted by an independent Certified Public Accountant (CPA) firm at the Company's expense to ensure that the financial data reported to us accurately represents the flood insurance activities of the Company. The CPA firm must conduct its audits in accordance with the generally accepted auditing standards (GAAS) and Government Auditing Standards issued by the Comptroller General of the United States (commonly known as "yellow book" requirements). The Company must file with us (the Federal Insurance Administration) a report of the CPA firm's detailed biennial audit, and, after our review of the audit report, we will convey our determination to the Standards Committee.

(2) Participate in a WYO Company/FIA Operation review. We will conduct a review of the WYO Company's flood insurance claims, underwriting, customer service, marketing, and litigation activities at least once every three (3) years. As part of these reviews, we will reconcile specific files with a listing of transactions submitted by the Company under the Transaction Record Reporting and Processing (TRPP) Plan (Part 5). We will file a report of the Operation Review with the Standards Committee.

(3) Meet the recording and reporting requirements of the WYO Transaction Record Reporting and Processing Plan and the WYO Accounting Procedures Manual. Transactions reported to the National Flood Insurance Program's

(NFIP's) Bureau and Statistical Agent by the WYO Company under the WYO Transaction Record Reporting and Processing Plan and the WYO Accounting Procedures Manual will be analyzed by the Bureau and Statistical Agent and a monthly report will be submitted to the WYO Company and the FIA. The analysis will cover the timeliness of the WYO Company submissions, the disposition of transactions which do not pass systems edits and the reconciliation of the totals generated from transaction reports with those submitted on WYO Company reconciliation reports.

(4) Cooperate with FEMA's Chief Financial Officer on Letter of Credit matters.

(5) Cooperate with FIA in the implementation of a claims reinspection program.

(6) Cooperate with FIA in the verification of risk rating information.

(7) Cooperate with DHS's Office of the Inspector General on matters pertaining to fraud.

(k) To facilitate the operation of the WYO Program and in order that a WYO Company can use its own customary standards, staff and independent contractor resources, as it would in the ordinary and necessary conduct of its own business affairs, subject to the Act, the Federal Insurance Administrator, for good cause shown, may grant exceptions to and waivers of the regulations contained in this title relative to the administration of the NFIP.

(l)(1) WYO Companies may, on a voluntary basis, elect to participate in the Mortgage Portfolio Protection Program (MPPP), under which they can offer, as a last resort, flood insurance at special high rates, sufficient to recover the full cost of this program in recognition of the uncertainty as to the degree of risk a given building presents due to the limited underwriting data required, to properties in a lending institution's mortgage portfolio to achieve compliance with the flood insurance purchase requirements of the Flood Disaster Protection Act of 1973. Flood insurance policies under the MPPP may only be issued for those properties that:

(i) Are determined to be located within special flood hazard areas of communities that are participating in the NFIP, and

(ii) Are not covered by a flood insurance policy even after a required series of notices have been given to the property owner (mortgagor) by the lending institution of the requirement for obtaining and maintaining such coverage, but the mortgagor has failed to respond.

(2) WYO Companies participating in the MPPP must provide a detailed implementation package to any lending institution that, on a voluntary basis, chooses to participate in the MPPP to ensure the lending institution has full knowledge of the criteria in that program and must obtain a signed receipt for that package from the lending institution. Participating WYO Companies must also maintain evidence of compliance with paragraph (l)(3) of this section for review during the audits and reviews required by the WYO Financial Control Plan contained in appendix B of this part.

(3) The mortgagor must be protected against the lending institution's arbitrary placing of flood insurance for which the mortgagor will be billed by being sent three notification letters as described in paragraphs (l)(4) through (6) of this section.

(4) The initial notification letter must:

(i) State the requirements of the Flood Disaster Protection Act of 1973, as amended;

(ii) Announce the determination that the mortgagor's property is in an identified special flood hazard area as delineated on the appropriate FEMA map, necessitating flood insurance coverage for the duration of the loan;

(iii) Describe the procedure to follow should the mortgagor wish to challenge the determination;

(iv) Request evidence of a valid flood insurance policy or, if there is none, encourage the mortgagor to obtain a Standard Flood Insurance Policy (SFIP) promptly from a local insurance agent (or WYO Company);

(v) Advise that the premium for a MPPP policy is significantly higher than a conventional SFIP policy and advise as to the option for obtaining less costly flood insurance; and

(vi) Advise that a MPPP policy will be purchased by the lender if evidence of flood insurance coverage is not received by a date certain.

(5) The second notification letter must remind the mortgagor of the previous notice and provide essentially the same information.

(6) The final notification letter must:

(i) Enclose a copy of the flood insurance policy purchased under the MPPP on the mortgagor's (insured's) behalf, together with the Declarations Page,

(ii) Advise that the policy was purchased because of the failure to respond to the previous notices, and

(iii) Remind the insured that similar coverage may be available at significantly lower cost and advise that the policy can be cancelled at any time during the policy year and a pro rata refund provided for the unearned portion of the premium in the event the insured purchases another policy that is acceptable to satisfy the requirements of the 1973 Act.

[61 FR 51219, Oct. 1, 1996, as amended at 64 FR 56176, Oct. 18, 1999; 67 FR 13549, Mar. 22, 2002; 69 FR 45610, July 30, 2004; 74 FR 15341, Apr. 3, 2009]

§ 62.24 WYO participation criteria.

New companies or organizations eligible for the pilot project we describe in paragraph (b) of this section that seek to participate in the WYO program, as well as former WYO companies seeking to return to the WYO program, must meet standards for financial capability and stability for statistical and financial reporting and for commitment to program objectives.

(a) To demonstrate the ability to meet the financial requirements, a private insurance company wishing to enter or reenter the WYO program must:

(1) Be a licensed property insurance company;

(2) Have a five (5) year history of writing property insurance;

(3) Disclose any legal proceedings, suspensions, judgments, settlements, or agreements reached with any State insurance department, State attorney general, State corporation commission, or the Federal Government during the

immediately prior five (5) years regarding the company's business practices;

(4) Submit its most recent National Association of Insurance Commissioners (NAIC) annual statement;

(5) Submit information, as data become available, to indicate that the company meets or exceeds NAIC standards for risk-based capital and surplus; and

(6) Submit its last State or regional audit, which should contain no material negative findings.

(b) To demonstrate the ability to meet the financial requirements, a public entity risk-sharing organization, an association of local governments, a State association of political subdivisions, a State-sponsored municipal league, and any other intergovernmental risk-sharing pool for covering public entity structures, wishing to enter the WYO program, which will end September 30, 2004, must:

(1) Have authority by a State to provide property coverage to its members;

(2) Have a five (5) year history of writing property coverage;

(3) Disclose any legal proceedings, suspensions, judgments, settlements, or agreements reached with any State insurance department, State attorney general, State corporation commission, or the Federal Government during the immediately prior five (5) years regarding the other insurer's business practices; and

(4) Submit its most recent two annual audits from an independent accounting firm performed in compliance with generally accepted accounting principles that show no material negative findings; and submit, as data become available, information to indicate that the other insurer meets or exceeds standards comparable to those of the NAIC for risk-based capital and surplus.

(c) An applicant for entry or reentry in the WYO program must also pass a test to determine the applicant's ability to process flood insurance and meet the Transaction Record Reporting and Processing (TRRP) Plan requirements of the WYO Financial Control Plan. Unless the test requirement is waived, e.g., where an already qualified performer will fulfill the applicant's reporting requirements, the applicant must prepare and submit test output monthly tape(s) and monthly financial statements and reconciliations for processing by the NFIP Bureau and Statistical Agent contractor. For test purposes, no error tolerance will be allowed. If the applicant fails the initial test, a second test will be run, which the applicant must pass to participate in the Program.

(d) To satisfy the requirement for commitment to Program goals, including marketing of flood insurance policies, the applicant will submit information concerning its plans for the WYO Program including plans for the training and support of producers and staff, marketing plans and sales targets, and claims handling and disaster response plans. Applicants must also identify those aspects of their planned flood insurance operations to be performed by another organization, managing agent, another WYO Company, a WYO vendor, a service bureau or related organization. Applicants will also name, in addition to a Principal Coordinator, a corporate officer point of contact—an individual, e.g., at the level of Senior Executive Vice President, who reports directly to the Chief Executive Officer or the Chief Operating Officer. Each applicant shall furnish the latest available information regarding the number of its fire, allied lines, farm-owners multiple peril, homeowners multiple peril, and commercial multiple peril policies or coverage documents in force, by line. A private insurance company applying for participation in the WYO program shall also furnish its Best's Financial Size Category for the purpose of setting marketing goals.

[67 FR 13550, Mar. 22, 2002]

APPENDIX A TO PART 62—FEDERAL EMERGENCY MANAGEMENT AGENCY, FEDERAL INSURANCE ADMINISTRATION, FINANCIAL ASSISTANCE/SUBSIDY ARRANGEMENT

Purpose: To assist the company in underwriting flood insurance using the Standard Flood Insurance Policy.

Accounting Data: Pursuant to Section 1310 of the Act, a Letter of Credit shall be issued for payment as provided for herein from the National Flood Insurance Fund.

Effective Date: October 1, 2004.

Issued By: Federal Emergency Management Agency, Federal Insurance Administration, Washington, DC 20472.

ARTICLE I—FINDINGS, PURPOSE, AND AUTHORITY

Whereas, the Congress in its "Finding and Declaration of Purpose" in the National Flood Insurance Act of 1968, as amended, ("the Act" or "Act") recognized the benefit of having the National Flood Insurance Program (the "Program" or "NFIP") "carried out to the maximum extent practicable by the private insurance industry"; and

Whereas the Federal Insurance Administration (FIA) within the Mitigation Division recognizes this Arrangement as coming under the provisions of Section 1345 of the Act (42 U.S.C. 4081); and

Whereas, the goal of the FIA is to develop a program with the insurance industry where, over time, some risk-bearing role for the industry will evolve as intended by the Congress (Section 1304 of the Act (42 U.S.C. 4011)); and

Whereas, the insurer (hereinafter the "Company") under this Arrangement shall charge rates established by the FIA; and

Whereas, FIA has promulgated regulations and guidance implementing the Act and the Write-Your-Own Program whereby participating private insurance companies act in a fiduciary capacity utilizing Federal funds to sell and administer the Standard Flood Insurance Policies, and has extensively regulated the participating companies' activities when selling or administering the Standard Flood Insurance Policies; and

Whereas, any litigation resulting from, related to, or arising from the Company's compliance with the written standards, procedures, and guidance issued by FEMA or FIA arises under the Act, regulations, or FIA guidance, and legal issues thereunder raise a federal question; and

Whereas, through this Arrangement, the Federal Treasury will back all flood policy claim payments by the Company; and

Whereas, this Arrangement has been developed to enable any interested qualified insurer to write flood insurance under its own name; and

Whereas, one of the primary objectives of the Program is to provide coverage to the maximum number of structures at risk and because the insurance industry has marketing access through its existing facilities not directly available to the FIA, it has been concluded that coverage will be extended to those who would not otherwise be insured under the Program; and

Whereas, flood insurance policies issued subject to this Arrangement shall be only that insurance written by the Company in its own name under prescribed policy conditions and pursuant to this Arrangement and the Act; and

Whereas, over time, the Program is designed to increase industry participation, and accordingly, reduce or eliminate Government as the principal vehicle for delivering flood insurance to the public; and

Whereas, the sole parties under this Arrangement are the WYO Companies and the Federal Government.

Now, therefore, the parties hereto mutually undertake the following:

ARTICLE II—UNDERTAKING OF THE COMPANY

A. Eligibility Requirements for Participation in the NFIP:

1. Policy Administration. All fund receipt, recording, control, timely deposit requirements, and disbursement in connection with all Policy Administration and any other related activities or correspondences, must meet all requirements of the Financial Control Plan. The Company shall be responsible for:

a. Compliance with the Community Eligibility/Rating Criteria

b. Making Policyholder Eligibility Determinations

c. Policy Issuance

d. Policy Endorsements

e. Policy Cancellations

f. Policy Correspondence

g. Payment of Agents' Commissions

2. Claims Processing. All claims processing must be processed in accordance with the processing of all the companies' insurance policies and with the Financial Control Plan. Companies will also be required to comply with FIA Policy Issuances and other guidance authorized by FIA or the Federal Emergency Management Agency ("FEMA").

3. Reports.

a. Monthly Financial Reporting and Statistical Transaction reporting requirements. All monthly financial reporting and statistical transaction reporting shall be in accordance with the requirements of the NFIP Transaction Record Reporting and Processing Plan for the Company Program and the Financial Control Plan for business written under the WYO (Write Your Own) Program. 44 CFR part 62, appendix B. These data shall be validated/edited/audited in detail and shall be compared and balanced against Company reports.

b. Monthly financial reporting procedure shall be in accordance with the WYO Accounting Procedures.

B. Time Standards. Time will be measured from the date of receipt through the date mailed out. All dates referenced are working days, not calendar days. In addition to the standards set forth below, all functions performed by the company shall be in accordance with the highest reasonably attainable quality standards generally utilized in the insurance and data processing field. Continual failure to meet these requirements

may result in limitations on the company's authority to write new business or the removal of the Company from the program. Applicable time standards are:

1. Application Processing—15 days (note: if the policy cannot be mailed due to insufficient or erroneous information or insufficient funds, a request for correction or added moneys shall be mailed within 10 days);

2. Renewal Processing—7 days.

3. Endorsement Processing—15 days.

4. Cancellation Processing—15 days.

5. Claims Draft Processing—7 days from completion of file examination.

6. Claims Adjustment—45 days average from the receipt of Notice of Loss (or equivalent) through completion of examination.

C. Single Adjuster Program. To ensure the maximum responsiveness to the NFIP policy holders following a catastrophic event, e.g., a hurricane, involving insured wind and flood damage to policyholders, the Company shall agree to the adjustment of the combined flood and wind losses utilizing one adjuster under an NFIP-approved Single Adjuster Program using procedures issued by the Federal Insurance Administrator. The Single Adjuster procedure shall be followed in the following cases:

1. Where the flood and wind coverage is provided by the Company;

2. Where the flood coverage is provided by the Company and the wind coverage is provided by a participating State Property Insurance Plan, Windpool Association, Beach Plan, Joint Underwriting Association, FAIR Plan, or similar property insurance mechanism; and

3. Where the flood coverage is provided by the Company and the wind coverage is provided by another property insurer and the State Insurance Regulator has determined that such property insurer shall, in the interest of consumers, facilitate the adjustment of its wind loss by the adjuster engaged to adjust the flood loss of the Company.

D. Policy Issuance.

1. The flood insurance subject to this Arrangement shall be only that insurance written by the Company in its own name pursuant to the Act.

2. The Company shall issue policies under the regulations prescribed by the Federal Insurance Administrator in accordance with the Act.

3. All such policies of insurance shall conform to the regulations prescribed by the Federal Insurance Administrator pursuant to the Act, and be issued on a form approved by the Federal Insurance Administrator.

4. All policies shall be issued in consideration of such premiums and upon such terms and conditions and in such States or areas or subdivisions thereof as may be designated by the Federal Insurance Administrator and only where the Company is licensed by State

law to engage in the property insurance business.

5. The Federal Insurance Administrator may require the Company to discontinue issuing policies subject to this Arrangement immediately in the event Congressional authorization or appropriation for the National Flood Insurance Program is withdrawn.

E. The Company shall separate Federal flood insurance funds from all other Company accounts, at a bank or banks of its choosing for the collection, retention and disbursement of Federal funds relating to its obligation under this Arrangement, less the Company's expenses as set forth in Article III, and the operation of the Letter of Credit established pursuant to Article IV. All funds not required to meet current expenditures shall be remitted to the United States Treasury, in accordance with the provisions of the WYO Accounting Procedures Manual.

F. The Company shall investigate, adjust, settle and defend all claims or losses arising from policies issued under this Arrangement. Payment of flood insurance claims by the Company shall be binding upon the FIA.

G. Compliance with Agency Standard and Guidelines.

1. The Company shall comply with written standards, procedures, and guidance issued by FEMA or FIA relating to the NFIP and applicable to the Company.

2. The Company shall market flood insurance policies in a manner consistent with marketing guidelines established by FIA.

3. The Company shall notify its agents of the requirement to comply with State regulations regarding flood insurance agent education, notify agents of flood insurance training opportunities, and assist FEMA in periodic assessment of agent training needs.

ARTICLE III—LOSS COSTS, EXPENSES, EXPENSE REIMBURSEMENT, AND PREMIUM REFUNDS

A. The Company shall be liable for operating, administrative and production expenses, including any State premium taxes, dividends, agents' commissions or any other expense of whatever nature incurred by the Company in the performance of its obligations under this Arrangement but excluding other taxes or fees, such as surcharges on flood insurance premium and guaranty fund assessments.

B. The Company may withhold as operating and administrative expenses, other than agents' or brokers' commissions, an amount from the Company's written premium on the policies covered by this Arrangement in reimbursement of all of the Company's marketing, operating, and administrative expenses, except for allocated and unallocated loss adjustment expenses described in C. of this article. This amount will equal the sum of the average of industry expense ratios for "Other Acq.", "Gen. Exp.",

and "Taxes" calculated by aggregating premiums and expense amounts for each of five property coverages using direct premium and expense information to derive weighted average expense ratios. For this purpose, we (the Federal Insurance Administration) will use data for the property/casualty industry published, as of March 15 of the prior Arrangement year, in Part III of the Insurance Expense Exhibit in A.M. Best Company's *Aggregates and Averages* for the following five property coverages: Fire, Allied Lines, Farmowners Multiple Peril, Homeowners Multiple Peril, and Commercial Multiple Peril (non-liability portion). In addition, this amount will be increased by one percentage point to reimburse expenses beyond regular property/casualty expenses.

The Company may retain fifteen percent (15%) of the Company's written premium on the policies covered by this Arrangement as the commission allowance to meet commissions or salaries of insurance agents, brokers, or other entities producing qualified flood insurance applications and other related expenses.

The amount of expense allowance retained by the Company may increase a maximum of two percentage points, depending on the extent to which the Company meets the marketing goals for the Arrangement year contained in marketing guidelines established pursuant to Article II.G. We will pay the company the amount of any increase after the end of the Arrangement year.

The Company, with the consent of the Federal Insurance Administrator as to terms and costs, may use the services of a national rating organization, licensed under state law, to help us undertake and carry out such studies and investigations on a community or individual risk basis, and to determine equitable and accurate estimates of flood insurance risk premium rates as authorized under the National Flood Insurance Act of 1968, as amended. We will reimburse the Company for the charges or fees for such services under the provisions of the WYO Accounting Procedures Manual.

C. Loss Adjustment Expenses shall be reimbursed as follows:

1. Unallocated loss adjustment expense shall be reimbursed to the Company pursuant to a "ULAE Schedule" coordinated with the Company and provided by the Federal Insurance Administrator.

2. Allocated loss adjustment expense shall be reimbursed to the Company pursuant to a "Fee Schedule" coordinated with the Company and provided by the Federal Insurance Administrator.

3. Special allocated loss expenses shall be reimbursed to the Company in accordance with guidelines issued by the Federal Insurance Administrator.

D. Loss Payments.

1. Loss payments under policies of flood insurance shall be made by the Company from Federal funds retained in the bank account(s) established under Article II, Section E and, if such funds are depleted, from Federal funds derived by drawing against the Letter of Credit established pursuant to Article IV.

2. Loss payments include payments as a result of litigation that arises under the scope of this Arrangement, and the Authorities set forth herein. All such loss payments and related expenses must meet the documentation requirements of the Financial Control Plan and of this Arrangement, and the Company must comply with the litigation documentation and notification requirements established by FEMA. Failure to meet these requirements may result in the Federal Insurance Administrator's decision not to provide reimbursement.

3. Limitation on Litigation Costs.

a. Following receipt of notice of such litigation, the FEMA Office of the Chief Counsel ("OCC") shall review the information submitted. If the FEMA OGC finds that the litigation is grounded in actions by the Company that are significantly outside the scope of this Arrangement, and/or involves issues of agent negligence, then the FEMA OCC shall make a recommendation to the Federal Insurance Administrator regarding whether all or part of the litigation is significantly outside the scope of the Arrangement.

b. In the event the Federal Insurance Administrator agrees with the determination of the FEMA OCC under Article III, Section D.3.a then the Company will be notified in writing within thirty (30) days of the Federal Insurance Administrator's decision that any award or judgment for damages and any costs to defend such litigation will not be recognized under Article III as a reimbursable loss cost, expense or expense reimbursement.

c. In the event a question arises whether only part of a litigation is reimbursable, the FEMA OCC shall make a recommendation to the Federal Insurance Administrator about the appropriate division of responsibility, if possible.

d. In the event that the Company wishes to petition for reconsideration of the determination that it will not be reimbursed for any part of the award or judgment or any part of the costs expended to defend such litigation made under Article III, Section D.3.a-c, it may do so by mailing, within thirty (30) days of the notice that reimbursement will not be made, a written petition to the Federal Insurance Administrator, who may request advice on other than legal matters of the WYO Standards Committee established under the WYO Financial Control Plan. The WYO Standards Committee will consider the request at its next regularly scheduled meeting or at a special meeting called for that purpose by the Chairman and issue a written recommendation to the Federal Insurance Administrator. The Federal Insurance Administrator's final determination will be made in writing within a reasonable time to the Company.

E. Premium refunds to applicants and policyholders required pursuant to rules contained in the National Flood Insurance Program (NFIP) "Flood Insurance Manual" shall be made by the Company from Federal flood insurance funds referred to in Article II, Section E, and, if such funds are depleted, from funds derived by drawing against the Letter of Credit established pursuant to Article IV. As fiscal agent, the Company shall not refund any premium to applicants or policyholders in any manner other than as specified in the NFIP's "Flood Insurance Manual" since flood insurance premiums are funds of the Federal Government.

ARTICLE IV—UNDERTAKINGS OF THE
GOVERNMENT

A. Letter(s) of Credit shall be established by the Federal Emergency Management Agency (FEMA) against which the Company may withdraw funds daily, if needed, pursuant to prescribed procedures implemented by FEMA. The amounts of the authorizations will be increased as necessary to meet the obligations of the Company under Article III, Sections C, D, and E. Request for funds shall be made only when net premium income has been depleted. The timing and amount of cash advances shall be as close as is administratively feasible to the actual disbursements by the recipient organization for allowable Letter of Credit expenses.

Request for payment on Letters of Credit shall not ordinarily be drawn more frequently than daily nor in amounts less than $5,000, and in no case more than $5,000,000 unless so stated on the Letter of Credit. This Letter of Credit may be drawn by the Company for any of the following reasons:

1. Payment of claim as described in Article III, Section D;

2. Refunds to applicants and policyholders for insurance premium overpayment, or if the application for insurance is rejected or when cancellation or endorsement of a policy results in a premium refund as described in Article III, Section E; and

3. Allocated and unallocated Loss Adjustment Expenses as described in Article III, Section C.

B. The FIA shall provide technical assistance to the Company as follows:

1. The FIA's policy and history concerning underwriting and claims handling.

2. A mechanism to assist in clarification of coverage and claims questions.

3. Other assistance as needed.

ARTICLE V—COMMENCEMENT AND
TERMINATION

A. The initial period of this Arrangement is from October 1, 2004 through September 30, 2005. Thereafter the Arrangement will be effective on an annual basis for the period October 1 through September 30. The FIA shall provide financial assistance only for policy applications and endorsements accepted by the Company during this period pursuant to the Program's effective date, underwriting and eligibility rules.

B. Each year, the FIA shall publish in the FEDERAL REGISTER and make available to the Company the terms for subscription or re-subscription to this Financial Assistance/ Subsidy Arrangement. The Company shall notify the FIA of its intent to re-subscribe or not re-subscribe within thirty days of publication.

C. In order to assure uninterrupted service to policyholders, the Company shall promptly notify the FIA in the event the Company elects not to participate in the Program during the Arrangement year. If so notified, or if the FIA chooses not to renew the Company's participation, the FIA, at its option, may require the continued performance of all or selected elements of this Arrangement for the period required for orderly transfer or cessation of business and settlement of accounts, not to exceed 18 months, and may either require Article V.C.1 or allow Article V.C.2:

1. The delivery to the FIA of:

a. A plan for the orderly transfer to the FIA of any continuing responsibilities in administering the policies issued by the Company under the Program including provisions for coordination assistance; and

b. All data received, produced, and maintained through the life of the Company's participation in the Program, including certain data, as determined by FIA, in a standard format and medium; and

c. All claims and policy files, including those pertaining to receipts and disbursements that have occurred during the life of each policy. In the event of a transfer of the services provided, the Company shall provide the FIA with a report showing, on a policy basis, any amounts due from or payable to insureds, agents, brokers, and others as of the transition date; and

d. All funds in its possession with respect to any policies transferred to FIA for administration and the unearned expenses retained by the Company.

2. Submission of plans for the renewal of the business by another WYO Company or Companies or the submission of detailed plans for another WYO Company to assume responsibility for the Company's NFIP policies. Such plans shall assure uninterrupted service to policyholders and shall be accompanied by a formal request for FIA approval of such transfers.

D. Financial assistance under this Arrangement may be canceled by the FIA in its entirety upon thirty (30) days written notice to the Company by certified mail stating one of the following reasons for such cancellation: (i) Fraud or misrepresentation by the Company subsequent to the inception of the Arrangement; or (ii) Nonpayment to the FIA of any amount due the FIA; or (iii) Material failure to comply with the requirements of this Arrangement or with the written standards, procedures, or guidance issued by FEMA or FIA relating to the NFIP and applicable to the Company. Under these specific conditions, the FIA may require the transfer of administrative responsibilities and the transfer of data and records as provided in Article V, Section C.1.a through d. If transfer is required, the unearned expenses retained by the Company shall be remitted to the FIA. In such event, the Government will assume all obligations and liabilities owed to policyholders under such policies, arising before and after the date of transfer. As an alternative to transfer of the policies to the Government, the FIA will consider a proposal, if it is made by the Company, for the assumption of responsibilities by another WYO Company as provided in Article V, Section C.2.

E. In the event that the Company is unable or otherwise fails to carry out its obligations under this Arrangement by reason of any order or directive duly issued by the Department of Insurance of any jurisdiction to which the Company is subject, the Company agrees to transfer, and the Government will accept, any and all WYO policies issued by the Company and in force as of the date of such inability or failure to perform. In such event the Government will assume all obligations and liabilities within the scope of the Arrangement owed to policyholders arising before and after the date of transfer, and the Company will immediately transfer to the Government all needed records and data and all funds in its possession with respect to all such policies transferred and the unearned expenses retained by the Company. As an alternative to transfer of the policies to the Government, the FIA will consider a proposal, if it is made by the Company, for the assumption of responsibilities by another WYO Company as provided by Article V, Section C.2.

F. In the event the Act is amended, or repealed, or expires, or if the FIA is otherwise without authority to continue the Program, financial assistance under this Arrangement may be canceled for any new or renewal business, but the Arrangement shall continue for policies in force that shall be allowed to run their term under the Arrangement.

ARTICLE VI—INFORMATION AND ANNUAL
STATEMENTS

The Company shall furnish to FEMA such summaries and analyses of information including claim file information, and property address, location, and/or site information in its records as may be necessary to carry out the purposes of the National Flood Insurance Act of 1968, as amended, in such form as the FIA, in cooperation with the Company, shall prescribe. The Company shall be a property/casualty insurer domiciled in a State or territory of the United States. Upon request, the Company shall file with the FIA a true and correct copy of the Company's Fire and Casualty Annual Statement, and Insurance Expense Exhibit or amendments thereof as filed with the State Insurance Authority of the Company's domiciliary State.

ARTICLE VII—CASH MANAGEMENT AND
ACCOUNTING

A. FEMA shall make available to the Company during the entire term of this Arrangement and any continuation period required by FIA pursuant to Article V, Section C., the Letter of Credit provided for in Article IV drawn on a repository bank within the Federal Reserve System upon which the Company may draw for reimbursement of its expenses as set forth in Article IV that exceed net written premiums collected by the Company from the effective date of this Arrangement or continuation period to the date of the draw. In the event that adequate Letter of Credit funding is not available to meet current Company obligations for flood policy claim payments issued, FIA shall direct the Company to immediately suspend the issuance of loss payments until such time as adequate funds are available. The Companies are not required to pay claims from their own funds in the event of such suspension.

B. The Company shall remit all funds, including interest, not required to meet current expenditures to the United States Treasury, in accordance with the provisions of the WYO Accounting Procedures Manual or procedures approved in writing by the FIA.

C. In the event the Company elects not to participate in the Program in this or any subsequent fiscal year, or is otherwise unable or not permitted to participate, the Company and FIA shall make a provisional settlement of all amounts due or owing within three months of the expiration or termination of this Arrangement. This settlement shall include net premiums collected, funds drawn on the Letter of Credit, and reserves for outstanding claims. The Company and FIA agree to make a final settlement, subject to audit, of accounts for all obligations arising from this Arrangement within 18 months of its expiration or termination, except for contingent liabilities that shall be listed by the Company. At the time of final settlement, the balance, if any, due the FIA or the Company shall be remitted by the other immediately and the operating year under this Arrangement shall be closed.

ARTICLE VIII—ARBITRATION

If any misunderstanding or dispute arises between the Company and the FIA with reference to any factual issue under any provisions of this Arrangement or with respect to the FIA's non-renewal of the Company's participation, other than as to legal liability under or interpretation of the standard flood insurance policy, such misunderstanding or dispute may be submitted to arbitration for a determination that shall be binding upon approval by the FIA. The Company and the FIA may agree on and appoint an arbitrator who shall investigate the subject of the misunderstanding or dispute and make a determination. If the Company and the FIA cannot agree on the appointment of an arbitrator, then two arbitrators shall be appointed, one to be chosen by the Company and one by the FIA.

The two arbitrators so chosen, if they are unable to reach an agreement, shall select a third arbitrator who shall act as umpire, and such umpire's determination shall become final only upon approval by the FIA.

The Company and the FIA shall bear in equal shares all expenses of the arbitration. Findings, proposed awards, and determinations resulting from arbitration proceedings carried out under this section, upon objection by FIA or the Company, shall be inadmissible as evidence in any subsequent proceedings in any court of competent jurisdiction.

This Article shall indefinitely succeed the term of this Arrangement.

ARTICLE IX—ERRORS AND OMISSIONS

In the event of negligence by the Company that has not resulted in litigation but has resulted in a claim against the Company, FEMA will not consider reimbursement of the Company for costs incurred due to that negligence unless the Company takes all reasonable actions to rectify the negligence and to mitigate any such costs as soon as possible after discovery of the negligence. Further, (i) if the claim against the Company is grounded in actions significantly outside the scope of this Arrangement or (ii) if there is negligence by the agent, FEMA will not reimburse any costs incurred due to that negligence. The Company will be notified in writing within thirty (30) days of a decision not to reimburse. In the event the Company wishes to petition for reconsideration of the decision not to reimburse, the procedure in Article III, Section D.3.d shall apply.

However, in the event that the Company has made a claim payment to an insured without including a mortgagee (or trustee) of which the Company had actual notice prior to making payment, and subsequently determines that the mortgagee (or trustee) is also entitled to any part of said claim payment, any additional payment shall not be paid by the Company from any portion of the premium and any funds derived from any Federal Letter of Credit deposited in the bank account described in Article II, section E. In addition, the Company agrees to hold the Federal Government harmless against any claim asserted against the Federal Government by any such mortgagee (or Trustee), as described in the preceding sentence, by reason of any claim payment made to any insured under the circumstances described above.

ARTICLE X—OFFICIALS NOT TO BENEFIT

No Member or Delegate to Congress, or Resident Commissioner, shall be admitted to any share or part of this Arrangement, or to any benefit that may arise therefrom; but this provision shall not be construed to extend to this Arrangement if made with a corporation for its general benefit.

ARTICLE XI—OFFSET

At the settlement of accounts the Company and the FIA shall have, and may exercise, the right to offset any balance or balances, whether on account of premiums, commissions, losses, loss adjustment expenses, salvage, or otherwise due one party to the other, its successors or assigns, hereunder or under any other Arrangements heretofore or hereafter entered into between the Company and the FIA. This right of offset shall not be affected or diminished because of insolvency of the Company.

All debts or credits of the same class, whether liquidated or unliquidated, in favor of or against either party to this Arrangement on the date of entry, or any order of conservation, receivership, or liquidation, shall be deemed to be mutual debts and credits and shall be offset with the balance only to be allowed or paid. No offset shall be allowed where a conservator, receiver, or liquidator has been appointed and where an obligation was purchased by or transferred to a party hereunder to be used as an offset.

Although a claim on the part of either party against the other may be unliquidated or undetermined in amount on the date of the entry of the order, such claim will be regarded as being in existence as of the date of such order and any credits or claims of the same class then in existence and held by the other party may be offset against it.

ARTICLE XII—EQUAL OPPORTUNITY

The Company shall not discriminate against any applicant for insurance because of race, color, religion, sex, age, handicap, marital status, or national origin.

ARTICLE XIII—RESTRICTION ON OTHER FLOOD INSURANCE

As a condition of entering into this Arrangement, the Company agrees that in any area in which the Federal Insurance Administrator authorizes the purchase of flood insurance pursuant to the Program, all flood insurance offered and sold by the Company to persons eligible to buy pursuant to the Program for coverages available under the Program shall be written pursuant to this Arrangement.

However, this restriction applies solely to policies providing only flood insurance. It does not apply to policies provided by the Company of which flood is one of the several perils covered, or where the flood insurance coverage amount is over and above the limits of liability available to the insured under the Program.

ARTICLE XIV—ACCESS TO BOOKS AND RECORDS

The FIA and the Comptroller General of The United States, or their duly authorized representatives, for the purpose of investigation, audit, and examination shall have access to any books, documents, papers and records of the Company that are pertinent to this Arrangement. The Company shall keep records that fully disclose all matters pertinent to this Arrangement, including premiums and claims paid or payable under policies issued pursuant to this Arrangement. Records of accounts and records relating to financial assistance shall be retained and available for three (3) years after final settlement of accounts, and to financial assistance, three (3) years after final adjustment of such claims. The FIA shall have access to policyholder and claim records at all times for purposes of the review, defense, examination, adjustment, or investigation of any claim under a flood insurance policy subject to this Arrangement.

ARTICLE XV—COMPLIANCE WITH ACT AND REGULATIONS

This Arrangement and all policies of insurance issued pursuant thereto shall be subject to the provisions of the National Flood Insurance Act of 1968, as amended, the Flood Disaster Protection Act of 1973, as amended, the National Flood Insurance Reform Act of 1994, and Regulations issued pursuant thereto and all Regulations affecting the work that are issued pursuant thereto, during the term hereof.

ARTICLE XVI—RELATIONSHIP BETWEEN THE PARTIES (FEDERAL GOVERNMENT AND COMPANY) AND THE INSURED

Inasmuch as the Federal Government is a guarantor hereunder, the primary relationship between the Company and the Federal Government is one of a fiduciary nature, *i.e.*, to assure that any taxpayer funds are accounted for and appropriately expended. The Company is a fiscal agent of the Federal Government, but is not a general agent of the Federal Government. The Company is solely responsible for its obligations to its insured under any policy issued pursuant hereto, such that the Federal Government is not a proper party to any lawsuit arising out of such policies.

ADDENDUM TO APPENDIX A TO PART 62—FEDERAL EMERGENCY MANAGEMENT AGENCY, FEDERAL INSURANCE AND MITIGATION ADMINISTRATION, FINANCIAL ASSISTANCE/SUBSIDY ARRANGEMENT

NOTE: This Addendum to Appendix A to Part 62 applies only to a public entity risk-sharing organization, an association of local governments, a State association of political subdivisions, a State-sponsored municipal league, and any other intergovernmental risk-sharing pool for covering public entity structures participating in the pilot project established in §62.24(b) that permits intergovernmental risk-sharing pools to provide flood insurance to public entities to cover public buildings.

(1) "Company" in the preceding Arrangement includes "a public entity risk-sharing organization, an association of local governments, a State association of political subdivisions, a State-sponsored municipal league, and any other intergovernmental risk-sharing pool for covering public entity structures."

(2) The references to "marketing guidelines" in Article II—Undertaking of the Company and to "marketing goals" in Article III—Loss Costs, Expenses, Expense Reimbursement, and Premium Refunds shall apply only to the private insurance companies participating in the WYO program.

[62 FR 39910, July 24, 1997, as amended at 63 FR 32761, June 16, 1998; 64 FR 27709, May 21, 1999; 65 FR 36634, June 9, 2000; 66 FR 40917, Aug. 6, 2001; 67 FR 13550, Mar. 22, 2002; 67 FR 51769, Aug. 9, 2002; 68 FR 52701, Sept. 5, 2003; 68 FR 75454, Dec. 31, 2003; 69 FR 23659, Apr. 30, 2004; 69 FR 45611, July 30, 2004; 73 FR 18187, 18188, Apr. 3, 2008]

APPENDIX B TO PART 62—NATIONAL FLOOD INSURANCE PROGRAM

A PLAN TO MAINTAIN FINANCIAL CONTROL FOR BUSINESS WRITTEN UNDER THE WRITE YOUR OWN PROGRAM.

(a) *In general.* Under the Write Your Own (WYO) Program, we (the Federal Insurance Administration (FIA), Federal Emergency Management Agency (FEMA)) may enter into an arrangement with individual private sector insurance companies licensed to engage in the business of property insurance. The arrangement allows these companies— using their customary business practices—to offer flood insurance coverage to eligible property owners. To assist companies in marketing flood insurance coverage, the Federal Government will be a guarantor of flood insurance coverage for WYO policies issued under the WYO Arrangement. To account for and ensure appropriate spending of any taxpayer funds, the WYO companies and we will implement this Financial Control Plan (Plan). Only the Federal Insurance Administrator may approve any departures from the requirements of this Plan.

(b) *Financial Control Plan.* (1) The WYO Companies are subject to audit, examination, and regulatory controls of the various States. Additionally, the operating department of an insurance company is customarily subject to examinations and audits performed by the company's internal audit or quality control departments, or both, and independent Certified Public Accountant (CPA) firms. This Plan will use to the extent possible the findings of these examinations and audits as they pertain to business written under the WYO Program.

(2) This Plan contains several checks and balances that can, if properly implemented by the WYO Company, significantly reduce the need for extensive on-site reviews of the Company's files by us or our designee. Furthermore, we believe that this process is consistent with customary reinsurance practices and avoids duplication of examinations performed under the auspices of individual State Insurance Departments, NAIC Zone examinations, and independent CPA firms.

(c) *Standards Committee established.* (1) We establish in this Plan a Standards Committee for the WYO Program to oversee the performance of WYO companies under this Plan and to recommend appropriate remedial actions to the Federal Insurance Administrator. The Standards Committee will review and recommend to the Federal Insurance Administrator remedies for any adverse action arising from the implementation of the Financial Control Plan. Adverse actions include, but are not limited to, not renewing a particular company's WYO Arrangement.

(2) The Federal Insurance Administrator appoints the members of the Standards Committee, which consists of five (5) members from FIA, one (1) member from FEMA's Office of Chief Financial Officer, and one (1) member from each of the six (6) designated WYO Companies, pools, or other entities.

(3) A WYO company must—

(A) Have a biennial audit of the flood insurance financial statements conducted by a CPA firm at the Company's expense to ensure that the financial data reported to us accurately represents the flood insurance activities of the Company. The CPA firm must conduct its audits in accordance with generally accepted auditing standards (GAAS) and the Government Auditing Standards issued by the Comptroller General of the United States (commonly known as "yellow book" requirements). The Company must file with us a report of the CPA firm's detailed biennial audit, and, after our review of the audit report, we will convey our determination to the Standards Committee.

(B) Participate in a WYO Company/FIA Operation review. We will conduct a review of the WYO Company's flood insurance claims, underwriting, customer service, marketing, and litigation activities at least once every three (3) years. As part of these reviews, we will reconcile specific files with a listing of transactions submitted by the Company under the Transaction Record Reporting and Processing Plan (Part 5). We will file a report of the Operation Review with the Standards Committee (Part 7).

(C) Meet the recording and reporting requirements of the WYO Transaction Record Reporting and Processing (TRRP) Plan and the WYO Accounting Procedures Manual. The National Flood Insurance Program's (NFIP) Bureau and Statistical Agent will analyze the transactions reported under the TRRP Plan and submit a monthly report to the WYO company and to us. The analysis will cover the timeliness of the WYO submissions, the disposition of transactions that do not pass systems edits, and the reconciliation of the totals generated from transaction reports with those submitted on the WYO Company's reports. (Parts 2 and 6).

(D) Cooperate with FEMA's Office of Financial Management on Letter of Credit matters.

(E) Cooperate with us in the implementation of a claims reinspection program (Part 3).

(F) Cooperate with us in the verification of risk rating information.

(G) Cooperate with DHS's Office of Inspector General on matters pertaining to fraud.

(d) This Plan incorporates by reference a separate document, "The Write Your Own Program Financial Control Plan Requirements and Procedures," that contains the following parts, each of which is incorporated by reference into and is applicable to the Financial Control Plan:

(1) Part 1—Financial Audits, Audits for Cause, and State Insurance Department Audits;

(2) Part 2—Transaction Record Reporting and Processing Plan Reconciliation Procedures;

(3) Part 3—Claims Reinspection Program;

(4) Part 4—Report Certifications and Signature Authorization;

(5) Part 5—Transaction Record Reporting and Processing Plan;

(6) Part 6—Write Your Own (WYO) Accounting Procedures Manual; and

(7) Part 7—Operation Review Procedures.

(e) Interested members of the public may obtain a copy of "The Write Your Own Program Financial Control Plan Requirements and Procedures" by contacting the FEMA Distribution Center, P.O. Box 2012, Jessup, MD 20794.''

[64 FR 56176, Oct. 18, 1999]

PART 63—IMPLEMENTATION OF SECTION 1306(c) OF THE NATIONAL FLOOD INSURANCE ACT OF 1968

Subpart A—General

Subpart B—State Certification of Structures Subject to Imminent Collapse

63.18 Review of State certification by the Federal Insurance Administrator.

AUTHORITY: 42 U.S.C. 4001 *et seq.*; Reorganization Plan No. 3 of 1978; E.O. 12127.

SOURCE: 53 FR 36975, Sept. 23, 1988, unless otherwise noted.

Subpart A—General

§ 63.1 Purpose of part.

The purpose of this part is to implement section 1306(c) of the National Flood Insurance Act of 1968, as amended (the Act). Section 544 of the Housing and Community Development Act of 1987 (Pub. L. 100–242) amended the Act by adding subsection (c) to section 1306 of the Act. Under this amendment, effective February 5, 1988, section 1306(c) of the Act provides for benefit payments under the Standard Flood Insurance Policy (SFIP) for demolition or relocation of a structure insured under the Act that is located along the shore of a lake or other body of water and that is certified by an appropriate State or local land use authority to be subject to imminent collapse or subsidence as a result of erosion or undermining caused by waves or currents of water exceeding anticipated cyclical levels. This part establishes criteria by which States can obtain the approval of the Federal Insurance Administrator to make these certifications and sets forth the procedures and data requirements to be used by those States in making these certifications. This part also contains provisions regarding other aspects of section 1306(c) of the Act. For example, there are provisions regarding section 1306(c)(6)(B) of the Act (which provides for condemnation in lieu of certification), including clarification as to the form of condemnation issued under a State or local law that is required.

§ 63.2 Condemnation in lieu of certification.

(a) The condemnation required by section 1306(c)(6)(B) of the Act in lieu of certification need not be grounded in a finding that the structure is subject to imminent collapse or subsidence as a result of erosion, but may be issued for other reasons deemed sufficient by the State or local authority.

(b) The condemnation may be in the form of a court order or other instrument authorized by State or local law, e.g., a notification to the property owner of an unsafe condition, or unsanitary condition, or other deficiency at the property address, coupled with a statement that the property owner must vacate the property if the condition giving rise to the condemnation notice is not cured by repair, removal, or demolition of the building by a date certain.

(c) In addition to a condemnation in accordance with paragraphs (a) and (b) of this section, a structure must be found by the Federal Insurance Administrator to be subject to imminent collapse or subsidence as a result of erosion or undermining caused by waves or currents of water exceeding anticipated cyclical levels to be eligible for benefits under section 1306(c) of the Act.

§ 63.3 Requirement to be covered by a contract for flood insurance by June 1, 1988.

The requirement in section 1306(c)(4)(C)(i) of the Act that a structure be "covered by a contract for flood insurance under this title—(i) on or before June 1, 1988" was met if presentation of the appropriate premium and a properly completed flood insurance application form was made to the National Flood Insurance Program or a Write Your Own (WYO) Company on or before June 1, 1988.

§ 63.4 Property not covered.

Benefits under section 1306(c) of the Act do not include compensation for items excluded under the provisions of the Standard Flood Insurance Policy (SFIP).

§ 63.5 Coverage for contents removal.

Whenever a structure is subject to imminent collapse or subsidence as a result of erosion or undermining caused by waves or currents of water exceeding anticipated cyclical levels and otherwise meets the requirements of section 1306(c) of the Act so that benefits are payable under those provisions, the coverage in the definition of "Direct Physical Loss by or from Flood" in the SFIP for the expense of removing contents, up to the minimum deductible of $500.00, to protect and preserve them from flood or from the imminent danger of flood, applies if contents coverage is in effect.

§ 63.6 Reimbursable relocation costs.

In addition to the coverage described in § 63.5 of this part, relocation costs for which benefits are payable under section 1306(c) of the Act include the costs of:

(a) Removing the structure from the site,

(b) Site cleanup,

(c) Debris removal,

(d) Moving the structure to a new site, and

(e) At the new site, a new foundation and related grading, including elevating the structure as required by local flood plain management ordinances, and sewer, septic, electric, gas, telephone, and water connections at the building.

§ 63.7 Amount of coverage and deductible on effective date of condemnation or certification.

The amount of building coverage and the deductible applicable to a claim for benefits under section 1306(c) of the Act are what was in effect on the date of condemnation or the date of application for certification.

[53 FR 36975, Sept. 23, 1988, as amended at 53 FR 44193, Nov. 2, 1988]

§ 63.8 Limitation on amount of benefits.

(a) In section 1306(c)(3)(C) of the Act, the phrase *under the flood insurance contract issued pursuant to this title* means the value of the structure under section 1306(c)(3)(C) of the Act is limited to the amount of building coverage provided by the insured's policy.

(b) Where the amount payable under section 1306(c)(1)(A)(ii) of the Act for the cost of demolition, together with the amount payable under section 1306(c)(1)(A) of the Act for the value of the structure under the demolition option, exceeds the amount of building coverage provided by the insured's policy, such amounts will be paid beyond the amount of that building coverage, even if this payment exceeds the limits of coverage otherwise authorized by

section 1306(a) of the Act for the particular class of property.

§ 63.9 Sale while claim pending.

If a claimant sells a structure prior to its demolition or relocation, no benefits are payable to that claimant under section 1306(c) of the Act, and any payments which may have been made under those provisions shall be reimbursed to the insurer making them.

§ 63.10 Demolition or relocation contractor to be joint payee.

If a demolition or relocation contractor is used, the instrument of payment for benefits under section 1306(c) of the Act for the fee of that contractor, shall include that contractor as a joint payee, unless that contractor has already been paid when the instrument of payment is issued.

§ 63.11 Requirement for a commitment before October 1, 1989.

The requirement in section 1306(c)(7) of the Act that a commitment be made on or before September 30, 1989 as a necessary condition to making any payments after September 30, 1989, is met if before October 1, 1989,

(a) There is either a condemnation in accordance with § 63.2 of this part or a certification in accordance with subpart B of this part, and

(b) A policyholder's notice of claim for benefits under section 1306(c) of the Act is received by the insurer.

§ 63.12 Setback and community flood plain management requirements.

(a) Where benefits have been paid under section 1306(c) of the Act, the setback requirements in section 1306(c)(5) of the Act, which if not met result in a prohibition against subsequently providing flood insurance or assistance under the Disaster Relief Act of 1974, shall apply:

(1) To the structure involved wherever it is located, and

(2) To any other structure subsequently constructed on or moved to the parcel of land on which the structure involved was located when the claim under section 1306(c) of the Act arose.

(b) In addition, any structures relocated under section 1306 of the Act must comply with the flood plain management criteria set forth in § 60.3 of this chapter.

Subpart B—State Certification of Structures Subject to Imminent Collapse

§ 63.13   Purpose of subpart.

The purpose of this subpart is to establish criteria under the provisions of section 1306(c) of the National Flood Insurance Act of 1968, as amended, by which States can obtain approval from the Federal Insurance Administrator to certify that structures are subject to imminent collapse or subsidence as a result of erosion or undermining caused by waves or currents of water exceeding anticipated cyclical levels. The subpart also sets forth the procedures and data requirements to be utilized by those States in certifying structures as subject to imminent collapse. The State certification procedure represents an option to the use of the procedure whereby a structure is condemned by a State or local authority as a prerequisite to consideration for imminent collapse insurance benefits.

§ 63.14   Criteria for State qualification to perform imminent collapse certifications.

In order to qualify under this subpart, the State must be administering a coastal zone management program which includes the following components, as a minimum:

(a) A state-wide requirement that prohibits new construction and the relocation of structures seaward of an adopted erosion setback. Such setback must be based in whole or in part on some multiple of the local mean annual erosion (recession) rate; and

(b) An established, complete and functional data base of mean annual erosion rates for all reaches of coastal shorelines subject to erosion in the State, which is used as the basis to enforce these setback requirements.

§ 63.15   State application for eligibility to certify structures subject to imminent collapse.

(a) Application pursuant to this part shall be made by the Governor or other duly authorized official of the State.

(b) The application must be submitted to the Federal Emergency Management Agency, Federal Insurance Administration, 500 C Street SW., Washington, DC 20472.

(c) Documents to be included in the application are as follows:

(1) Copies of all applicable State statutes and regulations verifying the existence of a coastal zone management program including setback requirements for new and relocated construction which are based in whole or in part on mean annual erosion rates established for the State's shorelines.

(2) A copy of the State's mean annual erosion rate data base, if not already provided, showing such rates for all reaches of coastal shorelines subject to erosion within the State.

(3) The title, address and phone number of a contact person within the State agency having authority for administering the coastal zone management program.

(4) A statement that adequate resources are available to carry out the certification services, and that certifications will be performed in accordance with the procedures described in § 63.17.

§ 63.16   Review of State application by the Federal Insurance Administrator.

(a) The Federal Insurance Administrator may return the application for eligibility upon finding it incomplete or upon finding that additional information is required in order to make a determination as to the adequacy of the coastal zone management program and erosion rate data base.

(b) Upon determining that the State's program and/or data base does not meet the criteria set forth in § 63.14, the Federal Insurance Administrator shall in writing reject the application for eligibility and indicate in what respects the State program and/or data base fails to comply with the criteria.

(c) Upon determining that the State program and data base meets the criteria set forth in §63.14, the Federal Insurance Administrator shall approve the State as eligible to certify structures subject to imminent collapse. Such approval, however, is in all cases provisional. The Federal Insurance Administrator shall review the State program and data base for continued compliance with the criteria set forth in this part and may request updated documentation for the purpose of such review. If the program and/or data base is found to be inadequate and is not corrected within ninety days from the date that such inadequacies were identified, the Federal Insurance Administrator may revoke his approval.

§ **63.17 Procedures and data requirements for imminent collapse certifications by States.**

Any State that has been determined to be eligible by the Federal Insurance Administrator may certify that a coastal structure is subject to imminent collapse. Such certification requires that the State collect scientific or technical information relative to the structure and its site and provide such information to the insured to be filed with a claim for insurance benefits under Section 1306 of the National Flood Insurance Act of 1968, as amended. The information which is provided to the insured shall include, but is not limited to, the following:

(a) Certification from the State agency that the structure is subject to imminent collapse. The certification shall cite the property address, legal description (e.g., lot, block), the date of application for certification, and the date of and basis for the certification, and

(b) Supporting scientific and technical data to substantiate the certification consisting of the following:

(1) Photographs of the structure in relation to the obvious peril. All photographs should be labeled with the location, direction, date and time from which they were taken. The collection of photographs should adequately display the following:

(i) Any evidence of existing damage. The damage can include loss or erosion of soil near or around the foundation, or structural damage to the foundation components.

(ii) Structure and waterbody. These photographs shall show both the structure and the waterbody that presents the peril. If the structure is on a high bluff or dune and not accessible from the water side, the top edge of the bluff or dune will be sufficient. These will usually be taken from one or both sides of the structure.

(iii) Physical reference features used in the measurements discussed below. The reference feature shall be in or near the area affected by normal tides, when applicable. If a reference is not clearly distinguishable on the photograph, it should be annotated to identify the feature. If possible, all reference features described below should be photographed showing their relationship to the site of the threatened structure.

(2) Identification and selection of reference features. The following reference features are presented according to priority. If the first feature is not present, the next feature shall be located and photographed, and so forth.

(i) Top edge of bluff (cliff top).

(ii) Top edge of escarpment on an eroding dune (i.e., a nearly vertical erosional cut at the seaward face of the dune). The normal high tide should be near the toe of the dune and there should be indications that the dune is actively eroding.

(iii) The normal high tide limit may be indicated by one of the following:

(A) Vegetation line (the seaward most edge of permanent vegetation).

(B) Beach scarp (erosion line on beach, usually a sharp, nearly vertical drop of 0.5 to 3.0 feet at the upper limit of high tide).

(C) Debris line deposited by the normal high tide, not by a recent storm.

(D) Upper limit of wet sand.

(3) Distance measurements from the threatened structure to the nearest points on the reference features. These measurements should be taken from all photographed reference features to the closest point on the supporting foundation. For purposes of making this measurement, decks, stairs, and other exterior attachments that do not contribute to the structural support of the building are not considered part of the

structure. The measurements shall be taken horizontally with a tape and recorded to the nearest foot. The date and time of the measurement shall be noted. The location of the measurements (i.e., reference feature and closest structural member) shall be identified on the appropriate photograph or sketch of the site. If some or all of the reference features coincide, this shall also be noted and identified on the photographs. Reference features landward of the structure need not be measured, but shall be noted on the photographs.

(4) A determination of the average annual erosion rate at the site and a copy of the pertinent section of the reference document used to obtain the annual erosion rate at the site.

(5) Copy of the effective Flood Insurance Rate Map panel annotated with the location of the threatened structure.

(6) In the event that a structure is not situated within a "zone of imminent collapse" using the criteria and procedures in paragraphs (b) (1) through (5) of this section, then the State may submit other scientific and technical data, in addition to the information described in paragraphs (b) (1) through (5) of this section, that would reveal unusual erosive or stability conditions at the site. Such data must include engineering analyses or reports performed on the structure or site which evaluates local rates of erosion, or the condition or stability of the structure's foundation including supporting soil.

(c) In the case of structures planned to be relocated, a certification as to whether the proposed relocation site is outside the 30-year setback for 1-4 family residential structures, or outside the 60-year setback for all other structures, must also be submitted by the State.

[53 FR 36975, Sept. 23, 1988, as amended at 53 FR 44193, Nov. 2, 1988]

§ 63.18   Review of State certification by the Federal Insurance Administrator.

The Federal Insurance Administrator, after a claim has been filed by the property owner, will review the certification and data prepared by the State. Upon completion of the review, the State will be notified that:

(a) The structure has been determined to be subject to imminent collapse, or

(b) The structure has not been determined to be subject to imminent collapse and the basis for such determination, or

(c) Additional data are needed to verify that the procedures and criteria for imminent collapse certification have been met.

PART 64—COMMUNITIES ELIGIBLE FOR THE SALE OF INSURANCE

AUTHORITY: 42 U.S.C. 4001 et seq., Reorganization Plan No. 3 of 1978, 3 CFR, 1978 Comp.; p. 329; E.O. 12127, 44 FR 19367, 3 CFR, 1979 Comp.; p. 376.

§ 64.1   Purpose of part.

(a) 42 U.S.C. 4012(c), 4022 and 4102 require that flood insurance in the maximum limits of coverage under the regular program shall be offered in communities only after the Federal Insurance Administrator has: (1) Identified the areas of special flood, mudslide (i.e., mudflow) or flood-related erosion hazards within the community; and/or (2) completed a risk study for the applicant community. The priorities for conducting such risk studies are set forth in §§ 59.23 and 60.25 of this subchapter. The purpose of this part is to define the types of zones which the Agency will use for identifying the hazard areas on maps.

(b) 42 U.S.C. 4056 authorizes an emergency implementation of the National Flood Insurance Program whereby the Federal Insurance Administrator may make subsidized coverage available to eligible communities prior to the completion of detailed risk studies for such areas. This part also describes procedures under the emergency program and lists communities which become eligible under the NFIP.

[48 FR 28278, June 21, 1983, as amended at 49 FR 4751, Feb. 8, 1984; 49 FR 33879, Aug. 27, 1984]

§ 64.2 Definitions.

The definitions set forth in part 59 of this subchapter are applicable to this part.

[41 FR 46986, Oct. 26, 1976. Redesignated at 44 FR 31177, May 31, 1979]

§ 64.3 Flood Insurance Maps.

(a) The following maps may be prepared by the Federal Insurance Administrator for use in connection with the sale of flood insurance:

(1) Flood Insurance Rate Map: This map is prepared after the flood hazard study for the community has been completed and the risk premium rates have been established. The FIRM indicates the risk premium rate zones applicable in the community and when those rates are effective. The FIRM also may indicate, at the request of the community, zones to identify areas of future-conditions flood hazards. The symbols used to designate the risk premium rate zones and future-conditions zones are as follows:

Zone symbol	
A	Area of special flood hazard without water surface elevations determined
A1–30, AE	Area of special flood hazard with water surface elevations determined
AO	Area of special flood hazards having shallow water depths and/or unpredictable flow paths between (1) and (3) ft
A99	Area of special flood hazard where enough progress has been made on a protective system, such as dikes, dams, and levees, to consider it complete for insurance rating purposes
AH	Areas of special flood hazards having shallow water depths and/or unpredictable flow paths between (1) and (3) feet, and with water surface elevations determined
AR	Area of special flood hazard that results from the decertification of a previously accredited flood protection system that is determined to be in the process of being restored to provide base flood protection
V	Area of special flood hazards without water surface elevations determined, and with velocity, that is inundated by tidal floods (coastal high hazard area)
V1–30, VE	Area of special flood hazards, with water surface elevations determined and with velocity, that is inundated by tidal floods (coastal high hazard area)

Zone symbol	
VO	Area of special flood hazards having shallow water depths and/or unpredictable flow paths between (1) and (3) ft. and with velocity
B, X	Areas of moderate flood hazards or areas of future-conditions flood hazard.
C, X	Area of minimal hazards
D	Area of undetermined but possible, flood hazards
M	Area of special mudslide (i.e., mudflow) hazards
N	Area of moderate mudslide (i.e., mudflow) hazards
P	Area of undetermined, but possible, mudslide hazards
E	Area of special flood-related erosion hazards.

Areas identified as subject to more than one hazard (flood, mudslide (i.e., mudflow), flood-related erosion) or potential hazard (i.e., future-conditions flooding) will be designated on the FIRM by use of the proper zone symbols in combination.

(2) Flood Hazard Boundary Map (FHBM). This map is issued by the Administrator delineating Zones A, M, and E within a community.

(b) Notice of the issuance of new or revised FHBMs or FIRMs is given in Part 65 of this subchapter. The mandatory purchase of insurance is required within designated Zones A, A1–30, AE, A99, AO, AH, AR, AR/A1–30, AR/AE, AR/AO, AR/AH, AR/A, V1–30, VE, V, VO, M, and E.

(c) The FHBM or FIRM shall be maintained for public inspection at the following locations:

(1) The information office of the State agency or agencies designated by statute or the respective Governors to cooperate with the Federal Insurance Administrator in implementing the Program whenever a community becomes eligible for Program participation and the sale of insurance pursuant to this section or is identified as flood prone.

(2) One or more official locations within the community in which flood insurance is offered.

(3) [Reserved]

(4) The official record copy of each official map shall be maintained in FEMA files in Washington, DC.

[41 FR 46986, Oct. 26, 1976. Redesignated at 44 FR 31177, May 31, 1979, as amended at 46 FR 1274, Jan. 6, 1981; 48 FR 28278, June 21, 1983; 48 FR 44544 and 44552, Sept. 29, 1983; 49 FR 4751, Feb. 8, 1984; 50 FR 36028, Sept. 4, 1985; 59 FR 53599, Oct. 25, 1994; 62 FR 55716, Oct. 27, 1997; 66 FR 59170, Nov. 27, 2001]

§ 64.4 Effect on community eligibility resulting from boundary changes, governmental reorganization, etc.

(a) When a community not participating in the Program acquires by means of annexation, incorporation, or otherwise, an area within another community participating in the Program, no new flood insurance shall be made available as of the effective date of annexation until the newly acquiring community participates in the Program. Until the effective date of participation, existing flood insurance policies remain in effect until the policy's date of expiration, but shall not be renewed.

(b) When a community participating in the Program acquires by means of annexation, incorporation, or otherwise, another area which was previously located in a community either participating or not participating in the Program, the community shall have six months from the date of acquisition to formally amend its flood plain management regulations in order to include all flood-prone areas within the newly acquired area. The amended regulations shall satisfy the applicable requirements in § 60.3 of this subchapter based on the data previously provided by the Administrator. In the event that the newly acquired area was previously located in a community participating in the Program, the provisions of this section shall only apply if the community, upon acquisition, and pending formal adoption of the amendment to its flood plain management regulations, certifies in writing over the signature of a community official that within the newly acquired area the flood plain management requirements previously applicable in the area remain in force. In the event that the newly-acquired area was previously located in a community not participating in the Program, the provisions

of the section shall only apply if the community, upon acquisition, and pending formal adoption of the amendments to its flood plain management regulations, certifies in writing over the signature of a community official that it shall enforce within the newly-acquired area the requirements of § 60.3(b) of this subchapter. During the six month period, existing flood insurance policies shall remain in effect until their date of expiration may be renewed, and new policies may be issued. Failure to satisfy the applicable requirements in § 60.3 shall result in the community's suspension from Program participation pursuant to § 59.24 of this subchapter.

(c) When an area previously a part of a community participating in the Program becomes autonomous or becomes a portion of a newly autonomous community resulting from boundary changes, governmental reorganization, changes in state statutes or constitution, or otherwise, such new community shall be given six months from the date of its independence, to adopt flood plain management regulations within the special hazard areas subject to its jurisdiction and to submit its application for participation as a separate community in order to retain eligibility for the sale of flood insurance. The regulations adopted by such new community shall satisfy the applicable requirements in § 60.3 of this subchapter based on the data previously provided by the Federal Insurance Administrator. The provisions of this section shall only apply where the new community upon the date of its independence certifies in writing over the signature of a community official that, pending formal adoption of flood plain management regulations, the flood plain management requirements previously applicable in that area remain in effect. During the six month period, existing flood insurance policies shall remain in effect until their dates of expiration may be renewed, and new policies may be issued. Failure to satisfy the applicable requirements in § 60.3 of this subchapter shall result in the community's suspension from Program participation pursuant to § 59.24 of this subchapter.

(d) Where any community or any area within a community had in effect a FHBM or FIRM, but all or a portion of that community has been acquired by another community, or becomes autonomous, that map shall remain in effect until it is superseded by the Federal Insurance Administrator, whether by republication as part of the map of the acquiring community, or otherwise.

(e) When a community described in paragraph (a), (b), (c), or (d) of this section has flood elevations in effect, no new appeal period under parts 66, 67, and 68 of this subchapter will begin except as new scientific and technical data are available.

[41 FR 46986, Oct. 26, 1976. Redesignated at 44 FR 31177, May 31, 1979, as amended at 48 FR 44552, Sept. 29, 1983; 49 FR 4751, Feb. 8, 1984]

§ 64.5 Relationship of rates to zone designations.

(a) In order to expedite a community's qualification for flood insurance under the emergency program, the Administrator may authorize the sale of such insurance without designating any Zones A, M, or E within a community, provided the community has previously adopted flood plain management regulations meeting the requirements of § 60.3(a), § 60.4(a) or § 60.5(a) of this subchapter. When the Administrator has obtained sufficient technical information to delineate Zones A, M, or E, he/she shall delineate the tentative boundaries on a FHBM.

(b) Upon the effective date of the FIRM, flood insurance will continue to be available throughout the entire community at chargeable rates (i.e., subsidized) for first layer coverage of existing structures, but will be only available at risk premium rates for all new construction and substantial improvements. Upon the effective date of a FIRM, second layer coverage is available only at risk premium rates for all structures.

(c) Detailed insurance information may be obtained from the servicing companies. See part 62 of this subchapter.

[41 FR 46986, Oct. 26, 1976. Redesignated at 44 FR 31177, May 31, 1979, as amended at 48 FR 44552, Sept. 29, 1983; 49 FR 4751, Feb. 8, 1984]

§ 64.6 List of eligible communities.

The sale of flood insurance pursuant to the National Flood Insurance Program (42 U.S.C. 4001–4128) is authorized for the communities set forth under this section. Previous listings under this part continue in effect until revised.

[41 FR 46986, Oct. 25, 1976]

EDITORIAL NOTE: For references to FR pages showing lists of eligible communities, see the List of CFR Sections Affected, which appears in the Finding Aids section of the printed volume and at *www.fdsys.gov.*

PART 65—IDENTIFICATION AND MAPPING OF SPECIAL HAZARD AREAS

AUTHORITY: 42 U.S.C. 4001 et seq.; Reorganization Plan No. 3 of 1978, 43 FR 41943, 3 CFR, 1978 Comp., p. 329; E.O. 12127 of Mar. 31, 1979, 44 FR 19367, 3 CFR, 1979 Comp., p. 376.

§ 65.1 Purpose of part.

42 U.S.C. 4104 authorizes the Administrator to identify and publish information with respect to all areas within the United States having special flood,

mudslide (i.e., mudflow) and flood-related erosion hazards. The purpose of this part is to óutline the steps a community needs to take in order to assist the Agency's effort in providing up-to-date identification and publication, in the form of the maps described in part 64, on special flood, mudslide (i.e., mudflow) and flood-related erosion hazards.

[48 FR 28278, June 21, 1983]

§ 65.2 Definitions.

(a) Except as otherwise provided in this part, the definitions set forth in part 59 of this subchapter are applicable to this part.

(b) For the purpose of this part, a certification by a registered professional engineer or other party does not constitute a warranty or guarantee of performance, expressed or implied. Certification of data is a statement that the data is accurate to the best of the certifier's knowledge. Certification of analyses is a statement that the analyses have been performed correctly and in accordance with sound engineering practices. Certification of structural works is a statement that the works are designed in accordance with sound engineering practices to provide protection from the base flood. Certification of "as built" conditions is a statement that the structure(s) has been built according to the plans being certified, is in place, and is fully functioning.

(c) For the purposes of this part, "reasonably safe from flooding" means base flood waters will not inundate the land or damage structures to be removed from the SFHA and that any subsurface waters related to the base flood will not damage existing or proposed buildings.

[51 FR 30313, Aug. 25, 1986, as amended at 66 FR 22442, May 4, 2001]

§ 65.3 Requirement to submit new technical data.

A community's base flood elevations may increase or decrease resulting from physical changes affecting flooding conditions. As soon as practicable, but not later than six months after the date such information becomes available, a community shall notify the Ad-ministrator of the changes by submitting technical or scientific data in accordance with this part. Such a submission is necessary so that upon confirmation of those physical changes affecting flooding conditions, risk premium rates and flood plain management requirements will be based upon current data.

[51 FR 30313, Aug. 25, 1986]

§ 65.4 Right to submit new technical data.

(a) A community has a right to request changes to any of the information shown on an effective map that does not impact flood plain or floodway delineations or base flood elevations, such as community boundary changes, labeling, or planimetric details. Such a submission shall include appropriate supporting documentation in accordance with this part and may be submitted at any time.

(b) All requests for changes to effective maps, other than those initiatedby FEMA, must be made in writing by the Chief Executive Officer of the community (CEO) or an official designated by the CEO. Should the CEO refuse to submit such a request on behalf of another party, FEMA will agree to review it only if written evidence is provided indicating the CEO or designee has been requested to do so.

(c) Requests for changes to effective Flood Insurance Rate Maps (FIRMs) and Flood Boundary and Floodway Maps (FBFMs) are subject to the cost recovery procedures described in 44 CFR part 72. As indicated in part 72, revisions requested to correct mapping errors or errors in the Flood Insurance Study analysis are not to be subject to the cost-recovery procedures.

[51 FR 30313, Aug. 25, 1986, as amended at 57 FR 29038, June 30, 1992; 61 FR 46331, Aug. 30, 1996; 62 FR 5736, Feb. 6, 1997]

EDITORIAL NOTE: For references to FR pages showing lists of eligible communities, see the List of CFR Sections Affected, which appears in the Finding Aids section of the printed volume and at *www.fdsys.gov.*

§ 65.5 Revision to special hazard area boundaries with no change to base flood elevation determinations.

(a) *Data requirements for topographic changes.* In many areas of special flood hazard (excluding V zones and floodways) it may be feasible to elevate areas with engineered earthen fill above the base flood elevation. Scientific and technical information to support a request to gain exclusion from an area of special flood hazard of a structure or parcel of land that has been elevated by the placement of engineered earthen fill will include the following:

(1) A copy of the recorded deed indicating the legal description of the property and the official recordation information (deed book volume and page number) and bearing the seal of the appropriate recordation official (*e.g.*, County Clerk or Recorder of Deeds).

(2) If the property is recorded on a plat map, a copy of the recorded plat indicating both the location of the property and the official recordation information (plat book volume and page number) and bearing the seal of the appropriate recordation official. If the property is not recorded on a plat map, FEMA requires copies of the tax map or other suitable maps to help in locating the property accurately.

(3) A topographic map or other information indicating existing ground elevations and the date of fill. FEMA's determination to exclude a legally defined parcel of land or a structure from the area of special flood hazard will be based upon a comparison of the base flood elevations to the lowest ground elevation of the parcel or the lowest adjacent grade to the structure. If the lowest ground elevation of the entire legally defined parcel of land or the lowest adjacent grade to the structure are at or above the elevations of the base flood, FEMA will exclude the parcel and/or structure from the area of special flood hazard.

(4) Written assurance by the participating community that they have complied with the appropriate minimum floodplain management requirements under § 60.3. This includes the requirements that:

(i) Existing residential structures built in the SFHA have their lowest floor elevated to or above the base flood;

(ii) The participating community has determined that the land and any existing or proposed structures to be removed from the SFHA are "reasonably safe from flooding", and that they have on file, available upon request by FEMA, all supporting analyses and documentation used to make that determination;

(iii) The participating community has issued permits for all existing and proposed construction or other development; and

(iv) All necessary permits have been received from those governmental agencies where approval is required by Federal, State, or local law.

(5) If the community cannot assure that it has complied with the appropriate minimum floodplain management requirements under § 60.3, of this chapter, the map revision request will be deferred until the community remedies all violations to the maximum extent possible through coordination with FEMA. Once the remedies are in place, and the community assures that the land and structures are "reasonably safe from flooding," we will process a revision to the SFHA using the criteria set forth in § 65.5(a). The community must maintain on file, and make available upon request by FEMA, all supporting analyses and documentation used in determining that the land or structures are "reasonably safe from flooding."

(6) Data to substantiate the base flood elevation. If we complete a Flood Insurance Study (FIS), we will use those data to substantiate the base flood elevation. Otherwise, the community may submit data provided by an authoritative source, such as the U.S. Army Corps of Engineers, U.S. Geological Survey, Natural Resources Conservation Service, State and local water resource departments, or technical data prepared and certified by a registered professional engineer. If base flood elevations have not previously been established, we may also request hydrologic and hydraulic calculations.

(7) A revision of floodplain delineations based on fill must demonstrate that any such fill does not result in a floodway encroachment.

(b) *New topographic data.* A community may also follow the procedures described in paragraphs (a)(1) through (6) of this section to request a map revision when no physical changes have occurred in the area of special flood hazard, when no fill has been placed, and when the natural ground elevations are at or above the elevations of the base flood, where new topographic maps are more detailed or more accurate than the current map.

(c) *Certification requirements.* A registered professional engineer or licensed land surveyor must certify the items required in paragraphs (a)(3) and (6) and (b) of this section. Such certifications are subject to the provisions under § 65.2.

(d) *Submission procedures.* Submit all requests to the appropriate address serving the community's geographic area or to the FEMA Headquarters Office in Washington, DC.

[66 FR 22442, May 4, 2001]

§ 65.6 Revision of base flood elevation determinations.

(a) *General conditions and data requirements.* (1) The supporting data must include all the information FEMA needs to review and evaluate the request. This may involve the requestor's performing new hydrologic and hydraulic analysis and delineation of new flood plain boundaries and floodways, as necessary.

(2) To avoid discontinuities between the revised and unrevised flood data, the necessary hydrologic and hydraulic analyses submitted by the map revision requestor must be extensive enough to ensure that a logical transition can be shown between the revised flood elevations, flood plain boundaries, and floodways and those developed previously for areas not affected by the revision. Unless it is demonstrated that it would not be appropriate, the revised and unrevised base flood elevations must match within one-half foot where such transitions occur.

(3) Revisions cannot be made based on the effects of proposed projects or future conditions. Section 65.8 of this subchapter contains provisions for obtaining conditional approval of proposed projects that may effect map changes when they are completed.

(4) The datum and date of releveling of benchmarks, if any, to which the

elevations are referenced must be indicated.

(5) Maps will not be revised when discharges change as a result of the use of an alternative methodology or data for computing flood discharges unless the change is statistically significant as measured by a confidence limits analysis of the new discharge estimates.

(6) Any computer program used to perform hydrologic or hydraulic analyses in support of a flood insurance map revision must meet all of the following criteria:

(i) It must have been reviewed and accepted by a governmental agency responsible for the implementation of programs for flood control and/or the regulation of flood plain lands. For computer programs adopted by non-Federal agencies, certification by a responsible agency official must be provided which states that the program has been reviewed, tested, and accepted by that agency for purposes of design of flood control structures or flood plain land use regulation.

(ii) It must be well-documented including source codes and user's manuals.

(iii) It must be available to FEMA and all present and future parties impacted by flood insurance mapping developed or amended through the use of the program. For programs not generally available from a Federal agency, the source code and user's manuals must be sent to FEMA free of charge, with fully-documented permission from the owner that FEMA may release the code and user's manuals to such impacted parties.

(7) A revised hydrologic analysis for flooding sources with established base flood elevations must include evaluation of the same recurrence interval(s) studied in the effective FIS, such as the 10-, 50-, 100-, and 500-year flood discharges.

(8) A revised hydraulic analysis for a flooding source with established base flood elevations must include evaluation of the same recurrence interval(s) studied in the effective FIS, such as the 10-, 50-, 100-, and 500-year flood elevations, and of the floodway. Unless the basis of the request is the use of an alternative hydraulic methodology or the requestor can demonstrate that the

data of the original hydraulic computer model is unavailable or its use is inappropriate, the analysis shall be made using the same hydraulic computer model used to develop the base flood elevations shown on the effective Flood Insurance Rate Map and updated to show present conditions in the flood plain. Copies of the input and output data from the original and revised hydraulic analyses shall be submitted.

(9) A hydrologic or hydraulic analysis for a flooding source without established base flood elevations may be performed for only the 100-year flood.

(10) A revision of flood plain delineations based on topographic changes must demonstrate that any topographic changes have not resulted in a floodway encroachment.

(11) Delineations of flood plain boundaries for a flooding source with established base flood elevations must provide both the 100- and 500-year flood plain boundaries. For flooding sources without established base flood elevations, only 100-year flood plain boundaries need be submitted. These boundaries should be shown on a topographic map of suitable scale and contour interval.

(12) If a community or other party seeks recognition from FEMA, on its FHBM or FIRM, that an altered or relocated portion of a watercourse provides protection from, or mitigates potential hazards of, the base flood, the Federal Insurance Administrator may request specific documentation from the community certifying that, and describing how, the provisions of §60.3(b)(7) of this subchapter will be met for the particular watercourse involved. This documentation, which may be in the form of a written statement from the Community Chief Executive Officer, an ordinance, or other legislative action, shall describe the nature of the maintenance activities to be performed, the frequency with which they will be performed, and the title of the local community official who will be responsible for assuring that the maintenance activities are accomplished.

(13) Notwithstanding any other provisions of §65.6, a community may submit, in lieu of the documentation specified in §65.6(a)(12), certification by a registered professional engineer that the project has been designed to retain its flood carrying capacity without periodic maintenance.

(14) The participating community must provide written assurance that they have complied with the appropriate minimum floodplain management requirements under §60.3 of this chapter. This includes the requirements that:

(i) Existing residential structures built in the SFHA have their lowest floor elevated to or above the base flood;

(ii) The participating community has determined that the land and any existing or proposed structures to be removed from the SFHA are "reasonably safe from flooding," and that they have on file, available upon request by FEMA, all supporting analyses and documentation used to make that determination;

(iii) The participating community has issued permits for all existing and proposed construction or other development; and

(iv) All necessary permits have been received from those governmental agencies where approval is required by Federal, State, or local law.

(15) If the community cannot assure that it has complied with the appropriate minimum floodplain management requirements under §60.3, of this chapter the map revision request will be deferred until the community remedies all violations to the maximum extent possible through coordination with FEMA. Once the remedies are in place, and the community assures that the land and structures are "reasonably safe from flooding," we will process a revision to the SFHA using the criteria set forth under §65.6. The community must maintain on file, and make available upon request by FEMA, all supporting analyses and documentation used in determining that the land or structures are "reasonably safe from flooding."

(b) *Data requirements for correcting map errors.* To correct errors in the original flood analysis, technical data submissions shall include the following:

(1) Data identifying mathematical errors.

(2) Data identifying measurement errors and providing correct measurements.

(c) *Data requirements for changed physical conditions.* Revisions based on the effects of physical changes that have occurred in the flood plain shall include:

(1) *Changes affecting hydrologic conditions.* The following data must be submitted:

(i) General description of the changes (e.g., dam, diversion channel, or detention basin).

(ii) Construction plans for as-built conditions, if applicable.

(iii) New hydrologic analysis accounting for the effects of the changes.

(iv) New hydraulic analysis and profiles using the new flood discharge values resulting from the hydrologic analysis.

(v) Revised delineations of the flood plain boundaries and floodway.

(2) *Changes affecting hydraulic conditions.* The following data shall be submitted:

(i) General description of the changes (e.g., channelization or new bridge, culvert, or levee).

(ii) Construction plans for as-built conditions.

(iii) New hydraulic analysis and flood elevation profiles accounting for the effects of the changes and using the original flood discharge values upon which the original map is based.

(iv) Revised delineations of the flood plain boundaries and floodway.

(3) *Changes involving topographic conditions.* The following data shall be submitted:

(i) General description of the changes (e.g., grading or filling).

(ii) New topographic information, such as spot elevations, cross sections grading plans, or contour maps.

(iii) Revised delineations of the flood plain boundaries and, if necessary, floodway.

(d) *Data requirements for incorporating improved data.* Requests for revisions based on the use of improved hydrologic, hydraulic, or topographic data shall include the following data:

(1) Data that are believed to be better than those used in the original analysis (such as additional years of stream gage data).

(2) Documentation of the source of the data.

(3) Explanation as to why the use of the new data will improve the results of the original analysis.

(4) Revised hydrologic analysis where hydrologic data are being incorporated.

(5) Revised hydraulic analysis and flood elevation profiles where new hydrologic or hydraulic data are being incorporated.

(6) Revised delineations of the flood plain boundaries and floodway where new hydrologic, hydraulic, or topographic data are being incorporated.

(e) *Data requirements for incorporating improved methods.* Requests for revisions based on the use of improved hydrologic or hydraulic methodology shall include the following data:

(1) New hydrologic analysis when an alternative hydrologic methodology is being proposed.

(2) New hydraulic analysis and flood elevation profiles when an alternative hyrologic or hydraulic methodology is being proposed.

(3) Explanation as to why the alternative methodologies are superior to the original methodologies.

(4) Revised delineations of the flood plain boundaries and floodway based on the new analysis(es).

(f) *Certification requirements.* All analysis and data submitted by the requester shall be certified by a registered professional engineer or licensed land surveyor, as appropriate, subject to the definition of "certification" given at § 65.2 of this subchapter.

(g) *Submission procedures.* All requests shall be submitted to the FEMA Regional Office servicing the community's geographic area or to the FEMA Headquarters Office in Washington, DC, and shall be accompanied by the appropriate payment, in accordance with 44 CFR part 72.

[51 FR 30314, Aug. 25, 1986, as amended at 53 FR 16279, May 6, 1988; 54 FR 33550, Aug. 15, 1989; 61 FR 46331, Aug. 30, 1996; 62 FR 5736, Feb. 6, 1997; 66 FR 22442, May 4, 2001]

§ 65.7   Floodway revisions.

(a) *General.* Floodway data is developed as part of FEMA Flood Insurance Studies and is utilized by communities to select and adopt floodways as part of the flood plain management program required by §60.3 of this subchapter. When it has been determined by a community that no practicable alternatives exist to revising the boundaries of its previously adopted floodway, the procedures below shall be followed.

(b) *Data requirements when base flood elevation changes are requested.* When a floodway revision is requested in association with a change to base flood elevations, the data requirements of §65.6 shall also be applicable. In addition, the following documentation shall be submitted:

(1) Copy of a public notice distributed by the community stating the community's intent to revise the floodway or a statement by the community that it has notified all affected property owners and affected adjacent jurisdictions.

(2) Copy of a letter notifying the appropriate State agency of the floodway revision when the State has jurisdiction over the floodway or its adoption by communities participating in the NFIP.

(3) Documentation of the approval of the revised floodway by the appropriate State agency (for communities where the State has jurisdiction over the floodway or its adoption by communities participating in the NFIP).

(4) Engineering analysis for the revised floodway, as described below:

(i) The floodway analysis must be performed using the hydraulic computer model used to determine the proposed base flood elevations.

(ii) The floodway limits must be set so that neither the effective base flood elevations nor the proposed base flood elevations if less than the effective base flood elevations, are increased by more than the amount specified under §60.3 (d)(2). Copies of the input and output data from the original and modified computer models must be submitted.

(5) Delineation of the revised floodway on the same topographic map used for the delineation of the revised flood boundaries.

(c) *Data requirements for changes not associated with base flood elevation changes.* The following data shall be submitted:

(1) Items described in paragraphs (b) (1) through (3) of this section must be submitted.

(2) Engineering analysis for the revised floodway, as described below:

(i) The original hydraulic computer model used to develop the established base flood elevations must be modified to include all encroachments that have occurred in the flood plain since the existing floodway was developed. If the original hydraulic computer model is not available, an alternate hydraulic computer model may be used provided the alternate model has been calibrated so as to reproduce the original water surface profile of the original hydraulic computer model. The alternate model must be then modified to include all encroachments that have occurred since the existing floodway was developed.

(ii) The floodway analysis must be performed with the modified computer model using the desired floodway limits.

(iii) The floodway limits must be set so that combined effects of the past encroachments and the new floodway limits do not increase the effective base flood elevations by more than the amount specified in §60.3(d)(2). Copies of the input and output data from the original and modified computer models must be submitted.

(3) Delineation of the revised floodway on a copy of the effective NFIP map and a suitable topographic map.

(d) *Certification requirements.* All analyses submitted shall be certified by a registered professional engineer. All topographic data shall be certified by a registered professional engineer or licensed land surveyor. Certifications are subject to the definition given at §65.2 of this subchapter.

(e) *Submission procedures.* All requests that involve changes to floodways shall be submitted to the appropriate FEMA Regional Office servicing the community's geographic area.

[51 FR 30315, Aug. 25, 1986]

§65.8 Review of proposed projects.

A community, or an individual through the community, may request FEMA's comments on whether a proposed project, if built as proposed, would justify a map revision. FEMA's comments will be issued in the form of a letter, termed a Conditional Letter of Map Revision, in accordance with 44 CFR part 72. The data required to support such requests are the same as those required for final revisions under §§ 65.5, 65.6, and 65.7, except as-built certification is not required. All such requests shall be submitted to the FEMA Headquarters Office in Washington, DC, and shall be accompanied by the appropriate payment, in accordance with 44 CFR part 72.

[62 FR 5736, Feb. 6, 1997]

§ 65.9 Review and response by the Administrator.

If any questions or problems arise during review, FEMA will consult the Chief Executive Officer of the community (CEO), the community official designated by the CEO, and/or the requester for resolution. Upon receipt of a revision request, the Federal Insurance Administrator shall mail an acknowledgment of receipt of such request to the CEO. Within 90 days of receiving the request with all necessary information, the Federal Insurance Administrator shall notify the CEO of one or more of the following:

(a) The effective map(s) shall not be modified;

(b) The base flood elevations on the effective FIRM shall be modified and new base flood elevations shall be established under the provisions of part 67 of this subchapter;

(c) The changes requested are approved and the map(s) amended by Letter of Map Revision (LOMR);

(d) The changes requested are approved and a revised map(s) will be printed and distributed;

(e) The changes requested are not of such a significant nature as to warrant a reissuance or revision of the flood insurance study or maps and will be deferred until such time as a significant change occurs;

(f) An additional 90 days is required to evaluate the scientific or technical data submitted; or

(g) Additional data are required to support the revision request.

(h) The required payment has not been submitted in accordance with 44 CFR part 72, no review will be conducted and no determination will be issued until payment is received.

[51 FR 30315, Aug. 25, 1986; 61 FR 46331, Aug. 30, 1996, as amended at 62 FR 5736, Feb. 6, 1997]

§ 65.10 Mapping of areas protected by levee systems.

(a) *General.* For purposes of the NFIP, FEMA will only recognize in its flood hazard and risk mapping effort those levee systems that meet, and continue to meet, minimum design, operation, and maintenance standards that are consistent with the level of protection sought through the comprehensive flood plain management criteria established by § 60.3 of this subchapter. Accordingly, this section describes the types of information FEMA needs to recognize, on NFIP maps, that a levee system provides protection from the base flood. This information must be supplied to FEMA by the community or other party seeking recognition of such a levee system at the time a flood risk study or restudy is conducted, when a map revision under the provisions of part 65 of this subchapter is sought based on a levee system, and upon request by the Federal Insurance Administrator during the review of previously recognized structures. The FEMA review will be for the sole purpose of establishing appropriate risk zone determinations for NFIP maps and shall not constitute a determination by FEMA as to how a structure or system will perform in a flood event.

(b) *Design criteria.* For levees to be recognized by FEMA, evidence that adequate design and operation and maintenance systems are in place to provide reasonable assurance that protection from the base flood exists must be provided. The following requirements must be met:

(1) *Freeboard.* (i) Riverine levees must provide a minimum freeboard of three feet above the water-surface level of the base flood. An additional one foot above the minimum is required within 100 feet in either side of structures (such as bridges) riverward of the levee or wherever the flow is constricted. An additional one-half foot above the minimum at the upstream end of the levee, tapering to not less than the minimum

at the downstream end of the levee, is also required.

(ii) Occasionally, exceptions to the minimum riverine freeboard requirement described in paragraph (b)(1)(i) of this section, may be approved. Appropriate engineering analyses demonstrating adequate protection with a lesser freeboard must be submitted to support a request for such an exception. The material presented must evaluate the uncertainty in the estimated base flood elevation profile and include, but not necessarily be limited to an assessment of statistical confidence limits of the 100-year discharge; changes in stage-discharge relationships; and the sources, potential, and magnitude of debris, sediment, and ice accumulation. It must be also shown that the levee will remain structurally stable during the base flood when such additional loading considerations are imposed. Under no circumstances will freeboard of less than two feet be accepted.

(iii) For coastal levees, the freeboard must be established at one foot above the height of the one percent wave or the maximum wave runup (whichever is greater) associated with the 100-year stillwater surge elevation at the site.

(iv) Occasionally, exceptions to the minimum coastal levee freeboard requirement described in paragraph (b)(1)(iii) of this section, may be approved. Appropriate engineering analyses demonstrating adequate protection with a lesser freeboard must be submitted to support a request for such an exception. The material presented must evaluate the uncertainty in the estimated base flood loading conditions. Particular emphasis must be placed on the effects of wave attack and overtopping on the stability of the levee. Under no circumstances, however, will a freeboard of less than two feet above the 100-year stillwater surge elevation be accepted.

(2) *Closures.* All openings must be provided with closure devices that are structural parts of the system during operation and design according to sound engineering practice.

(3) *Embankment protection.* Engineering analyses must be submitted that demonstrate that no appreciable erosion of the levee embankment can be expected during the base flood, as a result of either currents or waves, and that anticipated erosion will not result in failure of the levee embankment or foundation directly or indirectly through reduction of the seepage path and subsequent instability. The factors to be addressed in such analyses include, but are not limited to: Expected flow velocities (especially in constricted areas); expected wind and wave action; ice loading; impact of debris; slope protection techniques; duration of flooding at various stages and velocities; embankment and foundation materials; levee alignment, bends, and transitions; and levee side slopes.

(4) *Embankment and foundation stability.* Engineering analyses that evaluate levee embankment stability must be submitted. The analyses provided shall evaluate expected seepage during loading conditions associated with the base flood and shall demonstrate that seepage into or through the levee foundation and embankment will not jeopardize embankment or foundation stability. An alternative analysis demonstrating that the levee is designed and constructed for stability against loading conditions for Case IV as defined in the U.S. Army Corps of Engineers (COE) manual, "Design and Construction of Levees" (EM 1110–2–1913, Chapter 6, Section II), may be used. The factors that shall be addressed in the analyses include: Depth of flooding, duration of flooding, embankment geometry and length of seepage path at critical locations, embankment and foundation materials, embankment compaction, penetrations, other design factors affecting seepage (such as drainage layers), and other design factors affecting embankment and foundation stability (such as berms).

(5) *Settlement.* Engineering analyses must be submitted that assess the potential and magnitude of future losses of freeboard as a result of levee settlement and demonstrate that freeboard will be maintained within the minimum standards set forth in paragraph (b)(1) of this section. This analysis must address embankment loads, compressibility of embankment soils, compressibility of foundation soils, age of the levee system, and construction

compaction methods. In addition, detailed settlement analysis using procedures such as those described in the COE manual, "Soil Mechanics Design—Settlement Analysis" (EM 1100-2-1904) must be submitted.

(6) *Interior drainage.* An analysis must be submitted that identifies the source(s) of such flooding, the extent of the flooded area, and, if the average depth is greater than one foot, the water-surface elevation(s) of the base flood. This analysis must be based on the joint probability of interior and exterior flooding and the capacity of facilities (such as drainage lines and pumps) for evacuating interior floodwaters.

(7) *Other design criteria.* In unique situations, such as those where the levee system has relatively high vulnerability, FEMA may require that other design criteria and analyses be submitted to show that the levees provide adequate protection. In such situations, sound engineering practice will be the standard on which FEMA will base its determinations. FEMA will also provide the rationale for requiring this additional information.

(c) *Operation plans and criteria.* For a levee system to be recognized, the operational criteria must be as described below. All closure devices or mechanical systems for internal drainage, whether manual or automatic, must be operated in accordance with an officially adopted operation manual, a copy of which must be provided to FEMA by the operator when levee or drainage system recognition is being sought or when the manual for a previously recognized system is revised in any manner. All operations must be under the jurisdiction of a Federal or State agency, an agency created by Federal or State law, or an agency of a community participating in the NFIP.

(1) *Closures.* Operation plans for closures must include the following:

(i) Documentation of the flood warning system, under the jurisdiction of Federal, State, or community officials, that will be used to trigger emergency operation activities and demonstration that sufficient flood warning time exists for the completed operation of all closure structures, including necessary sealing, before floodwaters reach the base of the closure.

(ii) A formal plan of operation including specific actions and assignments of responsibility by individual name or title.

(iii) Provisions for periodic operation, at not less than one-year intervals, of the closure structure for testing and training purposes.

(2) *Interior drainage systems.* Interior drainage systems associated with levee systems usually include storage areas, gravity outlets, pumping stations, or a combination thereof. These drainage systems will be recognized by FEMA on NFIP maps for flood protection purposes only if the following minimum criteria are included in the operation plan:

(i) Documentation of the flood warning system, under the jurisdiction of Federal, State, or community officials, that will be used to trigger emergency operation activities and demonstration that sufficient flood warning time exists to permit activation of mechanized portions of the drainage system.

(ii) A formal plan of operation including specific actions and assignments of responsibility by individual name or title.

(iii) Provision for manual backup for the activation of automatic systems.

(iv) Provisions for periodic inspection of interior drainage systems and periodic operation of any mechanized portions for testing and training purposes. No more than one year shall elapse between either the inspections or the operations.

(3) *Other operation plans and criteria.* Other operating plans and criteria may be required by FEMA to ensure that adequate protection is provided in specific situations. In such cases, sound emergency management practice will be the standard upon which FEMA determinations will be based.

(d) *Maintenance plans and criteria.* For levee systems to be recognized as providing protection from the base flood, the maintenance criteria must be as described herein. Levee systems must be maintained in accordance with an officially adopted maintenance plan, and a copy of this plan must be provided to FEMA by the owner of the levee system when recognition is being sought or when the plan for a previously recognized system is revised in any manner. All maintenance activities must be under the jurisdiction of a Federal or State agency, an agency created by Federal or State law, or an agency of a community participating in the NFIP that must assume ultimate responsibility for maintenance. This plan must document the formal procedure that ensures that the stability, height, and overall integrity of the levee and its associated structures and systems are maintained. At a minimum, maintenance plans shall specify the maintenance activities to be performed, the frequency of their performance, and the person by name or title responsible for their performance.

(e) *Certification requirements.* Data submitted to support that a given levee system complies with the structural requirements set forth in paragraphs (b)(1) through (7) of this section must be certified by a registered professional engineer. Also, certified as-built plans of the levee must be submitted. Certifications are subject to the definition given at § 65.2 of this subchapter. In lieu of these structural requirements, a Federal agency with responsibility for levee design may certify that the levee has been adequately designed and constructed to provide protection against the base flood.

[51 FR 30316, Aug. 25, 1986]

§ 65.11 Evaluation of sand dunes in mapping coastal flood hazard areas.

(a) *General conditions.* For purposes of the NFIP, FEMA will consider storm-induced dune erosion potential in its determination of coastal flood hazards and risk mapping efforts. The criterion to be used in the evaluation of dune erosion will apply to primary frontal dunes as defined in § 59.1, but does not apply to artificially designed and constructed dunes that are not well-established with long-standing vegetative cover, such as the placement of sand materials in a dune-like formation.

(b) *Evaluation criterion.* Primary frontal dunes will not be considered as effective barriers to base flood storm surges and associated wave action where the cross-sectional area of the primary frontal dune, as measured perpendicular to the shoreline and above the 100-year stillwater flood elevation and seaward of the dune crest, is equal to, or less than, 540 square feet.

(c) *Exceptions.* Exceptions to the evaluation criterion may be granted where it can be demonstrated through authoritative historical documentation that the primary frontal dunes at a specific site withstood previous base flood storm surges and associated wave action.

[53 FR 16279, May 6, 1988]

§ 65.12 Revision of flood insurance rate maps to reflect base flood elevations caused by proposed encroachments.

(a) When a community proposes to permit encroachments upon the flood plain when a regulatory floodway has not been adopted or to permit encroachments upon an adopted regulatory floodway which will cause base flood elevation increases in excess of those permitted under paragraphs (c)(10) or (d)(3) of § 60.3 of this subchapter, the community shall apply to the Federal Insurance Administrator for conditional approval of such action prior to permitting the encroachments to occur and shall submit the following as part of its application:

(1) A request for conditional approval of map change and the appropriate initial fee as specified by § 72.3 of this subchapter or a request for exemption from fees as specified by § 72.5 of this subchapter, whichever is appropriate;

(2) An evaluation of alternatives which would not result in a base flood elevation increase above that permitted under paragraphs (c)(10) or (d)(3) of § 60.3 of this subchapter demonstrating why these alternatives are not feasible;

(3) Documentation of individual legal notice to all impacted property owners within and outside of the community, explaining the impact of the proposed action on their property.

(4) Concurrence of the Chief Executive Officer of any other communities impacted by the proposed actions;

(5) Certification that no structures are located in areas which would be impacted by the increased base flood elevation;

(6) A request for revision of base flood elevation determination according to the provisions of § 65.6 of this part;

(7) A request for floodway revision in accordance with the provisions of § 65.7 of this part;

(b) Upon receipt of the Federal Insurance Administrator's conditional approval of map change and prior to approving the proposed encroachments, a community shall provide evidence to the Federal Insurance Administrator of the adoption of flood plain management ordinances incorporating the increased base flood elevations and/or revised floodway reflecting the post-project condition.

(c) Upon completion of the proposed encroachments, a community shall provide as-built certifications in accordance with the provisions of § 65.3 of this part. The Federal Insurance Administrator will initiate a final map revision upon receipt of such certifications in accordance with part 67 of this subchapter.

[53 FR 16279, May 6, 1988]

§ 65.13 Mapping and map revisions for areas subject to alluvial fan flooding.

This section describes the procedures to be followed and the types of information FEMA needs to recognize on a NFIP map that a structural flood control measure provides protection from the base flood in an area subject to alluvial fan flooding. This information must be supplied to FEMA by the community or other party seeking recognition of such a flood control measure at the time a flood risk study or restudy is conducted, when a map revision under the provisions of part 65 of this subchapter is sought, and upon request by the Federal Insurance Administrator during the review of previously recognized flood control measures. The FEMA review will be for the sole purpose of establishing appropriate risk zone determinations for NFIP maps and shall not constitute a determination by FEMA as to how the flood control measure will perform in a flood event.

(a) The applicable provisions of §§ 65.2, 65.3, 65.4, 65.6, 65.8 and 65.10 shall also apply to FIRM revisions involving alluvial fan flooding.

(b) The provisions of § 65.5 regarding map revisions based on fill and the provisions of part 70 of this chapter shall not apply to FIRM revisions involving alluvial fan flooding. In general, elevations of a parcel of land or a structure by fill or other means, will not serve as a basis for removing areas subject to alluvial fan flooding from an area of special food hazards.

(c) FEMA will credit on NFIP maps only major structural flood control measures whose design and construction are supported by sound engineering analyses which demonstrate that the measures will effectively eliminate alluvial fan flood hazards from the area protected by such measures. The provided analyses must include, but are not necessarily limited to, the following:

(1) Engineering analyses that quantify the discharges and volumes of water, debris, and sediment movement associated with the flood that has a one-percent probability of being exceeded in any year at the apex under current watershed conditions and under potential adverse conditions (e.g., deforestation of the watershed by fire). The potential for debris flow and sediment movement must be assessed using an engineering method acceptable to FEMA. The assessment should consider the characteristics and availability of sediment in the drainage basin above the apex and on the alluvial fan.

(2) Engineering analyses showing that the measures will accommodate the estimated peak discharges and volumes of water, debris, and sediment, as determined in accordance with paragraph (c)(1) of this section, and will withstand the associated hydrodynamic and hydrostatic forces.

(3) Engineering analyses showing that the measures have been designed to withstand the potential erosion and scour associated with estimated discharges.

(4) Engineering analyses or evidence showing that the measures will provide protection from hazards associated with the possible relocation of flow paths from other parts of the fan.

(5) Engineering analyses that assess the effect of the project on flood hazards, including depth and velocity of floodwaters and scour and sediment deposition, on other areas of the fan.

(6) Engineering analyses demonstrating that flooding from sources other than the fan apex, including local runoff, is either insignificant or has been accounted for in the design.

(d) *Coordination.* FEMA will recognize measures that are adequately designed and constructed, provided that: evidence is submitted to show that the impact of the measures on flood hazards in all areas of the fan (including those not protected by the flood control measures), and the design and maintenance requirements of the measures, were reviewed and approved by the impacted communities, and also by State and local agencies that have jurisdiction over flood control activities.

(e) *Operation and maintenance plans and criteria.* The requirements for operation and maintenance of flood control measures on areas subject to alluvial fan flooding shall be those specified under § 65.10, paragraphs (c) and (d), when applicable.

(f) *Certification requirements.* Data submitted to support that a given flood control measure complies with the requirements set forth in paragraphs (c) (1) through (6) of this section must be certified by a registered professional engineer. Also, certified as-built plans of the flood control measures must be submitted. Certifications are subject to the definition given at § 65.2.

[54 FR 33551, Aug. 15, 1989, as amended at 74 FR 15342, Apr. 3, 2009]

§ 65.14 Remapping of areas for which local flood protection systems no longer provide base flood protection.

(a) *General.* (1) This section describes the procedures to follow and the types of information FEMA requires to designate flood control restoration zones. A community may be eligible to apply for this zone designation if the Federal Insurance Administrator determines that it is engaged in the process of restoring a flood protection system that was:

(i) Constructed using Federal funds;

(ii) Recognized as providing base flood protection on the community's effective FIRM; and

(iii) Decertified by a Federal agency responsible for flood protection design or construction.

(2) Where the Federal Insurance Administrator determines that a community is in the process of restoring its flood protection system to provide base flood protection, a FIRM will be prepared that designates the temporary flood hazard areas as a flood control restoration zone (Zone AR). Existing special flood hazard areas shown on the community's effective FIRM that are further inundated by Zone AR flooding shall be designated as a "dual" flood insurance rate zone, Zone AR/AE or AR/AH with Zone AR base flood elevations, and AE or AH with base flood elevations and Zone AR/AO with Zone AR base flood elevations and Zone AO with flood depths, or Zone AR/A with Zone AR base flood elevations and Zone A without base flood elevations.

(b) *Limitations.* A community may have a flood control restoration zone designation only once while restoring a flood protection system. This limitation does not preclude future flood control restoration zone designations should a fully restored, certified, and accredited system become decertified for a second or subsequent time.

(1) A community that receives Federal funds for the purpose of designing or constructing, or both, the restoration project must complete restoration or meet the requirements of 44 CFR 61.12 within a specified period, not to exceed a maximum of 10 years from the date of submittal of the community's application for designation of a flood control restoration zone.

(2) A community that does not receive Federal funds for the purpose of constructing the restoration project must complete restoration within a specified period, not to exceed a maximum of 5 years from the date of submittal of the community's application for designation of a flood control restoration zone. Such a community is not eligible for the provisions of § 61.12. The designated restoration period may not be extended beyond the maximum allowable under this limitation.

(c) *Exclusions.* The provisions of these regulations do not apply in a coastal high hazard area as defined in 44 CFR 59.1, including areas that would be subject to coastal high hazards as a result of the decertification of a flood protection system shown on the community's effective FIRM as providing base flood protection.

(d) *Effective date for risk premium rates.* The effective date for any risk premium rates established for Zone AR shall be the effective date of the revised FIRM showing Zone AR designations.

(e) *Application and submittal requirements for designation of a flood control restoration zone.* A community must submit a written request to the Federal Insurance Administrator, signed by the community's Chief Executive Officer, for a flood plain designation as a flood control restoration zone. The request must include a legislative action by the community requesting the designation. The Federal Insurance Administrator will not initiate any action to designate flood control restoration zones without receipt of the formal request from the community that complies with all requirements of this section. The Federal Insurance Administrator reserves the right to request additional information from the community to support or further document the community's formal request for designation of a flood control restoration zone, if deemed necessary.

(1) At a minimum, the request from a community that receives Federal funds for the purpose of designing, constructing, or both, the restoration project must include:

(i) A statement whether, to the best of the knowledge of the community's Chief Executive Officer, the flood protection system is currently the subject matter of litigation before any Federal, State or local court or administrative agency, and if so, the purpose of that litigation;

(ii) A statement whether the community has previously requested a determination with respect to the same subject matter from the Federal Insurance Administrator, and if so, a statement that details the disposition of such previous request;

(iii) A statement from the community and certification by a Federal agency responsible for flood protection design or construction that the existing flood control system shown on the effective FIRM was originally built using Federal funds, that it no longer provides base flood protection, but that it continues to provide protection from the flood having at least a 3-percent chance of occurrence during any given year;

(iv) An official map of the community or legal description, with supporting documentation, that the community will adopt as part of its flood plain management measures, which designates developed areas as defined in § 59.1 and as further defined in § 60.3(f).

(v) A restoration plan to return the system to a level of base flood protection. At a minimum, this plan must:

(A) List all important project elements, such as acquisition of permits, approvals, and contracts and construction schedules of planned features;

(B) Identify anticipated start and completion dates for each element, as well as significant milestones and dates;

(C) Identify the date on which "as built" drawings and certification for the completed restoration project will be submitted. This date must provide for a restoration period not to exceed the maximum allowable restoration period for the flood protection system, or;

(D) Identify the date on which the community will submit a request for a finding of adequate progress that meets all requirements of § 61.12. This date may not exceed the maximum allowable restoration period for the flood protection system;

(vi) A statement identifying the local project sponsor responsible for restoration of the flood protection system;

(vii) A copy of a study, performed by a Federal agency responsible for flood protection design or construction in consultation with the local project sponsor, which demonstrates a Federal interest in restoration of the system and which deems that the flood protection system is restorable to a level of base flood protection.

(viii) A joint statement from the Federal agency responsible for flood protection design or construction involved in restoration of the flood protection system and the local project sponsor certifying that the design and construction of the flood control system involves Federal funds, and that the restoration of the flood protection system will provide base flood protection;

(2) At a minimum, the request from a community that receives no Federal funds for the purpose of constructing the restoration project must:

(i) Meet the requirements of §65.14(e)(1)(i) through (iv);

(ii) Include a restoration plan to return the system to a level of base flood protection. At a minimum, this plan must:

(A) List all important project elements, such as acquisition of permits, approvals, and contracts and construction schedules of planned features;

(B) Identify anticipated start and completion dates for each element, as well as significant milestones and dates; and

(C) Identify the date on which "as built" drawings and certification for the completed restoration project will be submitted. This date must provide for a restoration period not to exceed the maximum allowable restoration period for the flood protection system;

(iii) Include a statement identifying the local agency responsible for restoration of the flood protection system;

(iv) Include a copy of a study, certified by registered Professional Engineer, that demonstrates that the flood protection system is restorable to provide protection from the base flood;

(v) Include a statement from the local agency responsible for restoration of the flood protection system certifying that the restored flood protection system will meet the applicable requirements of Part 65; and

(vi) Include a statement from the local agency responsible for restoration of the flood protection system that identifies the source of funds for the purpose of constructing the restoration project and a percentage of the total funds contributed by each source. The statement must demonstrate, at a minimum, that 100 percent of the total financial project cost of the completed flood protection system has been appropriated.

(f) *Review and response by the Federal Insurance Administrator.* The review and response by the Federal Insurance Administrator shall be in accordance with procedures specified in §65.9.

(g) *Requirements for maintaining designation of a flood control restoration zone.* During the restoration period, the community and the cost-sharing Federal agency, if any, must certify annually to the FEMA Regional Office having jurisdiction that the restoration will be completed in accordance with the restoration plan within the time period specified by the plan. In addition, the community and the cost-sharing Federal agency, if any, will update the restoration plan and will identify any permitting or construction problems that will delay the project completion from the restoration plan previously submitted to the Federal Insurance Administrator. The FEMA Regional Office having jurisdiction will make an annual assessment and recommendation to the Federal Insurance Administrator as to the viability of the restoration plan and will conduct periodic on-site inspections of the flood protection system under restoration.

(h) *Procedures for removing flood control restoration zone designation due to adequate progress or complete restoration of the flood protection system.* At any time during the restoration period:

(1) A community that receives Federal funds for the purpose of designing, constructing, or both, the restoration project shall provide written evidence of certification from a Federal agency having flood protection design or construction responsibility that the necessary improvements have been completed and that the system has been restored to provide protection from the base flood, or submit a request for a finding of adequate progress that meets all requirements of §61.12. If the Administrator determines that adequate progress has been made, FEMA will revise the zone designation from a flood control restoration zone designation to Zone A99.

303

(2) After the improvements have been completed, certified by a Federal agency as providing base flood protection, and reviewed by FEMA, FEMA will revise the FIRM to reflect the completed flood control system.

(3) A community that receives no Federal funds for the purpose of constructing the restoration project must provide written evidence that the restored flood protection system meets the requirements of Part 65. A community that receives no Federal funds for the purpose of constructing the restoration project is not eligible for a finding of adequate progress under § 61.12.

(4) After the improvements have been completed and reviewed by FEMA, FEMA will revise the FIRM to reflect the completed flood protection system.

(i) *Procedures for removing flood control restoration zone designation due to non-compliance with the restoration schedule or as a result of a finding that satisfactory progress is not being made to complete the restoration.* At any time during the restoration period, should the Federal Insurance Administrator determine that the restoration will not be completed in accordance with the time frame specified in the restoration plan, or that satisfactory progress is not being made to restore the flood protection system to provide complete flood protection in accordance with the restoration plan, the Federal Insurance Administrator shall notify the community and the responsible Federal agency, in writing, of the determination, the reasons for that determination, and that the FIRM will be revised to remove the flood control restoration zone designation. Within thirty (30) days of such notice, the community may submit written information that provides assurance that the restoration will be completed in accordance with the time frame specified in the restoration plan, or that satisfactory progress is being made to restore complete protection in accordance with the restoration plan, or that, with reasonable certainty, the restoration will be completed within the maximum allowable restoration period. On the basis of this information the Federal Insurance Administrator may suspend the decision to revise the FIRM to remove the flood control res-

toration zone designation. If the community does not submit any information, or if, based on a review of the information submitted, there is sufficient cause to find that the restoration will not be completed as provided for in the restoration plan, the Federal Insurance Administrator shall revise the FIRM, in accordance with 44 CFR Part 67, and shall remove the flood control restoration zone designations and shall redesignate those areas as Zone A1–30, AE, AH, AO, or A.

[62 FR 55717, Oct. 27, 1997]

§ 65.15 List of communities submitting new technical data.

This section provides a cumulative list of communities where modifications of the base flood elevation determinations have been made because of submission of new scientific or technical data. Due to the need for expediting the modifications, the revised map is already in effect and the appeal period commences on or about the effective date of the modified map. An interim rule, followed by a final rule, will list the revised map effective date, local repository and the name and address of the Chief Executive Officer of the community. The map(s) is (are) effective for both flood plain management and insurance purposes.

[51 FR 30317, Aug. 25, 1986. Redesignated at 53 FR 16279, May 6, 1988, and further redesignated at 54 FR 33551, Aug. 15, 1989. Redesignated at 59 FR 53599, Oct. 25, 1994]

EDITORIAL NOTE: For references to FR pages showing lists of eligible communities, see the List of CFR Sections Affected, which appears in the Finding Aids section of the printed volume and at *www.fdsys.gov.*

§ 65.16 Standard Flood Hazard Determination Form and Instructions.

(a) Section 528 of the National Flood Insurance Reform Act of 1994 (42 U.S.C. 1365(a)) directs FEMA to develop a standard form for determining, in the case of a loan secured by improved real estate or a mobile home, whether the building or mobile home is located in an area identified by the Director as an area having special flood hazards and in which flood insurance under this title is available. The purpose of the form is to determine whether a building or mobile home is located within an identified Special Flood Hazard Area (SFHA), whether flood insurance is required, and whether federal flood insurance is available. Use of this form will ensure that required flood insurance coverage is purchased for structures located in an SFHA, and will assist federal entities for lending regulation in assuring compliance with these purchase requirements.

(b) The form is available by written request to Federal Emergency Management Agency, PO Box 2012, Jessup, MD 20794; ask for the Standard Flood Hazard Determination form. It is also available by fax-on-demand; call (202) 646–3362, form #23103. Finally, the form is available through the Internet at *http://www.fema.gov/nfip/mpurfi.htm*.

[63 FR 27857, May 21, 1998]

§65.17 Review of determinations.

This section describes the procedures that shall be followed and the types of information required by FEMA to review a determination of whether a building or manufactured home is located within an identified Special Flood Hazard Area (SFHA).

(a) *General conditions.* The borrower and lender of a loan secured by improved real estate or a manufactured home may jointly request that FEMA review a determination that the building or manufactured home is located in an identified SFHA. Such a request must be submitted within 45 days of the lender's notification to the borrower that the building or manufactured home is in the SFHA and that flood insurance is required. Such a request must be submitted jointly by the lender and the borrower and shall include the required fee and technical information related to the building or manufactured home. Elevation data will not be considered under the procedures described in this section.

(b) *Data and other requirements.* Items required for FEMA's review of a determination shall include the following:

(1) Payment of the required fee by check or money order, in U.S. funds, payable to the National Flood Insurance Program;

(2) A request for FEMA's review of the determination, signed by both the borrower and the lender;

(3) A copy of the lender's notification to the borrower that the building or manufactured home is in an SFHA and that flood insurance is required (the request for review of the determination must be postmarked within 45 days of borrower notification);

(4) A completed Standard Flood Hazard Determination Form for the building or manufactured home, together with a legible hard copy of all technical data used in making the determination; and

(5) A copy of the effective NFIP map (Flood Hazard Boundary Map (FHBM) or Flood Insurance Rate Map (FIRM)) panel for the community in which the building or manufactured home is located, with the building or manufactured home location indicated. Portions of the map panel may be submitted but shall include the area of the building or manufactured home in question together with the map panel title block, including effective date, bar scale, and north arrow.

(c) *Review and response by FEMA.* Within 45 days after receipt of a request to review a determination, FEMA will notify the applicants in writing of one of the following:

(1) Request submitted more than 45 days after borrower notification; no review will be performed and all materials are being returned;

(2) Insufficient information was received to review the determination; therefore, the determination stands until a complete submittal is received; or

(3) The results of FEMA's review of the determination, which shall include the following:

(i) The name of the NFIP community in which the building or manufactured home is located;

(ii) The property address or other identification of the building or manufactured home to which the determination applies;

(iii) The NFIP map panel number and effective date upon which the determination is based;

(iv) A statement indicating whether the building or manufactured home is within the Special Flood Hazard Area;

(v) The time frame during which the determination is effective.

[60 FR 62218, Dec. 5, 1995]

PART 66—CONSULTATION WITH LOCAL OFFICIALS

Sec.
66.1 Purpose of part.
66.2 Definitions.
66.3 Establishment of community case file and flood elevation study docket.
66.4 Appointment of consultation coordination officer.
66.5 Responsibilities for consultation and coordination.

AUTHORITY: 42 U.S.C. 4001 *et seq.*; Reorganization Plan No. 3 of 1978; E.O. 12127.

§ 66.1 Purpose of part.

(a) The purpose of this part is to comply with section 206 of the Flood Disaster Protection Act of 1973 (42 U.S.C. 4107) by establishing procedures for flood elevation determinations of Zones A1–30, AE, AH, AO and V1–30, and VE within the community so that adequate consultation with the community officials shall be assured.

(b) The procedures in this part shall apply when base flood elevations are to be determined or modified.

(c) The Federal Insurance Administrator or his delegate shall:

(1) Specifically request that the community submit pertinent data concerning flood hazards, flooding experience, plans to avoid potential hazards, estimate of historical and prospective economic impact on the community, and such other appropriate data (particularly if such data will necessitate a modification of a base flood elevation).

(2) Notify local officials of the progress of surveys, studies, investigations, and of prospective findings, along with data and methods employed in reaching such conclusions; and

(3) Encourage local dissemination of surveys, studies, and investigations so that interested persons will have an opportunity to bring relevant data to the attention of the community and to the Federal Insurance Administrator.

(4) Carry out the responsibilities for consultation and coordination set forth in § 66.5 of this part.

[41 FR 46988, Oct. 26, 1976. Redesignated at 44 FR 31177, May 31, 1979, as amended at 47 FR 771, Jan. 7, 1982; 48 FR 44553, Sept. 29, 1983; 49 FR 4751, Feb. 8, 1984; 50 FR 36028, Sept. 4, 1985]

§ 66.2 Definitions.

The definitions set forth in part 59 of this subchapter are applicable to this part.

[41 FR 46988, Oct. 26, 1976. Redesignated at 44 FR 31177, May 31, 1979]

§ 66.3 Establishment of community case file and flood elevation study docket.

(a) A file shall be established for each community at the time initial consideration is given to studying that community in order to establish whether or not it contains flood-prone areas. Thereafter, the file shall include copies of all correspondence with officials in that community. As the community is tentatively identified, provided with base flood elevations, or suspended and reinstated, documentation of such actions by the Federal Insurance Administrator shall be placed in the community file. Even if a map is administratively rescinded or withdrawn after notice under part 65 of this subchapter or the community successfully rebuts its flood-prone designation, the file will be maintained indefinitely.

(b) A portion of the community file shall be designated a flood elevation study consultation docket and shall be established for each community at the time the contract is awarded for a flood elevation study. The docket shall include copies of (1) all correspondence between the Federal Insurance Administrator and the community concerning the study, reports of any meetings among the Agency representatives, property owners of the community, the state coordinating agency, study contractors or other interested persons, (2) relevant publications, (3) a copy of the completed flood elevation study, and (4) a copy of the Federal Insurance Administrator's final determination.

(c) A flood elevation determination docket shall be established and maintained in accordance with part 67 of this subchapter.

[41 FR 46988, Oct. 26, 1976. Redesignated at 44 FR 31177, May 31, 1979, as amended at 48 FR 44544 and 44553, Sept. 29, 1983; 49 FR 4751, Feb. 8, 1984]

§ 66.4 Appointment of consultation co-ordination officer.

The Federal Insurance Administrator may appoint an employee of the Federal Emergency Management Agency, or other designated Federal employee, as the Consultation Coordination Officer, for each community when an analysis is undertaken to establish or to modify flood elevations pursuant to a new study or a restudy. When a CCO is appointed by the Federal Insurance Administrator, the responsibilities for consultation and coordination as set forth in § 66.5 shall be carried out by the CCO. The Federal Insurance Administrator shall advise the community and the state coordinating agency, in writing, of this appointment.

[47 FR 771, Jan. 7, 1982, as amended at 49 FR 4751, Feb. 8, 1984]

§ 66.5 Responsibilities for consultation and coordination.

(a) Contact shall be made with appropriate officials of a community in which a proposed investigation is undertaken, and with the state coordinating agency.

(b) Local dissemination of the intent and nature of the investigation shall be encouraged so that interested parties will have an opportunity to bring relevant data to the attention of the community and to the Federal Insurance Administrator.

(c) Submission of information from the community concerning the study shall be encouraged.

(d) Appropriate officials of the community shall be fully informed of (1) The responsibilities placed on them by the Program, (2) the administrative procedures followed by the Federal Emergency Management Agency, (3) the community's role in establishing elevations, and (4) the responsibilities of the community if it participates in or continues to participate in the Program.

(e) Before the commencement of an initial Flood Insurance Study, the CCO or other FEMA representative, together with a representative of the organization undertaking the study, shall meet with officials of the community. The state coordinating agency shall be notified of this meeting and may attend. At this meeting, the local officials shall be informed of (1) The date when the study will commence, (2) the nature and purpose of the study, (3) areas involved, (4) the manner in which the study shall be undertaken, (5) the general principles to be applied, and (6) the intended use of the data obtained. The community shall be informed in writing if any of the six preceding items are or will be changed after this initial meeting and during the course of the ongoing study.

(f) The community shall be informed in writing of any intended modification to the community's final flood elevation determinations or the development of new elevations in additional areas of the community as a result of a new study or restudy. Such information to the community will include the data set forth in paragraph (e) of this section. At the discretion of the Regional Administrator in each FEMA Regional Office, a meeting may be held to accomplish this requirement.

[47 FR 771, Jan. 7, 1982, as amended at 49 FR 4751, Feb. 8, 1984]

PART 67—APPEALS FROM PROPOSED FLOOD ELEVATION DETERMINATIONS

AUTHORITY: 42 U.S.C. 4001 *et seq.*; Reorganization Plan No. 3 of 1978, 3 CFR, 1978 Comp., p. 329; E.O. 12127, 44 FR 19367, 3 CFR, 1979 Comp., p. 376.

SOURCE: 41 FR 46989, Oct. 26, 1976, unless otherwise noted. Redesignated at 44 FR 31177, May 31, 1979.

§ 67.1 Purpose of part.

The purpose of this part is to establish procedures implementing the provisions of section 110 of Flood Disaster Protection Act of 1973.

§ 67.2 Definitions.

The definitions set forth in part 59 of this subchapter are applicable to this part.

§ 67.3 Establishment and maintenance of a flood elevation determination docket (FEDD).

The Federal Insurance Administrator shall establish a docket of all matters pertaining to flood elevation determinations. The docket files shall contain the following information:

(a) The name of the community subject to the flood elevation determination;

(b) A copy of the notice of the proposed flood elevation determination to the Chief Executive Officer (CEO) of the Community;

(c) A copy of the notice of the proposed flood elevation determination published in a prominent local newspaper of the community;

(d) A copy of the notice of the proposed flood elevation determination published in the FEDERAL REGISTER;

(e) Copies of all appeals by private persons received by the Federal Insurance Administrator from the CEO;

(f) Copies of all comments received by the Federal Insurance Administrator on the notice of the proposed flood elevation determination published in the FEDERAL REGISTER.

(g) A copy of the community's appeal or a copy of its decision not to appeal the proposed flood elevation determination;

(h) A copy of the flood insurance study for the community;

(i) A copy of the FIRM for the community;

(j) Copies of all materials maintained in the flood elevation study consultation docket; and

(k) A copy of the final determination with supporting documents.

[41 FR 46989, Oct. 26, 1976. Redesignated at 44 FR 31177, May 31, 1979, as amended at 48 FR 44553, Sept. 29, 1983; 49 FR 4751, Feb. 8, 1984]

§ 67.4 Proposed flood elevation determination.

The Federal Insurance Administrator shall propose flood elevation determinations in the following manner:

(a) Publication of the proposed flood elevation determination for comment in the FEDERAL REGISTER;

(b) Notification by certified mail, return receipt requested, of the proposed flood elevation determination to the CEO; and

(c) Publication of the proposed flood elevation determination in a prominent local newspaper at least twice during the ten day period immediately following the notification of the CEO.

[41 FR 46989, Oct. 26, 1976. Redesignated at 44 FR 31177, May 31, 1979, as amended at 48 FR 44553, Sept. 29, 1983; 49 FR 4751, Feb. 8, 1984]

EDITORIAL NOTE: For references to FR pages showing lists of flood elevation determinations, see the List of CFR Sections Affected, which appears in the Finding Aids section of the printed volume and at *www.fdsys.gov*.

§ 67.5 Right of appeal.

(a) Any owner or lessee of real property, within a community where a proposed flood elevation determination has been made pursuant to section 1363 of the National Flood Insurance Act of 1968, as amended, who believes his property rights to be adversely affected by the Federal Insurance Administrator's proposed determination, may file a written appeal of such determination with the CEO, or such agency as he shall publicly designate, within ninety days of the second newspaper publication of the Federal Insurance Administrator's proposed determination.

(b) [Reserved]

[41 FR 46989, Oct. 26, 1976. Redesignated at 44 FR 31177, May 31, 1979, as amended at 48 FR 44553, Sept. 29, 1983; 49 FR 4751, Feb. 8, 1984]

§ 67.6 Basis of appeal.

(a) The sole basis of appeal under this part shall be the possession of knowledge or information indicating that the elevations proposed by FEMA are scientifically or technically incorrect. Because scientific and technical correctness is often a matter of degree rather than absolute (except where mathematical or measurement error or changed physical conditions can be demonstrated), appellants are required to demonstrate that alternative methods or applications result in more correct estimates of base flood elevations, thus demonstrating that FEMA's estimates are incorrect.

(b) *Data requirements.* (1) If an appellant believes the proposed base flood elevations are technically incorrect due to a mathematical or measurement error or changed physical conditions, then the specific source of the error must be identified. Supporting data must be furnished to FEMA including certifications by a registered professional engineer or licensed land surveyor, of the new data necessary for FEMA to conduct a reanalysis.

(2) If an appellant believes that the proposed base flood elevations are technically incorrect due to error in application of hydrologic, hydraulic or other methods or use of inferior data in applying such methods, the appeal must demonstrate technical incorrectness by:

(i) Identifying the purported error in the application or the inferior data.

(ii) Supporting why the application is incorrect or data is inferior.

(iii) Providing an application of the same basic methods utilized by FEMA but with the changes itemized.

(iv) Providing background technical support for the changes indicating why the appellant's application should be accepted as more correct.

(v) Providing certification of correctness of any alternate data utilized or measurements made (such as topographic information) by a registered professional engineer or licensed land surveyor, and

(vi) Providing documentation of all locations where the appellant's base flood elevations are different from FEMA's.

(3) If any appellant believes the proposed base flood elevations are scientifically incorrect, the appeal must demonstrate scientific incorrectness by:

(i) Identifying the methods, or assumptions purported to be scientifically incorrect.

(ii) Supporting why the methods, or assumptions are scientifically incorrect.

(iii) Providing an alternative analysis utilizing methods, or assumptions purported to be correct.

(iv) Providing technical support indicating why the appellant's methods should be accepted as more correct and

(v) Providing documentation of all locations where the appellant's base flood elevations are different from FEMA's.

[48 FR 31644, July 1, 1983]

§ 67.7 Collection of appeal data.

(a) Appeals by private persons to the CEO shall be submitted within ninety (90) days following the second newspaper publication of the Federal Insurance Administrator's proposed flood elevation determination to the CEO or to such agency as he may publicly designate and shall set forth scientific or technical data that tend to negate or contradict the Federal Insurance Administrator's findings.

(b) Copies of all individual appeals received by the CEO shall be forwarded, as soon as they are received, to the Federal Insurance Administrator for information and placement in the Flood Elevation Determination Docket.

(c) The CEO shall review and consolidate all appeals by private persons and issue a written opinion stating whether the evidence presented is sufficient to justify an appeal on behalf of such persons by the community in its own name.

(d) The decision issued by the CEO on the basis of his review, on whether an appeal by the community in its own name shall be made, shall be filed with the Federal Insurance Administrator not later than ninety days after the date of the second newspaper publication of the Federal Insurance Administrator's proposed flood elevation determination and shall be placed in the FEDD.

[41 FR 46989, Oct. 26, 1976. Redesignated at 44 FR 31177, May 31, 1979, as amended at 48 FR 44553, Sept. 29, 1983; 49 FR 4751, Feb. 8, 1984]

§ 67.8 Appeal procedure.

(a) If a community appeals the proposed flood elevation determination, the Federal Insurance Administrator shall review and take fully into account any technical or scientific data submitted by the community that tend to negate or contradict the information upon which his/her proposed determination is based.

(b) The Federal Insurance Administrator shall resolve such appeal by consultation with officials of the local government, or by administrative hearings under the procedures set forth in part 68 of this subchapter, or by submission of the conflicting data to an independent scientific body or appropriate Federal agency for advice.

(c) The final determination by the Federal Insurance Administrator where an appeal is filed shall be made within a reasonable time.

(d) Nothing in this section shall be considered to compromise an appellant's rights granted under § 67.12.

(e) The Federal Insurance Administrator shall make available for public inspection the reports and other information used in making the final determination. This material shall be admissible in a court of law in the event the community seeks judicial review in accordance with § 67.12.

[41 FR 46989, Oct. 26, 1976. Redesignated at 44 FR 31177, May 31, 1979, as amended at 48 FR 44553, Sept. 29, 1983; 49 FR 4751, Feb. 8, 1984]

§ 67.9 Final determination in the absence of an appeal by the community.

(a) If the Federal Insurance Administrator does not receive an appeal from the community within the ninety days provided, he shall consolidate and review on their own merits the individual appeals which, in accordance with § 67.7 are filed within the community and forwarded by the CEO.

(b) The final determination shall be made pursuant to the procedures in § 67.8 and, modifications shall be made of his proposed determination as may be appropriate, taking into account the written opinion, if any, issued by the community in not supporting such appeals.

[41 FR 46989, Oct. 26, 1976. Redesignated at 44 FR 31177, May 31, 1979, as amended at 48 FR 44553, Sept. 29, 1983; 49 FR 4751, Feb. 8, 1984]

§ 67.10 Rates during pendency of final determination.

(a) Until such time as a final determination is made and proper notice is given, no person within a participating community shall be denied the right to purchase flood insurance at the subsidized rate.

(b) After the final determination and upon the effective date of a FIRM, risk premium rates will be charged for new construction and substantial improvements. The effective date of a FIRM shall begin not later than six months after the final flood elevation determination.

§ 67.11 Notice of final determination.

The Federal Insurance Administrator's notice of the final flood elevation determination for a community shall be in written form and published in the FEDERAL REGISTER, and copies shall be sent to the CEO, all individual appellants and the State Coordinating Agency.

[41 FR 46989, Oct. 26, 1976. Redesignated at 44 FR 31177, May 31, 1979, as amended at 48 FR 44553, Sept. 29, 1983; 49 FR 4751, Feb. 8, 1984]

EDITORIAL NOTE: For the list of communities issued under this section, and not carried in the CFR, see the List of CFR Sections Affected, which appears in the Finding Aids section of the printed volume and at www.fdsys.gov.

§ 67.12 Appeal to District Court.

(a) An appellant aggrieved by the final determination of the Federal Insurance Administrator may appeal such determination only to the United States District Court for the District within which the community is located within sixty days after receipt of notice of determination.

(b) During the pendency of any such litigation, all final determinations of the Federal Insurance Administrator shall be effective for the purposes of this title unless stayed by the court for good cause shown.

(c) The scope of review of the appellate court shall be in accordance with the provisions of 5 U.S.C. 706, as modified by 42 U.S.C. 4104(b).

[41 FR 46989, Oct. 26, 1976. Redesignated at 44 FR 31177, May 31, 1979, as amended at 48 FR 44544 and 44553, Sept. 29, 1983; 49 FR 4751, Feb. 8, 1984; 49 FR 33879, Aug. 27, 1984]

PART 68—ADMINISTRATIVE HEARING PROCEDURES

AUTHORITY: 42 U.S.C. 4001 *et seq.*; Reorganization Plan No. 3 of 1978; E.O. 12127.

SOURCE: 47 FR 23449, May 29, 1982, unless otherwise noted.

§ 68.1 Purpose of part.

The purpose of this part is to establish procedures for appeals of the Federal Insurance Administrator's base flood elevation determinations, whether proposed pursuant to section 1363(e) of the Act (42 U.S.C. 4104) or modified because of changed conditions or newly acquired scientific and technical information.

[47 FR 23449, May 29, 1982, as amended at 49 FR 33879, Aug. 27, 1984]

§ 68.2 Definitions.

The definitions set forth in part 59 of this subchapter are applicable to this part.

[47 FR 23449, May 29, 1982, as amended at 49 FR 33879, Aug. 27, 1984]

§ 68.3 Right to administrative hearings.

If a community appeals the Federal Insurance Administrator's flood elevation determination established pursuant to §67.8 of this subchapter, and the Federal Insurance Administrator has determined that such appeal cannot be resolved by consultation with officials of the community or by submitting the conflicting data to an independent scientific body or appropriate Federal agency for advice, the Federal Insurance Administrator shall hold an administrative hearing to resolve the appeal.

[47 FR 23449, May 29, 1982, as amended at 49 FR 33879, Aug. 27, 1984]

§ 68.4 Hearing board.

(a) Each hearing shall be conducted by a three member hearing board (hereinafter "board"). The board shall consist of a hearing officer (hereinafter "Judge") appointed by the Administrator based upon a recommendation by the Office of Personnel Management and two members selected by the Judge who are qualified in the technical field of flood elevation determinations. The Judge shall consult with anyone he deems appropriate to determine the technical qualifications of individuals being considered for appointment to the board. The board members shall not be FEMA employees.

(b) The Judge shall be responsible for conducting the hearing, and shall make all procedural rulings during the course of the hearing. Any formal orders and the final decision on the merits of the hearing shall be made by a majority of the board. A dissenting member may submit a separate opinion for the record.

(c) A technically qualified alternate will be appointed by the Judge as a member of the board when a technically qualified appointed member becomes unavailable. The Administrator will appoint an alternate Judge if the appointed Judge becomes unavailable.

§ 68.5 Establishment of a docket.

The Chief Counsel shall establish a docket for appeals referred to him/her by the Federal Insurance Administrator for administrative hearings. This docket shall include, for each appeal, copies of all materials contained in the flood elevation determination docket (FEDD) file on the matter, copies of all correspondence in connection with the appeal, all motions, orders, statements, and other legal documents, a transcript of the hearing, and the board's final determination.

[47 FR 23449, May 29, 1982, as amended at 49 FR 33879, Aug. 27, 1984]

§ 68.6 Time and place of hearing.

(a) The time and place of each hearing shall be designated by the Judge for that hearing. The Federal Insurance Administrator and the Chief Counsel shall be promptly advised of such designations.

(b) The board's notice of the time and place of hearing shall be sent by the Flood Insurance Docket Clerk by registered or certified mail, return receipt requested, to all appellants. Such notice shall include a statement indicating the nature of the proceedings and their purpose and all appellants' entitlement to counsel. Notice of the hearing shall be sent no later than 30 days before the date of hearing unless such period is waived by all appellants.

[47 FR 23449, May 29, 1982, as amended at 49 FR 33879, Aug. 27, 1984]

§ 68.7   Conduct of hearings.

(a) The Judge shall be responsible for the fair and expeditious conduct of proceedings.

(b) The Federal Insurance Administrator shall be represented by the Chief Counsel or his/her designee.

(c) One administrative hearing shall be held for any one community unless the Federal Insurance Administrator for good cause shown grants a separate hearing or hearings.

(d) The Chief Executive Officer (CEO) of the community or his/her designee shall represent all appellants from that community; *Provided,* That any appellant may petition the board to allow such appellant to make an appearance on his/her own behalf. Such a petition shall be granted only upon a showing of good cause.

(e) Hearings shall be open to the public.

(f) A verbatim transcript will be made of the hearing. An appellant may order copies of the transcribed verbatim record directly from the reporter and will be responsible for payments.

[47 FR 23449, May 29, 1982, as amended at 49 FR 33879, Aug. 27, 1984]

§ 68.8   Scope of review.

Review at administrative hearings shall be limited to: An examination of any information presented by each appellant within the 90 day appeal period indicating that elevations proposed by the Federal Insurance Administrator are scientifically or technically incorrect; the FIRM; the flood insurance study; its backup data and the references used in development of the flood insurance study; and responses by

FEMA to the issues raised by the appellant(s).

[47 FR 23449, May 29, 1982, as amended at 49 FR 33879, Aug. 27, 1984]

§ 68.9   Admissible evidence.

(a) Legal rules of evidence shall not be in effect at adminstrative hearings. However, *only* evidence relevant to issues within the scope of review under § 68.8 shall be admissible.

(b) Documentary and oral evidence shall be admissible.

(c) Admissibility of non-expert testimony shall be within the discretion of the board.

(d) All testimony shall be under oath.

(e) *Res judicata/* collateral estoppel. Where there has been a previous determination, decision or finding of fact by the Director, one of his delegees, an administrative law judge, hearing officer, or hearing board regarding the base flood elevations of any other community, such determination, decision, or finding of fact shall not be binding on the board and may only be admissible into evidence if relevant.

§ 68.10   Burden of proof.

The burden shall be on appellant(s) to prove that the flood elevation determination is not scientifically or technically correct.

§ 68.11   Determination.

The board shall render its written decision within 45 days after the conclusion of the hearing. The entire record of the hearing including the board's decision will be sent to the Administrator for review and approval. The Administrator shall make the final base flood elevation determination by accepting in whole or in part or by rejecting the board's decision.

§ 68.12   Relief.

The final determination may be appealed by the appellant(s) to the United States district court as provided in section 1363(f) of the Act (42 U.S.C. 4104).

PART 69 [RESERVED]

PART 70—PROCEDURE FOR MAP CORRECTION

AUTHORITY: 42 U.S.C. 4001 *et seq.*; Reorganization Plan No. 3 of 1978, 43 FR 41943, 3 CFR, 1978 Comp., p. 329; E.O. 12127 of Mar. 31, 1979, 44 FR 19367, 3 CFR, 1979 Comp., p. 376.

MAPPING DEFICIENCIES UNRELATED TO COMMUNITY-WIDE ELEVATION DETERMINATIONS

§70.1 Purpose of part.

The purpose of this part is to provide an administrative procedure whereby the Federal Insurance Administrator will review the scientific or technical submissions of an owner or lessee of property who believes his property has been inadvertently included in designated A, AO, A1–30, AE, AH, A99, AR, AR/A1–30, AR/AE, AR/AO, AR/AH, AR/A, VO, V1–30, VE, and V Zones, as a result of the transposition of the curvilinear line to either street or to other readily identifiable features. The necessity for this part is due in part to the technical difficulty of accurately delineating the curvilinear line on either an FHBM or FIRM. These procedures shall not apply when there has been any alteration of topography since the effective date of the first NFIP map (i.e., FHBM or FIRM) showing the property within an area of special flood hazard. Appeals in such circumstances are subject to the provisions of part 65 of this subchapter.

[62 FR 55718, Oct. 27, 1997]

§70.2 Definitions.

The definitions set forth in part 59 of this subchapter are applicable to this part.

[41 FR 46991, Oct. 26, 1976. Redesignated at 44 FR 31177, May 31, 1979]

§70.3 Right to submit technical information.

(a) Any owner or lessee of property (applicant) who believes his property has been inadvertently included in a designated A, AO, A1–30, AE, AH, A99, AR, AR/A1–30, AR/AE, AR/AO, AR/AH, AR/A, VO, V1–30, VE, and V Zones on a FHBM or a FIRM, may submit scientific or technical information to the Federal Insurance Administrator for the Federal Insurance Administrator's review.

(b) Scientific and technical information for the purpose of this part may include, but is not limited to the following:

(1) An actual copy of the recorded plat map bearing the seal of the appropriate recordation official (e.g. County Clerk, or Recorder of Deeds) indicating the official recordation and proper citation (Deed or Plat Book Volume and Page Numbers), or an equivalent identification where annotation of the deed or plat book is not the practice.

(2) A topographical map showing (i) ground elevation contours in relation to the National Geodetic Vertical Datum (NVGD) of 1929, (ii) the total area of the property in question, (iii) the location of the structure or structures located on the property in question, (iv) the elevation of the lowest adjacent grade to a structure or structures and (v) an indication of the curvilinear line which represents the area subject to inundation by a base flood. The curvilinear line should be based upon information provided by any appropriate authoritative source, such as a Federal Agency, the appropriate state agency (e.g. Department of Water Resources), a County Water Control District, a County or City Engineer, a Federal Emergency Management Agency Flood Insurance Study, or a determination by a Registered Professional Engineer;

(3) A copy of the FHBM or FIRM indicating the location of the property in question;

(4) A certification by a Registered Professional Engineer or Licensed Land Surveyor that the lowest grade adjacent to the structure is above the base flood elevation.

[41 FR 46991, Oct. 26, 1976. Redesignated at 44 FR 31177, May 31, 1979, as amended at 48 FR 44544 and 44553, Sept. 29, 1983; 49 FR 4751, Feb. 8, 1984; 50 FR 36028, Sept. 4, 1985; 51 FR 30317, Aug. 25, 1986; 53 FR 16280, May 6, 1988; 59 FR 53601, Oct. 25, 1994; 62 FR 55719, Oct. 27, 1997]

§ 70.4 Review by the Administrator.

The Administrator, after reviewing the scientific or technical information submitted under the provisions of § 70.3, shall notify the applicant in writing of his/her determination within 60 days after we receive the applicant's scientific or technical information that we have compared either the ground elevations of an entire legally defined parcel of land or the elevation of the lowest adjacent grade to a structure with the elevation of the base flood and that:

(a) The property is within a designated A, A0, A1-30, AE, AH, A99, AR, AR/A1-30, AR/AE, AR/AO, AR/AH, AR/A, V0, V1-30, VE, or V Zone, and will state the basis of such determination; or

(b) The property should not be within a designated A, A0, A1-30, AE, AH, A99, AR, AR/A1-30, AR/AE, AR/AO, AR/AH, AR/A,V0, V1-30, VE, or V Zone and that we will modify the FHBM or FIRM accordingly; or

(c) The property is not within a designated A, A0, A1-30, AE, AH, A99, AR, AR/A1-30, AR/AE, AR/AO, AR/AH, AR/A,V0, V1-30, VE, or V Zone as shown on the FHBM or FIRM and no modification of the FHBM or FIRM is necessary; or

(d) We need an additional 60 days to make a determination.

[66 FR 33900, June 26, 2001]

§ 70.5 Letter of Map Amendment.

Upon determining from available scientific or technical information that a FHBM or a FIRM requires modification under the provisions of § 70.4(b), the Administrator shall issue a Letter of Map Amendment which shall state:

(a) The name of the Community to which the map to be amended was issued;

(b) The number of the map;

(c) The identification of the property to be excluded from a designated A, AO, A1-30, AE, AH, A99, AR, AR/A1-30, AR/AE, AR/AO, AR/AH, AR/A, VO, V1-30, VE, or V Zone.

[41 FR 46991, Oct. 26, 1976. Redesignated at 44 FR 31177, May 31, 1979, as amended at 48 FR 44553, Sept. 29, 1983; 49 FR 4751, Feb. 8, 1984; 50 FR 36028, Sept. 4, 1985; 59 FR 53601, Oct. 25, 1994; 62 FR 55719, Oct. 27, 1997]

§ 70.6 Distribution of Letter of Map Amendment.

(a) A copy of the Letter of Map Amendment shall be sent to the applicant who submitted scientific or technical data to the Federal Insurance Administrator.

(b) A copy of the Letter of Map Amendment shall be sent to the local map repository with instructions that it be attached to the map which the Letter of Map Amendment is amending.

(c) A copy of the Letter of Map Amendment shall be sent to the map repository in the state with instructions that it be attached to the map which it is amending.

(d) A copy of the Letter of Map Amendment will be sent to any community or governmental unit that requests such Letter of Map Amendment.

(e) [Reserved]

(f) A copy of the Letter of Map Amendment will be maintained by the Agency in its community case file.

[41 FR 46991, Oct. 26, 1976. Redesignated at 44 FR 31177, May 31, 1979, as amended at 48 FR 44544 and 44553, Sept. 29, 1983; 49 FR 4751, Feb. 8, 1984]

§ 70.7 Notice of Letter of Map Amendment.

(a) The Federal Insurance Administrator, shall not publish a notice in the FEDERAL REGISTER that the FIRM for a particular community has been amended by letter determination pursuant to this part unless such amendment includes alteration or change of base flood elevations established pursuant to part 67. Where no change of base flood elevations has occurred, the Letter of Map Amendment provided under

§§70.5 and 70.6 serves to inform the parties affected.

(b) [Reserved]

EDITORIAL NOTE: For a list of communities issued under this section and not carried in the CFR see the List of CFR Sections Affected, which appears in the Finding Aids Section of the printed volume and at www.fdsys.gov.

§70.8 **Premium refund after Letter of Map Amendment.**

A Standard Flood Insurance Policyholder whose property has become the subject of a Letter of Map Amendment under this part may cancel the policy within the current policy year and receive a premium refund under the conditions set forth in §62.5 of this subchapter.

[41 FR 46991, Oct. 26, 1976. Redesignated at 44 FR 31177, May 31, 1979]

§70.9 **Review of proposed projects.**

An individual who proposes to build one or more structures on a portion of property that may be included inadvertently in a Special Flood Hazard Area (SFHA) may request FEMA's comments on whether the proposed structure(s), if built as proposed, will be in the SFHA. FEMA's comments will be issued in the form of a letter, termed a Conditional Letter of Map Amendment. The data required to support such requests are the same as those required for final Letters of Map Amendment in accordance with §70.3, except as-built certification is not required and the requests shall be accompanied by the appropriate payment, in accordance with 44 CFR part 72. All such requests for CLOMAs shall be submitted to the FEMA Regional Office servicing the community's geographic area or to the FEMA Headquarters Office in Washington, DC.

[62 FR 5736, Feb. 6, 1997]

PART 71—IMPLEMENTATION OF COASTAL BARRIER LEGISLATION

Sec.

AUTHORITY: 42 U.S.C. 4001, et seq.; Reorganization Plan No. 3 of 1978, 3 CFR, 1978 Comp., p. 329; E.O. 12127, 44 FR 19367, 3 CFR, 1979 Comp., p. 376; 42 U.S.C. 4028; secs. 9 and 14, Pub. L. 101–591, 42 U.S.C. 4028(b).

SOURCE: 48 FR 37039, Aug. 16, 1983, unless otherwise noted.

§71.1 **Purpose of part.**

This part implements section 11 of the Coastal Barrier Resources Act (Pub. L. 97–348) and section 9 of the Coastal Barrier Improvement Act of 1990 (Pub. L. 101–591), as those Acts amend the National Flood Insurance Act of 1968 (42 U.S.C. 4001 et seq.).

[48 FR 37039, Aug. 16, 1983, as amended at 57 FR 22661, May 29, 1992]

§71.2 **Definitions.**

(a) Except as otherwise provided in this part, the definitions set forth in part 59 of this subchapter are applicable to this part.

(b) For the purpose of this part, a structure located in an area identified as being in the Coastal Barrier Resources System (CBRS) both as of October 18, 1982, and as of November 16, 1990, is "new construction" unless it meets the following criteria:

(1)(i) A legally valid building permit or equivalent documentation was obtained for the construction of such structure prior to October 18, 1982; and

(ii) The start of construction (see part 59) took place prior to October 18, 1982; or

(2)(i) A legally valid building permit or equivalent documentation was obtained for the construction of such structure prior to October 1, 1983; and

(ii) The structure constituted an insurable building, having walls and a roof permanently in place no later than October 1, 1983.

(c) For the purpose of this part, a structure located in an area newly identified as being in the CBRS as of November 16, 1990, is "new construction" unless it meets the following criteria:

(1) A legally valid building permit or equivalent documentation was obtained for the construction of such structure prior to November 16, 1990; and

(2) The start of construction (see 44 CFR part 59) took place prior to November 16, 1990.

(d) For the purpose of this part, a structure located in an "otherwise protected area" is "new construction" unless it meets the following criteria:

(1)(i) A legally valid building permit or equivalent documentation was obtained for the construction of such structure prior to November 16, 1990; and

(ii) The start of construction took place prior to November 16, 1990; or

(2)(i) A legally valid building permit or equivalent documentation was obtained for the construction of such structure prior to November 16, 1991; and

(ii) The structure constituted an insurable building, having walls and a roof permanently in place, no later than November 16, 1991.

(e) For the purpose of this part, a structure located in an area identified as being in the CBRS both as of October 18, 1982, and as of November 16, 1990, is a "substantial improvement" if the substantial improvement (see 44 CFR part 59) of such structure took place on or after October 1, 1983.

(f) For the purpose of this part, a structure located in an area newly identified as being in the CBRS as of November 16, 1990, is a "substantial improvement" if the substantial improvement of such structure took place on or after November 16, 1990.

(g) For the purpose of this part, a structure located in an "otherwise protected area" is a "substantial improvement" if the substantial improvement of such structure took place after November 16, 1991.

(h) For the purpose of this part, a *policy of flood insurance* means a policy issued pursuant to the National Flood Insurance Act of 1968, as amended. This includes a policy issued directly by the Federal Government as well as by a private sector insurance company under the Write Your Own Program as authorized by 44 CFR part 62.

(i) For the purpose of this part, *new policy of flood insurance* means a policy of flood insurance other than one issued by an insurer (Write Your Own insurer or the Federal Government as the direct insurer) effective upon the expiration of a prior policy of flood insurance issued by the same insurer without any lapse in coverage between these two policies.

(j) For the purpose of this part, *new flood insurance coverage* means a new or renewed policy of flood insurance.

(k) For the purpose of this part, *otherwise protected area* means an undeveloped coastal barrier within the boundaries of an area established under Federal, State, or local law, or held by a qualified organization, primarily for wildlife refuge, sanctuary, recreational, or natural resource conservation purposes and identified and depicted on the maps referred to in section 4(a) of the Coastal Barrier Resources Act, as amended by the Coastal Barrier Improvement Act of 1990, as an area that is:

(1) Not within the CBRS and

(2) In an "otherwise protected area."

[48 FR 37039, Aug. 16, 1983, as amended at 49 FR 33879, Aug. 27, 1984; 57 FR 22661, May 29, 1992]

§ 71.3   Denial of flood insurance.

(a) No new flood insurance coverage may be provided on or after October 1, 1983, for any new construction or substantial improvement of a structure located in an area identified as being in the CBRS both as of October 18, 1982, and as of November 16, 1990.

(b) No new flood insurance coverage may be provided on or after November 16, 1990, for any new construction or substantial improvement of a structure located in any area newly identified as being in the CBRS as of November 16, 1990.

(c) No new flood insurance coverage may be provided after November 16, 1991, for any new construction or substantial improvement of a structure which is located in an "otherwise protected area."

(d) Notwithstanding paragraph (c) of this section, new flood insurance coverage may be provided for a structure which is newly constructed or substantially improved in an "otherwise protected area" if the building is used in a manner consistent with the purpose for which the area is protected.

[57 FR 22662, May 29, 1992]

§71.4 Documentation.

(a) In order to obtain a new policy of flood insurance for a structure which is located in an area identified as being in the CBRS as of November 16, 1990, or in order to obtain a new policy of flood insurance after November 16, 1991, for a structure located in an "otherwise protected area," the owner of the structure must submit the documentation described in this section in order to show that such structure is eligible to receive flood insurance. However, if the new policy of flood insurance is being obtained from an insurer (Write Your Own or the Federal Government as direct insurer) that has previously obtained the documentation described in this section, the property owner need only submit a signed written certification that the structure has not been substantially improved since the date of the previous documentation.

(b) The documentation must be submitted along with the application for the flood insurance policy.

(c) For a structure located in an area identified as being in the CBRS both as of October 18, 1982, and as of November 16, 1990, where the start of construction of the structure took place prior to October 18, 1982, the documentation shall consist of:

(1) A legally valid building permit or its equivalent for the construction of the structure dated prior to October 18, 1982;

(i) If the community did not have a building permit system at the time the structure was built, a written statement to this effect signed by the responsible community official will be accepted in lieu of the building permit;

(ii) If the building permit was lost or destroyed, a written statement to this effect signed by the responsible community official will be accepted in lieu of the building permit. This statment must also include a certification that the official has inspected the structure and found no evidence that the structure was not in compliance with the building code at the time it was built; and

(2) A written statement signed by the community official responsible for building permits, attesting to the fact that he or she knows of his/her own knowledge or from official community records, that:

(i) The start of construction took place prior to October 18, 1982; and

(ii) The structure has not been substantially improved since September 30, 1983.

(d) For a structure located in an area identified as being in the CBRS both as of October 18, 1982, and as of November 16, 1990, where the start of construction of the structure took place on or after October 18, 1982, but the structure was completed (walls and roof permanently in place) prior to October 1, 1983, the documentation shall consist of:

(1) A legally valid building permit or its equivalent for the construction of the structure dated prior to October 1, 1983;

(i) If the community did not have a building permit system at the time the structure was built, a written statement to this effect signed by the responsible community official will be accepted in lieu of the building permit;

(ii) If the building permit was lost or destroyed, a written statement to this effect signed by the responsible community official will be accepted in lieu of the building permit. This statement must also include a certification that the official has inspected the structure and found no evidence that the structure was not in compliance with the building code at the time it was built; and

(2) A written statement signed by the community official responsible for building permits, attesting to the fact that he or she knows of his/her own knowledge or from official community records, that:

(i) The structure constituted an insurable building, having walls and a roof permanently in place no later than October 1, 1983; and

(ii) The structure has not been substantially improved since September 30, 1983; and

(3) A community issued final certificate of occupancy or other use permit or equivalent proof certifying the building was completed (walled and roofed) by October 1, 1983.

(e) For a structure located in an area newly identified as being in the CBRS as of November 16, 1990, where the start of construction of the structure took place prior to November 16, 1990, the documentation shall consist of:

(1) A legally valid building permit or its equivalent for the construction of the structure, dated prior to November 16, 1990.

(i) If the community did not have a building permit system at the time the structure was built, a written statement to this effect signed by the responsible community official will be accepted in lieu of the building permit;

(ii) If the building permit was lost or destroyed, a written statement to this effect signed by the responsible community official will be accepted in lieu of the building permit. This statement must also include a certification that the official has inspected the structure and found no evidence that the structure was not in compliance with the building code at the time it was built; and

(2) A written statement signed by the community official responsible for building permits, attesting to the fact that he or she knows of his or her own knowledge or from official community records, that:

(i) The start of construction took place prior to November 16, 1990; and

(ii) The structure has not been substantially improved since November 15, 1990.

(f) For a structure located in an area identified as an "otherwise protected area" where the start of construction of the structure took place prior to November 16, 1990, the documentation shall consist of:

(1) A legally valid building permit or its equivalent for the construction of the structure, dated prior to November 16, 1990.

(i) If the community did not have a building permit system at the time the structure was built, a written statement to this effect signed by the responsible community official will be accepted in lieu of the building permit;

(ii) If the building permit was lost or destroyed, a written statement to this effect signed by the responsible community official will be accepted in lieu of the building permit. This statement must also include a certification that the official has inspected the structure and found no evidence that the structure was not in compliance with the

building code at the time it was built; and

(2) A written statement signed by the community official responsible for building permits, attesting to the fact that he or she knows of his or her own knowledge or from official community records, that:

(i) The start of construction took place prior to November 16, 1990; and

(ii) The structure has not been substantially improved since November 16, 1991.

(g) For a structure located in an area identified as an "otherwise protected area" where the start of construction of the structure took place after November 15, 1990, but construction was completed with the walls and a roof permanently in place no later than November 16, 1991, the documentation shall consist of:

(1) A legally valid building permit or its equivalent for the construction of the structure, dated prior to November 16, 1991.

(i) If the community did not have a building permit system at the time the structure was built, a written statement to this effect signed by the responsible community official will be accepted in lieu of the building permit;

(ii) If the building permit was lost or destroyed, a written statement to this effect signed by the responsible community official will be accepted in lieu of the building permit. This statement must also include a certification that the official has inspected the structure and found no evidence that the structure was not in compliance with the building code at the time it was built; and

(2) A statement signed by the community official responsible for building permits, attesting to the fact that he or she knows of his or her own knowledge or from official community records that:

(i) The structure constituted an insurable building, having walls and a roof permanently in place, no later than November 16, 1991; and

(ii) The structure has not been substantially improved since November 16, 1991; and

(3) A community issued final certificate of occupancy or other use permit or equivalent proof certifying that the

building was completed (walled and roofed) by November 16, 1991.

(h) For a structure located in an area identified as an "otherwise protected area" for which the documentation requirements of neither paragraph (f) nor paragraph (g) of this section have been met, the documentation shall consist of a written statement from the governmental body or qualified organization overseeing the "otherwise protected area" certifying that the building is used in a manner consistent with the purpose for which the area is protected.

[48 FR 37039, Aug. 16, 1983, as amended at 57 FR 22662, May 29, 1992; 74 FR 15343, Apr. 3, 2009]

§ 71.5 Violations.

(a) Any flood insurance policy which has been issued where the terms of this section have not been complied with or is otherwise inconsistent with the provisions of this section, is void *ab initio* and without effect.

(b) Any false statements or false representations of any kind made in connection with the requirements of this part may be punishable by fine or imprisonment under 18 U.S. Code section 1001.

PART 72—PROCEDURES AND FEES FOR PROCESSING MAP CHANGES

Sec.

AUTHORITY: 42 U.S.C. 4001 *et seq.*; Reorganization Plan No. 3 of 1978, 43 FR 41943, 3 CFR, 1978 Comp., p. 329; E.O. 12127, 44 FR 19367, 3 CFR, 1979 Comp., p. 376.

§ 72.1 Purpose of part.

This part provides administrative and cost-recovery procedures for the engineering review and administrative processing associated with FEMA's response to requests for Conditional Letters of Map Amendment (CLOMAs), Conditional Letters of Map Revision (CLOMRs), Conditional Letters of Map Revision Based on Fill (CLOMR-Fs), Letters of Map Revision Based on Fill (LOMR-Fs), Letters of Map Revision (LOMRs), and Physical Map Revisions (PMRs). Such requests are based on proposed or actual manmade alterations within the floodplain, such as the placement of fill; modification of a channel; construction or modification of a bridge, culvert, levee, or similar measure; or construction of single or multiple residential or commercial structures on single or multiple lots.

[62 FR 5736, Feb. 6, 1997]

§ 72.2 Definitions.

Except as otherwise provided in this part, the definitions in 44 CFR part 59 are applicable to this part. For the purposes of this part, the products are defined as follows:

CLOMA. A CLOMA is FEMA's comment on a proposed structure or group of structures that would, upon construction, be located on existing natural ground above the base (1-percent-annual-chance) flood elevation on a portion of a legally defined parcel of land that is partially inundated by the base flood.

CLOMR. A CLOMR is FEMA's comment on a proposed project that would, upon construction, affect the hydrologic or hydraulic characteristics of a flooding source and thus result in the modification of the existing regulatory floodway, the effective base flood elevations, or the Special Flood Hazard Area (SFHA).

CLOMR-F. A CLOMR-F is FEMA's comment on a proposed project that would, upon construction, result in a modification of the SFHA through the placement of fill outside the existing regulatory floodway.

LOMR. A LOMR is FEMA's modification to an effective Flood Insurance Rate Map (FIRM), or Flood Boundary and Floodway Map (FBFM), or both. LOMRs are generally based on the implementation of physical measures that affect the hydrologic or hydraulic characteristics of a flooding source and thus result in the modification of the existing regulatory floodway, the effective base flood elevations, or the SFHA. The LOMR officially revises the FIRM or FBFM, and sometimes the Flood Insurance Study (FIS) report, and, when appropriate, includes a description of the modifications. The LOMR is generally accompanied by an annotated copy of the affected portions of the FIRM, FBFM, or FIS report.

LOMR-F. A LOMR-F is FEMA's modification of the SFHA shown on the FIRM based on the placement of fill outside the existing regulatory floodway.

PMR. A PMR is FEMA's physical revision and republication of an effective FIRM, FBFM, or FIS report. PMRs are generally based on physical measures that affect the hydrologic or hydraulic characteristics of a flooding source and thus result in the modification of the existing regulatory floodway, the effective base flood elevations, or the SFHA.

[62 FR 5737, Feb. 6, 1997]

§ 72.3 Fee schedule.

(a) For requests for CLOMRs, LOMRs, and PMRs based on structural measures on alluvial fans, an initial fee of $5,000, subject to the provisions of § 72.4, shall be paid to FEMA before FEMA begins its review of the request. The initial fee represents the minimum cost for reviewing these requests and is based on the prevailing private-sector labor rate. A revision to this initial fee, if necessary, will be published as a notice in the FEDERAL REGISTER.

(b) For requests for CLOMRs, LOMRs, and PMRs based on structural measures on alluvial fans, the total fee will be calculated based on the total hours by FEMA to review and process the request multiplied by an hourly rate based on the prevailing private-sector labor rate. The hourly rate is published as a notice in the FEDERAL REGISTER. A revision to the hourly rate, if necessary, shall be published as a notice in the FEDERAL REGISTER.

(c) For conditional and final map revision requests for the following categories, flat user fees, subject to the provisions of § 72.4, shall be paid to FEMA before FEMA begins its review of the request:

(1) Requests for CLOMAs, CLOMR-Fs, and LOMR-Fs for single structures or single lots;

(2) Requests for CLOMAs for multiple structures or multiple lots;

(3) Requests for CLOMR-Fs and LOMR-Fs for multiple structures or multiple lots;

(4) Requests LOMR-Fs for single structures or single lots based on as-built information for projects for which FEMA issued CLOMR-Fs previously;

(5) Requests for LOMR-Fs for multiple structures or multiple lots based on as-built information for projects for which FEMA issued CLOMR-Fs previously;

(6) Requests for LOMRs and PMRs based on projects involving bridges, culverts, or channels, or combinations thereof;

(7) Requests for LOMRs and PMRs based on projects involving levees, berms, or other structural measures;

(8) Requests for LOMRs and PMRs based on as-built information for projects for which FEMA issued CLOMRs previously, except those based on structural measures on alluvial fans;

(9) Requests for LOMRs and PMRs based solely on more detailed data;

(10) Requests for CLOMRs based on projects involving new hydrologic information, bridges, culverts, or channels, or combinations thereof; and

(11) Requests for CLOMRs based on projects involving levees, berms, or other structural measures.

(d) If a request involves more than one of the categories listed above, the highest applicable flat user fee must be submitted.

(e) The flat user fees for conditional and final map amendments and map revisions are based on the actual costs for reviewing and processing the requests. The fees for requests for LOMR-Fs, LOMRs, and PMRs also include a fee of $35 to cover FEMA's costs for physically revising affected FIRM and FBFM panels to reflect the map changes.

(f) Revisions to the fees, if necessary, shall be published as a notice in the FEDERAL REGISTER.

[62 FR 5737, Feb. 6, 1997]

§ 72.4 Submittal/payment procedures and FEMA response.

(a) The initial fee shall be submitted with a request for FEMA review and processing of CLOMRs, LOMRs, and PMRs based on structural measures on alluvial fans; the appropriate flat user fee shall be submitted with all other requests for FEMA review and processing.

(b) FEMA must receive initial or flat user fees before it will begin any review. The fee is non-refundable once FEMA begins its review.

(c) Following completion of FEMA's review for any CLOMR, LOMR, or PMR based on structural measures on alluvial fans, FEMA shall invoice the requester at the established hourly rate for any actual costs exceeding the initial fee incurred for review and processing. FEMA shall not issue a determination letter or revised map panel(s) until it receives the invoiced amount.

(d) For all map revision requests, FEMA shall bear the cost of reprinting and distributing the revised FIRM panel(s), FBFM panel(s), or combination.

(e) The entity that applies to FEMA through the local community for review is responsible for the cost of the review. The local community incurs no financial obligation under the reimbursement procedures of this part when another party sends the application to FEMA.

(f) Requesters shall submit payments by check or money order or by credit card. Checks or money orders, in U.S. funds, shall be made payable to the National Flood Insurance Program.

(g) For CLOMA, CLOMR-F, LOMA, and LOMR-F requests, FEMA shall:

(1) Notify the requester and community within 30 days as to the adequacy of the submittal, and

(2) Provide to the requester and the community, within 60 days of receipt of adequate information and fee, a determination letter or other written comment in response to the request.

(h) For CLOMR, LOMR, and PMR requests, FEMA shall:

(1) Notify the requester and community within 60 days as to the adequacy of the submittal; and

(2) Provide to the requester and the community, within 90 days of receipt of adequate information and fee, a CLOMR, a LOMR, other written comment in response to the request, or preliminary copies of the revised FIRM panels, FBFM panels, and/or affected portions of the FIS report for review and comment.

[62 FR 5737, Feb. 6, 1997]

§72.5 Exemptions.

Requesters are exempt from submitting review and processing fees for:

(a) Requests for map changes based on mapping or study analysis errors;

(b) Requests for map changes based on the effects of natural changes within SFHAs;

(c) Requests for a Letter of Map Amendment (LOMA);

(d) Requests for map changes based on federally sponsored flood-control projects where 50 percent or more of the project's costs are federally funded;

(e) Requests for map changes based on detailed hydrologic and hydraulic studies conducted by Federal, State, or local agencies to replace approximate studies conducted by FEMA and shown on the effective FIRM; and

(f) Requests for map changes based on flood hazard information meant to improve upon that shown on the flood map or within the flood study will be exempt from review and processing fees. Improvements to flood maps or studies that partially or wholly incorporate man-made modifications within the special flood hazard area will not be exempt from review and processing fees.

[64 FR 51462, Sept. 23, 1999]

§72.6 Unfavorable response.

(a) Requests for CLOMAs, CLOMRs, or CLOMR-Fs may be denied or the determinations may contain specific comments, concerns, or conditions regarding proposed projects or designs and their impacts on flood hazards in a community. Requesters are not entitled to any refund of fees paid if the determinations contain such comments, concerns, or conditions, or if the requests are denied. Requesters are not entitled to any refund of fees paid if the requesters are unable to provide the appropriate scientific or technical documentation or to obtain required authorizations, permits, financing, etc., for which requesters seek the CLOMAs, CLOMRs, or CLOMR-Fs.

(b) Requests for LOMRs, LOMR-Fs, or PMRs may be denied or the revisions to the FIRM, FBFM, or both, may not be in the manner or to the extent desired by the requesters. Requesters are not entitled to any refund of fees paid if the revision requests are denied or if the LOMRs, LOMR-Fs, or PMRs do not revise the map specifically as requested.

[62 FR 5738, Feb. 6, 1997]

§ 72.7 Resubmittals.

(a) Resubmittals of CLOMA, CLOMR, CLOMR-F, LOMR, LOMR-F, or PMR requests more than 90 days after FEMA notification that the requests were denied or after FEMA ended its review because the requester provided insufficient information will be treated as original submissions and subject to all submittal/payment procedures described in § 72.4. The procedure in § 72.4 also applies to a resubmitted request (regardless of when submitted) if the project on which the request is based has been altered significantly in design or scope other than as necessary to respond to comments, concerns, or other findings made by FEMA regarding the original submission.

(b) When LOMR, LOMR-F, or PMR requests are made after FEMA issues CLOMRs or CLOMR-Fs, the procedures in § 72.4 and the appropriate fee apply, as referenced in § 72.3(c). When the as-built conditions differ from the proposed conditions on which FEMA issued the CLOMRs or CLOMR-Fs, the reduced fee for as-built requests will not apply.

[62 FR 5738, Feb. 6, 1997]

PART 73—IMPLEMENTATION OF SECTION 1316 OF THE NATIONAL FLOOD INSURANCE ACT OF 1968

Sec.
73.1 Purpose of part.
73.2 Definitions.
73.3 Denial of flood insurance coverage.
73.4 Restoration of flood insurance coverage.

AUTHORITY: 42 U.S.C. 4001 *et seq.*; Reorganization Plan No. 3 of 1978; E.O. 12127.

SOURCE: 51 FR 30318, Aug. 25, 1986, unless otherwise noted.

§ 73.1 Purpose of part.

This part implements section 1316 of the National Flood Insurance Act of 1968.

§ 73.2 Definitions.

(a) Except as otherwise provided in this part, the definitions set forth in part 59 of this subchapter are applicable to this part.

(b) For the purpose of this part a *duly constituted State or local zoning authority or other authorized public body* means an official or body authorized under State or local law to declare a structure to be in violation of a law, regulation or ordinance.

(c) For the purpose of this part, *State or local laws, regulations or ordinances* intended to discourage or restrict development or occupancy of flood-prone areas are measures such as those defined as *Flood plain management regulations* in § 59.1 of this subchapter. Such measures are referred to in this part as State or local flood plain management regulations.

§ 73.3 Denial of flood insurance coverage.

(a) No new flood insurance shall be provided for any property which the Federal Insurance Administrator finds has been declared by a duly constituted State or local zoning authority or other authorized public body, to be in violation of State or local laws, regulations or ordinances which are intended to discourage or otherwise restrict land development or occupancy in flood-prone areas.

(b) New and renewal flood insurance shall be denied to a structure upon a finding by the Federal Insurance Administrator of a valid declaration of a violation.

(c) States and communities shall determine whether to submit a declaration to the Federal Insurance Administrator for the denial of insurance.

(d) A valid declaration shall consist of:

(1) The name(s) of the property owner(s) and address or legal description of the property sufficient to confirm its identity and location;

(2) A clear and unequivocal declaration that the property is in violation of

a cited State or local law, regulation or ordinance;

(3) A clear statement that the public body making the declaration has authority to do so and a citation to that authority;

(4) Evidence that the property owner has been provided notice of the violation and the prospective denial of insurance; and

(5) A clear statement that the declaration is being submitted pursuant to section 1316 of the National Flood Insurance Act of 1968, as amended.

§ 73.4 Restoration of flood insurance coverage.

(a) Insurance availability shall be restored to a property upon a finding by the Federal Insurance Administrator of a valid rescission of a declaration of a violation.

(b) A valid rescission shall be submitted to the Federal Insurance Administrator and shall consist of:

(1) The name of the property owner(s) and an address or legal description of the property sufficient to identify the property and to enable FEMA to identify the previous declaration;

(2) A clear and unequivocal statement by an authorized public body rescinding the declaration and giving the reason(s) for the rescission;

(3) A description of and supporting documentation for the measures taken in lieu of denial of insurance in order to bring the structure into compliance with the local flood plain management regulations; and

(4) A clear statement that the public body rescinding the declaration has the authority to do so and a citation to that authority.

PART 74 [RESERVED]

PART 75—EXEMPTION OF STATE-OWNED PROPERTIES UNDER SELF-INSURANCE PLAN

Subpart A—General

Subpart B—Standards for Exemption

AUTHORITY: 42 U.S.C. 4001 *et seq.*; Reorganization Plan No. 3 of 1978, 43 FR 41943, 3 CFR, 1978 Comp., p. 329; E.O. 12127 of Mar. 31, 1979, 44 FR 19367, 3 CFR, 1979 Comp., p. 376.

SOURCE: 41 FR 46991, Oct. 26, 1976, unless otherwise noted. Redesignated at 44 FR 31177, May 31, 1979.

Subpart A—General

§ 75.1 Purpose of part.

The purpose of this part is to establish standards with respect to the Federal Insurance Administrator's determinations that a State's plan of self-insurance is adequate and satisfactory for the purposes of exempting such State, under the provisions of section 102(c) of the Act, from the requirement of purchasing flood insurance coverage for State-owned structures and their contents in areas identified by the Federal Insurance Administrator as A, AO, AH, A1–30, AE, AR, AR/A1–30, AR/AE, AR/AO, AR/AH, AR/A, A99, M, V, VO, V1–30, VE, and E Zones, in which the sale of insurance has been made available, and to establish the procedures by which a State may request exemption under section 102(c).

[62 FR 55719, Oct. 27, 1997]

§ 75.2 Definitions.

The definitions set forth in part 59 of this subchapter are applicable to this part.

§ 75.3 Burden of proof.

In any application made by a State to the Administrator for certification of its self-insurance plan, the burden of proof shall rest upon the State making application to establish that its policy of self-insurance is adequate and equals or exceeds the standards provided in this part.

Subpart B—Standards for Exemption

§ 75.10 Applicability.

A State shall be exempt from the requirement to purchase flood insurance in respect to State-owned structures and, where applicable, their contents located or to be located in areas identified by the Federal Insurance Administrator as A, AO, AH, A1–30, AE, AR, AR/A1–30, AR/AE, AR/AO, AR/AH, AR/A, A99, M, V, VO, V1–30, VE, and E Zones, and in which the sale of flood insurance has been made available under the National Flood Insurance Act of 1968, as amended, provided that the State has established a plan of self-insurance determined by the Federal Insurance Administrator to equal or exceed the standards set forth in this subpart.

[62 FR 55719, Oct. 27, 1997]

§ 75.11 Standards.

(a) In order to be exempt under this part, the State's self-insurance plan shall, as a minimum:

(1) Constitute a formal policy or plan of self-insurance created by statute or regulation authorized pursuant to statute.

(2) Specify that the hazards covered by the self-insurance plan expressly include the flood and flood-related hazards which are covered under the Standard Flood Insurance Policy.

(3) Provide coverage to state-owned structures and their contents equal to that which would otherwise be available under a Standard Flood Insurance Policy.

(4) Consist of a self-insurance fund, or a commercial policy of insurance or reinsurance, for which provision is made in statute or regulation and that is funded by periodic premiums or charges allocated for state-owned structures and their contents in areas identified by the Federal Insurance Administrator as A, AO, AH, A1–30, AE, AR, AR/A1–30, AR/AE, AR/AO, AR/AH, AR/A, A99, M, V, VO, V1–30, VE, and E Zones. The person or persons responsible for such self-insurance fund shall report on its status to the chief executive authority of the State, or to the legislature, or both, not less frequently

than annually. The loss experience shall be shown for each calendar or fiscal year from inception to current date based upon loss and loss adjustment expense incurred during each separate calendar or fiscal year compared to the premiums or charges for each of the respective calendar or fiscal years. Such incurred losses shall be reported in aggregate by cause of loss under a loss coding system adequate, as a minimum, to identify and isolate loss caused by flood, mudslide (i.e., mudflow) or flood-related erosion. The Federal Insurance Administrator may, subject to the requirements of paragraph (a)(5) of this section, accept and approve in lieu of, and as the reasonable equivalent of the self-insurance fund, an enforceable commitment of funds by the State, the enforceability of which shall be certified to by the State's Attorney General, or other principal legal officer. Such funds, or enforceable commitment of funds in amounts not less than the limits of coverage that would be applicable under Standard Flood Insurance Policies, shall be used by the State for the repair or restoration of State-owned structures and their contents damaged as a result of flood-related losses occurring in areas identified by the Federal Insurance Administrator as A, AO, AH, A1–30, AE, AR, AR/A1–30, AR/AE, AR/AO, AR/AH, AR/A, A99, M, V, VO, V1–30, VE, and E Zones.

(5) Provide for the maintaining and updating by a designated State official or agency not less frequently than annually of an inventory of all State-owned structures and their contents within A, AO, AH, A1–30, AE, AR, AR/A1–30, AR/AE, AR/AO, AR/AH, AR/A, A99, M, V, VO, V1–30, VE, and E zones. The inventory shall:

(i) Include the location of individual structures;

(ii) Include an estimate of the current replacement costs of such structures and their contents, or of their current economic value; and

(iii) Include an estimate of the anticipated annual loss due to flood damage.

(6) Provide the flood loss experience for State-owned structures and their contents based upon incurred losses for

a period of not less than the 5 years immediately preceding application for exemption, and certify that such historical information shall be maintained and updated.

(7) Include, pursuant to §60.12 of this subchapter, a certified copy of the flood plain management regulations setting forth standards for State-owned properties within A, AO, AH, A1–30, AE, AR, AR/A1–30, AR/AE, AR/AO, AR/AH, AR/A, A99, M, V, VO, V1–30, VE, and E Zones.

(b) The Federal Insurance Administrator shall determine the adequacy of the insurance provisions whether they be based on available funds, an enforceable commitment of funds, commercial insurance, or some combination thereof, but has discretion to waive specific requirements under this part.

[41 FR 46991, Oct. 26, 1976. Redesignated at 44 FR 31177, May 31, 1979, as amended at 48 FR 44544, Sept. 29, 1983; 49 FR 4751, Feb. 8, 1984; 49 FR 5621, Feb. 14, 1984; 50 FR 36029, Sept. 4, 1985; 59 FR 53601, Oct. 25, 1994; 62 FR 55719, Oct. 27, 1997]

§75.12 Application by a State for exemption.

Application for exemption made pursuant to this part shall be made by the Governor or other duly authorized official of the State accompanied by sufficient supporting documentation which certifies that the plan of self-insurance upon which the application for exemption is based meets or exceeds the standards set forth in §75.11.

§75.13 Review by the Federal Insurance Administrator.

(a) The Federal Insurance Administrator may return the application for exemption upon finding it incomplete or upon finding that additional information is required in order to make a determination as to the adequacy of the self-insurance plan.

(b) Upon determining that the State's plan of self-insurance is inadequate, the Federal Insurance Administrator shall in writing reject the application for exemption and shall state in what respects the plan fails to comply with the standards set forth in §75.11 of this subpart.

(c) Upon determining that the State's plan of self-insurance equals or exceeds the standards set forth in §75.11 of this subpart, the Federal Insurance Administrator shall certify that the State is exempt from the requirement for the purchase of flood insurance for State-owned structures and their contents located or to be located in areas identified by the Federal Insurance Administrator as A, AO, AH, A1–30, AE, AR, AR/A1–30, AR/AE, AR/AO, AR/AH, AR/A, A99, M, V, VO, V1–30, VE, and E Zones. Such exemption, however, is in all cases provisional. The Federal Insurance Administrator shall review the plan for continued compliance with the criteria set forth in this part and may request updated documentation for the purpose of such review. If the plan is found to be inadequate and is not corrected within ninety days from the date that such inadequacies were identified, the Federal Insurance Administrator may revoke his certification.

(d) Documentation which cannot reasonably be provided at the time of application for exemption shall be submitted within six months of the application date. The Federal Insurance Administrator may revoke his certification for a State's failure to submit adequate documentation after the six month period.

[41 FR 46991, Oct. 26, 1976. Redesignated at 44 FR 31177, May 31, 1979, as amended at 48 FR 44544, Sept. 29, 1983; 49 FR 4751, Feb. 8, 1984; 49 FR 5621, Feb. 14, 1984; 50 FR 36029, Sept. 4, 1985; 59 FR 53601, Oct. 25, 1994; 62 FR 55719, Oct. 27, 1997]

§75.14 States exempt under this part.

The following States have submitted applications and adequate supporting documentation and have been determined by the Federal Insurance Administrator to be exempt from the requirement of flood insurance on State-owned structures and their contents because they have in effect adequate State plans of self-insurance: Florida, Georgia, Iowa, Kentucky, Maine, New Jersey, New York, North Carolina, Oregon, Pennsylvania, South Carolina, Tennessee, and Vermont.

[48 FR 44544, Sept. 29, 1983, as amended at 57 FR 19542, May 7, 1992]

PARTS 76–77 [RESERVED]

PART 78—FLOOD MITIGATION ASSISTANCE

AUTHORITY: 6 U.S.C. 101; 42 U.S.C. 4001 *et seq.*; 42 U.S.C. 4104c, 4104d; Reorganization Plan No. 3 of 1978, 43 FR 41943, 3 CFR, 1978 Comp., p. 329; E.O. 12127, 44 FR 19367, 3 CFR, 1979 Comp., p. 376; E.O. 12148, 44 FR 43239, 3 CFR, 1979 Comp., p. 412; E.O. 13286, 68 FR 10619, 3 CFR, 2003 Comp., p. 166.

SOURCE: 62 FR 13347, Mar. 20, 1997, unless otherwise noted.

§ 78.1 Purpose.

(a) The purpose of this part is to prescribe actions, procedures, and requirements for administration of the Flood Mitigation Assistance (FMA) program, authorized by Sections 1366 and 1367 of the National Flood Insurance Act of 1968, 42 U.S.C. 4104c and 4104d. The rules in this part apply to the administration of funds awarded under the FMA program for which the application period opened prior to December 3, 2007. On or after that date, the administration of funds awarded under FMA program shall be subject to the rules in part 79 of this subchapter.

(b) The purpose of FMA is to assist State and local governments in funding cost-effective actions that reduce or eliminate the long-term risk of flood damage to buildings, manufactured homes, and other insured structures. The long-term goal of FMA is to reduce or eliminate claims under the National Flood Insurance Program (NFIP) through mitigation activities. The program provides cost-shared grants for three purposes: Planning Grants to States and communities to assess the flood risk and identify actions to reduce that risk; Project Grants to execute measures to reduce flood losses;

and Technical Assistance Grants that States may use to assist communities to develop viable FMA applications and implement FMA projects. FMA also outlines a process for development and approval of Flood Mitigation Plans.

[62 FR 13347, Mar. 20, 1997, as amended at 72 FR 61552, 61738, Oct. 31, 2007]

§ 78.2 Definitions.

(a) Except as otherwise provided in this part, the definitions set forth in part 59 of this subchapter are applicable to this part.

(b) *Community* means:

(1) A political subdivision, including any Indian tribe or authorized tribal organization or Alaskan native village or authorized native organization, that has zoning and building code jurisdiction over a particular area having special flood hazards, and is participating in the NFIP; or

(2) A political subdivision of a State, or other authority, that is designated to develop and administer a mitigation plan by political subdivisions, all of which meet the requirements of paragraph (b)(1) of this section.

§ 78.3 Responsibilities.

(a) *Federal.* The Administrator will allocate available funds to each FEMA Region. The FEMA Regional Administrator will:

(1) Allocate Technical Assistance and Planning Grants to each State through the annual Cooperative Agreements;

(2) Approve Flood Mitigation Plans in accordance with § 78.6; and

(3) Award all FMA project grants, after evaluating applications for minimum eligibility criteria and ensuring compliance with applicable Federal laws.

(b) *State.* The State will serve as grantee through the State Point of Contact (POC) designated by the Governor. The POC must have working knowledge of NFIP goals and processes and will ensure that FMA is coordinated with other mitigation activities at the State level. If a Governor chooses not to identify a POC to coordinate the FMA, communities may follow alternative procedures as described in § 78.14. States will:

(1) Provide technical assistance to communities to assist them in developing applications and implementing approved applications;

(2) Award planning grants;

(3) Submit plans to the FEMA Regional Administrator for approval;

(4) Evaluate project applications, selecting projects to forward to the FEMA Regional Administrator for final approval; and

(5) Submit performance and financial reports to FEMA in compliance with 44 CFR 13.40 and 13.41.

(c) *Community*. The community will:

(1) Complete and submit applications to the State POC for the Planning and Projects Grants;

(2) Prepare and submit the Flood Mitigation Plan;

(3) Implement all approved projects;

(4) Comply with FMA requirements, 44 CFR part 13, the grant agreement, applicable Federal, State and local laws and regulations (as applicable); and

(5) Account for the appropriate use of grant funds to the State POC.

[62 FR 13347, Mar. 20, 1997, as amended at 74 FR 15343, Apr. 3, 2009]

§78.4 Applicant eligibility.

(a) The State is eligible to apply for grants for Technical Assistance.

(b) State agencies and communities are eligible to apply for Planning and Project Grants and to act as subgrantee. Communities on probation or suspended under 44 CFR part 60 of the NFIP are not eligible. To be eligible for Project Grants, an eligible applicant will develop, and have approved by the FEMA Regional Administrator , a Flood Mitigation Plan in accordance with §78.5.

§78.5 Flood Mitigation Plan development.

A Flood Mitigation Plan will articulate a comprehensive strategy for implementing technically feasible flood mitigation activities for the area affected by the plan. At a minimum, plans will include the following elements:

(a) Description of the planning process and public involvement. Public involvement may include workshops, public meetings, or public hearings.

(b) Description of the existing flood hazard and identification of the flood risk, including estimates of the number and type of structures at risk, repetitive loss properties, and the extent of flood depth and damage potential.

(c) The applicant's floodplain management goals for the area covered by the plan.

(d) Identification and evaluation of cost-effective and technically feasible mitigation actions considered.

(e) Presentation of the strategy for reducing flood risks and continued compliance with the NFIP, and procedures for ensuring implementation, reviewing progress, and recommending revisions to the plan.

(f) Documentation of formal plan adoption by the legal entity submitting the plan (e.g., Governor, Mayor, County Executive).

§78.6 Flood Mitigation Plan approval process.

The State POC will forward all Flood Mitigation Plans to the FEMA Regional Administrator for approval. The Regional Administrator will notify the State POC of the approval or disapproval of the plan within 120 days after submission. If the Regional Administrator does not approve a mitigation plan, the Regional Administrator will notify the State POC of the reasons for non-approval and offer suggestions for improvement.

§78.7 Grant application procedures.

States will apply for Technical Assistance and Planning Grants through the annual Cooperative Agreement between FEMA and the State. The State POC will be notified regarding their available funds for project grants each fiscal year. The State may forward project applications to FEMA for review at any time.

§78.8 Grant funding limitations.

(a) The Administrator will allocate the available funds for FMA each fiscal year. Each State will receive a base amount of $10,000 for Planning Grants and $100,000 for Project Grants, with the remaining funds distributed based on the number of NFIP policies, repetitive loss structures, and other such criteria as the Administrator may determine in furtherance of the disaster resistant community concept.

(b) A maximum of $1,500,000 may be allocated for Planning Grants nationally each fiscal year. A Planning Grant will not be awarded to a State or community more than once every 5 years, and an individual Planning Grant will not exceed $150,000 to any State agency applicant, or $50,000 to any community applicant. The total Planning Grant made in any fiscal year to any State, including all communities located in the State, will not exceed $300,000.

(c) A maximum of ten percent of the funds available for Project Grants will be allocated to Technical Assistance grants each fiscal year.

(d) The total amount of FMA Project Grant funds provided during any 5-year period will not exceed $10,000,000 to any State or $3,300,000 to any community. The total amount of Project Grant funds provided to any State, including all communities located in the State will not exceed $20,000,000 during any 5-year period.

§ 78.9 Planning grant approval process.

The State POC will evaluate and approve applications for Planning Grants. Funds will be provided only for the flood portion of any mitigation plan, and Planning Grants will not be awarded to develop new or improved floodplain maps. The performance period for each Planning Grant will not exceed 3 years.

§ 78.10 Project grant approval process.

The State POC will solicit applications from eligible applicants, review projects for eligibility, and select applications for funding. Those project applications will then be forwarded to FEMA for final approval. FEMA will provide funding on a project by project basis through a supplement to the annual Cooperative Agreement. The FEMA Regional Administrator will notify States regarding the program schedule at the beginning of each fiscal year.

§ 78.11 Minimum project eligibility criteria.

The identification of a project or activity in an approved Flood Mitigation Plan does not mean it meets FMA eligibility criteria. Projects must:

(a) Be cost-effective, not costing more than the anticipated value of the reduction in both direct damages and subsequent negative impacts to the area if future floods were to occur. Both costs and benefits are computed on a net present value basis.

(b) Be in conformance with 44 CFR part 9, Floodplain Management and Protection of Wetlands; Executive Order 12699, Seismic Safety of Federal and Federally Assisted or Regulated New Building Construction; 44 CFR part 10, Environmental Considerations; and any applicable environmental laws and regulations.

(c) Be technically feasible.

(d) Be in conformance with the minimum standards of the NFIP Floodplain Management Regulations at 44 CFR part 60.

(e) Be in conformance with the Flood Mitigation Plan; the type of project being proposed must be identified in the plan.

(f) Be located physically in a participating NFIP community that is not on probation or must benefit such community directly by reducing future flood damages.

§ 78.12 Eligible types of projects.

The following types of projects are eligible for funding through FMA, providing they meet all other eligibility criteria.

(a) Acquisition of insured structures and underlying real property in fee simple and easements restricting real property to open space uses.

(b) Relocation of insured structures from acquired or restricted real property to non hazard-prone sites.

(c) Demolition and removal of insured structures on acquired or restricted real property.

(d) Elevation of insured residential structures in accordance with 44 CFR 60.3.

(e) Elevation or dry floodproofing of insured non-residential structures in accordance with 44 CFR 60.3.

(f) Other activities that bring an insured structure into compliance with the floodplain management requirements at 44 CFR 60.3.

(g) Minor physical flood mitigation projects that reduce localized flooding problems and do not duplicate the flood prevention activities of other Federal agencies.

(h) Beach nourishment activities.

§ 78.13 Grant administration.

(a) FEMA may contribute up to 75 percent of the total eligible costs of each grant. At least 25 percent of the total eligible costs will be provided from a nonFederal source. Of this amount, not more than one half will be provided from in-kind contributions. Allowable costs will be governed by OMB Circular A-87 and 44 CFR part 13.

(b) The grantee must submit performance and financial reports to FEMA and must ensure that all subgrantees are aware of their responsibilities under 44 CFR part 13.

(c) FEMA will recapture any funds provided to a State or a community under FMA and deposit the amounts in the National Flood Mitigation Fund if the applicant has not provided the appropriate matching funds, the approved project has not been completed within the timeframes specified in the grant agreement, or the completed project does not meet the criteria specified in the regulations in this part.

[62 FR 13347, Mar. 20, 1997, as amended at 74 FR 15343, Apr. 3, 2009]

§ 78.14 Alternative procedures.

For the purposes of this part, alternative procedures are available which allow the community to coordinate directly with FEMA in implementing the program. These alternative procedures are available in the following circumstances. Native American tribes or authorized tribal organizations may submit plans and applications to the State POC or directly to the FEMA Regional Administrator . If a Governor chooses not to identify a POC to coordinate the FMA, communities may also submit plans and applications to the FEMA Regional Administrator.

PART 79—FLOOD MITIGATION GRANTS

Sec.

AUTHORITY: 6 U.S.C. 101; 42 U.S.C. 4001 et seq.; 42 U.S.C. 4104c, 4104d; Reorganization Plan No. 3 of 1978, 43 FR 41943, 3 CFR, 1978 Comp., p. 329; E.O. 12127, 44 FR 19367, 3 CFR, 1979 Comp., p. 376; E.O. 12148, 44 FR 43239, 3 CFR, 1979 Comp., p. 412; E.O. 13286, 68 FR 10619, 3 CFR, 2003 Comp., p. 166.

SOURCE: 72 FR 61738, Oct. 31, 2007, unless otherwise noted.

§ 79.1   Purpose.

(a) The purpose of this part is to prescribe actions, procedures, and requirements for administration of the hazard mitigation grant programs made available under the National Flood Insurance Act of 1968, as amended, and the Flood Disaster Protection Act of 1973, as amended, 42 U.S.C. 4001 et seq. The Severe Repetitive Loss (SRL) and Flood Mitigation Assistance (FMA) grant programs mitigate losses from floods, minimizing impacts to the National Flood Insurance Fund (NFIF). The rules in this part apply to the administration of funds under the SRL and FMA programs for which the application period opens on or after December 3, 2007. Prior to this date, the administration of funds under the FMA program shall be subject to the rules in part 78 of this subchapter.

(b) The purpose of the SRL program is to:

(1) Assist State and local governments in funding actions that reduce or eliminate the risk of flood damage to residential properties insured under the National Flood Insurance Program (NFIP) that meet the definition of severe repetitive loss property;

(2) Reduce the need to increase flood insurance premiums of NFIP policyholders that would otherwise be required to pay for potential future repetitive claims associated with severe repetitive loss properties; and

(3) Reduce loss of life, property damage, outlays for the NFIF, and Federal disaster assistance by reducing or eliminating the risk of flood damage to those insured properties that have historically experienced the most severe flood losses.

(c) The purpose of the FMA program is to assist State and local governments in funding cost-effective actions that reduce or eliminate the risk of flood damage to buildings, manufactured homes, and other structures insured under the NFIP.

§ 79.2 Definitions.

(a) Except as otherwise provided in this part, the definitions set forth in section 59.1 of this subchapter are applicable to this part.

(b) *Applicant* is the State or Indian tribal government applying to FEMA for a grant, and which will be accountable for the use of the funds.

(c) *Community* means:

(1) A political subdivision, including any Indian Tribe, authorized Tribal organization, Alaska Native village or authorized native organization, that has zoning and building code jurisdiction over a particular area having special flood hazards, and is participating in the NFIP; or

(2) A political subdivision of a State, or other authority that is designated by a political subdivision to develop and administer a mitigation plan.

(d) *Grantee* means the State or Indian tribal government to which FEMA awards a grant and which is accountable for the use of the funds provided. The grantee is the entire legal entity, even if only a particular component of the entity is designated in the grant award document.

(e) *Indian Tribal government* means any Federally recognized governing body of an Indian or Alaska Native Tribe, band, nation, pueblo, village, or community that the Secretary of Interior acknowledges to exist as an Indian Tribe under the Federally Recognized Indian Tribe List Act of 1994, 25 U.S.C.

479a. This does not include Alaska Native corporations, the ownership of which is vested in private individuals.

(f) *Market Value* is generally defined as the amount in cash, or on terms reasonably equivalent to cash, for which in all probability the property would have sold on the effective date of the valuation, after a reasonable exposure time on the open competitive market, from a willing and reasonably knowledgeable seller to a willing and reasonably knowledgeable buyer, with neither acting under any compulsion to buy or sell, giving due consideration to all available economic uses of the property at the time of the valuation.

(g) *Multifamily Property* means a property consisting of 5 or more residences.

(h) *Severe Repetitive Loss Properties* are defined as single or multifamily residential properties that are covered under an NFIP flood insurance policy and:

(1) That have incurred flood-related damage for which 4 or more separate claims payments have been made, with the amount of each claim (including building and contents payments) exceeding $5,000, and with the cumulative amount of such claims payments exceeding $20,000; or

(2) For which at least 2 separate claims payments (building payments only) have been made under such coverage, with cumulative amount of such claims exceeding the market value of the building.

(3) In both instances, at least 2 of the claims must be within 10 years of each other, and claims made within 10 days of each other will be counted as 1 claim.

(i) *Subapplicant* means a State agency, community, or Indian tribal government submitting an application for planning or project activity to the applicant for assistance under the FMA or SRL programs. Upon grant award, the subapplicant is referred to as the subgrantee.

(j) *Subgrant* means an award of financial assistance made under a grantee to an eligible subgrantee.

(k) *Subgrantee* means the State agency, community, or Indian tribal government or other legal entity to which a subgrant is awarded and which is accountable to the grantee for the use of the funds provided.

(l) *Administrator* means the head of the Federal Emergency Management Agency, or his/her designated representative.

(m) *Regional Administrator* means the head of a Federal Emergency Management Agency regional office, or his/her designated representative.

[72 FR 61738, Oct. 31, 2007, as amended at 74 FR 47480, Sept. 16, 2009]

§ 79.3 Responsibilities.

(a) *Federal Emergency Management Agency (FEMA).* Administer and provide oversight to all FEMA-related hazard mitigation programs and grants, including:

(1) Issue program implementation procedures, as necessary, which will include information on availability of funding;

(2) Allocate funds to States for the FMA and for the SRL programs;

(3) Award all grants to the grantee after evaluating subgrant applications for eligibility and ensuring compliance with applicable Federal laws, giving priority to such properties, or to the subset of such properties, as the Administrator may determine are in the best interest of the NFIF;

(4) Provide technical assistance and training to State, local and Indian tribal governments regarding the mitigation and grants management process;

(5) Review and approve State, Indian tribal, and local mitigation plans in accordance with part 201 of this chapter;

(6) Comply with applicable Federal statutory, regulatory, and Executive Order requirements related to environmental and historic preservation compliance, including reviewing and supplementing, if necessary, the environmental analyses conducted by the State and subgrantee in accordance with part 10 of this chapter;

(7) Establish and maintain an updated list of SRL properties and make such information available to States and communities; and

(8) Notify owners of SRL properties that their properties meet the definition of a severe repetitive loss property and provide a summary of the opportunities and implications of being identified as such.

(b) *State.* The State will serve as the applicant and grantee through a single Point of Contact (POC) for the FMA and SRL programs. The POC is a State agency that must have working knowledge of NFIP goals, requirements, and processes and ensure that the programs are coordinated with other mitigation activities at the State level. States will:

(1) Have a FEMA approved Mitigation Plan in accordance with part 201 of this chapter;

(2) Review and submit local mitigation plans to the FEMA Regional Administrator for final review and approval;

(3) Provide technical assistance and training to communities on mitigation planning, mitigation project activities, developing subgrant applications, and implementing approved subgrants;

(4) Prioritize and recommend subgrant applications to be approved by FEMA, based on the State Mitigation Plan, other State evaluation criteria and the eligibility criteria described in § 79.6;

(5) Award FEMA-approved subgrants; and

(6) Comply with program requirements under this part, grant management requirements identified under part 13 of this chapter, the grant agreement articles, and other applicable Federal, State, tribal and local laws and regulations.

(c) *Indian tribal governments.* The Indian tribal government will coordinate all tribal activities relating to hazard evaluation and mitigation including:

(1) Have a FEMA approved Tribal Mitigation Plan in accordance with § 201.7 of this chapter;

(2) A Federally Recognized Indian tribal government as defined by the Federally Recognized Indian Tribe List Act of 1994, 25 U.S.C. 479a, applying directly to FEMA for mitigation grant funding will assume the responsibilities of the "State" as the term is used in this part, as applicant or grantee, described in paragraphs (b)(3) through (6) of this section; and

(3) A Federally Recognized Indian tribal government as defined by the Federally Recognized Indian Tribe List

331

Act of 1994, 25 U.S.C. 479a, applying through the State, will assume the responsibilities of the community (as the subapplicant or subgrantee) described in paragraphs (d)(2) through (4) of this section.

(d) *Community.* The community (referred to as both subapplicant and subgrantee) will:

(1) Prepare and submit a FEMA-approved Local Mitigation Plan, consistent with the requirements of part 201 of this chapter;

(2) Complete and submit subgrant applications to the State POC for FMA planning, project and management cost subgrants, and for SRL project and management cost subgrants;

(3) Implement all approved subgrants; notifying each holder of a recorded interest in severe repetitive loss properties when an offer of mitigation assistance has been made under the SRL program, and when such offer has been refused; and

(4) Comply with program requirements under this part, grant management requirements identified under part 13 of this chapter, the grant agreement articles, and other applicable Federal, State, tribal and local laws and regulations.

§ 79.4 Availability of funding.

(a) *Allocation.* (1) For the amount made available for the SRL program, the Administrator will allocate the available funds to States each fiscal year based upon the percentage of the total number of severe repetitive loss properties located within that State. Ten percent of the total funds made available in any fiscal year will be made available to States and Indian tribal applicants that have at least 1 SRL property and that receive little or no allocation.

(2) For the amount made available for the FMA program, the Administrator will allocate the available funds each fiscal year. Funds will be distributed based upon the number of NFIP policies, repetitive loss structures, and any other such criteria as the Administrator may determine are in the best interests of the NFIF.

(i) A maximum of 7.5 percent of the amount made available in any fiscal year may be allocated for FMA planning grants nationally. A planning grant will not be awarded to a State or community more than once every 5 years, and an individual planning grant will not exceed $150,000 to any State agency applicant, or $50,000 to any community subapplicant. The total planning grant made in any fiscal year to any State, including all communities located in the State, will not exceed $300,000.

(ii) The total amount of FMA project grant funds provided during any 5-year period will not exceed $10,000,000 to any State agency(s) or $3,300,000 to any community. The total amount of project grant funds provided to any State, including all communities located in the State will not exceed $20,000,000 during any 5-year period. The Administrator may waive the limits of this subsection for any 5-year period when a major disaster or emergency is declared pursuant to the Robert T. Stafford Disaster Relief and Emergency Assistance Act for flood conditions.

(b) *Redistribution.* Funds allocated to States who choose not to participate in either the FMA or SRL program in any given year will be reallocated to participating States and Indian tribal applicants. Any funds allocated to a State, and the communities within the State, which have not been obligated within the timeframes established by the Administrator, shall be redistributed by the Administrator to other States and communities to carry out eligible activities in accordance with this part.

(c) *Cost Share.* All mitigation activities approved under the grant will be subject to the following cost-share provisions:

(1) FEMA may contribute up to 75 percent of the eligible cost of activities for grants approved for funding; or

(2) FEMA may contribute up to 90 percent of the cost of the eligible activities for each severe repetitive loss property for which grant amounts are provided if the applicant has an approved Mitigation Plan meeting the repetitive loss requirements identified in § 201.4(c)(3)(v) or § 201.7(c)(3)(vi) of this chapter, as applicable, at the time the project application is submitted;

(3) For the FMA program only, of the non-Federal contribution, not more than one half will be provided from in-kind contributions.

[72 FR 61738, Oct. 31, 2007, as amended at 74 FR 47481, Sept. 16, 2009]

§ 79.5 Application process.

(a) *Applicant or grantee.* (1) States will be notified of the amount allocated to them for the SRL and FMA programs each fiscal year, along with the application timeframes.

(2) The State will be responsible for soliciting applications from eligible communities, or subapplicants, and for reviewing and prioritizing applications prior to forwarding them to FEMA for review and award.

(3) Participation in these flood mitigation grant programs is voluntary, and States may elect not to participate in either the SRL or FMA program in any fiscal year without compromising their eligibility in future years.

(4) Indian tribal governments interested in applying directly to FEMA for either the FMA or SRL program grants should contact the appropriate FEMA Regional Administrator for application information.

(b) *Subapplicant or subgrantee.* Participation in the SRL and the FMA program is voluntary, and communities may elect not to apply. Communities or other subapplicants who choose to apply must develop applications within the timeframes and requirements established by FEMA and must submit applications to the State.

§ 79.6 Eligibility.

(a) *Eligible applicants and subapplicants.* (1) States, Indian tribal governments, and communities participating in the NFIP may apply for FMA planning and project grants and associated management costs.

(2) States, Indian tribal governments, and communities participating in the NFIP may apply for SRL project grants and associated management costs.

(3) Communities withdrawn, suspended, or not participating under part 60 of this subchapter of the NFIP are not eligible for either the FMA or SRL programs.

(b) *Plan requirement.* (1) States must have an approved State Mitigation Plan meeting the requirements of §§ 201.4 or 201.5 of this chapter in order to apply for grants through the FMA or SRL programs. Indian Tribal governments must have an approved plan meeting the requirements of § 201.7 of this chapter at the time of application.

(2) In order to be eligible for FMA and SRL project grants, subapplicants must have an approved mitigation plan at the time of application in accordance with part 201 of this chapter that, at a minimum, addresses flood hazards.

(c) *Eligible activities.* (1) *Planning.* FMA planning grants may be used to develop or update State, Indian tribal and/or local mitigation plans which meet the planning criteria outlined in part 201 of this chapter. FMA planning grants are limited to those activities necessary to develop or update the flood portion of any mitigation plan. Planning grants are not eligible for funding under the SRL program.

(2) *Projects.* Projects funded under the SRL program are limited to those activities that specifically reduce or eliminate flood damages to severe repetitive loss properties. Projects funded under the FMA program are limited to activities that reduce flood damages to properties insured under the NFIP. For either program, applications involving any activities for which implementation has already been initiated or completed are not eligible for funding, and will not be considered. Eligible activities are:

(i) Acquisition of real property from property owners, and demolition or relocation of buildings and/or structures to areas outside of the floodplain to convert the property to open space use in perpetuity, in accordance with part 80 of this subchapter;

(ii) Elevation of existing structures to at least base flood levels or higher, if required by FEMA or if required by any State or local ordinance, and in accordance with criteria established by the Administrator;

(iii) Floodproofing of existing non-residential structures in accordance with the requirements of the NFIP or higher standards if required by FEMA or if required by any State or local ordinance, and in accordance with criteria established by the Administrator;

(iv) Floodproofing of historic structures as defined in § 59.1 of this subchapter;

(v) For SRL only, demolition and rebuilding of properties to at least base flood levels or higher, if required by FEMA or if required by any State or local ordinance, and in accordance with criteria established by the Administrator; and

(vi) Minor physical localized flood reduction measures that lessen the frequency or severity of flooding and decrease predicted flood damages, and that do not duplicate the flood prevention activities of other Federal agencies. Major flood control projects such as dikes, levees, floodwalls, seawalls, groins, jetties, dams and large-scale waterway channelization projects are not eligible.

(d) *Minimum project criteria.* In addition to being an eligible project type, mitigation grant projects must also:

(1) Be in conformance with mitigation plans approved under part 201 of this chapter for the State and community where the project is located;

(2) Be in conformance with part 9 of this chapter, Floodplain management and protection of wetlands, part 10 of this chapter, Environmental considerations, § 60.3 of this subchapter, Flood plain management criteria for flood-prone areas, and other applicable Federal, State, tribal, and local laws and regulations;

(3) Be technically feasible;

(4) Solve a problem independently, or constitute a functional portion of a long-term solution where there is assurance that the project as a whole will be completed. This assurance will include documentation identifying the remaining funds necessary to complete the project, and the timeframe for completing the project;

(5) Be cost-effective and reduce the risk of future flood damage;

(6) Consider long-term changes to the areas and entities it protects, and have manageable future maintenance and modification requirements. The subgrantee is responsible for the continued maintenance needed to preserve the

hazard mitigation benefits of these measures; and

(7) Not duplicate benefits available from another source for the same purpose or assistance that another Federal agency or program has more primary authority to provide.

[72 FR 61738, Oct. 31, 2007, as amended at 74 FR 47481, Sept. 16, 2009]

§ 79.7 **Offers and appeals under the SRL program.**

(a) *Consultation.* States and communities shall consult, to the extent practicable, and in accordance with criteria determined by the Administrator, with owners of the severe repetitive loss properties to select the most appropriate eligible mitigation activity. These consultations shall be initiated in the early stages of the project development, and shall continue throughout the process. After FEMA awards the project grant, the subgrantee shall continue to consult with the property owners to determine the specific conditions of the offer.

(b) *Mitigation offer.* After FEMA awards the grant and the subgrantee completes final consultations with the property owners, the subgrantee shall develop and present official offers to the property owners participating in the mitigation activities.

(1) The offer shall include all pertinent information regarding the mitigation activity, including a detailed description of the activity (*e.g.* property acquisition, elevation), the responsibilities of and benefits to the property owner, a summary of the consultation process, timeframes, and the consequences of refusing such offer. For open space acquisitions, it will also include the market value of the property, the basis for the purchase offer, and the final offer amount. The offer will also clearly state that the property owner's participation in the SRL program is voluntary.

(2) The subgrantee will send the written offer to the property owner's current mailing address as a certified letter, along with a copy to the appropriate FEMA Regional Administrator. In addition, the subgrantee will notify each holder of a recorded interest on the property when such offer is extended, along with the identification of

the mitigation assistance being offered.

(3) The property owner will have 45 days from the date of the letter to accept or refuse the offer of mitigation assistance in writing. Failure to respond in writing within this time period will be deemed a refusal of the offer.

(c) *Insurance increases due to refusal of offer.* In any case in which the property owner refuses an offer of mitigation assistance made through the SRL program, the Administrator shall provide written notice that the chargeable insurance rates with respect to the property will increase effective on the next renewal of the policy.

(1) The chargeable insurance premium rate shall be increased to the amount equal to 150 percent of the chargeable rate for the property at the time that the offer was made, as adjusted by any other premium adjustments otherwise applicable to the property. Each time there is another claim payment in excess of $1,500, the chargeable premium rate for that property shall be the amount equal to 150 percent over the chargeable rate at the time of every such claim, as adjusted by any other premium adjustments otherwise applicable to the property. The increases shall end when the actuarial rate is reached.

(2) Upon each renewal or modification of the flood insurance coverage, the property owner will be able to accept the original mitigation offer, if the community, through the State, forwards the request to FEMA, and if sufficient funds are available.

(d) *Appeals of insurance rate increases.* Any owner of a severe repetitive loss property may appeal the decision to increase the chargeable insurance premium rate as described in paragraph (c) of this section by submitting a written appeal, including supporting documentation that is postmarked or delivered to the appropriate FEMA Regional Administrator within 90 days of the date of the notice of the insurance increase. The increase in the amount of chargeable premium rate for flood insurance coverage for the property will be suspended pending the outcome of the appeal.

(1) Appeals must be based upon one or more of the following grounds. The property owner must include documentation to support each ground serving as a basis for the appeal:

(i) The offered mitigation activity is an acquisition and the property owner would be unable to purchase a replacement of the primary residence that is of comparable value and that is functionally equivalent. The property owner must document the actions taken to locate such replacement dwelling and demonstrate that no such dwelling is available.

(ii)(A) The amount of Federal funds offered for a mitigation activity, when combined with funds from the required non-Federal sources, would not cover the actual eligible costs of the mitigation activity contained in the mitigation offer, based on independent information. In the case of an acquisition, the purchase offer is not an accurate estimation of the market value of the property, based on independent information.

(B) For a mitigation activity other than acquisition, the property owner must submit independent estimates from professional engineers or registered architects to support this claim. For an acquisition, the property owner must submit an appraisal from a qualified appraiser to support this claim, and valuations will be considered by a review appraiser.

(iii) The offered mitigation activity would diminish the integrity of a historic district, site, building, or object's significant historic characteristics to the extent where the historic resource would lose its status as listed or eligible for inclusion on the National Register of Historic Places. The property owner must submit appropriate documentation from the State Historic Preservation Officer/Tribal Historic Preservation Officer to support this claim.

(iv) For a multifamily property: Each of the flood insurance claims payments that served as the basis for its designation as a severe repetitive loss property must have resulted directly from the actions of a third party in violation of Federal, State, or local law, ordinance, or regulation. The property owner(s) must submit appropriate evidence, documentation, or data to support this claim.

(v) The property owner relied upon FEMA Flood Insurance Rate Maps (FIRMs) that were current at the time the property was purchased, and the effective FIRM and associated Flood Insurance Study (FIS) did not indicate that the property was located in an area having special flood hazards. The property owner must produce the dated FIRM and FIS in effect at the time the property was purchased to support this claim.

(vi) An alternative mitigation activity would be at least as cost effective as the offered mitigation activity. The property owner must submit documentation of the costs for a technically feasible and eligible alternative mitigation activity based on estimates from qualified appraisers, professional engineers, or registered architects, and information and documentation demonstrating the cost effectiveness using a FEMA approved methodology to support this claim.

(2) The FEMA Regional Administrator will conduct an initial review of each appeal that is filed on a timely basis to determine if the appeal complies with this section and includes sufficient documentation to be evaluated. The Regional Administrator may reject an appeal on initial review if it is made on a basis other than those listed in paragraph (d)(1) of this section; if the property owner does not provide sufficient documentation, including, if applicable, supplemental information requested by the Regional Administrator by the deadline established by the Regional Administrator, which shall not exceed the timeframe described in paragraph (d) of this section; or if the appeal otherwise fails to comply with this section.

(3) If, upon initial review, the Regional Administrator determines that the basis for the offered mitigation activity was erroneous on its face and the appeal can be resolved in favor of the property owner, the appeal will be closed and no insurance increase will apply to the property. All other cases will be referred to the Administrator for assignment to an independent third party for review. The independent third

party shall make a final determination on each appeal within 90 days of the date on which FEMA receives the appeal. As a low cost option, the property owner may request that the Administrator substitute a reviewer from FEMA's Alternative Dispute Resolution Office for the independent third party.

(4) A property owner who brings an appeal will be responsible for paying his/her attorneys' fees and costs to gather the necessary documentation and data to demonstrate the ground(s) for the appeal. Attorneys' fees and costs cannot be awarded by the independent third party.

(5) If the property owner prevails on appeal, the independent third party shall require the Administrator to charge the risk premium rate for flood insurance coverage of the property at the amount paid prior to the mitigation offer, as adjusted by any other premium adjustments otherwise applicable to the property. If the independent third party hearing the appeal is compensated for such service, the NFIF shall bear the costs of such compensation.

(6) If the property owner loses the appeal, the Administrator shall promptly increase the chargeable risk premium rate for flood insurance coverage of the property to the amount established pursuant to paragraph (c) of this section, and shall collect from the property owner the amount necessary to cover the stay of the applicability of such increased rates while the appeal was pending. If FEMA does not receive the additional premium by the date it is due, the amount of coverage will be reduced to match the amount of premium payment received. If the independent third party hearing the appeal is compensated for such service, the property owner shall bear the costs of such compensation.

§ 79.8 Allowable costs.

(a) *General.* General policies for determining allowable costs are addressed in §§ 13.4, 13.6, and 13.22 of this chapter. Allowable costs are explained in this paragraph.

(1) *Eligible Management Costs*—(i) Grantee. States are eligible to receive

management costs consisting of a maximum of 10 percent of the planning and project activities awarded to the State, each fiscal year under FMA and SRL, respectively. These costs must be included in the application to FEMA. An Indian tribal government applying directly to FEMA is eligible for management costs consisting of a maximum of 10 percent of grants awarded for planning and project activities under the SRL and FMA programs respectively.

(ii) Subgrantee. Subapplicants may include a maximum of 5 percent of the total funds requested for their subapplication for management costs to support the implementation of their planning or project activity. These costs must be included in the subapplication to the State.

(2) Indirect costs. Indirect costs of administering the FMA and SRL programs are eligible as part of the 10 percent management costs for the grantee or the 5 percent management costs of the subgrantee, but in no case do they make the recipient eligible for additional management costs that exceed the caps identified in paragraph (a)(1) of this section. In addition, all costs must be in accordance with the provisions of part 13 of this chapter and Office of Management and Budget Circular A–87.

(b) Pre-award costs. FEMA may fund eligible pre-award planning or project costs at its discretion and as funds are available. Grantees and subgrantees may be reimbursed for eligible pre-award costs for activities directly related to the development of the project or planning proposal. These costs can only be incurred during the open application period of the respective grant program. Costs associated with implementation of the activity but incurred prior to grant award are not eligible. Therefore, activities where implementation is initiated or completed prior to award are not eligible and will not be reimbursed.

(c) Duplication of benefits. Grant funds may not duplicate benefits received by or available to applicants, subapplicants and project participants from insurance, other assistance programs, legal awards, or any other source to address the same purpose. Such individual or entity must notify the grantee and FEMA of all benefits that it receives or anticipates from other sources for the same purpose. FEMA will reduce the subgrant award by the amounts available for the same purpose from another source.

(d) Negligence or other tortious conduct. FEMA grant funds are not available where an applicant, subapplicant, other project participant, or third party's negligence or intentional actions contributed to the conditions to be mitigated. If the applicant, subapplicant, or project participant suspects negligence or other tortious conduct by a third party for causing such condition, they are responsible for taking all reasonable steps to recover all costs attributable to the tortious conduct of the third party. FEMA generally considers such amounts to be duplicated benefits available for the same purpose, and will treat them consistent with paragraph (c) of this section.

(e) FEMA grant funds are not available to satisfy or reimburse for legal obligations, such as those imposed by a legal settlement, court order, or State law.

§ 79.9 Grant administration.

(a) The Grantee must follow FEMA grant requirements, including submission of performance and financial status reports, and shall follow adequate competitive procurement procedures. In addition, grantees are responsible for ensuring that all subgrantees are aware of and follow the requirements contained in part 13 of this chapter.

(b) During the implementation of an approved grant, the State POC may find that actual costs are exceeding the approved award amount. While there is no guarantee of additional funding, FEMA will only consider requests made by the State POC to pay for such overruns if:

(1) Funds are available to meet the requested increase in funding;

(2) The amended grant award meets the cost-share requirements identified in this section; and

(3) The total amount obligated to the State does not exceed the maximum funding amounts set in § 79.4(a)(2).

(c) Grantees may use cost underruns from ongoing subgrants to offset overruns incurred by another subgrant(s)

337

awarded under the same grant. All costs for which funding is requested must have been included in the original application's cost estimate.

(d) For all cost overruns that exceed the amount approved under the grant, and which require additional Federal funds, the State POC shall submit a written request with a recommendation, including a justification for the additional funding to the Regional Administrator for a determination. If approved, the Regional Administrator shall increase the grant through an amendment to the original award document.

(e) At the time of closeout, FEMA will recapture any funds provided to a State or a community under these programs if the applicant has not provided the appropriate matching funds, the approved project has not been completed within the timeframes specified in the grant agreement, or the completed project does not meet the criteria specified in this part.

PART 80—PROPERTY ACQUISITION AND RELOCATION FOR OPEN SPACE

Subpart A—General

AUTHORITY: Robert T. Stafford Disaster Relief and Emergency Assistance Act, 42 U.S.C. 5121 through 5207; the National Flood Insurance Act of 1968, as amended, 42 U.S.C. 4001 *et seq.*; Reorganization Plan No. 3 of 1978, 43 FR 41943, 3 CFR, 1978 Comp., p. 329; Homeland Security Act of 2002, 6 U.S.C. 101; E.O. 12127, 44 FR 19367, 3 CFR, 1979 Comp., p. 376; E.O. 12148, 44 FR 43239, 3 CFR, 1979 Comp., p.

412; E.O. 13286, 68 FR 10619, 3 CFR, 2003 Comp., p. 166.

SOURCE: 72 FR 61743, Oct. 31, 2007, unless otherwise noted.

Subpart A—General

§ 80.1 Purpose and scope.

This part provides guidance on the administration of FEMA mitigation assistance for projects to acquire property for open space purposes under all FEMA hazard mitigation assistance programs. It provides information on the eligibility and procedures for implementing projects for acquisition and relocation of at-risk properties from the hazard area to maintain the property for open space purposes. This part applies to property acquisition for open space project awards made under any FEMA hazard mitigation assistance program. This part supplements general program requirements of the funding grant program and must be read in conjunction with the relevant program regulations and guidance available at *http://www.fema.gov.* This part, with the exception of § 80.19 Land use and oversight, applies to projects for which the funding program application period opens or for which funding is made available pursuant to a major disaster declared on or after December 3, 2007. Prior to that date, applicable program regulations and guidance in effect for the funding program (available at *http://www.fema.gov*) shall apply. Section 80.19 Land use and oversight apply as of December 3, 2007 to all FEMA funded acquisitions for the purpose of open space.

§ 80.3 Definitions.

(a) Except as noted in this part, the definitions applicable to the funding program apply to implementation of this part. In addition, for purposes of this part:

(b) *Applicant* is the State or Indian tribal government applying to FEMA for a grant, and which will be accountable for the use of the funds.

(c) *Grantee* means the State or Indian tribal government to which FEMA awards a grant and which is accountable for the use of the funds provided. The grantee is the entire legal entity, even if only a particular component of the entity is designated in the grant award document.

(d) *Market Value* is generally defined as the amount in cash, or on terms reasonably equivalent to cash, for which in all probability the property would have sold on the effective date of the valuation, after a reasonable exposure time on the open competitive market, from a willing and reasonably knowledgeable seller to a willing and reasonably knowledgeable buyer, with neither acting under any compulsion to buy or sell, giving due consideration to all available economic uses of the property at the time of the valuation.

(e) *National of the United States* means a person within the meaning of the term as defined in the Immigration and Nationality Act, 8 U.S.C. section 1101(a)(22).

(f) *Purchase offer* is the initial value assigned to the property, which is later adjusted by applicable additions and deductions, resulting in a final offer amount to a property owner.

(g) *Qualified alien* means a person within the meaning of the term as defined at 8 U.S.C. 1641.

(h) "Qualified conservation organization" means a qualified organization with a conservation purpose pursuant to 26 CFR 1.170A–14 and applicable implementing regulations, that is such an organization at the time it acquires the property interest and that was such an organization at the time of the major disaster declaration, or for at least 2 years prior to the opening of the grant application period.

(i) *Subapplicant* means the entity that submits an application for FEMA mitigation assistance to the State or Indian tribal applicant/grantee. With respect to open space acquisition projects under the Hazard Mitigation Grant Program (HMGP), this term has the same meaning as given to the term "applicant" in part 206, subpart N of this chapter. Upon grant award, the subapplicant is referred to as the subgrantee.

(j) *Subgrant* means an award of financial assistance made under a grantee to an eligible subgrantee.

(k) *Subgrantee* means the State agency, community, or Indian tribal government or other legal entity to which a subgrant is awarded and which is accountable to the grantee for the use of the funds provided.

(l) *Administrator* means the head of the Federal Emergency Management Agency, or his/her designated representative.

(m) *Regional Administrator* means the head of a Federal Emergency Management Agency regional office, or his/her designated representative.

[72 FR 61743, Oct. 31, 2007, as amended at 74 FR 47481, Sept. 16, 2009]

§ 80.5 Roles and responsibilities.

The roles and responsibilities of FEMA, the State, the subapplicant/subgrantee, and participating property owners in the particular context of mitigation projects for the purpose of creating open space include the activities in this section. These are in addition to grants management roles and responsibilities identified in regulations and guidance of the program funding the project (available at *http://www.fema.gov*) and other responsibilities specified in this part.

(a) *Federal roles and responsibilities.* Oversee property acquisition activities undertaken under FEMA mitigation grant programs, including:

(1) Providing technical assistance to the applicant/grantee to assist in implementing project activities in compliance with this part;

(2) Reviewing applications for eligibility and compliance with this part;

(3) Reviewing proposals for subsequent transfer of a property interest and approving appropriate transferees;

(4) Making determinations on the compatibility of proposed uses with the open space purpose, in accordance with § 80.19;

(5) Complying with applicable Federal statutory, regulatory, and Executive Order requirements related to environmental and historic preservation compliance, including reviewing and supplementing, if necessary, environmental analyses conducted by the State and subgrantee in accordance with part 10 of this chapter;

(6) Providing no Federal disaster assistance, flood insurance claims payments, or other FEMA assistance with respect to the property or any open-space related improvements, after the property interest transfers; and

(7) Enforcing the requirements of this part and the deed restrictions to ensure that the property remains in open space use in perpetuity.

(b) *State (applicant/grantee) roles and responsibilities.* Serve as the point of contact for all property acquisition activities by coordinating with the subapplicant/subgrantee and with FEMA to ensure that the project is implemented in compliance with this part, including:

(1) Providing technical assistance to the subapplicant/subgrantee to assist in implementing project activities in compliance with this part;

(2) Ensuring that applications are not framed in a manner that has the effect of circumventing any requirements of this part;

(3) Reviewing the application to ensure that the proposed activity complies with this part, including ensuring that the property acquisition activities remain voluntary in nature, and that the subgrantee and property owners are made aware of such;

(4) Submitting to FEMA subapplications for proposed projects in accordance with the respective program schedule and programmatic requirements, and including all the requisite information to enable FEMA to determine the eligibility, technical feasibility, cost effectiveness, and environmental and historic preservation compliance of the proposed projects;

(5) Reviewing proposals for subsequent transfer of property interest and obtaining FEMA approval of such transfers; and ensuring that all uses proposed for the property are compatible with open space project purposes;

(6) Making no application for, nor providing, Federal disaster assistance or other FEMA assistance for the property or any open-space related improvements, after the property interest transfers;

(7) Enforcing the terms of this part and the deed restrictions to ensure that the property remains in open space use in perpetuity; and

(8) Reporting on property compliance with the open space requirements after the grant is awarded.

(c) *Subapplicant/Subgrantee roles and responsibilities.* Coordinate with the applicant/grantee and with the property owners to ensure that the project is implemented in compliance with this part, including:

(1) Submitting all applications for proposed projects in accordance with the respective program schedule and programmatic requirements, and including all the requisite information to enable the applicant/grantee and FEMA to determine the eligibility, technical feasibility, cost effectiveness, and environmental and historic preservation compliance of the proposed projects;

(2) Ensuring that applications are not framed in a manner that has the effect of circumventing any requirements of this part;

(3) Coordinating with the property owners to ensure they understand the benefits and responsibilities of participating in the project, including that participation in the project is voluntary, and that the property owner(s) are made aware of such;

(4) Developing the application and implementing property acquisition activities in compliance with this part, and ensuring that all terms of the deed restrictions and grant award are enforced;

(5) Ensuring fair procedures and processes are in place to compensate property owners and tenants affected by the purchase of property; such as determining property values and/or the amount of the mitigation offer, and reviewing property owner disputes regarding such offers;

(6) Making no application for Federal disaster assistance, flood insurance, or other FEMA benefits for the property or any open-space related improvements, after the property interest transfers;

(7) Taking and retaining full property interest, consistent with this part; or if transferring such interest, obtaining approval of the grantee and FEMA;

(8) Submitting to the grantee and FEMA proposed uses on the property for open space compatibility determinations; and

(9) Monitoring and reporting on property compliance after the grant is awarded.

(d) *Participating property owner roles and responsibilities.* Notify the subapplicant/subgrantee of its interest to participate, provide information to the subapplicant/subgrantee, and take all required actions necessary for the completion of the grant application and the implementation of property acquisition activities in accordance with this part.

Subpart B—Requirements Prior to Award

§ 80.7 General.

A project involving property acquisition or the relocation of structures for open space is eligible for hazard mitigation assistance only if the subapplicant meets the pre-award requirements set forth in this subpart. A project may not be framed in a manner that has the effect of circumventing the requirements of this subpart.

§ 80.9 Eligible and ineligible costs.

(a) *Allowable costs.* Eligible project costs may include compensation for the value of structures, for their relocation or demolition, for associated land, and associated costs. For land that is already held by an eligible entity, compensation for the land is not an allowable cost, but compensation for development rights may be allowable.

(b) *Pre-award costs.* FEMA may fund eligible pre-award project costs at its discretion and as funds are available. Grantees and subgrantees may be reimbursed for eligible pre-award costs for activities directly related to the development of the project proposal. These costs can only be incurred during the open application period of the respective grant program. Costs associated with implementation of the project but incurred prior to grant award are not eligible. Therefore, activities where implementation is initiated or completed prior to award are not eligible and will not be reimbursed.

(c) *Duplication of benefits.* Grant funds may not duplicate benefits received by or available to applicants, subapplicants and other project participants from insurance, other assistance programs, legal awards, or any other source to address the same purpose. Such individual or entity must notify the subapplicant and FEMA of all benefits that it receives, anticipates, or has available from other sources for the same purpose. FEMA will reduce the subgrant award by the amounts available for the same purpose from another source.

(d) *Negligence or other tortious conduct.* FEMA acquisition funds are not available where an applicant, subapplicant, other project participant, or third party's negligence or intentional actions contributed to the conditions to be mitigated. If the applicant, subapplicant, or project participant suspects negligence or other tortious conduct by a third party for causing such condition, they are responsible for taking all reasonable steps to recover all costs attributable to the tortious conduct of the third party. FEMA generally considers such amounts to be duplicated benefits available for the same purpose, and will treat them consistent with paragraph (c) of this section.

(e) FEMA mitigation grant funds are not available to satisfy or reimburse for legal obligations, such as those imposed by a legal settlement, court order, or State law.

§ 80.11 Project eligibility.

(a) *Voluntary participation.* Eligible acquisition projects are those where the property owner participates voluntarily, and the grantee/subgrantee will not use its eminent domain authority to acquire the property for the open space purposes should negotiations fail.

(b) *Acquisition of improved properties.* Eligible properties are those with at-risk structures on the property, including those that are damaged or destroyed due to an event. In some cases, undeveloped, at-risk land adjacent to an eligible property with existing structures may be eligible.

(c) *Subdivision restrictions.* The land may not be subdivided prior to acquisition except for portions outside the identified hazard area, such as the Special Flood Hazard Area or any risk zone identified by FEMA.

(d) *Subapplicant property interest.* To be eligible, the subapplicant must acquire or retain fee title (full property interest), except for encumbrances FEMA determines are compatible with open space uses, as part of the project implementation. A pass through of funds from an eligible entity to an ineligible entity must not occur.

(e) *Hazardous materials.* Eligible properties include only those that are not contaminated with hazardous materials, except for incidental demolition and household hazardous waste.

(f) *Open space restrictions.* Property acquired or from which a structure is removed must be dedicated to and maintained as open space in perpetuity consistent with this part.

[72 FR 61743, Oct. 31, 2007, as amended at 74 FR 47481, Sept. 16, 2009]

§ 80.13 Application information.

(a) An application for acquisition of property for the purpose of open space must include:

(1) A photograph that represents the appearance of each property site at the time of application;

(2) Assurances that the subapplicant will implement the project grant award in compliance with subparts C and D of this part;

(3) The deed restriction language, which shall be consistent with the FEMA model deed restriction that the local government will record with the property deeds. Any variation from the model deed restriction language can only be made with prior approval from FEMA's Office of General Counsel;

(4) The documentation of voluntary interest signed by each property owner, which must include that the subapplicant has informed them in writing that it will not use its eminent domain authority for the open space purpose; and

(5) Assurance that the subject property is not part of an intended, planned, or designated project area for which the land is to be acquired by a certain date, and that local and State governments have no intention to use the property for any public or private facility in the future inconsistent with this part;

(6) If the subapplicant is offering preevent value: the property owner's certification that the property owner is a National of the United States or qualified alien; and

(7) Other information as determined by the Administrator.

(b) *Consultation regarding other ongoing Federal activities.* (1) The subapplicant must demonstrate that it has consulted with the United States Army Corps of Engineers (USACE) regarding the subject land's potential future use for the construction of a levee system. The subapplicant must also demonstrate that it has, and will, reject any future consideration of such use if it accepts FEMA assistance to convert the property to permanent open space.

(2) The subapplicant must demonstrate that it has coordinated with its State Department of Transportation to ensure that no future, planned modifications, improvements, or enhancements to Federal aid systems are under consideration that will affect the subject property.

(c) *Restriction on alternate properties.* Changes to the properties in an approved mitigation project will be considered by FEMA but not approved automatically. The subapplicant must identify the alternate properties in the project application and each alternate property must meet eligibility requirements in order to be considered.

[72 FR 61743, Oct. 31, 2007, as amended at 74 FR 47481, Sept. 16, 2009]

Subpart C—Post-Award Requirements

§ 80.15 General.

A project involving property acquisition or the relocation of structures for open space must be implemented consistent with the requirements set forth in this subpart.

§ 80.17 Project implementation.

(a) *Hazardous materials.* The subgrantee shall take steps to ensure it does not acquire or include in the project properties contaminated with hazardous materials by seeking information from property owners and from other sources on the use and presence of contaminants affecting the property from owners of properties that are or were industrial or commercial, or adjacent to such. A contaminated property must be certified clean prior to participation. This excludes permitted disposal of incidental demolition and household hazardous wastes. FEMA mitigation grant funds may not be used for clean up or remediation of contaminated properties.

(b) *Clear title.* The subgrantee will obtain a title insurance policy demonstrating that fee title conveys to the subgrantee for each property to ensure that it acquires only a property with clear title. The property interest generally must transfer by a general warranty deed. Any incompatible easements or other encumbrances to the property must be extinguished before acquisition.

(c) *Purchase offer and supplemental payments.* (1) The amount of purchase offer is the current market value of the property or the market value of the property immediately before the relevant event affecting the property ("pre-event").

(i) The relevant event for Robert T. Stafford Disaster Relief and Emergency Assistance Act assistance under HMGP is the major disaster under which funds are available; for assistance under the Pre-disaster Mitigation program (PDM) (42 U.S.C. 5133), it is the most recent major disaster. Where multiple disasters have affected the same property, the grantee and subgrantee shall determine which is the relevant event.

(ii) The relevant event for assistance under the National Flood Insurance Act is the most recent event resulting in a National Flood Insurance Program (NFIP) claim of at least $5000.

(2) For acquisition of properties under the Severe Repetitive Loss program under part 79 of this subchapter, the purchase offer is not less than the greatest of the amount in paragraph (c)(1) of this section; the original purchase price paid by the participating property owner holding the flood insurance policy; or the outstanding amount of any loan to the participating property owner, which is secured by a recorded interest in the property at the time of the purchase offer.

(3) The grantee should coordinate with the subgrantee in their determination of whether the valuation should be based on pre-event or current market value. Generally, the same method to determine market value should be used for all participants in the project.

(4) A property owner who did not own the property at the time of the relevant event, or who is not a National

of the United States or qualified alien, is not eligible for a purchase offer based on pre-event market value of the property. Subgrantees who offer pre-event market value to the property owner must have already obtained certification during the application process that the property owner is either a National of the United States or a qualified alien.

(5) Certain tenants who must relocate as a result of the project are entitled to relocation benefits under the Uniform Relocation Assistance and Real Property Acquisition Policies Act (such as moving expenses, replacement housing rental payments, and relocation assistance advisory services) in accordance with 49 CFR part 24.

(6) If a purchase offer for a residential property is less than the cost of the homeowner-occupant to purchase a comparable replacement dwelling outside the hazard-prone area in the same community, the subgrantee for funding under the Severe Repetitive Loss program implemented at part 79 of this subchapter shall make available a supplemental payment to the homeowner-occupant to apply to the difference. Subgrantees for other mitigation grant programs may make such a payment available in accordance with criteria determined by the Administrator.

(7) The subgrantee must inform each property owner, in writing, of what it considers to be the market value of the property, the method of valuation and basis for the purchase offer, and the final offer amount. The offer will also clearly state that the property owner's participation in the project is voluntary.

(d) *Removal of Existing Buildings.* Existing incompatible facilities must be removed by demolition or by relocation outside of the hazard area within 90 days of settlement of the property transaction. The FEMA Regional Administrator may grant an exception to this deadline only for a particular property based upon written justification if extenuating circumstances exist, but shall specify a final date for removal.

(e) *Deed Restriction.* The subgrantee, upon settlement of the property transaction, shall record with the deed of

343

the subject property notice of applicable land use restrictions and related procedures described in this part, consistent with FEMA model deed restriction language.

[72 FR 61743, Oct. 31, 2007, as amended at 74 FR 47481, Sept. 16, 2009]

§ 80.19 Land use and oversight.

This section applies to acquisitions for open space projects to address flood hazards. If the Administrator determines to mitigate in other circumstances, he/she will adapt the provisions of this section as appropriate.

(a) *Open space requirements.* The property shall be dedicated and maintained in perpetuity as open space for the conservation of natural floodplain functions.

(1) These uses may include: Parks for outdoor recreational activities; wetlands management; nature reserves; cultivation; grazing; camping (except where adequate warning time is not available to allow evacuation); unimproved, unpaved parking lots; buffer zones; and other uses FEMA determines compatible with this part.

(i) Allowable uses generally do not include: Walled buildings, levees, dikes, or floodwalls, paved roads, highways, bridges, cemeteries, landfills, storage of any hazardous or toxic materials, above or below ground pumping and switching stations, above or below ground storage tanks, paved parking, off-site fill or other uses that obstruct the natural and beneficial functions of the floodplain.

(ii) In the rare circumstances where the Administrator has determined competing Federal interests were unavoidable and has analyzed floodplain impacts for compliance with § 60.3 of this subchapter or higher standards, the Administrator may find only USACE projects recognized by FEMA in 2000 and improvements to pre-existing Federal-aid transportation systems to be allowable uses.

(2) No new structures or improvements will be built on the property except as indicated below:

(i) A public facility that is open on all sides and functionally related to a designated open space or recreational use;

(ii) A public restroom; or

(iii) A structure that is compatible with open space and conserves the natural function of the floodplain, which the Administrator approves in writing before the construction of the structure begins.

(3) Any improvements on the property shall be in accordance with proper floodplain management policies and practices. Structures built on the property according to paragraph (a)(2) of this section shall be floodproofed or elevated to at least the base flood level plus 1 foot of freeboard, or greater, if required by FEMA, or if required by any State or local ordinance, and in accordance with criteria established by the Administrator.

(4) After the date of property settlement, no Federal entity or source may provide disaster assistance for any purpose with respect to the property, nor may any application for such assistance be made to any Federal entity or source.

(5) The property is not eligible for coverage under the NFIP for damage to structures on the property occurring after the date of the property settlement, except for pre-existing structures being relocated off the property as a result of the project.

(b) *Subsequent transfer.* After acquiring the property interest, the subgrantee, including successors in interest, shall convey any interest in the property only if the Regional Administrator, through the State, gives prior written approval of the transferee in accordance with this paragraph.

(1) The request by the subgrantee, through the State, to the Regional Administrator must include a signed statement from the proposed transferee that it acknowledges and agrees to be bound by the terms of this section, and documentation of its status as a qualified conservation organization if applicable.

(2) The subgrantee may convey a property interest only to a public entity or to a qualified conservation organization. However, the subgrantee may convey an easement or lease to a private individual or entity for purposes compatible with the uses described in paragraph (a), of this section, with the prior approval of the Regional Administrator, and so long as the conveyance

does not include authority to control and enforce the terms and conditions of this section.

(3) If title to the property is transferred to a public entity other than one with a conservation mission, it must be conveyed subject to a conservation easement that shall be recorded with the deed and shall incorporate all terms and conditions set forth in this section, including the easement holder's responsibility to enforce the easement. This shall be accomplished by one of the following means:

(i) The subgrantee shall convey, in accordance with this paragraph, a conservation easement to an entity other than the title holder, which shall be recorded with the deed, or

(ii) At the time of title transfer, the subgrantee shall retain such conservation easement, and record it with the deed.

(4) Conveyance of any property interest must reference and incorporate the original deed restrictions providing notice of the conditions in this section and must incorporate a provision for the property interest to revert to the subgrantee or grantee in the event that the transferee ceases to exist or loses its eligible status under this section.

(c) *Inspection.* FEMA, its representatives and assigns, including the grantee shall have the right to enter upon the property, at reasonable times and with reasonable notice, for the purpose of inspecting the property to ensure compliance with the terms of this part, the property conveyance and of the grant award.

(d) *Monitoring and reporting.* Every 3 years the subgrantee (in coordination with any current successor in interest) through the grantee, shall submit to the FEMA Regional Administrator a report certifying that the subgrantee has inspected the property within the month preceding the report, and that the property continues to be maintained consistent with the provisions of this part, the property conveyance and the grant award.

(e) *Enforcement.* The subgrantee, grantee, FEMA, and their respective representatives, successors and assigns, are responsible for taking measures to bring the property back into compliance if the property is not maintained according to the terms of this part, the conveyance, and the grant award. The relative rights and responsibilities of FEMA, the grantee, the subgrantee, and subsequent holders of the property interest at the time of enforcement, shall include the following:

(1) The grantee will notify the subgrantee and any current holder of the property interest in writing and advise them that they have 60 days to correct the violation.

(i) If the subgrantee or any current holder of the property interest fails to demonstrate a good faith effort to come into compliance with the terms of the grant within the 60-day period, the grantee shall enforce the terms of the grant by taking any measures it deems appropriate, including but not limited to bringing an action at law or in equity in a court of competent jurisdiction.

(ii) FEMA, its representatives, and assignees may enforce the terms of the grant by taking any measures it deems appropriate, including but not limited to 1 or more of the following:

(A) Withholding FEMA mitigation awards or assistance from the State and subgrantee; and current holder of the property interest.

(B) Requiring transfer of title. The subgrantee or the current holder of the property interest shall bear the costs of bringing the property back into compliance with the terms of the grant; or

(C) Bringing an action at law or in equity in a court of competent jurisdiction against any or all of the following parties: the grantee, the subgrantee, and their respective successors.

Subpart D—After the Grant Requirements

§80.21 Closeout requirements.

Upon closeout of the grant, the subgrantee, through the grantee, shall provide FEMA, with the following:

(a) A copy of the deed recorded for each property, demonstrating that each property approved in the original application was mitigated and that the deed restrictions recorded are consistent with the FEMA model deed restriction language to meet the requirements of this part;

(b) A photo of each property site after project completion;

(c) The latitude-longitude coordinates of each property site;

(d) Identification of each property as a repetitive loss property, if applicable; and

(e) Other information as determined by the Administrator.

PARTS 81–149 [RESERVED]

SUBCHAPTER C—FIRE PREVENTION AND CONTROL

PART 150—PUBLIC SAFETY AWARDS TO PUBLIC SAFETY OFFICERS

Sec.
150.1 Background and purpose.
150.2 Definitions.
150.3 Nomination process.
150.4 Nomination and selection criteria.
150.5 Joint Public Safety Awards Board.
150.6 Design and procurement of awards.
150.7 Selection process.
150.8 Presentation of awards.
150.9 Funding.
150.10 Date of submission of nominations.

AUTHORITY: Federal Fire Prevention and Control Act of 1974, sec. 15, 15 U.S.C. 2214; Reorg. Plan No. 3 of 1978, 3 CFR, 1978 Comp., p. 329, and E.O. 12127, dated Mar. 31, 1979, 3 CFR, 1979 Comp., p. 376.

SOURCE: 49 FR 39845, Oct. 11, 1984, unless otherwise noted.

§ 150.1 Background and purpose.

The regulations in this part are issued under the authority of the Federal Fire Prevention and Control Act of 1974 (the Act), 15 U.S.C. 2201 *et seq.* The Act establishes two classes of honorary awards for public safety officers and directs the issuance of the necessary joint regulations by the Administrator of the Federal Emergency Management Agency (FEMA) and the Attorney General. The functions of the Secretary of Commerce were transferred by Reorganization Plan No. 3 of 1978 to the Administrator , FEMA. Since initial passage of the Act, civil defense functions which then were delegated to the Secretary of Defense have been delegated to theAdministrator, FEMA. Section 15 of the Act has been amended to delete the Secretary of Defense from participating in the granting of awards. *See* Public Law 98–241, 98 Stat. 95, 96 (1984). The Administrator , FEMA, and the Attorney General are issuing this regulation to implement the statutory provisions for FEMA and the Department of Justice.

§ 150.2 Definitions.

Civil defense officer (or member of a recognized civil defense or emergency preparedness organization) means any individual who is assigned to and is performing the assigned tasks of the unit or organization which has been given a mission under the direction or operational control of a Civil Defense or Emergency Preparedness Director/ Coordinator in accordance with a Federal, State or local emergency plan and sanctioned by the government concerned. This also includes emergency management officers. This includes volunteers and paid employees for any governmental entity.

Distinguished Public Safety Service Award means the *Secretary's Award for Distinguished Public Safety Service*, presented by either the Attorney General or the Administrator of FEMA to public safety officers for distinguished service in the field of public safety.

FEMA means the Federal Emergency Management Agency.

Firefighter means a member, regardless of rank or duties, of any organization (including such Federal organizations) in any State consisting of personnel, apparatus, and equipment which has as its purpose protecting property and maintaining the safety and welfare of the public from the dangers of fire. This term includes volunteer or paid employees. The location of any such organization may include, but is not limited to, a Federal installation, a State, city, town, borough, parish, county, fire district, rural fire district or other special district.

Joint Board means the Joint Public Safety Awards Board established by the Administrator of the Federal Emergency Management Agency and the Attorney General to carry out the purposes of the Federal Fire Prevention and Control Act of 1974.

Law enforcement officer means a person involved in the control or reduction of crime and juvenile delinquency or enforcement of the criminal laws. This includes, but is not limited to, police, corrections, probation, parole, and court officers, and Federal civilian officers in such capacities.

Nominating official means the head of a Federal government department or agency, or his delegatee(s), the governor or other head of a State, or the chief executive or executives of any

347

general governmental unit within any State.

President's Award means the President's Award for Outstanding Public Safety Service, presented by the President of the United States to public safety officers for extraordinary valor in the line of duty or for outstanding contributions to public safety.

Public safety officer means a person serving a public agency, with or without compensation, as a firefighter, a civil defense officer (or member of a recognized civil defense or emergency preparedness organization), or a law enforcement officer, including a corrections or court officer.

State means any State, the District of Columbia, the Commonwealth of Puerto Rico, the Commonwealth of the Northern Mariana Islands, the Virgin Islands, Guam, American Samoa, the Trust Territory of the Pacific Islands and any other territory or possession of the United States.

§ 150.3   Nomination process.

(a) The Nominating Officials nominating Firefighters and Civil Defense Officers shall submit their nominations for the President's Award or Distinguished Public Safety Service Award to the Executive Secretary, Joint Public Safety Awards Board, National Emergency Training Center, Emmitsburg, MD 21727. Copies of all nominations shall also be forwarded, depending on the category of the nominee, as follows:

(1) *Firefighter:*

FEMA, Attention: Superintendent, National Fire Academy, Emmitsburg, MD 21727

(2) *Civil defense officer (or member of a recognized civil defense or emergency preparedness organization):*

FEMA, Attention: Superintendent, Emergency Management Institute, Emmitsburg, MD 21727

(b) The Nominating Officials nominating law enforcement, corrections or court officers shall submit their nominations for the President's Award or Distinguished Public Safety Service Awards to: Assistant Attorney General for Administration, U.S. Department of Justice, Washington, DC 20530.

(c) All nominations shall be submitted in writing in accordance with the requirements prescribed in this section and §150.4 at the earliest practicable date after the performance of the act or acts for which the nomination is made. Nominations for each year shall be made before November 15; any received thereafter will be considered as having been made for the following year. However, for the year 1983, nominations may be made by February 28, 1985.

(d) Nominations for the President's Award or the Distinguished Public Safety Service Award should include the name of the candidate, his/her position, title and address, and public agency served, the locale where the candidate performs his/her duties, the name, address and telephone number of the nominating official, a summary describing the outstanding contribution, distinguished service or extraordinary valor, and the dates relating thereto. The description should be sufficiently concise and specific to justify the request for recognition of the public safety officer through the presentation of either of the awards. Copies of any published factual accounts of the nominee's accomplishment should also be attached when available.

(e) An annual invitation shall be issued by the Joint Board for nominations for the President's Award and, on behalf of the Attorney General and the Administrator of FEMA, for the Distinguished Public Safety Service Award. The invitation shall be issued by letter or by notice in apporpriate publications of interest to the public safety community. However, nominating officials need not wait for such invitation but may nominate at the most appropriate time in accordance with the other provisions of this part.

[49 FR 39845, Oct. 11, 1984, as amended at 50 FR 3350, Jan. 24, 1985; 74 FR 15344, Apr. 3, 2009]

§ 150.4   Nomination and selection criteria.

(a) Nominations for the President's Award or the Distinguished Public Safety Service Award shall be made on the basis of, and in conformity with, the following uniform criteria.

(1) *President's Award.* Documentation accompanying the nomination for this Award must indicate not only that the

348

nominee unquestionably meets the standards established for the Distinguished Public Safety Service Award (see paragraph (a)(2) of this section), but also deserves greater public recognition because he/she has demonstrated unique qualities of courage, imagination or ability, which have resulted in outstanding contributions to the public safety.

(2) *Distinguished Public Safety Service Award.* Nomination for this award shall clearly show that the public safety officer's qualifying service or act is marked by courage, imagination or ability or has resulted in a significant contribution to the public safety accomplished through an originality of effort which far exceeds the expected quality of performance of the normal duties assigned to the nominee.

(b) A nomination shall specify whether it is being submitted for the President's Award or the Distinguished Public Safety Award.

[49 FR 39845, Oct. 11, 1984, as amended at 74 FR 15344, Apr. 3,2009]

§150.5 Joint Public Safety Awards Board.

(a) A Joint Public Safety Awards Board (Joint Board) is hereby established to fulfill the responsibilities of the Administrator of FEMA and the Attorney General by administering the process of nomination for the President's Award and by participating in the selection process with the Executive Office of the President. The Joint Board shall consist of ten representatives who are Federal employees and are of appropriate rank (at or equivalent to grades GM–14 or above). Five persons shall be named by and represent the Administrator of FEMA, and five persons shall be named by and represent the Attorney General. The representatives serving on the Joint Board shall select one of their number to act as the chairperson.

(b) Representatives on the Joint Board shall serve in addition to their regular duties and without additional compensation. Consistent with the requirements of this part, the members of the Joint Board shall establish the procedures by which the selections for the President's Award shall be made to assure the timely presentation of these awards.

(c) A National Emergency Training Center employee shall act as Executive Secretary of the Joint Board. The Executive Secretary shall perform such functions as are appropriate to the Board's responsibilities, including the receipt of all nominations and the communication of nomination information, for the purpose of receiving comments thereon, from members of the public safety community pursuant to §150.5(e). The Executive Secretary shall be appointed by the Associate Director, Training and Fire Programs of FEMA.

(d) The Joint Board shall review the nominations for the President's Award and shall recommend to the Administrator , FEMA, and the Attorney General by February 1 of each year, those nominees determined by it to merit consideration for the President's Award together with reasons therefor. The Administrator and the Attorney General shall then recommend to the President those nominees determined by them to merit the President's Award, together with the reasons therefor. Recommendations for 1983 shall be submitted on or before March 29, 1985.

(e) The Joint Board may request that persons representing a cross-section of the national public safety community comment upon nominations made to the Board for the President's Award. Both the request for comments and the comments themselves shall be made in writing.

[49 FR 39845, Oct. 11, 1984, as amended at 50 FR 3350, Jan. 24, 1985]

§150.6 Design and procurement of awards.

(a) The Joint Board shall consult with the Department of the Treasury and the Executive Office of the President in regard to the design and procurement of the appropriate citations and medal for the President's Award in accordance with applicable laws and regulations.

(b) Insofar as practicable, the designs for Distinguised Public Safety Service Awards of FEMA and the Department of Justice shall be coordinate so as to avoid distinctly different recognition of the various public safety officers.

§ 150.7 Selection process.

(a) *President's Award.* Nominations for the President's Award shall be reviewed, and winners selected by the President (or his designee) in accordance with the requirements of § 150.3, the criteria in § 150.4(a)(1), and the procedures of § 150.5.

(b) *Distinguished Public Safety Service Award.* Upon receipt of nominations for this Award, the Administrator of FEMA or the Attorney General shall cause an evaluation and selection of the nominees to be made in accordance with the requirements of § 150.3 and the criteria prescribed in § 150.4(a)(2). In reviewing nominations, the Attorney General or the Administrator of FEMA may request that persons representing the relevant segment of the national public safety community comment upon the nomination and accompanying documentation. Both the request for comments and the comments themselves shall be made in writing.

(c) Individuals nominated for the President's Award who are considered not to meet the criteria for the Award by the Joint Board or who are not recommended to or selected by the President shall be automatically considered by the appropriate authority for nomination for the Distinguished Public Safety Service Award.

(d) Individuals nominated for the Distinguished Public Safety Service Award may be considered by the Joint Board for the President's Award if the Administratorof FEMA or the Attorney General determines that consideration for the President's Award is merited.

§ 150.8 Presentation of awards.

(a) Presentation of the President's Award shall be made at such time, place and circumstances as the Executive Office of the President directs. There shall not be more twelve President's Awards given out during any calendar year.

(b) Presentation of the Distinguished Public Safety Service Award shall be made by the Attorney General or the Administrator of FEMA or a designee at such time, place and circumstances as the Administrator of FEMA or the Attorney General determines. There is no limit on the number of these awards made during any calendar year.

§ 150.9 Funding.

(a) *President's Award.* The costs involved in designing and striking the medal to be presented in conjunction with the President's Award shall be prorated among the agencies concerned. The cost of producing the medal and printing the certificate shall be borne by FEMA if the recipient is a firefighter or a civil defense officer. If the award recipient is a law enforcement officer, then such cost shall be borne by the Department of Justice.

(b) *Distinguished Public Safety Service Award.* All expenses in connection with this Award shall be borne by the appropriate Agency.

§ 150.10 Date of submission of nominations.

Nominations may only be submitted for acts, services, or contributions occurring within two years preceding the November 15 cut-off date described in § 150.3(c) of this part. However, nominations submitted prior to the February 28, 1985 cut-off date may be made for acts, services or contributions occurring on or after October 29, 1972 (two years before the effective date of the Act).

[50 FR 3350, Jan. 24, 1985]

PART 151—REIMBURSEMENT FOR COSTS OF FIREFIGHTING ON FEDERAL PROPERTY

Subpart A—Purpose, Scope, Definitions

151.23 Penalties.

AUTHORITY: Secs. 11 and 21(b)(5), Federal Fire Prevention and Control Act of 1974 (15 U.S.C. 2210 and 2218(b)(5)); Reorganization Plan No. 3 of 1978 (3 CFR, 1978 Comp., p. 379) and E.O. 12127, dated Mar. 31, 1979 (3 CFR, 1979 Comp., p. 376).

SOURCE: 49 FR 5929, Feb. 16, 1984, unless otherwise noted.

Subpart A—Purpose, Scope, Definitions

§ 151.01 Purpose.

Section 11 of the Federal Fire Prevention and Control Act of 1974, provides that "each fire service that engages in the fighting of a fire on property which is under the jurisdiction of the United States may file a claim with the Administrator of the Federal Emergency Management Agency for the amount of direct expenses and direct losses incurred by such fire service as a result of fighting such fire." This part, implements section 11 of the Act and governs the submission, determination, and appeal of claims under section 11.

§ 151.02 Scope.

Fire services, in any State, may file claims for reimbursement under section 11 and this part for the direct expenses and losses which are additional firefighting costs over and above normal operating costs incurred while fighting a fire on property which is under the jurisdiction of the United States. Section 11 requires that certain payments be deducted from those costs and that the Treasury Department will ordinarily pay the amount resulting from the application of that formula. Where the United States has entered into a contract (which is not a mutual aid agreement, defined in § 151.03) for the provision of fire protection, and it is the intent of the parties that reimbursement under section 11 is unavailable, this intent will normally govern. Where a mutual aid agreement is in effect between the claimant and an agency of the United States for the property upon which the fire occurred, reimbursement will be available in otherwise proper situations. However, any payments (including the value of services) rendered under the agreement during the term of the agreement (or the Federal fiscal year in which the fire occurred, if no term is discernible) shall be deducted from the costs claimed, pursuant to § 151.12.

§ 151.03 Definitions.

(a) *The Act* means the Federal Fire Prevention and Control Act of 1974, 15 U.S.C. 2201 *et seq.*

(b) *Additional firefighting costs over and above normal operating costs* means reasonable and authorized (or ratified by a responsible Federal official) costs ordinarily associated with the function of firefighting as performed by a fire service. Such costs would normally arise out of response of personnel and apparatus to the site of the fire, search and rescue, exposure protection, fire containment, ventilation, salvage, extinguishment, overhaul, and preparation of the equipment for further use. This would also include costs associated with emergency medical services to the extent normally rendered by a fire service in connection with a fire. Not included are administrative expenses, costs of employee benefits, insurance, disability, death, litigation or health care, and the costs associated with processing claims under section 11 of the Act and this part.

(c) *Administrator* means the Administrator of the Federal Emergency Management Agency, or his/her designee.

(d) *Claimant* means a fire service as defined in paragraph (g) of this section.

(e) *Direct expenses and losses* means expenses and losses which would not have been incurred had not the fire in question taken place. This includes salaries for specially employed personnel, overtime pay, the cost of supplies expended, and the depreciated value of equipment destroyed or damaged. It does not include such costs as the ordinary wages of firefighters, overhead costs, or depreciation (if based on other than hours of use during fires). Expenses as defined herein would normally be incurred after the first call or alarm and would normally cease upon the first of the following: Return to station, report in-service and ready for further operations, or commence response to another incident.

351

(f) *Fire* means any instance of destructive or uncontrolled burning, including scorch burns and explosions of combustible dusts or solids, flammable liquids, and gases. The definition does not include the following except where they cause fire or occur as a consequence of fire: Lightning or electrical discharge, explosion of steam boilers, hot water tanks, or other pressure vessels, explosions of ammunition or other detonating materials, overheating, mechanical failures, or breakdown of electrical equipment in power transmission facilities, and accidents involving ships, aircraft, or other vehicles. Not included in this definition are any costs associated with false alarms, regardless of cause.

(g) *Fire service* means any organization in any State consisting of personnel, apparatus, and equipment which has as its purpose protecting property and maintaining the safety and welfare of the public from the dangers of fire, including a private firefighting brigade. The personnel of any such organization may be paid employees or unpaid volunteers or any combination thereof. The location of any such organization and its responsibility for extinguishment and suppression of fires may include, but need not be limited to, a State, city, town, borough, parish, county, fire district, fire protection district, rural fire district, or other special district.

(h) *Mutual aid agreement* means any reciprocal agreement whether written or oral between a Federal agency and the claimant fire service, or its parent jurisdiction, for the purpose of providing fire protection for the property of the United States upon which the fire which gave rise to the claim occurred and for other property for which the claimant normally provides fire protection. Such agreement must be primarily one of service rendered for service, or must be entered into under 42 U.S.C. 1856 through 1856d. Not included are all other agreements and contracts, particularly those in which the intent of the parties is that the United States pays for fire protection.

(i) *FEMA* means the Federal Emergency Management Agency.

(j) *Over and above normal operating expenses* means costs, losses and expenses which are not ordinarily and necessarily associated with the maintenance, administration, and day-to-day operations of a fire service and which would not have been incurred absent the fire out of which the claim arises.

(k) *Payments to the fire service or its parent jurisdiction, including taxes or payments in lieu of taxes, the United States has made for the support of fire services on the property in question* means any Federal monies, or the value of services, including those made available through categorical or block grants, contracts, mutual aid agreements, taxes, and payments in lieu of taxes which the United States has paid to the fire service or its parent jurisdiction for fire protection and firefighting services. Such payments will be determined on the basis of the term of the arrangement, or if no such term is discernible, on the basis of the Federal fiscal year in which the fire occurred.

(l) *Property which is under the jurisdiction of the United States* means real property and Federal improvements thereon and appurtenances thereto in which the United States holds legal fee simple title. This excludes Federal leasehold interests. This likewise excludes Federal personal property on land in which the United States does not hold fee simple title.

(m) *State* means any State of the United States of America, the District of Columbia, the Commonwealth of Puerto Rico, the Virgin Islands, Guam, American Samoa, The Commonwealth of the Northern Mariana Islands, the Trust Territory of the Pacific Islands, and any other territory or possession of the United States.

[49 FR 5929, Feb. 16, 1984, as amended at 74 FR 15344, Apr. 3, 2009]

Subpart B—Submission, Determination, Appeal

§ 151.11 Submission of claims.

Any fire service in any State which believes it has a claim(s) cognizable under section 11 shall submit its claim(s) in writing within 90 days of the occurrence of the fire(s) for which a claim(s) is made. If the fire is of such duration that the claimant desires to submit a claim before its conclusion, it may do so, but only for the eligible costs actually incurred to date. Additional claims may be filed for costs later incurred. Claims shall be submitted to the Director, FEMA, Washington, DC, 20472. Each claim shall include the following information:

(a) Name, address, jurisdiction and nature (volunteer, private, municipal, etc.) of claimant's fire service organization;

(b) Name, title, address and telephone number of individual authorized by the claimant fire service to make this claim in its behalf and his/her certification as to the accuracy of the information provided;

(c) Name and telephone number of Federal employee familiar with the facts of the event and the name and address of the Federal agency having jurisdiction over the property on which the fire occurred;

(d) Proof of authority to fight the fire (source of alarm, whether fire service was requested by responsible Federal official or whether such an official accepted the assistance when offered);

(e) Personnel and equipment committed to fighting of fire (type of equipment and number of items); and an itemized list of direct expenses (e.g., hours of equipment operation, fuel costs, consumables, overtime pay and wages for any specially hired personnel) and direct losses (e.g., damaged or destroyed equipment, to include purchase cost, estimate of the cost of repairs, statement of depreciated value immediately preceding and subsequent to the damage or destruction and the extent of insurance coverage) actually incurred in fighting the fire. A statement should be included explaining why each such expense or loss is considered by the claimant not be a normal operating cost, or to be in excess of normal operating costs;

(f) Copy of fire report which includes the location of the fire, a description of the property burned, the time of alarm, etc.;

(g) Such other information or documentation as the Administrator considers relevant to those considerations to be made in determining the amount authorized for payment, as set forth in §151.12 of these regulations;

(h) Source and amount of any payments received or to be received for the fiscal year in which the fire occurred, including taxes or payments in lieu of taxes and including all monies received or receivable from the United States through any program or agreement including categorical or block grants, and contracts, by the claimant fire service or its parent jurisdiction for the support of fire services on the property on which the fire occurred. If this information is available when the claim is submitted, it should accompany the claim. If it is not, the information should be submitted as soon as practicable, but no later than 15 days after the end of the Federal fiscal year in which the fire occurred.

[49 FR 5929, Feb. 16, 1984, as amended at 74 FR 15344, Apr. 3, 2009]

§151.12 Determination of amount authorized for payment.

(a) The Administrator shall determine the amount to be paid on a claim (subject to payment by the Department of the Treasury). The amount to be paid is the total of eligible expenses, costs and losses under paragraph (a)(1) of this section which exceeds the amount of payments under paragraph (a)(2) of this section. The Administrator shall establish the reimbursable amount by determining:

(1) The extent to which the fire service incurred additional firefighting costs, over and above its normal operating costs, in connection with the fire which is the subject of the claim, i.e., the "amount of costs"; and

(2) What payments, if any, including taxes or payments in lieu of taxes, the fire service or its parent jurisdiction has received from the United States for the support of fire services on the property on which the fire occurred.

The reimbursable amount is the amount, if any, by which the amount of costs, determined under paragraph (a)(1) of this section exceeds the amount of payments determined under paragraph (a)(2) of this section. Where more than one claim is filed the aggregate reimbursable amount is the amount by which the total amount of costs, determined under paragraph (a)(1) of this section exceed the amount of Federal payments (in the case of a mutual aid agreement—its term or if none is determinable, the Federal fiscal year) determined under paragraph (a)(2) of this section.

(b) The Administrator will first determine the costs as contemplated in paragraph (a)(1) of this section. The Administrator will then notify the claimant as to that amount. The claimant must indicate within 30 days its acceptance or rejection of that amount.

(1) If the determination is accepted by the claimant, this will be the final and conclusive determination of the amount of costs by the claimant in conjunction with the fire for which the claims are submitted.

(2) If the claimant rejects this amount, it must notify the Administrator , within 30 days, of its reasons for its rejection. Upon receipt of notification of rejection, the Administrator shall reconsider his determination and notify the claimant of the results of the reconsideration. The amount determined on reconsideration will constitute the costs to be used by the Director in determining the reimbursable amount.

(c) Upon receipt of documentation from the claimant on the amount of payments the Federal Government has made for the support of fire services on the property in question, the Administrator will, following such verification or investigation as the Administrator may deem appropriate, calculate the full amount to be reimbursed under the section 11 formula as set forth in § 151.12(a). This calculation of the reimbursable amount is based upon the costs determined pursuant to § 151.12(b) and the documentation of Federal payments that the claimant submitted.

(d) The Administrator's determination of the reimbursable amount will be sent to the Secretary of the Treasury. The Secretary of the Treasury shall, upon receipt of the claim and determination made under § 151.12 (a), (b), and (c), determine the amount authorized for payment, which shall be the amount actually available for payment from any monies in the Treasury not otherwise appropriated but subject to reimbursement (from any appropriations which may be available or which may be made available for the purpose)

by the Federal department or agency under whose jurisdiction the fire occurred. This shall be a sum no greater, although it may be less, that the reimbursable amount determined by the Administrator , FEMA, with respect to the claim under § 151.12 (a), (b) and (c).

(e) Upon receipt of written notification from the claimant of its intention to accept the amount authorized as full settlement of the claim, accompanied by a properly executed document of release, the Administrator will forward the claim, a copy of the Administrator's determination and the claimant's document of release to the Secretary of the Treasury for payment of the claim in the amount authorized.

(f) Subject to the discovery of additional material evidence, the Administrator may reconsider any determination in this section, whether or not made as his final determination.

[49 FR 5929, Feb. 16, 1984, as amended at 49 FR 38119, Sept. 27, 1984]

§ 151.13 Reconsideration of amount authorized for payment.

(a) If the claimant elects to protest the amount authorized for payment, after the applicable procedures of § 151.12 have been followed, it must within 30 days of receipt of notification of the amount authorized notify the Administrator in writing of its objections and set forth the reasons why the Administrator should reconsider the determination. The Administrator will upon notice of protest and receipt of additional evidence reconsider the determination of the amount of Federal payments under § 151.12(a)(2) but not the determination of the amount of costs under § 151.12(a)(1). The Administrator shall cause a reconsideration by the Secretary of the Treasury of the amount actually available and authorized for payment by the Treasury. The Administrator, upon receipt of the Secretary of the Treasury's reconsidered determination, will notify the claimant in writing of the amount authorized, upon reconsideration, for payment in full settlement of the claim.

(b) If the claimant elects to accept the amount authorized, upon reconsideration, for payment in full settlement of its claims, it must within 30 days (or a longer period of time acceptable to the Administrator) of its receipt of that determination notify the Administrator of its acceptance in writing accompanied by a properly executed document of release. Upon receipt of such notice and document of release, the Administrator will forward the claim, a copy of the Administrator's final determination, and the claimant's document of release to the Secretary of the Treasury for payment of the claim in the amount of final authorization.

§ 151.14 Adjudication.

If the claimant, after written notice by the Administrator of the amount authorized for payment in full settlement of the claim and after all applicable procedures of §§ 151.12 and 151.13 have been followed elects to dispute the amount authorized, it may then initiate action in the United States Claims Court, which shall have jurisdiction to adjudicate the claim and enter judgment in accordance with section 11(d) of the Act.

Subpart C—Administration, Penalties

§ 151.21 [Reserved]

§ 151.22 Audits.

At the discretion of the Administrator, all claims submitted under section 11 of the Act and all records of the claimant will be subject to audit by the Administrator or his/her designee. In addition, the Comptroller General of the United States or his/her designee shall have access to all books and records of all claimants making claims under section 11.

§ 151.23 Penalties.

Claimant's officials or others who provide information or documentation under this part are subject to, among other laws, the criminal penalties of Title 18 of the United States Code, sections 287 and 1001, which punish the submission of false, fictitious or fraudulent claims and the making of false, fictitious or fraudulent statements and which provide for a fine of not more than $10,000 or imprisonment for not more than five years, or both. For such a violation, the person is likewise subject to the civil penalties set out in 31 U.S.C. 3729 and 3730.

PART 152—ASSISTANCE TO FIREFIGHTERS GRANT PROGRAM

Sec.
152.1 Purpose and eligible uses of grant funds.
152.2 Definitions.
152.3 Availability of funds.
152.4 Roles and responsibilities.
152.5 Review process and evaluation criteria.
152.6 Application review and award process.
152.7 Grant payment, reporting and other requirements.
152.8 Application submission and deadline.
152.9 Reconsideration.

AUTHORITY: Federal Fire Protection and Control Act, 15 U.S.C. 2201 *et seq.*

SOURCE: 68 FR 12547, Mar. 14, 2003, unless otherwise noted.

§ 152.1 Purpose and eligible uses of grant funds.

(a) This competitive grant program will provide funding directly to fire departments of a State for the purpose of enhancing departments abilities to protect the health and safety of the public, as well as that of firefighting personnel, facing fire and fire-related hazards. Eligible applicants can submit only one application per application period. Departments that submit multiple applications in one application period will have each of their applications deemed ineligible.

(b) Eligible applicants are fire departments or fire departments of a State which is defined as an agency or organization that has a "formally recognized arrangement" with a State, local or tribal authority (city, county, parish, fire district, township, town, or other non-Federal governing body) to provide fire suppression services within a fixed geographical area. A fire department can apply for assistance for its emergency medical services unit provided the unit falls organizationally under the auspices of the fire department. A municipality or fire district may submit an application on behalf of a fire department when the fire department lacks the legal status to do so, e.g., where the fire department falls within the auspices of the municipality. When a municipality or fire district submits an application on behalf of a fire department, the fire department is precluded from submitting an additional application. Non-Federal airport and/or port authority fire departments are eligible, but only if they have a formally recognized arrangement with the local jurisdiction to provide fire suppression, on a first-due basis, outside the confines of the airport or port facilities. Airport or port authority fire departments whose sole responsibility is suppression of fires on the airport grounds or port facilities are not eligible for this grant program. Fire departments that are Federal or contracted by the Federal government and whose sole responsibility is suppression of fires on Federal installations are not eligible for this grant program. Fire stations that are not independent but are part of, or controlled by a larger fire department or agency, are typically not eligible. Fire departments that are for-profit departments (*i.e.*, do not have specific non-profit status or are not municipally based) are not eligible to apply for assistance under this program. Also not eligible for this program are ambulance services, rescue squads, auxiliaries, dive teams, urban search and rescue teams, fire service organizations or associations, and State/local agencies such as a forest service, fire marshal, hospitals, and training offices.

(c) Congress included in the legislation a list of fourteen activities eligible for funding under this program. Those activities are as follows:

(1) To hire additional firefighting personnel;

(2) To train firefighting personnel in firefighting, emergency response (including response to a terrorism incident or use of a weapon of mass destruction), arson prevention and detection, or the handling of hazardous materials, or to train firefighting personnel to provide any of the training in this paragraph (c);

(3) To fund the creation of rapid intervention teams to protect firefighting personnel at scenes of fires and other emergencies;

(4) To certify fire inspectors;

(5) To establish wellness and fitness programs for firefighting personnel to ensure that the firefighting personnel can carry out their duties;

(6) To fund emergency medical services provided by fire departments;

(7) To acquire additional firefighting vehicles, including fire trucks;

(8) To acquire additional firefighting equipment, including equipment for communications, monitoring, and response to a terrorism incident or use of a weapon of mass destruction;

(9) To acquire personal protective equipment required for firefighting personnel by the Occupational Safety and Health Administration, and other personal protective equipment for firefighting personnel, including protective equipment to respond to a terrorism incident or the use of a weapon of mass destruction;

(10) To modify fire stations, fire training facilities, and other facilities to protect the health and safety of firefighting personnel;

(11) To enforce fire codes;

(12) To fund fire prevention programs;

(13) To educate the public about arson prevention and detection; and

(14) To provide incentives for the recruitment and retention of volunteer firefighting personnel for volunteer firefighting departments and other firefighting departments that utilize volunteers.

(d) The specific activities that will be eligible for funding will be announced in the Notice of Funding Availability (NOFA) that we will publish pursuant to the program's annual appropriation.

§ 152.2 Definitions.

Active firefighter is a member of a fire department or organization in good standing that is qualified to respond to and extinguish fires or perform other fire department emergency services and has actively participated in such activities during the past year.

Bay is the part or compartment of a building that provides parking for one or more pieces of firefighting apparatus.

Career department is a fire suppression agency or organization in which all active firefighters are considered full-time employees, are assigned regular duty shifts, and receive financial compensation for their services rendered on behalf of the department. Departments with active firefighters that are paid stipends on a per-call basis are not career departments. See the definition of combination department in this section.

Combination department is a fire suppression agency or organization in which at least one active firefighter receives financial compensation for his/her services rendered on behalf of the department and at least one active firefighter does not receive financial compensation for his/her services rendered on behalf of the department other than life/health insurance, workmen's compensation insurance, length of service awards, pay per-call or per-hour, or similar token compensation.

Construction is the creation of a new structure or any modification of the footprint or profile of an existing structure. Changes or renovations to an existing structure that do not change the footprint or profile of the structure but exceed either $10,000 or 50 percent of the value of the structure, are also considered construction for the purposes of this grant program. Changes that are less than $10,000 and/or 50 percent of the value of the structure are considered renovations, for the purposes of this grant program.

Direct delivery of training is training conducted within a training organization's own jurisdiction using the organization's own resources (trainers, facilities, equipment, etc.).

Fire boat is a vessel designed primarily for firefighting operations, however, may also be capable of water rescue and hazardous materials spills mitigation, etc. These vessels may also have the capability to pump a large volume of water from a drafting operation.

Fire department or fire department of a State is an agency or organization that has a "formally recognized arrangement" with a State, local or tribal authority (city, county, parish, fire district, township, town, or other non-Federal governing body) to provide fire suppression services within a fixed geographical area. A fire department can apply for assistance for its emergency medical services unit provided the unit

falls organizationally under the auspices of the fire department. A municipality or fire district may submit an application on behalf of a fire department when the fire department lacks the legal status to do so, e.g., where the fire department falls within the auspices of the municipality. When a municipality or fire district submits an application on behalf of a fire department, the fire department is precluded from submitting an additional application. Non-Federal airport and/or port authority fire departments are eligible, but only if they have a formally recognized arrangement with the local jurisdiction to provide fire suppression services, on a first-due basis, outside the confines of the airport or port facilities. Airport or port authority fire departments whose sole responsibility is suppression of fires on the airport grounds or port facilities are not eligible for this grant program. Fire departments that are Federal or contracted by the Federal government and whose sole responsibility is suppression of fires on Federal installations are not eligible for this grant program. Fire departments or fire stations that are not independent but are part of, or controlled by a larger fire department or agency, are typically not eligible. Fire departments that are for-profit departments (*i.e.*, do not have specific nonprofit status or are not municipally based) are not eligible to apply for assistance under this program. Also not eligible for this program are ambulance services, rescue squads, auxiliaries, dive teams, urban search and rescue teams, fire service organizations or associations, and State/local agencies such as a forest service, fire marshal, hospitals, and training offices.

Firefighter. See the definition of *Active firefighter* in this section.

First-due response area is a geographical area in proximity to a fire or rescue facility and normally served by the personnel and apparatus from that facility in the event of a fire or other emergency.

Formally recognized arrangement is an agreement between the fire department and a local jurisdiction such that the jurisdiction has publicly or otherwise formally deemed that the fire department has the first-due response responsibilities within a fixed geographical area of the jurisdiction. Often this agreement is recognized or reported to the appropriate State entity with cognizance over fire departments, such as registration with the State Fire Marshal's office, or the agreement is specifically contained in the fire department's or jurisdiction's charter.

Integrated communication systems and devices are equipment or systems for dispatch centers or communication infrastructure. Examples of these include 911 systems, computer-aided dispatch systems, global positioning systems, fixed repeaters, etc. Towers are an integral part of any communication system, but they are not eligible to be included in any award under this program.

New mission is a first-responder function that a department has never delivered in the past or that was once delivered but has since been abandoned by the department due to the lack of funding or community support. Examples include technical search and rescue, emergency medical services, hazardous materials response, etc. A new mission does not include services already provided from existing facilities. Opening additional stations to provide similar services would be considered an expansion of existing services.

Population means permanent residents in the first-due response area or jurisdiction served by the applicant. It would include students but does not include seasonal population or any population in area that the fire department responds to under mutual/automatic aid agreements.

Prop is something that can be held up in a classroom or moved from site to site in order to facilitate or enhance the training experience. A training tower (pre-fabricated or constructed) is not a prop.

Renovation is changes or alterations or modifications to an existing structure that do not exceed either $10,000 and/or 50 percent of the market value of the structure and do not involve a change in the footprint or profile of the structure.

Rural community is a community that has low population density, zoned agri-

cultural or parkland, and whose fire department has a relatively low volume of fire calls.

State means any of the fifty States, the District of Columbia, Puerto Rico, the U.S. Virgin Islands, Guam, American Samoa, and the Commonwealth of the Northern Mariana Islands.

Suburban community is a community that has a medium density population with a portion of their jurisdiction being zoned for industrial and/or commercial uses, and whose fire department has a high call volume relative to a rural community.

Supplies means any expendable property that typically has a one-time use limit and an expectation of being replaced within one year.

The United States Fire Administrator's (USFA) operational and performance objectives are to reduce losses of life and reduce economic losses due to fire and related emergencies. Specific target groups are children under 14 years old, seniors over 65 years old, and firefighters.

Urban community is a community with a high density population with a major proportion of its jurisdiction zoned for commercial and/or industrial use and a significant call volume.

Vehicle is a mechanized device used for carrying passengers, goods, or equipment. Examples of vehicles include, but are not limited to: pumpers, brush trucks, tankers, tenders, attack pumpers, rescue (transport and nontransport), ambulances, foam units, quints, aerials, ladders, hazmat vehicles, squads, crash rescue (ARFF), boats, hovercraft, planes, and helicopters. Details concerning vehicle eligibility will be provided in the NOFA that will be published pursuant to this program's annual appropriation.

Volunteer department is a fire suppression agency or organization in which no active firefighters are considered full-time employees, and which no members receive financial compensation for their services rendered on behalf of the department other than life/health insurance, workers' compensation insurance, length of service awards, pay per-call or per-hour, or similar token compensation.

Watercraft is a small boat (less than 13 feet in length) or other watercraft designed and equipped for water and/or ice rescue, rather than basic firefighting operations. Generally, these vessels will be equipped with water rescue equipment, flotation devices, and other basic medical and rescue equipment and their primary function will be rescue activities.

§ 152.3 Availability of funds.

(a) Fire departments that have received funding under the Assistance to Firefighter Grant Program in previous years are eligible to apply for funding in the current year. However, due to our responsibilities under this program to assure adequate distribution of awards amongst certain types of departments (career, combination and volunteer) and certain types of communities (urban, suburban or rural) as well as an equitable geographic distribution, we reserve the right to fund or not to fund previous recipients of grants under this program in order for us to fulfill these responsibilities.

(b) No applicant can receive more than $750,000 in Federal grant funds under this program in any fiscal year.

(c) No applicant can submit more than one application per fiscal year. Applicants that submit multiple applications will have each of their applications deemed ineligible.

(d) The scoring of the applications will determine the distribution of the funding across the eligible programs. Notwithstanding anything in this part, no more than twenty-five (25) percent of the funds appropriated for grants shall be used to assist grant recipients to purchase firefighting vehicles and not less than five (5) percent of the funds shall be used for fire prevention programs.

(e) We will not provide assistance under this part for activities for which another Federal agency has more specific or primary authority to provide assistance for the same purpose. We may disallow or recoup amounts that fall within other Federal agency's authority.

§ 152.4 Roles and responsibilities.

(a) Applicants must:

(1) Complete the application and certify to the accuracy of all the information contained therein;

(2) Certify that they are an eligible applicant, *i.e.*, a fire department, as defined in this part;

(3) Certify that the person submitting the application is duly authorized to do so, and

(b) Recipients (Grantees) must agree to:

(1) Share in the costs of the projects funded under this grant program. Fire departments in areas serving populations over 50,000 must agree to match the Federal grant funds with an amount of non-Federal funds equal to thirty (30) percent of the total project cost. Fire departments serving areas with a population of 50,000 or less will have to match the Federal grant funds with an amount of non-Federal funds equal to ten (10) percent of the total project cost. No waivers of this requirement will be granted except for fire departments of Insular Areas as provided for in 48 U.S.C. 1469a.

(2) Maintain operating expenditures during the grant's period of performance in the areas funded by a grant at a level equal to or greater than the average of their operating expenditures in the two years preceding the year in which this assistance is received.

(3) Obtain the appropriate Federal, State, or local permits necessary to fulfill the grant's scope of work including historical and/or environmental clearances as required.

(4) Retain grant files and supporting documentation for three years after the official closeout of the grant.

(5) Report to FEMA on the progress made on the grant and financial status of the grant. The award documents will detail the specific period of performance for each grantee and provide instructions on the frequency and timing of the required performance reports.

(6) Maintain documentation to support the expenditure of grant funds as well as pertinent grant decisions.

(7) Make their grant files and other books and records related to the grant, available if requested for an audit to ensure compliance with any requirement of the grant program.

(8) Agree to provide information to the U.S. Fire Administration's National Fire Incident Reporting System (NFIRS) for the period covered by the grant. If a grantee does not currently

participate in the incident reporting system and does not have the capacity to report at the time of the award, that grantee must agree to provide information to the system for a twelve-month period commencing as soon as they develop the capacity to report. Capacity to report to the NFIRS must be established prior to the termination of the one-year performance period.

(c) FEMA activities:

(1) We will ensure that the funds are awarded based on the priorities and expected benefits articulated in the statute, this part, USFA's strategic plan, and the Notice of Funds Availability.

(2) We will ensure that not more than twenty-five (25) percent of the appropriated funding will be used to purchase firefighting vehicles.

(3) We will ensure that not less than five (5) percent of the funds are made available to national, State, local, or community organizations, including fire departments, for the purpose of carrying out fire prevention programs.

(4) We will ensure that fire departments with volunteer staff, or staff comprised of a combination of career fire fighters and volunteers, receive a proportion of the total grant funding that is not less than the proportion of the United States population that those firefighting departments protect.

(5) We will ensure that grants are made to fire departments located in urban, suburban, and rural communities.

(6) We will strive to ensure geographic diversity of awards as stipulated in § 152.6.

(7) We will strive to ensure that activities funded under this grant program are consistent with the programs goals and intent, and generally in the government's best interest.

(8) We will provide the chief executives of the States with information concerning the total number and dollar amount of awards made to fire departments in their States; the program areas and activities supported by these grants; and other information about specific awards when generated and available.

[68 FR 12547, Mar. 14, 2003, as amended at 74 FR 15344, Apr. 3, 2009]

§ 152.5 Review process and evaluation criteria.

(a) Every application will be evaluated based on the answers to the activity-specific questions during our initial screening. The applications that are determined to best address the Assistance to Firefighters Grant Program's established priorities during this initial screening will be in the "competitive range" and subject to a second level of review. We will use the narratives/supplemental information provided by the applicants in their grant applications to evaluate, on a competitive basis, the merits and benefits of each request for funding. In selecting applications for award, we will evaluate each application for assistance independently based on established eligibility criteria and the program priorities. Eligible applicants that best address the priorities will advance to a second level of review. The second level of review involves an assessment of the financial needs of the applicant, and an analysis of the benefits that would result from the grant award.

(b) In order to be successful at this second level of the evaluation, an applicant must complete the narrative section of the application package. The narrative should include a detailed description of the planned program, uses for the grant funds including details of each budget line item. For example, if personnel costs are included in the budget, please provide a break down of what those costs are for. The narrative should explain why the grant funds are needed and why the department has not been able to obtain funding for the planned activities on its own. A discussion of financial need should include a discussion of any Federal funding received for similar activities. Finally, the applicant's narrative should detail the benefits the department or community will realize as a result of the grant award.

(c) This second level of review will be conducted using a panel of technical evaluation panelists. These panelists are largely made up of non-Federal experts with a fire service background. The panelists will assess the application's merits with respect to the clarity and detail provided in the narrative about the project, the applicant's financial need, and the project's purported benefit to be derived from the cost. Technical evaluation panelists will independently score each application before them and then discuss the merits/shortcomings of the application in an effort to reconcile any major discrepancies. A consensus on the score is not required. The highest scoring applications resulting from this second level of review will then be considered for award. We seek to maximize the benefits derived from the funding by crediting applicants with the greatest financial need and whose proposed activities provide the greatest benefit versus the cost.

(d) In addition to the project narrative, the applicant must provide an itemized budget detailing the use of the grant funds. If an applicant is seeking funds in more than one eligible activity within a program, separate budgets will have to be generated for each activity and then an overall or summary budget will have to be generated. For those applicants applying on line, the summary budget will be automatically generated by the e-grants system.

(e) Specific rating criteria for each of the eligible programs will be published in a Notice of Funding Availability that we will publish pursuant to the program's annual appropriation.

§ 152.6 **Application review and award process.**

(a) As stated in § 152.5, we will evaluate each application in the preliminary screening process to determine which applications best address the program's established priorities. The best applications as determined in this preliminary step will be deemed to be in the "competitive range." All applications in the competitive range will advance to a second level review by a technical evaluation panel. Using the evaluation criteria detailed in the Program Guidance and in the NOFA (both of which are published pursuant to this program's annual appropriation), the panelists will score each application they evaluate. The assigned score will reflect the degree to which the applicant: clearly relates their proposed project; demonstrates financial need; and, details a high benefit to cost value of the pro-

posed activities. We will provide the panelists the complete application content for their evaluation. We will also provide them with reference materials for national standards or regulations and guidelines with respect to typical costs for proposed apparatus and equipment purchases.

(b) Our award decisions will be based on the stated priorities of the grant program first, then on the demonstrated need of the applicant and the benefits to be derived from the proposed projects. We will make awards on a competitive basis, *i.e.*, we will fund the highest scored applications before considering lower scored applications.

(c) In a few cases, to fulfill our obligations under the law to make grants to a variety of departments, we may also make funding decisions using rank order as the preliminary basis, and then analyze the type of fire department (paid, volunteer, or combination fire departments), the size and character of the community it serves (urban, suburban, or rural), and/or the geographic location of the fire department. In these instances where we are making decisions based on geographic location, we will use States as the basic geographic unit. We may also base our funding decisions on previous grant awards funded by this program and/or grantees' performance on previous grants and a technical evaluation of reasonable costs for labor, services, materials or equipment.

§ 152.7 **Grant payment, reporting and other requirements.**

(a) Grantees will have twelve months to incur obligations and complete the scope of work to fulfill their responsibilities under this grant program. The performance period of each grant will be detailed in the Articles of Agreement that we provide each grantee. Grantees may request funds from FEMA as reimbursement for expenditures made under the grant program or they may request funds for immediate cash needs under FEMA regulations (44 CFR 13.21). Advances of funds may also be approved to meet immediate cash needs.

(b) Generally, fire departments cannot use grant funds to pay for products and services contracted for, or purchased prior to the effective date of the grant. However, we will consider requests for reimbursement for these on an exception basis. Expenses incurred after the application deadline but prior to award may be eligible for reimbursement if the expenses were justified, unavoidable (i.e., urgent and compelling), consistent with the scope of work, and specifically approved by the Assistance Officer. Expenses, obligations, commitments or contracts incurred or entered into prior to the application deadline are not eligible to be included as an expense.

(c) All grantees must follow their own established procurement process when buying anything with Federal grant funds (as provided in 44 CFR 13.26). If the grantee does not have an established procurement process, they must seek a minimum of two bids for any acquisition.

(d) When requesting funding, grantees can only request an amount that is necessary to satisfy their immediate cash needs directly related to the grant, i.e., an amount equal to the total eligible grant expenses due within 30 days. Grantees can request payments of up to one hundred (100) percent of the federal share of the award amount but only if delivery of the ordered products and/or services is imminent (approximately 30 days) and the resulting payment will require the entire amount of funds.

(e) A grantee may request sufficient funding for a down payment if required to do so by the seller, such as in grants involving some purchases of firefighting vehicles. The grantee may request as much as fifty (50) percent of the federal share of the award amount at the time of the order placement to pay the down payment. The grantee may request the balance of the federal share upon delivery of the ordered equipment or vehicle.

(f) The recipients of funding under this program must report to us on how the grant funding was used and the benefits that resulted. This will be accomplished via submission of performance reports. Details regarding the reporting requirements will be provided in the Articles of Agreement provided to each grantee.

(g) Fire departments that receive funding under this program must agree to provide information to the National Fire Incident Reporting System (NFIRS) for the period covered by the assistance. If a grantee does not currently participate in the incident reporting system and does not have the capacity to report at the time of the award, that grantee must agree to provide information to the system for a twelve-month period commencing as soon as possible after they develop the capacity to report. Capacity to report to the NFIRS must be established prior to the termination of the one-year performance period.

[68 FR 12547, Mar. 14, 2003, as amended at 74 FR 15344, Apr. 3, 2009]

§ 152.8 Application submission and deadline.

In each year that this program is authorized and receives an appropriation, we will announce the grants availability via Notice of Funds Availability. That Notice will contain all pertinent information concerning the eligible funding activities, funding priorities, funding levels, application period, timelines, and deadlines.

§ 152.9 Reconsideration.

(a) *Reconsideration of initial grant award decisions.* We will review our decision with respect to an initial grant award decision only when the applicant asserts that we have made a material technical or procedural error in the processing of the application and can substantiate such assertions. As grants are awarded on a competitive basis, in accordance with the findings of an independent panel of experts, we cannot consider requests for reconsideration based upon the merits of an original application. Similarly, we will not consider new information provided after the submission of the original application. In the case of new information, we encourage applicants to incorporate their changed circumstances into their applications for future grant cycles.

(b) *Reconsideration of other decisions.* We will consider requests for reconsideration of decisions other than those related to the initial grant award on their merits.

(c) We must receive a request for reconsideration under this section within 60 days of the date of the notice of the decision for which reconsideration is requested.

(d) Requests for reconsideration should be directed to: Assistant Administrator, Grant Programs Directorate, Assistance to Firefighters Grant Program, FEMA, 800 K Street, NW., South Tower 5th Floor, Washington, DC 20001.

PARTS 153–199 [RESERVED]

SUBCHAPTER D—DISASTER ASSISTANCE

PART 200 [RESERVED]

PART 201—MITIGATION PLANNING

Sec.
201.1 Purpose.
201.2 Definitions.
201.3 Responsibilities.
201.4 Standard State Mitigation Plans.
201.5 Enhanced State Mitigation Plans.
201.6 Local Mitigation Plans.
201.7 Tribal Mitigation Plans.

AUTHORITY: Robert T. Stafford Disaster Relief and Emergency Assistance Act, 42 U.S.C. 5121 through 5207; Reorganization Plan No. 3 of 1978, 43 FR 41943, 3 CFR, 1978 Comp., p. 329; Homeland Security Act of 2002, 6 U.S.C. 101; E.O. 12127, 44 FR 19367, 3 CFR, 1979 Comp., p. 376; E.O. 12148, 44 FR 43239, 3 CFR, 1979 Comp., p. 412; E.O. 13286, 68 FR 10619, 3 CFR, 2003 Comp., p. 166.

SOURCE: 67 FR 8848, Feb. 26, 2002, unless otherwise noted.

§ 201.1 Purpose.

(a) The purpose of this part is to provide information on the polices and procedures for mitigation planning as required by the provisions of section 322 of the Stafford Act, 42 U.S.C. 5165.

(b) The purpose of mitigation planning is for State, local, and Indian tribal governments to identify the natural hazards that impact them, to identify actions and activities to reduce any losses from those hazards, and to establish a coordinated process to implement the plan, taking advantage of a wide range of resources.

§ 201.2 Definitions.

Administrator means the head of the Federal Emergency Management Agency, or his/her designated representative.

Flood Mitigation Assistance (FMA) means the program authorized by section 1366 of the National Flood Insurance Act of 1968, as amended, 42 U.S.C. 4104c, and implemented at parts 78 and 79.

Grantee means the government to which a grant is awarded, which is accountable for the use of the funds provided. The grantee is the entire legal entity even if only a particular component of the entity is designated in the grant award document. Generally, the State is the grantee. However, after a declaration, an Indian tribal government may choose to be a grantee, or may act as a subgrantee under the State. An Indian tribal government acting as grantee will assume the responsibilities of a "state", as described in this part, for the purposes of administering the grant.

Hazard mitigation means any sustained action taken to reduce or eliminate the long-term risk to human life and property from hazards.

Hazard Mitigation Grant Program (HMGP) means the program authorized under section 404 of the Robert T. Stafford Disaster Relief and Emergency Assistance Act, 42 U.S.C. 5170c, and implemented at part 206, subpart N of this chapter.

Indian Tribal government means any Federally recognized governing body of an Indian or Alaska Native Tribe, band, nation, pueblo, village, or community that the Secretary of Interior acknowledges to exist as an Indian Tribe under the Federally Recognized Indian Tribe List Act of 1994, 25 U.S.C. 479a. This does not include Alaska Native corporations, the ownership of which is vested in private individuals.

Local government is any county, municipality, city, town, township, public authority, school district, special district, intrastate district, council of governments (regardless of whether the council of governments is incorporated as a nonprofit corporation under State law), regional or interstate government entity, or agency or instrumentality of a local government; any Indian tribe or authorized tribal organization, or Alaska Native village or organization; and any rural community, unincorporated town or village, or other public entity.

Managing State means a State to which FEMA has delegated the authority to administer and manage the HMGP under the criteria established by FEMA pursuant to 42 U.S.C. 5170c(c). FEMA may also delegate authority to tribal governments to administer and manage the HMGP as a Managing State.

364

Pre-Disaster Mitigation Program (PDM) means the program authorized under section 203 of the Robert T. Stafford Disaster Relief and Emergency Assistance Act, 42 U.S.C. 5133.

Regional Administrator means the head of a Federal Emergency Management Agency regional office, or his/her designated representative.

Repetitive Flood Claims (RFC) program means the program authorized under section 1323 of the National Flood Insurance Act of 1968, as amended, 42 U.S.C. 4011, which provides funding to reduce flood damages to individual properties for which 1 or more claim payments for losses have been made under flood insurance coverage and that will result in the greatest savings to the National Flood Insurance Program (NFIP) in the shortest period of time.

Severe Repetitive Loss (SRL) program means the program authorized under section 1361(a) of the National Flood Insurance Act of 1968, as amended, 42 U.S.C. 4102a, and implemented at part 79 of this chapter.

Severe Repetitive Loss properties are defined as single or multifamily residential properties that are covered under an NFIP flood insurance policy and:

(1) That have incurred flood-related damage for which 4 or more separate claims payments have been made, with the amount of each claim (including building and contents payments) exceeding $5,000, and with the cumulative amount of such claims payments exceeding $20,000; or

(2) For which at least 2 separate claims payments (building payments only) have been made under such coverage, with cumulative amount of such claims exceeding the market value of the property.

(3) In both instances, at least 2 of the claims must be within 10 years of each other, and claims made within 10 days of each other will be counted as 1 claim.

Small and impoverished communities means a community of 3,000 or fewer individuals that is identified by the State as a rural community, and is not a remote area within the corporate boundaries of a larger city; is economically disadvantaged, by having an average per capita annual income of residents not exceeding 80 percent of national, per capita income, based on best available data; the local unemployment rate exceeds by one percentage point or more, the most recently reported, average yearly national unemployment rate; and any other factors identified in the State Plan in which the community is located.

The Stafford Act refers to the Robert T. Stafford Disaster Relief and Emergency Assistance Act, Public Law 93–288, as amended (42 U.S.C. 5121–5206).

State is any State of the United States, the District of Columbia, Puerto Rico, the Virgin Islands, Guam, American Samoa, and the Commonwealth of the Northern Mariana Islands.

State Hazard Mitigation Officer is the official representative of State government who is the primary point of contact with FEMA, other Federal agencies, and local governments in mitigation planning and implementation of mitigation programs and activities required under the Stafford Act.

Subgrantee means the government or other legal entity to which a subgrant is awarded and which is accountable to the grantee for the use of the funds provided. Subgrantees can be a State agency, local government, private nonprofit organizations, or Indian tribal government. Indian tribal governments acting as a subgrantee are accountable to the State grantee.

[67 FR 8848, Feb. 26, 2002, as amended at 72 FR 61747, Oct. 31, 2007; 74 FR 15344, Apr. 3, 2009; 74 FR 47481, Sept. 16, 2009]

§201.3 Responsibilities.

(a) *General.* This section identifies the key responsibilities of FEMA, States, and local/tribal governments in carrying out section 322 of the Stafford Act, 42 U.S.C. 5165.

(b) *FEMA.* The key responsibilities of the Regional Administrator are to:

(1) Oversee all FEMA related pre- and post-disaster hazard mitigation programs and activities;

(2) Provide technical assistance and training to State, local, and Indian tribal governments regarding the mitigation planning process;

(3) Review and approve all Standard and Enhanced State Mitigation Plans;

(4) Review and approve all local mitigation plans, unless that authority has been delegated to the State in accordance with § 201.6(d);

(5) Conduct reviews, at least once every three years, of State mitigation activities, plans, and programs to ensure that mitigation commitments are fulfilled, and when necessary, take action, including recovery of funds or denial of future funds, if mitigation commitments are not fulfilled.

(c) *State.* The key responsibilities of the State are to coordinate all State and local activities relating to hazard evaluation and mitigation and to:

(1) Prepare and submit to FEMA a Standard State Mitigation Plan following the criteria established in § 201.4 as a condition of receiving non-emergency Stafford Act assistance and FEMA mitigation grants. In addition, a State may choose to address severe repetitive loss properties in their plan as identified in § 201.4(c)(3)(v) to receive the reduced cost share for the Flood Mitigation Assistance (FMA) and Severe Repetitive Loss (SRL) programs, pursuant to § 79.4(c)(2) of this chapter.

(2) In order to be considered for the 20 percent HMGP funding, prepare and submit an Enhanced State Mitigation Plan in accordance with § 201.5, which must be reviewed and updated, if necessary, every three years from the date of the approval of the previous plan.

(3) At a minimum, review and update the Standard State Mitigation Plan every 3 years from the date of the approval of the previous plan in order to continue program eligibility.

(4) Make available the use of up to the 7 percent of HMGP funding for planning in accordance with § 206.434.

(5) Provide technical assistance and training to local governments to assist them in applying for HMGP planning grants, and in developing local mitigation plans.

(6) For Managing States that have been approved under the criteria established by FEMA pursuant to 42 U.S.C. 5170c(c), review and approve local mitigation plans in accordance with § 201.6(d).

(d) *Local governments.* The key responsibilities of local governments are to:

(1) Prepare and adopt a jurisdiction-wide natural hazard mitigation plan as a condition of receiving project grant funds under the HMGP, in accordance with § 201.6.

(2) At a minimum, review and update the local mitigation plan every 5 years from date of plan approval of the previous plan in order to continue program eligibility.

(e) *Indian tribal governments.* The key responsibilities of the Indian tribal government are to coordinate all tribal activities relating to hazard evaluation and mitigation and to:

(1) Prepare and submit to FEMA a Tribal Mitigation Plan following the criteria established in § 201.7 as a condition of receiving non-emergency Stafford Act assistance as a grantee. This plan will also allow Indian tribal governments to apply through the State, as a subgrantee, for any FEMA mitigation project grant. Indian tribal governments with a plan approved by FEMA on or before October 1, 2008 under § 201.4 or § 201.6 will also meet this planning requirement. All Tribal Mitigation Plans approved after that date must follow the criteria identified in § 201.7. In addition, an Indian Tribal government applying to FEMA as a grantee may choose to address severe repetitive loss properties as identified in § 201.4(c)(3)(v) as a condition of receiving the reduced cost share for the FMA and SRL programs, pursuant to § 79.4(c)(2) of this chapter.

(2) Review and update the Tribal Mitigation Plan at least every 5 years from the date of approval of the previous plan in order to continue program eligibility.

(3) In order to be considered for the increased HMGP funding, the Tribal Mitigation Plan must meet the Enhanced State Mitigation Plan criteria identified in § 201.5. The plan must be reviewed and updated at least every 3 years from the date of approval of the previous plan.

[67 FR 8848, Feb. 26, 2002, as amended at 67 FR 61515, Oct. 1, 2002; 69 FR 55096, Sept. 13, 2004; 72 FR 61748, Oct. 31, 2007; 74 FR 47482, Sept. 16, 2009]

§201.4 Standard State Mitigation Plans.

(a) *Plan requirement.* States must have an approved Standard State Mitigation Plans meeting the requirements of this section as a condition of receiving non-emergency Stafford Act assistance and FEMA mitigation grants. Emergency assistance provided under 42 U.S.C. 5170a, 5170b, 5173, 5174, 5177, 5179, 5180, 5182, 5183, 5184, 5192 will not be affected. Mitigation planning grants provided through the Pre-disaster Mitigation (PDM) program, authorized under section 203 of the Stafford Act, 42 U.S.C. 5133, will also continue to be available. The mitigation plan is the demonstration of the State's commitment to reduce risks from natural hazards and serves as a guide for State decision makers as they commit resources to reducing the effects of natural hazards.

(b) *Planning process.* An effective planning process is essential in developing and maintaining a good plan. The mitigation planning process should include coordination with other State agencies, appropriate Federal agencies, interested groups, and be integrated to the extent possible with other ongoing State planning efforts as well as other FEMA mitigation programs and initiatives.

(c) *Plan content.* To be effective the plan must include the following elements:

(1) Description of the *planning process* used to develop the plan, including how it was prepared, who was involved in the process, and how other agencies participated.

(2) *Risk assessments* that provide the factual basis for activities proposed in the strategy portion of the mitigation plan. Statewide risk assessments must characterize and analyze natural hazards and risks to provide a statewide overview. This overview will allow the State to compare potential losses throughout the State and to determine their priorities for implementing mitigation measures under the strategy, and to prioritize jurisdictions for receiving technical and financial support in developing more detailed local risk and vulnerability assessments. The risk assessment shall include the following:

(i) An overview of the type and location of all natural hazards that can affect the State, including information on previous occurrences of hazard events, as well as the probability of future hazard events, using maps where appropriate;

(ii) An overview and analysis of the State's vulnerability to the hazards described in this paragraph (c)(2), based on estimates provided in local risk assessments as well as the State risk assessment. The State shall describe vulnerability in terms of the jurisdictions most threatened by the identified hazards, and most vulnerable to damage and loss associated with hazard events. State owned or operated critical facilities located in the identified hazard areas shall also be addressed;

(iii) An overview and analysis of potential losses to the identified vulnerable structures, based on estimates provided in local risk assessments as well as the State risk assessment. The State shall estimate the potential dollar losses to State owned or operated buildings, infrastructure, and critical facilities located in the identified hazard areas.

(3) A *Mitigation Strategy* that provides the State's blueprint for reducing the losses identified in the risk assessment. This section shall include:

(i) A description of State goals to guide the selection of activities to mitigate and reduce potential losses.

(ii) A discussion of the State's pre- and post-disaster hazard management policies, programs, and capabilities to mitigate the hazards in the area, including: an evaluation of State laws, regulations, policies, and programs related to hazard mitigation as well as to development in hazard-prone areas; a discussion of State funding capabilities for hazard mitigation projects; and a general description and analysis of the effectiveness of local mitigation policies, programs, and capabilities.

(iii) An identification, evaluation, and prioritization of cost-effective, environmentally sound, and technically feasible mitigation actions and activities the State is considering and an explanation of how each activity contributes to the overall mitigation strategy. This section should be linked to local plans, where specific local actions and projects are identified.

(iv) Identification of current and potential sources of Federal, State, local, or private funding to implement mitigation activities.

(v) A State may request the reduced cost share authorized under § 79.4(c)(2) of this chapter for the FMA and SRL programs, if it has an approved State Mitigation Plan meeting the requirements of this section that also identifies specific actions the State has taken to reduce the number of repetitive loss properties (which must include severe repetitive loss properties), and specifies how the State intends to reduce the number of such repetitive loss properties. In addition, the plan must describe the strategy the State has to ensure that local jurisdictions with severe repetitive loss properties take actions to reduce the number of these properties, including the development of local mitigation plans.

(4) A section on the *Coordination of Local Mitigation Planning* that includes the following:

(i) A description of the State process to support, through funding and technical assistance, the development of local mitigation plans.

(ii) A description of the State process and timeframe by which the local plans will be reviewed, coordinated, and linked to the State Mitigation Plan.

(iii) Criteria for prioritizing communities and local jurisdictions that would receive planning and project grants under available funding programs, which should include consideration for communities with the highest risks, repetitive loss properties, and most intense development pressures. Further, that for non-planning grants, a principal criterion for prioritizing grants shall be the extent to which benefits are maximized according to a cost benefit review of proposed projects and their associated costs.

(5) A *Plan Maintenance Process* that includes:

· (i) An established method and schedule for monitoring, evaluating, and updating the plan.

(ii) A system for monitoring implementation of mitigation measures and project closeouts.

(iii) A system for reviewing progress on achieving goals as well as activities and projects identified in the Mitigation Strategy.

(6) A *Plan Adoption Process.* The plan must be formally adopted by the State prior to submittal to us for final review and approval.

(7) *Assurances.* The plan must include assurances that the State will comply with all applicable Federal statutes and regulations in effect with respect to the periods for which it receives grant funding, in compliance with 44 CFR 13.11(c) of this chapter. The State will amend its plan whenever necessary to reflect changes in State or Federal statutes and regulations as required in 44 CFR 13.11(d) of this chapter.

(d) *Review and updates.* Plan must be reviewed and revised to reflect changes in development, progress in statewide mitigation efforts, and changes in priorities and resubmitted for approval to the appropriate Regional Administrator every three years. The Regional review will be completed within 45 days after receipt from the State, whenever possible. We also encourage a State to review its plan in the post-disaster timeframe to reflect changing priorities, but it is not required.

[67 FR 8848, Feb. 26, 2002, as amended at 67 FR 61515, Oct. 1, 2002; 69 FR 55096, Sept. 13, 2004; 72 FR 61565, 61738, Oct. 31, 2007]

§ 201.5 Enhanced State Mitigation Plans.

(a) A State with a FEMA approved Enhanced State Mitigation Plan at the time of a disaster declaration is eligible to receive increased funds under the HMGP, based on twenty percent of the total estimated eligible Stafford Act disaster assistance. The Enhanced State Mitigation Plan must demonstrate that a State has developed a comprehensive mitigation program, that the State effectively uses available mitigation funding, and that it is capable of managing the increased funding. In order for the State to be eligible for the 20 percent HMGP funding, FEMA must have approved the plan within three years prior to the disaster declaration.

(b) Enhanced State Mitigation Plans must include all elements of the Standard State Mitigation Plan identified in

§201.4, as well as document the following:

(1) Demonstration that the plan is integrated to the extent practicable with other State and/or regional planning initiatives (comprehensive, growth management, economic development, capital improvement, land development, and/or emergency management plans) and FEMA mitigation programs and initiatives that provide guidance to State and regional agencies.

(2) Documentation of the State's project implementation capability, identifying and demonstrating the ability to implement the plan, including:

(i) Established eligibility criteria for multi-hazard mitigation measures.

(ii) A system to determine the cost effectiveness of mitigation measures, consistent with OMB Circular A–94, Guidelines and Discount Rates for Benefit-Cost Analysis of Federal Programs, and to rank the measures according to the State's eligibility criteria.

(iii) Demonstration that the State has the capability to effectively manage the HMGP as well as other mitigation grant programs, including a record of the following:

(A) Meeting HMGP and other mitigation grant application timeframes and submitting complete, technically feasible, and eligible project applications with appropriate supporting documentation;

(B) Preparing and submitting accurate environmental reviews and benefit-cost analyses;

(C) Submitting complete and accurate quarterly progress and financial reports on time; and

(D) Completing HMGP and other mitigation grant projects within established performance periods, including financial reconciliation.

(iv) A system and strategy by which the State will conduct an assessment of the completed mitigation actions and include a record of the effectiveness (actual cost avoidance) of each mitigation action.

(3) Demonstration that the State effectively uses existing mitigation programs to achieve its mitigation goals.

(4) Demonstration that the State is committed to a comprehensive state mitigation program, which might include any of the following:

(i) A commitment to support local mitigation planning by providing workshops and training, State planning grants, or coordinated capability development of local officials, including Emergency Management and Floodplain Management certifications.

(ii) A statewide program of hazard mitigation through the development of legislative initiatives, mitigation councils, formation of public/private partnerships, and/or other executive actions that promote hazard mitigation.

(iii) The State provides a portion of the non-Federal match for HMGP and/or other mitigation projects.

(iv) To the extent allowed by State law, the State requires or encourages local governments to use a current version of a nationally applicable model building code or standard that addresses natural hazards as a basis for design and construction of State sponsored mitigation projects.

(v) A comprehensive, multi-year plan to mitigate the risks posed to existing buildings that have been identified as necessary for post-disaster response and recovery operations.

(vi) A comprehensive description of how the State integrates mitigation into its post-disaster recovery operations.

(c) *Review and updates.* (1) A State must review and revise its plan to reflect changes in development, progress in statewide mitigation efforts, and changes in priorities, and resubmit it for approval to the appropriate Regional Administrator every three years. The Regional review will be completed within 45 days after receipt from the State, whenever possible.

(2) In order for a State to be eligible for the 20 percent HMGP funding, the Enhanced State Mitigation plan must be approved by FEMA within the three years prior to the current major disaster declaration.

§201.6 Local Mitigation Plans.

The local mitigation plan is the representation of the jurisdiction's commitment to reduce risks from natural hazards, serving as a guide for decision makers as they commit resources to reducing the effects of natural hazards. Local plans will also serve as the basis for the State to provide technical assistance and to prioritize project funding.

(a) *Plan requirements.* (1) A local government must have a mitigation plan approved pursuant to this section in order to receive HMGP project grants. The Administrator may, at his discretion, require a local mitigation plan for the Repetitive Flood Claims Program. A local government must have a mitigation plan approved pursuant to this section in order to apply for and receive mitigation project grants under all other mitigation grant programs.

(2) Plans prepared for the FMA program, described at part 79 of this chapter, need only address these requirements as they relate to flood hazards in order to be eligible for FMA project grants. However, these plans must be clearly identified as being flood mitigation plans, and they will not meet the eligibility criteria for other mitigation grant programs, unless flooding is the only natural hazard the jurisdiction faces.

(3) Regional Administrator's may grant an exception to the plan requirement in extraordinary circumstances, such as in a small and impoverished community, when justification is provided. In these cases, a plan will be completed within 12 months of the award of the project grant. If a plan is not provided within this timeframe, the project grant will be terminated, and any costs incurred after notice of grant's termination will not be reimbursed by FEMA.

(4) Multi-jurisdictional plans (*e.g.* watershed plans) may be accepted, as appropriate, as long as each jurisdiction has participated in the process and has officially adopted the plan. State-wide plans will not be accepted as multi-jurisdictional plans.

(b) *Planning process.* An open public involvement process is essential to the development of an effective plan. In order to develop a more comprehensive approach to reducing the effects of natural disasters, the planning process shall include:

(1) An opportunity for the public to comment on the plan during the drafting stage and prior to plan approval;

(2) An opportunity for neighboring communities, local and regional agencies involved in hazard mitigation activities, and agencies that have the authority to regulate development, as well as businesses, academia and other private and non-profit interests to be involved in the planning process; and

(3) Review and incorporation, if appropriate, of existing plans, studies, reports, and technical information.

(c) *Plan content.* The plan shall include the following:

(1) Documentation of the *planning process* used to develop the plan, including how it was prepared, who was involved in the process, and how the public was involved.

(2) A *risk assessment* that provides the factual basis for activities proposed in the strategy to reduce losses from identified hazards. Local risk assessments must provide sufficient information to enable the jurisdiction to identify and prioritize appropriate mitigation actions to reduce losses from identified hazards. The risk assessment shall include:

(i) A description of the type, location, and extent of all natural hazards that can affect the jurisdiction. The plan shall include information on previous occurrences of hazard events and on the probability of future hazard events.

(ii) A description of the jurisdiction's vulnerability to the hazards described in paragraph (c)(2)(i) of this section. This description shall include an overall summary of each hazard and its impact on the community. All plans approved after October 1, 2008 must also address NFIP insured structures that have been repetitively damaged by floods. The plan should describe vulnerability in terms of:

(A) The types and numbers of existing and future buildings, infrastructure, and critical facilities located in the identified hazard areas;

(B) An estimate of the potential dollar losses to vulnerable structures identified in paragraph (c)(2)(ii)(A) of this section and a description of the methodology used to prepare the estimate;

(C) Providing a general description of land uses and development trends within the community so that mitigation options can be considered in future land use decisions.

(iii) For multi-jurisdictional plans, the risk assessment section must assess each jurisdiction's risks where they vary from the risks facing the entire planning area.

(3) *A mitigation strategy* that provides the jurisdiction's blueprint for reducing the potential losses identified in the risk assessment, based on existing authorities, policies, programs and resources, and its ability to expand on and improve these existing tools. This section shall include:

(i) A description of mitigation goals to reduce or avoid long-term vulnerabilities to the identified hazards.

(ii) A section that identifies and analyzes a comprehensive range of specific mitigation actions and projects being considered to reduce the effects of each hazard, with particular emphasis on new and existing buildings and infrastructure. All plans approved by FEMA after October 1, 2008, must also address the jurisdiction's participation in the NFIP, and continued compliance with NFIP requirements, as appropriate.

(iii) An action plan describing how the actions identified in paragraph (c)(3)(ii) of this section will be prioritized, implemented, and administered by the local jurisdiction. Prioritization shall include a special emphasis on the extent to which benefits are maximized according to a cost benefit review of the proposed projects and their associated costs.

(iv) For multi-jurisdictional plans, there must be identifiable action items specific to the jurisdiction requesting FEMA approval or credit of the plan.

(4) A *plan maintenance process* that includes:

(i) A section describing the method and schedule of monitoring, evaluating, and updating the mitigation plan within a five-year cycle.

(ii) A process by which local governments incorporate the requirements of the mitigation plan into other planning mechanisms such as comprehensive or capital improvement plans, when appropriate.

(iii) Discussion on how the community will continue public participation in the plan maintenance process.

(5) *Documentation* that the plan has been formally adopted by the governing body of the jurisdiction requesting approval of the plan (e.g., City Council, County Commissioner, Tribal Council). For multi-jurisdictional plans, each jurisdiction requesting approval of the plan must document that it has been formally adopted.

(d) *Plan review.* (1) Plans must be submitted to the State Hazard Mitigation Officer (SHMO) for initial review and coordination. The State will then send the plan to the appropriate FEMA Regional Office for formal review and approval. Where the State point of contact for the FMA program is different from the SHMO, the SHMO will be responsible for coordinating the local plan reviews between the FMA point of contact and FEMA.

(2) The Regional review will be completed within 45 days after receipt from the State, whenever possible.

(3) A local jurisdiction must review and revise its plan to reflect changes in development, progress in local mitigation efforts, and changes in priorities, and resubmit it for approval within 5 years in order to continue to be eligible for mitigation project grant funding.

(4) Managing States that have been approved under the criteria established by FEMA pursuant to 42 U.S.C. 5170c(c) will be delegated approval authority for local mitigation plans, and the review will be based on the criteria in this part. Managing States will review the plans within 45 days of receipt of the plans, whenever possible, and provide a copy of the approved plans to the Regional Office.

[67 FR 8848, Feb. 26, 2002, as amended at 67 FR 61515, Oct. 1, 2002; 68 FR 61370, Oct. 28, 2003; 69 FR 55096, Sept. 13, 2004; 72 FR 61748, Oct. 31, 2007 ; 74 FR 47482, Sept. 16, 2009]

§201.7 Tribal Mitigation Plans.

The Indian Tribal Mitigation Plan is the representation of the Indian tribal government's commitment to reduce risks from natural hazards, serving as a guide for decision makers as they commit resources to reducing the effects of natural hazards.

(a) *Plan requirement.* (1) Indian tribal governments applying to FEMA as a grantee must have an approved Tribal

Mitigation Plan meeting the requirements of this section as a condition of receiving non-emergency Stafford Act assistance and FEMA mitigation grants. Emergency assistance provided under 42 U.S.C. 5170a, 5170b, 5173, 5174, 5177, 5179, 5180, 5182, 5183, 5184, 5192 will not be affected. Mitigation planning grants provided through the PDM program, authorized under section 203 of the Stafford Act, 42 U.S.C. 5133, will also continue to be available.

(2) An Indian Tribal government applying to FEMA as a grantee may choose to address severe repetitive loss properties in their plan, as identified in § 201.4(c)(3)(v), to receive the reduced cost share for the FMA and SRL programs.

(3) Indian Tribal governments applying through the State as a subgrantee must have an approved Tribal Mitigation Plan meeting the requirements of this section in order to receive HMGP project grants and, the Administrator, at his discretion may require a Tribal Mitigation Plan for the Repetitive Flood Claims Program. A Tribe must have an approved Tribal Mitigation Plan in order to apply for and receive FEMA mitigation project grants, under all other mitigation grant programs. The provisions in § 201.6(a)(3) are available to Tribes applying as subgrantees.

(4) Multi-jurisdictional plans (*e.g.* county-wide or watershed plans) may be accepted, as appropriate, as long as the Indian tribal government has participated in the process and has officially adopted the plan. Indian tribal governments must address all the elements identified in this section to ensure eligibility as a grantee or as a subgrantee.

(b) An effective planning process is essential in developing and maintaining a good plan. The mitigation planning process should include coordination with other tribal agencies, appropriate Federal agencies, adjacent jurisdictions, interested groups, and be integrated to the extent possible with other ongoing tribal planning efforts as well as other FEMA mitigation programs and initiatives.

(c) *Plan content.* The plan shall include the following:

(1) Documentation of the *planning process* used to develop the plan, including how it was prepared, who was involved in the process, and how the public was involved. This shall include:

(i) An opportunity for the public to comment on the plan during the drafting stage and prior to plan approval, including a description of how the Indian tribal government defined "public;"

(ii) As appropriate, an opportunity for neighboring communities, tribal and regional agencies involved in hazard mitigation activities, and agencies that have the authority to regulate development, as well as businesses, academia, and other private and nonprofit interests to be involved in the planning process;

(iii) Review and incorporation, if appropriate, of existing plans, studies, and reports; and

(iv) Be integrated to the extent possible with other ongoing tribal planning efforts as well as other FEMA programs and initiatives.

(2) A *risk assessment* that provides the factual basis for activities proposed in the strategy to reduce losses from identified hazards. Tribal risk assessments must provide sufficient information to enable the Indian tribal government to identify and prioritize appropriate mitigation actions to reduce losses from identified hazards. The risk assessment shall include:

(i) A description of the type, location, and extent of all natural hazards that can affect the tribal planning area. The plan shall include information on previous occurrences of hazard events and on the probability of future hazard events.

(ii) A description of the Indian tribal government's vulnerability to the hazards described in paragraph (c)(2)(i) of this section. This description shall include an overall summary of each hazard and its impact on the tribe. The plan should describe vulnerability in terms of:

(A) The types and numbers of existing and future buildings, infrastructure, and critical facilities located in the identified hazard areas;

(B) An estimate of the potential dollar losses to vulnerable structures identified in paragraph (c)(2)(ii)(A) of this section and a description of the methodology used to prepare the estimate;

(C) A general description of land uses and development trends within the tribal planning area so that mitigation options can be considered in future land use decisions; and

(D) Cultural and sacred sites that are significant, even if they cannot be valued in monetary terms.

(3) A *mitigation strategy* that provides the Indian tribal government's blueprint for reducing the potential losses identified in the risk assessment, based on existing authorities, policies, programs and resources, and its ability to expand on and improve these existing tools. This section shall include:

(i) A description of mitigation goals to reduce or avoid long-term vulnerabilities to the identified hazards.

(ii) A section that identifies and analyzes a comprehensive range of specific mitigation actions and projects being considered to reduce the effects of each hazard, with particular emphasis on new and existing buildings and infrastructure.

(iii) An action plan describing how the actions identified in paragraph (c)(3)(ii) of this section will be prioritized, implemented, and administered by the Indian Tribal government.

(iv) A discussion of the Indian tribal government's pre- and post-disaster hazard management policies, programs, and capabilities to mitigate the hazards in the area, including: An evaluation of tribal laws, regulations, policies, and programs related to hazard mitigation as well as to development in hazard-prone areas; and a discussion of tribal funding capabilities for hazard mitigation projects.

(v) Identification of current and potential sources of Federal, tribal, or private funding to implement mitigation activities.

(vi) An Indian Tribal government applying to FEMA as a grantee may request the reduced cost share authorized under § 79.4(c)(2) of this chapter of the FMA and SRL programs if they have an approved Tribal Mitigation Plan meeting the requirements of this section that also identifies actions the Indian Tribal government has taken to reduce the number of repetitive loss properties (which must include severe repetitive loss properties), and specifies how the Indian Tribal government intends to reduce the number of such repetitive loss properties.

(4) A *plan maintenance process* that includes:

(i) A section describing the method and schedule of monitoring, evaluating, and updating the mitigation plan.

(ii) A system for monitoring implementation of mitigation measures and project closeouts.

(iii) A process by which the Indian tribal government incorporates the requirements of the mitigation plan into other planning mechanisms such as reservation master plans or capital improvement plans, when appropriate.

(iv) Discussion on how the Indian tribal government will continue public participation in the plan maintenance process.

(v) A system for reviewing progress on achieving goals as well as activities and projects identified in the mitigation strategy.

(5) *Plan Adoption Process.* The plan must be formally adopted by the governing body of the Indian tribal government prior to submittal to FEMA for final review and approval.

(6) *Assurances.* The plan must include assurances that the Indian tribal government will comply with all applicable Federal statutes and regulations in effect with respect to the periods for which it receives grant funding, in compliance with § 13.11(c) of this chapter. The Indian tribal government will amend its plan whenever necessary to reflect changes in tribal or Federal laws and statutes as required in § 13.11(d) of this chapter.

(d) *Plan review and updates.* (1) Plans must be submitted to the appropriate FEMA Regional Office for formal review and approval. Indian tribal governments who would like the option of being a subgrantee under the State must also submit their plan to the State Hazard Mitigation Officer for review and coordination.

(2) The Regional review will be completed within 45 days after receipt from the Indian tribal government, whenever possible.

(3) Indian tribal governments must review and revise their plan to reflect changes in development, progress in local mitigation efforts, and changes in priorities, and resubmit it for approval within 5 years in order to continue to be eligible for non-emergency Stafford Act assistance and FEMA mitigation grant funding, with the exception of the Repetitive Flood Claims program.

[72 FR 61749, Oct. 31, 2007, as amended at 74 FR 47482, Sept. 16, 2009]

PARTS 202-203 [RESERVED]

PART 204—FIRE MANAGEMENT ASSISTANCE GRANT PROGRAM

Subpart A—General

AUTHORITY: Robert T. Stafford Disaster Relief and Emergency Assistance Act, 42 U.S.C. 5121–5207; Reorganization Plan No. 3 of 1978, 43 FR 41943; 3 CFR, 1978 Comp., p. 329; E.O. 12127, 44 FR 19367, 3 CFR, 1979 Comp., p. 376; E.O. 12148, 44 FR 43239, 3 CFR, 1979 Comp., p. 412; and E.O. 12673, 54 FR 12571, 3 CFR, 1989 Comp., p. 214.

SOURCE: 66 FR 57347, Nov. 14, 2001, unless otherwise noted.

Subpart A—General

§ 204.1 Purpose.

This part provides information on the procedures for the declaration and grants management processes for the Fire Management Assistance Grant Program in accordance with the provisions of section 420 of the Stafford Act. This part also details applicant eligibility and the eligibility of costs to be considered under the program. We (FEMA) will actively work with State and Tribal emergency managers and foresters on the efficient delivery of fire management assistance as directed by this part.

§ 204.2 Scope.

This part is intended for those individuals responsible for requesting declarations and administering grants under the Fire Management Assistance Grant Program, as well as those applying for assistance under the program.

§ 204.3 Definitions used throughout this part.

Applicant. A State or Indian tribal government submitting an application to us for a fire management assistance grant, or a State, local, or Indian tribal government submitting an application to the Grantee for a subgrant under an approved fire management assistance grant.

Declared fire. An uncontrolled fire or fire complex, threatening such destruction as would constitute a major disaster, which the Administrator has approved in response to a State's request for a fire management assistance declaration and in accordance with the criteria listed in § 204.21.

Demobilization. The process and procedures for deactivating, disassembling, and transporting back to their point of origin all resources that had been provided to respond to and support a declared fire.

FEMA Form 90–91. See Project Worksheet.

Fire complex. Two or more individual fires located in the same general area, which are assigned to a single Incident Commander.

Governor's Authorized Representative (GAR). The person empowered by the Governor to execute, on behalf of the State, all necessary documents for fire management assistance, including the request for a fire management assistance declaration.

Grant. An award of financial assistance, including cooperative agreements, by FEMA to an eligible Grantee. The grant award will be based on the projected amount of total eligible costs for which a State submits an application and that FEMA approves related to a declared fire.

Grantee. The Grantee is the government to which a grant is awarded which is accountable for the use of the funds provided. The Grantee is the entire legal entity even if only a particular component of the entity is designated in the grant award document. Generally, the State, as designated in the FEMA-State Agreement for the Fire Management Assistance Grant Program, is the Grantee. However, after a declaration, an Indian tribal government may choose to be a Grantee, or it may act as a subgrantee under the State. An Indian tribal government acting as Grantee will assume the responsibilities of a "state", as described in this Part, for the purpose of administering the grant.

Hazard mitigation plan. A plan to develop actions the State, local, or tribal government will take to reduce the risk to people and property from all hazards. The intent of hazard mitigation planning under the Fire Management Assistance Grant Program is to identify wildfire hazards and cost-effective mitigation alternatives that produce long-term benefits. We address mitigation of fire hazards as part of the State's comprehensive Mitigation Plan, described in 44 CFR part 201.

Incident commander. The ranking official responsible for overseeing the management of fire operations, planning, logistics, and finances of the field response.

Incident period. The time interval during which the declared fire occurs. The Regional Administrator , in consultation with the Governor's Authorized Representative and the Principal Advisor, will establish the incident period. Generally, costs must be incurred during the incident period to be considered eligible.

Indian tribal government. An Indian tribal government is any Federally recognized governing body of an Indian or Alaska Native tribe, band, nation, pueblo, village, or community that the Secretary of Interior acknowledges to exist as an Indian tribe under the Federally Recognized Tribe List Act of 1994, 25 U.S.C. 479a. This does not include Alaska Native corporations, the ownership of which is vested in private individuals.

Individual assistance. Supplementary Federal assistance provided under the Stafford Act to individuals and families adversely affected by a major disaster or an emergency. Such assistance may be provided directly by the Federal Government or through State or local governments or disaster relief organizations. For further information, see subparts D, E, and F of part 206.

Local government. A local government is any county, municipality, city, town, township, public authority, school district, special district, intrastate district, council of governments (regardless of whether the council of governments is incorporated as a nonprofit corporation under State law), regional or interstate government entity, or agency or instrumentality of a local government; any Indian tribal government or authorized tribal organization, or Alaska Native village or organization; and any rural community, unincorporated town or village, or other public entity, for which an application for assistance is made by a State or political subdivision of a State.

Mitigation, management, and control. Those activities undertaken, generally during the incident period of a declared fire, to minimize immediate adverse effects and to manage and control the fire. Eligible activities may include associated emergency work and pre-positioning directly related to the declared fire.

Mobilization. The process and procedures used for activating, assembling, and transporting all resources that the Grantee requested to respond to support a declared fire.

Performance period. The time interval designated in block 13 on the Application for Federal Assistance (Standard Form 424) for the Grantee and all subgrantees to submit eligible costs and have those costs processed, obligated, and closed out by FEMA.

Pre-positioning. Moving existing fire prevention or suppression resources from an area of lower fire danger to one of higher fire danger in anticipation of an increase in fire activity likely to constitute the threat of a major disaster.

Principal advisor. An individual appointed by the Forest Service, United States Department of Agriculture, or Bureau of Land Management, Department of the Interior, who is responsible for providing FEMA with a technical assessment of the fire or fire complex for which a State is requesting a fire management assistance declaration. The Principal Advisor also frequently participates with FEMA on other wildland fire initiatives.

Project worksheet. FEMA Form 90–91, which identifies actual costs incurred by eligible applicants as a result of the eligible firefighting activities.

Public assistance. Supplementary Federal assistance provided under the Stafford Act to State and local governments or certain private, nonprofit organizations for eligible emergency measures and repair, restoration, and replacement of damaged facilities. For further information, see Subparts G and H of Part 206.

Regional Administrator. The administrator of a regional office of FEMA, or his/her designated representative.

Request for Federal Assistance. See Standard Form (SF) 424.

Standard Form (SF) 424. The SF 424 is the Request for Federal Assistance. This is the form the State submits to apply for a grant under a fire management assistance declaration.

Subgrant. An award of financial assistance under a grant by a Grantee to an eligible subgrantee.

Subgrantee. An applicant that is awarded a subgrant and is accountable to the Grantee for the use of grant funding provided.

Threat of a major disaster. The potential impact of the fire or fire complex is of a severity and magnitude that would result in a presidential major disaster declaration for the Public Assistance Program, the Individual Assistance Program, or both.

Uncontrolled fire. Any fire not safely confined to predetermined control lines as established by firefighting resources.

We, our, us mean FEMA.

[66 FR 57347, Nov. 14, 2001, as amended at 68 FR 61370, Oct. 28, 2003; 74 FR 15345, Apr. 3, 2009; 75 FR 50715, Aug. 17, 2010]

§§ 204.4–204.20 [Reserved]

Subpart B—Declaration Process

§ 204.21 Fire management assistance declaration criteria.

(a) *Determinations.* We will approve declarations for fire management assistance when the Administrator determines that a fire or fire complex threatens such destruction as would constitute a major disaster.

(b) *Evaluation criteria.* We will evaluate the threat posed by a fire or fire complex based on consideration of the following specific criteria:

(1) Threat to lives and improved property, including threats to critical facilities/infrastructure, and critical watershed areas;

(2) Availability of State and local firefighting resources;

(3) High fire danger conditions, as indicated by nationally accepted indices such as the National Fire Danger Ratings System;

(4) Potential major economic impact.

[66 FR 57347, Nov. 14, 2001, as amended at 75 FR 50715, Aug. 17, 2010]

§ 204.22 Submitting a request for a fire management assistance declaration.

The Governor of a State, or the Governor's Authorized Representative (GAR), may submit a request for a fire management assistance declaration.

The request must be submitted while the fire is burning uncontrolled and threatens such destruction as would constitute a major disaster. The request must be submitted to the Regional Administrator and should address the relevant criteria listed in §204.21, with supporting documentation that contains factual data and professional estimates on the fire or fire complex. To ensure that we can process a State's request for a fire management assistance declaration as expeditiously as possible, the State should transmit the request by telephone, promptly followed by written documentation (FEMA Form 90–58).

§204.23 Processing a request for a fire management assistance declaration.

(a) In processing a State's request for a fire management assistance declaration, the Regional Administrator, in coordination with the Principal Advisor, will verify the information submitted in the State's request.

(b) The Principal Advisor, at the request of the Regional Administrator, is responsible for providing FEMA a technical assessment of the fire or fire complex for which the State is requesting a fire management assistance declaration. The Principal Advisor may consult with State agencies, usually emergency management or forestry, as well as the Incident Commander, in order to provide FEMA with an accurate assessment.

[75 FR 50715, Aug. 17, 2010]

§204.24 Determination on request for a fire management assistance declaration.

The Administrator will review all information submitted in the State's request along with the Principal Advisor's assessment and render a determination. The determination will be based on the conditions of the fire or fire complex existing at the time of the State's request. When possible, the Administrator will evaluate the request and make a determination within several hours. Once the Administrator renders a determination, FEMA will promptly notify the State of the determination.

[75 FR 50715, Aug. 17, 2010]

§204.25 FEMA–State agreement for fire management assistance grant program.

(a) After a State's request for a fire management assistance declaration has been approved, the Governor and Regional Administrator will enter into a standing FEMA–State Agreement (the Agreement) for the declared fire and for future declared fires in that calendar year. The State must have a signed and up-to-date FEMA–State Agreement before receiving Federal funding for fire management assistance grants. FEMA will provide no funding absent a signed and up-to-date Agreement. An Indian tribal government serving as Grantee, must sign a FEMA–Tribal Agreement, modeled upon the FEMA–State Agreement.

(b) The Agreement states the understandings, commitments, and conditions under which we will provide Federal assistance, including the cost share provision and articles of agreement necessary for the administration of grants approved under fire management assistance declarations. The Agreement must also identify the State legislative authority for firefighting, as well as the State's compliance with the laws, regulations, and other provisions applicable to the Fire Management Assistance Grant Program.

(c) For each subsequently declared fire within the calendar year, the parties must add a properly executed amendment, which defines the incident period and contains the official declaration number. Other amendments modifying the standing Agreement may be added throughout the year to reflect changes in the program or signatory parties.

§204.26 Appeal of fire management assistance declaration denial.

(a) *Submitting an appeal.* When a State's request for a fire management assistance declaration is denied, the Governor or GAR may appeal the decision in writing within 30 days after the date of the letter denying the request. The State should submit this one-time request for reconsideration in writing, with appropriate additional information to the Administrator through the

Regional Administrator. The Administrator will reevaluate the State's request and notify the State of the final determination within 90 days of receipt of the appeal or the receipt of additional requested information.

(b) *Requesting a time-extension.* The Administrator may extend the 30-day period for filing an appeal, provided that the Governor or the GAR submits a written

(c) *Request for such an extension within the 30-day period.* The Administrator will evaluate the need for an extension based on the reasons cited in the request and either approve or deny the request for an extension.

[75 FR 50715, Aug. 17, 2010]

§§ 204.27-204.40 [Reserved]

Subpart C—Eligibility

§ 204.41 Applicant eligibility.

(a) The following entities are eligible to apply through a State Grantee for a subgrant under an approved fire management assistance grant:

(1) State agencies;

(2) Local governments; and

(3) Indian tribal governments.

(b) Entities that are not eligible to apply for a subgrant as identified in (a), such as privately owned entities and volunteer firefighting organizations, may be reimbursed through a contract or compact with an eligible applicant for eligible costs associated with the fire or fire complex.

(c) Eligibility is contingent upon a finding that the Incident Commander or comparable State official requested the applying entity's resources.

(d) The activities performed must be the legal responsibility of the applying entity, required as the result of the declared fire, and located within the designated area.

§ 204.42 Eligible costs.

(a) *General.* (1) All eligible work and related costs must be associated with the incident period of a declared fire.

(2) Before obligating Federal funds the Regional Administrator must review and approve the initial grant application, along with Project Worksheets submitted with the application

and any subsequent amendments to the application.

(3) Grantees will award Federal funds to subgrantees under State law and procedure and complying with 44 CFR part 13.

(b) *Equipment and supplies.* Eligible costs include:

(1) Personal comfort and safety items normally provided by the State under field conditions for firefighter health and safety, including:

(2) Firefighting supplies, tools, materials, expended or lost, to the extent not covered by reasonable insurance, will be replaced with comparable items.

(3) Operation and maintenance costs of publicly owned, contracted, rented, or volunteer firefighting department equipment used in eligible firefighting activities to the extent any of these costs are not included in applicable equipment rates.

(4) Use of U.S. Government-owned equipment based on reasonable costs as billed by the Federal agency and paid by the State. (Only direct costs for use of Federal Excess Personal Property (FEPP) vehicles and equipment on loan to State Forestry and local cooperators may be eligible.)

(5) Repair of equipment damaged in firefighting activities to the extent not covered by reasonable insurance. We will use the lowest applicable equipment rates, or other rates that we determine, to calculate the eligible cost of repairs.

(6) Replacement of equipment lost or destroyed in firefighting activities, to the extent not covered by reasonable insurance, will be replaced with comparable equipment.

(c) *Labor costs.* Eligible costs include:

(1) Overtime for permanent or reassigned State and local employees.

(2) Regular time and overtime for temporary and contract employees hired to perform fire-related activities.

(d) *Travel and per diem costs.* Eligible costs include:

(1) Travel and per diem of employees who are providing services directly associated with eligible fire-related activities may be eligible.

(2) Provision of field camps and meals when made available in place of per diem;

378

(e) *Pre-positioning costs.* (1) The actual costs of pre-positioning Federal, out-of-State (including compact), and international resources for a limited period may be eligible when those resources are used in response to a declared fire.

(2) The Regional Administrator must approve all pre-positioning costs.

(i) Upon approval of a State's request for a fire management assistance declaration by the Assistant Administrator for the Disaster Assistance Directorate , the State should immediately notify the Regional Administrator of its intention to seek funding for pre-positioning resources.

(ii) The State must document the number of pre-positioned resources to be funded and their respective locations throughout the State, estimate the cost of the pre-positioned resources that were used on the declared fire and the amount of time the resources were pre-positioned, and provide a detailed explanation of the need to fund the pre-positioned resources.

(iii) The State will base the detailed explanation on recognized scientific indicators, that include, but are not limited to, drought indices, short-term weather forecasts, the current number of fires burning in the State, and the availability of in-State firefighting resources. The State may also include other quantitative indicators with which to measure the increased risk of the threat of a major disaster.

(iv) Based on the information contained in the State's notification, the Regional Administrator will determine the number of days of pre-positioning to be approved for Federal funding, up to a maximum of 21 days before the fire declaration.

(3) Upon rendering his/her determination on pre-positioning costs, the Regional Administrator will notify the Assistant Administrator for the Disaster Assistance Directorate of his/her determination.

(f) *Emergency work.* We may authorize the use of section 403 of the Stafford Act, Essential Assistance, under an approved fire management assistance grant when directly related to the mitigation, management, and control of the declared fire. Essential assistance activities that may be eligible include, but are not limited to, police barricading and traffic control, extraordinary emergency operations center expenses, evacuations and sheltering, search and rescue, arson investigation teams, public information, and the limited removal of trees that pose a threat to the general public.

(g) *Temporary repair of damage caused by firefighting activities.* Temporary repair of damage caused by eligible firefighting activities listed in this subpart involves short-term actions to repair damage directly caused by the firefighting effort or activities. This includes minimal repairs to bulldozer lines, camps, and staging areas to address safety concerns; as well as minimal repairs to facilities damaged by the firefighting activities such as fences, buildings, bridges, roads, etc. All temporary repair work must be completed within thirty days of the close of the incident period for the declared fire.

(h) *Mobilization and demobilization.* Costs for mobilization to, and demobilization from, a declared fire may be eligible for reimbursement. Demobilization may be claimed at a delayed date if deployment involved one or more declared fires. If resources are being used on more than one declared fire, mobilization and demobilization costs must be claimed against the first declared fire.

(i) *Fires on co-mingled Federal/State lands.* Reasonable costs for the mitigation, management, and control of a declared fire burning on co-mingled Federal and State land may be eligible in cases where the State has a responsibility for suppression activities under an agreement to perform such action on a non-reimbursable basis. (This provision is an exception to normal FEMA policy under the Stafford Act and is intended to accommodate only those rare instances that involve State firefighting on a Stafford Act section 420 fire incident involving co-mingled Federal/State and privately-owned forest or grassland.)

§ 204.43 Ineligible costs.

Costs not directly associated with the incident period are ineligible. Ineligible costs include the following:

(a) Costs incurred in the mitigation, management, and control of undeclared fires;

(b) Costs related to planning, pre-suppression (*i.e.*, cutting fire-breaks without the presence of an imminent threat, training, road widening, and other similar activities), and recovery (*i.e.*, land rehabilitation activities, such as seeding, planting operations, and erosion control, or the salvage of timber and other materials, and restoration of facilities damaged by fire);

(c) Costs for the straight or regular time salaries and benefits of a subgrantee's permanently employed or reassigned personnel;

(d) Costs for mitigation, management, and control of a declared fire on co-mingled Federal land when such costs are reimbursable to the State by a Federal agency under another statute (See 44 CFR part 51);

(e) Fires fought on Federal land are generally the responsibility of the Federal Agency that owns or manages the land. Costs incurred while fighting fires on federally owned land are not eligible under the Fire Management Assistance Grant Program except as noted in § 204.42(i).

§§ 204.44–204.50　[Reserved]

Subpart D—Application Procedures

§ 204.51　Application and approval procedures for a fire management assistance grant.

(a) *Preparing and submitting an application.* (1) After the approval of a fire management assistance declaration, the State may submit an application package for a grant to the Regional Administrator . The application package must include the SF 424 (Request for Federal Assistance) and FEMA Form 20–16a (Summary of Assurances—Non-construction Programs), as well as supporting documentation for the budget.

(2) The State should submit its grant application within 9 months of the declaration. Upon receipt of the written request from the State, the Regional Administrator may grant an extension for up to 3 months. The State's request must include a justification for the extension.

(b) *Fire cost threshold.* (1) We will approve the initial grant award to the State when we determine that the State's application demonstrates either of the following:

(i) Total eligible costs for the declared fire meet or exceed the individual fire cost threshold; or

(ii) Total costs of all declared and non-declared fires for which a State has assumed responsibility in a given calendar year meet the cumulative fire cost threshold.

(2) The individual fire cost threshold for a State is the greater of the following:

(i) $100,000; or

(ii) Five percent × $1.07 × the State population, adjusted annually for inflation using the Consumer Price Index for All Urban Consumers published annually by the Department of Labor.

(3) The cumulative fire cost threshold for a State is the greater of the following:

(i) $500,000; or

(ii) Three times the five percent × $1.07 × the State population as described in § 204.51(b)(2)(ii).

(4) States must document the total eligible costs for a declared fire on Project Worksheets, which they must submit with the grant application.

(5) We will not consider the costs of pre-positioning resources for the purposes of determining whether the grant application meets the fire cost threshold.

(6) When the State's total eligible costs associated with the fire management assistance declaration meet or exceed the fire cost threshold eligible costs will be cost shared in accordance with § 204.61.

(c) *Approval of the State's grant application.* The Regional Administrator has 45 days from receipt the State's grant application or an amendment to the State's grant application, including attached supporting Project Worksheet(s), to review and approve or deny the grant application or amendment; or to notify the Grantee of a delay in processing funding.

(d) *Obligation of the grant.* Before we approve the State's grant application, the State must have an up-to-date

State Administrative Plan and a Hazard Mitigation Plan that has been reviewed and approved by the Regional Administrator . Once these plans are approved by the Regional Administrator , the State's grant application may be approved and we may begin to obligate the Federal share of funding for subgrants to the Grantee.

(1) *State administrative plan.*(i) The State must develop an Administrative Plan (or have a current Administrative Plan on file with FEMA) that describes the procedures for the administration of the Fire Management Assistance Grant Program. The Plan will include, at a minimum, the items listed below:

(A) The designation of the State agency or agencies which will have responsibility for program administration.

(B) The identification of staffing functions for the Fire Management Assistance Program, the sources of staff to fill these functions, and the management and oversight responsibilities of each.

(C) The procedures for:

(*1*) Notifying potential applicants of the availability of the program;

(*2*) Assisting FEMA in determining applicant eligibility;

(*3*) Submitting and reviewing subgrant applications;

(*4*) Processing payment for subgrants;

(*5*) Submitting, reviewing, and accepting subgrant performance and financial reports;

(*6*) Monitoring, close-out, and audit and reconciliation of subgrants;

(*7*) Recovering funds for disallowed costs;

(*8*) Processing appeal requests and requests for time extensions; and

(*9*) Providing technical assistance to applicants and subgrant recipients, including briefings for potential applicants and materials on the application procedures, program eligibility guidance and program deadlines.

(ii) The Grantee may request the Regional Administrator to provide technical assistance in the preparation of the State Administrative Plan.

(2) *Hazard Mitigation Plan.* As a requirement of receiving funding under a fire management assistance grant, a State, or tribal organization, acting as Grantee, must:

(i) Develop a Mitigation Plan in accordance with 44 CFR part 201 that addresses wildfire risks and mitigation measures; or

(ii) Incorporate wildfire mitigation into the existing Mitigation Plan developed and approved under 44 CFR part 201 that also addresses wildfire risk and contains a wildfire mitigation strategy and related mitigation initiatives.

[66 FR 57347, Nov. 14, 2001, as amended at 68 FR 61371, Oct. 28, 2003]

§ **204.52 Application and approval procedures for a subgrant under a fire management assistance grant.**

(a) *Request for Fire Management Assistance.* (1) State, local, and tribal governments interested in applying for subgrants under an approved fire management assistance grant must submit a Request for Fire Management Assistance to the Grantee in accordance with State procedures and within timelines set by the Grantee, but no longer than 30 days after the close of the incident period.

(2) The Grantee will review and forward the Request to the Regional Administrator for final review and determination. The Grantee may also forward a recommendation for approval of the Request to the Regional Administrator when appropriate.

(3) The Regional Administrator will approve or deny the request based on the eligibility requirements outlined in § 204.41.

(4) The Regional Administrator will notify the Grantee of his/her determination; the Grantee will inform the applicant.

(b) *Preparing a Project Worksheet.* (1) Once the Regional Administrator approves an applicant's Request for Fire Management Assistance, the Regional Administrator's staff may begin to work with the Grantee and local staff to prepare Project Worksheets (FEMA Form 90–91).

(2) The Regional Administrator may request the Principal Advisor to assist in the preparation of Project Worksheets.

(3) The State will be the primary contact for transactions with and on behalf of the applicant.

(c) *Submitting a Project Worksheet.* (1) Applicants should submit all Project Worksheets through the Grantee for approval and transmittal to the Regional Administrator as amendments to the State's application.

(2) The Grantee will determine the deadline for an applicant to submit completed Project Worksheets, but the deadline must be no later than six months from close of the incident period.

(3) At the request of the Grantee, the Regional Administrator may grant an extension of up to three months. The Grantee must include a justification in its request for an extension.

(4) Project Worksheets will not be accepted after the deadline and extension specified in paragraphs (c)(2) and (c)(3) of this section has expired.

(5) *$1,000 Project Worksheet minimum.* When the costs reported are less than $1,000, that work is not eligible and we will not approve that Project Worksheet.

§ 204.53 **Certifying costs and payments.**

(a) By submitting applicants' Project Worksheets to us, the Grantee is certifying that all costs reported on applicant Project Worksheets were incurred for work that was performed in compliance with FEMA laws, regulations, policy and guidance applicable to the Fire Management Assistance Grant Program, as well as with the terms and conditions outlined for the administration of the grant in the FEMA-State Agreement for the Fire Management Assistance Grant Program.

(b) Advancement/Reimbursement for State grant costs will be processed as follows:

(1) Through the U.S. Department of Health and Human Services SMARTLINK system; and

(2) In compliance with 44 CFR 13.21 and U. S. Treasury 31 CFR part 205, Cash Management Improvement Act.

§ 204.54 **Appeals.**

An eligible applicant, subgrantee, or grantee may appeal any determination we make related to an application for the provision of Federal assistance according to the procedures below.

(a) *Format and content.* The applicant or subgrantee will make the appeal in writing through the grantee to the Regional Administrator . The grantee will review and evaluate all subgrantee appeals before submission to the Regional Administrator . The grantee may make grantee-related appeals to the Regional Administrator . The appeal will contain documented justification supporting the appellant's position, specifying the monetary figure in dispute and the provisions in Federal law, regulation, or policy with which the appellant believes the initial action was inconsistent.

(b) *Levels of appeal.* (1) The Regional Administrator will consider first appeals for fire management assistance grant-related decisions under subparts A through E of this part.

(2) The Assistant Administrator for the Disaster Assistance Directorate will consider appeals of the Regional Administrator's decision on any first appeal under paragraph (b)(1) of this section.

(c) *Time limits.* (1) Appellants must file appeals within 60 days after receipt of a notice of the action that is being appealed.

(2) The grantee will review and forward appeals from an applicant or subgrantee, with a written recommendation, to the Regional Administrator within 60 days of receipt.

(3) Within 90 days following receipt of an appeal, the Regional Administrator (for first appeals) or Assistant Administrator for the Disaster Assistance Directorate (for second appeals) will notify the grantee in writing of the disposition of the appeal or of the need for additional information. A request by the Regional Administrator or Assistant Administrator for the Disaster Assistance Directorate for additional information will include a date by which the information must be provided. Within 90 days following the receipt of the requested additional information or following expiration of the period for providing the information, the Regional Administrator or Assistant Administrator for the Disaster Assistance Directorate will notify the grantee in writing of the disposition of the appeal. If the decision is to grant the appeal,

the Regional Administrator will take appropriate implementing action.

(d) *Technical advice.* In appeals involving highly technical issues, the Regional Administrator or may, at his or her discretion, submit the appeal to an independent scientific or technical person or group having expertise in the subject matter of the appeal for advice or recommendation. The period for this technical review may be in addition to other allotted time periods. Within 90 days of receipt of the report, the Regional Administrator or Assistant Administrator for the Disaster Assistance Directorate will notify the grantee in writing of the disposition of the appeal.

(e) The decision of the Assistant Administrator for the Disaster Assistance Directorate at the second appeal level will be the final administrative decision of FEMA.

§§ 204.55–204.60 [Reserved]

Subpart E—Grant Administration

§ 204.61 Cost share.

(a) All fire management assistance grants are subject to a cost share. The Federal cost share for fire management assistance grants is seventy-five percent (75%).

(b) As stated in § 204.25, the cost share provision will be outlined in the terms and conditions of the FEMA-State Agreement for the Fire Management Assistance Grant Program.

§ 204.62 Duplication and recovery of assistance.

(a) *Duplication of benefits.* We provide supplementary assistance under the Stafford Act, which generally may not duplicate benefits received by or available to the applicant from insurance, other assistance programs, legal awards, or any other source to address the same purpose. An applicant must notify us of all benefits that it receives or anticipates from other sources for the same purpose, and must seek all such benefits available to them. We will reduce the grant by the amounts available for the same purpose from another source. We may provide assistance under this Part when other benefits are available to an applicant, but the applicant will be liable to us for any duplicative amounts that it receives or has available to it from other sources, and must repay us for such amounts.

(b) *Duplication of programs.* We will not provide assistance under this part for activities for which another Federal agency has more specific or primary authority to provide assistance for the same purpose. We may disallow or recoup amounts that fall within another Federal agency's authority. We may provide assistance under this part, but the applicant must agree to seek assistance from the appropriate Federal agency and to repay us for amounts that are within another Agency's authority.

(c) *Negligence.* We will provide no assistance to an applicant for costs attributable to applicant's own negligence. If the applicant suspects negligence by a third party for causing a condition for which we made assistance available under this Part, the applicant is responsible for taking all reasonable steps to recover all costs attributable to the negligence of the third party. We generally consider such amounts to be duplicated benefits available to the Grantee or subgrantee, and will treat them consistent with (a) of this section.

(d) *Intentional acts.* Any person who intentionally causes a condition for which assistance is provided under this part shall be liable to the United States to the extent that we incur costs attributable to the intentional act or omission that caused the condition. We may provide assistance under this part, but it will be conditioned on an agreement by the applicant to cooperate with us in efforts to recover the cost of the assistance from the liable party. A person shall not be liable under this section as a result of actions the person takes or omits in the course of rendering care or assistance in response to the fire.

§ 204.63 Allowable costs.

44 CFR 13.22 establishes general policies for determining allowable costs.

(a) We will reimburse direct costs for the administration of a fire management assistance grant under 44 CFR part 13.

383

(b) We will reimburse indirect costs for the administration of a fire management assistance grant in compliance with the Grantee's approved indirect cost rate under OMB Circular A–87.

§ 204.64 Reporting and audit requirements

(a) *Reporting.* Within 90-days of the Performance Period expiration date, the State will submit a final Financial Status Report (FEMA Form 20–10), which reports all costs incurred within the incident period and all administrative costs incurred within the performance period; and

(b) *Audit.* (1) Audits will be performed, for both the Grantee and the subgrantees, under 44 CFR 13.26.

(2) FEMA may elect to conduct a program-specific Federal audit on the Fire Management Assistance Grant or a subgrant.

PART 205 [RESERVED]

PART 206—FEDERAL DISASTER ASSISTANCE

Subpart A—General

Subpart B—The Declaration Process

Subpart C—Emergency Assistance

Subpart D—Federal Assistance to Individuals and Households

Subpart E—Individual and Family Grant Programs

AUTHORITY: Robert T. Stafford Disaster Relief and Emergency Assistance Act, 42 U.S.C. 5121 through 5207; Reorganization Plan No. 3 of 1978, 43 FR 41943, 3 CFR, 1978 Comp., p. 329; Homeland Security Act of 2002,

6 U.S.C. 101; E.O. 12127, 44 FR 19367, 3 CFR, 1979 Comp., p. 376; E.O. 12148, 44 FR 43239, 3 CFR, 1979 Comp., p. 412; and E.O. 13286, 68 FR 10619, 3 CFR, 2003 Comp., p. 166.

SOURCE: 54 FR 11615, Mar. 21, 1989, unless otherwise noted.

Subpart A—General

SOURCE: 55 FR 2288, Jan. 23, 1990, unless otherwise noted.

§ 206.1 Purpose.

(a) *Purpose.* The purpose of this subpart is to prescribe the policies and procedures to be followed in implementing those sections of Public Law 93–288, as amended, delegated to the Administrator, Federal Emergency Management Agency (FEMA). The rules in this subpart apply to major disasters and emergencies declared by the President on or after November 23, 1988, the date of enactment of the Robert T. Stafford Disaster Relief and Emergency Assistance Act, 42 U.S.C. 5121 *et seq.*

(b) *Prior regulations.* Prior regulations relating to major disasters and emergencies declared by the President before November 23, 1988 were published in 44 CFR part 205 (see 44 CFR part 205 as contained in the CFR edition revised as of October 1, 1994).

[59 FR 53363, Oct. 24, 1994]

§ 206.2 Definitions.

(a) *General.* The following definitions have general applicability throughout this part:

(1) *The Stafford Act:* The Robert T. Stafford Disaster Relief and Emergency Assistance Act, Public Law 93–288, as amended.

(2) *Applicant:* Individuals, families, States and local governments, or private nonprofit organizations who apply for assistance as a result of a declaration of a major disaster or emergency.

(3) [Reserved]

(4) *Concurrent, multiple major disasters:* In considering a request for an advance, the term concurrent multiple major disasters means major disasters which occur within a 12-month period immediately preceding the major disaster for which an advance of the non-

Federal share is requested pursuant to section 319 of the Stafford Act.

(5) *Contractor:* Any individual, partnership, corporation, agency, or other entity (other than an organization engaged in the business of insurance) performing work by contract for the Federal Government or a State or local agency.

(6) *Designated area:* Any emergency or major disaster-affected portion of a State which has been determined eligible for Federal assistance.

(7) *Administrator:* The Administrator, FEMA.

(8) *Disaster Recovery Manager (DRM):* The person appointed to exercise the authority of a Regional Administrator for a particular emergency or major disaster.

(9) *Emergency:* Any occasion or instance for which, in the determination of the President, Federal assistance is needed to supplement State and local efforts and capabilities to save lives and to protect property and public health and safety, or to lessen or avert the threat of a catastrophe in any part of the United States.

(10) *Federal agency:* Any department, independent establishment, Government corporation, or other agency of the executive branch of the Federal Government, including the United States Postal Service, but shall not include the American National Red Cross.

(11) *Federal Coordinating Officer (FCO):* The person appointed by the Administrator, or in his absence, the Deputy Director, to coordinate Federal assistance in an emergency or a major disaster.

(12) *Governor:* The chief executive of any State or the Acting Governor.

(13) *Governor's Authorized Representative (GAR):* The person empowered by the Governor to execute, on behalf of the State, all necessary documents for disaster assistance.

(14) *Hazard mitigation:* Any cost effective measure which will reduce the potential for damage to a facility from a disaster event.

(15) *Individual assistance:* Supplementary Federal assistance provided under the Stafford Act to individuals and families adversely affected by a major disaster or an emergency. Such

assistance may be provided directly by the Federal Government or through State or local governments or disaster relief organizations. For further information, see subparts D, E, and F of these regulations.

(16) *Local government:*

(i) A county, municipality, city, town, township, local public authority, school district, special district, intrastate district, council of governments (regardless of whether the council of governments is incorporated as a nonprofit corporation under State law), regional or interstate government entity, or agency or instrumentality of a local government;

(ii) An Indian tribe or authorized tribal organization, or Alaska Native village or organization; and

(iii) A rural community, unincorporated town or village, or other public entity, for which an application for assistance is made by a State or political subdivision of a State.

(17) *Major disaster:* Any natural catastrophe (including any hurricane, tornado, storm, high water, winddriven water, tidal wave, tsunami, earthquake, volcanic eruption, landslide, mudslide, snowstorm, or drought), or, regardless of cause, any fire, flood, or explosion, in any part of the United States, which in the determination of the President causes damage of sufficient severity and magnitude to warrant major disaster assistance under this Act to supplement the efforts and available resources of States, local governments, and disaster relief organizations in alleviating the damage, loss, hardship, or suffering caused thereby.

(18) *Mission assignment:* Work order issued to a Federal agency by the Regional Administrator, Assistant Administrator for the Disaster Operations Directorate, or Administrator, directing completion by that agency of a specified task and citing funding, other managerial controls, and guidance.

(19) *Private nonprofit organization:* Any nongovernmental agency or entity that currently has:

(i) An effective ruling letter from the U.S. Internal Revenue Service granting tax exemption under section 501 (c), (d), or (e) of the Internal Revenue Code of 1954; or

(ii) Satisfactory evidence from the State that the organization or entity is a nonprofit one organized or doing business under State law.

(20) *Public Assistance:* Supplementary Federal assistance provided under the Stafford Act to State and local governments or certain private, nonprofit organizations other than assistance for the direct benefit of individuals and families. For further information, see subparts G and H of this part. Fire Management Assistance Grants under section 420 of the Stafford Act are also considered Public Assistance. See subpart K of this part and part 204 of this chapter.

(21) *Regional Administrator:* An administrator of a regional office of FEMA, or his/her designated representative. As used in these regulations, Regional Administrator also means the Disaster Recovery Manager who has been appointed to exercise the authority of the Regional Administrator for a particular emergency or major disaster.

(22) *State:* Any State of the United States, the District of Columbia, Puerto Rico, the Virgin Islands, Guam, American Samoa, and the Commonwealth of the Northern Mariana Islands.

(23) *State Coordinating Officer (SCO):* The person appointed by the Governor to act in cooperation with the Federal Coordinating Officer to administer disaster recovery efforts.

(24) *State emergency plan:* As used in section 401 or section 501 of the Stafford Act means that State plan which is designated specifically for State-level response to emergencies or major disasters and which sets forth actions to be taken by the State and local governments, including those for implementing Federal disaster assistance.

(25) *Temporary housing:* Temporary accommodations provided by the Federal Government to individuals or families whose homes are made unlivable by an emergency or a major disaster.

(26) *United States:* The 50 States, District of Columbia, Puerto Rico, the Virgin Islands, Guam, American Samoa, and the Commonwealth of the Northern Mariana Islands.

(27) *Voluntary organization:* Any chartered or otherwise duly recognized tax-

exempt local, State, or national organization or group which has provided or may provide needed services to the States, local governments, or individuals in coping with an emergency or a major disaster.

(b) *Additional definitions.* Definitions which apply to individual subparts are found in those subparts.

[54 FR 11615, Mar. 21, 1989, as amended at 63 FR 17110, Apr. 8, 1998; 66 FR 57352, 57353, Nov. 14, 2001; 69 FR 24083, May 3, 2004; 74 FR 15346, Apr. 3, 2009]

§ 206.3   Policy.

It is the policy of FEMA to provide an orderly and continuing means of assistance by the Federal Government to State and local governments in carrying out their responsibilities to alleviate the suffering and damage that result from major disasters and emergencies by:

(a) Providing Federal assistance programs for public and private losses and needs sustained in disasters;

(b) Encouraging the development of comprehensive disaster preparedness and assistance plans, programs, capabilities, and organizations by the States and local governments;

(c) Achieving greater coordination and responsiveness of disaster preparedness and relief programs;

(d) Encouraging individuals, States, and local governments to obtain insurance coverage and thereby reduce their dependence on governmental assistance; and

(e) Encouraging hazard mitigation measures, such as development of land-use and construction regulations, floodplain management, protection of wetlands, and environmental planning, to reduce losses from disasters.

§ 206.4   State emergency plans.

The State shall set forth in its emergency plan all responsibilities and actions specified in the Stafford Act and these regulations that are required of the State and its political subdivisions to prepare for and respond to major disasters and emergencies and to facilitate the delivery of Federal disaster assistance. Although not mandatory, prior to the adoption of the final plan, the State is encouraged to circulate the plan to local governments for review and comment.

[55 FR 2288, Jan. 23, 1990, 55 FR 5458, Feb. 15, 1990]

§ 206.5   Assistance by other Federal agencies.

(a) In any declared major disaster, the Administrator, Assistant Administrator for the Disaster Operations Directorate, or the Regional Administrator may direct any Federal agency to utilize its authorities and the resources granted to it under Federal law (including personnel, equipment, supplies, facilities, and managerial, technical, and advisory services) to support State and local assistance efforts.

(b) In any declared emergency, the Administrator, Assistant Administrator for the Disaster Operations Directorate, or the Regional Administrator may direct any Federal agency to utilize its authorities and the resources granted to it under Federal law (including personnel, equipment, supplies, facilities, and managerial, technical, and advisory services) to support emergency efforts by State and local governments to save lives; protect property, public health and safety; and lessen or avert the threat of a catastrophe.

(c) In any declared major disaster or emergency, the Administrator, Assistant Administrator for the Disaster Operations Directorate, or the Regional Administrator may direct any Federal agency to provide emergency assistance necessary to save lives and to protect property, public health, and safety by:

(1) Utilizing, lending, or donating to State and local governments Federal equipment, supplies, facilities, personnel, and other resources, other than the extension of credit, for use or distribution by such governments in accordance with the purposes of this Act;

(2) Distributing medicine, food, and other consumable supplies; or

(3) Performing work or services to provide emergency assistance authorized in the Stafford Act.

(d) Disaster assistance by other Federal agencies is subject to the coordination of the FCO. Federal agencies shall provide any reports or information about disaster assistance rendered under the provisions of these regulations or authorities independent of the Stafford Act, that the FCO or Regional Administrator considers necessary and requests from the agencies.

(e) Assistance furnished by any Federal agency under paragraphs (a), (b), or (c) of this section is subject to the criteria provided by the Assistant Administrator for the Disaster Operations Directorate under these regulations.

(f) Assistance under paragraphs (a), (b), or (c) of this section, when directed by the Administrator, Assistant Administrator for the Disaster Operations Directorate, or the Regional Administrator, does not apply to nor shall it affect the authority of any Federal agency to provide disaster assistance independent of the Stafford Act.

(g) In carrying out the purposes of the Stafford Act, any Federal agency may accept and utilize, with the consent of the State or local government, the services, personnel, materials, and facilities of any State or local government, agency, office, or employee. Such utilization shall not make such services, materials, or facilities Federal in nature nor make the State or local government or agency an arm or agent of the Federal Government.

(h) Any Federal agency charged with the administration of a Federal assistance program may, if so requested by the applicant State or local authorities, modify or waive, for a major disaster, such administrative conditions for assistance as would otherwise prevent the giving of assistance under such programs if the inability to meet such conditions is a result of the major disaster.

§206.6 Donation or loan of Federal equipment and supplies.

(a) In any major disaster or emergency, the Administrator, Assistant Administrator for the Disaster Operations Directorate, or the Regional Administrator may direct Federal agencies to donate or loan their equipment and supplies to State and local governments for use and distribution by them for the purposes of the Stafford Act.

(b) A donation or loan may include equipment and supplies determined under applicable laws and regulations to be surplus to the needs and responsibilities of the Federal Government. The State shall certify that the surplus property is usable and necessary for current disaster purposes in order to receive a donation or loan. Such a donation or loan is made in accordance with procedures prescribed by the General Services Administration.

§206.7 Implementation of assistance from other Federal agencies.

All directives, known as mission assignments, to other Federal agencies shall be in writing, or shall be confirmed in writing if made orally, and shall identify the specific task to be performed and the requirements or criteria to be followed. If the Federal agency is to be reimbursed, the letter will also contain a dollar amount which is not to be exceeded in accomplishing the task without prior approval of the issuing official.

§206.8 Reimbursement of other Federal agencies.

(a) Assistance furnished under §206.5 (a) or (b) of this subpart may be provided with or without compensation as considered appropriate by the Administrator, Assistant Administrator for the Disaster Assistance Directorate, or the Regional Administrator or Regional Director.

(b) The Administrator, Assistant Administrator for the Disaster Assistance Directorate, or the Regional Administrator or the Regional Director may not approve reimbursement of costs incurred while performing work pursuant to disaster assistance authorities independent of the Stafford Act.

(c) *Expenditures eligible for reimbursement.* The Administrator, Assistant Administrator for the Disaster Assistance Directorate, or the Regional Administrator or the Regional Director may approve reimbursement of the following costs which are incurred in providing requested assistance.

(1) Overtime, travel, and per diem of permanent Federal agency personnel.

(2) Wages, travel, and per diem of temporary Federal agency personnel assigned solely to performance of services directed by the Administrator, Assistant Administrator for the Disaster Assistance Directorate, or the Regional Administrator or the Regional Director

389

in the major disaster or emergency area designated by the Regional Director.

(3) Travel and per diem of Federal military personnel assigned solely to the performance of services directed by the Administrator, Assistant Administrator for the Disaster Assistance Directorate, or the Regional Administrator or the Regional Director in the major disaster or emergency area designated by the Regional Director.

(4) Cost of work, services, and materials procured under contract for the purposes of providing assistance directed by the Administrator, Assistant Administrator for the Disaster Assistance Directorate, or the Regional Administrator or the Regional Director.

(5) Cost of materials, equipment, and supplies (including transportation, repair, and maintenance) from regular stocks used in providing directed assistance.

(6) All costs incurred which are paid from trust, revolving, or other funds, and whose reimbursement is required by law.

(7) Other costs submitted by an agency with written justification or otherwise agreed to in writing by the Administrator, Assistant Administrator for the Disaster Assistance Directorate, or the Regional Administrator or the Regional Director and the agency.

(d) *Procedures for reimbursement.* Federal agencies performing work under a mission assignment will submit requests for reimbursement, as follows:

(1) Federal agencies may submit requests for reimbursement of amounts greater than $1,000 at any time. Requests for lesser amounts may be submitted only quarterly. An agency shall submit a final accounting of expenditures after completion of the agency's work under each directive for assistance. The time limit and method for submission of reimbursement requests will be stipulated in the mission assignment letter.

(2) An agency shall document its request for reimbursement with specific details on personnel services, travel, and all other expenses by object class as specified in OMB Circular A-12 and by any other subobject class used in the agency's accounting system. Where contracts constitute a significant portion of the billings, the agency shall provide a listing of individual contracts and their associated costs.

(3) Reimbursement requests shall cite the specific mission assignment under which the work was performed, and the major disaster or emergency identification number. Requests for reimbursement of costs incurred under more than one mission assignment may not be combined for billing purposes.

(4) Unless otherwise agreed, an agency shall direct all requests for reimbursement to the Regional Administrator of the region in which the costs were incurred.

(5) A Federal agency requesting reimbursement shall retain all financial records, supporting documents, statistical records, and other records pertinent to the provision of services or use of resources by that agency. These materials shall be accessible to duly authorized representatives of FEMA and the U.S. Comptroller General, for the purpose of making audits, excerpts, and transcripts, for a period of 3 years starting from the date of submission of the final billing.

§ 206.9 **Nonliability.**

The Federal Government shall not be liable for any claim based upon the exercise or performance of, or the failure to exercise or perform a discretionary function or duty on the part of a Federal agency or an employee of the Federal Government in carrying out the provisions of the Stafford Act.

§ 206.10 **Use of local firms and individuals.**

In the expenditure of Federal funds for debris removal, distribution of supplies, reconstruction, and other major disaster or emergency assistance activities which may be carried out by contract or agreement with private organizations, firms, or individuals, preference shall be given, to the extent feasible and practicable, to those organizations, firms, and individuals residing or doing business primarily in the area affected by such major disaster or emergency. This shall not be considered to restrict the use of Department of Defense resources in the provision of major disaster assistance under the Stafford Act.

§ 206.11 Nondiscrimination in disaster assistance.

(a) Federal financial assistance to the States or their political subdivisions is conditioned on full compliance with 44 CFR part 7, Nondiscrimination in Federally-Assisted Programs.

(b) All personnel carrying out Federal major disaster or emergency assistance functions, including the distribution of supplies, the processing of the applications, and other relief and assistance activities, shall perform their work in an equitable and impartial manner, without discrimination on the grounds of race, color, religion, nationality, sex, age, or economic status.

(c) As a condition of participation in the distribution of assistance or supplies under the Stafford Act, or of receiving assistance under the Stafford Act, government bodies and other organizations shall provide a written assurance of their intent to comply with regulations relating to nondiscrimination.

(d) The agency shall make available to employees, applicants, participants, beneficiaries, and other interested parties such information regarding the provisions of this regulation and its applicability to the programs or activities conducted by the agency, and make such information available to them in such manner as the head of the agency finds necessary to apprise such persons of the protections against discrimination assured them by the Act and this regulation.

§ 206.12 Use and coordination of relief organizations.

(a) In providing relief and assistance under the Stafford Act, the FCO or Regional Administrator may utilize, with their consent, the personnel and facilities of the American National Red Cross, the Salvation Army, the Mennonite Disaster Service, and other voluntary organizations in the distribution of medicine, food, supplies, or other items, and in the restoration, rehabilitation, or reconstruction of community services and essential facilities, whenever the FCO or Regional Ad-

ministrator finds that such utilization is necessary.

(b) The Administrator is authorized to enter into agreements with the American Red Cross, The Salvation Army, the Mennonite Disaster Service, and other voluntary organizations engaged in providing relief during and after a major disaster or emergency. Any agreement shall include provisions assuring that use of Federal facilities, supplies, and services will be in compliance with § 206.11, Nondiscrimination in Disaster Assistance, and § 206.191, Duplication of Benefits, of these regulations and such other regulations as the Administrator may issue. The FCO may coordinate the disaster relief activities of the voluntary organizations which agree to operate under his/her direction.

(c) Nothing contained in this section shall be construed to limit or in any way affect the responsibilities of the American National Red Cross as stated in Public Law 58–4.

§ 206.13 Standards and reviews.

(a) The Administrator shall establish program standards and assess the efficiency and effectiveness of programs administered under the Stafford Act by conducting annual reviews of the activities of Federal agencies and State and local governments involved in major disaster or emergency response efforts.

(b) In carrying out this provision, the Administrator may direct Federal agencies to submit reports relating to their disaster assistance activities. The Administrator may request similar reports from the States relating to these activities on the part of State and local governments. Additionally, the Administrator may conduct independent investigations, studies, and evaluations as necessary to complete the reviews.

[55 FR 2288, Jan. 23, 1990; 55 FR 5458, Feb. 15, 1990]

§ 206.14 Criminal and civil penalties.

(a) *Misuse of funds.* Any person who knowingly misapplies the proceeds of a loan or other cash benefit obtained under the Stafford Act shall be fined an amount equal to one and one-half times the misapplied amount of the proceeds or cash benefit.

(b) *Civil enforcement.* Whenever it appears that any person has violated or is about to violate any provision of the Stafford Act, including any civil penalty imposed under the Stafford Act, the Attorney General may bring a civil action for such relief as may be appropriate. Such action may be brought in an appropriate United States district court.

(c) *Referral to Attorney General.* The Office of Chief Counsel shall expeditiously refer to the Attorney General for appropriate action any evidence developed in the performance of functions under the Stafford Act that may warrant consideration for criminal prosecution.

(d) *Civil penalty.* Any individual who knowingly violates any order or regulation shall be subject to a civil penalty of not more than $5,500 for each violation.

[55 FR 2288, Jan. 23, 1990, as amended at 74 FR 15346, Apr. 3, 2009; 74 FR 58850, Nov. 16, 2009]

§ 206.15   Recovery of assistance.

(a) *Party liable.* Any person who intentionally causes a condition for which Federal assistance is provided under this Act or under any other Federal law as a result of a declaration of a major disaster or emergency under this Act shall be liable to the United States for the reasonable costs incurred by the United States in responding to such disaster or emergency to the extent that such costs are attributable to the intentional act or omission of such person which caused such condition. Such action shall be brought in an appropriate United States District Court.

(b) *Rendering of care.* A person shall not be liable under this section for costs incurred by the United States as a result of actions taken or omitted by such person in the course of rendering care or assistance in response to a major disaster or emergency.

§ 206.16   Audit and investigations.

(a) Subject to the provisions of chapter 75 of title 31, United States Code, and 44 CFR part 13, relating to requirements for single audits, the Administrator, the Assistant Administrator for the Disaster Operations Directorate, or the Regional Administrator shall conduct audits and investigations as necessary to assure compliance with the Stafford Act, and in connection therewith may question such persons as may be necessary to carry out such audits and investigations.

(b) For purposes of audits and investigations under this section, FEMA or State auditors, the Governor's Authorized Representative, the Administrator, the Regional Administrator, the Assistant Administrator for the Disaster Assistance Directorate, the DHS Inspector General, and the Comptroller General of the United States, or their duly authorized representatives, may inspect any books, documents, papers, and records of any person relating to any activity undertaken or funded under the Stafford Act.

[55 FR 2288, Jan. 23, 1990, as amended at 74 FR 15346, Apr. 3, 2009]

§ 206.17   Effective date.

These regulations are effective for all major disasters or emergencies declared on or after November 23, 1988.

§§ 206.18–206.30   [Reserved]

Subpart B—The Declaration Process

SOURCE: 55 FR 2292, Jan. 23, 1990, unless otherwise noted.

§ 206.31   Purpose.

The purpose of this subpart is to describe the process leading to a Presidential declaration of a major disaster or an emergency and the actions triggered by such a declaration.

§ 206.32   Definitions.

All definitions in the Stafford Act and in § 206.2 apply. In addition, the following definitions apply:

(a) *Appeal:* A request for reconsideration of a determination on any action related to Federal assistance under the Stafford Act and these regulations. Specific procedures for appeals are contained in the relevant subparts of these regulations.

(b) *Commitment:* A certification by the Governor that the State and local governments will expend a reasonable amount of funds to alleviate the effects of the major disaster or emergency, for which no Federal reimbursement will be requested.

(c) *Disaster Application Center:* A center established in a centralized location within the disaster area for individuals, families, or businesses to apply for disaster aid.

(d) *FEMA-State Agreement:* A formal legal document stating the understandings, commitments, and binding conditions for assistance applicable as the result of the major disaster or emergency declared by the President.

(e) *Incident:* Any condition which meets the definition of major disaster or emergency as set forth in §206.2 which causes damage or hardship that may result in a Presidential declaration of a major disaster or an emergency.

(f) *Incident period:* The time interval during which the disaster-causing incident occurs. No Federal assistance under the Act shall be approved unless the damage or hardship to be alleviated resulted from the disaster-causing incident which took place during the incident period or was in anticipation of that incident. The incident period will be established by FEMA in the FEMA-State Agreement and published in the FEDERAL REGISTER.

§206.33 Preliminary damage assessment.

The preliminary damage assessment (PDA) process is a mechanism used to determine the impact and magnitude of damage and the resulting unmet needs of individuals, businesses, the public sector, and the community as a whole. Information collected is used by the State as a basis for the Governor's request, and by FEMA to document the recommendation made to the President in response to the Governor's request. It is in the best interest of all parties to combine State and Federal personnel resources by performing a joint PDA prior to the initiation of a Governor's request, as follows:

(a) *Preassessment by the State.* When an incident occurs, or is imminent, which the State official responsible for disaster operations determines may be beyond the State and local government capabilities to respond, the State will request the Regional Administrator to perform a joint FEMA-State preliminary damage assessment. It is not anticipated that all occurrences will result in the requirement for assistance; therefore, the State will be expected to verify their initial information, in some manner, before requesting this support.

(b) *Damage assessment teams.* Damage assessment teams will be composed of at least one representative of the Federal Government and one representative of the State. A local government representative, familiar with the extent and location of damage in his/her community, should also be included, if possible. Other State and Federal agencies, and voluntary relief organizations may also be asked to participate, as needed. It is the State's responsibility to coordinate State and local participation in the PDA and to ensure that the participants receive timely notification concerning the schedule. A FEMA official will brief team members on damage criteria, the kind of information to be collected for the particular incident, and reporting requirements.

(c) *Review of findings.* At the close of the PDA, FEMA will consult with State officials to discuss findings and reconcile any differences.

(d) *Exceptions.* The requirement for a joint PDA may be waived for those incidents of unusual severity and magnitude that do not require field damage assessments to determine the need for supplemental Federal assistance under the Act, or in such other instances determined by the Regional Administrator upon consultation with the State. It may be necessary, however, to conduct an assessment to determine unmet needs for managerial response purposes.

§206.34 Request for utilization of Department of Defense (DOD) resources.

(a) *General.* During the immediate aftermath of an incident which may ultimately qualify for a Presidential declaration of a major disaster or emergency, when threats to life and property are present which cannot be effectively dealt with by the State or local governments, the Assistant Administrator for the Disaster Assistance Directorate may direct DOD to utilize DOD personnel and equipment for removal of debris and wreckage and temporary restoration of essential public facilities and services.

(b) *Request process.* The Governor of a State, or the Acting Governor in his/her absence, may request such DOD assistance. The Governor should submit the request to the Assistant Administrator for the Disaster Assistance Directorate through the appropriate Regional Administrator to ensure prompt acknowledgment and processing. The request must be submitted within 48 hours of the occurrence of the incident. Requests made after that time may still be considered if information is submitted indicating why the request for assistance could not be made during the initial 48 hours. The request shall include:

(1) Information describing the types and amount of DOD emergency assistance being requested;

(2) Confirmation that the Governor has taken appropriate action under State law and directed the execution of the State emergency plan;

(3) A finding that the situation is of such severity and magnitude that effective response is beyond the capabilities of the State and affected local governments and that Federal assistance is necessary for the preservation of life and property;

(4) A certification by the Governor that the State and local government will reimburse FEMA for the non-Federal share of the cost of such work; and

(5) An agreement:

(i) To provide all lands, easements and rights-of-way necessary to accomplish the approved work without cost to the United States;

(ii) To hold and save the United States free from damages due to the requested work, and to indemnify the Federal government against any claims arising from such work; and

(iii) To assist DOD in all support and local jurisdictional matters.

(c) *Processing the request.* Upon receipt of the request, the Regional Administrator shall gather adequate information to support a recommendation and forward it to the Assistant Administrator for the Disaster Assistance Directorate. If the Assistant Administrator for the Disaster Assistance Directorate determines that such work is essential to save lives and protect property, he/she will issue a mission assignment to DOD authorizing direct Federal assistance to the extent deemed appropriate.

(d) *Implementation of assistance.* The performance of emergency work may not exceed a period of 10 days from the date of the mission assignment.

(e) *Limits.* Generally, no work shall be approved under this section which falls within the statutory authority of DOD or another Federal agency. However, where there are significant unmet needs of sufficient severity and magnitude, not addressed by other assistance, which could appropriately be addressed under this section of the Stafford Act, the involvement of other Federal agencies would not preclude the authorization of DOD assistance by the Assistant Administrator for the Disaster Assistance Directorate.

(f) *Federal share.* The Federal share of assistance under this section shall be not less than 75 percent of the cost of eligible work.

(g) *Project management.* DOD shall ensure that the work is completed in accordance with the approved scope of work, costs, and time limitations in the mission assignment. DOD shall also keep the Regional Administrator and the State advised of work progress and other project developments. It is the responsibility of DOD to ensure compliance with applicable Federal, State and local legal requirements. A final report will be submitted to the Regional Administrator upon termination of all direct Federal assistance work. Final reports shall be signed by a representative of DOD and the State. Once the final eligible cost is determined, DOD will request reimbursement from FEMA and FEMA will submit a bill to the State for the non-Federal share of the mission assignment.

(h) *Reimbursement of DOD.* Reimbursement will be made in accordance with § 206.8 of these regulations.

§ 206.35 Requests for emergency declarations.

(a) When an incident occurs or threatens to occur in a State, which would not qualify under the definition of a major disaster, the Governor of a State, or the Acting Governor in his/her absence, may request that the President declare an emergency. The Governor should submit the request to the President through the appropriate Regional Administrator to ensure prompt acknowledgment and processing. The request must be submitted within 5 days after the need for assistance under title V becomes apparent, but no longer than 30 days after the occurrence of the incident, in order to be considered. The period may be extended by the Assistant Administrator for the Disaster Assistance Directorate provided that a written request for such extension is made by the Governor, or Acting Governor, during the 30-day period immediately following the incident. The extension request must stipulate the reason for the delay.

(b) The basis for the Governor's request must be the finding that the situation:

(1) Is of such severity and magnitude that effective response is beyond the capability of the State and the affected local government(s); and

(2) Requires supplementary Federal emergency assistance to save lives and to protect property, public health and safety, or to lessen or avert the threat of a disaster.

(c) In addition to the above findings, the complete request shall include:

(1) Confirmation that the Governor has taken appropriate action under State law and directed the execution of the State emergency plan;

(2) Information describing the State and local efforts and resources which have been or will be used to alleviate the emergency;

(3) Information describing other Federal agency efforts and resources which have been or will be used in responding to this incident; and

(4) Identification of the type and extent of additional Federal aid required.

(d) *Modified declaration for Federal emergencies.* The requirement for a Governor's request under paragraph (a) of this section can be waived when an emergency exists for which the primary responsibility rests in the Federal government because the emergency involves a subject area for which, under the Constitution or laws of the United States, the Federal government exercises exclusive or preeminent responsibility and authority. Any party may bring the existence of such a situation to the attention of the FEMA Regional Administrator. Any recommendation for a Presidential declaration of emergency in the absence of a Governor's request must be initiated by the Regional Administrator or transmitted through the Regional Administrator by another Federal agency. In determining that such an emergency exists, the Assistant Administrator for the Disaster Assistance Directorate or Regional Administrator shall consult the Governor of the affected State, if practicable.

(e) *Other authorities.* It is not intended for an emergency declaration to preempt other Federal agency authorities and/or established plans and response mechanisms in place prior to the enactment of the Stafford Act.

§ 206.36 Requests for major disaster declarations.

(a) When a catastrophe occurs in a State, the Governor of a State, or the Acting Governor in his/her absence, may request a major disaster declaration. The Governor should submit the request to the President through the appropriate Regional Administrator to ensure prompt acknowledgment and processing. The request must be submitted within 30 days of the occurrence of the incident in order to be considered. The 30-day period may be extended by the Assistant Administrator for the Disaster Assistance Directorate, provided that a written request for an extension is submitted by the Governor, or Acting Governor, during this 30-day period. The extension request will stipulate reasons for the delay.

(b) The basis for the request shall be a finding that:

(1) The situation is of such severity and magnitude that effective response is beyond the capabilities of the State and affected local governments; and

(2) Federal assistance under the Act is necessary to supplement the efforts and available resources of the State, local governments, disaster relief organizations, and compensation by insurance for disaster-related losses.

(c) In addition to the above findings, the complete request shall include:

(1) Confirmation that the Governor has taken appropriate action under State law and directed the execution of the State emergency plan;

(2) An estimate of the amount and severity of damages and losses stating the impact of the disaster on the public and private sector;

(3) Information describing the nature and amount of State and local resources which have been or will be committed to alleviate the results of the disaster;

(4) Preliminary estimates of the types and amount of supplementary Federal disaster assistance needed under the Stafford Act; and

(5) Certification by the Governor that State and local government obligations and expenditures for the current disaster will comply with all applicable cost sharing requirements of the Stafford Act.

(d) For those catastrophes of unusual severity and magnitude when field damage assessments are not necessary to determine the requirement for supplemental Federal assistance, the Governor or Acting Governor may send an abbreviated written request through the Regional Administrator for a declaration of a major disaster. This may be transmitted in the most expeditious manner available. In the event the FEMA Regional Office is severely impacted by the catastrophe, the request may be addressed to the Administrator of FEMA. The request must indicate a finding in accordance with § 206.36(b), and must include as a minimum the information requested by § 206.36 (c)(1), (c)(3), and (c)(5). Upon receipt of the request, FEMA shall expedite the processing of reports and recommendations to the President. Notification to the Governor of the Presidential declaration shall be in accordance with 44 CFR 206.39. The Assistant Administrator for the Disaster Assistance Directorateshall assure that documentation of the declaration is later assembled to comply fully with these regulations.

§ 206.37 Processing requests for declarations of a major disaster or emergency.

(a) *Acknowledgment.* The Regional Administrator shall provide written acknowledgment of the Governor's request.

(b) *Regional summary.* Based on information obtained by FEMA/State preliminary damage assessments of the affected area(s) and consultations with appropriate State and Federal officials and other interested parties, the Regional Administrator shall promptly prepare a summary of the PDA findings. The data will be analyzed and submitted with a recommendation to the Assistant Administrator for the Disaster Assistance Directorate. The Regional Analysis shall include a discussion of State and local resources and capabilities, and other assistance available to meet the major disaster or emergency-related needs.

(c) *FEMA recommendation.* Based on all available information, the Administrator shall formulate a recommendation which shall be forwarded to the President with the Governor's request.

(1) *Major disaster recommendation.* The recommendation will be based on a finding that the situation is or is not of such severity and magnitude as to be beyond the capabilities of the State and its local governments. It will also contain a determination of whether or not supplemental Federal assistance under the Stafford Act is necessary and appropriate. In developing a recommendation, FEMA will consider such factors as the amount and type of damages; the impact of damages on affected individuals, the State, and local governments; the available resources of the State and local governments, and other disaster relief organizations; the extent and type of insurance in effect to cover losses; assistance available from other Federal programs and other sources; imminent threats to public health and safety; recent disaster history in the State; hazard mitigation measures taken by the State or local governments, especially implementation of measures required as a

result of previous major disaster declarations; and other factors pertinent to a given incident.

(2) *Emergency recommendation.* The recommendation will be based on a report which will indicate whether or not Federal emergency assistance under section 502 of the Stafford Act is necessary to supplement State and local efforts to save lives, protect property and public health and safety, or to lessen or avert the threat of a catastrophe. Only after it has been determined that all other resources and authorities available to meet the crisis are inadequate, and that assistance provided in section 502 of the Stafford Act would be appropriate, will FEMA recommend an emergency declaration to the President.

(d) *Modified Federal emergency recommendation.* The recommendation will be based on a report which will indicate that an emergency does or does not exist for which assistance under section 502 of the Stafford Act would be appropriate. An emergency declaration will not be recommended in situations where the authority to respond or coordinate is within the jurisdiction of one or more Federal agencies without a Presidential declaration. However, where there are significant unmet needs of sufficient severity and magnitude, not addressed by other assistance, which could appropriately be addressed under the Stafford Act, the involvement of other Federal agencies would not preclude a declaration of an emergency under the Act.

§ 206.38 Presidential determination.

(a) The Governor's request for a major disaster declaration may result in either a Presidential declaration of a major disaster or an emergency, or denial of the Governor's request.

(b) The Governor's request for an emergency declaration may result only in a Presidential declaration of an emergency, or denial of the Governor's request.

[55 FR 2292, Jan. 23, 1990; 55 FR 5458, Feb. 15, 1990]

§ 206.39 Notification.

(a) The Governor will be promptly notified by the Administrator or his/her designee of a declaration by the President that an emergency or a major disaster exists. FEMA also will notify other Federal agencies and other interested parties.

(b) The Governor will be promptly notified by the Administrator or his/her designee of a determination that the Governor's request does not justify the use of the authorities of the Stafford Act.

(c) Following a major disaster or emergency declaration, the Regional Administrator or the Assistant Administrator for the Disaster Assistance Directorate will promptly notify the Governor of the designations of assistance and areas eligible for such assistance.

§ 206.40 Designation of affected areas and eligible assistance.

(a) *Eligible assistance.* The Assistant Administrator for the Disaster Assistance Directorate has been delegated authority to determine and designate the types of assistance to be made available. The initial designations will usually be announced in the declaration. Determinations by the Assistant Administrator for the Disaster Assistance Directorate of the types and extent of FEMA disaster assistance to be provided are based upon findings whether the damage involved and its effects are of such severity and magnitude as to be beyond the response capabilities of the State, the affected local governments, and other potential recipients of supplementary Federal assistance. The Assistant Administrator for the Disaster Assistance Directorate may authorize all, or only particular types of, supplementary Federal assistance requested by the Governor.

(b) *Areas eligible to receive assistance.* The Assistant Administrator for the Disaster Assistance Directorate also has been delegated authority to designate the affected areas eligible for supplementary Federal assistance under the Stafford Act. These designations shall be published in the FEDERAL REGISTER. An affected area designated by the Assistant Administrator for the Disaster Assistance Directorate includes all local government jurisdictions within its boundaries. The Assistant Administrator for the Disaster Assistance Directorate may, based upon damage assessments in any given area, designate all or only some of the areas requested by the Governor for supplementary Federal assistance.

(c) *Requests for additional designations after a declaration.* After a declaration by the President, the Governor, or the GAR, may request that additional areas or types of supplementary Federal assistance be authorized by the Assistant Administrator for the Disaster Assistance Directorate. Such requests shall be accompanied by appropriate verified assessments and commitments by State and local governments to demonstrate that the requested designations are justified and that the unmet needs are beyond State and local capabilities without supplementary Federal assistance. Additional assistance or areas added to the declaration will be published in the FEDERAL REGISTER.

(d) *Time limits to request.* In order to be considered, all supplemental requests under paragraph (c) of this section must be submitted within 30 days from the termination date of the incident, or 30 days after the declaration, whichever is later. The 30-day period may be extended by the Assistant Administrator for the Disaster Assistance Directorate provided that a written request is made by the appropriate State official during this 30-day period. The request must include justification of the State's inability to meet the deadline.

[55 FR 2292, Jan. 23, 1990, as amended at 74 FR 60213, Nov. 20, 2009]

§ 206.41 Appointment of disaster officials.

(a) *Federal Coordinating Officer.* Upon a declaration of a major disaster or of an emergency by the President, the Administrator or Deputy Administrator shall appoint an FCO who shall initiate action immediately to assure that Federal assistance is provided in accordance with the declaration, applicable laws, regulations, and the FEMA-State Agreement.

(b) *Disaster Recovery Manager.* The Regional Administrator shall designate a DRM to exercise all the authority of the Regional Administrator in a major disaster or an emergency.

(c) *State Coordinating Officer.* Upon a declaration of a major disaster or of an emergency, the Governor of the affected State shall designate an SCO who shall coordinate State and local disaster assistance efforts with those of the Federal Government.

(d) *Governor's Authorized Representative.* In the FEMA-State Agreement, the Governor shall designate the GAR, who shall administer Federal disaster assistance programs on behalf of the State and local governments and other grant or loan recipients. The GAR is responsible for the State compliance with the FEMA-State Agreement.

§ 206.42 Responsibilities of coordinating officers.

(a) Following a declaration of a major disaster or an emergency, the FCO shall:

(1) Make an initial appraisal of the types of assistance most urgently needed;

(2) In coordination with the SCO, establish field offices and Disaster Application Centers as necessary to coordinate and monitor assistance programs, disseminate information, accept applications, and counsel individuals, families and businesses concerning available assistance;

(3) Coordinate the administration of relief, including activities of State and local governments, activities of Federal agencies, and those of the American Red Cross, the Salvation Army, the Mennonite Disaster Service, and other voluntary relief organizations which agree to operate under the FCO's advice and direction;

(4) Undertake appropriate action to make certain that all of the Federal agencies are carrying out their appropriate disaster assistance roles under their own legislative authorities and operational policies; and

(5) Take other action, consistent with the provisions of the Stafford Act, as necessary to assist citizens and public officials in promptly obtaining assistance to which they are entitled.

(b) The SCO coordinates State and local disaster assistance efforts with those of the Federal Government working closely with the FCO. The SCO is the principal point of contact regarding coordination of State and local disaster relief activities, and implementation of the State emergency plan. The functions, responsibilities, and authorities of the SCO are set forth in the State emergency plan. It is the responsibility of the SCO to ensure that all affected local jurisdictions are informed of the declaration, the types of assistance authorized, and the areas eligible to receive such assistance.

§ 206.43 Emergency support teams.

The Federal Coordinating Officer may activate emergency support teams, composed of Federal program and support personnel, to be deployed into an area affected by a major disaster or emergency. These emergency support teams assist the FCO in carrying out his/her responsibilities under the Stafford Act and these regulations. Any Federal agency can be directed to detail personnel within the agency's administrative jurisdiction to temporary duty with the FCO. Each detail shall be without loss of seniority, pay, or other employee status.

§ 206.44 FEMA-State Agreements.

(a) *General.* Upon the declaration of a major disaster or an emergency, the Governor, acting for the State, and the FEMA Regional Administrator or his/her designee, acting for the Federal Government, shall execute a FEMA-State Agreement. The FEMA-State Agreement states the understandings, commitments, and conditions for assistance under which FEMA disaster assistance shall be provided. This Agreement imposes binding obligations on FEMA, States, their local governments, and private nonprofit organizations within the States in the form of conditions for assistance which are legally enforceable. No FEMA funding will be authorized or provided to any grantees or other recipients, nor will direct Federal assistance be authorized by mission assignment, until such time as this Agreement for the Presidential declaration has been signed, except where it is deemed necessary by the Regional Administrator to begin the process of providing essential emergency services or housing assistance under the Individuals and Households Program.

(b) *Terms and conditions.* This Agreement describes the incident and the incident period for which assistance will be made available, the type and extent of the Federal assistance to be made available, and contains the commitment of the State and local government(s) with respect to the amount of funds to be expended in alleviating damage and suffering caused by the major disaster or emergency. The Agreement also contains such other terms and conditions consistent with the declaration and the provisions of applicable laws, Executive Order and regulations.

(c) *Provisions for modification.* In the event that the conditions stipulated in the original Agreement are changed or modified, such changes will be reflected in properly executed amendments to the Agreement, which may be signed by the GAR and the Regional Administrator or his/her designee for the specified major disaster or emergency. Amendments most often occur to close or amend the incident period, to add forms of assistance not originally authorized, or to designate additional areas eligible for assistance.

(d) In a modified declaration for a Federal emergency, a FEMA-State Agreement may or may not be required based on the type of assistance being provided.

[55 FR 2292, Jan. 23, 1990, as amended at 67 FR 61460, Sept. 30, 2002]

§ 206.45 Loans of non-Federal share.

(a) *Conditions for making loans.* At the request of the Governor, the Assistant Administrator for the Disaster Assistance Directorate together with the Chief Financial Officer may lend or advance to a State, either for its own use or for the use of public or private nonprofit applicants for disaster assistance under the Stafford Act, the portion of assistance for which the State or other eligible disaster assistance applicant is responsible under the cost-sharing provisions of the Stafford Act in any case in which:

(1) The State or other eligible disaster assistance applicant is unable to assume their financial responsibility under such cost sharing provisions:

(i) As a result of concurrent, multiple major disasters in a jurisdiction, or

(ii) After incurring extraordinary costs as a result of a particular disaster;

(2) The damages caused by such disasters or disaster are so overwhelming and severe that it is not possible for the State or other eligible disaster assistance applicant to immediately assume their financial responsibility under the Act; and

(3) The State and the other eligible disaster applicants are not delinquent in payment of any debts to FEMA incurred as a result of Presidentially declared major disasters or emergencies.

(b) *Repayment of loans.* Any loan made to a State under paragraph (a) of this section must be repaid to the United States. The Governor must include a repayment schedule as part of the request for advance.

(1) The State shall repay the loan (the principal disbursed plus interest) in accordance with the repayment schedule approved by the Assistant Administrator for the Disaster Assistance Directorate together with the Chief Financial Officer.

(2) If the State fails to make payments in accordance with the approved repayment schedule, FEMA will offset delinquent amounts against the current, prior, or any subsequent disasters, or monies due the State under other FEMA programs, in accordance with the established Claims Collection procedures.

(c) *Interest.* Loans or advances under paragraph (a) of this section shall bear interest at a rate determined by the Secretary of the Treasury, taking into consideration the current market yields on outstanding marketable obligations of the United States with remaining periods to maturity comparable to the reimbursement period of the loan or advance. Simple interest will be computed from the date of the disbursement of each drawdown of the loan/advance by the State based on 365 days/year.

§ 206.46 Appeals.

(a) *Denial of declaration request.* When a request for a major disaster declaration or for any emergency declaration is denied, the Governor may appeal the decision. An appeal must be made within 30 days after the date of the letter denying the request. This one-time request for reconsideration, along with appropriate additional information, is submitted to the President through the appropriate Regional Administrator. The processing of this request is similar to the initial request.

(b) *Denial of types of assistance or areas.* In those instances when the type of assistance or certain areas requested by the Governor are not designated or authorized, the Governor, or the GAR, may appeal the decision. An appeal must be submitted in writing within 30 days of the date of the letter denying the request. This one-time request for reconsideration, along with justification and/or additional information, is sent to the Assistant Administrator for the Disaster Assistance Directorate through the appropriate Regional Administrator.

(c) *Denial of advance of non-Federal share.* In those instances where the Governor's request for an advance is denied, the Governor may appeal the decision. An appeal must be submitted in writing within 30 days of the date of the letter denying the request. This one-time request for reconsideration, along with justification and/or additional information, is sent to the Assistant Administrator for the Disaster Assistance Directorate through the appropriate Regional Administrator.

(d) *Extension of time to appeal.* The 30-day period referred to in paragraphs (a), (b), or (c) of this section may be extended by the Assistant Administrator for the Disaster Assistance Directorate provided that a written request for such an extension, citing reasons for the delay, is made during this 30-day period, and if the Assistant Administrator for the Disaster Assistance Directorate agrees that there is a legitimate basis for extension of the 30-day period. Only the Governor may request a time extension for appeals covered in paragraphs (a) and (c) of this section. The Governor, or the GAR if one has been named, may submit the time extension request for appeals covered in paragraph (b) of this section.

400

§ 206.47 Cost-share adjustments.

(a) We pay seventy-five percent (75%) of the eligible cost of permanent restorative work under section 406 of the Stafford Act and for emergency work under section 403 and section 407 of the Stafford Act, unless the Federal share is increased under this section.

(b) We recommend an increase in the Federal cost share from seventy-five percent (75%) to not more than ninety percent (90%) of the eligible cost of permanent work under section 406 and of emergency work under section 403 and section 407 whenever a disaster is so extraordinary that actual Federal obligations under the Stafford Act, excluding FEMA administrative cost, meet or exceed a qualifying threshold of:

(1) Beginning in 1999 and effective for disasters declared on or after May 21, 1999, $75 per capita of State population;

(2) Effective for disasters declared after January 1, 2000, and through December 31, 2000, $85 per capita of State population;

(3) Effective for disasters declared after January 1, 2001, $100 per capita of State population; and,

(4) Effective for disasters declared after January 1, 2002 and for later years, $100 per capita of State population, adjusted annually for inflation using the Consumer Price Index for All Urban Consumers published annually by the Department of Labor.

(c) When we determine whether to recommend a cost-share adjustment we consider the impact of major disaster declarations in the State during the preceding twelve-month period.

(d) If warranted by the needs of the disaster, we recommend up to one hundred percent (100%) Federal funding for emergency work under section 403 and section 407, including direct Federal assistance, for a limited period in the initial days of the disaster irrespective of the per capita impact.

[64 FR 19498, Apr. 21, 1999]

§ 206.48 Factors considered when evaluating a Governor's request for a major disaster declaration.

When we review a Governor's request for major disaster assistance under the Stafford Act, these are the primary factors in making a recommendation to the President whether assistance is warranted. We consider other relevant information as well.

(a) *Public Assistance Program.* We evaluate the following factors to evaluate the need for assistance under the Public Assistance Program.

(1) *Estimated cost of the assistance.* We evaluate the estimated cost of Federal and nonfederal public assistance against the statewide population to give some measure of the per capita impact within the State. We use a figure of $1 per capita as an indicator that the disaster is of such size that it might warrant Federal assistance, and adjust this figure annually based on the Consumer Price Index for all Urban Consumers. We are establishing a minimum threshold of $1 million in public assistance damages per disaster in the belief that we can reasonably expect even the lowest population States to cover this level of public assistance damage.

(2) *Localized impacts.* We evaluate the impact of the disaster at the county and local government level, as well as impacts at the American Indian and Alaskan Native Tribal Government levels, because at times there are extraordinary concentrations of damages that might warrant Federal assistance even if the statewide per capita is not met. This is particularly true where critical facilities are involved or where localized per capita impacts might be extremely high. For example, we have at times seen localized damages in the tens or even hundreds of dollars per capita though the statewide per capita impact was low.

(3) *Insurance coverage in force.* We consider the amount of insurance coverage that is in force or should have been in force as required by law and regulation at the time of the disaster, and reduce the amount of anticipated assistance by that amount.

(4) *Hazard mitigation.* To recognize and encourage mitigation, we consider the extent to which State and local government measures contributed to the reduction of disaster damages for the disaster under consideration. For example, if a State can demonstrate in its disaster request that a Statewide building code or other mitigation

measures are likely to have reduced the damages from a particular disaster, we consider that in the evaluation of the request. This could be especially significant in those disasters where, because of mitigation, the estimated public assistance damages fell below the per capita indicator.

(5) *Recent multiple disasters.* We look at the disaster history within the last twelve-month period to evaluate better the overall impact on the State or locality. We consider declarations under the Stafford Act as well as declarations by the Governor and the extent to which the State has spent its own funds.

(6) *Programs of other Federal assistance.* We also consider programs of other Federal agencies because at times their programs of assistance might more appropriately meet the needs created by the disaster.

(b) *Factors for the Individual Assistance Program.* We consider the following factors to measure the severity, magnitude and impact of the disaster and to evaluate the need for assistance to individuals under the Stafford Act.

(1) *Concentration of damages.* We evaluate the concentrations of damages to individuals. High concentrations of damages generally indicate a greater need for Federal assistance than widespread and scattered damages throughout a State.

(2) *Trauma.* We consider the degree of trauma to a State and to communities.

Some of the conditions that might cause trauma are:

(i) Large numbers of injuries and deaths;

(ii) Large scale disruption of normal community functions and services; and

(iii) Emergency needs such as extended or widespread loss of power or water.

(3) *Special populations.* We consider whether special populations, such as low-income, the elderly, or the unemployed are affected, and whether they may have a greater need for assistance. We also consider the effect on American Indian and Alaskan Native Tribal populations in the event that there are any unique needs for people in these governmental entities.

(4) *Voluntary agency assistance.* We consider the extent to which voluntary agencies and State or local programs can meet the needs of the disaster victims.

(5) *Insurance.* We consider the amount of insurance coverage because, by law, Federal disaster assistance cannot duplicate insurance coverage.

(6) *Average amount of individual assistance by State.* There is *no set threshold* for recommending Individual Assistance, but the following averages may prove useful to States and voluntary agencies as they develop plans and programs to meet the needs of disaster victims.

AVERAGE AMOUNT OF ASSISTANCE PER DISASTER

[July 1994 to July 1999]

	Small states (under 2 million pop.)	Medium states (2–10 million pop.)	Large states (over 10 million pop.)
Average Population (1990 census data)	1,000,057	4,713,548	15,522,791
Number of Disaster Housing Applications Approved	1,507	2,747	4,679
Number of Homes Estimated Major Damage/Destroyed	173	582	801
Dollar Amount of Housing Assistance	$2.8 million	$4.6 million	$9.5 million
Number of Individual and Family Grant Applications Approved	495	1,377	2,071
Dollar Amount of Individual and Family Grant Assistance	1.1 million	2.9 million	4.6 million
Disaster Housing/IFG Combined Assistance	3.9 million	7.5 million	14.1 million

NOTE: The high 3 and low 3 disasters, based on Disaster Housing Applications, are not considered in the averages. Number of Damaged/Destroyed Homes is estimated based on the number of owner-occupants who qualify for Eligible Emergency Rental Resources. Data source is FEMA's National Processing Service Centers. Data are only available from July 1994 to the present.

,*Small Size States (under 2 million population, listed in order of 1990 population):* Wyoming, Alaska, Vermont, District of Columbia, North Dakota, Delaware, South Dakota, Montana, Rhode Island, Idaho, Hawaii, New

Hampshire, Nevada, Maine, New Mexico, Nebraska, Utah, West Virginia, U.S. Virgin Islands and all Pacific Island dependencies.

Medium Size States (2–10 million population, listed in order of 1990 population): Arkansas, Kansas, Mississippi, Iowa, Oregon, Oklahoma, Connecticut, Colorado, South Carolina, Arizona, Kentucky, Alabama, Louisiana, Minnesota, Maryland, Washington, Tennessee, Wisconsin, Missouri, Indiana, Massachusetts, Virginia, Georgia, North Carolina, New Jersey, Michigan. Puerto Rico.

Large Size States (over 10 million population, listed in order of 1990 population): Ohio, Illinois, Pennsylvania, Florida, Texas, New York, California.

[64 FR 47698, Sept. 1, 1999]

§§ 206.49–206.60 [Reserved]

Subpart C—Emergency Assistance

SOURCE: 55 FR 2296, Jan. 23, 1990, unless otherwise noted.

§ 206.61 Purpose.

The purpose of this subpart is to identify the forms of assistance which may be made available under an emergency declaration.

§ 206.62 Available assistance.

In any emergency declaration, the Regional Administrator or Administrator may provide assistance, as follows:

(a) Direct any Federal agency, with or without reimbursement, to utilize its authorities and the resources granted to it under Federal law (including personnel, equipment, supplies, facilities, and managerial, technical and advisory services) in support of State and local emergency assistance efforts to save lives, protect property and public health and safety, and lessen or avert the threat of a catastrophe;

(b) Coordinate all disaster relief assistance (including voluntary assistance) provided by Federal agencies, private organizations, and State and local governments;

(c) Provide technical and advisory assistance to affected State and local governments for:

(1) The performance of essential community services;

(2) Issuance of warnings of risks or hazards;

(3) Public health and safety information, including dissemination of such information;

(4) Provision of health and safety measures; and

(5) Management, control, and reduction of immediate threats to public health and safety;

(d) Provide emergency assistance under the Stafford Act through Federal agencies;

(e) Remove debris in accordance with the terms and conditions of section 407 of the Stafford Act;

(f) Provide assistance in accordance with section 408 of the Stafford Act; and

(g) Assist State and local governments in the distribution of medicine, food, and other consumable supplies, and emergency assistance.

[55 FR 2296, Jan. 23, 1990, as amended at 67 FR 61460, Sept. 30, 2002]

§ 206.63 Provision of assistance.

Assistance authorized by an emergency declaration is limited to immediate and short-term assistance, essential to save lives, to protect property and public health and safety, or to lessen or avert the threat of a catastrophe.

§ 206.64 Coordination of assistance.

After an emergency declaration by the President, all Federal agencies, voluntary organizations, and State and local governments providing assistance shall operate under the coordination of the Federal Coordinating Officer.

§ 206.65 Cost sharing.

The Federal share for assistance provided under this title shall not be less than 75 percent of the eligible costs.

§ 206.66 Limitation on expenditures.

Total assistance provided in any given emergency declaration may not exceed $5,000,000, except when it is determined by the Administrator that:

(a) Continued emergency assistance is immediately required;

(b) There is a continuing and immediate risk to lives, property, public health and safety; and

(c) Necessary assistance will not otherwise be provided on a timely basis.

§ 206.67 Requirement when limitation is exceeded.

Whenever the limitation described in § 206.66 is exceeded, the Administrator must report to the Congress on the nature and extent of continuing emergency assistance requirements and shall propose additional legislation if necessary.

§§ 206.68–206.100 [Reserved]

Subpart D—Federal Assistance to Individuals and Households

§ 206.101 Temporary housing assistance for emergencies and major disasters declared on or before October 14, 2002.

(a) *Purpose.* This section prescribes the policy to be followed by the Federal Government or any other organization when implementing section 408 of the Stafford Act for Presidentially-declared emergencies and major disasters declared on or before October 14, 2002 (Note that the reference to section 408 of the Stafford Act refers to prior legislation amended by the Disaster Mitigation Act 2000).

(b) *Program intent.* Assistance under this program is made available to applicants who require temporary housing as a result of a major disaster or emergency that is declared by the President. Eligibility for assistance is based on need created by disaster-related unlivability of a primary residence or other disaster-related displacement, combined with a lack of adequate insurance coverage. Eligible applicants may be paid for authorized accommodations and/or repairs. In the interest of assisting the greatest number of people in the shortest possible time, applicants who are able to do so will be encouraged to make their own arrangements for temporary housing. Although numerous instances of minor damage may cause some inconvenience to the applicant, the determining eligibility factor must be the livability of the primary residence. FEMA has also determined that it is reasonable to expect applicants or their landlords to make some repairs of a minor nature. Temporary housing will normally consist of a check to cover housing-related costs wherever possible.

(c) *Definitions*—(1) *Adequate alternate housing* means housing that:

(i) Accommodates the needs of the occupants.

(ii) Is within reasonable commuting distance of work, school, or agricultural activities which provide over 25% of the household income.

(iii) Is within the financial ability of the occupant in the realization of a permanent housing plan.

(2) *Effective date of assistance* means the date the eligible applicant received temporary housing assistance but, where applicable, only after appropriate insurance benefits are exhausted.

(3) *Essential living area* means that area of the residence essential to normal living, i.e., kitchen, one bathroom, dining area, living room, entrances and exits, and essential sleeping areas. It does not include family rooms, guest rooms, garages, or other nonessential areas, unless hazards exist in these areas which impact the safety of the essential living area.

(4) *Fair market rent* means a reasonable amount to pay in the local area for the size and type of accommodations which meets the applicant's needs.

(5) *Financial ability* is the determination of the occupant's ability to pay housing costs. The determination is based upon the amount paid for housing before the disaster, provided the household income has not changed subsequent to or as a result of the disaster or 25 percent of gross post disaster income if the household income changed as a result of the disaster. When computing financial ability, extreme or unusual financial circumstances may be considered by the Regional Administrator.

(6) *Household* means all residents of the predisaster residence who request temporary housing assistance, plus any additions during the temporary housing period, such as infants, spouses, or part-time residents who were not present at the time of the disaster but who are expected to return during the temporary housing period.

(7) *Housing costs* means shelter rent and mortgage payments including principal, interest, real estate taxes, real

property insurance, and utility costs, where appropriate.

(8) *Occupant* means an eligible applicant residing in temporary housing provided under this section.

(9) *Owner-occupied* means that the residence is occupied by: the legal owner; a person who does not hold formal title to the residence and pays no rent but is responsible for the payment of taxes, or maintenance of the residence; or a person who has lifetime occupancy rights with formal title vested in another.

(10) *Primary residence* means the dwelling where the applicant normally lives during the major portion of the calendar year, a dwelling which is required because of proximity to employment, or to agricultural activities as referenced in paragraph (c)(1)(ii) of this section.

(d) *Duplication of benefits*—(1) *Requirement to avoid duplication.* Temporary housing assistance shall not be provided to an applicant if such assistance has been provided by any other source. If any State or local government or voluntary agency has provided temporary housing, the assistance under this section begins at the expiration of such assistance, and may continue for a period not to exceed 18 months from the date of declaration, provided the criteria for continued assistance in paragraph (k)(3) of this section are met. If it is determined that temporary housing assistance will be provided under this section, notification shall be given those agencies which have the potential for duplicating such assistance. In the instance of insured applicants, temporary housing assistance shall be provided only when:

(i) Payment of the applicable benefits has been significantly delayed;

(ii) Applicable benefits have been exhausted;

(iii) Applicable benefits are insufficient to cover the temporary housing need; or

(iv) Housing is not available on the private market.

(2) *Recovery of funds.* Prior to provision of assistance, the applicant must agree to repay to FEMA from insurance proceeds or recoveries from any other source an amount equivalent to the value of the temporary housing assistance provided. In no event shall the amount repaid to FEMA exceed the amount recovered by the applicant. All claims shall be collected in accordance with agency procedures for debt collection.

(e) *Applications*—(1) *Application period.* The standard FEMA application period is the 60 days following the date the President declares an incident a major disaster or an emergency. The Regional Administrator may, however, extend the application period, when we anticipate that we need more time to collect applications from the affected population or to establish the same application deadline for contiguous Counties or States. After the application period has ended, FEMA will accept and process applications for an additional 60 days only from persons who can provide an acceptable explanation (and documentation to substantiate their explanation) for why they were not able to contact FEMA before the application period ended.

(2) *Household composition.* Members of a household shall be included on a single application and be provided one temporary housing residence unless it is determined by the Regional Administrator that the size of the household requires that more than one residence be provided.

(f) *General eligibility guidelines.* Temporary housing assistance may be made available to those applicants who, as a result of a major disaster or emergency declared by the President, are qualified for such assistance.

(1) *Conditions of eligibility.* Temporary housing assistance may be provided only when *both* of the following conditions are met:

(i) The applicant's primary residence has been made unlivable or the applicant has been displaced as the result of a major disaster or emergency because:

(A) The residence has been destroyed, essential utility service has been interrupted, or the essential living area has been damaged as a result of the disaster to such an extent as to constitute a serious health or safety hazard which did not exist prior to the disaster. The Regional Administrator shall prepare additional guidelines when necessary to respond to a particular disaster;

405

(B) The residence has been made inaccessible as a result of the incident to the extent that the applicant cannot reasonably be expected to gain entry due to the disruption or destruction of transportation routes, other impediments to access, or restrictions placed on movement by a responsible official due to continued health and safety problems;

(C) The owner of the applicant's residence requires the residence to meet their personal needs because the owner's predisaster residence was made unlivable as a result of the disaster;

(D) Financial hardship resulting from the disaster has led to eviction or dispossession; or

(E) Other circumstances resulting from the disaster, as determined by the Regional Administrator, prevent the applicant from occupying their predisaster primary residence.

(ii) Insured applicants have made every reasonable effort to secure insurance benefits, and the insured has agreed to repay FEMA from whatever insurance proceeds are later received, pursuant to paragraph (d)(2) of this section.

(2) *Conditions of ineligibility.* Except as provided for in section 408(b), Temporary Housing Assistance shall not be provided:

(i) To an applicant who is displaced from other than their primary residence; or

(ii) When the residence in question is livable, i.e., only minor damage exists and it can reasonably be expected to be repaired by the applicant/owner or the landlord; or

(iii) When the applicant owns a secondary or vacation residence, or unoccupied rental property which meets their temporary housing needs; or

(iv) To an applicant who has adequate rent-free housing accommodations; or

(v) To an applicant who has adequate insurance coverage and there is no indication that benefits will be delayed; or

(vi) When a late application is not approved for processing by the Regional Administrator; or

(vii) To an applicant who evacuated the residence in response to official warnings solely as a precautionary measure, and who is able to return to the residence immediately after the incident (i.e., the applicant is not otherwise eligible for temporary housing assistance).

(g) *Forms of Temporary Housing Assistance.* All proceeds received or receivable by the applicant under § 206.101 shall be exempt from garnishment, seizure, encumbrance, levy, execution, pledge, attachment, release, or waiver. No rights under this provision are assignable or transferable.

(1) Temporary Housing Assistance is normally provided in the form of a check to cover the cost of rent or essential home repairs. The exceptions to this are when existing rental resources are not available and repairs to the home will not make it livable in a reasonable period of time, or when the eligible applicant is unable to physically leave the home due to the need to tend crops or livestock.

(i) *Government-owned, private, and commercial properties.* When an eligible applicant is unable to obtain an available temporary housing unit, FEMA may enter into a leasing agreement for the eligible applicant. Rent payments shall be in accordance with the fair market rent (FMR) rates established for each operation for the type and size residence.

(ii) *Transient accommodations.* Immediately following a Presidentially declared major disaster or emergency, disaster victims are expected to stay with family or friends without FEMA assistance, or to make use of mass shelters to the fullest extent possible for short-term housing. Transient accommodations may be provided when individual circumstances warrant such assistance for only a short period of time or pending provision of other temporary housing resources. Transient accommodations may be provided for up to 30 days unless this period is extended by the Regional Administrator. Authorized expenditures for transient accommodations shall be restricted to the rental cost including utilities except for those which are separately metered. Payment for food, telephone, or other similar services is not authorized under this section.

(2) Mobile homes, travel trailers, and other manufactured housing units.

Government-owned or privately owned mobile homes, travel trailers, and other manufactured housing units may be placed on commercial, private, or group sites. The placement must comply with applicable State and local codes and ordinances as well as FEMA'S regulations at 44 CFR part 9, Floodplain Management and Protection of Wetlands, and the regulations at 44 CFR part 10, Environmental Considerations.

(i) A commercial site is a site customarily leased for a fee because it is fully equipped to accommodate a housing unit. In accordance with section 408(a)(2)(B), the Assistant Administrator for the Disaster Assistance Directorate has determined that leasing commercial sites at Federal expense is in the public interest. When the Regional Administrator determines that upgrading of commercial sites or installation of utilities on such sites will provide more cost-effective, timely, and suitable temporary housing than other types of resources, they may authorize such action at Federal expense.

(ii) A private site is a site provided or obtained by the applicant at no cost to the Federal Government. Also in accordance with section 408(a)(2)(B), the Assistant Administrator for the Disaster Assistance Directorate has determined that the cost of installation or repairs of essential utilities on private sites is authorized at Federal expense when such actions will provide more cost-effective, timely, and suitable temporary housing than other types of resources.

(iii) A group site is a site which accommodates two or more units. In accordance with section 408(a)(2)(A), locations for group sites shall be provided by State or local government complete with utilities. However, the Assistant Administrator for the Disaster Assistance Directorate may authorize development of group sites, including installation of essential utilities, by the Federal Government, based on a recommendation from the Regional Administrator; provided, however, that the Federal expense is limited to 75 percent of the cost of construction and development (including installation of utilities). In accordance with section 408(a)(4) of the Stafford Act, the State

or local government shall pay any cost which is not paid for from the Federal share, including long-term site maintenance such as snow removal, street repairs and other services of a governmental nature.

(3) *Temporary mortgage and rental payments.* Assistance in the form of mortgage or rental payments may be paid to or be provided on behalf of eligible applicants who, as a result of a major disaster or emergency, have received written notice of dispossession or eviction from their primary residence by foreclosure of any mortgage or lien, cancellation of any contract of sale, or termination of any lease entered into prior to the disaster. Written notice, for the purpose of this paragraph, means a communication in writing by a landlord, mortgage holder, or other party authorized under State law to file such notice. The purpose of such notice is to notify a person of impending termination of a lease, foreclosure of a mortgage or lien, or cancellation of any contract of sale, which would result in the person's dispossession or eviction. Applications for this type of assistance may be filed for up to 6 months following the date of declaration. This assistance may be provided for a period not to exceed 18 months or for the duration of the period of financial hardship, as determined by the Regional Administrator, whichever is less. The location of the residence of an applicant for assistance under this section shall not be a consideration of eligibility.

(4) *Home repairs.* Repairs may be authorized to quickly repair or restore to a livable condition that portion of or areas affecting the essential living area of, or private access to, an owner-occupied primary residence which was damaged as a result of the disaster. Installation of utilities or conveniences not available in the residence prior to the disaster shall not be provided. However, repairs which are authorized shall conform to applicable local and/or State building codes; upgrading of existing damaged utilities may be authorized when required by these codes.

(i) *Options for repairs.* Eligible applicants approved for repairs may be assisted through one or a combination of the following methods:

(A) *Cash payment.* Payment shall be limited to the reasonable costs for the repairs and replacements in the locality, as determined by the Regional Administrator. This will be the method normally used, unless unusual circumstances warrant the methods listed under paragraph (g)(4), (i) (B) or (C) of this section.

(B) Provision of materials and replacement items.

(C) Government awarded repair contracts when authorized by the Assistant Administrator for the Disaster Assistance Directorate.

(ii) *Feasibility.* Repairs may be provided to those eligible applicants:

(A) Who are owner-occupants of the residence to be made livable;

(B) Whose residence can be made livable by repairs to the essential living area within 30 days following the feasibility determination. The Regional Administrator may extend this period for extenuating circumstances by determining that this type of assistance is still more cost effective, timely and otherwise suitable than other forms for temporary housing; and

(C) Whose residence can be made livable by repairs to the essential living area, the cost of which do not exceed the dollar limitations established by the Assistant Administrator for the Disaster Assistance Directorate. The Regional Administrator may, on a case-by-case basis, waive the dollar limitations when repairs are more cost effective and appropriate than other forms of housing assistance or when extenuating circumstances warrant.

(iii) *Scope of work.* The type of repair or replacement authorized may vary depending upon the nature of the disaster. Items will be repaired where feasible or replaced only when necessary to insure the safety or health of the occupant. Replacement items shall be of average quality, size, and capacity taking into consideration the needs of the occupant. Repairs shall be disaster related and shall be limited to:

(A) Repairs to the plumbing system, including repairs to or replacement of fixtures, providing service to the kitchen and one bathroom;

(B) Repairs to the electrical system providing service to essential living areas, including repairs to or replacement of essential fixtures;

(C) Repairs to the heating unit, including repairs to duct work, vents, and integral fuel and electrical systems. If repair or replacement through other forms of assistance cannot be accomplished before the start of the season requiring heat, home repairs may be authorized by the Regional Administrator when an inspection shows that the unit has been damaged beyond repair, or when the availability of necessary parts or components makes repair impossible;

(D) Repairs to or replacement of essential components of the fuel system to provide for cooking;

(E) Pumping and cleaning of the septic system, repairs to or replacement of the tank, drainfield, or repairs to sewer lines;

(F) Flushing and/or purifying the water well, and repairs to or replacement of the pump, controls, tank, and pipes;

(G) Repairs to or replacement of exterior doors, repair of windows and/or screens needed for health purposes;

(H) Repairs to the roof, when the damages affect the essential living area;

(I) Repairs to interior floors, when severe buckling or deterioration creates a serious safety hazard;

(J) Blocking, leveling, and anchoring of a mobile home; and reconnecting and/or resetting mobile home sewer, water, electrical and fuel lines, and tanks;

(K) Emergency repairs to private access routes, limited to those repairs that meet the minimum safety standards and using the most economical materials available. Such repairs are provided on a one-time basis when no alternative access facilities are immediately available and when the repairs are more cost effective, timely or otherwise suitable than other forms of temporary housing.

(L) Repairs to the foundation piers, walls or footings when the damages affect the structural integrity of the essential living area;

(M) Repairs to the stove and refrigerator, when feasible; and

(N) Elimination of other health and safety hazards or performance of essential repairs which are authorized by the Regional Administrator as not available through emergency services provided by voluntary or community agencies, and cannot reasonably be expected to be completed on a timely basis by the occupant without FEMA assistance.

(iv) Requirements of the Flood Disaster Protection Act. FEMA has determined that flood insurance purchase requirements need not be imposed as a condition of receiving assistance under paragraph (g)(4) of this section. Repair recipients will normally receive assistance for further repairs from other programs which will impose the purchase and maintenance requirements. Home repairs may not be provided in Zones A or V of a sanctioned or suspended community except for items that are not covered by flood insurance.

(h) *Appropriate form of temporary housing.* The form of temporary housing provided should not exceed occupants' minimum requirements, taking into consideration items such as timely availability, cost effectiveness, permanent housing plans, special needs (handicaps, the location of crops and livestock, etc.) of the occupants, and the requirements of FEMA'S floodplain management regulations at 44 CFR part 9. An eligible applicant shall receive one form of temporary housing, except for transient accommodations or when provision of an additional form is in the best interest of the Government. An eligible applicant is expected to accept the first offer of temporary housing; unwarranted refusal shall result in forfeiture of temporary housing assistance. Existing rental resources and home repairs shall be utilized to the fullest extent practicable prior to provision of government-owned mobile homes.

(i) *Utility costs and security deposits.* All utility costs shall be the responsibility of the occupant except where utility services are not metered separately and are therefore a part of the rental charge. Utility use charges and deposits shall always be the occupants responsibility. When authorized by the Regional Administrator, the Federal Government may pay security depos-

its; however, the owner or occupant shall reimburse the full amount of the security deposit to the Federal Government before or at the time that the temporary housing assistance is terminated.

(j) *Furniture.* An allowance for essential furniture may be provided to occupants when such assistance is required to occupy the primary or temporary housing residence. However, loss of furniture does not in and of itself constitute eligibility for temporary housing assistance. Luxury items shall not be provided.

(k) *Duration of assistance*—(1) *Commencement.* Temporary housing assistance may be provided as of the date of the incident of the major disaster or emergency as specified in the FEDERAL REGISTER notice and may continue for 18 months from the date of declaration. An effective date of assistance shall be established for each applicant.

(2) *Continued assistance.* Predisaster renters normally shall be provided no more than 1 month of assistance unless the Regional Administrator determines that continued assistance is warranted in accordance with paragraph (k)(3) of this section. All other occupants of temporary housing shall be certified eligible for continued assistance in increments not to exceed 3 months. Recertification of eligibility for continued assistance shall be in accordance with paragraph (k)(3) of this section, taking into consideration the occupant's permanent housing plan. A realistic permanent housing plan shall be established for each occupant requesting additional assistance no later than at the time of the first recertification.

(3) *Criteria for continued assistance.* A temporary housing occupant shall make every effort to obtain and occupy permanent housing at the earliest possible time. A temporary housing occupant will be required to provide receipts documenting disaster related housing costs and shall be eligible for continued assistance when:

(i) Adequate alternate housing is not available;

(ii) The permanent housing plan has not been realized through no fault of the occupant; or

(iii) In the case of FEMA-owner leases, the occupant is in compliance with the terms of the lease/rental agreement.

(l) *Period of assistance.* Provided the occupant is eligible for continued assistance, assistance shall be provided for a period not to exceed 18 months from the declaration date.

(m) *Appeals.* Occupants shall have the right to appeal a program determination in accordance with the following:

(1) An applicant declared ineligible for temporary housing assistance, an applicant whose application has been cancelled for cause, an applicant whose application has been refused because of late filing, and an occupant who received a direct housing payment but is not eligible for continued assistance in accordance with paragraph (k) of this section, shall have the right to dispute such a determination within 60 calendar days following notification of such action. The Regional Administrator shall reconsider the original decision within 15 calendar days after its receipt. The appellant shall be given a written notice of the disposition of the dispute. The decision of the Regional Administrator is final.

(2) An occupant who has been notified that his/her request to purchase a mobile home or manufactured housing unit or that a request for an adjustment to the sales price has been denied shall have the right to dispute such a determination within 60 business days after receipt of such notice. The Regional Administrator shall reconsider the original decision within 15 calendar days after receipt of the appeal. The appellant shall receive written notice of the disposition of the dispute. The decision of the Regional Administrator is final.

(3) Termination of assistance provided through a FEMA lease agreement shall be initiated with a 15-day written notice after which the occupant shall be liable for such additional charges as are deemed appropriate by the Regional Administrator including, but not limited to, the fair market rental for the temporary housing residence.

(i) *Grounds for termination.* Temporary housing assistance may be terminated for reasons including, but not limited to the following:

(A) Adequate alternate housing is available to the occupant(s);

(B) The temporary housing assistance was obtained either through misrepresentation or fraud; or

(C) Failure to comply with any term of the lease/rental agreement.

(ii) *Termination procedures.* These procedures shall be utilized in all instances except when a State is administering the Temporary Housing Assistance program. States shall be subject to their own procedures provided they afford the occupant(s) with due process safeguards described in paragraph (m)(2)(v)(B) of this section.

(A) *Notification to occupant.* Written notice shall be given by FEMA to the occupant(s) at least 15 days prior to the proposed termination of assistance. This notice shall specify: the reasons for termination of assistance/occupancy; the date of termination, which shall be not less than 15 days after receipt of the notice; the administrative procedure available to the occupant if they wish to dispute the action; and the occupant's liability after the termination date for additional charges.

(B) *Filing of appeal.* If the occupant desires to dispute the termination, upon receipt of the written notice specified in paragraph (m)(2)(i) of this section, he/she shall present an appeal in writing to the appropriate office in person or by mail within 60 days from the date of the termination notice. The appeal must be signed by the occupant and state the reasons why the assistance or occupancy should not be terminated. If a hearing is desired, the appeal should so state.

(C) *Response to appeal.* If a hearing pursuant to paragraph (m)(2)(ii) of this section has not been requested, the occupant has waived the right to a hearing. The appropriate program official shall deliver or mail a written response to the occupant within 5 business days after the receipt of the appeal.

(D) *Request for hearing.* If the occupant requests a hearing pursuant to paragraph (m)(2)(ii) of this section, FEMA shall schedule a hearing date within 10 business days from the receipt of the appeal, at a time and place reasonably convenient to the occupant, who shall be notified promptly thereof in writing. The notice of hearing shall specify the procedure governing the hearing.

410

(E) *Hearing*—(1) *Hearing officer.* The hearing shall be conducted by a Hearing Officer, who shall be designated by the Regional Administrator, and who shall not have been involved with the decision to terminate the occupant's temporary housing assistance, nor be a subordinate of any individual who was so involved.

(2) *Due process.* The occupant shall be afforded a fair hearing and provided the basic safeguards of due process, including cross-examination of the responsible official(s), access to the documents on which FEMA is relying, the right to counsel, the right to present evidence, and the right to a written decision.

(3) *Failure to appear.* If an occupant fails to appear at a hearing, the Hearing Officer may make a determination that the occupant has waived the right to a hearing, or may, for good cause shown, postpone the hearing for no more than 5 business days.

(4) *Proof.* At the hearing, the occupant must first attempt to establish that continued assistance is appropriate; thereafter, FEMA must sustain the burden of proof in justifying that termination of assistance is appropriate. The occupant shall have the right to present evidence and arguments in support of their complaint, to controvert evidence relied on by FEMA, and to cross examine all witnesses on whose testimony or information FEMA relies. The hearing shall be conducted by the Hearing Officer, and any evidence pertinent to the facts and issues raised may be received without regard to its admissibility under rules of evidence employed in formal judicial proceedings.

(F) *Decision.* The decision of the Hearing Officer shall be based solely upon applicable Federal and State law, and FEMA regulations and requirements promulgated thereunder. The Hearing Officer shall prepare a written decision setting forth a statement of findings and conclusions together with the reasons therefor, concerning all material issues raised by the complainant within 5 business days after the hearing. The decision of the Hearing Officer shall be binding on FEMA, which shall take all actions necessary to carry out the decision or refrain from any actions prohibited by the decision.

(1) The decision shall include a notice to the occupant that he/she must vacate the premises within 3 days of receipt of the written notice or on the termination date stated in the original notice of termination, as required in paragraph (m)(2)(i) of this section, whichever is later. If the occupant does not quit the premises, appropriate action shall be taken and, if suit is brought, the occupant may be required to pay court costs and attorney fees.

(2) If the occupant is required to give a specific number of days' notice which exceeds the number of days in the termination notice, the Regional Administrator may approve the payment of rent for this period of time if requested by the occupant.

(n) *Disposition of temporary housing units*—(1) *Acquisition.* The Assistant Administrator for the Disaster Assistance Directorate may purchase mobile homes or other manufactured housing units for those who require temporary housing. After such temporary housing is vacated, it shall be returned to one of the FEMA-operated Strategic Storage Centers for refurbishment and storage until needed in a subsequent major disaster or emergency. When returning the unit to a Strategic Storage Center is not feasible or cost effective, the Assistant Administrator for the Disaster Assistance Directorate may prescribe a different method of disposition in accordance with applicable Federal statutes and regulations.

(2) *Sales*—(i) *Eligibility.* When adequate alternate housing is not available, the Regional Administrator shall make available for sale directly to a temporary housing occupant(s) any mobile home or manufactured housing unit acquired by purchase, in accordance with the following:

(A) The unit is to be used as a primary residence;

(B) The purchaser has a site that complies with local codes and ordinances as well as FEMA's floodplain management regulations at 44 CFR part 9 (in particular §9.13(e)); and

(C) The purchaser has sufficient funds to purchase and, if necessary, relocate the unit. The Assistant Administrator for the Disaster Assistance Directorate may approve the sale of a mobile home or manufactured housing unit to a temporary housing occupant when adequate alternate housing is available but only when such sales are clearly in the best interest of the Government.

(ii) *Sales price.* Units shall be sold at prices that are fair and equitable to the purchaser and to the Government, as determined by the Assistant Administrator for the Disaster Assistance Directorate. The purchaser shall pay the total sales price at the time of sale.

(iii) Adjustment to the sales price.

(A) Adjustments to the sales price may be provided only when both of the following conditions are met:

(*1*) There is a need to purchase the unit for use as the purchaser's primary residence because other adequate alternate housing is unavailable. Adequate alternate housing must meet the criteria in paragraph (c)(1) of this section, and may consist of:

(*i*) Existing housing;

(*ii*) Additional resources such as disaster-damaged rental accommodations which can reasonably be expected to be repaired and become available in the near future;

(*iii*) New housing construction or housing to be made available through Government subsidy which is included in the immediate recovery plans for the area; and

(*iv*) Residences which can be repaired by the predisaster owner/occupant through funds available from insurance, other disaster assistance programs, or through their own resources.

(*2*) In addition to his/her resources, the purchaser cannot obtain sufficient funds through insurance proceeds, disaster loans, grants, and commercial lending institutions to cover the sales price.

(B) To determine the adjusted sales price, the current available financial resources of the purchaser shall be calculated. If the financial resources are equal to or greater than the basic sales price, then no adjustment shall be approved. If the purchaser's financial resources are less than the basic sales price, the sales price shall be adjusted to take into consideration the financial resources available but shall include some consideration. Deviations from this rule may be reviewed on a case-by-case basis by the Assistant Administrator for the Disaster Assistance Directorate.

(C) The Regional Administrator must approve all adjustments to the sales price of a mobile home.

(iv) Other conditions of sale.

(A) A unit shall be sold "as is, where is" except for repairs necessary to protect health or safety, which are to be completed prior to sale. There shall be no implied warranties. In addition, the purchaser must be informed that he/she may have to bring the unit up to codes and standards which are applicable at the proposed site.

(B) In accordance with the Flood Disaster Protection Act of 1973, Public Law 93–234, as amended, the sale of a unit for the purpose of meeting the permanent housing need of an individual or family may not be approved where the unit would be placed in a designated special flood hazard area which has been identified by the Administrator for at least 1 year as floodprone unless the community in which the unit is to be located after the sale is, at the time of approval, participating in the National Flood Insurance Program. The purchaser must agree to buy and maintain an adequate flood insurance policy for as long as the unit is occupied by the purchaser. An adequate policy for purposes of this paragraph shall mean one which provides coverage for the basic sales price of the unit. The purchaser must provide proof of purchase of the initial flood insurance policy.

(3) *Transfer.* The Assistant Administrator for the Disaster Assistance Directorate may lend temporary housing units purchased under section 408(a) of the Act directly to States, other Governmental entities, or voluntary organizations. Such transfers may be made only in connection with a Presidential declaration of a major disaster or emergency. Donations may be made only when it is in the best interest of the Government, such as when future re-use by the Federal Government would not be economically feasible. As

a condition of such transfers, the Assistant Administrator for the Disaster Assistance Directorate shall require that the recipient:

(i) Utilize the units for the purpose of providing temporary housing for victims of major disasters or emergencies in accordance with the written agreement; and

(ii) Comply with the current applicable FEMA policies and regulations, including this section; 44 CFR part 9 (especially §§ 9.13 and 9.14), Floodplain Management and Protection of Wetlands; 44 CFR part 10, Environmental Considerations. The Assistant Administrator for the Disaster Assistance Directorate may order returned any temporary housing unit made available under this section which is not used in accordance with the terms of transfer.

(o) *Reports.* The Assistant Administrator for the Disaster Assistance Directorate, Regional Administrator, or Federal Coordinating Officer may require from field operations such reports, plans, and evaluations as they deem necessary to carry out their responsibilities under the Act and these regulations.

(p) *Federal responsibility.* The Federal financial and operational responsibility for the Temporary Housing Assistance program shall not exceed 18 months from the date of the declaration of the major disaster or emergency. This period may be extended in writing by the Assistant Administrator for the Disaster Assistance Directorate, based on a determination that an extension is necessary and in the public interest. The Regional Administrator may authorize continued use on a non-reimbursable basis of Government property, office space, and equipment by a State, other Government entity, or voluntary organization after the 18 month period.

(q) *Applicant notification*—(1) *General.* All applicants for temporary housing assistance will be notified regarding the type and amount of assistance for which they are qualified. Whenever practicable, such notification will be provided within 7 days of their application and will be in writing.

(2) Eligible applicants for temporary housing assistance will be provided information regarding:

(i) All forms of housing assistance available;

(ii) The criteria which must be met to qualify for each type of assistance;

(iii) Any limitations which apply to each type of assistance; and

(iv) The address and telephone number of offices responsible for responding to appeals and requests for changes in the type or amount of assistance provided.

(r) *Location.* In providing temporary housing assistance, consideration will be given to the location of:

(1) The eligible applicants' home and place of business;

(2) Schools which the eligible applicant or members of the household attend; and

(3) Agricultural activities which provide 25 percent or more of the eligible applicants' annual income.

(s) *NonFederal administration of temporary housing assistance.* A State may request authority to administer all or part of the temporary housing assistance program in the Governor's request for a declaration or in a subsequent written request to the Regional Administrator from the Governor or his/her authorized representative. The Associate Director shall approve such a request based on the Regional Administrator's recommendation and based on a finding that State administration is both in the interest of the Federal Government and those needing temporary housing assistance. The State must have an approved plan prior to the incident and an approved operational annex within 3 days of the declaration in order to administer the program. When administering the program the State must comply with FEMA program regulations and policies.

(1) *State temporary housing assistance plan.* (i) States which have an interest in administering the Temporary Housing Assistance program shall be required to develop a plan that includes, at a minimum, the items listed below:

(A) Assignment of temporary housing assistance responsibilities to State and/or local officials and agencies;

(B) A description of the program, its functions, goals and objectives of the program, and proposed organization and staffing plan;

(C) Procedures for:

(1) Accepting applications at Disaster Application Centers and subsequently at a State established disaster housing office;

(2) Determining eligibility utilizing FEMA's habitability contract and notifying applicants of the determination;

(3) Preventing duplication of benefits between temporary housing assistance and assistance from other means, as well as a recoupment procedure when duplication occurs;

(4) Providing the various types of assistance (home repairs, existing rental resources, transient accommodations, and mobile homes);

(5) Providing furniture assistance;

(6) Recertifying occupants for continued assistance;

(7) Terminating assistance;

(8) Contracting for services and/or supplies;

(9) Quality control;

(10) Maintaining a management information system;

(11) Financial management;

(12) Public information;

(13) Processing appeals; and

(14) Arranging for a program review.

(ii) The Governor or his/her designee may request the Regional Administrator to provide technical assistance in the preparation of an administrative plan.

(iii) The Governor or designee shall submit the plan to the Regional Administrator for approval. Plans shall be revised, as necessary, and shall be reviewed at least annually by the Regional Administrator.

(2) *Operational annex.* Prior to the State administering the program, the state must submit an operational annex which tailors the approved State plan to the particular disaster or emergency. The annex must be reviewed and approved by the Regional Administrator within 3 days of the declaration or the State shall not be permitted to administer the program. The operational annex shall include but not be limited to:

(i) Organization and staffing specific to the major disaster or emergency;

(ii) Pertinent goals and management objectives;

(iii) A proposed budget; and

(iv) A narrative which describes methods for orderly tracking and processing of applications; assuring timely delivery of assistance; identification of potential problem areas; and any deviations from the approved plan. The Regional Administrator may require additional annexes as necessary for subsequent phases of the operation.

(3) *Evaluation of capability.* State and local government assumption of the temporary housing assistance program for a particular disaster shall be approved by the Assistant Administrator for the Disaster Assistance Directorate based on an evaluation of the capabilities and commitment of the entity by the Regional Administrator. At a minimum, the evaluation shall include a review of the following:

(i) The State temporary housing assistance plan which has been approved by the Regional Administrator prior to the incident, and the specific operational annex which has been approved in accordance with paragraph (s)(2) of this section.

(ii) Past performance in administration of temporary housing assistance or other similar operations;

(iii) Management and staff capabilities; and

(iv) Demonstrated understanding of the tasks to be performed.

(4) *Grant application.* Approval of funding shall be obtained through submission of a project application by the State or local government through the Governor's Authorized Representative. The State shall maintain adequate documentation according to the requirements of 44 CFR part 13, Uniform Administrative Requirements for Grants and Cooperative Agreements to State and Local Governments, to enable analysis of the program. Final reimbursement to the State, or final debt collection, shall be based on an examination of the voucher filed by the State.

(5) *Authorized costs.* All expenditures associated with administering the program are authorized if in compliance with 44 CFR 13.22, Allowable Costs, and the associated OMB Circular A-87, Cost Principles for State and Local Governments. Examples of program costs allowable under the Temporary Housing Assistance program include home repairs, costs associated with rental payments, reimbursements for temporary

housing including transient accommodations and commercial site rental, mobile home installation and maintenance, mobile home private site development, cost of supplemental assistance, mortgage and rental payments, other necessary costs, when approved by the Assistant Administrator for the Disaster Assistance Directorate. All contracts require the review and approval of the Regional Administrator prior to award, in order to be considered as an authorized expenditure.

(6) *Federal monitoring and oversight.* The Regional Administrator shall monitor State-administered activities since he/she remains responsible for the overall delivery of temporary housing assistance. In addition, policy guidance and interpretations to meet specific needs of a disaster shall be provided through the oversight function.

(7) *Technical assistance.* The Regional Administrator shall provide technical assistance as necessary to support State-administered operations through training, procedural issuances, and by providing experienced personnel to assist the State and local staff.

(8) *Operational resources.* The Regional Administrator shall make available for use in State or locally administered temporary housing programs Federal stand-by contracts, memoranda of understanding with Government and voluntary agencies, and Federal property, such as government-owned mobile homes and travel trailers.

(9) *Program reviews and audits.* The State shall conduct program review of each operation. All operations are subject to Federal audit.

[55 FR 2296, Jan. 23, 1990, as amended at 61 FR 7224, Feb. 27, 1996; 64 FR 46853, Aug. 27, 1999; 67 FR 61460, Sept. 30, 2002; 74 FR 15347, Apr. 3, 2009]

§§ 206.102–206.109 [Reserved]

§ 206.110 Federal assistance to individuals and households.

(a) *Purpose.* This section implements the policy and procedures set forth in section 408 of the Robert T. Stafford Disaster Relief and Emergency Assistance Act, 42 U.S.C. 5174, as amended by the Disaster Mitigation Act of 2000. This program provides financial assistance and, if necessary, direct assistance to eligible individuals and households who, as a direct result of a major disaster or emergency, have uninsured or under-insured, necessary expenses and serious needs and are unable to meet such expenses or needs through other means.

(b) *Maximum amount of assistance.* No individual or household will receive financial assistance greater than $25,000 under this subpart with respect to a single major disaster or emergency. FEMA will adjust the $25,000 limit annually to reflect changes in the Consumer Price Index (CPI) for All Urban Consumers that the Department of Labor publishes.

(c) *Multiple types of assistance.* One or more types of housing assistance may be made available under this section to meet the needs of individuals and households in the particular disaster situation. FEMA shall determine the appropriate types of housing assistance to be provided under this section based on considerations of cost effectiveness, convenience to the individuals and households and the suitability and availability of the types of assistance. An applicant is expected to accept the first offer of housing assistance; unwarranted refusal of assistance may result in the forfeiture of future housing assistance. Temporary housing and repair assistance shall be utilized to the fullest extent practicable before other types of housing assistance.

(d) *Date of eligibility.* Eligibility for Federal assistance under this subpart will begin on the date of the incident that results in a presidential declaration that a major disaster or emergency exists, except that reasonable lodging expenses that are incurred in anticipation of and immediately preceding such event may be eligible for Federal assistance under this chapter.

(e) *Period of assistance.* FEMA may provide assistance under this subpart for a period not to exceed 18 months from the date of declaration. The Assistant Administrator for the Disaster Assistance Directorate may extend this period if he/she determines that due to extraordinary circumstances an extension would be in the public interest.

(f) *Assistance not counted as income.* Assistance under this subpart is not to be counted as income or a resource in the determination of eligibility for welfare, income assistance or income-tested benefit programs that the Federal Government funds.

(g) *Exemption from garnishment.* All assistance provided under this subpart is exempt from garnishment, seizure, encumbrance, levy, execution, pledge, attachment, release or waiver. Recipients of rights under this provision may not reassign or transfer the rights. These exemptions do not apply to FEMA recovering assistance fraudulently obtained or misapplied.

(h) *Duplication of benefits.* In accordance with the requirements of section 312 of the Stafford Act, 42 U.S.C. 5155, FEMA will not provide assistance under this subpart when any other source has already provided such assistance or when such assistance is available from any other source. In the instance of insured applicants, we will provide assistance under this subpart only when:

(1) Payment of the applicable benefits are significantly delayed;

(2) Applicable benefits are exhausted;

(3) Applicable benefits are insufficient to cover the housing or other needs; or

(4) Housing is not available on the private market.

(i) *Cost sharing.* (1) Except as provided in paragraph (i)(2) of this section, the Federal share of eligible costs paid under this subpart shall be 100 percent.

(2) Federal and State cost shares for "Other Needs" assistance under subsections 408 (e) and (f) of the Stafford Act will be as follows;

(i) The Federal share shall be 75 percent; and

(ii) The non-federal share shall be paid from funds made available by the State. If the State does not provide the non-Federal share to FEMA before FEMA begins to provide assistance to individuals and households under subsection 408(e) of the Stafford Act, FEMA will still process applications. The State will then be obliged to reimburse FEMA for the non-Federal cost share of such assistance on a monthly basis. If the State does not provide such reimbursement on a monthly basis, then FEMA will issue a Bill for Collection to the State on a monthly

basis for the duration of the program. FEMA will charge interest, penalties, and administrative fees on delinquent Bills for Collection in accordance with the Debt Collection Improvement Act. Cost shared funds, interest, penalties and fees owed to FEMA through delinquent Bills for Collections may be offset from other FEMA disaster assistance programs (*i.e.* Public Assistance) from which the State is receiving, or future grant awards from FEMA or other Federal Agencies. Debt Collection procedures will be followed as outlined in 44 CFR part 11.

(j) *Application of the Privacy Act.* (1) All provisions of the Privacy Act of 1974, 5 U.S.C. 552a, apply to this subpart. FEMA may not disclose an applicant's record except:

(i) In response to a release signed by the applicant that specifies the purpose for the release, to whom the release is to be made, and that the applicant authorizes the release;

(ii) In accordance with one of the published routine uses in our system of records; or

(iii) As provided in paragraph (j)(2) of this section.

(2) Under section 408(f)(2) of the Stafford Act, 42 U.S.C. 5174(f)(2), FEMA must share applicant information with States in order for the States to make available any additional State and local disaster assistance to individuals and households.

(i) States receiving applicant information under this paragraph must protect such information in the same manner that the Privacy Act requires FEMA to protect it.

(ii) States receiving such applicant information shall not further disclose the information to other entities, and shall not use it for purposes other than providing additional State or local disaster assistance to individuals and households.

(k) *Flood Disaster Protection Act requirement.* (1) The Flood Disaster Protection Act of 1973, Public Law 93–234, as amended (42 U.S.C. 4106), imposes certain restrictions on federal financial assistance for acquisition and construction purposes. For the purpose of this paragraph, *financial assistance for acquisition or construction purposes* means assistance to an individual or household to buy, receive, build, repair or improve insurable portions of a home and/or to purchase or repair insurable contents. For a discussion of what elements of a home and contents are insurable, *See* 44 CFR part 61, Insurance Coverage and Rates.

(2) Individuals or households that are located in a special flood hazard area may not receive Federal Assistance for National Flood Insurance Program (NFIP)—insurable real and/or personal property, damaged by a flood, unless the community in which the property is located is participating in the NFIP (*See* 44 CFR part 59.1), or the exception in 42 U.S.C. 4105(d) applies. However, if the community in which the damaged property is located qualifies for and enters the NFIP during the six-month period following the declaration, the Governor's Authorized Representative may request a time extension for FEMA (*See* § 206.112) to accept registrations and to process assistance applications in that community.

(3) *Flood insurance purchase requirement:* (i) As a condition of the assistance and in order to receive any Federal assistance for future flood damage to any insurable property, individuals and households named by FEMA as eligible recipients under section 408 of the Stafford Act who receive assistance, due to flood damages, for acquisition or construction purposes under this subpart must buy and maintain flood insurance, as required in 42 U.S.C. 4012a, for at least the assistance amount. This applies only to real and personal property that is in or will be in a designated Special Flood Hazard Area and that can be insured under the National Flood Insurance Program.

(A) If the applicant is a homeowner, flood insurance coverage must be maintained at the address of the flood-damaged property for as long as the address exists. The flood insurance requirement is reassigned to any subsequent owner of the flood-damaged address.

(B) If the applicant is a renter, flood insurance coverage must be maintained on the contents for as long as the renter resides at the flood-damaged rental unit. The restriction is lifted once the renter moves from the rental unit.

(C) When financial assistance is used to purchase a dwelling, flood insurance coverage must be maintained on the dwelling for as long as the dwelling exists and is located in a designated Special Flood Hazard Area. The flood insurance requirement is reassigned to any subsequent owner of the dwelling.

(ii) FEMA may not provide financial assistance for acquisition or construction purposes to individuals or households who fail to buy and maintain flood insurance required under paragraph (k)(3)(i) of this section or required by the Small Business Administration.

(l) *Environmental requirements.* Assistance provided under this subpart must comply with the National Environmental Policy Act (NEPA) and other environmental laws and Executive Orders, consistent with 44 CFR part 10.

(m) *Historic preservation.* Assistance provided under this subpart generally does not have the potential to affect historic properties and thus is exempted from review in accordance with section 106 of the National Historic Preservation Act, with the exception of ground disturbing activities and construction related to §§ 206.117(b)(1)(ii) (Temporary housing), 206.117(b)(3) (Replacement housing), and 206.117(b)(4) (Permanent housing construction).

[67 FR 61452, Sept. 30, 2002; 67 FR 62896, Oct. 9, 2002]

§ 206.111 Definitions.

Adequate, alternate housing means housing that accommodates the needs of the occupants; is within the normal commuting patterns of the area or is within reasonable commuting distance of work, school, or agricultural activities that provide over 50 percent of the household income; and is within the financial ability of the occupant.

Alternative housing resources means any housing that is available or can quickly be made available in lieu of permanent housing construction and is cost-effective when compared to permanent construction costs. Some examples are rental resources, mobile homes and travel trailers.

Applicant means an individual or household who has applied for assistance under this subpart.

Assistance from other means includes monetary or in-kind contributions from voluntary or charitable organizations, insurance, other governmental programs, or from any sources other than those of the applicant.

Dependent means someone who is normally claimed as such on the Federal tax return of another, according to the Internal Revenue Code. It may also mean the minor children of a couple not living together, where the children live in the affected residence with the parent or guardian who does not actually claim them on the tax return.

Displaced applicant means one whose primary residence is uninhabitable, inaccessible, made unavailable by the landlord (to meet their disaster housing need) or not functional as a direct result of the disaster and has no other housing available in the area, *i.e.*, a secondary home or vacation home.

Effective date of assistance means the date that the applicant was determined eligible for assistance.

Eligible hazard mitigation measures are home improvements that an applicant can accomplish in order to reduce or prevent future disaster damages to essential components of the home.

Fair market rent means housing market-wide estimates of rents that provide opportunities to rent standard quality housing throughout the geographic area in which rental housing units are in competition. The fair market rent rates applied are those identified by the Department of Housing and Urban Development as being adequate for existing rental housing in a particular area.

Financial ability means the applicant's capability to pay housing costs. If the household income has not changed subsequent to or as a result of the disaster then the determination is based upon the amount paid for housing before the disaster. If the household income is reduced as a result of the disaster then the applicant will be deemed capable of paying 30 percent of gross post disaster income for housing. When computing financial ability, extreme or unusual financial circumstances may be considered by the Regional Administrator.

Financial assistance means cash that may be provided to eligible individuals and households, usually in the form of a check or electronic funds transfer.

Functional means an item or home capable of being used for its intended purpose.

Household means all persons (adults and children) who lived in the pre-disaster residence who request assistance under this subpart, as well as any persons, such as infants, spouse, or part-time residents who were not present at the time of the disaster, but who are expected to return during the assistance period.

Housing costs means rent and mortgage payments, including principal, interest, real estate taxes, real property insurance, and utility costs.

Inaccessible means as a result of the incident, the applicant cannot reasonably be expected to gain entry to his or her pre-disaster residence due to the disruption, or destruction, of access routes or other impediments to access, or restrictions placed on movement by a responsible official due to continued health, safety or security problems.

In-kind contributions mean something other than monetary assistance, such as goods, commodities or services.

Lodging expenses means expenses for reasonable short-term accommodations that individuals or households incur in the immediate aftermath of a disaster. Lodging expenses may include but are not limited to the cost of brief hotel stays.

Manufactured housing sites means those sites used for the placement of government or privately owned mobile homes, travel trailers, and other manufactured housing units, including:

(1) *Commercial site*, a site customarily leased for a fee, which is fully equipped to accommodate a housing unit;

(2) *Private site*, a site that the applicant provides or obtains at no cost to the Federal Government, complete with utilities; and

(3) *Group site*, a site provided by the State or local government that accommodates two or more units and is complete with utilities.

Necessary expense means the cost associated with acquiring an item or items, obtaining a service, or paying for any other activity that meets a serious need.

Occupant means a resident of a housing unit.

Owner-occupied means that the residence is occupied by:

(1) The legal owner;

(2) A person who does not hold formal title to the residence and pays no rent, but is responsible for the payment of taxes or maintenance of the residence; or

(3) A person who has lifetime occupancy rights with formal title vested in another.

Permanent housing plan means a realistic plan that, within a reasonable timeframe, puts the disaster victim back into permanent housing that is similar to the victim's pre-disaster housing situation. A reasonable timeframe includes sufficient time for securing funds, locating a permanent dwelling, and moving into the dwelling.

Primary residence means the dwelling where the applicant normally lives, during the major portion of the calendar year; or the dwelling that is required because of proximity to employment, including agricultural activities, that provide 50 percent of the household's income.

Reasonable commuting distance means a distance that does not place undue hardship on an applicant. It also takes into consideration the traveling time involved due to road conditions, *e.g.*, mountainous regions or bridges out and the normal commuting patterns of the area.

Safe means secure from disaster-related hazards or threats to occupants.

Sanitary means free of disaster-related health hazards.

Serious need means the requirement for an item, or service, that is essential to an applicant's ability to prevent, mitigate, or overcome a disaster-related hardship, injury or adverse condition.

Significantly delayed means the process has taken more than 30 days.

Uninhabitable means the dwelling is not safe, sanitary or fit to occupy.

We, our, and *us* mean FEMA.

[67 FR 61452, Sept. 30, 2002; 67 FR 62896, Oct. 9, 2002]

§ 206.112 **Registration period.**

(a) *Initial period.* The standard FEMA registration period is 60 days following the date that the President declares an incident a major disaster or an emergency.

(b) *Extension of the registration period.* The regional administrator or his/her designee may extend the registration period when the State requests more time to collect registrations from the affected population. The Regional Administrator or his/her designee may also extend the standard registration period when necessary to establish the same registration deadline for contiguous counties or States.

(c) *Late registrations.* After the standard or extended registration period ends, FEMA will accept late registrations for an additional 60 days. We will process late registrations for those registrants who provide suitable documentation to support and justify the reason for the delay in their registration.

[67 FR 61452, Sept. 30, 2002; 67 FR 62896, Oct. 9, 2002]

§ 206.113 **Eligibility factors.**

(a) *Conditions of eligibility.* In general, FEMA may provide assistance to individuals and households who qualify for such assistance under section 408 of the Stafford Act and this subpart. FEMA may only provide assistance:

(1) When the individual or household has incurred a disaster-related necessary expense or serious need in the state in which the disaster has been declared, without regard to their residency in that state;

(2) In a situation where the applicant has insurance, when the individual or household files a claim with their insurance provider for all potentially applicable types of insurance coverage and the claim is denied;

(3) In a situation where the applicant has insurance, when the insured individual or household's insurance proceeds have been significantly delayed through no fault of his, her or their own, and the applicant has agreed to repay the assistance to FEMA or the State from insurance proceeds that he, she or they receive later;

(4) In a situation where the applicant has insurance, when the insured individual or household's insurance proceeds are less than the maximum

419

amount of assistance FEMA can authorize and the proceeds are insufficient to cover the necessary expenses or serious needs;

(5) In a situation where the applicant has insurance, when housing is not available on the private market;

(6) In a situation where the applicant has insurance, when the insured individual or household has accepted all assistance from other sources for which he, she, or they are eligible, including insurance, when the insured individual or household's insurance proceeds and all other assistance are less than the maximum amount of assistance FEMA can authorize and the proceeds are insufficient to cover the necessary expense or serious needs;

(7) When the applicant agrees to refund to FEMA or the State any portion of the assistance that the applicant receives or is eligible to receive as assistance from another source;

(8) With respect to housing assistance, if the primary residence has been destroyed, is uninhabitable, or is inaccessible; and

(9) With respect to housing assistance, if a renter's primary residence is no longer available as a result of the disaster.

(b) *Conditions of ineligibility.* We may not provide assistance under this subpart:

(1) For housing assistance, to individuals or households who are displaced from other than their pre-disaster primary residence;

(2) For housing assistance, to individuals or households who have adequate rent-free housing accommodations;

(3) For housing assistance, to individuals or households who own a secondary or vacation residence within reasonable commuting distance to the disaster area, or who own available rental property that meets their temporary housing needs;

(4) For housing assistance, to individuals or households who evacuated the residence in response to official warnings solely as a precautionary measure and who are able to return to the residence immediately after the incident;

(5) For housing assistance, for improvements or additions to the pre-disaster condition of property, except those required to comply with local and State ordinances or eligible mitigation measures;

(6) To individuals or households who have adequate insurance coverage and where there is no indication that insurance proceeds will be significantly delayed, or who have refused assistance from insurance providers;

(7) To individuals or households whose damaged primary residence is located in a designated special flood hazard area, and in a community that is not participating in the National Flood Insurance Program, except that financial assistance may be provided to rent alternate housing and for medical, dental, funeral expenses and uninsurable items to such individuals or households. However, if the community in which the damaged property is located qualifies for and enters the NFIP during the six-month period following the declaration then the individual or household may be eligible;

(8) To individuals or households who did not fulfill the condition to purchase and maintain flood insurance as a requirement of receiving previous Federal disaster assistance;

(9) For business losses, including farm businesses and self-employment; or

(10) For any items not otherwise authorized by this section.

[67 FR 61452, Sept. 30, 2002; 67 FR 62896, Oct. 9, 2002]

§ 206.114 Criteria for continued assistance.

(a) FEMA expects all recipients of assistance under this subpart to obtain and occupy permanent housing at the earliest possible time. FEMA may provide continued housing assistance during the period of assistance, but not to exceed the maximum amount of assistance for the program, based on need, and generally only when adequate, alternate housing is not available or when the permanent housing plan has not been fulfilled through no fault of the applicant.

(b) *Additional criteria for continued assistance.* (1) All applicants requesting continued rent assistance must establish a realistic permanent housing plan no later than the first certification for continued assistance. Applicants will be required to provided documentation showing that they are making efforts to obtain permanent housing.

(2) Applicants requesting continued rent assistance must submit rent receipts to show that they have exhausted the FEMA rent funds, and provide documentation identifying the continuing need.

(3) FEMA generally expects that pre-disaster renters will use their initial rental assistance to obtain permanent housing. However, we may certify them, during the period of assistance, for continued rent assistance when adequate, alternate housing is not available, or when they have not realized a permanent housing plan through no fault of their own.

(4) FEMA may certify pre-disaster owners for continued rent assistance, during the period of assistance, when adequate, alternate housing is not available, or when they have not realized a permanent housing plan through no fault of their own.

(5) Individuals or households requesting additional repair assistance will be required to submit information and/or documentation identifying the continuing need.

(6) Individuals or households requesting additional assistance for personal property, transportation, medical, dental, funeral, moving and storage, or other necessary expenses and serious needs will be required to submit information and/or documentation identifying the continuing need.

[67 FR 61452, Sept. 30, 2002; 67 FR 62896, Oct. 9, 2002]

§ 206.115 Appeals.

(a) Under the provisions of section 423 of the Stafford Act, applicants for assistance under this subpart may appeal any determination of eligibility for assistance made under this subpart. Applicants must file their appeal within 60 days after the date that we notify the applicant of the award or denial of assistance. Applicants may appeal the following:

(1) Eligibility for assistance, including recoupment;

(2) Amount or type of assistance;

(3) Cancellation of an application;

(4) The rejection of a late application;

(5) The denial of continued assistance under § 206.114, Criteria for continued assistance;

(6) FEMA's intent to collect rent from occupants of a housing unit that FEMA provides;

(7) Termination of direct housing assistance;

(8) Denial of a request to purchase a FEMA-provided housing unit at the termination of eligibility;

(9) The sales price of a FEMA-provided housing unit they want to purchase; or

(10) Any other eligibility-related decision.

(b) Appeals must be in writing and explain the reason(s) for the appeal. The applicant or person who the applicant authorizes to act on his or her behalf must sign the appeal. If someone other than the applicant files the appeal, then the applicant must also submit a signed statement giving that person authority to represent him, her or them.

(c) Applicants must appeal to the Regional Administrator or his/her designee for decisions made under this subpart, unless FEMA has made a grant to the State to provide assistance to individuals and households under § 206.120(a), State administration of other needs assistance; then the applicant must appeal to the State.

(d) An applicant may ask for a copy of information in his or her file by writing to FEMA or the State as appropriate. If someone other than the applicant is submitting the request, then the applicant must also submit a signed statement giving that person authority to represent him or her.

(e) The appropriate FEMA or State program official will notify the applicant in writing of the receipt of the appeal.

(f) The Regional Administrator or his/her designee or appropriate State official will review the original decision after receiving the appeal. FEMA or the State, as appropriate, will give the appellant a written notice of the disposition of the appeal within 90 days of the receiving the appeal. The decision of the appellate authority is final.

[67 FR 61452, Sept. 30, 2002; 67 FR 62896, Oct. 9, 2002]

§ 206.116 Recovery of funds.

(a) The applicant must agree to repay to FEMA (when funds are provided by FEMA) and/or the State (when funds are provided by the State) from insurance proceeds or recoveries from any other source an amount equivalent to the value of the assistance provided. In no event must the amount repaid to FEMA and/or the State exceed the amount that the applicant recovers from insurance or any other source.

(b) An applicant must return funds to FEMA and/or the State (when funds are provided by the State) when FEMA and/or the State determines that the assistance was provided erroneously, that the applicant spent the funds inappropriately, or that the applicant obtained the assistance through fraudulent means.

[67 FR 61452, Sept. 30, 2002; 67 FR 62896, Oct. 9, 2002]

§ 206.117 Housing assistance.

(a) *Purpose.* FEMA may provide financial or direct assistance under this section to respond to the disaster-related housing needs of individuals and households.

(b) *Types of housing assistance*—(1) *Temporary housing assistance*—(i) *Financial assistance.* Eligible individuals and households may receive financial assistance to rent alternate housing resources, existing rental units, manufactured housing, recreational vehicles, or other readily fabricated dwellings. FEMA may also provide assistance for the reasonable cost of any transportation, utility hookups, or installation of a manufactured housing unit or recreational vehicle to be used for housing. This includes reimbursement for reasonable short-term lodging expenses that individuals or households incur in the immediate aftermath of a disaster.

(A) FEMA will include all members of a pre-disaster household in a single registration and will provide assistance for one temporary housing residence, unless the Regional Administrator or his/her designee determines that the size or nature of the household requires that we provide assistance for more than one residence.

(B) FEMA will base the rental assistance on the Department of Housing and Urban Development's current fair market rates for existing rental units. FEMA will further base the applicable rate on the household's bedroom requirement and the location of the rental unit.

(C) All utility costs and utility security deposits are the responsibility of the occupant except where the utility does not meter utility services separately and utility services are a part of the rental charge.

(D) The occupant is responsible for all housing security deposits. In extraordinary circumstances, the Regional Administrator or his/her designee may authorize the payment of security deposits; however, the owner or occupant must reimburse the full amount of the security deposit to the Federal Government before or at the time that the temporary housing assistance ends.

(ii) *Direct assistance.* (A) FEMA may provide direct assistance in the form of purchased or leased temporary housing units directly to individuals or households who lack available housing resources and would be unable to make use of the assistance provided under paragraph (b)(1)(i) of this section.

(B) FEMA will include all members of a pre-disaster household in a single application and will provide assistance for one temporary housing residence, unless the Regional Administrator or his/her designee determines that the size or nature of the household requires that we provide assistance for more than one residence.

(C) Any site upon which a FEMA-provided housing unit is placed must comply with applicable State and local codes and ordinances, as well as 44 CFR part 9, Floodplain Management and Protection of Wetlands, and 44 CFR part 10, Environmental Considerations, and all other applicable environmental laws and Executive Orders.

(D) All utility costs and utility security deposits are the responsibility of the occupant except where the utility does not meter utility services separately and utility services are a part of the rental charge.

(E) FEMA-provided or funded housing units may be placed in the following locations:

(1) A commercial site that is complete with utilities; when the Regional Administrator or his/her designee determines that the upgrading of commercial sites, or installation of utilities on such sites, will provide more cost-effective, timely and suitable temporary housing than other types of resources, then Federal assistance may be authorized for such actions.

(2) A private site that an applicant provides, complete with utilities; when the Regional Administrator or his/her designee determines that the cost of installation or repairs of essential utilities on private sites will provide more cost effective, timely, and suitable temporary housing than other types of resources, then Federal assistance may be authorized for such actions.

(3) A group site that the State or local government provides that accommodates two or more units and is complete with utilities; when the Regional Administrator or his/her designee determines that the cost of developing a group site provided by the State or local government, to include installation or repairs of essential utilities on the sites, will provide more cost effective, timely, and suitable temporary housing than other types of resources, then Federal assistance may be authorized for such actions.

(4) A group site provided by FEMA, if the Regional Administrator or his/her designee determines that such a site would be more economical or accessible than one that the State or local government provides.

(F) After the end of the 18-month period of assistance, FEMA may begin to charge up to the fair market rent rate for each temporary housing unit provided. We will base the rent charged on the number of bedrooms occupied and needed by the household. When establishing the amount of rent, FEMA will take into account the financial ability of the household.

(G) We may terminate direct assistance for reasons that include, but are not limited to, the following:

(1) The period of assistance expired under §206.110(e) and has not been extended;

(2) Adequate alternate housing is available to the occupant(s);

(3) The occupant(s) obtained housing assistance through either misrepresentation or fraud;

(4) The occupant(s) failed to comply with any term of the lease/rental agreement or other rules of the site where the unit is located.

(5) The occupant(s) does not provide evidence documenting that they are working towards a permanent housing plan.

(H) FEMA will provide a 15 day written notice when initiating the termination of direct assistance that we provide under our lease agreements. This notice will specify the reasons for termination of assistance and occupancy, the date of termination, the procedure for appealing the determination, and the occupant's liability for such additional charges as the Regional Administrator or his/her designee deems appropriate after the termination date, including fair market rent for the unit.

(I) Duplication of benefits may occur when an applicant has additional living expense insurance benefits to cover the cost of renting alternate housing. In these instances, FEMA may provide a temporary housing unit if adequate alternate housing is not available, or if doing so is in the best interest of the household and the government. We will establish fair market rent, not to exceed insurance benefits available.

(2) *Repairs.* (i) FEMA may provide financial assistance for the repairs of uninsured disaster-related damages to an owner's primary residence. The funds are to help return owner-occupied primary residences to a safe and sanitary living or functioning condition. Repairs may include utilities and residential infrastructure (such as private access routes, privately owned bridge, wells and/or septic systems) damaged by a major disaster.

(ii) The type of repair FEMA authorizes may vary depending upon the nature of the disaster. We may authorize repair of items where feasible or replacement when necessary to insure the safety or health of the occupant and to make the residence functional.

(iii) FEMA may also provide assistance for eligible hazard mitigation measures that reduce the likelihood of future damage to damaged residences, utilities or infrastructure.

(iv) Eligible individuals or households may receive up to $5,000 under this paragraph, adjusted annually to reflect changes in the CPI, to repair damages to their primary residence without first having to show that the assistance can be met through other means, except insurance proceeds.

(v) The individual or household is responsible for obtaining all local permits or inspections that applicable State or local building codes may require.

(3) *Replacement.* FEMA may provide financial assistance under this paragraph to replace the primary residence of an owner-occupied dwelling if the dwelling was damaged by the disaster and there was at least $10,000 of damage (as adjusted annually to reflect changes in the CPI). The applicant may either replace the dwelling in its entirety for $10,000 (as adjusted annually to reflect changes in the CPI) or less, or may use the assistance toward the cost of acquiring a new permanent residence that is greater in cost than $10,000 (as adjusted annually to reflect changes in the CPI). All replacement assistance awards must be individually approved by the Assistant Administrator for the Disaster Assistance Directorate. The Assistant Administrator for the Disaster Assistance Directorate may approve replacement assistance for applicants whose damages are less than $10,000 in extraordinary circumstances where replacement assistance is more appropriate than other forms of housing assistance.

(4) *Permanent housing construction.* FEMA may provide financial or direct assistance to applicants for the purpose of constructing permanent housing in insular areas outside the continental United States and in other remote locations when alternative housing resources are not available and the types of financial or direct temporary housing assistance described at paragraph (b)(1) of this section are unavailable, infeasible, or not cost-effective.

(c) *Eligible costs.* (1) Repairs to the primary residence or replacement of items must be disaster-related and must be of average quality, size, and capacity, taking into consideration the needs of the occupant. Repairs to the primary residence are limited to restoration of the dwelling to a safe and sanitary living or functioning condition and may include:

(i) Repair or replacement of the structural components, including foundation, exterior walls, and roof;

(ii) Repair or replacement of the structure's windows and doors;

(iii) Repair or replacement of the structure's Heating, Ventilation and Air Conditioning System;

(iv) Repair or replacement of the structure's utilities, including electrical, plumbing, gas, water and sewage systems;

(v) Repair or replacement of the structure's interior, including floors, walls, ceilings, doors and cabinetry;

(vi) Repair to the structure's access and egress, including privately owned access road and privately owned bridge;

(vii) Blocking, leveling, and anchoring of a mobile home, and reconnecting or resetting mobile home sewer, water, electrical and fuel lines and tanks; and

(viii) Items or services determined to be eligible hazard mitigation measures.

(2) Replacement assistance, will be based on the verified disaster-related level of damage to the dwelling, or the statutory maximum, whichever is less.

(3) Permanent housing construction, in general, must be consistent with current minimal local building codes and standards where they exist, or minimal acceptable construction industry standards in the area, including reasonable hazard mitigation measures, and federal environmental laws and regulations Dwellings will be of average quality, size and capacity, taking into consideration the needs of the occupant.

[67 FR 61452, Sept. 30, 2002; 67 FR 62896, Oct. 9, 2002]

§ 206.118 Disposal of housing units.

(a) FEMA may sell housing units purchased under § 206.117(b)(1)(ii), Temporary housing, direct assistance, as follows:

(1) Sale to an applicant.

(i) Sale to the individual or household occupying the unit, if the occupant lacks permanent housing, has a site that complies with local codes and ordinances and part 9 of this Title.

(ii) Adjustment to the sales price. FEMA may approve adjustments to the sales price when selling a housing unit to the occupant of a unit if the purchaser is unable to pay the fair market value of the home or unit and when doing so is in the best interest of the applicant and FEMA.

(iii) FEMA may sell a housing unit to the occupant only on the condition that the purchaser agrees to obtain and maintain hazard insurance, as well as flood insurance on the unit if it is or will be in a designated Special Flood Hazard Area.

(2) Other methods of disposal:

(i) FEMA may sell, transfer, donate, or otherwise make a unit available directly to a State or other governmental entity, or to a voluntary organization, for the sole purpose of providing temporary housing to disaster victims in major disasters and emergencies. As a condition of the sale, transfer, or donation, or other method of provision, the State, governmental entity, or voluntary organization must agree to:

(A) Comply with the nondiscrimination provisions of the Stafford Act, 42 U.S.C. 5151; and

(B) Obtain and maintain hazard insurance on the unit, as well as flood insurance if the housing unit is or will be in a designated Special Flood Hazard Area.

(ii) FEMA may also sell housing units at a fair market value to any other person.

(b) A unit will be sold "as is, where is", except for repairs FEMA deems necessary to protect health or safety, which are to be completed before the sale. There will be no implied warranties. In addition, FEMA will inform the purchaser that he/she may have to bring the unit up to codes and standards that are applicable at the proposed site.

[67 FR 61452, Sept. 30, 2002; 67 FR 62896, Oct. 9, 2002]

§ 206.119 Financial assistance to address other needs.

(a) *Purpose.* FEMA and the State may provide financial assistance to individuals and households who have other disaster-related necessary expenses or serious needs. To qualify for assistance under this section, an applicant must also:

(1) Apply to the United States Small Business Administration's (SBA) Disaster Home Loan Program for all available assistance under that program; and

(2) Be declined for SBA Disaster Home Loan Program assistance; or

(3) Demonstrate that the SBA assistance received does not satisfy their total necessary expenses or serious needs arising out of the major disaster.

(b) *Types of assistance.* (1) Medical, dental, and funeral expenses. FEMA may provide financial assistance for medical, dental and funeral items or services to meet the disaster-related necessary expenses and serious needs of individuals and households.

(2) Personal property, transportation, and other expenses.

(i) FEMA may provide financial assistance for personal property and transportation items or services to meet the disaster-related necessary expenses and serious needs of individuals and households.

(ii) FEMA may provide financial assistance for other items or services that are not included in the specified categories for other assistance but which FEMA approves, in coordination with the State, as eligible to meet unique disaster-related necessary expenses and serious needs of individuals and households.

(c) *Eligible costs—*(1) *Personal property.* Necessary expenses and serious needs for repair or replacement of personal property are generally limited to the following:

(i) Clothing;

(ii) Household items, furnishings or appliances;

(iii) Tools, specialized or protective clothing, and equipment required by an employer as a condition of employment;

(iv) Computers, uniforms, schoolbooks and supplies required for educational purposes; and

(v) Cleaning or sanitizing any eligible personal property item.

(2) *Transportation.* Necessary expenses or serious needs for transportation are generally limited to the following:

(i) Repairing or replacing vehicles; and

425

(ii) Financial assistance for public transportation and any other transportation related costs or services.

(3) *Medical expenses.* Medical expenses are generally limited to the following:

(i) Medical costs;

(ii) Dental costs; and

(iii) Repair or replacement of medical equipment.

(4) *Funeral expenses.* Funeral expenses are generally limited to the following

(i) Funeral services;

(ii) Burial or cremation; and

(iii) Other related funeral expenses.

(5) *Moving and storage expenses.* Necessary expenses and serious needs related to moving and storing personal property to avoid additional disaster damage generally include storage of personal property while disaster-related repairs are being made to the primary residence, and return of the personal property to the individual or household's primary residence.

(6) *Other.* Other disaster-related expenses not addressed in this section may include:

(i) The purchase of a Group Flood Insurance Policy as described in paragraph (d) of this section.

(ii) Other miscellaneous items or services that FEMA, in consultation with the State, determines are necessary expenses and serious needs.

(d) *Group Flood Insurance purchase.* Individuals identified by FEMA as eligible for "Other Needs" assistance under section 408 of the Stafford Act as a result of flood damage caused by a Presidentially-declared major disaster and who reside in a special flood hazard area (SFHA) may be included in a Group Flood Insurance Policy (GFIP) established under the National Flood Insurance Program (NFIP) regulations at 44 CFR 61.17.

(1) The premium for the GFIP is a necessary expense within the meaning of this section. FEMA or the State shall withhold this portion of the Other Needs award and provide it to the NFIP on behalf of individuals and households who are eligible for coverage. The coverage shall be equivalent to the maximum assistance amount established under section 408 of the Stafford Act.

(2) FEMA or the State IHP staff shall provide the NFIP with records of individuals who received an "Other Needs"

award and are to be insured through the GFIP. Records of "Other Needs" applicants to be insured shall be accompanied by payments to cover the premium amounts for each applicant for the 3-year policy term. The NFIP will then issue a Certificate of Flood Insurance to each applicant. Flood insurance coverage becomes effective on the 30th day following the receipt of records of GFIP insureds and their premium payments from the State or FEMA, and such coverage terminates 36 months from the inception date of the GFIP, which is 60 days from the date of the disaster declaration.

(3) Insured applicants would not be covered if they are determined to be ineligible for coverage based on a number of exclusions established by the NFIP. Therefore, once applicants/policyholders receive the Certificate of Flood Insurance that contains a list of the policy exclusions, they should review that list to see if they are ineligible for coverage. Those applicants who fail to do this may find that their property is, in fact, not covered by the insurance policy when the next flooding incident occurs and they file for losses. Once the applicants find that their damaged buildings, contents, or both, are ineligible for coverage, they should notify the NFIP in writing in order to have their names removed from the GFIP, and to have the flood insurance maintenance requirement expunged from the data-tracking system.

[67 FR 61452, Sept. 30, 2002; 67 FR 62896, Oct. 9, 2002]

§ 206.120 State administration of other needs assistance.

(a) *State administration of other needs assistance.* A State may request a grant from FEMA to provide financial assistance to individuals and households in the State under § 206.119. The State may also expend administrative costs not to exceed 5 percent of the amount of the grant in accordance with section 408(f)(1)(b) of the Stafford Act. Any State that administers the program to provide financial assistance to individuals and households must administer the program consistent with § 206.119 and the State Administrative Option and the State Administrative Plan that we describe at paragraph (b) and (c) of this section.

(b) *State administrative options.* The delivery of assistance under § 206.119 is contingent upon the State choosing an administrator for the assistance. The State may either request that FEMA administer the assistance or the State may request a grant from FEMA for State administration. The Governor or designee will execute the State Administrative Option annually. During non-disaster periods the State may submit any proposed amendments to the administrative option in writing to the FEMA Regional Administrator. FEMA shall review the request and respond to the Governor or his/her designee within 45 days of receipt of the proposed amendment;

(c) *State Administrative Plan (SAP).* The delivery of assistance by a State under this section is contingent upon approval of a SAP, which describes the procedures the State will use to deliver assistance under section 408 of the Stafford Act, 42 U.S.C. 5174, when a State requests a grant to administer Other Needs assistance. All implementation procedures must be in compliance with Federal laws and requirements, State laws and procedures, and paragraphs (c) and (d) of this section.

(1) *Timeframe for submission of SAP.* A signed SAP, or renewal, must be provided to the FEMA Regional Administrator prior to November 30 of each year. A SAP shall be effective for at least one year, and must be resubmitted in full every three years.

(2) *Renewals.* Annual updates/revisions to the SAP must be submitted by November 30 of each year for FEMA's review and approval by December 31. If the SAP does not need to be updated/revised, a letter from the State stating the SAP is still current must be submitted by November 30 to document the SAP submission requirement.

(3) *Amendments.* The State may request amendments to the SAP at any time. An amendment is effective upon signature by the FEMA Regional Administrator and the Governor or his/her designee. The State may request an amendment to the administrative plan as follows:

(i) *During non-disaster periods.* The State may submit any proposed amend-ments to the SAP in writing to the FEMA Regional Administrator. FEMA shall review the request and respond to the Governor or his/her designee within 45 days of receipt of the proposed amendment;

(ii) *During Presidentially-declared disasters.* The State shall submit any proposed amendments to the SAP in writing to FEMA within three days after disaster declaration. FEMA shall review the request and respond to the Governor or his/her designee within three days of receipt.

(d) *State administrative plan requirements.* The State shall develop a plan for the administration of the Other Needs assistance that describes, at a minimum, the following items:

(1) Assignment of grant program responsibilities to State officials or agencies.

(2) Staffing Schedule that identifies the position, salary and percent of time for each staff person assigned to program administration and/or implementation.

(3) Procedures for interaction with applicants:

(i) Procedures for notifying potential applicants of the availability of the program, to include the publication of application deadlines, pertinent program descriptions, and further program information on the requirements which must be met by the applicant in order to receive assistance;

(ii) Procedures for registration and acceptance of applications, including late applications, up to the prescribed time limitations as described in § 206.112;

(iii) Procedures for damage inspection and/or other verifications.

(iv) Eligibility determinations.

(A) *Under a cooperative agreement:* The procedure for eligibility determinations when the FEMA application and inspection systems are used by the State but additional eligibility criteria are necessary to make State eligibility determinations.

(B) *Under a grant:* The procedure for eligibility determinations when the FEMA application and inspection systems are not used by the State, including the method for determination of costs for personal property and provision of a standard list for personal property items with allowable costs identified for each item.

(v) Procedures for checking compliance for mandated flood insurance in accordance with § 206.110(k);

(vi) Procedures for notifying applicants of the State's eligibility decision;

(vii) Procedures for disbursement of funds to applicants;

(viii) Procedures for applicant appeal processing. Procedures must provide for any appealable determination as identified in § 206.115(a);

(ix) Procedures for expeditious reporting of allegations of fraud, waste or abuse to DHS Office of Inspector General.

(x) Capacity to investigate allegations of waste, fraud and abuse independently if requested by DHS OIG, or in conjunction with DHS OIG.

(xi) Provisions for safeguarding the privacy of applicants and the confidentiality of information, in accordance with § 206.110(j).

(xii) Provisions for complying with § 206.116(b), Recovery of funds.

(4) Procedures for financial management, accountability and oversight.

(i) Procedures for verifying by random sample that assistance funds are meeting applicants' needs, are not duplicating assistance from other means, and are meeting flood insurance requirements.

(ii) Provisions for specifically identifying, in the accounts of the State, all Federal and State funds committed to each grant program; and for immediately returning, upon discovery, all Federal funds that are excess to program needs.

(iii) Provisions for accounting for cash in compliance with State law and procedure and the Cash Management Improvement Act of 1990, as amended.

(iv) Reports.

(A) Procedures for preparing and submitting quarterly and final Financial Status Reports in compliance with 44 CFR 13.41.

(B) Procedures for submitting Program Status Reports in compliance with paragraph (f)(2)(iii) of this section.

(C) Procedures for preparing and submitting the PSC 272, Federal Cash Transactions Report.

(v) Procedures for inventory control, including a system for identifying and tracking placement of equipment purchased with grant funds or loaned by FEMA to the State for purposes of administering the Individuals and Households Program.

(vi) Procedures for return of funds to FEMA.

(vii) State criteria and requirements for closing out Federal grants.

(viii) Process for retention of records.

(e) *Application for assistance procedure.* This section describes the procedures that must be followed by the State to submit an application to administer the Individuals and Households Program through a Grant Award or a Cooperative Agreement.

(1) The State must submit an Other Needs assistance application to the Regional Administrator within 72 hours of the major disaster declaration before IHP assistance may be provided. FEMA will work with the State to approve the application or to modify it so it can be approved.

(2) The application shall include:

(i) Standard Form (SF) 424, Application for Federal Assistance;

(ii) FEMA Form (FF) 20-20 Budget Information—Non Construction Programs;

(iii) Copy of approved indirect cost rate from a Federal cognizant agency if indirect costs will be charged to the grant. Indirect costs will be included in the administrative costs of the grant allowed under paragraph (a) of this section; and

(iv) Disaster specific changes to the State Administrative Plan, if applicable.

(f) *Grants management oversight*—(1) *Period of assistance.* All costs must be incurred within the period of assistance, which is 18 months from the date of the disaster declaration. This period of assistance may be extended if requested in writing by the State and approved in writing by the Assistant Administrator for the Disaster Assistance Directorate. The State must include a justification for an extension of the assistance period.

(2) *Reporting requirements.* (i) The State shall provide financial status reports, as required by 44 CFR 13.41.

(ii) The State shall provide copies of PSC 272, Federal Cash Transactions Report to FEMA. The PSC 272 is required quarterly by the Department of Health and Human Services from users of its SMARTLINK service.

(iii) The State shall provide weekly program status reports which include the number and dollar amount of applications approved, the amount of assistance disbursed and the number of appeals received.

(3) *Ineligible costs.* Funds provided to the State for the administrative costs of administering Other Needs assistance shall not be used to pay regular time for State employees, but may be used to pay overtime for those employees.

(4) *Closeout.* The State has primary responsibility to closeout the tasks approved under the Grant Award. In compliance with the period of assistance, as identified in the award, the State must reconcile costs and payments, resolve negative audit findings, and submit final reports within 90 days of the end of the period of assistance. The State must also provide an inventory of equipment purchased with grant funds and loaned to it by FEMA for purposes of administering IHP, which lists the items, dates, and costs of equipment purchased.

(5) *Recovery of funds.* The State is responsible for recovering assistance awards from applicants obtained fraudulently, expended for unauthorized items or services, expended for items for which assistance is received from other means, and awards made in error.

(i) Adjustments to expenditures will be made as funding is recovered and will be reported quarterly on the Financial Status Report.

(ii) A list of applicants from whom recoveries are processed will be submitted on the quarterly progress report to allow FEMA to adjust its program and financial information systems.

(iii) The State will reimburse FEMA for the Federal share of awards not recovered through quarterly financial adjustments within the 90 day close out liquidation period of the grant award.

(iv) If the State does not reimburse FEMA within the 90 day close out liquidation period, a bill for collection will be issued. FEMA will charge interest, penalties, and administrative fees on delinquent bills for collection in accordance with the Debt Collection Improvement Act. Recovered funds, interest, penalties, and fees owed to FEMA through delinquent bills for collection may be offset from other FEMA disaster assistance programs from which the State is receiving funds or future grant awards from FEMA or other Federal agencies. Debt collection procedures will be followed as outlined in 44 CFR part 11.

(6) *Audit requirements.* Pursuant to 44 CFR 13.26, uniform audit requirements apply to all grants provided under this subpart.

(7) *Document retention.* Pursuant to 44 CFR 13.42, States are required to retain records, including source documentation, to support expenditures/costs incurred against the grant award, for 3 years from the date of submission to FEMA of the final Financial Status Report. The State is responsible for resolving questioned costs that may result from an audit conducted during the three-year record retention period and for returning disallowed costs from ineligible activities.

[67 FR 61452, Sept. 30, 2002; 67 FR 62896, 62897, Oct. 9, 2002]

§§ 206.121–206.130 [Reserved]

Subpart E—Individual and Family Grant Programs

§ 206.131 Individual and Family Grant Program for major disasters declared on or before October 14, 2002.

(a) *General.* The Governor may request that a Federal grant be made to a State for the purpose of such State making grants to individuals or families who, as a result of a major disaster, are unable to meet disaster-related necessary expenses or serious needs for Presidentially-declared major disasters declared on or before October 14, 2002 (Note that the reference to section 411 of the Stafford Act refers to prior legislation amended by the Disaster Mitigation Act 2000). The total Federal grant under this section will be equal to 75 percent of the actual cost of meeting necessary expenses or serious needs of individuals and families, plus

State administrative expenses not to exceed 5 percent of the Federal grant (see paragraph (g) of this section). The total Federal grant is made only on condition that the remaining 25 percent of the actual cost of meeting individuals' or families' necessary expenses or serious needs is paid from funds made available by the State. With respect to any one major disaster, an individual or family may not receive a grant or grants under this section totaling more than $10,000 including both the Federal and State shares. The $10,000 limit will be adjusted annually, at the beginning of each fiscal year, to reflect changes in the Consumer Price Index for all Urban Consumers. IFG assistance for damages or losses to real or personal property, or both, will be provided to individuals or families with those IFG-eligible losses totaling $201 or more; those individuals with damages or losses of $200 or less to real or personal property, or both, are ineligible. The Governor or his/her designee is responsible for the administration of the grant program. The provisions of this regulation are in accordance with 44 CFR Part 13, Uniform Administrative Requirements for Grants and Cooperative Agreements to State and Local Governments.

(b) *Purpose.* The grant program is intended to provide funds to individuals or families to permit them to meet those disaster-related necessary expenses or serious needs for which assistance from other means is either unavailable or inadequate. Meeting those expenses and needs as expeditiously as possible will require States to make an early commitment of personnel and resources. States may make grants in instances where the applicant has not received other benefits to which he/she may be entitled by the time of application to the IFG program, and if the applicant agrees to repay all duplicated assistance to the State. The grant program is not intended to indemnify disaster losses or to permit purchase of items or services which may generally be characterized as nonessential, luxury, or decorative. Assistance under this program is not to be counted as income or a resource in the determination of eligibility for welfare or other income-tested programs supported by the Federal Government, in that IFG assistance is intended to address only disaster-related needs.

(c) *Definitions used in this section.* (1) *Necessary expense* means the cost of a serious need.

(2) *Serious need* means the requirement for an item or service essential to an individual or family to prevent, mitigate, or overcome a disaster-related hardship, injury, or adverse condition.

(3) *Family* means a social unit living together and composed of:

(i) Legally married individuals or those couples living together as if they were married and their dependents; or

(ii) A single person and his/her dependents; or

(iii) Persons who jointly own the residence and their dependents.

(4) *Individual* means anyone who is not a member of a family as described above.

(5) *Dependent* means someone who is normally claimed as such on the Federal tax return of another, according to the Internal Revenue Code. It may also mean the minor children of a couple not living together where the children live in the affected residence with the parent who does not actually claim them on the tax return.

(6) *Expendable items* means consumables, as follows: linens, clothes, and basic kitchenware (pots, pans, utensils, dinnerware, flatware, small kitchen appliances).

(7) *Assistance from other means* means assistance including monetary or in-kind contributions, from other governmental programs, insurance, voluntary or charitable organizations, or from any sources other than those of the individual or family. It does not include expendable items.

(8) *Owner-occupied* means that the residence is occupied by: The legal owner; a person who does not hold formal title to the residence but is responsible for payment of taxes, maintenance of the residence, and pays no rent; or a person who has lifetime occupancy rights in the residence with formal title vested in another. In States where documentation proving ownership is not recorded or does not exist, the State is required to include in its administrative plan a State Attorney

General approved set of conditions describing adequate proof of ownership.

(9) *Flowage easement* means an area where the landowner has given the right to overflow, flood, or submerge the land to the government or other entity for a public purpose.

(d) *National eligibility criteria.* In administering the IFG program, a State shall determine the eligibility of an individual or family in accordance with the following criteria;

(1) *General.* (i) To qualify for a grant under this section, an individual or family representative must:

(A) Make application to all applicable available governmental disaster assistance programs for assistance to meet a necessary expense or serious need, and be determined not qualified for such assistance, or demonstrate that the assistance received does not satisfy the total necessary expense or serious need;

(B) Not have previously received or refused assistance from other means for the specific necessary expense or serious need, or portion thereof, for which application is made; and

(C) Certify to refund to the State that part of the grant for which assistance from other means is received, or which is not spent as identified in the grant award document.

(ii) Individuals and families who incur a necessary expense or serious need in the major disaster area may be eligible for assistance under this section without regard to their alienage, their residency in the major disaster area, or their residency within the State in which the major disaster has been declared except that for assistance in the "housing" category, ownership and residency in the declared disaster area are required (see paragraph (d)(2)(i) of this section).

(iii) The Flood Disaster Protection Act of 1973, Public Law 93–234, as amended, imposes certain restriction on approval of Federal financial assistance for acquisition and construction purposes. This paragraph states those requirements for the IFG program.

(A) For the purpose of this paragraph, *financial assistance for acquisition or construction purposes* means a grant to an individual or family to repair, replace, or rebuild the insurable portions of a home, and/or to purchase or repair insurable contents. For a discussion of what elements of a home and contents are insurable, see 44 CFR part 61, Insurance Coverage and Rates.

(B) A State may not make a grant for acquisition or construction purposes where the structure to which the grant assistance relates is located in a designated special flood hazard area which has been identified by the Assistant Administrator for Mitigation for at least 1 year as floodprone, unless the community in which the structure is located is participating in the National Flood Insurance Program (NFIP). However, if a community qualifies for and enters the NFIP during the 6-month period following the major disaster declaration, the Governor's Authorized Representative (GAR) may request a time extension (see paragraph (j)(1)(ii) of this section) from the Regional Administrator for the purpose of accepting and processing grant applications in that community. The Regional Administrator or Assistant Administrator for the Disaster Assistance Directorate, as appropriate, may approve the State's request if those applicable governmental disaster assistance programs which were available during the original application period are available to the grant applicants during the extended application period.

(C)(*1*) The State may not make a grant for acquisition or construction purposes in a designated special flood hazard area in which the sale of flood insurance is available under the NFIP unless the individual or family obtains adequate flood insurance and maintains such insurance for as long as they live at that property address. The coverage shall equal the maximum grant amount established under § 411(f) of the Stafford Act. If the grantee is a homeowner, flood insurance coverage must be maintained on the residence at the flood-damaged property address for as long as the structure exists if the grantee, or any subsequent owner of that real estate, ever wishes to be assisted by the Federal government with any subsequent flood damages or losses to real or personal property, or both. If the grantee is a renter, flood insurance coverage must be maintained on the

431

contents for as long as the renter resides at the flood-damaged property address. The restriction is lifted once the renter moves from the rental unit.

(2) Individuals named by a State as eligible recipients under § 411 of the Stafford Act for an IFG program award for flood damage as a result of a Presidential major disaster declaration will be included in a Group Flood Insurance Policy (GFIP) established under the National Flood Insurance Program (NFIP) regulations, at 44 CFR 61.17.

(*i*) The premium for the GFIP is a necessary expense within the meaning of this section. The State shall withhold this portion of the IFG award and provide it to the NFIP on behalf of individuals and families who are eligible for coverage. The coverage shall be equivalent to the maximum grant amount established under § 411(f) of the Stafford Act.

(*ii*) The State IFG program staff shall provide the NFIP with records of individuals who received an IFG award and are, therefore, to be insured. Records of IFG grantees to be insured shall be accompanied by payments to cover the premium amounts for each grantee for the 3-year policy term. The NFIP will then issue a Certificate of Flood Insurance to each grantee. Flood insurance coverage becomes effective on the 30th day following the receipt of records of GFIP insureds and their premium payments from the State, and terminates 36 months from the inception date of the GFIP, i.e., 60 days from the date of the disaster declaration.

(*iii*) Insured grantees would not be covered if they are determined to be ineligible for coverage based on a number of exclusions established by the NFIP. Therefore, once grantees/policyholders receive the Certificate of Flood Insurance that contains a list of the policy exclusions, they should review that list to see if they are ineligible for coverage. Those grantees who fail to do this may find that their property is, in fact, not covered by the insurance policy when the next flooding incident occurs and they file for losses. Once the grantees find that their damaged buildings, contents, or both, are ineligible for coverage, they should notify the NFIP in writing in order to have their names removed from the GFIP, and to have the flood insurance maintenance requirement expunged from the NFIP data-tracking system. (If the grantee wishes to refer to or review a Standard Flood Insurance Policy, it will be made available by the NFIP upon request.)

(D) A State may not make a grant to any individual or family who received Federal disaster assistance for flood damage occurring after September 23, 1994, if that property has already received Federal flood-disaster assistance in a disaster declared after September 23, 1994, a flood insurance purchase and maintenance requirement was levied as a condition or result of receiving that Federal disaster assistance, and flood insurance was, in fact, not maintained in an amount at least equal to the maximum IFG grant amount. However, if that property was determined to be ineligible for NFIP flood insurance coverage and is in a special flood hazard area located in a community participating in the NFIP, then the State may continue to make grants to those individuals or families that receive additional damage in all subsequent Presidentially declared major disasters involving floods.

(iv) In order to comply with the President's Executive Orders on Floodplain Management (E.O. 11988) and Protection of Wetlands (E.O. 11990), the State must implement the IFG program in accordance with FEMA regulations 44 CFR part 9. That part specifies which IFG program actions require a floodplain management decision-making process before a grant may be made, and also specifies the steps to follow in the decisionmaking process. Should the State determine that an individual or family is otherwise eligible for grant assistance, the State shall accomplish the necessary steps in accordance with that section, and request the Regional Administrator to make a final floodplain management determination.

(2) *Eligible categories.* Assistance under this section shall be made available to meet necessary expenses or serious needs by providing essential items or services in the following categories:

(i) Housing. With respect to primary residences (including mobile homes) which are owner-occupied at the time of the disaster, grants may be authorized to:

(A) Repair, replace, or rebuild;

(B) Provide access. When an access serves more than one individual or family, an owner-occupant whose primary residence is served by the access may be eligible for a proportionate share of the cost of jointly repairing or providing such access. The owner-occupant may combine his/her grant funds with funds made available by the other individuals or families if a joint use agreement is executed (with no cost or charge involved) or if joint ownership of the access is agreed to;

(C) Clean or make sanitary;

(D) Remove debris from such residences. Debris removal is limited to the minimum required to remove health or safety hazards from, or protect against additional damage to the residence;

(E) Provide or take minimum protective measures required to protect such residences against the immediate threat of damage, which means that the disaster damage is causing a potential safety hazard and, if not repaired, will cause actual safety hazards from common weather or environmental events (example: additional rain, flooding, erosion, wind); and

(F) Minimization measures required by owner-occupants to comply with the provision of 44 CFR part 9 (Floodplain Management and Protection of Wetlands), to enable them to receive assistance from other means, and/or to enable them to comply with a community's floodplain management regulations.

(ii) Personal property. Proof of ownership of personal property is not required. This category includes:

(A) Clothing;

(B) Household items, furnishings, or appliances. If a predisaster renter receives a grant for household items, furnishings, or appliances and these items are an integral part of mobile home or other furnished unit, the predisaster renter may apply the funds awarded for these specific items toward the purchase of the furnished unit, and toward mobile home site development, towing, set-up, connecting and/or reconnecting;

(C) Tools, specialized or protective clothing, and equipment which are required by an employer as a condition of employment;

(D) Repairing, cleaning or sanitizing any eligible personal property item; and

(E) Moving and storing to prevent or reduce damage.

(iii) Transportation. Grants may be authorized to repair, replace, or provide privately owned vehicles or to provide public transportation.

(iv) Medical or dental expenses.

(v) Funeral expenses. Grants may include funeral and burial (and/or cremation) and related expenses.

(vi) Cost of the first year's flood insurance premium to meet the requirement of this section.

(vii) Costs for estimates required for eligibility determinations under the IFG program. Housing and personal property estimates will be provided by the government. However, an applicant may appeal to the State if he/she feels the government estimate is inaccurate. The cost of an applicant-obtained estimate to support the appeal is not an eligible cost.

(viii) Other. A State may determine that other necessary expenses and serious needs are eligible for grant assistance. If such a determination is made, the State must summarize the facts of the case and thoroughly document its findings of eligibility. Should the State require technical assistance in making a determination of eligibility, it may provide a factual summary to the Regional Administrator and request guidance. The Assistant Administrator for the Disaster Assistance Directorate also may determine that other necessary expenses and serious needs are eligible for grant assistance. Following such a determination, the Assistant Administrator for the Disaster Assistance Directorate shall advise the State, through the Regional Administrator, and provide the necessary program guidance.

(3) *Ineligible categories.* Assistance under this section shall not be made available for any item or service in the following categories:

(i) Business losses, including farm businesses and self-employment;

(ii) Improvements or additions to real or personal property, except those

433

required to comply with paragraph (d)(2)(i)(F) of this section;

(iii) Landscaping;

(iv) Real or personal property used exclusively for recreation; and

(v) Financial obligations incurred prior to the disaster.

(4) *Verification.* The State will be provided most verification data on IFG applicants who were not required to first apply to the SBA. The FEMA Regional Administrator shall be responsible for performing most of the required verifications in the categories of housing (to include documentation of home ownership and primary residency); personal property; and transportation (to include notation of the plate or title number of the vehicle; the State may wish to follow up on this). Certain verifications may still be required to be performed by the State, such as on late applicants or reverifications, when FEMA or its contractors are no longer available, and on medical/dental, funeral and "other" categories. Eligibility determination functions shall be performed by the State. The SBA will provide copies of verification performed by SBA staff on housing and personal property (including vehicles) for those applicants who were first required to apply to SBA. This will enable the State to make an eligibility determination on those applicants. When an applicant disagrees with the grant award, he/she may appeal to the State. The cost of any estimate provided by the applicant in support of his/her appeal is not eligible under the program.

(e) *State administrative plan.* (1) The State shall develop a plan for the administration of the IFG program that includes, as a minimum, the items listed below.

(i) Assignment of grant program responsibilities to State officials or agencies.

(ii) Procedures for:

(A) Notifying potential grant applicants of the availability of the program, to include the publication of application deadlines, pertinent program descriptions, and further program information on the requirements which must be met by the applicant in order to receive assistance;

(B) Participating with FEMA in the registration and acceptance of applications, including late applications, up to the prescribed time limitations;

(C) Reviewing verification data provided by FEMA and performing verifications for medical, dental, funeral, and "other" expenses, and also for all grant categories in the instance of late applications and appeals. FEMA will perform any necessary reverifications while its contract personnel are in the disaster area, and the State will perform any others;

(D) Determining applicant eligibility and grant amounts, and notifying applicants of the State's decision;

(E) Determining the requirement for flood insurance;

(F) Preventing duplication of benefits between grant assistance and assistance from other means;

(G) At the applicant's request, and at the State's option, reconsidering the State's determinations;

(H) Processing applicant appeals, recognizing that the State has final authority. Such procedures must provide for:

(1) The receipt of oral or written evidence from the appellate or representative;

(2) A determination on the record; and

(3) A decision by an impartial person or board;

(I) Disbursing grants in a timely manner;

(J) Verifying by random sample that grant funds are meeting applicants' needs, are not duplicating assistance from other means, and are meeting floodplain management and flood insurance requirements. Guidance on the sample size will be provided by the Regional Administrator;

(K) Recovering grant funds obtained fraudulently, expended for unauthorized items or services, expended for items for which assistance is received from other means, or authorized for acquisition or construction purposes where proof of purchase of flood insurance is not provided to the State. Except for those mentioned in the previous sentence, grants made properly by the State on the basis of federally sponsored verification information are not subject to recovery by the State, i.e., FEMA will not hold the State responsible for repaying to FEMA the Federal share of those grants. The State is responsible for its 25 percent share of those grants. As an attachment to its voucher, the State must identify each case where recovery actions have been taken or are to be taken, and the steps taken or to be taken to accomplish recovery;

(L) Conducting any State audits that might be performed in compliance with the Single Audit Act of 1984; and ensuring that appropriate corrective action is taken within 6 months after receipt of the audit report in instances of noncompliance with Federal laws and regulations;

(M) Reporting to the Regional Administrator, and to the Federal Coordinating Officer as required; and

(N) Reviewing and updating the plan each January.

(iii) National eligibility criteria as defined in paragraph (d) of this section.

(iv) Provisions for compliance with 44 CFR part 13, Uniform Administrative Requirements for Grants and Cooperative Agreements to State and Local Governments; 44 CFR part 11, Claims; the State's own debt collection procedures; and all applicable Federal laws and regulations.

(v) Pertinent time limitations for accepting applications, grant award activities, and administrative activities, to comply with Federal time limitations.

(vi) Provisions for specifically identifying, in the accounts of the State, all Federal and State funds committed to each grant program; for repaying the loaned State share as of the date agreed upon in the FEMA-State Agreement; and for immediately returning, upon discovery, all Federal funds that are excess to program needs.

(vii) Provisions for safeguarding the privacy of applicants and the confidentiality of information, except that the information may be provided to agencies or organizations who require it to make eligibility decisions for assistance programs, or to prevent duplication of benefits, to State agencies responsible for audit or program review, and to FEMA or the Government Accountability Office for the purpose of making audits or conducting program reviews.

(viii) A section identifying the management and staffing functions in the IFG program, the sources of staff to fill these functions, and the management and oversight responsibilities of:

(A) The GAR;

(B) The department head responsible for the IFG program;

(C) The Grant Coordinating Officer, i.e., the State official assigned management responsibility for the IFG program; and

(D) The IFG program manager, where management responsibilities are assigned to such a person on a day-to-day basis.

(2) The Governor or his/her designee may request the Regional Administrator to provide technical assistance in the preparation of an administrative plan to implement this program.

(3) The Governor shall submit a revised State administrative plan each January to the Regional Administrator. The Regional Administrator shall review and approve the plan annually. In each disaster for which assistance under this section is requested, the Regional Administrator shall request the State to prepare any amendments required to meet current policy guidance. The Regional Administrator must then work with the State until the plan and amendment(s) are approved.

(4) The State shall make its approved administrative plan part of the State emergency plan, as described in subpart A of these regulations.

(f) *State initiation of the IFG program.* To make assistance under this section available to disaster victims, the Governor must, either in the request of the President for a major disaster declaration or by separate letter to the Regional Administrator, express his/her intention to implement the program. This expression of intent must include an estimate of the size and cost of the program. In addition, this expression of intent represents the Governor's agreement to the following:

(1) That the program is needed to satisfy necessary expenses and serious needs of disaster victims which cannot otherwise be met;

(2) That the State will pay its 25 percent share of all grants to individuals and families;

(3) That the State will return immediately upon discovery advanced Federal funds that exceed actual requirements;

(4) To implement an administrative plan as identified in paragraph (e) of this section;

(5) To implement the grant program throughout the area designated as eligible for assistance by the Assistant Administrator for the Disaster Assistance Directorate; and

(6) To maintain close coordination with and provide reports to the Regional Administrator.

(g) *Funding.* (1) The Regional Administrator may obligate the Federal share of the IFG program based upon the determination that:

(i) The Governor has indicated the intention to implement the program, in accordance with paragraph (f) of this section;

(ii) The State's administrative plan meets the requirements of this section and current policy guidance; and

(iii) There is no excess advance of the Federal share due FEMA from a prior IFG program. The State may eliminate any such debt by paying it immediately, or by accepting an offset of the owed funds against other funds payable by FEMA to the State. When the excess Federal share has been repaid, the Regional Administrator may then obligate funds for the Federal share for the current disaster.

(2) The Regional Administrator may increase the State's letter of credit to meet the Federal share of program needs if the above conditions are met. The State may withdraw funds for the Federal share in the amount made available to it by the Regional Administrator. Advances to the State are governed by 44 CFR 13.21, Payment.

(3) The Regional Administrator may lend to the State its share in accordance with subpart A of these regulations.

(4) Payable costs are governed by 44 CFR 13.22, Allowable Costs, and the associated OMB Circular A–87, Cost Principles for State and Local Governments. Also, the costs must be in accordance with the national eligibility criteria stated in paragraph (d) of this section, and the State's administrative plan, as stated in paragraph (e) of this section. The Federal contribution to this program shall be 75 percent of program costs and shall be made in accordance with 44 CFR 13.25, Matching or Cost-Sharing.

(h) *Final payment.* Final payment to the State for the Federal share of the IFG program plus administrative costs, is governed by 44 CFR 13.21, Payment, and 44 CFR 13.50, Closeout. The voucher is Standard Form 270, Request for Advance or Reimbursement). A separate voucher for the State share will be prepared, to include all disaster programs for which the State is requesting a loan of the nonFederal share. The FEMA Regional Administrator will analyze the voucher and approve, disapprove, or suspend approval until deficiencies are corrected.

(i) *Audits.* The State should perform the audits required by the Single Audit Act of 1984. Refer to 44 CFR part 13. All programs are subject to Federal audit.

(j) *Time limitations.* (1) In the administration of the IFG program:

(i) The Governor shall indicate his/ her intention to implement the IFG program no later than 7 days following the day on which the major disaster was declared and in the manner set forth in paragraph (f) of this section;

(ii) Applications shall be accepted from individuals or families for a period of 60 days following the declaration, and for no longer than 30 days thereafter when the State determines that extenuating circumstances beyond the applicants' control (such as, but not limited to, hospitalization, illness, or inaccessibility to application centers) prevented them from applying in a timely manner. *Exception:* If applicants exercising their responsibility to first apply to the Small Business Administration do so after SBA's deadline, and SBA accepts their case for processing because of "substantial causes essentially beyond the control of the applicant," and provides a formal decline or insufficient loan based on lack of repayment ability, unsatisfactory credit, or unsatisfactory experience with prior loans (i.e., the reasons a loan denial client would normally be eligible for IFG assistance), then such an application referred to the State by the SBA is considered as meeting the IFG filing deadline. The State may then apply its own criteria in determining whether to process the case for grant assistance. The State automatically has an extension of time to complete the processing, eligibility, and disbursement functions. However, the State must still complete all administrative activity within the 270-day period described in this section.

(iii) The State shall complete all grant award activity, including eligibility determinations, disbursement, and disposition of State level appeals, within 180 days following the declaration date. The Regional Administrator shall suspend all grant awards disbursed after the specified completion date; and

(iv) The State shall complete all administrative activities and submit final reports and vouchers to the Regional Administrator within 90 days of the completion of all grant award activity.

(2) The GAR may submit a request with appropriate justification for the extension of any time limitation. The Regional Administrator may approve the request for a period not to exceed 90 days. The Assistant Administrator for the Disaster Assistance Directorate may approve any request for a further extension of the time limitations.

(k) *Appeals*—(1) *Bills for collection (BFC's).* The State may appeal the issuance of a BFC by the Regional Administrator. Such an appeal shall be made in writing within 60 days of the issuance of the bill. The appeal must include information justifying why the bill is incorrect. The Regional Administrator shall review the material submitted and notify the State, in writing, within 15 days of receipt of the appeal, of his/her decision. Interest on BFC's starts accruing on the date of issuance of the BFC, but is not charged if the State pays within 30 days of issuance. If the State is successful in its appeal, interest will not be charged; if unsuccessful, interest is due and payable, as above.

(2) *Other appeals.* The State may appeal any other decision of the regional Administrator. Such appeals shall be made in writing within 60 days of the

Regional Administrator 's decision. The appeal must include information justifying a reversal of the decision. The Regional Administrator shall review the material submitted and notify the State, in writing, within 15 days of receipt of the appeal, of his/her decision.

(3) *Appeals to the Assistant Administrator for the Disaster Assistance Directorate.* The State may further appeal the Regional Administrator 's decisions to the Assistant Administrator for the Disaster Assistance Directorate. This appeal shall be made in writing within 60 days of the Regional Administrator 's decision. The appeal must include information justifying a reversal of the decision. The Assistant Administrator for the Disaster Assistance Directorate shall review the material submitted and notify the State, in writing, within 15 days of receipt of the appeal, of his/her decision.

(l) *Exemption from garnishment.* All proceeds received or receivable under the IFG program shall be exempt from garnishment, seizure, encumbrance, levy, execution, pledge, attachment, release, or waiver. No rights under this provision are assignable or transferable. The above exemptions will not apply to the requirement imposed by paragraph (e)(1)(ii)(K) of this section.

(m) *Debt collection.* If the State has been unable to recover funds as stated in paragraph (e)(1)(k) of this section, the Regional Administrator shall institute debt collection activities against the individual according to the procedures outlined in 44 CFR part 11, Claims, and 44 CFR 13.52, Collection of Amounts Due.

[54 FR 11615, Mar. 21, 1989, as amended at 55 FR 28627, July 12, 1990; 60 FR 7130, Feb. 7, 1995; 61 FR 19201, May 1, 1996; 67 FR 61460, Sept. 30, 2002; 74 FR 15348, Apr. 3, 2009]

§§ 206.132–206.140 [Reserved]

Subpart F—Other Individual Assistance

§ 206.141 Disaster unemployment assistance.

The authority to implement the disaster unemployment assistance (DUA) program authorized by section 410 of the Stafford Act, and the authority to issue regulations, are currently delegated to the Secretary of Labor.

§§ 206.142–206.150 [Reserved]

§ 206.151 Food commodities.

(a) The Administrator will assure that adequate stocks of food will be ready and conveniently available for emergency mass feeding or distribution in any area of the United States which suffers a major disaster or emergency.

(b) In carrying out the responsibilities in paragraph (a) of this section, the Administrator may direct the Secretary of Agriculture to purchase food commodities in accordance with authorities prescribed in section 413(b) of the Stafford Act.

§§ 206.152–206.160 [Reserved]

§ 206.161 Relocation assistance.

Notwithstanding any other provision of law, no person otherwise eligible for any kind of replacement housing payment under the Uniform Relocation Assistance and Real Property Acquisition Policies Act of 1970 (Pub. L. 91–646) shall be denied such eligibility as a result of his being unable, because of a major disaster as determined by the President, to meet the occupancy requirements set by such Act.

§§ 206.162–206.163 [Reserved]

§ 206.164 Disaster legal services.

(a) Legal services, including legal advice, counseling, and representation in non fee-generating cases, except as provided in paragraph (b) of this section, may be provided to low-income individuals who require them as a result of a major disaster. For the purpose of this section, *low-income individuals* means those disaster victims who have insufficient resources to secure adequate legal services, whether the insufficiency existed prior to or results from the major disaster. In cases where questions arise about the eligibility of an individual for legal services, the Regional Administrator or his/her representative shall make a determination.

(b) Disaster legal services shall be provided free to such individuals. Fee-generating cases shall not be accepted by lawyers operating under these regulations. For purposes of this section, a fee-generating case is one which would not ordinarily be rejected by local lawyers as a result of its lack of potential remunerative value. Where any question arises as to whether a case is fee-generating as defined in this section, the Regional Administrator or his/her representative, after any necessary consultation with local or State bar associations, shall make the determination. Any fee-generating cases shall be referred by the Regional Administrator or his/her representative to private lawyers, through existing lawyer referral services, or, where that is impractical or impossible, the Regional Director may provide a list of lawyers from which the disaster victim may choose. Lawyers who have rendered voluntary legal assistance under these regulations are not precluded from taking fee-generating cases referred to them in this manner while in their capacity as private lawyers.

(c) When the Regional Administrator determines after any necessary consultation with the State Coordinating Officer, that implementation of this section is necessary, provision of disaster legal services may be accomplished by:

(1) Use of volunteer lawyers under the terms of appropriate agreements;

(2) Use of Federal lawyers, provided that these lawyers do not represent an eligible disaster victim before a court or Federal agency in a matter directly involving the United States, and further provided that these lawyers do not act in a way which will violate the standards of conduct of their respective agencies or departments;

(3) Use of private lawyers who may be paid by the Federal Emergency Management Agency when the Regional Administrator has determined that there is no other means of obtaining adequate legal assistance for qualified disaster victims; or

(4) Any other arrangement the Regional Administrator deems appropriate.

The Assistant Administrator for the Disaster Assistance Directorate shall coordinate with appropriate Federal agencies and the appropriate national, state and local bar associations, as necessary, in the implementation of the disaster legal services programs.

(d) In the event it is necessary for FEMA to pay lawyers for the provision of legal services under these regulations, the Regional Administrator, in consultation with State and local bar associations, shall determine the amount of reimbursement due to the lawyers who have provided disaster legal services at the request of the Regional Administrator. At the Regional Administrator 's discretion, administrative costs of lawyers providing legal services requested by him or her may also be paid.

(e) Provision of disaster legal services is confined to the securing of benefits under the Act and claims arising out of a major disaster.

(f) Any disaster legal services shall be provided in accordance with subpart A of these regulations, Non-discrimination in disaster assistance.

§§ 206.165–206.170 [Reserved]

§ 206.171 Crisis counseling assistance and training.

(a) *Purpose.* This section establishes the policy, standards, and procedures for implementing section 416 of the Act, Crisis Counseling Assistance and Training. FEMA will look to the Director, National Institute of Mental Health (NIMH), as the delegate of the Secretary of the Department of Health and Human Services (DHHS).

(b) *Definitions.* (1) *Assistant Administrator* means the head of the Disaster Assistance Directorate; the official who approves or disapproves a request for assistance under section 416 of the Act, and is the final appeal authority.

(2) *Crisis* means any life situation resulting from a major disaster or its aftermath which so affects the emotional and mental equilibrium of a disaster victim that professional mental health counseling services should be provided to help preclude possible damaging physical or psychological effects.

(3) *Crisis counseling* means the application of individual and group treatment procedures which are designed to ameliorate the mental and emotional crises and their subsequent psychological and behavioral conditions re-

sulting from a major disaster or its aftermath.

(4) *Federal Coordinating Officer (FCO)* means the person appointed by the Administrator or Deputy Administrator to coordinate Federal assistance in an emergency or a major disaster.

(5) *Grantee* means the State mental health agency or other local or private mental health organization which is designated by the Governor to receive funds under section 416 of the Act.

(6) *Immediate services* means those screening or diagnostic techniques which can be applied to meet mental health needs immediately after a major disaster. Funds for immediate services may be provided directly by the Regional Administrator to the State or local mental health agency designated by the Governor, prior to and separate from the regular program application process of crisis counseling assistance.

(7) *Major disaster* means any natural catastrophe (including any hurricane, tornado, storm, high water, winddriven water, tidal wave, tsunami, earthquake, volcanic eruption, landslide, mudslide, snowstorm or drought), or, regardless of cause, any fire, flood, or explosion, in any part of the United States, which in the determination of the President causes damage of sufficient severity and magnitude to warrant major disaster assistance under this Act to supplement the efforts and available resources of States, local governments, and disaster relief organizations in alleviating the damage, loss, hardship, or suffering caused thereby.

(8) *Project Officer* means the person assigned by the Secretary, DHHS, to monitor a crisis counseling program, provide consultation, technical assistance, and guidance, and be the contact point within the DHHS for program matters.

(9) *Regional Administrator* means the director of a regional office of FEMA, or the Disaster Recovery Manager, as the delegate of the Regional Administrator.

(10) *Secretary* means the Secretary of DHHS or his/her delegate.

(11) *State Coordinating Officer (SCO)* means the person appointed by the

439

Governor to act in cooperation with the FCO.

(c) *Agency policy.* (1) It is agency policy to provide crisis counseling services, when required, to victims of a major disaster for the purpose of relieving mental health problems caused or aggravated by a major disaster or its aftermath. Assistance provided under this section is short-term in nature and is provided at no cost to eligible disaster victims.

(2) The Regional Administrator and Assistant Administrator for the Disaster Assistance Directorate, in fulfilling their responsibilities under this section, shall coordinate with the Secretary.

(3) In meeting the responsibilities under this section, the Secretary or his/her delegate will coordinate with the Assistant Administrator for the Disaster Assistance Directorate.

(d) *State initiation of the crisis counseling program.* To obtain assistance under this section, the Governor or his/her authorized representative must initiate an assessment of the need for crisis counseling services within 10 days of the date of the major disaster declaration. The purpose of the assessment is to provide an estimate of the size and cost of the program needed and to determine if supplemental Federal assistance is required. The factors of the assessment must include those described in paragraphs (f)(2) (ii) and (iii) and (g)(2) (iii) and (iv) of this section.

(e) *Public or private mental health agency programs.* If the Governor determines during the assessment that because of unusual circumstances or serious conditions within the State or local mental health network, the State cannot carry out the crisis counseling program, he/she may identify a public or private mental health agency or organization to carry out the program or request the Regional Administrator to identify, with the assistance of the Secretary, such an agency or organization. Preference should be given to the extent feasible and practicable to those public and private agencies or organizations which are located in or do business primarily in the major disaster area.

(f) *Immediate services.* If, during the course of the assessment, the State determines that immediate mental health services are required because of the severity and magnitude of the disaster, and if State or local resources are insufficient to provide these services, the State may request and the Regional Administrator, upon determining that State resources are insufficient, may provide funds to the State, separate from the application process for regular program funds (described at paragraph (g) of this section).

(1) The application must be submitted to the Regional Administrator no later than 14 days following the declaration of the major disaster. This application represents the Governor's agreement and/or certification:

(i) That the requirements are beyond the State and local governments' capabilities;

(ii) That the program, if approved, will be implemented according to the plan contained in the application approved by the Regional Administrator;

(iii) To maintain close coordination with and provide reports to the Regional Administrator; and

(iv) To include mental health disaster planning in the State's emergency plan prepared under title II of the Stafford Act.

(2) The application must include:

(i) The geographical areas within the designated disaster area for which services will be provided;

(ii) An estimate of the number of disaster victims requiring assistance;

(iii) A description of the State and local resources and capabilities, and an explanation of why these resources cannot meet the need;

(iv) A description of response activities from the date of the disaster incident to the date of application;

(v) A plan of services to be provided to meet the identified needs; and

(vi) A detailed budget, showing the cost of proposed services separately from the cost of reimbursement for any eligible services provided prior to application.

(3) *Reporting requirements.* The State shall submit to the Regional Administrator:

(i) A mid-program report only when a regular program grant application is being prepared and submitted. This report will be included as part of the regular program grant application;

(ii) A final program report, a financial status report, and a final voucher 90 days after the last day of immediate services funding.

(4) Immediate services program funding:

(i) Shall not exceed 60 days following the declaration of the major disaster, except when a regular program grant application has been submitted;

(ii) May continue for up to 30 additional days when a regular program grant application has been submitted;

(iii) May be extended by the Regional Administrator, upon written request from the State, documenting extenuating circumstances; and

(iv) May reimburse the State for documented, eligible expenses from the date of the occurrence of the event or incurred in anticipation of and immediately preceding the disaster event which results in a declaration.

(v) Any funds granted pursuant to an immediate services program, paragraph (f) of this section, shall be expended solely for the purposes specified in the approved application and budget, these regulations, the terms and conditions of the award, and the applicable principles prescribed in 44 CFR part 13.

(5) *Appeals.* There are two levels of appeals. If a State submits appeals at both levels, the first appeal must be submitted early enough to allow the latter appeal to be submitted within 60 days following the date of the funding determination on the immediate services program application.

(i) The State may appeal the Regional Administrator 's decision. This appeal must be submitted in writing within 60 days of the date of notification of the application decision, but early enough to allow for further appeal if desired. The appeal must include information justifying a reversal of the decision. The Regional Director shall review the material submitted, and after consultation with the Secretary, notify the State, in writing within 15 days of receipt of the appeal, of his/her decision;

(ii) The State may further appeal the Regional Administrator 's decision to the Assistant Administrator for the Disaster Assistance Directorate. This appeal shall be made in writing within 60 days of the date of the Regional Administrator 's notification of the decision on the immediate services application. The appeal must include information justifying a reversal of the decision. The Assistant Administrator for the Disaster Assistance Directorate, or other impartial person, shall review the material submitted, and after consultation with the Secretary and Regional Administrator, notify the State, in writing, within 15 days of receipt of the appeal, of his/her decision.

(g) *Regular program.* (1) The application must be submitted by the Governor or his/her authorized representative to the Assistant Administrator for the Disaster Assistance Directorate through the Regional Administrator, and simultaneously to the Secretary no later than 60 days following the declaration of the major disaster. This application represents the Governor's agreement and/or certification:

(i) That the requirements are beyond the State and local governments' capabilities;

(ii) That the program, if approved, will be implemented according to the plan contained in the application approved by the Assistant Administrator for the Disaster Assistance Directorate;

(iii) To maintain close coordination with and provide reports to the Regional Administrator, the Assistant Administrator for the Disaster Assistance Directorate, and the Secretary; and

(iv) To include mental health disaster planning in the State's emergency plan prepared under title II of the Stafford Act.

(2) The application must include:

(i) Standard Form 424, Application for Federal Assistance;

(ii) The geographical areas within the designated disaster area for which services will be supplied;

(iii) An estimate of the number of disaster victims requiring assistance. This documentation of need should include the extent of physical, psychological, and social problems observed, the types of mental health problems encountered by victims, and a description of how the estimate was made;

(iv) A description of the State and local resources and capabilities, and an explanation of why these resources cannot meet the need;

(v) A plan of services which must include at a minimum:

(A) The manner in which the program will address the needs of the affected population, including the types of services to be offered, an estimate of the length of time for which mental health services will be required, and the manner in which long-term cases will be handled;

(B) A description of the organizational structure of the program, including designation by the Governor of an individual to serve as administrator of the program. If more than one agency will be delivering services, the plan to coordinate services must also be described;

(C) A description of the training program for project staff, indicating the number of workers needing such training;

(D) A description of the facilities to be utilized, including plans for securing office space if necessary to the project; and

(E) A detailed budget, including identification of the resources the State and local governments will commit to the project, proposed funding levels for the different agencies if more than one is involved, and an estimate of the required Federal contribution.

(3) *Reporting requirements.* The State shall submit the following reports to the Regional Administrator, the Secretary, and the State Coordinating Officer:

(i) Quarterly progress reports, as required by the Regional Administrator or the Secretary, due 30 days after the end of the reporting period. This is consistent with 44 CFR 13.40, Monitoring and Reporting Program Performance;

(ii) A final program report, to be submitted within 90 days after the end of the program period. This is also consistent with 44 CFR 13.40, Monitoring and Reporting Program Performance;

(iii) An accounting of funds, in accordance with 44 CFR 13.41, Financial Reporting, to be submitted with the final program report; and

(iv) Such additional reports as the Regional Administrator, Secretary, or SCO may require.

(4) Regular program funding:

(i) Shall not exceed 9 months from the date of the DHHS notice of grant award, except that upon the request of the State to the Regional Administrator and the Secretary, the Assistant Administrator for the Disaster Assistance Directorate may authorize up to 90 days of additional program period because of documented extraordinary circumstances. In limited circumstances, such as disasters of a catastrophic nature, the Assistant Administrator for the Disaster Assistance Directorate may extend the program period for more than 90 days where he or she deems it to be in the public interest.

(ii) The amount of the regular program grant award will take into consideration the Secretary's estimate of the sum necessary to carry out the grant purpose.

(iii) Any funds granted pursuant to a regular program, paragraph (g) of this section, shall be expended solely for the purposes specified in the approved application and budget, these regulations, the terms and conditions of the award, and the applicable cost principles prescribed in subpart Q of 45 CFR part 92.

(5) *Appeals.* The State may appeal the Assistant Administrator for the Disaster Assistance Directorate 's decision, in writing, within 60 days of the date of notification of the decision. The appeal must include information justifying a reversal of the decision. The Assistant Administrator for the Disaster Assistance Directorate, or other impartial person, in consultation with the Secretary and Regional Administrator, shall review the material submitted and notify the State, in writing within 15 days of receipt of the appeal, of his/her decision.

(h) *Eligibility guidelines.* (1) For services. An individual may be eligible for crisis counseling services if he/she was a resident of the designated major disaster areas or was located in the area at the time of the disaster event and if:

(i) He/she has a mental health problem which was caused or aggravated by the major disaster or its aftermath; or

(ii) He/she may benefit from preventive care techniques.

(2) For training. (i) The crisis counseling project staff or consultants to the project are eligible for the specific instruction that may be required to enable them to provide professional mental health crisis counseling to eligible individuals;

(ii) All Federal, State, and local disaster workers responsible for assisting disaster victims are eligible for general instruction designed to enable them to deal effectively and humanely with disaster victims.

(i) *Assignment of responsibilities.* (1) The Regional Administrator shall:

(i) In the case of an immediate services program application, acknowledge receipt of the request, verify (with assistance from the Secretary) that State resources are insufficient, approve or disapprove the State's application, obligate and advance funds for this purpose, review appeals, make a determination (with assistance from the Secretary), and notify the State;

(ii) In the case of a regular program grant application:

(A) Acknowledge receipt of the request;

(B) Request the Secretary to conduct a review to determine the extent to which assistance requested by the Governor or his/her authorized representative is warranted;

(C) Considering the Secretary's recommendation, recommend approval or disapproval of the application for assistance under this section; and forward the Regional Administrator 's and Secretary's recommendations and documentation to the Assistant Administrator for the Disaster Assistance Directorate;

(D) Assist the State in preliminary surveys and provide guidance and technical assistance if requested to do so; and

(E) Maintain liaison with the Secretary and look to the Secretary for program oversight and monitoring.

(2) The Secretary shall:

(i) Provide technical assistance, consultation, and guidance to the Regional Administrator in reviewing a State's application, to a State during program implementation and development, and

to mental health agencies, as appropriate;

(ii) At the request of the Regional Administrator, conduct a review to verify the extent to which the requested assistance is needed and provide a recommendation on the need for supplementary Federal assistance. The review must include:

(A) A verification of the need for services with an indication of how the verification was conducted;

(B) Identification of the Federal mental health programs in the area, and the extent to which such existing programs can help alleviate the need;

(C) An identification of State, local, and private mental health resources, and the extent to which these resources can assume the workload without assistance under this section and the extent to which supplemental assistance is warranted;

(D) A description of the needs; and

(E) A determination of whether the plan adequately addresses the mental health needs;

(iii) If the application is approved, provide grant assistance to States or the designated public or private entities;

(iv) If the application is approved, monitor the progress of the program and perform program oversight;

(v) Coordinate with, and provide program reports to, the Regional Administrator, and the Assistant Administrator for the Disaster Assistance Directorate;

(vi) Make the appeal determination, for regular program grants, involving allowable costs and termination for cause as described in paragraph (j)(2) of this section;

(vii) As part of the project monitoring responsibilities, report to the Regional Administrator and Assistant Administrator for the Disaster Assistance Directorate at least quarterly on the progress of crisis counseling programs, in a report format jointly agreed upon by the Secretary and FEMA; provide special reports, as requested by the Regional Administrator, FCO, or Assistant Administrator for the Disaster Assistance Directorate;

(viii) Require progress reports and other reports from the grantee to facilitate his/her project monitoring responsibilities;

(ix) Properly account for all Federal funds made available to grantees under this section. Submit to the Assistant Administrator for the Disaster Assistance Directorate, within 120 days of completion of a program, a final accounting of all expenditures for the program and return to FEMA all excess funds. Attention is called to the reimbursement requirements of this part.

(3) The Assistant Administrator for the Disaster Assistance Directorate shall:

(i) Approve or disapprove a State's request for assistance based on recommendations of the Regional Administrator and the Secretary;

(ii) Obligate funds and authorize advances of funds to the DHHS;

(iii) Request that the Secretary designate a Project Officer;

(iv) Maintain liaison with the Secretary and Regional Administrator; and

(v) Review and make determinations on appeals, except for regular program appeals involving allowable costs and termination for cause as described in paragraph (j)(2) of this section, and notify the State of the decision.

(j) *Grant awards.* (1) Neither the approval of any application nor the award of any grant commits or obligates the United States in any way to make any additional, supplemental, continuation, or other award with respect to any approved application or portion of any approved application.

(2) Several other regulations of the DHHS apply to grants under this section. These include, but are not limited to:

45 CFR part 16—DHHS grant appeals procedures

42 CFR part 50, subpart D—PHS grant appeals procedures

45 CFR part 74—Administration of grants

45 CFR part 75—Informal grant appeals procedures (indirect cost rates and other cost allocations)

45 CFR part 80—Nondiscrimination under programs receiving Federal assistance through the DHHS (effectuation of Title VI of the Civil Rights Act of 1964)

45 CFR part 81—Practice and procedure for hearings under part 80

45 CFR part 84—Nondiscrimination on the basis of handicap in federally assisted programs

45 CFR part 86—Nondiscrimination on the basis of sex in federally assisted programs

45 CFR part 91—Nondiscrimination on the basis of age in federally assisted programs

45 CFR part 92—Uniform administrative requirements for grants and cooperative agreements to State and local governments

(k) *Federal audits.* The crisis counseling program is subject to Federal audit. The Assistant Administrator for the Disaster Assistance Directorate, the Regional Administrator, the DHS Inspector General, The Secretary, and the Comptroller General of the United States, or their duly authorized representatives, shall have access to any books, documents, papers, and records that pertain to Federal funds, equipment, and supplies received under this section for the purpose of audit and examination.

[54 FR 11615, Mar. 21, 1989, as amended at 68 FR 9900, Mar. 3, 2003]

§§ 206.172–206.180 [Reserved]

§ 206.181 Use of gifts and bequests for disaster assistance purposes.

(a) *General.* FEMA sets forth procedures for the use of funds made possible by a bequest of funds from the late Cora C. Brown of Kansas City, Missouri, who left a portion of her estate to the United States for helping victims of natural disasters and other disasters not caused by or attributable to war. FEMA intends to use the funds, and any others that may be bequeathed under this authority, in the manner and under the conditions described below.

(b) *Purposes for awarding funds.* Money from the Cora Brown Fund may only be used to provided for disaster-related needs that have not been or will not be met by governmental agencies or any other organizations which have programs to address such needs; however, the fund is not intended to replace or supersede these programs. For example, if assistance is available from another source, including the Individual and Family Grant program and government-sponsored disaster loan assistance, then money from the Cora Brown Fund will not be available to the applicant for the same purpose. Listed below are the general categories of assistance which can be provided by the Cora Brown Fund:

(1) Disaster-related home repair and rebuilding assistance to families for permanent housing purposes, including site acquisition and development, relocation of residences out of hazardous areas, assistance with costs associated with temporary housing or permanent rehousing (e.g., utility deposits, access, transportation, connection of utilities, etc.);

(2) Disaster-related unmet needs of families who are unable to obtain adequate assistance under the Act or from other sources. Such assistance may include but is not limited to: health and safety measures; evacuation costs; assistance delineated in the Act or other Federal, State, local, or volunteer programs; hazard mitigation or floodplain management purposes; and assistance to self-employed persons (with no employees) to reestablish their businesses; and

(3) Other services which alleviate human suffering and promote the well being of disaster victims. For example, services to the elderly, to children, or to handicapped persons, such as transportation, recreational programs, provision of special ramps, or hospital or home visiting services. The funds may be provided to individual disaster victims, or to benefit a group of disaster victims.

(c) *Conditions for use of the Cora Brown Fund.* (1) The Cora Brown Fund is available only when the President declares that a major disaster or emergency exists under the Act, only in areas designated as eligible for Federal disaster assistance through notice in the FEDERAL REGISTER, and only at the discretion of the Assistant Administrator for the Disaster Assistance Directorate. The fund is limited to the initial endowment plus accrued interest, and this assistance program will cease when the fund is used up.

(2) A disaster victim normally will receive no more than $2,000 from this fund in any one declared disaster unless the Assistant Administrator for the Disaster Assistance Directorate determines that a larger amount is in the best interest of the disaster victim and

the Federal Government. Funds to provide service which benefit a group may be awarded in an amount determined by the Assistant Administrator for the Disaster Assistance Directorate, based on the Regional Administrator 's recommendation.

(3) The fund may not be used in a way that is inconsistent with other federally mandated disaster assistance or insurance programs, or to modify other generally applicable requirements.

(4) Funds awarded to a disaster victim may be provided by FEMA jointly to the disaster victim and to a State or local agency, or volunteer organization, to enable such an agent to assist in providing the approved assistance to an applicant. Example: Repair funds may be provided jointly to an applicant and the Mennonite Disaster Service, who will coordinate the purchase of supplies and provide the labor.

(5) Money from this fund will not duplicate assistance for which a person is eligible from other sources.

(6) In order to comply with the Flood Disaster Protection Act of 1973 (Pub. L. 93–234), as amended, any award for acquisition or construction purposes shall carry a requirement that any adequate flood insurance policy be purchased and maintained. The Assistant Administrator for the Disaster Assistance Directorate shall determine what is adequate based on the purpose of the award.

(7) The fund shall be administered in an equitable and impartial manner without discrimination on the grounds of race, color, religion, national origin, sex, age, or economic status.

(8) Funds awarded to a disaster victim from this fund may be combined with funds from other sources.

(d) *Administrative procedures.* (1) The Assistant Administrator for the Disaster Assistance Directorate, shall be responsible for awarding funds and authorizing disbursement.

(2) The Chief Financial Officer shall be responsible for fund accountability and, in coordination with the Assistant Administrator for the Disaster Assistance Directorate, for liaison with the Department of the Treasury concerning the investment of excess

money in the fund pursuant to the provisions contained in section 601 of the Act.

(3) Each FEMA Regional Administrator may submit requests to the Assistant Administrator for the Disaster Assistance Directorate on a disaster victim's behalf by providing documentation describing the needs of the disaster victim, a verification of the disaster victim's claim, a record of other assistance which has been or will be available for the same purpose, and his/her recommendation as to the items and the amount. The Assistant Administrator for the Disaster Assistance Directorate shall review the facts and make a determination. If the award amount is below $2,000, the Assistant Administrator for the Disaster Assistance Directorate may appoint a designee to have approval authority; approval authority of $2,000 or above shall be retained by the Assistant Administrator for the Disaster Assistance Directorate. The Assistant Administrator for the Disaster Assistance Directorate shall notify the Chief Financial Officer of a decision for approval, and the Chief Financial Officer shall order a check to be sent to the disaster victim (or jointly to the disaster victim and an assistance organization), through the Regional Administrator. The Assistant Administrator for the Disaster Assistance Directorate shall also notify the Regional Administrator of the decision, whether for approval or disapproval. The Regional Administrator shall notify the disaster victim in writing, identify any award as assistance from the Cora Brown Fund, and advise the recipient of appeal procedures.

(4) If the award is to be for a service to a group of disaster victims, the Regional Administrator shall submit his/her recommendation and supporting documentation to the Assistant Administrator for the Disaster Assistance Directorate (or his/her designee if the award is below $2,000), who shall review the information and make a determination. In cases of approval, the Assistant Administrator for the Disaster Assistance Directorate shall request the Chief Financial Officer to send a check to the intended recipient or provider, as appropriate. The Assistant

Administrator for the Disaster Assistance Directorate shall notify the Regional Administrator of the decision. The Regional Administrator shall notify a representative of the group in writing.

(5) The Chief Financial Officer shall process requests for checks, shall keep records of disbursements and balances in the account, and shall provide the Assistant Administrator for the Disaster Assistance Directorate with quarterly reports.

(e) *Audits.* The Inspector General of DHS may audit the use of money in this account to determine whether the funds are being administered according to these regulations and whether the financial management of the account is adequate. The Inspector General shall provide his/her findings to the Administrator, for information, comments and appropriate action. A copy shall be provided to the Chief Financial Officer for the same purpose.

§§ 206.182–206.190 [Reserved]

§ 206.191 Duplication of benefits.

(a) *Purpose.* This section establishes the policies for implementing section 312 of the Stafford Act, entitled Duplication of Benefits. This section relates to assistance for individuals and families.

(b) *Government policy.* (1) Federal agencies providing disaster assistance under the Act or under their own authorities triggered by the Act, shall cooperate to prevent and rectify duplication of benefits, according to the general policy guidance of the Federal Emergency Management Agency. The agencies shall establish appropriate agency policies and procedures to prevent duplication of benefits.

(2) Major disaster and emergency assistance provided to individuals and families under the Act, and comparable disaster assistance provided by States, local governments, and disaster assistance organizations, is not considered as income or a resource when determining eligibility for or benefit levels under federally funded income assistance or resource-tested programs. Examples of federally funded income assistance or resource-tested programs are the food

stamp program and welfare assistance programs.

(c) *FEMA policy.* It is FEMA policy:

(1) To prevent duplication of benefits between its own programs and insurance benefits, and between its own programs and other disaster assistance. Assistance under the Act may be provided in instances where the applicant has not received other benefits to which he/she may be entitled by the time of application and if the applicant agrees to repay all duplicated assistance to the agency providing the Federal assistance;

(2) To examine a debt resulting from duplication to determine that the likelihood of collecting the debt and the best interests of the Federal Government justify taking the necessary recovery actions to remedy duplication which has occurred when other assistance has become available;

(3) To assure uniformity in preventing duplication of benefits, by consulting with other Federal agencies and by performing selected quality control reviews, that the other disaster relief agencies establish and follow policies and procedures to prevent and remedy duplication among their programs, other programs, and insurance benefits; and

(4) To coordinate the effort of agencies providing assistance so that each agency understands the prevention and remedial policies of the others and is able to fulfill its own responsibilities regarding duplication of benefits.

(d) *Guidance to prevent duplication of benefits.* (1) Delivery sequence. FEMA provides the following policy and procedural guidance to ensure uniformity in preventing duplication of benefits.

(i) Duplication occurs when an agency has provided assistance which was the primary responsibility of another agency, and the agency with primary responsibility later provides assistance. A delivery sequence establishes the order in which disaster relief agencies and organizations provide assistance. The specific sequence, in accordance with the mandates of the assistance programs, is to be generally followed in the delivery of assistance.

(ii) When the delivery sequence has been disrupted, the disrupting agency is responsible for rectifying the dupli-

cation. The delivery sequence pertains to that period of time in the recovery phase when most of the traditional disaster assistance programs are available.

(2) The delivery sequence is, in order of delivery:

(i) Volunteer agencies' emergency assistance (except expendable items such as clothes, linens, and basic kitchenware); insurance (including flood insurance);

(ii) Housing assistance pursuant to section 408 of the Stafford Act.

(iii) Small Business Administration and Farmers Home Administration disaster loans;

(iv) Other Needs assistance, pursuant to section 408 of the Stafford Act or its predecessor program, the Individual and Family Grant Program.

(v) Volunteer agencies' "additional assistance" programs; and

(vi) The "Cora Brown Fund."

(3) Two significant points about the delivery sequence are that:

(i) Each assistance agency should, in turn, offer and be responsible for delivering assistance without regard to duplication with a program later in the sequence; and

(ii) The sequence itself determines what types of assistance can duplicate other assistance (i.e., a Federal program can duplicate insurance benefits, however, insurance benefits cannot duplicate the Federal assistance). An agency's position in the sequence determines the order in which it should provide assistance and what other resources it must consider before it does so.

(4) If following the delivery sequence concept would adversely affect the timely receipt of essential assistance by a disaster victim, an agency may offer assistance which is the primary responsibility of another agency. There also may be cases when an agency (Agency B) delivers assistance which is normally the primary responsibility of another agency (Agency A) because Agency A has, for good cause, denied assistance. After the assistance is delivered, Agency A reopens the case. If the primary response Agency A then provides assistance, that Agency A is responsible for coordinating with Agency B to either:

447

(i) Assist Agency B in preventing the duplication of benefits, or

(ii) In the case where the disaster victim has refused assistance from Agency A, notify Agency B that it must recover assistance previously provided.

(e) *Program guidance*—(1) *Programs under the Act vs. other agency assistance.*
(i) In making an eligibility determination, the FEMA Regional Administrator, in the case of federally operated programs, or the State, in the case of State operated programs, shall determine whether assistance is the primary responsibility of another agency to provide, according to the delivery sequence; and determine whether that primary response agency can provide assistance in a timely way.

(ii) If it is determined that timely assistance can be provided by the agency with primary responsibility, refrain from providing assistance under the Act. If it is determined that assistance from the agency with primary responsibility will be delayed, assistance under the Act may be provided, but then must be recovered from the applicant when the other assistance becomes available.

(2) *Programs under the Act vs. insurance.* In making an eligibility determination, the FEMA Regional Administrator or State shall:

(i) Remind the applicant about his/her responsibility to pursue an adequate settlement. The applicant must provide information concerning insurance recoveries.

(ii) Determine whether the applicant's insurance settlement will be sufficient to cover the loss or need without disaster assistance; and

(iii) Determine whether insurance benefits (including flood insurance) will be provided in a timely way. Where flood insurance is involved, the Regional Administrator shall coordinate with the Federal Insurance Administration. The purpose of this coordination is to obtain information about flood insurance coverage and settlements.

(3) *Random sample.* Each disaster assistance agency is responsible for preventing and rectifying duplication of benefits under the coordination of the Federal Coordinating Officer (FCO) and the general authority of section 312. To

determine whether duplication has occurred and established procedures have been followed, the Regional Administrator shall, within 90 days after the close of the disaster assistance programs application period, for selected disaster declarations, examine on a random sample basis, FEMA's and other government and voluntary agencies' case files and document the findings in writing.

(4) *Duplication when assistance under the Act is involved.* If duplication is discovered, the Regional Administrator shall determine whether the duplicating agency followed its own remedial procedures.

(i) If the duplicating agency followed its procedures and was successful in correcting the duplication, the Regional Administrator will take no further action. If the agency was not successful in correcting the duplication, and the Regional Administrator is satisfied that the duplicating agency followed its remedial procedures, no further action will be taken.

(ii) If the duplicating agency did not follow its duplication of benefits procedures, or the Regional Administrator is not satisfied that the procedures were followed in an acceptable manner, then the Regional Administrator shall provide an opportunity for the agency to take the required corrective action. If the agency cannot fulfill its responsibilities for remedial action, the Regional Administrator shall notify the recipient of the excess assistance, and after examining the debt, if it is determined that the likelihood of collecting the debt and the best interests of the Federal Government justify taking the necessary recovery actions, then take those recovery actions in conjunction with agency representatives for each identified case in the random sample (or larger universe, at the Regional Administrator's discretion).

(5) *Duplication when assistance under other authorities is involved.* When the random sample shows evidence that duplication has occurred and corrective action is required, the Regional Administrator and the FCO shall urge the duplicating agency to follow its own procedures to take corrective action, and shall work with the agency toward that end. Under his/her authority in section

Federal Emergency Management Agency, DHS

§ 206.201

312, the Regional Administrator shall require the duplicating agency to report to him/her on its attempt to correct the duplications identified in the sample.

(f) *Recovering FEMA funds: debt collection.* Funds due to FEMA are recovered in accordance with the Department of Homeland Security's Debt Collection Regulations (6 CFR part 11—Claims).

[54 FR 11615, Mar. 21, 1989, as amended at 67 FR 61460, Sept. 30, 2002; 74 FR 15350, Apr. 3, 2009]

§§ 206.192–206.199   [Reserved]

Subpart G—Public Assistance Project Administration

SOURCE: 55 FR 2304, Jan. 23, 1990, unless otherwise noted.

§ 206.200   General.

(a) *Purpose.* This subpart establishes procedures for the administration of Public Assistance grants approved under the provisions of the Stafford Act.

(b) *What policies apply to FEMA public assistance grants?* (1) The Stafford Act requires that we deliver eligible assistance as quickly and efficiently as possible consistent with Federal laws and regulations. We expect the Grantee and the subgrantee to adhere to Stafford Act requirements and to these regulations when administering our public assistance grants.

(2) The regulations entitled "Uniform Requirements for Grants and Cooperative Agreements to State and Local Governments," published at 44 CFR part 13, place requirements on the State in its role as Grantee and gives the Grantee discretion to administer federal programs under their own procedures. We expect the Grantee to:

(i) Inform subgrantees about the status of their applications, including notifications of our approvals of Project Worksheets and our estimates of when we will make payments;

(ii) Pay the full amounts due to subgrantees as soon as practicable after we approve payment, including the State contribution required in the FEMA-State Agreement; and

(iii) Pay the State contribution consistent with State laws.

[55 FR 2304, Jan. 23, 1990, as amended at 63 FR 64425, Nov. 20, 1998; 64 FR 55160, Oct. 12, 1999]

§ 206.201   Definitions used in this subpart.

(a) *Applicant* means a State agency, local government, or eligible private nonprofit organization, as identified in Subpart H of this regulation, submitting an application to the Grantee for assistance under the State's grant.

(b) *Emergency work* means that work which must be done immediately to save lives and to protect improved property and public health and safety, or to avert or lessen the threat of a major disaster.

(c) *Facility* means any publicly or privately owned building, works, system, or equipment, built or manufactured, or an improved and maintained natural feature. Land used for agricultural purposes is not a facility.

(d) *Grant* means an award of financial assistance. The grant award shall be based on the total eligible Federal share of all approved projects.

(e) *Grantee.* Grantee means the government to which a grant is awarded, and which is accountable for the use of the funds provided. The grantee is the entire legal entity even if only a particular component of the entity is designated in the grant award document. Generally, except as provided in § 206.202(f), the State for which the emergency or major disaster is declared is the grantee. However, an Indian Tribal government may choose to be a grantee, or it may act as a subgrantee under the State. If an Indian Tribal government is the grantee, it will assume the responsibilities of the "grantee" or "State" as described in this part with respect to administration of the Public Assistance program.

(f) *Hazard mitigation* means any cost effective measure which will reduce the potential for damage to a facility from a disaster event.

(g) *Host-State.* A State or Indian Tribal government that by agreement with

449

FEMA provides sheltering and/or evacuation support to evacuees from an impact-State. An Indian Tribal government may also be referred to as a "Host-Tribe."

(h) *Impact-State.* The State for which the President has declared an emergency or major disaster and that, due to a need to evacuate and/or shelter affected individuals outside the State, requests such assistance from FEMA pursuant to § 206.208.

(i) *Indian Tribal government* means any federally recognized governing body of an Indian or Alaska Native Tribe, band, nation, pueblo, village, or community that the Secretary of the Interior acknowledges to exist as an Indian Tribe under the Federally Recognized Tribe List Act of 1994, 25 U.S.C. 479a. This does not include Alaska Native corporations, the ownership of which is vested in private individuals.

(j) *Permanent work* means that restorative work that must be performed through repairs or replacement, to restore an eligible facility on the basis of its predisaster design and current applicable standards.

(k) *Predisaster design* means the size or capacity of a facility as originally designed and constructed or subsequently modified by changes or additions to the original design. It does not mean the capacity at which the facility was being used at the time the major disaster occurred if different from the most recent designed capacity.

(l) A *project* is a logical grouping of work required as a result of the declared major disaster or emergency. The scope of work and cost estimate for a project are documented on a Project Worksheet (FEMA Form 90–91).

(1) We must approve a scope of eligible work and an itemized cost estimate before funding a project.

(2) A project may include eligible work at several sites.

(m) *Project approval* means the process in which the Regional Administrator, or designee, reviews and signs an approval of work and costs on a Project Worksheet or on a batch of Project Worksheets. Such approval is also an obligation of funds to the Grantee.

(n) *Subgrant* means an award of financial assistance under a grant by a grantee to an eligible subgrantee.

(o) *Subgrantee* means the government or other legal entity to which a subgrant is awarded and which is accountable to the grantee for the use of the funds provided.

[55 FR 2304, Jan. 23, 1990, as amended at 63 FR 64425, Nov. 20, 1998; 64 FR 55160, Oct. 12, 1999; 74 FR 60213, Nov. 20, 2009]

§ 206.202 Application procedures.

(a) *General.* This section describes the policies and procedures that we use to process public assistance grants to States. Under this section the State is the Grantee. As Grantee you are responsible for processing subgrants to applicants under 44 CFR parts 13 and 206, and your own policies and procedures.

(b) *Grantee.* You are the grant administrator for all funds provided under the Public Assistance grant program. Your responsibilities under this section include:

(1) Providing technical advice and assistance to eligible subgrantees;

(2) Providing State support for project identification activities to include small and large project formulation and the validation of small projects;

(3) Ensuring that all potential applicants are aware of available public assistance; and

(4) Submitting documents necessary for the award of grants.

(c) *Request for Public Assistance (Request).* The Grantee must send a completed *Request* (FEMA Form 90–49) to the Regional Administrator for each applicant who requests public assistance. You must send *Requests* to the Regional Administrator within 30 days after designation of the area where the damage occurred.

(d) *Project Worksheets.* (1) An applicant's authorized local representative is responsible for representing the applicant and for ensuring that the applicant has identified all eligible work and submitted all costs for disaster-related damages for funding.

(i) We or the applicant, assisted by the State as appropriate, will prepare a Project Worksheet (FEMA Form 90–91) for each project. The Project Worksheet must identify the eligible scope of work and must include a quantitative estimate for the eligible work.

(ii) The applicant will have 60 days following its first substantive meeting with us to identify and to report damage to us.

(2) When the estimated cost of work on a project is less than $1,000, that work is not eligible and we will not approve a Project Worksheet for the project. Periodically we will review this minimum approval amount for a Project Worksheet and, if needed, will adjust the amount by regulation.

(e) *Grant approval.* (1) Before we obligate any funds to the State, the Grantee must complete and send to the Regional Administrator a Standard Form (SF) 424, Application for Federal Assistance, and a SF 424D, Assurances for Construction Programs. After we receive the SF 424 and SF 424D, the Regional Administrator will obligate funds to the Grantee based on the approved Project Worksheets. The Grantee will then approve subgrants based on the Project Worksheets approved for each applicant.

(2) When the applicant submits the Project Worksheets, we will have 45 days to obligate Federal funds. If we have a delay beyond 45 days we will explain the delay to the Grantee.

(f) *Exceptions.* The following are exceptions to the procedures and time limitations outlined in this section.

(1) *Host-State Evacuation and/or Sheltering.* (i) *General.* A grant to a host-State for sheltering and/or evacuation support is available under this section when an impact-State requests direct Federal assistance for sheltering and/or evacuation support pursuant to §206.208. To receive this grant, a host-State must enter into a FEMA–Host-State Agreement, amend its State Administrative Plan pursuant to §206.207, and submit a Standard Form SF424 *Application for Federal Assistance* directly to FEMA to apply for reimbursement of eligible costs for evacuating and/or sheltering individuals from an impact-State. Upon award, the host-State assumes the responsibilities of the "grantee" or "State" under this part with respect to its grant award.

(ii) *Force Account Labor Costs.* For the performance of eligible evacuation and sheltering support under sections 403 or 502 of the Stafford Act, the straight-time salaries and benefits of a host-State's permanently employed personnel are eligible for reimbursement. This is an exception to §206.228(a)(2).

(2) *Time limitations.* The Regional Administrator may extend the time limitations shown in paragraphs (c) and (d) of this section when the Grantees justifies and makes a request in writing. The justification must be based on extenuating circumstances beyond the grantee's or subgrantee's control.

[64 FR 55160, Oct. 12, 1999, as amended at 74 FR 15350, Apr. 3, 2009; 74 FR 60213, Nov. 20, 2009]

§ 206.203 Federal grant assistance.

(a) *General.* This section describes the types and extent of Federal funding available under State disaster assistance grants, as well as limitations and special procedures applicable to each.

(b) *Cost sharing.* All projects approved under State disaster assistance grants will be subject to the cost sharing provisions established in the FEMA-State Agreement and the Stafford Act.

(c) *Project funding*—(1) *Large projects.* When the approved estimate of eligible costs for an individual project is $35,000 or greater, Federal funding shall equal the Federal share of the actual eligible costs documented by a grantee. Such $35,000 amount shall be adjusted annually to reflect changes in the Consumer Price Index for All Urban Consumers published by the Department of Labor.

(2) *Small projects.* When the approved estimate of costs for an individual project is less than $35,000, Federal funding shall equal the Federal share of the approved estimate of eligible costs. Such $35,000 amount shall be adjusted annually as indicated in paragraph (c)(1) of this section.

(d) *Funding options*—(1) *Improved projects.* If a subgrantee desires to make improvements, but still restore the predisaster function of a damaged facility, the Grantee's approval must be obtained. Federal funding for such improved projects shall be limited to the Federal share of the approved estimate of eligible costs.

(2) *Alternate projects.* In any case where a subgrantee determines that the public welfare would not be best served by restoring a damaged public facility or the function of that facility, the Grantee may request that the Regional Administrator approve an alternate project.

(i) The alternate project option may be taken only on permanent restorative work.

(ii) Federal funding for alternate projects for damaged public facilities will be 90 percent of the Federal share of the Federal estimate of the cost of repairing, restoring, reconstructing, or replacing the facility and of management expenses.

(iii) Federal funding for alternate projects for damaged private nonprofit facilities will be 75 percent of the Federal share of the Federal estimate of the cost of repairing, restoring, reconstructing, or replacing the facility and of management expenses.

(iv) Funds contributed for alternate projects may be used to repair or expand other selected public facilities, to construct new facilities, or to fund hazard mitigation measures. These funds may not be used to pay the nonFederal share of any project, nor for any operating expense.

(v) Prior to the start of construction of any alternate project the Grantee shall submit for approval by the Regional Administrator the following: a description of the proposed alternate project(s); a schedule of work; and the projected cost of the project(s). The Grantee shall also provide the necessary assurances to document compliance with special requirements, including, but not limited to floodplain management, environmental assessment, hazard mitigation, protection of wetlands, and insurance.

[55 FR 2304, Jan. 23, 1990, as amended at 66 FR 22444, May 4, 2001; 73 FR 20551, Apr. 16, 2008]

§ 206.204 Project performance.

(a) *General.* This section describes the policies and procedures applicable during the performance of eligible work.

(b) *Advances of funds.* Advances of funds will be made in accordance with 44 CFR 13.21, Payment.

(c) *Time limitations for completion of work*—(1) *Deadlines.* The project completion deadlines shown below are set from the date that a major disaster or emergency is declared and apply to all projects approved under State disaster assistance grants.

COMPLETION DEADLINES

Type of work	Months
Debris clearance	6
Emergency work	6
Permanent work	18

(2) *Exceptions.* (i) The Grantee may impose lesser deadlines for the completion of work under paragraph (c)(1) of this section if considered appropriate.

(ii) Based on extenuating circumstances or unusual project requirements beyond the control of the subgrantee, the Grantee may extend the deadlines under paragraph (c)(1) of this section for an additional 6 months for debris clearance and emergency work and an additional 30 months, on a project by project basis for permanent work.

(d) *Requests for time extensions.* Requests for time extensions beyond the Grantee's authority shall be submitted by the Grantee to the Regional Administrator and shall include the following:

(1) The dates and provisions of all previous time extensions on the project; and

(2) A detailed justification for the delay and a projected completion date. The Regional Administrator shall review the request and make a determination. The Grantee shall be notified of the Regional Administrator's determination in writing. If the Regional Administrator approves the request, the letter shall reflect the approved completion date and any other requirements the Regional Administrator may determine necessary to ensure that the new completion date is met. If the Regional Administrator denies the time extension request, the grantee may, upon completion of the project, be reimbursed for eligible project costs incurred only up to the latest approved completion date. If the project is not completed, no Federal funding will be provided for that project.

(e) *Cost Overruns.* (1) During the execution of approved work a subgrantee may find that the actual project costs exceed the approved Project Worksheet estimates. Such cost overruns normally fall into the following three categories:

(i) Variations in unit prices;

(ii) Change in the scope of eligible work; or

(iii) Delays in timely starts or completion of eligible work.

(2) The subgrantee must evaluate each cost overrun and, when justified, submit a request for additional funding through the Grantee to the Regional Administrator for a final determination. All requests for the Regional Administrator's approval will contain sufficient documentation to support the eligibility of all claimed work and costs. The Grantee must include a written recommendation when forwarding the request. The Regional Administrator will notify the Grantee in writing of the final determination. FEMA will not normally review an overrun for an individual small project. The normal procedure for small projects will be that when a subgrantee discovers a significant overrun related to the total final cost for all small projects, the subgrantee may submit an appeal for additional funding in accordance with § 206.206, within 60 days following the completion of all its small projects.

(f) *Progress reports.* Progress reports will be submitted by the Grantee to the Regional Administrator quarterly. The Regional Administrator and Grantee shall negotiate the date for submission of the first report. Such reports will describe the status of those projects on which a final payment of the Federal share has not been made to the grantee and outline any problems or circumstances expected to result in noncompliance with the approved grant conditions.

[55 FR 2304, Jan. 23, 1990; 55 FR 5458, Feb. 15, 1990, as amended at 64 FR 55161, Oct. 12, 1999]

§ 206.205 Payment of claims.

(a) *Small Projects.* Final payment of the Federal share of these projects will be made to the Grantee upon approval of the Project Worksheet. The Grantee will make payment of the Federal share to the subgrantee as soon as practicable after Federal approval of funding. Before the closeout of the disaster contract, the Grantee must certify that all such projects were completed in accordance with FEMA approvals and that the State contribution to the non-Federal share, as specified in the FEMA-State Agreement, has been paid to each subgrantee. Such certification is not required to specify the amount spent by a subgrantee on small projects. The Federal payment for small projects shall not be reduced if all of the approved funds are not spent to complete a project. However, failure to complete a project may require that the Federal payment be refunded.

(b) *Large projects.* (1) The Grantee shall make an accounting to the Regional Administrator of eligible costs for each approved large project. In submitting the accounting the Grantee shall certify that reported costs were incurred in the performance of eligible work, that the approved work was completed, that the project is in compliance with the provisions of the FEMA-State Agreement, and that payments for that project have been made in accordance with 44 CFR 13.21, Payments. Each large project shall be submitted as soon as practicable after the subgrantee has completed the approved work and requested payment.

(2) The Regional Administrator shall review the accounting to determine the eligible amount of reimbursement for each large project and approve eligible costs. If a discrepancy between reported costs and approved funding exists, the Regional Administrator may conduct field reviews to gather additional information. If discrepancies in the claim cannot be resolved through a field review, a Federal audit may be conducted. If the Regional Administrator determines that eligible costs exceed the initial approval, he/she will obligate additional funds as necessary.

[55 FR 2304, Jan. 23, 1990, as amended at 64 FR 55161, Oct. 12, 1999]

§ 206.206 Appeals.

An eligible applicant, subgrantee, or grantee may appeal any determination previously made related to an application for or the provision of Federal assistance according to the procedures below.

(a) *Format and Content.* The applicant or subgrantee will make the appeal in writing through the grantee to the Regional Administrator. The grantee shall review and evaluate all subgrantee appeals before submission to the Regional Administrator. The grantee may make grantee-related appeals to the Regional Administrator. The appeal shall contain documented justification supporting the appellant's position, specifying the monetary figure in dispute and the provisions in Federal law, regulation, or policy with which the appellant believes the initial action was inconsistent.

(b) *Levels of Appeal.* (1) The Regional Administrator will consider first appeals for public assistance-related decisions under subparts A through L of this part.

(2) The Assistant Administrator for the Disaster Assistance Directorate will consider appeals of the Regional Administrator's decision on any first appeal under paragraph (b)(1) of this section.

(c) *Time Limits.* (1) Appellants must file appeals within 60 days after receipt of a notice of the action that is being appealed.

(2) The grantee will review and forward appeals from an applicant or subgrantee, with a written recommendation, to the Regional Administrator within 60 days of receipt.

(3) Within 90 days following receipt of an appeal, the Regional Administrator (for first appeals) or Assistant Administrator for the Disaster Assistance Directorate (for second appeals) will notify the grantee in writing of the disposition of the appeal or of the need for additional information. A request by the Regional Administrator or Assistant Administrator for the Disaster Assistance Directorate for additional information will include a date by which the information must be provided. Within 90 days following the receipt of the requested additional information or following expiration of the period for providing the information, the Regional Administrator or Assistant Administrator for the Disaster Assistance

Directorate will notify the grantee in writing of the disposition of the appeal. If the decision is to grant the appeal, the Regional Administrator will take appropriate implementing action.

(d) *Technical Advice.* In appeals involving highly technical issues, the Regional Administrator or Assistant Administrator for the Disaster Assistance Directorate may, at his or her discretion, submit the appeal to an independent scientific or technical person or group having expertise in the subject matter of the appeal for advice or recommendation. The period for this technical review may be in addition to other allotted time periods. Within 90 days of receipt of the report, the Regional Administrator or Assistant Administrator for the Disaster Assistance Directorate will notify the grantee in writing of the disposition of the appeal.

(e) *Transition.* (1) This rule is effective for all appeals pending on and appeals from decisions issued on or after May 8, 1998, except as provided in paragraph (e)(2) of this section.

(2) Appeals pending from a decision of an Assistant Administrator for the Disaster Assistance Directorate before May 8, 1998 may be appealed to the Administrator in accordance with 44 CFR 206.440 as it existed before May 8, 1998 (44 CFR, revised as of October 1, 1997).

(3) The decision of the FEMA official at the next higher appeal level shall be the final administrative decision of FEMA.

[63 FR 17110, Apr. 8, 1998; 63 FR 24970, May 6, 1998]

§ 206.207 Administrative and audit requirements.

(a) *General.* Uniform administrative requirements which are set forth in 44 CFR part 13 apply to all disaster assistance grants and subgrants.

(b) *State administrative plan.* (1) The State shall develop a plan for the administration of the Public Assistance program that includes at a minimum, the items listed below:

(i) The designation of the State agency or agencies which will have the responsibility for program administration.

(ii) The identification of staffing functions in the Public Assistance program, the sources of staff to fill these functions, and the management and oversight responsibilities of each.

(iii) Procedures for:

(A) Notifying potential applicants of the availability of the program;

(B) Conducting briefings for potential applicants and application procedures, program eligibility guidance and program deadlines;

(C) Assisting FEMA in determining applicant eligibility;

(D) Participating with FEMA in conducting damage surveys to serve as a basis for obligations of funds to subgrantees;

(E) Participating with FEMA in the establishment of hazard mitigation and insurance requirements;

(F) Processing appeal requests, requests for time extensions and requests for approval of overruns, and for processing appeals of grantee decisions;

(G) Compliance with the administrative requirements of 44 CFR parts 13 and 206;

(H) Compliance with the audit requirements of 44 CFR part 13;

(I) Processing requests for advances of funds and reimbursement; and

(J) Determining staffing and budgeting requirements necessary for proper program management.

(K) Determining the reasonable percentage or amount of pass-through funds for management costs provided under 44 CFR part 207 that the grantee will make available to subgrantees, and the basis, criteria, or formula for determining the subgrantee percentage or amount.

(2) The Grantee may request the Regional Administrator to provide technical assistance in the preparation of such administrative plan.

(3) In accordance with the Interim Rule published March 21, 1989, the Grantee was to have submitted an administrative plan to the RD for approval by September 18, 1989. An approved plan must be on file with FEMA before grants will be approved in a future major disaster. Thereafter, the Grantee shall submit a revised plan to the Regional Administrator annually. In each disaster for which Public Assistance is included, the Regional Administrator shall request the Grantee to prepare any amendments required to meet current policy guidance.

(4) The Grantee shall ensure that the approved administrative plan is incorporated into the State emergency plan.

(c) *Audit*—(1) *Nonfederal audit.* For grantees or subgrantees, requirements for nonfederal audit are contained in FEMA regulations at 44 CFR part 13 or OMB Circular A–110 as appropriate.

(2) *Federal audit.* In accordance with 44 CFR part 13, FEMA may elect to conduct a Federal audit of the disaster assistance grant or any of the subgrants.

[55 FR 2304, Jan. 23, 1990; 55 FR 5458, Feb. 15, 1990, as amended at 72 FR 57875, Oct. 11, 2007; 74 FR 15350, Apr. 3, 2009]

§ 206.208 **Direct Federal assistance.**

(a) *General.* When the State and local government lack the capability to perform or to contract for eligible emergency work and/or debris removal, under sections 402(1) and (4), 403, 407, 502(a)(1), (5) and (7) of the Act, the Grantee may request that the work be accomplished by a Federal agency. Such assistance is subject to the cost sharing provisions outlined in § 206.203(b) of this subpart. Direct Federal assistance is also subject to the eligibility criteria contained in Subpart H of these regulations. FEMA will reimburse other Federal agencies in accordance with Subpart A of these regulations.

(b) *Requests for assistance.* All requests for direct Federal assistance shall be submitted by the Grantee to the Regional Administrator and shall include:

(1) A written agreement that the State will:

(i) Provide without cost to the United States all lands, easements and rights-of-ways necessary to accomplish the approved work;

(ii) Hold and save the United States free from damages due to the requested work, and shall indemnify the Federal Government against any claims arising from such work;

(iii) Provide reimbursement to FEMA for the nonFederal share of the cost of such work in accordance with the provisions of the FEMA-State Agreement; and

(iv) Assist the performing Federal agency in all support and local jurisdictional matters.

(2) A statement as to the reasons the State and the local government cannot perform or contract for performance of the requested work.

(3) A written agreement from an eligible applicant that such applicant will be responsible for the items in subparagraph (b)(1) (i) and (ii) of this section, in the event that a State is legally unable to provide the written agreement.

(c) *Implementation.* (1) If the Regional Administrator approves the request, a mission assignment will be issued to the appropriate Federal agency. The mission assignment letter to the agency will define the scope of eligible work, the estimated cost of the eligible work and the billing period frequency. The Federal agency must not exceed the approved funding limit without the authorization of the Regional Administrator.

(2) If all or any part of the requested work falls within the statutory authority of another Federal agency, the Regional Administrator shall not approve that portion of the work. In such case, the unapproved portion of the request will be referred to the appropriate agency for action.

(3) If an impact-State requests assistance in providing evacuation and sheltering support outside an impact-State, FEMA may directly reimburse a host-State for such eligible costs through a grant to a host-State under an impact-State's declaration, consistent with § 206.202(f)(1). FEMA may award a grant to a host-State when FEMA determines that a host-State has sufficient capability to meet some or all of the sheltering and/or evacuation needs of an impact-State, and a host-State agrees in writing to provide such support to an impact-State.

(d) *Time limitation.* The time limitation for completion of work by a Federal agency under a mission assignment is 60 days after the President's declaration. Based on extenuating circumstances or unusual project requirements, the Regional Administrator may extend this time limitation.

(e) *Project management.* (1) The performing Federal agency shall ensure that the work is completed in accordance with the Regional Administrator's approved scope of work, costs and time limitations. The performing Fed-

eral agency shall also keep the Regional Administrator and Grantee advised of work progress and other project developments. It is the responsibility of the performing Federal agency to ensure compliance with applicable Federal, State and local legal requirements. A final inspection report will be completed upon termination of all direct Federal assistance work. Final inspection reports shall be signed by a representative of the performing Federal agency and the State. Once the final eligible cost is determined (including Federal agency overhead), the State will be billed for the nonFederal share of the mission assignment in accordance with the cost sharing provisions of the FEMA-State Agreement.

(2) Pursuant to the agreements provided in the request for assistance the Grantee shall assist the performing Federal agency in all State and local jurisdictional matters. These matters include securing local building permits and rights of entry, control of traffic and pedestrians, and compliance with local building ordinances.

[55 FR 2304, Jan. 23, 1990, as amended at 64 FR 55161, Oct. 12, 1999; 74 FR 60214, Nov. 20, 2009]

§ 206.209 Arbitration for Public Assistance determinations related to Hurricanes Katrina and Rita (Major disaster declarations DR–1603, DR–1604, DR–1605, DR–1606, and DR–1607).

(a) *Scope.* Pursuant to section 601 of the American Recovery and Reinvestment Act of 2009, Public Law 111–5, this section establishes procedures for arbitration to resolve disputed Public Assistance applications under the following major disaster declarations: DR–1603, DR–1604, DR–1605, DR–1606, and DR–1607.

(b) *Applicability.* An applicant or subgrantee (hereinafter "applicant" for purposes of this section) may request arbitration of a determination made by FEMA on an application for Public Assistance, provided that the total amount of the project is greater than $500,000, and provided that:

(1) the applicant is eligible to file an appeal under § 206.206; or

(2) the applicant had a first or second level appeal pending with FEMA pursuant to § 206.206 on or after February 17, 2009.

(c) *Governing rules.* An applicant that elects arbitration agrees to abide by this section and applicable guidance. The arbitration will be conducted pursuant to procedure established by the arbitration panel.

(d) *Limitations*—(1) *Election of remedies.* A request for arbitration under this section is in lieu of filing or continuing an appeal under § 206.206.

(2) *Final agency action under § 206.206.* Arbitration is not available for any matter that obtained final agency action by FEMA pursuant to § 206.206 prior to February 17, 2009. Arbitration is not available for determinations for which the applicant failed to file a timely appeal under the provisions of § 206.206 prior to August 31, 2009, or for determinations which received a decision on a second appeal from FEMA prior to February 17, 2009.

(e) *Request for arbitration*—(1) *Content of request.* The request for arbitration must contain a written statement and all documentation supporting the position of the applicant, the disaster number, and the name and address of the applicant's authorized representative or counsel.

(2) *Submission by the applicant to the Grantee, the FEMA Regional Administrator, and the arbitration administrator.* An applicant under paragraph (b)(1) of this section must submit its request for arbitration in writing simultaneously to the Grantee, the FEMA Regional Administrator, and the arbitration administrator within 30 calendar days after receipt of notice of the determination that is the subject of the arbitration request or by September 30, 2009, whichever is later. An applicant under paragraph (b)(2) of this section must make a request for arbitration in writing and, if FEMA has not issued a decision on the appeal, submit a withdrawal of the pending appeal, simultaneously to the Grantee, the FEMA Regional Administrator, and the arbitration administrator by October 30, 2009.

(3) *Submission by the Grantee to the arbitration administrator and FEMA.* Within 15 calendar days of receipt of the applicant's request for arbitration, the Grantee must forward the name and address of the Grantee's authorized representative or counsel, and may forward a written recommendation in support or opposition to the applicant's request for arbitration, simultaneously to the FEMA Regional Administrator, the arbitration administrator, and the applicant.

(4) *Submission of FEMA's response.* FEMA will submit a memorandum in support of its position, a copy of the Project Worksheet(s), and any other supporting information, as well as the name and address of its authorized representative or counsel, simultaneously to the arbitration administrator, the Grantee, and the applicant, within 30 calendar days of receipt of the applicant's request for arbitration.

(5) *Process for submissions.* When submitting a request for arbitration, the applicant should describe its claim with sufficient detail so that the circumstances of the dispute are clear to the arbitration panel. All papers, notices, or other documents submitted to the arbitration administrator under this section by the applicant, the Grantee, or FEMA will be served on each party's authorized representative or counsel. The submitting party will make such service by courier or overnight delivery service (such as Federal Express, DHL, United Parcel Service, or the United States Postal Service overnight delivery), addressed to the party, representative, or counsel, as applicable, at its last known address.

(f) *Selection of arbitration panel.* The arbitration administrator will select the arbitration panel for arbitration and notify the applicant, FEMA, and the Grantee of the names and identities of the arbitrators selected for the panel.

(g) *Preliminary conference.* The arbitration panel will hold a preliminary conference with the parties and/or representatives of the parties within 10 business days of the panel's receipt of FEMA's response to the request for arbitration. The panel and the parties will discuss the future conduct of the arbitration, including clarification of the disputed issues, request for disqualification of an arbitrator (if applicable), and any other preliminary matters. The date and place of any oral

457

hearing will be set at the preliminary conference. The preliminary conference will be conducted by telephone.

(h) *Hearing*—(1) *Request for hearing.* The panel will provide the applicant and FEMA with an opportunity to make an oral presentation on the substance of the applicant's claim in person, by telephone conference, or other means during which all the parties may simultaneously hear all other participants. If the applicant or FEMA would like to request an oral hearing, the request must be made no later than the preliminary conference.

(2) *Location of hearing.* If an in-person hearing is authorized, it will be held at a hearing facility of the arbitration panel's choosing.

(3) *Conduct of hearing.* Each party may present its position through oral presentations by individuals designated in advance of the hearing. These presentations may reference documents submitted pursuant to paragraph (e) of this section; the parties may not provide additional paper submissions at the hearing. If the panel deems it appropriate or necessary, it may request additional written materials from either or both parties or seek the advice or expertise of independent scientific or technical subject matter experts.

(4) *Closing of hearing.* The panel will inquire of each party whether it has any further argument. When satisfied that the record is complete, the panel will declare the hearing closed, unless a post-hearing submission of additional information or a memorandum of law is to be provided in accordance with this paragraph. The hearing will be declared closed as of the date set by the panel for the submission of the additional information or the memorandum of law.

(5) *Time limits.* The panel will endeavor to hold the hearing within 60 calendar days of the preliminary conference.

(6) *Postponement.* The arbitration panel may postpone a hearing upon agreement of the parties, or upon request of a party for good cause shown. Within 10 business days of the postponement, the arbitration panel will notify the parties of the rescheduled date of the hearing.

(7) *Record of the hearing.* There will be no recording of the hearing, unless a party specifically requests and arranges for such recording at its own expense.

(8) *Post-hearing submission of additional information.* A party may file with the arbitration panel additional information or a memorandum of law after the hearing upon the arbitration panel's request or upon the request of one of the parties with the panel's consent. The panel will set the time for submission of the additional information or the memorandum of law.

(9) *Reopening of hearing.* The hearing may be reopened on the panel's initiative under compelling circumstances at any time before the decision is made.

(i) *Review by the arbitration panel.* (1) *Determination of timeliness.* Upon notification by FEMA, or on its own initiative, the arbitration panel will determine whether the applicant timely filed a request for arbitration.

(2) *Substantive review.* The arbitration panel will consider all relevant written materials provided by the applicant, the Grantee, and FEMA, as well as oral presentations, if any. If the panel deems it appropriate or necessary, it may request additional written materials from either or both parties or seek the advice or expertise of independent scientific or technical subject matter experts.

(j) *Ex parte communications.* No party and no one acting on behalf of any party will engage in ex parte communications with a member of the arbitration panel. If a party or someone acting on behalf of any party engages in ex parte communications with a member of the arbitration panel, the party that engaged in such communication will provide a summary or a transcript of the entire communication to the other parties.

(k) *Decision*—(1) *Time limits.* The panel will make every effort to issue a written decision within 60 calendar days after the panel declares the hearing closed pursuant to paragraph (h)(4) of this section, or, if a hearing was not requested, within 60 calendar days following the receipt of FEMA's response to the request for arbitration. A decision of the panel may take longer than

60 calendar days if the arbitration involves a highly technical or complex matter.

(2) *Form and content.* The decision of the panel will be in writing and signed by each member of the panel. The panel will issue a reasoned decision that includes a brief and informal discussion of the factual and legal basis for the decision.

(3) *Finality of decision.* A decision of the majority of the panel shall constitute a final decision, binding on all parties. Final decisions are not subject to further administrative review. Final decisions are not subject to judicial review, except as permitted by 9 U.S.C. 10.

(4) *Delivery of decision.* Notice and delivery of the decision will be by facsimile or other electronic means and by regular mail to each party or its authorized representative or counsel.

(l) *Costs.* FEMA will pay the fees associated with the arbitration panel, the costs of any expert retained by the panel, and the arbitration facility costs, if any. The expenses for each party, including attorney's fees, representative fees, copying costs, costs associated with attending any hearing, or any other fees not listed in this paragraph will be paid by the party incurring such costs.

(m) *Guidance.* FEMA may issue separate guidance as necessary to supplement this section.

[FR 44767, Aug. 31, 2009]

§§ 206.210–206.219　[Reserved]

Subpart H—Public Assistance Eligibility

SOURCE: 55 FR 2307, Jan. 23, 1990, unless otherwise noted.

§ 206.220　General.

This subpart provides policies and procedures for determinations of eligibility of applicants for public assistance, eligibility of work, and eligibility of costs for assistance under sections 402, 403, 406, 407, 418, 419, 421(d), 502, and 503 of the Stafford Act. Assistance under this subpart must also conform to requirements of 44 CFR part 201, Mitigation Planning, and 44 CFR part 206, subparts G—Public Assistance Project Administration, I—Public Assistance Insurance Requirements, J—Coastal Barrier Resources Act, and M—Minimum Standards. Regulations under 44 CFR part 9—Floodplain Management and 44 CFR part 10—Environmental Considerations, also apply to this assistance.

[67 FR 8854, Feb. 26, 2002]

§ 206.221　Definitions.

(a) *Educational institution* means:

(1) Any elementary school as defined by section 801(c) of the Elementary and Secondary Education Act of 1965; or

(2) Any secondary school as defined by section 801(h) of the Elementary and Secondary Education Act of 1965; or

(3) Any institution of higher education as defined by section 1201 of the Higher Education Act of 1965.

(b) *Force account* means an applicant's own labor forces and equipment.

(c) *Immediate threat* means the threat of additional damage or destruction from an event which can reasonably be expected to occur within five years.

(d) *Improved property* means a structure, facility or item of equipment which was built, constructed or manufactured. Land used for agricultural purposes is not improved property.

(e) *Private nonprofit facility* means any private nonprofit educational, utility, emergency, medical, or custodial care facility, including a facility for the aged or disabled, and other facility providing essential governmental type services to the general public, and such facilities on Indian reservations. Further definition is as follows:

(1) *Educational facilities* means classrooms plus related supplies, equipment, machinery, and utilities of an educational institution necessary or appropriate for instructional, administrative, and support purposes, but does not include buildings, structures and related items used primarily for religious purposes or instruction.

(2) *Utility* means buildings, structures, or systems of energy, communication, water supply, sewage collection and treatment, or other similar public service facilities.

(3) *Irrigation facility* means those facilities that provide water for essential services of a governmental nature to

the general public. Irrigation facilities include water for fire suppression, generating and supplying electricity, and drinking water supply; they do not include water for agricultural purposes.

(4) *Emergency facility* means those buildings, structures, equipment, or systems used to provide emergency services, such as fire protection, ambulance, or rescue, to the general public, including the administrative and support facilities essential to the operation of such emergency facilities even if not contiguous.

(5) *Medical facility* means any hospital, outpatient facility, rehabilitation facility, or facility for long term care as such terms are defined in section 645 of the Public Health Service Act (42 U.S.C. 2910) and any similar facility offering diagnosis or treatment of mental or physical injury or disease, includng the administrative and support facilities essential to the operation of such medical facilities even if not contiguous.

(6) *Custodial care facility* means those buildings, structures, or systems including those for essential administration and support, which are used to provide institutional care for persons who require close supervision and some physical constraints on their daily activities for their self-protection, but do not require day-to-day medical care.

(7) *Other essential governmental service facility* means museums, zoos, community centers, libraries, homeless shelters, senior citizen centers, rehabilitation facilities, shelter workshops and facilities which provide health and safety services of a governmental nature. All such facilities must be open to the general public.

(f) *Private nonprofit organization* means any nongovernmental agency or entity that currently has:

(1) An effective ruling letter from the U.S. Internal Revenue Service, granting tax exemption under sections 501(c), (d), or (e) of the Internal Revenue Code of 1954, or

(2) Satisfactory evidence from the State that the nonrevenue producing organization or entity is a nonprofit one organized or doing business under State law.

(g) *Public entity* means an organization formed for a public purpose whose direction and funding are provided by one or more political subdivisions of the State.

(h) *Public facility* means the following facilities owned by a State or local government: any flood control, navigation, irrigation, reclamation, public power, sewage treatment and collection, water supply and distribution, watershed development, or airport facility; any non-Federal aid, street, road, or highway; and any other public building, structure, or system, including those used for educational, recreational, or cultural purposes; or any park.

(i) *Standards* means codes, specifications or standards required for the construction of facilities.

[55 FR 2307, Jan. 23, 1990, as amended at 58 FR 47994, Sept. 14, 1993; 66 FR 22445, May 4, 2001]

§ 206.222 Applicant eligibility.

The following entities are eligible to apply for assistance under the State public assistance grant:

(a) State and local governments.

(b) Private non-profit organizations or institutions which own or operate a private nonprofit facility as defined in § 205.221(e).

(c) Indian tribes or authorized tribal organizations and Alaska Native villages or organizations, but not Alaska Native Corporations, the ownership of which is vested in private individuals.

§ 206.223 General work eligibility.

(a) *General.* To be eligible for financial assistance, an item of work must:

(1) Be required as the result of the emergency or major disaster event;

(2) Be located within the designated area of a major disaster or emergency declaration, except that sheltering and evacuation activities may be located outside the designated area; and

(3) Be the legal responsibility of an eligible applicant.

(b) *Private nonprofit facilities.* To be eligible, all private nonprofit facilities must be owned and operated by an organization meeting the definition of a private nonprofit organization [see § 206.221(f)].

(c) *Public entities.* Facilities belonging to a public entity may be eligible for assistance when the application is submitted through the State or a political subdivision of the State.

(d) *Facilities serving a rural community or unincorporated town or village.* To be eligible for assistance, a facility not owned by an eligible applicant, as defined in § 206.222, must be owned by a private nonprofit organization; and provide an essential governmental service to the general public. Applications for these facilities must be submitted through a State or political subdivision of the State.

(e) *Negligence.* No assistance will be provided to an applicant for damages caused by its own negligence. If negligence by another party results in damages, assistance may be provided, but will be conditioned on agreement by the applicant to cooperate with FEMA in all efforts necessary to recover the cost of such assistance from the negligent party.

[55 FR 2307, Jan. 23, 1990, as amended at 71 FR 40027, July 14, 2006; 74 FR 60214, Nov. 20, 2009]

§ 206.224 Debris removal.

(a) *Public interest.* Upon determination that debris removal is in the public interest, the Regional Administrator may provide assistance for the removal of debris and wreckage from publicly and privately owned lands and waters. Such removal is in the public interest when it is necessary to:

(1) Eliminate immediate threats to life, public health, and safety; or

(2) Eliminate immediate threats of significant damage to improved public or private property; or

(3) Ensure economic recovery of the affected community to the benefit of the community-at-large; or

(4) Mitigate the risk to life and property by removing substantially damaged structures and associated appurtenances as needed to convert property acquired through a FEMA hazard mitigation program to uses compatible with open space, recreation, or wetlands management practices. Such removal must be completed within two years of the declaration date, unless the Assistant Administrator for the Disaster Assistance Directorate extends this period.

(b) *Debris removal from private property.* When it is in the public interest for an eligible applicant to remove debris from private property in urban, suburban and rural areas, including large lots, clearance of the living, recreational and working area is eligible except those areas used for crops and livestock or unused areas.

(c) *Assistance to individuals and private organizations.* No assistance will be provided directly to an individual or private organization, or to an eligible applicant for reimbursement of an individual or private organization, for the cost of removing debris from their own property. Exceptions to this are those private nonprofit organizations operating eligible facilities.

[55 FR 2307, Jan. 23, 1990, as amended at 66 FR 33901, June 26, 2001]

§ 206.225 Emergency work.

(a) *General.* (1) Emergency protective measures to save lives, to protect public health and safety, and to protect improved property are eligible.

(2) In determining whether emergency work is required, the Regional Administrator may require certification by local State, and/or Federal officials that a threat exists, including identification and evaluation of the threat and recommendations of the emergency work necessary to cope with the threat.

(3) In order to be eligible, emergency protective measures must:

(i) Eliminate or lessen immediate threats to live, public health or safety; or

(ii) Eliminate or lessen immediate threats of significant additional damage to improved public or private property through measures which are cost effective.

(b) *Emergency access.* An access facility that is not publicly owned or is not the direct responsibility of an eligible applicant for repair or maintenance may be eligible for emergency repairs or replacement provided that emergency repair or replacement of the facility economically eliminates the need for temporary housing. The work will be limited to that necessary for the access to remain passable through

461

events which can be considered an immediate threat. The work must be performed by an eligible applicant and will be subject to cost sharing requirements.

(c) *Emergency communications.* Emergency communications necessary for the purpose of carrying out disaster relief functions may be established and may be made available to State and local government officials as deemed appropriate. Such communications are intended to supplement but not replace normal communications that remain operable after a major disaster. FEMA funding for such communications will be discontinued as soon as the needs have been met.

(d) *Emergency public transportation.* Emergency public transportation to meet emergency needs and to provide transportation to public places and such other places as necessary for the community to resume its normal pattern of life as soon as possible is eligible. Such transportation is intended to supplement but not replace predisaster transportation facilities that remain operable after a major disaster. FEMA funding for such transportation will be discontinued as soon as the needs have been met.

§ 206.226 Restoration of damaged facilities.

Work to restore eligible facilities on the basis of the design of such facilities as they existed immediately prior to the disaster and in conformity with the following is eligible:

(a) *Assistance under other Federal agency (OFA) programs.* (1) Generally, disaster assistance will not be made available under the Stafford Act when another Federal agency has specific authority to restore facilities damaged or destroyed by an event which is declared a major disaster.

(2) An exception to the policy described in paragraph (a)(1) of this section exists for public elementary and secondary school facilities which are otherwise eligible for assistance from the Department of Education (ED) under 20 U.S.C. 241-1 and 20 U.S.C. 646. Such facilities are also eligible for assistance from FEMA under the Stafford Act, and grantees shall accept applica-

tions from local educational agencies for assistance under the Stafford Act.

(3) The exception does not cover payment of increased current operating expenses or replacement of lost revenues as provided in 20 U.S.C. 241-1(a) and implemented by 34 CFR 219.14. Such assistance shall continue to be granted and administered by the Department of Education.

(b) *Mitigation planning.* In order to receive assistance under this section, the State or Indian Tribal government applying to FEMA as a grantee must have in place a FEMA approved State or Tribal Mitigation Plan, as applicable, in accordance with 44 CFR part 201.

(c) *Private nonprofit facilities.* Eligible private nonprofit facilities may receive funding under the following conditions:

(1) The facility provides critical services, which include power, water (including water provided by an irrigation organization or facility in accordance with § 206.221(e)(3)), sewer services, wastewater treatment, communications, emergency medical care, fire department services, emergency rescue, and nursing homes; or

(2) The private nonprofit organization not falling within the criteria of § 206.226(c)(1) has applied for a disaster loan under section 7(b) of the Small Business Act (15 U.S.C.636(b)) and

(i) The Small Business Administration has declined the organization's application; or

(ii) Has eligible damages greater than the maximum amount of the loan for which it is eligible, in which case the excess damages are eligible for FEMA assistance.

(d) *Standards.* For the costs of Federal, State, and local repair or replacement standards which change the predisaster construction of facility to be eligible, the standards must:

(1) Apply to the type of repair or restoration required;

(Standards may be different for new construction and repair work)

(2) Be appropriate to the predisaster use of the facility;

(3)(i) Be found reasonable, in writing, and formally adopted and implemented by the State or local government on or before the disaster declaration date or be a legal Federal requirement applicable to the type of restoration.

(ii) This paragraph (d) applies to local governments on January 1, 1999 and to States on January 1, 2000. Until the respective applicability dates, the standards must be in writing and formally adopted by the applicant prior to project approval or be a legal Federal or State requirement applicable to the type of restoration.

(4) Apply uniformly to all similar types of facilities within the jurisdiction of owner of the facility; and

(5) For any standard in effect at the time of a disaster, it must have been enforced during the time it was in effect.

(e) *Hazard mitigation.* In approving grant assistance for restoration of facilities, the Regional Administrator may require cost effective hazard mitigation measures not required by applicable standards. The cost of any requirements for hazard mitigation placed on restoration projects by FEMA will be an eligible cost for FEMA assistance.

(f) *Repair vs. replacement.* (1) A facility is considered repairable when disaster damages do not exceed 50 percent of the cost of replacing a facility to its predisaster condition, and it is feasible to repair the facility so that it can perform the function for which it was being used as well as it did immediately prior to the disaster.

(2) If a damaged facility is not repairable in accordance with paragraph (d)(1) of this section, approved restorative work may include replacement of the facility. The applicant may elect to perform repairs to the facility, in lieu of replacement, if such work is in conformity with applicable standards. However, eligible costs shall be limited to the less expensive of repairs or replacement.

(3) An exception to the limitation in paragraph (d)(2) of this section may be allowed for facilities eligible for or on the National Register of Historic Properties. If an applicable standard requires repair in a certain manner, costs associated with that standard will be eligible.

(g) *Relocation.* (1) The Regional Administrator may approve funding for and require restoration of a destroyed facility at a new location when:

(i) The facility is and will be subject to repetitive heavy damage;

(ii) The approval is not barred by other provisions of title 44 CFR; and

(iii) The overall project, including all costs, is cost effective.

(2) When relocation is required by the Regional Administrator, eligible work includes land acquisition and ancillary facilities such as roads and utilities, in addition to work normally eligible as part of a facility reconstruction. Demolition and removal of the old facility is also an eligible cost.

(3) When relocation is required by the Regional Administrator, no future funding for repair or replacement of a facility at the original site will be approved, except those facilities which facilitate an open space use in accordance with 44 CFR part 9.

(4) When relocation is required by the Regional Administrator, and, instead of relocation, the applicant requests approval of an alternate project [see § 206.203(d)(2)], eligible costs will be limited to 90 percent of the estimate of restoration at the original location excluding hazard mitigation measures.

(5) If relocation of a facility is not feasible or cost effective, the Regional Administrator shall disapprove Federal funding for the original location when he/she determines in accordance with 44 CFR parts 9, 10, 201, or subpart M of this part 206, that restoration in the original location is not allowed. In such cases, an alternative project may be applied for.

(h) *Equipment and furnishings.* If equipment and furnishings are damaged beyond repair, comparable items are eligible as replacement items.

(i) *Library books and publications.* Replacement of library books and publications is based on an inventory of the quantities of various categories of books or publications damaged or destroyed. Cataloging and other work incidental to replacement are eligible.

(j) *Beaches.* (1) Replacement of sand on an unimproved natural beach is not eligible.

(2) Improved beaches. Work on an improved beach may be eligible under the following conditions:

(i) The beach was constructed by the placement of sand (of proper grain size) to a designed elevation, width, and slope; and

(ii) A maintenance program involving periodic renourishment of sand must have been established and adhered to by the applicant.

(k) *Restrictions*—(1) *Alternative use facilities.* If a facility was being used for purposes other than those for which it was designed, restoration will only be eligible to the extent necessary to restore the immediate predisaster alternate purpose.

(2) *Inactive facilities.* Facilities that were not in active use at the time of the disaster are not eligible except in those instances where the facilities were only temporarily inoperative for repairs or remodeling, or where active use by the applicant was firmly established in an approved budget or the owner can demonstrate to FEMA's satisfaction an intent to begin use within a reasonable time.

[55 FR 2307, Jan. 23, 1990, as amended at 58 FR 55022, Oct. 25, 1993; 63 FR 5897, Feb. 5, 1998; 66 FR 22445, May 4, 2001; 67 FR 8854, Feb. 26, 2002; 68 FR 61371, Oct. 28, 2003; 69 FR 55097, Sept. 13, 2004; 74 FR 15350, Apr. 3, 2009; 74 FR 47482, Sept. 16, 2009]

§ 206.227 Snow assistance.

Emergency or major disaster declarations based on snow or blizzard conditions will be made only for cases of record or near record snowstorms, as established by official government records. Federal assistance will be provided for all costs eligible under 44 CFR 206.225 for a specified period of time which will be determined by the circumstances of the event.

[62 FR 45330, Aug. 27, 1997]

§ 206.228 Allowable costs.

General policies for determining allowable costs are established in 44 CFR 13.22. Exceptions to those policies as allowed in 44 CFR 13.4 and 13.6 are explained below.

(a) *Eligible direct costs*—(1) *Applicant-owned equipment.* Reimbursement for ownership and operation costs of applicant-owned equipment used to perform eligible work shall be provided in accordance with the following guidelines:

(i) *Rates established under State guidelines.* In those cases where an applicant uses reasonable rates which have been established or approved under State guidelines, in its normal daily operations, reimbursement for applicant-owned equipment which has an hourly rate of $75 or less shall be based on such rates. Reimbursement for equipment which has an hourly rate in excess of $75 shall be determined on a case by case basis by FEMA.

(ii) *Rates established under local guidelines.* Where local guidelines are used to establish equipment rates, reimbursement will be based on those rates or rates in a Schedule of Equipment Rates published by FEMA, whichever is lower. If an applicant certifies that its locally established rates do not reflect actual costs, reimbursement may be based on the FEMA Schedule of Equipment Rates, but the applicant will be expected to provide documentation if requested. If an applicant wishes to claim an equipment rate which exceeds the FEMA Schedule, it must document the basis for that rate and obtain FEMA approval of an alternate rate.

(iii) *No established rates.* The FEMA Schedule of Equipment Rates will be the basis for reimbursement in all cases where an applicant does not have established equipment rates.

(2) *Force Account Labor Costs.* The straight- or regular-time salaries and benefits of a subgrantee's permanently employed personnel are not eligible in calculating the cost of eligible work under sections 403 and 407 of the Stafford Act, 42 U.S.C. 5170b and 5173. For the performance of eligible permanent restoration under section 406 of the Stafford Act, 42 U.S.C. 5172, straight-time salaries and benefits of a subgrantee's permanently employed personnel are eligible.

(3) Administrative and management costs for major disasters and emergencies will be paid in accordance with 44 CFR part 207.

(b) [Reserved]

[55 FR 2307, Jan. 23, 1990, as amended at 58 FR 47996, Sept. 14, 1993; 63 FR 64426, Nov. 20, 1998; 64 FR 55161, Oct. 12, 1999; 72 FR 57875, Oct. 11, 2007]

§§ 206.229–206.249 [Reserved]

Subpart I—Public Assistance Insurance Requirements

SOURCE: 56 FR 64560, Dec. 11, 1991, unless otherwise noted.

§ 206.250 General.

(a) Sections 311 and 406(d) of the Stafford Act, and the Flood Disaster Protection Act of 1973, Public Law 93–234, set forth certain insurance requirements which apply to disaster assistance provided by FEMA. The requirements of this subpart apply to all assistance provided pursuant to section 406 of the Stafford Act with respect to any major disaster declared by the President after November 23, 1988.

(b) Insurance requirements prescribed in this subpart shall apply equally to private nonprofit (PNP) facilities which receive assistance under section 406 of the Act. PNP organizations shall submit the necessary documentation and assurances required by this subpart to the Grantee.

(c) Actual and anticipated insurance recoveries shall be deducted from otherwise eligible costs, in accordance with this subpart.

(d) The full coverage available under the standard flood insurance policy from the National Flood Insurance Program (NFIP) will be subtracted from otherwise eligible costs for a building and its contents within the special flood hazard area in accordance with § 206.252.

(e) The insurance requirements of this subpart should not be interpreted as a substitute for various hazard mitigation techniques which may be available to reduce the incidence and severity of future damage.

§ 206.251 Definitions.

(a) *Assistance* means any form of a Federal grant under section 406 of the Stafford Act to replace, restore, repair, reconstruct, or construct any facility and/or its contents as a result of a major disaster.

(b) *Building* means a walled and roofed structure, other than a gas, or liquid storage tank, that is principally above ground and affixed to a permanent site, as well as a manufactured home on a permanent foundation.

(c) *Community* means any State or political subdivision thereof, or any Indian tribe or authorized tribal organization, or Alaskan Native Village or authorized native organization which has authority to adopt and enforce floodplain management regulations for the areas within its jurisdiction.

(d) *National Flood Insurance Program* (NFIP) means the program authorized by the National Flood Insurance Act of 1968, as amended, 42 U.S.C. 4001 *et seq.*

(e) *Special flood hazard area* means an area having special flood, mudslide, and/or flood-related erosion hazards, and shown on a Flood Hazard Boundary map (FHBM) or the Flood Insurance Rate Map (FIRM) issued by FEMA as Zone A, AO, A1–30, AE, A99, AH, VO, V1–30 VE, V, M, or E. "Special flood hazard area" is synonymous with "special hazard area", as defined in 44 CFR part 59.

(f) *Standard Flood Insurance Policy* means the flood insurance policy issued by the Federal Insurance Administrator, or by a Write-Your-Own Company pursuant to 44 CFR 62.23.

§ 206.252 Insurance requirements for facilities damaged by flood.

(a) Where an insurable building damaged by flooding is located in a special flood hazard area identified for more than one year by the Administrator, assistance pursuant to section 406 of the Stafford Act shall be reduced. The amount of the reduction shall be the maximum amount of the insurance proceeds which would have been received had the building and its contents been fully covered by a standard flood insurance policy.

(b) The reduction stated above shall not apply to a PNP facility which could not be insured because it was located in a community not participating in the NFIP. However, the provisions of the Flood Disaster Protection Act of 1973 prohibit approval of assistance for the PNP unless the community agrees to participate in the NFIP within six months after the major disaster declaration date, and the required flood insurance is purchased.

(c) Prior to approval of a Federal grant for the restoration of a facility and its contents which were damaged by a flood, the Grantee shall notify the Regional Administrator of any entitlement to an insurance settlement or recovery. The Regional Administrator shall reduce the eligible costs by the amount of insurance proceeds which the grantee receives.

(d) The grantee or subgrantee is required to obtain and maintain flood insurance in the amount of eligible disaster assistance, as a condition of receiving Federal assistance that may be available. This requirement also applies to insurable flood damaged facilities located outside a special flood hazard area when it is reasonably available, adequate, and necessary. However, the Regional Administrator shall not require greater types and amounts of insurance than are certified as reasonable by the State Insurance Commissioner. The requirement to purchase flood insurance is waived when eligible costs for an insurable facility do not exceed $5,000.

§ 206.253 Insurance requirements for facilities damaged by disasters other than flood.

(a) Prior to approval of a Federal grant for the restoration of a facility and its contents which were damaged by a disaster other than flood, the Grantee shall notify the Regional Administrator of any entitlement to insurance settlement or recovery for such facility and its contents. The Regional Administrator shall reduce the eligible costs by the actual amount of insurance proceeds relating to the eligible costs.

(b)(1) Assistance under section 406 of the Stafford Act will be approved only on the condition that the grantee obtain and maintain such types and amounts of insurance as are reasonable and necessary to protect against future loss to such property from the types of hazard which caused the major disaster. The extent of insurance to be required will be based on the eligible damage that was incurred to the damaged facility as a result of the major disaster. The Regional Administrator shall not require greater types and extent of insurance than are certified as

reasonable by the State Insurance Commissioner.

(2) Due to the high cost of insurance, some applicants may request to insure the damaged facilities under a blanket insurance policy covering all their facilities, an insurance pool arrangement, or some combination of these options. Such an arrangement may be accepted for other than flood damages. However, if the same facility is damaged in a similar future disaster, eligible costs will be reduced by the amount of eligible damage sustained on the previous disaster.

(c) The Regional Administrator shall notify the Grantee of the type and amount of insurance required. The grantee may request that the State Insurance Commissioner review the type and extent of insurance required to protect against future loss to a disaster-damaged facility, the Regional Administrator shall not require greater types and extent of insurance than are certified as reasonable by the State Insurance Commissioner.

(d) The requirements of section 311 of the Stafford Act are waived when eligible costs for an insurable facility do not exceed $5,000. The Regional Administrator may establish a higher waiver amount based on hazard mitigation initiatives which reduce the risk of future damages by a disaster similar to the one which resulted in the major disaster declaration which is the basis for the application for disaster assistance.

(e) The Grantee shall provide assurances that the required insurance coverage will be maintained for the anticipated life of the restorative work or the insured facility, whichever is the lesser.

(f) No assistance shall be provided under section 406 of the Stafford Act for any facility for which assistance was provided as a result of a previous major disaster unless all insurance required by FEMA as a condition of the previous assistance has been obtained and maintained.

§§ 206.254–206.339 [Reserved]

Subpart J—Coastal Barrier Resources Act

SOURCE: 55 FR 2311, Jan. 23, 1990, unless otherwise noted.

§ 206.340 Purpose of subpart.

This subpart implements the Coastal Barrier Resources Act (CBRA) (Pub. L. 97–348) as that statute applies to disaster relief granted to individuals and State and local governments under the Stafford Act. CBRA prohibits new expenditures and new financial assistance within the Coastal Barrier Resources System (CBRS) for all but a few types of activities identified in CBRA. This subpart specifies what actions may and may not be carried out within the CBRS. It establishes procedures for compliance with CBRA in the administration of disaster assistance by FEMA.

§ 206.341 Policy.

It shall be the policy of FEMA to achieve the goals of CBRA in carrying out disaster relief on units of the Coastal Barrier Resources System. It is FEMA's intent that such actions be consistent with the purpose of CBRA to minimize the loss of human life, the wasteful expenditure of Federal revenues, and the damage to fish, wildlife and other natural resources associated with coastal barriers along the Atlantic and Gulf coasts and to consider the means and measures by which the long-term conservation of these fish, wildlife, and other natural resources may be achieved under the Stafford Act.

§ 206.342 Definitions.

Except as otherwise provided in this subpart, the definitions set forth in part 206 of subchapter D are applicable to this subject.

(a) *Consultation* means that process by which FEMA informs the Secretary of the Interior through his/her designated agent of FEMA proposed disaster assistance actions on a designated unit of the Coastal Barrier Resources System and by which the Secretary makes comments to FEMA about the appropriateness of that ac-

tion. Approval by the Secretary is not required in order that an action be carried out.

(b) *Essential link* means that portion of a road, utility, or other facility originating outside of the system unit but providing access or service through the unit and for which no alternative route is reasonably available.

(c) *Existing facility* on a unit of CBRS established by Public Law 97–348 means a publicly owned or operated facility on which the start of a construction took place prior to October 18, 1982, and for which this fact can be adequately documented. In addition, a legally valid building permit or equivalent documentation, if required, must have been obtained for the construction prior to October 18, 1982. If a facility has been substantially improved or expanded since October 18, 1982, it is not an existing facility. For any other unit added to the CBRS by amendment to Public Law 97–348, the enactment date of such amendment is substituted for October 18, 1982, in this definition.

(d) *Expansion* means changing a facility to increase its capacity or size.

(e) *Facility* means "public facility" as defined in § 206.201. This includes any publicly owned flood control, navigation, irrigation, reclamation, public power, sewage treatment and collection, water supply and distribution, watershed development, or airport facility; and nonfederal-aid street, road, or highway; and any other public building, structure, or system, including those used for educational, recreational, or cultural purposes, or any park.

(f) *Financial assistance* means any form of Federal loan, grant guaranty, insurance, payment rebate, subsidy or any other form of direct or indirect Federal assistance.

(g) *New financial assistance* on a unit of the CBRS established by Public Law 97–348 means an approval by FEMA of a project application or other disaster assistance after October 18, 1982. For any other unit added to the CBRS by amendment to Public Law 97–348, the enactment date such amendment is substituted for October 18, 1982, in this definition.

(h) *Start of construction* for a structure means the first placement of permanent construction, such as the placement of footings or slabs or any work beyond the stage of excavation. Permanent construction for a structure does not include land preparation such as clearing, grading, and placement of fill, nor does it include excavation for a basement, footings, or piers. For a facility which is not a structure, start of construction means the first activity for permanent construction of a substantial part of the facility. Permanent construction for a facility does not include land preparation such as clearing and grubbing but would include excavation and placement of fill such as for a road.

(i) *Structure* means a walled and roofed building, including a gas or liquid storage tank, that is principally above ground, as well as a mobile home.

(j) *Substantial improvement* means any repair, reconstruction or other improvement of a structure or facility, that has been damaged in excess of, or the cost of which equals or exceeds, 50 percent of the market value of the structure or placement cost of the facility (including all "public facilities") as defined in the Stafford Act) either:

(1) Before the repair or improvement is started; or

(2) If the structure or facility has been damaged and is proposed to be restored, before the damage occurred. If a facility is a link in a larger system, the percentage of damage will be based on the relative cost of repairing the damaged facility to the replacement cost of that portion of the system which is operationally dependent on the facility. The term *substantial improvement* does not include any alternation of a structure or facility listed on the National Register of Historic Places or a State Inventory of Historic Places.

(k) *System unit* means any undeveloped coastal barrier, or combination of closely related undeveloped coastal barriers included within the Coastal Barrier Resources System as established by the section 4 of the CBRA, or as modified by the Secretary in accordance with that statute.

§ 206.343 Scope.

(a) The limitations on disaster assistance as set forth in this subpart apply only to FEMA actions taken on a unit of the Coastal Barrier Resources System or any conduit to such unit, including, but not limited to a bridge, causeway, utility, or similar facility.

(b) FEMA assistance having a social program orientation which is unrelated to development is not subject to the requirements of these regulations. This assistance includes:

(1) Individual and Family Grants that are not for acquisition or construction purposes;

(2) Crisis counseling;

(3) Disaster Legal services; and

(4) Disaster unemployment assistance.

§ 206.344 Limitations on Federal expenditures.

Except as provided in §§ 206.345 and 206.346, no new expenditures or financial assistance may be made available under authority of the Stafford Act for any purpose within the Coastal Barrier Resources System, including but not limited to:

(a) Construction, reconstruction, replacement, repair or purchase of any structure, appurtenance, facility or related infrastructure;

(b) Construction, reconstruction, replacement, repair or purchase of any road, airport, boat landing facility, or other facility on, or bridge or causeway to, any System unit; and

(c) Carrying out of any project to prevent the erosion of, or to otherwise stabilize, any inlet, shoreline, or inshore area, except that such assistance and expenditures may be made available on units designated pursuant to Section 4 on maps numbered S01 through S08 for purposes other than encouraging development and, in all units, in cases where an emergency threatens life, land, and property immediately adjacent to that unit.

§ 206.345 Exceptions.

The following types of disaster assistance actions are exceptions to the prohibitions of § 206.344.

(a) After consultation with the Secretary of the Interior, the Regional Administrator may make disaster assistance available within the CBRS for:

(1) Replacement, reconstruction, or repair, but not the expansion, of publicly owned or publicly operated roads, structures, or facilities that are essential links in a larger network or system;

(2) Repair of any facility necessary for the exploration, extraction, or transportation of energy resources which activity can be carried out only on, in, or adjacent to coastal water areas because the use or facility requires access to the coastal water body; and

(3) Restoration of existing channel improvements and related structures, such as jetties, and including the disposal of dredge materials related to such improvements.

(b) After consultation with the Secretary of the Interior, the Regional Administrator may make disaster assistance available within the CBRS for the following types of actions, provided such assistance is consistent with the purposes of CBRA;

(1) Emergency actions essential to the saving of lives and the protection of property and the public health and safety, if such actions are performed pursuant to sections 402, 403, and 502 of the Stafford Act and are limited to actions that are necessary to alleviate the impacts of the event;

(2) Replacement, reconstruction, or repair, but not the expansion, of publicly owned or publicly operated roads, structures, or facilities, except as provided in §206.347(c)(5);

(3) Repair of air and water navigation aids and devices, and of the access thereto;

(4) Repair of facilities for scientific research, including but not limited to aeronautical, atmospheric, space, geologic, marine, fish and wildlife and other research, development, and applications;

(5) Repair of facilities for the study, management, protection and enhancement of fish and wildlife resources and habitats, including but not limited to, acquisition of fish and wildlife habitats and related lands, stabilization projects for fish and wildlife habitats, and recreational projects; and

(6) Repair of nonstructural projects for shoreline stabilization that are designed to mimic, enhance, or restore natural stabilization systems.

§206.346 Applicability to disaster assistance.

(a) *Emergency assistance.* The Regional Administrator may approve assistance pursuant to sections 402, 403, or 502 of the Stafford Act, for emergency actions which are essential to the saving of lives and the protection of property and the public health and safety, are necessary to alleviate the emergency, and are in the public interest. Such actions include but are not limited to:

(1) Removal of debris from public property;

(2) Emergency protection measures to prevent loss of life, prevent damage to improved property and protect public health and safety;

(3) Emergency restoration of essential community services such as electricity, water or sewer;

(4) Provision of access to a private residence;

(5) Provision of emergency shelter by means of providing emergency repair of utilities, provision of heat in the season requiring heat, or provision of minimal cooking facilities;

(6) Relocation of individuals or property out of danger, such as moving a mobile home to an area outside of the CBRS (but disaster assistance funds may not be used to relocate facilities back into the CBRS);

(7) Home repairs to private owner-occupied primary residences to make them habitable;

(8) Housing eligible families in existing resources in the CBRS; and

(9) Mortgage and rental payment assistance.

(b) *Permanent restoration assistance.* Subject to the limitations set out below, the Regional Administrator may approve assistance for the repair, reconstruction, or replacement but not the expansion of the following publicly owned or operated facilities and certain private nonprofit facilities.

(1) Roads and bridges;

(2) Drainage structures, dams, levees;

469

(3) Buildings and equipment;

(4) Utilities (gas, electricity, water, etc.); and

(5) Park and recreational facilities.

§ 206.347 Requirements.

(a) *Location determination.* For each disaster assistance action which is proposed on the Atlantic or Gulf Coasts, the Regional Administrator shall:

(1) Review a proposed action's location to determine if the action is on or connected to the CBRS unit and thereby subject to these regulations. The appropriate Department of Interior map identifying units of the CBRS will be the basis of such determination. The CBRS units are also identified on FEMA Flood Insurance Maps (FIRM's) for the convenience of field personnel.

(2) If an action is determined not to be on or connected to a unit of the CBRS, no further requirements of these regulations needs to be met, and the action may be processed under other applicable disaster assistance regulations.

(3) If an action is determined to be on or connected to a unit of the CBRS, it is subject to the consultation and consistency requirements of CBRA as prescribed in §§ 206.348 and 206.349.

(b) *Emergency disaster assistance.* For each emergency disaster assistance action listed in § 206.346(a), the Regional Administrator shall perform the required consultation. CBRA requires that FEMA consult with the Secretary of the Interior before taking any action on a System unit. The purpose of such consultation is to solicit advice on whether the action is or is not one which is permitted by section 6 of CBRA and whether the action is or is not consistent with the purposes of CBRA as defined in section 1 of that statute.

(1) FEMA has conducted advance consultation with the Department of the Interior concerning such emergency actions. The result of the consultation is that the Secretary of the Interior through the Assistance Secretary for Fish and Wildlife and Parks has concurred that the emergency work listed in § 206.346(a) is consistent with the purposes of CBRA and may be approved by FEMA without additional consultation.

(2) *Notification.* As soon as practicable, the Regional Administrator will notify the designated Department of the Interior representative at the regional level of emergency projects that have been approved. Upon request from the Secretary of the Interior, the Director, Office of Environmental Planning and Historic Preservation, Mitigation Directorate will supply reports of all current emergency actions approved on CBRS units. Notification will contain the following information:

(i) Identification of the unit in the CBRS;

(ii) Description of work approved;

(iii) Amount of Federal funding; and

(iv) Additional measures required.

(c) *Permanent restoration assistance.* For each permanent restoration assistance action including but not limited to those listed in § 206.346(b), the Regional Administrator shall meet the requirements set out below.

(1) *Essential links.* For the repair or replacement of publicly owned or operated roads, structures or facilities which are essential links in a larger network or system:

(i) No facility may be expanded beyond its predisaster design.

(ii) Consultation in accordance with § 206.348 shall be accomplished.

(2) *Channel improvements.* For the repair of existing channels, related structures and the disposal of dredged materials:

(i) No channel or related structure may be repaired, reconstructed, or replaced unless funds were appropriated for the construction of such channel or structure before October 18, 1982;

(ii) Expansion of the facility beyond its predisaster design is not permitted;

(iii) Consultation in accordance with § 206.348 shall be accomplished.

(3) *Energy facilities.* For the repair of facilities necessary for the exploration, extraction or transportation of energy resources:

(i) No such facility may be repaired, reconstructed or replaced unless such function can be carried out only in, on, or adjacent to a coastal water area because the use or facility requires access to the coastal water body;

(ii) Consultation in accordance with § 206.348 shall be accomplished.

(4) *Special-purpose facilities.* For the repair of facilities used for the study, management, protection or enhancement of fish and wildlife resources and habitats and related recreational projects; air and water navigation aids and devices and access thereto; and facilities used for scientific research, including but not limited to aeronautical, atmospheric, space, geologic, marine, fish and wildlife and other research, development, and applications; and, nonstructural facilities that are designed to mimic, enhance or restore natural shoreline stabilization systems:

(i) Consultation in accordance with § 206.348 shall be accomplished;

(ii) No such facility may be repaired, reconstructed, or replaced unless it is otherwise consistent with the purposes of CBRA in accordance with § 206.349.

(5) *Other public facilities.* For the repair, reconstruction, or replacement of publicly owned or operated roads, structures, or facilities that do not fall within the categories identified in paragraphs (c)(1), (2), (3), and (4) of this section:

(i) No such facility may be repaired, reconstructed, or replaced unless it is an "existing facility;"

(ii) Expansion of the facility beyond its predisaster design is not permitted;

(iii) Consultation in accordance with § 206.348 shall be accomplished;

(iv) No such facility may be repaired, reconstructed, or replaced unless it is otherwise consistent with the purposes of CBRA in accordance with § 206.349.

(6) *Private nonprofit facilities.* For eligible private nonprofit facilities as defined in these regulations and of the type described in paragraphs (c)(1), (2), (3), and (4) of this section:

(i) Consultation in accordance with § 206.348 shall be accomplished.

(ii) No such facility may be repaired, reconstructed, or replaced unless it is otherwise consistent with the purposes of CBRA in accordance with § 206.349.

(7) *Improved project.* An improved project may not be approved for a facility in the CBRS if such grant is to be combined with other funding, resulting in an expansion of the facility beyond the predisaster design. If a facility is exempt from the expansion prohibitions of CBRA by virtue of falling into one of the categories identified in paragraph (c)(1), (2), (3), or (4) of this section, then an improved project for such facilities is not precluded.

(8) *Alternate project.* A new or enlarged facility may not be constructed on a unit of the CBRS under the provisions of the Stafford Act unless the facility is exempt from the expansion prohibition of CBRA by virtue of falling into one of the categories identified in paragraph (c)(1), (2), (3), or (4) of this section.

§ 206.348 Consultation.

As required by section 6 of the CBRA, the FEMA Regional Administrator will consult with the designated representative of the Department of the Interior (DOI) at the regional level before approving any action involving permanent restoration of a facility or structure on or attached to a unit of the CBRS.

(a) The consultation shall be by written memorandum to the DOI representative and shall contain the following:

(1) Identification of the unit within the CBRS;

(2) Description of the facility and the proposed repair or replacement work; including identification of the facility as an exception under section 6 of CBRA; and full justification of its status as an exception;

(3) Amount of proposal Federal funding;

(4) Additional mitigation measures required; and

(5) A determination of the action's consistency with the purposes of CBRA, if required by these regulations, in accordance with § 206.349.

(b) Pursuant to FEMA understanding with DOI, the DOI representative will provide technical information and an opinion whether or not the proposed action meets the criteria for a CBRA exception, and on the consistency of the action with the purposes of CBRA (when such consistency is required). DOI is expected to respond within 12 working days from the date of the FEMA request for consultation. If a response is not received within the time limit, the FEMA Regional Administrator shall contact the DOI representative to determine if the request for consultation was received in a timely manner. If it was not, an appropriate extension for response will be given. Otherwise, he or she may assume DOI concurrence and proceed with approval of the proposed action.

(c) For those cases in which the regional DOI representative believes that the proposed action should not be taken and the matter cannot be resolved at the regional level, the FEMA Regional Administrator will submit the issue to the Director, Office of Environmental Planning and Historic Preservation, Mitigation Directorate. In coordination with the Office of Chief Counsel (OCC), consultation will be accomplished at the FEMA National Office with the DOI consultation officer. After this consultation, the Director, Office of Environmental Planning and Historic Preservation, Mitigation Directorate, determines whether or not to approve the proposed action.

§ 206.349 Consistency determinations.

Section 6(a)(6) of CBRA requires that certain actions be consistent with the purposes of that statute if the actions are to be carried out on a unit of the CBRA. The purpose of CBRA, as stated in section 2(b) of that statute, is to minimize the loss of human life, wasteful expenditure of Federal revenues, and the damage to fish, wildlife, and other natural resources associated with the coastal barriers along with Atlantic and Gulf coasts. For those actions where a consistency determination is required, the FEMA Regional Administrator shall evaluate the action according to the following procedures, and the evaluation shall be included in the written request for consultation with DOI.

(a) *Impact identification.* FEMA shall identify impacts of the following types that would result from the proposed action:

(1) Risks to human life;

(2) Risks of damage to the facility being repaired or replaced;

(3) Risks of damage to other facilities;

(4) Risks of damage to fish, wildlife, and other natural resources;

(5) Condition of existing development served by the facility and the degree to which its redevelopment would be encouraged; and

(6) Encouragement of new development.

(b) *Mitigation.* FEMA shall modify actions by means of practicable mitigation measures to minimize adverse effects of the types listed in paragraph (a) of this section.

(c) *Conservation.* FEMA shall identify practicable measures that can be incorporated into the proposed action and will conserve natural and wildlife resources.

(d) *Finding.* For those actions required to be consistent with the purposes of CBRA, the above evaluation must result in a finding of consistency with CBRA by the Regional Administrator before funding may be approved for that action.

§§ 206.350–206.359   [Reserved]

Subpart K—Community Disaster Loans

Source: 55 FR 2314, Jan. 23, 1990, unless otherwise noted.

§ 206.360   Purpose.

This subpart provides policies and procedures for local governments and State and Federal officials concerning the Community Disaster Loan program under section 417 of the Stafford Act. Sections 206.360 through 206.367 of the subpart do not implement the Community Disaster Loan Act of 2005. (see § 206.370).

[70 FR 60446, Oct. 18, 2005]

§ 206.361   Loan program.

(a) *General.* The Assistant Administrator for the Disaster Assistance Directorate may make a Community Disaster Loan to any local government which has suffered a substantial loss of tax and other revenues as a result of a major disaster and which demonstrates a need for Federal financial assistance in order to perform its governmental functions.

(b) *Amount of loan.* The amount of the loan is based upon need, not to exceed 25 percent of the operating budget of the local government for the fiscal year in which the disaster occurs, but shall not exceed $5 million. The term *fiscal year* as used in this subpart means the local government's fiscal year.

(c) *Interest rate.* The interest rate is the rate for five year maturities as determined by the Secretary of the Treasury in effect on the date that the Promissory Note is executed. This rate is from the monthly Treasury schedule of certified interest rates which takes into consideration the current average yields on outstanding marketable obligations of the United States, adjusted to the nearest ⅛ percent.

(d) *Time limitation.* The Assistant Administrator for the Disaster Assistance Directorate may approve a loan in either the fiscal year in which the disaster occurred or the fiscal year immediately following that year. Only one loan may be approved under section 417(a) for any local government as the result of a single disaster.

(e) *Term of loan.* The term of the loan is 5 years, unless otherwise extended by the Assistant Administrator for the Disaster Assistance Directorate. The Assistant Administrator for the Disaster Assistance Directorate may consider requests for an extensions of loans based on the local government's financial condition. The total term of any loan under section 417(a) normally may not exceed 10 years from the date the Promissory Note was executed. However, when extenuating circumstances exist and the Community Disaster Loan recipient demonstrates an inability to repay the loan within the initial 10 years, but agrees to repay such loan over an extended period of time, additional time may be provided for loan repayment. (See § 206.367(c).)

(f) *Use of loan funds.* The local government shall use the loaned funds to carry on existing local government functions of a municipal operation character or to expand such functions to meet disaster-related needs. The funds shall not be used to finance capital improvements nor the repair or restoration of damaged public facilities. Neither the loan nor any cancelled portion of the loans may be used as the nonFederal share of any Federal program, including those under the Act.

(g) *Cancellation.* The Assistant Administrator for the Disaster Assistance Directorate shall cancel repayment of all or part of a Community Disaster Loan to the extent that he/she determines that revenues of the local government during the 3 fiscal years following the disaster are insufficient to meet the operating budget of that local government because of disaster-related revenue losses and additional unreimbursed disaster-related municipal operating expenses.

(h) *Relation to other assistance.* Any community disaster loans including cancellations made under this subpart shall not reduce or otherwise affect any commitments, grants, or other assistance under the Act or these regulations.

[55 FR 2314, Jan. 23, 1990, as amended at 66 FR 22445, May 4, 2001]

§ 206.362   **Responsibilities.**

(a) The local government shall submit the financial information required by FEMA in the application for a Community Disaster Loan and in the application for loan cancellation, if submitted, and comply with the assurances on the application, the terms and conditions of the Promissory Note, and these regulations. The local government shall send all loan application, loan administration, loan cancellation, and loan settlement correspondence through the GAR and the FEMA Regional Office to the FEMA Assistant Administrator for the Disaster Assistance Directorate.

(b) The GAR shall certify on the loan application that the local government can legally assume the proposed indebtedness and that any proceeds will be used and accounted for in compliance with the FEMA-State Agreement for the major disaster. States are encouraged to take appropriate pre-disaster action to resolve any existing State impediments which would preclude a local government from incurring the increased indebtedness associated with a loan in order to avoid protracted delays in processing loan application requests in major disasters or emergencies.

(c) The Regional Administrator or designee shall review each loan application or loan cancellation request received from a local government to ensure that it contains the required documents and transmit the application to the Assistant Administrator for the

473

Disaster Assistance Directorate. He/she may submit appropriate recommendations to the Assistant Administrator for the Disaster Assistance Directorate.

(d) The Assistant Administrator for the Disaster Assistance Directorate, or a designee, shall execute a Promissory Note with the local government, and the FEMA Finance Center, shall administer the loan until repayment or cancellation is completed and the Promissory Note is discharged.

(e) The Assistant Administrator for the Disaster Assistance Directorate or designee shall approve or disapprove each loan request, taking into consideration the information provided in the local government's request and the recommendations of the GAR and the Regional Administrator. The Assistant Administrator for the Disaster Assistance Directorate or designee shall approve or disapprove a request for loan cancellation in accordance with the criteria for cancellation in these regulations.

(f) The Chief Financial Officer shall establish and maintain a financial account for each outstanding loan and disburse funds against the Promissory Note.

§ 206.363 Eligibility criteria.

(a) *Local government.* (1) The local government must be located within the area designated by the Assistant Administrator for the Disaster Assistance Directorate as eligible for assistance under a major disaster declaration. In addition, State law must not prohibit the local government from incurring the indebtedness resulting from a Federal loan.

(2) Criteria considered by FEMA in determining the eligibility of a local government for a Community Disaster Loan include the loss of tax and other revenues as result of a major disaster, a demonstrated need for financial assistance in order to perform its governmental functions, the maintenance of an annual operating budget, and the responsibility to provide essential municipal operating services to the community. Eligibility for other assistance under the Act does not, by itself, establish entitlement to such a loan.

(b) *Loan eligibility*—(1) *General.* To be eligible, the local government must show that it may suffer or has suffered a substantial loss of tax and other revenues as a result of a major disaster or emergency, must demonstrate a need for financial assistance in order to perform its governmental functions, and must not be in arrears with respect to any payments due on previous loans. Loan eligibility is based on the financial condition of the local government and a review of financial information and supporting documentation accompanying the application.

(2) *Substantial loss of tax and other revenues.* The fiscal year of the disaster or the succeeding fiscal year is the base period for determining whether a local government may suffer or has suffered a substantial loss of revenue. Criteria used in determining whether a local government has or may suffer a substantial loss of tax and other revenue include the following disaster-related factors:

(i) Whether the disaster caused a large enough reduction in cash receipts from normal revenue sources, excluding borrowing, which affects significantly and adversely the level and/or categories of essential municipal services provided prior to the disaster;

(ii) Whether the disaster caused a revenue loss of over 5 percent of total revenue estimated for the fiscal year in which the disaster occurred or for the succeeding fiscal year;

(3) *Demonstrated need for financial assistance.* The local government must demonstrate a need for financial assistance in order to perform its governmental functions. The criteria used in making this determination include the following:

(i) Whether there are sufficient funds to meet current fiscal year operating requirements;

(ii) Whether there is availability of cash or other liquid assets from the prior fiscal year;

(iii) Current financial condition considering projected expenditures for governmental services and availability of other financial resources;

(iv) Ability to obtain financial assistance or needed revenue from State and other Federal agencies for direct program expenditures;

(v) Debt ratio (relationship of annual receipts to debt service);

(vi) Ability to obtain financial assistance or needed revenue from State and other Federal agencies for direct program expenditures;

(vii) Displacement of revenue-producing business due to property destruction;

(viii) Necessity to reduce or eliminate essential municipal services; and

(ix) Danger of municipal insolvency.

[55 FR 2314, Jan. 23, 1990, as amended at 66 FR 22445, May 4, 2001]

§ 206.364 Loan application.

(a) *Application.* (1) The local government shall submit an application for a Community Disaster Loan through the GAR. The loan must be justified on the basis of need and shall be based on the actual and projected expenses, as a result of the disaster, for the fiscal year in which the disaster occurred and for the 3 succeeding fiscal years. The loan application shall be prepared by the affected local government and be approved by the GAR. FEMA has determined that a local government, in applying for a loan as a result of having suffered a substantial loss of tax and other revenue as a result of a major disaster, is not required to first seek credit elsewhere (see § 206.367(c)).

(2) The State exercises administrative authority over the local government's application. The State's review should include a determination that the applicant is legally qualified, under State law, to assume the proposed debt, and may include an overall review for accuracy for the submission. The Governor's Authorized Representative may request the Regional Administrator to waive the requirement for a State review if an otherwise eligible applicant is not subject to State administration authority and the State cannot legally participate in the loan application process.

(b) *Financial requirements.* (1) The loan application shall be developed from financial information contained in the local government's annual operating budget (see § 206.364(b)(2)) and shall include a Summary of Revenue Loss and Unreimbursed Disaster-Related Expenses, a Statement of the Applicant's Operating Results—Cash Posi-

tion, a Debt History, Tax Assessment Data, Financial Projections, Other Information, a Certification, and the Assurances listed on the application.

(i) Copies of the local government's financial reports (Revenue and Expense and Balance Sheet) for the 3 fiscal years immediately prior to the fiscal year of the disaster and the applicant's most recent financial statement must accompany the application. The local government's financial reports to be submitted are those annual (or interim) consolidated and/or individual official annual financial presentations for the General Fund and all other funds maintained by the local government.

(ii) Each application for a Community Disaster Loan must also include:

(A) A statement by the local government identifying each fund (i.e. General Fund, etc.) which is included as its annual Operating budget, and

(B) A copy of the pertinent State statutes, ordinance, or regulations which prescribe the local government's system of budgeting, accounting and financial reporting, including a description of each fund account.

(2) *Operating budget.* For loan application purposes, the operating budget is that document or documents approved by an appropriating body, which contains an estimate of proposed expenditures, other than capital outlays for fixed assets for a stated period of time, and the proposed means of financing the expenditures. For loan cancellation purposes, FEMA interprets the term "operating budget" to mean actual revenues and expenditures of the local government as published in the official financial statements of the local government.

(3) *Operating budget increases.* Budget increases due to increases in the level of, or additions to, municipal services not rendered at the time of the disaster or not directly related to the disaster shall be identified.

(4) *Revenue and assessment information.* The applicant shall provide information concerning its method of tax assessment including assessment dates and the dates payments are due. Tax revenues assessed but not collected, or

other revenues which the local government chooses to forgive, stay, or otherwise not exercise the right to collect, are not a legitimate revenue loss for purposes of evaluating the loan application.

(5) *Estimated disaster-related expense.* Unreimbursed disaster-related expenses of a municipal operating character should be estimated. These are discussed in § 206.366(b).

(c) *Federal review.* (1) The Assistant Administrator for the Disaster Assistance Directorate or designee shall approve a community disaster loan to the extent it is determined that the local government has suffered a substantial loss of tax and other revenues and demonstrates a need for financial assistance to perform its governmental function as the result of the disaster.

(2) *Resubmission of application.* If a loan application is disapproved, in whole or in part, by the Assistant Administrator for the Disaster Assistance Directorate because of inadequacy of information, a revised application may be resubmitted by the local government within sixty days of the date of the disapproval. Decision by the Assistant Administrator for the Disaster Assistance Directorate on the resubmission is final.

(d) *Community disaster loan.* (1) The loan shall not exceed the lesser of:

(i) The amount of projected revenue loss plus the projected unreimbursed disaster-related expenses of a municipal operating character for the fiscal year of the major disaster and the subsequent 3 fiscal years, or

(ii) 25 percent of the local government's annual operating budget for the fiscal year in which the disaster occurred.

(2) *Promissory note.* (i) Upon approval of the loan by the Assistant Administrator for the Disaster Assistance Directorate or designee, he or she, or a designated Loan Officer will execute a Promissory Note with the applicant. The Note must be co-signed by the State (see § 206.364(d)(2)(ii)). The applicant should indicate its funding requirements on the Schedule of Loan Increments on the Note.

(ii) If the State cannot legally cosign the Promissory Note, the local government must pledge collateral security, acceptable to the Assistant Administrator for the Disaster Assistance Directorate, to cover the principal amount of the Note. The pledge should be in the form of a resolution by the local governing body identifying the collateral security.

[55 FR 2314, Jan. 23, 1990, as amended at 74 FR 15351, Apr. 3, 2009]

§ 206.365   Loan administration.

(a) *Funding.* (1) FEMA will disburse funds to the local government when requested, generally in accordance with the Schedule of Loan Increments in the Promissory Note. As funds are disbursed, interest will accrue against each disbursement.

(2) When each incremental disbursement is requested, the local government shall submit a copy of its most recent financial report (if not submitted previously) for consideration by FEMA in determining whether the level and frequency of periodic payments continue to be justified. The local government shall also provide the latest available data on anticipated and actual tax and other revenue collections. Desired adjustments in the disbursement schedule shall be submitted in writing at least 10 days prior to the proposed disbursement date in order to ensure timely receipt of the funds. A sinking fund should be established to amortize the debt.

(b) *Financial management.* (1) Each local government with an approved Community Disaster Loan shall establish necessary accounting records, consistent with local government's financial management system, to account for loan funds received and disbursed and to provide an audit trail.

(2) FEMA auditors, State auditors, the GAR, the Regional Administrator, the Assistant Administrator for the Disaster Assistance Directorate, and the Comptroller General of the United States or their duly authorized representatives shall, for the purpose of audits and examination, have access to any books, documents, papers, and records that pertain to Federal funds, equipments, and supplies received under these regulations.

(c) *Loan servicing.* (1) The applicant annually shall submit to FEMA copies of its annual financial reports (operating statements, balance sheets, etc.) for the fiscal year of the major disaster, and for each of the 3 subsequent fiscal years.

(2) The Disaster Assistance Directorate, will review the loan periodically. The purpose of the reevaluation is to determine whether projected revenue losses, disaster-related expenses, operating budgets, and other factors have changed sufficiently to warrant adjustment of the scheduled disbursement of the loan proceeds.

(3) The Disaster Assistance Directorate, shall provide each loan recipient with a loan status report on a quarterly basis. The recipient will notify FEMA of any changes of the responsible municipal official who executed the Promissory Note.

(d) *Inactive loans.* If no funds have been disbursed from the Treasury, and if the local government does not anticipate a need for such funds, the note may be cancelled at any time upon a written request through the State and Regional Office to FEMA. However, since only one loan may be approved, cancellation precludes submission of a second loan application request by the same local government for the same disaster.

§ 206.366   Loan cancellation.

(a) *Policies.* (1) FEMA shall cancel repayment of all or part of a Community Disaster Loan to the extent that the Assistant Administrator for the Disaster Assistance Directorate determines that revenues of the local government during the full three fiscal year period following the disaster are insufficient, as a result of the disaster, to meet the operating budget for the local government, including additional unreimbursed disaster-related expenses for a municipal operating character. For loan cancellation purposes, FEMA interprets that term *operating budget* to mean actual revenues and expenditures of the local government as published in the official financial statements of the local government.

(2) If the tax and other revenues rates or the tax assessment valuation of property which was not damaged or destroyed by the disaster are reduced during the 3 fiscal years subsequent to

the major disaster, the tax and other revenue rates and tax assessment valuation factors applicable to such property in effect at the time of the major disaster shall be used without reduction for purposes of computing revenues received. This may result in decreasing the potential for loan cancellations.

(3) If the local government's fiscal year is changed during the "full 3 year period following the disaster" the actual period will be modified so that the required financial data submitted covers an inclusive 36-month period.

(4) If the local government transfers funds from its operating funds accounts to its capital funds account, utilizes operating funds for other than routine maintenance purposes, or significantly increases expenditures which are not disaster related, except increases due to inflation, the annual operating budget or operating statement expenditures will be reduced accordingly for purposes of evaluating any request for loan cancellation.

(5) It is not the purpose of this loan program to underwrite predisaster budget or actual deficits of the local government. Consequently, such deficits carried forward will reduce any amounts otherwise eligible for loan cancellation.

(b) *Disaster-related expenses of a municipal operation character.* (1) For purpose of this loan, unreimbursed expenses of a municipal operating character are those incurred for general government purposes, such as police and fire protection, trash collection, collection of revenues, maintenance of public facilities, flood and other hazard insurance, and other expenses normally budgeted for the general fund, as defined by the Municipal Finance Officers Association.

(2) Disaster-related expenses do not include expenditures associated with debt service, any major repairs, rebuilding, replacement or reconstruction of public facilities or other capital projects, intragovernmental services, special assessments, and trust and agency fund operations. Disaster expenses which are eligible for reimbursement under project applications or other Federal programs are not eligible for loan cancellation.

477

(3) Each applicant shall maintain records including documentation necessary to identify expenditures for unreimbursed disaster-related expenses. Examples of such expenses include but are not limited to:

(i) Interest paid on money borrowed to pay amounts FEMA does not advance toward completion of approved Project Applications.

(ii) Unreimbursed costs to local governments for providing usable sites with utilities for mobile homes used to meet disaster temporary housing requirements.

(iii) Unreimbursed costs required for police and fire protection and other community services for mobile home parks established as the result of or for use following a disaster.

(iv) The cost to the applicant of flood insurance required under Public Law 93-234, as amended, and other hazard insurance required under section 311, Public Law 93-288, as amended, as a condition of Federal disaster assistance for the disaster under which the loan is authorized.

(4) The following expenses are not considered to be disaster-related for Community Disaster Loan purposes:

(i) The local government's share for assistance provided under the Act including flexible funding under section 406(c)(1) of the Act.

(ii) Improvements related to the repair or restoration of disaster public facilities approved on Project Applications.

(iii) Otherwise eligible costs for which no Federal reimbursement is requested as a part of the applicant's disaster response commitment, or cost sharing as specified in the FEMA-State Agreement for the disaster.

(iv) Expenses incurred by the local government which are reimbursed on the applicant's project application.

(c) *Cancellation application.* A local government which has drawn loan funds from the Treasury may request cancellation of the principal and related interest by submitting an Application for Loan Cancellation through the Governor's Authorized Representative to the Regional Administrator prior to the expiration date of the loan.

(1) Financial information submitted with the application shall include the following:

(i) Annual Operating Budgets for the fiscal year of the disaster and the 3 subsequent fiscal years;

(ii) Annual Financial Reports (Revenue and Expense and Balance Sheet) for each of the above fiscal years. Such financial records must include copies of the local government's annual financial reports, including operating statements balance sheets and related consolidated and individual presentations for each fund account. In addition, the local government must include an explanatory statement when figures in the Application for Loan Cancellation form differ from those in the supporting financial reports.

(iii) The following additional information concerning annual real estate property taxes pertaining to the community for each of the above fiscal years:

(A) The market value of the tax base (dollars);

(B) The assessment ratio (percent);

(C) The assessed valuation (dollars);

(D) The tax levy rate (mils);

(E) Taxes levied and collected (dollars).

(iv) Audit reports for each of the above fiscal years certifying to the validity of the Operating Statements. The financial statements of the local government shall be examined in accordance with generally accepted auditing standards by independent certified public accountants. The report should not include recommendations concerning loan cancellation or repayment.

(v) Other financial information specified in the Application for Loan Cancellation.

(2) *Narrative justification.* The application may include a narrative presentation to amplify the financial material accompanying the application and to present any extenuating circumstances which the local government wants the Assistant Administrator for the Disaster Assistance Directorate to consider in rendering a decision on the cancellation request.

(d) *Determination.* (1) If, based on a review of the Application for Loan Cancellation and FEMA audit, when determined necessary, the Assistant Administrator for the Disaster Assistance Directorate determines that all or part of the Community Disaster Loan funds should be canceled, the principal amount which is canceled will become a grant, and the related interest will be forgiven. The Assistant Administrator for the Disaster Assistance Directorate's determination concerning loan cancellation will specify that any uncancelled principal and related interest must be repaid immediately and that, if immediate repayment will constitute a financial hardship, the local government must submit for FEMA review and approval, a repayment schedule for settling the indebtedness on timely basis. Such repayments must be made to the Treasurer of the United States and be sent to FEMA, Attention: Chief Financial Officer.

(2) A loan or cancellation of a loan does not reduce or affect other disaster-related grants or other disaster assistance. However, no cancellation may be made that would result in a duplication of benefits to the applicant.

(3) The uncancelled portion of the loan must be repaid in accordance with § 206.367.

(4) *Appeals.* If an Application for Loan Cancellation is disapproved, in whole or in part, by the Assistant Administrator for the Disaster Assistance Directorate or designee, the local government may submit any additional information in support of the application within 60 days of the date of disapproval. The decision by the Assistant Administrator for the Disaster Assistance Directorate or designee on the submission is final.

[55 FR 2314, Jan. 23, 1990, as amended at 74 FR 15351, Apr. 3, 2009]

§ 206.367 Loan repayment.

(a) *Prepayments.* The local government may make prepayments against loan at any time without any prepayment penalty.

(b) *Repayment.* To the extent not otherwise cancelled, Community Disaster Loan funds become due and payable in accordance with the terms and conditions of the Promissory Note. The note shall include the following provisions:

(1) The term of a loan made under this program is 5 years, unless extended by the Assistant Administrator for the Disaster Assistance Directorate. Interest will accrue on outstanding cash from the actual date of its disbursement by the Treasury.

(2) The interest amount due will be computed separately for each Treasury disbursement as follows: $I=P \times R \times T$, where I=the amount of simple interest, P=the principal amount disbursed; R=the interest rate of the loan; and, T=the outstanding term in years from the date of disbursement to date of repayment, with periods less than 1 year computed on the basis of 365 days/year. If any portion of the loan is cancelled, the interest amount due will be computed on the remaining principal with the shortest outstanding term.

(3) Each payment made against the loan will be applied first to the interest computed to the date of the payment, and then to the principal. Prepayments of scheduled installments, or any portion thereof, may be made at any time and shall be applied to the installments last to become due under the loan and shall not affect the obligation of the borrower to pay the remaining installments.

(4) The Assistant Administrator for the Disaster Assistance Directorate may defer payments of principal and interest until FEMA makes its final determination with respect to any Application for Loan Cancellation which the borrower may submit. However, interest will continue to accrue.

(5) Any costs incurred by the Federal Government in collecting the note shall be added to the unpaid balance of the loan, bear interest at the same rate as the loan, and be immediately due without demand.

(6) In the event of default on this note by the borrower, the FEMA claims collection officer will take action to recover the outstanding principal plus related interest under Federal debt collection authorities, including administrative offset against other Federal funds due the borrower and/or referral to the Department of Justice for judicial enforcement and collection.

(c) *Additional time.* In unusual circumstances involving financial hardship, the local government may request an additional period of time beyond the original 10 year term to repay the indebtedness. Such request may be approved by the Assistant Administrator for the Disaster Assistance Directorate subject to the following conditions:

(1) The local government must submit documented evidence that it has applied for the same credit elsewhere and that such credit is not available at a rate equivalent to the current Treasury rate.

(2) The principal amount shall be the original uncancelled principal plus related interest.

(3) The interest rate shall be the Treasury rate in effect at the time the new Promissory Note is executed but in no case less than the original interest rate.

(4) The term of the new Promissory Note shall be for the settlement period requested by the local government but not greater than 10 years from the date the new note is executed.

§§ 206.368–206.369 **[Reserved]**

§ 206.370 **Purpose and scope.**

(a) *Purpose.* Sections 206.370 through 206.377 provide procedures for local governments and State and Federal officials concerning the Special Community Disaster Loans program under section 417 of the Stafford Act (42 U.S.C. 5184), the Community Disaster Loan Act of 2005, Public Law 109–88, and the Emergency Supplemental Appropriations Act for Defense, the Global War on Terror, and Hurricane Recovery, 2006, Public Law 109–234.

(b) *Scope.* Sections 206.370 through 206.377 apply only to Special Community Disaster Loans issued under the Community Disaster Loan Act of 2005, Public Law 109–88, and the Emergency Supplemental Appropriations Act for Defense, the Global War on Terror, and Hurricane Recovery, 2006, Public Law 109–234.

[70 FR 60446, Oct. 18, 2005, as amended at 75 FR 2817, Jan. 19, 2010]

§ 206.371 **Loan program.**

(a) *General.* The Assistant Administrator for the Disaster Assistance Directorate may make a Special Community Disaster Loan to any local government which has suffered a substantial loss of tax and other revenues as a result of a major disaster and which demonstrates a need for Federal financial assistance in order to provide essential services.

(b) *Amount of loan.* The amount of the loan is based upon need, not to exceed 25 percent of the operating budget of the local government for the fiscal year in which the disaster occurs. The term fiscal year as used in this subpart means the local government's fiscal year.

(c) *Interest rate.* The interest rate is the rate for five year maturities as determined by the Secretary of the Treasury in effect on the date that the Promissory Note is executed. This rate is from the monthly Treasury schedule of certified interest rates which takes into consideration the current average yields on outstanding marketable obligations of the United States. If an applicant can demonstrate *unusual circumstances involving financial hardship,* the Assistant Administrator for the Disaster Assistance Directorate may approve a rate equal to the five year maturity rate plus 1 per centum, adjusted to the nearest ⅛ percent, and further reduced by one-half.

(d) *Time limitation.* The Assistant Administrator for the Disaster Assistance Directorate may approve a loan in either the fiscal year in which the disaster occurred or the fiscal year immediately following that year.

(e) *Term of loan.* The term of the loan is 5 years, unless otherwise extended by the Assistant Administrator for the Disaster Assistance Directorate. The Assistant Administrator for the Disaster Assistance Directorate may consider a request for an extension of a loan based on the local government's financial condition. The total term of any loan under section 417(a) of the Stafford Act normally may not exceed 10 years from the date the Promissory Note was executed. However, when extenuating circumstances exist and the recipient demonstrates an inability to repay the loan within the initial 10 years, but agrees to repay such loan over an extended period of time, additional time may be provided for loan repayment (see §206.377(c)).

(f) *Use of loan funds.* The local government shall use the loaned funds to assist in providing essential services. The funds shall not be used to finance capital improvements nor the repair or restoration of damaged public facilities. Neither the loan nor any cancelled portion of the loans may be used as the non-Federal share of any Federal program, including those under the Stafford Act.

(g) *Relation to other assistance.* Any Special Community Disaster Loans including cancellations of loans made under this subpart shall not reduce or otherwise affect any commitments, grants, or other assistance provided under the authority of the Stafford Act or this part.

(h) *Cancellation.* The Director of the Public Assistance Division shall cancel repayment of all or part of a Special Community Disaster Loan to the extent that he/she determines that revenues of the local government during the three full fiscal years following the disaster are insufficient to meet the operating budget of that local government because of disaster-related revenue losses and additional unreimbursed disaster-related municipal operating expenses.

[70 FR 60446, Oct. 18, 2005, as amended at 75 FR 2817, Jan. 19, 2010]

§ 206.372 Responsibilities.

(a) The local government shall submit the financial information required by FEMA in the application for a Community Disaster Loan or other format specified by FEMA and comply with the assurances on the application, the terms and conditions of the Promissory Note, the application for loan cancellation, if submitted, and §§206.370 through 206.377. The local government shall send all loan application, loan administration, loan cancellation, and loan settlement correspondence through the Governor's Authorized Representative (GAR) and the FEMA Regional Office to the Director of the Public Assistance Division.

(b) The GAR shall certify on the loan application that the local government can legally assume the proposed indebtedness and that any proceeds will be used and accounted for in compliance with the FEMA-State Agreement for the major disaster. States are encouraged to take appropriate pre-disaster action to resolve any existing State impediments which would preclude a local government from incurring the increased indebtedness associated with a loan in order to avoid protracted delays in processing loan application requests resulting from major disasters.

(c) The Regional Administrator or designee shall review each loan application or loan cancellation request received from a local government to ensure that it contains the required documents and transmit the application to the Director of the Public Assistance Division. He/she may also submit appropriate recommendations to the Director of the Public Assistance Division.

(d) The Director of the Public Assistance Division or a designee, shall execute a Promissory Note with the local government and shall administer the loan until repayment or cancellation is completed and the Promissory Note is discharged.

(e) The Director of the Public Assistance Division shall approve or disapprove each loan request, taking into consideration the information provided in the local government's request and the recommendations of the GAR and the Regional Administrator. The Director of the Public Assistance Division shall approve or disapprove a request for loan cancellation in accordance with the criteria for cancellation in these regulations.

(f) The FEMA Chief Financial Officer shall establish and maintain a financial account for each outstanding loan and disburse funds against the Promissory Note.

[70 FR 60446, Oct. 18, 2005, as amended at 75 FR 2818, Jan. 19, 2010]

§ 206.373 Eligibility criteria.

(a) *Local government.* (1) The local government must be located within the area eligible for assistance under a major disaster declaration. In addition, State law must not prohibit the local government from incurring the indebtedness resulting from a Federal loan.

481

(2) Criteria considered by FEMA in determining the eligibility of a local government for a Special Community Disaster Loan include the loss of tax and other revenues as result of a major disaster, a demonstrated need for financial assistance in order to perform essential governmental functions, the maintenance of an annual operating budget, and the responsibility to provide essential services to the community. Eligibility for other assistance under the Stafford Act does not, by itself, establish entitlement to such a loan.

(b) *Loan eligibility*—(1) *General.* To be eligible, the local government must show that it may suffer or has suffered a substantial loss of tax and other revenues as a result of a major disaster or emergency, and it must demonstrate a need for financial assistance in order to provide essential municipal services. Loan eligibility is based on the financial condition of the local government and a review of financial information and supporting documentation accompanying the application.

(2) *Substantial loss of tax and other revenues.* The fiscal year of the disaster or the succeeding fiscal year is the base period for determining whether a local government may suffer or has suffered a substantial loss of revenue. Criteria used in determining whether a local government has or may suffer a substantial loss of tax and other revenue include the following disaster-related factors:

(i) Whether the disaster caused a large enough reduction in cash receipts from normal revenue sources, excluding borrowing, which affects significantly and adversely the level and/or categories of essential services provided prior to the disaster;

(ii) Whether the disaster caused a revenue loss of over 5 percent of total revenue estimated for the fiscal year in which the disaster occurred or for the succeeding fiscal year.

(3) *Demonstrated need for financial assistance.* The local government must demonstrate a need for financial assistance in order to perform essential governmental functions. The criteria used in making this determination may include some or all of the following factors:

(i) Whether there are sufficient funds to meet current fiscal year operating requirements;

(ii) Whether there is availability of cash or other liquid assets from the prior fiscal year;

(iii) Current financial condition considering projected expenditures for governmental services and availability of other financial resources;

(iv) Ability to obtain financial assistance or needed revenue from State and other Federal agencies for direct program expenditures;

(v) Debt ratio (relationship of annual receipts to debt service);

(vi) Displacement of revenue-producing business due to property destruction;

(vii) Necessity to reduce or eliminate essential services; and

(viii) Danger of municipal insolvency.

[70 FR 60446, Oct. 18, 2005]

§ 206.374   Loan application.

(a) *Application.* (1) The local government shall submit an application for a Special Community Disaster Loan through the GAR. The loan must be justified on the basis of need and shall be based on the actual and projected expenses, as a result of the disaster, for the fiscal year in which the disaster occurred and for the 3 succeeding fiscal years. The loan application shall be prepared by the affected local government and be approved by the GAR. FEMA has determined that a local government, in applying for a loan as a result of having suffered a substantial loss of tax and other revenue as a result of a major disaster, is not required to first seek credit elsewhere (see § 206.377(c)).

(2) The State exercises administrative authority over the local government's application. The State's review should include a determination that the applicant is legally qualified, under State law, to assume the proposed debt, and may include an overall review for accuracy of the submission. The GAR may request the Regional Administrator to waive the requirement for a State review if an otherwise eligible applicant is not subject to State administration authority and the State

cannot legally participate in the loan application process.

(b) *Financial requirements.* (1) The loan application shall be developed from financial information contained in the local government's annual operating budget (see paragraph (b)(2) of this section) and shall include a Summary of Revenue Loss and Unreimbursed Disaster-Related Expenses, a Statement of the Applicant's Operating Results—Cash Position, and certification and assurances requested by the Assistant Administrator for the Disaster Assistance Directorate.

(i) Copies of the local government's financial reports (Revenue and Expense and Balance Sheet) for the 3 fiscal years immediately prior to the fiscal year of the disaster and the applicant's most recent financial statement must, unless impracticable, accompany the application. The local government's financial reports to be submitted are those annual (or interim) consolidated and/or individual official annual financial presentations for the General Fund and all other funds maintained by the local government.

(ii) Each application for a Special Community Disaster Loan must also include:

(A) A statement by the local government identifying each fund (i.e. General Fund, etc.) which is included as its annual Operating budget, and

(B) A copy of the pertinent State statutes, ordinances, or regulations which prescribe the local government's system of budgeting, accounting and financial reporting, including a description of each fund account.

(2) *Operating budget.* For loan application purposes, the operating budget is that document or documents approved by an appropriating body, which contains an estimate of proposed expenditures, other than capital outlays for fixed assets for a stated period of time, and the proposed means of financing the expenditures. For loan cancellation purposes, FEMA interprets the term "operating budget" to mean actual revenues and expenditures of the local government as published in the official financial statements of the local government.

(3) *Operating budget increases.* Budget increases due to increases in the level

of, or additions to, municipal services not rendered at the time of the disaster or not directly related to the disaster shall be identified.

(4) *Revenue and assessment information.* The applicant shall provide information concerning its method of tax assessment including assessment dates and the dates payments are due.

(5) *Estimated disaster-related expense.* Unreimbursed disaster-related expenses of a municipal operating character should be estimated.

(c) *Federal review.* (1) The Assistant Administrator for the Disaster Assistance Directorate or designee shall approve a Special Community Disaster Loan to the extent it is determined that the local government has suffered a substantial loss of tax and other revenues and demonstrates a need for financial assistance as the result of the disaster to provide essential municipal services.

(2) *Resubmission of application.* If a loan application is disapproved, in whole or in part, by the Assistant Administrator for the Disaster Assistance Directorate because of inadequacy of information, a revised application may be submitted by the local government within sixty days of the date of the disapproval. Decision by the Assistant Administrator for the Disaster Assistance Directorate on the resubmission is final.

(d) *Special Community Disaster Loan.* (1) The loan shall not exceed the lesser of:

(i) The amount of projected revenue loss plus the projected unreimbursed disaster-related expenses of a municipal operating character for the fiscal year of the major disaster and the subsequent 3 fiscal years, or

(ii) 25 percent of the local government's annual operating budget for the fiscal year in which the disaster occurred.

(2) *Promissory note.* (i) Upon approval of the loan by the Assistant Administrator for the Disaster Assistance Directorate or designee, he or she, or a designated Loan Officer will execute a Promissory Note with the applicant. The Note must be co-signed by the State (see paragraph (d)(2)(ii) of this section). The applicant should indicate

its funding requirements on the Schedule of Loan Increments on the Note.

(ii) If the State cannot legally cosign the Promissory Note, the local government must pledge collateral security, acceptable to the Assistant Administrator for the Disaster Assistance Directorate, to cover the principal amount of the Note. The pledge should be in the form of a resolution by the local governing body identifying the collateral security.

(e) *Waiver of requirements.* Notwithstanding any other provision of this or other sections promulgated pursuant to Public Law 109–88, the Assistant Administrator for the Disaster Assistance Directorate may, upon the request of an applicant or loan recipient, waive any specific application requirement or financial reporting requirement (see, e.g., § 206.375(a)(2)) upon a finding by the Assistant Administrator for the Disaster Assistance Directorate that the effects of the major disaster prevent the applicant from fulfilling the application requirement and that waiving the requirements would be consistent with the purposes of the Community Disaster Loan Act of 2005.

[70 FR 60446, Oct. 18, 2005, as amended at 75 FR 2818, Jan. 19, 2010]

§ 206.375 Loan administration.

(a) *Funding.* (1) FEMA will disburse funds to the local government when requested, generally in accordance with the Schedule of Loan Increments in the Promissory Note. As funds are disbursed, interest will accrue against each disbursement.

(2) When each incremental disbursement is requested, the local government shall submit a copy of its most recent financial report (if not submitted previously) for consideration by FEMA in determining whether the level and frequency of periodic payments continue to be justified. The local government shall also provide the latest available data on anticipated and actual tax and other revenue collections. Desired adjustments in the disbursement schedule shall be submitted in writing at least 10 days prior to the proposed disbursement date in order to ensure timely receipt of the funds.

(b) *Financial management.* (1) Each local government with an approved Special Community Disaster Loan shall establish necessary accounting records, consistent with local government's financial management system, to account for loan funds received and disbursed and to provide an audit trail.

(2) FEMA auditors, State auditors, the GAR, the Regional Administrator, the Assistant Administrator for the Disaster Assistance Directorate, the Department of Homeland Security Inspector General, and the Comptroller General of the United States or their duly authorized representatives shall, for the purpose of audits and examination, have access to any books, documents, papers, and records that pertain to Federal funds, equipments, and supplies received under §§ 206.370 through 206.377.

(c) *Loan servicing.* (1) The applicant annually shall submit to FEMA copies of its annual financial reports (operating statements, balance sheets, etc.) for the fiscal year of the major disaster, and for each of the 3 subsequent fiscal years.

(2) FEMA will review the loan periodically. The purpose of the reevaluation is to determine whether projected revenue losses, disaster-related expenses, operating budgets, and other factors have changed sufficiently to warrant adjustment of the scheduled disbursement of the loan proceeds.

(3) FEMA shall provide each loan recipient with a loan status report on a quarterly basis. The recipient will notify FEMA of any changes of the responsible municipal official who executed the Promissory Note.

(d) *Inactive loans.* If no funds have been disbursed from the loan program, and if the local government does not anticipate a need for such funds, the note may be cancelled at any time upon a written request through the State and Regional Office to FEMA.

[70 FR 60446, Oct. 18, 2005]

§ 206.376 Loan cancellation.

(a) FEMA shall cancel repayment of all or part of a Special Community Disaster Loan to the extent that the Director of the Public Assistance Division determines that revenues of the local government during the three-full-fiscal-year period following the disaster are insufficient, as a result of the disaster, to meet the operating budget for the local government, including additional unreimbursed disaster-related expenses of a municipal operating character.

(b) *Definitions.* For loan cancellation purposes,

(1) "Operating budget" means actual revenues and expenditures of the local government as published in the official financial statements of the local government.

(2) "Revenue" means any source of income from taxes, fees, fines, and other sources of income, and will be recognized only as they become susceptible to accrual (measurable and available).

(3) "Three-full-fiscal-year period following the disaster" means either a 36-month period beginning on September 1, 2005, or the 36 months of the applicant's fiscal year as established before the disaster, at the applicant's discretion.

(4) "Operating expenses" means those expenses and expenditures incurred as a result of performing services, including salaries and benefits, contractual services, and commodities. Capital expenditures and debt service payments and capital leases are not considered operating expenses. Under accrual accounting, expenses are recognized as soon as a liability is incurred, regardless of the timing of related cash flows.

(c) *Revenue Calculation procedures.* (1) If the tax rates and other revenues or the tax assessment valuation of property which was not damaged or destroyed by the disaster are reduced during the three full fiscal years subsequent to the major disaster, the tax rates and other revenues and tax assessment valuation factors applicable to such property in effect at the time of the major disaster shall be used without reduction for purposes of computing revenues received.

(2) At the applicant's discretion, the three-full-fiscal-year period following the disaster is either a 36-month period beginning on September 1, 2005 or the 36 months of the applicant's fiscal year as established before the disaster. If the applicant's fiscal year is changed within the 36 months immediately following the disaster, the actual period will be modified so that the required financial data submitted covers an inclusive 36-month period. Should the applicant elect the 36-month period beginning September 1, 2005, FEMA will prorate the revenues and expenses for the partial years based on the applicant's annual financial statements.

(3) If the local government transfers funds from its operating funds accounts to its capital funds account, utilizes operating funds for other than routine maintenance purposes, or significantly increases expenditures which are not disaster related, except increases due to inflation, the annual operating budget or operating statement expenditures will be reduced accordingly for purposes of evaluating any request for loan cancellation.

(4) Notwithstanding paragraph (c)(3) of this section, the amount of property taxes that are transferred to other funds for Debt Service or Pension Obligations funding will not be excluded from the calculation of the operating budget or from expenditures in calculation of the operating deficit, to the extent that the property tax revenues in the General Fund are less than they were pre-disaster. FEMA will consider the impact of the loss of property tax revenue in Debt Service or Pension Funds (non-operating funds) if all of the following conditions are met:

(i) The entity experienced a loss of property tax revenue as a result of the disaster and the assessed value during the three years following the disaster, in the aggregate, is less than the pre-disaster assessed value;

(ii) the entity has a property tax cap limitation on the ability to raise property taxes post-disaster; and

(iii) the property taxes are levied through the General Operating Fund and transfers for obligations mandated by law are made to fund Debt Service or Pension Obligations which result in the entity experiencing a reduction of property tax revenues in the General Fund.

(5) It is not the purpose of this loan program to underwrite pre-disaster budget or actual deficits of the local government. Consequently, such deficits carried forward will reduce any

amounts otherwise eligible for loan cancellation.

(6) The provisions of this section apply to all Special Community Disaster loans issued from the dates of enactment of Public Law 109-88 and Public Law 109-234.

(d) *Disaster-related expenses of a municipal operation character.* (1) For purposes of this loan, unreimbursed expenses of a municipal operating character are those incurred for general government purposes, including but not limited to police and fire protection, trash collection, collection of revenues, maintenance of public facilities, flood and other hazard insurance.

(2) Disaster-related expenses do not include expenditures associated with debt service, any major repairs, rebuilding, replacement or reconstruction of public facilities or other capital projects, intragovernmental services, special assessments, and trust and agency fund operations. Disaster expenses which are eligible for reimbursement under project applications or other Federal programs are not eligible for loan cancellation.

(3) Each applicant shall maintain records including documentation necessary to identify expenditures for unreimbursed disaster-related expenses. Examples of such expenses include but are not limited to:

(i) Interest paid on money borrowed to pay amounts FEMA does not advance toward completion of approved Project Applications.

(ii) Unreimbursed costs to local governments for providing usable sites with utilities for mobile homes used to meet disaster temporary housing requirements.

(iii) Unreimbursed costs required for police and fire protection and other community services for mobile home parks established as the result of or for use following a disaster.

(iv) The cost to the applicant of flood insurance required under Public Law 93-234, as amended, and other hazard insurance required under section 311, Public Law 93-288, as amended, as a condition of Federal disaster assistance for the disaster under which the loan is authorized.

(4) The following expenses are not considered to be disaster-related for Special Community Disaster Loan purposes:

(i) The local government's share for assistance provided under the Stafford Act including flexible funding under section 406(c)(1) of the Act (42 U.S.C. 5172).

(ii) Improvements related to the repair or restoration of disaster public facilities approved on Project Applications.

(iii) Otherwise eligible costs for which no Federal reimbursement is requested as a part of the applicant's disaster response commitment, or cost sharing as specified in the FEMA-State Agreement for the disaster.

(iv) Expenses incurred by the local government which are reimbursed on the applicant's Project Application.

(e) *Cancellation application.* A local government which has drawn loan funds from the U.S. Treasury may request cancellation of the principal and related interest by submitting an Application for Loan Cancellation through the Governor's Authorized Representative to the Regional Administrator prior to the expiration date of the loan.

(1) Financial information submitted with the application shall include the following:

(i) Annual Operating Budgets for the fiscal year of the disaster and the three subsequent fiscal years;

(ii) Annual Financial Reports (Revenue and Expense and Balance Sheet) for each of the above fiscal years. Such financial records must include copies of the local government's annual financial reports, including operating statements and balance sheets and related consolidated and individual presentations for each fund account. In addition, the local government must include an explanatory statement when figures in the Application for Loan Cancellation form differ from those in the supporting financial reports.

(iii) The following additional information concerning annual real estate property taxes pertaining to the community for each of the above fiscal years:

(A) The market value of the tax base (dollars);

(B) The assessment ratio (percent);

(C) The assessed valuation (dollars);

(D) The tax levy rate (mils);

(E) Taxes levied and collected (dollars).

(iv) Audit reports for each of the above fiscal years certifying to the validity of the Operating Statements. The financial statements of the local government shall be examined in accordance with generally accepted auditing standards by independent certified public accountants. The report should not include recommendations concerning loan cancellation or repayment.

(v) Other financial information specified in the Application for Loan Cancellation.

(2) *Narrative justification.* The application may include a narrative presentation to supplement the financial material accompanying the application and to present any extenuating circumstances which the local government wants the Director of the Public Assistance Division to consider in rendering a decision on the cancellation request.

(f) *Determination.* (1) The Director of the Public Assistance Division will make a cancellation determination within 60 days of the date the applicant submits all required and requested information, including documentation in support of un-reimbursed disaster related expenses.

(2) If, based on a review of the Application for Loan Cancellation and FEMA audit, the Director of the Public Assistance Division determines that all or part of the Special Community Disaster Loan funds should be canceled, the amount of principal canceled and the related interest will be forgiven. The Director of the Public Assistance Division's determination concerning loan cancellation will specify that any uncancelled principal and related interest must be repaid in accordance with the terms and conditions of the Promissory Note, and that, if repayment will constitute a financial hardship, the local government must submit for FEMA review and approval, a repayment schedule for settling the indebtedness on a timely basis. Such repayments must be made to the Treasurer of the United States and be sent to FEMA, Attention: Office of the Chief Financial Officer.

(3) A loan or cancellation of a loan does not reduce or affect other disaster-related grants or other disaster assistance. However, no cancellation may be made that would result in a duplication of benefits to the applicant.

(4) The uncancelled portion of the loan must be repaid in accordance with §206.377.

(5) *Appeals.* If an Application for Loan Cancellation is disapproved, in whole or in part, by the Director of the Public Assistance Division, the local government may submit any additional information in support of the application within 60 days of the date of disapproval. The decision by the Assistant Administrator for the Disaster Assistance Directorate on the additional information is final.

[75 FR 2818, Jan. 19, 2010]

§206.377 **Loan repayment.**

(a) *Prepayments.* The local government may make prepayments against loan at any time without any prepayment penalty.

(b) *Repayment.* To the extent not otherwise cancelled, loan funds become due and payable in accordance with the terms and conditions of the Promissory Note. The note shall include the following provisions:

(1) The term of a loan made under this program is 5 years, unless extended by the Assistant Administrator for the Disaster Assistance Directorate. Interest will accrue on outstanding cash from the actual date of its disbursement by FEMA or FEMA's designated Disbursing Agency.

(2) The interest amount due will be computed separately for each Treasury disbursement as follows: $I = P \times R \times T$, where I = the amount of simple interest, P = the principal amount disbursed; R = the interest rate of the loan; and, T = the outstanding term in years from the date of disbursement to date of repayment, with periods less than 1 year computed on the basis of 365 days/year. If any portion of the loan is cancelled, the interest amount due will be computed on the remaining principal with the shortest outstanding term.

(3) Each payment made against the loan will be applied first to the interest computed to the date of the payment,

487

and then to the principal. Prepayments of scheduled installments, or any portion thereof, may be made at any time and shall be applied to the installments last to become due under the loan and shall not affect the obligation of the borrower to pay the remaining installments.

(4) The Assistant Administrator for the Disaster Assistance Directorate may defer payments of principal and interest until FEMA makes its final determination with respect to any Application for Loan Cancellation which the borrower may submit. However, interest will continue to accrue.

(5) Any costs incurred by the Federal Government in collecting the note shall be added to the unpaid balance of the loan, bear interest at the same rate as the loan, and be immediately due without demand.

(6) In the event of default on this note by the borrower, the FEMA claims collection officer will take action to recover the outstanding principal plus related interest under Federal debt collection authorities, including administrative offset against other Federal funds due the borrower and/or referral to the Department of Justice for judicial enforcement and collection.

(c) *Additional time.* In unusual circumstances involving financial hardship, the local government may request an additional period of time beyond the original 10 year term to repay the indebtedness. Such request may be approved by the Assistant Administrator for the Disaster Assistance Directorate subject to the following conditions:

(1) The local government must submit documented evidence that it has applied for the same credit elsewhere and that such credit is not available at a rate equivalent to the current Treasury rate.

(2) The principal amount shall be the original uncancelled principal plus related interest less any payments made.

(3) The interest rate shall be the Treasury rate in effect at the time the new Promissory Note is executed but in no case less than the original interest rate. A reduced rate may not be applied if was it was not previously applied to the loan.

(4) The term of the new Promissory Note shall be for the settlement period requested by the local government but not greater than 10 years from the date the new note is executed.

[70 FR 60446, Oct. 18, 2005, as amended at 75 FR 2820, Jan. 19, 2010]

§§ 206.378–206.389   [Reserved]

Subpart L—Fire Suppression Assistance

SOURCE: 55 FR 2318, Jan. 23, 1990, unless otherwise noted.

§ 206.390   General.

When the Assistant Administrator for the Disaster Assistance Directorate determines that a fire or fires threaten such destruction as would constitute a major disaster, assistance may be authorized, including grants, equipment, supplies, and personnel, to any State for the suppression of any fire on publicly or privately owned forest or grassland.

§ 206.391   FEMA-State Agreement.

Federal assistance under section 420 of the Act is provided in accordance with a continuing FEMA-State Agreement for Fire Suppression Assistance (the Agreement) signed by the Governor and the Regional Administrator. The Agreement contains the necessary terms and conditions, consistent with the provisions of applicable laws, Executive Orders, and regulations, as the Assistant Administrator for the Disaster Assistance Directorate may require and specifies the type and extent of Federal assistance. The Governor may designate authorized representatives to execute requests and certifications and otherwise act for the State during fire emergencies. Supplemental agreements shall be executed as required to update the continuing Agreement.

§ 206.392   Request for assistance.

When a Governor determines that fire suppression assistance is warranted, a request for assistance may be initiated. Such request shall specify in detail the factors supporting the request for assistance. In order that all actions in processing a State request are executed as rapidly as possible, the

State may submit a telephone request to the Regional Administrator, promptly followed by a confirming telegram or letter.

[55 FR 2318, Jan. 23, 1990, as amended at 74 FR 15352, Apr. 3, 2009]

§ 206.393 **Providing assistance.**

Following the Assistant Administrator for the Disaster Assistance Directorate's decision on the State request, the Regional Administrator will notify the Governor and the Federal firefighting agency involved. The Regional Administrator may request assistance from Federal agencies if requested by the State. For each fire or fire situation, the State shall prepare a separate Fire Project Application based on Federal Damage Survey Reports and submit it to the Regional Administrator for approval.

§ 206.394 **Cost eligibility.**

(a) *Cost principles.* See 44 CFR 13.22, Allowable Costs, and the associated OMB Circular A–87, Cost Principles for State and Local Governments.

(b) *Program specific eligible costs.* (1) Expenses to provide field camps and meals when made available to the eligible employees in lieu of per diem costs.

(2) Costs for use of publicly owned equipment used on eligible fire suppression work based on reasonable State equipment rates.

(3) Costs to the State for use of U.S. Government-owned equipment based on reasonable costs as billed by the Federal agency and paid by the State. Only direct costs for use of Federal Excess Personal Property (FEPP) vehicles and equipment on loan to State Forestry and local cooperators, can be paid.

(4) Cost of firefighting tools, materials, and supplies expended or lost, to the extent not covered by reasonable insurance.

(5) Replacement value of equipment lost in fire suppression, to the extent not covered by reasonable insurance.

(6) Costs for personal comfort and safety items normally provided by the State under field conditions for firefighter health and safety.

(7) Mobilization and demobilization costs directly relating to the Federal fire suppression assistance approved by the Assistant Administrator for the Disaster Assistance Directorate.

(8) Eligible costs of local governmental firefighting organizations which are reimbursed by the State pursuant to an existing cooperative mutual aid agreement, in suppressing an approved incident fire.

(9) State costs for suppressing fires on Federal land in cases in which the State has a responsibility under a cooperative agreement to perform such action on a nonreimbursable basis. This provision is an exception to normal FEMA policy under the Act and is intended to accommodate only those rare instances that involve State fire suppression of section 420 incident fires involving co-mingled Federal/State and privately owned forest or grassland.

(10) In those instances in which assistance under section 420 of the Act is provided in conjunction with existing Interstate Forest Fire Protection Compacts, eligible costs are reimbursed in accordance with eligibility criteria established in this section.

(c) *Program specific ineligible costs.* (1) Any costs for presuppression, salvaging timber, restoring facilities, seeding and planting operations.

(2) Any costs not incurred during the incident period as determined by the Regional Administrator other than reasonable and directly related mobilization and demobilization costs.

(3) State costs for suppressing a fire on co-mingled Federal land where such costs are reimbursable to the State by a Federal agency under another statute (see 44 CFR part 151).

§ 206.395 **Grant administration.**

(a) Project administration shall be in accordance with 44 CFR part 13, and applicable portions of subpart G, 44 CFR part 206.

(b) In those instances in which reimbursement includes State fire suppression assistance on co-mingled State and Federal lands (§ 206.394(b)(9)), the Regional Administrator shall coordinate with other Federal programs to preclude any duplication of payments. (See 44 CFR part 151.)

(c) Audits shall be in accordance with the Single Audit Act of 1984, Pub. L. 98–502. (See subpart G of this part.)

(d) A State may appeal a determination by the Regional Administrator on any action related to Federal assistance for fire suppression. Appeal procedures are contained in 44 CFR 206.206.

§§ 206.396–206.399　[Reserved]

Subpart M—Minimum Standards

SOURCE: 67 FR 8852, Feb. 26, 2002, unless otherwise noted.

§ 206.400　General.

(a) As a condition of the receipt of any disaster assistance under the Stafford Act, the applicant shall carry out any repair or construction to be financed with the disaster assistance in accordance with applicable standards of safety, decency, and sanitation and in conformity with applicable codes, specifications and standards.

(b) Applicable codes, specifications, and standards shall include any disaster resistant building code that meets the minimum requirements of the National Flood Insurance Program (NFIP) as well as being substantially equivalent to the recommended provisions of the National Earthquake Hazards Reduction Program (NEHRP). In addition, the applicant shall comply with any requirements necessary in regards to Executive Order 11988, Floodplain Management, Executive Order 12699, Seismic Safety of Federal and Federally Assisted or Regulated New Building Construction, and any other applicable Executive orders.

(c) In situations where there are no locally applicable standards of safety, decency and sanitation, or where there are no applicable local codes, specifications and standards governing repair or construction activities, or where the Regional Administrator determines that otherwise applicable codes, specifications, and standards are inadequate, then the Regional Administrator may, after consultation with appropriate State and local officials, require the use of nationally applicable codes, specifications, and standards, as well as safe land use and construction practices in the course of repair or construction activities.

(d) The mitigation planning process that is mandated by section 322 of the Stafford Act and 44 CFR part 201 can assist State and local governments in determining where codes, specifications, and standards are inadequate, and may need to be upgraded.

§ 206.401　Local standards.

The cost of repairing or constructing a facility in conformity with minimum codes, specifications and standards may be eligible for reimbursement under section 406 of the Stafford Act, as long as such codes, specifications, and standards meet the criteria that are listed at 44 CFR 206.226(d).

[74 FR 47482, Sept. 16, 2009]

§ 206.402　Compliance.

A recipient of disaster assistance under the Stafford Act must document for the Regional Administrator its compliance with this subpart following the completion of any repair or construction activities.

Subpart N—Hazard Mitigation Grant Program

SOURCE: 55 FR 35537, Aug. 30, 1990, unless otherwise noted.

§ 206.430　General.

This subpart provides guidance on the administration of hazard mitigation grants made under the provisions of section 404 of the Robert T. Stafford Disaster Relief and Emergency Assistance Act, 42 U.S.C. 5170c, hereafter Stafford Act, or the Act.

[59 FR 24356, May 11, 1994]

§ 206.431　Definitions.

Activity means any mitigation measure, project, or action proposed to reduce risk of future damage, hardship, loss or suffering from disasters.

Applicant means a State agency, local government, Indian tribal government, or eligible private nonprofit organization, submitting an application to the grantee for assistance under the HMGP.

Enhanced State Mitigation Plan is the hazard mitigation plan approved under 44 CFR part 201 as a condition of receiving increased funding under the HMGP.

Grant application means the request to FEMA for HMGP funding, as outlined in § 206.436, by a State or tribal government that will act as grantee.

Grant award means total of Federal and non-Federal contributions to complete the approved scope of work.

Grantee means the government to which a grant is awarded and which is accountable for the use of the funds provided. The grantee is the entire legal entity even if only a particular component of the entity is designated in the grant award document. Generally, the State for which the major disaster is declared is the grantee. However, an Indian tribal government may choose to be a grantee, or it may act as a subgrantee under the State. An Indian tribal government acting as a grantee will assume the responsibilities of a "state", under this subpart, for the purposes of administering the grant.

Indian Tribal government means any Federally recognized governing body of an Indian or Alaska Native Tribe, band, nation, pueblo, village, or community that the Secretary of Interior acknowledges to exist as an Indian Tribe under the Federally Recognized Indian Tribe List Act of 1994, 25 U.S.C. 479a. This does not include Alaska Native corporations, the ownership of which is vested in private individuals.

Local Mitigation Plan is the hazard mitigation plan required of a local government acting as a subgrantee as a condition of receiving a project subgrant under the HMGP as outlined in 44 CFR 201.6.

Standard State Mitigation Plan is the hazard mitigation plan approved under 44 CFR part 201, as a condition of receiving Stafford Act assistance as outlined in § 201.4.

State Administrative Plan for the Hazard Mitigation Grant Program means the plan developed by the State to describe the procedures for administration of the HMGP.

Subgrant means an award of financial assistance under a grant by a grantee to an eligible subgrantee.

Subgrant application means the request to the grantee for HMGP funding by the eligible subgrantee, as outlined in § 206.436.

Subgrantee means the government or other legal entity to which a subgrant is awarded and which is accountable to the grantee for the use of the funds provided. Subgrantees can be a State agency, local government, private nonprofit organizations, or Indian tribal government as outlined in § 206.433. Indian tribal governments acting as a subgrantee are accountable to the State grantee.

Tribal Mitigation Plan is the hazard mitigation plan required of an Indian Tribal government acting as a grantee or subgrantee as a condition of receiving a project grant or subgrant under the HMGP as outlined in 44 CFR 201.7.

[67 FR 8852, Feb. 26, 2002, as amended at 74 FR 47482, Sept. 16, 2009; 74 FR 60214, Nov. 20, 2009]

§ 206.432 **Federal grant assistance.**

(a) *General.* This section describes the extent of Federal funding available under the State's grant, as well as limitations and special procedures applicable to each.

(b) *Amounts of Assistance.* The total Federal contribution of funds is based on the estimated aggregate grant amount to be made under 42 U.S.C. 5170b, 5172, 5173, 5174, 5177, and 5183 of the Stafford Act for the major disaster (less associated administrative costs), and shall be as follows:

(1) *Standard percentages.* Not to exceed 15 percent for the first $2,000,000,000 or less of such amounts; not to exceed 10 percent of the portion of such amounts over $2,000,000,000 and not more than $10,000,000,000; and not to exceed 7.5 percent of the portion of such amounts over $10,000,000,000 and not more than $35,333,000,000.

(2) *Twenty (20) percent.* A State with an approved Enhanced State Mitigation Plan, in effect before the disaster declaration, which meets the requirements outlined in § 201.5 of this subchapter shall be eligible for assistance under the HMGP not to exceed 20 percent of such amounts, for amounts not more than $35.333 billion.

(3) The estimates of Federal assistance under this paragraph (b) shall be based on the Regional Administrator's estimate of all eligible costs, actual grants, and appropriate mission assignments.

(c) *Cost sharing.* All mitigation measures approved under the State's grant will be subject to the cost sharing provisions established in the FEMA-State Agreement. FEMA may contribute up to 75 percent of the cost of measures approved for funding under the Hazard Mitigation Grant Program for major disasters declared on or after June 10, 1993. FEMA may contribute up to 50 percent of the cost of measures approved for funding under the Hazard Mitigation Grant Program for major disasters declared before June 10, 1993. The nonFederal share may exceed the Federal share. FEMA will not contribute to costs above the Federally approved estimate.

[55 FR 35537, Aug. 30, 1990, as amended at 59 FR 24356, May 11, 1994; 67 FR 8853, Feb. 26, 2002; 67 FR 61515, Oct. 1, 2002; 69 FR 55097, Sept. 13, 2004; 72 FR 61750, Oct. 31, 2007; 74 FR 47482, Sept. 16, 2009]

§ 206.433   State responsibilities.

(a) *Grantee.* The State will be the Grantee to which funds are awarded and will be accountable for the use of those funds. There may be subgrantees within the State government.

(b) *Priorities.* The State will determine priorities for funding. This determination must be made in conformance with § 206.435.

(c) *Hazard Mitigation Officer.* The State must appoint a Hazard Mitigation Officer who serves as the responsible individual for all matters related to the Hazard Mitigation Grant Program.

(d) *Administrative plan.* The State must have an approved administrative plan for the Hazard Mitigation Grant Program in conformance with § 206.437.

[55 FR 35537, Aug. 30, 1990, as amended at 72 FR 61750, Oct. 31, 2007]

§ 206.434   Eligibility.

(a) *Applicants.* The following are eligible to apply for the Hazard Mitigation Program Grant:

(1) State and local governments;

(2) Private nonprofit organizations that own or operate a private nonprofit facility as defined in § 206.221(e). A qualified conservation organization as defined at § 80.3(h) of this chapter is the only private nonprofit organization eligible to apply for acquisition or relocation for open space projects;

(3) Indian tribes or authorized tribal organizations and Alaska Native villages or organizations, but not Alaska native corporations with ownership vested in private individuals.

(b) *Plan requirement.* (1) Local and Indian Tribal government applicants for project subgrants must have an approved local or Tribal Mitigation Plan in accordance with 44 CFR part 201 before receipt of HMGP subgrant funding for projects.

(2) Regional Administrators may grant an exception to this requirement in extraordinary circumstances, such as in a small and impoverished community when justification is provided. In these cases, a plan will be completed within 12 months of the award of the project grant. If a plan is not provided within this timeframe, the project grant will be terminated, and any costs incurred after notice of grant's termination will not be reimbursed by FEMA.

(c) *Minimum project criteria.* To be eligible for the Hazard Mitigation Grant Program, a project must:

(1) Be in conformance with the State Mitigation Plan and Local or Tribal Mitigation Plan approved under 44 CFR part 201; or for Indian Tribal governments acting as grantees, be in conformance with the Tribal Mitigation Plan approved under 44 CFR 201.7;

(2) Have a beneficial impact upon the designated disaster area, whether or not located in the designated area;

(3) Be in conformance with 44 CFR part 9, Floodplain Management and Protection of Wetlands, and 44 CFR part 10, Environmental Considerations;

(4) Solve a problem independently or constitute a functional portion of a solution where there is assurance that the project as a whole will be completed. Projects that merely identify or analyze hazards or problems are not eligible;

(5) Be cost-effective and substantially reduce the risk of future damage, hardship, loss, or suffering resulting from a major disaster. The grantee must demonstrate this by documenting that the project;

(i) Addresses a problem that has been repetitive, or a problem that poses a significant risk to public health and safety if left unsolved,

(ii) Will not cost more than the anticipated value of the reduction in both direct damages and subsequent negative impacts to the area if future disasters were to occur,

(iii) Has been determined to be the most practical, effective, and environmentally sound alternative after consideration of a range of options,

(iv) Contributes, to the extent practicable, to a long-term solution to the problem it is intended to address,

(v) Considers long-term changes to the areas and entities it protects, and has manageable future maintenance and modification requirements.

(d) *Eligible activities*—(1) *Planning.* Up to 7% of the State's HMGP grant may be used to develop State, tribal and/or local mitigation plans to meet the planning criteria outlined in 44 CFR part 201.

(2) *Types of projects.* Projects may be of any nature that will result in protection to public or private property. Activities for which implementation has already been initiated or completed are not eligible for funding. Eligible projects include, but are not limited to:

(i) Structural hazard control or protection projects;

(ii) Construction activities that will result in protection from hazards;

(iii) Retrofitting of facilities;

(iv) Property acquisition or relocation, as defined in paragraph (e) of this section;

(v) Development of State or local mitigation standards;

(vi) Development of comprehensive mitigation programs with implementation as an essential component;

(vii) Development or improvement of warning systems.

(e) *Property acquisitions and relocation requirements.* Property acquisitions and relocation projects for open space proposed for funding pursuant to a major disaster declared on or after December 3, 2007 must be implemented in accordance with part 80 of this chapter. For major disasters declared before December 3, 2007, a project involving property acquisition or the relocation of structures and individuals is eligible for assistance only if the applicant enters into an agreement with the FEMA Regional Administrator that provides assurances that:

(1) The following restrictive covenants shall be conveyed in the deed to any property acquired, accepted, or from which structures are removed (hereafter called in section (d) the property):

(i) The property shall be dedicated and maintained in perpetuity for uses compatible with open space, recreational, or wetlands management practices; and

(ii) No new structure(s) will be built on the property except as indicated below:

(A) A public facility that is open on all sides and functionally related to a designated open space or recreational use;

(B) A rest room; or

(C) A structure that is compatible with open space, recreational, or wetlands management usage and proper floodplain management policies and practices, which the Administrator approves in writing before the construction of the structure begins.

(iii) After completion of the project, no application for additional disaster assistance will be made for any purpose with respect to the property to any Federal entity or source, and no Federal entity or source will provide such assistance.

(2) In general, allowable open space, recreational, and wetland management uses include parks for outdoor recreational activities, nature reserves, cultivation, grazing, camping (except where adequate warning time is not available to allow evacuation), temporary storage in the open of wheeled vehicles which are easily movable (except mobile homes), unimproved, previous parking lots, and buffer zones.

(3) Any structures built on the property according to paragraph (d)(1) of this section, shall be floodproofed or elevated to the Base Flood Elevation plus one foot of freeboard.

(f) *Duplication of programs.* Section 404 funds cannot be used as a substitute or replacement to fund projects or programs that are available under other Federal authorities, except under limited circumstances in which there are extraordinary threats to lives, public health or safety or improved property.

(g) *Packaging of programs.* Section 404 funds may be packaged or used in combination with other Federal, State, local, or private funding sources when appropriate to develop a comprehensive mitigation solution, though section 404 funds cannot be used as a match for other Federal funds.

[55 FR 35537, Aug. 30, 1990, as amended at 59 FR 24356, May 11, 1994; 67 FR 8853, Feb. 26, 2002; 67 FR 61515, Oct. 1, 2002; 69 FR 55097, Sept. 13, 2004; 72 FR 61750, Oct. 31, 2007; 74 FR 47483, Sept. 16, 2009]

§ 206.435 Project identification and selection criteria.

(a) *Identification.* It is the State's responsibility to identify and select eligible hazard mitigation projects. All funded projects must be consistent with the State Mitigation Plan. Hazard Mitigation projects shall be identified and prioritized through the State, Indian tribal, and local planning process.

(b) *Selection.* The State will establish procedures and priorities for the selection of mitigation measures. At a minimum, the criteria must be consistent with the criteria stated in § 206.434(c) and include:

(1) Measures that best fit within an overall plan for development and/or hazard mitigation in the community, disaster area, or State;

(2) Measures that, if not taken, will have a severe detrimental impact on the applicant, such as potential loss of life, loss of essential services, damage to critical facilities, or economic hardship on the community;

(3) Measures that have the greatest potential impact on reducing future disaster losses;

(c) *Other considerations.* In addition to the selection criteria noted above, consideration should be given to measures that are designed to accomplish multiple objectives including damage reduction, environmental enhancement, and economic recovery, when appropriate.

[55 FR 35537, Aug. 30, 1990, as amended at 66 FR 8853, Feb. 26, 2002; 68 FR 63738, Nov. 10, 2003]

§ 206.436 Application procedures.

(a) *General.* This section describes the procedures to be used by the grantee in submitting an application for HMGP funding. Under the HMGP, the State or Indian tribal government is the grantee and is responsible for processing subgrants to applicants in accordance with 44 CFR part 13 and this part 206. Subgrantees are accountable to the grantee.

(b) *Governor's Authorized Representative.* The Governor's Authorized Representative serves as the grant administrator for all funds provided under the Hazard Mitigation Grant Program. The Governor's Authorized Representative's responsibilities as they pertain to procedures outlined in this section include providing technical advice and assistance to eligible subgrantees, and ensuring that all potential applicants are aware of assistance available and submission of those documents necessary for grant award.

(c) *Hazard mitigation application.* Upon identification of mitigation measures, the State (Governor's Authorized Representative) will submit its Hazard Mitigation Grant Program application to the FEMA Regional Administrator. The application will identify one or more mitigation measures for which funding is requested. The application must include a Standard Form (SF) 424, Application for Federal Assistance, SF 424D, Assurances for Construction Programs, if appropriate, and a narrative statement. The narrative statement will contain any pertinent project management information not included in the State's administrative plan for Hazard Mitigation. The narrative statement will also serve to identify the specific mitigation measures for which funding is requested. Information required for each mitigation measure shall include the following:

(1) Name of the subgrantee, if any;

(2) State or local contact for the measure;

(3) Location of the project;

(4) Description of the measure;

(5) Cost estimate for the measure;

(6) Analysis of the measure's cost-effectiveness and substantial risk reduction, consistent with § 206.434(c);

(7) Work schedule;

(8) Justification for selection;

494

(9) Alternatives considered;

(10) Environmental information consistent with 44 CFR part 9, Floodplain Management and Protection of Wetlands, and 44 CFR part 10, Environmental Considerations.

(d) *Application submission time limit.* The State's application may be amended as the State identifies and selects local project applications to be funded. The State must submit all local HMGP applications and funding requests for the purpose of identifying new projects to the Regional Administrator within 12 months of the date of disaster declaration.

(e) *Extensions.* The State may request the Regional Administrator to extend the application time limit by 30 to 90 day increments, not to exceed a total of 180 days. The grantee must include a justification in its request.

(f) *FEMA approval.* The application and supplement(s) will be submitted to the FEMA Regional Administrator for approval. FEMA has final approval authority for funding of all projects.

(g) *Indian tribal grantees.* Indian tribal governments may submit a SF 424 directly to the Regional Administrator.

[67 FR 8853, Feb. 26, 2002]

§ 206.437 State administrative plan.

(a) *General.* The State shall develop a plan for the administration of the Hazard Mitigation Grant Program.

(b) *Minimum criteria.* At a minimum, the State administrative plan must include the items listed below:

(1) Designation of the State agency will have responsibility for program administration;

(2) Identification of the State Hazard Mitigation Officer responsible for all matters related to the Hazard Mitigation Grant Program.

(3) Determination of staffing requirements and sources of staff necessary for administration of the program;

(4) Establishment of procedures to:

(i) Identify and notify potential applicants (subgrantees) of the availability of the program;

(ii) Ensure that potential applicants are provided information on the application process, program eligibility and key deadlines;

(iii) Determine applicant eligibility;

(iv) Conduct environmental and floodplain management reviews;

(v) Establish priorities for selection of mitigation projects;

(vi) Process requests for advances of funds and reimbursement;

(vii) Monitor and evaluate the progress and completion of the selected projects;

(viii) Review and approve cost overruns;

(ix) Process appeals;

(x) Provide technical assistance as required to subgrantee(s);

(xi) Comply with the administrative and audit requirements of 44 CFR parts 13 and 206;

(xii) Provide quarterly progress reports to the Regional Administrator on approved projects.

(xiii) Determine the percentage or amount of pass-through funds for management costs provided under 44 CFR part 207 that the grantee will make available to subgrantees, and the basis, criteria, or formula for determining the subgrantee percentage or amount.

(c) *Format.* The administrative plan is intended to be a brief but substantive plan documenting the State's process for the administration of the Hazard Mitigation Grant Program and management of the section 404 funds. This administrative plan should become a part of the State's overall emergency response or operations plan as a separate annex or chapter.

(d) *Approval.* The State must submit the administrative plan to the Regional Administrator for approval. Following each major disaster declaration, the State shall prepare any updates, amendments, or plan revisions required to meet current policy guidance or changes in the administration of the Hazard Mitigation Grant Program. Funds shall not be awarded until the State administrative plan is approved by the FEMA Regional Administrator.

[55 FR 35537, Aug. 30, 1990, as amended at 55 FR 52172, Dec. 20, 1990; 72 FR 57875, Oct. 11, 2007; 74 FR 15352, Apr. 3, 2009]

§ 206.438 Project management.

(a) *General.* The State serving as grantee has primary responsibility for project management and accountability of funds as indicated in 44 CFR part 13. The State is responsible for ensuring that subgrantees meet all program and administrative requirements.

(b) *Cost overruns.* During the execution of work on an approved mitigation measure the Governor's Authorized Representative may find that actual project costs are exceeding the approved estimates. Cost overruns which can be met without additional Federal funds, or which can be met by offsetting cost underruns on other projects, need not be submitted to the Regional Administrator for approval, so long as the full scope of work on all affected projects can still be met. For cost overruns which exceed Federal obligated funds and which require additional Federal funds, the Governor's Authorized Representative shall evaluate each cost overrun and shall submit a request with a recommendation to the Regional Administrator for a determination. The applicant's justification for additional costs and other pertinent material shall accompany the request. The Regional Administrator shall notify the Governor's Authorized Representative in writing of the determination and process a supplement, if necessary. All requests that are not justified shall be denied by the Governor's Authorized Representative. In no case will the total amount obligated to the State exceed the funding limits set forth in § 206.432(b). Any such problems or circumstances affecting project costs shall be identified through the quarterly progress reports required in paragraph (c) of this section.

(c) *Progress reports.* The grantee shall submit a quarterly progress report to FEMA indicating the status and completion date for each measure funded. Any problems or circumstances affecting completion dates, scope of work, or project costs which are expected to result in noncompliance with the approved grant conditions shall be described in the report.

(d) *Payment of claims.* The Governor's Authorized Representative shall make a claim to the Regional Administrator for reimbursement of allowable costs for each approved measure. In submitting such claims the Governor's Authorized Representative shall certify that reported costs were incurred in the performance of eligible work, that

the approved work was completed and that the mitigation measure is in compliance with the provisions of the FEMA-State Agreement. The Regional Administrator shall determine the eligible amount of reimbursement for each claim and approve payment. If a mitigation measure is not completed, and there is not adequate justification for noncompletion, no Federal funding will be provided for that measure.

(e) *Audit requirements.* Uniform audit requirements as set forth in 44 CFR part 13 apply to all grant assistance provided under this subpart. FEMA may elect to conduct a Federal audit on the disaster assistance grant or on any of the subgrants.

[55 FR 35537, Aug. 30, 1990, as amended at 74 FR 15352, Apr. 3, 2009]

§ 206.439   Allowable costs.

(a) General requirements for determining allowable costs are established in 44 CFR 13.22. Exceptions to those requirements as allowed in 44 CFR 13.4 and 13.6 are explained in paragraph (b) of this section.

(b) Administrative and management costs for major disasters will be paid in accordance with 44 CFR part 207.

(c) *Pre-award costs.* FEMA may fund eligible pre-award planning or project costs at its discretion and as funds are available. Grantees and subgrantees may be reimbursed for eligible pre-award costs for activities directly related to the development of the project or planning proposal. These costs can only be incurred during the open application period of the grant program. Costs associated with implementation of the activity but incurred prior to grant award are not eligible. Therefore, activities where implementation is initiated or completed prior to award are not eligible and will not be reimbursed.

[72 FR 57875, Oct. 11, 2007, as amended at 72 FR 61750, Oct. 31, 2007]

§ 206.440   Appeals.

An eligible applicant, subgrantee, or grantee may appeal any determination previously made related to an application for or the provision of Federal assistance according to the procedures below.

(a) *Format and Content.* The applicant or subgrantee will make the appeal in writing through the grantee to the Regional Administrator. The grantee shall review and evaluate all subgrantee appeals before submission to the Regional Administrator. The grantee may make grantee-related appeals to the Regional Administrator. The appeal shall contain documented justification supporting the appellant's position, specifying the monetary figure in dispute and the provisions in Federal law, regulation, or policy with which the appellant believes the initial action was inconsistent.

(b) *Levels of Appeal.* (1) The Regional Administrator will consider first appeals for hazard mitigation grant program-related decisions under subparts M and N of this part.

(2) The Assistant Administrator for the Mitigation Directorate will consider appeals of the Regional Administrator's decision on any first appeal under paragraph (b)(1) of this section.

(c) *Time Limits.* (1) Appellants must make appeals within 60 days after receipt of a notice of the action that is being appealed.

(2) The grantee will review and forward appeals from an applicant or subgrantee, with a written recommendation, to the Regional Administrator within 60 days of receipt.

(3) Within 90 days following receipt of an appeal, the Regional Administrator (for first appeals) or Assistant Administrator for the Mitigation Directorate (for second appeals) will notify the grantee in writing of the disposition of the appeal or of the need for additional information. A request by the Regional Administrator or Assistant Administrator for the Mitigation Directorate for additional information will include a date by which the information must be provided. Within 90 days following the receipt of the requested additional information or following expiration of the period for providing the information, the Regional Administrator or Assistant Administrator for the Mitigation Directorate will notify the grantee in writing of the disposition of the appeal. If the decision is to grant the appeal, the Regional Administrator will take appropriate implementing action.

(d) *Technical Advice.* In appeals involving highly technical issues, the Regional Administrator or Assistant Administrator for the Mitigation Directorate may, at his or her discretion, submit the appeal to an independent scientific or technical person or group having expertise in the subject matter of the appeal for advice or recommendation. The period for this technical review may be in addition to other allotted time periods. Within 90 days of receipt of the report, the Regional Administrator or Assistant Administrator for the Mitigation Directorate will notify the grantee in writing of the disposition of the appeal.

(e) *Transition.* (1) This rule is effective for all appeals pending on and appeals from decisions issued on or after May 8, 1998, except as provided in paragraph (e)(2) of this section.

(2) Appeals pending from a decision of an Assistant Administrator for the Mitigation Directorate before May 8, 1998 may be appealed to the Administrator in accordance with 44 CFR 206.440 as it existed before May 8, 1998.

(3) The decision of the FEMA official at the next higher appeal level shall be the final administrative decision of FEMA.

[63 FR 17111, Apr. 8, 1998]

PART 207—MANAGEMENT COSTS

Sec.
207.1 Purpose.
207.2 Definitions.
207.3 Applicability and eligibility.
207.4 Responsibilities.
207.5 Determination of management cost funding.
207.6 Use of funds.
207.7 Procedures for requesting management cost funding.
207.8 Management cost funding oversight.
207.9 Declarations before November 13, 2007.
207.10 Review of management cost rates.

AUTHORITY: Robert T. Stafford Disaster Relief and Emergency Assistance Act, 42 U.S.C. 5121 through 5206; Reorganization Plan No. 3 of 1978, 43 FR 41943, 3 CFR, 1978 Comp., p. 329; Homeland Security Act of 2002, 6 U.S.C. 101; E.O. 12127, 44 FR 19367, 3 CFR, 1979 Comp., p. 376; E.O. 12148, 44 FR 43239, 3 CFR, 1979 Comp., p. 412; E.O. 13286, 68 FR 10619, 3 CFR, 2003 Comp., p. 166.

SOURCE: 72 FR 57875, Oct. 11, 2007, unless otherwise noted.

§ 207.1 Purpose.

The purpose of this part is to implement section 324 of the Robert T. Stafford Disaster Relief and Emergency Assistance Act (Stafford Act), 42 U.S.C. 5165b.

§ 207.2 Definitions.

Cap means the maximum dollar amount that may be provided to a grantee for management cost funds for a single declaration pursuant to § 207.5(c) of this part.

Chief Financial Officer (CFO) is the Chief Financial Officer of FEMA, or his/her designated representative.

Cognizant Agency means the Federal agency responsible for reviewing, negotiating, and approving cost allocation plans or indirect cost proposals developed on behalf of all Federal agencies. The Office of Management and Budget (OMB) publishes a listing of cognizant agencies.

Grant means an award of financial assistance making payment in cash, property, or in kind for a specified purpose, by the Federal Government to an eligible grantee.

Grantee for purposes of this part means the government to which a Public Assistance (PA) or Hazard Mitigation Grant Program (HMGP) grant is awarded that is accountable for the use of the funds provided. The grantee is the entire legal entity even if only a particular component of the entity is designated in the grant award document. Generally, the State is the grantee. However, after a declaration, an Indian tribal government may choose to be a grantee, or may act as a subgrantee under the State for purposes of administering a grant under PA, HMGP, or both. When an Indian tribal government has chosen to act as grantee, it will also assume the responsibilities of a "grantee" under this part for the purposes of administering management cost funding.

Hazard Mitigation Grant Program (HMGP) means the program implemented at part 206, subpart N of this chapter.

HMGP lock-in ceiling means the level of HMGP funding available to a grantee for a particular disaster declaration.

HMGP project narrative refers to the request submitted for HMGP funding.

Indian tribal government is a Federally recognized governing body of an Indian or Alaska Native tribe, band, nation, pueblo, village, or community that the Secretary of Interior acknowledges to exist as an Indian tribe under the Federally Recognized Tribe List Act of 1994, 25 U.S.C. 479a. This does not include Alaska Native corporations, the ownership of which is vested in private individuals.

Indirect Costs means costs that are incurred by a grantee for a common or joint purpose benefiting more than one cost objective that are not readily assignable to the cost objectives specifically benefited.

Lock-in means the amount of management cost funds available to a grantee for PA or HMGP, respectively, for a particular major disaster or emergency, as FEMA determines at 30 days, 6 months, and 12 months or upon calculation of the final HMGP lock-in ceiling, whichever is later.

Management Costs means any indirect costs, administrative expenses, and any other expenses not directly chargeable to a specific project that are reasonably incurred by a grantee or subgrantee in administering and managing a PA or HMGP grant award. For HMGP, management cost funding is provided outside of Federal assistance limits defined at § 206.432(b) of this chapter.

Project refers to a project as defined at § 206.201(i) of this chapter for PA or eligible activities as defined at § 206.434(d) of this chapter for HMGP.

Project Worksheet (PW) refers to FEMA Form 90–91, or any successor form, on which the scope of work and cost estimate for a logical grouping of work required under the PA program as a result of a declared major disaster or emergency is documented.

Public Assistance (PA) means the program implemented at part 206, subparts G and H of this chapter.

Regional Administrator is the head of a FEMA regional office, or his/her designated representative, appointed under section 507 of the Post-Katrina Emergency Management Reform Act of 2006 (Pub. L. 109–295). The term also refers to Regional Directors as discussed in part 2 of this chapter.

Stafford Act refers to the Robert T. Stafford Disaster Relief and Emergency Assistance Act, as amended (42 U.S.C. 5121–5206).

State is any State of the United States, the District of Columbia, Puerto Rico, the Virgin Islands, Guam, American Samoa, and the Commonwealth of the Northern Mariana Islands.

Subgrantee means the government or other legal entity to which a grantee awards a subgrant and which is accountable to the grantee for the use of the funds provided. Subgrantees can be a State agency, local government, private nonprofit organization, or Indian tribal government.

§ 207.3 Applicability and eligibility.

Only PA and HMGP grantees with PA and HMGP grants awarded pursuant to major disasters and emergencies declared by the President on or after November 13, 2007 are eligible to apply to FEMA for management cost funding under this part.

§ 207.4 Responsibilities.

(a) *General.* This section identifies key responsibilities of FEMA and grantees in carrying out section 324 of the Stafford Act, 42 U.S.C. 5165b. These responsibilities are unique to the administration of this part and are in addition to common Federal Government requirements of grantees and subgrantees, consistent with OMB circulars and other applicable requirements, such as part 13 of this chapter.

(b) *FEMA.* FEMA is responsible for:

(1) Determining the lock-in amount for management costs in accordance with § 207.5.

(2) Obligating funds for management costs in accordance with § 207.5(b).

(3) Deobligating funds provided for management costs not disbursed in accordance with § 207.8(b).

(4) Reviewing management cost rates not later than 3 years after this rule is in effect and periodically thereafter.

(c) *Grantee.* The grantee must:

(1) Administer management cost funds to ensure that PA and HMGP, as applicable, are properly implemented and closed out in accordance with program timeframes and guidance.

(2) Determine the reasonable amount or percentage of management cost funding to be passed through to subgrantees for contributions to their costs for administering PA and HMGP projects and ensure that it provides such funds to subgrantees.

(3) Address procedures for subgrantee management costs amount or percentage determination, pass through, closeout, and audit in the State administrative plan required in § 206.207(b) of this chapter for PA and § 206.437 of this chapter for HMGP.

§ 207.5 Determination of management cost funding.

(a) *General.* This section describes how FEMA determines the amount of funds that it will contribute under this part for management costs for PA and/or HMGP for a particular major disaster or emergency.

(b) *Lock-in.* FEMA will determine the amount of funds that it will make available for management costs by a lock-in, which will act as a ceiling for funds available to a grantee, including its subgrantees.

(1) Not earlier than 30 days and not later than 35 days from the date of declaration, FEMA will provide the grantee preliminary lock-in amount(s) for management costs based on the projections at that time of the Federal share for financial assistance for PA and HMGP, as applicable. In accordance with § 207.7(c), FEMA will obligate 25 percent of the estimated lock-in amount(s) to the grantee.

(2) For planning purposes, FEMA will revise the lock-in amount(s) at 6 months after the date of the declaration. In accordance with § 207.7(e), FEMA may obligate interim amount(s) to the grantee.

(3) FEMA will determine the final lock-in amount(s) 12 months after date of declaration or after determination of the final HMGP lock-in ceiling, whichever is later. FEMA will obligate the remainder of the lock-in amount(s) to the grantee in accordance with § 207.7(f).

(4) *Rates.* (i) For major disaster declarations, FEMA will determine the

lock-in for PA based on a flat percentage rate of the Federal share of projected eligible program costs for financial assistance pursuant to sections 403, 406, and 407 of the Stafford Act, 42 U.S.C. 5170b, 5172, and 5173, respectively, but not including direct Federal assistance. For major disaster declarations on or after November 13, 2007, the PA rate will be 3.34 percent.

(ii) For major disaster declarations, FEMA will determine the lock-in for HMGP based on a flat percentage rate of the Federal share of projected eligible program costs under section 404 of the Stafford Act, 42 U.S.C. 5170c. For major disaster declarations on or after November 13, 2007, the HMGP rate will be 4.89 percent.

(iii) For emergency declarations, FEMA will determine the lock-in for PA based on a flat percentage rate of the Federal share of projected eligible program costs for financial assistance (sections 502 and 503 of the Stafford Act, 42 U.S.C. 5192 and 5193, respectively), but not including direct Federal assistance. For emergency declarations on or after November 13, 2007 the rate will be 3.90 percent.

(c) The dollar amount provided to a grantee for management cost funds for a single declaration will not exceed 20,000,000, except as described in paragraphs (d) and (e) of this section.

(d) The grantee must justify in writing to the Regional Administrator any requests to change the amount of the lock-in or the cap, extend the time period before lock-in, or request an interim obligation of funding at the time of the 6-month lock-in adjustment. The Regional Administrator will recommend to the Chief Financial Officer whether to approve the extension, change, or interim obligation. Extensions, changes to the lock-in, or interim obligations will not be made without the approval of the Chief Financial Officer.

(e) The Chief Financial Officer may change the amount of the lock-in or the cap, or extend the time before lock-in, if the Chief Financial Officer determines that the projections used to determine the lock-in were inaccurate to such a degree that the change to the lock-in would be material, or for other reasons in his or her discretion that

may reasonably warrant such changes. The Chief Financial Officer will not make such changes without consultation with the grantee and the Regional Administrator.

§ 207.6 Use of funds.

(a) The grantee or subgrantee must use management cost funds provided under this part in accordance with § 13.22 of this chapter and only for costs related to administration of PA or HMGP, respectively. All charges must be properly documented in accordance with § 207.8(f).

(b) Indirect costs may not be charged directly to a project or reimbursed separately, but rather are considered to be eligible management costs under this part.

(c) Activities and costs that can be directly charged to a project with proper documentation are not eligible for funding under this part.

§ 207.7 Procedures for requesting management cost funding.

(a) *General.* This section describes the procedures to be used by the grantee in requesting management cost funding.

(b) *State Administrative Plan Requirements.* State administrative plans, as required in § 206.207(b) of this chapter for PA and § 206.437 of this chapter for HMGP, must be amended to include procedures for subgrantee management costs amount or percentage determination, pass through, closeout, and audit, as required by § 207.4(c)(3) before management cost funds will be provided under this part.

(c) *Initial Funding Request Submission.* Upon notification of the preliminary lock-in amount(s) for management costs based on the Federal share of the projected eligible program costs for financial assistance at that time for PA and HMGP, as applicable, the grantee must submit its initial management cost funding request to the Regional Administrator. FEMA must receive the initial funding request before it will provide any management cost funds under this part.

(1) For PA management costs, funding requests shall be submitted using a PW.

(2) For HMGP management costs, funding requests shall be submitted using an HMGP project narrative.

(d) *Request Documentation.* The grantee is required to submit, no later than 120 days after the date of declaration, documentation to support costs and activities for which the projected lock-in for management cost funding will be used. In extraordinary circumstances, FEMA may approve a request by a grantee to submit support documentation after 120 days. FEMA will work with the grantee to approve or reject the request within 30 days of receipt of the request. If the request is rejected, the grantee will have 30 days to resubmit it for reconsideration and approval. FEMA will not obligate the balance of the management costs lock-in pursuant to a final funding request as described in paragraph (f) of this section or any interim amounts as allowed under paragraph (e) of this section unless the grantee's documentation is approved. The documentation must include:

(1) A description of activities, personnel requirements, and other costs for which the grantee will use management cost funding provided under this part;

(2) The grantee's plan for expending and monitoring the funds provided under this part and ensuring sufficient funds are budgeted for grant closeout; and

(3) An estimate of the percentage or amount of pass-through funds for management costs provided under this part that the grantee will make available to subgrantees, and the basis, criteria, or formula for determining the subgrantee percentage or amount (*e.g.*, number of projects, complexity of projects, X percent to any subgrantee).

(e) *Interim Funding Request.* If the grantee can justify a bona fide need for an additional obligation of management cost funds at 6 months, the grantee may submit a request to the Regional Administrator. Any interim obligations by FEMA must be approved by the Chief Financial Officer and will not exceed an amount equal to 10 percent of the 6-month lock-in amount, except in extraordinary circumstances.

(f) *Final Funding Request.* Upon notification of the final lock-in amount(s),

the grantee must submit a final management cost funding request to the Regional Administrator. Any necessary revisions to supporting documentation must be attached to the final funding request.

§ 207.8 Management cost funding oversight.

(a) *General.* The grantee has primary responsibility for grants management activities and accountability of funds provided for management costs as required by part 13 of this chapter, especially §§ 13.20 and 13.36. The grantee is responsible for ensuring that subgrantees meet all program and administrative requirements.

(b) *Period of availability.* (1) For major disaster declarations, the grantee may expend management cost funds for allowable costs for a maximum of 8 years from the date of the major disaster declaration or 180 days after the latest performance period date of a non-management cost PA PW or HMGP project narrative, respectively, whichever is sooner.

(2) For emergency declarations, the grantee may expend management cost funds for allowable costs for a maximum of 2 years from the date of the emergency declaration or 180 days after the latest performance period of a non-management cost PA PW, whichever is sooner.

(3) The period of availability may be extended only at the written request of the grantee, with the recommendation of the Regional Administrator, and with the approval of the Chief Financial Officer. The grantee must include a justification in its request for an extension, and must demonstrate that there is work in progress that can be completed within the extended period of availability. In no case will an extended period of availability allow more than 180 days after the expiration of any performance period extensions granted under PA or HMGP for project completion. FEMA will deobligate any funds not liquidated by the grantee in accordance with § 13.23 of this chapter.

(c) *Reporting requirements.* The grantee must provide quarterly progress reports on management cost funds to the Regional Administrator as required by the FEMA-State Agreement.

(d) *Closeout.* The grantee has primary responsibility for the closeout tasks associated with both the program and subgrantee requirements. Complying with each program's performance period requirement, the grantee must conduct final inspections for projects, reconcile subgrantee expenditures, resolve negative audit findings, obtain final reports from subgrantees and reconcile the closeout activities of subgrantees with PA and HMGP grant awards.

(e) *Audit requirements.* Uniform audit requirements in § 13.26 of this chapter apply to all assistance provided under this part.

(f) *Document Retention.* In compliance with State law and procedures and with § 13.42 of this chapter, grantees must retain records, including source documentation to support expenditures/costs incurred for management costs, for 3 years from the date of submission of the final Financial Status Report to FEMA that is required for PA and HMGP. The grantee is responsible for resolving questioned costs that may result from audit findings during the 3-year-record-retention period and returning any disallowed costs from ineligible activities.

§ 207.9 Declarations before November 13, 2007.

(a) *General.* This section describes how FEMA provides administrative and management cost funding for PA and HMGP for major disasters or emergencies declared before November 13, 2007.

(b) *Eligible direct costs.* Eligible direct costs to complete approved activities are governed by part 13 of this chapter. The eligible direct costs for administration and management of the program are divided into two categories as follows:

(1) *Grantee.* (i) *Statutory administrative costs.* FEMA may provide funds to the grantee to cover the extraordinary costs incurred in preparing project worksheets or applications, final inspection reports, quarterly reports, final audits, and related field inspections by State employees, including overtime pay and per diem and travel expenses, but not including regular time for such employees. FEMA will base the funds on the following percentages of the total amount of assistance provided (Federal share) for all subgrantees in the State under sections 403, 404, 406, 407, 502, and 503 of the Stafford Act (42 U.S.C. 5170b, 5170c, 5172, 5173, 5192, and 5193, respectively):

(A) For the first 100,000 of total assistance provided (Federal share), 3 percent of such assistance.

(B) For the next 900,000, 2 percent of such assistance.

(C) For the next 4,000,000, 1 percent of such assistance.

(D) For assistance over $5,000,000, one-half of 1 percent of such assistance.

(ii) *State management administrative costs.* Except for the items listed in paragraph (b)(1)(i) of this section, other administrative costs will be paid in accordance with § 13.22 of this chapter. The grantee and FEMA will share such costs under the cost share provisions of applicable PA and HMGP regulations.

(2) *Subgrantee.* The grantee may provide funds to the subgrantee to cover necessary costs of requesting, obtaining, and administering Federal disaster assistance subgrants, based on the following percentages of net eligible costs under sections 403, 404, 406, 407, 502, and 503 of the Stafford Act (42 U.S.C. 5170b, 5170c, 5172, 5173, 5192, and 5193, respectively), for an individual applicant (applicants in this context include State agencies):

(i) For the first $100,000 of net eligible costs, 3 percent of such costs.

(ii) For the next $900,000, 2 percent of such costs.

(iii) For the next $4,000,000, 1 percent of such costs.

(iv) For those costs over $5,000,000, one-half of 1 percent of such costs.

(c) *Eligible indirect costs:* (1) *Grantee.* Indirect costs of administering the disaster program are eligible in accordance with the provisions of part 13 of this chapter and OMB Circular No. A–87, if the grantee provides FEMA with a current Indirect Cost Rate Agreement approved by its Cognizant Agency.

(2) *Subgrantee.* No indirect costs of a subgrantee are separately eligible because the percentage allowance in paragraph (b)(2) of this section covers

necessary costs of requesting, obtaining and administering Federal assistance.

(d) *Availability.* (1) For major disaster declarations, FEMA will reimburse grantee eligible costs as described in this section at (b)(1)(ii) and (c)(1) for a maximum of 8 years from the date of the major disaster declaration or 180 days after the latest performance period date of a non-management cost PA PW or predecessor form or HMGP project narrative, respectively, whichever is sooner.

(2) For emergency declarations, FEMA will reimburse grantee eligible costs as described in this section at (b)(1)(ii) and (c)(1) for a maximum of 2 years from the date of the emergency declaration or 180 days after the latest performance period of a non-management cost PA PW or predecessor form, whichever is sooner.

(3) The reimbursement of grantee eligible costs as described in this section at (b)(1)(ii) and (c)(1) may be provided by FEMA after the periods of availability described in this section only at the written request of the grantee, with the recommendation of the Regional Administrator, and with the approval of the Chief Financial Officer. The grantee must include a justification in its request for further reimbursement, and must demonstrate that there is work in progress that can be completed within the extended period of reimbursement. In no case will reimbursement be provided after 180 days after the expiration of any performance period extensions granted under PA or HMGP for project completion.

§ 207.10 Review of management cost rates.

(a) FEMA will review management cost rates not later than 3 years after this rule is in effect and periodically thereafter.

(b) In order for FEMA to review the management cost rates established, and in accordance with part 13 of this chapter, the grantee and subgrantee must document all costs expended for management costs (including cost overruns). After review of this documentation, FEMA will determine whether the established management cost rates are adequate for the administration and closeout of the PA and HMGP programs.

PART 208—NATIONAL URBAN SEARCH AND RESCUE RESPONSE SYSTEM

Subpart A—General

Subpart B—Preparedness Cooperative Agreements

Subpart C—Response Cooperative Agreements

208.44 Reimbursement for other costs.
208.45 Advance of funds.
208.46 Title to equipment.
208.47–208.50 [Reserved]

Subpart D—Reimbursement Claims and Appeals

208.51 General.
208.52 Reimbursement procedures.
208.53–208.59 [Reserved]
208.60 Determination of claims.
208.61 Payment of claims.
208.62 Appeals.
208.63 Request by DHS for supplemental information.
208.64 Administrative and audit requirements.
208.65 Mode of transmission.
208.66 Reopening of claims for retrospective or retroactive adjustment of costs.
208.67–208.70 [Reserved]

AUTHORITY: Robert T. Stafford Disaster Relief and Emergency Assistance Act, 42 U.S.C. 5121 through 5206; Reorganization Plan No. 3 of 1978, 43 FR 41943, 3 CFR, 1978 Comp., p. 329; Homeland Security Act of 2002, 6 U.S.C. 101; E.O. 12127, 44 FR 19367, 3 CFR, 1979 Comp., p. 376; E.O. 12148, 44 FR 43239, 3 CFR, 1979 Comp., p. 412; E.O. 13286, 68 FR 10619, 3 CFR, 2003 Comp., p. 166.

SOURCE: 70 FR 9194, Feb. 24, 2005, unless otherwise noted.

Subpart A—General

§ 208.1 Purpose and scope of this part.

(a) *Purpose.* The purpose of this part is to prescribe policies and procedures pertaining to the Department of Homeland Security's (DHS) National Urban Search and Rescue Response System.

(b) *Scope.* This part applies to Sponsoring Agencies and other participants in the National Urban Search and Rescue Response System that have executed agreements governed by this part. Part 206 of this chapter does not apply to activities undertaken under this part, except as provided in §§ 208.5 and 208.10 of this part. This part does not apply to reimbursement under part 206, subpart H, of this chapter.

§ 208.2 Definitions of terms used in this part.

(a) *General.* Any capitalized word in this part is a defined term unless such capitalization results from the application of standard capitalization or style rules for Federal regulations. The fol-

lowing definitions have general applicability throughout this part:

Activated or *Activation* means the status of a System resource placed at the direction, control and funding of DHS in response to, or in anticipation of, a presidential declaration of a major disaster or emergency under the Stafford Act.

Activation Order means the DHS communication placing a System resource under the direction, control, and funding of DHS.

Advisory means a DHS communication to System resources indicating that an event has occurred or DHS anticipates will occur that may require Alert or Activation of System resources.

Alert means the status of a System resource's readiness when triggered by an Alert Order indicating that DHS may Activate the System resource.

Alert Order means the DHS communication that places a System resource on Alert status.

Assistant Administrator means the Assistant Administrator for the Disaster Operations Directorate.

Assistance Officer means the DHS employee who has legal authority to bind DHS by awarding and amending Cooperative Agreements.

Backfill means the personnel practice of temporarily replacing a person in his or her usual position with another person.

Cooperating Agency means a State or Local Government that has executed a Cooperative Agreement to provide Technical Specialists.

Cooperative Agreement means a legal instrument between DHS and a Sponsoring Agency or Cooperating Agency that provides funds to accomplish a public purpose and anticipates substantial Federal involvement during the performance of the contemplated activity.

Daily Cost Estimate means a Sponsoring Agency's estimate of Task Force personnel compensation, itemized fringe benefit rates and amounts including calculations, and Backfill expenditures for a 24-hour period of Activation.

Deputy Assistant Administrator means the Deputy Assistant Administrator for the Disaster Operations Directorate, or other person the Assistant Administrator designates.

DHS means the Department of Homeland Security.

Disaster Search Canine Team means a disaster search canine and handler who have successfully completed the written examination and demonstrated the performance skills required by the Disaster Search Canine Readiness Evaluation Process. A disaster search canine is a dog that has successfully completed the DHS Disaster Search Canine Readiness Evaluation criteria for Type II or both Type II and Type I.

Emergency means any occasion or instance for which, in the determination of the President, Federal assistance is needed to supplement State and local efforts and capabilities to save lives and to protect property and public health and safety, or to lessen or avert the threat of a catastrophe in any part of the United States.

Equipment Cache List means the DHS-issued list that defines:

(1) The equipment and supplies that US & R will furnish to Sponsoring Agencies; and

(2) The maximum quantities and types of equipment and supplies that a Sponsoring Agency may purchase and maintain with DHS funds.

Federal Excess Property means any Federal personal property under the control of a Federal agency that the agency head or a designee determines is not required for its needs or for the discharge of its responsibilities.

Federal Response Plan means the signed agreement among various Federal departments and agencies that provides a mechanism for coordinating delivery of Federal assistance and resources to augment efforts of State and Local Governments overwhelmed by a Major Disaster or Emergency, supports implementation of the Stafford Act, as well as individual agency statutory authorities, and supplements other Federal emergency operations plans developed to address specific hazards.

Joint Management Team or *JMT* means a multi-disciplinary group of National Disaster Medical System (NDMS), Urban Search and Rescue (US&R), and other specialists combined to provide operations, planning, logistics, finance and administrative support for US&R and NDMS resources, and to provide technical advice and assistance to States and Local Governments.

Local Government means any county, city, village, town, district, or other political subdivision of any State; any federally recognized Indian tribe or authorized tribal organization; and any Alaska Native village or organization.

Major Disaster means any natural catastrophe (including any hurricane, tornado, storm, high water, wind driven water, tidal wave, tsunami, earthquake, volcanic eruption, landslide, mudslide, snowstorm, or drought), or regardless of cause, any fire, flood, or explosion, in any part of the United States, that in the determination of the President, causes damage of sufficient severity and magnitude to warrant major disaster assistance under the Stafford Act to supplement the efforts and available resources of States, Local Governments, and disaster relief organizations in alleviating the damage, loss, hardship, or suffering caused thereby.

Memorandum of Agreement (MOA) means the document signed by DHS, a Sponsoring Agency and its State that describes the relationship of the parties with respect to the National Urban Search & Rescue Response System.

Participating Agency means a State or Local Government, non-profit organization, or private organization that has executed an agreement with a Sponsoring Agency to participate in the National US&R Response System.

Personnel Rehabilitation Period means the period allowed by DHS for a person's rehabilitation to normal conditions of living following an Activation.

Preparedness Cooperative Agreement means the agreement between DHS and a Sponsoring Agency for reimbursement of allowable expenditures incurred by the Sponsoring Agency to develop and maintain System capabilities and operational readiness.

Program Directive means guidance and direction for action to ensure consistency and standardization across the National US&R Response System.

Program Manager means the individual, or his or her designee, within DHS who is responsible for day-to-day administration of the National US&R Response System.

Program Office means the organizational entity within DHS that is responsible for day-to-day administration of the National US&R Response System.

Response Cooperative Agreement means an agreement between DHS and a Sponsoring Agency for reimbursement of allowable expenditures incurred by the Sponsoring Agency as a result of an Alert or Activation.

Sponsoring Agency means a State or Local Government that has executed an MOA with DHS to organize and administer a Task Force.

Stafford Act means the Robert T. Stafford Disaster Relief and Emergency Assistance Act, 42 U.S.C. 5121 through 5206.

State means any State of the United States, the District of Columbia, Puerto Rico, the Virgin Islands, Guam, American Samoa, the Commonwealth of the Northern Mariana Islands, the Federated States of Micronesia or the Republic of the Marshall Islands.

Support Specialist means a person participating in the System who assists the Task Force with administrative or other support during mobilization, ground transportation and demobilization as directed.

System or *National US&R Response System* means the national US&R response capability administered by DHS.

System Member means any Task Force Member, JMT Member, Technical Specialist, Support Specialist or Disaster Search Canine Team.

Task Force means an integrated US&R organization of multi-disciplinary resources with common communications and a leader, organized and administered by a Sponsoring Agency and meeting DHS standards.

Task Force Member means a person occupying a position on a Task Force.

Technical Specialist means a person participating in the System contributing technical knowledge and skill who may be placed on Alert or Activated as a single resource and not as a part of a JMT or a Task Force.

US&R means urban search and rescue, the process of searching for, extricating, and providing for the imme-

diate medical stabilization of victims who are entrapped in collapsed structures.

(b) *Additional definitions.* Definitions for certain terms that apply only to individual subparts of this part are located in those subparts.

[70 FR 9194, Feb. 24, 2005, as amended at 74 FR 15353, Apr. 3, 2009]

§ 208.3   Authority for the National US&R Response System.

(a) *Enabling legislation.* The Federal Emergency Management Agency established and operated the System under the authority of §§ 303, 306(a), 306(b), 403(a)(3)(B) and 621(c) of the Stafford Act, 42 U.S.C. 5144, 5149(a), 5149(b), 5170b(a)(3)(B) and 5197(c), respectively. Section 503 of the Homeland Security Act of 2002, 6 U.S.C. 313, transferred the functions of the Administrator of FEMA to the Secretary of Homeland Security. The President redelegated to the Secretary of Homeland Security in Executive Order 13286 those authorities of the President under the Stafford Act that had been delegated previously to the Administrator of FEMA under Executive Order 12148.

(b) *Implementing plan.* The National Response Plan identifies DHS as the primary Federal agency with responsibility for Emergency Support Function 9, Urban Search and Rescue.

§ 208.4   Purpose for System.

It is DHS policy to develop and provide a national system of standardized US&R resources to respond to Emergencies and Major Disasters that are beyond the capabilities of affected State and Local Governments.

§ 208.5   Authority of the Assistant Administrator for the Disaster Operations Directorate.

(a) *Participation in activities of the System.* The Assistant Administrator is responsible for determining participation in the System and any activity thereof, including but not limited to whether a System resource is operationally ready for Activation.

(b) *Standards for and measurement of System efficiency and effectiveness.* In addition to the authority provided in § 206.13 of this chapter, the Assistant

Administrator may establish performance standards and assess the efficiency and effectiveness of System resources.

§ 208.6   System resource reports.

(a) *Reports to Assistant Administrator.* The Assistant Administrator may request reports from any System resource relating to its activities as part of the System.

(b) *Reports to FEMA Regional Administrators.* Any FEMA Regional Administrator may request through the Assistant Administrator reports from any System resource used within or based within the Regional Administrator's jurisdiction.

(c) *Audits, investigations, studies and evaluations.* DHS and the General Accounting Office may conduct audits, investigations, studies, and evaluations as necessary. Sponsoring Agencies, Participating Agencies and System Members are expected to cooperate fully in such audits, investigations, studies and evaluations.

§ 208.7   Enforcement.

(a) *Remedies for noncompliance.* In accordance with the provisions of 44 CFR 13.43, if a Sponsoring Agency, Participating Agency, Affiliated Personnel or other System Member materially fails to comply with a term of a Cooperative Agreement, Memorandum of Agreement, System directive or other Program Directive, the Assistant Administrator may take one or more of the actions provided in 44 CFR 13.43(a)(1) through (5). Any such enforcement action taken by the Assistant Administrator will be subject to the hearings, appeals, and effects of suspension and termination provisions of 44 CFR 13.43(b) and (c).

(b) The enforcement remedies identified in this section, including suspension and termination, do not preclude a Sponsoring Agency, Participating Agency, Affiliated Personnel or other System Member from being subject to "Debarment and Suspension" under E.O. 12549, as amended, in accordance with 44 CFR 13.43(d).

(c) *Other authority for sanctions.* Nothing in this section limits or precludes the application of other authority to impose civil or criminal sanctions, including 42 U.S.C. 5156.

§ 208.8   Code of conduct.

The Assistant Administrator will develop and implement a code of conduct for System Members acting under DHS's direction and control. Nothing in this section or the DHS code of conduct will limit the authority of a Sponsoring Agency, Participating Agency or Cooperating Agency to apply its own code of conduct to its System Members or employees. If the DHS code is more restrictive, it controls.

§ 208.9   Agreements between Sponsoring Agencies and Participating Agencies.

Every agreement between a Sponsoring Agency and a Participating Agency regarding the System must include a provision making this part applicable to the Participating Agency and its employees who engage in System activities.

§ 208.10   Other regulations.

The following provisions of title 44 CFR, Chapter I also apply to the program in this part:

(a) Section 206.9, which deals with the non-liability of DHS in certain circumstances.

(b) Section 206.11, which prescribes nondiscrimination in the provision of disaster assistance.

(c) Section 206.14, which deals with criminal and civil penalties.

(d) Section 206.15, which permits recovery of assistance by DHS.

§ 208.11   Federal status of System Members.

The Assistant Administrator will appoint all Activated System Members as temporary excepted Federal volunteers. The Assistant Administrator may appoint a System Member who participates in Alert activities as such a Federal volunteer. The Assistant Administrator may also appoint each System Member who participates in DHS-sanctioned preparedness activities as a temporary excepted Federal volunteer. DHS intends these appointments to secure protection for such volunteers under the Federal Employees Compensation Act and the Federal Tort

507

Claims Act and do not intend to interfere with any preexisting employment relationship between a System Member and a Sponsoring Agency, Cooperating Agency or Participating Agency. System Members whom DHS appoints as temporary excepted Federal volunteers will not receive any compensation or employee benefit directly from the United States of America for their service, but will be compensated through their Sponsoring Agency.

§ 208.12 Maximum Pay Rate Table.

(a) *Purpose.* This section establishes the process for creating and updating the Maximum Pay Rate Table (Table), and the Table's use to reimburse Affiliated Personnel (Task Force Physicians, Task Force Engineers, and Canine Handlers) and Backfill for Activated System Members employed by or otherwise associated with a for-profit Participating Agency. Section 208.32 defines the "Maximum Pay Rate Table" as "the DHS-issued table that identifies the maximum pay rates for selected System positions that may be used for reimbursement of Affiliated Personnel compensation and Backfill for Activated System Members employed by or otherwise associated with a for-profit Participating Agency." In that same section, the term "Affiliated Personnel" is defined as "individuals not normally employed by a Sponsoring Agency or Participating Agency and individuals normally affiliated with a Sponsoring Agency or Participating Agency as volunteers."

(b) *Scope of this section.* (1) The Maximum Pay Rate Table applies to those individuals who are not normally employed by a Sponsoring Agency or Participating Agency, or whose affiliation with a Sponsoring Agency or Participating Agency is as a volunteer; that is, an individual whom the Sponsoring Agency or Participating Agency does not normally compensate in any way, at any rate.

(2) The Table also applies to Backfill for Activated System Members employed by or otherwise associated with a for-profit Participating Agency.

(c) *Method for determining maximum pay rates.* (1) DHS uses the United States Office of Personnel Management's salary rates, computed under 5

U.S.C. 5504, as the basis for the maximum pay rate schedule. DHS considers System members' experience and sets maximum pay rates at the maximum grade, middle step for each position, which demonstrates an experience level of five years.

(2) The Office of Personnel Management (OPM) publishes salary and locality pay schedules each calendar year.

(i) *Physicians.* DHS uses the latest Special Salary Rate Table Number 0290 for Medical Officers (Clinical) Worldwide for physicians. The rates used in the initial Table can be found at *http://www.opm.gov/oca/03 tables/SSR/HTML/0290.asp.*

(ii) *Engineers and Canine Handlers.* DHS uses the latest General Schedule pay scale for both positions. Both specialties are compared to the General Schedule pay scale to ensure parity with like specialties on a task force (canine handlers are equated with rescue specialists). The rates used in the initial Table can be found at *http://www.opm.gov/oca/03tables/html/gs.asp.*

(iii) *Locality Pay.* To determine adjustments for locality pay DHS uses the latest locality pay areas (including the "Rest of U.S." area) established by OPM. The rates used in the initial Table can be found at *http://www.opm.gov/oca/03tables/locdef.asp.*

(3) *Review and update.* DHS will review and update the Table periodically, at least annually. The comments of Sponsoring and Participating Agencies and their experience with the Table will be considered and evaluated in the course of the reviews.

(4) *Initial rates and subsequent revisions.* DHS will publish the initial maximum pay rate table in the FEDERAL REGISTER as a notice with request for comments. Subsequent revisions will be made to the pay rate table as OPM changes salary rates as described in this section. When subsequent revisions are made to the maximum pay rate table DHS will publish the new maximum pay rate table in the FEDERAL REGISTER. The rates will be effective for the latest year indicated by OPM.[1]

---

[1] In some years the latest year may not be the current calendar year. For instance,

(d) *Application of the maximum pay rate table*—(1) *Applicability.* The Maximum Pay Rate Table sets forth maximum rates for which DHS will reimburse the Sponsoring Agency for compensation paid to Activated Affiliated Personnel and as Backfill for Activated System Members employed by or otherwise associated with a for-profit Participating Agency.

(2) *Higher rates.* The Sponsoring Agency may choose to pay Affiliated Personnel at a higher rate, but DHS will not reimburse the increment above the maximum rate specified in the Maximum Pay Rate Table. Likewise, the Sponsoring Agency may choose to enter into a Participating Agency agreement with the individual's employer, rather than use the individual as an Affiliated Personnel, in which case the Maximum Pay Rate Table would not apply.

(3) *Compensation for Sponsoring Agency employees serving as Affiliated Personnel.* An employee of a Sponsoring Agency serving on a Task Force in a capacity other than his or her normal job, *e.g.*, a fire department dispatcher affiliated with the Task Force as a canine search specialist, as an Affiliated Personnel, would not necessarily be subject to the Maximum Pay Rate Table for reimbursement for salary and benefits for that individual. However, Sponsoring Agencies may use the rates in the Maximum Pay Rate Table as a guide for establishing compensation levels for such individuals.

(4) *Backfill expenses for Affiliated Personnel under § 208.39(g).* (i) The only way that DHS can reimburse for Backfill costs incurred for Affiliated Personnel is through Participating Agencies. If reimbursement for Backfill expenses is needed for Affiliated Personnel, DHS encourages them to urge their employers or professional association to seek Participating Agency status.

(ii) *Private, for-profit organizations.* Participating Agency status is available to private, for-profit organizations, *e.g.*, HMOs or medical or engineering professional associations, under the revised definition of "Participating Agency" set forth in this In-

terim rule. (See Definitions, § 208.2, *Participating Agency*, and § 208.32, *Maximum Pay Rate Table*). When a for-profit Participating Agency must backfill an Activated System Member's position we will compensate that Participating Agency up to the maximum rate provided in the Table.

(iii) *Compensation costs.* DHS will reimburse for-profit organizations, for purposes of reimbursement and Backfill, for the System Member's actual compensation or the actual compensation of the individual who Backfills a position (which includes salary and benefits, as described in §§ 208.39 and 208.40), but will not reimburse for billable or other rates that might be charged for services rendered to commercial clients or patients.

§§ 208.13–208.20 [Reserved]

Subpart B—Preparedness Cooperative Agreements

§ 208.21 **Purpose.**

Subpart B of this part provides guidance on the administration of Preparedness Cooperative Agreements.

§ 208.22 **Preparedness Cooperative Agreement process.**

(a) *Application.* To obtain DHS funding for an award or amendment of a Preparedness Cooperative Agreement, the Sponsoring Agency must submit an application. Standard form SF–424 "Application for Federal Assistance" generally will be used. However, the application must be in a form that the Assistance Officer specifies.

(b) *Award.* DHS will award a Preparedness Cooperative Agreement to each Sponsoring Agency to provide Federal funding to develop and maintain System resource capabilities and operational readiness. For the purposes of the Preparedness Cooperative Agreement, the Sponsoring Agency will be considered the "recipient."

(c) *Amendment*—(1) *Procedure.* Absent special circumstances, DHS will fund and amend Preparedness Cooperative Agreements on an annual basis. Before amendment, the Assistance Officer will issue a call for Cooperative Agreement

OPM did not change its pay rates for calendar year 2004, and the 2003 schedules apply.

amendment applications. The Assistance Officer will specify required application forms and supporting documentation to be submitted with the application.

(2) *Period of performance.* Absent special circumstances, the period of performance for Preparedness Cooperative Agreements will be 1 year from the date of award. The Assistance Officer may allow for an alternate period of performance with the approval of the Assistant Administrator.

(3) *Assistance Officer.* The Assistance Officer is the only individual authorized to award or modify a Preparedness Cooperative Agreement.

(d) *Award amounts.* The Assistant Administrator will determine award amounts on an annual basis. A Task Force is eligible for an annual award only if the Program Manager receives and approves the Task Force's current-year Daily Cost Estimate.

(e) *DHS priorities.* The Assistant Administrator will establish overall priorities for the use of Preparedness Cooperative Agreement funds taking into consideration the results of readiness evaluations and actual Activations, overall priorities of DHS, and other factors, as appropriate.

(f) *Cost sharing.* The Assistant Administrator may subject Preparedness Cooperative Agreement awards to cost sharing provisions. In the call for Preparedness Cooperative Agreement amendment applications, the Assistance Officer must inform Sponsoring Agencies about any cost sharing obligations.

(g) *Sponsoring Agency priorities.* The Sponsoring Agency should indicate its spending priorities in the application. The Program Manager will review these priorities and will make recommendations to the Assistance Officer for negotiating the final agreement.

(h) *Responsibility to maintain integrity of the equipment cache.* The Sponsoring Agency is responsible to maintain the integrity of the equipment cache, including but not limited to, maintenance of the cache, replacement of equipment or supplies expended in training, activations, or local use of the cache, and timely availability of the cache for Task Force Activations.

§ 208.23 Allowable costs under Preparedness Cooperative Agreements.

System Members may spend Federal funds that DHS provides under any Preparedness Cooperative Agreement and any required matching funds under 44 CFR 13.22 and this section to pay reasonable, allowable, necessary and allocable costs that directly support System activities, including the following:

(a) Administration, including:

(1) Management and administration of day-to-day System activities such as personnel compensation and benefits relating to System maintenance and development, record keeping, inventory of equipment, and correspondence;

(2) Travel to and from System activities, meetings, conferences, training, drills and exercises;

(3) Tests and examinations, including vaccinations, immunizations and other tests that are not normally required or provided in the course of a System Member's employment, and that DHS requires to meet its standards.

(b) Training:

(1) Development and delivery of, and participation in, System-related training courses, exercises, and drills;

(2) Construction, maintenance, lease or purchase of System-related training facilities or materials;

(3) Personnel compensation expenses, including overtime and other related expenses associated with System-related training, exercises, or drills;

(4) System-required evaluations and certifications other than the certifications that DHS requires System Members to possess at the time of entry into the System. For instance, DHS will not pay for a medical school degree, paramedic certification or recertification, civil engineering license, etc.

(c) Equipment:

(1) Procurement of equipment and supplies specifically identified on the then-current DHS-approved Equipment Cache List;

(2) Maintenance and repair of equipment included on the current Equipment Cache List;

(3) Maintenance and repair of equipment acquired with DHS approval through the Federal Excess Property

program, except as provided in § 208.25 of this part;

(4) Purchase, construction, maintenance or lease of storage facilities and associated equipment for System equipment and supplies.

(d) Disaster search canine expenses limited to:

(1) Procurement for use as a System resource;

(2) Training and certification expenses;

(3) Veterinary care.

(e) Management and administrative costs, actually incurred but not otherwise specified in this section that directly support the Sponsoring Agency's US&R capability, provided that such costs do not exceed 7.5 percent of the award/amendment amount.

§ 208.24 Purchase and maintenance of items not listed on Equipment Cache List.

(a) Requests for purchase or maintenance of equipment and supplies not appearing on the Equipment Cache List, or that exceed the number specified in the Equipment Cache List, must be made in writing to the Program Manager. No Federal funds provided under any Preparedness Cooperative Agreement may be expended to purchase or maintain any equipment or supply item unless:

(1) The equipment and supplies directly support the Sponsoring Agency's US&R capability;

(2) The Program Manager approves the expenditure and gives written notice of his or her approval to the Sponsoring Agency before the Sponsoring Agency purchases the equipment or supply item.

(b) Maintenance of items approved for purchase under this section is eligible for reimbursement, except as provided in § 208.26 of this subpart.

§ 208.25 Obsolete equipment.

(a) The Assistant Administrator will periodically identify obsolete items on the Equipment Cache List and provide such information to Sponsoring Agencies.

(b) Neither funds that DHS provides nor matching funds required under a Preparedness Cooperative Agreement may be used to maintain or repair items that DHS has identified as obsolete.

§ 208.26 Accountability for use of funds.

The Sponsoring Agency is accountable for the use of funds as provided under the Preparedness Cooperative Agreement, including financial reporting and retention and access requirements according to 44 CFR 13.41 and 13.42.

§ 208.27 Title to equipment.

Title to equipment purchased by a Sponsoring Agency with funds provided under a DHS Preparedness Cooperative Agreement vests in the Sponsoring Agency, provided that DHS reserves the right to transfer title to the Federal Government or a third party that DHS may name, under 44 CFR 13.32(g), for example, when a Sponsoring Agency indicates or demonstrates that it cannot fulfill its obligations under the Memorandum of Agreement.

§§ 208.28–208.30 [Reserved]

Subpart C—Response Cooperative Agreements

§ 208.31 Purpose.

Subpart C of this part provides guidance on the administration of Response Cooperative Agreements.

§ 208.32 Definitions of terms used in this subpart.

Affiliated Personnel means individuals not normally employed by a Sponsoring Agency or Participating Agency and individuals normally affiliated with a Sponsoring Agency or Participating Agency as volunteers.

Demobilization Order means a DHS communication that terminates an Alert or Activation and identifies cost and time allowances for rehabilitation.

Exempt means any System Member who is exempt from the requirements of the Fair Labor Standards Act, 29 U.S.C. 201 *et seq.*, pertaining to overtime compensation and other labor standards.

Maximum Pay Rate Table means the DHS-issued table that identifies the maximum pay rates for selected System positions that may be used for reimbursement of Affiliated Personnel compensation and Backfill for Activated System Members employed by or otherwise associated with a for-profit Participating Agency. The Maximum Pay Rate Table does not apply to a System member whom a Sponsoring Agency or Participating Agency employs.

Mobilization means the process of assembling equipment and personnel in response to an Alert or Activation.

Non-Exempt means any System Member who is covered by 29 U.S.C. 201 *et seq.*

Rehabilitation means the process of returning personnel and equipment to a pre-incident state of readiness after DHS terminates an Activation.

§ 208.33 Allowable costs.

(a) *Cost neutrality.* DHS policy is that an Alert or Activation should be as cost neutral as possible to Sponsoring Agencies and Participating Agencies. To make an Alert or Activation cost-neutral, DHS will reimburse under this subpart all reasonable, allowable, necessary and allocable costs that a Sponsoring Agency or Participating Agency incurs during the Alert or Activation.

(b) *Actual costs.* Notwithstanding any other provision of this chapter, DHS will not reimburse a Sponsoring Agency or Participating Agency for any costs greater than those that the Sponsoring Agency or Participating Agency actually incurs during an Alert, Activation.

(c) *Normal or predetermined practices.* Consistent with Office of Management and Budget (OMB) Circulars A–21, A–87, A–102 and A–110 (2 CFR part 215), as applicable, Sponsoring Agencies and Participating Agencies must adhere to their own normal and predetermined practices and policies of general application when requesting reimbursement from DHS except as it sets out in this subpart.

(d) *Indirect costs.* Indirect costs beyond the administrative and management costs allowance established by § 208.41 of this part are not allowable.

§ 208.34 Agreements between Sponsoring Agencies and others.

Sponsoring Agencies are responsible for executing such agreements with Participating Agencies and Affiliated Personnel as may be necessary to implement the Sponsoring Agency's Response Cooperative Agreement with DHS. Those agreements must identify established hourly or daily rates of pay for System Members. The hourly or daily rates of pay for Affiliated Personnel must be in accordance with, and must not exceed, the maximum pay rates contained in the then-current Maximum Pay Rate Table.

§ 208.35 Reimbursement for Advisory.

DHS will not reimburse costs incurred during an Advisory.

§ 208.36 Reimbursement for Alert.

(a) *Allowable costs.* DHS will reimburse costs incurred during an Alert, up to the dollar limit specified in the Alert Order, for the following activities:

(1) Personnel costs, including Backfill, incurred to prepare for Activation.

(2) Transportation costs relating to hiring, leasing, or renting vehicles and drivers.

(3) The administrative allowance provided in § 208.41 of this part.

(4) Food and beverages for Task Force Members and Support Specialists when DHS does not provide meals during the Alert. DHS will limit food and beverage reimbursement to the amount of the then-current Federal meals daily allowance published in the FEDERAL REGISTER for the locality where such food and beverages were provided, multiplied by the number of personnel who received them.

(b) *Calculation of Alert Order dollar limit.* The Alert Order dollar limit will equal:

(1) An allowance of 10 percent of the Task Force's Daily Cost Estimate; and

(2) A supplemental allowance of 1 percent of the Task Force's Daily Cost Estimate for each 24-hour period beyond the first 72 hours of Alert.

(c) *Non-allowable costs.* DHS will not reimburse costs incurred or relating to the leasing, hiring or chartering of aircraft or the purchase of any equipment, aircraft, or vehicles.

§ 208.37 Reimbursement for equipment and supply costs incurred during Activation.

(a) *Allowable costs.* DHS will reimburse costs incurred for the emergency procurement of equipment and supplies in the number, type, and up to the cost specified in the current approved Equipment Cache List, and up to the aggregate dollar limit specified in the Activation Order. The Assistant Administrator may determine emergency procurement dollar limits, taking into account previous Activation history, available funding, the extent and nature of the incident, and the current state of Task Force readiness.

(b) *Non-Allowable costs.* DHS will not reimburse costs incurred for items that are not listed on the Equipment Cache List; for items purchased greater than the cost or quantity identified in the Equipment Cache List; or for any purchase of non-expendable items that duplicate a previous purchase under a Preparedness or Response Cooperative Agreement.

§ 208.38 Reimbursement for re-supply and logistics costs incurred during Activation.

With the exception of emergency procurement authorized in the Activation Order, and replacement of consumable items provided for in § 208.43(a)(2) of this subpart, DHS will not reimburse costs incurred for re-supply and logistical support during Activation. Re-supply and logistical support of Task Forces needed during Activation are the responsibility of the Joint Management Team.

§ 208.39 Reimbursement for personnel costs incurred during Activation.

(a) *Compensation.* DHS will reimburse the Sponsoring Agency for costs incurred for the compensation of each Activated System Member during Activation. Reimbursement of compensation costs for Activated Support Specialists will be limited to periods of time during which they were actively supporting the Activation or traveling to or from locations at which they were actively supporting the Activa-

tion. The provisions of § 208.40 of this part govern costs incurred for providing fringe benefits to System Members.

(b) *Public Safety Exemption not applicable.* DHS will reimburse Sponsoring Agencies for costs incurred by Non-Exempt System Members in accordance with 29 U.S.C. 207(a) of the Fair Labor Standards Act, without regard to the public safety exemption contained in 29 U.S.C. 207(k). In other words, DHS will reimburse Sponsoring Agencies on an overtime basis for any hours worked by Non-Exempt System Members greater than 40 hours during a regular workweek.

(c) *Tour of duty.* The tour of duty for all Activated System Members will be 24 hours. DHS will reimburse the Sponsoring Agency for salary and overtime costs incurred in compensating System Members for meal periods and regularly scheduled sleep periods during Activation. Activated System Members are considered "on-duty" and must be available for immediate response at all times during Activation.

(d) *Regular rate.* The regular rate for purposes of calculating allowable salary and overtime costs is the amount determined in accordance with § 208.39(e)(1) through (3) of this subpart.

(e) *Procedures for calculating compensation during Activation.* A Sponsoring Agency or Participating Agency must:

(1) Convert the base hourly wage of any Non-Exempt System Member regularly paid under 29 U.S.C. 207(k) to its equivalent for a 40-hour work week;

(2) Convert the annual salary of any salaried Non-Exempt System Member to its hourly equivalent for a 40-hour workweek;

(3) Calculate the daily compensation of Exempt System Members based on their current annual salary, exclusive of fringe benefits;

(4) Calculate the total number of hours worked by each System Member to be included in the Sponsoring Agency's request for reimbursement; and

(5) Submit a request for reimbursement under § 208.52 of this part according to the following table:

If the Sponsoring Agency or Participating Agency * * *	And the Sponsoring Agency or Participating Agency * * *	Then the following compensation costs are allowable:
(i) Customarily and usually compensates Exempt System Members by paying a salary, but not overtime,	Does not customarily and usually grant compensatory time or other form of overtime substitute to Exempt System members.	The daily compensation equivalent calculated under § 208.39(e)(3) of this part for each Activated Exempt System Member for each full or partial day during Activation.
(ii) Customarily and usually compensates Exempt System Members by paying a salary but not overtime	Customarily and usually awards compensatory time or other overtime substitute for Exempt System Members for hours worked above a predetermined hours threshold (for example, the Sponsoring Agency customarily and usually grants compensatory time for all hours worked above 60 in a given week).	The daily compensation equivalent calculated under § 208.39(e)(3) of this part for each Activated Exempt System Member for each full or partial day during Activation AND the dollar value at the time of accrual of the compensatory time or other overtime substitute for each Activated Exempt System Member based on the duration of the Activation.
(iii) Customarily and usually compensates Exempt System Members by paying a salary and overtime,	Customarily and usually calculates overtime for Exempt System Members by paying a predetermined overtime payment for each hour worked above a predetermined hours threshold,.	The daily compensation equivalent calculated under § 208.39(e)(3) of this part for each Activated Exempt System Member for each full or partial day during Activation AND the predetermined overtime payment for each hour during the Activation above the previously determined hours threshold for each Activated Exempt System Member.
(iv) Customarily and usually compensates Non-Exempt System Members by paying overtime after 40 hours per week,	Does not customarily and usually grant compensatory time or other form of overtime substitute to Non-Exempt System members,.	For each seven-day period during the Activation, the hourly wage of each Activated Non-Exempt System Member for the first 40 hours AND the overtime payment for each Activated Non-Exempt System Member for every hour over 40.
(v) Customarily and usually compensates Non-Exempt System Members according to a compensation plan established under 29 U.S.C. 207(k),	Does not customarily and usually grant compensatory time or other form of overtime substitute to Non-Exempt System Members,.	For each seven-day period during the Activation, the hourly wage equivalent of each Activated Non-Exempt System Member calculated under § 208.39(e)(1) of this part for the first 40 hours AND the overtime payment equivalent for each Activated Non-Exempt System Member calculated under § 208.39(e)(1) of this part for every hour over 40.
(vi) Activates Personnel, who are customarily and usually paid an hourly wage according to the Maximum Pay Rate Table,	....	For each seven-day period during the Affiliated Activation, the hourly wage for each Activated Affiliated Personnel for the first 40 hours and one and one-half times the hourly wage for each Activated Affiliated Personnel for every hour over 40.
(vii) Activates Affiliated Personnel who are customarily and usually paid a daily compensation rate according to the Maximum Pay Rate Table,	....	The daily compensation rate for each Activated Affiliated Personnel for each full or partial day during the Activation.

(f) *Reimbursement of additional salary and overtime costs.* DHS will reimburse any identified additional salary and overtime cost incurred by a Sponsoring Agency as a result of the temporary conversion of a Non-Exempt System Member normally compensated under 29 U.S.C. 207(k) to a 40-hour work week under 29 U.S.C. 207(a).

(g) *Reimbursement for Backfill costs upon Activation.* DHS will reimburse the cost to Backfill System Members. Backfill costs consist of the expenses generated by filling the position in which the Activated System Member should have been working. These costs are calculated by subtracting the non-overtime compensation, including fringe benefits, of Activated System Members from the total costs (non-overtime and overtime compensation, including fringe benefits) paid to Backfill the Activated System Members. Backfill reimbursement is available only for those positions that are normally Backfilled by the Sponsoring Agency or Participating Agency during Activation. Employees exempt under the Fair Labor Standards Act (FLSA) not normally Backfilled by the Sponsoring Agency or Participating Agency are not eligible for Backfill during Activation.

§ 208.40 Reimbursement of fringe benefit costs during Activation.

(a) Except as specified in § 208.40 (c) of this subpart, DHS will reimburse the

Sponsoring Agency for fringe benefit costs incurred during Activation according to the following table:

If the Sponsoring Agency or Participating Agency * * *	Then the Sponsoring Agency or Participating Agency must * * *	Example
(1) Incurs a fringe benefit cost based on the number of base hours worked by a System Member,	Bill DHS for a pro-rata share of the premium based on the number of base hours worked during Activation.	The City Fire Department incurs a premium of 3 percent for dental coverage based on the number of base hours worked in a week (53 hours). The City should bill DHS an additional 3 percent of the firefighter's converted compensation for the first 40 hours Activation.
(2) Incurs a fringe benefit cost based on the number of hours a System Member actually worked (base hours and overtime),	Bill DHS for a pro-rata share of the premium based on the number of hours each System Member worked during Activation.	The City Fire Department pays a premium of 12 percent for retirement based on the number of hours worked by a firefighter. The City should bill DHS an additional 12 percent of the firefighter's total compensation during Activation.
(3) Incurs a fringe benefit cost on a yearly basis based on the number of people employed full-time during the year,	Bill DHS for a pro-rata share of those fringe benefit costs based on the number of non-overtime hours worked during Activation by System Members employed full time.	The City Fire Department pays workers compensation premiums into the City risk fund for the following year, based on the number of full-time firefighters employed during the current year. The City should bill DHS for workers compensation premium costs by multiplying the hourly fringe benefit rate or amount by the number of non-overtime hours worked during Activation by full time firefighters who are System Members.

(b) *Differential pay.* DHS will reimburse the Sponsoring Agency for direct costs incurred because of any separate differential compensation paid for work performed during an Activation including, but not limited to, differentials paid for holidays, night work, hazardous duty, or other paid fringe benefits, provided such differentials are not otherwise reimbursed under paragraph (a) of this section. A detailed explanation of the differential payment for which the Sponsoring Agency seeks reimbursement must accompany any request for reimbursement under this section together with identification of every fringe benefit sought under § 208.40(a) of this part and the method used to calculate each such payment and the reimbursement sought from DHS.

(c) DHS will not reimburse the Sponsoring Agency for fringe benefit costs for Affiliated Personnel.

§ 208.41 **Administrative allowance.**

(a) The administrative allowance is intended to defray costs of the following activities, to the extent provided in paragraph (b) of this section:

(1) Collecting expenditure information from Sponsoring Agencies and Participating Agencies;

(2) Compiling and summarizing cost records and reimbursement claims;

(3) Duplicating cost records and reimbursement claims; and

(4) Submitting reimbursement claims, including mailing, transmittal, and related costs.

(b) The administrative allowance will be equal to the following:

(1) If total allowable costs are less than $100,000, 3 percent of total allowable costs included in the reimbursement claim;

(2) If total allowable costs are $100,000 or more but less than $1,000,000, $3,000 plus 2 percent of costs included in the reimbursement claim greater than $100,000;

(3) If total allowable costs are $1,000,000 or more, $21,000 plus 1 percent of costs included in the reimbursement claim greater than $1,000,000.

§ 208.42 **Reimbursement for other administrative costs.**

Costs incurred for conducting after-action meetings and preparing after-action reports must be billed as direct costs in accordance with DHS administrative policy.

§ 208.43 **Rehabilitation.**

DHS will reimburse costs incurred to return System equipment and personnel to a state of readiness following Activation as provided in this section.

515

(a) *Costs for Equipment Cache List items*—(1) *Non-consumable items.* DHS will reimburse costs incurred to repair or replace any non-consumable item on the Equipment Cache List that was lost, damaged, destroyed, or donated at DHS direction to another entity, during Activation. For each such item, the Sponsoring Agency must document, in writing, the circumstances of the loss, damage, destruction, or donation.

(2) *Consumable items.* DHS will reimburse costs incurred to replace any consumable item on the Equipment Cache List that was consumed during Activation.

(3) *Personnel costs associated with equipment cache rehabilitation.* DHS will reimburse costs incurred for the compensation, including benefits, payable for actual time worked by each person engaged in rehabilitating the equipment cache following Activation, in accordance with the standard pay policy of the Sponsoring Agency or Participating Agency and without regard to the provisions of § 208.39(e)(1) of this part, up to the number of hours specified in the Demobilization Order. Fringe benefits are reimbursed under the provisions of § 208.40 of this part.

(b) *Costs for personnel rehabilitation.* DHS will reimburse costs incurred for the compensation, including benefits and Backfill, of each Activated System Member regularly scheduled to work during the rehabilitation period specified in the Demobilization Order, in accordance with the standard pay policy of the Sponsoring Agency or Participating Agency and without regard to the provisions of § 208.39(e)(1) of this part.

(c) *Other allowable costs*—(1) *Local transportation.* DHS will reimburse costs incurred for transporting Task Force Members from the point of assembly to the point of departure and from the point of return to the location where they are released from duty. DHS will also reimburse transportation costs incurred for assembling and moving the equipment cache from its usual place(s) of storage to the point of departure, and from the point of return to its usual place(s) of storage. Such reimbursement will include costs to return the means of transportation to its point of origin.

(2) *Ground transportation.* When DHS orders a Sponsoring Agency to move its Task Force Members and equipment cache by ground transportation, DHS will reimburse costs incurred for such transportation, including but not limited to charges for contract carriers, rented vehicles, contract vehicle operators, fleet vehicles, fuel and associated transportation expenses. The Assistant Administrator has authority to issue schedules of maximum hourly or per mile reimbursement rates for fleet and contract vehicles.

(3) *Food and beverages.* DHS will reimburse expenditures for food and beverages for Activated Task Force Members and Support Specialists when the Federal government does not provide meals during Activation. Reimbursement of food and beverage costs for Activated Support Specialists will be limited to periods of time during which they were actively supporting the Activation or traveling to or from locations at which they were actively supporting the Activation. Food and beverage reimbursement will be limited to the amount of the then-current Federal meals and incidental expenses daily allowance published in the FEDERAL REGISTER for the locality where such food and beverages were provided, multiplied by the number of personnel who received the same.

§ 208.44   Reimbursement   for   other costs.

(a) Except as allowed under paragraph (b) of this section, DHS will not reimburse other costs incurred preceding, during or upon the conclusion of an Activation unless, before making the expenditure, the Sponsoring Agency has requested, in writing, permission for a specific expenditure and has received written permission from the Program Manager or his or her designee to make such expenditure.

(b) At the discretion of the Program Manager or his or her designee, a request for approval of costs presented after the costs were incurred must be in writing and establish that:

(1) The expenditure was essential to the Activation and was reasonable;

(2) Advance written approval by the Program Manager was not feasible; and

(3) Advance verbal approval by the Program Manager had been requested and was given.

§ 208.45 Advance of funds.

At the time of Activation of a Task Force, the Task Force will develop the documentation necessary to request an advance of funds be paid to such Task Force's Sponsoring Agency. Upon approval, DHS will submit the documentation to the Assistance Officer and will request an advance of funds up to 75 percent of the estimated personnel costs for the Activation. The estimated personnel costs will include the salaries, benefits, and Backfill costs for Task Force Members and an estimate of the salaries, benefits and Backfill costs required for equipment cache rehabilitation. The advance of funds will not include any costs for equipment purchase.

§ 208.46 Title to equipment.

Title to equipment purchased by a Sponsoring Agency with funds provided under a DHS Response Cooperative Agreement vests in the Sponsoring Agency, provided that DHS reserves the right to transfer title to the Federal Government or a third party that DHS may name, under 44 CFR 13.32(g), when a Sponsoring Agency indicates or demonstrates that it cannot fulfill its obligations under the Memorandum of Agreement.

§§ 208.47–208.50 [Reserved]

Subpart D—Reimbursement Claims and Appeals

§ 208.51 General.

(a) *Purpose.* This subpart identifies the procedures that Sponsoring Agencies must use to request reimbursement from DHS for costs incurred under Response Cooperative Agreements.

(b) *Policy.* It is DHS policy to reimburse Sponsoring Agencies as expeditiously as possible consistent with Federal laws and regulations.

§ 208.52 Reimbursement procedures.

(a) *General.* A Sponsoring Agency must present a claim for reimbursement to DHS in such manner as the Assistant Administrator specifies .

(b) *Time for submission.* (1) Claims for reimbursement must be submitted within 90 days after the end of the Personnel Rehabilitation Period specified in the Demobilization Order.

(2) The Assistant Administrator may extend and specify the time limitation in paragraph (b)(1) of this section when the Sponsoring Agency justifies and requests the extension in writing.

§§ 208.53–208.59 [Reserved]

§ 208.60 Determination of claims.

When DHS receives a reviewable claim for reimbursement, DHS will review the claim to determine whether and to what extent reimbursement is allowable. Except as provided in § 208.63 of this part, DHS will complete its review and give written notice to the Sponsoring Agency of its determination within 90 days after the date DHS receives the claim. If DHS determines that any item of cost is not eligible for reimbursement, its notice of determination will specify the grounds on which DHS disallowed reimbursement.

§ 208.61 Payment of claims.

DHS will reimburse all allowable costs for which a Sponsoring Agency requests reimbursement within 30 days after DHS determines that reimbursement is allowable, in whole or in part, at any stage of the reimbursement and appeal processes identified in this subpart.

§ 208.62 Appeals.

(a) *Initial appeal.* The Sponsoring Agency may appeal to the Program Manager any determination made under § 208.60 of this part to disallow reimbursement of an item of cost:

(1) The appeal must be in writing and submitted within 60 days after receipt of DHS's written notice of disallowance under § 208.60 of this part.

(2) The appeal must contain legal and factual justification for the Sponsoring Agency's contention that the cost is allowable.

(3) Within 90 days after DHS receives an appeal, the Program Manager will review the information submitted, make such additional investigations as

necessary, make a determination on the appeal, and submit written notice of the determination of the appeal to the Sponsoring Agency.

(b) *Final appeal.* (1) If the Program Manager denies the initial appeal, in whole or in part, the Sponsoring Agency may submit a final appeal to the Deputy Assistant Administrator. The appeal must be made in writing and must be submitted not later than 60 days after receipt of written notice of DHS's determination of the initial appeal.

(2) Within 90 days following the receipt of a final appeal, the Deputy Assistant Administrator will render a determination and notify the Sponsoring Agency, in writing, of the final disposition of the appeal.

(c) *Failure to file timely appeal.* If the Sponsoring Agency does not file an appeal within the time periods specified in this section, DHS will deem that the Sponsoring Agency has waived its right to appeal any decision that could have been the subject of an appeal.

§ 208.63 Request by DHS for supplemental information.

(a) At any stage of the reimbursement and appeal processes identified in this subpart, DHS may request the Sponsoring Agency to provide supplemental information that DHS considers necessary to determine either a claim for reimbursement or an appeal. The Sponsoring Agency must exercise its best efforts to provide the supplemental information and must submit to DHS a written response that includes such supplemental information as the Sponsoring Agency is able to provide within 30 days after receiving DHS's request.

(b) If DHS makes a request for supplemental information at any stage of the reimbursement and appeal processes, the applicable time within which its determination of the claim or appeal is to be made will be extended by 30 days. However, without the consent of the Sponsoring Agency, no more than one such time extension will be allowed for any stage of the reimbursement and appeal processes.

§ 208.64 Administrative and audit requirements.

(a) *Non-Federal audit.* For Sponsoring Agencies and States, requirements for non-Federal audit are contained in 44 CFR 13.26, in accordance with OMB Circular A–133, Audits of States, Local Governments, and Non-Profit Organizations.

(b) *Federal audit.* DHS or the Government Accountability Office may elect to conduct a Federal audit of any payment made to a Sponsoring Agency or State.

§ 208.65 Mode of transmission.

When sending all submissions, determinations, and requests for supplemental information under this subpart, all parties must use a means of delivery that permits both the sender and addressee to verify the dates of delivery.

§ 208.66 Reopening of claims for retrospective or retroactive adjustment of costs.

(a) Upon written request by the Sponsoring Agency DHS will reopen the time period for submission of a request for reimbursement after the Sponsoring Agency has submitted its request for reimbursement, if:

(1) The salary or wage rate applicable to the period of an Activation is retroactively changed due to the execution of a collective bargaining agreement, or due to the adoption of a generally applicable State or local law, ordinance or wage order or a cost-of-living adjustment;

(2) The Sponsoring Agency or any Participating Agency incurs an additional cost because of a legally-binding determination; or

(3) The Deputy Director determines that other extenuating circumstances existed that prevented the Sponsoring Agency from including the adjustment of costs in its original submission.

(c) The Sponsoring Agency must notify DHS as early as practicable that it anticipates such a request.

§§ 208.67–208.70 [Reserved]

PART 209—SUPPLEMENTAL PROPERTY ACQUISITION AND ELEVATION ASSISTANCE

Sec.
209.1 Purpose.
209.2 Definitions.
209.3 Roles and responsibilities.
209.4 Allocation and availability of funds.
209.5 Applicant eligibility.
209.6 Project eligibility.
209.7 Priorities for project selection.
209.8 Application and review process.
209.9 Appeals.
209.10 Project implementation requirements.
209.11 Grant administration.
209.12 Oversight and results.

AUTHORITY: Pub. L. 106–113, Div. B, sec. 1000(a)(5) (enacting H.R. 3425 by cross-reference), 113 Stat. 1501, 1536; Pub. L. 106–246, 114 Stat. 511, 568; Robert T. Stafford Disaster Relief and Emergency Assistance Act, 42 U.S.C. 5121, Reorganization Plan No. 3 of 1978, 43 FR 41943, 3 CFR, 1978 Comp., p. 329; E.O. 12127, 44 FR 19367, 3 CFR, 1979 Comp., p. 376; E.O. 12148, 44 FR 43239, 3 CFR, 1979 Comp., p. 412.

SOURCE: 66 FR 32669, June 15, 2001, unless otherwise noted.

§ 209.1 Purpose.

This part provides guidance on the administration of a program to provide supplemental property acquisition and elevation assistance made available by Congress to provide funds for the acquisition or elevation, for hazard mitigation purposes, of properties that have been made uninhabitable by floods in areas that were declared major disasters in federal fiscal years 1999 and 2000.

§ 209.2 Definitions.

Except as noted in this part, the definitions listed at §§ 206.2 and 206.431 apply to the implementation of this part.

Allowable open space uses means recreational and wetland management uses including: Parks for outdoor recreational activities; nature reserves; cultivation; grazing; camping (except where adequate warning time is not available to allow evacuation); temporary storage in the open of wheeled vehicles which are easily movable (ex-cept mobile homes); unimproved, permeable parking lots; and buffer zones. Allowable uses generally do not include walled buildings, flood reduction levees, highways or other uses that obstruct the natural and beneficial functions of the floodplain.

Applicant means a State agency, local government, or qualified private non-profit organization that submits an application for acquisition or elevation assistance to the State or to FEMA.

Cost-effective means that the mitigation activity will not cost more than the anticipated value of the reduction in both direct damages and subsequent negative impacts to the area if future disasters were to occur. Both costs and benefits will be computed on a net present value basis. The State will complete an analysis of the cost effectiveness of the project, in accordance with FEMA guidance and using a FEMA-approved methodology. FEMA will review the State's analysis.

Pre-event fair market value means the value a willing buyer would have paid and a willing seller would have sold a property for had the disaster not occurred.

Principal residence means a residence that is occupied by the legal owner and is the dwelling where the legal owner normally lives during the major portion of the calendar year.

Qualified alien means an alien who meets one of the following criteria:

(1) An alien lawfully admitted for permanent residence under the Immigration and Nationality Act (INA);

(2) An alien granted asylum under section 208 of the INA;

(3) A refugee admitted to the United States under section 207 of the INA;

(4) An alien paroled into the United States under section 212(d)(5) of the INA for at least one year;

(5) An alien whose deportation is being withheld under section 243(h) of the INA as in effect prior to April 1, 1997, or section 241(b)(3) of the INA;

(6) An alien granted conditional entry pursuant to section 203(a)(7) of the INA as in effect prior to April 1, 1980;

(7) An alien who is a Cuban and Haitian entrant (as defined in section 501(e) of the Refugee Education Assistance Act of 1980); or

(8) An alien who (or whose child or parent) has been battered and meets the requirements of 8 U.S.C. 1641(c).

Qualified private nonprofit organization means an organization with a conservation mission as qualified under section 170(h) of the Internal Revenue Code of 1954, as amended, and the regulations applicable under that section.

Repetitive Loss Structure means a structure covered by a contract for flood insurance under the National Flood Insurance Program (NFIP) that has incurred flood-related damage on two occasions during a 10-year period, each resulting in at least a $1000 claim payment;

State Hazard Mitigation Plan means the hazard mitigation plan that reflects the State's systematic evaluation of the nature and extent of vulnerability to the effects of natural hazards typically present in the State and includes a description of actions needed to minimize future vulnerability to hazards.

Subgrantee means the government or other legal entity to which a subgrant is awarded and which is accountable to the grantee for the use of the funds provided. Subgrantees can be a State agency, local government, qualified private nonprofit organizations, or Indian tribes as outlined in 44 CFR 206.434;

Substantial Damage means damage of any origin sustained by a structure whereby the cost of restoring the structure to its before-damage condition would equal or exceed 50 percent of the market value of the structure before the damage occurred;

Uninhabitable means that properties are certified by the appropriate State or local official normally empowered to make such certifications as meeting one or more of the following criteria:

(1) Determined by an authorized local government official to be substantially damaged, according to National Flood Insurance Program criteria contained in 44 CFR 59.1;

(2) Have been red- or yellow-tagged and declared uninhabitable due to environmental contamination by floodwaters, or otherwise determined to be uninhabitable by a State or local official in accordance with current codes or ordinances; or

(3) Have been demolished due to damage or environmental contamination by floodwaters.

We, our, or *us* means FEMA.

[66 FR 32669, June 15, 2001; 66 FR 49554, Sept. 28, 2001]

§ 209.3 **Roles and responsibilities.**

The following describes the general roles of FEMA, the State, local communities or other organizations that receive grant assistance, and participating homeowners.

(a) *Federal.* We will notify States about the availability of funds, and will allocate available funding to States that received major disaster declarations during the period covered by the supplemental authority. Our Regional Administrators will verify project eligibility, provide technical assistance to States upon request, make grant awards, and oversee program implementation.

(b) *State.* The State will be the Grantee to which we award funds and will be accountable for the use of those funds. The State will determine priorities for funding within the State. This determination must be made in conformance with the HMGP project identification and selection criteria (44 CFR 206.435). The State also will provide technical assistance and oversight to applicants for project development and to subgrantees for project implementation. The State will report program progress and results to us. The States also will recover and return to us any funds made available from other sources for the same purposes. When Native American tribes apply directly to us, they will be the grantee and carry out "state" roles.

(c) *Applicant (pre-award) and subgrantee (post-award).* The applicant (a State agency, local government, or qualified private nonprofit organization) will coordinate with interested homeowners to complete an application to the State. The subgrantee implements all approved projects, generally takes title to all property, and agrees to dedicate and maintain the property in perpetuity for uses compatible with open-space, recreational, or wetlands management practices. The subgrantee will receive, review and make final decisions about any appraisal disputes that are brought by participating homeowners. The subgrantee is accountable to the State, as well as to us, for the use of funds.

(d) *Participating homeowners.* The participating homeowners will notify the community of their interest to participate; provide necessary information to the community coordinator about property ownership, disaster damage, and other disaster benefits received or available; review the offer made from the community; and accept it or request a review appraisal.

§ 209.4 **Allocation and availability of funds.**

(a) We will allocate available funds based on the number and value of properties that meet the eligibility criteria and whose owners want to participate in an acquisition or elevation project.

(b) We may reallocate funds for which we do not receive and approve adequate applications. We will obligate most available funds within 12 months following the deadline for submitting applications, unless extenuating circumstances exist.

§ 209.5 **Applicant eligibility.**

The following are eligible to apply to the State for a grant:

(a) State and local governments;

(b) Indian tribes or authorized tribal organizations. A tribe may apply either to the State or directly to us; and

(c) Qualified private nonprofit organizations.

§ 209.6 **Project eligibility.**

(a) *Eligible types of project activities.* This grant authority is for projects to acquire floodprone properties and demolish or relocate structures per § 209.10(i), or to elevate floodprone structures. Approved projects must meet the following criteria and comply with all other program requirements described in this rule;

(b) *Eligibility criteria.* To be eligible, projects must:

(1) Be cost effective. The State will complete an analysis of the cost-effectiveness of the project, in accordance with our guidance and using a methodology that we approve. We will review the State's analysis;

(2) Include only properties that:

(i) For acquisition, the owner agrees to sell voluntarily;

(ii) Are within the 100-year floodplain based on best available data or as identified by a FIRM or FEMA-approved Disaster Recovery Map;

(iii) Were made uninhabitable (as certified by an appropriate State or local official) by the effects of a declared major disaster during federal fiscal years 1999 or 2000;

(iv) For acquisition, had a pre-event fair market value of less than $300,000 just before the disaster event. Properties submitted for buyout under Pub. L. 106–113 (the original Hurricane Floyd supplemental buyout program) are exempt from this policy, with the limitation that in no case does the Federal share or offer for any such property exceed $225,000; and

(v) Served as the principal residence for the owner. For multifamily units such as condominium buildings, all units within the structure should be principal residences of the owners and not sublet.

(3) Conform with 44 CFR part 9, Floodplain Management and Protection of Wetlands; 44 CFR part 10, Environmental Considerations; and any applicable environmental and historic preservation laws and regulations.

(c) For acquisition projects, an owner who is not a United States citizen or qualified alien may receive current fair market value for his or her property. He or she may not receive additional amounts for pre-event fair market value.

(d) Funds available under Pub. L. 106–113 (the original Floyd supplemental appropriation) are limited to use for acquisition purposes only.

§ 209.7 **Priorities for project selection.**

(a) It is the State's responsibility to identify and select eligible buyout projects for funding under the supplemental grant program. All funded projects must be consistent with the State Hazard Mitigation Plan. The mitigation planning process or any other appropriate means may identify buyout and elevation projects.

(b) States will set priorities in their State mitigation plan to use as the basis for selecting projects for funding.

The State's priorities will address, at a minimum, substantially damaged properties, repetitive loss target properties, and such other criteria that the State deems necessary to comply with the law. States and subgrantees are to give priority consideration to projects for acquisition or elevations of repetitive loss properties, and must include all eligible repetitive loss properties in the projects submitted to us for funding.

[66 FR 32669, June 15, 2001; 66 FR 49554, Sept. 28, 2001, as amended at 74 FR 15353, Apr. 3, 2009]

§ 209.8 Application and review process.

(a) *General.* This section describes the procedures to be used by the State in submitting an application for funding under the Supplemental Property Acquisition and Elevation Assistance program. Under this program, the State is the grantee and is responsible for processing subgrants to applicants in accordance with 44 CFR part 13 and this part.

(b) *Timeframes.* We will establish deadlines for States to submit applications, and States will set local application deadlines. States may begin forwarding applications to us immediately upon Notice of Availability of Funds and must forward all applications not later than the date set by the Regional Administrator. States must provide to us the information described below in paragraph (c) of this section for each property proposed for acquisition or elevation in support of the supplemental allocation requested and within the timeframe that we establish. We will verify project eligibility estimates provided by States in order to assure that all projects meet the criteria for the supplemental grant awards. We will perform an independent verification of this information for not less than 50 percent of the properties submitted.

(c) *Format.* The State will forward its application to the Regional Administrator. The Application will include: a Standard Form (SF) 424, Application for Federal Assistance; FEMA form 20–15, Budget Information—Construction Programs; Project Narrative (section 209.8(c)—community project applications (buyout plans) selected by the

State); FEMA form 20–16, 20–16b and 20–16c Assurances and Certifications; Standard Form LLL, Disclosure of Lobbying Activities; FEMA form 20–10, Financial Status Report; the Performance/Progress Report format; and the State's certification that the State has reviewed all applications and that they meet program eligibility criteria. The Project Narrative (community project applications) will include:

(1) Community applicant information, including contact names and numbers;

(2) Description of the problem addressed by the proposed project;

(3) Description of the applicant's decision-making process, including alternatives considered;

(4) Project description, including property locations/addresses and scope of activities;

(5) Project cost estimate and match source;

(6) For acquisition projects, open space use description and maintenance assurance;

(7) Risk and cost-effectiveness information, or State's benefit-cost analysis;

(8) Environmental and historic preservation information including

(i) Whether the property is now or ever has been used for commercial or industrial purposes, and

(ii) Any information regarding historic preservation that is readily available;

(9) Attachments for each property as follows:

(i) A photograph of the structure from the street;

(ii) Owner's name;

(iii) Complete address, including zip code;

(iv) Latitude and longitude;

(v) The date of construction;

(vi) Proximity to the 100-year floodplain;

(vii) Panel and date of the applicable Flood Insurance Rate Map, if any;

(viii) The elevation of the first habitable floor and an estimate of the depth of flooding in the structure;

(ix) The estimated pre-event fair market value of the home. Applicants will estimate the value of properties using the best available information, such as inspections, public records and market values of similar properties in similar neighborhoods to arrive at a pre-event fair market value that reflects what a willing buyer would have paid a willing seller had the disaster not occurred. If tax assessment data are used as the basis, the applicant should add the relevant adjustment percentage for that jurisdiction to adjust the tax assessment to the current fair market value. These adjustment data should be obtained from the jurisdiction's tax assessor's office. For any jurisdictions where the adjustment factor is over 25 percent, applicants should include a justification for the high adjustment factor. Applicants should not include any other project costs in the property values. These costs will be reflected elsewhere;

(x) Indication whether flood insurance was in force at the time of the loss, and policy number, if available.

(xi) Indications that the property will meet the definition of uninhabitable:

(A) Substantial damage determination, and name and title of determining official, or if not yet determined then:

(1) For manufactured homes (mobile homes), inundation of 1 foot or more of water above the first habitable floor or other evidence of substantial damage; or

(2) For permanent structures other than manufactured homes, inundation of 5 feet or more of water above the first above-ground habitable floor or other evidence of substantial damage. Habitable floors do not include basements.

(B) Were red- or yellow-tagged and declared uninhabitable due to environmental contamination by floodwaters, or otherwise determined to be uninhabitable by a State or local official under current codes or ordinances; or

(C) Were demolished due to damage or environmental contamination by floodwaters.

(xii) Information regarding whether the structure is on the NFIP repetitive loss list (provide NFIP Repetitive Loss Property Locator Number, if available); and

(xiii) Observations on whether acquisition or elevation of the structure may result in a mixture of vacant lots

and lots with structures remaining on them; and

(10) *FEMA review and approval.* We will review and verify the State's eligibility determination and either approve, deny, or request additional information within 60 days. The Regional Administrator may extend this timeframe if complicated issues arise. We have final approval authority for funding of all projects.

[66 FR 32669, June 15, 2001; 66 FR 49554, Sept. 28, 2001; 74 FR 15353, Apr. 3, 2009]

§209.9 Appeals.

The State may appeal any decision that we make regarding projects submitted for funding in the Supplemental Property Acquisition and Elevation Assistance program. The State must submit the appeal in writing to the Regional Administrator and must include documentation that justifies the request for reconsideration. The appeal must specify the monetary figure in dispute and the provisions in Federal law, regulation, or policy with which the appellant believes the initial action was inconsistent. The applicant must appeal within 60 days of the applicant's receipt of our funding decision. The State must forward any appeal from an applicant or subgrantee with a written recommendation to the Regional Administrator within 60 days of receipt. Within 90 days following the receipt of an appeal, the Regional Administrator will notify the State in writing as to the new decision or the need for more information.

§209.10 Project implementation requirements.

Subgrantees must enter into an agreement with the State, with the written concurrence of the Regional Administrator, that provides the following assurances:

(a) The subgrantee will administer the grant and implement the project in accordance with program requirements, 44 CFR part 13, the grant agreement, and with applicable Federal, State, and local laws and regulations.

(b) The State and subgrantee will administer the grant in an equitable and impartial manner, without discrimination on the grounds or race, color, religion nationality, sex, age, or economic status in compliance with section 308 of the Stafford Act (42 U.S.C. 5151) and Title VI of the Civil Rights Act. In implementing the grant, the State and the subgrantee will ensure that no discrimination is practiced.

(c) The State and subgrantee will ensure that projects involving alterations to existing structures comply with all applicable State and local codes.

(d) The State and subgrantee will ensure that projects comply with applicable State and local floodplain management requirements. Structures will be elevated to the Base Flood Elevation.

(e) Property owners participating in acquisition projects may receive assistance up to the pre-event fair market value of their real property, except as limited by the eligibility criteria.

(f) The subgrantee will establish a process, which we must approve, whereby property owners participating in acquisition projects may request a review of the appraisal for their property, or request a second appraisal.

(g) The State will reduce buyout assistance by any duplication of benefits from other sources. Such benefits include, but are not limited to, payments made to the homeowner for repair assistance; insurance settlements; legal settlements; Small Business Administration loans; and any other payments made by any source to address the property loss unless the property owner can provide receipts showing that the benefits were used for their intended purpose to make repairs to the property.

(h) Increased Cost of Compliance coverage benefits under the National Flood Insurance Program (NFIP) may be used to match elevation or acquisition and relocation projects. Increased Cost of Compliance claims can only be used for NFIP-approved costs; these can then be applied to the project grant match. This coverage does not pay for property acquisition, but can pay demolition or structure relocation.

(i) The following restrictive covenants must be conveyed in the deed to any property acquired, accepted, or from which structures are removed ("the property"):

(1) The property must be dedicated and maintained in perpetuity for uses compatible with open space, recreational, or wetlands management practices; and

(2) No new structure(s) will be built on the property except as indicated in this paragraph:

(A) A public facility that is open on all sides and functionally related to a designated open space or recreational use;

(B) A public rest room; or

(C) A structure that is compatible with open space, recreational, or wetlands management usage and proper floodplain management policies and practices, which the Administrator of FEMA approves in writing before the construction of the structure begins.

(D) In general, allowable open space, recreational, and wetland management uses include parks for outdoor recreational activities, nature reserves, cultivation, grazing, camping (except where adequate warning time is not available to allow evacuation), temporary storage in the open of wheeled vehicles that are easily movable (except mobile homes), unimproved, permeable parking lots and buffer zones. Allowable uses generally do not include walled buildings, flood reduction levees, highways or other uses that obstruct the natural and beneficial functions of the floodplain.

(3) After completing the acquisition project, no application for future disaster assistance will be made for any purpose with respect to the property to any Federal entity or source, and no Federal entity or source will provide such assistance, even for the allowable uses of the property described above.

(4) Any structures built on the property according to paragraph (i)(2) of this section, must be: Located to minimize the potential for flood damage; floodproofed; or elevated to the Base Flood Elevation plus one foot of freeboard.

(5) The subgrantee or other public property owner will seek the approval of the State grantee agency and our Regional Administrator before conveying any interest in the property to any other party. The subgrantee or other public entity or qualified private nonprofit organization must retain all development rights to the property. Our Regional Administrator will only approve the transfer of properties that

meet the criteria identified in this paragraph.

(6) In order to carry out tasks associated with monitoring, we, the subgrantee, or the State have the right to enter the parcel, with notice to the parcel owner, to ensure compliance with land use restrictions. Subgrantees may identify the open space nature of the property on local tax maps to assist with monitoring. Whether the subgrantee obtains full title or a conservation easement on the parcel, the State must work with subgrantees to ensure that the parcel owner maintains the property in accordance with land use restrictions. Specifically, the State may:

(i) Monitor and inspect the parcel every two years and certify that the owner continues to use the inspected parcel for open space or agricultural purposes; and

(ii) Take measures to bring a noncompliant parcel back into compliance within 60 days of notice.

(7) Only as a last resort, we reserve the right to require the subgrantee to bring the property back into compliance and transfer the title and easement to a qualified third party for future maintenance.

(8) Every 2 years on October 1st, the subgrantee will report to the State, certifying that the property continues to be maintained consistent with the provisions of the agreement. The State will report the certification to us.

[66 FR 32669, June 15, 2001, as amended at 74 FR 15353, Apr. 3, 2009]

§209.11   Grant administration.

(a) *Cost share.* We may contribute up to 75 percent of the total eligible costs. The State must ensure that non-Federal sources contribute not less than 25 percent of the total eligible costs for the grant. The State or any subgrantee cannot use funds that we provide under this Act as the non-Federal match for other Federal funds nor can the State or any subgrantee use other Federal funds as the required non-Federal match for these funds, except as provided by statute.

(b) *Allowable costs.* A State may find guidance on allowable costs for States and subgrantees in Office of Management and Budget (OMB) Circulars A-87

and A-122 on Cost Principles. States may use up to 7 percent of the grant funds for management costs of the grant. The State should include management costs in its application. Subgrantees must include reasonable costs to administer the grant as a direct project cost in their budget.

(c) *Progress reports.* The State must provide a quarterly progress report to us under 44 CFR 13.40, indicating the status and completion date for each project funded. The report will include any problems or circumstances affecting completion dates, scope of work, or project costs that may result in non-compliance with the approved grant conditions.

(d) *Financial reports.* The State must provide a quarterly financial report to us under 44 CFR 13.41.

(e) *SMARTLINK Drawdowns.* The State will make SMARTLINK drawdowns to reimburse or advance allowable costs to subgrantees for approved projects.

(f) *Audit requirements.* Uniform audit requirements as set forth in 44 CFR part 13 apply to all grant assistance provided under this subpart. We may elect to conduct a Federal audit on the disaster assistance grant or on any of the subgrants.

(g) If a mitigation measure is not completed, and there is not adequate justification for non-completion, no Federal funding will be provided for that project.

[66 FR 32669, June 15, 2001, as amended at 74 FR 15353, Apr. 3, 2009]

§209.12   Oversight and results.

(a) *FEMA oversight.* Our Regional Administrators are responsible for overseeing this grant authority and for ensuring that States and subgrantees meet all program requirements. Regional Administrators will review program progress quarterly.

(b) *Monitoring and enforcement.* We, subgrantees, and States will monitor the properties purchased under this authority and ensure that the properties are maintained in open space use. We and the State may enforce the agreement by taking any measures that we or they deem appropriate.

(c) *Program results.* The State will review the effectiveness of approved projects after each future flood event in the affected area to monitor whether projects are resulting in expected savings. The State will report to us on program effectiveness after project completion and after each subsequent flood event.

PARTS 210–294 [RESERVED]

SUBCHAPTER E—CERRO GRANDE FIRE ASSISTANCE

PART 295—CERRO GRANDE FIRE ASSISTANCE

Subpart A—General

AUTHORITY: Pub. L. 106–246, 114 Stat. 511, 584; Reorganization Plan No. 3 of 1978, 43 FR 41493, 3 CFR, 1978 Comp., p. 329; E.O. 12127, 44 FR 19367, 3 CFR, 1979 Comp., p. 376; E.O. 12148, 44 FR 43239, 3 CFR, 1979 Comp., p. 412.

SOURCE: 66 FR 15959, Mar. 21, 2001, unless otherwise noted.

Subpart A—General

§ 295.1 Purpose.

This part implements the Cerro Grande Fire Assistance Act (CGFAA), Public Law 106–246, 114 Stat. 584, which requires that the Federal Emergency Management Agency (FEMA) establish a process to evaluate, process and pay claims injuries and property damage resulting from the Cerro Grande Fire.

§ 295.2 Policy.

It is our policy to provide for the expeditious resolution of meritorious claims through a process that is administered with sensitivity to the burdens placed upon Claimants by the Cerro Grande Fire.

§ 295.3 Information and assistance.

Information and assistance concerning the CGFAA is available from the Office of Cerro Grande Fire Claims (OCGFC), Federal Emergency Management Agency, P.O. Box 1480, Los Alamos, New Mexico, 87544–1480, or telephone 1–888–748–1853 (toll free). The Cerro Grande Fire Assistance site on the World Wide Web can be accessed at *http://www.fema.gov/cerrogrande*. In the interest of brevity, we do not restate the provisions of the CGFAA in most instances. Our website has a copy of the CGFAA and we will provide a copy upon request.

§ 295.4 Organization of this part 295.

This part contains six subparts. Subpart A provides an overview of the CGFAA process. Subpart B describes the procedures for bringing a claim. Subpart C explains what compensation is available. Subpart D discusses the claims evaluation process. Subpart E explains the dispute resolution process. Subpart F contains a glossary in which various terms used in the rule are defined.

§ 295.5 Overview of the claims process.

(a) The CGFAA is intended to provide persons who suffered losses from the Cerro Grande Fire with a simple, expedited process to seek redress from the

United States. This section provides a brief explanation of the claims process for claims other than subrogation claims. It is not intended to supersede the more specific regulations that follow and explain the claims process in greater detail. In order to obtain benefits under this legislation, a person must submit all Cerro Grande Fire related claims against the United States to FEMA. A person who elects to proceed under the CGFAA is barred from bringing a claim under the Federal Tort Claims Act or filing a civil action against the United States for damages resulting from the Cerro Grande Fire. Judicial review of our decisions under the CGFAA is available.

(b) The first step in the process is to file a Notice of Loss with OCGFC. OCGFC will provide the Claimant with a written acknowledgement that the claim has been filed and the claim number.

(c) Shortly thereafter, a Claims Reviewer will contact the Claimant to review the claim. The Claims Reviewer will help the Claimant formulate a strategy for obtaining any necessary documentation or other support. This assistance does not relieve the Claimant of his or her responsibility for establishing all elements of the Loss and the compensatory damages that are sought, including that the Cerro Grande Fire caused the Loss. After the Claimant has had an opportunity to discuss the claim with the Claims Reviewer, a Proof of Loss will be presented to the Claimant for signature. After any necessary documentation has been obtained and the claim has been fully evaluated, the Claims Reviewer will submit a report to the Authorized Official. The Claims Reviewer is responsible for providing an objective evaluation of the claim to the Authorized Official.

(d) The Authorized Official will review the report and determine whether compensation is due to the Claimant. The Claimant will be notified in writing of the Authorized Official's Determination. If the Claimant is satisfied with the decision payment will be made after the Claimant returns a completed Release and Certification Form. If the Claimant is dissatisfied with the Authorized Official's Deter-

mination an Administrative Appeal may be filed with the Director of OCGFC. If the Claimant remains dissatisfied after the appeal is decided, the dispute may be resolved through binding arbitration or heard in the United States District Court for the District of New Mexico.

§ 295.6   Partial payments.

OCGFC, on its own initiative, or in response to a request by a Claimant, may make one or more partial payments on the claim. A partial payment can be made if OCGFC has a reasonable basis to estimate the Claimant's damages. Acceptance of a partial payment in no way affects a Claimant's ability to pursue an Administrative Appeal of the Authorized Official's Determination or to pursue other rights afforded by the CGFAA. Partial payment decisions cannot be appealed.

§ 295.7   Authority to settle or compromise claims.

Notwithstanding any other provision of these regulations, the Director of OCGFC may extend an offer to settle or compromise a claim or any portion of a claim, which if accepted by the Claimant will be binding on the Claimant and on the United States, except that the United States may recover funds improperly paid to a Claimant due to fraud or misrepresentation on the part of the Claimant or the Claimant's representative, a material mistake on our part or the Claimant's failure to cooperate in an audit as required by § 295.35.

Subpart B—Bringing a Claim Under the CGFAA

§ 295.10   Bringing a claim under the CGFAA.

(a) Any Injured Person may bring a claim under the CGFAA by filing a Notice of Loss. A claim submitted on any form other than a Notice of Loss will not be accepted. The Claimant must provide a brief description of each Loss on the Notice of Loss.

(b) A single Notice of Loss may be submitted on behalf of a Household containing Injured Persons provided that all Injured Persons on whose behalf the claim is presented are identified.

(c) The Notice of Loss must be signed by each Claimant, if the Claimant is an individual or by a duly authorized legal representative of each Claimant, if the Claimant is an entity or an individual who lacks the legal capacity to sign the Notice of Loss. If one is signing a Notice of Loss as the legal representative of a Claimant, the signer must disclose his or her relationship to the Claimant. FEMA may require a legal representative to submit evidence of authority.

(d) Notice of Loss forms are available from OCGFC by request. They may be obtained through the mail, in person at the OCGFC office or by telephone request. The Notice of Loss form can also be downloaded from the Internet at *http://www.fema.gov/cerrogrande.*

(e) Notices of Loss may be filed with OCGFC by mail to P.O. Box 1480, Los Alamos, NM 87544–1480. OCGFC is unable to accept Notices of Loss submitted by facsimile or e-mail.

(f) A Notice of Loss that is completely filled out and properly signed is deemed to be filed on the date it is received by OCGFC.

§ 295.11 Deadline for notifying FEMA of losses.

The deadline for filing a Notice of Loss is August 28, 2002. Except as provided in § 295.21(d) with respect to mitigation and in § 295.31(b) with respect to the lump sum payment described therein, a Loss that has not been described: on a Notice of Loss, on a supplement to a Notice of Loss or a request to supplement a Notice of Loss under § 295.33, or a request to reopen a claim under § 295.34, received by OCGFC on or before August 28, 2002 cannot be compensated under the CGFAA. The CGFAA establishes this deadline and does not provide any extensions of the filing deadline.

§ 295.12 Election of remedies.

(a) By filing a Notice of Loss, an Injured Person waives the right to seek redress for Cerro Grande Fire related claims against the United States through the Federal Tort Claims Act or by filing a civil action authorized by any other provision of law.

(b) An Injured Person who files a Federal Tort Claims Act claim or who initiates a civil action against the United States or any officer, employee or agent of the United States relating to the Cerro Grande Fire on or after August 28, 2000 is not eligible under the CGFAA to file a Notice of Loss.

(c) An Injured Person who filed before August 28, 2000 a Federal Tort Claims Act claim or a civil action against the United States for injuries, losses or damages relating to the Cerro Grande Fire may file a Notice of Loss provided that the Federal Tort Claims Act claim is withdrawn or the Injured Person is dismissed as a party to the civil action with prejudice not later than October 27, 2000. The withdrawal of a Federal Tort Claims Act claim must be in the form of a signed, written statement on a form provided by OCGFC that is filed with OCGFC not later than October 27, 2000. OCGFC will promptly forward the original notice of withdrawal to the applicable federal agency and retain a copy in the Claimant's file.

§ 295.13 Subrogation.

An insurer or other third party with the rights of a subrogee, who has compensated an Injured Person for Cerro Grande Fire related losses, may file a Subrogation Notice of Loss under the CGFAA for the subrogated claim. An insurer or other third party with the rights of a subrogee may file a Subrogation Notice of Loss without regard to whether the Injured Party who received payment from the insurer or third party filed a Notice of Loss. A Subrogation Notice of Loss may not be filed until the insurer or other party with the rights of a subrogee has made all payments that it believes the Injured Person is entitled to receive for Cerro Grande Fire related losses under the terms of the insurance policy or other agreement between the insurer or other party with the rights of a subrogee and the Injured Person. By filing a Subrogation Notice of Loss for any subrogated claim, the insurer or third party elects the CGFAA as its exclusive remedy against the United States for all subrogated claims arising out of the Cerro Grande Fire. Subrogation claims must be made on a Subrogation Notice of Loss form furnished by OCGFC. FEMA will evaluate subrogation claims on their merits. FEMA may reimburse insurers and other third parties with the rights of a subrogee for reasonable payments made to an Injured Party on or before October 25, 2000, which exceeded or were not required by the terms of the insurance policy or other agreement creating a right of subrogation. FEMA will not reimburse insurers and other third parties with the rights of a subrogee for payments made to an Injured Party after October 25, 2000 that exceeded or are not required by the terms of the insurance policy or other agreement creating a right of subrogation.

§ 295.14 Assignments.

Assignment of claims and the right to receive compensation for claims under the CGFAA is prohibited and will not be recognized by FEMA.

Subpart C—Compensation Available Under the CGFAA

§ 295.20 Prerequisite to compensation.

In order to receive compensation under the CGFAA a Claimant must be an Injured Person who suffered a Loss as a result of the Cerro Grande Fire and sustained damages.

§ 295.21 Allowable compensation.

(a) *Allowable compensation.* The CGFAA provides for the payment of compensatory damages. Compensatory damages are "real, substantial and just money damages established by the Claimant in compensation for actual or real injury or loss." In general, an Injured Person will be compensated for Losses to the same extent that the plaintiff in a successful tort action brought against a private party under the laws of the State of New Mexico would be compensated. In addition the CGFAA permits FEMA to compensate Injured Parties for certain categories of "loss of property," "business loss," and "financial loss," which are enumerated in the CGFAA. Damages must be reasonable in amount. Claimants must take reasonable steps to mitigate

(reduce) their damages, if possible, as required by New Mexico tort law.

(b) *Exclusions.* Except as otherwise provided in the CGFAA, a Claimant will not receive compensation for any injury or damage that is not compensable under the Federal Tort Claims Act and New Mexico law. Punitive damages, statutory damages under § 30-32-4 of the New Mexico Statutes Annotated (1978), interest on claims, attorney's fees and agents' fees incurred in prosecuting a claim under the CGFAA or an insurance policy, adjusting costs incurred by an insurer or other third party with the rights of a subrogee, and taxes that may be owed by a Claimant as a consequence of receiving an award are not recoverable from FEMA. The cost to a Claimant of prosecuting a claim under the CGFAA does not constitute compensatory damages and is not recoverable from FEMA, except as provided in § 295.31(b).

(c) *Damages arising in the future.* In the event that a lump sum payment is awarded to a Claimant for future damages the amount of the payment will be Discounted to Present Value.

(d) *Destruction of home*—(1) *Home and contents.* Compensatory damages for the Destruction of a Home may include the reasonable cost of reconstructing a home comparable in design, construction materials, size and improvements to the home that was lost taking into account post-fire construction costs in the community in which the home existed before the fire and current building codes and standards. Compensatory damages may also include the cost of removing debris and burned trees, stabilizing the land, replacing household contents, and compensation for any decrease in the value of land on which the structure sat pursuant to paragraph (e) of this section. (2) *Trees and landscaping.* Compensation for the Replacement Cost of destroyed trees and landscaping will be limited to 25% of the pre-fire value of the structure and lot.

(3) *Mitigation.* If requested by a Claimant, FEMA may compensate a Claimant for the reasonable cost of mitigation measures that will reduce the property's vulnerability to the future risk of wildfire, flood or other natural hazards related to the Cerro

Grande Fire. Mitigation compensation made available under this section may not exceed fifteen percent of payments from all sources (i.e., CGFAA, insurance proceeds, FEMA assistance under the Stafford Act) for damage to the structure and lot. The Claimant must obtain all government permits, approvals and clearances required by applicable law, ordinance or regulation before constructing the mitigation measures. The mitigation measures must be reviewed by FEMA under applicable environmental and historic preservation laws. Claimants must construct the mitigation measures for which they have received compensation.

(e) *Reduction in the value of real property.* Compensatory damages may be awarded for reduction in the value of real property that a Claimant owned before the fire if:

(1) The Claimant sells the real property in a good faith arm's length transaction that is closed no later than August 28, 2002 and realizes a loss in the pre-fire value; or

(2) The Claimant can establish that the value of the real property was permanently diminished as a result of the Cerro Grande Fire.

(f) *Destruction of unique items of personal property.* Compensatory damages may be awarded for unique items of personal property that were destroyed as a result of the Cerro Grande Fire. If the item can be replaced in the current market, the cost to replace the item will be awarded. If the item cannot be replaced in the current market, its fair market value on the date it was destroyed will be awarded.

(g) *Disaster recovery loans.* FEMA will reimburse Claimants awarded compensation under the CGFAA for interest paid on Small Business Administration disaster loans and similar loans obtained after May 4, 2000. Interest will be reimbursed for the period beginning on the date that the loan was taken out and ending on the date when the Claimant receives a compensation award (other than a partial payment). Claimants are required to use the proceeds of their compensation awards to repay Small Business Administration disaster loans. FEMA will cooperate with the Small Business Administration to formulate procedures for assur-

ing that Claimants repay Small Business Administration disaster loans contemporaneously with the receipt of CGFAA compensation awards.

(h) *Mitigation.* FEMA may compensate Claimants for the cost of reasonable and cost-effective efforts incurred on or before August 28, 2003 to mitigate the heightened risks of wildfire, flood or other natural disaster resulting from the Cerro Grande Fire that are consistent with a OCGFC-approved Mitigation Compensation Plan. No more than 15% of the total amount appropriated by Congress for the payment of Cerro Grande fire related claims may be allocated for mitigation compensation under this subsection. Claimants seeking compensation under this provision must file a Notice of Loss under §295.10 or amend a Notice of Loss previously filed under §295.33 or §295.34. The Notice of Loss or amendment must specify that compensation for mitigation is sought. The Notice of Loss must be filed or a proposed amendment under §295.33 or §295.34 submitted no later than August 28, 2002. A separate request for mitigation assistance must be filed with OCGFC no later than August 28, 2003. Claimants must construct the mitigation measures for which they have received compensation.

(i) *Subsistence*—(1) *Allowable damages.* FEMA may reimburse an Indian tribe, a Tribal Member or a Household Including Tribal Members for the reasonable cost of replacing Subsistence Resources customarily and traditionally used by the Claimant on or before May 4, 2000, but no longer available to the Claimant as a result of the Cerro Grande Fire. For each category of Subsistence Resources, the Claimant must elect to receive compensatory damages either for the increased cost of obtaining Subsistence Resources from lands not damaged by the Cerro Grande Fire or for the cost of procuring substitute resources in the cash economy. Long-term damage awards will be made in the form of lump sum cash payments to eligible Claimants.

(2) *Proof of subsistence use.* FEMA may consider evidence submitted by Claimants, Indian Tribes and other knowledgeable sources in determining

the nature and extent of a Claimant's subsistence uses.

(3) *Duration of damages.* Compensatory damages for subsistence losses will be paid for the period between May 4, 2000 and the date when Subsistence Resources can reasonably be expected to return to the level of availability that existed before the Cerro Grande Fire. FEMA may rely upon the advice of experts in making this determination.

(j) *Flood insurance.* A Claimant that owned or leased real property in the counties of Los Alamos, Rio Arriba, Sandoval or Santa Fe at the time of the Cerro Grande Fire who was not required by law to maintain flood insurance before the fire and who did not maintain flood insurance before the fire may be reimbursed by FEMA for reasonable flood insurance premiums incurred during the period beginning May 12, 2000 and ending May 12, 2002 on the owned or leased real property. Alternatively, FEMA may provide flood insurance to such Claimants directly through a group or blanket policy.

(k) *Out of pocket expenses for treatment of mental health conditions.* FEMA may reimburse an individual Claimant for reasonable out of pocket expenses incurred for treatment of a mental health condition rendered by a licensed mental health professional, which condition resulted from the Cerro Grande Fire and which could not be effectively addressed through no-cost crisis counseling services available in the community. FEMA will not reimburse for treatment rendered after December 31, 2001.

(l) *Donations.* FEMA will compensate individual or business Claimants in the counties of Los Alamos, Rio Arriba, Sandoval and Santa Fe (including those located on pueblos and Indian reservations) for the cost of merchandise, use of equipment or other nonpersonal services, directly or indirectly donated to survivors of the Cerro Grande Fire not later than June 19, 2000. Donations will be valued at cost. FEMA will also compensate businesses located in the counties of Los Alamos, Rio Arriba, Sandoval and Santa Fe (including those located on pueblos and Indian reservations) for discounts offered to fire survivors on goods and services not later than June 19, 2000 provided that actual revenues earned by the business during the period May 1–June 30, 2000 did not exceed reasonable projections for the period and the shortfall between actual revenues and reasonable projections resulted from the Cerro Grande Fire. Compensation will be the difference between the Claimant's established post-fire price for the good or service actually charged to the general public and the post-fire discounted price charged to fire survivors.

(m) *Duplication of benefits.* The CGFAA allows FEMA to compensate Injured Parties only if their damages have not been paid or will not be paid by insurance or a third party.

(1) *Insurance.* Claimants who carry insurance will be required to disclose the name of the insurer(s) and the nature of the insurance and provide OCGFC with such insurance documentation as OCGFC reasonably requests.

(2) *Coordination with our Public Assistance Program.* Injured Parties eligible for disaster assistance under our Public Assistance Program are expected to apply for all available assistance. Compensation will not be awarded under the CGFAA for:

(i) Emergency costs that are eligible for reimbursement under the Public Assistance Program; or

(ii) Losses that are eligible for repair, restoration or replacement under the Public Assistance Program; or

(iii) Costs or charges determined excessive under the Public Assistance Program.

(3) *Benefits provided by non-governmental organizations and individuals.* Unless otherwise provided by these regulations, disaster relief payments made to a Claimant by a non-governmental organization or an individual, other than wages paid by the Claimant's employer or insurance payments, will be disregarded in evaluating claims and need not be disclosed to OCGFC by Claimants.

(4) *Benefits provided by our Individual Assistance program.* Compensation under the CGFAA will not be awarded

for losses or costs that have been reimbursed under the Individual and Family Grant Program or any other FEMA Individual Assistance Program.

(5) *Worker's compensation claims.* Individuals who have suffered injuries that are compensable under State or Federal worker's compensation laws must apply for all benefits available under such laws.

Subpart D—Claims Evaluation

§295.30 Establishing losses and damages.

(a) *Burden of proof.* The burden of proving Losses and damages rests with the Claimant. A Claimant may submit for the Administrative Record a statement explaining why the Claimant believes that the Losses and damages are compensable and any documentary evidence supporting the claim. Claimants will provide documentation, which is reasonably available, to corroborate the nature, extent and value of their losses and/or to execute affidavits in a form established by OCGFC. FEMA may compensate a Claimant for a Loss in the absence of supporting documentation, in its discretion, on the strength of an affidavit or Proof of Loss executed by the Claimant, if documentary evidence substantiating the loss is not reasonably available. FEMA may request that a business Claimant execute an affidavit, which states that the Claimant will provide documentary evidence, including but not limited to income tax returns, if requested by our DHS Office of the Inspector General or the Government Accountability Office during an audit of the claim.

(b) *Proof of Loss.* All Claimants are required to attest to the nature and extent of each Loss for which compensation is sought in the Proof of Loss. The Proof of Loss, which will be in a form specified by OCGFC, must be signed by the Claimant or the Claimant's legal representative if the Claimant is a not an individual or is an individual who lacks the legal capacity to execute the Proof of Loss. The Proof of Loss must be signed under penalty of perjury and subject to the provisions of 18 U.S.C.1001, which establishes penalties for false statements. Non-subrogation Claimants who filed a Notice of Loss

before January 1, 2001 should submit a signed Proof of Loss to OCGFC not later than June 19, 2001. Non-subrogation Claimants who file a Notice of Loss on or after January 1, 2001 should submit a signed Proof of Loss to OCGFC not later than 150 days after the date when the Notice of Loss was submitted. These deadlines may be extended at the discretion of the Director of OCGFC for good cause. If a non-subrogation Claimant fails to submit a signed Proof of Loss within the timeframes set forth in this section and does not obtain an extension from the Director of OCGFC, OCGFC may administratively close the claim and require the Claimant to repay any partial payments made on the claim. Subrogation Claimants will submit the Proof of Loss contemporaneously with filing the Notice of Loss.

(c) *Release and Certification Form.* All Claimants who receive compensation under the CGFAA are required to sign a Release and Certification Form. The Release and Certification Form must be executed by the Claimant or the Claimant's legal representative if the Claimant is an entity or lacks the legal capacity to execute the Release and Certification Form. The Release and Certification Form must be received by OCGFC within 120 days of the date when the Authorized Official's Determination is rendered under §295.32, or if subsequent proceedings occur under Subpart E of these regulations, not later than 60 days after the date when further review of the decision (if available) is precluded. The United States will not attempt to recover compensatory damages paid to a Claimant who has executed and returned a Release and Certification Form within the periods provided above, except in the case of fraud or misrepresentation by the Claimant or the Claimant's representative, failure of the Claimant to cooperate with an audit as required by §295.35 or a material mistake by FEMA.

§295.31 Reimbursement of claim expenses.

(a) FEMA will reimburse Claimants for the reasonable costs they incur in copying documentation requested by OCGFC. FEMA will also reimburse Claimants for the reasonable costs they incur in providing appraisals, or other third-party opinions, requested by OCGFC. FEMA will not reimburse Claimant for the cost of appraisals, or other third party opinions, not requested by OCGFC.

(b) FEMA will provide a lump sum payment for incidental expenses incurred in claims preparation to individual and business Claimants that are awarded compensatory damages under the CGFAA after a properly executed Release and Certification Form has been returned to OCGFC. The amount of the lump sum payment will be the greater of $100 or 5% of CGFAA compensatory damages and insurance proceeds recovered by the Claimant for Cerro Grande Fire related losses (not including the lump sum payment or monies reimbursed under the CGFAA for the purchase of flood insurance), but will not exceed $15,000. No more than one lump sum payment will be made to all Claimants in a Household, regardless of whether the Household filed separate or combined Notices of Loss. The following Claimants will not be eligible to receive the lump sum payment: subrogation Claimants and Claimants whose only Cerro Grande Fire related loss is for flood insurance premiums.

§ 295.32 Determination of compensation due to claimant.

(a) *Authorized Official's report.* After OCGFC has evaluated all elements of a claim as stated in the Proof of Loss, the Authorized Official will issue, and provide the Claimant with a copy of, the Authorized Official's Determination.

(b) *Claimant's options upon issuance of the Authorized Official's determination.* Not later than 120 days after the date that appears on the Authorized Official's Determination, the Claimant must either accept the findings by submitting a Release and Certification Form to FEMA or initiate an Administrative Appeal in accordance with § 295.41. The CGFAA requires that Claimants sign the Release and Certification Form to receive payment on their claims (except for partial payments). The Claimant will receive payment of compensation awarded by the Authorized Official after FEMA re-

ceives the completed Release and Certification Form. If the Claimant does not either submit a Release and Certification Form to FEMA or initiate an Administrative Appeal no later than 120 Days after the date that appears on the Authorized Official's Determination, he or she will be conclusively presumed to have accepted the Authorized Official's Determination. The Director of OCGFC may modify the deadlines set forth in this subsection at the request of a Claimant for good cause shown.

§ 295.33 Supplementing claims.

A Claimant may amend the Notice of Loss to include additional claims at any time before signing a Proof of Loss. After the Claimant has submitted a Proof of Loss and before submission of the Release and Certification Form, a Claimant may request that the Director of OCGFC consider one or more Losses not addressed in the Proof of Loss. The request must be submitted in writing to the Director of OCGFC and received not later than the deadline for filing an Administrative Appeal under § 295.32 or August 28, 2002, whichever is earlier. It must be supported by the Claimant's explanation of why the Loss was not previously reported. If good cause is found to consider the additional loss, the Director will determine whether compensation is due to the Claimant for the Loss under the Administrative Appeal procedures described in § 295.41.

§ 295.34 Reopening a claim.

(a) The Director of OCGFC may reopen a claim if requested to do so by the Claimant, notwithstanding the submission of the Release and Certification Form, for the limited purpose of considering issues raised by the request to reopen if:

(1) The Claimant desires mitigation compensation and the request to reopen is filed not later than August 28, 2003 in accordance with § 295.21(d) or (h); or

(2) The Claimant closed the sale of real property not later than August 28, 2002 and wishes to present a claim for reduction in the value of the real property under § 295.21(e) and the request to

reopen is filed not later than August 28, 2002; or

(3) The Claimant has incurred Replacement Costs under §295.21(d) in excess of those previously awarded and is not prohibited by the terms of an agreement pertaining to home replacement with OCGFC from requesting that the case be reopened; or

(4) The Director of OCGFC otherwise determines that Claimant has demonstrated good cause.

(b) The Director of OCGFC may establish a deadline by which requests to reopen under paragraphs (a)(3) or (4) of this section must be submitted. The deadline will be published as a notice in the FEDERAL REGISTER and broadly disseminated throughout the communities, pueblos and Indian reservations in Los Alamos, Rio Arriba, Sandoval, and Santa Fe Counties.

§295.35 Access to records.

For purpose of audit and investigation, a Claimant will grant the FEMA DHS Office of the Inspector General and the Comptroller General of the United States access to any property that is the subject of a claim and to any and all books, documents, papers, and records maintained by a Claimant or under the Claimant's control pertaining or relevant to the claim.

§295.36 Confidentiality of information.

Confidential information submitted by individual Claimants is protected from disclosure to the extent permitted by the Privacy Act. These protections are described in the Privacy Act Notice provided with the Notice of Loss. Other Claimants should consult with FEMA concerning the availability of confidentiality protection under exemptions to the Freedom of Information Act and other applicable laws before submitting confidential, proprietary or trade secret information.

Subpart E—Dispute Resolution

§295.40 Scope.

This subpart describes a Claimant's right to bring an Administrative Appeal in response to the Authorized Official's Determination. It also describes the Claimant's right to pursue arbitration or seek judicial review following an Administrative Appeal.

§295.41 Administrative appeal.

(a) *Notice of appeal.* A Claimant may request that the Director of OCGFC review the Authorized Official's Determination by written request to the Appeals Docket, Office of Cerro Grande Claims, P.O. Box 1480, Los Alamos, NM 87544–1480, postmarked or delivered within 120 Days after the date that appears on the Authorized Official's Determination. The Claimant will submit along with the notice of appeal a statement explaining why the Authorized Official's Determination was incorrect.

(b) *Acknowledgement of appeal.* OCGFC will acknowledge the receipt of appeals that are timely filed. Following the receipt of a timely filed appeal, the Director of OCGFC will obtain the Administrative Record from the Authorized Official and transmit a copy to the Claimant.

(c) *Supplemental filings.* The Claimant may supplement the statement of reasons and provide any additional documentary evidence supporting the appeal within 60 Days after the date when the appeal is filed. The Director of OCGFC may extend these timeframes or authorize additional filings either on his or her own initiative or in response to a request by the Claimant for good cause shown.

(d) *Admissible evidence.* The Claimant may rely upon any relevant evidence to support the appeal, regardless of whether the evidence was previously submitted to the Claims Reviewer for consideration by the Authorized Official.

(e) *Obtaining evidence.* The Director of OCGFC may request from the Claimant or from the Authorized Official any additional information that is relevant to the issues posed by the appeal in his or her discretion.

(f) *Conferences.* The Director of OCGFC may schedule a conference to gain a better understanding of the issues or to explore settlement possibilities.

(g) *Hearings.* The Director of OCGFC may exercise the discretion to convene an informal hearing to receive oral testimony from witnesses or experts. The rules under which hearings will be conducted will be established by the Director of OCGFC. Formal rules of evidence applicable to court proceedings will not be used in hearings under this subsection. Hearings will be transcribed and the transcript will be entered in the Administrative Record.

(h) *Decision on appeal.* After the allotted time for submission of evidence has passed, the Director of OCGFC will close the Administrative Record and render a written decision on the Administrative Appeal. The Director of OCGFC's decision on the Administrative Appeal will constitute the final decision of the Administrator of FEMA under §§ 104(d)(2)(B) and 104(i)(1) of the CGFAA.

(i) *Claimant's options following appeal.* The Claimant's concurrence with the decision in the Administrative Appeal will be conclusively presumed unless the Claimant initiates arbitration in accordance with § 295.42 or seeks judicial review in accordance with § 295.43. If the Claimant concurs with the Director's determination, payment of any additional damages awarded by the Director will be made to the Claimant upon receipt of a properly executed Release and Certification Form.

§ 295.42 Arbitration.

(a) *Initiating arbitration.* A Claimant who is dissatisfied with the outcome of the Administrative Appeal may initiate binding arbitration by submitting a written request for arbitration to the Arbitration Administrator for Cerro Grande Claims, Alternate Dispute Resolution Office, Federal Emergency Management Agency, 500 C Street, SW., room 214, Washington, DC 20472 on a form provided by OCGFC. The written request for arbitration must be received not later than 60 days after the date that appears on the Administrative Appeal decision.

(b) *Permissible claims.* A Claimant may not arbitrate an issue unless it was raised and decided in the Administrative Appeal. Arbitration will be conducted on the evidence in the Administrative Record. Evidence not previously entered into the Administrative Record will not be considered.

(c) *Settlement and mediation alternatives.* At any time after a request for arbitration is filed and before the time a decision is rendered, either party may request in writing that the Alternate Dispute Resolution Office stay further proceedings in the arbitration to facilitate settlement discussions. A mediator may be appointed (if requested by the parties) to facilitate settlement discussions. If both parties concur in the request, the Alternate Dispute Resolution Office will stay the arbitration and appoint a mediator at our expense. The stay may be terminated and the arbitration resumed upon written request of either party to the Alternate Dispute Resolution Office. If the dispute is settled, the Alternate Dispute Resolution Office will issue an order terminating the arbitration and provide the Claimant with a Release and Certification Form.

(d) *Selection of arbitrator.* Arbitrators will be selected from a list of qualified arbitrators who have agreed to serve provided by the Alternate Dispute Resolution Office. If the amount in dispute is $300,000 or less, the arbitration will be decided by one arbitrator selected by the Claimant from the list. If the amount in dispute exceeds $300,000, a panel of three arbitrators selected at random by the Alternate Dispute Resolution Office will decide the arbitration.

(e) *Conduct of arbitration.* The arbitration will be conducted in a manner determined by the arbitrator consistent with guidelines established by the Alternate Dispute Resolution Office. The Alternate Dispute Resolution Office will provide these guidelines upon request.

(f) *Hearings.* The arbitrator may convene a hearing at a location designated by the Alternate Dispute Resolution Office. Whenever possible hearings will be held in Los Alamos, New Mexico unless the parties jointly agree to a different location.

(g) *Decision.* After reviewing the evidence, the arbitrator(s) will render a decision in writing to the Alternate Dispute Resolution Office. The Alternate Dispute Resolution Office will transmit the decision to the Claimant and the Director of OCGFC. If a panel of three arbitrators conducts the arbitration, at least two of the three arbitrators must sign the decision. The decision will be rendered no later than 10 Days after a hearing is concluded or 60 Days after the arbitration is initiated, whichever is earlier. The Alternate Dispute Resolution Office may extend the time for a decision. The decision will establish the compensation due to the Claimant, if any, and the reasons therefore.

(h) *Action on arbitration decision.* The Alternate Dispute Resolution Office will forward the arbitration decision and a Release and Certification Form to the Claimant. A Claimant who has received or who has been awarded any compensation under the CGFAA must sign and return the Release and Certification Form, regardless of whether any additional compensation is awarded by the arbitration. Additional compensation awarded in the arbitration will be paid to the Claimant after the signed Release and Certification Form is received.

(i) *Final decision.* The decision of the arbitrator will be final and binding on all parties and will not be subject to any administrative or judicial review. The arbitrator may correct clerical, typographical or computational errors as requested by the Alternate Dispute Resolution Office.

(j) *Administration of arbitration.* The Alternate Dispute Resolution Office will serve as arbitration administrator and will conclusively resolve any procedural disputes arising in the course of the arbitration. The Alternate Dispute Resolution Office will pay the fees of the arbitrator and reimburse the arbitrator for arbitration related expenses unless the parties jointly agree otherwise.

§ 295.43 Judicial review.

As an alternative to arbitration, a Claimant dissatisfied with the outcome of an Administrative Appeal may seek judicial review of the decision by bringing a civil lawsuit against FEMA in the United States District Court for the District of New Mexico. This lawsuit must be brought within 60 Days of the date that appears on the Administrative Appeal decision. The court may only consider evidence in the Adminis-

trative Record. The court will uphold our decision if it is supported by substantial evidence on the record considered as a whole. If the judge has awarded damages over and above those previously paid, FEMA will cause the damages to be paid to the Claimant upon receipt of the Release and Certification Form or as otherwise specified by order of the court. Claimants who have received any compensation under the CGFAA must return a Release and Certification Form as provided in § 295.30(c), regardless of whether a court awards additional compensation.

Subpart F—Glossary

§ 295.50 Definitions.

Administrative Appeal means an appeal of the Authorized Official's Determination to the Director of OCGFC in accordance with the provisions of Subpart E of these regulations.

Administrative Record means all information submitted by the Claimant and all information collected by FEMA concerning the claim, which is used to evaluate the claim and to formulate the Authorized Official's Determination. It also means all information that is submitted by the Claimant or FEMA in an Administrative Appeal and the decision of the Administrative Appeal. It excludes the opinions, memoranda and work papers of our attorneys and drafts of documents prepared by OCGFC personnel and contractors.

Alternate Dispute Resolution Office means the Office established by FEMA to promote use of Alternative Dispute Resolution as a means of resolving disputes. The address of the Alternate Dispute Resolution Office is Federal Emergency Management Agency, 500 C Street, SW., Washington, DC 20472.

Authorized Official means an employee of the United States who is delegated with authority by the Director of OCGFC to render binding determinations on claims and to determine compensation due to Claimants under the CGFAA.

Authorized Official's Determination means a report signed by an Authorized Official and mailed to the Claimant evaluating each element of the claim as stated in the Proof of Loss and determining the compensation, if any, due to the Claimant.

Claimant means a person who has filed a Notice of Loss under the CGFAA.

Claims Reviewer means an employee of the United States or an OCGFC contractor or subcontractor who is authorized by the Director of OCGFC to review and evaluate claims submitted under the CGFAA.

Days means calendar days, including weekends and holidays.

Destruction of a Home means destruction or physical damage to a residence or the land upon which it sat, resulting from the Cerro Grande Fire.

Discount to Net Present Value means a reduction of an award for damages arising in the future by making allowance for the fact that such award, if properly invested would earn interest.

Household means a group of people, related or unrelated, who live together on a continuous basis and does not include members of an extended family who do not regularly and continuously cohabit.

Household Including Tribal Members means a Household that existed on May 4, 2000, which included one or more Tribal Members as continuous residents.

Indian tribe means an entity listed on the most recent list of federally recognized tribes published in the FEDERAL REGISTER by the Secretary of the Interior pursuant to the Federally Recognized Indian Tribe List Act, 25 U.S.C. 479a, or successor legislation.

Injured Person means an individual, regardless of citizenship or alien status, an Indian tribe, corporation, tribal corporation, partnership, company, association, cooperative, joint venture, limited liability company, estate, trust, county, city, State, school district, special district or other non-Federal entity that suffered Loss resulting from the Cerro Grande Fire and any entity that provided insurance to an Injured Person. The term Injured Person includes an Indian tribe with respect to any claim relating to property or natural resources held in trust for the Indian tribe by the United States. Lenders holding mortgages or security interests on property affected by the Cerro Grande fire and lien holders are not "Injured Persons" for purposes of the CGFAA.

Loss means "injury or loss of property, or personal injury or death," as that phrase appears in the Federal Tort Claims Act, 28 U.S.C. 1346(b)(1), and the several categories of "property loss," "business loss" or "financial loss" set out in the § 104(d) of the CGFAA.

Mitigation Compensation Plan means a written mitigation plan submitted by a local government with land use regulatory authority or by an Indian tribe that recommends specific mitigation measures to reduce the heightened risks of wildfire, flood or other natural hazards resulting from the Cerro Grande Fire or seeks compensation for the cost of such measures expended before August 28, 2000, or both. The Mitigation Compensation Plan may address property specific mitigation measures and community level mitigation measures.

Notice of Loss means a form supplied by OCGFC through which an Injured Person makes a binding, conclusive and irrevocable election to have all Losses resulting from the Cerro Grande Fire reviewed by FEMA for possible compensation under the CGFAA.

Proof of Loss means a statement, signed by a Claimant under penalty of perjury and subject to the provisions of 18 U.S.C.1001 that the claim is true and correct, attesting to the nature and extent of the Claimant's injuries.

Public Assistance Program means the FEMA program establish under Subchapter IV of the Robert T. Stafford Disaster Relief and Emergency Assistance Act, as amended, 42 U.S.C. 5121, *et seq.*, which provides grants to States, local governments, Indian tribes and private nonprofit organizations for emergency measures and repair, restoration and replacement of damaged facilities.

Replacement Cost means the cost of replacing an item that is damaged or destroyed with an item that is comparable in quality and utility.

Release and Certification Form means a document in the manner prescribed by § 104(e) of the CGFAA that all Claimants who have received or are awarded compensatory damages under the CGFAA must execute and return to OCGFC as required by § 295.30(c).

Subsistence Resources means food and other items obtained through hunting, fishing, firewood and other resource gathering, timbering, grazing or agricultural activities undertaken by the Claimant without financial remuneration.

Tribal Member means an enrolled member of an Indian Tribe.

PARTS 296–299 [RESERVED]

SUBCHAPTER F—PREPAREDNESS

PART 300—DISASTER PREPAREDNESS ASSISTANCE

Sec.
300.1 Definitions.
300.2 Technical assistance.
300.3 Financial assistance.

AUTHORITY: 42 U.S.C. 5121 *et seq.*; Reorganization Plan No. 3 of 1978; E.O. 12148.

SOURCE: 45 FR 13464, Feb. 29, 1980, unless otherwise noted.

§ 300.1 Definitions.

As used in this part:

(a) *The Act* means the Robert T. Stafford Disaster Relief and Emergency Assistance Act, 42 U.S.C. 5121 *et seq.*

(b) *Disaster assistance plans* means those plans which identify tasks needed to deliver disaster assistance and to avoid, reduce, or mitigate natural hazards; make assignments to execute those tasks; reflect State authorities for executing disaster assignments; and provide for adequate training of personnel in their disaster or mitigation assignments.

(c) *Mitigation* means the process of systematically evaluating the nature and extent of vulnerability to the effects of natural hazards present in society and planning and carrying out actions to minimize future vulnerability to those hazards to the greatest extent practicable.

(d) *State* means any State of the United States, the District of Columbia, Puerto Rico, the Virgin Islands, Guam, American Samoa, Commonwealth of the Northern Mariana Islands, the Trust Territory of the Pacific Islands, the Federated States of Micronesia, or the Republic of the Marshall Islands.

[54 FR 2128, Jan. 19, 1989]

§ 300.2 Technical assistance.

Requests for technical assistance under section 201(b) of the Act shall be made by the Governor or his/her designated representative to the Regional Director.

(a) The request for technical assistance shall indicate as specifically as possible the objectives, nature, and duration of the requested assistance; the recipient agency or organization within the State; the State official responsible for utilizing such assistance; the manner in which such assistance is to be utilized; and any other information needed for a full understanding of the need for such requested assistance.

(b) The request for assistance requires participation by the State in the technical assistance process. As part of its request for such assistance, the State shall agree to facilitate coordination among FEMA, local governments, State agencies and the businesses and industries in need of assistance in the areas of disaster preparedness and mitigation.

[54 FR 2129, Jan. 19, 1989]

§ 300.3 Financial assistance.

(a) The Regional Administrator may provide to States upon written request by the State Governor or an authorized representative, an annual improvement grant up to $50,000, but not to exceed 50 percent of eligible costs, except where separate legislation requires or permits a waiver of the State's matching share, e.g., with respect to "insular areas", as that term is defined at 48 U.S.C. 1469a(d). The nonFederal share in all cases may exceed the Federal share.

(b) The improvement grant shall be product-oriented; that is, it must produce something measurable in a way that determines specific results, to substantiate compliance with the grant workplan objectives and to evidence contribution to the State's disaster capability. The following list, *which is neither exhaustive nor ranked in priority order*, offers examples of eligible products under the Disaster Preparedness Improvement Grant Program:

(1) Evaluations of natural hazards and development of the programs and actions required to mitigate such hazards;

(2) Hazard mitigation activities, including development of predisaster natural hazard mitigation plans, policies, programs and strategies for State-level multi-hazard mitigation;

540

(3) Updates to State disaster assistance plans, including plans for the Individual and Family Grant (IFG) Program, Public Assistance Program, Hazard Mitigation Grant Program, Disaster Application Center operations, damage assessment, etc.;

(4) Handbooks to implement State disaster assistance program activities;

(5) Exercise materials (EXPLAN, scenario, injects, etc.) to test and exercise procedures for State efforts in disaster response, including provision of individual and public assistance;

(6) Standard operating procedures for individual State agencies to execute disaster responsibilities for IFG, crisis counseling, mass care or other functional responsibilities;

(7) Training for State employees in their responsibilities under the State's disaster assistance plan;

(8) Report of formal analysis of State enabling legislation and other authorities to ensure efficient processing by the State of applications by governmental entities and individuals for Federal disaster relief;

(9) An inventory of updated inventory of State/local critical facilities (including State/local emergency operations centers) and their proximity to identified hazard areas;

(10) A tracking system of critical actions (identified in postdisaster critiques) to be executed by State or local governments to improve disaster assistance capabilities or reduce vulnerability to natural hazards.

(11) Plans or procedures for dealing with disasters not receiving supplementary Federal assistance;

(12) Damage assessment plans or procedures;

(13) Procedures for search and rescue operations; and,

(14) Disaster accounting procedures.

(c) The State shall provide quarterly financial and performance reports to the Regional Administrator. Reporting shall be by program quarter unless otherwise agreed to by the Regional Administrator.

[54 FR 2129, Jan. 19, 1989]

PART 301 [RESERVED]

PART 302—CIVIL DEFENSE-STATE AND LOCAL EMERGENCY MANAGEMENT ASSISTANCE PROGRAM (EMA)

Sec.
302.1 Purpose.
302.2 Definitions.
302.3 Documentation of eligibility.
302.4 Merit personnel systems.
302.5 Allocations and reallocations.
302.6 Fiscal year limitation.
302.7 Use of funds, materials, supplies, equipment, and personnel.
302.8 Waiver of "single" State agency requirements.

AUTHORITY: 50 U.S.C. app. 2251 et seq. Reorganization Plan No. 3 of 1978; E.O. 12148.

SOURCE: 48 FR 44211, Sept. 28, 1983, unless otherwise noted.

§ 302.1 Purpose.

(a) The regulations in this part prescribe the requirements applicable to the Emergency Management Assistance (EMA) program for Federal financial contributions to the States, and through the States to their political subdivisions, for up to one half of the necessary and essential State and local civil defense personnel and administrative expenses, under section 205 of the Federal Civil Defense Act of 1950, as amended, and set forth the conditions under which such contributions will be made.

(b) The intent of this program is to increase civil defense operational capability at the State and local levels of government by providing Federal financial assistance so that personnel and other resources can be made available for essential planning and other administrative functions and activities required in order to accomplish this objective.

§ 302.2 Definitions.

Except as otherwise stated or clearly apparent by context, the definitions ascribed in this section to each of the listed terms shall constitute their meaning when used in the regulations in this part. Terms not defined in this part shall have the meaning set forth in their definition, if any, in the Federal Civil Defense Act of 1950, as amended.

(a) *Act.* The Federal Civil Defense Act of 1950, as amended (50 U.S.C. App. 2251 *et seq.*).

(b) *Administrative expenses.* Necessary and essential expenses, other than personnel expenses as defined in this section, of a grantee and its subgrantees incurred in the administration of their civil defense programs, as detailed in CPG 1–3, Federal Assistance Handbook, and in CPG 1–32, FEMA Financial Assistance Guidelines.

(c) *Annual submission.* The State's annual request for participation in the contributions program authorized by section 205 of the Act. As specified in CPG 1–3, it includes staffing patterns (including job description changes), budget requirements, and any amendments to the State administrative plan, a request for funds covering the State and its subgrantees and program statements of work for the grantee and subgrantees under the Comprehensive Cooperative Agreement.

(d) *Approval.* All approvals by the Federal Emergency Management Agency (FEMA) as grantor agency required under the regulations in this part mean prior approval in writing signed by an authorized FEMA official. When failure to obtain prior approval of an action has not resulted and is not expected to result in any failure of compliance with a substantive requirement, and approval after the fact is not contrary to law (or regulation having the effect of law), written approval after the fact may be granted at the discretion of the authorized official.

(e) *CPG 1–3.* Civil Preparedness Guide entitled "Federal Assistance Handbook," which sets forth detailed guidance on procedures that a State and, where applicable, its political subdivisions must follow in order to request financial assistance from the grantor agency. It also sets forth detailed requirements, terms, and conditions upon which financial assistance is granted under these regulations. Included are amendments by numbered changes. References to CPG 1–3 include provisions of any other volumes of the CPG series specifically referenced in CPG 1–3. Copies of the Civil Preparedness Guides and the Civil Preparedness Circulars may be ordered by FEMA Regional Offices using FEMA Form 60–8

transmitted to FEMA, P.O. Box 8181, Washington, DC, 20024. One or more copies of CPG 1–3 have been distributed to each State and to each local government participating in the program under the regulations in this part. Copies of revisions and amendments are distributed to participating governments (addressed to the Emergency Management Coordinator) upon issuance.

(f) *Comprehensive Cooperative Agreement (CCA).* Provides for each State a single vehicle for applying for and receiving financial assistance for several discrete FEMA programs and for organizing and reporting on emergency management objectives and accomplishments, particularly under the funded programs.

(g) *Emergency management.* Refers to the activities and measures undertaken by a State, or one of its political subdivisions, to manage a "civil defense program" as defined and provided for by the Federal Civil Defense Act of 1950, as amended, including without limitation Title V, added by Public Law 96–342, and section 207, added by Public Law 97–86. Title V calls for an improved civil defense program that includes:

(1) A program structure for the resources to be used for attack-related civil defense; (2) a program structure for the resources to be used for disaster-related civil defense; and (3) criteria and procedures under which those resources planned for attack-related civil defense and those planned for disaster-related civil defense can be used interchangeably. Thus, emergency management includes "civil defense" for and operations in either attack-related or disaster-related emergencies. Section 207 allows Federal Civil Defense Act funds to be used for disaster preparedness and response if such use "is consistent with, contributes to, and does not detract from attack-related civil defense preparedness." Also 44 CFR part 312, Use of Civil Defense Personnel, Materials, and Facilities for Natural Disaster Purposes, provides terms and conditions for such use.

(h) *Administrator.* The head of the grantor agency or another official of the Agency authorized in writing by

542

the Administrator to act officially on behalf of the Administrator.

(i) *Forms prescribed by the grantor agency.* Forms prescribed by the grantor agency are identified in CPG 1–3 and may be ordered by FEMA Regional Offices using FEMA Form 60–8 transmitted to FEMA, P.O. Box 8181, Washington, DC, 20024.

(j) *Grantee.* A State that has received EMA funds as a result of having a State administrative plan, a statement of work, and an annual submission, all approved by the grantor agency as meeting the requirements prescribed in this part and in CPG 1–3 for necessary and essential State and local civil defense personnel and administrative expenses for a current Federal fiscal year.

(k) *Grantor agency.* The Federal Emergency Management Agency (FEMA).

(l) *Interstate civil defense authority.* Any civil defense authority established by interstate compact pursuant to section 201(g) of the Act.

(m) *Necessary and essential civil defense expenses.* Necessary and essential civil defense expenses are those required for the proper and efficient administration of the civil defense program of a grantee or a subgrantee as described in a State administrative plan and statement of work approved by the Regional Administrator as being consistent with the national plan (i.e., program) for civil defense and as meeting other requirements for civil defense prescribed by or under provisions of the Act.

(n) *OMB Circular A–87.* "Cost Principles Applicable to Grants and Contracts with State and Local Governments," promulgated by the Office of Management and Budget, Executive Office of the President, as published in the FEDERAL REGISTER (46 FR 9548) and subsequent amendments or revisions. (See CPG 1–32, Financial Assistance Guidelines).

(o) *OMB Circular A–102.* "Uniform Administrative Requirements for Grants-in-aid to State and Local Governments," promulgated by the Office of Management and Budget, Executive Office of the President (42 FR 45828) including amendments or revisions as published in the FEDERAL REGISTER.

(See CPG 1–32, Financial Assistance Guidelines).

(p) *Emergency Operations Plan (EOP).* State or local government Emergency Operations Plans identify the available personnel, equipment, facilities, supplies, and other resources in the jurisdiction and states the method or scheme for coordinated actions to be taken by individuals and government services in the event of natural, manmade and attack-related disasters.

(q) *Personnel expenses.* Necessary and essential civil defense expenses for personnel on the approved staffing pattern of a grantee or subgrantee (including but not necessarily limited to salaries, wages, and supplementary compensation and fringe benefits) for such employees appointed in accordance with State and local government laws and regulations under a system which meets Federal merit system and other applicable Federal requirements. Such expenses must be supported by job descriptions, payrolls, time distribution records, and other documentation as detailed in CPG 1–3. Personnel compensation and other costs incurred with regard to employees who are not on the civil defense staff but whose work serves the civil defense agency (e.g., State's budget and accounting office) may be charged as civil defense expense to the extent covered therefore in a federally approved indirect cost allocation plan.

(r) *Political subdivisions.* Local governments, including but not limited to cities, towns, incorporated communities, counties or parishes, and townships.

(s) *Regional Administrator.* A FEMA official delegated authority to exercise specified functions as they apply to grantees and subgrantees, within the geographical area of a particular region as identified (including address) in 44 CFR part 2.

(t) *State.* Any of the actual States, the District of Columbia, the Commonwealth of Puerto Rico, the Commonwealth of the Northern Mariana Islands, and the territories of American Samoa, Guam, and the Virgin Islands.

(u) *State administrative plan.* A one-time submission with amendments as necessary to keep it current, the plan is a formal description of each participating State's total civil defense program and of related State and local laws, executive directives, rules, and plans and procedures, including personnel standards administered on a merit basis, updated emergency operations plans, travel regulations, indirect cost allocation plans and other information necessary to reflect the total civil defense program throughout the State. The plan also includes without limitation documentation as to administrative and financial systems to assure compliance with uniform grant-in-aid administrative requirements for States and subgrantees as required under OMB Circular A–102 and with other requirements relevant to the eligibility of the State and its political subdivisions for participation in financial assistance programs for civil defense purposes. Detailed requirements are prescribed in CPG 1–3. (Also see § 302.3.)

(v) *Statement of work.* Formal identification of specific actions to be accomplished by a State and its political subdivisions during the fiscal year for which Federal funds are being requested by the State. Submission is made to the FEMA Regional Administrator as part of the CCA Program Narrative.

(w) *Subgrantee.* A political subdivision of a State listed in the State's annual submission (or amendments thereto) as approved by the grantor agency (including any grantor agency-approved amendments thereto) as eligible to receive a portion of the Federal financial contribution provided for use within the State. The term includes Indian tribes when the State has assumed jurisdiction pursuant to State law and tribal regulations.

[48 FR 44211 Sept. 28, 1983, as amended at 51 FR 12520, Apr. 11, 1986; 74 FR 15354, Apr. 3, 2009]

§ 302.3 Documentation of eligibility.

In order to remain eligible for Federal financial contributions under the regulations in this part, each State must have on file with FEMA a current State administrative plan, an emergency operations plan for civil defense, and an annual submission (including a statement of work) which have been approved by the Regional Administrator as being consistent with the national plan (i.e., program) for civil defense and as meeting the requirements of the regulations in this part and CPG 1–3. A State may allocate a portion of its EMA funds to an Indian tribe as a subgrantee where the State has assumed jurisdiction pursuant to State law and tribal regulations.

(a) *State administrative plans.* Every State has a State administrative plan file with FEMA and is required to keep the plan current through amendments as necessary. Such plans and amendments shall be reviewed by the Regional Administrator, who will advise the State in writing as to the effect, if any, changes will have on the continued eligibility of the State and its subgrantees. The Regional Administrator shall not, however, approve any amendments that would result in failure of the plan to meet these criteria:

(1) Provides for and is, pursuant to State law, in effect in all political subdivision of the State, mandatory on them, and, unless waived by the Administrator under section 204 of the Intergovernmental Cooperation Act of 1968 (42 U.S.C. 4214), administered or supervised by a single State administrative agency. In demonstrating that the State administrative plan for civil defense is in effect in all political subdivisions of the State and mandatory on them, the plan shall contain references to the applicable State statutes and local ordinances, executive orders and directives, and rules and regulations at the State and local level that establish the civil defense authority, structure, plans, and procedures, including those relating to emergency operations, throughout the State.

(2) Provides assurance of nonFederal contributions at least equal to Federal funding for necessary and essential costs eligible under this program from any source consistent with State law, but not from another Federal source unless Federal law specifically authorizes the use of funds from such Federal source as part of the State's share.

(3) Provides for the development of State and local government civil defense emergency operations plans pursuant to the standards approved by the Administrator.

(4) Provides for the employment by the State of full-time civil defense director or deputy director.

(5) Provides for the establishment and maintenance of methods of personnel administration in public agencies administering or supervising the civil defense program, at both the State and local government levels, in conformity with the Standards for a Merit System of Personnel Administration (5 CFR part 900), which incorporate the Intergovernmental Personnel Act Merit Principles (Pub. L. 91–648, section 2, 84 Stat. 1908) prescribed by the Office of Personnel Management pursuant to section 208 of the Intergovernmental Personnel Act of 1970, as amended.

(6) Provides for the establishment of safeguards to prohibit State and local government employees from using their positions for a purpose that is or gives the appearance of being motivated by desire for private gain for themselves or others, particularly those with whom they have family, business, or other ties.

(7) Provides that the State shall make such reports (including without limitation financial reports) in such form and content as the Administrator may require.

(8) Provides that the State and all subgrantees shall retain, in accordance with OMB Circular A–102, and make available to duly authorized representatives of the Administrator and the U.S. Comptroller General all books, records, and papers pertinent to the grant program for the purpose of making audits, examinations, excerpts, and transcripts necessary to conduct audits.

(9) Provides for establishment and maintenance of a financial management system of grant-supported activities of the State and all subgrantees which meets the federally prescribed standards promulgated in "Standards for Grantee Financial Management Systems," Attachment G of OMB Circular A–102.

(10) Provides for establishment and maintenance of procedures for monitoring and reporting grant program and project performance of the State and its subgrantees which meet the federally prescribed standards promul-

gated in Attachment I of OMB Circular A–102.

(11) Provides for the establishment and maintenance at the State level and by subgrantees of property management systems in accordance with the federally prescribed standards set forth in Attachment N of OMB Circular A–102.

(12) Provides for the establishment and maintenance at the State level and by subgrantees of systems for the procurement of supplies, equipment, construction, and other services, with the assistance of grant funds, in accordance with federally prescribed standards set forth in Attachment O of OMB Circular A–102.

(13) Provides for disbursement of the appropriate share of the Federal grant to the State's subgrantees in accordance with requirements detailed in CPG 1–3.

(14) Provides for the State's supervision and review of the civil defense plans, programs, and operations of its subgrantees to obtain conformity and compliance with Federal requirements and goals set forth or referenced in the regulations in this part and as detailed in CPG 1–3.

(15) Contains a Statement of Compliance with grantor agency regulations relating to nondiscrimination in FEMA programs (see 44 CFR part 7).

(16) Provides for timely submission to the appropriate Regional Administrator of amendments to the administrative plan as necessary to reflect the current laws, regulation, criteria, plans, methods, practices, and procedures for administration of the State's civil defense program and those of its subgrantees.

(17) Conforms to other Federal standards and requirements set forth or referenced in the regulations in this part and as detailed in CPG 1–3.

(18) Provides for performance of independent organizationwide audits by State and local governments that receive EMA funds of their financial operations, including compliance with certain provisions of Federal law and regulation.

(b) *Emergency Operations Plans (EOP's).* (1) Each participating State shall have an EOP approved by the Regional Administrator and conforming with the requirements for plan content set forth in this part and in CPG 1–3, and in CPG 1–8 "Guide for the Development of State and Local Emergency Operations Plans" and in CPG 1–8A, "Guide for the Review of State and Local Emergency Operations Plans," which plan must provide for coordinated actions to be undertaken throughout the State in the event of attack and in the event of other disasters.

(2) Each subgrantee jurisdiction shall have a local EOP which conforms with the requirements for plan content as set forth in CPG 1–3 and CPG 1–8 and CPG 1–8A, and which has been approved by the local chief executive or other authorized official and accepted by the Governor or other authorized State official as being consistent with the State's EOP.

(c) *Annual submission.* Each State should include in its annual CCA application the amount of EMA funding requested (see § 302.5(c)). In order to participate for a particular Federal fiscal year, however, each State must also, within 60 days of receipt or notice of a formal allocation made pursuant to the criteria set forth in § 302.5 and in accordance with procedures and criteria specified in CPG 1–3, submit to the Regional Administrator an approvable annual submission which includes:

(1) A request or amended request for a financial contribution from FEMA in a specified amount for civil defense personnel and administrative expenses; (see § 302.5 (d) through (h)).

(2) Unless previously submitted for the particular Federal fiscal year, a statement of work for the State and proposed subgrantees or amendments to a statement of work previously submitted under the CCA.

(3) Staffing patterns (including new or revised job descriptions not previously submitted) on forms prescribed by FEMA for the civil defense organizations of the State and proposed subgrantees; and

(4) Any amendments to the State administrative plan required to reflect current status.

(d) *Approval of State administrative plan and annual submission.* If the State administrative plan and the annual submission are determined to be ap-

provable, the Regional Administrator will so notify the State in writing. The State administrative plan is a one-time submission. Unless amendments are necessary to meet Federal standards prescribed in the regulations in this part or in CPG 1–3 or to reflect changes in the State's administrative structure, procedures, criteria, or activities, or unless a portion were conditionally approved by the Regional Administrator as provided for in paragraph (e) of this section, no approval regarding the State administrative plan will be required for a State which participated for the preceding Federal fiscal year.

(e) *Agreement for contribution.* Approval pursuant to procedures and criteria described in this part and in CPG 1–3 of an annual submission of a State whose administrative plan is approved and current shall constitute agreement between FEMA and the State as grantee for its participation and that of its subgrantees in this program during the Federal fiscal year covered by the approved annual submission on the basis of the requirements and conditions prescribed in this part, in CPG 1–3, and in other federally promulgated criteria referenced in this part. Refusal or failure to comply with such requirements and conditions may result in the grantor agency cancelling, terminating, or suspending the grant, in whole or in part, and refraining from extending any further assistance to the grantee or subgrantee until satisfactory assurance of future compliance has been received.

(f) *Disapproval or conditional approval.* If a State's administrative plan or annual submission is disapproved, the Regional Administrator will advise the State in writing, including the reasons for such disapproval and the revisions required for approval. The State shall have 30 days from date of such notification in which to submit its revisions. In the event more time is required in which to place the revisions into effect, the Regional Administrator may conditionally approve the State administrative plan or annual submission subject to the specified conditions to be met within a specified time, as agreed by the State and FEMA.

(g) *Appeals.* (1) Appeal from a Regional Administrator's disapproval of a

State administrative plan or an annual submission or other final action as unjustified under the criteria in CPG 1–3 may be made by letter to the Deputy Administrator for the National Preparedness Directorate, signed by an authorized State official and submitted through the Regional Administrator. Such appeal letter shall be mailed or otherwise transmitted so as to reach the Regional Administrator within 30 days after receipt of the notification of disapproval. Failure to file its appeal on time may result in withdrawal of the State's allocation and the proposed funding being reallocated by the Administrator.

(2) A local jurisdiction that regards the final action on its subgrant made by a State as unjustified under the criteria in CPG 1–3 may submit an appeal through the State to the Regional Administrator. Upon receipt of such an appeal, the RegionalAdministrator shall forward the letter, together with all available pertinent documentation from the Regional Administrator's files and any additional documentation submitted by the local jurisdiction in support of its appeal, to the Deputy Administrator for the National Preparedness Directorate, for review and determination. The appeal shall contain all of the exceptions being taken by the State or local jurisdiction, and no exceptions will be determined piecemeal.

(3) No portion of the appellant State's allocation shall be reallocated by FEMA, and no portion of a local jurisdiction's allocation shall be reallocated by the State, pending determination of its appeal by the Administrator. The State and local jurisdiction (if applicable) will be notified in writing of the Administrator's decision, including a statement of the reasons therefor.

[48 FR 44211 Sept. 28, 1983, as amended at 51 FR 12520, Apr. 11, 1986; 74 FR 15354, Apr. 3, 2009]

§ 302.4 **Merit personnel systems.**

(a) *Background.* Section 208 of the Intergovernmental Personnel Act, as amended (42 U.S.C. 4728) authorizes Federal agencies to require, as a condition of participation in Federal assistance programs, systems of a personnel administration consistent with personnel standards prescribed by the Of-fice of Personnel Management (OPM). OPM has promulgated Standards for a System of Personnel Administration (5 CFR part 900) which prescribe intergovernmental personnel standards on a merit basis as a condition of eligibility in the administration of grant programs. OPM has approved FEMA adoption of these standards by the regulations in this part.

(b) *Standard.* Participation by each grantee and each subgrantee under the program covered in this part is subject to compliance with the following conditions regarding merit personnel systems:

Methods of personnel administration will be established and maintained in public agencies administering or supervising the administration of the civil defense program in conformity with the Standards for a Merit System of Personnel Administration 5 CFR part 900, which incorporate the Intergovernmental Personnel Act Merit Principles (Pub. L. 91–648, section 2, 84 Stat. 1909) prescribed by the Office of Personnel Management pursuant to section 208 of the Intergovernmental Personnel Act of 1970 as amended.

Section 302.3(a)(5) of this part provides, in part, that State administrative plans that fail to provide for fulfilling this condition are not approvable.

§ 302.5 **Allocations and reallocations.**

(a) The Administrator shall allocate the entire amount of funds available for the purposes of this program from the appropriation for each fiscal year. The allocation made to each State represents the total amount of funds available to pay the Federal share of necessary and essential civil defense personnel and administrative expenses of the State and its participating subdivisions during the fiscal year.

(b) The first calculation for developing the allocation for each State will be a formula distribution in accordance with section 205(d) of the Act, made by applying the following percentages to the total sum of Emergency Management Assistance in the President's budget request to Congress:

(1) Fifty (50) percent will be allocated on the basis of the prior-year State allocations, in fulfilment of the statutory requirement to give due regard to "the relative state of development of

547

civil defense readiness of the State" (State and local levels).

(2) Thirty-three (33) percent will be allocated on the basis of the ratio of the State's population to the national population (50 States, District of Columbia, and Puerto Rico), in fulfilment of the statutory requirements to give due regard to "population" and to "the criticality of target and support areas and the areas which may be affected by natural disasters with respect to the development of the total civil defense readiness of the Nation."

(3) Fifteen (15) percent will be divided equally among the 50 States, the District of Columbia, and Puerto Rico.

(4) In consonance with the statutory provision allowing the Administrator to prescribe other factors concerning the State allocations, the remaining two (2) percent will be held temporarily in reserve, to be used first to fund the four territories of the Virgin Islands, American Samoa, Guam, and the Commonwealth of the Northern Mariana Islands. Conditions peculiar to those areas make strict application of the mathematical formula in § 302.5(b) inequitable. Therefore, the Administrator will consider prior-year allocations, percentage of total United States population, and the factors set out in § 302.5(e) (1), (2), (4), and (5) in determining their allocations. The remaining balance of the reserve fund will then be used to restore any State which would receive less by formula share than its formula share for the previous fiscal year, provided that the reserve balance is sufficient to do this for all such States. Any remaining balance after this has been done will constitute a supplemental fund from which the Administrator will consider State requests for additional funding and the needs of any interstate civil defense authorities.

(c) For initial planning purposes only, each State will then be informed of the figure by the Regional Administrator. The State will base its initial EMA application upon that figure but may request a smaller amount or with appropriate justification a larger amount.

(d) The amount requested by the State shall not exceed 50 percent of its estimate of necessary and essential State and local personnel and administrative expenses for the fiscal year.

(e) The formula distribution shall be reviewed and evaluated, and adjusted as appropriate, by the Administrator, based on the current situation in each State, the requests of all States, and recommendations by the Regional Administrators. The Administrator will consider the following five factors:

(1) The ability of the State and its subgrantees to effectively expend such an amount for necessary and essential civil defense personnel and administrative purposes. Past performance is a factor in this determination.

(2) Special circumstances existing in the State at the time of allocating which require unusual expenditures for civil defense.

(3) Conditions peculiar to the State which make strict application of mathematical formula inequitable either to that State or other States.

(4) The relative cost of civil defense personnel and administrative services in that State; that is, whether such costs are considerably above or below the national average for similar services and expenses.

(5) Substantial changes in the civil defense readiness of the State not reflected by its recent civil defense expenditures.

(f) In September of each year, based on applications received and recommendations by the Regional Administrators, the Administrator will make a tentative allocation to the States. This will include adjustments for States that have indicated they will not be using the total of the formula distribution amount. States can then revise their earlier plans and applications to more nearly reflect the level of funding expected to become available.

(g) A State may provide to the Regional Administrator a preliminary annual submission in an amount not to exceed its tentative allocation.

(h) By September 30 (or as soon thereafter as feasible), the Administrator will make a formal allocation based on, or subject to, appropriation by Congress and allotment of the funds. This allocation for each State may include any additional amounts from the reserve portion of the EMA funds, and shall be in accordance with the regulations in this part and CPG 1-3.

(i) Upon the appropriation becoming available, and if requested by a State, the Regional Administrator may approve such State's preliminary annual submission (if found to meet all requirements in this part and CPG 1-3) in an appropriate amount which does not exceed the amount of the State's share of the Administrator's formal allocation of the Federal appropriation. An award document obligating Federal funds on the basis of the approved preliminary annual submission may be executed in accordance with the provisions of CPG 1-3.

(j) Based on and within 60 days after notification of its formal allocation, each State must provide to the Regional Administrator a final annual submission which meets all requirements in this part and CPG 1-3. If no changes are necessary, a State and the Regional Administrator may adopt in writing the State's preliminary annual submission as its final annual submission. If no award document was executed based on a State's preliminary annual submission, such document will be executed on the basis of that State's approved final annual submission.

(k) With regard to any State whose award document was executed pursuant to a preliminary annual submission covering only part of its formal allocation, upon approval (by the Regional Administrator) of the final annual submission (including a revised statement of work supporting the additional funding request) the Regional Administrator shall execute an amended award document obligating the balance of such State's formal allocation.

(l) After being advised of its annual formal allocation, if a State fails to submit, within 60 days, an approvable annual submission in the amount of its allocation, the Regional Administrator may reallocate the unused portion to other States in the region in such amounts as in his/her judgment will best assure adequate development of the civil defense capability of the Nation. The exception to this authority is in the event a State, or local jurisdiction, refuses to participate in attack preparedness activities. EMA funds withheld or returned for that reason are to be released to headquarters for reallocation on a national basis. In addition, the Regional Administrator may from time to time reallocate the amounts released by a State from its allocation as no longer being required for utilization in accordance with an approved annual submission and award document.

(m) Immediate notice to the headquarters EMA Program Manager of State reallocations is required in the form of copies of EMA-approved Annual Submission amendment documents, accompanied by copies of assistance award/amendment documents signed by regional and State authorized officials of both the releasing and recipient States.

(n) There is no dollar ceiling on the amount of funds that may be reallocated among States in a region. However, at any time that there are funds surplus to the eligible needs of the States within a region, those funds should be promptly released to headquarters for reallocation to other States with unfunded additional requirements.

(o) On July 1 of each fiscal year, the authority to reallocate EMA funds shall revert to the Administrator. In addition, any excess EMA funds available on that date, or that become available during the remainder of the fiscal year, are to be promptly released to headquarters for reallocation by the Administrator.

[48 FR 44211 Sept. 28, 1983, as amended at 51 FR 12521, Apr. 11, 1986; 51 FR 43924, Dec. 5, 1986; 56 FR 29905, July 1, 1991]

§ 302.6 Fiscal year limitation.

Federal appropriations for the program covered by the regulations in this part are limited for obligation on a Federal fiscal year basis. Each annual submission (or amendment thereto) which results in a change in scope (e.g., an increase in the amount of funds other than a cost overrun) must be approved during the Federal Fiscal year for which the funds to be charged were appropriated. Valid expenses incurred by a State or its subgrantee during the fiscal year but before obligation by FEMA of funds under this program may qualify for payment of a Federal financial contribution out of the funds subsequently appropriated for that fiscal year.

§ 302.7 **Use of funds, materials, supplies, equipment, and personnel.**

Financial contributions provided under the authority of section 205 of the Act are provided for necessary and essential State and local civil defense personnel and administrative expenses as prescribed by the regulations in this part and the provisions of CPG 1-3, and are obligated only on the basis of documentation justifying such need.

(a) *Emergencies.* In addition to such civil defense use, Federal funds obligated under a grantee's approved annual submission may be used, to the extent and under such terms and conditions as prescribed by the Administrator in CPG 1-3, for providing emergency assistance, including the use of civil defense personnel, organizational equipment, materials, and facilities, in preparation for and response to actual attack-related events or natural disasters (including manmade catastrophies).

(b) *Limitations.* Section 207 of the Act allows use of funds under the Act, including those for this program, for natural (including manmade) disaster preparedness and response purposes only to the extent that such use is consistent with, contributes to, and does not detract from attack-related preparedness (reference 44 CFR part 312).

§ 302.8 **Waiver of "single" State agency requirements.**

Section 205 of the Act requires that plans for civil defense of the United States be administered or supervised by a single State agency (50 U.S.C. App. 2286). Notwithstanding such law, section 204 of the Intergovernmental Cooperation Act of 1968 (42 U.S.C. 4214) provides authority for the Administrator as head of the grantor agency, upon the State's request, to waive the single State agency requirement and to approve other State administrative structure or arrangements, upon adequate showing that the requirement prevents the establishment of the most effective and efficient organizational arrangements within the State government. First, however, the Administrator must have found that the objec-

tives of the Act (50 U.S.C. app. 2251 *et seq.*) will not be endangered by the use of such other State structure or arrangements. Attachment D of OMB Circular A-102 requires that such requests be given expeditious handling by the grantor agency and that, whenever possible, an affirmative response be made.

[48 FR 44211 Sept. 28, 1983, as amended at 51 FR 12521, Apr. 11, 1986]

PART 303 [RESERVED]

PART 304—CONSOLIDATED GRANTS TO INSULAR AREAS

Sec.
304.1 Purpose.
304.2 Definitions.
304.3 Conditions for a consolidated grant.
304.4 Allocations.
304.5 Audits and records.

AUTHORITY: 50 U.S.C. app. 2251 *et seq.*; Reorganization Plan No. 3 of 1978; E.O. 12148.

SOURCE: 43 FR 39776, Sept. 7, 1978, unless otherwise noted. Redesignated at 44 FR 56173, Sept. 28, 1979.

§ 304.1 **Purpose.**

The purpose of the regulations in this part is to prescribe the basis under which the Federal Emergency Management Agency (FEMA) contributes Federal funds to an insular area through a consolidated grant.

§ 304.2 **Definitions.**

Except as otherwise stated when used in the regulations of this part, the meaning of the listed terms are as follows:

(a) *Insular areas.* The Virgin Islands, Guam, American Samoa, and the Government of the Northern Mariana Islands.

(b) *Consolidated grant.* A grant by FEMA to any insular area through an allocation which combines funds for the State and local management program and the State and local maintenance and services program for a single Federal fiscal year.

(c) *FEMA guidance material.* FEMA regulations (44 CFR chapter I), Civil Preparedness Guide (CPG) 1-3, and Civil Preparedness Circulars (CPC) as presently providing or hereafter amended or revised.

[43 FR 39776, Sept. 7, 1978. Redesignated at 44 FR 56173, Sept. 28, 1979, as amended at 48 FR 44554, Sept. 29, 1983]

§ 304.3 Conditions for a consolidated grant.

(a) In order to participate, an insular area must submit a (one-time) administrative plan as provided for in FEMA guidance material (to be maintained in current status) and must sign a (one-time) civil rights assurance and a (one-time) grant agreement agreeing to comply with Federal requirements.

(b) An insular area need not submit an application for a consolidated grant, but must submit an annual program paper which meets the requirements prescribed in FEMA guidance material.

(c) Funds made available under a consolidated grant must be expended for State and local management program expenses and/or State and local maintenance and services program expenses as defined and described in FEMA guidance material. Each participating insular area will determine the proportion in which funds granted to it will be allocated between the two programs.

(d) Participating insular areas need not provide matching funds for consolidated grants.

[43 FR 39776, Sept. 7, 1978. Redesignated at 44 FR 56173, Sept. 28, 1979, as amended at 50 FR 40007, Oct. 1, 1985]

§ 304.4 Allocations.

For each Federal fiscal year concerned, the Administrator, FEMA, shall allocate to each participating insular area an amount not less than the sum of grants for the two programs which the Administrator, FEMA, has determined such insular area would otherwise be entitled to receive for such fiscal year.

§ 304.5 Audits and records.

(a) *Audits.* FEMA will maintain adequate auditing, accounting and review procedures as outlined in FEMA guidance material and OMB Circulars No. A–73 and A–102.

(b) *Records.* Financial records, supporting documents, statistical records, and all other records pertinent to a consolidated grant shall be retained for a period of three years from submission of final billing and shall be available to the Administrator, FEMA, and the Comptroller General of the United States, all as prescribed in FEMA guidance material and in accordance with OMB Circular A–102 (42 FR 45828–45891).

PARTS 305–311 [RESERVED]

PART 312—USE OF CIVIL DEFENSE PERSONNEL, MATERIALS, AND FACILITIES FOR NATURAL DISASTER PURPOSES

Sec.
312.1 Purpose.
312.2 Definitions.
312.3 Policy.
312.4 General.
312.5 Personnel.
312.6 Materials and facilities.

AUTHORITY: Sec. 803(a)(3) Pub. L. 97–86; sec. 401, Federal Civil Defense Act of 1950, as amended, 50 U.S.C. app. 2253; Reorganization Plan No. 3 of 1978; 3 CFR, 1978 Comp., p. 329; and E.O. 12148 of July 20, 1979, 44 FR 43239.

SOURCE: 47 FR 43381, Oct. 1, 1982, unless otherwise noted.

§ 312.1 Purpose.

The purpose of the regulations in this part is to prescribe the terms and conditions under which civil defense personnel, materials, and facilities, supported in whole or in part through contributions under the Federal Civil Defense Act of 1950, as amended, 50 U.S.C. App. 2251, *et seq.*, hereinafter referred to as "the Act", may be used for natural disasters, to the extent that such usage is consistent with, contributes to, and does not detract from attack-related civil defense preparedness.

§ 312.2 Definitions.

Except as otherwise stated, when used in the regulations in this part, the meaning of the listed terms are as follows:

(a) The term *attack* means any attack or series of attacks by an enemy of the United States causing, or which may cause, substantial damage or injury to civilian property or persons in the United States in any manner by sabotage or by use of bombs, shellfire, or atomic-radiological, chemical, bacteriological, or biological means or other weapons or processes;

(b) The term *natural disaster* means any hurricane, tornado, storm, flood, high water, wind-driven water, tidal wave, tsunami, earthquake, volcanic eruption, landslide, mudslide, snowstorm, drought, fire, or other catastrophe in any part of the United States which causes, or which may cause, substantial damage or injury to civilian property or persons and, for the purposes of the Act, any explosion, civil disturbance, or any other manmade catastrophe shall be deemed to be a natural disaster;

(c) The term *civil defense* means all those activities and measures designed or undertaken (1) to minimize the effects upon the civilian population caused, or which would be caused, by an attack upon the United States, or by natural disaster, (2) to deal with the immediate emergency conditions which would be created by any such attack, or natural disaster, and (3) to effectuate emergency repairs to, or the emergency restoration of vital utilities and facilities destroyed or damaged by any such attack or natural disaster. Such term shall include, but shall not be limited to, (i) measures to be taken in preparation for anticipated attack or natural disaster (including the establishment of appropriate organizations, operational plans, and supporting agreements; the recruitment and training of personnel; the conduct of research; the procurement and stockpiling of necessary materials and supplies; the provision of suitable warning systems; the construction or preparation of shelter areas, and control centers; and, when appropriate, the non-military evacuation of civil population); (ii) measures to be taken during attack or natural disaster (including the enforcement of passive defense regulations prescribed by duly established military or civil authorities; the evacuation of personnel to shelter areas; the control of traffic and panic; and the control and use of lighting and civil communications); and (iii) measures to be taken following attack or natural disaster (including activities for firefighting; rescue, emergency medical, health and sanitation serv-

ices; monitoring for specific hazards of special weapons; unexploded bomb reconnaissance; essential debris clearance; emergency welfare measures; and immediately essential emergency repair or restoration of damaged vital facilities);

(d) The word *materials* shall include raw materials, supplies, medicines, equipment, component parts and technical information and processes necessary for civil defense;

(e) The word *facilities*, except as otherwise provided herein, shall include buildings, shelters, utilities, and land;

(f) The term *United States* or *States* shall include the several States, the District of Columbia, the Territories, and the possessions of the United States;

(g) The term *political subdivisions* shall include local governments, including but not limited to cities, towns, incorporated communities, counties, parishes, and townships; and

(h) The term *CPG 1-3* refers to FEMA's "Federal Assistance Handbook" promulgated as Civil Preparedness Guide (CPG) 1-3, as amended, by numbered changes thereto and by Civil Preparedness Circulars (CPC). CPG 1-3 sets forth detailed guidance on procedures which a State and, where applicable, its political subdivisions must follow in order to request financial assistance from FEMA. It also sets forth detailed requirements, terms, and conditions upon which financial assistance is granted.

(Reorganization Plan No. 3 of 1978, E.O. 12127 and E.O. 12148)

[47 FR 43381, Oct. 1, 1982, as amended at 48 FR 44545, Sept. 29, 1983]

§ 312.3 Policy.

(a) It is the policy of FEMA to provide a means of assistance to States and their political subdivisions in their carrying out responsibilities to alleviate the suffering and damage from attack-related or natural disasters by:

(1) Providing contributions for personnel, equipment, materials and facilities that may be used in preparing for or responding to disasters, provided that the use of such funds for natural disasters is consistent with, contributes to, and does not detract from attack-related civil defense preparedness.

(2) Encouraging the development of comprehensive disaster preparedness and assistance plans, programs, capabilities, and organizations by the State and its political subdivisions.

(3) Assisting in achieving greater coordination of disaster preparation and response programs.

(4) Providing technical advice and guidance to States and their political subdivisions for organizing and preparing to meet the effects of disasters.

(b) These regulations are not to be interpreted as authorizing States and their political subdivisions to request or receive additional assistance relating to particular disaster incidents.

§312.4 General.

(a) The Administrator, FEMA, will provide statements to States and their political subdivisions concerning Agency mission and goals, Annual Program Emphasis, and other directions, instructions, and technical guidance which together specify preparedness and response activities for both attack-related and natural disasters.

(b) States and their political subdivisions may apply to FEMA for financial assistance under the Act in a manner prescribed by Federal Regulations governing grants and cooperative agreements. Such applications must be compatible with FEMA's goals and requirements described in paragraph (a) of this section.

(c) Financial contributions to States and their political subdivisions are made by FEMA based on approval of the activities and projects described in the Annual Program Paper, and/or Comprehensive Cooperative Agreement, and which are in conformance with provisions of CPG 1–3, and applicable FEMA regulations set forth in chapter 1 of this title 44, chapter 1, subchapter E, of the Code of Federal Regulations. Financial contributions will not be made unless substantive activities and projects in preparation for and response to attack-related disasters are identified, and progress is indicated in the submissions, and recorded in program reporting systems. The presence of unavoidable circumstances, and the good faith effort of the applicant, will be considered if certain objectives are not met.

(d) State and local officials may use personnel, equipment, and facilities for natural disasters outside the physical boundaries of the jurisdiction and under the conditions stated within this regulation.

(e) Specific criteria relating to the preparedness and response activities are given in §§312.5 and 312.6 of this part.

§312.5 Personnel.

FEMA contributes to the development and support of emergency management organizations in the States and their political subdivisions, and to the development, operation, and maintenance of specific programs, through payment of salaries and benefits of State and local civil defense staff, and the payment of administrative expenses and travel, not to exceed 50 percent. FEMA also provides contributions for training and education expenses. The following use of such personnel for natural disaster purposes is allowable provided that such usage is consistent with, contributes to, and does not detract from attack-related civil defense preparedness:

(a) In developing, maintaining, testing and exercising plans, systems, and procedures for the protection of people and property from the effects of attack-related disasters, States and their political subdivisions may include and provide for natural disasters.

(b) Personnel supported in part through contributions under the Act may be assigned responsibilities for preparation for and response to natural disasters in any specific emergency occurring in a State or its political subdivisions as determined by the responsible State or local officials, respectively.

(c) Personnel supported in whole under the Act, may be assigned to emergency response operations for 15 days at the discretion of State officials; approval of the FEMA Regional Administrator is required for the use of these personnel in excess of 15 days. An assignment to emergency response operations does not preclude the accomplishment of program work and objectives. Failure to accomplish such work may subject the State to the withholding of funds contributed under the

Act, or to collection of funds already obligated, not to exceed the estimated cost of the work not performed, as determined by the Regional Administrator.

(d) In the event of an emergency or major disaster declared under the Disaster Relief Act of 1974, as amended, personnel will not be provided overtime compensation and expenses under the Act.

§ 312.6 Materials and facilities.

FEMA also contributes to the development and support of emergency management in the States and their political subdivisions, and to the development, operation, and maintenance of specific programs, through providing certain materials and facilities. The following may be used for natural disaster purposes provided that such usage is consistent with, contributes to, and does not detract from attack-related civil defense preparedness:

(a) Materials provided and maintained through contributions under the Act.

(b) Technical information, guidance through which technical assistance is provided, and training courses, may contain examples, illustrations, discussion, suggested applications and uses of material.

(c) Equipment loaned under provisions of the Contributions Project Loan Program.

(d) Facilities, such as Emergency Operating Centers, provided and maintained through contributions under the Act.

(e) Equipment loaned or granted to the States for civil defense purposes (e.g., radiological instruments, shelter supplies).

PARTS 313–320 [RESERVED]

PART 321—MAINTENANCE OF THE MOBILIZATION BASE (DEPARTMENT OF DEFENSE, DEPARTMENT OF ENERGY, MARITIME ADMINISTRATION)

Sec.
321.1 General.
321.2 Selection of the mobilization base.
321.3 Maintaining the mobilization base.
321.4 Achieving production readiness.
321.5 Retention of industrial facilities.
321.6 Participation of small business.
321.7 [Reserved]
321.8 Reports.

AUTHORITY: National Security Act of 1947, as amended 50 U.S.C. 404; Defense Production Act of 1950, as amended; 50 U.S.C. app. 2061 *et seq.;* Reorganization Plan No. 3 of 1978, 3 CFR, 1978 Comp., p. 329; E.O. 12148 (44 FR 43239).

SOURCE: 45 FR 44576, July 1, 1980, unless otherwise noted.

§ 321.1 General.

A sustained state of mobilization production readiness is necessary to place the United States in a defense posture which will enable the nation to defend itself against aggression in peripheral conflicts or general war involving nuclear attacks on this country. Therefore, the facilities, machine tools, production equipment, and skilled workers necessary to produce the wartime requirements of the Department of Defense, Department of Energy, and the Maritime Administration shall be maintained in a state of readiness which will facilitate their immediate use or conversion in time of emergency, with especial emphasis on measures to maximize the probability of continued post-attack production of those items judged to be vital to survival and victory.

§ 321.2 Selection of the mobilization base.

(a) The Department of Defense shall select, for its mobilization base, facilities which produce or are capable of producing critically important military items or components (military class A components used entirely in the production, maintenance, or repair of military items) which meet one of the following:

(1) Those items which would be so urgent to the defense of this country that utmost effort must be exerted to produce them even in case of general war involving severe damage to the facilities necessary to produce these items and the components thereof.

(2) Those items essential to survival and retaliation, maintenance of health, or combat efficiency required to support peripheral war and which meet one or more of the following criteria:

(i) Items requiring a long lead-time or long manufacturing cycle.

(ii) Items currently not in production or which are required in quantities far in excess of peacetime production.

(iii) Items requiring the conversion of an industry or a number of plants within an industry.

(iv) Items requiring materials or manufacturing processes essentially different from those in current use.

(v) Items for which industry does not have production experience.

Paragraph (a)(2) of this section is inclusive of the Department of Defense Preferential Planning List of End Items.

(b) In selecting facilities for the Department of Defense mobilization base, consideration shall be given to their vulnerability to nuclear attack, with particular attention to the possibility of (1) minimizing vulnerability of facilities producing "urgent" items under paragraph (a)(1) of this section, including the need for dispersal, protective construction, and special security measures to safeguard against sabotage of clandestine attack, and (2) reducing concentration of uncommon critical production facilities so that a productive segment of each critical industry would be likely to survive a nuclear attack.

(c) The Department of Energy and the Maritime Administration, in cooperation with the Federal Emergency Management Agency, shall determine the items and facilities which meet the above criteria for their respective programs for maintaining the mobilization base.

§ 321.3 Maintaining the mobilization base.

(a) Facilities selected to produce "urgent" items shall be maintained within limits of existing procurement authority and funds available by the Department of Defense, the Department of Energy, and the Maritime Administration in the following manners to the maximum practical degree:

(1) Current procurement shall be placed in these facilities to the extent which will maintain them in a state of readiness compatible with the plans of the procuring agency.

(2) Machine tools and production equipment will be installed in these facilities to the extent found necessary by the procuring agency.

(3) Develop and maintain plans for alternate production capacity in case disaster destroys current facilities, such capacity to be located to the maximum extent possible away from highly concentrated industrial areas and major military installations.

(b) Other facilities selected as part of the mobilization base, shall be maintained to the fullest extent possible.

(1) Procurement agencies shall integrate current procurement with their industrial mobilization plans to the greatest possible extent with the objective of supporting the mobilization base within authorities and funds available.

(2) Data assembled on essential mobilization suppliers by the industrial mobilization planning of these agencies shall be used in planning current procurement. The policy of using contractors and facilities essential to the mobilization base is considered to be in the best interest of the Government.

(3) Planned producers that are deemed to be a part of the mobilization base will be invited to participate in appropriate current procurement.

(4) Upon expiration of current procurement contracts in a facility, the procuring agency shall take such of the following actions as are compatible with its plans for maintaining a state of readiness:

(i) *Government-owned facilities and tools.* Within the limitations that may be imposed by Congressional appropriations, place government-owned facilities and tools in standby status and establish provisions for their adequate maintenance. This does not preclude the use of government-owned production equipment, on a loan basis, to enable the military departments to meet current production schedules, as provided in DMO–VII–4, Amendment 1.

(ii) *Privately-owned facilities and government-owned tools.* (A) Arrange with management of privately-owned facilities, wherever possible, to place government-owned tools and production equipment in the status provided by DMO–VII–4, as amended, taking into

555

account the desirability of safe location.

(B) Arrange with management, on a voluntary basis, to keep a group of key managers, engineers, and skilled workers familiar with the items planned for mobilization production.

(C) Determine the gaps which exist in government-owned packages of tools and production equipment needed to produce mobilization requirements in privately-owned plants. Within the limit of fund availability, plan the procurement of such tools and equipment with priority being given to long lead-time tools and equipment or those not used in general manufacturing. These tools and equipment, when procured, should be placed in the status provided by DMO–VII–4, as amended, taking into account the desirability of safe locations.

(D) Determine which government-owned tools and equipment have become obsolete, or which would not be used in event of mobilization, and plan for their disposal in accordance with the provisions of DMO–VII–4, as amended.

§ 321.4 Achieving production readiness.

(a) In order to achieve a capability for maximum production of "urgent" items during the initial phase of war, the following readiness measures shall be taken where advisable for facilities producing such items:

(1) Establishment of emergency production schedules.

(2) Development of a production capability which would function under widespread disruption and damage imposed by enemy attack, including, where necessary:

(i) Maintenance of an increased inventory of finished components and related production supplies at assembly plants, or arrangements for alternative supply lines where increased inventories are not feasible.

(ii) A capability to carry on urgent production without dependence on additional personnel, external sources of power, fuel, and water, or on long-distance communications; with spare replacements for highly vulnerable or unreliable parts of production equipment.

(iii) Protection of production facilities from enemy sabotage through adequate physical security measures.

(iv) Protection of personnel from widespread radiological fallout through provisions for decontamination and shelter.

§ 321.5 Retention of industrial facilities.

(a) Industrial properties, owned by the Department of Defense, the Department of Energy, and the Maritime Administration, shall be retained in the Industrial reserves (National Industrial Reserve, Departmental Industrial Reserve for the Department of Defense) of the department and agencies to the extent the capacity of said reserves is necessary for the production of defense or defense-supporting end items, materials or components in a mobilization period.

(b) Each idle plant in the reserves shall be reviewed annually by the heads of the respective agencies to determine if the capacity of the plant continues necessary for mobilization purposes.

(c) Upon the determination by the head of the agency that the capacity of a plant is excess to the mobilization requirements of the agency immediate steps will be taken to dispose of the plant through existing government channels for surplus disposal. The Federal Emergency Management Agency shall be informed by General Services Administration of each proposed surplus action prior to final determination.

§ 321.6 Participation of small business.

The agencies concerned with the order shall, in all of their programs for maintaining the mobilization base, be mindful of the national policy to protect the interests of small business, and to assure the maximum participation of small business in the mobilization base, including current procurement.

§ 321.7 [Reserved]

§ 321.8 Reports.

The Department of Defense, Department of Energy, and Maritime Administration shall furnish the Administrator of the Federal Emergency Management Agency with reports on items and facilities for programs under § 321.2 (a) and (b) of this part, and with such other periodic and special reports as he may require affecting the maintenance of the mobilization base.

PART 322 [RESERVED]

PART 323—GUIDANCE ON PRIORITY USE OF RESOURCES IN IMMEDIATE POST ATTACK PERIOD (DMO-4)

Sec.
323.1 Purpose.
323.2 General policy.
323.3 Responsibilities.
323.4 Priority activities in immediate postattack period.
323.5 Assignment of resources.
APPENDIX 1 TO PART 323—LIST OF ESSENTIAL SURVIVAL ITEMS

AUTHORITY: National Security Act of 1947, as amended, 50 U.S.C. 404; Defense Production Act of 1950, as amended, 50 U.S.C. app. 2061 *et seq.*; Reorganization Plan No. 3 of 1978, 3 CFR, 1978 Comp., p. 329; E.O. 12148 of July 20, 1979, 44 FR 43239.

SOURCE: 45 FR 44579, July 1, 1980, unless otherwise noted.

§ 323.1 Purpose.

This part:

(a) States the policy of the Federal Government on use of resources in the period immediately following a nuclear attack on the United States;

(b) Provides general guidance for Federal, State, and local government officials on activities to be accorded priority in the use of postattack resources; and

(c) Lists those items essential to national survival in the immediate postattack period.

§ 323.2 General policy.

(a) In an immediate postattack period all decisions regarding the use of resources will be directed to the objective of national survival and recovery.

In order to achieve this objective, postattack resources will be assigned to activities concerned with the maintenance and saving of lives, immediate military defense and retaliatory operations, economic activities essential to continued survival and recovery.

(b) This guidance is designed to achieve a degree of national equity in the use of resources and to assign and conserve resources effectively in the immediate postattack period. Until more specific instructions are available, these are the general guidelines within which managerial judgment and common sense must be used to achieve national objectives under widely differing emergency conditions.

§ 323.3 Responsibilities.

(a) As stated in The National Plan for Emergency Preparedness, the direction of resources mobilization is a Federal responsibility. However, in the period immediately following an attack, certain geographical areas may be temporarily isolated, and State and local governments will assume responsibility for the use of resources remaining in such areas until effective Federal authority can be restored. State and local governments will not assume responsibility for resources under the jurisdiction of a Federal agency where the Federal agency is able to function.

(b) As soon as possible after an attack and until specific national direction and guidance on the use of resources is provided, Federal, State, and local officials will determine what resources are available, to what needs they can be applied, how they are to be used, and the extent to which resources are deficient or in excess of survival needs. They will base determinations as to the relative urgency for use of resources primarily upon the importance of specific needs of defense, survival, and recovery.

§ 323.4 Priority activities in immediate postattack period.

The following activities are to be accorded priority over all other claims for resources. There is no significance in the order of the listing—all are important. The order in which and the extent to which they are supported locally may vary with local conditions and circumstances. If local conditions necessitate the establishment of an order of priority among these activities, that order shall be based on determinations of relative urgency among the activities listed, the availability of resources for achieving the actions required, and the feasibility and timeliness of the activities in making the most rapid and effective contribution to national survival.

(a) The immediate defense and retaliatory combat operations of the Armed Forces of the United States and its Allies: This includes support of military personnel and the production and distribution of military and atomic weapons, materials and equipment required to carry out these immediate defense and retaliatory combat operations.

(b) Maintenance or reestablishment of Government authority and control to restore and preserve order and to assure direction of emergency operations essential for the safety and protection of the people. This includes:

(1) Police protection and movement direction;

(2) Fire defense, rescue and debris clearance;

(3) Warnings;

(4) Emergency information and instructions;

(5) Radiological detection, monitoring and decontamination.

(c) Production and distribution of survival items and provision of services essential to continued survival and rapid recovery. (For list of survival items, see appendix 1 to this part.) These include:

(1) Expedient shelter;

(2) Food, including necessary processing and storage;

(3) Feeding, clothing, lodging, and other welfare services;

(4) Emergency housing and community services;

(5) Emergency health services, including medical care, public health and sanitation;

(6) Water, fuel, and power supply;

(7) Emergency repair and restoration of damaged vital facilities.

(d) Essential communications and transportation services needed to carry out the above activities.

(e) Provision of supplies, equipment, and repair parts to produce and distribute goods needed for the above activities.

§ 323.5 Assignment of resources.

Resources required for essential uses, including manpower, will be assigned to meet the emergency requirements of the priority activities indicated above. The principal objectives are to use available resources to serve essential needs promptly and effectively, and to:

(a) Protect and to prevent waste or dissipation of resources prior to their assignment to priority activities;

(b) Support production of essential goods. Other production will be permitted to continue only from inventories on hand and when there is no emergency requirement for the resources vital to this production.

(c) Support construction for emergency repair and restoration, construction of facilities needed for survival, or the conversion of facilities to survival use, where this can be accomplished quickly. Other construction already under way should be stopped, and no new construction started unless it can be used immediately for essential purposes upon completion.

APPENDIX 1 TO PART 323—LIST OF
ESSENTIAL SURVIVAL ITEMS

This document contains a list of items considered essential to sustain life at a productive level to assure national survival in an emergency. The list identifies items to which major attention should be given in all phases of preattack planning to insure the availability of basic essentials for a productive economy in the event of a nuclear attack. Supply-requirements studies and assessments for these items will be made to disclose critical deficiencies or other problems that can be anticipated. Revisions will be made as necessary to keep the items as up-to-date as possible.

The items are arranged by seven major groups:

(1) Health Supplies and Equipment,

(2) Food,

(3) Body Protection and Household Operations,

(4) Electric Power and Fuels,

(5) Sanitation and Water Supply,

(6) Emergency Housing and Construction Materials and Equipment, and

(7) General Use Items.

Survival items are defined as "those items without which large segments of the population would die or have their health so seriously impaired as to render them both burdensome and non-productive." The items have been classified into Group A or Group B, with Group A representing end products consumed or used directly by the population, and Group B consisting of those items essential to the effective production and utilization of the Group A items, which are consumed or used directly by the people.

There are no Group B items in the categories of Health Supplies and Equipment, Body Production and Household Operations, and Emergency Housing and Construction Materials and Equipment. All of these items are considered to be consumed directly and any attempt to separate them in to A and B groupings would be too arbitrary to be meaningful.

It is important to keep in mind the fact that while the items listed are the basic essentials necessary for maintaining a viable economy during the first six months following an attack, not all of them would create problems that would require government action preattack to insure adequate supplies. The aforementioned supply-requirements studies will be undertaken to identify the problem areas. In developing supply data, all available production capacity, existing inventories, and possible substitutions will be considered. For example, in analyzing clothing items, all available supplies would be considered from sport to dress shirts, from overalls to dress suits. However, new production would be limited to the simplest form of the basic item which can be produced. The final determination as to which of the items are most critical and which may require preattack actions by the Government, as well as the type of actions which must be taken, can be made only after a comprehensive supply-requirements analysis is completed.

LIST OF ESSENTIAL SURVIVAL ITEMS

I. HEALTH SUPPLIES AND EQUIPMENT

Group A

1. *Pharmaceuticals:*
Alcohol.
Analgesics, non-narcotic.
Antibiotics and antibacterials.
Antidiabetic agents, oral.
Antihistamines.
Antimalarials.
Atropine.
Blood derivatives.
Carbon dioxide absorbent.
Cardiovascular depressants.
Cardiovascular stimulants.
Corticosteriods.
Diuretics.
General anesthetics.
Hypnotics.
Insulin.
Intravenous solutions for replacement therapy.
Local anesthetics.
Lubricant, surgical.
Morphine and substitutes.
Oral electrolytes.
Oxygen.
Surgical antiseptics.
Sulfa drugs.
Synthetic plasma volume expanders.
Vitamin preparations, pediatric.
Water for injection.

2. *Blood Collecting and Dispensing Supplies:*
Blood collecting and dispensing containers.
Blood donor sets.
Blood grouping and typing sera.
Blood recipient sets.
Blood shipping containers.

3. *Biologicals:*
Diphtheria toxoid.
Diphtheria antitoxin.
Diphtheria and tetanus toxoids and pertussis vaccine.
Gas gangrene antitoxin.
Poliomyelitis vaccine, oral.
Rabies vaccine.
Smallpox vaccine.
Tetanus antitoxin.
Tetanus toxoid, absorbed.
Typhoid vaccine.
Typhus vaccine, epidemic.
Yellow fever vaccine.

4. *Surgical Textiles:*
Adhesive plaster.
Bandage, gauze.
Bandage, muslin.
Bandage, plaster of paris.
Cotton, USP.
Surgical pads.
Stockinette, surgical.
Wadding, cotton sheet.

5. *Emergency Surgical Instruments and Supplies:*
Airway, pharyngeal.
Anesthesia apparatus.
Basin, wash, solution.
Blade, surgical knife.
Brush, scrub, surgical.
Catheter, urethral.
Containers for sterilization.
Chisel, bone.
Drain, Penrose.
Dusting powder.
Forceps, dressing.
Forceps, hemostatic.
Forceps, obstetrical.
Forceps, tissue.
Gloves, surgeon's.
Handles, surgical knife.
Holder, suture needle.
Inhaler, anesthesia, Yankauer (ether mask).
Intravenous injection sets.
Knife, cast cutting.
Lamps, for diagnostic instruments.

Lamps, for surgical lights.
Laryngoscope.
Light, surgical, portable.
Litter.
Mallet, bone surgery.
Needles, hypodermic, reusable.
Needles, suture, eyed.
Otoscope and ophthalmoscope set.
Probe, general operating.
Razor and blades (for surgical preparation).
Retractor, rib.
Retractor set, general operating.
Rongeur, bone.
Saw, amputating.
Saw, bone cutting, wire (Gigli).
Scissors, bandage.
Scissors, general surgical.
Sigmoidoscope.
Speculum, vaginal.
Sphygmomanometer.
Splint, leg, Thomas.
Splint, wire, ladder.
Sterilizer, pressure, portable.
Stethoscope.
Sutures, absorbable.
Sutures, absorbable, with attached needle.
Sutures, nonabsorbable.
Sutures, nonabsorbable, with attached needle.
Syringes, Luer, reusable (hypodermic syringes).
Thermometers, clinical.
Tracheotomy tube.
Tube, nasogastric.
Tubing, rubber or plastic, and connectors.
Vascular prostheses.
Webbing, textile, with buckle.

6. *Laboratory Equipment and Supplies:*
Bacteriological culture media and apparatus.
Balance, laboratory with weights.
Blood and urine analysis instruments, equipment and supplies.
Chemical reagents, stains and apparatus.
Glassware cleaning equipment.
Laboratory glassware.
Microscope and slides.
Water purification apparatus.

Group B

None.

II. FOOD

Group A

1. *Milk group.* Milk in all forms, milk products. Important for calcium, riboflavin, protein, and other nutrients.

2. *Meat and meat alternate group.* Meat, poultry, fish, eggs; also dry beans, peas, nuts. Important for protein, iron, and B-vitamins.

3. *Vegetable-fruit group.* Including 1. Dark Green and yellow vegetables. Important for Vitamin A. 2. Citrus fruit or other fruit or vegetables. Important for Vitamin C. 3. Other fruits and vegetables, including potatoes.

4. *Grain products.* Especially enriched, restored, cereal and cereal products, and bread, flours, and meals. Important for energy, protein, iron, and B-vitamins.

5. *Fats and oils.* Including butter, margarine, lard, and other shortening oils. Important for palatability and food energy; some for Vitamin A and essential fatty acids.

6. *Sugars and syrups.* Important for palatability and food energy.

7. *Food adjuncts.* Certain food adjuncts should be provided to make effective use of available foods. These include antioxidants and other food preservatives, yeast, baking powder, salt, soda, seasonings and other condiments. In addition, coffee, tea, and cocoa are important for morale support.

Group B

Food containers.
Nitrogenous fertilizers.
Seed and livestock feed.
Salt for livestock.
Veterinary Medical Items:
Anthrax vaccine.
Black leg vaccine.
Hog cholera vaccine.
Newcastle vaccine.

III. BODY PROTECTION AND HOUSEHOLD OPERATIONS

Group A

1. *Clothing:*
Gloves and mittens.
Headwear.
Hosiery.
Outerwear.
Shoes and other footwear.
Underwear.
Waterproof outer garments.

2. *Personal Hygiene Items:*
Diapers, all types.
Disposable tissues.
First aid items (included on Health Supplies and Equipment List).
Nipples.
Nursing bottles, all types.
Pins.
Sanitary napkins.
Soaps, detergents, and disinfectants.
Toilet tissue.

3. *Household Equipment:*
Bedding.
Canned heat.
Cots.
Hand sewing equipment.
Heating and cooking stoves.
Incandescent hand portable lighting equipment (including flashlights, lamps, batteries).
Kitchen, cooking, and eating utensils.
Lamps (incandescent medium base) and lamp holders.
Matches.

Nonelectric lighting equipment.
Sleeping bags.

Group B

None.

IV. ELECTRIC POWER AND FUELS

1. *Electric Power.*

Group A

Electricity.

Group B

Conductors (copper and/or aluminum), including bare cable for high voltage lines and insulated wire or cable for lower voltage distribution circuits.
Switches and circuit breakers.
Insulators.
Pole line hardware.
Poles and crossarms.
Transformers (distribution, transmission, and mobile).
Tools for live-circuit operations, including rubber protective equipment, and linemen's tools.
Utility repair trucks, fully equipped.
Prime mover generator sets up to 501 kilowatts and 2400 volts, including portable and mobile sets up to 150 kilowatts and 110/220/440 volts, 3-phase, 60-cycle complete with fuel tank and switchgear in self-contained units.

2. *Petroleum Products.*

Group A

Gasoline.
Kerosene.
Distillate fuel oil.
Residual fuel oil.
Liquefied petroleum oil.
Lubricating oil.
Grease.

Group B

Storage tanks.
Pumps for loading and unloading.
Pressure containers and fittings for liquefied petroleum gas.

3. *Gas.*

Group A

Natural gas.
Manufactured gas.

Group B

Various sizes of pipe (mostly steel).
Various sizes of valves, fittings, and pressure regulators.
Specialized repair trucks and equipment.

4. *Solid Fuels.*

Group A

Coal and coke.

Group B

Conveyor belting.
Insulated trail cables.
Trolley feeder wire.
Roof bolts.

V. SANITATION AND WATER SUPPLY

Group A

1. *Water.*
2. *Water Supply Materials:*
   a. *Coagulation:*
Ferric chloride.
Ferrous sulfate.
Ferric sulfate.
Chlorinated copperas.
Filter alum.
Hydrated lime.
Pulverized limestone.
Soda ash.
   b. *Disinfection Chemicals:*
High-test hypochlorites (70 percent) in drums, cans, ampules.
Iodine tablets.
Liquid chlorine, including containers.
Chlorine compounds (not gas).
   c. *Miscellaneous Materials:*
Diatomaceous earth.
Activated carbon.
3. *Chemical Biological, and Radiological CBR Detection, Protection, and Decontamination Items:*
Calibrators.
Chemical agent detection kits, air, food, and water.
Dosimeters and chargers.
Protective masks, clothing, helmets.
Survey meters (Alpha, Beta, Gamma).
Warning signs—biological, chemical, and radiological contamination.
4. *Insect and Rodent Control Items:*
   a. *Insecticides:*
DDT, water dispersible powder (75 percent).
Lindane powder, dusting (1 percent).
Malathion, liquid, emulsifiable concentrate (57 percent).
Deet (diethyltoluamide) 75 percent in denatured alcohol.
Pyrethrum.
   b. *Rodenticides:*
Anticoagulant type, ready-mixed bait.
"1080" (sodium monofluoroacetate) (for controlled use only).
5. *General Sanitation:*
Lye.

Group B

1. *General Supplies and Equipment:*
Chemical feeders.
Mobile and portable pressure filters.
Chlorinators (gas and hypochlorites).
Pumps and appurtenances, Hand—Electric—Gasoline—Diesel.
Well-drilling equipment, including well casing, drive pipe and drive points.

2. *Storage and Transport Equipment:*
Lyster bags.
Storage tanks, collapsible and portable.
Storage tanks, rigid, transportable.
Storage tanks, wood stave, knock-down.

3. *Laboratory Equipment and Supplies:*
Membrane filter kits with filters and media.
Chlorine and pH determination equipment.

4. *Sanitation Equipment:*
Hand sprayer, continuous type.
Hand sprayer, compression type.
Hand duster, plunger type.
Spraying equipment for use with helicopter, fixed-wing light aircraft, high-speed fixed-wing attack aircraft, and cargo-type aircraft.

VI. EMERGENCY HOUSING AND CONSTRUCTION MATERIALS AND EQUIPMENT

Group A

Asphalt and tar roofing and siding products.
Builders hardware—hinges, locks, handles, etc.
Building board, including insulating board, laminated fiberboard, hardpressed fiberboard, gypsum board, and asbestos cement (flat sheets and wallboard).
Building papers.
Plastic patching, couplings, clamps, etc. for emergency repairs.
Plumbing fixtures and fittings.
Prefabricated emergency housing.
Rough hardware—nails, bolts, screws, etc.
Sewer pipe and fittings.
Tents and tarpaulins; canvas, plastics, and other similar materials.
Lumber and allied products; Lumber, principally 1-inch and 2-inch, minor quantities of small and large timbers; siding and flooring; plywood; millwork, doors, and windows.
Masonry products—brick, cement, lime, concrete block, hollow tile, etc.
Translucent window coverings.
Water pipe and hose, plus fittings—all types including fire hose.

Group B

None.

VII. GENERAL USE ITEMS

Group A

None.

Group B

Batteries, wet and dry cell.
Bulldozers.
Fire fighting equipment.
Light equipment and hand tools (including electric powered) for carpentry, masonry, plumbing, and excavation.
Pipe installation materials and equipment.
Refrigerators, mechanical.

Rigging tools—cables, ropes, tackles, hoists, etc.
Tank railroad cars.
Tank Trucks and trailers.
Tires.
Trenching equipment.
Truck tractors and trailers, including low bed.
Trucks up to five tons (25 percent equipped with power takeoff).
Welding equipment and supplies (electric and acetylene).

PARTS 324–326 [RESERVED]

PART 327—POLICY ON USE OF GOVERNMENT-OWNED INDUSTRIAL PLANT EQUIPMENT BY PRIVATE INDUSTRY (DMO-10A)

Sec.
327.1   Purpose.
327.2   Scope and applicability.
327.3   Policy.
327.4   Disputes.
327.5   Reports.

AUTHORITY: National Security Act of 1947, as amended, 50 U.S.C. 404; Defense Production Act of 1950, as amended, 50 U.S.C. app. 2061 *et seq.;* Reorganization Plan No. 3 of 1978, 3 CFR, 1978 Comp., p. 329; E.O. 12148 of July 20, 1979, 44 FR 43239.

SOURCE: 45 FR 44583, July 1, 1980, unless otherwise noted.

§ 327.1   Purpose.

This part establishes policy on the use by private industry of Government-owned industrial plant equipment. This policy is necessary to maintain a highly effective and immediately available reserve of such equipment for the emergency preparedness programs of the U.S. Government.

§ 327.2   Scope and applicability.

(a) This part applies to all Federal departments and agencies having, for purposes of mobilization readiness, Government-owned industrial plant equipment under their jurisdiction or control and having emergency preparedness functions assigned by Executive orders concerning use of that equipment.

(b) As used herein, *industrial plant equipment* means those items of equipment, each with an acquisition cost of $1,000 or more, that fall within specified classes of equipment listed in DOD regulations. Classes of equipment may from time to time be added to or deleted from this list.

§327.3 Policy.

(a) *General.* (1) Primary reliance for defense production shall be placed upon private industry.

(2) When it is determined by an agency that, because of the lack of specific industrial plant equipment, private industry of the United States cannot be relied upon for needed Government production, that agency may provide to private industry such Government-owned industrial plant equipment as is deemed necessary to ensure required production capability. Requirements for such equipment should be reviewed at least annually to ascertain the continuing need, particularly with a view toward private industry furnishing the equipment for long term requirements.

(3) When it is necessary for Federal agencies to supply Government-owned industrial plant equipment to private industry, these agencies will maintain uniformity and fairness in the arrangements for the use of this equipment by following regulations for the use of such equipment as developed and published by the Secretary of Defense pursuant to section 809 of Public Law 93–155. The regulations to be developed by the Secretary of Defense shall be in consonance with this order. These regulations will attempt to ensure that no Government contractor is afforded an advantage over his competitors and that Government-owned industrial plant equipment is maintained properly and kept immediately available for the emergency preparedness needs of the United States.

(b) *Interagency use of idle equipment.* In any instances in which a Government contractor cannot meet Government production schedules because necessary industrial plant equipment is not available from private industry or from the contracting Federal department or agency, idle industrial plant equipment under the control of other Federal agencies may be made available for this purpose through existing authorities on a transfer, loan, or replacement basis by interagency agreement.

(c) *Availability of equipment for emergency use.* Government-owned industrial plant equipment may be provided by controlling agencies for emergency use by essential Government contractors whose facilities have been damaged or destroyed.

(d) *Uniform rental rates.* All new agreements entered into by any agency of the Federal Government under which private business establishments are provided with Government-owned industrial plant equipment shall be subject to rental rates established by the Secretary of Defense pursuant to section 809 of Public Law 93–155. The rental rates shall ensure a fair and equitable return to the U.S. Government and be generally competitive with commercial rates for like equipment.

(e) *Use of Government-owned industrial plant equipment for commercial (non-Government) purposes.* Subject to adequate controls being established under DOD regulations pursuant to Public Law 93–155, and statutory authority for leasing, Government-owned industrial plant equipment may be authorized for commercial use by contractors performing contracts or subcontracts for the Government agency if it is necessary to keep the equipment in a high state of operational readiness through regular usage to support the emergency preparedness programs of the U.S. Government.

§327.4 Disputes.

In the event of an interagency dispute about the regulations developed by the Department of Defense in accordance with this order, the Administrator, Federal Emergency Management Agency, shall adjudicate.

§327.5 Reports.

Such reports of operations under this order as may be required by the Federal Emergency Management Agency, shall be submitted to the Administrator.

PART 328 [RESERVED]

PART 329—USE OF PRIORITIES AND ALLOCATION AUTHORITY FOR FEDERAL SUPPLY CLASSIFICATION (FSC) COMMON USE ITEMS (DMO-12)

Sec.
329.1 Purpose.
329.2 Policies.
329.3 Procedures.
329.4 Implementation.

AUTHORITY: Defense Production Act of 1950, as amended, 50 U.S.C. app. 2061 *et seq.*; Reorganization Plan No. 3 of 1978, 3 CFR, 1978 Comp., p. 329; E.O. 12148 of July 20, 1979, 44 FR 43239; E.O. 10480 of Aug. 14, 1953, (18 FR 4939) as amended.

SOURCE: 45 FR 44585, July 1, 1980, unless otherwise noted.

§ 329.1 Purpose.

This part provides policy guidance concerning the use of priorities and allocation authority under title I of the Defense Production Act of 1950, as amended, for the procurement of common use items in the Federal Supply Classification (FSC).

§ 329.2 Policies.

The following guidance is provided pursuant to the Defense Production Act of 1950, as amended; section 201 of Executive Order 10480, and § 322.2 of this chapter (DMO-3).

(a) Priority ratings under title I of the Defense Production Act of 1950, as amended, are not authorized for certain FSC Groups, Classes, and Items:

(1) Which are of the types commonly available in commercial markets for general consumption,

(2) Which do not require major modification when purchased for military or other ratable government use, and

(3) Which are in sufficient supply as to cause no hindrance to the accomplishment of military or other national defense objectives.

Such Groups, Classes, and Items will be as specified from time to time by the Department of Commerce with the approval of the Federal Emergency Management Agency. Procurement in these Groups, Classes, and Items is to be made without priority assistance, including single service procurement that may include defense and defense-supporting needs. In the event procurement difficulties are encountered which threaten timely delivery, application for special assistance may be made for those categories of supply authorized special assistance in existing lists, and must be accompanied by full justification to support the need for such assistance.

(b) Priority ratings may be used for the procurement of other authorized FSC Groups, Classes, and Items only in quantities required to meet the needs of approved programs of ratable agencies. The quantities of current procurement of each Group, Class, and Item shall be based on and shall not exceed the ratio of rated purchases to total purchases for that Group, Class, and Item that was consummated in the 6-month period preceding the first day of January and July in each year. Any other periodic cycle considered suitable and agreed to by the Domestic and International Business Administration, Department of Commerce, and the procuring agency may be substituted.

(c) In the interest of minimizing administrative costs, where rated procurement under paragraph (b)(2) of this section, constitutes 97 percent or more of the total procurement of a Group, Class, or Item, all of the Group, Class, or Item may be bought on ratings.

§ 329.3 Procedures.

Requests for additional authorizations of Classes, Groups, or Items should be presented to General Services Administration (AP), Washington, DC, 20405, accompanied by a statement of justification indicating why the Class, Group, or Item should be regarded as necessary or appropriate to promote the national defense and why defense-related requirements cannot be met without the use of priorities.

§ 329.4 Implementation.

Departments and agencies involved with this program shall issue implementing instructions and directives no later than 30 work days from the effective date of this order. Copies of such instructions, directives, and related documents shall be furnished to the General Services Administration (AP) on a routine basis as issued.

PART 330—POLICY GUIDANCE AND DELEGATION OF AUTHORITIES FOR USE OF PRIORITIES AND ALLOCATIONS TO MAXIMIZE DOMESTIC ENERGY SUPPLIES IN ACCORDANCE WITH SUBSECTION 101(c) OF THE DEFENSE PRODUCTION ACT OF 1950, AS AMENDED (DMO-13)

Sec.
330.1 Purpose.
330.2 Policies.
330.3 Delegation of authority.

AUTHORITY: Defense Production Act of 1950, as amended, including amendment to sec. 101(c) by sec. 104 of the Energy Policy and Conservation Act (Pub. L. 94–163) 50 U.S.C. app. 2061 et seq.; Reorganization Plan No. 3 of 1978, 3 CFR, 1978 Comp., p. 329; E.O. 12148 of July 20, 1979, 44 FR 43239; E.O. 11912 of April 13, 1976.

SOURCE: 45 FR 44586, July 1, 1980, unless otherwise noted.

§ 330.1 Purpose.

This part:

(a) Establishes policy guidance on determination and use of priorities and allocations for materials and equipment to maximize domestic energy supplies pursuant to section 104 of the Energy Policy and Conservation Act (Pub. L. 94–163, 89 Stat. 878), which added subsection 101(c) to the Defense Production Act of 1950, as amended (the Act); and

(b) Delegates authority and assigns responsibility related thereto pursuant to sections 7 and 8 of Executive Order 11912, dated April 13, 1976.

§ 330.2 Policies.

(a) The authority of subsection 101(c) of the Act to require the allocation of, or priority performance under contracts or orders relating to, supplies of materials and equipment to maximize domestic energy supplies shall be limited to those exceptional circumstances when it is found that:

(1) Such supplies of material and equipment are scarce, critical, and essential; and

(2) The maintenance or furtherance of exploration, production, refining, transportation, or conservation of energy supplies, or the construction and maintenance of energy facilities, cannot reasonably be accomplished without exercising this authority.

(b) The authority contained in subsection 101(c) shall not be used to require priority performance under contracts or orders relating to, or the allocation of, any supplies of materials and equipment except for programs or projects to maximize domestic energy supplies as specifically determined by the Secretary of Energy, after coordination with the Administrator, Federal Emergency Management Agency.

(c) The allocation of, or priority performance under contracts or orders relating to, supplies of materials and equipment in support of authorized programs or projects shall be so undertaken as to ensure that:

(1) Supplies of the specified materials and equipment are available to the extent practicable on time and in proper quantity to authorized programs or projects.

(2) The demands of these authorized programs or projects are distributed among suppliers on a fair and equitable basis.

(3) Allotments of supplies of materials and equipment are not made in excess of actual current requirements of these authorized programs or projects.

(4) Fulfillment of the needs of these authorized programs and projects are achieved in such manner and to such degree as to minimize hardship in the market place.

(d) The authority of subsection 101(c) of the Act will not be used to control the general distribution of any supplies of material and equipment in the civilian market, as that phrase is used in subsection 101(b) of the Act, except after Presidential approval as required by subsection 7(d) of Executive Order 11912.

§ 330.3 Delegation of authority.

(a) The functions of the Administrator of the Federal Management Agency under subsection 101(c) of the Act are hereby delegated to the Secretary of Commerce with respect to the areas of responsibility designated and subject to the limitations prescribed and section 7 of Executive Order 11912. Specifically:

(1) The Secretary of Commerce is delegated the function, provided in subsection 101(c)(1) of the Act, of requiring the allocation of, or priority performance under contracts or orders (other than contracts of employment) relating to, supplies of materials and equipment to maximize domestic energy supplies, if the findings specified in subsection 101(c)(3) of the Act are made.

(2) The Secretary of Commerce is delegated those functions provided in subsection 101(c)(3) of the Act, but shall redelegate to the Secretary of Energy the function of making the findings that supplies of materials and equipment are critical and essential to maximize domestic energy supplies. The Secretary of Commerce shall retain the functions of finding that supplies of materials and equipment are scarce, and that the purposes described in subsection 101(c)(3)(B) of the Act cannot reasonably be accomplished without exercising the authority specified in subsection 101(c)(1). This finding will include, to the extent practicable, an assessment of the effects of using the authority for the project in question on other significantly impacted projects.

(b) The Administrator of the Federal Emergency Management Agency shall be responsible for the overall coordination and direction of the functions provided by subsection 101(c) of the Act in a manner similar to the exercise of functions under subsections 101(a) and 101(b) of the Act. In line with these functions, the Administrator is also responsible for resolving any conflicts between claimant agencies regarding particular supplies of materials and equipment. In addition, the Federal Emergency Management Agency will monitor the impact of the implementation of the authorities of subsection 101(c) and other authorities under section 101 of the Defense Production Act on each other and on the national economy.

(c) The functions assigned, delegated, or required to be redelegated by this order to the Secretary of Commerce and the Secretary of Energy may not be redelegated to other agencies without first being coordinated with the Administrator, Federal Emergency Management Agency.

(d) Procedures to execute the above delegations will be carried out in accordance with guidance provided by the Administrator, Federal Emergency Management Agency, pursuant to this order and Executive Order 11912.

PART 331—PRESERVATION OF THE MOBILIZATION BASE THROUGH THE PLACEMENT OF PROCUREMENT AND FACILITIES IN LABOR SURPLUS AREAS

Sec.
331.1 Purpose.
331.2 Policy.
331.3 Scope and applicability.
331.4 Special consideration.
331.5 Production facilities.

AUTHORITY: Reorganization Plan No. 3 of 1978, E.O. 10480, as amended, E.O. 12148.

SOURCE: 45 FR 34885, May 23, 1980, unless otherwise noted. Redesignated at 45 FR 44575, July 1, 1980.

§ 331.1 Purpose.

Success of the national defense program depends upon efficient use of all of our resources, including the labor force and production facilities, which are preserved through utilizing the skills of both management and labor. A primary aim of Federal manpower policy is to encourage full utilization of existing production facilities and workers in preference to creating new plants or moving workers, thus assisting in the maintenance of economic balance and employment stability. When large numbers of new workers move to labor surplus areas, heavy burdens are placed on community facilities, such as schools, hospitals, housing, transportation, and utilities. On the other hand, when unemployment develops in certain areas, unemployment costs increase the total cost to the Government, and plants, tools, and workers' skills remain idle and unable to contribute to our national defense program. Consequently, it is the purpose of Defense Manpower Policy No. 4B to direct attention to the potential of labor surplus areas when awarding appropriate procurement contracts and when locating new plants or facilities.

§ 331.2   Policy.

(a) It is the policy of the Federal Government to award appropriate contracts to eligible labor surplus area concerns, to place production facilities in labor surplus areas, and to make the best use of our natural, industrial and labor resources in order to achieve the following objectives:

(1) To preserve management and employee skills necessary to the fulfillment of Government contracts and purchases;

(2) To maintain productive facilities;

(3) To improve utilization of the Nation's total economic potential by making use of the labor force resources of each area; and

(4) To help ensure timely delivery of required goods and services and to promote readiness for mobilization by locating procurement where the needed labor force and facilities are fully available.

(b) This policy is consonant with the intent of Public Law 95–89 and Public Law 95–507 as implemented by E.O. 12073. In carrying out this policy, Federal departments and agencies shall be guided by E.O. 12073, the policy direction of the Office of Federal Procurement Policy and implementing regulations.

§ 331.3   Scope and applicability.

The provisions of this policy apply to all Federal departments and agencies, except as otherwise prohibited by law. In addition to these normal duties;

(a) The Secretary of Commerce shall:

(1) In cooperation with State economic development agencies, the Secretary of Defense, the Administrator of General Services, and the Administrator of Small Business Administration, assist concerns which have agreed to perform contracts in labor surplus areas in obtaining Government procurement business by providing such concerns with timely information on proposed Government procurements.

(2) Urge concerns planning new production facilities to consider the advantages of locating in labor surplus areas.

(3) Provide technical advice and counsel to groups and organizations in labor surplus areas on planning industrial parks, industrial development organizations, expanding tourist business, and available Federal aids.

(b) The Administrator of the Small Business Administration shall make available to small business concerns in labor surplus areas all of its services, endeavor to ensure opportunity for maximum participation by such concerns in Government procurement, and give consideration to the needs of these concerns in the making of joint small business set-asides with Government procurement agencies.

(c) OFPP shall coordinate the maintenance by Federal agencies of current information on the manufacturing capabilities of labor surplus area concerns with respect to Government procurement and disseminate such information to Federal departments and agencies.

§ 331.4   Special consideration.

When an entire industry that sells a significant proportion of its production to the Government is generally depressed or has a significant proportion of its production, manufacturing and service facilities located in a labor surplus area, the Administrator, Federal Emergency Management Agency, or successor in function, after notice to and hearing of interested parties, will give consideration to appropriate measures applicable to the entire industry.

§ 331.5   Production facilities.

All Federal departments and agencies shall give consideration to labor surplus areas in the selection of sites for Government-financed production facilities, including expansion, to the extent that such selection is consistent with existing law and essential economic and strategic factors.

PART 332—VOLUNTARY AGREEMENTS UNDER SECTION 708 OF THE DEFENSE PRODUCTION ACT OF 1950, AS AMENDED

AUTHORITY: Sec. 708, Defense Production Act of 1950, as amended (50 U.S.C. app. 2158); E.O. 10480, 3 CFR, 1949–1953 Comp., p. 961, as amended; E.O. 12148, 44 FR 43239.

SOURCE: 46 FR 2350, Jan. 9, 1981, unless otherwise noted.

§ 332.1 General provisions.

(a) Pursuant to section 708 of the Defense Production Act of 1950, as amended (50 U.S.C. App. 2158), the President may consult with representatives of industry, business, financing, agriculture, labor, or other interests, and may approve the making of voluntary agreements to help provide for the defense of the United States by developing preparedness programs and expanding productive capacity and supply beyond levels needed to meet essential civilian demand.

(b) *Sponsor.* (1) As used in this part, "sponsor" of a voluntary agreement is an officer of the Government who, pursuant to a delegation or redelegation of the functions given to the President by section 708 of the Defense Production Act (DPA) of 1950, as amended, proposes or otherwise provides for the development or carrying out of a voluntary agreement.

(2) The use of voluntary agreements, as authorized by section 708 of the DPA to help provide for the defense of the United States through the development of preparedness programs, is an activity coordinated by the Administrator of the Federal Emergency Management Agency, as provided by sections 101 and 501(a) of Executive Order 10480, as amended.

(3) The sponsor of a voluntary agreement shall carry out sponsorship functions subject to the direction and control of the Administrator of the Federal Emergency Management Agency.

(c) This part applies to the development and carrying out under section 708 of the DPA, as amended, of all voluntary agreements, and the carrying out of any voluntary agreement which was entered into under former section 708 of the DPA and in effect immediately prior to April 14, 1976, and which is in a period of extension as authorized by subsection 708(f)(2) of the DPA.

(d) The rules in the part void any provision of a voluntary agreement to which they apply, if that provision is contrary to or inconsistent with them. Each voluntary agreement shall be construed as containing every substantive provision that these rules require, whether or not a particular provision is included in the agreement.

(e) Pursuant to subsection 708(d) of the DPA, the sponsor may establish such advisory committees as he deems to be necessary for developing or carrying out voluntary agreements. Such advisory committees shall comply with this part as well as with the requirements and procedures of the Federal Advisory Committee Act (Pub. L. 92–463, as amended).

§ 332.2 Developing voluntary agreements.

(a) *Purpose and scope.* This section establishes the standards and procedures by which voluntary agreements may be developed through consultation, pursuant to subsection 708(c) of the DPA.

(b) *Proposal to develop an agreement.* (1) A sponsor who wishes to develop a voluntary agreement shall submit to the Attorney General and the Administrator of the Federal Emergency Management Agency a document proposing the agreement. The proposal will include statements as to: The purpose of the agreement; the factual basis for making the finding required in subsection 708(c)(1) of the DPA; the proposed participants in the agreement; and any coordination with other Federal agencies accomplished in connection with the proposal.

(2) If the Attorney General, after consultation with the Chairman of the Federal Trade Commission, approves this proposal, the sponsor shall then initiate one or more meetings of interested persons to develop the agreement.

(c) *Conduct of meetings held to develop the agreement.* (1) The sponsor shall give to the Attorney General, the Chairman of the Federal Trade Commission, and the Administrator of the Federal Emergency Management Agency adequate written notice of each meeting to develop a voluntary agreement. The sponsor shall also publish in the FEDERAL REGISTER notice of the time, place, and nature of each meeting at least seven days prior to the meeting.

(2) The sponsor shall chair each meeting held to develop a voluntary agreement. Both the Attorney General and the Chairman of the Federal Trade Commission, or their delegates, shall attend each of these meetings.

(3) Any interested person may attend a meeting held to develop a voluntary agreement, unless the sponsor of the agreement limits attendance pursuant to §332.5 of this part.

(4) Any interested person may, as set out in the FEDERAL REGISTER meeting notice, submit written data and views concerning the proposed voluntary agreement, and at the discretion of the Chairman of the meeting, may be given the opportunity for oral presentation.

(d) *Maintenance of records.* (1) The sponsor is responsible for the making of a full and verbatim transcript of each meeting. The Chairman shall send this transcript, and any voluntary agreement resulting from the meeting, to the Attorney General, the Chairman of the Federal Trade Commission, the Administrator of the Federal Emergency Management Agency, and any other party or repository required by law.

(2) The sponsor of a voluntary agreement shall maintain each meeting transcript and voluntary agreement, and make them available for public inspection and copying the extent required by §332.5 of this part.

(e) *Effectiveness of agreements.* The following steps must occur before a new voluntary agreement or an extension of an existing agreement may become effective:

(1) The sponsor must approve the agreement and certify in writing that it is necessary to carry out the purposes of subsection 708(c)(1) of the DPA;

(2) The Director of the Federal Emergency Management Agency must approve this certification, and submit it to the Attorney General with a request for a written finding; and

(3) The Attorney General, after consulting with the Chairman of the Federal Trade Commission, must issue a written finding that the purposes of subsection 708(c)(1) can not reasonably be achieved through a voluntary agreement having less anti-competitive effects or without any voluntary agreement.

§332.3 **Carrying out voluntary agreements.**

(a) *Purpose and scope.* This section establishes the standards and procedures by which the participants in each approved voluntary agreement shall carry out the agreement.

(b) *Participants.* The participants in each voluntary agreement shall be reasonably representative of the appropriate industry or segment of that industry.

(c) *Conduct of meetings held to carry out an agreement.* (1) The sponsor of a voluntary agreement shall initiate, or approve in advance, each meeting of the participants in the agreement held to discuss problems, determine policies, recommend actions, and make decisions necessary to carry out the agreement.

(2) The sponsor shall provide to the Attorney General, the Chairman of the Federal Trade Commission, and the Administrator of the Federal Emergency Management Agency adequate prior notice of the time, place, and nature of each meeting, and a proposed agenda of each meeting. The sponsor shall also publish in the FEDERAL REGISTER, reasonably in advance of each meeting, a notice of time, place, and nature of the meeting. If the sponsor has determined, pursuant to §332.5 of this part, to limit attendance at the meeting, the sponsor shall publish this FEDERAL REGISTER notice within ten days of the meeting.

(3) Any interested person may attend a meeting held to carry out a voluntary agreement unless the sponsor has restricted attendance pursuant to §332.5 of this part. A person attending a meeting under this section may present oral or written data, views, and arguments to any limitations on the manner of presentation that the sponsor may impose.

(4) No meeting shall be held to carry out any voluntary agreement unless a Federal employee, other than an individual employed pursuant to 5 U.S.C. 3109, is in attendance. Any meeting to carry out a voluntary agreement may be attended by the sponsor of the agreement, the Attorney General, the

Chairman of the Federal Trade Commission, the Administrator of the Federal Emergency Management Agency, or their delegates.

(5) Notwithstanding any other provision of this section, a meeting between a single participant and the sponsor solely to deliver or exchange information is not subject to the requirements and procedures of this section, provided that a copy of the information is promptly delivered to the Attorney General, the Chairman of the Federal Trade Commission, and the Administrator of the Federal Emergency Management Agency.

(d) *Maintenance of records.* (1) The participants in any voluntary agreement shall maintain for five years all minutes of meetings, transcripts, records, documents, and other data, including any communications among themselves or with any other member of their industry, related to the carrying out of the voluntary agreement. The participants shall agree, in writing, to make available to the sponsor, the Attorney General, the Chairman of the Federal Trade Commission and the Administrator of the Federal Emergency Management Agency for inspection and copying at reasonable times and upon reasonable notice any item that this section requires them to maintain.

(2) Any person required by this paragraph to maintain records shall indicate specific portions, if any, that such person believes should not be disclosed to the public pursuant to § 332.5 of this part, and the reasons therefor. Any item made available to a Government official named in this paragraph shall be available from that official for public inspection and copying to the extent set forth in § 332.5 of this part.

§ 332.4 Termination or modifying voluntary agreements.

The Attorney General may terminate or modify a voluntary agreement, in writing, after consultation with the Chairman of the Federal Trade Commission and the sponsor of the agreement. The sponsor of the agreement, with the concurrence of or at the direction of the Administrator of the Federal Emergency Management Agency, may terminate or modify a voluntary agreement, in writing, after consultation with the Attorney General and the Chairman of the Federal Trade Commission. Any person who is a party to a voluntary agreement may terminate his participation in the agreement upon written notice to the sponsor. Any antitrust immunity conferred upon the participants in that agreement by subsection 708(j) of the DPA shall not apply to any act or omission occurring after the termination of the voluntary agreement. Immediately upon modification of a voluntary agreement, no antitrust immunity shall apply to any subsequent act or omission that is beyond the scope of the modified agreement.

§ 332.5 Public access to records and meetings.

(a) Interested persons may, pursuant to 5 U.S.C. 552, inspect or copy any voluntary agreement, minutes of meetings, transcripts, records, or other data maintained pursuant to these rules.

(b) Except as provided by paragraph (c) of this section, interested persons may attend any part of a meeting held to develop or carry out a voluntary agreement pursuant to these rules.

(c) The sponsor of a voluntary agreement may withhold material described in this section from disclosure and restrict attendance at meetings only on the grounds specified in:

(1) Section 552(b)(1) of 5 U.S.C., which applies to matter specifically required by Executive Order to be kept secret in the interest of the national defense or foreign policy. This section shall be interpreted to included matter protected under Executive Order 12065, dated June 28, 1978 (3 CFR 1979–1975 Comp. p. 678), establishing categories and criteria for classification; and

(2) Section 552(b)(3) of 5 U.S.C., which applies to matter specifically exempted from disclosure by statute; and

(3) Section 552(b)(4) of 5 U.S.C., which applies to trade secrets and commercial or financial information obtained from a person as privileged and confidential.

PART 333 [RESERVED]

PART 334—GRADUATED MOBILIZATION RESPONSE

Sec.
334.1 Purpose.
334.2 Policy.
334.3 Background.
334.4 Definitions.
334.5 GMR system description.
334.6 Department and agency responsibilities.
334.7 Reporting.

AUTHORITY: National Security Act of 1947, as amended, 50 U.S.C. 404; Defense Production Act of 1950, as amended, 50 U.S.C. app. 2061 *et seq;* E.O. 12148 of July 20, 1979, 3 CFR, 1979 Comp., p. 412; E.O. 10480 of Aug. 14, 1953, 3 CFR, 1949–53 Comp., p. 962; E.O. 12472 of Apr. 3, 1984; 3 CFR, 1984 Comp., p. 193; E.O. 12656 of Nov. 18, 1988, 53 FR 47491.

SOURCE: 55 FR 1821, Jan. 19, 1990, unless otherwise noted.

§ 334.1 Purpose.

(a) Provides policy guidance pursuant to the Defense Production Act of 1950, as amended; section 1–103 of Executive Order 12148, as amended, which includes functions continued from E.O. 11051; section 104(f) of Executive Order 12656; and part 2 of Executive Order 10480.

(b) Establishes a Graduated Mobilization Response (GMR) system for developing and implementing mobilization actions that are responsive to a wide range of national security threats and ambiguous or specific warning indicators. GMR provides for a coherent decision making process with which to proceed with specific responses to an identified crisis or emergency.

(c) Provides guidance to the Federal departments and agencies for developing plans that are responsive to a GMR system and for preparing costed option packages, as appropriate, to implement the plans.

§ 334.2 Policy.

(a) As established in Executive Order 12656, the policy of the United States is to have sufficient emergency response capabilities at all levels of government to meet essential defense and civilian needs during any national security emergency. Accordingly, each Federal department and agency shall prepare its national security emergency preparedness plans and programs to respond adequately and in a timely manner to all national security emergencies.

(b) As part of emergency response, the GMR system should be incorporated in each department's and agency's emergency preparedness plans and programs to provide appropriate and effective response options for consideration in reacting to ambiguous and specific warnings.

(c) Departments and agencies will be provided early warning information developed by the intelligence community and policy statements of the President.

(d) Emergency resource preparedness planning is essential to ensure that the nation is adequately prepared to respond to potential national emergencies. Such emergency resource preparedness planning requires an exchange of information and planning factors among the various departments and agencies responsible for different resource preparedness actitivities.

(e) To carry out their emergency planning activities, civilian departments and agencies require the Department of Defense's (DOD) assessment of potential military demands that would be made on the economy in a full range of possible national security emergencies. Similarly, DOD planning should be conducted using planning regimes consistent with the policies and plans of the civilian resource departments and agencies.

(f) Under section 104(c) of Executive Order 12656, FEMA is responsible for coordinating the implementation of national emergency preparedness policy with Federal departments and agencies and with state and local governments and, therefore, is responsible for developing a system of planning procedures for integrating the emergency preparedness actions of federal, state and local governments.

(g) Federal departments and agencies shall design their preparedness measures to permit a rapid and effective transition from routine to emergency operations, and to make effective use of the period following initial indication of a probable national security emergency. This will include:

(1) Development of a system of emergency actions that defines alternatives, processes, and issues to be considered

during various stages of national security emergencies; and

(2) Identification of actions that could be taken at the Federal and local levels of government in the early stages of a national security emergency or pending national security emergency to mitigate the impact of or reduce significantly the leadtime associated with full emergency action implementation.

§ 334.3 Background.

(a) The GMR system is designed to take into account the need to mobilize the Nation's resources in response to a wide range of crisis or emergency situations. GMR is a flexible decision making process of preparedness and response actions which are appropriate to warning indicators or an event. Thus, GMR allows the government, as a whole, to take small or large, often reversible, steps to increase its national security emergency preparedness posture.

(b) Crises, especially those resulting in major military activities, always have some political or economic context. As the risks of military action increase, nations undertake more extensive preparations over a longer period of time to increase their military power. Such preparations by potential adversaries shape the nature and gravity of the threat as well as its likelihood and timing of occurrence. These measures permit the development of reliable indicators of threat at an early time in the evolution of a crisis. Depending on the nature of the situation or event and the nation involved, these early warning indicators may emanate from the political, socio-economic and/or industrial sectors.

(c) The GMR system enables the nation to approach mobilization planning and actions as part of the deterrent response capability and to use it to reduce the probability of conflict. Alternatively, if deterrence should fail, the GMR system would enable the nation to undertake a series of phased actions intended to increase its ability to meet defense and essential civilian requirements. The GMR system integrates the potential strength of the national economy into U.S. national security strategy.

§ 334.4 Definitions.

(a) *Graduated Mobilization Response* (GMR) is a system for integrating mobilization actions designed to respond to ambiguous and/or specific warnings. These actions are designed to mitigate the impact of an event or crisis and reduce significantly the lead time associated with a full national emergency action implementation.

(b) *National security emergency* is any occurrence, including natural disaster, military attack, technological emergency, or other emergency, that seriously degrades or threatens the national security of the United States.

(c) *Mobilization* is the process of marshalling resources, both civil and military, to respond to and manage a national security emergency.

(d) *GMR Plans* are those agency documents that describe, in general, the actions that an agency could take in the early stages of a national security emergency, or upon receipt of warning information about a possible national security emergency. These actions would be designed to mitigate the impact of, or reduce significantly, the lead times associated with full emergency action implementation. Such plans are required by section 201(4)(b) of Executive Order 12656.

(e) *A Costed Option Package* is a document that describes in detail a particular action that an agency could take in the early stages of a national security emergency. The general content of a GMR costed option package includes alternative response options; the resource implications of each option; shortfalls, costs, timeframes and political feasibility.

§ 334.5 GMR system description.

The GMR system contains three stages of mobilization activity (additional intermediate GMR stages may be developed). For example, a Federal department or agency might divide "Crisis Management" into two, three, or more levels as suits its needs.

(a) *Stage 3, Planning and Preparation.* During the planning and preparation stage, Federal departments and agencies develop their GMR plans and maintain capability to carry out their mobilization-related responsibilities in accordance with section 201 of Executive Order 12656. General types of problems likely to arise in a crisis situation are identified along with possible methods for dealing with them. Investment programs can be undertaken to overcome identified problems.

(b) *Stage 2, Crisis Management.* During the crisis management stage, GMR plans are reviewed and capabilities will be re-examined in light of an actual event or crisis perceived to be emerging.

(1) Federal departments and agencies may need to gather additional data on selected resources or increase their preparedness activities. Costed Option Packages may need to be updated or new ones prepared for the response option measures in each of the department's and agency's area of responsibility. For example, when it appears likely that increased national resources may be required, resource readiness could be improved through the procurement of essential long lead time items, especially those that can be used even if the situation does not escalate. In general, long lead time preparedness actions would be considered for implementation at this time.

(2) Many preparedness actions at this stage would be handled through reprogramming, but the Costed Option Packages may also require new funding.

(3) If the crisis worsens, and prior to the declaration of national emergency, it may be necessary to surge certain production and stockpile items for future use.

(c) *Stage 1, National Emergency/War.* During a national emergency or declaration of war, mobilization of all national resources escalates and GMR will be subsumed into the overall mobilization effort. As military requirements increase, the national resources would increasingly be focused on the national security emergency. This would involve diverting non-essential demand for scarce resources from peacetime to defense uses, and converting industry from commercial to military production. Both surge production and expansion of the nation's productive capacity may also be necessary. Supplemental appropriations may be required for most Federal departments and agencies having national security emergency responsibilities.

§334.6 **Department and agency responsibilities.**

(a) During Stage 3, each Federal department and agency with mobilization responsibilities will develop GMR plans as part of its emergency preparedness planning process in order to meet possible future crisis. Costed Option Packages will be developed for actions that may be necessary in the early warning period. Option packages will be reviewed, focused and refined during Stage 2 to meet the particular emergency.

(b) Each department and agency should identify response actions appropriate for the early stage of any crisis or emergency situation, which then will be reviewed, focused and refined in Stage 2 for execution, as appropriate. GMR plans should contain a menu of costed option packages that provide details of alternative measures that may be used in an emergency situation.

(c) FEMA will provide guidance pursuant to Executive Order 12656 and will coordinate GMR plans and option packages of DOD and the civilian departments and agencies to ensure consistency and to identify areas where additional planning or investment is needed.

(d) During State 2, FEMA will coordinate department and agency recommendations for action and forward them to the National Security Advisor to make certain that consistency with the overall national strategy planning is achieved.

(e) Departments and agencies will refine their GMR plans to focus on the specific crisis situation. Costed option packages should be refined to identify the resources necessary for the current crisis, action taken to obtain those resources, and GMR plans implemented consistent with the seriousness of the crisis.

(f) At Stage 1, declaration of national emergency or war, the crisis is under the control of NSC or other central authority, with GMR being integrated into partial, full or total mobilization. At this point the more traditional mechanisms of resource mobilization are pursued, focusing on resource allocation and adjudication with cognizance of the essential civilian demand.

(g) Programs and plans developed by the departments and agencies under this guidance should be shared, as appropriate, with States, local governments and the private sector to provide a baseline for their development of supporting programs and plans.

§ 334.7 Reporting.

The Administrator of FEMA shall provide the President with periodic assessments of the Federal departments and agencies capabilities to respond to national security emergencies and periodic reports to the National Security Council on the implementation of the national security emergency preparedness policy. Pursuant to section 201(15) of Executive Order 12656, departments and agencies, as appropriate, shall consult and coordinate with the Administrator of FEMA to ensure that their activities and plans are consistent with current National Security Council guidelines and policies. An evaluation of the Federal departments and agencies participation in the graduated mobilization response program may be included in these reports.

PARTS 335-349 [RESERVED]

PART 350—REVIEW AND APPROVAL OF STATE AND LOCAL RADIOLOGICAL EMERGENCY PLANS AND PREPAREDNESS

AUTHORITY: 42 U.S.C. 5131, 5201, 50 U.S.C. app. 2253(g); Sec. 109 Pub. L. 96–295; Reorganization Plan No. 3 of 1978; E.O. 12127; E.O. 12148.

SOURCE: 48 FR 44335, Sept. 28, 1983, unless otherwise noted.

§ 350.1 Purpose.

The purpose of the regulation in this part is to establish policy and procedures for review and approval by the Federal Emergency Management Agency (FEMA) of State and local emergency plans and preparedness for the offsite effects of a radiological emergency which may occur at a commercial nuclear power facility. Review and approval of these plans and preparedness involves preparation of findings and determinations of the adequacy of the plans and capabilities of State and local governments to effectively implement the plans.

§ 350.2 Definitions.

As used in this part, the following terms are defined:

(a) *Administrator* means the Administrator, FEMA, or designee;

(b) *Regional Administrator* means a Regional Administrator of FEMA, or designee;

(c) *Deputy Administrator* means the , National Preparedness Directorate, FEMA, or designee;

(d) *FEMA* means the Federal Emergency Management Agency;

(e) *NRC* means the Nuclear Regulatory Commission;

(f) *EPZ* means Emergency Planning Zone.

(g) *Emergency Planning Zone (EPZ)* is a generic area around a commercial nuclear facility used to assist in offsite emergency planning and the development of a significant response base. For commercial nuclear power plants, EPZs of about 10 and 50 miles are delineated for the plume and ingestion exposure pathways respectively.

(h) *Plume Exposure Pathway* refers to whole body external exposure to gamma radiation from the plume and from deposited materials and inhalation exposure from the passing radioactive plume. The duration of primary exposures could range in length from hours to days.

(i) *Ingestion Exposure Pathway* refers to exposure primarily from ingestion of water or foods such as milk and fresh vegetables that have been contaminated with radiation. The duration of primary exposure could range from hours to months.

(j) *Full participation* refers to an exercise in which: (1) State and local government emergency personnel are engaged in sufficient numbers to verify the capability to respond to the actions required by the accident scenario; (2) the integrated capability to adequately assess and respond to an accident at a commercial nuclear power plant is tested; and (3) the implementation of the observable portions of State and/or local plans is tested.

(k) *Partial participation* refers to the engagement of State and local government emergency personnel in an exercise sufficient to adequately test direction and control functions for protective action decisionmaking related to emergency action levels and communication capabilities among affected State and local governments and the licensee.

(l) *Remedial exercise* is one that tests deficiencies of previous joint exercise that are considered significant enough to impact on the public health and safety.

(m) *Local government* refers to boroughs, cities, counties, municipalities, parishes, towns, townships and other local jurisdictions within the plume exposure pathway EPZ when any of these entities has specific roles in emergency planning and preparedness in the EPZ.

(n) *Site* refers to the location at which there is one or more commercial nuclear power plants. A nuclear power plant is synonymous with a nuclear power facility.

§350.3 Background.

(a) On December 7, 1979, the President directed the Administrator of FEMA to take the lead in State and local emergency planning and preparedness activities with respect to nuclear power facilities. This included a review of the existing emergency plans both in States with operating reactors and those with plants scheduled for operation in the near future.

(b) This assignment was given to FEMA because of its responsibilities under Executive Order 12148 to establish Federal policies for and coordinate civil emergency planning, management and assistance functions and to represent the President in working with State and local governments and the private sector to stimulate vigorous participation in civil emergency preparedness programs. Under section 201 of the Disaster Relief Act of 1974 (42 U.S.C. 5131), and other statutory functions, the Administrator of FEMA is charged with the responsibility to develop and implement plans and programs of disaster preparedness.

(c) There are two sections in the NRC's fiscal year 1982/1983 Appropriation Authorization (Pub. L. 97–415) that pertain to the scope of this rule.

(1) Section 5 provides for the issuance of an operating license for a commercial nuclear power plant by the NRC if it is determined that there exists a State, local or utility plan which provides assurance that public health and safety is not endangered by the operation of the facility. This section would allow the NRC to issue an operating license for such plants without FEMA-approved State and local government plans.

(2) Section 11 provides for the issuance of temporary licenses for operating a utilization facility at a specific power level to be determined by the Commission, pending final action by the Commission on the application. Also, this section authorizes the NRC to issue temporary operating licenses for these facilities without the completion of the required (NRC) Commission hearing process. A petition for such a temporary license may not be filed until certain actions are completed including the submission of a State, local or utility emergency response plan for the facility.

(d) To carry out these responsibilities, FEMA is engaged in a cooperative effort with State and local governments and other Federal agencies in the development of State and local plans and preparedness to cope with the offsite effects resulting from radiological emergencies at commercial nuclear power facilities. FEMA developed and published the Federal Radiological Emergency Response Plan 50 FR 46542 Nov. 8, 1985, to provide the overall support to State and local governments, for all types of radiological incidents including those occurring at nuclear power plants.

(e) FEMA has entered into a Memorandum of Understanding (MOU) with the NRC to which it will furnish assessments, findings and determinations as to whether State and local emergency plans and preparedness are adequate and continue to be capable of implementation (e.g., adequacy and maintenance of procedures, training, resources, staffing levels and qualification and equipment adequacy). These findings and determinations will be used by NRC under its own rules in connection with its licensing and regulatory requirements and FEMA will support its findings in the NRC licensing process and related court proceedings.

(f) Notwithstanding the procedures set forth in these rules for requesting and reaching a FEMA administrative approval of State and local plans, findings and determinations on the current status of emergency preparedness around particular sites may be requested by the NRC and provided by FEMA for use as needed in the NRC licensing process. These findings and determinations may be based upon plans currently available to FEMA or furnished to FEMA by the NRC through the NRC/FEMA Steering Committee.

(g) An environmental assessment has been prepared on which FEMA has determined that this rule will not have a significant impact on the quality of the human environment.

[48 FR 44335, Sept. 28, 1983, as amended at 51 FR 34606, Sept. 30, 1986]

§ 350.4 Exclusions.

The regulation in this part does not apply to, nor will FEMA apply any criteria with respect to, any evaluation, assessment or determination regarding the NRC licensee's emergency plans or preparedness, nor shall FEMA make any similar determination with respect to the integration of offsite and NRC licensee emergency preparedness except as these assessments and determinations affect the emergency preparedness of State and local governments. The regulation in this part applies only to State and local planning and preparedness with respect to emergencies at commercial nuclear power facilities and does not apply to other facilities which may be licensed by NRC, nor to United States Government-owned, non-licensed facilities nor the jurisdictions surrounding them.

§ 350.5 Criteria for review and approval of State and local radiological emergency plans and preparedness.

(a) Section 50.47 of NRC's Emergency Planning Rule (10 CFR parts 50 (appendix E) and 70 as amended) and the joint FEMA–NRC *Criteria for Preparation and Evaluation of Radiological Emergency Response Plans and Preparedness in Support of Nuclear Power Plants* (NUREG–0654/FEMA–REP–1, Rev. 1, November 1980) which apply insofar as FEMA is concerned to State and local governments, are to be used in reviewing, evaluating and approving State and local radiological emergency plans and preparedness and in making any findings and determinations with respect to the adequacy of the plans and the capabilities of State and local governments to implement them. Both the planning and preparedness standards and related criteria contained in NUREG–0654/ FEMA–REP–1, Rev. 1 are to be used by FEMA and the NRC in reviewing and evaluating State and local government radiological emergency plans and preparedness. For brevity, only the planning standards contained in NUREG–0654/ FEMA–REP–1, Rev. 1 are presented below.

(1) Primary responsibilities for emergency response by the nuclear facility licensee, and by State and local organizations within the Emergency Planning Zones have been assigned, the emergency responsibilities of the various supporting organizations have been specifically established and each principal response organization has staff to respond to and augment its initial response on a continuous basis.

(2) On-shift facility licensee responsibilities for emergency response are

unambiguously defined, adequate staffing to provide initial facility accident response in key functional areas is maintained at all times, timely augmentation of response capabilities is available and the interfaces among various onsite response activities and offsite support and response activities are specified. (This standard applies only to NRC licensees but is included here for completeness.)

(3) Arrangements for requesting and effectively using assistance resources have been made, arrangements to accommodate State and local staff at the licensee's near-site Emergency Operations Facility have been made and other organizations capable of augmenting the planned response have been identified.

(4) A standard emergency classification and action level scheme, the bases of which include facility system and effluent parameters, is in use by the nuclear facility licensee, and State and local response plans call for reliance on information provided by facility licensees for determinations of minimum initial offsite response measures.

(5) Procedures have been established for notification, by the licensee, of State and local response organizations and for the notification of emergency personnel by all response organizations; the content of initial and followup messages to response organizations and the public has been established; and means to provide early notification and clear instruction to the populace within the plume exposure pathway Emergency Planning Zone have been established.

(6) Provisions exist for prompt communications among principal response organizations to emergency personnel and to the public.

(7) Information is made available to the public on a periodic basis on how they will be notified and what their initial actions should be in an emergency (e.g., listening to a local broadcast station and remaining indoors), the principal points of contact with the news media for dissemination of information during an emergency (including the physical location or locations) are established in advance and procedures for coordinated dissemination of information to the public are established.

(8) Adequate emergency facilities and equipment to support the emergency response are provided and maintained.

(9) Adequate methods, systems and equipment for assessing and monitoring actual or potential offsite consequences of a radiological emergency condition are in use.

(10) A range of protective actions has been developed for the plume exposure pathway EPZ for emergency workers and the public. Guidelines for the choice of protective actions during an emergency, consistent with Federal guidance, are developed and in place and protective actions for the ingestion exposure pathway EPZ appropriate to the locale have been developed.

(11) Means for controlling radiological exposures, in an emergency, are established for emergency workers. The means for controlling radiological exposures shall include exposure guidelines consistent with EPA Emergency Worker and Lifesaving Activity Protective Action Guides.

(12) Arrangements are made for medical services for contaminated injured individuals.

(13) General plans for recovery and reentry are developed.

(14) Periodic exercises are (will be) conducted to evaluate major portions of emergency response capabilities, periodic drills are (will be) conducted to develop and maintain key skills and deficiencies identified as a result of exercises or drills are (will be) corrected.

(15) Radiological emergency response training is provided to those who may be called upon to assist in an emergency.

(16) Responsibilities for plan development and review and for distribution of emergency plans are established, and planners are properly trained.

(b) In order for State of local plans and preparedness to be approved, such plans and preparedness must be determined to adequately protect the public health and safety by providing reasonable assurance that appropriate protective measures can be taken offsite in the event of a radiological emergency.

§ 350.6 Assistance in development of State and local plans.

(a) An integrated approach to the development of offsite radiological emergency plans by States, localities and the licensees of NRC with the assistance of the Federal Government is the approach most likely to provide the best protection to the public. Hence, Federal agencies, including FEMA Regional staff, will be made available upon request to assist States and localities in the development of plans.

(b) There now exists in each of the ten standard Federal Regions a Regional Assistance Committee (RAC) (formerly the Regional Advisory Committee) chaired by a FEMA Regional official and having members from the Nuclear Regulatory Commission, Department of Health and Human Services, Department of Energy, Department of Transportation, Environmental Protection Agency, the United States Department of Agriculture and Department of Commerce. Whereas in 44 CFR part 351, the Department of Defense is listed as a potential member of the RACs, it is not listed in this rule because military nuclear facilities are not the subject of concern. The RACs will assist State and local government officials in the development of their radiological emergency response plans, and will review plans and observe exercises to evaluate the adequacy of these plans and related preparedness. This assistance does not include the actual writing of State and local government plans by RAC members.

(c) In accomplishing the foregoing, the RACs will use the standards and criteria in NUREG–0654/FEMA–REP–1, Rev. 1, and will render such technical assistance as may be required, appropriate to their agency mission and expertise. In observing and evaluating exercises, the RACs will identify, soon after an exercise, any deficiencies observed in the planning and preparedness effort including deficiencies in resources, training of staff, equipment, staffing levels and deficiencies in the qualifications of personnel.

§ 350.7 Application by State for review and approval.

(a) A State which seeks formal review and approval by FEMA of the State's radiological emergency plan shall submit an application for such review and approval to the FEMA Regional Administrator of the Region in which the State is located. The application, in the form of a letter from the Governor or from such other State official as the Governor may designate, shall contain one copy of the completed State plan, including coverage of response in the ingestion exposure pathway EPZ. The application will also include plans of all appropriate local governments. The application shall specify the site or sites for which plan approval is sought. For guidance on the local government plans that should be included with an application, refer to Part I.E. NUREG–0654/FEMA–REP–1, Rev. 1, entitled Contiguous Jurisdiction Governmental Emergency Planning (see (e)). Only a State may request formal review of State or local radiological emergency plans.

(b) Generally, the plume exposure pathway EPZ for nuclear power facilities shall consist of an area about 10 miles (16 Km) in radius and the ingestion exposure pathway EPZ shall consist of an area about 50 miles (80 Km) in radius. The exact size and configuration of the EPZs surrounding a particular nuclear power facility shall be determined by State and local governments in consultation with FEMA and NRC taking into account such local conditions as demography, topography, land characteristics, access routes and local jurisdiction boundaries. The size of the EPZs may be determined by NRC in consultation with FEMA on a case-by-case basis for gas cooled reactors and for reactors with an authorized power level less than 250 Mw thermal. The plans for the ingestion exposure pathway shall focus on such actions as are appropriate to protect the public from ingesting contaminated food and water.

(c) A State may submit separately its plans for the EPZs and the local government plans related to individual nuclear power facilities. The purpose of separate submissions is to allow approval of a State plan, and of the plans necessary for specific nuclear power facilities in a multiple-facility State, while not approving or acting on the plans necessary for other nuclear power facilities within the State. If separate submissions are made, appropriate adjustments in the State plan may be necessary. In any event, FEMA approval of State plans and appropriate local government plans shall be site specific.

(d) The applications shall contain a statement that the State plan, together with the appropriate local plans, is, in the opinion of the State, adequate to protect the public health and safety of its citizens living within the emergency planning zones for the nuclear power facilities included in the submission by providing reasonable assurance that State and local governments can and intend to effect appropriate protective measures offsite in the event of a radiological emergency.

(e) FEMA and the States will make suitable arrangements in the case of overlapping or adjacent jurisdictions to permit an orderly assessment and approval of interstate or interregional plans.

§ 350.8 Initial FEMA action on State plan.

(a) The Regional Administrator shall acknowledge in writing within ten days the receipt of the State application.

(b) FEMA shall publish a notice signed by the Regional Administrator or designee in the FEDERAL REGISTER within 30 days after receipt of the application, that an application from a State has been received and that copies are available at the Regional Office for review and copying in accordance with 44 CFR 5.26.

(c) The Regional Administrator shall furnish copies of the plan to members of the RAC for their analysis and evaluation.

(d) The Regional Administrator shall make a detailed review of the State plan, including those of local governments, and assess the capability of State and local governments to effectively implement the plan (e.g., adequacy and maintenance of procedures, training, resources, staffing levels and qualification and equipment adequacy). Evaluation and comments of the RAC members will be used as part of the review process.

(e) In connection with the review, the Regional Administrator may make

suggestions to States concerning perceived gaps or deficiencies in the plans, and the State may amend the plan at any time prior to forwarding to the Deputy Administrator for the National Preparedness Directorate.

(f) Two conditions for FEMA approval of State plans (including local government plans) are the requirements for an exercise (see § 350.9), and for public participation (see §§ 350.9 and 350.10.). These activities occur during the Regional review and prior to the forwarding of the plan to the Deputy Administrator for the National Preparedness Directorate.

§ 350.9 Exercises.

(a) Before a Regional Administrator can forward a State plan to the Deputy Administrator for the National Preparedness Directorate for approval, the State, together with all appropriate local governments, must conduct a joint exercise of that State plan, involving full participation[1] of appropriate local government entities, the State and the appropriate licensee of the NRC. To the extent achievable, this exercise shall include participation by appropriate Federal agencies. This exercise shall be observed and evaluated by FEMA and by representatives of other Federal agencies with membership on the RACs and by NRC with respect to licensee response. Within 48 hours of the completion of the exercise, a briefing involving the exercise participants and Federal observers shall be conducted by the Regional Administrator to discuss the preliminary results of the exercise. If the exercise discloses any deficiencies in the State and local plans, or the ability of the State and local governments to implement the plans, the FEMA representatives shall make them known promptly in writing to appropriate State officials. To the extent necessary, the State shall amend the plan to incorporate recommended changes or improvements or take other corrective measures, such as remedial exercises,[1] to

---

[1] See § 350.2 for definitions of "full participation" and "remedial exercises".

demonstrate to the Regional Administrator that identified weaknesses have been corrected.

(b) The Regional Administrator shall be the FEMA official responsible for certifying to the Deputy Administrator for the National Preparedness Directorate that an exercise of the State plan has been conducted, and that changes and corrective measures in accordance with paragraph (a) of this section have been made.

(c) State and local governments that have fully participated in a joint exercise within one year prior to the effective date of this final rule will have continuing approval of their radiological emergency plans and preparedness by following the frequency indicated in paragraphs (c) (1) through (4) of this section. State and local governments that have not fully participated in a joint exercise within one year prior to the effective date of this final rule will follow the frequency indicated in paragraphs (c) (1) through (4) of this section after completion of a joint exercise in which they have fully participated. If, in developing exercise schedules with State and local governments to implement the requirements in paragraphs (c) (1) through (4) of this section, the Regional Administrator finds that unusual hardships would result, he may seek relief from the Deputy Administrator for the National Preparedness Directorate.

(1) Each State which has a commercial nuclear power site within its boundaries or is within the 10-mile plume exposure pathway Emergency Planning Zone of such site shall fully participate in an exercise jointly with the nuclear power plant licensee and appropriate local governments at least every two years.

(2) Each State with multiple sites within its boundaries shall fully participate in a joint exercise at some site on a rotational basis at least every 2 years. When not fully participating in an exercise at a site, the State shall partially participate[2] at that site to support the full participation of appropriate local governments. Priority shall be given to new facilities seeking

_____

[2] See § 350.2 for definition of "partial exercise".

an operating license from the NRC and which have not fully participated in a joint exercise involving the State, local governments and the licensee at that site. State and local governments will coordinate the scheduling of these exercises with the appropriate FEMA and NRC Regional Offices and the affected licensees.

(3) Each appropriate local government which has a site within its boundaries or is within the 10-mile emergency planning zone shall fully participate in a joint exercise with the licensee and the State at least every two years. For those local governments that have planning and preparedness responsibilities for more than one facility, the Regional Administrator may seek an exemption from this requirement by recommending alternative arrangements for approval by the Associate Director.

(4) States within the 50-mile emergency planning zone of a site shall exercise their plans and preparedness related to ingestion exposure pathway measures at least once every five years in conjunction with a plume exposure pathway exercise for that site.

(5) Remedial exercises may be required to correct deficiencies observed in exercises conducted for continued FEMA approval. Should this occur, the FEMA Regional Administrator will determine the participation required from the States and/or local governments.

(d) Within 48 hours of the completion of an exercise conducted for continued FEMA approval, a briefing involving the exercise participants and Federal observers shall be conducted by the Regional Administrator to discuss the preliminary results of the exercise. If the exercise discloses any deficiencies in the State and local plans, or the ability of the State and local governments to implement the plans, the FEMA representatives shall make them known promptly in writing to appropriate State officials. To the extent necessary, the State shall amend the plan to incorporate recommended changes or improvements or take other corrective measures, such as remedial exercises, to demonstrate to the Regional Administrator that identified weaknesses have been corrected. The

Regional Administrator shall forward his or her evaluation of the exercise conducted for continued FEMA approval to the Deputy Administrator for the National Preparedness Directorate including the certification that changes and corrective measures have been made.

(e) Following the exercise conducted for continued FEMA approval, the Regional Administrator shall conduct a meeting in the vicinity of the nuclear power facility which will include the exercise participants, representatives from the NRC and other appropriate Federal agencies and the public and media as observers. The purpose of this meeting is to discuss the evaluation of the exercise. At the discretion of the Regional Administrator, written comments from the public and media may be submitted at or after the meeting. These comments will be taken into consideration by the Regional Administrator in his or her evaluation.

(f) After FEMA approval of a State and local plan has been granted, failure to exercise the State and local plans at the frequency and participation described in this section shall be grounds for withdrawing FEMA approval. (See §350.13.)

§350.10 Public meeting in advance of FEMA approval.

(a) During the FEMA Regional Office review of a State plan and prior to the submission by the Regional Administrator of the evaluation of the plan and exercise to the Deputy Administrator for the National Preparedness Directorate, the FEMA Regional Administrator shall assure that there is at least one public meeting conducted in the vicinity of the nuclear power facility. The purpose of such a meeting, which may be conducted by the State or by the Regional Administrator, shall be to:

(1) Acquaint the members of the public in the vicinity of each facility with the content of the State and related local plans, and with the conduct of the joint exercise which tested the plans;

(2) Answer any questions about FEMA review of the plan and the exercise;

(3) Receive suggestions from the public concerning improvements or changes that may be necessary; and

(4) Describe to the public the way in which the plan is expected to function in the event of an actual emergency.

(b) The Regional Administrator should assure that representatives from appropriate State and local government agencies, and the affected utility appear at such meetings to make presentations and to answer questions from the public. The public meeting should be held after the first joint (utility, State and local governments) exercise at a time mutually agreed to by State and local authorities, licensee and FEMA and NRC Regional officials. This meeting shall be noticed in the local newspaper with the largest circulation in the area, or other such media as the Regional Administrator may select, on at least two occasions, one of which is at least two weeks before the meeting takes place and the other is within a few days of the meeting date. Local radio and television stations should be notified of the scheduled meeting at least one week in advance. Representatives from NRC and other appropriate Federal agencies should also be invited to participate in these meetings. If, in the judgment of the FEMA Regional Administrator, the public meeting or meetings reveal deficiencies in the State plan and/or the joint exercise, the Regional Administrator shall inform the State of the fact together with recommendations for improvement. No FEMA approval of State and local plans and preparedness shall be made until a meeting described in this paragraph shall have been held at or near the nuclear power facility site for which the State is seeking approval.

§350.11 Action by FEMA Regional Administrator.

(a) Upon completion of his or her review, including conduct of the exercise required by §350.9 and after the public meeting required by §350.10, the Regional Administrator shall prepare an evaluation of the State plan, including plans for local governments. Such evaluation shall be specific with respect to the plans applicable to each nuclear facility so that findings and determinations can be made by the Deputy Administrator for the National Preparedness Directorate on a site-specific basis.

(b) The Regional Administrator shall evaluate the adequacy of State and local plans and preparedness on the basis of the criteria set forth in § 350.5, and shall report the evaluation with respect to each of the planning standards mentioned therein as such apply to State and local plans and preparedness.

(c) The Regional Administrator shall forward the State plan together with his or her evaluation and other relevant record material to the Deputy Administrator for the National Preparedness Directorate. Relevant record material will include the results of the exercise (i.e., deficiencies noted and corrections made), a summary of the deficiencies identified during the public meeting, recommendations made to the State and commitments made by the State for effecting improvements in its plans and preparedness and actions taken by the State.

§ 350.12 FEMA Headquarters review and approval.

(a) Upon receipt from a Regional Administrator of a State plan, the Deputy Administrator for the National Preparedness Directorate shall conduct such review of the State plan as he or she shall deem necessary. The Deputy Administrator for the National Preparedness Directorate shall arrange for copies of the plan, together with the Regional Administrator's evaluation, to be made available to the members of the Federal Radiological Preparedness Coordinating Committee (FRPCC) and to other offices of FEMA with appropriate guidance relative to any assistance that may be needed in the FEMA review and approval process.

(b) If, after formal submission of the State plan and the Regional Director's evaluation, the Deputy Administrator for the National Preparedness Directorate determines that the State plans and preparedness:

(1) Are adequate to protect the health and safety of the public living in the vicinity of the nuclear power facility by providing reasonable assurance

that appropriate protective measures can be taken offsite in the event of a radiological emergency; and

(2) Are capable of being implemented (e.g. adequacy and maintenance of procedures, training, resources, staffing levels and qualification and equipment adequacy); the Deputy Administrator for the National Preparedness Directorate shall approve in writing the State plan. The Deputy Administrator for the National Preparedness Directorate shall concurrently communicate this FEMA approval to the Governor of the State(s) in question, the NRC and the pertinent Regional Administrator(s) and immediately shall publish in the FEDERAL REGISTER a notice of this effect.

(c) If, after formal submission of the State plan, the Deputy Administrator for the National Preparedness Directorate is not satisfied with the adequacy of the plan or preparedness with respect to a particular site, he or she shall concurrently communicate that decision to the Governor(s) of the State(s), the NRC and the pertinent Regional Administrator(s), together with a statement in writing explaining the reasons for the decision and requesting appropriate plan or preparedness revision. Such statement shall be transmitted to the Governor(s) through the appropriate Regional Administrator(s). The Deputy Administrator for the National Preparedness Directorate shall immediately publish a notice to this effect in the FEDERAL REGISTER.

(d) The approval shall be of the State plan together with the local plans for each nuclear power facility (including out-of-State facilities) for which approval has been requested. FEMA may withhold approval of plans applicable to a specific nuclear power facility in a multi-facility State, but nevertheless approve the State plan and associated local plans applicable to other facilities in a State. Approval may be withheld for a specific site until plans for all jurisdictions within the emergency planning zones of that site have been reviewed and found adequate.

(e) Within 30 days after the date of notification of approval for a particular nuclear power facility or within 30 days of any statement of disapproval of a State plan, any interested person may appeal the decision of the Deputy Administrator for the National Preparedness Directorate to the Administrator; however, such an appeal must be made solely upon the ground that the Deputy Administrator for the National Preparedness Directorate's decision, based on the available record, was unsupported by substantial evidence. (See §350.15 for appeal procedures.)

§350.13 Withdrawal of approval.

(a) If, at any time after granting approval of a State plan, the Deputy Administrator for the National Preparedness Directorate determines, on his or her own initiative, motion or on the basis of information another person supplied, that the State or local plan is no longer adequate to protect public health and safety by providing reasonable assurance that appropriate protective measures can be taken, or is no longer capable of being implemented, he or she shall immediately advise the Governor of the affected State, through the appropriate Regional Administrator and the NRC of that initial determination in writing. FEMA shall spell out in detail the reasons for its initial determination, and shall describe the deficiencies in the plan or the preparedness of the State. If, after four months from the date of such an initial determination, the State in question has not either:

(1) Corrected the deficiencies noted, or (2) submitted an acceptable plan for correcting those deficiencies, the Deputy Administrator for the National Preparedness Directorate shall withdraw approval and shall immediately inform the NRC and the Governor of the affected State, of the determination to withdraw approval and shall publish in the FEDERAL REGISTER and the local newspaper having the largest daily circulation in the affected State notice of its withdrawal or approval. The basis upon which the Deputy Administrator for the National Preparedness Directorate makes the determination for withdrawal of approval is the same basis used for reviewing plans and exercises, i.e., the planning standards and related criteria in NUREGO654/FEMA/REP–1, Rev. 1.

(b) In the event that the State in question shall submit a plan for correcting the deficiencies, the Deputy Administrator for the National Preparedness Directorate shall negotiate a schedule and a timetable under which the State shall correct the deficiencies. If, on the agreed upon date, the deficiencies have been corrected, the Deputy Administrator for the National Preparedness Directorate shall withdraw the initial determination and the approval previously granted shall remain valid. He or she shall inform the Governor(s), the NRC, the pertinent Regional Administrator(s) and notify the public as stated in paragraph (a) of this section. If, however, on the agreed upon date, the deficiencies are not corrected, FEMA shall withdraw its approval and shall communicate its decision to the Governor of the State whose plan is in question, the NRC, the appropriate Federal agencies and notify the public as indicated above.

(c) Within 30 days after the date of notification of withdrawal of approval of a State or local plan, any interested person may appeal the decision of the Deputy Administrator for the National Preparedness Directorate to the Administrator; however, such an appeal must be made solely upon the ground that the Deputy Administrator for the National Preparedness Directorate's decision, based on the available record, was unsupported by substantial evidence. (See §350.15 for appeal procedures.)

§350.14 Amendments to State plans.

(a) The State may amend a plan submitted to FEMA for review and approval under §350.7 at any time during the review process or may amend a plan at any time after FEMA approval has been granted under §350.12. A State must amend its plan in order to extend the coverage of the plan to any new nuclear power facility which becomes operational after a FEMA approval or in case of any other significant change. The State plan shall remain in effect as approved while any significant change is under review.

(b) A significant change is one which involves the evaluation and assessment of a planning standard or which involves a matter which, if presented with the plan, would need to have been considered by the Deputy Administrator for the National Preparedness Directorate in making a decision that State or local plans and preparedness are:

(1) Adequate to protect the health and safety of the public living in the vicinity of the nuclear power facility by providing reasonable assurance that appropriate protective measures can be taken offsite in the event of a radiological emergency; and

(2) Capable of being implemented.

(c) A significant change will be processed in the same manner as if it were an initial plan submission. However, the Regional Administrator may determine that certain procedures, such as holding a public meeting or a complete exercise, would be unnecessary. The existing FEMA approval shall remain in effect while any significant changes are under review.

(d) Changes, such as a change in a telephone number, that are not significant as defined in paragraphs (b) and (c) of this section, but are necessary to maintain currency of the plan, should be forwarded to the Regional Administrator.

§ 350.15 Appeal procedures.

(a) Any interested person may appeal a decision made under §§ 350.12 and 350.13 of this part, by submitting to the Administrator, FEMA, a written notice of appeal, within 30 days after the appearance in the FEDERAL REGISTER, of the notice of decision relating to the matter being appealed. The appeal must be addressed to the Administrator, Federal Emergency Management Agency, 500 C Street, SW., Washington, DC, 20472. The appeal letter shall state specific reasons for the appeal and include an offer to provide documentation supporting appellate arguments.

(b) Upon receipt of an appeal, the Administrator or the Administrator's designee shall review the file, as submitted to the Deputy Administrator for the National Preparedness Directorate, by the Regional Administrator of the FEMA Region concerned, based on the information contained in the file and the appeal letter, with supporting documentation. The Adminis-

trator or the Administrator's designee shall decide whether or not the Associate Director's initial decision was supported by substantial evidence in the file and is consistent with FEMA policy.

(c) The decision of the Administrator or the Administrator's designee shall be published in the FEDERAL REGISTER as the final agency decision on the matter and shall not be reviewable within FEMA, except upon a showing that it was procured by fraud or misrepresentation. In addition to publication in the FEDERAL REGISTER, copies of the decision shall be forwarded to the appellant, the Governor(s) of the State(s) affected, the NRC and the affected licensee of the involved power facility.

PART 351—RADIOLOGICAL EMERGENCY PLANNING AND PREPAREDNESS

Subpart A—General

Subpart B—Federal Radiological Preparedness Coordinating Committee and Regional Assistance Committees

Subpart C—Interagency Assignments

AUTHORITY: 5 U.S.C. 552, Reorganization Plan No. 3 of 1978, E.O. 12127, E.O. 12148, E.O. 12241; Presidential Directive of Dec. 7, 1979.

SOURCE: 47 FR 10759, Mar. 11, 1982, unless otherwise noted.

Subpart A—General

§351.1 Purpose.

This part sets out Federal agency roles and assigns tasks regarding Federal assistance to State and local governments in their radiological emergency planning and preparedness activities. Assignments in this part are applicable to radiological accidents at fixed nuclear facilities and transportation accidents involving radioactive materials.

§351.2 Scope.

The emergency planning and preparedness responsibilities covered by this part relate to consequences and activities which extend beyond the boundaries of any fixed nuclear facility with a potential for serious consequences and the area affected by a transportation accident involving radioactive materials.

§351.3 Limitation of scope.

(a) This part covers Federal agency assignments and responsibilities in connection with State and local emergency plans and preparedness measures. It does not set forth criteria used in the review and approval of these plans and does not include any of the requirements associated with FEMA findings and determinations on the adequacy of State and local government radiological emergency preparedness. FEMA has published a separate rule on procedures and criteria for reviewing and approving these plans and preparedness capabilities. Furthermore, this part does not set forth Federal agency responsibilities or capabilities for *responding to an accident* at a fixed nuclear facility or a transportation accident involving radioactive materials. These responsibilities are addressed in the "Federal Radiological Emergency Response Plan" (50 FR 46542, November 8, 1985).

(b) Nothing in this part authorizes access to or disclosure of classified information required to be protected in accordance with Federal law or regulation in the interest of national security.

[47 FR 10759, Mar. 11, 1982, as amended at 51 FR 34606, Sept. 30, 1986]

Subpart B—Federal Radiological Preparedness Coordinating Committee and Regional Assistance Committees

§351.10 Establishment of committees.

(a) The Federal Radiological Preparedness Coordinating Committee (FRPCC) consists of the Federal Emergency Management Agency, which chairs the Committee, Nuclear Regulatory Commission, Environmental Protection Agency, Department of Health and Human Services, Department of Energy, Department of Transportation, Department of Defense, United States Department of Agriculture, Department of Commerce and, where appropriate and on an ad hoc basis, other Federal departments and agencies. In chairing the committee, FEMA will be responsible for assuring that all agency assignments described in this rule are coordinated through the Committee and carried out with or on behalf of State and local governments.

(b) The Regional Assistance Committees (RACs), one in each of 10 standard Federal regions,[1] consist of a FEMA Regional Representative who chairs the Committee and representatives from the Nuclear Regulatory Commission, Environmental Protection Agency, Department of Health and Human Services, Department of Energy, Department of Transportation, United States Department of Agriculture, Department of Commerce and other Federal departments and agencies such as the Department of Defense, as appropriate. The FEMA Chairperson of the RACs will provide guidance and orientation to other agency members to assist them in carrying out their functions.

§351.11 Functions of committees.

(a) The FRPCC shall assist FEMA in providing policy direction for the program of Federal assistance to State and local governments in their radiological emergency planning and preparedness activities. The FRPCC will

[1] I (Boston); II (New York); III (Philadelphia); IV (Atlanta); V (Chicago); VI (Dallas); VII (Kansas City); VIII (Denver); IX (San Francisco) and X (Seattle).

establish subcommittees to aid in carrying out its functions; e.g., research, training, emergency instrumentation, transportation, information, education and Federal response. The FRPCC will assist FEMA in resolving issues relating to granting of final FEMA approval of a State plan. The FRPCC will coordinate research and study efforts of its member agencies related to State and local government radiological emergency preparedness to assure minimum duplication and maximum benefits to State and local governments. The FRPCC will also assure that the research efforts of its member agencies are coordinated with the Interagency Radiation Research Committee.

(b) The RACs will assist State and local government officials in the development of their radiological emergency plans and will review these plans and observe exercises to evaluate adequacy of the plans. Each Federal agency member of the RACs will support the functions of these committees by becoming knowledgeable of Federal planning and guidance related to State and local radiological emergency plans, of their counterpart State organizations and personnel, where their agency can assist in improving the preparedness and by participating in RAC meetings.

Subpart C—Interagency Assignments

§ 351.20 The Federal Emergency Management Agency.

(a) Establish policy and provide leadership via the FRPCC in the coordination of all Federal assistance and guidance to State and local governments for developing, reviewing, assessing and testing the State and local radiological emergency plans.

(b) Issue guidance in cooperation with other Federal agencies concerning their responsibilities for providing radiological emergency planning and preparedness assistance to State and local governments.

(c) Foster cooperation of industry, technical societies, Federal agencies and other constituencies in the radiological emergency planning and preparedness of State and local governments.

(d) Develop and promulgate preparedness criteria and guidance to State and local governments, in coordination with other Federal agencies, for the preparation, review and testing of State and local radiological emergency plans.

(e) Provide assistance to State and local governments in the preparation, review and testing of radiological emergency plans.

(f) Assess, with the assistance of other Federal agencies, the adequacy of State and local government emergency plans and the capability of the State and local government officials to implement them (e.g., adequacy and maintenance of equipment, procedures, training, resources, staffing levels and qualifications) and report the findings and determinations to NRC.

(g) Review and approve State radiological emergency plans and preparedness in accordance with FEMA procedures in 44 CFR part 350.

(h) Develop, implement and maintain a program of public education and information to support State and local radiological emergency plans and preparedness.

(i) Develop and manage a radiological emergency response training program to meet State and local needs, using technical expertise and resources of other involved agencies. Develop and field test exercise materials and coordinate the Federal assistance required by States and localities in conducting exercises, including guidance for Federal observers.

(j) Develop, with NRC and other Federal Agencies, representative scenarios from which NRC licensed facility operators and State and local governments may select for use in testing and exercising radiological emergency plans.

(k) Issue guidance for establishment of State and local emergency instrumentation systems for radiation detection and measurement.

(l) Provide guidance and assistance, in coordination with NRC and HHS, to State and local governments concerning the storage and distribution of radioprotective substances and prophylactic use of drugs (e.g., potassium iodide) to reduce the radiation dose to specific organs as a result of radiological emergencies.

§351.21 The Nuclear Regulatory Commission.

(a) Assess NRC nuclear facility (e.g., commercial power plants, fuel processing centers and research reactors) licensee emergency plans for adequacy to protect the health and safety of the public.

(b) Verify that nuclear facility licensee emergency plans can be adequately implemented (e.g., adequacy and maintenance of equipment, procedures, training, resources, staffing levels and qualifications).

(c) Review FEMA's findings and determinations of State and local radiological emergency plans for areas surrounding NRC licensed nuclear facilities.

(d) Take into account the overall state of emergency preparedness in making decisions to issue operating licenses or shut down licensed operating reactors, including the integration of assessments of emergency preparedness onsite by the NRC and offsite by FEMA.

(e) Where not already established, determine, in cooperation with other Federal agencies, the appropriate planning bases for NRC licensed nuclear facilities including distances, times and radiological characteristics.

(f) Assist FEMA in developing and promulgating guidance to State and local governments for the preparation of radiological emergency plans.

(g) Participate with FEMA in assisting State and local governments in developing their radiological emergency plans, evaluating exercises to test plans and evaluating the plans and preparedness.

(h) Assist FEMA and DOT in the preparation and promulgation of guidance to State and local governments for their use in developing the transportation portions of radiological emergency plans.

(i) Provide representation to and support for the FRPCC and the RACs.

(j) Assist FEMA in the development, implementation and maintenance of public information and education programs.

(k) Assist FEMA with other Federal agencies in the development of representative scenarios from which nuclear facility operators and State and local governments may select for use in testing and exercising radiological emergency plans.

(l) Assist FEMA in the development of guidance for State and local governments on emergency instrumentation systems for radiation detection and measurement.

(m) Assist FEMA with the development, implementation and presentation to the extent that resources permit of training programs for Federal, State and local radiological emergency preparedness personnel.

(n) Assist FEMA in providing guidance and assistance to State and local governments concerning the storage and distribution of radioprotective substances and prophylactic use of drugs (e.g., potassium iodide) to reduce the radiation dose to specific organs as a result of radiological emergencies.

§351.22 The Environmental Protection Agency.

(a) Establish Protective Action Guides (PAGs) for all aspects of radiological emergency planning in coordination with appropriate Federal agencies.

(b) Prepare guidance for State and local governments on implementing PAGs, including recommendations on protective actions which can be taken to mitigate the potential radiation dose to the population. This guidance will be presented in the Environmental Protection Agency (EPA) "Manual of Protective Action Guides and Protective Actions for Nuclear Incidents." (The preparation of PAGs related to human food and animal feed will be done in coordination with the Department of Health and Human Services (HHS)/Food and Drug Administration.)

(c) Assist FEMA in developing and promulgating guidance to State and local governments for the preparation of radiological emergency plans.

(d) Assist FEMA with the development, implementation and presentation to the extent that resources permit of technical training for State and local officials regarding PAGs and protective actions, radiation dose assessment and decisionmaking.

(e) Participate with FEMA in assisting State and local governments in developing their radiological emergency plans, evaluating exercises to test plans and evaluating the plans and preparedness.

(f) Assist FEMA in the development of guidance for State and local governments on emergency instrumentation systems for radiation detection and measurement.

(g) Provide representation to and support for the FRPCC and the RACs.

(h) Assist FEMA in developing representative scenarios from which nuclear facility operators and State and local governments may select for use in testing and exercising radiological emergency plans.

(i) Assist FEMA in the development, implementation and maintenance of public information and education programs.

§ 351.23 The Department of Health and Human Services.

(a) Develop and specify protective actions and associated guidance to State and local governments for human food and animal feed (in cooperation with the Environmental Protection Agency).

(b) Provide guidance and assistance to State and local governments in preparing programs related to mental health, behavioral disturbances and epidemiology associated with radiological emergencies.

(c) Assist FEMA in the development, implementation and maintenance of public information and education programs to support State and local government radiological emergency plans and preparedness.

(d) Assist FEMA with the development, implementation and presentation to the extent that resources permit of a radiological emergency training program to support State and local government personnel in accident assessment, protective actions and decisionmaking.

(e) Develop and assist in providing the requisite training programs for State and local health, mental health and social service agencies.

(f) Provide guidance to State and local governments on the use of radioprotective substances and prophylactic use of drugs (e.g., potassium iodide) to reduce the radiation dose to specific organs including dosage and projected radiation exposures at which such drugs should be used.

(g) Assist FEMA in developing and promulgating guidance to State and local governments for the preparation of radiological emergency plans.

(h) Participate with FEMA in assisting State and local governments in developing their radiological emergency plans, evaluating exercises to test plans and evaluating the plans and preparedness.

(i) Provide representation to and support for the FRPCC and the RACs.

(j) Assist FEMA in developing representative scenarios from which nuclear facility operators and State and local governments may select for use in testing and exercising radiological emergency plans.

(k) Assist FEMA in the development of guidance for State and local governments on emergency instrumentation systems for radiation detection and measurement.

(l) Assist, in cooperation with the United States Department of Agriculture (USDA), the State and local governments in the planning for the safe production, during radiological emergencies, of human food and animal feed in the emergency planning zones around fixed nuclear facilities.

(m) Assist FEMA, through the Interagency Radiation Research Committee, chaired by the Department of Health and Human Services, in the coordination of Federal research efforts, primarily in areas related to the bioeffects of radiation, applicable to State and local plans and preparedness.

§ 351.24 The Department of Energy.

(a) Determine the appropriate planning bases for the Department of Energy (DOE) owned and contractor operated nuclear facilities (e.g., research and weapon production facilities) including distances, time and radiological characteristics.

(b) Assess DOE nuclear facility emergency plans for adequacy in contributing to the health and safety of the public.

(c) Verify that DOE nuclear facility emergency plans can be adequately implemented (e.g., adequacy and maintenance of equipment, procedures, training, resources, staffing levels and qualifications).

(d) Assist State and local governments, within the constraints of national security and in coordination with FEMA, in the preparation of those portions of their radiological emergency plans related to DOE owned and contractor operated nuclear facilities and radioactive materials in transit.

(e) Review and assess FEMA's findings and determinations on the adequacy of and capability to implement State and local radiological emergency plans for areas surrounding DOE nuclear facilities. Make independent assessments of the overall State of plans and preparedness.

(f) Serve as the lead agency for coordinating the development and issuance of interagency instructions and guidance to implement the Federal Radiological Monitoring and Assessment Plan (FRMAP), which will replace the Interagency Radiological Assistance Plan. The FRMAP provides the framework through which participating Federal agencies will coordinate their emergency radiological monitoring and assessment activities with those of State and local governments.

(g) Develop, maintain and improve capability to detect and assess hazardous levels of radiation.

(h) Assist FEMA in developing and promulgating guidance to State and local governments for the preparation of radiological emergency plans.

(i) Assist FEMA with the development, implementation and presentation to the extent that resources permit of training programs for Federal, State and local radiological emergency response personnel.

(j) Participate with FEMA in assisting State and local governments in developing their radiological emergency plans, evaluating exercises to test plans and evaluating the plans and preparedness.

(k) Develop, with FEMA, representative scenarios from which DOE facility operators and State and local governments may select for use in testing and exercising radiological emergency plans.

(l) Provide representation to and support for the FRPCC and the RACs.

(m) Assist FEMA in the development of guidance for State and local governments on emergency instrumentation systems for radiation detection and measurement.

§ 351.25 The Department of Transportation.

(a) Assist FEMA, along with NRC, in the preparation and promulgation of guidance to State and local governments for their use in developing the transportation portions of radiological emergency plans.

(b) Assist FEMA in its review and approval of State and local radiological emergency plans and in the evaluation of exercises to test such plans.

(c) Provide guidance and materials for use in training emergency services and other response personnel for transportation accidents involving radioactive materials and participate in interagency planning for such training.

(d) Provide representation to and support for the FRPCC and the RACs.

§ 351.26 The United States Department of Agriculture.

(a) Assist FEMA in developing and promulgating guidance to State and local governments for the preparation of radiological emergency plans.

(b) Participate with FEMA in assisting State and local governments in developing their radiological emergency plans, evaluating exercises to test plans and reviewing and evaluating the plans and preparedness.

(c) Assist State and local governments in preparing to implement protective actions in food ingestion pathway emergency planning zones around fixed nuclear facilities.

(d) Develop, in coordination with FEMA, the HHS and other Federal agencies, guidance for assisting State and local governments in the production, processing and distribution of food resources under radiological emergency conditions.

(e) Assist FEMA with the development, implementation and presentation to the extent that resources permit of training programs of Federal,

State and local radiological emergency personnel.

(f) Provide representation to and support for the FRPCC and the RACs.

§ 351.27 The Department of Defense.

(a) Determine appropriate planning bases for Department of Defense (DOD) nuclear facilities and installations (e.g., missile bases, nuclear submarine facilities and weapon storage sites) including distances, time and radiological characteristics.

(b) Develop, with FEMA, representative scenarios from which DOD nuclear facility commanders and State and local governments may select for use in testing and exercising radiological emergency plans.

(c) Assist State and local governments, within the constraints of national security and in coordination with FEMA, in the development, review and assessment of those portions of their radiological emergency plans related to DOD nuclear facilities and assist State officials with planning for response to accidents involving DOD controlled radioactive materials in transit.

(d) Provide representation to and support for the FRPCC and the RACs when appropriate.

§ 351.28 The Department of Commerce.

(a) Assist State and local governments in determining their requirements for meteorological and hydrological services for radiological emergencies and assist State and local governments in preparing to meet these requirements within the limits of available resources.

(b) Assist FEMA in developing and promulgating guidance to State and local governments for the preparation of radiological emergency plans.

(c) Participate with FEMA in assisting State and local governments in developing their radiological emergency plans, evaluating exercises to test plans and evaluating the plans and preparedness.

(d) Assist FEMA with the development, implementation and presentation to the extent that resources permit of technical training for State and local officials in the use of

meterological information in responding to radiological emergencies.

(e) Provide representation to and support for the FRPCC and the RACs.

(f) Assist FEMA in the development of guidance for State and local governments on the exposure and location of emergency instrumentation systems for radiation detection and measurement.

(g) The Federal Coordinator for Meteorological Services and Supporting Research will, consistent with the provisions of the Office of Management and Budget Circular A-62, serve as the coordinating agent for any multi-agency meteorological aspects of assisting State and local governments in their radiological emergency planning and preparedness.

PART 352—COMMERCIAL NUCLEAR POWER PLANTS: EMERGENCY PREPAREDNESS PLANNING

AUTHORITY: Federal Civil Defense Act of 1950, as amended (50 U.S.C. app. 2251 et seq.;)

Robert T. Stafford Disaster Relief and Emergency Assistance Act, 42 U.S.C. 5121 *et seq.*; 31 U.S.C. 9701; Executive Order 12657; Executive Order 12148; Executive Order 12127 and Executive Order 12241.

SOURCE: 54 FR 31925, Aug. 2, 1989, unless otherwise noted.

§ 352.1 Definitions.

As used in this part, the following terms and concepts are defined:

(a) *Deputy Administrator* means the Deputy Administrator, National Preparedness Directorate, FEMA or designee.

(b) *Administrator* means the Administrator, FEMA or designee.

(c) *EPZ* means Emergency Planning Zone.

(d) *FEMA* means the Federal Emergency Management Agency.

(e) *NRC* means the Nuclear Regulatory Commission.

(f) *Regional Administrator* means the Regional Administrator of FEMA or designee.

(g) *Local government* means boroughs, cities, counties, municipalities, parishes, towns, townships or other local jurisdictions within the plume and ingestion exposure pathway EPZs that have specific roles in emergency planning and preparedness.

(h) *Decline or fail* means a situation where State or local governments do not participate in preparing offsite emergency plans or have significant planning or preparedness inadequacies and have not demonstrated the commitment or capabilities to correct those inadequacies in a timely manner so as to satisfy NRC licensing requirements.

(i) *Governor* means the Governor of a State or his/her designee.

(j) *Certification* means the written justification by a licensee of the need for Federal compensatory assistance. This certification is required to activate the Federal assistance under this part.

(k) *Responsible local official* means the highest elected official of an appropriate local government.

(l) *Technical assistance* means services provided by FEMA and other Federal agencies to facilitate offsite radiological emergency planning and preparedness such as: Provision of support for the preparation off site radiological

emergency response plans and procedures; FEMA coordination of services from other Federal agencies; provision and interpretation of Federal guidance; provision of Federal and contract personnel to offer advice and recommendations for specific aspects of preparedness such as alert and notification and emergency public information.

(m) *Federal facilities and resources* means personnel, property (land, buildings, vehicles, equipment), and operational capabilities controlled by the Federal government related to establishing and maintaining radiological emergency response preparedness.

(n) *Licensee* means the utility which has applied for or has received a license from the NRC to operate a commercial nuclear power plant.

(o) *Reimbursement* means the payment to FEMA/Federal agencies, jointly or severally, by a licensee and State and local governments for assistance and services provided in processing certifications and implementing Federal compensatory assistance under this part 352.

(p) *Host FEMA Regional Office* means the FEMA Regional Office that has primary jurisdiction by virtue of the nuclear power plant being located within its geographic boundaries.

(q) *Command and control* means making and issuing protective action decisions and directing offsite emergency response resources, agencies, and activities.

§ 352.2 Scope, purpose and applicability.

(a) This part applies whenever State or local governments, either individually or together, decline or fail to prepare commercial nuclear power plant offsite radiological emergency preparedness plans that are sufficient to satisfy NRC licensing requirements or to participate adequately in the preparation, demonstration, testing, exercise, or use of such plans. In order to request the assistance provided for in this part, an affected nuclear power plant applicant or licensee shall certify in writing to FEMA that the above situation exists.

(b) The purposes of this part are as follows: (1) To establish policies and

591

procedures for the submission of a licensee certification for Federal assistance under Executive Order 12657; (2) set forth policies and procedures for FEMA's determination to accept, accept with modification, or reject the licensee certification; (3) establish a framework for providing Federal assistance to licensees; and (4) provide procedures for the review and evaluation of the adequacy of offsite radiological emergency planning and preparedness. Findings and determinations on offsite planning and preparedness made under this part are provided to the NRC for its use in the licensing process.

(c) This part applies only in instances where Executive Order 12657 is used by a licensee and its provisions do not affect the validity of the emergency preparedness developed by the licensee independent of or prior to Executive Order 12657.

Subpart A—Certifications and Determinations

§ 352.3 Purpose and scope.

This subpart establishes policies and procedures for submission by a commercial nuclear power plant licensee of a certification for Federal assistance under Executive Order 12657. It contains policies and procedures for FEMA's determinations, with respect to a certification. It establishes a framework for providing Federal assistance to licensees. It also provides procedures for review and evaluation of the adequacy of licensee offsite radiological emergency planning and preparedness.

§ 352.4 Licensee certification.

(a) A licensee which seeks Federal assistance under this part shall submit a certification to the host FEMA Regional Administrator that a decline or fail situation exists. The certification shall be in the form of a letter from the chief executive officer of the licensee. The contents of this letter shall address the provisions set forth in paragraphs (b) and (c) of this section.

(b) The licensee certification shall delineate why such assistance is needed based on the criteria of decline or fail for the relevant State or local governments.

(c) The licensee certification shall document requests to and responses from the Governor(s) or responsible local official(s) with respect to the efforts taken by the licensee to secure their participation, cooperation, commitment of resources or timely correction of planning and preparedness failures.

[54 FR 31925, Aug. 2, 1989, as amended at 74 FR 15357, Apr. 3, 2008]

§ 352.5 FEMA action on licensee certification.

(a) Upon receiving a licensee certification, the host Regional Administrator shall immediately notify FEMA Headquarters of the licensee certification. Within 5 days the host Regional Administrator shall notify the Governor of an affected State and the chief executive officer of any local government that a certification has been received, and make a copy of the certification available to such persons. Within 10 days, the host Regional Administrator shall acknowledge in writing the receipt of the certification to the licensee.

(b) Within 15 days of receipt of the certification, the Regional Administrator shall publish a notice in the FEDERAL REGISTER that a certification from the licensee has been received, and that copies are available at the Regional Office for review and copying in accordance with 44 CFR 5.26.

(c) FEMA Headquarters shall notify the NRC of receipt of the certification and shall request advice from the NRC on whether a decline or fail situation exists.

(d) State and local governments may submit written statements to the host Regional Administrator outlining their position as to the facts stated in the letter of certification. Such statements shall be submitted to FEMA within 10 days of the date of notification provided to State and local government under § 352.5(a). Any such statements shall be a part of the record and will be considered in arriving at recommendations or determinations made under the provisions of this part.

(e) The host FEMA Regional Office shall provide, after consulting with

State and responsible local officials, a recommended determination on whether a decline or fail situation exists to the FEMA Deputy Administrator for the National Preparedness Directorate within 30 days of receipt of the licensee certification.

(f) The FEMA Deputy Administrator for the National Preparedness Directorate shall make a determination on whether a decline or fail situation exists within 45 days of receipt of the licensee certification and shall advise the licensee, NRC, and State and local officials.

(g) The times for actions set out above may be extended up to an aggregate of 30 days by the host Regional Administrator or Deputy Administrator for the National Preparedness Directorate, as appropriate.

§ 352.6 FEMA determination on the commitment of Federal facilities and resources.

(a) A licensee request for Federal facilities and resources shall document the licensee's maximum feasible use of its resources and its efforts to secure the use of State and local government and volunteer resources.

(b) Upon a licensee request for Federal facilities and resources, FEMA headquarters shall notify NRC and request advice from the NRC as to whether the licensee has made maximum use of its resources and the extent to which the licensee has complied with 10 CFR 50.47(c)(1). The host FEMA Regional Administratorshall make a recommendation to the FEMA Deputy Administrator for the National Preparedness Directorate on whether the provision of these facilities and resources is warranted. The FEMA Deputy Administrator for the National Preparedness Directorate shall make a final determination as to whether Federal facilities and resources are needed.

(c) In making the determination under paragraph (b) of this section, FEMA:

(1) Shall work actively with the licensee, and before relying upon any Federal resources, shall make maximum feasible use of the licensee's own resources, which may include agreements with volunteer organizations

and other government entities and agencies; and

(2) Shall assume that, in the event of an actual radiological emergency or disaster, State and local authorities would contribute their full resources and exercise their authorities in accordance with their duties to protect the public and would act generally in conformity with the licensee's radiological emergency preparedness plan.

(d) The FEMA Deputy Administrator for the National Preparedness Directorate shall make a determination on the need for and commitment of Federal facilities and resources. The FEMA determination shall be made in consultation with affected Federal agencies and in accordance with 44 CFR 352.21. FEMA shall inform the licensee, the States and affected local governments in writing of the Federal support which will be provided. This information shall identify Federal agencies that are to provide Federal support, the extent and purpose of the support to be provided, the Federal facilities and resources to be committed and the limitations on their use. The provision of the identified Federal support shall be made under the policies and procedures of subpart B of this part.

§ 352.7 Review and evaluation.

FEMA shall conduct its activities and make findings under this part in a manner consistent with 44 CFR part 350 to the extent that those procedures are appropriate and not inconsistent with the intent and procedures required by E.O. 12657. This Order shall take precedence, and any inconsistencies shall be resolved under the procedures in the NRC/FEMA Memorandum of Understanding (MOU) on planning and preparedness. (50 FR 15485, April 18, 1985)

Subpart B—Federal Participation

§ 352.20 Purpose and scope.

This subpart establishes policy and procedures for providing support for offsite radiological emergency planning and preparedness in a situation where Federal support under Executive Order 12657 (E.O. 12657) has been requested. This subpart:

(a) Describes the process for providing Federal technical assistance to the licensee for developing its offsite emergency response plan after an affirmative determination on the licensee certification under subpart A (44 CFR 352.5(f));

(b) Describes the process for providing Federal facilities and resources to the licensee after a determination under subpart A (44 CFR 352.6(d)) that Federal resources are required;

(c) Describes the principal response functions which Federal agencies may be called upon to provide;

(d) Describes the process for allocating responsibilities among Federal agencies for planning site-specific emergency response functions; and

(e) Provides for the participation of Federal agencies, including the members of the FRPCC and the RACs.

§ 352.21 Participating Federal agencies.

(a) FEMA may call upon any Federal agency to participate in planning for the use of Federal facilities and resources in the licensee offsite emergency response plan.

(b) FEMA may call upon the following agencies, and others as needed, to provide Federal technical assistance and Federal facilities and resources:

(1) Department of Commerce;

(2) Department of Defense;

(3) Department of Energy;

(4) Department of Health and Human Services;

(5) Department of Housing and Urban Development;

(6) Department of the Interior;

(7) Department of Transportation;

(8) Environmental Protection Agency;

(9) Federal Communications Commission;

(10) General Services Administration;

(11) National Communications System;

(12) Nuclear Regulatory Commission;

(13) United States Department of Agriculture; and

(14) Department of Veterans Affairs.

(c) FEMA is the Federal agency primarily responsible for coordinating Federal assistance. FEMA may enter into Memorandums of Understanding (MOU) and other instruments with Federal agencies to provide technical assistance and to arrange for the commitment and utilization of Federal facilities and resources as necessary. FEMA also may use a MOU to delegate to another Federal agency, with the consent of that agency, any of the functions and duties assigned to FEMA. Following review and approval by OMB, FEMA will publish such documents in the FEDERAL REGISTER.

§ 352.22 Functions of the Federal Radiological Preparedness Coordinating Committee (FRPCC).

Under 44 CFR part 351, the role of the FRPCC is to assist FEMA in providing policy direction for the program of technical assistance to State and local governments in their radiological emergency planning and preparedness activities. Under this subpart, the role of the FRPCC is to provide advice to FEMA regarding Federal assistance and Federal facilities and resources for implementing subparts A and B of this part. This assistance activity is extended to licensees. The FRPCC will assist FEMA in revising the Federal Radiological Emergency Response Plan (FRERP).

§ 352.23 Functions of a Regional Assistance Committee (RAC).

(a) Under 44 CFR part 351, the role of a RAC is to assist State and local government officials to develop their radiological emergency plans, to review the plans, and to observe exercises to evaluate the plans. Under subparts A and B of this part, these technical assistance activities are extended to the licensee.

(b) Prior to a determination under subpart A (44 CFR 352.6(d)) that Federal facilities and resources are needed, the designated RAC for the specific site will assist the licensee, as necessary, in evaluating the need for Federal facilities and resources, in addition to providing technical assistance under § 352.23(a).

(c) In accomplishing the foregoing, the RAC will use the standards and evaluation criteria in NUREG–0654/ FEMA–REP–1, Rev. 1 and Supp. 1.[1] or approved alternative approaches, and

---

[1] Copy available from FEMA Distribution Center, P.O. Box 70274 Washington, DC 20024

RAC members shall render such technical assistance as appropriate to their agency mission and expertise.

(d) Following determination under subpart A (44 CFR 352.6(d)) that Federal facilities and resources are needed, the RAC will assist FEMA in identifying agencies and specifying the Federal facilities and resources which the agencies are to provide.

§ 352.24 Provision of technical assistance and Federal facilities and resources.

(a) Under a determination under subpart A (44 CFR 352.5(f) and 352.4(e)) that a decline or fail situation exists, FEMA and other Federal agencies will provide technical assistance to the licensee. Such assistance may be provided during the pendency of an appeal under § 352.29.

(b) The applicable criteria for the use of Federal facilities and resources are set forth in subpart A (44 CFR 352.6(c)(1)(2)). Upon a determination under subpart A (44 CFR 352.6(d)) that Federal resources or facilities will be required, FEMA will consult with the FRPCC, the RAC, the individual Federal agencies, and the licensee, to determine the extent of Federal facilities and resources that the government could provide, and the most effective way to do so. After such consultation, FEMA will specifically request Federal agencies to provide those Federal facilities and resources. The Federal agencies, in turn, will respond to confirm the availability of such facilities and resources and provide estimates of their costs.

(c) FEMA will inform the licensee in writing of the Federal support which will be provided. This information will identify Federal agencies which are to be included in the plan, the extent and purpose of technical assistance to be provided and the Federal facilities and resources to be committed, and the limitations of their use. The information will also describe the requirements for reimbursement to the Federal Government for this support.

(d) FEMA will coordinate the Federal effort in implementing the determinations made under subpart A (44 CFR 352.5(f) and 352.6(d)) so that each Federal agency maintains the committed

technical assistance, facilities, and resources after the licensee offsite emergency response plan is completed. FEMA and other Federal agencies will participate in training, exercises, and drills, in support of the licensee offsite emergency response plan.

(e) In carrying out paragraphs (a) through (c) of this section, FEMA will keep affected State and local governments informed of actions taken.

[54 FR 31925, Aug. 2, 1989, as amended at 74 FR 15357, Apr. 3, 2009]

§ 352.25 Limitation on committing Federal facilities and resources for emergency preparedness.

(a) The commitment of Federal facilities and resources will be made through the authority of the affected Federal agencies.

(b) In implementing a determination under subpart A (44 CFR 352.6(d)), that Federal facilities and resources are necessary for emergency preparedness, FEMA shall take care not to supplant State and local resources. Federal facilities and resources shall be substituted for those of the State and local governments in the licensee offsite emergency response plan only to the extent necessary to compensate for the nonparticipation or inadequate participation of those governments, and only as a last resort after consultation with the Governor(s) and responsible local officials in the affected area(s) regarding State and local participation.

(c) All Federal planning activities described in this subpart will be conducted under the assumption that, in the event of an actual radiological emergency or disaster, State and local authorities would contribute their full resources and exercise their authorities in accordance with their duties to protect the public from harm and would act, generally, in conformity with the licensee's offsite emergency response plan.

§ 352.26 Arrangements for Federal response in the licensee offsite emergency response plan.

Federal agencies may be called upon to assist the licensee in developing a licensee offsite emergency response plan in areas such as:

(a) Arrangements for use of Federal facilities and resources for response functions such as:

(1) Prompt notification of the emergency to the public;

(2) Assisting in any necessary evacuation;

(3) Providing reception centers or shelters and related facilities and services for evacuees;

(4) Providing emergency medical services at Federal hospitals; and

(5) Ensuring the creation and maintenance of channels of communication from commercial nuclear power plant licensees to State and local governments and to surrounding members of the public.

(b) Arrangements for transferring response functions to State and local governments during the response in an actual emergency; and

(c) Arrangements which may be necessary for FEMA coordination of the response of other Federal agencies.

§ 352.27 Federal role in the emergency response.

In addition to the Federal component of the licensee offsite emergency response plan described in subpart B (§ 352.26), and after complying with E.O. 12657, Section 2(b)(2), which states that FEMA:

(2) Shall take care not to supplant State and local resources and that FEMA shall substitute its own resources for those of State and local governments only to the extent necessary to compensate for the non-participation or inadequate participation of those governments, and only as a last resort after appropriate consultation with the Governors and responsible local officials in the affected area regarding State and local participation;

FEMA shall provide for initial Federal response activities, including command and control of the offsite response, as may be needed. Any Federal response role, undertaken pursuant to this section, shall be transferred to State and local governments as soon as feasible after the onset of an actual emergency.

§ 352.28 Reimbursement.

In accordance with Executive Order 12657, Section 6(d), and to the extent permitted by law, FEMA will coordinate full reimbursement, either jointly or severally, to the agencies performing services or furnishing resources, from any affected licensee and from any affected nonparticipating or inadequately participating State or local government.

§ 352.29 Appeal process.

(a) Any interested party may appeal a determination made by the Deputy Administrator for the National Preparedness Directorate, under §§ 352.5 and 352.6 of this part, by submitting to the Administrator, FEMA, a written notice of appeal, within 30 days after issuance. The appeal is to be addressed to the Administrator, Federal Emergency Management Agency, 500 C Street SW., Washington, DC 20472. The appeal letter shall state the specific reasons for the appeal and include documentation to support appellant arguments. The appeal is limited to matters of record under §§ 352.5 and 352.6.

(b) Within 30 days of receipt of this letter, the FEMA Administrator or designee will review the record and make a final determination on the matter.

(c) Copies of this determination shall be furnished to the Appellant, the State(s), affected local governments, and the NRC.

(d) For purposes of this section, the term *interested party* means only a licensee, a State or a local government, as defined in § 352.1(g).

PART 353—FEE FOR SERVICES IN SUPPORT, REVIEW AND APPROVAL OF STATE AND LOCAL GOVERNMENT OR LICENSEE RADIOLOGICAL EMERGENCY PLANS AND PREPAREDNESS

Sec.
353.1 Purpose.
353.2 Scope.
353.3 Definitions.
353.4 Payment of fees.
353.5 Average cost per FEMA professional staff-hour.
353.6 Schedule of services.
353.7 Failure to pay.
APPENDIX A TO PART 353—MEMORANDUM OF UNDERSTANDING BETWEEN FEDERAL EMERGENCY MANAGEMENT AGENCY AND NUCLEAR REGULATORY COMMISSION

AUTHORITY: 31 U.S.C. 9701; E.O. 12657 of Nov. 18, 1988; 3 CFR, 1988 Comp., p. 611; 50

U.S.C. app. 2251 note; E.O. 12148 of July 20, 1979; 3 CFR, 1979 Comp., p. 412, 50 U.S.C. app. 2251 note.

SOURCE: 56 FR 9455, March 6, 1991, unless otherwise noted.

§ 353.1 Purpose.

This part sets out fees charged for site-specific radiological emergency planning and preparedness services rendered by the Federal Emergency Management Agency, as authorized by 31 U.S.C. 9701.

§ 353.2 Scope.

The regulation in this part applies to all licensees who have applied for or have received a license from the Nuclear Regulatory Commission to operate a commercial nuclear power plant.

§ 353.3 Definitions.

As used in this part, the following terms and concepts are defined:

(a) *FEMA* means the Federal Emergency Management Agency.

(b) *NRC* means the Nuclear Regulatory Commission.

(c) *Certification* means the written justification by a licensee of the need for Federal compensatory assistance, as authorized in 44 CFR part 352 and E.O. 12657.

(d) *Technical assistance* means services provided by FEMA to facilitate offsite radiological emergency planning and preparedness such as provision of support for the preparation of offsite radiological emergency response plans and procedures; provision of advice and recommendations for specific aspects of preparedness such as alert and notification and emergency public information.

(e) *Licensee* means the utility which has applied for or has received a license from the NRC to operate a commercial nuclear power plant.

(f) *Governor* means the Governor of a State or his/her designee.

(g) *RAC* means Regional Assistance Committee chaired by FEMA with representatives from the Nuclear Regulatory Commission, Environmental Protection Agency, Department of Health and Human Services, Department of Energy, Department of Agriculture, Department of Transportation, Department of Commerce and other

Federal Departments and agencies as appropriate.

(h) *REP* means FEMA's Radiological Emergency Preparedness Program.

(i) *Fiscal Year* means Federal fiscal year commencing on the first day of October through the thirtieth day of September.

(j) *Federal Radiological Preparedness Coordinating Committee* is the national level committee chaired by FEMA with representatives from the Nuclear Regulatory Commission, Environmental Protection Agency, Department of Health and Human Services, Department of Interior, Department of Energy, Department of Transportation, United States Department of Agriculture, Department of Commerce and other Federal Departments and agencies as appropriate.

§ 353.4 Payment of fees.

Fees for site-specific offsite radiological emergency plans and preparedness services and related site-specific legal services are payable upon notification by FEMA. FEMA services will be billed at 6-month intervals for all accumulated costs on a site-specific basis. Each bill will identify the costs related to services for each nuclear power plant site.

§ 353.5 Average cost per FEMA professional staff-hour.

Fees for FEMA services rendered will be calculated based upon the costs for such services using a professional staff rate per hour equivalent to the sum of the average cost to the agency of maintaining a professional staff member performing site-specific services related to the Radiological Emergency Preparedness Program, including salary, benefits, administrative support, travel and overhead. This rate will be charged when FEMA performs such services as: Development of exercise objectives and scenarios, pre-exercise logistics, exercise conduct and participation, evaluation, meetings and reports; review and approval of Plan revisions that are utility-requested or exercise inadequacy related; remedial exercise, medical drill or any other exercise or drill upon which a license is predicated, with regard to preparation, review, conduct, participation, evaluation, meetings and reports; the issuance of interim findings pursuant to the FEMA/NRC Memorandum of Understanding (MOU) (App. A of this part); review of utility plan submissions through the NRC under the MOU; utility certification submission review under 44 CFR part 352 and follow-on activities; site-specific adjudicatory proceedings and any other site-specific legal costs and technical assistance that is utility requested or exercise inadequacy related. The professional staff rate for FY 91 is $39.00 per hour. The referenced FEMA/NRC MOU is provided in this rule as appendix A. The professional staff rate for the REP Program and related legal services will be revised on a fiscal year basis using the most current fiscal data available and the revised hourly rate will be published as a notice in the FEDERAL REGISTER for each fiscal year if the rate increases or decreases.

§ 353.6 Schedule of services.

Recipients shall be charged the full cost of site-specific services based upon the appropriate professional hourly staff rate for the FEMA services described in this Section and for related contractual services which will be charged to the licensee by FEMA, at the rate and cost incurred.

(a) When a State seeks formal review and approval by FEMA of the State's radiological emergency response plan pursuant to 44 CFR part 350 (Review and Approval Process of State and Local Radiological Emergency Plans and Preparedness), FEMA shall provide the services as described in 44 CFR part 350 in regard to that request and fees will be charged for such services to the licensee, which is the ultimate beneficiary of FEMA services. This provision does not apply where an operating license has been granted or the application denied or withdrawn, except as necessary to support biennial exercises and related activities. Fees will be charged for all FEMA, but not other Federal agency activities related to such services, including but not limited to the following:

(1) Development of exercise objectives and scenarios, preexercise logis-

tics, exercise conduct and participation, evaluation, meetings and reports.

(2) Review of plan revisions that are exercise-inadequacy related;

(3) Technical assistance that is exercise-inadequacy related;

(4) Remedial exercise, medical drill, or any other exercise or drill upon which maintenance of a license is predicated, with regard to preparation, review, conduct, participation, evaluation, meetings and reports.

(b) Interim findings. Where the NRC seeks from FEMA under the FEMA/NRC MOU an interim finding of the status of radiological emergency planning and preparedness at a particular time for a nuclear power plant, FEMA shall assess a fee to the licensee for providing this service. The provision of this service consists of making a determination whether the plans are adequate to protect the health and safety of the public living in the vicinity of the nuclear power facility by providing reasonable assurance that appropriate protective measures can be taken offsite in the event of a radiological emergency and that such plans are capable of being implemented.

(c) NRC utility plan submissions. Fees will be charged for all FEMA but not other Federal agency activities related to such services, including but not limited to the following:

(1) Development of exercise objectives and scenarios, preexercise logistics, exercise conduct and participation, evaluation and post-exercise meetings and reports.

(2) Notice and conduct of public meeting.

(3) Regional finding and determination of adequacy of plans and preparedness followed by review by FEMA Headquarters resulting in final FEMA determination of adequacy of plans and preparedness,

(4) Remedial exercise, medical drill, or any other exercise or drill upon which maintenance of a license is predicated, with regard to preparation, review, conduct, participation, evaluation, meetings and reports.

(d) Utility certification submission review. When a licensee seeks Federal assistance within the framework of 44 CFR part 352 due to the decline or failure of a State or local government to adequately prepare an emergency plan, FEMA shall process the licensee's certification and make the determination whether a decline or fail situation exists. Fees will be charged for services rendered in making the determination. Upon the determination that a decline or fail situation does exist, any services provided or secured by FEMA consisting of assistance to the licensee, as described in 44 CFR part 352, will have a fee charged for such services.

(e) FEMA participation in site-specific NRC adjudicatory proceedings and any other site-specific legal costs. Where FEMA participates in NRC licensing proceedings and any related court actions to support FEMA findings as a result of its review and approval of offsite emergency plans and preparedness, or provides legal support for any other site specific FEMA activities comprised in this rule, fees will be charged to the licensee for such participation.

(f) Rendering technical assistance. Where FEMA is requested by a licensee to provide any technical assistance, or where a State or local government requests technical assistance in order to correct an inadequacy identified as a result of a biennial exercise or any other drill or exercise upon which maintenance of a license is predicated, FEMA will charge such assistance to the licensee for the provision of such service.

§ 353.7 Failure to pay.

In any case where there is a dispute over the FEMA bill or where FEMA finds that a licensee has failed to pay a prescribed fee required under this part, procedures will be implemented in accordance with 44 CFR part 11 subpart C to effectuate collections under the Debt Collection Act of 1982 (31 U.S.C. 3711 et seq.).

APPENDIX A TO PART 353—MEMORANDUM OF UNDERSTANDING BETWEEN FEDERAL EMERGENCY MANAGEMENT AGENCY AND NUCLEAR REGULATORY COMMISSION

The Federal Emergency Management Agency (FEMA) and the Nuclear Regulatory Commission (NRC) have entered into a new Memorandum of Understanding (MOU) Relating to Radiological Emergency Planning

and Preparedness. This supersedes a memorandum entered into on November 1, 1980 (published December 16, 1980, 45 FR 82713), revised April 9, 1985 (published April 18, 1985, 50 FR 15485), and published as Appendix A to 44 CFR part 353. The substantive changes in the new MOU are: (1) Self-initiated review by the NRC; (2) Early Site Permit process; (3) adoption of FEMA exercise time-frames; (4) incorporation of FEMA definition of exercise deficiency; (5) NRC commitment to work with licensees in support of State and local governments to correct exercise deficiencies; (6) correlation of FEMA actions on withdrawal of approvals under 44 CFR part 350 and NRC enforcement actions; and (7) disaster-initiated reviews in situations that affect offsite emergency infrastructures. The text of the MOU follows.

MEMORANDUM OF UNDERSTANDING BETWEEN NRC AND FEMA RELATING TO RADIOLOGICAL EMERGENCY PLANNING AND PREPAREDNESS

I. Background and Purposes

This Memorandum of Understanding (MOU) establishes a framework of cooperation between the Federal Emergency Management Agency (FEMA) and the U.S. Nuclear Regulatory Commission (NRC) in radiological emergency response planning matters so that their mutual efforts will be directed toward more effective plans and related preparedness measures at and in the vicinity of nuclear reactors and fuel cycle facilities which are subject to 10 CFR part 50, appendix E, and certain other fuel cycle and materials licensees which have potential for significant accidental offsite radiological releases. The memorandum is responsive to the President's decision of December 7, 1979, that FEMA will take the lead in offsite planning and response, his request that NRC assist FEMA in carrying out this role, and the NRC's continuing statutory responsibility for the radiological health and safety of the public.

On January 14, 1980, the two agencies entered into a "Memorandum of Understanding Between NRC and FEMA to Accomplish a Prompt Improvement in Radiological Emergency Preparedness," that was responsive to the President's December 7, 1979, statement. A revised and updated Memorandum of Understanding became effective November 1, 1980. The MOU was further revised and updated on April 9, 1985. This MOU is a further revision to reflect the evolving relationship between NRC and FEMA and the experience gained in carrying out the provisions of the previous MOU's. This MOU supersedes these two earlier versions of the MOU.

The general principles agreed to in the previous MOU's and reaffirmed in this MOU, are as follows: FEMA coordinates all Federal planning for the offsite impact of radiological emergencies and takes the lead for assessing offsite radiological emergency response plans[1] and preparedness, makes findings and determinations as to the adequacy and capability of implementing offsite plans, and communicates those findings and determinations to the NRC. The NRC reviews those FEMA findings and determinations in conjunction with the NRC onsite findings for the purpose of making determinations on the overall state of emergency preparedness. These overall findings and determinations are used by NRC to make radiological health and safety decisions in the issuance of licenses and the continued operation of licensed plants to include taking enforcement actions as notices of violations, civil penalties, orders, or shutdown of operating reactors. This delineation of responsibilities avoids duplicative efforts by the NRC staff in offsite preparedness matters. However, if FEMA informs the NRC that an emergency, unforeseen contingency, or other reason would prevent FEMA from providing a requested finding in a reasonable time, then, in consultation with FEMA, the NRC might initiate its own review of offsite emergency preparedness.

A separate MOU dated October 22, 1980, deals with NRC/FEMA cooperation and responsibilities in response to an actual or potential radiological emergency. Operations Response Procedures have been developed that implement the provisions of the Incident Response MOU. These documents are intended to be consistent with the Federal Radiological Emergency Response Plan which describes the relationships, roles, and responsibilities of Federal Agencies for responding to accidents involving peacetime nuclear emergencies. On December 1, 1991, the NRC and FEMA also concluded a separate MOU in support of Executive Order 12657 (FEMA Assistance in Emergency Preparedness Planning at Commercial Nuclear Power Plants).

II. Authorities and Responsibilities

FEMA-Executive Order 12148 charges the Director, FEMA, with the responsibility to "* * * establish Federal policies for, and coordinate, all civil defense and civil emergency planning, management, mitigation, and assistance functions of Executive agencies" (Section 2–101) and "* * * represent the President in working with State and local governments and the private sector to stimulate vigorous participation in civil emergency preparedness, mitigation, response, and recovery programs" (Section 2–104.).

On December 7, 1979, the President, in response to the recommendations of the Kemeny Commission on the Accident at Three Mile Island, directed that FEMA assume lead responsibility for all offsite nuclear emergency planning and response.

Specifically, the FEMA responsibilities with respect to radiological emergency preparedness as they relate to NRC are:

1. To take the lead in offsite emergency planning and to review and assess offsite emergency plans and preparedness for adequacy.

2. To make findings and determinations as to whether offsite emergency plans are adequate and can be implemented (e.g., adequacy and maintenance of procedures, training, resources, staffing levels and qualifications, and equipment). Notwithstanding the procedures which are set forth in 44 CFR part 350 for requesting and reaching a FEMA administrative approval of State and local plans, findings, and determinations on the current status of emergency planning and preparedness around particular sites, referred to as interim findings, will be provided by FEMA for use as needed in the NRC licensing process. Such findings will be provided by FEMA on mutually agreed to schedules or on specific NRC request. The request and findings will normally be by written communications between the co-chairs of the NRC/FEMA Steering Committee. An interim finding provided under this arrangement will be an extension of FEMA's procedures for review and approval of offsite radiological emergency plans and preparedness set forth in 44 CFR part 350. It will be based on the review of currently available plans and, if appropriate, joint exercise results related to a specific nuclear power plant site.

If the review involves an application under 10 CFR part 52 for an early site permit, the NRC will forward to FEMA pertinent information provided by the applicant and consult with FEMA as to whether there is any significant impediment to the development of offsite emergency plans. As appropriate, depending upon the nature of information provided by the applicant, the NRC will also request that FEMA determine whether major features of offsite emergency plans submitted by the applicant are acceptable, or whether offsite emergency plans submitted by the applicant are adequate, as discussed below.

An interim finding based only on the review of currently available offsite plans will include an assessment as to whether these plans are adequate when measured against the standards and criteria of NUREG–0654/FEMA–REP–1, and, pending a demonstration

---

[1] Assessments of offsite plans may be based on State and local government plans submitted to FEMA under its rule (44 CFR Part 350), and as noted in 44 CFR 350.3(f), may also be based on plans currently available to FEMA or furnished to FEMA through the NRC/FEMA Steering Committee.

through an exercise, whether there is reasonable assurance that the plans can be implemented. The finding will indicate one of the following conditions: (1) Plans are adequate and there is reasonable assurance that they can be implemented with only limited or no corrections needed; (2) plans are adequate, but before a determination can be made as to whether they can be implemented, corrections must be made to the plans or supporting measures must be demonstrated (e.g., adequacy and maintenance of procedures, training, resources, staffing levels and qualifications, and equipment) or (3) plans are inadequate and cannot be implemented until they are revised to correct deficiencies noted in the Federal review.

If, in FEMA's view, the plans that are available are not completed or are not ready for review, FEMA will provide NRC with a status report delineating milestones for preparation of the plan by the offsite authorities as well as FEMA's actions to assist in timely development and review of the plans.

An interim finding on preparedness will be based on review of currently available plans and joint exercise results and will include an assessment as to (1) whether offsite emergency plans are adequate as measured against the standards and criteria of NUREG–0654/FEMA–REP–1 and (2) whether the exercise(s) demonstrated that there is reasonable assurance that the plans can be implemented.

An interim finding on preparedness will indicate one of the following conditions: (1) There is reasonable assurance that the plans are adequate and can be implemented as demonstrated in an exercise; (2) there are deficiencies that must be corrected; or (3) FEMA is undecided and will provide a schedule of actions leading to a decision.

3. To assume responsibility, as a supplement to State, local, and utility efforts, for radiological emergency preparedness training of State and local officials.

4. To develop and issue an updated series of interagency assignments which delineate respective agency capabilities and responsibilities and define procedures for coordination and direction for emergency planning and response. [Current assignments are in 44 CFR part 351, March 11, 1982. (47 FR 10758)]

NRC-The Atomic Energy Act of 1954, as amended, requires that the NRC grant licenses only if the health and safety of the public is adequately protected. While the Atomic Energy Act does not specifically require emergency plans and related preparedness measures, the NRC requires consideration of overall emergency preparedness as a part of the licensing process. The NRC rules (10 CFR 50.33, 50.34, 50.47, 50.54, and appendix E to 10 CFR part 50, and 10 CFR part 52) include requirements for the licensee's emergency plans.

Specifically, the NRC responsibilities for radiological emergency preparedness are:

1. To assess licensee emergency plans for adequacy. This review will include organizations with whom licensees have written agreements to provide onsite support services under emergency conditions.

2. To verify that licensee emergency plans are adequately implemented (e.g., adequacy and maintenance of procedures, training, resources, staffing levels and qualifications, and equipment).

3. To review the FEMA findings and determinations as to whether offsite plans are adequate and can be implemented.

4. To make radiological health and safety decisions with regard to the overall state of emergency preparedness (i.e., integration of emergency preparedness onsite as determined by the NRC and offsite as determined by FEMA and reviewed by NRC) such as assurance for continued operation, for issuance of operating licenses, or for taking enforcement actions, such as notices of violations, civil penalties, orders, or shutdown of operating reactors.

III. Areas of Cooperation

A. NRC Licensing Reviews

FEMA will provide support to the NRC for licensing reviews related to reactors, fuel facilities, and materials licensees with regard to the assessment of the adequacy of offsite radiological emergency response plans and preparedness. This will include timely submittal of an evaluation suitable for inclusion in NRC safety evaluation reports.

Substantially prior to the time that a FEMA evaluation is required with regard to fuel facility or materials license review, NRC will identify those fuel and materials licensees with potential for significant accidental offsite radiological releases and transmit a request for review to FEMA as the emergency plans are completed.

FEMA routine support will include providing assessments, findings and determinations (interim and final) on offsite plans and preparedness related to reactor license reviews. To support its findings and determinations, FEMA will make expert witnesses available before the Commission, the NRC Advisory Committee on Reactor Safeguards, NRC hearing boards and administrative law judges, for any court actions, and during any related discovery proceedings.

FEMA will appear in NRC licensing proceedings as part of the presentation of the NRC staff. FEMA counsel will normally present FEMA witnesses and be permitted, at the discretion of the NRC licensing board, to cross-examine the witnesses of parties other than the NRC witnesses, on matters involving FEMA findings and determinations, policies, or operations; however, FEMA will not be asked to testify on status reports.

FEMA is not a party to NRC proceedings and, therefore, is not subject to formal discovery requirements placed upon parties to NRC proceedings. Consistent with available resources, however, FEMA will respond informally to discovery requests by parties. Specific assignment of professional responsibilities between NRC and FEMA counsel will be primarily the responsibility of the attorneys assigned to a particular case. In situations where questions of professional responsibility cannot be resolved by the attorneys assigned, resolution of any differences will be made by the General Counsel of FEMA and the General Counsel of the NRC or their designees. NRC will request the presiding Board to place FEMA on the service list for all litigation in which it is expected to participate.

Nothing in this MOU shall be construed in any way to diminish NRC's responsibility for protecting the radiological health and safety of the public.

B. FEMA Review of Offsite Plans and Preparedness

NRC will assist in the development and review of offsite plans and preparedness through its membership on the Regional Assistance Committees (RAC). FEMA will chair the Regional Assistance Committees. Consistent with NRC's statutory responsibility, NRC will recognize FEMA as the interface with State and local governments for interpreting offsite radiological emergency planning and preparedness criteria as they affect those governments and for reporting to those governments the results of any evaluation of their radiological emergency plans and preparedness.

Where questions arise concerning the interpretation of the criteria, such questions will continue to be referred to FEMA Headquarters, and when appropriate, to the NRC/FEMA Steering Committee to assure uniform interpretation.

C. Preparation for and Evaluation of Joint Exercises

FEMA and NRC will cooperate in determining exercise requirements for licensees, and State and local governments. They will also jointly observe and evaluate exercises. NRC and FEMA will institute procedures to enhance the review of objectives and scenarios for joint exercises. This review is to assure that both the onsite considerations of NRC and the offsite considerations of FEMA are adequately addressed and integrated in a manner that will provide for a technically sound exercise upon which an assessment of preparedness capabilities can be based. The NRC/FEMA procedures will provide for the availability of exercise objectives and scenarios sufficiently in advance of scheduled exercises to allow enough time for adequate review by NRC and FEMA and correction of any deficiencies by the licensee. The failure of a licensee to develop a scenario that adequately addresses both onsite and offsite considerations may result in NRC taking enforcement actions.

The FEMA reports will be a part of an interim finding on emergency preparedness; or will be the result of an exercise conducted pursuant to FEMA's review and approval procedures under 44 CFR part 350 and NRC's requirement under 10 CFR part 50, appendix E, Section IV.F. Exercise evaluations will identify one of the following conditions: (1) There is reasonable assurance that the plans are adequate and can be implemented as demonstrated in the exercise; (2) there are deficiencies that must be corrected; or (3) FEMA is undecided and will provide a schedule of actions leading to a decision. The schedule for issuance of the draft and final exercise reports will be as shown in FEMA-REP–14 (Radiological Emergency Preparedness Exercise Manual).

The deficiency referred to in (2) above is defined as an observed or identified inadequacy of organizational performance in an exercise that could cause a finding that offsite emergency preparedness is not adequate to provide reasonable assurance that appropriate protective measures can be taken in the event of a radiological emergency to protect the health and safety of the public living in the vicinity of a nuclear power plant. Because of the potential impact of deficiencies on emergency preparedness, they should be corrected within 120 days through appropriate remedial actions, including remedial exercises, drills, or other actions.

Where there are deficiencies of the types noted above, and when there is a potential for remedial actions, FEMA Headquarters will promptly (1–2 days) discuss these with NRC Headquarters. Within 10 days of the exercise, official notification of identified deficiencies will be made by FEMA to the State, NRC Headquarters, and the RAC with an information copy to the licensee. NRC will formally notify the licensee of the deficiencies and monitor the licensee's efforts to work with State and local authorities to correct the deficiencies. Approximately 60 days after official notification of the deficiency, the NRC, in consultation with FEMA, will assess the progress being made toward resolution of the deficiencies.

D. Withdrawal of Reasonable Assurance Finding

If FEMA determines under 44 CFR 350.13 of its regulations that offsite emergency plans or preparedness are not adequate to provide reasonable assurance that appropriate protective measures can be taken in the event of radiological emergency to protect the health and safety of the public, FEMA shall, as described in its rule, withdraw approval.

Federal Emergency Management Agency, DHS

Pt. 353, App. A

Upon receiving notification of such action from FEMA, the NRC will promptly review FEMA's findings and determinations and formally document the NRC's position. When, as described in 10 CFR 50.54(s)(2)(ii) and 50.54(s)(3) of its regulations, the NRC finds the state of emergency preparedness does not provide reasonable assurance that adequate protective measures can and will be taken in the event of a radiological emergency, the NRC will notify the affected licensee accordingly and start the "120-day clock."[2]

E. Emergency Planning and Preparedness Guidance

NRC has lead responsibility for the development of emergency planning and preparedness guidance for licensees. FEMA has lead responsibility for the development of radiological emergency planning and preparedness guidance for State and local agencies. NRC and FEMA recognize the need for an integrated, coordinated approach to radiological emergency planning and preparedness by NRC licensees and State and local governments. NRC and FEMA will each, therefore, provide opportunity for the other agency to review and comment on such guidance (including interpretations of agreed joint guidance) prior to adoption as formal agency guidance.

F. Support for Document Management System

FEMA and NRC will each provide the other with continued access to those automatic data processing support systems which contain relevant emergency preparedness data.

G. Ongoing NRC Research and Development Programs

Ongoing NRC and FEMA research and development programs that are related to State and local radiological emergency planning and preparedness will be coordinated. NRC and FEMA will each provide opportunity for the other agency to review and comment on relevant research and development programs prior to implementing them.

---

[2] Per 10 CFR 50.54(s)(2)(ii), the Commission will determine whether the reactor shall be shut down or other appropriate enforcement actions if such conditions are not corrected within four months. The NRC is not limited by this provision of the rule, for, as stated in 10 CFR 50.54(s)(3), "Nothing in this paragraph shall be construed as limiting the authority of the Commission to take action under any other regulation or authority of the Commission *or at any time other than that specified in this paragraph*" (emphasis added).

H. Public Information and Education Programs

FEMA will take the lead in developing public information and educational programs. NRC will assist FEMA by reviewing for accuracy educational materials concerning radiation, and its hazards and information regarding appropriate actions to be taken by the general public in the event of an accident involving radioactive materials.

I. Recovery from Disasters Affecting Offsite Emergency Preparedness

Disasters that destroy roads, buildings, communications, transportation resources or other offsite infrastructure in the vicinity of a nuclear power plant can degrade the capabilities of offsite response organizations in the 10-mile plume emergency planning zone. Examples of events that could cause such devastation are hurricanes, tornadoes, earthquakes, tsunamis, volcanic eruptions, major fires, large explosions, and riots.

If a disaster damages the area around a licensed operating nuclear power plant to an extent that FEMA seriously questions the continued adequacy of offsite emergency preparedness, FEMA will inform the NRC promptly. Likewise, the NRC will inform FEMA promptly of any information it receives from licensees, its inspectors, or others, that raises serious questions about the continued adequacy of offsite emergency preparedness. If FEMA concludes that a disaster-initiated review of offsite radiological emergency preparedness is necessary to determine if offsite emergency preparedness is still adequate, it will inform the NRC in writing, as soon as practicable, including a schedule for conduct of the review. FEMA will also give the NRC (1) interim written reports of its findings, as appropriate, and (2) a final written report on the results of its review.

The disaster-initiated review is performed to reaffirm the radiological emergency preparedness capabilities of affected offsite jurisdictions located in the 10-mile emergency planning zone and is not intended to be a comprehensive review of offsite plans and preparedness.

The NRC will consider information provided by FEMA Headquarters and pertinent findings from FEMA's disaster-initiated review in making decisions regarding the restart or continued operation of an affected operating nuclear power reactor. The NRC will notify FEMA Headquarters, in writing, of the schedule for restart of an affected reactor and keep FEMA Headquarters informed of changes in that schedule.

IV. NRC/FEMA Steering Committee

The NRC/FEMA Steering Committee on Emergency Preparedness will continue to be

603

the focal point for coordination of emergency planning and preparedness. As discussed in Section I of this agreement, response activities between these two agencies are addressed in a separate MOU. The Steering Committee will consist of an equal number of members to represent each agency with one vote per agency. When the Steering Committee cannot agree on the resolution of an issue, the issue will be referred to NRC and FEMA management. The NRC members will have lead responsibility for licensee planning and preparedness and the FEMA members will have lead responsibility for offsite.planning and preparedness. The Steering Committee will assure coordination of plans and preparedness evaluation activities and revise, as necessary, acceptance criteria for licensee, State and local radiological emergency planning and preparedness. NRC and FEMA will then consider and adopt criteria, as appropriate, in their respective jurisdictions. (See Attachment 1).

V. Working Arrangements

A. The normal point of contact for implementation of the points in this MOU will be the NRC/FEMA Steering Committee.

B. The Steering Committee will establish the day-to-day procedures for assuring that the arrangements of this MOU are carried out.

VI. Memorandum of Understanding

A. This MOU shall be effective as of date of signature and shall continue in effect unless terminated by either party upon 30 days notice in writing.

B. Amendments or modifications to this MOU may be made upon written agreement by both parties.

Approved for the U.S. Nuclear Regulatory Commission.

Dated: June 17, 1993.

James M. Taylor,

Executive Director for Operations.

Dated: June 17, 1993.

Approved for the Federal Emergency Management Agency.

Richard W. Krimm,

Acting Associate Director, State and Local Programs and Support.

ATTACHMENT 1—FEMA/NRC STEERING COMMITTEE

Purpose

Assure coordination of efforts to maintain and improve emergency planning and preparedness for nuclear power reactors as described in the NRC and FEMA rules and the NRC/FEMA MOU on Radiological Emergency Planning and Preparedness. Coordinate consistent criteria for licensee, State and local emergency plans and preparedness.

Membership

The NRC and FEMA consignees of this MOU will designate respective co-chairs for the Steering Committee. The designated co-chairs will, in turn, appoint their respective members to the Committee.

Membership Changes

Changes to the membership of the NRC/FEMA Steering Committee may be made by the co-chairs representing the agency whose member is being changed.

Operating Procedures

The Steering Committee will maintain a record of each meeting to include identification of issues discussed and conclusions reached. No meeting will be held without the attendance and participation of at least the co-chairs or two assigned members of each agency.

Coordination

When items involving responsibilities of other NRC or FEMA offices are discussed, the affected offices will be contacted as appropriate.

[58 FR 47997, Sept. 14, 1993]

PART 354—FEE FOR SERVICES TO SUPPORT FEMA'S OFFSITE RADIOLOGICAL EMERGENCY PREPAREDNESS PROGRAM

AUTHORITY: Reorganization Plan No. 3 of 1978, 43 FR 41943, 3 CFR, 1978 Comp., p. 329; Sec. 109, Pub. L. 96–295, 94 Stat. 780; Sec. 2901, Pub. L. 98–369, 98 Stat. 494; Title III, Pub. L. 103–327, 108 Stat. 2323–2325; Pub. L. 105–276, 112 Stat. 2502; EO 12148, 44 FR 43239, 3 CFR, 1979 Comp., p. 412; EO 12657, 53 FR 47513, 3 CFR, 1988 Comp., p. 611.

SOURCE: 66 FR 32577, June 15, 2001, unless otherwise noted.

§ 354.1   Purpose.

This part establishes the methodology for FEMA to assess and collect user fees from Nuclear Regulatory

Commission (NRC) licensees of commercial nuclear power plants to recover at least 100 percent of the amounts that we anticipate to obligate for our Radiological Emergency Preparedness (REP) Program as authorized under Title III, Public Law 105–276, 112 Stat. 2461, 2502. Public Law 105–276 established in the Treasury a Radiological Emergency Preparedness Fund, to be available under the Atomic Energy Act of 1954, as amended (42 U.S.C. 2011 et. seq.), and under Executive Order 12657 (3 CFR, 1988 Comp., p. 611), for offsite radiological emergency planning, preparedness, and response. Beginning in fiscal year 1999 and thereafter, the Administrator of FEMA must publish fees to be assessed and collected, applicable to persons subject to FEMA's radiological emergency preparedness regulations. The methodology for assessment and collection of fees must be fair and equitable and must reflect the full amount of costs of providing radiological emergency planning, preparedness, response and associated services. Our assessment of fees include our costs for use of agency resources for classes of regulated persons and our administrative costs to collect the fees. Licensees deposit fees by electronic transfer into the Radiological Emergency Preparedness Fund in the U.S. Treasury as offsetting collections.

§ 354.2 Scope of this regulation.

The regulation in this part applies to all persons or licensees who have applied for or have received from the NRC:

(a) A license to construct or operate a commercial nuclear power plant;

(b) A possession-only license for a commercial nuclear power plant, with the exception of licensees that have received an NRC-approved exemption to 10 CFR 50.54(q) requirements;

(c) An early site permit for a commercial nuclear power plant;

(d) A combined construction permit and operating license for a commercial nuclear power plant; or

(e) Any other NRC licensee that is now or may become subject to requirements for offsite radiological emergency planning and preparedness.

§ 354.3 Definitions.

The following definitions of terms and concepts apply to this part:

Biennial exercise means the joint licensee/State and local government exercise, evaluated by FEMA, conducted around a commercial nuclear power plant site once every two years in conformance with 44 CFR part 350.

EPZ means emergency planning zone.

Federal Radiological Preparedness Coordinating Committee (FRPCC) means a committee chaired by FEMA with representatives from the Nuclear Regulatory Commission, Environmental Protection Agency, Department of Health and Human Services, Department of Interior, Department of Energy, Department of Transportation, Department of Agriculture, Department of Commerce, Department of State, Department of Veterans Affairs, General Services Administration, National Communications System, the National Aeronautics and Space Administration and other Federal departments and agencies as appropriate.

FEMA means the Federal Emergency Management Agency.

Fiscal Year means the Federal fiscal year, which begins on the first day of October and ends on the thirtieth day of September.

NRC means the U. S. Nuclear Regulatory Commission.

Obligate or *obligation* means a legal reservation of appropriated funds for expenditure.

Persons or *Licensee* means the utility or organization that has applied for or has received from the NRC:

(1) A license to construct or operate a commercial nuclear power plant;

(2) A possession-only license for a commercial nuclear power plant, with the exception of licensees that have received an NRC-approved exemption to 10 CFR 50.54(q) requirements;

(3) An early site permit for a commercial nuclear power plant;

(4) A combined construction permit and operating license for a commercial nuclear power plant; or

(5) Any other NRC license that is now or may become subject to requirements for offsite radiological emergency planning and preparedness activities.

Plume pathway EPZ means for planning purposes, the area within approximately a 10-mile radius of a nuclear plant site.

RAC means Regional Assistance Committee chaired by FEMA with representatives from the Nuclear Regulatory Commission, Environmental Protection Agency, Department of Health and Human Services, Department of Energy, Department of Agriculture, Department of Transportation, Department of Commerce, Department of Interior, and other Federal departments and agencies as appropriate.

REP means Radiological Emergency Preparedness, as in FEMA's REP Program.

Site means the location at which one or more commercial nuclear power plants (reactor units) have been, or are planned to be built.

Site-specific services mean offsite radiological emergency planning, preparedness and response services provided by FEMA personnel and by FEMA contractors that pertain to a specific commercial nuclear power plant site.

Technical assistance means services provided by FEMA to accomplish offsite radiological emergency planning, preparedness and response, including provision of support for the preparation of offsite radiological emergency response plans and procedures, and provision of advice and recommendations for specific aspects of radiological emergency planning, preparedness and response, such as alert and notification and emergency public information.

We, our, us, means and refers to FEMA.

§ 354.4 Assessment of fees.

(a)(1) We assess user fees from licensees using a methodology that includes charges for REP Program services provided by both our personnel and our contractors. Beginning in FY 1995, established a four-year cycle from FY 1995–1998 with predetermined user fee assessments that were collected each year of the cycle. The following six-year cycle will run from FY 1999 through FY 2004. The fee for each site consists of two distinct components:

(i) A *site-specific, biennial exercise-related component* to recover the portion of the REP program budget associated only with plume pathway emergency planning zone (EPZ) biennial exercise-related activities. We determine this component by reviewing average biennial exercise-related activities/hours that we use in exercises conducted since the inception of our REP user fee program in 1991. We completed an analysis of REP Program activities/hours used during the FY 1991–1995 cycle at the end of that four-year cycle. We will make adjustments to the site-specific user fees for the next proposed FY 1999–2004 six-year cycle.

(ii) A *flat fee component* that is the same for each site and recovers the remaining portion of the REP Program budgeted funding that does not include biennial exercise-related activities.

(2) We will assess fees only for REP Program services provided by our personnel and by our contractors, and we will not assess fees for those services that other Federal agencies involved in the FRPCC or the RAC's provide.

(b) *Determination of site-specific, biennial exercise-related component for our personnel.* We will determine an average biennial exercise-related cost for our personnel for each commercial nuclear power plant site in the REP Program. We base this annualized cost (dividing the average biennial exercise-related cost by two) on the average number of hours spent by our personnel in REP exercise-related activities for each site. We will determine the average number of hours using an analysis of site-specific exercise activity spent since the beginning of our user fee program (1991). We determine the actual user fee assessment for this component by multiplying the average number of REP exercise-related hours that we determine and annualize for each site by the average hourly rate in effect for the fiscal year for a REP Program employee. We will revise the hourly rate annually to reflect actual budget and cost of living factors, but the number of annualized, site-specific exercise hours will remain constant for user fee calculations and assessments throughout the six-year cycle. We will continue to track and monitor exercise activity during the six-year cycle, FY

1999–2004. We will make appropriate adjustments to this component to calculate user fee assessments for later six-year cycles.

(c) *Determination of site-specific, biennial exercise-related component for FEMA contract personnel.* We have determined an average biennial exercise-related cost for REP contractors for each commercial nuclear power plant site in the REP Program. We base this annualized cost (dividing the average biennial exercise-related cost by two) on the average costs of contract personnel in REP site-specific exercise-related activities since the beginning of our user fee program (1991). We will continue to track and monitor activity during the initial six-year cycle, FY 1999–2004, and we will make appropriate adjustments to this component for calculation of user fee assessments during subsequent six-year cycles.

(d) *Determination of flat fee component.* For each year of the six-year cycle, we recover the remainder of REP Program budgeted funds as a flat fee component. Specifically, we determine the flat fee component by subtracting the total of our personnel and contractor site-specific, biennial exercise-related components, as outlined in paragraphs (a) and (b) of this section, from the total REP budget for that fiscal year. We then divide the resulting amount equally among the total number of licensed commercial nuclear power plant sites (defined under 354.2) to arrive at each site's flat fee component for that fiscal year.

(e) *Discontinuation of charges.* When we receive a copy from the NRC of their approved exemption to 10 CFR 50.54(q) requirements stating that offsite radiological emergency planning and preparedness are no longer required at a particular commercial nuclear power plant site, we will discontinue REP Program services at that site. We will no longer assess a user fee for that site from the beginning of the next fiscal year.

§ 354.5 Description of site-specific, plume pathway EPZ biennial exercise-related component services and other services.

Site-specific and other REP Program services provided by FEMA and FEMA contractors for which FEMA will assess fees on licensees include the following:

(a) *Site-specific, plume pathway EPZ biennial exercise-related component services.* (1) Schedule plume pathway EPZ biennial exercises.

(2) Review plume pathway EPZ biennial exercise objectives and scenarios.

(3) Provide pre-plume pathway EPZ biennial exercise logistics.

(4) Conduct plume pathway EPZ biennial exercises, evaluations, and post exercise briefings.

(5) Prepare, review and finalize plume pathway EPZ biennial exercise reports, give notice and conduct public meetings.

(6) Activities related to Medical Services and other drills conducted in support of a biennial, plume pathway exercise.

(b) *Flat fee component services.* (1) Evaluate State and local offsite radiological emergency plans and preparedness.

(2) Schedule other than plume pathway EPZ biennial exercises.

(3) Develop other than plume pathway EPZ biennial exercise objectives and scenarios.

(4) Pre-exercise logistics for other than the plume pathway EPZ.

(5) Conduct other than plume pathway EPZ biennial exercises and evaluations.

(6) Prepare, review and finalize other than plume pathway EPZ biennial exercise reports, notice and conduct of public meetings.

(7) Prepare findings and determinations on the adequacy or approval of plans and preparedness.

(8) Conduct the formal 44 CFR part 350 review process.

(9) Provide technical assistance to States and local governments.

(10) Review licensee submissions pursuant to 44 CFR part 352.

(11) Review NRC licensee offsite plan submissions under the NRC/FEMA Memorandum of Understanding on Planning and Preparedness, and NUREG–0654/FEMA–REP–1, Revision 1, Supplement 1. You may obtain copies of the NUREG–0654 from the Superintendent of Documents, U.S. Government Printing Office.

(12) Participate in NRC adjudication proceedings and any other site-specific legal forums.

(13) Alert and notification system reviews.

(14) Responses to petitions filed under 10 CFR 2.206.

(15) Congressionally-initiated reviews and evaluations.

(16) Responses to licensee's challenges to FEMA's administration of the fee program.

(17) Respond to actual radiological emergencies.

(18) Develop regulations, guidance, planning standards and policy.

(19) Coordinate with other Federal agencies to enhance the preparedness of State and local governments for radiological emergencies.

(20) Coordinate REP Program issues with constituent organizations such as the National Emergency Management Association, Conference of Radiation Control Program Directors, and the Nuclear Energy Institute.

(21) Implement and coordinate REP Program training with FEMA's Emergency Management Institute (EMI) to assure effective development and implementation of REP training courses and conferences.

(22) Participation of REP personnel as lecturers or to perform other functions at EMI, conferences and workshops.

(23) Any other costs that we incur resulting from our REP Program Strategic Review implementation and oversight working group activities.

(24) Costs associated with a transition phase should we decide to advertise and award a contract for technical support to the REP Program. Transition phase activities may include training new contractor personnel in the REP Exercise Evaluation and Planning courses, and on-the-job training for new evaluators at a select number of REP exercises.

(25) Services associated with the assessment of fees, billing, and administration of this part.

(26) Disaster-initiated reviews and evaluations.

§ 354.6 Billing and payment of fees.

(a) *Electronic billing and payment.* We will deposit all funds collected under this part to the Radiological Emergency Preparedness Fund as offsetting collections, which will be available for our REP Program. The Department of the Treasury revisions to section 8025.30 of publication I–TFM 6–8000 require Federal agencies to collect funds by electronic funds transfer when such collection is cost-effective, practicable, and consistent with current statutory authority. Working with the Department of the Treasury we now provide for payment of bills by electronic transfers through Automated Clearing House (ACH) credit payments.

(b) We will send bills that are based on the assessment methodology set out in § 354.4 to licensees to recover the full amount of the funds that we budget to provide REP Program services. Licensees that have more than one site will receive consolidated bills. We will forward one bill to each licensee during the first quarter of the fiscal year, with payment due within 30 days. If we exceed our original budget for the fiscal year and need to make minor adjustments, the adjustment will appear in the bill for the next fiscal year.

§ 354.7 Failure to pay.

Where a licensee fails to pay a prescribed fee required under this part, we will implement procedures under 44 CFR part 11, subpart C, to collect the fees under the Debt Collection Act of 1982 (31 U.S.C. 3711 *et seq.*).

PARTS 355–359 [RESERVED]

PART 360—STATE ASSISTANCE PROGRAMS FOR TRAINING AND EDUCATION IN COMPREHENSIVE EMERGENCY MANAGEMENT

AUTHORITY: Reorganization Plan No. 3 (3 CFR, 1978 Comp., p. 329); E.O. 12127 (44 FR 19367); E.O. 12148 (44 FR 43239).

SOURCE: 46 FR 1271, Jan. 6, 1981, unless otherwise noted.

§ 360.1 Purpose.

The Emergency Management Training Program is designed to enhance the States' emergency management training program to increase State capabilities and those of local governments in this field, as well as to give States the opportunity to develop new capabilities and techniques. The Program is an ongoing intergovernmental endeavor which combines financial and human resources to fill the unique training needs of local government, State emergency staffs and State agencies, as well as the general public. States will have the opportunity to develop, implement and evaluate various approaches to accomplish FEMA emergency objectives as well as goals and objectives of their own. The intended result is an enhanced capability to protect lives and property through planning, mitigation, operational skill, and rapid response in case of disaster or attack on this country.

§ 360.2 Description of program.

(a) The program is designed for all States regardless of their present level of involvement in training or their degree of expertise in originating and presenting training courses in the past. The needs of individual States, difference in numbers to be trained, and levels of sophistication in any previous training program have been recognized. It is thus believed that all States are best able to meet their own unique situations and those of local government by being given this opportunity and flexibility.

(b) Each State is asked to submit an acceptable application, to be accompanied by a Training and Education (T&E) plan for a total of three years, only the first year of which will be required to be detailed. The remaining two year program should be presented in terms of ongoing training objectives and programs. In the first year plan applicants shall delineate their objectives in training and education, including a description of the programs to be offered, and identify the audiences and numbers to be trained. Additionally, the State is asked to note the month in which the activity is to be presented, the location, and cost estimates including instructional costs and partici-

pant's travel and per diem. These specifics of date, place, and costs will be required for the first year of any three year plan. A three year plan will be submitted each year with an application. Each negotiated agreement will include a section of required training (Radiological Defense), and a section including optional courses to be conducted in response to State and local needs.

(c) FEMA support to the States in their training program for State and local officials, has been designed around three Program elements. Each activity listed in the State Training and Education (T&E) Plan will be derived from the following three elements:

(1) *Government Conducted Courses:* Such courses require the least capability on the part of the State. They are usually conducted through provisions in a FEMA Regional Support Contract and/or FEMA or other Federal agency staff. The State's responsibilities fall primarily into administrative areas of recruiting participants, making all arrangements for the facilities needed for presentation of the course, and the handling of the cost reimbursement to participants, though State staff may participate as instructors. These courses for example include:

(i) Career Development Courses: Phases I, II, and III,

(ii) Radiological Officer and Instructor Courses,

(iii) Technical Workshops on Disaster Recovery or Hazard Mitigation.

(2) *Government and recipient conducted courses:* Responsibilities in these courses fall jointly upon Federal and State government as agreed in the planning for the course. Courses in this category might include:

(i) Emergency Management Workshops,

(ii) Multijurisdictional Emergency Operations Simulation Training.

In this category also, it is expected that the State will be responsible for administrative and logistical requirements, plus any instructional activity as agreed upon prior to the conduct of the course.

(3) *Recipient conducted courses:* This element requires the greatest degree of

sophistication in program planning and delivery on the part of the State. Training events proposed by the State must be justified as addressing Emergency Management Training Program objectives. Additionally, they must address State or community needs and indicate the State's ability to present and carry out the Program of Instruction. Courses in this category could include:

(i) Radiological Monitoring,

(ii) Emergency Operations Simulating Training,

(iii) Shelter Management.

(d) In order that this three year comprehensive Training and Education Program planning can proceed in a timely and logical manner, each State will be provided three target appropriation figures, one for each of the three program years. States will develop their proposals, using the target figure to develop their scope of work. Adjustments in funding and the scope of work will be subject to negotiation before finalization. Both the funding and the scope of work will be reviewed each year and adjustments in the out years will reflect increased sophistication and expertise of the States as well as changing training needs within each State.

(e)(1) FEMA funding through the State Cooperative Agreement for the training activities is to be used for travel and per diem expenses of students selected by the States for courses reflecting individually needed or required training. Additionally funds may be expended for course materials and instructor expenses. The funding provided in the State Cooperative Agreement is not for the purpose of conducting ongoing State activities or for funding staff positions to accomplish work to be performed under this Agreement. Nor is the Agreement for the purpose of purchasing equipment which may be obtained with the help of Personnel and Administrative funds. In cases where equipment has been identified as needed in the scope of work submitted with the application, and where it serves as an outreach to a new audience or methodology, equipment purchase may be approved at the time of initial application approval.

(2) Allowable cost will be funded at 100%.

[46 FR 1271, Jan. 6, 1981, as amended at 48 FR 9646, Mar. 8, 1983]

§ 360.3 Eligible applicants.

Each of the 50 States, independent commonwealths, and territories is eligible to participate in a State Cooperative Agreement with FEMA. The department, division, or agency of the State government assigned the responsibility for State training in comprehensive emergency management should file the application.

§ 360.4 Administrative procedures.

(a) *Award.* Each State desiring to participate will negotiate the amount of financial support for the training and education program. Deciding factors will be the scope of the program, a prudent budget, the number of individuals to be trained, and variety of audiences included which are in need of training. All these factors are part of the required application as discussed in § 360.2.

(b) *Period of agreement.* Agreements will be negotiated annually and will be in effect for a period of 12 months. Each agreement, however, will include a scope of work for three years as reflected in § 360.2(b) to give continuity to the total training and education program.

(c) *Submission procedure.* Each State applicant shall comply with the following procedures:

(1) *Issuance of a request for application:* Each State emergency management agency will receive a Request for Application Package from the State's respective FEMA Regional Administrator.

(2) *How to submit:* Each State shall submit the completed application package to the Regional Administrator of the Appropriate Region.

(3) *Application package:* The Application Package should include:

(i) A transmittal letter signed by the State Director of the agency tasked with emergency management responsibilities for that State.

(ii) A three year projected training and education scope of work including both "required" training and "optional" courses. The first of the projected three year program is to be detailed as to list of courses, description of training to be offered, audiences to be reached and numbers to be trained. Dates and locations of training as well as costs of delivery and student travel and per diem are to be estimated. Special instructions for this portion of the submittal will be included in the Application Package.

(iii) Standard Form 270 "Request for Advance or Reimbursement" as required by OMB Circular A–102 and FEMA General Provisions for Cooperative Agreements.

(d) *Reporting agreements.* Recipients of State Agreement benefits will report quarterly during the Federal Fiscal year, directly to the Regional Administrator of their respective Regions. The report should include a narrative of the training programs conducted accompanied by rosters for each event, agenda, and a summary financial statement on the status of the Agreement funds. Any course or training activity included in the Scope of Work and not presented as scheduled should be explained in detail as to the reason for cancellation in the quarterly report. The costs allocated to this cancelled activity should be reprogrammed to another training activity approved by the Regional Administrator no later than the last day of the 3rd quarter, or released to the Region. An evaluation of the degree to which objectives were met, the effectiveness of the methodology, and the appropriateness of the resources and references used should also be included in the quarterly report. The report is due in the Regional Office no later than the 15th day of January, April, and July. A final report for the year is due the 15th of October.

§ **360.5 General provisions for State Cooperative Agreement.**

The legal funding instrument for the State Assistance Program for Training and Education FEMA is the State Cooperative Agreement. All States will be required to comply with FEMA General Provisions for the State Cooperative Agreement. The General Provisions for the State Cooperative Agreement will be provided to the States as part of the Request for Application package. The General Provisions will become part of the Cooperative Agreement.

PART 361—NATIONAL EARTHQUAKE HAZARDS REDUCTION ASSISTANCE TO STATE AND LOCAL GOVERNMENTS

Subpart A—Earthquake Hazards Reduction Assistance Program

Sec.
361.1 Purpose.
361.2 Definitions.
361.3 Project description.
361.4 Matching contributions.
361.5 Criteria for program assistance, matching contributions, and return of program assistance funds.
361.6 Documentation of matching contributions.
361.7 General eligible expenditures.
361.8 Ineligible expenditures.

Subpart B [Reserved]

AUTHORITY: Reorganization Plan No. 3 of 1978, 43 FR 41943, 3 CFR, 1978 Comp., p. 329; Earthquake Hazards Reduction Act of 1977, as amended, 42 U.S.C. 7701 *et seq.*; E.O. 12148, 44 FR 43239, 3 CFR, 1979 Comp., p. 412; and E.O. 12381, 47 FR 39795, 3 CFR, 1982 Comp., p. 207.

SOURCE: 57 FR 34869, Aug. 7, 1992, unless otherwise noted.

Subpart A—Earthquake Hazards Reduction Assistance Program

§ **361.1 Purpose.**

This part prescribes the policies to be followed by the Federal Emergency Management Agency (FEMA) and States in the administration of FEMA's earthquake hazards reduction assistance program, and establishes the criteria for cost-sharing.

§ **361.2 Definitions.**

Cash Contribution means the State cash outlay (expenditure), including the outlay of money contributed to the State by other public agencies and institutions, and private organizations and individuals. All expenditures must be listed in the project's approved budget.

611

Certification represents the Governor's written assurance describing the steps State agencies will take toward meeting the 50 percent cash contribution required following the third year of program funding. The letter of certification is intended to assist the State maintain a commitment to and plan for securing the future cash match with the long-range goal of developing an ongoing, rather than a short-term, State program.

Cost Sharing and *Matching* represent that portion of project costs not borne by the Federal Government.

Eligible Activities are activities for which FEMA may provide funding to States under this section. They include specific activities or projects related to earthquake hazards reduction which fall into one or more of the following categories: Preparedness and response planning; mitigation planning and implementation, including inventories preparation, seismic safety inspections of critical structures and lifelines, updating building and zoning codes and ordinances to enhance seismic safety; and public awareness and education. The activities that will actually be funded shall be determined through individual negotiations between FEMA and the States (see criteria in § 361.3(3)).

In-kind contributions represent the value of non-cash contributions provided by the States and other non-Federal parties. In-kind contributions may be in the form of charges for real property and non-expendable personal property and the value of goods and services directly benefiting and specifically identifiable to the States' earthquake hazards reduction projects.

Project means the complete set of approved earthquake hazards reduction activities undertaken by a State, or other jurisdiction, on a cost-shared basis with FEMA in a given Federal fiscal year.

Project Period is the duration of time over which an earthquake hazards reduction project is implemented.

State refers to the States of the United States of America, individually or collectively, the District of Columbia, the Commonwealth of Puerto Rico, the Virgin Islands, Guam, American Samoa, the Mariana Islands, and any other territory or possession of the United States. It also means local units of government or substate areas that include a number of local government jurisdictions.

State Assistance means the funding provided under this subpart by FEMA through the National Earthquake Hazards Reduction Program (NEHRP) to States to develop State programs specifically related to earthquake hazards reduction. The term also includes assistance to local units of government or substate areas, such as a group of several counties.

Target Allocation is the maximum amount of FEMA earthquake program funds presumably available to an eligible State in a fiscal year. It is based primarily upon the total amount of State assistance funds available to FEMA annually, the number of eligible States, and a nationally standardized comparison of these States' seismic hazard and population-at-risk. The target allocation is not necessarily the amount of funding that a State will actually receive from FEMA. Rather, it represents a planning basis of negotiations between the State and its FEMA Regional Office which will ultimately determine the actual amount of earthquake State assistance to be provided by FEMA.

§ 361.3 Project description.

(a) An objective of the Earthquake Hazards Reduction Act is to develop, in areas of seismic risk, improved understanding of and capability with respect to earthquake-related issues, including methods of mitigating earthquake damage, planning to prevent or minimize earthquake damage, disseminating warnings of earthquakes, organizing emergency services, and planning for post-earthquake recovery. To achieve this objective, FEMA has implemented an earthquake hazards reduction assistance program for State and local governments in seismic risk areas.

(b) This assistance program provides funding for earthquake hazards reduction activities which are eligible according to the definition in § 361.2. The categories, or program elements, listed therein comprise a comprehensive earthquake hazards reduction project for any given seismic hazard area. Key aspects of each of these elements are as follows:

(1) *Mitigation* involves developing and implementing strategies for reducing losses from earthquakes by incorporating principles of seismic safety into public and private decisions regarding the siting, design, and construction of structures (i.e., updating building and zoning codes and ordinances to enhance seismic safety), and regarding buildings' nonstructural elements, contents and furnishings. Mitigation includes preparing inventories of and conducting seismic safety inspections of critical structures and lifelines, and developing plans for identifying and retrofitting existing structures that pose threats to life or would suffer major damage in the event of a serious earthquake.

(2) *Preparedness/response planning* are closely related and usually considered as one comprehensive activity. They do differ, however, in that preparedness planning involves those efforts undertaken before an earthquake to prepare for or improve capability to respond to the event, while response planning can be defined as the planning necessary to implement an effective response once the earthquake has occurred. Preparedness/response planning usually considers functions related to the following:

(i) Rescue and fire services;

(ii) Medical services;

(iii) Damage assessments;

(iv) Communications;

(v) Security;

(vi) Restoration of lifeline and utility services;

(vii) Transportation;

(viii) Sheltering, food and water supplies;

(ix) Public health and information services;

(x) Post-disaster recovery and the return of economic stability;

(xi) Secondary impacts, such as dam failures, toxic releases, etc.; and

(xii) Organization and management.

(3) *Public awareness/earthquake education* activities are designed to increase public awareness of earthquakes and their associated risks, and to stimulate behavioral changes to foster a self-help approach to earthquake preparedness, response, and mitigation. Audiences that may be targeted for such efforts include:

(i) The general public;

(ii) School populations (administrators, teachers, students, and parents);

(iii) Special needs groups (e.g., elderly, disabled, non-English speaking);

(iv) Business and industry;

(v) Engineers, architects, builders;

(vi) The media; and

(vii) Public officials.

(4) *Other Activities* in support of those listed in §361.3(b)(1), (b)(2), and (b)(3) may include, but are not limited to, State seismic advisory boards which provide State and local officials responsible for implementing earthquake hazards reduction projects with expert advice in a variety of fields; hazard identification which defines the potential for earthquakes and their related geological hazards in a particular area; and vulnerability assessments, also known as loss estimation studies, which provide information on the impacts and consequences of an earthquake on an area's resources, as well as opportunities for earthquake hazards mitigation.

(c) State eligibility for financial assistance to States under this section is determined by FEMA based on a combination of the following criteria:

(1) Seismic hazard, including the historic occurrence of damaging earthquakes, as well as probable seismic activity;

(2) Total population and major urban concentrations exposed to such risk; and

(3) Other factors, the loss, damage, or disruption of which by a severe earthquake would have serious national impacts upon national security, such as industrial concentrations, concentrations or occurrences of natural resources, financial/economic centers and national defense facilities.

(d) Each fiscal year, FEMA will establish a target allocation of earthquake program funds for each eligible State.

(e) The specific activities, and the distribution of funds among them, that will be undertaken with this assistance will be determined during the annual Comprehensive Cooperative Agreement (CCA) negotiations between FEMA and the State, and will be based upon the following:

(1) The availability of information regarding identification of seismic hazards and vulnerability to those hazards;

(2) Earthquake hazards reduction accomplishments of the State to date;

(3) State and Federal priorities for needed earthquake hazards reduction activities; and

(4) State and local capabilities with respect to staffing, professional expertise, and funding.

(f) As a condition of receiving FEMA funding, a percentage of the amount of the total State project (FEMA State assistance, combined with the State match) must be spent for activities under the Mitigation Planning element. The percentage, to be determined by FEMA, may be increased by no more than 5 percent annually, beginning at 15 percent in fiscal year 1991 with a limit of 50 percent of the total State project. The increase will take into account the amount of time a State has been participating in the program. States may expend more than the required percentage of funding on eligible mitigation activities.

(g) The State match may be distributed among the eligible activities in any manner that is mutually agreed upon by FEMA and the State in the CCA negotiations.

(h) Negotiations between FEMA and the State regarding the scope of work and the determination of the amount of State assistance to be awarded shall consider earthquake hazards reduction activities previously accomplished by the State, as well as the quality of their performance.

§ 361.4 Matching contributions.

(a) All State assistance will be cost shared after the first year of funding. States which received a grant before October 1, 1990, which included the 50 percent non-Federal contribution to the State program, will continue to match the Federal funds on a 50 percent cash match basis.

(b) States which did not receive a grant before October 1, 1990, will assume cost sharing on a phased-in basis over a period of four years with the full cost sharing requirements being implemented in the fourth year. The sequence is as follows:

(1) For the first fiscal year, cost sharing will be voluntary. FEMA will provide State assistance without requiring a State match. Those States that are able to cost-share are encouraged to do so (on either a cash or in-kind basis).

(2) For the second fiscal year, the minimum acceptable non-Federal contribution is 25 percent of the total project cost, which may be satisfied through an in-kind contribution. Those States that are able to cost-share on a cash-contribution basis are encouraged to do so.

(3) For the third fiscal year, the minimum acceptable non-Federal contribution is 35 percent of the total project cost, which may be satisfied through an in-kind contribution. Those States that are able to cost-share on a cash-contribution basis are encouraged to do so.

(4) For the fourth and subsequent fiscal years, full cost sharing will be implemented, requiring a minimum of a 50 percent non-Federal contribution to a State program, with this share required to be cash. In-kind matching will no longer be acceptable. Thus, every dollar FEMA provides to a State must be matched by one dollar from the State. States that can contribute an amount greater than that required by the match are permitted and encouraged to do so. However, State assistance will not exceed the established target allocation.

(c) The State contribution need not be applied at the exact time of the obligation of the Federal funds. However, the State full matching share must be obligated by the end of the project period for which the State assistance has been made available for obligation under an approved program or budget.

(d) In the event a State interrupts its participation in this program, if it later elects to participate again, the nature and amount of that State's cost sharing shall be determined by the regulations then in effect, taking into account the number of years in which the State previously participated.

§ 361.5 Criteria for program assistance, matching contributions, and return of program assistance funds.

(a) In order to qualify for assistance, a State must:

(1) Demonstrate that the assistance will result in enhanced seismic safety in the State;

(2) Provide a share of the costs of the activities for which assistance is being given, in accordance with §361.4; and

(3) Demonstrate that it is taking actions to ensure its ability to meet the 50 percent cash contribution commitment either on an ongoing basis or for new States, by the fourth year of funding.

(i) The Governor of newly participating State must certify to the FEMA Regional Administrator the State will take steps to meet the 50 percent cash contribution requirement after the third year of funding. The specific steps to be taken will be outlined in the certification which must be submitted prior to the State receiving program funds.

(ii) The Governor must certify the State's continued commitment in the second and third years of funding. The certification will describe the progress made on the steps contained in the previous year's certification and steps to be taken in the future. The certification must be submitted to the Regional Administrator before the State will receive program funds.

(iii) If a State encounters difficulties meeting the 50 percent cash contribution requirement for the target allocation following the fourth year of funding, the Regional Administrator may require the Governor to continue certifying the State is working to resolve the difficulty.

(iv) A State will not receive Federal funds if it cannot provide the required cash contribution.

(b) The value of any resources accepted as a matching share under one Federal agreement or program cannot be counted again as a contribution under another.

(c) The State seeking the match shall submit documentation sufficient for FEMA to determine that the contribution meets the following requirements. The match shall be:

(1) Necessary and reasonable for proper, cost-effective and efficient administration of the project, allocable solely thereto, and except as specifically provided herein, not be a general expense required to carry out the overall responsibilities of State and local governments;

(2) Verifiable from the recipient State's records;

(3) Not allocable to or included as a cost of any other Federally financed program in either the current or a prior period;

(4) Authorized under State law;

(5) Consistent with any limitations or exclusions set forth in these regulations, Federal laws or other governing limitations as to types of cost items;

(6) Accorded consistent treatment through application of generally accepted accounting principles appropriate to the circumstances;

(7) Provided for in the approved budget/workplan of the State; and

(8) Consistent with OMB Circular A-87, "Cost Principles for State and Local Governments," and with 44 CFR part 13, Uniform Administrative Requirements for Grants and Cooperative Agreements to State and Local Governments.

(d) A State must submit and FEMA must approve a statement of work before the State receives any grant funds. The statement of work and target allocation of funds are based on a 12-month performance period. Except under extenuating circumstances, the funds initially obligated to the State will be based on the amount of time remaining in the performance period at the time the statement of work is approved. (Approved by the Office of Management and Budget under OMB control number 3067–0170)

(e) States are expected to perform activities and therefore expend funds on a quarterly basis in accordance with the approved statement of work. At the end of the third quarter, State and FEMA regional office staff will review the State's accomplishments to date. Funds not expended in accordance with the approved statement of work by the end of the third quarter of the performance period will not be made available to the State unless the State can demonstrate, and FEMA approves, its ability to perform activities adequately resulting in the expenditure of the funds by the end of the performance period.

§ 361.6 Documentation of matching contributions.

(a) The statement of work provided by the State to FEMA describing the specific activities comprising its earthquake hazards reduction project, including the project budget, shall reflect a level of effort commensurate with the total of the State and FEMA contributions.

(b) The basis by which the State determines the value of an in-kind match must be documented and a copy retained as part of the official record.

(c) The State shall maintain all records pertaining to matching contributions for a three-year period after the date of submission of the final financial report required by the CCA, or date of audit, whichever date comes first.

§ 361.7 General eligible expenditures.

(a) Expenditures must be for activities described in the statement of work mutually agreed to by FEMA and the State during the annual negotiation process, or for activities that the State agrees to perform as a result of subsequent modifications to that statement of work. These activities shall be consistent with the definition of eligible activities in § 361.2.

(b) The following is a list of eligible expenditures. When items do not appear on the list they will be considered on a case-by-case basis for policy determinations, based on criteria set forth in § 361.5. All costs must be reasonable, and consistent with OMB Circular A–87.

(1) Direct and indirect salaries or wages (including overtime) of employees hired specifically for carrying out earthquake hazards reduction activities are eligible when engaged in the performance of eligible work.

(2) Reasonable costs for work performed by private contractors on eligible projects contracted for by the State.

(3) Travel costs and per diem costs of State employees not to exceed the actual subsistence expense basis for the permanent or temporary activity, as determined by the State's cost principles governing travel.

(4) Non-expendable personal property, office supplies, and supplies for workshops; exhibits.

(5) A maximum of $8,000 or 10 percent of the total project allocation, whichever is less, may be expended for personal computer equipment in the first year of program funding. A full-time earthquake staff person must be employed and the equipment must be dedicated entirely to the earthquake project.

(6) Meetings and conferences, when the primary purpose is dissemination of information relating to the earthquake hazards reduction project.

(7) Training which directly benefits the conduct of earthquake hazards reduction activities.

§ 361.8 Ineligible expenditures.

(a) Expenditures for anything defined as an unallowable cost by OMB Circular A–87.

(b) Federal funds may not be used for the purchase or rental of any equipment such as radio/telephone communications equipment, warning systems, and computers and other related information processing equipment, except as stated in § 361.7(b)(5). If a State wishes to use its matching funds for this purpose, it must:

(1) Document during the annual negotiation process with FEMA how this equipment will support the earthquake hazards reduction activities in its scope of work (see § 361.7(a)); and

(2) Claim as credit for its match, if the equipment is to be used for purposes in addition to support of earthquake hazards reduction activities, only that proportion of costs directly related to its earthquake hazards reduction project.

Subpart B [Reserved]

PART 362—CRITERIA FOR ACCEPTANCE OF GIFTS, BEQUESTS, OR SERVICES

362.3 Criteria for determining acceptance.

AUTHORITY: 42 U.S.C. 7701, 7705c.

SOURCE: 59 FR 35631, July 13, 1994, unless otherwise noted.

§362.1 Purpose.

This part establishes criteria for determining whether the Administrator may accept gifts, bequests, or donations of services, money or property for the National Earthquake Hazards Reduction Program (NEHRP), under section 9 of the National Earthquake Hazards Reduction Program Reauthorization Act, 42 U.S.C. 7705c.

§362.2 Definitions.

As used in this part—

Gifts of property means a gratuitous, voluntary transfer or conveyance of ownership in property by one person to another without any consideration, including transfer by donation, devise or bequest.

Gifts of services means a gratuitous, voluntary offer of labor or professional work by one person to another without any compensation for that labor or professional work.

Program Agencies means the Federal Emergency Management Agency, the United States Geological Survey, the National Science Foundation, and the National Institute of Standards and Technology.

Property means real or personal property, tangible or intangible, including money, certificates of stocks, bonds, or other evidence of value.

Services means labor or professional work performed for the benefit of another or at another's command.

Solicit means to endeavor to obtain by asking or pleading.

§362.3 Criteria for determining acceptance.

The following criteria shall be applied whenever a gift of property or gift of services is offered to the Administrator for the benefit of the National Earthquake Hazards Reduction Program.

(a) The gift of property or gift of services must clearly and directly further the objectives of the National Earthquake Hazards Reduction Program, as defined in 42 U.S.C. 7702.

(b) All gifts of property must be offered unconditionally, with sole discretion of use, administration and disposition of such property to be determined by the Administrator or his designee.

(c) The Administrator may accept and use gifts of services of voluntary and uncompensated personnel, and may provide transportation and subsistence as authorized by 5 U.S.C. 5703 for persons serving without compensation.

(d) Employees of FEMA or the Program agencies may not solicit gifts of property, or gifts of services.

(e) Acceptance of gifts of property, or gifts of services must first be approved by the Office of the Chief Counsel, FEMA, for conformance with all applicable laws and regulations.

(f) In all cases where it is determined that the acceptance of a gift may create a conflict of interest, or the appearance of a conflict of interest, the gift will be declined.

PARTS 363–399 [RESERVED]

CHAPTER IV—DEPARTMENT OF COMMERCE AND DEPARTMENT OF TRANSPORTATION

619

PART 401—SHIPPING RESTRICTIONS (T-1)

AUTHORITY: Sec. 704, 64 Stat. 816, as amended; 50 U.S.C. app. 2154, as amended; Interpret or apply secs. 101, 705, 64 Stat. 799, as amended; 50 U.S.C. app. 2071; E.O. 10480, 3 CFR, 1949–1953 Comp., p. 962.

SOURCE: Transportation Order T-1, 30 FR 9092, July 21, 1965; 32 FR 15831, Nov. 17, 1967, unless otherwise noted. Redesignated at 45 FR 44574, July 1, 1980.

§ 401.1 Prohibited transportation and discharge.

No person shall transport in any ship documented under the laws of the United States or in any aircraft registered under the laws of the United States any commodity at the time not identified by the Symbol B in the last column of the Commodity Control List (339.1 of the Comprehensive Export Schedule, issued by the Bureau of International Commerce, Department of Commerce (15 CFR parts 368 through 399), any article designated as arms, ammunition, and implements of war in the United States Munitions List (22 CFR parts 121 through 128), or any commodity, including fissionable, materials controlled for export under the Atomic Energy Act of 1954, as amended, to any destination at the time in country groups X, Y, or Z as set forth in the Comprehensive Export Schedule (15 CFR 370.1(g)(2)), and no person shall discharge from any such ship or any such aircraft any such commodity or article at any such port or place or at any other port or place in transit to any such destination, unless a validated export license under the Export Control Act of 1949, as amended, under section 414 of the Mutual Security Act of 1954, as amended, or under the Atomic Energy Act of 1954, as amended, has been obtained for the shipment, or unless authorization for the shipment has been obtained from the Assistant Secretary for Domestic and International Business. This prohibition applies to the owner of the ship or aircraft, the master of the ship or aircraft, or any other officer, employee or agent of the owner of the ship or aircraft who participates in the transportation. The consular officers of the United States are furnished with current copies of the Commodity Control List.

§ 401.2 Application for adjustment or exceptions.

Any person affected by any provisions of this order may file an application for an adjustment or exception upon the ground that such provision works an exceptional hardship upon him, not suffered by others, or that its enforcement against him would not be in the interest of the national defense program. Such an application may be made by letter or telegram addressed to the Assistant Secretary for Domestic and International Business, Department of Commerce, Washington, DC, 20230, reference T-1. If authorization is requested, any such application should specify in detail the material to be shipped, the name and address of the shipper and of the recipient of the shipment, the ports or places from which and to which the shipment is being made and the use to which the material shipped will be put. The application should also specify in detail the facts which support the applicant's claim for an exception.

§ 401.3 Reports.

Persons subject to this order shall submit such reports to the Assistant Secretary for Domestic and International Business as he shall require, subject to the terms of the Federal Reports Act.

§ 401.4 Records.

Each person participating in any transaction covered by this order shall retain in his possession, for at least 2 years, records of shipments in sufficient detail to permit an audit that determines for each transaction that the provisions of this order have been met. This does not specify any particular accounting method and does not require alteration of the system of records customarily maintained, provided such records supply an adequate basis for audit. Records may be retained in the form of microfilm or other photographic copies instead of the originals.

§ 401.5 Defense against claims for damages.

No person shall be held liable for damages or penalties for any default under any contract or order which shall result directly or indirectly from compliance with this order or any provision thereof, notwithstanding that this order or such provision shall thereafter be declared by judicial or other competent authority to be invalid.

§ 401.6 Violations.

Any person who wilfully violates any provisions of this order or wilfully conceals a material fact or furnishes false information in the course of operation under this order is guilty of a crime and upon conviction may be punished by fine or imprisonment or both. In addition, administrative action may be taken against any such person, denying him the privileges generally accorded under this order.

PART 402—SHIPMENTS ON AMERICAN FLAG SHIPS AND AIRCRAFT (T-1, INT. 1)

Sec.
402.1 Shipments from the United States.
402.2 Restricted commodities.
402.3 Addition of commodities to the Positive List.
402.4 Calls at restricted ports en route to an unrestricted port with restricted cargo.
402.5 Forwarding commodities previously shipped.
402.6 Relation to Transportation Order T-2.

AUTHORITY: Sec. 704, 64 Stat. 816, as amended; 50 U.S.C. app. 2154. Interpret or apply sec. 101, 64 Stat. 799, as amended; 50 U.S.C. app. 2071, E.O. 10480, 3 CFR, 1949–1953 Comp., p. 962.

SOURCE: Transportation Order T-1, Interpretation 1, 15 FR 9145, Dec. 21, 1950; 32 FR 15831, Nov. 17, 1967, unless otherwise noted. Redesignated at 45 FR 44574, July 1, 1980.

§ 402.1 Shipments from the United States.

Transportation Order T-1 applies to shipments from the United States, as well as to shipments from foreign ports, on American flag ships and aircraft.

§ 402.2 Restricted commodities.

The restrictions of Transportation Order T-1 apply to the transportation or discharge of (a) commodities on the Positive List (15 CFR part 399) (as amended from time to time) of the Comprehensive Export Schedule of the Office of International Trade, Department of Commerce, (b) articles on the list of arms, ammunition and implements of war coming within the meaning of Proclamation No. 2776 of March 26, 1948, and (c) commodities, including fissionable materials, controlled for export under the Atomic Energy Act of 1946. The restrictions imposed by Transportation Order T-1 do not apply to other commodities, not within these restricted classes at the time of transportation or discharge, even though authorization for the export of the commodity from the United States to the particular destination is required under regulations of the Office of International Trade or under other Federal law or regulation. In this respect Order T-1 is different from Order T-2 which applies to all commodities destined to Communist China. Order T-1 does not relax or modify any of the requirements of any other regulation or law.

§ 402.3 Addition of commodities to the Positive List.

Order T-1 applies to the transportation or discharge of commodities which are restricted at the time of transportation or discharge. Accordingly, if a commodity is added to the Positive List while the commodity is being transported on an American flag ship or aircraft, the restrictions of Order T-1 immediately apply and the commodity may not be transported to or discharged at any of the restricted ports or discharged in transit to one of the restricted ports, unless authorization under Order T-1 is obtained.

§ 402.4 Calls at restricted ports en route to an unrestricted port with restricted cargo.

Order T-1 does not prohibit an American flag ship or aircraft from going to or calling at one of the restricted ports, even though it has on board a commodity which could not be discharged at that port. (Note, however, that Order T–2 prohibits American flag ships and aircraft from calling at any port or other place in Communist China.) For example, an American flag ship may call at one of the restricted ports (except one in Communist China), even though it has on board the following classes of commodities:

(a) A Positive List commodity manifested to a destination outside the restricted area, with an export license and an export declaration showing the unrestricted destination at the ultimate destination, (b) a Positive List commodity destined for the restricted port of call which cannot be discharged there because there is no export license or authorization from the Assistant Secretary for Domestic and International Business permitting discharge at the restricted port of call, (c) a commodity of any kind destined for Communist China (the transportation and discharge of which is covered by Order T–2). None of these commodities may be discharged at the restricted port of call. Discharge of any of these commodities at the port covered by the restrictions of Order T–1 is prohibited and subject to penalty, regardless of the circumstances under which the discharge of the cargo at the restricted port occurs, unless appropriate authorization is obtained.

§402.5 Forwarding commodities previously shipped.

Order T–1 applies to transportation on or discharge from ships documented under the laws of the United States and aircraft registered under the laws of the United States. These restrictions apply either in the case of a discharge at one of the restricted ports or to discharge at any other port in transit to a restricted destination. The restrictions of Order T–1 do not apply to transportation by foreign carriers, as long as there is no prohibited transportation or discharge by or from a United States flag ship or aircraft after the issuance of Order T–1. Accordingly, if an American flag ship or aircraft, before the issuance of Order T–1, had transported restricted commodities manifested to restricted destinations, and had completed the transportation to a foreign intermediate point and had completed the discharge from the American flag ship or aircraft before the issuance of Order T–1, no violation of that order would have occurred, but Order T–1 would prohibit further shipment on an American flag ship or aircraft unless authorization under Order T–1 is obtained.

§402.6 Relation to Transportation Order T–2.

Transportation Order T–1 applies to the transportation of commodities to, or in transit to, destinations in Sub-Group A, Hong Kong or Macao. It applies, however, only to commodities on the Positive List of the Office of International Trade, arms and ammunition, and commodities controlled under the Atomic Energy Act (see section 2 of this interpretation). Transportation Order T–2 applies to the transportation of commodities of any kind which are destined to Communist China (Order T–2 also prohibits American ships and aircraft from calling at any port or place in Communist China). Since Communist China is in Sub-Group A, the restrictions of both orders apply to the transportation of commodities to Communist China or to any other point in transit to Communist China.

PARTS 403–499 [RESERVED]

FINDING AIDS

A list of CFR titles, subtitles, chapters, subchapters and parts and an alphabetical list of agencies publishing in the CFR are included in the CFR Index and Finding Aids volume to the Code of Federal Regulations which is published separately and revised annually.

Table of CFR Titles and Chapters

(Revised as of October 1, 2011)

Title 1—General Provisions

Title 2—Grants and Agreements

629

630

Title 7—Agriculture—Continued

Title 8—Aliens and Nationality

Title 9—Animals and Animal Products

Title 10—Energy

Title 11—Federal Elections

Title 12—Banks and Banking

Title 13—Business Credit and Assistance

Title 13—Business Credit and Assistance—Continued
Chap.

III Economic Development Administration, Department of Commerce (Parts 300—399)

IV Emergency Steel Guarantee Loan Board (Parts 400—499)

V Emergency Oil and Gas Guaranteed Loan Board (Parts 500—599)

Title 14—Aeronautics and Space

I Federal Aviation Administration, Department of Transportation (Parts 1—199)

II Office of the Secretary, Department of Transportation (Aviation Proceedings) (Parts 200—399)

III Commercial Space Transportation, Federal Aviation Administration, Department of Transportation (Parts 400—499)

V National Aeronautics and Space Administration (Parts 1200—1299)

VI Air Transportation System Stabilization (Parts 1300—1399)

Title 15—Commerce and Foreign Trade

SUBTITLE A—OFFICE OF THE SECRETARY OF COMMERCE (PARTS 0—29)

SUBTITLE B—REGULATIONS RELATING TO COMMERCE AND FOREIGN TRADE

I Bureau of the Census, Department of Commerce (Parts 30—199)

II National Institute of Standards and Technology, Department of Commerce (Parts 200—299)

III International Trade Administration, Department of Commerce (Parts 300—399)

IV Foreign-Trade Zones Board, Department of Commerce (Parts 400—499)

VII Bureau of Industry and Security, Department of Commerce (Parts 700—799)

VIII Bureau of Economic Analysis, Department of Commerce (Parts 800—899)

IX National Oceanic and Atmospheric Administration, Department of Commerce (Parts 900—999)

XI Technology Administration, Department of Commerce (Parts 1100—1199)

XIII East-West Foreign Trade Board (Parts 1300—1399)

XIV Minority Business Development Agency (Parts 1400—1499)

SUBTITLE C—REGULATIONS RELATING TO FOREIGN TRADE AGREEMENTS

XX Office of the United States Trade Representative (Parts 2000—2099)

SUBTITLE D—REGULATIONS RELATING TO TELECOMMUNICATIONS AND INFORMATION

XXIII National Telecommunications and Information Administration, Department of Commerce (Parts 2300—2399)

634

Title 21—Food and Drugs

Title 22—Foreign Relations

Title 23—Highways

Title 24—Housing and Urban Development

Title 25—Indians

Title 25—Indians—Continued

Title 26—Internal Revenue

Title 27—Alcohol, Tobacco Products and Firearms

Title 28—Judicial Administration

Title 29—Labor

Title 45—Public Welfare—Continued

Title 46—Shipping

Title 47—Telecommunication

Title 48—Federal Acquisition Regulations System

643

Title 49—Transportation

Alphabetical List of Agencies Appearing in the CFR

(Revised as of October 1, 2011)

Agency	CFR Title, Subtitle or Chapter
Management and Budget, Office of	5, III, LXXVII; 14, VI; 48, 99
National Drug Control Policy, Office of	21, III
National Security Council	32, XXI; 47, 2
Presidential Documents	3
Science and Technology Policy, Office of	32, XXIV; 47, II
Trade Representative, Office of the United States	15, XX
Export-Import Bank of the United States	2, XXXV; 5, LII; 12, IV
Family Assistance, Office of	45, II
Farm Credit Administration	5, XXXI; 12, VI
Farm Credit System Insurance Corporation	5, XXX; 12, XIV
Farm Service Agency	7, VII, XVIII
Federal Acquisition Regulation	48, 1
Federal Aviation Administration	14, I
Commercial Space Transportation	14, III
Federal Claims Collection Standards	31, IX
Federal Communications Commission	5, XXIX; 47, I
Federal Contract Compliance Programs, Office of	41, 60
Federal Crop Insurance Corporation	7, IV
Federal Deposit Insurance Corporation	5, XXII; 12, III
Federal Election Commission	11, I
Federal Emergency Management Agency	44, I
Federal Employees Group Life Insurance Federal Acquisition Regulation	48, 21
Federal Employees Health Benefits Acquisition Regulation	48, 16
Federal Energy Regulatory Commission	5, XXIV; 18, I
Federal Financial Institutions Examination Council	12, XI
Federal Financing Bank	12, VIII
Federal Highway Administration	23, I, II
Federal Home Loan Mortgage Corporation	1, IV
Federal Housing Enterprise Oversight Office	12, XVII
Federal Housing Finance Agency	5, LXXX; 12, XII
Federal Housing Finance Board	12, IX
Federal Labor Relations Authority	5, XIV, XLIX; 22, XIV
Federal Law Enforcement Training Center	31, VII
Federal Management Regulation	41, 102
Federal Maritime Commission	46, IV
Federal Mediation and Conciliation Service	29, XII
Federal Mine Safety and Health Review Commission	5, LXXIV; 29, XXVII
Federal Motor Carrier Safety Administration	49, III
Federal Prison Industries, Inc.	28, III
Federal Procurement Policy Office	48, 99
Federal Property Management Regulations	41, 101
Federal Railroad Administration	49, II
Federal Register, Administrative Committee of	1, I
Federal Register, Office of	1, II
Federal Reserve System	12, II
Board of Governors	5, LVIII
Federal Retirement Thrift Investment Board	5, VI, LXXVI
Federal Service Impasses Panel	5, XIV
Federal Trade Commission	5, XLVII; 16, I
Federal Transit Administration	49, VI
Federal Travel Regulation System	41, Subtitle F
Financial Crimes Enforcement Network	31, X
Financial Research Office	12, XVI
Financial Stability Oversight Council	12, XIII
Fine Arts, Commission on	45, XXI
Fiscal Service	31, II
Fish and Wildlife Service, United States	50, I, IV
Food and Drug Administration	21, I
Food and Nutrition Service	7, II
Food Safety and Inspection Service	9, III
Foreign Agricultural Service	7, XV
Foreign Assets Control, Office of	31, V
Foreign Claims Settlement Commission of the United States	45, V
Foreign Service Grievance Board	22, IX
Foreign Service Impasse Disputes Panel	22, XIV

Agency	CFR Title, Subtitle or Chapter
Foreign Service Labor Relations Board	22, XIV
Foreign-Trade Zones Board	15, IV
Forest Service	36, II
General Services Administration	5, LVII; 41, 105
Contract Appeals, Board of	48, 61
Federal Acquisition Regulation	48, 5
Federal Management Regulation	41, 102
Federal Property Management Regulations	41, 101
Federal Travel Regulation System	41, Subtitle F
General	41, 300
Payment From a Non-Federal Source for Travel Expenses	41, 304
Payment of Expenses Connected With the Death of Certain Employees	41, 303
Relocation Allowances	41, 302
Temporary Duty (TDY) Travel Allowances	41, 301
Geological Survey	30, IV
Government Accountability Office	4, I
Government Ethics, Office of	5, XVI
Government National Mortgage Association	24, III
Grain Inspection, Packers and Stockyards Administration	7, VIII; 9, II
Harry S. Truman Scholarship Foundation	45, XVIII
Health and Human Services, Department of	2, III; 5, XLV; 45, Subtitle A,
Centers for Medicare & Medicaid Services	42, IV
Child Support Enforcement, Office of	45, III
Children and Families, Administration for	45, II, III, IV, X
Community Services, Office of	45, X
Family Assistance, Office of	45, II
Federal Acquisition Regulation	48, 3
Food and Drug Administration	21, I
Human Development Services, Office of	45, XIII
Indian Health Service	25, V
Inspector General (Health Care), Office of	42, V
Public Health Service	42, I
Refugee Resettlement, Office of	45, IV
Homeland Security, Department of	2, XXX; 6, I
Coast Guard	33, I; 46, I; 49, IV
Coast Guard (Great Lakes Pilotage)	46, III
Customs and Border Protection	19, I
Federal Emergency Management Agency	44, I
Human Resources Management and Labor Relations Systems	5, XCVII
Immigration and Customs Enforcement Bureau	19, IV
Immigration and Naturalization	8, I
Transportation Security Administration	49, XII
HOPE for Homeowners Program, Board of Directors of	24, XXIV
Housing and Urban Development, Department of	2, XXIV; 5, LXV; 24, Subtitle B
Community Planning and Development, Office of Assistant Secretary for	24, V, VI
Equal Opportunity, Office of Assistant Secretary for	24, I
Federal Acquisition Regulation	48, 24
Federal Housing Enterprise Oversight, Office of	12, XVII
Government National Mortgage Association	24, III
Housing—Federal Housing Commissioner, Office of Assistant Secretary for	24, II, VIII, X, XX
Housing, Office of, and Multifamily Housing Assistance Restructuring, Office of	24, IV
Inspector General, Office of	24, XII
Public and Indian Housing, Office of Assistant Secretary for	24, IX
Secretary, Office of	24, Subtitle A, VII
Housing—Federal Housing Commissioner, Office of Assistant Secretary for	24, II, VIII, X, XX
Housing, Office of, and Multifamily Housing Assistance Restructuring, Office of	24, IV
Human Development Services, Office of	45, XIII
Immigration and Customs Enforcement Bureau	19, IV

652

653

Agency	CFR Title, Subtitle or Chapter
National Park Service	36, I
National Railroad Adjustment Board	29, III
National Railroad Passenger Corporation (AMTRAK)	49, VII
National Science Foundation	2, XXV; 5, XLIII; 45, VI
Federal Acquisition Regulation	48, 25
National Security Council	32, XXI
National Security Council and Office of Science and Technology Policy	47, II
National Telecommunications and Information Administration	15, XXIII; 47, III, IV
National Transportation Safety Board	49, VIII
Natural Resources Conservation Service	7, VI
Natural Resource Revenue, Office of	30, XII
Navajo and Hopi Indian Relocation, Office of	25, IV
Navy Department	32, VI
Federal Acquisition Regulation	48, 52
Neighborhood Reinvestment Corporation	24, XXV
Northeast Interstate Low-Level Radioactive Waste Commission	10, XVIII
Nuclear Regulatory Commission	2, XX; 5, XLVIII; 10, I
Federal Acquisition Regulation	48, 20
Occupational Safety and Health Administration	29, XVII
Occupational Safety and Health Review Commission	29, XX
Offices of Independent Counsel	28, VI
Office of Workers' Compensation Programs	20, VII
Oklahoma City National Memorial Trust	36, XV
Operations Office	7, XXVIII
Overseas Private Investment Corporation	5, XXXIII; 22, VII
Patent and Trademark Office, United States	37, I
Payment From a Non-Federal Source for Travel Expenses	41, 304
Payment of Expenses Connected With the Death of Certain Employees	41, 303
Peace Corps	22, III
Pennsylvania Avenue Development Corporation	36, IX
Pension Benefit Guaranty Corporation	29, XL
Personnel Management, Office of	5, I, XXXV; 45, VIII
Human Resources Management and Labor Relations Systems, Department of Defense	5, XCIX
Human Resources Management and Labor Relations Systems, Department of Homeland Security	5, XCVII
Federal Acquisition Regulation	48, 17
Federal Employees Group Life Insurance Federal Acquisition Regulation	48, 21
Federal Employees Health Benefits Acquisition Regulation	48, 16
Pipeline and Hazardous Materials Safety Administration	49, I
Postal Regulatory Commission	5, XLVI; 39, III
Postal Service, United States	5, LX; 39, I
Postsecondary Education, Office of	34, VI
President's Commission on White House Fellowships	1, IV
Presidential Documents	3
Presidio Trust	36, X
Prisons, Bureau of	28, V
Procurement and Property Management, Office of	7, XXXII
Productivity, Technology and Innovation, Assistant Secretary	37, IV
Public Contracts, Department of Labor	41, 50
Public and Indian Housing, Office of Assistant Secretary for	24, IX
Public Health Service	42, I
Railroad Retirement Board	20, II
Reclamation, Bureau of	43, I
Recovery Accountability and Transparency Board	4, II
Refugee Resettlement, Office of	45, IV
Relocation Allowances	41, 302
Research and Innovative Technology Administration	49, XI
Rural Business-Cooperative Service	7, XVIII, XLII, L
Rural Development Administration	7, XLII
Rural Housing Service	7, XVIII, XXXV, L

List of CFR Sections Affected

All changes in this volume of the Code of Federal Regulations that were made by documents published in the FEDERAL REGISTER since January 1, 2001, are enumerated in the following list. Entries indicate the nature of the changes effected. Page numbers refer to FEDERAL REGISTER pages. The user should consult the entries for chapters and parts as well as sections for revisions.

For the period before January 1, 1986, see the "List of CFR Sections Affected, 1949–1963, 1964–1972, 1973–1985, and 1986–2000" published in 11 separate volumes.

44 CFR—Continued

44 CFR—Continued

2003

44 CFR

List of CFR Sections Affected

2010

44 CFR

75 FR Page

44 CFR—Continued

75 FR Page

2011

(Regulations published from January 1,
2011, through October 1, 2011)

44 CFR

76 FR Page